Management

QUALITY AND COMPETITIVENESS

Management

QUALITY AND COMPETITIVENESS

Second Edition

JOHN M. IVANCEVICH

UNIVERSITY OF HOUSTON

PETER LORENZI

LOYOLA COLLEGE IN MARYLAND

STEVEN J. SKINNER

UNIVERSITY OF KENTUCKY

with

PHILIP B. CROSBY

CAREER IV, INC.

Irwin
McGraw-Hill

Boston, Massachusetts   Burr Ridge, Illinios   Dubuque, Iowa
Madison, Wisconsin   New York, New York   San Francisco, California   St. Louis, Missouri

Irwin/McGraw-Hill

A Division of The **McGraw·Hill** Companies

Irwin Book Team

Publisher: *Rob Zwettler*
Sponsoring editor: *John E. Biernat*
Senior developmental editor: *Laura Hurst Spell*
Marketing manager: *Michael Campbell*
Senior project supervisor: *Mary Conzachi*
Production supervisor: *Dina L. Genovese*
Senior designer: *Heidi J. Baughman*
Interior designer: *Paul C. Uhl/Design Associates, Inc.*
Assistant manager, desktop services: *Jon Christopher*
Coordinator, Graphics and Desktop Services: *Keri Johnson*
Compositor: *Precision Graphics*
Typeface: *9.5/12 pt. Cheltenham Light*
Printer: *Quebecor Printing/Dubuque*

Library of Congress Cataloging-in-Publication Data

Ivancevich, John M.
    Management : quality and competitiveness / John M. Ivancevich,
Peter Lorenzi, Steven J. Skinner ; with Philip B. Crosby. — 2nd ed.
      p.   cm.
    Includes bibliographical references and index.
    ISBN 0-256-18939-0
    1. Decision-making. 2. Management. 3. Quality of products.
4. Competition. I. Lorenzi, Peter. II. Skinner, Steven J.
III. Title.
HD30.23.I9   1997
658—dc20   96–26410

To Dana Louise, our sun, mountain, and water.

—

To Dena Adrienne Lorenzi, for her love and support. She makes all the late nights on the Mac worthwhile.

—

To my parents, John and Dorothy Skinner, for their love and support.

About the Authors

JOHN M. IVANCEVICH

John M. Ivancevich, the Cullen Professor of Management, has spent 21 years at the University of Houston, teaching, conducting research, participating in professional associations, and consulting with many different enterprises in an outside the United States. In his academic career (which includes a B.S. degree from Purdue University and master's and doctor's degrees from the University of Maryland) he has taught management, organizational behavior, and human resource management courses. He has written, coauthored, or coedited over 45 books and published over 130 refereed papers.

During his academic career Ivancevich has consulted with over 100 firms on such topics as reward system implementation, performance appraisal plans, goal-setting programs, merging divergent organizational cultures, new business start-ups, team building, and leadership training. He's currently involved in a number of management research projects involving stress and health-related lawsuits and diversity management concepts as applied in organizations.

PETER LORENZI

Peter Lorenzi has been dean of the Joseph A. Sellinger, S. J. School of Business and Management of Loyola College in Maryland since July 1995. Before coming to Loyola, Lorenzi was dean of the College of Business Administration at the University of Central Arkansas (1992–95). Lorenzi earned his B.S. in Administration Science in 1973 and M.B.A. in 1975 from Binghamton University. He earned his Ph.D. (1978) in organizational behavior from The Pennsylvania State University.

Lorenzi coauthored *The New Leadership Paradigm* (Sage, 1992). He has lectured extensively across the United States and in Europe, Russia, and Malaysia. Lorenzi has presented management development and executive education programs on topics such as motivation, quality, and leadership, for construction executives, marketing managers, insurance executives, young presidents, municipal clerks, city managers, newspaper editors, health care facility managers, university administrators and civic leaders around the world. In the late 1980s he taught a program for General Motors employees on global competitiveness. He has authored numerous newspaper columns on management, business, and government. Lorenzi has earned excellence in teaching honors at three universities.

STEVEN J. SKINNER

Steven J. Skinner is the Rosenthal Professor and director of the School of Management at the University of Kentucky, where he has taught for 15 years. He was previously on the faculty at Illinois State University and was formerly a research administrator for State Farm Insurance Companies. He has also consulted with a variety of large and small firms.

Dr. Skinner is the coauthor of *The New Banker* (a business trade book published by Irwin Professional Publishing), and *The Business Environment* (a college textbook published by South-Western). His research has been published in *Academy of Management*

Journal, Journal of Marketing Research, Journal of Retailing, Journal of Business Research, Public Opinion Quarterly, and the *Journal of Risk and Insurance.* He is on the editorial review board of the *Journal of Business Research.*

PHILIP B. CROSBY

Philip B. Crosby began his professional career as a test technician on an assembly line at the Crosely Corporation in Richmond, Indiana. He then became interested in management and in causing quality in an organization. Over the next 27 years he was a reliability engineer at the Bendix Corporation, a quality manager at Martin-Marietta—where he created the zero defects concept—and, for 14 of those, vice president of ITT Corporation responsible for quality worldwide. Based on this experience, Mr. Crosby developed the concepts and systems that led him to write *Quality Is Free* in 1979. Upon the success of this book, he founded Philip Crosby Associates, Inc. (PCA) in Winter Park, Florida, which became the largest quality management education and consulting firm in the world. In 1985 he made PCA the first consulting firm to go public.

In trying to help managers understand the reality of quality management, Mr. Crosby wrote several other books (13 books in all). They include: *Quality without Tears, Running Things, The Eternally Successful Organization, Leading, Let's Talk Quality,* and *Completeness.* In 1991 he retired from PCA and formed Career IV, Inc., to manage his speeches and publications. He has since developed "To Be an Executive, by Choice," a video package to help those who seek successful careers. He has also had three new books released—*Quality Is Still Free, Reflections,* and *The Absolutes of Leadership.* He lives in Winter Park, Florida, and spends his summers in Highlands, North Carolina.

Foreword
by Philip B. Crosby

When I was asked to participate in creating this book I was delighted to accept. I looked at it as an opportunity to reach those who will be managing our world in the 21st century. If those individuals are going to succeed in this challenge, they have to understand how to manage quality as a real part of their professional and personal lives. Most of what comes down as gospel in the teaching of quality is based on conventional wisdom rather than on experience in the real world. But there will not be time to chase fairy dust in the competitive business world we are entering as managers. We have to be certain about what we are doing.

If I've learned nothing else from my 42 years of management experience, I know that an organization's quality (meaning ability to do what it agreed to do) is a direct reflection of the leader's personal integrity and intensity about getting things done properly. The output of a business looks exactly like the attitude of the management. Suppliers, customers, and the general public can read that attitude exactly.

I've also learned that causing quality is a matter of understanding the philosophy behind it, and quality cannot be made to happen by applying some assigned set of rules and regulations. For that reason I have written several books and innumerable articles on the quality of philosophy and its application. I also set up the Quality College at Philip Crosby Associates, Inc. (PCA), to teach executives and managers their responsibility to understand quality.

The third thing I've learned is that education and training are what make the difference in companies and, for that matter, individuals. When people understand the requirements of their job and when they know how their job fits into the overall world of their organization, then they can contribute.

All of this happens when managers know that quality is an integral part of the operation, rather than some add-on or a special task done by a little group of people over in the corner. Quality should be taught in college as part of every other subject, not as a separate entity. We need to learn how to do everything right the first time in all fields. We need to learn how to communicate meaningfully with people regardless of the product or service involved. We need to learn how to prevent problems, rather than becoming experts at fixing them, if we want to be thought useful.

The format chosen for my participation in the book was to read each chapter written by the authors and then write a "reflection" on the subject. I tried to share my experience on each subject through on anecdote or observation. I thought this was the best way to share with the students. The life of business is mostly relationships and understanding. We learn from those relationships as they grow.

Today many of those who would be business leaders try to pick up prepackaged components of management thoughts and applications to apply to their organizations, but they are often disappointed in the results. Leaders must deal with ideas and with action. They must develop a personal philosophy of management based on their own experiences through these reflections. I wish all of you the very best in your careers and your life.

Philip B. Crosby, Winter Park, Florida

Preface

The growing integration of the world economy is causing managers to pay closer attention to human resources, the quality of goods and services, and the need to adapt to change. In the past four decades, most firms pursued the "economies of scale" approach to managing organizations. Big corporations, the Fortune 500s, were the preferred way of doing business. As the 1990s come to an end, change is so much a part of a manager's world that he or she is constantly searching for ways to cope.

Today, managers are concerned about competitiveness, globalization, falling trade barriers, computerization, automation, ethical behavior, workforce diversity, and total quality management. World interest has shifted to using efficient approaches for managing human resources in all sizes of firms. Firms of all sizes are using computers. Quality improvements are considered important in a growing number of countries. Examples of ethical behavior are finally beginning to appear in the headlines because customers, clients, and consumers expect managers to treat them honestly, fairly, and with respect. As these changes in managerial practices and marketplace transactions occur, a need to reorient management teaching has become obvious. Management instructional materials, therefore, must change to keep up with or even to stay ahead of a transforming world.

We believe the job of managing is one of the most exciting, challenging, and personally rewarding positions a person can possibly hold. The manager's job is critically important because managers make a difference in how our society functions and in the standard of living we enjoy. *Management: Quality and Competitiveness*, Second Edition, is about the manager's job in a changing world. It describes how men and women go about managing so that quality and competitiveness are conveyed as the ultimate goals of managing organizations in any country.

In this text, the student (reader) is considered to be a potential manager. The book's tone is purposefully positive about the manager's job. Managerial thinking, practice, and evaluation are themes that are woven into the content, examples, problems, and issues. Managers can't give "maybe" answers. They usually have to say yes or no and then implement their response. This book attempts to help the reader clearly understand how, why, and when managers make decisions. It will become obvious very early in the book that most managers must carefully diagnose situations, use their abilities, skills, and knowledge to weigh facts and fiction, work with other people, and evaluate the results of their choices every day. Yes, the job of managing and working with people is difficult. But few careers are as stimulating as that of a manager.

The Book Concept

During the past three decades business schools have been regarded as educational centers for the development of professional skills for future managers. This important responsibility has placed business educators in the spotlight. Consequently, educators have often been asked whether they're teaching students about what's being talked about by managers, and a number of critics have claimed that what's being taught has little practical relevance. Then, in 1992, an open letter in the *Harvard Business Review,* the leaders of several U.S. corporations reached out and called for a partnership between academia and business in advancing total quality management.

In conceptualizing this book, we listened to the critics, agreed with some of what was being said, and decided that a management book that focuses on relevance, quality, and competitiveness would help students understand the changes taking place in the world around them. Quality and competitiveness are topics that have unusual appeal and interest. Even the nations of Eastern Europe, the People's Republic of China, and Central and Latin America understand that, without producing or providing high-quality products and services, they won't be able to compete in the global marketplace.

Instead of simply putting together a text in the traditional way, we decided that the author partnership team should include both academic and quality experts. Since quality was a major part of what we wanted to present, the idea of teaming up with a quality expert became a top priority. We reviewed the quality literature, videos, annual reports, and training materials and talked to publishers, business executives, and training experts. The notion of a text being prepared by an academic/quality expert team appealed to every person who discussed the idea with us.

Our homework and analysis led to the identification of Philip B. Crosby. In our opinion, Phil is America's premier management consultant in the quality area. He has been an executive for 40 years, working for corporations such as Martin-Marietta and ITT. He founded Philip Crosby Associates (PCA) in 1979 and built it into the world's largest management consulting firm. He retired from PCA in 1991 and founded Career IV, Inc., to concentrate on helping executives become better leaders. Phil Crosby has the background, experience, and knowledge to fit our needs for a quality expert. A number of discussions about this text resulted in forming an author team that had real-world experience, teaching experience, dedication to the quality concept, and an interest in providing management knowledge that was current, needed, and relevant. Phil joined our team and has been a guiding light in developing the text. He has become a friend who continually provides straightforward advice. We believe that our unique team, with the able help of our Richard D. Irwin associates, has produced an up-to-date, teachable, and stimulating book.

In this text, the planning, organizing, leading, and control functions are covered with a distinct emphasis on quality and competitiveness issues, problems, and solutions. Contrary to popular belief, we propose that the United States still has a preeminent competitive position in many industries relative to any other nation. In fact, we believe that, in most service industries, American firms have no equals. In part, this preeminence is sustained because of how managers do their jobs. It isn't an American birthright to have an advantage in some industries, and there's no guarantee that other nations won't become dominant. Managers in other nations are rapidly catching up to Americans in how they use their skills and knowledge to diagnose situations, to solve problems, to work with other people, and to evaluate their applications. In fact, there are now numerous examples of non-American managers who are more proficient at planning, organizing, leading, and controlling than their American counterparts. Whether the student reading this book is an American or a non-American, he or she will learn that quality and competitiveness are goals that must become ingrained in the job of managing for organizations to be successful.

This new edition updates and provides new examples, illustrates new workplace trends, and introduces new cases and realistic situations that managers face daily. The changes were made with improved student understanding and appreciation of the challenges that occur continuously within organizations of all sizes in every industry. For managers to deal with these challenges, they must understand the need to problem solve. Managers are not able to passively sit and wait for solutions to appear. Instead, as this edition emphasizes with example after example, proactive managing is the rule rather than the exception.

Learning Tools

This book attempts to build vocabulary, to improve understanding about the job of management, and to provide applications that illustrate the manager's involvement with other people both inside and outside the organization.

Each chapter is filled with real-world examples and elements to make the reading and learning more enjoyable and more interactive. Thus the student is encouraged to become involved with the chapter content and the elements. In keeping with the spirit of the text, the chapter elements will place in the forefront quality and competitiveness, the global nature of management, the workforce's increasing diversity, the ethical context of managing, the relevance of managing effectively in any society, and the role managing will play in the 21st century.

The emphasis on student learning starts with the specific learning objectives that open each chapter. The learning objectives are followed by the various elements listed below, which are designed to reinforce learning and provide real-world applications.

OPENING QUALITY ISSUE - Each chapter begins with a real-world story that relates to quality. These vignettes are intended to help students pause and focus on matters that managers constantly have to think about. There are no specific answers provided—only thoughts and dilemmas. A few of the opening quality issues are:

❖ TQM and Ethics: A Natural Fit, p. 57
❖ CAI Successfully Launches Service Quality Program, p. 151
❖ Getting Started with Less: Today's Entrepreneurs Use Outsourcing, p. 501

GLOBAL EXCHANGE - In each chapter the *Global Exchange* highlights a global situation, issue, problem, or decision faced by managers. Examples include:

❖ Practicing Porter's Competitive Advantage Strategies, p. 51
❖ Global Network Organizations, p. 233
❖ Software Innovation: America versus Europe, p. 547

WHAT MANAGERS ARE READING - Managers attend workshops and seminars and, somehow, occasionally find time to read books to help them do a better job. New in this edition is an element that introduces some of the popular press books that managers have found interesting and helpful. Some of the featured titles are:

❖ *Paradigms and Parables: The Ten Commandments for Ethics in Business*, by Brother Louis Dethomasis and William Ammentorp, p. 82
❖ *The World in 2020: Power Culture and Prosperity*, by Hamish McRae, p. 107
❖ *The Road Ahead*, by Bill Gates, p. 538

ETHICS SPOTLIGHT - Managers constantly face ethical dilemmas and situations. Ethical standards can be established by an organization, but ethical behaviors are exerted by people. The differences in how people face or see a situation are important to consider when evaluating how well a manager performs. A few of the *Ethics Spotlights* are:

❖ Are Layoffs Necessary? p. 227
❖ Driving Out Fear, p. 243
❖ Microsoft's Strategy Unethical? p. 546

DIVERSITY SCOPE - Today's workforce doesn't look, think, or behave like the workforce of the past, nor does it hold the same values. Managing these differences and being able to achieve world-class product and service quality is a significant challenge. *Diversity Scopes* include:

❖ Three Important Questions about Affirmative Action, p. 265
❖ New Multicultural Workplace Raises Morality Issues, p. 476

REFLECTIONS BY PHILIP B. CROSBY - In various chapters a brief experience or story has been written by Philip B. Crosby expressly for this textbook. Phil Crosby has consulted with hundreds of firms, worked as a quality vice president, and trained thousands of individuals. The *Reflections* element provides the reader with Phil Crosby's no-nonsense, straightforward viewpoints. His relevant, real-world-anchored, stimulating discussions bring the quality and competitiveness theme to life. As the *Reflections* will illustrate, Phil Crosby insists that quality has to be woven into the very fabric of the operation. He firmly believes that a firm's management cadre can make quality the core of the firm or they can cause the absolute failure of any work and effort to instill quality. As you read the *Reflections*, think carefully about what Phil Crosby is encouraging future managers to do in terms of quality.

WORKPLACE OF TOMORROW - Selected features and/or concluding paragraphs in many chapters explore new trends that are reshaping today's workplace, such as:

❖ Ethics in the Digital Age, p. 71
❖ Here comes the Horizontal Organization, p. 172
❖ The Informated Workplace, p. 201

SUMMARY OF LEARNING OBJECTIVES - These summaries provide clear, concise views of the learning objectives, giving students a quick reference point for reviewing the major concepts included in the chapter.

REVIEW, DISCUSSION, AND APPLICATION QUESTIONS - These questions are also keyed to the learning objectives. Students can test themselves in terms of their recall and understanding of the chapter concepts, as well as their ability to apply them in realistic situations.

CASES - There are generally two cases in each chapter. One case is a standard case that presents information about a firm and managerial problems that must be solved. The second case is accompanied by a video for in-class viewing and discussion. The video case brings into clear view how problems occur and are addressed by managers. The cases, like the chapters, deal with dilemmas managers face. There are no "canned" or "right" answers for any of the questions. Instead the cases are intended to help students probe, diagnose, and creatively face dilemmas and problems.

APPLICATION EXERCISE - Each chapter includes an *Application Exercise*. These student involvement exercises should increase student self-assessment, self-learning, and team interaction. Each exercise relates to a topic in the chapter. Samples include:

❖ Managerial Behavior Assessment: A Look at Yourself, p. 27
❖ Rokeach Value Survey, p. 87
❖ Team Planning, p. 180

KEY TERMS - Throughout the chapters, glossary entries appear in the margin. These highlight key terms and are part of the vocabulary-building objective. A list of key terms with page references appears at the end of each chapter. A complete glossary is included at the end of the book.

SUPPLEMENTS

The value of supplements to improve understanding and learning is a major concern of the author team. Thus developing a stimulating, integrative, and user-friendly supplement package was a top priority. As experienced authors and teachers of management, we know how instructors and students benefit from a well-integrated supplement package. Each part of the package was developed with the student and instructor in mind.

INSTRUCTOR'S MANUAL - Prepared by Jon Kalinowski of Mankato State University. The Instructor's Manual contains a lecture outline for each chapter as well as answer keys and support materials for all questions, cases, and exercises in the student text. Supplemental cases are also provided for each chapter.

TEST BANK - Prepared by Anna M. McCormick, West Virginia Institute of Technology. The test bank contains over 2,500 true/false, multiple choice, scenario, and essay questions. Each question carries a text page reference and is classified according to level of difficulty.

COMPUTERIZED TESTING SOFTWARE - The most recent version of Irwin's test-generation software, this program includes advanced features such as allowing the instructor to add and edit questions on-line, save and reload tests, create up to 99 versions of each test, attach graphics to questions, import and export ASCII files, and select questions based on type, level of difficulty, or key word. The program allows password protection of saved test and question databases, and is networkable. This software will be available for use on IBM, IBM compatibles, and Macintosh computers.

VIDEOS - A set of 20 videos is available to complement individual text chapters. Many of these videos feature companies students will recognize and relate to, such as Ben & Jerry's, Specialized Bicycle, and Heavenly Ski Resort. In addition, a set of quality videos created by Philip Crosby Associates, Inc., is available exclusively to adopters of this text. These videos show Philip Crosby in a recent public appearance and examine eight organizations that have benefited from the application of his concepts.

POWERPOINT® PRESENTATION SOFTWARE - Prepared by Kim A. Stewart, University of Denver. Over 200 slides are provided, containing key elements from the text as well as additional lecture material. These slides are also available in a color acetate and transparency master package.

Acknowledgments

Excellent books and supplements don't simply happen. It takes a lot of hard work by the authors, publisher, and reviewers to produce a quality product. The authors had a concept, and Richard D. Irwin's managers had the confidence to review, help modify, and produce the book. We want to personally thank a number of Irwin partners on this project. Kurt Strand helped steer the entire course.

One Irwin partner stands out as a beacon light showing the way as she removed obstacles and insisted on a package that can make a difference. Laura Hurst Spell was invaluable in guiding each edition of this book from its inception to its use in classrooms.

One final thank you is extended to Jeff Cunningham, publisher, *Forbes* magazine, who expressed interest in the original idea. He also helped us make contact with Phil Crosby.

Our expression of thanks for all the help, suggestions, and reviews includes many people. Reviewers of various drafts and parts of the manuscript include:

Mary Jo Boehms, Jackson State Community College

C. Richard Bartlett, Muskingum Tech

Donna E. Bush, Middle Tennessee State University

David Chown, Mankato State University

Ron A DiBattista, Bryant College

Joseph Gray, Nassau Community College

Stanley D. Guzell, Youngstown State University

Nell Tabor Hartley, Robert Morris College

Ken Hess, Anoka-Ramsey Community College

Donna Leonowich, Middlesex Community College

Linda Livingstone, Baylor University

Diana Page, The University of West Florida

Leonard Reich, Colby College

Mary L. Tucker, Colorado State University

Richard J. Vorwerk, Governor's State University

A special thanks to Tom Duening, who made contributions to many chapters and parts of the finished product. Tom did exceptional work updating and working on various chapters and elements making them up to date and interesting.

We also would like to thank our assistants, each of whom put up with pressing requests, telephone and fax messages by the hundreds, mailing schedules, and, at times, specific deadlines. Thank you, Jacque Franco, Ginger Roberts, and Eva Azzam (all of the University of Houston), and Ernestine Barnes (University of Kentucky).

Unfortunately, any list of acknowledgments is usually incomplete and inadequate. We hope that everyone who helped or contributed to this new edition knows that his or her efforts are appreciated. The authors, as with any book, are responsible for not only acknowledgment oversights, but also for any errors in the text.

Brief Table of Contents

Table of Contents

PART 2

Planning 113

6. PLANNING 150

7. STRATEGY 182

PART 3

Organizing 209

8. ORGANIZATIONAL STRUCTURE AND DESIGN 210

PART 4

Leading 291

PART 5   # Controlling 387

15. CONTROL SYSTEMS 388

PART 6   Growth, Technology, and Innovation 499

19. ENTREPRENEURSHIP AND GROWTH 500

20. TECHNOLOGY AND INNOVATION 526

APPENDIX A   THE BALDRIGE AWARD 557

APPENDIX B   SEVEN TOOLS OF QUALITY CONTROL 565

GLOSSARY 569

ENDNOTES 583

PHOTO CREDITS 603

INDEXES 605

PART 1

Managing and the Environment

CHAPTER 1

The Management Challenge

After studying this chapter, you should be able to:

❖ Define the terms management, competitiveness. and quality.

❖ Explain why a quality focus has become imperative in a globalizing world.

❖ Identify what are called the traditional functions of management.

❖ Describe how competitiveness (at the national level) is impacted by the quality of products produced in a country.

❖ Explain the types of skills that managers need to achieve their goals.

❖ List the types of managers within organizations.

❖ Discuss the suggestion that management's traditional methods must be changed.

❖ Define zero defects and tell at what stage of organizational maturity this concept becomes part of a firm's culture.

Quality Management Is Still a Winning Managerial Practice

Books, CDs, technical reports, consulting reports, seminars, professional meetings, and speeches about business management usually point to a panacea to solve problems. Since about 1945, the material written about new management labels, fads, and quick fixes could fill entire rooms. Some of the broader concepts that have found their way into common acceptance are: (1) management involves using art and science, (2) people are the most crucial resource in an institution, (3) quality pays for itself, and (4) stick to what you do well in terms of a product or a service. It is difficult to measure the precise impact of most management ideas, but there appear to be some valuable lessons embedded in most of the management communication that practicing managers are asked to consider.

The idea that studying management could help managers and was a practice, like medicine, didn't even exist in the early 1950s. Peter Drucker, a management professor and consultant published a classic book in 1955, *The Practice of Management.* Once companies such as General Electric and DuPont started to think about management as a practice, changes were made in the way people were recruited, selected, motivated, and trained. Drucker's writings influenced managers to consider strategy, delegation of authority, and managing people—not just the business. Drucker's work influenced a shift away from top-down authoritarian management. Empowering employees to think and work on job design and workflow improvements became a new way of managing.

In his book *The Fifth Discipline,* Pete Senge, a management consultant in the 1990s, provided a plan for empowering people in organizations and discussed why motivating people is good for a firm.

An idea that had an apostle and has had a lasting impact on how managers practice is quality pays for itself. W. Edwards Deming, an

W. Edwards Deming

American engineer and consultant, emphasized the importance of quality. On June 24, 1980, he appeared on the NBC show about Japanese quality programs called "If Japan Can, Why Can't We?" A manager at Ford Motors happened to be watching and brought many of Deming's quality improvement ideas to Ford. The result was Team Taurus, a quality-driven project that helped Ford turn itself around. This project eventually resulted in the development of the company's best-selling car.

After this 1980 wake-up call, quality as an important concept spread throughout the Untied States. Deming passed away in 1994; Joseph Juran, another co-founder of the quality improvement concept in the United States, gave his last lecture tour in 1995. Is quality now a forgotten or declining issue. Not according to customers of products and service firms who claim again and again that quality is an important attribute in making a purchase or use decision.

This book will illustrate that quality management and improvement are important management practices that are crucial for survival. Customers have demanded that quality be designed into products before they are manufactured and that quality be a part of every service delivery system. Today, throughout the world, quality is a managerial priority that must be continually reviewed and improved.

Source: Adapted from Robin Cooper and W. Bruce Chew, "Control Tomorrow's Costs Through Today's Designs," *Harvard Business Review,* January-February 1996, 88–97; Brian Dumaine, "Distilled Wisdom: Buddy, Can You Paradigm?" *Fortune,* May 15, 1995, 205–206; and "The Straining of Quality," *The Economist,* January 14, 1995, 55–56.

The opening vignette sets up the quality concept as a centerpiece for this chapter and the rest of the book. Managers have historically played a significant role in Western organizations and must now be at the forefront in Eastern Europe and other developing countries. A nation's economic strength is tied to the talents, knowledge, and understanding of managers. The exact mix of needed talent is changing. This chapter blends traditional management thinking with a new, needed emphasis on quality and competitiveness. The study and practice of management have moved beyond simply presenting the principles of planning, organizing, controlling, and leading. It now focuses on understanding and coping with competition and the demands for better-quality products and services. This change in emphasis to global competition and quality is highlighted in this chapter and throughout the book.

Here's a little story to help us begin. On an aircraft carrier on the high seas, a little blip suddenly appeared in the radar screen. The admiral on the carrier instructed the radio operator, "Tell that ship to change its course 15 degrees." A message came back on the radio. "You change your course 15 degrees." The admiral said, "Tell that ship that we are the United States Navy and to change its course 15 degrees." Again the message came back, "You change your course 15 degrees." Now flustered, the admiral himself got on the radio and said, "I am an admiral in the U.S. Navy. Change your course 15 degrees." The word came back, "You change your course 15 degrees—I am a lighthouse."

This parable reflects the views presented throughout this text. We believe that managers in the United States—once the undisputed power of the high seas of economic competition—must shift their course. Organizations, management practices, and management education must all be changed to meet the challenges of our increasingly globalized world. A new pattern of transacting business, operating organizations, and servicing customers has emerged throughout the world. U.S. managers must learn new skills, adapt traditional techniques, and become much more flexible to cope with competition from other nations and foreign managers. To be competitive, American institutions must become revitalized and committed to quality.

Rather than focusing on U.S. problems such as soaring national debt, crime, and legal and health care costs, not to mention a deteriorating infrastructure, we'll focus on management. These significant problems all require management and leadership, but they aren't the focus of this book. The United States today is still the country the rest of the world emulates. By most measures, the past 50 years have shown solid economic achievement for the United States in total growth, industrial production, job creation, and increase in personal income. But this achievement has slowed down in the past 10 years. Japan, Germany, and a handful of other nations have competed effectively with the United States. In the past 50 years, the militarily vanquished (Japan and Germany) and economically weak (South Korea, Taiwan, Hong Kong, and Singapore) have become economic powers.

COMPETITIVENESS

competitiveness
The degree to which a nation/organization can, under free and fair market conditions, produce goods and services that meet the test of domestic and/or international markets while simultaneously maintaining or expanding the real incomes of its citizens.

Japan and Germany's emergence as major economic powers has led to much discussion of competitiveness. Can the United States compete effectively with these new powers? First, let's define national and organizational **competitiveness** as *the degree to which a nation can, under free and fair market conditions, produce goods and services that meet the test of international markets while simultaneously maintaining or expanding the real incomes of its citizens.*[1]

Then we can alter the national definition to fit an individual organization such as IBM, Nike, The Limited, or General Electric by inserting the company's name for *nation* and the words *employees and owners* for *citizens*. Our new, company-specific definition of competitiveness converts the focus to the factory, office, or shop. How effectively can workers produce a car? Can they produce a high-quality product with the resources on hand? Is one firm's service better than service from the business across the street or across the ocean?

Since World War II the world has been shrinking. Transportation systems have speeded up. Telecommunications advances have linked all parts of the world electronically. National companies serving domestic markets have accepted the reality of a global marketplace. Global interconnectedness is the result of the shrinking world.

Two significant events have set the stage for our entry into the 21st century. First, due to growing foreign competition, *quality* became a major competitive approach. Excellent products and services became the standard established in Japan as well as Singapore, Germany, and France. In such industries as computers, telecommunications, machine tools, robots, medicine, and aerospace quality is vital to an organization's success and survival. Domestic and global markets demand that the highest quality and best price be top priorities.

The Soviet Union and Eastern Europe's collapse in the early 1990s is the second significant event. Their political and social collapse uncovered poor-quality products and services and environmental degradation. Russia and other Eastern European countries must address the quality factor if they are ever to become world-class competitors.

Chapter 20 details the link between quality and competitiveness in terms of technology and innovation. Quality's importance in a rapidly globalizing world appears throughout the book. Whether to improve quality is no longer an option for firms that want to remain competitive. The only option is how to properly manage the shift to quality so that opportunities to remain competitive are taken in a timely fashion.

To be globally competitive, managers must be aware of competition, allocate time and attention to quality, and maintain an organizational environment conducive to flexibility and change. In the United States, Japan, Germany, and elsewhere, competition is maintained via sound management with an emphasis on quality. It is not enough to think in terms of only applying management principles. Competition is now so intense that it stimulates a more aggressive approach to managing employees and improving quality. Unfortunately, rising competition can result in unethical behavior. The Ethics Spotlight illustrates this danger. Managers must learn how to compete ethically with domestic and foreign firms.

Competitiveness and Ethics

Ethics and competitiveness are inseparable. No society can compete globally while its people are stealing from each other, with every squabble ending in litigation or with threats that the end of our way of living is close at hand. Some Americans have turned the competitiveness issue into a litmus test of economic loyalty, by urging us to "buy American." The United States is suggested to be the bastion of democracy, free enterprise, and confidence. When we're told to buy American, is it an ethical imperative, a moral obligation, or a patriotic assignment?[2]

Technological prowess is no longer synonymous with good old Yankee know-how. But America remains one of the world's most innovative countries, as seen from its success in many high-tech businesses from satellites to software. The United States spends more on science than any other country; its scientists publish more scientific papers than the European Community and Japan combined.

So why is there a call to buy American? Are Americans who make these calls knowledgeable about global economy? What is an American product? Secretary of Labor Robert B. Reich believes that almost any product weighing more than 10 pounds and costing more than $10 is a global composite, combining parts or services from many different nations.

Competition has created combative adversaries in many industries. No-holds-barred competition for human resources, ideas, innovations, data, and market information has led to numerous instances of illegal behavior and many unethical procedures. Beating "them" (e.g., a competitor, the Japanese, the government, the Internal Revenue Service) is an obsession in some organizations.

It came as a shock to a large U.S. manufacturer of medical supplies when a Japanese competitor, Kokoku Rubber Industry, was boosting output at a new plant in Kentucky. The U.S. firm had to cut prices drastically as it struggled to survive. Kokoku had gathered information (intelligence) for years from legal sources (newspapers) about its U.S. competitor. Kokoku used information gathering to gain an edge and beat the competition.

Intelligence involves gathering information about competitors and customers. It ranges from Kokoku's methods (reading, filing, and analyzing published reports and data) to illegal spying. The heat of competition unfortunately has spawned more and more illegal and unethical intelligence gathering.

Companies have been known to sift through competitors' garbage to find information. Others have instructed executives (using disguised names or positions) to take competitors' plant tours just to acquire information. Kellogg has stopped granting plant tours because competitors were observing and collecting information on manufacturing technology.

Is intelligence gathering necessary? Most firms would state that gathering intelligence in a legal manner is part of management's fiduciary responsibility to its employees, shareholders, and customers.

Ethical methods of intelligence gathering include review of public documents, financial report analysis, legitimate employment interviews with people who worked for a competitor, attending trade fairs, market surveys, and analyzing competitors' products and services.

Unethical intelligence gathering has taken many routes: bribery, planting spies in a competitor's business, wire tapping, theft, blackmail, and extortion.

Cordis Corporation, a Miami-based heart pacemaker manufacturer, introduced a superior product. Sales, however, worsened. Cordis management was baffled by the lack of positive response to its superior product, but found that competitors were offering physicians cars, boats, and trips to use their pacemakers. Cordis responded by increasing educational support for doctors, by adding salespeople so that more time could be spent explaining the product to physicians, and by giving doctors additional medical equipment if they purchased the pacemakers. This dramatically increased sales. Cordis took the high road and responded to unethical behavior with a set of steps that by most standards were ethical.

Intelligence gathering is now part of competition. But will the methods be ethical or unethical? Each person making a decision on how to conduct intelligence gathering must answer this question.

Source: Adapted from Richard S. Teitebaum, "The New Race for Intelligence," *Forbes*, November 2, 1992, pp. 104–7; and Patrick E. Murphy and Gene R. Lacznack, "Emerging Ethical Issues Facing Marketing Researchers," *Marketing Research*, June 1992, pp. 6–11.

Today talking about buying American is a deceptive statement. If you want to buy American, you can't drive a Chevrolet Lumina sedan (assembled in Canada), eat at Burger King (British-owned), or watch a Columbia Pictures movie (Japanese-owned). A Chrysler Eagle Summit made at Mitsubishi's Diamond-Star Motors plant in Normal, Illinois, contains 52 percent U.S. parts, while a Toyota Camry made in Georgetown, Kentucky, has 74 percent American parts. What constitutes an American part? The question can become ridiculous. Is it where the ore was mined or where the steel was forged?

The "buy American" argument is hard to resolve. Making it a patriotic issue seems farfetched in a rapidly globalizing world. "Which is better," Reich asks, "a product involving 100 workers, 80 of whom are in Singapore making $100 a month or 20 of whom are in Tennessee making $500 a week?" Or a product in which 80 jobs are in the United States paying minimum wages or 20 in Japan involving high-tech research and development, paying good wages? Location means jobs and standard of living.

Quality Standards and the Baldrige Award

Managing effectively is important in achieving or sustaining competitive advantages. Certainly a host of national problems need to be solved to make the United States more competitive globally. However, management and managers also must ethically address competition among firms. Quality appears to be a competitive standard that managers need to continuously address. With the support of American industry, in 1988 Congress established the Malcolm Baldrige National Quality Award. This award stresses that American managers need to pay more attention to the quality of products and services that their enterprises sell or provide. (See Appendix A at the end of this book.) U.S. companies that excel in quality achievement and quality management receive the award. Past winners include Globe Metallurgical, Inc., IBM Rochester, Federal Express, and Milliken Co.

Congressman Don Fuqua (D-Florida) first introduced a bill to establish a national quality award in 1986. This later became the Baldrige Award, whose purpose is to stimulate American business, government, and other organizations to attain excellence through improved and superior quality. The award was named after Secretary of Commerce Malcolm Baldrige, who constantly wanted to improve the U.S. competitive position in the world.

Malcolm Baldrige was nominated as secretary of commerce by President Ronald Reagan on December 11, 1980, and confirmed by the United States Senate on January 22, 1981.

During his tenure, Baldrige played a major role in developing and carrying out administration trade policy. He took the lead in resolving difficulties in technology transfers with China and India. Baldrige held the first cabinet-level talks with the Soviet Union in seven years, which paved the way for increased access by U.S. firms to the Soviet market. He was highly regarded by the world's preeminent leaders.

Leading the administration's effort to pass the Export Trading Company Act of 1982, Baldrige was named by the president to chair a cabinet-level trade strike force to search out unfair trading practices and recommend ways to end those practices. He was the leader in the reform of the nation's antitrust laws.

Baldrige's award-winning managerial excellence contributed to long-term improvement in the economy and the efficiency and effectiveness of government. Within the Commerce Department, Baldrige reduced the budget by more than 30 percent and administrative personnel by 25 percent.

Baldrige worked during his boyhood as a ranch hand and earned several awards as a professional team roper on the rodeo circuit. He was Professional Rodeo Man of the Year in 1980 and was installed in the National Cowboy Hall of Fame in Oklahoma City in 1984.

Malcolm Baldrige died July 25, 1987, in a rodeo accident in California. His service as secretary of commerce was one of the longest in history. He was possibly the most colorful secretary of commerce and one of the most beloved.[3]

The Baldrige Award has stimulated debate over its impact on organizational practices and customer satisfaction.[4] The award was designated (1) to raise the consciousness level of enterprise leaders regarding quality and (2) to provide a comprehensive framework for measuring quality efforts of businesses. On both counts, the Baldrige Award has been exceptionally good. Yet some critics urge expanding the judging criteria to include innovation, financial performance, ethics, and environmental management.[5]

As with any award or change, there are going to be critics. It's generally agreed, however, that the Baldrige Award has focused more attention on quality among business leaders, government officials, academics, and administrators in nonprofit organizations. The criteria of the award have influenced American management's 21st-century agenda like no other quality idea, technique, or program.

ISO 9000

ISO 9000 is a quality guideline established by the International Organization for Standardization (ISO). The European Community has set formal quality standards such as ISO 9000 as a baseline for designing products and receiving certification that products meet these quality standards. These standards indicate whether manufacturing plants and service organizations implement and document sound quality procedures.

Fifty trading countries, including the United States, now use ISO 9000. It's expected that certification based on these international quality standards will eventually become mandatory for most manufacturers seeking global markets. Companies that don't adopt the ISO

9000 standards risk their ability to trade with foreign partners. Manufacturers in the United States making products for the National Aeronautics and Space Administration, Department of Defense, Federal Aviation Administration, and Food and Drug Administration must meet ISO 9000 standards, discussed further in Chapter 3.

Awards and standards are excellent as stimuli, but it's managers and workers who create competitive, high-quality products and services. Developed nations and organizations must compete through their human resources, technology, and innovations. If we had to choose which is more crucial, the answer would be human resources—the managers and workers in organizations.

MANAGEMENT AND MANAGERS DEFINED

organization
An administrative and functional structure that can be as small as a one-person operation or as large as more than 1 million employees.

The three dominant world economies—the United States, Japan, and Germany—are propelled by organizations operated by managers. An **organization** can be a one-person operation or have more than 700,000 employees, like General Motors. The urban industrial economy that emerged in the United States in this century relied on extensive investments in both machine and human capital. **Managers** helped to plan, organize, lead, and control the organizations that led to the urban industrial economy. Today they direct or oversee the work and performance of other individuals.

managers
The individuals who guide, direct, or oversee the work and performance of other individuals.

Management as a Process
Have you ever said, "This is a poorly managed firm," "Management is totally incompetent," or "Management is really on top of everything"? If so, what did your statements mean? They imply that (1) management is some type of work and (2) sometimes the activities are performed quite well and sometimes not so well.

Management is a *process* involving certain functions and work activities that managers must perform to achieve the goals of an enterprise. Managers use principles in managing that guide them in this process.

Management as a Discipline
Designating management as a discipline implies that it's an accumulated body of knowledge that can be learned by study. Thus management is a subject with principles, concepts, and theories. We study management to understand these principles, concepts, and theories and to learn how to apply them in the process of managing.

Management as People
Whether you say, "That company has an entirely new management team," or "She's the best manager I've ever worked for," you're referring to the people who guide, direct, and thus manage organizations. The word *management* used in this manner refers to the people (*managers*) who engage in the process of management. Managers are the people primarily responsible for seeing that work gets done in an organization.

The perspective of management as people has another meaning. It refers to and emphasizes the importance of the workers whom managers work with and manage in accomplishing an organization's objectives. People are an organization's lifeblood. Without people, there's no such thing as a profitable firm or a successful new product launch.

Management as a Career
"Joe Cardenas is on the fast track in our quality improvement division. He has held three management positions and is now, after 10 years, being promoted to the vice president level." Joe has moved through a sequence of jobs on a career path. He has a management career.

The different meanings and interpretation of the term *management* can be related as follows: *People* who wish to have a *career* as a manager must study the *discipline* of management as a means toward practicing the *process* of management. Thus, we define **management** as the process undertaken by one or more persons to coordinate the work activities of other persons, capital, materials, and technologies to achieve high-*quality* results not attainable by any one person acting alone.

QUALITY

The definition of management includes the term *quality*. The quality concept will be at the core of this entire book. A Gallup survey of top executives showed that they viewed improving product and service quality as the most critical challenge facing companies.[6] These executives ranked quality improvement ahead of such issues as product liability, government regulations, and labor relations. Quality is now viewed as a major weapon in restoring and improving global competitive position of the United States. But note that *quality* is a globally accepted term and practice. The Global Exchange points out the international flavor of the original quality pioneers.

The word *quality* seems to trigger a multitude of definitions, so selecting a single definition is difficult. Table 1–1 presents an array of definitions, each of which is concise and meaningful. There seems to be no single correct or best definition. Each firm needs to

management
The process undertaken by one or more persons, capital, materials, and technologies to coordinate other persons' activities to achieve high-quality results not attainable by any one person acting alone.

GLOBAL EXCHANGE　　PIONEERS IN QUALITY

As indicated in this chapter's opening vignette, on June 24, 1980, NBC-TV aired "If Japan Can, Why Can't We?" The program examined how, from the ashes of World War II, Japan has risen to become an economic powerhouse. The show set America on a course to discover, rediscover, and incorporate quality. Long before NBC-TV broadcast it, a number of international pioneers had explained, discussed, and promoted quality. Their contributions have bettered products and services while encouraging leaders across all industries to make new commitments to quality.

- B. A. Fisher (British scientist and statistician) developed speedier and more productive crop-growing methods in the early 1900s.
- Walter A. Shewhart (American physicist) transformed Fisher's methods into a quality control discipline for factories.
- W. Edwards Deming (American mathematician and physicist) began making an impact in Japan in 1950. His view—published in *Out of the Crisis*—is based on 14 points including three quality ingredients: continual

improvement, constancy of purpose, and profound knowledge.
- Philip B. Crosby (American businessman and consultant) created the zero-defects movement at Martin Marietta in the 1960s and promotes the concept of doing it correctly the first time, which he states was used in the mid-1930s at Western Electric. He worked for ITT as vice president for quality and wrote the best-seller *Quality is Free* in 1979.
- J. M. Juran (American engineer and lawyer) first described his methods of total quality control in Japan in 1954. He claims that the three most important items in a quality program are that the top people be in charge, that people be trained in how to manage for quality, and that quality be improved at an unprecedented pace.
- Kaoru Ishikawa (Japanese businessman and consultant) instituted quality control circles in 1962 in Japan. His father (Ichiro Ishikawa) arranged for Deming to present quality ideas to Japanese leaders in 1950.
- Genichi Taguchi (Japanese consultant) produced the concept referred to as the Taguchi Loss Function: The further away a product is from being perfect, the greater the loss will be

from defects. (In contrast, the traditional view is that there's no loss so long as parts are within engineering specifications. For example, a part should be 500 millimeters wide, but the engineer states that if it's 495 to 505 millimeters wide, it's good enough.)
- Armand V. Feigenbaum (American businessman) was in charge of quality at General Electric. He developed the concepts of the cost of quality and total quality control beginning in the 1940s. He stressed the importance of the customer defining quality.

These and other quality gurus are widely published and some are often found on the lecture circuit. Hopefully, 10 years from now a list of globally oriented business leaders who implemented quality programs that met the test of time can be assembled.

Source: Adapted from R. Ray Gehani, "Quality Value-Chain: A Meta-Synthesis of Frontiers of Quality Movement." *Academy of Management Executive*, 27, no. 2, 1993, pp. 29–42: Lloyd Dobyns and Clare Crawford-Mason. *Quality or Else* (Boston: Houghton Mifflin, 1991), pp. 52–87; Ronald Yates, "Prophet of Boom," *Chicago Tribune Magazine*, February 16, 1992, pp. 16, 18, 20 and 22; and "The Quality Imperative," *Business Week* (bonus issue), October 25, 1991.

TABLE 1–1	DEFINITIONS OF QUALITY

Definitions of quality are personal and idiosyncratic. These concise, clear, and meaningful definitions are arranged by category of focus.

1. Manufacturing-based

"Quality [means] conformance to requirements."
   Philip B. Crosby

"Quality is the degree to which a specific product conforms to a design or specification."
   Harold L. Gilmore

2. Customer-based

"Quality is fitness for use."
   J. M. Juran

"Total Quality is performance leadership in meeting customer requirements by doing the right things right the first time."
   Westinghouse

Quality is meeting customer expectations. The Quality Improvement Process is a set of principles, policies, support structures, and practices designed to continually improve the efficiency and effectiveness of our way of life.
   AT&T

"You achieve customer satisfaction when you sell merchandise that doesn't come back and a customer who does."
   Stanley Marcus

3. Product-based

"Differences in quality amount to differences in the quantity of some desired ingredient or attribute."
   Lawrence Abbott

"Quality refers to the amount of the unpriced attribute contained in each unit of the priced attribute."
   Keith B. Leffler

4. Value-based

"Quality is the degree of excellence at an acceptable price and the control of variability at an acceptable cost."
   Robert A. Broh

"Quality means best for certain customer conditions. These conditions are (a) the actual use and (b) the selling price of the product."
   Armand V. Feigenbaum

5. Transcendent

"Quality is neither mind nor matter, but a third entity independent of the other two . . . even though Quality cannot be denied, you know what it is."
   Robert Pirsig

"A condition of excellence implying fine quality as distinct from poor quality . . . Quality is achieving or reaching the highest standard as against being satisfied with the sloppy or fraudulent."
   Barbara W. Tuchman

Source: *Fortune,* March 22, 1993. p. 21: and V. Daniel Hunt, *Quality in America* (Burr Ridge, Il.: Business One Irwin, 1992), p. 21.

quality

The totality of features and characteristics of a product or service that bear on the ability to satisfy stated or implied needs.

develop its own company-specific definition. For the purpose of this text, we will use the following definition: **Quality** is the totality of features and characteristics of a product or service that bear on the ability to satisfy stated or implied needs.[7] This definition suggests that quality must conform to requirements to satisfy the needs of users or anyone in contact with the product or service.

Eight Dimensions of Quality

Author and Harvard professor David A. Garvin developed a meaningful conceptual view of quality.[8] He suggested that the quality of a product or service is composed of the eight dimensions in Table 1–2.

Garvin's eight dimensions broaden the perspective of the quality concept. Customers, managers, engineers, line operators, and clerks at every level of an organization's hierarchy must be involved in enhancing and managing quality. Renowned quality expert W. Edwards Deming explains top managers' role in improving quality:

> *The job of top management is not supervision, but leadership. Management must work on sources of improvement, the intent of quality of product and of service, and on the translation of the intent into design and actual product. The required transformation of Western style of management requires that managers be leaders.[9]*

Philip B. Crosby and Zero Defects

Philip B. Crosby, who has taught more than 1,500 companies about quality, believes that it's the responsibility of management to improve quality. He introduced the **zero defects** concept as a way of making management believe that it doesn't have to accept defects. He proposes that no defects are acceptable. Crosby suggests that top management must make the commitment about zero defects and quality for the entire company. He proposes establishing quality improvement teams, quality measures for every activity, training in quality management, quality councils, and even a zero-defects day. The zero-defects day signals employees that the company has a new standard of quality.[10]

Table 1–3 presents Crosby's grid, which is a first step in determining a firm's current quality management profile. Six measures on the left examine the management's current style. Across the top are five levels or stages of quality management maturity—Stage I (Uncertainty) to Stage V (Certainty). Crosby believes that only at Stage V is conformance to a zero-defect culture (a set of beliefs, rituals, norms, and values) held throughout the firm. He believes that if the job is done correctly the first time (zero defects), quality's cost will be reduced to its lowest possible level.

The premise proposed by Crosby is that when managers practice the process of management (planning, organizing, controlling, and leading), they must include the quality concept. Quality must be considered, discussed, and learned like management's traditional functions. For example, a plan to develop and market a new product is incomplete without attention to quality dimensions such as conformance, performance, reliability, and perceptions of customers.

zero defects
A concept proposed by Philip Crosby whereby management believes that no defects are acceptable.

TABLE 1–2	GARVIN'S DIMENSIONS OF QUALITY

1. Performance—a product's/service's primary operating characteristic (e.g., a car's acceleration performance, the comfort of a user using long-wear contact lenses).

2. Features—add-ons or supplements (e.g., the student study guide for a course, power locks on a car).

3. Reliability—A probability of not malfunctioning or breaking down for a specified period of time (e.g., a 5-year, 60,000-mile warranty).

4. Conformance—the degree to which a product's design and operating characteristics meet established standards (e.g., a product test shows that the product is within 0.001 inches of the standard).

5. Durability—a measure of a product's life (e.g., 10 years).

6. Serviceability—the speed and ease of repair (e.g., a panel that can be replaced by an untrained user).

7. Aesthetics—a product's look, feel, taste, and smell (e.g., a rose has a delicate feel, a desired color, and a distinctive scent).

8. Perceived quality—quality as viewed by a customer, client or student (e.g., a parent uses a disposable diaper because it's sanitary, convenient, and reasonably priced).

TABLE 1-3	CROSBY'S QUALITY MANAGEMENT MATURITY GRID				
Measurement Categories	Stage I: Uncertainty	Stage II: Awakening	Stage III: Enlightenment	Stage IV: Wisdom	Stage V: Certainty
Management understanding and attitude	Fails to see quality as a management tool.	Supports quality management in theory but is unwilling to provide the necessary money or time.	Learns about quality management and becomes supportive.	Participates personally in quality activities.	Regards quality management as essential to the company's success.
Quality organization status	Quality activities are limited to the manufacturing or engineering department and are largely appraisal and sorting.	A strong quality leader has been appointed, but quality activities remain focused on appraisal and sorting and are still limited to manufacturing and engineering.	Quality department reports to top management. Its leader is active in company management.	Quality manager is an officer of the company. Prevention activities have become important.	Quality manager is on the board of directors. Prevention is the main quality activity.
Problem handling	Problems are fought as they occur and are seldom fully resolved; "fire-fighting" dominates.	Teams are established to attack major problems, but the approach remains short-term.	Problems are resolved in an orderly fashion, and corrective action is a regular event.	Problems are identified early in their development.	Except in the most unusual cases, problems are prevented.
Cost of quality as percentage of sales	Reported: unknown. Actual: 20%	Reported: 5% Actual: 18%	Reported: 8% Actual: 12%	Reported: 6.5% Actual: 8%	Reported: 2.5% Actual: 2.5%
Quality improvement actions	No organized activities.	Activities are motivational and short-term.	Implements the 14-step program with full understanding.	Continues the 14-step program and starts Make Certain	Quality improvement is a regular and continuing activity.
Summation of company quality posture	"We don't know why we have quality problems."	"Must we always have quality problems?"	"Because of management commitment and quality improvement programs, we are identifying and resolving our quality problems."	"We routinely prevent defects from occurring."	"We know why we don't have quality problems."

Source: Adapted from Philip B. Crosby, *Quality is Free* (New York: McGraw-Hill, 1979).

THE PROCESS OF MANAGEMENT PLUS QUALITY

The process of management usually consists of basic *management functions*. The traditional process of management identifies the functions as *planning, organizing*, and *controlling*, linked together by *leading*. Planning determines *what* results the organization will achieve; organizing specifies *how* it will achieve the results; and controlling determines *whether* the results are achieved.

Planning

The planning function is the capstone activity of management. **Planning** activities determine an organization's objectives and establish appropriate strategies for achieving them. A

planning
The function of management that determines an organization's objectives and establishes the appropriate strategies for achieving those objectives.

top-priority planning objective must be quality. The organizing, controlling, and leading functions all derive from planning in that these functions carry out the planning decisions.

Managers at every level of the organization do planning. Through their plans, managers outline what the organization must do to be successful. Although plans may differ in focus, they all concern achieving short- and long-term organizational goals. The authors of this text propose that short- and long-term quality goals must be paramount concerns. If quality goals are achieved, related goals (such as improved market share, cost containment, and return on investment) are easier to accomplish. Taken as a whole, an organization's plans are the primary tools for preparing for and dealing with changes in its environment.

Strategy is a multidimensional concept that provides a firm with direction, a sense of unity, and purpose. It's the integrative blueprint for the organization. Strategy gives rise to the plans that assure that quality and other goals are accomplished. Strategy is intended to achieve a sustainable competitive advantage over competitors. Strategy serves to obtain a match between the firm's external environment and internal capabilities. If a competing firm raises its quality, then the firm's strategy must address that environmental force.[11]

Organizing

After managers develop a strategy, objectives, and plans to achieve the objectives, they must design and develop an organization that can accomplish the objectives. Thus, the organizing function is to create a structure of task and authority relationships that improves and sustains quality.

The **organizing** function takes the tasks identified during planning and assigns them to individuals and groups within the organization so that objectives set by planning can be achieved. Organizing, then, involves turning plans into action. The organizing function also provides an organizational structure that enables the organization to function effectively as a cohesive whole and to achieve quality objectives.

organizing
The function of management that assigns the tasks identified during planning to individuals and groups within the organization so that objectives set by planning can be achieved.

Leading

Sometimes called *directing* or *motivating*, **leading** involves influencing organization members to perform in ways that accomplish the organization's objectives. As Deming pointed out, managers must be leaders who guide the way to improve product and service quality through workers' efforts.

The leading function focuses directly on the employees in the organization, since its major purpose is to channel human behavior toward organizational goals such as improved quality. Effective leadership is important in organizations. Some managers especially must develop this skill as global competitiveness grows.

leading
A function of managers who, by directing and motivating, influence organization members to perform in ways that accomplish the organization's objectives.

Controlling

Finally, a manager must make sure that the organization's actual performance conforms with the performance that was planned for it. This **controlling** function of management requires three elements: (1) established *standards* of performance, (2) *information* that indicates deviations between actual performance and the established standards, and (3) *action* to correct performance that doesn't meet the standards. Simply speaking, the purpose of management control is to make sure the organization stays on the quality path that it planned to follow.

controlling
A function of management that makes sure that the organization's actual performance conforms with the performance that was planned for it.

The four functions of management must be learned in the context of quality improvement and maintenance. Management functions and quality are related and shouldn't be separated. Performance of one function depends on the performance of the other functions. A plan requires leaders, an organization, and control to be properly carried out. If a plan fails to incorporate quality considerations, it will only be a matter of time until failure becomes the reality.

The Ford Edsel's failure highlights this point.[12] Plans for the Edsel's entry into the medium-price auto field were elaborate. The 1950s saw a growing trend toward medium-price cars: Pontiac, Oldsmobile, Buick, and Dodge. Marketing research led Ford to introduce

The Management Challenge: Quality and Competitiveness

Getting an organization to do things right the first time is obviously a good idea. Naturally it's cheapest to do something only once. Along those lines, it seems apparent that happy customers are a company's primary objective. Yet the conventional way of managing isn't automatically tilted toward these objectives. Management is full of "old wives tales"—ideas that are accepted as true without investigation. Management has its own agenda, which is usually very short-term oriented.

Executives used to tell me that I would bankrupt the company if I insisted on getting everything perfect. They had a vision of work slowing to a crawl while each step was inspected and tested several times. They talked about the perils of babying the customer. They wanted to grant permission to deliver materials and services that weren't absolutely correct—merely fit to be used.

People who talk about the good old days, when everything was done better, have selective memories. Nothing was made right the first time years ago—it was reworked until it was acceptable, which was part of the plan. Management knew in its heart that the problem was the workers, so they kept making systems to reduce labor's effect. This discouraged people and led to a self-fulfilling prophecy of even more separation of the workforce from product and service quality. I found myself trying to explain the people to the management and vice versa.

One day, when I was a quality engineer, I was asked to attend the monthly management review and say a few words about quality. I put on my good suit and appeared at the proper time, sitting in the back of the room. The meeting began with the comptroller breaking down revenue by product line and services. There was an animated discussion about each item, particularly those not meeting their objectives. Charts and discussion on profitability, inventory, employee compensation, purchasing, accounts receivable, and debt followed for three hours. Then the personnel director presented a new hospitalization plan. Next the industrial relations director talked about labor negotiations and the possibility of a strike. Then there was a pause.

The general manager checked his watch and noted that they had "invited Phil Crosby to come and talk about quality."

"We've used up most of the time, Phil," he said. "Could you limit your remarks to five minutes or so?"

I noticed that the attendees were busily putting their papers away and checking things out with each other. This wasn't going to be an attentive group, I thought, but I nodded and stood up.

When they quieted down I smiled and said, "Quality can be measured by money also. If we added up the expenses of doing things wrong and over—like rework, customer service, inspection, excess inventory, unplanned overtime, accounts receivable overdue, engineering change notices purchasing change notices, and such—it comes to over 20 percent of revenue. These are my figures put together without benefit of the accounting department, but I think if they're calculated properly the number will be much higher. Roughly the price of nonconformance, as I call it, is five times the pretax profit I saw reported earlier. Thank you."

When I sat down the group just stared at me. The general manager turned to the comptroller, "Five times pretax profits'?" he asked.

"Anyway," said the comptroller, "I've mentioned it before."

The meeting continued for another hour and ended with the price of nonconformance (PONC) becoming a regular part of the accounting and reporting process. From that moment on, management's interest in quality was focused; the old beliefs disappeared and were replaced by management attention on a management subject. They reduced the PONC expense by half in a year just by changing their attitude and attacking problems that measurement showed to be important. They even started talking to their employees.

Measure quality by money, not by statistics. Be real.

---

the Ford Edsel in 1958. But a $350 million loss on the Edsel resulted from such factors as a recession, poor promotion, and changing consumer preferences for even smaller cars. However, lack of quality was the Achilles heel of Ford's plans for the Edsel. Production was rushed to get the Edsel to market on schedule before numerous defects had been cleared up. Brakes failed, oil leaked, there were rattles, and the car didn't start properly. Edsel owners were driving an inferior product. Before these defects were corrected, the car became known as a lemon. The Edsel's poor quality became the storyline in many jokes, the standard for poor quality to many Americans.

Planning, organizing, controlling, and leading were all done at Ford. These functions were followed to the letter—a textbook example of "how to manage a product from an idea to the market." Unfortunately, quality wasn't the primary objective or the driving focal point in the management process. The Edsel clearly illustrates the need to integrate the functions of management with an overriding quality umbrella.

MANAGERS

A successful manager possesses certain qualities in applying skills and carrying out various managerial roles. A study by Harbridge House, a Boston consulting firm, identified 10 qualities of a successful manager regardless of age, sex, industry, organization size, or corporate culture.[13]

1. *Provides clear direction.* An effective manager needs to establish explicit goals and standards for people. Managers must communicate group goals, not just individual goals. The manager must involve people in setting these goals and not simply state them to workers. Managers must be clear and thorough in delegating responsibility.

2. *Encourages open communication.* Managers must be candid in dealing with people. They must be honest and direct. "People want straight information from their bosses," the study says, "and managers must establish a climate of openness and trust."

3. *Coaches and supports people.* This means being helpful to others, working constructively to correct performance problems, and going to bat with superiors for subordinates.

4. *Provides objective recognition.* Managers must recognize employees for good performance more often than they criticize them for problems. Rewards must be related to the quality of job performance, not seniority or personal relationships. "Most managers don't realize how much criticism they give," the study says. "They do it to be helpful, but positive recognition is what really motivates people."

5. *Establishes ongoing controls.* This means following up on important issues and actions and giving subordinates feedback.

6. *Selects the right people to staff the organization.* Attracting and selecting the best people in terms of skills and competencies to accomplish the firm's mission and goals.

7. *Understands the financial implications of decisions.* This quality is considered important even for functional managers, such as those in personnel/human resources and research and development, who have no direct responsibility for the profit margin.

8. *Encourages innovation and new ideas.* Employees rate this quality important in even the most traditional or conservative organizations.

9. *Gives subordinates clear-cut decisions when they're needed.* "Employees want a say in things," the report says, "but they don't want endless debate. There's a time to get on with things, and the best managers know when that time comes."

10. *Consistently demonstrates a high level of integrity.* The study shows that most employees want to work for a manager they can respect.

TYPES OF MANAGERS

The history of Dell Computers in Austin, Texas, reveals management's evolution from one entrepreneur (Michael Dell) to a team of many managers with many subordinates. The development of different types of managers is a result of this evolution. Let's assume that the firm is successful, and the manager decides to add some new products and sell them to new markets. As the manager becomes overworked because of his or her job's increased complexity, he or she may decide to specialize *vertically* by assigning the task of supervising subordinates to another person (Figure 1–1) or *horizontally* by assigning certain tasks, such as production or marketing, to another person (Figure 1–2). Whichever method is chosen, the management process is now shared, specialized, and thus more complex.

First-Line Management

These managers coordinate the work of others—workers—who aren't themselves managers. People at the **first-line management** level are often called *supervisors, office managers, or foremen.* The first-line manager may oversee the work of blue-collar workers, salespeople, accounting clerks, or scientists, depending on the subunit's particular tasks (for example, production, marketing, accounting, or research). First-line managers are responsible for the organization's basic work and are in daily or near-daily contact with

first-line management
Managers, also known as supervisors, office managers, or foremen, who coordinate the work of others who aren't managers (subordinates).

Since the beginning of Dell Computers, Michael Dell's role has changed dramatically—from one entrepreneur to the leader of several levels of managers.

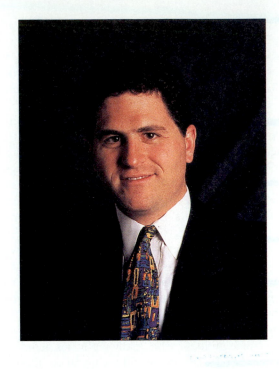

workers. They must work with their own workers and with other first-line supervisors whose tasks are related to their own.

Middle Management

The middle manager is known in many organizations as the department manager, plant manager, or director of operations. Unlike first-line managers, those in **middle management** plan, organize, control, and lead other managers' activity; yet, like first-line managers, they're subject to the managerial efforts of a superior. The middle manager coordinates the work activity (for example, marketing) of a subunit.

In the past ten years many middle managers in firms such as Sears, General Motors, Xerox, IBM, and General Dynamics have been laid off. Organizations like these have downsized the management cadre especially at the middle management level. Changes in the environment, competitive pressures, cost overruns, lost market share, and inefficiencies in operations have resulted in the move to downsize. The shrinkage of management in large companies is expected to continue into the 21st century.

middle management
Managers, also known as departmental managers, plant managers, or directors of operations, who plan, organize, lead, and control other managers' activities and who themselves are subject to a supervisor's managerial efforts.

FIGURE 1—1
Vertical Specialization of the Management Process

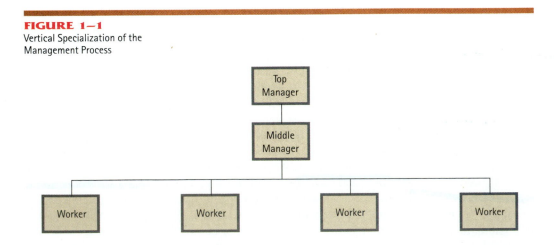

FIGURE 1–2
Horizontal Specialization
of the Management Process

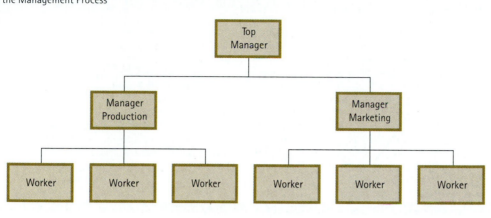

Top Management

A small cadre of managers (usually including a chief executive officer, president, or vice president) constitutes **top management**. Top management is responsible for the performance of the entire organization through the middle managers. Unlike other managers, the top manager is accountable to none other than the owners of the resources used by the organization.[14] Of course, top-level managers depend on the work of all their subordinates to accomplish the organization's goals and mission.

The designations *top, middle,* and *first-line* classify managers on the basis of their vertical rank in the organization. Completing a task usually requires completing several interrelated activities. As these activities are identified, and as the responsibility for completing each task is assigned, that manager becomes a functional manager.

As the management process becomes horizontally specialized, a functional manager is responsible for a particular activity. The management functions in a manufacturing firm could include quality and operations, marketing, and accounting.

Thus, one manager may be a first-line manager in quality and operations, while another may be a middle manager in marketing. The function refers to what *activities* the manager oversees as a result of horizontal specialization of the management process. A manager's **management level** refers to the *right to act and use resources* within specified limits as a result of vertical specialization of the management process.

MANAGERIAL SKILLS

Regardless of the level at which managers perform, they must learn and develop many skills.[15] A **skill** is an ability or proficiency in performing a particular task. Various skills classifications are important in performing managerial roles.

Technical Skills

Technical skills are the ability to use *specific* knowledge, techniques, and resources in performing work. Accounting supervisors, engineering directors, and nursing supervisors need technical skills to perform their management jobs. Technical skills are especially important at the first-line management level, since daily work-related problems must be solved. The technical skill of measuring quality performance is especially important for firms competing with international companies. The array of techniques available to managers working on quality improvement includes control charts, cause-and-effect diagrams, Pareto charts, and quality action plans, which are discussed in detail in Appendix B.

top management
A small cadre of managers, usually including a CEO, president, or vice president, that is responsible for the performance of the entire organization through the middle managers.

management level
The right to act and use resources within specified limits as a result of vertical specialization of the management process.

skill
An ability or proficiency in performing a particular task.

technical skills
The ability to use specific knowledge, techniques, and resources in performing work.

WHAT MANAGERS ARE READING

LIFE AND DEATH IN THE EXECUTIVE FAST LANE

Books on management and leadership often describe what a person did, where he or she learned, and other background information. Usually, how a manager acts and behaves is overlooked. Manfred Kets de Vries, in *Life and Death in the Executive Fast Lane*, examines the emotions and behaviors of executives. It is the author's belief that executives fail to understand their behavior and that of others. Executives know numbers and can analyze data, but they come up short on understanding people.

The author presents an interesting array of topics in chapters including managing change, working abroad, women as leaders, family companies, and creativity in organizations. In a clinical and careful manner, Kets de Vries examines executives in specific situations and analyzes their behavior and consequences.

The author stresses that executives have significantly improved their analytical skills over the years. What he is concerned about is the lagging development of interpersonal skills among managers. This book brings to the forefront the importance of more carefully considering the emotional make-up of managers in dissecting the decisions being made in organizational settings.

Source: Manfred F.R. Kets de Vries, *Life and Death in the Executive Fast Lane*, San Francisco: Jossey-Bass, 1995.

Analytical Skills

analytical skills
The ability to use specific approaches or techniques in solving managerial problems.

Analytical skills involve using approaches or techniques such as materials requirement planning, inventory control models, activity-based cost accounting, forecasting, and human resource information systems to solve management problems. In essence, they're the ability to identify key factors, to understand how they interrelate, and to realize their roles in a situation. Analytical skill is actually an ability to diagnose and evaluate. It's needed to understand the problem and to develop a plan of action. Without analytical proficiency, there's little hope for long-term success.

Decision-Making Skills

All managers must make decisions or choose from among alternatives. The quality of these decisions determines their effectiveness. Managers' decision-making skill in selecting a course of action is greatly influenced by their analytical skill. Poor analytical proficiency inevitably results in poor decision making.

Patricia Stonesifer put Microsoft's Consumer Division on the map by making timely decisions and by launching 20 new CD-ROMs and software products for the home. She stepped ahead of competitors by deciding to address pent-up demand for products to use at home. Selecting a course of action before others is especially important in the highly competitive CD-ROM and software markets.[16]

Computer Skills

computer skills
The ability to use computer software applications and have a conceptual understanding of how computers work.

Managers with **computer skills** have a conceptual understanding of computers and, in particular, know how to use the computer and software to perform many aspects of their jobs. Computer ability is a valuable managerial skill. In one study of 100 personnel directors from America's largest corporations, 7 of every 10 directors believed that computer skills are important, very important, or essential for advancement in management.[17]

Computer abilities are important since computers can substantially increase a manager's productivity. In minutes computers can perform tasks in financial analysis, human resource planning, and other areas that otherwise take hours—even days—to complete. The computer is exceedingly helpful for decision making as it instantly places at a manager's fingertips a vast array of information in a flexible, usable form. Software enables managers to manipulate the data and perform "what if" scenarios, looking at the projected impact of different decision alternatives.

People Skills

people skills
The ability to work with, communicate with, and understand others.

Since managers must accomplish much of their work through other people, their ability to work with, communicate with, and understand others is vital. **People skills** are essential at every organizational level of management; they reflect a manager's leadership abilities.

Recognizing the growing demand for in-home software, Patricia Stonesifer made timely decisions that helped Microsoft beat its competitors to the punch.

Effective communication—the written and oral transmission of common understanding—is critical to success in every field, but it's crucial to managers who must achieve results through others' efforts. **Communication skills** involve the ability to communicate in ways that other people understand and to seek and use feedback from employees to ensure that you're understood.

Lewis Lehr, chairman and CEO of 3M, emphasizes open communication among managers and employees. Lehr spends six months of every year away from 3M's headquarters in St. Paul, Minnesota, visiting the company's numerous plants. There, he participates in question-and-answer sessions with employees. Lehr believes that frequent communication is the only way to build employee trust and cooperation, which is essential to 3M's success. He also requires that executives who run 3M operations frequently visit with media, government, and education officials in their regions to talk about 3M.[18]

Conceptual Skills

Conceptual skills consist of the ability to see the big picture, the complexities of the overall organization, and how the various parts fit together. Conceptualizing how each part of the organization fits and interacts with other parts to accomplish goals and operate in an ever-changing environment is needed to keep an organization focused.

Warren Buffett, chief executive officer of the investment firm Berkshire Hathaway, is concerned with making decisions about creating wealth in the future for employees and stockholders. He looks at mergers, acquisitions, and investments with an eye toward a decade or a few decades ahead. He uses logic and a conceptual approach to predict future winners.[19]

Although the preceding skills are all important, each one's relative importance will vary according to the level of the manager in the organization. Figure 1–3 illustrates the skills required at each level. For example, note that technical and human relations skills are more important at lower levels of management. These managers have greater contact with the work being done and the people doing the work. Communication and computer skills are equally important at all levels of management. Analytical skills are slightly more important at higher levels of management where the environment is less stable and problems are less predictable. Finally, decision making and conceptual skills are extremely critical to top

communication skills
The ability to communicate in ways that other people understand, and to seek and use feedback from employees to ensure that one is understood.

conceptual skills
Visualizing how each part of an organization fits and interacts with other parts to accomplish goals and objectives.

FIGURE 1–3
Managerial Skills and
Management Level

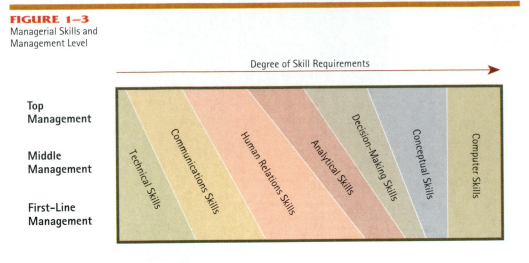

managers' performance. Top management's primary responsibility is to make decisions that are implemented at lower levels.

MANAGERIAL ROLES

role
A behavior pattern expected of an individual within a unit or position.

A **role** is a behavior pattern expected of an individual within a unit or position. One of the most frequently cited studies of *managerial roles* was conducted by Henry Mintzberg. He observed and interviewed five chief executives from different industries for a two-week period. He determined that managers serve in 10 different but closely related roles.[20] Figure 1–4 indicates that the 10 activities can be placed into the three roles: interpersonal roles, informational roles, and decisional roles.[21]

Interpersonal Roles

interpersonal roles
The figurehead, leader, and liaison roles assumed by managers that subsequently enable them to perform informational and decisional roles.

The three **interpersonal roles** of figurehead, leader, and liaison grow out of the manager's formal authority and focus on interpersonal relationships. By assuming these roles, the manager can also perform informational roles which, in turn, lead directly to performing decisional roles.

All managerial jobs require some duties that are symbolic or ceremonial in nature. Examples of the *figurehead role* include a college dean who hands out diplomas at graduation, a manager who attends the wedding of a worker's daughter, and the mayor of Houston who presents the key to the city to a NASA space shuttle crew.

The manager's *leadership role* involves directing and coordinating subordinates' activities. This may involve staffing (hiring, training, promoting, dismissing) and motivating workers. The leadership role also involves controlling, or making sure that things are going according to plan.

The *liaison role* involves managers in interpersonal relationships outside their area of command. This role may involve contacts both inside and outside the organization. Within the organization, managers must interact with numerous other managers and other individuals. They must maintain good relations with the managers who send work to the unit as well as those who receive work from the unit.

Informational Roles

informational roles
The roles assumed by managers that establish them as the central point for receiving and sending nonroutine information.

The **informational role** establishes the manager as the central point for receiving and sending information. As a result of the three interpersonal roles just discussed, managers build a network of interpersonal contacts. These contacts aid them in gathering and receiving information as a monitor and transmitting that information as the disseminator and spokesperson.

FIGURE 1—4
Mintzberg's 10
Management Roles

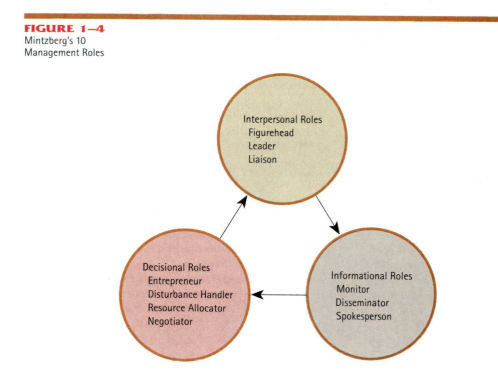

The *monitor role* involves examining the environment to discover information, changes, opportunities, and problems that may affect the unit. Formal and informal contacts developed in the liaison role are often useful here. The information gathered may concern competitive moves that could influence the entire organization, such as observing young people at a mall wearing a new fashion that suggests a change in a product line.

The *disseminator role* involves providing important or privileged information to subordinates. During a lunch conversation a firm's president learns that a large customer is upset because of quality defects in the firm's products. Returning to the office, the president asks the vice president of operations and quality about the quality problem. He also instructs the vice president to personally assure him of the quality of the orders sent to the customer.

In the *spokesperson role*, the manager represents the unit to other people. This representation may be internal when a manager makes the case for salary increases to top management. It may also be external when an executive represents the organization's views on a particular issue of public interest to a local civic organization.

Decisional Roles

Developing interpersonal relationships and gathering information are important, but they aren't ends in themselves. They serve as the basic inputs to the process of decision making. Some people believe **decisional roles**—entrepreneur, disturbance handler, resource allocator, and negotiator—are a manager's most important roles.

The purpose of the *entrepreneurial role* is to improve the unit. The effective first-line supervisor continually seeks new quality improvement methods to boost his or her unit's performance. A bank president is continually planning changes that will improve banking services. The effective marketing manager continually seeks new customer tastes.

In the *disturbance handler role*, managers make decisions or take corrective action in response to pressure beyond their control. Usually decisions must be made quickly, so this role takes priority over other roles. The immediate goal is to bring about stability. When an emergency room supervisor responds quickly to a local disaster, when a plant manager reacts to a strike, or when a first-line manager responds to a breakdown in a key piece of equipment, they're dealing with disturbances in their environments. They must respond quickly and must return the environment to stability.

decisional roles
The roles assumed by managers that establish them as decision makers after receiving interpersonal and information input. Other decisional roles include entrepreneur, disturbance handler, resource allocator, and negotiator.

In the *resource allocator role*, a manager decides who'll get what resources (money, people, time, equipment). Invariably, there aren't enough resources to go around, so the manager must allocate scarce goods in many directions. Resource allocation, therefore, is one of the manager's most critical decisional roles. A first-line supervisor must decide whether to set up overtime schedules or hire part-time workers. A worker with three projects must decide how much time to spend on each project daily. The president of the United States must decide whether to allocate more to defense and less to social programs.

In the *negotiator role*, managers must bargain with other units and individuals to obtain advantages for their unit. Negotiations may concern work, performance, objectives, resources, or anything else influencing the unit. A sales manager may negotiate with the production department over a special order for a large customer. A first-line supervisor may negotiate for new work schedules for workers. A top-level manager may negotiate with a labor union representative.

Mintzberg suggests that recognizing these 10 roles serves three important functions. First, they help explain the job of managing while emphasizing that all the roles are interrelated. Neglecting one or more of the roles hinders the manager's total progress. Second, a team of employees can't function effectively if any of the roles is neglected. Teamwork in an organizational setting requires that each role be performed consistently. Finally, the magnitude of the 10 roles points out the importance of managing time effectively if managers are to successfully perform each of the 10 roles.

PLAN FOR THE BOOK

The lighthouse parable at the beginning of the chapter portrays what this book intends to accomplish. Management is a process, a discipline—it's in a constant state of change. Managers at all levels—top, middle, and lower—performing the interpersonal, informational, and decision roles must be well grounded in understanding and applying principles of quality improvement. This book proposes that if quality is maintained and/or improved, the organization has a greater opportunity to remain competitive. Although the American auto industry has lost market share to foreign competitors, imagine where it would be today if quality improvement programs weren't initiated at General Motors, Ford, and Chrysler.

Peter Drucker aptly describes what managers do on the job:

> *Managers practice management. They do not practice economics. They do not practice quantification. They do not practice behavior science. These are tools for the manager . . . As a specific discipline, management has its own basic problems. . . . Specific approaches. . . . distinct concerns. . . . a man who only knows the skills and techniques, without understanding the fundamentals of management, is not a manager. He is, at best, only a technician.[22]*

We don't want to provide only technical tools in this book. Instead, readers should understand how management, competition, and quality are inextricably linked. There are tools and techniques that can make this linkage successful and productive. However, like Drucker, we believe that knowledge and appreciation of the fundamentals is the important point.

Figure 1–5 graphically presents this book's format. The core theme of the book is the management of quality and competitiveness. Chapters are established on the basis of the four traditional functions of management: planning, organizing, leading, and controlling. It will become evident that these functions are interrelated and that each plays a role in improving an enterprise's quality and competitiveness. Quality of products and services simply does not happen without a distinct strategy, plans, organization, control mechanisms, and leadership. As you read, analyze, and discuss the chapter content, think about the lighthouse parable.

FIGURE 1–5
Plan for the Book

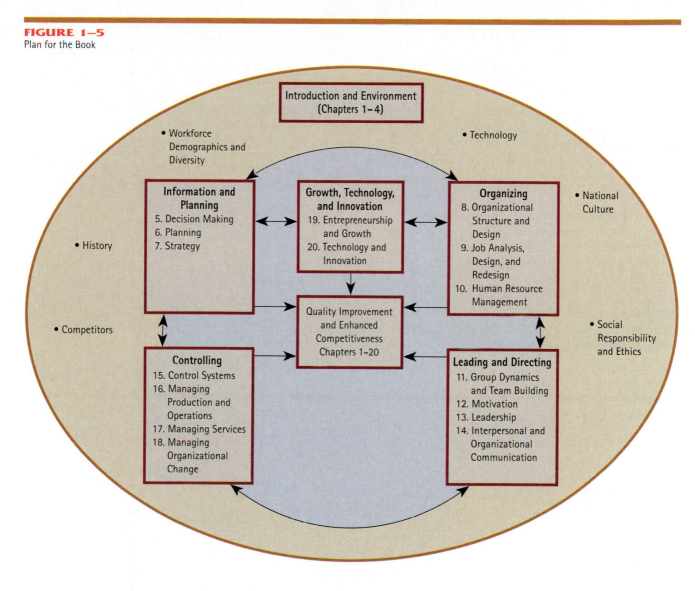

SUMMARY OF LEARNING OBJECTIVES

DEFINE THE TERMS MANAGEMENT, COMPETITIVENESS, AND QUALITY.

This chapter defines a number of key terms used throughout the book. **Management** is the process undertaken by one or more persons to coordinate the activities of other persons to achieve high-quality results not attainable by any one person acting alone. **Competitiveness** at the organizational level is defined as the degree to which a company can, under free and fair market conditions, produce goods and services that meet the test of domestic and/or international markets while simultaneously maintaining or expanding the real incomes of its employees and owners. **Quality** is defined as the totality of features and characteristics of a product or service that bear on its ability to satisfy stated or implied needs.

EXPLAIN WHY A QUALITY FOCUS HAS BECOME IMPERATIVE IN A GLOBALIZING WORLD.

U.S. industry has finally begun to recognize the cost of relegating quality to a separate function. Only by integrating quality in all management processes, all systems, and all practices can quality improvement continuously occur.

IDENTIFY WHAT ARE CALLED THE TRADITIONAL FUNCTIONS OF MANAGEMENT.

The traditional functions of management are all needed, and they must be practiced efficiently. However, we propose that they must be practiced with quality improvement as the primary goal. **Planning** involves activities that lead to the determination of objectives and the appropriate actions needed to achieve these objectives. **Organizing** results in the design of the structure that clarifies the authority, responsibility, and tasks in an organization. **Controlling** is the managerial activity that assures that the work or operation proceeds according to plan. **Leading** involves influencing others in the organization in ways that result in the accomplishment of goals.

DESCRIBE HOW COMPETITIVENESS AT THE NATIONAL LEVEL IS IMPACTED BY THE QUALITY OF PRODUCTS PRODUCED IN A COUNTRY.

Survival is the impetus for quality improvement, as foreign competition challenges American firms. The improved quality of goods and services means being able to compete better domestically and globally.

EXPLAIN THE TYPES OF SKILLS THAT MANAGERS NEED TO ACHIEVE THEIR GOALS.

To compete and perform their jobs, managers need technical, analytical, decision making, computer, people, communication, and conceptual skills.

LIST THE TYPES OF MANAGERS WITHIN ORGANIZATIONS.

Managers are typically categorized as first-line (supervisors), middle, and top (vice president and above). The level and title suggest where in the hierarchy the person works, as well as for whom and with whom he works.

DISCUSS THE SUGGESTION THAT MANAGEMENT'S TRADITIONAL METHODS MUST BE CHANGED.

Management has been viewed as a rather static, technique-oriented approach emphasizing rules, procedures, and policies. U.S. enterprises that haven't been able to create high-quality products and services increasingly went out of business. Competition became intense and consumers became sophisticated and demanding. The static, by-the-book approach won't work in a changing world. The nondynamic emphasis of simply stating a plan and organizing to accomplish the plan without considering the "messiness" of the real world is doomed to fail. The world is messy in that there's little certainty of what the competition is or will be doing, although consumers want the best buy and value they can get. Whether the product is American, French, or a global composite doesn't really matter to most consumers. This new era suggests that management must be alert, responsive, up to date, and able to move quickly.

DEFINE ZERO DEFECTS AND TELL AT WHAT STAGE OF ORGANIZATIONAL MATURITY THIS CONCEPT BECOMES PART OF THE FIRM'S CULTURE.

Zero defects is a performance standard based on doing the job correctly the first time. The emphasis is on preventing defects rather than just finding them and fixing them. Crosby's five-stage quality management maturity grid suggests that zero defects can become a part of a firm's culture at the most mature stage of certainty (Stage V). The firm doesn't have quality problems except in very unusual cases because defects have been prevented.

KEY TERMS

analytical skills, p. 18
communication skills, p. 19
competitiveness, p. 4
computer skills, p. 18
conceptual skills, p. 19
controlling, p. 13
decisional roles, p. 21
first-line management, p. 15
informational roles, p. 20

interpersonal roles, p. 20
leading, p. 13
management, p. 9
management level, p. 17
managers, p. 8
middle management, p. 16
organization, p. 8
organizing, p. 13
people skills, p. 18

planning, p. 12
quality, p. 10
role, p. 20
skill, p. 17
technical skills, p. 17
top management, p. 17
zero defects, p. 11

REVIEW AND DISCUSSION QUESTIONS

Recall

1. What is the difference between a national view and an organizational view of competitiveness?
2. At what level in the management hierarchy would managers be concerned about quality issues?
3. How can managers performing the roles described by Mintzberg address the quality and competitiveness concepts?
4. Name some international pioneers of quality who have encouraged increased attention to quality.

Understanding

5. Was it necessary to establish a Malcolm Baldrige National Quality Award in the United States? Explain.
6. Some individuals state that intense competition forces them to consider or use questionable practices to compete. Do you accept or support this position on ethics? Why?

7. Is it possible to deliver a service such as mail, legal advice, or air travel without having a single glitch or defect? Explain.

Application

8. Visit a service organization and prepare a brief report on the services that it provides that would improve a customer's satisfaction with the business.
9. Interview a manager and ask him/her to describe how they plan, organize, control, and lead. Can the manager describe these functions without your helping him/her or giving them examples? Why?
10. What are the four best products that you purchased in the past three months? What characteristics encouraged you to cite them as the best? Do any of these characteristics fit Garvin's eight quality dimensions in Table 1–2?

CASE STUDY

The Journey to Trust and Belief: 1979–1994

The quality record of Wainwright Industries is built from a comprehensive set of strategies and tactics woven throughout the enterprise. But it was not always that way.

The company, founded in 1947, initially produced components for internal combustion engines. The move to expand the business began in 1979. That's when second-generation family members Don Wainwright, chairman and chief executive officer, and his brother, Nelson Wainwright, president, decided to build a new plant and diversify into new business areas.

"The timing couldn't have been worse," said Don Wainwright. "We based our business projections on what we thought was the worst-case scenario. But we didn't anticipate one of the worst recessions in history, and no one imagined how much the domestic automobile market would suffer."

In 1980, only one year after moving into their new plant, annual sales dipped from $5 million to $3 million. Operations were down to three days a week, and a large portion of the workforce was laid off. The brothers feared they might have to close the doors, but they had a plan and managed to keep the business afloat. Shortly after that, a series of events was set in motion that would change Wainwright Industries forever and for the better.

The journey that eventually led to winning the Malcolm Baldridge National Quality Award has been marked by a number of key turning points, but three significant emotional events—as Don Wainwright calls them—stand out.

EVENT NO. 1: "THESE PARTS AREN'T FLAT." (1981)

"We were called to a meeting in Detroit with General Motors [GM]," recalled Don Wainwright. "GM told us that they were losing market share and they had to change the way they were doing things. They challenged us to apply statistical process control and to stop production when bad parts began to show up."

The company's determination to follow GM's challenge came to an abrupt halt one day when St. Louis plant manager Mike Simms, who was then a quality manager, came to management and said, "These parts aren't flat."

"We all just looked at each other," Don Wainwright recalled. "I said, 'What do you mean? We've been making those parts for 25 years. The customer has always taken them that way. What do you mean they're not flat? Ship them.'"

Simms responded, "I thought we were committed to quality around here."

Simms' initiative marked a major crossroads for the organization. "We decided not to ship the parts," said Don Wainwright. "Instead, we reworked them. When you see the costs involved in a decision like that, you seriously question the whole thing. But when your reject rate goes down, you begin to appreciate the value."

"That's when you understand that you don't improve quality just to improve quality," added David Robbins, chief operating officer. "You improve quality so you can lower cost. That means lower prices for a better product, and that's one of the main reasons we're succeeding with our customers."

As evidence of that success, Wainwright Industries was one of six companies supplying piston inserts to the domestic automobile industry in 1979. Today, it is the only one.

EVENT NO. 2: "WE WANTED TO BUILD TRUST." (1984)

In the late 1970s and early 1980s, tensions between the company and its associates were running high. "We decided that this kind of relationship was not in the best long-term interest of the company," said Robbins. "We set out to actively open communication, build bridges, and bury hatchets. We wanted to build trust."

Management's efforts led to reduced tensions over the next few years. In 1984, several key events occurred to significantly improve the nature of the relationship between management and associates.

"First, we started calling people associates instead of employees," said Robbins. "Then we made some substantive changes. To reflect the new relationship of mutual trust, everyone was put on salary. All associates today are salaried, nonexempt. They are paid when they miss work for any reason, and they are paid time-and-a-half for overtime."

The company also started a profit-sharing program. In keeping with its commitment to associate participation and responsibility, the 401K profit-sharing plan was designed by a team of seven non-management associates and one senior manager. "The team invited four mutual fund companies to make presentations, and we chose the one we thought would be best for the associates," said Nelson Wainwright. "I only had one vote, like everyone else on the team. Our form might be corporate, but our attitude is partnership."

Another important change concerned the clothing that people wore to work. Since 1984, everyone in the organization—chairman and line worker alike—has worn the same uniform: black slacks and a white pinstripe shirt with the person's name on one side and "Team Wainwright" on the other.

"That was a tough change for some of the professional office people," said Susan Cutler, chief financial officer. "It doesn't phase me now, but it did at one time. Matter of fact, I used to change before I'd go out someplace. Now I don't know what I'd do if I had to go back. It's more comfortable, and it's a constant reminder of the climate we want around here."

Cutler also recalls when she was first instructed to share financial information that previously had been viewed as highly confidential. It was 1989, and she was told to provide specific financial data to a select group of about 15 supervisors.

"One of the supervisors who was going to receive the information came over and asked what I was doing," said Cutler. "When I told him, he asked, 'Are you sure you know what you're doing?' I felt a cold sweat come over me. So I shut my book, ran to David Robbins' office, and asked him if I really knew what I was doing. He said, 'Yes,' and that launched the open-book philosophy in our organization. Since 1991, we have shared our financial records with everyone in the company."

The overall effect of these efforts to build trust can be seen in many ways throughout the company, but perhaps none is more striking than the attendance rate. Since 1984, it has run consistently at 99 percent. Last year it was 98.9 percent. "The snowstorm wrecked our average," said Don Wainwright, only partly joking. "The fact is that people just like to work here. They know they're needed and appreciated and they feel a strong personal responsibility to be here and get the job done."

EVENT NO. 3: "WE TOLD ASSOCIATES WE NEEDED THEIR HELP."
(1991)

When the improvement process began several years ago, it was far from the success it is today. The reason is that it was driven by management. "It was a classic suggestion system," said Robbins. "We had a box on the wall, and cobwebs were in it. People had to go through an extensive process, determining financial justification, amount of rewards, and more. It was all counterproductive."

So, in 1991, management called all associates together to announce a change in procedures. "We told them we couldn't do it the old way anymore, and we couldn't do it without them," said Don Wainwright. "We told them we needed their help, and we were going to let them tell us what to do and how to do it. It really was an emotional experience for us."

That was the beginning of the company's CIP (continuous improvement process) system, and the response was overwhelming right from the start. "When we started listening, the associates started talking," said Don Wainwright. Almost overnight, improvements were being implemented at a rate dozens of times greater than before.

"I discovered an important lesson from that experience," said Don Wainwright. "You can delegate authority, but you cannot delegate responsibility. Responsibility comes from within. If you create an environment where people aren't motivated to exercise that personal sense of responsibility, you can give them all the authority in the world and they won't do anything with it.

"The experience also helped me understand something else very important," he added. "You just can't push 275 people and expect to get the best performance from them. The real finesse of effective management is to make growth come from within."

The CIP system has some limits that everyone has agreed on. Improvements that require significant capital investment have to go through a different process, for example. But Don Wainwright said it's the little things that make the biggest difference anyway.

"A thousand raindrops make an ocean, and all these little ideas add up," he said. "But more important, it's helping us create the kind of mind-set we need for a culture of continuous improvement. We don't stop the momentum by taking time to evaluate every little idea throughout the process. We train people right and let them go."

The change to the CIP system also shifted relationships between managers and other associates. "My title is plant manager," said Simms, "but I'm viewed now more as a plant adviser than a manager. The people on the line are running the operation, and I provide them with advice and support when they need it. It's a reflection of our emphasis on trust and belief."

Still a Student, Not a Master

In his presentation remarks at the Baldrige Award ceremony in Washington, D.C., on December 5, 1994, Don Wainwright recounted the story of a parable told by James C. Collins in his book *Built to Last*.

As Collins tells the story, a martial arts student goes to his master to receive the black belt after completing the highest level of training and demonstrating his proficiency. But the student, believing that he has reached the end of his journey, is turned away by the master. It is not until years later that the student finally understands the true meaning of the black belt: It is the beginning of discipline, work, and commitment to ever-higher standards of performance. At that moment, the master says the student is ready and confers the ultimate honor of the black belt upon him.

"It's the perfect analogy for our company," said Don Wainwright. "We are only beginning. As much as we cherish the Baldrige Award, we are more excited about the extensive feedback report we expect from the examiners telling us where we can improve."

QUESTIONS

1. What people-oriented steps did Don Wainwright take to motivate employees to think and take quality seriously?
2. When Don Wainwright stated that "You can delegate authority, but you cannot delegate responsibility," what did he mean?
3. What management lessons or principles are pointed out in the case of Wainwright Industries?

Source: Les Landes, "The Journey to Trust and Belief: 1979–1994," Quality Progress, July 1995, 46–47; and James C. Collins, Built to Last (New York: Harper Collins, 1994).

VIDEO CASE

Management Challenge

This video focuses on the management style of United Airlines, headquartered just outside of Chicago. It looks at the company's recent change to becoming employee-owned and what effect that has had on management philosophy as it relates to quality and competitiveness.

On July 12, 1994, United Airlines (UAL) became the world's largest employee-owned company. In their new role as owners and investors, employees must take advantage of this distinction to position the company for long-term competitiveness in the airline industry. The new owners are working to create an organizational culture that fosters high commitment to employee involvement, open and honest communication, sharing of ideas, trust, respect for diversity, and teamwork.

One innovation already developed by the new owners is "customer problem resolution teams," a new customer-satisfaction initiative. These teams illustrate the point that, to be successful in an intensely competitive global environment, UAL feels it can no longer operate in the traditional ways of having only management involved in the business. Because United is an employee-owned company, now more than ever, it needs the commitment of ideas and the decision making of each "owner" to become a world class competitor.

UAL's new management style views employee participation, customer focus, and continuous improvement as essential factors to its success and profitability. Management is confronted with the task of becoming more involved in encouraging and empowering employees to solve problems immediately, by themselves. In this regard they have instituted several aggressive new programs emanating from their Culture Change division.

The overarching campaign of this new management approach is their Mission United program, a one day event for all employees for the purpose of gaining an understanding of how they must work together differently in achieving their primary goal: To become the worldwide airline of choice.

Each Mission United event is planned for approximately 150 employees from all departments, levels, and job groups within the company. The enrollment process is designed to ensure a maximum mix of employee job groups as well as a cross-function of departments and divisions at each event. At Mission United events, each participant is challenged to:

- ❖ Become thoroughly acquainted with United's mission, vision, and values;
- ❖ Gain a better understanding of how business decisions are made;
- ❖ Heighten awareness of their individual impact on the customer;
- ❖ Take a look at the strengths and weaknesses of the company;
- ❖ Interact with fellow employees;
- ❖ Examine the concept of ownership; and
- ❖ Share breakthrough successes and learn how employees are working differently.

Through Mission United, employees are oriented to focus on the company's "core values" of teamwork, safety, integrity, respect, community service, customer satisfaction, and profitability. Basically, the company feels that these values are going to help them achieve their goal to be the worldwide airline of choice, with the top priority of providing a safe airline.

As an outgrowth of this new kind of management approach to employee involvement, United has instituted a new employee participation process to focus on customer service, organizational concerns, and profitability. Taking the best practices from the most successful companies with high commitment to employee involvement, they created the "Best of Best" process. The main thrust of this process involves employees working together in teams to identify and resolve local operational and quality issues that impact the customer. The focus of Best of Best teams is for continuous improvement of services within the boundaries of the team's control. Teams will have a clear understanding of their goals and are empowered at the local level to work on creative new ways of doing business.

The Best of Best program was the first attempt by United to bridge all divisions together to solve problems. It represents the beginning of a long-term cultural transformation to a collaborative, decision-making, learning organization in which employees are encouraged to gain new skills and work differently. Teamwork is valued and rewarded, responsibility and accountability are maximized, personal and professional growth are continuous, and hierarchy is minimized. Self-determination, self-motivation, and self-management are expected, and management is providing the leadership necessary to drive and sustain the empowerment.

Managers have become more visible to the United employees as well. They are spending time on the front lines of the business to do a better job leading and planning for culture change. In many cases, they are leading by *doing* and are certainly much more open and available to their employees than they were in the past. The managers have been conducting "road shows" that become interactive question-and-answer sessions to encourage open communication with staff members.

Since becoming an employee-owned company, United Airlines has had to do a lot of internal soul-searching to discover a better way of doing things. This major cultural change has served to accelerate the company's strategic shift to becoming more competitive on a global scale. Fortunately, as owners employees were forced to focus on new and dynamic ways of doing things. They realized that exceeding the customer's expectations is the only way to compete and achieve their goals. By turning to greater employee involvement and more responsive management, they appear to be headed in the right direction.

QUESTIONS

1. United Airlines managers use an approach called Mission United to orient employees throughout the organization to new initiatives, goals, and competitive position. Discuss in class how managers should conduct these one-day sessions to get maximum employee buy-in and commitment.

2. Best of Best programs consist of cross-functional teams aimed at creating changes based on identified best practices. Why do you think United organized these teams cross-functionally?

3. Employee ownership has been attempted before in the airline industry through a company called People Express. That company didn't survive, although it was initially successful. What are some steps UAL can take to improve its chances of success?

APPLICATION EXERCISE

Managerial Behavior Assessment: A Look at Yourself

Below are 20 general statements that managers are likely to use in various situations. Indicate how often you would behave as asked by each statement. As a reader, you may actually be working as a manager or you might be a student. If you're a student, think about how you would behave or how you do behave on projects when you serve as manager.

Place a number from 1 to 9 in the space for each statement. There are no right or wrong answers.

1	2	3	4	5	6	7	8	9

Not very often   Not often   Occasionally   Very often

When (If) I work as a manager, I (will):

_____ 1. Carefully set clear goals for the group.
_____ 2. Represent the group with enthusiasm to outsiders.
_____ 3. Carefully review the group's performance.
_____ 4. Intervene to handle internal conflicts.
_____ 5. Attempt to receive the best work schedules for my group.
_____ 6. Motivate the group to perform at optimum level.
_____ 7. Examine the group's past and present performance.
_____ 8. Transmit relevant information to the group.
_____ 9. Positively influence how top managers view the group.
_____ 10. Find opportunities for the group to excel.
_____ 11. Take on difficult projects with risks so that the group can make an impact.
_____ 12. Make sure that the group is represented at important social events.

_____ 13. Pass along relevant group information to top managers.

_____ 14. Discipline individuals who purposely disrupt the group.

_____ 15. Reward good performers equitably.

_____ 16. Bring recognition to outstanding group members.

_____ 16. Provide needed time, materials, or resources upon member's(s') request.

_____ 18. Provide needed data to help members complete a project.

_____ 19. Represent the group when requests for information are made.

_____ 20. Help group members with other groups' and outsiders' requests.

Source: Exercise is based on the Mintzberg management role study and description.

Scoring the Self-Assessment

Place all your scores in the appropriate space. Divide the total by 2 to calculate the average.

Interpersonal

Figurehead	Leader	Liaison
#12 _____	#1 _____	#2 _____
#19 _____	#6 _____	#20 _____
Total _____	Total _____	Total _____

Informational

Monitor	Disseminator	Spokesperson
#3 _____	#8 _____	#9 _____
#7 _____	#18 _____	#13 _____
Total _____	Total _____	Total _____

Decisional

Entrepreneur	Disturbance handler	Resources allocator	Negotiator
#10 _____	#4 _____	#15 _____	#5 _____
#11 _____	#14 _____	#17 _____	#16 _____
Total _____	Total _____	Total _____	Total _____

Your Profile: A Picture

Fill in your average scores in the Mintzberg role profile diagram. Connect the scores with a color pen to show your patterns.

Would the people working with you (subordinates, classmates, friends) rate you the same way? Try this exercise with someone who works with you. Plot that person's profile for you. What does it show?

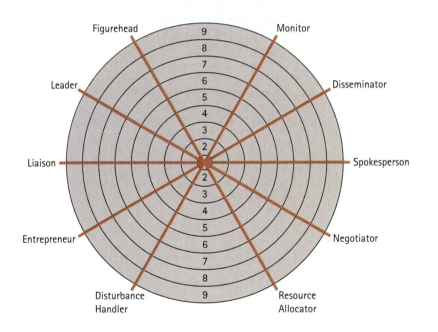

CHAPTER 2

The Evolution of Management

After studying this chapter, you should be able to:

❖ List some of the influential management thinkers and describe their contributions.

❖ Differentiate between the efficiency emphasis of the classical approach to management and the people emphasis of the behavioral approach to management.

❖ Describe what Frederick W. Taylor meant by the term <u>scientific methods</u>.

❖ Describe the decision and information sciences approach.

❖ Describe the systems approach.

❖ Explain the significance of the contingency approach to management.

The Gilbreths Study and Live for Efficiency

In the evolution of American management practice, Frank and Lillian Gilbreth stand out as major contributors. Born in 1868, Frank Gilbreth could have attended MIT, but decided instead to go to work as a bricklayer. He was intrigued by the motion that workers used to lay brick, and originated the concept of the "time and motion" study of jobs. This work also resulted in establishing meaningful work standards (how much brick could be laid in a specified work period) and incentive wage plans.

The Gilbreths

In 1904 Gilbreth married Lillian Moller, a woman with a unique background in psychology and management. The Gilbreths formed a team that studied work efficiency, used motion picture films for the first time in history to analyze and improve worker motions performing a job, and invented the microchronometer, a clock capable of recording time to 1/2000th of a second.

Frank and Lillian applied three principles of efficiency and time and motion in their personal life. Two of their children related their parents' interests, style, and ethic in a book, *Cheaper by the Dozen.* One interesting excerpt from the book states:

> *Our house was sort of a school for scientific management and the elimination of wasted motions—or "motion study," as Dad and Mother named it. Dad took pictures of us children washing dishes, so that he could figure out how we could reduce our motions and thus hurry through the task. . . .*

> *Yes, at home or on the job, Dad was always the efficiency expert. He buttoned his vest from the bottom up, instead of from the top down, because the bottom-to-top process took him only 3 seconds, while the top-to-bottom took 7. He used two shaving brushes to lather his face, because he found that by so doing he could cut 17 seconds off his shaving time.*

The Gilbreths studied and practiced efficiency improvements. They believed that human resources could be trained, developed, and motivated to be efficient contributors to organizations. They applied scientific procedures to the art of managing. The practical application of scientific study and analysis was a top priority of the Gilbreths.

The Gilbreths are not well-known, but their legacy can be found in many organizations around the world. Motion study, job simplification, efficiency, and optimizing the potential of workers are principles and procedures practiced at such admired and successful firms as Ford Motor, Volvo, Nestlé, Sumitomo, and Nucor.

Nucor, a steel manufacturer based in Charlotte, North Carolina, has practiced many of the Gilbreths' motion analysis and efficiency principles to compete with much larger, world-renown steel manufacturers. Nucor has been able to produce steel at five times the labor efficiency of competitors. Efficiency improvements and incentive pay practices tied to business success have been major reasons for which Nucor is profitable and growing. The firm intends to use efficiency of production as an important driving force as it expands its operations.

The Gilbreths continue to contribute to the practice of management. They knew early in the 20th century, what is today an accepted principle of practicing managers—scientific inquiry can help find a better way to complete a job or a task.

Source: Francis J. Gouillart and James N. Kelly, *Transforming the Organization* (New York: McGraw-Hill, 1995), pp. 123–125; F.B. Gilbreth, Jr., and E.G. Carey, *Cheaper by the Dozen* (New York: Thomas Cromwell, (1948), pp. 2–3; Claude S. George, Jr., *The History of Management Thought* (Englewood Cliffs, NJ: Prentice-Hall, 1968), pp. 96–99; and Frank B. Gilbreth and Lillian M. Gilbreth, *Applied Motion Study* (New York: Sturges & Walton, 1907).

Knowledge of past management history offers insight into how managerial theory and practice has evolved. Although the history of management goes back thousands of years, little is known about management history in the past 100 to 150 years. The Gilbreths made significant contributions to the practice of management in the 20th century and yet few students or practitioners of management recognize or appreciate their legacy.[1]

Historical perspective is the study of a subject in light of its earliest phases and subsequent evolution. Historical perspective differs from history in that the object of historical perspective is to sharpen one's vision of the present, not the past.[2]

This chapter presents a concise historical perspective of management. A number of contributors, approaches, and practices of the past provide insight, lessons, and techniques to current managers attempting to improve in quality and competitiveness. Interestingly, contributors have come from around the world. As Figure 2–1 shows, management as we know and practice it today has a global flavor.

MANAGEMENT: A FIELD OF STUDY

The systematic recording and reporting of management practice is primarily a 20th-century phenomenon. Yet the most magnificent feat of management practice and application of management principles is probably the construction of the Egyptian pyramids. The planning, organizing, leading, and control functions were applied to the work of over 100,000 people constructing the great pyramid of Cheops in 4000 BC. Remember, there was no modern technology to move heavy stones great distances, and there were no laws about the length of the workday or safety procedures.

Although the trials and tribulations of management today are not as dramatic as those that faced the Egyptians thousands of years ago, management still offers plenty of excitement and challenges. These challenges were launched with the Industrial Revolution, particularly in the United Kingdom in the mid-1700s. The Industrial Revolution shifted manufacturing to a factory setting from a household setting. One individual who recognized the significance of human resources was Robert Owen (1771–1858), a Scottish factory owner who refused to use child labor, which was a common practice of this era. Owen also emphasized good working conditions, cooperation, and tolerance for differences in worker capabilities. Andrew Ure (1778–1857) also recognized the importance of human resources. He provided workers with tea at breaks, medical treatment, and sickness payments. Owen and Ure saw the importance of human beings in producing products. Workers were considered to be more than simply cogs or a factor of necessary input. Workers were the livelihood of factories and, if treated well, could perform excellently.

FIGURE 2–1
Modern Management
Is a Global Affair:
Selected Contributors
to Management Theory

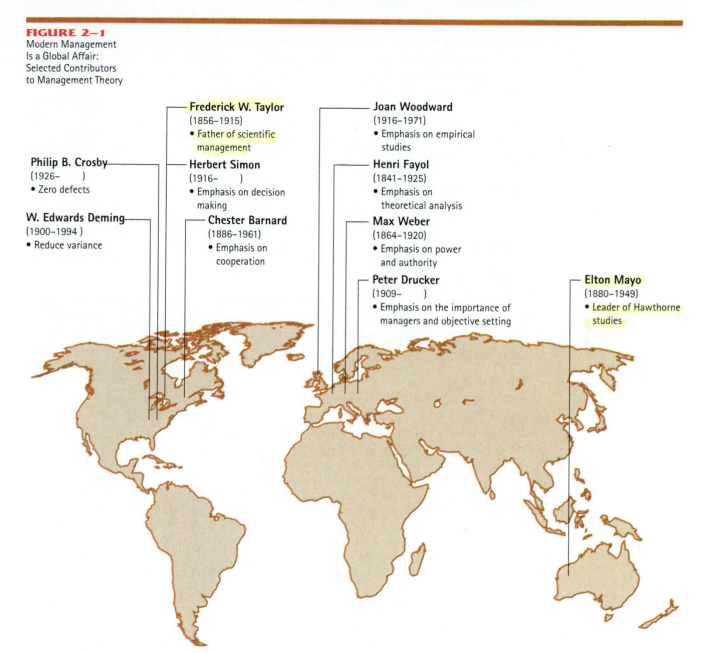

Frederick W. Taylor
(1856–1915)
• Father of scientific management

Joan Woodward
(1916–1971)
• Emphasis on empirical studies

Philip B. Crosby
(1926–   )
• Zero defects

Herbert Simon
(1916–   )
• Emphasis on decision making

Henri Fayol
(1841–1925)
• Emphasis on theoretical analysis

W. Edwards Deming
(1900–1994)
• Reduce variance

Chester Barnard
(1886–1961)
• Emphasis on cooperation

Max Weber
(1864–1920)
• Emphasis on power and authority

Peter Drucker
(1909–   )
• Emphasis on the importance of managers and objective setting

Elton Mayo
(1880–1949)
• Leader of Hawthorne studies

Modern societies depend on human resources within organizations to provide the goods and services customers seek. These organizations, large and small, are headed by one or more individuals designated "managers." Even the sole proprietor of a business is a manager. It's the cadre of managers and the workers who have, since the Industrial Revolution, created organizations of all sizes that enhance the standard of living and quality of life in societies around the world.

Managers are the people who allocate society's resources to various (often competing) ends. Managers have the authority and responsibility to build safe or unsafe products, seek war or peace, build or destroy cities, and clean up or pollute the environment. Managers establish the conditions under which we're provided jobs, incomes, lifestyles, products, services, protection, health care, and knowledge. It would be difficult to find anyone in a developed or developing nation who is neither a manager nor affected by a manager's decisions.

The endless list of 20th-century management scholars, consultants, and practitioners who have made lasting contributions to how management is practiced and will be practiced in the 21st century could be prepared. A few unique contributors, however, should be introduced so that readers can better understand many of the management practices that will be covered in this book. The Gilbreths are unique and have been introduced earlier. Two other important contributors that transcend time and geographical boundaries are Peter Drucker and W. Edwards Deming.

Born in 1909 in Austria, Peter Drucker was educated as a lawyer and worked as a journalist in Germany. He's now an educator, consultant, and philosopher. His work emphasizes managers' importance in organizational societies. Managers must always make economic performance the top priority. Drucker's central issue is how best to manage a business so that it is successful over time.

Drucker has argued that profits aren't the major objective of business:

> There is only one valid definition of business purpose: to create a customer. . . . What the business thinks it produces is not of first importance—especially not to the future of the business and to its success. What the customer thinks he is buying, what he considers "value" is decisive—it determines what a business is, what it produces, and whether it will prosper.[3]

Drucker considers the present era of management to be a period of transformation. The modern organization must be organized for constant changes. He proposes that to stay current and up to speed, management must engage in three practices. The first is continuing improvement of everything the organization does (the process the Japanese refer to as *kaizen*). Continuous improvement in services, product design, and product use has to become part of daily organizational life. Second, every organization must learn to exploit its knowledge. Taking the knowledge and developing one product after another from the same invention is one of the most successful practices of Japanese business. Finally, every firm must innovate. Every organization can accomplish these practices only by acquiring the most essential resource: qualified, knowledgeable people.[4]

In today's organizations individuals who weren't trained as managers often find themselves in managerial positions. Many people presently training to be teachers, engineers, accountants, musicians, salespersons, artists, physicians, or lawyers will one day earn their livings as managers. They'll manage schools, accounting firms, symphonies, sales organizations, museums, hospitals, and government agencies. The United States and other countries are organizational societies that rely on managers to manage work, operations, and people to efficiently accomplish goals. Because the growth in the number and size of organizations is relatively new in history, the study of management is also relatively new.

W. Edwards Deming was born in 1900 in Sioux City, Iowa. He received a Ph.D. in mathematical physics and worked for the U.S. Census Bureau during and after World War II.[5] In 1950, Deming went to Japan to help conduct a population census and lectured to Japanese business managers on statistical quality control. The Japanese were impressed with Deming and listened carefully to his views about quality. Deming stressed that quality is whatever the customer needs and wants. Deming was extremely critical of American management and its failure to properly address quality. He claimed that managers were responsible for 94 percent of quality problems.

Deming proposed 14 points of total quality management that reveal an emphasis on learning, worker involvement, leadership, and continuous improvement (Table 2–1). Deming stated: "People are born with intrinsic motivation. . . . People are born with a need for relationships with other people and with a need to be loved and esteemed by others. . . . One is born with a natural inclination to learn and to be innovative. One inherits a right to enjoy his work."[6] The three key ingredients of these 14 points, according to Deming, are continual improvement, constancy of purpose, and profound knowledge.

The Gilbreths, Drucker, and Deming have provided unique contributions to practicing managers. Each has offered suggestions, methods, and a philosophical orientation that warrants pause and consideration. As 21st-century managers search for answers and methods for solving problems, it is likely that the work and ideas of Frank and Lillian Gilbreth, Peter Drucker, and W. Edwards Deming will be consulted.[7] There are other approaches and contributors to the knowledge base of management that will also be considered.

TABLE 2–1	DEMING'S 14 POINTS OF TOTAL QUALITY MANAGEMENT

1. *Create constancy of purpose for improvement of product and service*. Deming suggests a radical new definition of a company's role. Rather than to make money, it's to stay in business and provide jobs through innovation, research, constant improvement, and maintenance.

2. *Adopt the new philosophy.* Americans are too tolerant of poor workmanship and sullen service. We need a new religion in which mistakes and negativism are unacceptable.

3. *Cease dependence on mass inspection*. American firms typically inspect a product as it comes off the assembly line or at major stages long the way; defective products are either thrown out or re-worked. Both practices are unnecessarily expensive. In effect, a company is paying workers to make defects and then to correct them. Quality comes not from inspection but from improvement of the process. With instruction, workers can be enlisted in this improvement.

4. *End the practice of awarding business on price tag alone*. Purchasing departments customarily operate on orders to see the lowest-priced vendor. Frequently, this leads to low-quality supplies. Instead, buyers should seek the best quality in a long-term relationship with a single supplier for any one item.

5. *Improve constantly the system of production and service*. Improvement isn't a one-time effort. Management is obligated to continually look for ways to reduce waste and improve quality.

6. *Institute training.* Too often, workers have learned their job from another worker who was never trained properly. They're forced to follow unintelligible instructions. They can't do their jobs well because no one tells them how to do so.

7. *Institute leadership.* The supervisor's job isn't to tell people what to do nor to punish them but to lead. Leading consists of (1) helping people do a better job and (2) learning by objective methods who needs individual help.

8. *Drive out fear.* Many employees are afraid to ask questions or to take a position, even when they don't understand what their job is or what's right or wrong. They will continue to do things the wrong way or not do them at all. Economic losses from fear are appalling. To ensure better quality and productivity, people must feel secure.

9. *Break down barriers between staff areas.* Often a company's departments or units are competing with each other or have goals that conflict. They don't work as a team so they can solve or foresee problems. Worse, one department's goals may cause trouble for another.

10. *Eliminate slogans, exhortations, and targets for the workforce*. These never helped anybody do a good job. Let workers formulate their own slogans.

11. *Eliminate numerical quotas.* Quotas take into account only numbers, not quality of methods. They're usually a guarantee of inefficiency and high cost. To hold their jobs, people meet quotas at any cost, without regard to damage to their company.

12. *Remove barriers to pride of workmanship.* People are eager to do a good job and distressed when they can't. Too often, misguided supervisors, faulty equipment, and defective materials stand in the way of good performance. These barriers must be removed.

13. *Institute a vigorous program of education and retraining.* Both management and the workforce must be educated in the new methods, including teamwork and statistical techniques.

14. *Take action to accomplish the transformation.* A special top management team with a plan of action is needed to carry out the quality mission. Workers can't do it on their own, nor can managers. A critical mass of people in the company must understand the 14 points.

Source: Adapted from W. Edwards Deming. *Out of the Crisis,* 2nd ed. (Cambridge, Mass.: MIT Center for Advanced Engineering Study, 1986); and Lloyd Dobyns and Clare Crawford-Mason. *Quality or Else* (Boston: Houghton Mifflin, 1991).

THE CLASSICAL MANAGEMENT APPROACH

A critical problem facing managers at the turn of the 20th century was how to increase the efficiency and productivity of the workforce. The effort to resolve these issues marked the beginning of the study of modern management. It was eventually labeled *the classical approach,* as is usually the case with the beginning effort of every field of study.

We believe that the classical approach to management can be best understood by examining it from two perspectives based on the problems each perspective examined. One perspective, *scientific management*, concentrated on lower-level managers dealing with everyday problems of the workforce. The other perspective, *classical organization theory*, concentrated on top-level managers dealing with the everyday problems of managing the entire organization. For management students, the contributions of the classical approach are critical. These insights, in fact, constitute the core of the discipline of management and the process of management and comprise a major part of this book. Let's briefly examine each perspective.

Scientific Management

At the turn of the 20th century, business was expanding and creating new products and new markets, but labor was in short supply. Two solutions were available: (1) substitute capital for labor or (2) use labor more efficiently. **Scientific management** concentrated on the second solution.

FREDERICK WINSLOW TAYLOR (1856–1915) - Frederick W. Taylor, called the Father of Scientific Management, was an engineer by training. He joined Midvale Steel Works as a laborer and rose through the ranks to become a chief engineer.[8] Taylor believed that management's principal object should be to secure the maximum prosperity for the employer, coupled with the maximum prosperity of each employee. The mutual interdependence of management and workers was a common message he expressed.

Taylor's view of "science" insisted upon the systematic observation and measurement of worker activities. He was driven by the notion of applying science to answer questions about efficiency, cooperation, and motivation. Taylor believed that inefficient rules of thumb of management inevitably lead to inefficiency, low productivity, and low-quality work. He recommended developing a science of management, the scientific selection and development of human resources, and personal cooperation between management and workers. Taylor believed that conflict among employees would obstruct productivity and so should be eliminated.

Taylor advocated maximum specialization of labor. He believed the person should become a specialist and master of specific tasks. Also, he assumed that increased efficiency would result from specialization. Taylor was unhappy with anything short of the one best way. He searched through the use of scientific methods for the one best way to manage.

Taylor tried to find a way to combine the interests of both management and labor to avoid the necessity for sweatshop management. He believed that the key to harmony was seeking to discover the one best way to do a job, determine the optimum work pace, train people to do the job properly, and reward successful performance by using an incentive pay system. Taylor believed that cooperation would replace conflict if workers and managers knew what was expected and saw the positive benefits of achieving mutual expectations.[9]

To the modern student of management, Taylor's ideas may not appear to be insightful. Given the times in which he developed them, however, his ideas were lasting contributions to how work is done at the shop floor level. He urged managers to take a more systematic approach in performing their job of coordination. His experiments with stopwatches and work methods stimulated many others at that time to undertake similar studies.[10]

Interestingly, if scientific management were evaluated in terms of its impact on management practice at the time of its development, it would receive a low grade. Although some firms adopted scientific management, the methods of Taylor and his followers were largely ignored. One cause of the seeming failure was the failure of Taylor and other scientific management supporters to understand fully the psychological and sociological aspects of work. For example, scientific management made the implicit assumption that people are motivated to work primarily by money. In the late 19th century, this was undoubtedly a valid assumption. To assume this today, however, is far too simplistic.

Classical Organization Theory

Another body of ideas developed at the same time as scientific management. These ideas focused on the problems faced by top managers of large organizations. Since this branch

scientific management
Practices introduced by Frederick W. Taylor to accomplish the management job. Taylor advocated the use of scientific procedures to find the one best way to do a job.

of the classical approach focused on the management of organizations (while scientific management focused on the management of work), it was labeled *classical organization theory*. Its two major purposes were (1) to develop basic principles that could guide the design, creation, and maintenance of large organizations and (2) to identify the basic functions of managing organizations.

An area receiving little mention in early classical literature was ethics within the work setting. Managers were involved in efficiency and applying the principles of management, but weren't considered promoters of an ethical society. Today, however, firms and managers are involved in promoting ethical behavior, as the Ethics Spotlight illustrates.

Engineers constitute many of the prime contributors to scientific management; numerous practicing executives were the major contributors to classical organization theory.

HENRI FAYOL (1841–1925) – A French mining engineer by training, Henri Fayol (1841–1925) eventually became a managing director of a French mining and metallurgical combine, Commentary-Fourchamboult-Decazeville. Besides many articles on administration, his most famous writing was the book *General and Industrial Management*, translated by Constance Storrs and first issued in 1949.[11] Fayol divided an organization's activities into six categories:

1. Technical (production, manufacturing).
2. Commercial (buying, selling).
3. Financial.
4. Security (protecting property and persons).
5. Accounting.
6. Managerial (planning, organizing, commanding, coordinating, and controlling).

These six categories in varying degrees are essential and present in all organizations.

PRINCIPLES OF MANAGEMENT – Fayol proposed 14 principles to guide the thinking of managers in resolving problems (Table 2–2). He never recommended total obedience to the principles but suggested that a manager's "experience and sense of proportion" should guide the degree of application of any principle in a particular situation. As

---

ETHICS SPOTLIGHT — ETHICAL GUIDELINES CAN HELP EMPLOYEES

The human resources of an organization are so crucial to the competitive success of a firm that ethical behavior has finally become a top priority in many firms. A strong ethics program can help guide employees in making decisions. Hercules, Inc., a supplier of specialty chemicals, provides an ethics policy that employees like and use. Before the policy was implemented, many employees were frustrated. Now Hercules workers have guidelines that help them make daily decisions. Employees have some boundaries on what is acceptable financial transaction behavior, operational behavior, and human resource management behavior.

In addition, employees can use a hotline to discuss workplace actions they think may be unethical. Although employees are encouraged to first meet with their managers, the hotline provides another option.

Texas Instruments (TI) is a firm that has used a formal ethics program to guide behavior. TI's expectations and what is acceptable behavior for many situations and issues are spelled out in an ethics policy provided to each employee. TI expects each employee to know what's right and to behave accordingly. Guidelines on abusing drugs or alcohol, stealing and theft, lying to a supervisor, falsifying reports, and conflicts of interest are available.

Texas Instruments teaches the employees seven steps they can use to determine whether a decision is ethical.
1. Is the action legal?
2. Does it comply with TI values?
3. If you do it, will you feel bad?
4. How will it look in the newspaper?
5. If you know its wrong, don't do it.
6. If you're not sure, ask.
7. Keep asking until you get an answer.

In addition to the code of ethics guidelines, which has been translated into 10 languages for worldwide use, TI has a series of Cornerstone Booklets. Each booklet covers a single subject, such as personal rights, travel and entertainment, and conducting business with the U.S. government.

Many organizations are paying more attention to the ethical behavior of their employees. Hercules and TI have found that their programs cost very little and are worth the expense.

Sources: Gillain Flynn, "Make Employee Ethics Your Business," *Personnel Journal*, June 1995, pp. 30–41; Robert E. Calem, "To Catch A Thief," *Forbes ASAP*, June 5, 1995, pp. 44–45.

TABLE 2-2	FAYOL'S 14 PRINCIPLES OF MANAGEMENT

1. *Division of work.* Specialization of labor is necessary for organizational success.

2. *Authority.* The right to give orders must accompany responsibility.

3. *Discipline.* Obedience and respect help an organization run smoothly.

4. *Unity of command.* Each employee should receive orders from only one superior.

5. *Unity of direction.* The efforts of everyone in the organization should be coordinated and focused in the same direction.

6. *Subordination of individual interests to the general interest.* Resolving the tug of war between personal and organizational interests in favor of the organization is one of the management's greatest difficulties.

7. *Remuneration.* Employees should be paid fairly in accordance with their contribution.

8. *Centralization.* The relationship between centralization and decentralization is a matter of proportion; the optimum balance must be found for each organization.

9. *Scalar chain.* Subordinates should observe the formal chain of command unless expressly authorized by their respective superiors to communicate with each other.

10. *Order.* Both material things and people should be in their proper places.

11. *Equity.* Fairness that results from a combination of kindliness and justice will lead to devoted and loyal service.

12. *Stability and tenure of personnel.* People need time to learn their jobs.

13. *Initiative.* One of the greatest satisfactions if formulating and carrying out a plan.

14. *Esprit de corps.* Harmonious effort among individuals is the key to organizational success.

with scientific management, the reader should keep in mind the time in which Fayol developed his principles and his intent. He probably was the first major thinker to address problems of managing large-scale business organizations, which were a relatively new phenomenon then.

FUNCTIONS OF MANAGEMENT - Fayol was perhaps the first individual to discuss management as a process with specific functions that all managers must perform. He proposed four management functions.

1. *Planning.* Fayol believed that managers should (a) make the best possible forecast of events that could affect the organization and (b) draw up an operating plan to guide future decisions.

2. *Organizing.* Fayol believed that managers must determine the appropriate combination of machines, material, and humans necessary to accomplish the task.

3. *Commanding.* In Fayol's scheme, commanding involved directing the subordinates' activities. He believed that managers should set a good example and have direct, two-way communication with subordinates. Finally, managers must continually evaluate both the organizational structure and their subordinates, and they shouldn't hesitate to change the structure if they consider it faulty, or to fire incompetent subordinates.

4. *Controlling.* Controlling ensures that actual activities are consistent with planned activities. Fayol didn't expand the idea except to state that everything should be "subject to control."

Authority of Management

Born in Germany, Max Weber (1864–1920) studied law and then entered an academic career at Berlin University. He studied and reported on the theory of authority structures in organizations. He made a distinction between power (the ability to force people to obey) and authority (where orders are voluntarily obeyed by those receiving them). In an authority system, those in the subordinate role (workers) see the issuing of directives by those in the authority role (managers) as legitimate.

The first mode of exercising authority is based on the qualities of the leader. Weber used the Greek term *charisma* to mean any quality of the individual's personality that sets him apart from ordinary people. A second mode of exercising authority is through precedent and usage. Managers in such an interpretation have authority by virtue of the status and the position they've achieved or inherited.

Weber believed that the "bureaucratic" organization is the dominant institution in society because it's the most efficient. Precision, speed, unambiguity, continuity, unity, and strict subordination are results of bureaucratic arrangements. As used by Weber, **bureaucracy** refers to a management approach based on formal organizational structure with set rules and regulations that rely on specialization of labor, an authority hierarchy, and rigid promotion and selection criteria.

bureaucracy
An organizational design that relies on specialization of labor, a specific authority hierarchy, a formal set of rules and procedures, and rigid promotion and selection criteria.

Contributions and Limitations of the Classical Approach

The greatest contribution of the classical approach was that it identified management as an important element of organized society. Management has, if anything, increased in importance in today's more global and competitive world. Advocates of the classical approach believe that management—like law, medicine, and other occupations—should be practiced according to principles that managers can learn. It's these principles that managers in Central and Eastern Europe and in the Commonwealth of Independent States (e.g., Russia, Latvia, Belarus, etc.) must now learn in order to compete with the West and around the world.

The identification of management functions such as planning, organizing, commanding and controlling provided the basis for training new managers. How management functions are presented often differs, depending upon who's presenting them. But any listing of management functions acknowledges that managers are concerned with *what* the organization is doing, *how* it's to be done, and *whether* it was done.

Contributions of the classical approach, however, go beyond the important work of identifying the field of management and its process and functions. Many management techniques used today (for example, time and motion analysis, work simplification, incentive wage systems, production scheduling, personnel testing, and budgeting) are derived from the classical approach.

One major criticism of the classical approach is that the majority of its insights are too simplistic for today's complex organizations in a constantly changing world. Critics argue that scientific management and classical organization theory are more appropriate for the past, when most organizations' environments were stable and predictable. The changing environment, shifting expectations of workers, increasing competition, growing diversity of the workforce, rising government regulations, and changing public responsibility and ethical expectations of society today are discussed in the next chapter.

THE BEHAVIORAL APPROACH

The behavioral approach to management developed partly because practicing managers found that the ideas of the classical approach didn't lead to total efficiency and workplace harmony. Managers still encountered problems because subordinates didn't always behave as they were supposed to. Thus, interest grew in helping managers become more efficient.

The behavioral approach to management has two branches. The first branch, the *human relations approach*, became popular in the 1940s and 1950s. The second branch, the *behavioral science approach*, became popular in the 1950s and still receives a great deal of attention today.

human relations approach
An approach describing how managers interact with subordinates. Attention is focused on the individual worker's needs, goals, and expectations.

The Human Relations Approach

The term **human relations approach** focuses on individuals working in group settings. Managers and workers are studied in terms of what occurs with the group.

An Australian, Elton Mayo (1880–1949), has been called the founder of both the human relations and the industrial sociology movements. The research work that he directed at Harvard University showed the importance of groups in affecting individuals' behavior at work.

Mayo's initial research in textile mills was on reorganizing the work schedule to include more rest pauses for workers to use in completing their jobs. The major effects of adding rest pauses were to reduce turnover. Mayo and his team acquired a new application for rest pauses and took their experience to the Hawthorne Works of the Western Electric Company (more explanation below).

Mayo's writings and thinking led to a fuller realization and understanding of the human factor in work situations. Central to this was the discovery of the informal group as an outlet and source of motivation for workers. His work also led to an emphasis on the importance of an adequate upward-flowing communication system.

A prominent human relations contributor was Hugo Munsterberg (1863–1916), a German psychologist and philosopher. He published a book that linked scientific management and human behavior. Mary Parker Follett (1868–1933), another contributor to the human relations approach, laid the foundation for studies in group dynamics, conflict management, and political processes in organizations.

Followers of this approach believe that to develop good human relations, managers must know why their workers behave as they do and what psychological and social factors influence them.

Students of human relations bring to management's attention the important role individuals play in determining an organization's success or failure. They try to show how the process and functions of management are affected by differences in individual behavior and the influence of groups in the workplace. Thus, while scientific management concentrates on the job's *physical* environment, human relations concentrates on the *social* environment.

Human relations experts believe that management should recognize employees' needs for recognition and social acceptance. They suggested that since groups provide members with feelings of acceptance and dignity, management should look upon the work group as a positive force that could be utilized productively. Therefore, managers should be trained in people skills as well as technical skills.

The Behavioral Science Approach and the Hawthorne Studies

Other individuals who were university trained in the social sciences such as psychology, sociology, and cultural anthropology began to study people at work. They had advanced training in applying the scientific approach to the study of human behavior. These individuals have become known as *behavioral* scientists, and their approach is considered to be distinct from the human relations approach.

behavioral science approach
Using the techniques, attitudes, and opinions of psychologists, sociologists, and anthropologists to study and understand individuals in the workplace.

Individuals using the **behavioral science approach** believe that workers are much more complex than the "economic man" described in the classical approach or the "social man" described in the human relations approach. The behavioral science approach concentrates more on the nature of work itself and the degree to which it can fulfill the human need to use skills and abilities. Behavioral scientists believe that an individual is motivated to work for many reasons in addition to making money and forming social relationships.

Hawthorne Studies
The most famous studies ever conducted in the field of management. Done at Western Electric's Hawthorne plant in a suburb of Chicago.

As mentioned above, the **Hawthorne Studies** (1927–1932, in a Western Electric Plant) are the most famous in management literature.[12] The company (which manufactured equipment for the telephone company) was known for its concern for its employees' welfare. It had maintained high standards in wages and hours. The study's original aim was to determine the relationship between intensity of illumination and two groups of workers' efficiency, measured in output. The intensity of light under which one group worked was varied, but was held constant for the other group.

Before Mayo and his Harvard research team arrived, the initial illumination studies were completed by another research group. Mayo and his team were presented with the findings that when illumination increased, productivity increased. However, when illumination decreased, productivity increased. It appeared that workers reacted more to the concern of the researchers about illumination than to the actual increase or decrease in illumination. This phenomenon is called the **Hawthorne Effect**.

The Harvard researchers also set up a relay assembly test room experiment at the Hawthorne plant. Six women were selected to work on assembling telephone relays in the test room. The women were studied over a long period of time as working conditions were altered (e.g., method of payment, rest period length). There were 12 different changes introduced. It was determined that in each experimental period, output was higher than in the preceding one.

The researchers concluded that changes and improvement in output were less affected by any of the 12 changes in work conditions that were introduced than by the attitudes of the six work team individuals. The cohesiveness and friendships among the team members were found to be significant. The group developed leadership and a common purpose—an increase in the output rate.

The Hawthorne Studies pointed out that workers are motivated by more than economic factors. Workers' attitudes are affected by their feelings about each other and a common purpose. Today this is a commonsense thought, but in 1927 to 1932, it wasn't a common belief.[13] The research was conducted before the era of collective bargaining and safety regulations, when workdays averaged 10 to 12 hours and 12-year-olds worked alongside adults.

Hawthorne Effect
The tendency of people being observed in a research effort to react more to the observer than to the actual working condition.

The Impact of Technology on Structure: A Behavioral Science Approach

The scientific study of the structure and technology of an organization was popularized through the work of industrial sociologist Joan Woodward. Her work encouraged managers to not seriously consider "one best way" claims of consultants and other managers. A number of writers and others were proposing "one best way" solutions to structure decisions. That is, there were claims that a particular structure should be used because it is the "one best way." Woodward's research and writing challenged this view.[14]

While a professor of industrial sociology in London, Joan Woodward, from 1953 to 1957, led the South-East Essex research team studying manufacturing firms. She investigated characteristics such as span of control (number of workers reporting to a manager), number of levels of authority, amount of written communications, and clarity of job definitions. She found significant differences across firms.

Woodward's research work and additional case studies showed that a firm's technology plays a significant role in its structure. She, unlike Frederick W. Taylor, found that there is no best way to manage or structure an organization. She warned against accepting principles of management as universally applicable.

Woodward's work pioneered an improved understanding of how empirical research can be used to change organizations' structure. She elevated empirical work to a level whereby managers could derive value from the results. Woodward also illustrated how comparisons of a large number of firms could be managed so that generalizations could be made to other organizations.

Contributions and Limitations of the Behavioral Approach

For the student of management, the behavioral approach has contributed a wealth of important ideas and research results on the people-managing aspect of management. The basic rationale is that since management must get work done through others, management is really applied behavioral science because a manager must motivate, lead, and understand interpersonal relations.

The efficiency emphasis of the classical management approach was supplemented with a focus on people and their needs, emotions, and thoughts. The work of the behavioral management approach resulted in organizations being considered as social systems with both formal and informal patterns of authority and communications. Workers, their skills, and their involvement in groups and motivation were proposed to be at the core of any success that management achieves.

The basic assumption that managers must know how to deal with people appears valid. But management is more than applied behavioral science. For the behavioral approach to be useful to managers, it must make them better practitioners of the process of management. It must help them in problem situations. In many cases, this objective hasn't been achieved because of the tendency of some behavioral scientists to use technical terms when trying to introduce their research findings to practicing managers. Also, in some situations, one behavioral scientist (a psychologist) may have a different suggestion from another (a sociologist) for the same management problem. Human behavior is complex and is studied from a variety of viewpoints. This complicates the problem for a manager trying to use insights from the behavioral sciences.

THE DECISION AND INFORMATION SCIENCES (DISC) APPROACH

decision and information sciences approach
In working with people, this approach uses mathematics, statistics, decision-making principles, and information systems to resolve problems.

The **decision and information sciences (DISC) approach** to management is in one sense a modern version of early emphasis on the "management of work" by those interested in scientific management. Its key feature is the use of decision making, information systems, mathematics, and statistics to aid in resolving production and operations problems. Thus, the approach focuses on solving technical rather than human behavior problems.

Origins of the DISC Approach

The DISC approach has only existed formally for approximately 50 years. It began during the early part of World War II when England was confronted with some complex military problems that had never been faced before, such as antisubmarine warfare strategy. To try to solve these problems, the English formed teams of scientists, mathematicians, and physicists. The units, named *operations research* teams, proved to be extremely valuable. When the war was over, American firms began to use the approach.

Herbert Simon, a distinguished American political and social scientist, influenced the thinking and practice of decision- and information-science-based management.[15] He viewed management as equivalent to decision making, and his major interest has been how decisions are made and how they might be made more effectively.

Simon describes three stages of decision making:

1. Finding occasions requiring a decision (intelligence).
2. Inventing, developing, and analyzing possible courses of action (design).
3. Selecting a course of action (choice).

In Simon's thinking, all managerial action is decision making. Economists' traditional theory is that decisions are made on the basis of rationality. However, in the real world, there are limits to rationality such as the emotions of the decision maker. In place of the "economically rational" decision maker, Simon proposes a "satisficing" decision maker. That is, decisions are made that are satisfactory or "good enough." Instead of searching for a decision to maximize profits, an adequate profit is sought.

Simon views decisions on a continuum ranging from programmed, or routinely occurring, to nonprogrammed, or nonroutine and unstructured. Because many decisions are toward the nonprogrammed end of the continuum, techniques such as mathematical analysis, operations research, and computer simulation have gained prominence. These techniques were first used for programmed decisions. However, with the use of computers and mathematics, more and more elements of judgment can now be incorporated into the decision-making process. As computer technology becomes more advanced, more complex decisions will become programmed.

Contributions and Limitations of the DISC Approach

Today the most important contributions of decision and information sciences management approach are in the areas of production management and operations management and information systems. *Production management* focuses on manufacturing technology and the flow of material in a manufacturing plant. Here, management science has contributed techniques that help solve production scheduling problems, product and service quality improvement problems, budgeting problems, and maintenance of optimal inventory levels.

Operations management is similar to production management except that it focuses on a wide class of problems and includes organizations such as hospitals, banks, government, and the military, which have operations problems but don't manufacture tangible products. For such organizations, management science has contributed techniques to solve such problems as budgeting, planning for workforce development programs, and aircraft scheduling.

Information systems refers to the use of computers in helping managers make better decisions and increase an organization's efficiency. The computer now permits managers to gather and accurately process large volumes of data, produce reports in a timely manner, make projections about the future, communicate with geographically separate parts of the organization, and apply quantitative techniques to improve the enterprise's efficiency and performance.

Information is a chief ingredient used by managers. It is data evaluated or processed for a particular use. Information is disseminated up, down, and across an enterprise's units. Large volumes of information are now commonly stored in databases (centralized collections of data and/or information for a particular subject). Organizations of all sizes now depend on the flow of information and the availability of databases to make more informed and more timely decisions. Planning, organization, commanding, and controlling decisions have been enhanced because of the availability of information systems.

We noted in our discussion of the behavioral approach that management is more than applied behavioral science. At this point, we should stress that decision and information sciences can't substitute for management. DISC approach techniques are especially useful to the manager performing the management process. If there's a flaw in the DISC approach, it's that too little emphasis has been placed on people and how they can use the tools and techniques available. What good is information provided by a computer if it's not interpretable, relevant, or specific? What good is a new statistical quality control chart if the worker can't interpret its meaning or even produce the chart? What good is the mathematically oriented inventory model if the data entered are inaccurate? Workers, customers, and managers using DISC techniques and approaches need to be viewed as users, interpreters, and benefactors. Their needs, reactions, and understanding must be weighed in deciding on an appropriate DISC approach.

THE SYSTEMS MANAGEMENT APPROACH

The systems approach to management is essentially a way of thinking about organizations and management problems. A **system** is a collection of parts that operates interdependently to achieve common goals.[16] The whole of the system is considered to be greater than the sum of its parts. 3M (Minnesota Mining and Manufacturing Co.) is more than a research and development, marketing, and production unit.

system
A collection of parts that operate interdependently to achieve common goals.

From the systems perspective, management involves managing and solving problems in each part of the organization, but doing so with the understanding that actions taken in one part of the organization affect other parts of the organization. For example, implementing a solution to a problem in a firm's production department will likely affect other aspects of the company such as marketing, finance, and personnel. Each part is tightly linked to other organizational parts; no single part of an organization exists and operates in isolation from the others. Thus, in solving problems, managers must view the organization as a dynamic whole and try to anticipate their decision's unintended as well as intended impacts.

Chester Barnard (1886–1961) was president of New Jersey Bell Telephone and a systems advocate. He viewed an organization as an aggregation of units that interact. He introduced the concept of the "system of coordination." Barnard was the first major theorist after the Hawthorne studies to emphasize the importance and variability of individuals in the work setting.

Barnard believed that an essential element of organizations is people's willingness to contribute their individual efforts to the cooperative system. The need for cooperation and interdependence is clearly presented in Barnard's classic management book *The Functions of the Executive,* in the following:

> *A cooperative system is a complex of physical, biological, personal, and social components which are in a specific systematic relationship by reason of the cooperation of two or more persons for at least one definite end.*[17]

Open Systems

According to the systems approach, the elements of an organization are interconnected. The approach also views the organization as linked to its environment. Organizational effectiveness, even survival, depends on the organization's interaction with its environment. A battery-powered digital watch would be considered a relatively closed system. The installation of the battery is the only outside intervention. Once in place the watch operates without any input from the external environment[18] To further your understanding of these ideas, let's consider Compaq Computers, Inc., as an example. As a computer manufacturer, Compaq Computer is an **open system** that actively interacts with its environment. (For now, consider the environment as comprised of such factors as customers, competitors, financial institutions, suppliers, and the government. The environment is detailed in Chapter 3.) Figure 2–2 shows Compaq Computer's basic elements as an open system.

Active interaction means that Compaq both obtains resources from and provides resources to its environment. For example, in order to function, Compaq must obtain *inputs* from the environment. The company needs motivated, skilled employees who can design and manufacture innovative, high-quality personal and business computers. Compaq obtains this resource from the environment—specifically, from the graduating classes of universities nationwide, from competitors, and from other organizations.

Financial resources (money) are needed to build manufacturing facilities, to fund Compaq's R&D efforts, and to meet any number of other expenses. Compaq obtains the funds from the environment—from banks, other lending institutions, and people who buy shares of Compaq's stock. Raw materials (e.g., computer parts) are obtained from outside suppliers in the environment. Information about the latest computer product technology and about the latest products developed by Compaq's competitors is also needed. This information substantially influences the design and manufacture of Compaq's computers. Information is obtained from the environment—from research journals, computer conferences, and other external contacts.[19]

These inputs are used, coordinated, and managed in a *transformation* process that produces *output*—in this case, personal and business computers. However, the company's task isn't complete. Compaq provides this resource (output) to the environment by deliv-

open system
An organization that interacts with its environment and uses the feedback received to make changes and modifications.

FIGURE 2–2
The Four Parts of an Open System Organization
(Compaq Computer, Inc.)

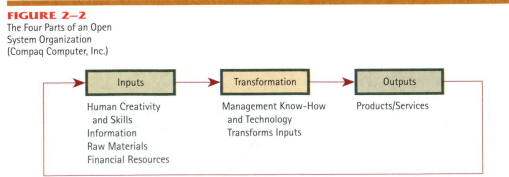

Environmental Feedback Serves as a Response to Products/Services

ering its computers to retail outlets for sale to customers. Does the company survive? Only if the customer reacts to Compaq's computers and decides to purchase the product. The customer's decision to buy or look elsewhere (for an IBM, Apple, or Hewlett-Packard computer) provides Compaq with *feedback*.

If the feedback is positive (customers buy Compaq), the environment provides a critical input to Compaq—cash that the company uses to obtain other inputs from the environment such as top-quality employees, materials, and knowledge. Negative feedback (no sales) provides Compaq with a serious problem. Regardless, Compaq Computer must closely monitor feedback and act upon it (e.g., changing a failing product's design or features based on customer responses). As an open system in a dynamic environment, Compaq can't afford to ignore the environment. Neglecting development in the environment (e.g., technological innovations, competitors' moves) will, over time, doom the company.[20]

Contributions and Limitations of the Systems Management Approach

Importantly, most organizations today operate as open systems to survive and utilize a systems perspective of management. Managers must think broadly about a problem and not concentrate only on the desired results, because these results will impact other problems and parts of the organization as well as the environment beyond the organization. The age-old confrontation between the production objective of low manufacturing costs (achieved

TABLE 2–3	MANAGEMENT MILESTONES	
5000 BC	4000 BC	500 BC
Sumerians recognized record keeping.	Egyptians recognized need for planning, organizing, and conducting.	Chinese introduced principle of specialization.
1750 ad	1799	1871
The Industrial Revolution.	Eli Whitney. Use of cost accounting and control.	Joseph Wharton established first college course in business management at the University of Pennsylvania.
1898	1911	1916
Mary Parker Follett discussed the benefits of group participation.	Frederick W. Taylor published Principle of Scientific Management.	Henri Fayol, French industrialist, published his master work.
1927	1936	1950
Elton Mayo and his Harvard colleagues began their study of the Hawthrone works of Western Electric.	The Academy of Management was founded to advance the study of management.	W. Edwards Deming first introduced quality control ideas to Japanese business managers, which helped Japan to become world-class quality leaders.
1965	1970s	1981
Joan Woodward published her findings on technology's impact on organizations.	Contingency theories were introduced.	William G. Ouchi introduced the concept of Theory Z management.
1982	1990	1993
Tom Peters and Robert Waterman identified aspects of excellently managed firms and stimulated thinking about management practices.	Harvard professor Michael Porter combined economic theory and strategy development to analyze competitive advantage.	Michael Hammer and James Champy introduced the concept of reengineering the organization or the redesign of the processes of an organization.

by making one product in one color and style) and the marketing objective of a broad product line (requiring high production costs) is a good example. Both objectives can't be achieved at the same time. In this situation, a compromise is necessary for the overall system to achieve its objective. And in seeking a compromise, the organization must always be mindfully aware of the environment (e.g., will customers accept the product's price or design?). The objectives of the individual parts must be compromised for the objective of the entire firm.

Using the systems approach in the preceding example, individual managers must adopt a broad perspective. With a systems perspective, managers can more easily achieve coordination between the objectives of the organization's various parts and the objectives of the organization as a whole.[21]

Critics consider the systems approach to be abstract and not very practical. Talking about inputs, transformations, and outputs isn't how everyday managers discuss problems, make decisions, and face reality. The Compaq manager must think, respond, and observe. He or she doesn't consider how transformation will occur or what the production unit will think about the decision made to go head-to-head with the competition and reduce personal computer prices. The systems concept is good for classroom analysis, but being in the middle of daily decision making precludes deep systems-like analysis and thinking.

THE CONTINGENCY MANAGEMENT APPROACH

contingency management approach
An approach that considers an organization's objectives, organizational and job design, human resources, environment, and managerial skills as interacting and affecting management decisions about planning, organizing, commanding, and controlling.

The systems approach to management advocates that managers recognize that organizations are systems comprised of interdependent parts and that a change in one part affects other parts. This insight is important. Beyond this, however, managers need to see how the parts fit together. The **contingency management approach** can help you better understand their interdependence.

The contingency view of organizations and their management suggests that the organization is a system composed of subsystems and delineated by identifiable boundaries from its environmental suprasystem. The contingency view seeks to understand the interrelationships within and among subsystems, as well as between the organization and its environment, and to define patterns of relationships or configurations of variables. It emphasizes the multivariate nature of organizations and attempts to understand how organizations operate under varying conditions and in specific circumstances. Contingency views are ultimately directed toward suggesting organizational designs and managerial systems most appropriate for specific situations.[22]

Universalist versus Situationalist Theories

In the early years of management theory, some individuals, like Frederick W. Taylor, advocated the "universalist" view of management effectiveness. Universalists argued that there indeed exists a one best way to perform different management functions. In their view, the task of management theorists is to identify these superior management prescriptions by developing and then testing theory via research.

However, other management theorists, called *situationalists*, disagreed. In their view, no one best approach to management exists because each situation is too different. No one principle or prescription is supremely applicable across totally unique situations. In fact, very few principles and concepts are useful across situations. Because each managerial situation is unique, a manager must approach each situation with few if any guidelines to follow. Management effectiveness first requires that a manager evaluate each situation from scratch before deciding which action to take.

The contingency approach attempts to bridge the extreme points on this continuum of views. Like the situationalists, contingency theorists don't subscribe to any one best approach to management. In their view, the situations that managers face do differ and thus prohibit any one best prescription. Ray Kroc, in the fast food industry, used contingency thinking in always searching for innovations to stay ahead of competition.

Identifying and Evaluating Contingency Variables

Contingency theorists stop short of asserting that all managerial situations are totally unique. Rather, they argue that situations are often similar to the extent that some principles of management can be effectively applied. However, the appropriate principles must be identified. This is done by first identifying the relevant *contingency variables* in the situation and then evaluating those factors.[23]

L-S Electro-Galvanizing (L-SE), a small firm in Cleveland, Ohio, has applied the contingency management approach.[24] Faced with competition in the specialty steel business, the firm decided to devise a system that was most appropriate for a small unionized firm. Before steel can be transformed into hoods and other car parts, it must first be electrogalvanized to prevent corrosion. That requires feeding rolls of steel into a machine that essentially coats the steel with the right mix of zinc and other chemicals before rerolling it and producing the finished product. Unfortunately, even barely discernible blemishes result in customers sending back bad steel. The managers thought about many different ways, structures, procedures, and incentives to reduce the number of blemishes and returned products.

REFLECTIONS BY PHILIP B. CROSBY

The Evolution of Management

Soon after I gained employment as a quality technician back in 1952, the company sent me to quality control school. There I learned that each process had its own lifestyle and results based on the laws of probability. I also learned that we should assign acceptable quality levels (AQL) to know how many good things would emerge from the process. But the people conducting the process weren't to be trusted, so all output had to examined carefully and protected from use if it was to found wanting. Little work was done properly the first time ,but this was attributed to humans' built-in error factor. All in all, error was inevitable and it was up to the science of quality control to protect the world.

My education and military experience were in medicine where the main effort was to keep people from getting sick. For this reason, vaccines had been developed to spare people smallpox, diphtheria, polio, and other disagreeable diseases. So all of this scientific determination that things could never be done right the first time on a regular basis didn't make sense to me. But my teachers and coworkers believed it all and so were upset with my deductions. They would point to the statistics and results.

Sure enough, the manufacturing operations were struggling to raise their quality to the AQLs assigned—indicating that more charts and more control were necessary. However, I thought things should be the other way around. The human element was completely missing: these beliefs assumed that "people were no damn good" and that was the end of it.

I felt that the concepts of quality control and of quality assurance (which checks upon quality control) were fatally flawed. I felt that the defect rates were self-fulfilling, caused by the concept rather than the process.

Since I was on the absolute bottom of the organization chart, my concerns had little effect except to generate some fatherly lectures from my superiors. But these only encouraged me since they were offering advice, not hemlock.

I felt that the main problem was that "quality" was considered to be "goodness" and as therefore negotiable. I proposed that we define the word as meaning "conformance to requirements." That way we could spend our time teaching and helping people to do their jobs right the first time, rather than just treating the wounded. As we learned, we could then improve the requirements. Requirements, I thought, originated when we determined what the customers needed and described the actions necessary to produce that. We weren't talking just about the shop workers here—most of the expensive problems were caused by errors originating in the white-collar and other service areas.

A paper I wrote on these ideas met with a complete lack of support. The conventional wisdom of quality control couldn't accept it. A few years later when I brought the idea of zero defects as a performance standard, it was completely rejected—even though it worked.

But ideas that deserve to live, live. And now we see that the concept of preventing has become a normal part of management's lifestyle. Relationships with employees, suppliers, and customers are beginning to be a priority of management. The old "do a good job and you get to keep it" style is gone. But there are those who still think doing things right the first time costs more.

We need to continually test the concepts put forth by business practitioners and philosophers. People who would become effective and prosper can't just accept whatever has been believed before. Personal success comes from applying an open mind to current attitudes. A large chest of unsound concepts is waiting to be challenged.

After all, not too long ago tomatoes were considered poisonous.

A team of 13 L-SE workers was given the task of addressing the quality problem. The team was motivated by the belief that greater worker responsibility is the best way to reduce complaints and blemishes. L-SE employees, on a volunteer basis, actually run the company. There are seven employee committees that handle everything from hiring and pay schedules to quality checks and handling social events. The quality system and committee begin with training. Management pays higher wages to workers who successfully complete advanced courses in quality systems and controls. The firm's goal is to train all employees for every job. In addition, employees can earn bonuses of up to 25 percent of their salaries if they reach goals set for the L-SE employee quality committee. Customer satisfaction is a top priority. Each month L-SE surveys its customers about quality. The company also decided to send line employees to meet with customers to discuss how quality can be improved. L-SE didn't adopt a standard management approach. The firm considered its competition, customers, technological competencies, and employees' skills and then decided on the seven-employee committee structure. The result was a savings of $2.2 million for fewer blemishes, and a higher level of morale among proud employees. L-SE managers assumed at the outset that a design and managerial system appropriate for their situation could result from employee involvement.

CONTEMPORARY INFLUENCES ON THE EVOLUTION OF MANAGEMENT

Frederick W. Taylor, Herbert Simon, Henri Fayol, and other pioneers of 20th-century management thinking and practice are historical reference beacons that management students read about. These pioneers set the course for reporting about, understanding, and studying management and workers. In addition to these historical giants, there are a number of contemporary philosophers and advocates of management practices. They may eventually stand beside the early pioneers for their shaping of how management is practiced.

Tom Peters: Excellent Companies

Management consultant Tom Peters was a principal in the consulting firm of McKinsey & Company when his first book, *In Search of Excellence*[25] (with Robert Waterman), became a runaway best-seller. His other best-sellers have been *A Passion for Excellence*,[26] *Thriving on*

Chaos: Handbook for Management Revolution,[27] and *Liberation Management*.[28] Today Peters travels around the world giving advice and inspirational talks about managing. He identifies nine aspects of excellently run companies:

1. *Managing ambiguity and paradox.* Chaos is the rule of businesses, not the exception. The business climate is always uncertain and always ambiguous. The rational, numerical approach doesn't always work because we live in irrational times.

2. *A bias for action.* Do it, try it, fix it. The point is to try something, without fear of failure. Sochiro Honda, founder of Honda, said that only 1 out of 100 of his ideas worked. Fortunately for him, he kept trying after his 99th failure.

3. *Close to the customer.* Excellent companies have an almost uncanny feel for what their customers want. This is because they're a customer of their own product or they closely listen to their customers.

4. *Autonomy and entrepreneurship.* Ownership of a department, tasking, or problem is essential in motivating employees. It's the most cited reason for entering into self-employment. Excellent companies allow and encourage autonomy and within-company entrepreneurship.

5. *Productivity through people.* Not surprisingly, people act in accordance with their treatment. Treat them as being untrustworthy, and they will be. Treat them as business partners, and they will be. Excellent companies have taken the leap of faith required to trust their employees to do the right thing right.

6. *Hands-on, value-driven.* Practice management by walking around. Constantly ask the value added of every process and procedure.

7. *Stick to the knitting.* Stay close to your organization's basic industry. The skills or culture involved in a different industry may be a shock that's fatal to the organization.

8. *Simple form, lean staff.* Organizations with few layers of management unencumbered by a bloated headquarters characterize the excellent companies.

9. *Loose-tight properties.* Tight control is maintained while at the same time allowing staff far more flexibility than is the norm.

Peters believes that he made a modest, close-to-the-customer plan in *In Search of Excellence*. His latest book, *Liberation Management*, states that being close to the customer isn't really enough. Management must remove structural impediments to being close to the customer. Liberating the organization from rigid rules, hierarchies, stilted policies, and stifling demands are steps in the direction of developing what Peters calls a "symbiosis" with both domestic and foreign customers.

Peters' contribution isn't found in his methods of study, the ability to replicate his conclusions, or attempts to conform to practices he recommends. In fact, researchers have determined that the excellent firms identified by Peters and Waterman may not have applied the principles called for by the authors.[29] Peters' contribution is that he has stimulated managers, researchers, and theorists to think more seriously about organizations, the tasks of managers and workers, and how to improve management practices. He and his coauthors literally put management on the front burner. Prior to the publication of *In Search of Excellence*, few people paid much attention to management practices, managerial dilemmas, or managerial excellence.

William Ouchi: Theory Z

Given the success of many Japanese organizations in the 1980s and early 1990s, many researchers and management practitioners have analyzed the factors behind these successes. One set of recommendations for American managers was introduced by UCLA management professor William Ouchi in 1981.[30] He introduced what was called *Theory Z* or the combining of American and Japanese management practices. Ouchi based his Theory Z on studies conducted in U.S. and Japanese organizations. Figure 2–3 presents Ouchi's findings about how management practices differ and how Theory Z would look.

Ouchi visualized a Theory Z organization as having a distinct American flavor (e.g., individual responsibility) and a unique Japanese emphasis (e.g., collective decision making). The Theory Z approach won't work in every situation, but it encourages managers to consider combining philosophy, methods, and tools to create a more effective organization.

FIGURE 2–3
Organization Principles

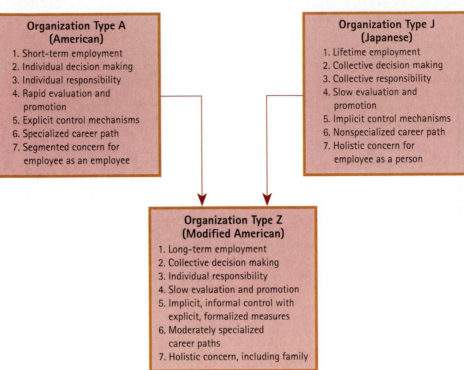

Michael Porter: Competitive Advantage

Michael Porter (a Harvard Business School professor of industrial organization and a consultant) was one of the first contemporary scholars to apply traditional economic thinking to management problems.[31] Porter explains corporate strategy in terms of a competitive marketplace. He identifies four generic strategies: (1) cost leadership, (2) differentiation, (3) cost focus, and (4) focused differentiation, as shown in the Porter generic strategy matrix (Figure 2–4). The two axes reflect competitive advantage and competitive scope. Competitive advantage can be gained through lower cost and differentiation. The term

FIGURE 2–4
Porter's Generic Competitive
Strategies

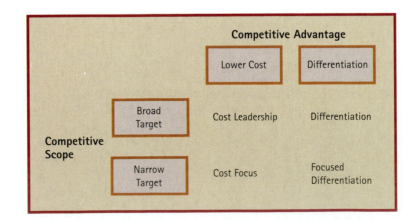

Source: Reprinted with permission of *The Free Press*, a Division of MacMillan, Inc., from *The Competitive Advantage of Nations* by Michael E. Porter. Copyright © 1990 by Michael E. Porter.

differentiation refers to the ability to provide unique and superior value to customers in terms of product quality, special features, or after-sale service.

The Japanese, long before Porter introduced his competitive advantage concept, attempted to gain market share in the world's automobile industry. The following Global Exchange explores how the Japanese gained entry into America's auto market in the 1950s and what they are now doing in Japan.

Competitive scope designates the breadth of the firm's target within its industry. A firm must choose the range of product variables it will produce, the way to distribute its products, the geographic area it will serve, and the array of industries in which it will compete.

The cost leadership strategy involves keeping costs and prices lower than competitors. Korean shipyards produce ships at lower costs and lower prices than their main competitors, Japanese firms.

Differentiation is a strategy that attempts to improve a firm's competitive position by developing unique products. Nike's Air Jordan shoes are unique because of their high-technology "air" construction; Coca-Cola has a unique taste and can be bought anyplace in the world; and Benneton sweaters have unique color and patterns.

A cost focus target emphasizes gaining competitive advantage through cost control in a narrow market area. Atlantic Richfield (ARCO) adopted this strategy in the early 1980s when it decided to service customers west of the Rocky Mountains. The fast-growing western states were close to the resource base, Alaska. Therefore, ARCO was able to cut distribution and transportation costs. The result was a lower price of gas and paying attention to a narrower western states market area.

GLOBAL EXCHANGE

PRACTICING PORTER'S COMPETITIVE ADVANTAGE STRATEGIES

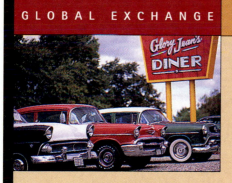

Americans and Europeans are learning that the Japanese not only understand what Michael Porter discusses in terms of competitive advantage, but Japanese firms practice what he discusses. In 1955 three companies made 95 percent of the cars that were sold in America. The cars that poured out of Detroit in those days were styled for vanity. Even today people like to be seen in them on a Saturday night—two-seat Ford Thunderbirds and two-tone Chevrolet Bel Airs, clear-topped Mercury's, and understated Chrysler 300s.

General Motors, Ford, and Chrysler could have produced every car sold, but antitrust legislation threats kept them away from controlling a 5 percent mar-

ket share. The Big Three controlled the distribution system except for the 5 percent segment. They had a competitive advantage. They sold cars to a captive market of exclusive dealerships. The United States dominated the industry.

One small crack in the network of dealerships permitted the Japanese to enter the American market. For America's Big Three, the exclusive-dealership rule was interpreted as a violation of the Clayton Antitrust Act in 1949. This is when auto imports from Japan, Germany, Britain, and France started to compete for a piece of the U.S. market. Volkswagen was the early leader of foreign car imports to America. Around 1958 the Nissan Datsun started to enter the U.S. market in a significant way. The Japanese, long before Porter wrote about and discussed corporate strategy in terms of gaining a competitive advantage, worked on lowering prices, controlling costs, increasing gas mileage, and improving their dealer base. The Japanese concluded in the late 1950s that the small-car category was where they could gain a competitive advantage over the Big Three. In 1993 the Big Three accounted for about 65 percent of domestic car sales; the 95 percent of the market monopoly is gone.

The Japanese in the early 1990s adopted a European competitive advantage strategy. Western European car sales slumped, and the European Community requested that Japan hold the line on price reductions of imported autos and those made in Japanese-owned plants in Europe. Japanese autos (imported and produced in Europe) made up about 10 percent of the 1995 European auto market.

The Japanese car makers certainly understand Porter's competitive advantage concept. They have practiced it around the world, beginning earnestly around 1958 to gain market share. Consumers around the world have gained a new range of competitively priced and high-quality vehicles because the Japanese have worked at gaining competitive advantages in the auto industry. Japanese competition has helped make the Big Three in the United States aware of the strategies that Porter so eloquently writes, lectures, and consults about throughout the world.

Source: Adapted from "Car Wars," *The Economist*, May 20, 1995, p. 59; J.M. Fenster, "Detroit Opens the Door for Japan," *Audacity* (Winter 1993), pp. 28–37; and "The Enemy Within," *The Economist*, June 12, 1993, pp. 67–68.

A focused differentiation strategy involves providing a competitive and unique product and/or service to a narrow market area.[32] Fiesta Food Mart has adopted a focused differentiation strategy in Houston and San Antonio. The store provides a unique array of foods for the different ethnic groups in the two cities. The food products aren't found in the natural chains and other competitors. Fiesta's customers find the normal array of goods, but immigrants from Vietnam, El Salvador, Mexico, Peru, and Brazil also find familiar ethnic foods.

Porter's approach is insightful and provocative. He is unique in concluding that the best analytical focus for explaining economic performance is neither the individual firm nor macroeconomic forces. Porter proposes that the explanation about performance is found in studying why nations succeed in particular industries. A handful of nations dominate any one industry. Also, competitors tend to be tightly bunched in a geographic area within a nation (e.g., Silicon Valley in California).

SUMMARY OF LEARNING OBJECTIVES

LIST SOME OF THE MANAGEMENT THINKERS AND DESCRIBE THEIR CONTRIBUTIONS.

This chapter refers to six specific individuals as pioneers. Frederick W. Taylor is called the Father of Scientific Management. He introduced the scientific study and observation of workers. Max Weber studied power, authority, and bureaucracy. Henri Fayol (a practitioner) proposed a theoretical analysis of management and also presented management as a process with specific functions. Elton Mayo founded the human relations and industrial sociology approaches to management. Joan Woodward determined through her research that technology plays a significant role in how an organization is structured. Woodward's empirical work and conclusions showed that research can be used by practicing managers. She provided an applied set of empirical findings that could be incorporated in actual organizations. Peter Drucker offered suggestions on how best to manage in a rapidly changing world. He stressed continuous improvement, the exploitation of knowledge, and innovation.

DIFFERENTIATE BETWEEN THE EFFICIENCY EMPHASIS OF THE CLASSICAL APPROACH TO MANAGEMENT AND THE PEOPLE EMPHASIS OF THE BEHAVIORAL APPROACH TO MANAGEMENT.

In the classical approach, efficiency of operation, behavior, and work flow is the focal point. In the behavioral approach, the individual or group in human terms is the focal point. Both approaches are important and need to be considered by managers.

DESCRIBE WHAT FREDERICK W. TAYLOR MEANT BY THE TERM SCIENTIFIC METHODS.

Taylor believed in using scientific methods to study work, to set up experiments, and to observe workers. He was an advocate of applying science to studying and answering questions about efficiency, cooperation, and motivation.

DESCRIBE THE DECISION AND INFORMATION SCIENCES APPROACH.

This approach emphasizes the management of work. It uses decision making, information systems, mathematics, and statistics to study and solve management problems. Techniques, tools, and models are provided to managers to help them solve operations and production problems.

DESCRIBE THE SYSTEMS APPROACH.

This approach provides a framework for viewing organizations as a collection of parts that operate interdependently to accomplish common goals. It points out that each part, unit, individual, and goal of an organization is linked to others. A change in one area will result in a change in other areas.

EXPLAIN THE SIGNIFICANCE OF THE CONTINGENCY APPROACH TO MANAGEMENT.

This view is termed multivariate in that a number of variables are examined to understand how an organization operates under varying conditions and in specific circumstances.

KEY TERMS

behavioral science approach, p. 40
bureaucracy, p. 39
contingency management approach, p. 46
decision and information sciences (DISC)
  approach, p. 42

Hawthorne Effect, p. 41
Hawthorne Studies, p. 40
human relations approach, p. 39

open system, p. 44
scientific management, p. 36
system, p. 43

REVIEW AND DISCUSSION QUESTIONS

Recall

1. What role did Elton Mayo play in advancing the understanding and practice of management?
2. Is there a universal contingency explanation of what motivates workers? Explain.
3. How did Frederick Taylor's background influence his approach to studying management?
4. How did the Hawthorne Studies influence thinking about work groups and motivation in the workplace?

Understanding

5. Why is there no best way to manage office employees?
6. Why is it accurate to consider a firm such as General Mills to be an open system?
7. Tom Peters has been criticized as offering only anecdotes to practitioners. Are anecdotes of any value? How did Peters and Waterman's In Search of Excellence affect interest in management?

Application

8. Examine additional historical accounts about early management pioneers. Whom would you include in a list of pioneers that isn't mentioned in this chapter? Tell us about a missing pioneer.
9. Select an individual pioneer presented in the chapter and prepare an analysis of three contributions to contemporary management he/she made that were not introduced in the chapter.
10. Select three specific techniques that the decision and information sciences approach to management has contributed to practitioners. After you select three techniques, ask a manager whether the techniques you selected are being used and, if so, where?

CASE STUDY

A Competitive Advantage: Treating Women Fairly

The evolution of management has been presented in this chapter. As management knowledge and practice have evolved so have the composition of the workforce. Significant shifts in demographics in the United States and Europe especially have created a different workplace setting at the close of the 20th century. Managers today are faced with people who are different in many ways—age, education, values, gender, experiences, personality, and work ethic attitudes. We have moved in the past century from an era in which large portions of the workforce were assured to be similar, to an era in which the workforce consists of many diverse individuals, each of whom wants to be valued.

Today's workforce doesn't look, behave, and think like the workforce Frederick Taylor or the Gilbreths studied and learned about. Many culturally diverse groups from around the world are spread throughout the American, European, and Canadian workforces. Gaining competitive advantage will require that managers must understand, address, and respect diversity. Although many challenges exist, there are numerous opportunities at hand for managers that understand history and chart the course for future generations. The proper management of diverse work populations is a reality that managers must cope with to be successful.

Women have increasingly entered the U.S. workforce and in the past few years accounted for 60 percent of the total increase in employment. A survey conducted in a workshop reported by John Fernandez collected comments of participants. A few of the comments are as follows:

It seems like women discriminate against women quite often. (white woman)
Pregnant women seem to be more discriminated against. There is an inadequate attitude about mothers as employees. (white woman)
Personal discussions between men and women often center on the distrust between the sexes. Until this is relieved, both sexes will reflect discrimination within the company. (white man)
I believe many women feel more discriminated against than they actually are; they sometimes look at events and issues, trying (perhaps unconsciously), to find a prejudice that may not really exist. (white man)

These comments point to workplace realities about diversity in attitudes and opinions. Why should managers be concerned about or interested in developing the talents of women? There are a host of opinions about this, ranging from obtaining the best talent you can and developing it to men and women are so different in their managerial talents that determining whether it is worthwhile to learn about and utilize the differences is questionable.

The "glass ceiling" or the invisible barrier that prohibits women from rising up the managerial hierarchy still exists. Whether the "glass ceiling" and overt gender bias stereotyping of women will be removed in the foreseeable future is an issue that managers need to debate and consider. Gender bias or preconceptions that result in unequal treatment of women are documented in recruitment, selection, promotion, salary allocation, performance appraisal, and management development.

As management continues to evolve and become more relevant and effective, the employment, retention, and motivation of women will have to become a top priority. Being listed as a top priority and achieving significant changes in perception, attitudes, and behavior are challenging tasks for 21st-century managers. Just as the Gilbreths, Taylor, and Fayol focused on improving the efficiency of managers and workers, a new cadre of management thinkers and practitioners will have to focus on diversity and unravel the mysteries of how to optimize the potential of each man or woman in the workforce.

QUESTIONS:

1. Was the Gilbreth and Taylor era of management so different from today's era in terms of diversity among workers? Explain.

2. What are three obvious reasons for utilizing the talents of women?

3. Do you believe that there should be laws prohibiting men's groups or women's groups from informally meeting to discuss work problems and issues?

Sources: Diane C. Harris, "Grease the Gears of Equality," *Personnel Journal*, September 1995, 120–127; John P. Fernandez and Mary Barr, *The Diversity Advantage* (New York: Lexington Books, 1993); and the entire issue of *Business and the Contemporary World*, Summer 1993, 1–197.

VIDEO CASE

The Evolution of Management

The management profession, as we know it today, is relatively new, even though the issues and problems that confront managers have existed for thousands of years. Management emerged as a formal discipline at the turn of the century, when rapid industrialization called for better-skilled management of natural resources, capital, and labor. The various management approaches that have been developed can be divided into two major groups: classical and contemporary approaches.

The classical approaches, which extended from the mid-19th century through the early 1950s, emerged as managers tried to cope with the growth of American industry. These approaches were systematic management, scientific management, administrative management, human relations, and bureaucracy.

Systematic management represented the beginning of formal management thought in the United States. It emphasized the way in which manufacturing firms operated because most management problems were focused on manufacturing.

Scientific management was introduced around the turn of the century by Frederick Taylor, an engineer who applied scientific methods to analyze work and determine the best way to complete production tasks. Taylor stressed the importance of hiring and training the proper workers to do those tasks. One of the most famous examples o the application of scientific management is the factory Henry Ford built to produce the Model T. Ford used scientific management principles to yield higher productivity and efficiency. For example, by 1914, chassis assembly line had been trimmed from almost 13 hours to 1.5 hours.

Administrative management emerged at about the same time and emphasized the perspective of senior managers within the organization. It viewed management as a profession that could be taught.

The human relations approach to management evolved from the Hawthorne studies conducted from 1924 to 1932 at the Western Electric Company outside Chicago. Various working conditions, particularly lighting, were altered to determine the effects of these changes on productivity. But researchers, led by Harvard professor Elton Mayo, were ultimately unable to determine any relationship between factory lighting and productivity levels. This led the researchers to believe the productivity was affected more by psychological and social factors. This approach highlighted the importance of the human element in the organization. However, critics believed the human relations philosophy of "the happy worker as a productive worker" was too simplistic.

The bureaucracy approach to management was developed by Max Weber, a German sociologist and social historian. He attempted to establish an overall management system by focusing on a structured, formal network of relationships among specialized positions in an organization. Bureaucracy allowed efficient performance of many routine activities.

The contemporary approaches to management, which have been developed since World War II, attempted to overcome the limitations of the classical approaches. The contemporary approaches include quantitative management, organizational behavior, systems theory, and the contingency perspective.

Quantitative management was aided by the development of modern computers. It emphasizes the application of a formal, mathematical model to management decisions and problems.

The organizational behavior approach to management promotes employee effectiveness through an understanding of the complex nature of individual, group, and organizational processes.

The systems theory of management, which originated in the 1950s, was a major effort to overcome the limitations of the earlier approaches by attempting to view the organization as a whole system. Systems theory introduced the concept of equifinality—that there is not "one best way" to reach a goal. And it stresses the notion of synergy—that the whole is greater that the sum of its parts.

The contingency perspective has most recently dominated the study of management. It asserts that situational characteristics, or contingencies, determine the management strategies that will be most effective. This approach argues that no universal principle should always be applied. Rather, managers, like those at Trek Bicycle, analyze situations and then, based on their analysis of key contingencies, make decisions regarding the most appropriate ways to manage. Trek, based in rural Wisconsin, has a very open-minded approach to managing and meeting customer needs.

But the evolution of management doesn't end there. Management thought and practice continues to evolve. Current events and trends are shaping the future of business and management. Among the major forces now revolutionizing management are: globalization, learning organization, total quality management, and reengineering.

Globalization refers to the rise of multinational enterprises in the ever-expanding global marketplace. Even small firms that don't operate on a global scale must make important strategic decisions based on international considerations.

The learning organization is committed to openness, new ideas, generating new knowledge, and spreading information and knowledge to others. Continuing dialogue and open-mindedness with an eye toward achieving the organization's goals are the foremost concern. Tellabs' stock has increased by more than 1,600 percent over the last five years, outperforming every other publicly traded stock in the nation.

Total quality management refers to an approach to management that produces customer satisfaction by providing high-quality goods and services. Its goal is to solve and the eliminate all quality-related problems. First National Bank of Chicago has an aggressive quality program that includes weekly performance review meetings. In the meetings, managers analyze dozens of charts that are designed to monitor the quality of their performance.

First National's Rich Gilgan said, "You can't manage what you don't understand. And you don't understand what you don't measure."

Finally, business reengineering is the process of starting all over to rebuild the company and overhaul its ways of doing business. The goal of reengineering is to achieve dramatic improvements in critical performance measures including cost, quality innovation, and speed. Reengineering requires a way of thinking that's quite different from traditional management practices.

From the classical approaches through the contemporary approaches and into the forces now revolutionizing management, the history of past efforts, triumphs, and failures has become the guide to future management practices. Since the mid-19th century, change has been the constant in the evolution of management. The marketplace keeps changing, the technology keeps changing, and the workforce keeps changing. Today's manager must learn how to deal with the forces of change affecting management. Only by understanding the implications of change and the challenges it presents will you be prepared to meet them head-on.

QUESTIONS

1. In general, how do contemporary approaches to management differ from classical approaches?
2. What are some modern organizational problems that are a result of classical approaches to managing?
3. The Hawthorne studies are frequently cited as a turning point in management thought. What is the significance of this research?

APPLICATION EXERCISE

This exercise is designed to have students apply the principles of excellence recommended by Tom Peters and Robert Waterman in their book *In Search of Excellence*. This 1982 book was a powerful motivator for practicing managers to closely examine their view of organizational processes. The principles presented by Peters and Waterman weren't intended to be the answer to every management problem or issue. Instead, they were to provide guidelines to help managers gauge how well their firms were operating. Each of the nine principles sends a special message that needs to be heard.

In reviewing the nine principles, comment on how you've been influenced by them, if at all, in a job and in college. Is your school really applying the type of principles that Peters and Waterman brought to the forefront?

A. In groups of four to six, go over the principles as applied to your college. Is there agreement on any of the principles?
B. In the group, develop an action plan for your school to improve its performance in the areas you determined to be weakest.

CHAPTER 3

Environment, Social Responsibility, and Ethics

After studying this chapter, you should be able to:

❖ Define the terms <u>internal environment</u> and <u>external environment</u>.

❖ Explain why workforce culture is such an important issue for managers to understand.

❖ Discuss how a person's values are formed.

❖ Explain social responsibility as social obligation, social reaction, and social responsiveness.

❖ Discuss why firms are growing more interested in producing environmentally friendly products.

❖ Discuss the distinction between deontological ethics and utilitarian ethics.

❖ Explain what is meant by virtue ethics.

TQM and Ethics: A Natural Fit

Ethics is the foundation and hallmark of any world-class, competitive organization. As the president and chief operating officer of Martin Marietta Corp., A. Thomas Young, states, "Ethics and quality have a common characteristic—both are attitudes—attitudes of doing things right."

Total Quality Management (TQM) is most effective in an environment that encourages openness, trust, and ethics. Advocates of TQM hold that management has an ethical obligation to support employees' right to fulfill their self-defined potential. Employees must be treated honestly and fairly, and be provided with opportunities to reach their potential.

Similarly, employees have an ethical obligation to do what's right. Ethics is the glue of the corporate culture. When all employees understand and internalize the company's ground rules, the corporate culture will drive quality in the workplace. Ethics is driven by internal forces; in other words, ethics means something different to each person. There is, however, one common thread: self-control in the absence of external pressure.

According to Ronald C. Arnett, chairman and professor of communication at Duquesne University, "Ethics is putting on the brakes. It's knowing when to stop, allowing our conscience to be our brakes. It's thinking out the consequences before acting. It is a form of thoughtful, deliberative restraint." With corporate ethics, management has to consider the differing values that employees, customers, and stockholders share and develop a standard that all entities can understand, own, and live by.

Like many other aspects of the modern organization, business ethics is undergoing significant change. What is driving the change in ethics? One ethics researcher states that changes in society and in the workplace are driving new corporate ethical standards, including:

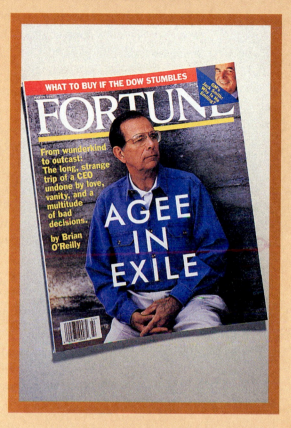

- ❖ Growing public demand for greater corporate accountability
- ❖ Leadership that is under fire in all sectors
- ❖ Global competition and the need to "win" at any cost
- ❖ Increasingly complex decisions and competing demands of multiple stakeholders
- ❖ Employee empowerment and an emphasis on service excellence, quality, and continuous improvement
- ❖ Growing emphasis on corporate culture
- ❖ Less (if any) teaching of values in schools, families, and churches
- ❖ Growing diversity in the workforce, reflecting a society with differing value systems and beliefs

❖ Employees must believe that the public's perception of the company's ethical behavior will have a direct influence on bottom-line results.

❖ Employees must understand that for the company to be recognized as ethical and as acting in the public interest, it might have to take action to separate itself from the industry. For example, ARCO decided that credit cards increased the price of gasoline, so it told customers that it was eliminating credit cards and cutting prices—a gutsy move. ARCO made it work because it simultaneously created a convenience store network that gave dealers a good source of high-profit-margin products and it effectively communicated the change. ARCO held the price line on gasoline longer than most other companies during the 1990 Middle East crisis.

❖ Employees must have enough courage to make tough decisions that separate the organization from the crowd.

❖ Employees must build a consensus of alliances and public support before there is a crisis. This is done by serving public interest in important, exciting, and publicly perceived ways.

❖ Management must plan far into the future.

❖ Management must continually lobby legislators, public administrators, and media.

❖ Management must be convinced and constantly reassured that the benefits of ethical measures more than merit their expense. The fact that the benefits outweigh the cost can be conveyed through messages such as this one used by educational institutions: "If you think education costs a lot, try ignorance."

The gap between what is said about ethics and what is done will never be closed completely because human behavior inevitably falls short of the highest ideals. For example, W.C. Fields once was deeply immersed in a book just before he was about to begin a performance. A friend saw him reading, and to his amazement, he noticed it was the Bible. The friend asked, "Bill, what are you doing reading the Bible?" Fields replied, "I'm looking for loopholes." But company executives can narrow this gap by reinforcing employees' personal values, strictly enforcing the code of conduct, and factoring ethics into the TQM equation, which will build prevention into all processes.

Sources: Adapted from Margaret Buban, "Factoring Ethics into the TQM Equation," *Quality Progress,* October 1995, pp. 97-99; A. Thomas Young, "Ethics in Business," a presentation to the Conference Board on May 5, 1992, New York; Terry Thompson, "Rhetoric and Reality," *CA Magazine,* August 1992.

Organizations are affected by a host of internal and external environmental factors ranging from ethical behavior of employees to a competitor's new, technologically sophisticated product. This chapter deals primarily with five of the most significant environmental forces that managers face in making decisions: social-cultural, economic, technological, political-legal, and ecological forces. Managers, in seizing opportunities, must analyze as many external and internal environmental forces as possible to develop a sustainable competitive advantage.

Some forces that shape how a company and its resources are managed can't be controlled. Managers must learn to adapt to these uncontrollable external environmental forces as they plan, organize, control, and direct strategies, workers, and resources. Sometimes unexpected events require businesses to radically change the way they operate. For example, in 1993 four children died after eating hamburgers tainted with the deadly *E. coli* bacterium. More than two years later, a long-promised overhaul of the federal meat inspection system has barely left the station and could be completely derailed by a proposed Congressional moratorium on new regulations. This poses a serious potential health threat. Big states like California, for example, still allow undercooked beef to be served. However, the restaurant industry is taking steps to ensure the safety of the meat it serves. Fast-food businesses have been telling their suppliers that either they implement more stringent safety measures or find other customers. Fast-food burger chains spend about $3 billion per year on ground beef, so they do command the attention of meat packers. Some restaurant chains have even developed techniques for detecting and killing off *E. coli.*[1]

Besides the external environment, an internal environment also exists in every firm. In many firms today, the internal environment is guided by the principles of total quality management. As the opening vignette discusses, TQM is a natural fit with a company's commitment to ethics.

This chapter first examines the internal environment and then reviews the external environment. It then discusses social responsibility and ethics. To acquire a framework for conducting business domestically and globally, managers must consider and understand ethical dilemmas and violations.

THE INTERNAL ENVIRONMENT

An organization's **internal environment** refers to the factors within the enterprise that immediately influence how work is done and how goals are accomplished. Factors that make up the internal environment include employees, work flow, office or plant layout, managers' style, and reward system. The most descriptive example of feel or orientation is provided by the notion of an organization's culture.

An enterprise's **culture** refers to a system of behavior, rituals, and shared meaning held by the employees that distinguishes the group, or organization, from other similar units.[2] Families, work groups, organizations, and entire nations possess cultures. Managers act to develop employees by training them, setting goals, and rewarding good performance. Every member of the organization, from the chief executive officer to the office clerk, shares responsibility for the firm's products and services. The unique patterns with which they carry out their responsibilities is part of their culture and distinguishes their firm from competitors. To perpetuate the culture, each employee passes valued knowledge along to new employees.

Culture serves as a guideline for what's appropriate and acceptable behavior because it provides an identity for employees. Culture establishes the rules that employees must follow.

> *Culture by definition is elusive, intangible, implicit, and taken for granted. But every organization develops a core set of assumptions, understandings, and implicit rules that govern day-to-day behavior in the workplace. . . Until newcomers learn the rules, they are not accepted as full-fledged members of the organization.*[3]

Total quality improvement efforts and activities have become an integral way of life for many organizations around the globe. The attempt to achieve systemwide changes of quality, and to maintain them, is generally considered to depend on cultural transformation.[4] However, according to some studies there is no clear causal chain from organizational culture to overall performance.[5] On the other hand, there are studies that have shown a clear relationship between certain elements of an organization's culture and its ability to successfully launch a TQM program. For example, a study of 61 U.S. hospitals found that a participative, flexible, risk-taking organizational culture was significantly related to quality improvement implementation.[6] Other research has linked elements of organizational culture to innovation. For example, the following seven characteristics of organizational culture were found to be related to innovation:

1. A stated and working strategy of innovation.
2. The use of workplace teams.
3. Rewards and recognition for employee creativity and innovation.
4. An environment in which managers allow people to make mistakes and take risks.
5. A setting in which training in creativity is provided to employees.
6. A carefully managedorganizational culture.
7. An atmosphere in which new opportunities are actively created.[7]

internal environment
The factors within an enterprise (such as employees, structure, policies, and rewards) that influence how work is done and how goals are accomplished.

culture
A system of behavior, rituals, and shared meaning held by employees that distinguishes the group of organization from other similar units.

And clearly, there are some organizational cultures that are hostile to the implementation of total quality initiatives.[8] Some of these could include: "turfism," a problem where people are afraid of losing control over certain organizational processes; organizational "silos," a problem where organizational functions don't communicate adequately; or employees may simply be fearful of any change effort that has the magnitude of a TQM implementation.

When a strong culture emerges, organizational commitment, loyalty, and cooperation are benefits to the organization. However, culture can be a liability when behaviors and work patterns aren't congruent with values and actions that enhance performance. Changes in the external environment may require rapid responses and adaptation. However, a culture that obstructs change may inhibit or block organizational growth. IBM developed a strong culture that simply wouldn't budge when new competitors created the need for rapid changes. The resistance of the IBM culture slowed the firm's ability to respond to strong competitors like Apple and Compaq, which were able to capture market share. IBM is still attempting to gain back some of the market share it lost to quicker-responding competitors.

Multiple Cultures

dominant culture
An organization's core values that are shared by the majority of employees.

Research suggests that most organizations have a dominant culture and a set of subcultures.[9] A **dominant culture** designates the core values shared by the majority of employees. This represents the distinct mark of a firm such as Disney's, which emphasizes quality products and services. *Subcultures* tend to develop because of common situations or problems that a group of employees faces. Subcultures are likely to be unit-, group-, or section-oriented. The finance department, for example, can create a subculture shared by members of the unit.

There are strong and weak dominant cultures.[10] In a strong culture, core values are intensely held and widely shared. In a firm with a strong culture, employees' or members' behavior can be dramatically affected by the values of other employees and role models. In Apple Computer's early days, it was a common practice to work long after the shift was over to complete the job. The clock at Apple meant very little, especially when a group was attempting to solve a problem.

Cultures vary from organization to organization. For example, Bausch & Lomb is a company with a very strong dominant culture, reflecting the personality of its tenacious CEO Dan Gill. Gill came to B&L in 1978 to head the company's fast-growing soft contact lens division. He immediately made his mark on the company as contact lens profits soared. Gill won the president's job in 1980, and the following year was named CEO and chairman. The culture Gill has created at B&L is a mirror image of himself: tenacious, demanding, and very numbers oriented. Gill began his career as an auditor and still closely examines each division's financial report every month. Once financial goals are set, Gill and his top executives rarely accept excuses for shortfalls.[11]

In contrast to B&L, Microsoft's culture is more laid back and entrepreneurial, although it too is reflective of its CEO, Bill Gates. Microsoft has a more casual culture, but it's just as competitive as B&L's. Gate's relationship to his company has been described as "more like a headmaster or supervisor than a tycoon. To be questioned by him is like a final university examination. But behind that discipline is the ultimate motivation of profit."[12]

Building Culture

Management success at culture building involves selecting, motivating, rewarding, and retaining high-performing employees. Managers, by examining companies such as Disney, will find three distinct actions that result in culture building: commitment, competence, and consistency.

In building a positive culture, managers must continually strive to instill commitment to a common philosophy and service, to develop and reward competence, and to find and retain the right people. *Organizational socialization* is a process through which a newcomer is transformed into an accepted member of the team. Proper socialization of a newcomer involves other staff (e.g., managers and co-workers) instilling commitment, rewarding competence, and giving consistent help to develop skills.

Values represent convictions that a specific mode of conduct is personally or socially preferable to another mode of conduct. Values are held by individuals. Some values are extremely important, while others aren't. Values are important because they help managers interpret workers' attitudes and motivations.

The values employees bring to the workplace were largely established in their early years by parents, teachers, relatives, and friends. The discussions a young person hears at home, in the street, or at school provide a basis for values later in life. Values are relatively stable and enduring. A workforce that includes recent immigrants, Hispanics, African-Americans, Asian-Americans, Caucasians, and other ethnic groups will possess a variety of values spanning economic, social, religious, and political issues.

Managers today deal with a workforce holding an array of values. Some employees value economic recognition for performance; others value time off to be with their families. Some value making a career commitment to their organizations; others value making a commitment to their profession. Sometimes Caucasians and Hispanics value the opportunity to socially interact on the job, but hold different values about joining a union. Often, what people have been lacking (such as the opportunity for promotion, respect, autonomy, and power) will be highly valued. Values often change with aging, significant life experiences, increased education, and achieving success. Since values differ, managers mustn't assume what employees' values are on a particular issue.

A survey of managers, human resource professionals, and organizational practitioners on workforce values suggests that nine values are important to employees:[13]

1. *Recognition for competence*—Employees want to be recognized for their accomplishments.
2. *Respect and dignity*—Employees want to be treated with respect.
3. *Personal choice and freedom*—Employees want to be more autonomous and able to rely on their own judgment.
4. *Involvement*—Employees want to be kept informed, included, and involved in important decisions at work.
5. *Pride in one's work*—Employees want to do a good job and exercise good-quality workmanship.
6. *Lifestyle quality*—Employees want time for family and leisure.
7. *Financial security*—Employees want some security in their retirement years from inflation, economic cycles, or catastrophic financial events.
8. *Self-development*—Employees want to personally improve to further themselves.
9. *Health and wellness*—Employees want to organize life and work in ways that are healthy.

These nine values appear to be important to men and women in any majority or minority group. Managers are challenged to apply procedures, principles, and approaches that balance the wishes and values of an increasingly diverse workforce with the need to recognize individual differences. Managers must become more proficient in listening to and observing workers as the work shifts in age, race, gender, and values.

THE EXTERNAL ENVIRONMENT

Learning about coping with an enterprise's internal culture and subcultures isn't managers' only challenge. They must also deal with external environmental factors. Figure 3–1 presents the components of environment, both internal and external, that managers face. Each external factor is important and is often in a state of change. In addition to change, the external environment consists of largely uncontrollable factors that influence an organization. The external factors in Figure 3–1 are divided into two interrelated categories: *remote factors* (forces that impact a number of firms) and *task factors* in proximity that can directly impact a particular enterprise. All five of the remote factors will be discussed.

values
Convictions that a specific mode of conduct is personally or socially preferable to another mode of conduct.

FIGURE 3—1
The External Environmental
Factors Facing Managers

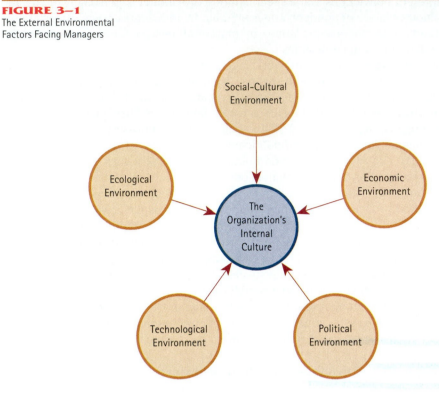

Input and Output

external environment
All factors such as laws, competition, technology, social-cultural norms and trends, and ecology that may affect the organization directly or indirectly.

An organization's **external environment** includes those factors that may affect the organization directly or indirectly in any noticeable way. Environmental factors affect organizations from two directions: input and output. Such environmental factors (people with values, needs, and goals), limited natural resources, and technology (equipment and procedures) are major parts of its input.

The organization transforms inputs and produces an output. The output (Nike shoes, a CD, an airline ticket to the Bahamas) goes back into the environment, is consumed, utilized, and evaluated. Thus, organizations and their environments are inseparable—each affects the other. It will also become apparent that *managerial skills* in observing, analyzing, and forecasting the environment may mean the difference between success, failure, or survival.

Environmental Analysis and Diagnosis

environmental analysis
The monitoring of external environmental forces to determine the firm's opportunities and threats.

environmental diagnosis
The process of making managerial and strategic decisions by assessing and interpreting data collected in the environmental analysis.

Environmental analysis is the monitoring of external environmental forces. It's designed to determine the source of a firm's opportunities and threats. **Environmental diagnosis** is the process of making managerial and strategic decisions by assessing the significance of the data (opportunities and threats) in the environmental analysis. The diagnosis is an opinion resulting from an evaluation of the available facts. The enterprise's decision makers must consider the firm's strategy and the environmental forces.

Many companies have developed corporate database systems, and some have established intelligence units, but these systems often fail to scan the external environment. To address the information needs of top managers, the environmental factors that have immediate effects on the company's operation should be identified and regularly monitored. Computer-based information systems can play an important role in collecting environmental information from various sources. However, in interpreting data and disseminating intelligence to managers, a human-computer mixed system is essential.[14] Strategic managers need to be aware that the modern environments in which they work are comprised of powerful forces for change that offer opportunities but also pose potential threats. Managers should adopt an objective, rational view of their position in their competitive environment, and adapt accordingly as changes arise.[15]

TABLE 3–1	SOME IMPORTANT EXTERNAL ENVIRONMENTAL FACTORS			
Social-Cultural	Economic	Technological	Political-Legal	Ecological
Lifestyle changes	Interest rates	New products	Antitrust laws	Environmental protection
Life expectancies	Deficit	Patent laws	Product liability laws	Waste management
Birth rate	Gross Domestic Product	Productivity measurement and growth	Tax laws	Public image in terms of environmental responsibility
Population growth rate (immigration included)	Unemployment levels	Industry R&D	Import/Export trade	
Family arrangements	Energy sources and costs	Federal support of R&D	Trade regulations	Product safety
Consumer activism	Inflation rates	Robotics	Investment tax credits	Packaging procedures
Shifts in population	Money supply	Computer technology	Corporate responsibility	
Ethical behavior				
Changing women's roles				

Table 3–1 identifies some key factors in the external environment that are likely to be important to managers. Any decision must be made after carefully weighing and evaluating these factors. Each of these external environmental factors is largely uncontrollable from a management perspective. The discussion that follows points out how little control a manager actually has over the external environment. Nevertheless, the manager must be up-to-date on trends and information associated with the external environment.

THE SOCIAL-CULTURAL ENVIRONMENT

The social-cultural environment involves institutions, people, their values, and the norms of behavior that are learned and shared. Managers make decisions that take into account the present and anticipated social structure and culture. Since social structures and culture are ever-changing, managers must examine trends, forecasts, and other forms of information. Specific social-cultural dimensions that are important to managing for better quality and remaining competitive include workforce composition, employees' family responsibilities, the nature of work, and employees' health.

The North American workforce is changing in terms of structure and composition. More women, minorities, and immigrants are entering the workforce. The workforce is aging, and the number of younger, entry-level workers available is shrinking. Table 3–2 shows these demographic changes.

Workforce Composition

In bygone years large portions of the workforce were similar; workers who were different were expected to adapt. But now differences abound. Today's workforce doesn't look, think, or behave like the workforce of the past, nor does it hold the same values. Managing these differences and being able to achieve world-class product and service quality is a significant challenge. The "one best way" that worked for Frederick W. Taylor won't work for an increasingly diverse workforce that managers must attempt to develop, motivate, and retain. The diversity spans age, race, gender, and values.

The aging of the baby boom generation is raising the median age of the U.S. population. The median age, about 33 in 1990, will be 36 by the year 2000. By 2010, one-quarter of the U.S. population will be at least 55, and one in seven Americans will be at least 65.

Older Americans are becoming a larger segment of the population, enjoying better health and longer life, and exercising economic and political power. The aging of the population will change buying habits and consumer preferences. Also, rehired retirees, health

TABLE 3-2	THE U.S. LABOR FORCE, 1976-2000
	(All population numbers in thousands)

	U.S. LABOR FORCE			NET CHANGE		% CHANGE/YEAR	
	1976	1988	2000	1976–88	1988–2000	1976–88	1988–2000
Total, age 16 & over	96,158	121,669	141,134	25,511	19,465	2.0%	1.2%
Men, age 16 & over	57,174	66,927	74,324	9,753	7,397	1.3	0.9
16–24 years	12,572	11,753	11,352	−999	−401	−0.7	−0.3
25–54 years	35,576	46,383	53,155	10,807	6,772	2.2	1.1
55+ years	8,846	8,791	9,817	−55	1,026	−0.1	0.9
Women, age 16 & over	38,984	54,742	66,810	15,758	12,068	2.9	1.7
16–24 years	10,588	10,782	11,104	194	322	0.2	0.2
25–54 years	22,925	37,659	48,112	14,734	10,453	4.2	2.1
55+ years	5,471	6,301	7,594	830	1,293	1.2	1.6
White	84,767	104,755	118,981	19,988	14,226	1.8	1.1
Black	9,565	13,205	16,465	3,640	3,260	2.7	1.9
Asian/Other	1,826	3,709	5,688	1,883	1,979	6.1	3.6
Hispanics*	4,289	8,982	14,321	4,693	5,339	6.4	4.0

*Persons of Hispanic origin may be of any race.
Source: U.S. Dept. of Labor.

care needs, and the issue of aging workers and productivity need to be evaluated by managers.

Although diversity in the workplace has become a popular buzzword in corporate America, it's difficult to determine what the notion really means. Today, any number of initiatives may be labeled as diversity management. The details vary, but the programs frequently include employee support groups and sensitivity training to promote tolerance. Diversity management is a direct result of the shifting demographics of the labor force. Many businesses, anticipating a shortfall in the traditional labor pool, started to see diversity as critical to their competitiveness. They began to implement programs to recruit diverse employees and move them along the company pipeline and to make their workplaces more receptive to nontraditional workers. Meanwhile, many experts agree that diversity initiatives give businesses a competitive advantage in the battle to attract and keep talented employees and gain market share.[16]

Because managing diversity is a relatively new concept, there is no right answer or formula for delivering the perfect diversity program. Companies, like people, are different. Thus, in formulating a diversity program, each company must assess its organizational goals and human resource problems. All companies should take certain steps:

1. Identify specific program objectives and goals;
2. Establish a program to meet these objectives;
3. Evaluate institutional cultural practices by conducting attitudinal surveys of employees; and
4. Develop realistic expectations.[17]

African-Americans currently make up 10 percent of the labor force. However, their participation is noticeably absent in high-tech fields where African-Americans make up less than 3 percent of the labor force. There are several reasons for this gap, and they all circle back to the reality that preparation for most careers in the sciences is best begun early. Most black children are not encouraged in these careers early enough. There are programs that address this gap, including the National Consortium for Graduate Degrees for Minorities in Engineering and Sciences. This program, working through colleges and universities, sponsors summer and weekend outreach programs for minority high school and middle school children.[18] Many companies that see the value of workforce diversity are also getting involved in helping minority children get started in technical fields.

Affirmative action programs have dramatically affected the make-up of the modern workforce. An estimated 6 million women wouldn't have the jobs they have today were it not for affirmative action, according to a 1995 study done at Rutgers University. By the Labor Department's calculations, the federal government's official equal-opportunity edicts now affect some 193,000 businesses, and some 26 million workers; nearly 25 percent of the U.S. labor force.[19] In 1995, several states have confronted affirmative action policies. The University of California system of higher education, for example, voted to abolish affirmative action from its hiring policies. This action met with great criticism from many, but was also widely supported—including support from some groups that traditionally had benefited from affirmative action policies. It's not clear what the future holds for affirmative action policies and programs. What's clear is that over the past 25 years affirmative action has radically changed the make-up of the American workforce.[20]

Another significant change in the American workforce is that there are fewer unionized workers. Today, only about 11 percent of the workforce belong to labor unions, compared to a high of 36 percent in 1953. One contributing factor to this is that the gap in pay levels between unionized and nonunionized workers has narrowed.

Union power is also eroding in other parts of the industrialized world. In Germany, cracks in the labor movement are starting to appear. Unique among major industrial countries, the share of organized workers in Sweden's labor force rose to nearly 90 percent over the last few years. However, Sweden's nearly 13 percent unemployment rate is poor public relations for near universal unionization.[21]

One trend that has swept through a number of industries in the United States is the rise of the contingent workforce. The term *contingent* is used to refer to workers who don't have permanent jobs.[22] The temporary employment industry has exploded in the last 10 years. Between the years 1993 and 1994, the industry experienced a 26 percent increase in its payroll. Temp agencies, as they're called, are now among the largest employers in the nation. They provide people with the opportunity to work between full-time appointments. Often a temporary assignment will lead to a full-time position. Many companies now use temporary services to meet the fluctuating demand for products and services. Experts predict that the temporary help industry will continue to expand for some time.

A decrease in the number of available younger workers and appropriately skilled workers will likely prompt more organizations to explore new programs to recruit more women. The rising number of working women will result in more women in executive positions, more men working for women, and more women working for other women. To attract and retain high-performing women, firms must adjust work schedules and develop good, affordable child care programs.

Family Responsibilities of Employees

In the last decade, many businesses have created policies and programs to help employees manage their home and work roles. The heightened interest in an employer work–family agenda is fueled by changing workforce demographics as well as by a growing understanding of the bottom-line benefits to employers for acknowledging and supporting people's personal lives. In determining the costs of a failure to have family–friendly policies, studies have found that problems with dependent care arrangements affected productivity and job effectiveness for both men and women. The benefits are measurable. Dependent care assistance has been proven to increase staff availability; work–family programs affect employee retention and reduce related stress.

Workplace needs assessments have shown that more than 33 percent of mothers with children under 12 years had a sick child in the last month; 51 percent missed work to care

A Stride Rite employee breaks up his workday by having lunch with his children, who are enrolled in the company's on-site day care program.

for the child but, equally important, 49 percent went to work and worried about the child. Of staff with children under 12 years old, one-quarter experienced child care breakdowns two to five times in a three-month period. These breakdowns were linked to higher absenteeism and tardiness, lower concentration on the job, and less marital and parental satisfaction. And while dependent care issues once were considered women's domain, the rapid growth of two-income families means men increasingly are affected. Consider the following statistics:

❖ Family and personal issues are a widespread source of stress in every workplace. The Families and Work Institutes' 1993 National Study of the Changing Workforce found that 87 percent of the U.S. workforce had some day-to-day family responsibility. In professional service firms, well over half the employees can be expected to experience some kind of work-family stress in a three-month period.

❖ Conflicts between work and personal life affect productivity and general well-being. A 1992 study by the St. Paul Companies found that staff who believed work was causing problems in their personal lives were much more likely to make mistakes than those who had few job-related personal problems (30 percent compared with 19 percent).

❖ Work–family conflict contributes to turnover and its related costs. Workplace research finds repeated evidence of the link between perceived ability to balance work and family issues and staff intentions to stay at a firm. Employees who experience work-family conflict are three times as likely to think about quitting their jobs as those who don't (43 percent compared to 14 percent). When work–life issues lead to turnover, the resulting costs consist of not only the visible expenses of recruiting and training a replacement but also the hidden inefficiencies of delays, suboptimal performance of new staff and ripple effects on co-workers. Researchers concur that turnover costs between 93 percent and 150 percent of a departing employee's salary—and up to 200 percent of salary for a highly skilled or senior person.

Some of the benefits of effective work–family programs include such hard-to-measure end points as improved morale, employee loyalty, and public relations image. Other, more tangible benefits include the following:

❖ Dependent care assistance increases staff ability. The surge in company-supported, short-term and back-up child care is due to the direct payback these programs offer in reducing absenteeism. In a cost-benefit analysis of its sick-child care programs, Honeywell determined that it saved $45,000 over and above the cost of the program in the first nine months of operation. Similarly, the 38-person CPA firm of Brown, Armstrong, Randall & Reyes estimated that by providing seasonal on-site child care, the firm netted an additional $25,000 annual income through increased staff availability.

❖ Work–family programs affect employee retention. Johnson & Johnson found that policies regarding time and leave were very significant in employees' decisions to stay, even if they personally had not used them. This isn't atypical; in one group of employers with family-supportive programs, 78 percent reported that the program helped their company retain valuable employees. At NationsBank, two-thirds of employees on flexible schedules said they would have left without these policies.

❖ Work–family initiatives reduce associated stress. In a study of companies with and without work–family programs, Northwestern Mutual Life found that employees in companies that didn't have supportive policies were twice as likely to report burnout and stress. Employer programs don't erase the difficulties of balancing responsibilities, but they do provide resources for employees to manage and solve their own problems.[23]

Nature of Work

The U.S. Dept. of Labor and the American Society for Training and Development (ASTD) conducted a project to identify the basic skills employers want their workers to possess. They found that employers want workers with a solid basic education plus relationship skills and skills in self-management. The researchers lumped the desired skills into seven categories:

1. Learning to learn (an aptitude for learning).
2. Competence (reading, writing, and computation).
3. Communication.
4. Personal management.
5. Adaptability.
6. Group effectiveness.
7. Influence.

These skills are assumed to be critical, but, unfortunately, are in short supply.

APTITUDE FOR LEARNING - This skill consists of a person's ability to acquire the self-knowledge to perform a job. Learning to learn means that each person must have enough "learning experience" and pay close enough attention to the methods of learning that work best for her. Since change is inevitable, workers must continuously learn new skills. Continuous reeducation and retraining are needed to stay current and to perform a high-quality job.

Increasingly, aptitude is measured by what people can do, not on what schools they went to. According to a survey conducted in 1994 by Recruit Research, 73.7 percent of 1,200 enterprises coming under the survey replied that they no longer insist on the graduates of well-known universities as a standard for selecting their new employees. Character and perceptive power have replaced academic careers as standards of selection.[24]

COMPETENCE - This refers to the basic skills of reading, writing, and math. Not only must workers know how to read a memo or set of instructions: they must also know how to read and interpret graphs, charts, and diagrams. Workers need writing skills so they can communicate clearly, concisely, and accurately. An ability to scan and interpret computer-generated results and a knowledge of business statistics will be essential.

COMMUNICATION - This refers to speaking and listening skills. Since workers in the future will be members of teams, increased communication will be the rule. Many instructions to perform the job come from oral comments, so good listening skills are important.

PERSONAL MANAGEMENT - This skill refers to a person's self-esteem and self-motivation. There's likely to be minimal supervision of the future workforce. Thus, workers who are self-starters, take pride in the quality of every job they perform, and are proud of themselves will be sought. The ability to set and accomplish personal and career goals will be valued in workers.

ADAPTABILITY - This refers to creative thinking and problem-solving skills. Due to increased emphasis on individual self-motivation, problem solving will be an important ability. The creative thinker appears to be well suited for increased problem-solving responsibilities.

GROUP EFFECTIVENESS - This refers to interpersonal and team skills. Employees need the skills to work effectively as part of a team. The ability to understand how their individual behavior and values impact others will be important. The abilities to negotiate, handle stress, and deal with undesirable behavior in others are part of this skill mix.

INFLUENCE - This refers to leadership skills—how to be an effective leader who can influence others. Being able to articulate a vision, maintain high ethical standards, and serve as a role model are part of the leadership mix.

The greater use of total quality management techniques, information technologies, computer-mediated processes, available knowledge, and a diverse workforce will make such skills essential. School dropouts and uneducated people will be left further behind as the nature of jobs change and these fundamental skills become essential.

Employees' Health

The United States has become an increasingly sedentary society. Our shift to postindustrial society means an increase in indoor working and living. Americans spend about 90 percent of their time indoors, usually sleeping, eating, dressing, or watching television. Bad habits associated with a sedentary lifestyle include smoking, snacking, and soda and coffee drinking. It's generally accepted that healthy workers lose less time and have fewer accidents than unhealthy ones.

The United States spends over $800 billion a year in health care—more than 13 percent of the Gross National Product. In the workplace, the employee is responsible for his own personal health and safety as well as that of fellow workers. Every year, 2.2 million people in the U.S. suffer ill health either caused or aggravated by workplace activities.[25] A growing number of firms are trying to improve workers' knowledge about health, lifestyles, and disease prevention. Issues such as mental stress, substance abuse, eyestrain from computer use, and proper use of equipment are covered in training programs, employee assistance programs, and new employee orientation sessions.

Workplace safety should be managed, and the responsibility to do so lies primarily with managers. Once the cause of an injury or accident is identified, a means of prevention becomes possible. The trick is to identify likely causes, and the means of preventing them, before accidents occur.

In the U.S., the federal Organizational Safety and Health Administration (OSHA) provides guidelines designed to protect the health and safety of workers in the workplace. However, OSHA can't possibly write policies that cover all possible workplace accidents or health problems. Therefore, OSHA requires all employers and employees to be on the lookout for hazards and act to prevent or eliminate them, even when OSHA has not promulgated specific standards to cover those areas.[26]

Managers need to adopt a safety philosophy that can be given practical application. It's important that all employees understand the consequences of changing to a safe system of work and becoming part of an organization's safety management program. Employers must teach employees about safety through induction and on-the-job training. In workplace health and safety, the foundation to any program is a clear policy supported by systems, procedures, training, and monitoring.[27]

These examples of social-cultural factors point out the uncontrollable nature of the external environment. Managers need to be aware of trends, values, and forecasts to be prepared for changes in the mix of employees, consumer preferences, and availability of skilled employees.

THE ECONOMIC ENVIRONMENT

The economic environment impacts management decisions and plans in many areas. An expanding economy directly affects demand for a firm's products or services. If demand increases, the workforce will probably need to be expanded or new shifts may have to be added to the work day. In a recessionary economy, decisions may have to be made about layoffs, downsizing, cutting back on the size of the firm, or even plant and office closings.

Economic uncertainty and changes in the economy must be carefully monitored and interpreted by managers to make informed decisions. Two prevalent economic environmental characteristics—uncertainty and change—are difficult to assess accurately.

One important first step in understanding the economic environment is to carefully define a few terms. *Macroeconomics* is the area of study that deals with big problems and issues such as inflation, recession, underemployment, and economic growth. *Microeconomics* involves the study of supply and demand and how particular individual prices are determined in the arena called the marketplace. **Gross National Product (GNP)** is the total market value of an economy's final goods and services produced over a one-year period. The goods and services included in the GNP are items produced as end products for final use rather than for use as materials, parts, or services to be incorporated in the value of other items that will then be resold as final products. **Gross Domestic Product (GDP)** is the measure of output attributable to all factors of production (labor and property) physically located within a country. GDP, therefore, excludes net property income from abroad (such as the earnings of U.S. nationals working abroad) that is included in the GNP.

Many persistent economic environment issues and problems affect management decision making and planning. Three in particular are significant: productivity, global economics, and the importance of small firms.

Productivity

Most economists agree that inflation is worsened by decreasing productivity. A sluggish, or flat, productivity rate can slow the growth of the entire economy. During most of the 1960s the American economy grew rapidly, with low unemployment and inflation. But in the 1970s and 1980s the economy grew much less rapidly, with high unemployment and inflation. Productivity rose at a rate of only about 1.2 percent annually from 1980 to 1990.

Productivity is an estimate of output per labor-hour worked. Certainly it's a crude measure, subject to short-term error. But over the long term, productivity measures can clearly show trends. For years, U.S. productivity increased at an annual rate of 2.5 to 3.0 percent. However, the rate of productivity growth slid to an anemic 2.0 percent from 1970 to 1978. Productivity in durable goods industries has started to rise at an annual rate of over 2 percent (actually 3.3 percent through the third quarter of 1995).[28]

The implications of sluggish, or flat, productivity growth concern managers. When workers produce more, total output grows and employers can increase wages without raising prices. The rise in revenue from increased output offsets the higher wage costs. But if productivity is flat, almost every dollar of wage gains is translated into price boosts. Goods and services that cost more won't be purchased because consumers don't have the dollars to purchase them.

Across different industries, it's interesting to examine white-collar and blue-collar productivity rates. White-collar employment in the past decade has increased by over 30 percent, while blue-collar employment has grown at only 2 percent. However, blue-collar productivity has increased by 28 percent, and white-collar productivity has decreased by 3 percent. Blue-collar American employees have kept up with the rest of the world in terms of productivity.

Gross National Product (GNP)
The market value of an economy's final goods and services produced over a one-year period.

Gross Domestic Product (GDP)
The measure of output attributable to all factors of production (labor and property) physically located within a country.

productivity
An estimate of output per labor-hour worked.

The Global Economy

In today's borderless economy, the workings of Adam Smith's invisible hand have a reach beyond anything Smith could have imagined. In Smith's day, economic activity took place within well-defined and circumscribed political borders of nation-states. Now, by contrast, economic activity is what defines the landscape on which all other institutions, including political institutions, must operate.

Today, governments large and small feel under siege. The biggest challenge comes from global capital markets, where money moves faster than people or goods ever can. But challenges are also coming from the proliferation of international administrative bodies, such as the World Trade Organization.[29] The very survival of the nation-state is being questioned by many.[30] What may replace the nation-state is an economic entity called the *region-state.*

There are now three main economic regions in the world: North America, Asia, and the European Union. Region-states differ from nation-states in that they are able to put global logic ahead of national interest. Since they are primarily economic rather than political units, they welcome foreign investment and foreign products. In fact, they welcome whatever will employ their people productively, improve their quality of life, and give them access to the best and cheapest products in the world.

Region-states have learned that people often have better access to low-cost, high-quality products when they don't try to produce them at home. Singaporeans, for example, enjoy better and cheaper agricultural products than do the Japanese, even though Singapore has no farms of its own.[31]

One of the major driving forces of the global economy is the liberalization of international trade. A key component of this liberalization is the development of free-trade agreements allowing for the virtual free flow of goods between countries bound by the agreement. The move toward free trade in North America began in the 1980s.[32] In 1992 leaders of the United States, Canada, and Mexico signed a North American Free Trade Agreement (NAFTA). NAFTA is expected to reduce consumer prices, increase competitiveness, and create export-related jobs by allowing companies in all three nations to produce for a market of 360 million people. The NAFTA nations' trading area and population is larger than the 340 million people in the 12-nation European Community.

General Agreement on Tariffs and Trade (GATT) An agreement setting rules of conduct for fair and equitable international trade. social responsibility.

In the aftermath of World War II, the 1948 **General Agreement on Tariffs and Trade (GATT)**–Bretton Woods trading system was built to prevent financial crashes like the Great Depression of the late 1920s and early 1930s.[33] Trade restrictions and tariff barriers between nations were gradually reduced. Under the rules, each of the member countries has to treat all other member countries in exactly the same way—the most favored nation principle.

GATT had become increasingly cumbersome over the years and a new round of trade talks, known as the Uruguay Round, resulted in the establishment of new international trade accords. No other international trade negotiations have been so comprehensive as the Uruguay Round, in which participants agreed to liberalize trade in agricultural products, to reduce tariffs on industrial products by an average of more than one-third, and to establish the World Trade Organization (WTO).[34]

The WTO is unique in that international dispute settlement mechanisms have become more innovative. On January 1, 1995, WTO's Rules and Procedures Governing the Settlement of Disputes were annexed to the trade agreements.[35] In contrast to GATT, which provided rough outlines of dispute settlement mechanisms, the WTO understanding codifies detailed rules and procedures for dispute settlement. This mechanism will be a central element in providing security and predictability to the multilateral trading system.[36]

Small Firms

From 1881 to 1973 American business dominated world commerce because of its sheer size. The big country and big corporations led the emphasis on quantity of goods and services produced and consumed. Quality wasn't given much attention. Because of the American penchant for bigness, the small business and individual proprietor were largely ignored. Except for a few small-to-big stories, bigness still predominates the teaching of business administration.

Today, the jobs being created in the United States are being created by small and new businesses. The number of self-employed persons has increased from just over 5 million in 1970 to over 10 million in 1991.

The 18 million new jobs created by smaller firms in the 1980s literally saved America's economy from disaster. They gave a massive boost to Chicago, Youngstown, Pittsburg, Houston, Denver, Orlando, and hundreds of other cities. By 1993, big companies couldn't promise stability around which employees could build careers. Millions of jobs have disappeared from large corporate firms. Today individuals have a number of career options. They can join large or small firms, work for the government, or start their own businesses. Creating new job opportunities still appears to be centered on smaller and start-up firms.

THE TECHNOLOGICAL ENVIRONMENT

Technological changes are the most visible of all the environmental changes, but public pride in controlled progress in the early 1900s appears to have changed to apprehension, or even fear, as we enter the mid-1990s. After two world wars, a depression, and many unresolved economic problems, few people believe that all change is positive and that increasing technical knowledge will produce still better technology that will undoubtedly improve the human condition.

Technology has touched almost every aspect of life in the industrialized nations. In the process, it has made widespread affluence possible. It has also created a host of new ethical dilemmas, as the Workplace of Tomorrow segment describes.

WORKPLACE OF TOMORROW

ETHICS IN THE DIGITAL AGE

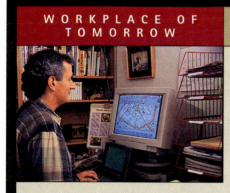

Microsoft Corporation's dominance in the software industry has inspired more than its share of critics. On the Internet, those potshots are beginning to attain a new level of polish and professionalism, due in part to technology offered by the World Wide Web. The kinds of messages—positive or negative—made possible by new Internet technologies raise concerns about decency, responsibility, and competitive ethics.

A prime example of the technical sophistication and scope of company bashing on the Internet is a World Wide Web site called the "Microsoft Hate Page," which invites people worldwide to submit comments, essays, jokes, graphics, and criticism related to the Redmond-based software company. The Web site was designed with a professional look and feel that provides color graphics, "hot" links to other pages, games, and e-mail capabilities to communicate with the site's creator. The site's content harshly criticizes Microsoft, in some instances with censurable language and graphics.

A Microsoft spokeswoman said that the company's position about complaints against it is that people have the right to voice their opinions. If they have problems with specific products, they should contact the company's customer support group, she said. Regarding the company's on-line detractors, the spokeswoman said Microsoft has not pursued any legal action against them; nor does it have any official policy in the matter.

The high level of commitment and resources needed to create a Web site easily may fuel suspicions about the motives behind certain Web sites and the messages they are sending. Hence, even though Web sites such as the Microsoft Hate Page may be created by individuals exercising their freedom of speech, the World Wide Web has given those messages a similar weight and reach to those of large corporations. Thus, the Internet has created a channel for market parity that may be used by companies and individuals to undermine their competition.

As one Internet engineer pointed out, the Internet is considered by many to be "the largest functioning anarchy in the world"—an anarchy that already has attracted debates about regulation, ethics, responsibility, and accountability.

Rushworth M. Kidder, president of the Institute of Global Ethics, believes we are moving into an age of greater self-regulation of digital technology. He suggests that the answer may lie in both moral strictures as well as legal injunctions. "As we move from tangible assets to intangible ideas, truth will become more crucial," Kidder declares. "How can we use the information highway when we can't tell what's true on it?"

Sources: Adapted from Ken Yamada, "World Wide Web Raises Issues of Decency, Ethics," *Computer Reseller News*, September 4, 1995, pp. 43–44; Eileen McMorrow, "Will Digital Technology Impact Ethics?" *Facilities Design & Management*, May 1995, p. 9.

technology
The accumulated competence to provide goods and services for people.

Technology is the totality of the means employed by people to provide comfort and human sustenance. Technology is a part of nature, and is given meaning, substance, and function by people. So it's hardly valid to think of technology itself as being a problem or the reason for problems occurring. Cartoon character Pogo's wry statement, "We have met the enemy and he is us," can apply to people misusing technology as much as to people electing a bad government. We can either help ourselves or hurt ourselves with technology. And we will almost certainly continue to expand our technology. Technology enables organizations to meet consumers' needs.

Technological Innovation

technological innovation
All those activities translating technical knowledge into a physical reality that can be used in a societal scale.

Technological innovation involves all those activities translating technical knowledge into a physical reality that can be used. The process of technological innovation progresses from basic research to marketing. The automobile was a technological innovation that had a long-term effect on the mobility of society and the purchasing patterns of consumers. The telephone, airplane, radio, television, computers, and various medical technologies have also significantly influenced society.

It takes time and money to carry out technological innovation and marketing. Years may pass before an innovation in biomedicine, energy, or any other sector reaches the marketing stage. A significant environmental force, technology drives change in industries and relationships between firms and customers, and it creates new competitors. To continue in business, managers must use technology properly. Astute managers employ technology to improve their services to customers, find new customers, lower cost, and speed the introduction of new products.

THE POLITICAL–LEGAL ENVIRONMENT

The political–legal environment consists of government rules and regulations that apply to organizations. The very words *rules and regulations* often make managers uneasy and resentful. No one likes being regulated. For years, the American manager has generally been a staunch theoretical supporter of a "hands-off" government policy (a policy of not interfering with business activity). Yet most managers know that the business system can't work without some government rules and regulations to organize and monitor the external environment.

The number and variety of government regulations affecting business are huge. Some are directed toward goals as disparate as economic growth, job security, and environmental pollution control. These regulations and government programs can be divided into those that are designed specifically to support business and those intended to control various business activities.

The business support programs can be divided into classifications such as subsidies, promotion, contracts, and research. *Subsidy* once meant directing the flow of resources to preferred users (for example, to stimulate agriculture and commerce). Today a subsidy involves the flow of money to politically determined business activities. The government provides subsidies in the form of guaranteed and insured loans, funds to keep the maritime industry afloat and the airlines in the air, and money for constructing highways to move people and products. Loans in 1971 to Lockheed, in 1979 to Chrysler, and in 1984 to Continental Illinois are among the most publicized subsidies to business. The government's $4.5 billion loan to Continental Illinois National Bank was the largest ever to a private firm.

The government is actively involved in *promoting* business through such devices as protecting home industries from foreign competition. The promotion effort has involved placing tariffs on imports and also supporting small business owners through the Small Business Administration.

A third type of support takes the form of government *contracts* for construction, production, service, or analysis. This type of contract support is supposed to stimulate business. Over 60,000 full-time government employees administer the billions of dollars spent annually on government contracts.

The federal government supports nearly one-fourth of all industrial scientists and engineers. In addition, it provides over half of all money spent annually for R&D. Much of the research output is of potential use by the business system. The future development and overall health of the nation's security and economy depend on adequate government support for *research*.

Government Control

There are three distinct areas of government control: investigation, antitrust, and direct regulation. By means of hearings, reports, and news conferences, the government attempts to pressure managers' behavior and attitudes. For example, by *investigating* and *publicizing* findings about cigarettes, the government has influenced public opinion about the tobacco industry.

Unlike investigation, control procedures (the second type of government control) are based on law. The philosophy behind antitrust laws is the belief in free and open competition. Such laws are designed to protect the small business from the large business in the marketplace. Bigness, if it reduces competition, is considered undesirable. The U.S. Department of Justice, for example, has been keeping a very close eye on the business practices of Microsoft. In July 1994, Microsoft and the Justice Department signed a consent decree in which Microsoft agreed to change some of its licensing practices. The battle is far from over, however. With its ubiquitous Windows operating system, the federal government is concerned that Microsoft has an unfair advantage in producing software products compatible with that system. Certainly there will be more battles over fairness and definitions of monopoly as the information age continues to unfold.[37]

The third type of control—regulation—refers to prescribing standards of business conduct, operation, or service. Regulations are designed to (1) protect the interests of consumers and employees from business exploitation, (2) protect health, morals, and safety, (3) protect the interests of inventors and competitors, or (4) control entry into certain markets like transportation or broadcasting.

Changes in the technological, social-cultural, and economic environment set off reactions. These reactions have brought us to our present state of government involvement through supports and controls in business and society. Once an opinion gains political support, it can become law or public policy. The public has demanded that government, to some extent, be involved in business activities. Government has complied with this opinion and has established the support-control framework illustrated in Figure 3–2.

FIGURE 3–2
Government Interaction
with Business

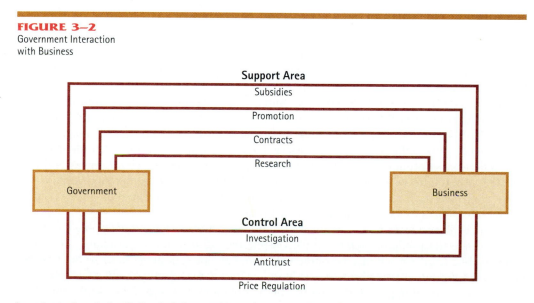

Source: Based on Grover Starling, *The Changing Environment of Business* (Boston: Kent, 1988), p. 197.

THE ECOLOGICAL ENVIRONMENT

ecology
The branch of natural science devoted to the relationship between living things and their environment.

The ecological environment consists of our natural surroundings. **Ecology** is the branch of natural science devoted to the relationship between living things and their environment.

Wastes, shortages, and other abuses to the natural environment are generated as a by-product of producing goods and services. Rachel Carson's best-selling book *Silent Spring* (1962) first alerted the world to the dangers of widely used chemical pesticides, particularly the organochlorine types of DDT and its related DDE and dieldrin. These agents interfere with life processes. She maintained that their uncontrolled use, without concern for harmful effects, promised future soil, water, and human health problems.

The tragic impact of some chemicals on the ecological environment and on human life was brought into focus when a cloud of poisonous methyl isocyanate gas was accidentally released from the Union Carbide Company plant in Bhopal, India, in December 1984. Over 3,000 people from the surrounding community were killed, and 200,000 were injured. The methyl isocyanate was used to manufacture Sevin, a plant pesticide distributed throughout India for corn, rice, soybean, cotton, and alfalfa crops.

The ecological problems of energy shortages, pollution, and poor planning didn't arise overnight. They result from years of economic growth, affluent lifestyles, urbanization, and technological development without concern for ecological consequences.

No nation is free of responsibilities and some criticism concerning humankind's ecological problems. The "consume and throw away" culture in developed countries and unchecked population growth in developing countries are endangering critical natural resources. Unfortunately, environmentalists have pointed their fingers primarily at the United States as the culprit in causing environmental damage. Certainly, in some areas, the American public and firms are guilty of mineral and water pollution, improper waste disposal, and ozone depletion. But many other nations endanger critical natural resources and pollute the environment too.

The world now faces problems in deforestation, species loss, soil erosion, and water and air pollution. In June 1992, 140 world leaders and 30,000 other participants met in Rio de Janeiro for the Earth Summit to discuss and find solutions for ecological problems. The world has changed dramatically since the first Earth Summit in 1972 in Stockholm. Since the first summit, 115 nations have created environmental agencies and ministries. The United States created the National Environmental Act, the Clean Air Act, and the Environmental Protection Agency. But much more must still be done to solve environmental problems. Here managers will play a prominent role.

Ecological decisions are not always easy to make. Usually, there's a significant trade-off to consider. For example, petroleum is the lifeblood of the former Soviet Union, providing one of the only remaining sources of hard currency. But like blood in a critical artery, crude oil flowing by pipeline can't be shut off without consequences. So when a line connecting Moscow to the Vozey oil field in the northern Komi Republic began hemorrhaging late in 1994, managers at Komineft, the pipeline's operators, were reluctant to shut it down. And the assault on the fragile Arctic environment went on for weeks. The incentive to keep oil flowing was enormous: not only would an interruption cost dearly in the short term, but if the channel were cut off for too long, oil in the pipeline might have cooled and hardened during the frigid Arctic winter. Flow might have been impossible to resume.[38] Managers are often faced with difficult decisions regarding the natural environment. Unfortunately, there's no easy solution to many issues concerning business and the environment. For now, managers should do what they can to monitor and influence environmental regulation. It's safe to say, however, that most businesses will look better to their customers if they behave in a manner that is friendly to the natural environment.

Table 3–3's survey of American public opinion about the environment points out areas of concern. Water pollution heads the list. Despite the controversy about many unresolved issues, public concern about environmental problems appears likely to grow. Support for increased environmental legislation and more environmental management strategies is expressed by diverse groups: young and old, liberal and conservative, and rich and poor.

TABLE 3–3	HOW THE GENERAL PUBLIC RANKED THE SERIOUSNESS OF U.S. ENVIRONMENTAL PROBLEMS, 1990
Water pollution from waste products of manufacturing plants	77%
Oil spillage from tankers	77
Environmental contamination from chemical waste disposal	75
Air pollution from industrial plants and factories	74
Destruction of the ozone layer	69
Contaminated drinking water	67
Environmental contamination from nuclear waste disposal	67
Air pollution from auto exhaust	62
Acid rain	60
Landfills for disposal of garbage from household and industry	58
Worker exposure to toxic chemicals	56
Water pollution caused by sewage from homes and offices	53
Radiation from nuclear power plants	52
Pesticide residues on food eaten by humans	51
The "greenhouse effect"	49
Litter of streets, parks, highways, and the countryside by careless people	44
Indoor air pollution	32
Strip mining of coal, iron, and copper	30
Radiation from X-rays, microwave ovens, and so on	26

Source: "The Environment: Public Attitudes and Individual Behavior," a public opinion study by the Roper Organization, commissioned by S. C. Johnson & Son Inc.

SOCIAL RESPONSIBILITY AND ETHICS

Laws set the minimum standards for responsible and ethical business practices and employer and employee behavior. Within an organization, there is a philosophy that becomes part of the culture that reflects the firm's approach to social responsibility. The firm's **social responsibility** is its practices with other parties such as customers, competitors, the government, employees, suppliers, and creditors. What it means to be socially responsible differs across industries and from firm to firm. There's no specific standard that a firm follows since managers think quite differently about what constitutes socially responsible behavior. Some managers view social responsibility as an obligation; others view it as a reactive situation; still others consider proactive behavior to be the proper position.

social responsibility
A firm's practices with other parties such as customers, competitors, the government, employees, suppliers, and creditors.

Social Responsibility as Social Obligation

This view holds that a corporation engages in socially responsible behavior when it pursues profit only within the constraints of law. Because society supports business by allowing it to exist, business is obligated to repay society by making profits. Thus, according to this view, legal behavior in pursuit of profit is socially responsible behavior, and any behavior that is illegal or is not in pursuit of profit is socially irresponsible.

This view is particularly associated with economist Milton Friedman and others who believe that society creates firms to pursue two primary purposes—to produce goods and services efficiently and to maximize profits.[39] As Friedman has stated, "There is one and only one social responsibility of business—to use its resources and engage in activities designed to increase its profits so long as it stays within the rules of the game, which is to say, engages in open and free competition without deception or fraud."[40]

Proponents of social responsibility as social obligation offer four primary arguments in support of their views. First, they assert, businesses are accountable to their shareholders, the owners of the corporation. Thus, management's sole responsibility is to serve the shareholders' interests by managing the company to produce profits from which shareholders benefit.

Secondly, socially responsible activities such as social improvement programs should be determined by law, by public policy, and by the actions and contributions of private individuals. As representatives of the people, the government (via legislation and allocation of tax revenues) is best equipped to determine the nature of social improvements and to realize those improvements in society. Businesses contribute in this regard by paying taxes to the government, which rightfully determines how they should be spent.

Third, if management allocates profits to social improvement activities, it's abusing its authority. As Friedman notes, these actions amount to taxation without representation. Management is taxing the shareholders by taking their profits and spending them on activities that have no immediate profitable return to the company. And management is doing so without input from shareholders. Because managers are not elected public officials, they are also taking actions that affect society without being accountable to society. Further, this type of non-profitseeking activity may be both unwise and unworkable because managers aren't trained to make noneconomic decisions.

Fourth, these actions by management may hurt society. In this sense, the financial costs of social activities may, over time, cause the price of the company's goods and services to increase, and customers must pay the bill. Thus, managers have acted in a manner contrary to the interests of the customers and, ultimately, the shareholders.

Social Responsibility as Social Reaction

A second view of social responsibility is behavior that is in reaction to "currently prevailing social norms, values, and performance expectations."[41] This pervasive view emphasizes that society is entitled to more than the mere provision of goods and services. At a minimum, business must be accountable for the ecological, environmental, and social costs incurred by its actions. At a maximum, business must react and contribute to solving society's problems (even those that can't be directly attributed to business). Thus, according to this viewpoint, corporate contribution to charity is socially responsible.

A somewhat restrictive interpretation of social responsibility as social reaction is that it involves only voluntary actions. This interpretation seeks to separate corporate actions that are required by economic or legal imperative from those that are initiated by voluntary, altruistic motives. This narrower view implies that a corporation pursuing only socially obligated behavior is not socially responsible because its behavior is required, not voluntary.

Whether the firm's actions are voluntary or not, a broader interpretation of the social reaction view identifies actions that exceed legal requirements as socially responsible. Typically, these actions are reactions to expectations of specific groups—for example, unions, stockholders, social activists, and consumerists. Because these groups expect more than legal minimums, firms can simply decide not to react. Favorable reaction, however, is considered the socially responsible response.

The essence of this view of social responsibility is that firms are reactive. Certain groups make demands of them, and forms are socially responsible when they react, voluntarily or involuntarily, to satisfy these demands.

Social Responsibility as Social Responsiveness

According to this view, socially responsible behaviors are anticipatory and preventive, rather than reactive and restorative.[42] The term *social responsiveness* has become widely used in recent years to refer to actions that exceed social obligation and social reaction.

These characteristics of socially responsive behavior include taking stands on public issues, accounting willingly for actions to any group, anticipating society's future needs and moving toward satisfying them, and communicating with the government about existing and potential legislation that's socially desirable.

A socially responsive corporation actively seeks solutions to social problems. Progressive managers, according to this view, apply corporate skills and resources to every problem—from run-down housing to youth employment and from local schools to small-business job creation. Such behavior reflects the "true" meaning of social responsibility for social-responsiveness advocates. Corporate executives who commit their organizations to such endeavors are likely to receive substantial public approval.

The social responsiveness view is the broadest meaning of social responsibility. It removes managers and their organizations from the traditional position of singular concern with economic means and ends. This view rests on two premises: (1) organizations should be involved in preventing, as well as solving, social problems, and (2) firms "are perhaps the most effective problem-solving organizations in a capitalist society."[43] As discussed in the Ethics Spotlight, Reebok is involved in solving social problems on a global scale.

These three viewpoints of social responsibility still leave managers with an abstract set of guidelines. Those who define social responsibility determine what is considered responsible. The importance of the concept of social responsibility has increased the attention paid to ethics and ethical dilemmas. The concept of social responsibility deals primarily with the external environment, while ethics deals with both the internal and external environments of the organization.

Somebody, presumably Groucho Marx, once offered the following advice: "The secret of success is honesty and fair dealing. If you can fake these, you've got it made."[44]

What is and isn't ethical behavior on the job is often in the eye of the beholder, it seems. And while most people consider themselves highly principled, they're beholding their co-workers more suspiciously.

A 1994 survey conducted by the Ethics Resource Center, a not-for-profit educational organization in Washington, DC, yielded that tidbit within its detailed look at ethics at work. More than half of the 4,035 respondents said that their own standards of ethics were higher than those of co-workers.

Although a little more than half of respondents thought their own companies were more ethical than the average U.S. company, nearly two-thirds agreed that ethical conduct is not rewarded in business today. Even more emphatically, 82 percent said that, in general, U.S. managers choose profits over doing the right thing.

One-third of respondents worked for companies that had ethics offices. Of that number, 23 percent had used the ethics office to ask advice or to report wrongdoing. More than 80 percent of those who used the ethics office were satisfied with the results and an equal number said they would use the office again.

When asked specific questions about the ethics displayed in their own companies, respondents described workplaces that were less than upstanding. About one-quarter said their companies look the other way or ignore unethical conduct in order to meet business objectives. Twenty-nine percent said that they sometimes feel pressure to act in ways that violate their own companies' codes of behavior. The top forces cited by respondents as leading to unethical behavior were schedule pressures (54 percent) and overly aggressive financial or business objectives (39 percent).

Nearly one-third of respondents reported having seen misconduct at work in the preceding year. The top three misdeeds were lying to supervisors, lying on reports or falsifying records, and stealing. Of those who observed misconduct, fewer than half reported it. Immediate supervisors were the individuals most often told. More than half who reported misconduct were unhappy with the resolution.

Those who observed misconduct but didn't report it gave these three top reasons: I didn't believe corrective action would be taken; I feared retribution or retaliation from my supervisor or management; I didn't trust the organization to keep my report confidential.[45]

Richard Nsanzabaganwa of Rwanda receives the Reebok Human Rights Award. At right is Reebok Chairman and CEO Paul Fireman, and behind is musician Peter Gabriel, a member of the Reebok Award Board of Advisors.

—

Ethics is a tough enough subject when we confine it to the U.S., where hostile takeovers, insider trading scandals, restructuring, and downsizing have posed their own ethical quandaries in recent years. Businesspeople are under the microscope as never before. But the struggle for ethical conduct gets even more complex abroad. Although great ethical challenges remain for companies in America, the world beyond presents some unfamiliar and daunting challenges—provoked by very different values and cultures, very different governments, regulations, and ways of communicating and doing business.

The ethics of doing business in foreign countries is framed by two potentially conflicting positions—what is an acceptable business practice in India, China, or Vietnam for the Indians, Chinese, or Vietnamese may not be acceptable to an American manager. A manager's ethics, values, and moral standards are shaped by his own cultural frame of reference.

At Reebok, senior managers are building a vision and charting a course that they think will work for their company, and that will ground these standards in their organization. Reebok's senior managers believe that, as a public company, they have an ethical responsibility to build value for shareholders—but not at all possible costs. What they seek is harmony between the profit-maximizing demands of the free-market system and the legitimate needs of shareholders, and the needs and aspirations of the larger world community.

Duerden, former President and CEO at Reebok, said, "Some 12 years ago, when Paul Fireman purchased the North American rights to a Reebok brand unknown to anyone except for a few cult runners in the U.K., the company probably didn't even know the word 'social responsibility.'" What it did know was that it wanted to make a difference—and that making a difference wasn't limited only to the product and the profits, but to people, both inside and outside the company.

By 1986, Reebok had grown incredibly: from $1.5 million in 1981 to $64 million in 1984 to $300 million in 1985 to just short of $916 million in 1986. That year, 1986, was also the year Reebok decided to sponsor Amnesty International's "Human Rights Now" World Concert Tour which would take place two years hence. The sponsoring fee, $20 million dollars, represented much more than the company's entire advertising program. Nonetheless, a rock concert to make young people aware of human rights, featuring celebrities such as Bruce Springsteen, Peter Gabriel, and Sting, fit the Reebok brand, and its consumer. Duerden said, "Amnesty opened our eyes, and we became passionate about human rights. What started as one summer's rock tour became an ongoing commitment at Reebok which shapes our thoughts and actions today."

Already involved in giving to the local community, after the tour, Reebok decided to allocate approximately 50 percent of its giving to the human rights community worldwide. In addition to its monetary donations, the company now sponsors an annual human rights award, honoring four young activists from around the world.

On December 8th, 1994, 3,000 people joined Reebok in Boston to celebrate that year's award winners. Duerden said, "I know that the pride the Reebok employees feel that day and all year—through this, through foundation involvement, through our volunteer programs—makes them proud to be part of Reebok. Proud to be part of a company which is truly making a difference. And, pride and productivity go hand-in-hand."

In 1992, Reebok became one of a very few companies to initiate a formal, worldwide code of conduct governing the treatment of workers who are employed by third parties. Called the Reebok Human Rights Production Standards, they were developed over six months by a high-level task force that relied heavily on guidance from the United Nations, human rights organizations, academia, and others.

Reebok's production managers are responsible for identifying gaps between the codes of conduct and factory conditions, and ensuring that steps are being taken to improve areas where a factory exhibits shortcomings. The company also uses an internal audit team to monitor working conditions abroad. In the spring of 1993, the internal audit team toured 45 factories, looking for specific ways to improve their conditions. It developed a 14-point checklist for all factories. The 14 points cover issues such as fair wages, child labor, working hours, and overtime. They also include a long list of mandatory safety and health items such as fire extinguishers, emergency exits, exhaust fans, and protective equipment.

Duerden reported, "In the almost two years since we implemented the Reebok Human Rights Production Standards, our audits have concluded that the standards are not only benefiting workers' overall well-being, they're also improving the quality of the products being produced."

Sources: Adapted from John Duerden, "Walking the Walk on Global Ethics," *Directors & Boards*, Spring 1995, pp. 42–45; also see the Planet Reebok Web site on the Internet's World Wide Web at http://www.planetreebok.com/".

Are corporate CEOs concerned about ethics? The Conference Board, a New York-based association of major corporations, says yes. Its "Corporate Ethics Practices" survey of 1,900 corporations in the United States, Canada, Mexico, and Europe found that:

❖ Codes are most common in the United States. Some 84 percent of U.S. respondents have corporate ethics codes, while only 58 percent of non-U.S. firms have them. A parallel study by the Institute of Business Ethics in London found that 71 percent of its sample of United Kingdom companies had codes of ethics in 1991—up from 55 percent in 1987.

❖ Chief executive officers are commenting "openly and often" on business ethics. Among respondents in the United States, 31 percent of CEOs spoke out on ethics in the prior year; in Europe, traditionally more reticent on the subject, the figure was a surprisingly high 40 percent.

❖ Ethics is increasingly popular in corporations. Nearly half (45 percent) of the respondents' codes of ethics had been enacted since an earlier Conference Board survey in 1987. Financial firms, however, are still much less likely (57 percent) to have codes than companies in other industries (82 percent).

❖ The United States and Europe have different views on codes. In the United States, where codes tend to be seen as legal documents, the corporate legal counsel is often central to the drafting process. In Europe, where the code is more often viewed as a social compact between the company and its workers, boards of directors play a central role and are far more apt to bring employee representatives into the drafting process.

❖ Ethics training is on the rise. Some 25 percent of the respondents have set up new ethics training programs, ethics committees, or ombudsmen's offices in the past three years.

The Conference Board cites three major reasons for these practices:

1. **Global management issues.** Companies operating internationally "want to determine their company's 'core' values while simultaneously showing respect for local customs and practices."

2. **Workforce diversity.** Corporations are concerned about minority representation. In addition, they find that in an era of downsizing, "new and less experienced workers and managers are now responsible for decisions"—and need an ethical handle on decision making.

3. **Inadequate education and training.** In addition to deficiencies in science, math, and literacy, graduates of public secondary education lack ethical literacy.[46]

Consumers are also concerned about corporate ethics. A study released by Porter/Novelli, a Chicago-based PR firm, found that corporate public relations executives underestimate how much consumers care about how managers run their companies. Consumers were asked to rate what influences their purchase decisions, and corporate PR executives were asked to reply how consumers would respond.

The two groups had similar philosophies in a few categories, including quality of a product (named among the three most important factors by 78 percent of the consumers and 87 percent of the executives) and handling consumer complaints (60 percent of consumers versus 54 percent of executives). However, PR executives underestimated how consumers would rank fairness and equality in hiring (24 percent of consumers, 4 percent of executives), environmental issues (20 percent of consumers, 4 percent of executives), and worker safety (16 percent of consumers, 1 percent of executives).

There were even larger discrepancies between consumers and PR executives in the company's record of worker safety (48 percent of consumers said it was a major influence, compared with 16 percent of executives), number of lawsuits against a company (39 percent of consumers, 16 percent of executives), and how a company handles a crisis that isn't its fault (42 percent of consumers, 63 percent of executives).

"Companies should broaden their dialogue with consumers," said Bob Druckenmiller, president of Porter/Novelli, "Most of the conversations companies have with their customers are related to their products and services. Now it's clear that some consumers also want to hear about how companies operate and what values guide their business decisions."

The top five factors that had a "major influence" on consumers were product quality (96 percent rated this first), a company's method of handling complaints (85 percent), the way a company handles a crisis in which it is at fault (73 percent), a challenge by a government agency about the safety of a company's products (60 percent), and an accusation of illegal or unethical trading practices (59 percent).

The factors least important to the consumers in the survey produced some surprises. The three choices, each named by 5 percent of the consumers surveyed, were openness in dealing with the media, support of charitable causes, and a boycott by animal rights activists. See Figure 3–3.

In weighing purchase decisions, women were more likely than men to consider whether a company had been accused of bias against women (48 percent of women, 30 percent of men), a company's fairness and equality in hiring (58 percent of women, 42 percent of men), and a company's record on worker safety (55 percent of women, 40 percent of men). People with higher educational levels were less likely to be influenced by a company's fairness and equality in hiring, its financial strength, worker safety, and the number of lawsuits it faces.

As people grow older, the study showed, they are more likely to be influenced by a company's financial strength, worker safety, management's reputation, openness in dealing with the media, the kind of programs it advertises on, the way it handles a crisis, and accusations of illegal or unethical trading practices. Younger people tend to be more concerned about boycotts of a company by animal rights activists, and challenges by consumer groups or the government about product and worker safety.[47]

Ethics is a major consideration for organizations today. As the above figures indicate, it's an area fraught with uncertainty, ambiguity, and occasionally anxiety. Managers can get a better handle on ethical issues in the workplace if they have some framework for thinking about the issues. As the Ethics Spotlight shows, many Mary Kay Cosmetics workers think that ethical behavior is good business.

FIGURE 3–3
Factors Considered Important
by Consumers when Dealing
with a Business

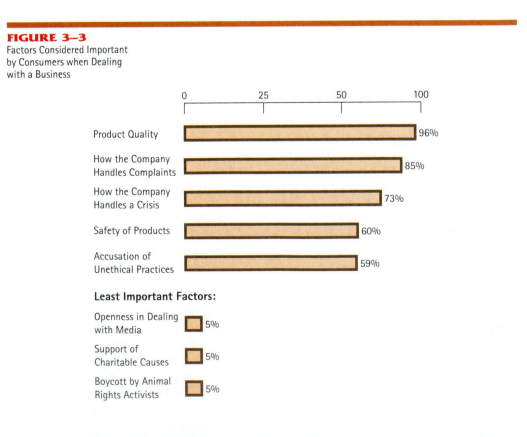

Mary Kay Ash founded her company on the Golden Rule—do unto others as you would have others do unto you. She believes that to apply the golden rule, to make it powerful in your life, you must develop a sense of empathy for other people. Empathy is an essential ingredient of ethics as well as an important attribute of leadership. Ethical leaders can create an ethical corporate culture that brings out the best in people. Ethical behavior takes on a life of its own and grows, if given a chance.

Mary Kay Ash believes that ethics is good business. However, an ethical company doesn't exist in a vacuum. To make ethical decisions, businesses must consider the impact on the larger society of which they are a part.

In the case of Mary Kay Cosmetics, the larger society includes independent entrepreneurs—the company's beauty consultants, its employees, the communities in which the company is located, and business partners such as suppliers, scientists, medical professionals, the cosmetics industry, the pharmaceutical industry, and the direct-selling industry.

All of these factored into a decision Mary Kay made in May 1989. The company announced a moratorium on animal testing while it developed and evaluated new testing technology. Mary Kay Cosmetics was one of the first companies to take such a step. The corporate goal was to take the high ground. The decision meant putting a hold on new products for a while, which meant lost sales. It also meant additional investment in evaluating alternatives.

Ethical corporate conduct is not easy and can be costly, but Mary Kay believes that ethics is good business. And the company believes that ethical conduct can be measured. Although CPAs have given the company many ways to measure goodwill for the balance sheet, loyalty and trust of employees, shareholders, and business partners are important measures, too. Mary Kay believes that loyalty and trust are probably the greatest assets a company can have, especially a company where independent entrepreneurs are not tied to the corporation through a paycheck. Loyalty and trust are built on a base of everyday ethical conduct. The ethics of people management has to be based on the fact that the truth is the only way people can trust each other.

Mary Kay Cosmetics prides itself on being a "caring" organization. People still laugh, even as they admire her success, when Mary Kay tells them that her ideas on people management are based on the Golden Rule—management by caring and sharing. Mary Kay's "core values" are a foundation for that approach:

- We believe in integrity and fairness in every aspect of our lives as expressed by the Golden Rule.
- We believe that service and quality are essential to our success.
- We believe that enthusiasm produces a positive, can-do attitude, which is a real source of inspiration in working toward our goals.
- We believe that leadership among our sales force and employees is the key to personal and corporate growth.
- We believe the priorities of faith, family, and career lead to a balanced life.

People want to work, they want to create, they want to produce, they want families, and they want their families to live well. They want to live in peace, in a clean, safe world. They want someone to care for; they want someone to care about them, to recognize them and reward them for their contributions. Caring competence allows Mary Kay Cosmetics to quickly take the high ground, to use its ethical framework to influence constituents, and to help make its communities better.

Sources: Adapted from Richard C. Bartlett, "Mary Kay's Foundation," *Journal of Business Strategy*, July/August 1995, pp. 16–19; Alan Farnham, "Mary Kay's Lessons In Leadership," *Fortune*, September 20, 1993, pp. 68–77.

Ethical Frameworks

The two major traditions that have dominated thinking in moral philosophy are **deontology** and **utilitarianism.** Of the two traditions, deontology is favored by many moral philosophers today. Utilitarianism has been attacked by moral philosophers because it seems to suggest certain untenable outcomes when applied to particular hypothetical situations. Utilitarian arguments are historically used to provide ethical justification for the modern economic systems in capitalistic democracies.

DEONTOLOGY - The reasoning found in deontological analyses suggests that there are self-evident ideals which can direct managers' thinking. Modern interpretations of these ideals suggest that they may be considered "universal" in character, but not necessarily "absolute." The difference between absolute and universal is the recognition that sometimes situations arise in which one or more universal statements of "right" and "wrong" may be inappropriate. Early deontological thinking would not admit the nonabsolute character of rules, but more modern versions perceive these statements as universal in character and allow exceptions. In general, the main concept is that these rules or duties are required, and a burden of proof lies with any exception to them. The "What Managers Are Reading" segment reviews a book that argues for "ten commandments" of business ethics.

deontological ethics
An approach to ethics that assumes certain ethical ideals are universal; that is, they apply in all situations regardless of the consequences.

utilitarian ethics
An approach to ethics that assumes that ethical judgments depend upon the consequences of an action. A familiar utilitarian measure is that an action is good if it results in the greatest good for the greatest number.

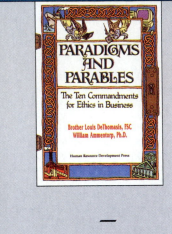
UTILITARIANISM – The utilitarian ideal can be summarized by the phrase, "the greatest good for the greatest number." There are many variations of utilitarianism, as there are variations of deontology. The primary way of assessing "the greatest good for the greatest number" is by performing a social cost/benefit analysis and acting on it. All benefits and all costs of a particular act are considered and summarized as the net of all benefits minus all costs. If the net result is positive, the act is morally acceptable; if the net result is negative, the act is not morally acceptable.

Utilitarianism seems to have been readily accepted in business, in part because of its tradition in economics. Adam Smith and much of the ensuing economic philosophy of capitalism provide a rich traditional heritage for the utilitarian concepts. Capitalistic systems, by providing the greatest material good for the greatest number, are considered ethical from the perspective of economic philosophy. It should be noted that the utilitarian analyses of moral philosophers extend beyond "material good" to the much broader concept of "utility" from which the term is derived.

Two criticisms are relevant to the discussion of utilitarianism. One is the problem of "unjust" distribution of utility. Summarizing the costs and benefits as described above can conceal major negative occurrences to people in small segments of a society by allowing them to be offset by relatively minor increases in utility to larger segments of society. For example, most of the arguments in support of the continued sale of Nestlé infant formula to the third world countries were utilitarian. In this case, it was suggested that the greatest good to the society was derived from the continued sale of the product. Other arguments, primarily deontological, seem to have prevailed because Nestlé agreed to severe marketing restrictions.

An additional problem for utilitarianism is the concern for individual acts. If each act is judged solely by its own cost/benefit outcome, there is lack of consistency and of ability to generalize. Marketers may argue that fraudulent advertising is all right if no one is worse off, and a rule against such practices becomes less tenable. However, in spite of the weaknesses of utilitarianism, it is still a major tradition in moral philosophy and receives substantial support.

A concluding point about the two major traditions is necessary. Deontology has the individual as its major concern and unit of analysis, whereas utilitarianism is decidedly social in character and focuses on the welfare of society as a unit. This focus can, in many situations, put the two traditions at odds with each other, as in the Nestlé case. There is no totally accepted, absolute statement of what is ethical and what is not ethical, only important and carefully reasoned traditions.

Virtue Ethics

A third tradition in the ethics literature, called **virtue ethics** is emerging. This tradition emphasizes that an individual's professional role in society often calls for behaviors that conflict with generally accepted social mores. This is not necessarily a bad thing. Professional work often requires far more complex decisions than are faced by the average individual in society. Consider a professional lawyer, for example. We'd think it unethical for a lawyer to not defend her client to the best of her ability, even though the case against the client is overwhelming. It's the professional duty of the lawyer to defend her client.

virtue ethics
An approach to ethics that assumes professional norms to be the measure of ethical status. If an act is appropriate within professional norms, it is considered to be ethically good or right.

All professional activities can be understood as guided by some special "artificial" virtues. This approach is needed because generalized moral considerations and psychological descriptions are usually irrelevant when applied to professional life, e.g., to acts of professional marketers. Professionals typically deal with ethically problematic areas. Their virtues are probably different from general virtues.

Professional virtues are those tendencies to act in ways that serve the goals of professions. An ideal professional may be described as one whose typical behavioral tendencies, values, and other relevant features are such that they serve professional goals. This approach creates a gap between general moral considerations and professional duties and values. For some professions, such a gap is typical and very wide. In the "world of professionals," professional goals are seen as "good" in some way or another.

Professional virtues are those individual character traits that serve the professional goals as well as possible. Professional virtues may be different from general virtues (like honesty, fairness, and impartiality), but may still be justifiable through the goals they serve.[48]

One researcher has argued that ethical decision rules presented in the literature have been limited to the citation of simple ethical maxims. Typically, these maxims include:

Deontological Principle: Act in such a way that the action taken under the circumstances could be a universal law or rule of behavior.

Utilitarian Principle: Act in a way that results in the greatest good for the greatest number.

Virtue Ethics: Take on actions that would be viewed as proper by a disinterested panel of professional colleagues.

Several questions can be presented which, given that they can be answered negatively, show that the action is probably ethical. These questions are:

Does action A violate the law?

Does Action A violate any general moral obligations:

❖ Duties of fidelity?
❖ Duties of gratitude?
❖ Duties of justice?
❖ Duties of beneficence?
❖ Duties of self-improvement?
❖ Duties of nonmaleficence?[49]

If a manager is able to answer "no" to these self-administered questions, the action in question may not violate any ethical standards. However, no test is foolproof. Managers must be able to foresee the consequences of any action to make an assessment of its ethical implications. Will anyone be hurt? Will other people agree with the action taken? In addition, managers must be honest with themselves and their motivations for their decisions. Was the decision made with the best interest of the company in mind? Was it made for selfish interests? Ethical questions can be raised not only regarding the consequences of an action, but also its motivation.

In the end, managers must be comfortable with the fact that they will constantly face questions about the ethics of their actions. To function under these conditions requires that managers be confident about the motivations of their actions. If a manager truly believes that he's acting in the best interests of the firm and the society in which it operates, then he's won half the battle. The other half, of course, is to closely monitor the consequences of a decision to determine whether they produce the intended ethical results.

SUMMARY OF LEARNING OBJECTIVES

DEFINE THE TERMS INTERNAL ENVIRONMENT AND EXTERNAL ENVIRONMENT.

The internal environment refers to the factors such as rules, people, structure, and reward system that influence how employees work to accomplish goals. The external environment refers to all factors such as social-cultural trends, laws, technology, and environmental issues that directly or indirectly impact the organization.

EXPLAIN WHY WORKFORCE CULTURE IS SUCH AN IMPORTANT ISSUE FOR MANAGERS TO UNDERSTAND.

Workforce culture affects the behavior of every employee in the workplace. The unique way in which employees carry out their responsibilities, as determined by the culture, distinguishes a firm from its competitors.

DISCUSS HOW A PERSON'S VALUES ARE FORMED.

Values (a person's convictions) are typically formed in the early years. Teachers, friends, relatives, and parents—by example, discus-

sions, and responses—illustrate various values that are observed, copied, and/or modified.

DISCUSS THE DISTINCTION BETWEEN DEONTOLOGICAL ETHICS AND UTILITARIAN ETHICS.

Deontological ethics assumes that ethical ideas are universal. That is, they apply in all situations regardless of the consequences. Utilitarian ethics, on the other hand, is situational. An act is considered ethical if it results in a predetermined outcome. This is usually stated as "the greatest good for the greatest number."

EXPLAIN WHAT IS MEANT BY "VIRTUE ETHICS."

Virtue ethics assumes that professional values determine ethical behavior. If a certain behavior is deemed to be professionally incorrect, it is deemed to be bad or wrong from an ethical perspective. Conversely, correct professional behavior is deemed ethically right or good.

KEY TERMS

culture, p. 59
deontological ethics, p. 81
dominant culture, p. 60
ecology, p. 74
environmental analysis, p. 62
environmental diagnosis, p. 62
external environment, p. 62

General Agreement on Tariffs and Trade (GATT), p. 70
Gross Domestic Product (GDP), p. 69
Gross National Product (GNP), p. 69
internal environment, p. 59
productivity, p. 69

social responsibility, p. 75
technological innovation, p. 72
technology, p. 72
utilitarian ethics, p. 81
values, p. 61
virtue ethics, p. 83

REVIEW AND DISCUSSION QUESTIONS

Recall

1. What is an organizational culture and how does it influence employees' performance?
2. In ecological terms, how can a product be environmentally friendly?
3. What are the implications of a sluggish productivity rate for a manager facing employees' demands for wage and salary increases?

Understanding

4. Values are important to every individual. Why would the values of an increasingly diverse workforce be difficult to determine?
5. What does the concept of learning to learn have to do with the need for a workforce that must use a range of skills to perform their jobs?
6. Explain why codes of ethics aren't always effective.

7. Many organizations are considered to be socially reactive. What does this mean in practical terms?

Application

8. Conduct your own informal poll of 10 businesspersons and 10 students. Ask them to rank the seriousness of environmental problems listed in Table 3–3. What did you determine? Are there differences? Why?

9. Ask a few businesspersons, friends, and peers to describe what they think comprises an organization's culture. What did you find in the terms and phrases they use? Is there confusion about what you meant by the term culture?

10. Conduct your own study of the understanding of workforce diversity in your school or workplace. Are any emotions expressed? Is there an understanding of the concept? Who provided you with the best insight about the concept?

CASE STUDY

Some Question Stride Rite's Social Responsibility Record

"If you're pro-business, you also have to be concerned about things like jobs in the inner city and the 38 million Americans living below the poverty line," proclaimed Arthur Hiatt, Stride Rite's (now former) chairman. With such sentiments in its executive suite, it should come as no surprise that Stride Rite is a darling of the corporate social responsibility movement and has won 14 social responsibility awards in recent years. Stride Rite allots 4 to 5 percent of its pretax profits to the Stride Rite Charitable Foundation, sent 100,000 pairs of sneakers to Mozambique, paid for Harvard University graduate students to work in a Cambodian refugee camp, gave scholarships to inner-city youth, and pioneered setting up on-site day care and elderly care facilities. But Stride Rite's concern for jobs in the inner city does not apply when its own bottom line is at stake.

The company may have joined 54 others in forming Businesses for Social Responsibility, but it joined hundreds more in moving production overseas in the search for cheap labor, laying off thousands of workers in America. As a result, Stride Rite managed to achieve its high profile for social responsibility while also pleasing stockholders: the company consistently posted profits.

Like most of its competitors in the shoe industry, Stride Rite began closing plants in the U.S. in the late 1960s. In the past decade alone, Stride Rite has closed 15 factories, mostly in the Northeast, several in depressed areas. Most of its shoes are now manufactured in Asia. The company doesn't own the overseas plants or directly employ the workers; instead, it contracts with local companies, and shifts the locus of production—for example, from South Korea to Indonesia and China—when local wages begin to rise. The wage differential is so substantial that, according to Carl Steidtmann, chief economist at Price Waterhouse, "It has become virtually impossible to manufacture sneakers in the U.S." Skilled workers in China, for example, earn $100 to 150 per month, and work 50- to 65-hour weeks; unskilled workers earn half that. By comparison, Stride Rite's U.S. workers average $1,200 to 1,400 per month in wages alone.

Stride Rite's search for lower costs takes place within the 48 contiguous states as well. Not long ago Stride Rite closed its facilities in Roxbury, Massachusetts, an area with 30 percent unemployment, which once was the home of its corporate headquarters and a plant that employed 2,500 workers (pushed out, former chairman Hiatt says, by the reluctance of its more skilled workers to go to Roxbury's deteriorating neighborhood). The new headquarters opened in Cambridge, Massachusetts. The company then moved what was left—a distribution center employing 175 workers, along with a center in New Bedford (14 percent unemployment)—to Kentucky, a site chosen because of its lower wages and a $24 million tax break, a more generous deal than the $3 million offered by Massachusetts.

Struck by the apparent contradiction between Stride Rite's actions, *The Wall Street Journal* writer Joseph Pereira asks: "What makes a company socially responsible? . . . Is it sufficient to do good deeds as everyone agrees Stride Rite has done? . . . Or is something more basic needed, such as providing jobs in depressed areas at the expense of profits?" But for Stride Rite this contradiction between good deeds and cost-cutting measures is no contradiction at all: Stride Rite's primary responsibility, says its former chairman, "is to [our] stockholders". Ervin Shames, Stride Rite's current chairman, echoes his predecessor's sentiments: "Putting jobs into places where it doesn't make economic sense is a dilution of corporate and community wealth."

Indeed, Stride Rite can be celebrated for its good deeds precisely because its own labor practices generate the profits that make its corporate generosity possible. But Stride Rite is celebrated for another reason as well: its cost economizing measures take place largely outside the official discourse of business ethics. Within that discourse there are no penalties for corporations like Stride Rite which, on the one hand, benefit from the positive public relations associated with doing good deeds abroad and, on the other hand, act in ways that create controversy and ethical questions at home.

Nonetheless, Stride Rite's decisions to relocate its facilities conform to existing fiduciary and legal obligations to its shareholders. To Stride Rite, these decisions are assumed to be unavoidable responses to the pressures of the marketplace, not matters of choice, and hence of ethics, at all.

Stride Rite contends that it has been socially responsible but nevertheless has to balance the demands of two masters—shareholders and society. If a company doesn't stay competitive, its executives contend, it can't grow, it would provide even fewer jobs, it would earn too little to afford its community programs, and, at worst, it might jeopardize its survival.

QUESTIONS

1. Do you think Stride Rite should be honored for its social responsibility given that the company has shifted so many jobs overseas? Explain your answer.

2. Is there any difference between reducing costs by using foreign labor or by corporate downsizing? Is either of these tactics ethical? What would make them unethical?

3. Do you think companies have greater ethical responsibility to shareholders or to the communities in which they operate? Explain your answer.

Sources: Adapted from Marilyn Kleinberg Neimark, "The Selling of Ethics: The Ethics of Business Meets the Business of Ethics," *Accounting Auditing & Accountability Journal*, 8(3): 1995, pp. 81-96; Joseph Pereira, "Social Responsibility and Need for Low Cost Clash at Stride Rite," *The Wall Street Journal*, May 28, 1993, pp. A1.

VIDEO EXERCISE

The High Bid Dilemma
Purpose
This exercise provides students with the opportunity to view the possibility of conflict of interest when dealing with an outside vendor.

A purchasing agent (PA) and his assistant are reviewing bids from seven companies to determine which company should receive a contract for bronze facing a clutch. The PA's assistant proposes that the bid should be awarded to Metaltech, the low bidder, which is located some 300 miles away. His boss, the PA agent, leans toward Spin Cast Systems, a nearby company, which has submitted a much higher bid. Both companies submitting bids have the ability to provide a quality product complete with delivery and support capabilities.

The PA attempts to persuade his assistant that the contract award should be given to Spin Cast Systems despite its higher bid that will create a budgetary problem. He informs his assistant that he has used Spin Cast's services previously. Moreover, Greg Sommers, the president of Spin Cast, is his personal friend, his fraternity brother, and his sailing companion. the PA tells his assistant, "You take care of your suppliers and they'll take care of you." In fact, to show his assistant that Sommers is a "nice guy," the PA will ask Sommers to invite the assistant to a house party.

QUESTIONS
1. Does the issue of a "conflict of interest" surface in this exercise? If so, how? If not, why not?
2. Will the purchasing assistant compromise his own ethics if he allows his boss to award the bid to Spin Cast Systems even though such an award will create a budget overrun and does not follow company regulations?
3. Does the purchasing agent's assistant have any possible options if his boss decides to award the bid to Spin Cast?

A Very Friendly Fellow
Purpose
This exercise demonstrates the problems of sexual harassment on the job.

Bill and Shelly are having a conversation in the hallway. Shelly feels a certain degree of discomfort because Bill is standing very close to her. Ginny, another worker, meets them in the hallway, and Bill begins talking about the good time he had at a night club. He tells Shelly and Ginny that they should meet him and his friends after work at the Steak and Cap. Although Shelly, upset by his invitation, tells him she is busy and cannot make it, Ginny sees his invitation as a friendly social gesture from a co-worker.

When Shelly tells Ginny that she has to talk with her about a work project, Bill decides to return to his office. Shelly informs Ginny that Bill will not leave her alone. She believes that he has been making sexual advances toward her and that she will be unable to work with him. The problem is that he cannot seem to keep his hands off of her. He "touches" her by massaging her neck or by squeezing her arm even though she has repeatedly told him to stop.

QUESTIONS
1. What should Shelly do when she meets Bill at work?
2. What impact will Bill's "advances" have on their ability to work together on a new project?
3. Does Shelly have responsibility to report Bill's actions to the human resource management office?

Compensation Issue
Purpose
This exercise discusses the possible problems that can occur when employees discuss their pay levels among themselves, and presents some of the possible issues of pay discrimination.

After Brenda, an African-American woman, and Sandy, a white woman, exchange pleasantries early on Friday morning, Brenda reveals to Sandy that she has just learned that another employee, June, who works in bookkeeping, receives $.30 an hour more pay. Brenda is upset by this information because both she and June began their employment with the company at the same time and they both perform similar functions.

Brenda believes that the company has "discriminated" against her because she is an African-American woman. She tells Sandy that she will hire an attorney to sue the company. Sandy suggests that the difference in pay, even for performing the same job functions, may be a result of other considerations. For example, even though both women were hired at the same time, June may have had previous experience that allows the company to pay her a slightly higher salary. Brenda counters Sandy's argument by saying that a similar job within the same company should mean that each employee receives the same salary.

QUESTIONS
1. Is it ethical for employees to compare salaries when working for the same company? If so, why? If not, why not?
2. Do you believe that Brenda has been discriminated against by her company? If so, what type of discrimination?
3. Are there times when people working in the same company, hired at the same time, and doing the same work should be paid different salaries? Explain your answer.

Competition or Revenge
Purpose
This exercise questions the ethics of an ex-employee to compete with his former employer for the same client.

A group of salespeople are discussing the impact a former employee is having on their current sales. Jack Rebeck, who was recently fired from his position, is now soliciting former clients. In one instance he has been successful in underbidding his old firm. The members of the sales group are concerned with Rebeck's competing for the same client pool.

Because Rebeck has limited financial resources, George, one member of the sales group, suggests that the company underbid Rebeck on projects. Jean, another former colleague, suggests that the group spread stories within the industry about the reasons Rebeck was terminated by the company, and finally, Jeff, the last member of the sales group, believes that bad-mouthing and undermining Rebeck is fruitless and will not have an impact on the company's business.

QUESTIONS

1. Is it ethical for an ex-employee to compete with a former company? If so, when? Under what circumstances?
2. Is it ethical for a company to attempt to undermine a former employee who is now a competitor?
3. If a company discusses the reason(s) an employee was terminated, does it violate employee confidentially?

Creative Expense Reporting
Purpose
This video raises the issues of padding the expense account by submitting unsubstantiated expense vouchers to a company for reimbursement.

Jim, a salesperson, enters Ken's workstation to discuss the problem. He apparently has lost the hotel room receipt for his last stay in New York. Ken tells him the cost of his larger suite. Jim also asks Ken about the cost of a taxi ride so that he can prepare his expense voucher. Ken informs him of the cost of his taxi ride.

Jim, after some deliberation, decides to pad both his hotel room and his taxi ride by settling on an "odd-dollar" amount that will appear more realistic to those reviewing the submission of his voucher. Finally, Jim informs Ken of his intention to pad the lunch and dinner bills to cover entertainment costs he incurred during the trip. Since Jim considers entertainment as a part of conducting business, no one would question an expense of a few extra dollars on the voucher.

QUESTIONS

1. Should Ken tell his superiors that Jim has padded the expense voucher?
2. Is padding a business expense ever justified? If so, when?
3. If he wanted to submit an accurate expense voucher, what possible options are available to Jim to secure the correct information?

APPLICATION EXERCISE

Rokeach Value Survey

The individual researcher who has done the most in terms of explaining and measuring values is Milton Rokeach. He separates values into two categories: instrumental and terminal. An instrumental value is a belief that a way of behaving fits every situation. For example, "being logical" no matter what the situation is an instrumental value. A terminal value is a belief that a certain end state (terminal) is worth attaining. One person may strive for "happiness," while another strives to be "socially recognized." Each individual has a set of instrumental and terminal values.

The Rokeach Value Study is presented here. Rank order the values in each column and determine how you view your value structure.

The Rokeach Value Survey

Instructions: Study the two lists of values presented below. Then rank the instrumental values in order of importance to you (1 = most important, 18 = least important). Do the same with the list of terminal values.

Instrumental values
RANK

_____ Ambitious (hard-working, aspiring)
_____ Broadminded (open-minded)
_____ Capable (competent, effective)
_____ Cheerful (lighthearted, joyful)
_____ Clean (neat, tidy)
_____ Courageous (standing up for your beliefs)
_____ Forgiving (willing to pardon others)
_____ Helpful (working for the welfare of others)
_____ Honest (sincere, truthful)
_____ Imaginative (daring, creative)
_____ Independent (self-sufficient)
_____ Intellectual (intelligent, reflective)
_____ Logical (consistent, rational)
_____ Loving (affectionate, tender)
_____ Obedient (dutiful, respectful)
_____ Polite (courteous, well-mannered)
_____ Responsible (dependable, reliable)
_____ Self-controlled (restrained, self-disciplined)

Terminal values
RANK

_____ A comfortable life (a prosperous life)
_____ An exciting life (a stimulating, active life)
_____ A sense of accomplishment (lasting contribution)
_____ A world at peace (free of war and conflict)
_____ A world of beauty (beauty of nature and the arts)
_____ Equality (brotherhood, equal opportunity for all)
_____ Family security (taking care of loved ones)
_____ Freedom (independence, free choice)
_____ Happiness (contentedness)
_____ Inner harmony (freedom from inner conflict)
_____ Mature love (sexual and spiritual intimacy)
_____ National security (protection from attack)
_____ Pleasure (an enjoyable, leisurely life)
_____ Salvation (saved, eternal life)
_____ Self-respect (self-esteem)
_____ Social recognition (respect, admiration)
_____ True friendship (close companionship)
_____ Wisdom (a mature understanding of life)

Try the Rokeach Value Survey again in about three months and compare your rankings. Are they the same? Are you surprised at your rankings? Do you think that reading about ethics and social responsibility in this chapter had any influence on your rankings?

CHAPTER 4

The Global Management Environment

After studying this chapter, you should be able to:

❖ Discuss the nature and importance of the global economy.

❖ Define the terms multinational company and global corporation.

❖ Identify the approaches to international business.

❖ Describe the environment for global business.

❖ Explain how regulations influence international management activities.

❖ List some international organizations and their functions.

❖ Describe the different multinational market groups.

❖ Discuss major challenges facing organizations in the global environment.

World War III

Throughout the world, managers are facing the same challenge—competitors that come from nowhere scrambling for business. Not only large companies like IBM and AT&T, but smaller ones like Bicknell Manufacturing and Lucerne Farms are fighting for customers by venturing beyond domestic borders, spurred on by deregulation, privatization, and rapid technological change. A survey of nearly 750 companies by Arthur Andersen & Co. and National Small Business United reports that 20 percent of firms with fewer than 500 employees exported products in 1994, up from 16 percent in 1993. Global fever has now reached the ranks of U.S. entrepreneurs as well as the huge firms of corporate America.

As a result of this intense scramble to enter foreign markets, companies around the world are at war. Any one company has no idea where its next challenge may originate. Car companies compete with banks in credit card wars, while software firms fight with cable companies over rights on the information highway. And the target in these wars, the competitor, is always moving. Giants like Coca-Cola and Pepsi have to fight off private label brands sold in copycat cans, and Six Flags taunts rival Disney in television ads claiming "Disney is a great vacation destination. So is Australia."

Today, size and experience count for much less than they once did. Speed and execution are critical, and battles between firms are fierce. Perhaps nothing illustrates this more in the U.S. than the war between the three major long-distance carriers—AT&T, MCI, and Sprint. In Thailand, the Japanese firms Sony and Matsushita are fighting for the electronics market. And whether they're trying to escape flat domestic markets or building on their successes, more and more companies are looking to foreign markets for growth opportunities.

Source: Adapted from Jaclyn Fierman, "When Genteel Rivals Become Mortal Enemies," *Fortune*, May 15, 1995, pp. 90-100; and Amy Barrett, "It's A Small (Business) World," *Business Week*, April 17, 1995, pp. 96-101.

More than ever before, people throughout the world want the same things, whether Disney theme parks, the latest in fashion, or fast-food restaurants. Sooner than most of us believed possible, our belief in the "nationality" of most corporations is out of date.[1] Says quality expert Philip B. Crosby, "We live in a boundaryless economy now . . . where we're headed for is a place where you can compete with anybody."[2] Only a decade ago, the world economy was the sum of the individual economies of many nations, but this is no longer the case. Thanks to joint ventures, technology, the cross-fertilization of cultures, and many other factors, a truly global economy has been created. This new global economy poses many challenges for today's managers.

This chapter examines the global management environment in terms of (1) the nature and importance of the global economy, (2) types of organizations in the global economy, (3) the environment for global business, (4) regulation of international business, (5) multi-national market groups, and (6) challenges facing organizations in the global environment.

THE NATURE AND IMPORTANCE OF THE GLOBAL ECONOMY

In the global economy, any product made anywhere has to compete with any product made anywhere else. U.S. automakers learned this the hard way. Cars made in Detroit compete with cars made in Japan; flowers grown in Florida compete with flowers grown in Colombia; wine bottled in California competes with wine bottled in France. The question facing firms in the United States and throughout the world isn't whether we should compete with foreign firms, but how we can survive in the global economy.

The answer to this question, of course, is complex. We know that customers are demanding better products, improved service, and lower prices, and the way to compete is through quality. Global competition means that consumers have a better choice of products for less money; management's common goal must be customer satisfaction. In the past decade America's dominance in the world economy has faltered because of the decline in competitiveness of American goods. A major factor in this decline has been consumer perception about the quality of these goods. The inevitable conclusion is that our economic status in the new global economy will depend upon our ability to meet new competitive standards.

Quality and the Status of a Nation

Much has been written about the quality of a product and its implications for a nation's status. In the 19th century, Britain was the world's economic leader. Today Britain finds itself at the bottom among developed nations. Many experts have attributed its economic fall to a drop in the quality of goods the British produced. Consider the following passage:

> The quality of product turned out has international, cold war status as well as personal, local, and national status. That this is a practical everyday kind of consideration is already very clear, even though America doesn't realize this as much as other countries do. The stereotype in most of the world is that an American fountain pen is more likely to be a good, workable, efficient fountain pen than if it comes from another country. And we have the recent example of the self-conscious cooperation between the government of Japan and its industries in deliberately shifting over to higher-quality products. The stereotype of Japanese products before the war was that they were shoddy and cheap or low-quality imitations. But already, we are getting to think of Japanese products in about the same way that we used to think of a German product in the old days, that is, as being of very high quality and of excellent workmanship. Countries to some extent get judged by the quality of automobiles or cameras that they turn out. I am told that German quality has gone down. If this is so, then the status of West Germany in the eyes of the whole world will go down. It will be considered in an unconscious way to have less status, to have poorer quality as a nation. This, of course, since every West German tends to identify with his country and tends to introject it, means a loss of self-esteem in every single citizen, just as the increased Japanese quality and the general respect for their products means an increase in the

self-esteem of every Japanese citizen. The same thing is true for the United States in a very general way.[3]

When do you think that passage was written? Noted psychologist Abraham Maslow wrote it in 1965. In retrospect, it almost seems like a warning. Several decades ago, "made in Japan" signified poor-quality products to be avoided. Today numerous Japanese products are known for their quality and dependability. According to Maslow, Japan's status in the eyes of the world should also go up, and it has. Japan worked for many years to shed its negative stereotype; Maslow noted decades ago that we were already thinking of the high quality of Japanese products. Similarly, the rest of the world judges America according to the quality of the goods we produce, whether they be cars or TVs. Maslow said Americans haven't realized this as much as other peoples have, but we *must* today.

Perhaps the most important part of Maslow's message is that citizens tend to identify with the status of their country. If the quality of a nation's products increases, so does the self-esteem of its citizens. Higher self-esteem of course translates into more motivated and committed workers. Likewise, as a nation's status falls, so does its citizens' self-esteem.

The Global Boom

International business is the performance of business activities across national boundaries. Every nation in the world participates in international business to some extent. Involvement in international business has increased steadily since World War II. It's expected to continue growing as we move into the 21st century. More than $2 trillion is spent annually on trade between nations. By the year 2000 a key requirement for chief executives of American firms will be experience in international business. And worldwide employment will increase in nearly 75 percent of American firms.[4] This growth will be due in part to the global boom and new business opportunities throughout the world.

international business Performance of business activities across national boundaries.

Today Japan is one of the world's leading economic powers. Only 50 years ago the country was left devastated by American bombing raids during World War II. Tokyo was burned to the ground; atomic bombs leveled Hiroshima and Nagasaki. When the war ended, Japan's economy existed no longer. But Japan learned from this disaster. Ever since, the Japanese have invested in people. Current changes in Eastern Europe, South Korea, Vietnam, and Taiwan also suggest a global environment in which market power, not military power, will prevail. Learning how to manage organizations in this new environment will be critical to American firms as well as firms throughout the world.

International management is the performance of the management process in an international business setting. The global boom has increased the importance of international management. As larger portions of the world desire quality goods at lower prices, managers must be prepared to compete in an increasingly interdependent global economy. Firms that choose not to compete in this global environment will be affected by U.S. and foreign competitors that do. In reality, organizations can't avoid competing in the global economy.

international management Performance of the management process in an international business setting.

Transportation, communication, and technology have fueled the global boom. In 18th-century America all economies were local. Little emphasis was placed on regional competition, let alone national competition. With the advent of the railroad and the telegraph, 19th-century economies became regional or national. Firms began to compete with others in distant parts of the country. Often the firm producing the greatest quantity won out; thus the first firms to adopt assembly-line techniques survived. In the 1950s fiberoptics, satellites, improved transistors, and air travel made geographic distance less relevant. Firms began to compete with firms in other parts of the world. As the 20th century progressed, firms competed still more on quality as well as quantity. In the 21st century the firm that offers high-quality products is most likely to succeed.

Global Opportunities

The global boom has resulted in a customer-driven world economy. Harvard professor Rosabeth Moss Kanter says information, the computer, and transportation advances caused the global market. She contends that many of the changes taking place in Europe today are occurring because people in Eastern Europe wanted to go shopping. Through TV and other mass media, people can learn about lifestyles in the rest of the world. It's interesting to think that Levi Strauss and Bon Jovi—not just U.S. military strength—helped cause the Soviet bloc's breakup.[5]

A customer-driven economy means new opportunities throughout the world. For example, Russians know that their standard of living is lower than that of citizens in the West and other parts of the world. As Russia's economy changes, demand will rise for products of all types—food, clothing, appliances, leisure items, medical care, and so on. Countless new opportunities will arise for firms to offer goods and services that meet these demands. In short, the global economy means global opportunities for firms that simply need the vision to act upon them. Argentina has experienced one of the fastest and most successful processes of privatization ever. The state-owned oil company, railroads, telephones, airline, utilities, and television and radio stations have been privatized. Inflation has dropped from 4,000 percent in the late 1980s to 17.5 percent, while growth is exceeding 6 percent annually.[6] Foreign investors, including such U.S. firms as Motorola, AT&T, Chrysler, IBM, and Apple, are flocking to China to invest in that country's double-digit growth.[7] China's flagrant piracy of American products ranging from pop music to computer software presents a clear risk to Western and Asian companies doing business there.[8] Western firms also are finding new opportunities in India, the world's fifth-largest economy, with a middle class of approximately 300 million people eager for new products.[9]

Taking advantage of global opportunities won't be easy. Firms throughout the world are poised to offer products to emerging markets. More competition means more choices, which drive the need for quality even higher. In 1980 there were approximately seven competitors in the luxury car market. By 1990 the number rose to 15, including companies in the United States, Japan, Germany, and other European countries. Competition in other industries is following the same pattern. The increased globalization of markets has led to greater competition among corporations throughout the world and an erosion in the world dominance of U.S. firms—a trend that's expected to continue.[10] Firms that supply high-quality products will be in the best position to survive and prosper in the global economy. The Ethics Spotlight illustrates how nations around the world also share environmental concerns.

TYPES OF ORGANIZATIONS IN THE GLOBAL ECONOMY

Any organization, large or small, can become involved in international business. While international firms are perceived to be large and well known (like Sony and IBM), numerous smaller firms also sell products in foreign markets. This section discusses multinational and global corporations and their approaches to becoming involved in international business.

Multinational and Global Corporations

multinational company (MNC)
An organization conducting business in two or more countries.

Firms involved in international business are commonly referred to as multinational companies. A **multinational company (MNC)** is an organization conducting business in two or more countries. MNCs are often based in one country, with operations, production facilities, and/or sales subsidiaries in other countries. KLM Royal Dutch Airliner's strategy is to use global alliances to serve airline passengers around the world.[11] Auto companies Volkswagen and General Motors have each invested over $2 billions in production facilities in Brazil.[12] MNCs are traditionally viewed as domestic firms that carry out activities in other parts of the world; IBM is an American firm, Grand Metropolitan is British, and Nestlé is Swiss. Table 4–1 lists the world's largest MNCs.

global corporation
A corporation operating as if the world were a single market, with corporate headquarters, manufacturing facilities, and marketing operations throughout the world.

Another term used to describe a type of organization emerging in the global economy is *global corporation*. In contrast to an MNC, a **global corporation** operates as if the world were a single market, and it has corporate headquarters, manufacturing facilities, and marketing operations throughout the world. At Ford Motor Co., North American and European units were combined into a single company; global product teams now design cars to be sold around the world.[13] Although similar to an MNC, a global corporation is different in that it isn't anchored in a single country; national boundaries are meaningless. Global cor-

ETHICS SPOTLIGHT   GLOBAL CATASTROPHE OR FALSE ALARM?

Overcrowding at the weekly market in the village of Qutur in the Nile Delta.

—

Donella and Dennis Meadows sparked intense debate in 1972 with the release of their book Limits to Growth. Through the use of computer models, the authors predicted that population growth would collide with the earth's ability to absorb pollution and regenerate itself. Some saw this as a serious warning of a potential global catastrophe; others passed it off as a false alarm. Twenty years later, leaders and negotiators from 170 countries met in Rio de Janeiro for the U.N. Conference on Environment and Development (UNCED). The major topic was a controversial agenda to protect the earth's atmosphere and inhabitants, attack poverty, and foster less destructive industrialization. A number of ecological trends are seen as likely to occur, resulting in increased levels of environmental regulation worldwide. The problems are far from simple:

- World population is expected to double, reaching 11 billion within 40 years. Industrial output would have to quintuple to meet the needs of all these people.
- Industrialized nations make up only 25 percent of the world's population, yet they consume 70 percent of the resources. As more nations become developed and boost economic growth, resources will be scarce.
- Seven industrial countries, including the United States, are responsible for 45 percent of human-caused greenhouse gas emissions. As developing nations industrialize, worldwide pollution will skyrocket.
- Human activities are destroying the earth's soils, forests, wetlands, and grasslands. Over 40 million acres of tropical forests are destroyed each year, and the ozone layer is thinning, increasing the potential for global warming.
- Damage to the environment costs industrialized nations 1 to 5 percent of their GNP (gross national product). Forest damage in Western Europe is cutting GNP by $30 billion a year.
- In places like Mexico City and Eastern Europe, millions breathe toxic air. China will soon deplete all its harvestable forests. The Baltic Sea is dying from sewage and other pollution.

Source: Adopted from Gene R. Laczniak, Anthony Pecotich and Angela Spadaccini, "Toward 2000: A Tougher Future For Australian Businesses," *Asian Pacific Journal of Management*, April 1994, pp. 67–90; Emily T. Smith, "Growth vs. Environment," *Business Week*, May 11, 1992, pp. 66–75; and Peter Hong and Michele Galen, "The Toxic Mess Called Superfund," *Business Week*, May 11, 1992, pp. 32–34.

porations pursue integrated strategies on a worldwide basis, while MNCs pursue separate strategies on a country-by-country basis.[14] Thus a truly global corporation isn't seen as Japanese or American, for instance, but as a global company. ABB is a global electrical equipment giant, larger than Westinghouse, and is able to take on GE. The world leader in high-speed trains, robotics, and environmental control, ABB isn't Japanese or American. The company's 13 top managers meet in different countries, and do not share a common first language. ABB is truly a global corporation.[15]

In reality, we haven't quite reached the point where global corporations are common. Most international firms are MNCs that have expanded their operations to other parts of the world. Toyota, with a large Camry plant in Georgetown, Kentucky, is considered a Japanese firm. Yet Camrys are made with predominantly American parts by American workers, have fewer defects than those made in Japan, and have actually been exported to Japan. While the Big Three automakers in the United States ask consumers to "buy American," some observers argue that Camry is more American than Fords made in Mexico with non-American parts. Confusion over the nationality of products is indicative of the emergence of global corporations. By the year 2000 global corporations will no longer be the exception. Firms that don't recognize their emerging presence face a serious threat.

Approaches to International Business

Depending on the level of commitment an organization is willing to make, it can take any of several approaches to international business. Some approaches represent a low level of commitment, while others represent a true global commitment. These approaches include

TABLE 4–1	THE 20 LARGEST MULTINATIONAL COMPANIES		
Rank	Company	Country	Revenues (in billions of U.S. dollars)
1	Mitsubishi	Japan	175.8
2	Mitsui	Japan	171.5
3	Itochu	Japan	167.8
4	Sumitomo	Japan	162.5
5	General Motors	U.S.	155.0
6	Marubeni	Japan	150.2
7	Ford Motor	U.S.	128.4
8	Exxon	U.S.	101.5
9	Nissho Iwai	Japan	100.9
10	Royal Dutch/Shell Group	Britain/Neth.	94.9
11	Toyota Motor	Japan	88.2
12	Wal-Mart Stores	U.S.	83.4
13	Hitachi	Japan	76.4
14	Nippon Life Insurance	Japan	75.3
15	AT&T	U.S.	75.1
16	Nippon Telegraph & Telephone	Japan	70.8
17	Matsushita Electric Industrial	Japan	69.9
18	Tomen	Japan	69.9
19	General Electric	U.S.	64.7
20	Daimler-Benz	Germany	64.2

Source: "The World's Largest Corporations," *Fortune*, August 7, 1995, p. F1.

exporting, licensing, trading companies, countertrading, joint ventures, strategic alliances, and direct investment.

exporting

Selling of domestic goods to a foreign country.

EXPORTING - The simplest way to enter international business is **exporting,** selling domestic goods to a foreign country. (*Importing* is purchasing goods made in another country.) Exporting requires the lowest level of resources and commitment. More than half of the U.S. firms involved in international trade do so through exporting.[16] In many cases a firm can locate an export agency that can provide assistance in selling products to foreign countries, thereby avoiding significant upfront investments.[17]

American exports are making a strong comeback and have reduced the *trade deficit*, which results when a country imports more than it exports. The United States trade deficit was a record $151 billion in 1994.[18] In 1994, for the fourth year in a row, the United States ranked as the top merchandise exporter in the world, with $512.7 billion in exports.[19] Many products once considered in serious trouble domestically are selling well in foreign markets. U.S. exports are on the rise, up 25 percent since 1993.[20] The major growth in exports is taking place in Canada, Japan, Mexico, Taiwan, Korea, and Germany. The fastest-growing U.S. exports are music, video, and computer tapes; cigarettes and tobacco products; meat; pulp and wastepaper; and synthetic resins, rubber, and plastics.[21] Table 4–2 lists the 20 largest

TABLE 4–2	THE 20 LARGEST U.S. EXPORTERS		
Rank	Company	Export Sales (in millions)	Exports as a Percentage of Sales
1	General Motors	$16,127	10.4
2	Ford Motor	11,892	9.3
3	Boeing	11,844	54.0
4	Chrysler	9,400	18.0
5	General Electric	8,110	12.5
6	Motorola	7,370	33.1
7	IBM	6,336	9.9
8	Phillip Morris	4,942	9.2
9	Archer Daniels Midland	4,625	41.1
10	Hewlett-Packard	4,653	18.6
11	Intel	4,561	39.6
12	Caterpillar	4,510	31.5
13	McDonnell Douglas	4,235	32.1
14	Du Pont	3,625	10.4
15	United Technologies	3,108	14.7
16	Eastman Kodak	2,600	15.4
17	Lockheed	2,079	15.8
18	Compaq Computer	2,018	18.6
19	Raytheon	1,867	18.6
20	Digital Equipment	1,831	13.6

Source: "Top 50 U.S. Industrial Exporters," *Fortune*, November 13, 1995, p. 74.

U.S. exporters. If exports continue to grow, the United States could see a *trade surplus*, which results when exports exceed imports.

Exports are a key to growth, especially when domestic markets are saturated. Many large and small U.S. firms are growing via exports. For instance, the United States is the leading exporter of food to Japan, with annual sales exceeding $10 billion.[22] General Motors markets a minivan manufactured in the United States and sold in Europe under the Opel name. GM expects to export about $750 million worth of vans in 1996.[23] Small companies also rely on exports for growth and sales. Treatment Products exports $5 million in auto wax, Sharper Finish exports $3 million in laundry and ironing equipment, and Midwest Tropical exports $5.5 million in aquariums.[24]

LICENSING ~ In a **licensing** agreement, one firm (the licensor) agrees to allow another firm (the licensee) to sell the licensor's product and use its brand name. In return, the licensee pays the licensor a commission or royalty. For example, a beverage company such as Pepsico might enter into a licensing agreement with a firm in Taiwan. The Taiwanese firm would have the right to sell Pepsi products in Taiwan and would pay Pepsico a specified percentage of the income from sales of Pepsi products. Playboy Enterprises has licensed 20 mainland Chinese sportswear boutiques operated by the Chinese government. The boutiques sell a variety of outerwear and other products with the rabbit logo.[25] Licensing offers

licensing
An agreement through which one firm (the licensor) allows another firm (the licensee) to sell the licensor's product and use its brand name.

advantages for both licensor and licensee. The licensor can become involved in international trade with little financial risk. The licensee gains products and technology that may otherwise be too costly to produce. But licensing doesn't result in a large payoff for the licensor—usually only about 5 percent of sales. Some American executives and managers believe that licensing agreements merely give away trade secrets for a meager 5 percent of sales; after the agreement expires (usually in less than 10 years), the licensee may continue to market the product without paying the licensor.

trading company
4 link between buyers and sellers indifferent countries.

TRADING COMPANIES - Businesses wishing to sell their products overseas may choose to sell through a **trading company,** which serves as a link between buyers and sellers in different countries. Trading companies aren't involved in manufacturing products. They're simply intermediaries that take title to products and undertake all the activities required to move products from the domestic country to customers in a foreign country. In addition, they provide sellers with information about markets, product quality and price expectations, distribution, and foreign exchange in domestic or international markets. Trading companies assume much of the manufacturer's risk in international business.

Because they're usually favored by their governments, trading companies can facilitate entrance into foreign markets. Some countries (Brazil, for one) give trading companies tax advantages. In the United States, the 1982 *Export Trading Company Act* encourages the efficient operation of trading companies, helps to finance international trade, and provides limited protection from antitrust laws when conducting export activities. After the act was passed, many major companies (such as General Electric, Kmart, and Sears, Roebuck) developed their own export trading companies.

countertrading
Complex bartering agreements between two or more parties.

COUNTERTRADING - **Countertrading** involves complex bartering agreements between two or more countries. (Bartering refers to the exchange of merchandise between countries.) Countertrading allows a nation with limited cash to participate in international trade. The country wishing to trade requires the exporting country to purchase products from it before allowing its products to be sold there. For instance, McDonnell Douglas sold $25 million worth of commercial helicopters to Uganda and financially supported a plant that catches and processes Nile perch and a factory to turn pineapples into concentrate in order for Uganda to earn hard currency and pay McDonnell Douglas; the factories were sold to buyers in Europe. Agreements like this account for an estimated 20 percent of U.S. exports, or $110 billion; the use of countertrade agreements is expected to grow during the 1990s.[26] Countertrading provides an established trading vehicle for the former Soviet bloc and other developing and Third World countries that want U.S. goods but lack currency to pay for them.[27] Although many U.S. companies still don't use countertrading, firms will find they have no choice if they wish to compete in global markets.

Countertrading has several drawbacks. First, it's often difficult to determine the true value of goods offered in a countertrade agreement. Second, it may be difficult to dispose of bartered goods after they're accepted. These problems can be reduced or eliminated through market analysis and negotiation. Companies have been developed to assist firms in handling countertrade agreements. Despite these drawbacks, companies that choose not to countertrade may miss significant opportunities.

joint venture
A partnership between a domestic firm and a firm in a foreign country.

JOINT VENTURES - Firms may also conduct international business through a **joint venture,** in this case a partnership between a domestic firm and a firm in a foreign country. Because of government restrictions on foreign ownership of corporations, joint ventures are often the only way a firm can purchase facilities in another country. For instance, General Motors formed a joint venture with China's Jinbei Automobile to build light trucks. GM owns 30 percent of the venture, which plans to produce 50,000 trucks by 1998 for the world's largest market.[28] Mitsubishi Motors Corp. has developed 10 joint ventures in Asia, giving the auto maker low-cost parts and access to restricted markets.[29]

Joint ventures are becoming more common because of cost advantages and the number of inexperienced firms entering foreign markets. Sometimes joint ventures are a political necessity because of nationalism and government restrictions on foreign ownership of property or industry. In environments with scarce resources, rapid technological changes, and massive capital requirements, joint ventures may be the best way for smaller firms with limited resources to attain better positions in global industries. Joint ventures may also be created to gain access to distributors, suppliers, and technology.

One major drawback to international joint ventures is that organizations may lose control of their operations. For example, because India doesn't allow foreign companies to own industries, Coca-Cola once entered into a joint venture with the Indian government. Despite India's huge soft drink market, Coca-Cola pulled out over a decade ago rather than risk giving up majority control and its secret formula.

STRATEGIC ALLIANCE - A recent strategy for entering foreign markets is a strategic alliance. A **strategic alliance** occurs when two firms combine their resources in a partnership that goes beyond the limits of a joint venture. Strategic alliances have been growing in the highly competitive global marketplace at an annual rate of 27 percent since 1985.[30] IBM alone has established over 400 strategic alliances with U.S. and foreign firms. Trust is the major requirement for an effective partnership. If a firm can't trust its prospective partners, it shouldn't enter into a strategic alliance with them. Trust generally evolves over time, so firms must give strategic alliances adequate time to prosper. Ford and Mazda formed a strategic alliance nearly 15 years ago to cooperate on new vehicles and exchange expertise. Ford is the best-selling foreign auto in Japan, and building trust over the years was a major factor in this success.[31]

strategic alliance
A combination of two firms' resources in a partnership that goes beyond the limits of a joint venture.

DIRECT OWNERSHIP - A much more involved approach to international business is **direct ownership** (purchasing one or more business operations in a foreign country). Direct ownership requires a large investment in production facilities, research, personnel, and marketing activities. General Electric, for example, invested $150 million to purchase 12 light bulb plants in Hungary that were once owned by the Hungarian government. GE planned to spend at least $140 million over five years to modernize the plants with no expectation of getting back its investment for some time.[32] Many MNCs such as Ford, Polaroid, and 3M own facilities outside the United States. Through direct ownership, a firm has greater control over a foreign subsidiary.

direct ownership
Purchasing of one or more business operations in a foreign country.

Some well-known firms operating in the United States are actually subsidiaries owned by foreign firms. Magnavox, Pillsbury, Saks Fifth Avenue, and Baskin-Robbins are wholly owned subsidiaries of foreign multinational companies. Nonprofit organizations (such as the Red Cross) and the U.S. Army also own foreign subsidiaries or divisions.

Firms invest in foreign subsidiaries for a number of reasons. Direct ownership can reduce manufacturing costs because of lower labor and operating costs. Direct ownership also enables a firm to avoid paying tariffs and other costs associated with exporting. Additionally, by paying taxes in the host country and providing employment for local residents, a foreign company can build good relations with the host government. The greatest danger of direct ownership is that a firm may lose a sizable investment because of market failure or nationalization of its interests by a foreign government. When problems arise in a foreign country, it's often very difficult and expensive to move operations out of the country.

THE ENVIRONMENT FOR GLOBAL BUSINESS

There are usually significant differences between the business environments of domestic and foreign markets. A detailed analysis of these differences is critical in determining whether to enter a foreign market. If a manager of an MNC or global corporation is to be effective in a global environment, differences in cultural, social, economic, political, legal, and technological environments must be understood.

Cultural Environment

Appreciating the differences among cultures is a basic requirement for successful international management.[33] **Cultural diversity** refers to the differences that exist both within and among cultures.[34] Meanings attached to body language, time, greetings, spatial patterns, and

cultural diversity
Differences both within and between cultures.

REFLECTIONS BY PHILIP B. CROSBY

The Global Management Environment

I spent the first 11 years of my career working for companies whose customer was the U.S. Department of Defense. My thoughts rarely strayed from the nation's borders. Then I moved to the ITT Corporation, which did business all over the world. Suddenly I was responsible for quality in a company where English was the official language, but the employees spoke in 15 or 20 different tongues and their work was done in accordance with as many different cultures.

ITT management (headed by Harold Geneen, who invented the conglomerate concept) took extraordinary steps to build communications. Each month senior executives from all from all over gathered in New York for a general meeting of status and action. The following week a detailed meeting was held in Brussels to review all the European operations. It was very hard to hide anything—and completely unnecessary.

I organized the quality management professionals into 28 Quality Councils all around the ITT world. Then these people were brought to a special school to learn the language of quality. They also learned how to communicate with colleagues who had completely different customs and situations. Their management was taught in school and in the general conversation of company business. The price of nonconformance was put into the reporting system and this assured management's continual attention to the subject. Those who have trouble keeping executives interested in quality only need to transfer it into financial terms. The one thing managers all have in common worldwide, is that they care about money first—above all, believe me. It is the only way they are measured and rewarded or denied.

We issued a corporate policy on quality that said, "It is the quality policy of the company that each employee will perform according to the agreed requirements or cause those requirements to be officially changed to what we and our customers really need. Quality is defined as conformance to the requirements.

Also, each unit of the corporation was required to have a quality management entity to the extent agreed by the unit president and the corporate vice president of quality (me). Thus in the late 1960s, service companies like Avis, Sheraton, and Hartford Insurance began to embrace the concepts of quality management as a normal part of doing business. As in the manufacturing companies, employees at all levels could now talk about quality and understand each other. They spent their time getting the "requirements" right rather than seeing what could be acceptable although not correct.

In my consulting years I often heard client CEOs say that the only thing everyone in the company understood the same was quality. They had all been to my "Quality College;" they all agreed that quality was conformance to requirements, that it was achieved by prevention, that the performance standard was zero defects, and that the measurement was money.

Translating concepts from English to some other language is not easily done. I found it necessary to hire someone to translate my material back into English in order to check it out. Once I found that a German translator had turned the word prevention into one that referred to birth control devices. Nevertheless, the message here is that any subject can be made comprehensible to all regardless of their location, culture, or business if it is patiently described and taught.

Communication, not control, is what builds world class quality.

other symbols differ significantly across cultures. When products are introduced into one nation from another, acceptance is far more likely if differences between cultures are recognized and accommodated. For example, the first McDonald's in Mecca, Saudi Arabia, used meat from animals slaughtered according to Islamic rules.[35] Conversely, Yokohama Rubber Co., based in Tokyo, had to recall auto tires with a tread pattern that resembled the Arabic word for Allah after Islamic customers protested. Yokohama apologized for its lack of knowledge of Islam, discontinued the tires, and replaced them free of charge in Islamic nations.[36]

Managers must be willing and able to adjust to cultural differences when doing business in foreign countries. How managers communicate in different countries varies greatly. For example, managers doing business in Japan know that the Japanese value saving face and achieving harmony. Thus, to be successful, managers never put a Japanese businessperson in a position where he or she must admit failure. They approach a Japanese manager at the highest level possible in the organization (the first person approached will be involved throughout the negotiation). Direct communication about money is avoided if feasible. Finally, and perhaps most difficult of all, American managers must wait patiently for Japanese meetings to move forward before an agreement is reached.[37]

Culture can also impact the most fundamental role of CEOs in a society. In the United States, CEOs are viewed much like celebrities, are featured in TV ads, and are paid high salaries (an average of $2 million a year) plus additional benefits or perks that go along with the position.[38] In contrast, CEOs in Japan and Korea are important social leaders.[39]

GLOBAL EXCHANGE · THE WORKERS AREN'T THE PROBLEM

Are American workers too lazy to compete in the global economy? It seems that when something goes wrong, you hear about poor workmanship, not poor management. Years ago, long before the threat of foreign cars became apparent, a joke about American cars made the rounds: Try to buy a car made on a Tuesday, Wednesday, or Thursday. Don't buy one made on a Monday (since the workers were recovering from the weekend) or a Friday (when they were getting ready for the weekend).

Maybe the joke has a ring of truth to it, maybe not, but that's not the point. Lemons were never thought to be a management problem; they were the workers' fault. This belief held not only for cars, but for TVs, banks, airlines, and virtually any other good or service. Customers blamed problems with banks on the tellers, not the managers. Putting responsibility for success or failure on the worker is still evident. We regularly hear about workers taking pay cuts, but it's rare to hear about executives cutting their pay, even after their firms have lost millions of dollars. So are the workers the problem?

The answer is a plain and simple no. Like everyone else in the new global economy, workers in America are adjusting to conditions they aren't familiar with. A recent survey conducted by Watson Wyatt Worldwide of Washington, D.C., reports that workers feel less secure about their jobs today than they did in 1987. But they aren't lazy. The productivity of American workers remains the highest in the industrial world, 25 percent higher than it is in Japan. Ironically, as American workers have maintained a high level of productivity, their real wages have stagnated, even declined.

In short, when given the training needed to do their jobs, American workers measure up. The problem is how their skills and talents are organized and nurtured. Managers must provide workers with the training they need to compete in the global economy and the freedom to use their intelligence and creativity on the job. According to Lord White, CEO of Hanson PLC's U.S. operations, workers "can only be as good as their leaders." Increasingly it's recognized that workers aren't the problem; it's the managers.

A major problem facing American workers is that the physical skills that made them successful in decades past are inadequate today when mental skills are needed. Worker training and retraining are critical to U.S. industry. Frontline workes in American factories, offices, and stores often receive little or no training. While American firms are reluctant to invest in their workers, firms like Germany and Japan invest heavily in them. At major Japanese corporations, workers receive extensive training, few change jobs, and layoffs are rare. U.S. workers are the first to be affected by problems in either the economy or their own companies. Some experts say that since managers can save a firm's short-term profits by laying off workers, they don't have to know how to manage. Workers are treated as expendable or replaceable parts, a situation that doesn't encourage much commitment on their part.

Commitment is the goal, and all quality experts agree that active worker participation leads to greater commitment. At Northern Telecom's plant in Morrisville, North Carolina, 420 people work in teams, act as their own bosses, and make their own decisions. Revenue is up 86 percent since management introduced this system. At a Honda assembly plant in Liberty, Ohio, the assembly line worker is treated like a professional because that person knows what's best and how to make it better. Honda management listens and often turns significant decisions over to workers. At Federal Express each employee is told that 100 percent customer satisfaction is the goal. After each worker is taught how to work both as a member of a team and independently, he or she is given the right to do anything necessary to satisfy a customer. No management approval is necessary.

Many similar stories could be told, proving that it's the manager's job to provide an environment in which workers can do their best work. Employees deserve this dignity as do customers. A study of workplace practices conducted by Ernst & Young found that investing in workers pays off in bottom-line profits. If managers fail to do this, the result is poor workmanship—a management problem.

Source: Adapted from Michael Reinemer, "Work Happy," *American Demographics*, July 1995, pp. 26–31; Susana Barciela, "Lip Service Paid on Valuing Workers," *Lexington Herald-Leader*, June 18, 1995, p. B6; Myron Magnet, "The Truth about the American Worker," *Fortune*, May 4, 1992, pp. 48–65; Jim Barnett, "Workers Manage to Make Decisions," *News and Observer* (Raleigh, N.C.), March 8, 1991, p. 6C; and Lloyd Dobyns and Clare Crawford-Mason, *Quality or Else* (Boston: Houghton Mifflin, 1991), pp. 105–26.

They receive only one fourth as much compensation as American CEOs, but take more responsibility for company failure.[40] To save face, Japanese CEOs often resign when their company loses money. For many years American CEOs have attributed failures to workers rather than to management. As a result many people in the United States and abroad view American workers as inferior. A controversy over this issue erupted several years ago when a high-level Japanese government official called American workers lazy and illiterate. But many experts on quality argue that managers, not workers, often are the problem. Furthermore, they say, we must recognize where the blame lies and make adjustments if we're to compete in the global economy. The Global Exchange on the next page deals with this subject.

Business customs also play a major role in international management. In some countries, one major goal in business is to be accepted by others. Japanese workers, for instance, are more concerned with being accepted by their fellow employees than with making a profit. In the Middle Eastern oil markets, companies frequently have to do business via a "connector," who has access to the oil producers and receives a commission for this role. Differences in ethical standards influence marketing activities. Price fixing, payoffs, and bribes are acceptable behavior in some countries. In Mexico, bribes and payoffs are sometimes a way of doing business.

Many U.S. firms provide cross-cultural training to help managers prepare for assignments involving international business. Training covers language, culture, and history of the foreign country plus how to conduct business there. Employees are screened carefully before they're given international assignments. Firms might require that candidates for international positions speak one or more foreign languages, have lived outside the United States, and have prior international work experience. American Express's global-management exchange program enables managers with at least two years of experience to transfer abroad for 18 months.[41]

Economic Environment

The process of international management is also influenced by a country's economic environment. Foreign economies are unfamiliar and often fluctuate even when the domestic economy is stable. Thus the stability of the nation's economy must be determined before managers can assess market potential for their products. Developed nations like the United States, Canada, and Japan tend to have more stable economies than less developed countries such as Ethiopia and Ecuador.

The size of the foreign market is another economic factor that must be understood before engaging in international management. A firm should verify that a market is large enough to justify the costs of introducing products there. Two factors are used to access the size of a foreign market: population and income. A country's population must be large enough to attract a firm's interest. The acceptable size varies considerably from one company to another. Some firms market only to the largest nations (Table 4–3). Other firms market products in countries with populations below one million. Managers must also investigate population trends to determine if the country is growing.

Next, managers must examine the prospective market's income, as measured by output. The United States has a gross national product (GNP) of more than $5.4 trillion, the largest in the world. Gross national product per capita, which takes into account a nation's GNP in relation to its population, is a measure of a nation's **standard of living.** U.S. per capita GNP is $20,910. Japan's GNP is $2.91 trillion, but per capita GNP is 22,900.[42] Thus, the average citizen in Japan has about the same standard of living as his or her American counterpart. But in China, fewer than 15 percent of households have income sufficient to buy a refrigerator.[43]

Gross domestic product (GDP) is another useful indicator of a market's income, as it measures the purely domestic output of a country. Some countries only report GDP data. International organizations often prefer it as a comparison of output between nations because it excludes net property income from abroad, giving a more realistic measure of domestic output.

If a foreign market is large enough to capture a firm's interest, the nation's economic condition should be examined. Developed countries have high literacy rates, modern technology, and high GDP. These nations often provide the greatest marketing opportunities. In developing countries, especially in Latin America, education and technology are improving. And while GDP is fairly low, it shows the highest growth rates in Asia, Latin America, and Eastern Europe.[44] Many less developed countries in Africa and South Asia have lower education levels, limited technology, and very low GDP. Although current business opportunities are limited in developing and less developed countries, long-term opportunities may be extremely favorable as these nations progress.

A nation's **infrastructure** (the communications, transportation, and energy facilities that mobilize the country) also indicates its economic condition.[45] The extent to which a firm can successfully promote a product in different countries partially depends on the communications media available. Similarly, the quantity and quality of transportation facilities affect a firm's ability to distribute its products. In a developed country like Italy, managers use sophisticated telecommunications systems to conduct business. In sharp contrast, many less developed nations have neither a sizable newspaper circulation nor an adequate road or railway system. Another good measure of economic conditions is a country's energy consumption: the higher the level of consumption, the greater the market potential.

standard of living
Gross National Product per capita, which takes into account a nation's GNP in relation to its population.

infrastructure
Communications, transportation, and energy facilities that mobilize the country and also indicate its economic condition.

TABLE 4-3	THE 25 LARGEST COUNTRIES	
Rank	Country	Population (in millions)
1	China	1,203
2	India	937
3	United States	264
4	Indonesia	204
5	Brazil	161
6	Russia	150
7	Pakistan	132
8	Bangladesh	128
9	Japan	126
10	Nigeria	101
11	Mexico	94
12	Germany	82
13	Viet Nam	74
14	Philippines	73
15	Iran	65
16	Turkey	63
17	Egypt	62
18	Thailand	60
19	United Kingdom	58
20	Italy	58
21	France	58
22	Ethiopia	56
23	Ukraine	52
24	South Korea	46
25	Burma	45

Source: *Statistical Abstract of the United States*, 1995, pp. 845–847.

Political–Legal Environment

Political and legal forces also shape a firm's international business activities. Managers must consider the political stability of foreign nations. Countries with intense political unrest may change their policies toward outside firms at any time. This creates an unfavorable environment for international business. In some political power struggles, production facilities have been destroyed, corporate assets seized, and personal security of employees and their families jeopardized. Yugoslavia and Somalia provide recent examples.

A government's policies toward public and private enterprise, consumers, and foreign firms influence firms' decisions to enter a foreign market and also affect the conduct of business across national boundaries. Some countries encourage and seek out foreign investors. Other countries develop barriers to prevent companies from doing business there.

A **quota** limits the amount of a product that can leave or enter a country. Some quotas are voluntary, such as Japan setting a target to buy 20 percent of its computer chips from U.S. firms. An **embargo** prohibits the import or export of certain goods. For instance, Muslim nations have embargoes on the importation of alcoholic beverages because alcohol consumption is a violation of Muslim values. A **duty** is a tax on an import or export Soon after taking office, President Clinton used such a tax to double the price of European steel, starting talk of possible retaliation from Europe.[46] An **exchange control** limits how much profit a foreign-based firm can return to its home country.

Many countries rely on customs and entry procedures to restrict the entry of foreign products. **Customs and entry procedures** govern the inspection, documentation, and licensing of imports. The documents that governments require are often extensive and complex. Japan requires six volumes of standards for each car that enters the country. Without proper documentation, products don't clear Japanese customs. In France, customs

quota
A limit to the amount of a product that can leave or enter a country.

embargo
A prohibition of the import or export of certain goods.

duty
A tax on an import or export.

exchange control
A limit on how much profit a foreign-based firm can return to its home country.

customs and entry procedures
Inspection, documentation, and licensing of foods entering a country.

documentation must be in French, which often slows product clearance. Beer can't be imported into Mexico without a license. To obtain a license, the importer must prove that domestic demand can't be met by Mexican brewers alone. India requires licenses for all imported goods.[47]

The highest risks for international firms are found in countries such as El Salvador, Afghanistan, and Iran, which are politically unstable and place many restrictions on business. On the other hand, countries such as the United States, Australia, and South Korea are considered attractive because they're politically stable and place fewer restrictions on business.

Technological Environment

Technology is also a major consideration when becoming involved in international business. Not all countries are at the same level of technological development. For instance, electricity isn't readily available in some parts of the world so demand isn't high for products requiring electricity to operate. Communications systems also differ throughout the world. Some countries lack modern broadcasting and postal services; much of the technology used for advertising can't be used in these nations.

REGULATION OF INTERNATIONAL BUSINESS

As business between nations grows, so does the number of laws and organizations involved in regulating international trade, which this section examines.

Legislation

The major U.S. laws affecting American firms engaged in international business are summarized in Table 4–4. The *Webb-Pomerene Export Trade Act* of 1918 exempts U.S. firms from certain antitrust laws if they're working together to develop export markets. The Webb-Pomerene Act doesn't allow companies to reduce competition in the United States or to use unfair methods of competition. The *Foreign Corrupt Practices Act*, passed in 1977, prohibits American firms from making bribes to foreign officials. This law spells out the penalties for companies and individuals who are in violation: companies may be fined up to $1 million, and individuals may receive a fine up to $10,000 and a prison sentence of up to five years. The *Export Trading Companies Act* of 1982 eliminates some antitrust barriers and allows banks to participate in joint ventures. (An export trading company is an organization that attempts to create exports.)

Unfortunately, many firms can take advantage of weak regulation in foreign countries. For example (as Chapter 3 pointed out), products that are regulated in the United States, such as dangerous pesticides and drugs, may not be regulated in other countries so firms look to these foreign markets to sell dangerous products. Third World nations are often the target of dangerous products because they have the weakest regulation.

TABLE 4–4	U.S. LAWS AFFECTING INTERNATIONAL BUSINESS
Law	Purpose
Webb-Pomerene Export Trade Act (1918)	Exempts U.S. firms from antitrust laws if they're acting together to develop international trade.
Foreign Corrupt Practices Act (1977)	Forbids bribing foreign officials to obtain sales for American firms.
Export Trading Companies Act (1982)	Encourages the formation of export trading companies by eliminating antitrust barriers and allowing banks to participate in such ventures.

International Organizations

Several international organizations exist to facilitate world trade. The major ones include GATT, IMF, and the World Bank.

GATT - Signed in 1947, the General Agreement on Tariffs and Trade (GATT) formed an international organization of 23 nations, including the United States. GATT works to reduce or eliminate tariffs and other barriers to international trade. Today nearly 100 countries agree to the guidelines established by GATT. As the previous chapter said, GATT's *most favored nation (MFN)* principle requires that any tariff reduction negotiated between any member countries be extended to all members.

Since it was organized, GATT has sponsored several "rounds" of negotiations to reduce trade barriers. President John F. Kennedy, through authority granted by the Trade Expansion Act of 1962, called for the reduction of tariffs through GATT. The Kennedy Round, which began in 1964, led to a nearly 40 percent reduction in tariffs. The Tokyo Round, held from 1973 to 1979, led to a reduction of more than 30 percent. Some nontariff restrictions, such as import quotas and unnecessary red tape in customs procedures, were also removed. In 1989 more than 100 countries agreed to halt farm subsidies and to institute a new system of arbitration for handling disputes between countries. Known as the Uruguay Round, this recent set of talks is expected to boost U.S. output by more than $1 trillion in a 10-year span following the conclusion of the Round.[48]

THE IMF AND WORLD BANK - Two international organizations have been established to help finance international trade. The **International Monetary Fund (IMF)** was founded in 1944 to promote cooperation among member nations by eliminating trade barriers. IMF lends money to countries that need short-term loans to conduct international trade. The **World Bank** was formed in 1946 to lend money to underdeveloped and developing countries for various projects such as the development of roads, factories, and medical facilities.

International Monetary Fund (IMF)
Founded in 1944, it promotes cooperation among member nations by eliminating trade barriers.

World Bank
Formed in 1946, it lends money to underdeveloped and developing countries for various projects.

multinational market group
An agreement by two or more countries to reduce trade and tariff barriers between them.

MULTINATIONAL MARKET GROUPS

Companies operating in the global business environment must recognize that economic cooperation among nations is increasing. A **multinational market group** is created when two or more countries agree to reduce trade and tariff barriers between them. This section covers several current and emerging markets in North America, the European Community, the Pacific Rim, and Eastern Europe and the Commonwealth of Independent States (the former Soviet Union).

The United States, Canada, and Mexico

The United States and Canada signed the *Free Trade Agreement (FTA)* in 1989, providing for the eventual elimination of tariffs and other trade barriers. The agreement essentially merged the U.S. and Canadian markets and made them the largest free trade zone in the world. Trade between the United States and Canada was nearly $170 billion annually before the FTA was signed.[49] Even greater commercial activity is expected after barriers to trade are removed. Some experts predict that the two countries' GNPs could increase by 1 to 5 percent annually.

The agreement calls for most trade restrictions to be removed in stages over a 10-year period. Tariffs were removed immediately on some products. Trade barriers for business personnel and restrictions on financial services are being phased out as quickly as possible.[50] This agreement should help both U.S. and Canadian firms compete more effectively with companies in Europe and Asia. The tariff reductions will be of special benefit to smaller American and Canadian firms because they'll allow them to create more efficient economies of scale for the unified market and to earn higher profit margins.

Even more far reaching is the *North American Free Trade Agreement (NAFTA)*, a three-nation alliance of the United States, Canada, and Mexico, agreed to on August 12, 1992. The

United States needs resources and a source of new labor; Canada is resource-rich but small in population; and Mexico has an abundance of oil and workers but desperately needs exports to fuel its economy. The three nations combined comprise a $6 trillion market of nearly 360 million consumers.[51] Thus, the agreement, which was approved by the respective governments in 1994, makes sense to many. Trade among the three nations, $237 billion a year before NAFTA, could increase dramatically once trade barriers are removed.[52] But many fear that the agreement will mean more U.S. jobs lost to Mexico, where wages are about 10 percent of those in the U.S.[53] Still, some economists argue that lower labor costs should put U.S. firms in a better position to take on global competitors, providing a long-range benefit to the economy.[54] Furthermore, they feel the treaty will keep U.S. exports to Mexico booming and result in more jobs in several industries, including automobile, textile, and telecommunications.[55]

The European Union

The 12-nation European Community (EC), created by the Treaty of Rome in 1957, called for eliminating most trade barriers between its members (Germany, France, Italy, the United Kingdom, Spain, the Netherlands, Belgium, Denmark, Greece, Portugal, Ireland, and Luxembourg) in 1992. Historically the member nations have primarily been separate markets and couldn't compete with the giant resources of Japan and the United States. When the barriers are dissolved, however, more competitive European companies will likely be tapping the unified European market. With over 340 million consumers, unified Europe will be one of the largest markets in the world.[56]

The elimination of trade barriers has already meant big gains for Europe in several industries, including airlines, telecommunications, and financial services. However, the broad monetary and political union of the 12 nations has yet to occur.[57] While single-market reform has generally been successful, the monetary unification has been less of a success. The Maastrict Treaty, an amendment to the original Treaty of Rome, mandates a single European currency by 1999 and a framework for coordinating defense and foreign policies. Denmark rejected the treaty early in 1992, and France nearly rejected it several months later. Failure to establish a single currency would be a major setback. Establishing one currency would eliminate expensive currency transactions (which can cost firms billions of dollars), make it easier for companies to sell products across borders, and enable customers to compare prices better.[58]

Before unification, European industry was fairly inefficient; firms are redesigning themselves to take advantage of a unified European market. Dutch manufacturer Philips Electronics is closing plants and has cut 20 percent of its workforce to concentrate production at its most efficient sites. French steelmaker Usinon-Sacilor eliminated half of its jobs and invested in new technology to become the second largest steelmaker in the world. British Telecommunications PLC, after cutting 170,000 jobs and investing $17 billion in new technology, is taking business from U.S. firms.[59] U.S. companies such as IBM, GM, and Coca-Cola already had a presence in Europe, and should also benefit from unification.

The Pacific Rim

The Pacific Rim nations include Japan, China, Taiwan, South Korea, Singapore, Hong Kong, the Philippines, Malaysia, Indonesia, Indochina, and Australia. Firms from these nations, especially Japan, have become increasingly competitive in comparison to U.S. firms. Names like Toyota, Sony, and Canon aren't only household worlds; they also represent firms that have eroded the market share of their U.S. counterparts General Motors, Zenith, and Kodak. Firms from Taiwan, South Korea, Hong Kong, and Singapore are expected to be even more competitive in the future. The fastest-growing economy in the world, the Pearl River Delta region of southern China, demonstrates the Pacific Rim's economic potential. Firms from around the world (including Procter & Gamble, Pabst Brewing, and GEC Alsthom of France) are doing business there.[60] China takes over the British colony of Hong Kong in 1997, and promises to support capitalism. This could make Hong Kong an open international business hub.[61] And with the economy growing 12 percent annually, China's economic boom is spreading rapidly from the coastal regions inland to areas of massive population.[62] Singapore has also transformed itself into an efficient island nation in which 3,000 multinationals make computer chips, televisions, aircraft parts, and many other products.[63]

Although no formal alliances exist among nations in the Pacific Rim, there's much speculation about future alliances. An alliance between the United States, Japan, Taiwan, China, and Hong Kong is possible. Although there's talk of a U.S.–Japanese free trade agreement, any such arrangement is years away. Lack of such an agreement has led many U.S. leaders to criticize Japan's trade restrictions on products from the United States and other nations. Although the Japanese government has removed some trade barriers, foreign firms trying to do business in Japan are still confronted with barriers including high cost of doing business and delays in receiving patents (during which time Japanese companies examine patent applications and copy new technologies), corruption (including collusion among Japanese bidders), and purchasing agents who are part of old-boy networks and refuse to buy foreign goods.[64]

Eastern Europe and the Commonwealth of Independent States

In 1985 the Soviet Union's Communist party secretary Mikhail Gorbachev began a new program called *perestroika* (or economic restructuring), which reduced government control and regulations. The Soviet Union and the Eastern European nations of Poland, Hungary, Yugoslavia, Czechoslovakia, Romania, and Bulgaria, under *perestroika*, underwent great changes. The changes climaxed in a stunning bloodless coup with the new Commonwealth of Independent States ending the rule of the Soviet Union's central government and prompting the resignation of Gorbachev on Christmas day, 1991. As a result, the former Soviet republics (including Russia, Ukraine, and Kazakhstan) became independent countries, replacing the staggering Soviet Union and instigating a loose economic and political alliance. Borders between the states are open, but there's no central government. The Commonwealth agreement does commit the independent states to coordinate economic policies. One year after launching his bid to create a market-oriented democracy, Russia's president Boris Yeltsin faced a deep recession and many layoffs.[65] On March 12, 1993, opponents in parliament slashed Yeltsin's presidential powers, and moved to impeach him in September. But in a violent confrontation, Yeltsin overcame parliament hardliners and he still prevails as the Commonwealth struggles toward economic unity.[66] And while Russia continues to feel the negative impact of economic restructuring—corruption, crime, and political uncertainty—many experts feel that capitalism is slowly taking root.[67]

Most of the rationale behind the changes in the former Soviet Union and Eastern Europe is to improve their economic conditions. The result is a more market-oriented society in which businesses formerly owned by the government have been granted independence. Economic and political restructurings also mean marketing opportunities for American and other foreign firms, either through exporting, joint ventures with native firms, or through direct ownership. General Motors Corporation's Trinity Motors, a Russia–United States–United Kingdom joint venture, opened its first car dealership in downtown Moscow across the street from McDonald's.[68] U.S. exports to Poland, Czechoslovakia, and Bulgaria increased 25 percent in 1992.[69]

Several of the reforming nations, including the former Soviet Union and Poland, want to reduce trade restrictions to encourage trade with other countries. The Russians have found that joint ventures, such as the one between the Moscow City Council's division of food service and McDonald's, can be rewarding. For example, McDonald's is helping the Russians learn new agricultural and food processing systems and a new appreciation for capitalism. These sweeping changes will increase Eastern European nations' opportunities. There's already speculation that some of these nations will join the European Community or eventually form their own multinational market group. Reunification of East and West Germany, for example, has resulted in a single Germany that is a major force in the European Community.

THE GLOBAL CHALLENGES

Throughout this chapter we've noted that the world will continue to change at a rapid pace. Change doesn't come easily—it brings problems and challenges—but it's inevitable. Firms risk failure if they don't acknowledge the changes taking place and don't adapt to them. The following chapters discuss these challenges, including quality and competitiveness.

The Quality Challenge

total quality management
A management approach to long-term success through customer satisfaction, based on the participation of all members of an organization in improving processes, products, service, and the culture in which they work.

Perhaps no greater challenge has grown out of the global economy than quality. In Chapter 1, we noted that *quality* is the totality of features and characteristics of a good or service that bear on its ability to satisfy stature or implied needs. The challenge facing managers is to manage in such a way that the outcome is a quality product. **Total quality management (TQM)** is a management approach to long-term success through customer satisfaction, based on the participation of all members of an organization in improving processes, products, services, and the culture in which they work.[70] TQM was initially used to describe the Japanese-style management approach to quality improvement; the global marketplace has led companies throughout the world to adopt TQM. Continuous improvement is the major focus of any successful quality program. Methods for implementing this approach are found in the teachings of such quality leaders as Crosby, Deming, Feigenbaum, Juran, and Ishikawa, and will be discussed throughout the book.

For TQM to work, managers must believe in quality for customers as a primary organizational aim and they must act to achieve this aim.[71] Their challenge is to create a pattern of shared values and beliefs throughout the organization so that all members work toward quality. Some quality experts have described TQM as a dream or a passion; unless *every* member of the organization fully believes in quality for the customer, success through TQM is nearly impossible to achieve. The most important parts of this system of total quality are (1) people's skills and talents and (2) how people are managed.

The Competitiveness Challenge

The quality of many products made in the United States has improved in a wide variety of industries ranging from computer chips to toilet paper made from recycled paper. But competitors throughout the world have also been improving product quality, in some cases at a faster pace than U.S. firms.[72] One outcome of the global economy is a change in the competitive structure within industries. Firms no longer compete on a local, regional, or national basis; they compete on a global basis. As we noted at the beginning of the chapter, any product made anywhere has to compete with like products made anywhere else. Remaining competitive in this environment is a major challenge facing managers.

What do Xerox and L. L. Bean have in common? Both handle products of various sizes and shapes. Xerox estimated that 3 to 5 percent of its recent productivity gains are the result of benchmarking activities focused on L. L. Bean.

Quality and competitiveness are closely related. To remain competitive, a firm must work toward continual improvement. Yet as American firms have experienced, competitors are also constantly improving quality. Such intense competition has increased interest in **benchmarking**, the continuous process of measuring a firm's goods, practices, and services against those of its toughest competitors and leading firms in other industries.[73] Through benchmarking, a firm can find the best way to do something and implement it. For instance, Xerox found that competitors were selling their products for what it cost Xerox to manufacture them. Clearly, Xerox couldn't stay in business this way, so it began benchmarking. Xerox focused on L.L. Bean, Inc., because of its superiority in warehousing and materials handling. L.L. Bean handles products of various sizes and shapes, just like Xerox. Xerox incorporated some of L.L. Bean's logistics practices to modernize its warehousing activities. Xerox estimates that 3 to 5 percent of its gains in productivity were the result of benchmarking activities.[74]

> **benchmarking**
> The continuous process of measuring a firm's goods, practices, and services against those of its toughest competitors and leading firms in other industries.

THE WORKPLACE OF TOMORROW

By the year 2000, nearly all organizations will be involved in some form of international business. The increased trend toward globalization will mean greater opportunities, as well as challenges. Companies are already establishing ties in Vietnam, China, Russia, and other areas of the world once closed to private firms. Domestic companies from many of these countries also hope to develop their products to a level that can compete in world markets. This, of course, means even greater competition throughout the world.

Joint ventures, strategic alliances, and acquisitions will be the most common vehicles used to enter foreign markets. In some instances, companies will find it most feasible to buy their way into foreign markets by acquiring or merging with another firm. Many countries, guarding against an invasion from companies located in the United States or Japan, will look most favorable on joint ventures.

Managers will also face new challenges in the global environment. In the years ahead, managers will need to be multilingual, multicultural, and multidimensional. They will speak several languages, and more importantly, have solid grounding in foreign cultures. Beyond cross-cultural training, managers will have spent time in foreign countries and thus

---

WHAT MANAGERS ARE READING

THE WORLD IN 2020: POWER, CULTURE AND PROSPERITY

As we approach the 21st century, authors, economists, and politicians alike are offering predictions about the world in the decade ahead. Some see a world entirely networked and borderless leading to a new international class. Others debate whether it will be a "Pacific Century" or if Asia's potential is overrated. British journalist Hamish McRae, in *The World in 2020: Power, Culture and Prosperity*, sees three major regions of influence—North America, Europe, and Asia (including Japan). He also predicts that by 2020, China will be emerging as a superpower that challenges America for economic superiority.

McRae suggests that prosperity can only endure in stable societies that are ordered and honest. This poses challenges for many nations. The U.S. will be struggling with stagnating living standards and a deteriorating society. East Asia and China, where individual rights are overlooked in pursuit of economic growth, will also face significant social problems. Those societies that can blend economic goals with social progress will prosper.

Source: Hamish McRae, *The World in 2020: Power, Culture, and Prosperity* (Boston: Harvard Business School Press, 1995).

"experienced" the cultures first-hand. And managers will need to develop a variety of skills that will enable them to do their jobs effectively. Some of these skills include the ability to deal with a diverse workforce, teach, coach, and manage operations that will span the globe. Finally, managers will have to think globally, by providing products that meet the needs of emerging and lucrative global markets.

SUMMARY OF LEARNING OBJECTIVES

DISCUSS THE NATURE AND IMPORTANCE OF THE GLOBAL ECONOMY.

Today any product made anywhere has to compete with similar products made nearly anywhere else. This has increased competition. A nation's economic status depends upon its ability to meet these new competitive standards. More than $2 trillion is spent annually on trade between nations. But taking advantage of opportunities will not be easy, as more and more firms throughout the world are offering quality products in the marketplace.

DEFINE THE TERMS MULTINATIONAL COMPANY AND GLOBAL CORPORATION.

A multinational company (MNC) is an organization that conducts business in two or more countries. A global corporation operates as if the world were a single market; national boundaries are meaningless to it.

IDENTIFY THE APPROACHES TO INTERNATIONAL BUSINESS.

Firms can take several approaches to international business. Exporting is selling domestic goods to a foreign country. Through a licensing agreement, one firm (the licensor) agrees to allow another firm (the licensee) to sell the licensor's product and use its brand name in return for a commission or royalty. Trading companies serve as links between buyers and sellers in different countries. Complex agreements between two or more countries are involved in countertrading. A joint venture is a partnership between a domestic and foreign firm. A strategic alliance occurs when two firms pool their resources in a partnership that goes beyond the limits of a joint venture. Direct ownership involves purchasing one or more business operations in a foreign country.

DESCRIBE THE ENVIRONMENT FOR GLOBAL BUSINESS.

The environment for global business includes cultural, economic, political, legal, and technological forces that differ among countries. Culture is all the learned values, behaviors, and other meaningful symbols shared by a society. Managers must adjust to cultural differences when doing business in a foreign country. International management is also influenced by economic factors, including a country's stability, market size, income, economic condition, and infrastructure. Political stability and government regulations also impact a firm's decision to enter a foreign market. Some countries encourage foreign investors; others develop barriers to entry. Fi-

nally, firms must assess the technology of foreign countries in making international management decisions.

EXPLAIN HOW REGULATIONS INFLUENCE INTERNATIONAL MANAGEMENT ACTIVITIES.

Major laws influencing the conduct of international managers include the Webb-Pomerene Export Trade Act, which exempts U.S. firms from antitrust laws if they're acting together to develop international trade. The Foreign Corrupt Practices Act makes bribing foreign officials to obtain sales illegal for U.S. firms. The Export Trading Companies Act encourages the formation of export trading companies by eliminating antitrust barriers and allowing banks to participate in such ventures.

LIST SOME INTERNATIONAL ORGANIZATIONS AND THEIR FUNCTIONS.

Several international organizations facilitate world trade. The General Agreement on Tariffs and Trade (GATT) was formed to reduce or eliminate tariffs and other barriers to international trade. The International Monetary Fund (IMF) promotes cooperation among members by eliminating trade barriers and offering short-term loans for international trade. The World Bank lends money to underdeveloped and developing countries for various projects.

DESCRIBE THE DIFFERENT MULTINATIONAL MARKET GROUPS.

A multinational market group is created when two or more countries agree to reduce trade and tariff barriers among themselves. The United States and Canada have signed the Free Trade Agreement (FTA) removing trade barriers over a 10-year period. The North American Free Trade Agreement (NAFTA) between the United States, Canada, and Mexico was approved by the respective governments in 1994. The European Community (EC) is removing all trade barriers between member nations. The Pacific Rim hasn't developed a formal alliance, but there's speculation about future alliances. Changes in Eastern Europe and the Commonwealth of Independent States (the former Soviet Union) will eventually lead to reduced trade restrictions among some of the reforming nations.

DISCUSS MAJOR CHALLENGES FACING ORGANIZATIONS IN THE GLOBAL ENVIRONMENT.

The major challenges, quality and competitiveness, are closely related issues. Foreign and U.S. competitors are constantly improving the quality of products. The challenge to managers is to develop an organization committed to quality.

KEY TERMS

benchmarking, p. 107
countertrading, p. 96
cultural diversity, p. 97
customs and entry procedures, p. 101
direct ownership, p. 97
duty, p. 101
embargo, p. 101
exchange control, p. 101

exporting, p. 94
global corporation, p. 94
infrastructure, p. 100
international business, p. 91
international management, p. 91
International Monetary Fund (IMF), p. 103
joint venture, p. 96
licensing, p. 95

multinational company (MNC), p. 93
multinational market group, p. 103
quota, p. 101
standard of living, p. 100
strategic alliance, p. 96
total quality management (TQM), p. 106
trading company, p. 95
World Bank, p. 103

REVIEW AND DISCUSSION QUESTIONS

Recall

1. What is international business? International management?
2. Describe the different approaches an organization can use to become involved in international business.
3. What types of trade barriers are used by some nations to discourage entry of foreign organizations or products?
4. How do international organizations facilitate world trade?
5. What is NAFTA, and how does it benefit the United States, Canada, and Mexico?
6. What are two major challenges facing firms operating in the global environment?

Understanding

7. What's the difference between a multinational company and a global corporation?
8. Why must a firm consider the business environment when determining whether to enter a foreign market?
9. What's the significance of multinational market groups to companies operating in the global environment?

Application

10. In a recent business magazine (e.g., *Business Week, Fortune,* or *Forbes*), read an article about a multinational market group, such as the Pacific Rim or the Economic Community. Describe some current issues confronting this market group.

CASE STUDY

Mickey Comes to Europe

Since opening in April 1992, Euro Disney is still fighting to prove that it can attract enough customers to pay off the loans it incurred during development. The $3.9 billion theme park and resort complex is one of Europe's largest construction projects. The French government assumed the bulk of the financial risk; Disney put up only $160 million of its own capital for the project. Some French intellectuals are outraged at the thought of Mickey Mouse in their back yard. But the Socialist government reasoned that Euro Disney would bring in tourist dollars, create thousands of jobs, and attract many other investors to the area. The Disney company can be counted on to deliver a quality service that consumers will buy. In fact, Euro Disney is so extravangantly designed that some have said it surpasses Disney's parks in Florida and California. Chairman Michael Eisner himself made many of the detailed decisions, such as the placement of 35 fireplaces in hotel lobbies and restaurants, and the design of a salad bar in the back of an old pickup truck. This eye to detail has made Disney one of the world's highest-quality organizations. Emphasis on service quality starts at the top at Disney (as it does in most organizations committed to quality) and filters down to every individual in the firm, even those on clean-up duty in the parks. Ask any park attendant or ticket taker where to find the restrooms or when the next parade begins and you'll get the answer. That's why it takes four days

for employees to learn how to take tickets at a Disney park. The initial response of Europeans to the park that's mostly American in theme was somewhat below expectations. Disney expected 11 million visitors to Euro Disney in the first year; the park drew less than 10 million and saddled Disney with $120 million in losses. Europe's sluggish economy and competition from Spain's World's Fair and Olympics were blamed for the rocky start. But many observers feel the attendance forecasts were optimistic, and they expect the French park to be a big success (Disney even plans to add a Disney-MGM Studios theme park to Euro Disney by 1997). Most of the usual Disney attractions can be found, such as Sleeping Beauty's castle, Main Street USA, and even the fast-food restaurants, but without the wine customary at French meals. Some attractions have been updated. Tomorrowland, with its 1950s images of the space age, has been replaced by Discoveryland based on European themes by Jules Verne and Leonardo da Vinci. And despite talk of cultural differences between the French and Americans, Eisner has said that the only real difference is that visitors pay with francs.

It seems he was right. In 1995, after three years in the red, Euro Disney finally reported its first quarterly profit. Boosted by a new Space Moutain ride, lower admissions prices (20 percent cut), and the gradual end to Europe's deep recession, the theme park once called a "cultural Chernobyl" is out of the red.

Source: Adapted from "A Faint Squeak From Euro-Mickey," *Economist*, July 29, 1995, p. 44; William J. Kole, "Disneyland Paris Digs Itself Out of the Red," *Lexington Herald-Leader*, July 29, 1995, p. A9; Ronald Glover, Stewart Toy, Gail DeGeorge, and Robert Neff, "Thrills and Chills at Disney," *Business Week*, June 21, 1993, pp. 73-74; Stewart Toy, Patrick Oster, and Ronald Glover, "The Mouse Isn't Roaring," *Business Week*, August 24, 1992, p. 38; Richard Turner and Peter Gumbel, "As Euro Disney Braces for Its Grand Opening, the French Go Goofy," *The Wall Street Journal*, April 10, 1992, pp. A1, A8; and Thomas J. Peters and Robert H. Waterman, Jr., *In Search of Excellence* (New York: Warner Books, 1982), pp. 167–68.

QUESTIONS

1. What are some of the cultural differences between French and Americans?
2. How did these differences impact Disney's venture in Europe?
3. What did Disney do to overcome the problems it faced?
4. How important was price in determining Disney's ultimate fate?

VIDEO CASE

Forces Affecting International Business

Although most of the business practices of one country work in other nations, there are eight forces that may dictate a need for change or adaptation in the way some foreign business is conducted. Among these are financial forces, which include such factors as inflation and currency exchange rate. There are economic and socioeconomic forces such as unemployment and population, as well as physical forces, which include the country's location, climate, and natural resources. One must also consider cultural forces involving the beliefs and religions of another nation. Politics is also a major force, especially when dealing with different ideologies like communism or socialism. There are legal issues such as tariffs, labor laws, and types of taxation, and competitive forces involving trade balance of imports and exports. The final force one must consider is labor, which involves union and employee–employer relationships.

At times dealing with these forces can be overwhelming. However, successful international business is conducted everyday despite these potential stumbling blocks. As we compare American and Japanese ways of life it will become clear how these forces play a roll in international business between the two nations.

From an early age life experience in each country is different. Japanese children attend school five and a half days a week. The hectic academic schedule continues year around. Starting around fourth grade, pressure increases for Japanese students. Expectations continue to rise throughout high school. Masauki Umai, a professor at Shiizuoka University, said, "My first son is in the 9th grade. He leaves the house at 7:30 in the morning and comes home at 5. He eats at 6. He goes to cram school at 7, returning home at 10 when he studies till he goes to sleep at 2 AM. This hard time for my son is only for a few years. If he has good marks and enters a good high school he will be able to go to a top industry and expect a good future."

Although the Japanese education system does an impressive job of preparing students for a good job, some Japanese feel this system does not promote individualism and creativity, American traits admired by the Japanese. Shihoko Ogawa, a Japanese housewife, said, "You are creating children with originality for expressing themselves freely. In Japan, our children are not very original, they are not very creative. They are sort of forced to sit still and memorize things and accumulate the knowledge and wisdom from other people. They are not creating their own thing."

American classrooms on the other hand usually promote interaction. For example, American high schools are far less regimented than their Japanese counterparts. However, they must deal with such problems as violence and dropouts. This is virtually nonexistent in Japan. As American teacher Linda Christiansen put it, "For a lot of students they see that education has not helped people in their neighborhood get better jobs. I think the lack of opportunity through education has become more apparent to them. So they are less willing to sit still and be contained for eight hours a day."

After completing the challenging requirements of an education in Japan, an individual usually dives into the workforce spending 12 to 15 hours a day, six days a week on a job. Unlike America where an individual may work for one division of a large company, the Japanese work for the company as a whole. In Japanese companies, no one makes decisions on their own, not even managers. This creates a lot of middlemen, making creativity and innovation difficult.

Even with tremendous business success and employee loyalty, some Japanese find a lack of creativity a problem in their culture. By comparison the American business environment is much more relaxed. Americans place a higher priority on family and life outside the workplace. Rob Bartel, an employee at Mentor Graphics, said, "My father worked very hard. I think that whole generation was a lot different than the generation we have now. In this country, we have made perhaps a tradeoff where we have said it's not that important to us to have quite that many goods and services. Rather, we prefer to have the incredible rewards and satisfaction that come from raising children and being with them and watching them grow."

The entire country of Japan is smaller than the state of California, so with a population of over 100 million, Japanese cities are very crowded. However, there are few homeless or unemployed. The Japanese say it's because they're willing to work and take pride in any job. Their devotion to work leaves less leisure time than the average American. Salaries in both countries are about the same, but items are priced higher in Japan due to their penchant for quality. A $4.00 apple is not out of line as long as it is the perfect color. The Japanese farmer goes to great lengths to grow food that is aesthetically pleasing.

Unfortunately farming is another area in which America and the Japanese have problems. The Japanese farmer considers his work an art form and is very enthusiastic about growing rice—a staple food in that country. There is friction over America's desire to sell surplus rice in Japan. Japanese farmer Momoru Saiki expressed his concern about American rice: "Japanese farmers produce less but still we have a rice surplus so I wonder why we would want to import American rice. I understand that Japanese export cost America and America has been hurt by this. They think Japan should buy something in return. The only thing they can sell to us in return is rice because rice is a staple food here and America has surplus rice. I understand this, but as a farmer I can't accept this."

An American rice farm is huge by Japanese standards, but due to a rice surplus and low prices many have trouble surviving. For this reason the average U.S. farmer thinks that Japan should import their rice. American farmer Dennis Gallagher said, "We should be able to export some of our rice into Japan and I think that it should happen in that direction. I don't necessarily feel that we need to control the entire Japanese rice market, but just a small niche of it. Five to 10 percent or something like that. Which to me doesn't seem like a whole lot." Without the ability to export the American farmer suffers greatly. In addition to farm trade, Japan and America have a lot to work on.

Despite such differences, both countries have much in common. This gives them a solid base upon which to build good business relationships. However, nothing is accomplished without first considering the forces that affect each country. That includes adapting or changing business practices to better serve each others' needs.

QUESTIONS

1. What are the eight forces that affect international business? Briefly discuss each force.
2. Japanese children spend long hours in school during their primary education, while the American system is more relaxed. Explain how differences in primary education practices between the two countries could have an affect on the differences in innovation and creativity at the corporate level.
3. Trade controversies between the United States and Japan have been going on for years and will likely continue. The video tape used the example of rice exports to highlight the different opinions of Japanese and Americans. Discuss the current state of trade between the United States and Japan. Has it gotten better or worse over the past year? Why? What barriers remain to free and fair trade?

APPLICATION EXERCISE

The first column below lists 10 characteristics of jobs in general. In the second column, rank order these characteristics from 1 to 10, with 1 as the most important job characteristic to you and 10 as the least important. In the third column, rank order the characteristics from 1 to 10 based on your perceptions of Japanese workers, with 1 representing your perception of the most important job characteristic to Japanese workers and 10 the least important.

Job Characteristic	Ranking of Importance to You	Rank of Importance to Japanese Worker
Variety in the job		
Good pay		
Opportunity to advance		
Interesting work		
Job security		
Autonomy		
Good co-workers		
Knowledgeable supervisor or mentor		
Freedom to make choices		
Opportunity to learn		

Now take a look at what's important to you and your perceptions of what's important to Japanese workers. There are probably some differences. Realizing your ranking is based on perceptions, consider the following to help explain the differences:

1. What cultural factors might explain some of the differences in your rankings?

2. Do these differences say anything about the quality of work? About global competition?

3. Do you think your parents or grandparents would rank the job characteristics differently than you did? Why? (You might ask them.)

Planning

CHAPTER 5

Decision Making

After studying this chapter, you should be able to:

❖ Compare programmed and nonprogrammed decisions.

❖ Contrast intuitive and systematic decision making.

❖ Identify and explain the nine steps in the decision-making process.

❖ Explain the difference between individual and group decision making.

❖ Define the terms cognitive dissonance and escalation of commitment.

❖ Describe brainstorming, the Delphi technique, and the nominal group technique.

❖ Explain the team approach to decision making in a quality environment.

❖ Explain how an MIS can help decision making.

❖ Explain how a decision support system works.

❖ Explain the benefits and costs of telecommuting.

Manufactures Use Simulations to Aid Decision Making

One of the rapidly expanding industrial technologies is manufacturing simulation. Simulation allows managers, engineers, and shop floor employees to make decisions based on information about how systems would behave under various conditions. Reliable new simulation tools enable manufacturers to generate "what-if?" scenarios on their computer screens. This ability reduces the costs traditionally involved in developing full working prototypes, and also saves time.

Nissan's Erwin Boer monitors a driver steering through a simulated course.

Research has indicated that the main reasons for the recent rise in using simulation in manufacturing are due to the:

❖ Development of powerful new micro-computers;

❖ Development of simulation software that can tackle almost any engineering project;

❖ Advances in computer graphics and solid modeling that provide animation so that designers and engineers can visualize systems in operation in real time;

❖ General industrial effort to link "islands of automation" through computer networks into flexible manufacturing systems (FMS); and

❖ Development of techniques to transfer simulation results into off-line programming for industrial robots.

Manufacturing industries worldwide are integrating FMS and flexible manufacturing cells (FMC) with existing manufacturing facilities. The integration gives more manufacturing flexibility and better work center utilization, which results in less cost per piece produced.

As an example of how manufacturers have turned to simulation to assist in the decision making required for the development of new products, five automakers—Audi, BMW, Ford, Renault, and Volvo—have teamed with Mechanical

Dynamics Inc. (MDI), in Ann Arbor, Michigan, to incorporate their specialized design and analytical expertise in MDI's ADAMS mechanical system simulation software. The resulting advanced vehicle simulation system, calls ADAMS/Car, will be used throughout member companies' engineering organizations and marketed worldwide MDI.

ADAMS/Car is intended to create a foundation, based on virtual prototyping technology, to support almost all aspects of automotive design. For example, it will enable designers, product engineers, and test engineers to build computer models of vehicle designs, animate vehicle motion, display graphs of key parameters, and generate test reports for each simulation.

The project reflects a growing trend in the engineering software industry, in which software developers and manufacturers customize existing software for specific industries. Currently, many manufacturers gain a competitive edge by being the first in their industry to adapt general-purpose tools to their engineering needs or by adapting such tools more effectively than the competition. The trend toward customized software is being driven by manufacturers' desire to focus more on the product development process and less on pioneering the use of computer-aided tools to gain a competitive advantage.

Further, now that "point solutions" (programs for specific applications) have revolutionized the way engineers in specific disciplines work, many engineers see an opportunity to reconfigure the engineering process at their companies from the ground up. According to Horst Walter Gonska, manager of computer-aided processes at Munich-based BMW, ADAMS/Car will support such a reorganization.

One of the keys to the new engineering process that will emerge, Gonska said, is making virtual prototyping technology available early in the design cycle. With ADAMS/Car, engineers will accurately represent entire vehicles, including assemblies such as suspensions, power trains, engines, and steering mechanisms. They will also be able to simulate traction control, antilock braking, and other control systems.

Additionally, engineers will use the software to take their designs for a test drive on a virtual test track. Such virtual test drives will help engineers predict their designs' handling characteristics, ride quality, and safety long before prototypes are built.

Questions

1. What are some of the potential problems with relying on computer simulations in the prototyping process?
2. What other industries besides manufacturing can benefit from using computer simulations of work process? Explain how simulations might be applied in those industries.
3. Manufacturers have been using simulations primarily in the manufacturing process. Think of some other areas of a manufacturing business (e.g., marketing, sales, logistics) in which simulations might be useful. Explain your response.

Sources: Adapted from Dan Deitz, "Automakers Retool Engineering Processes," *Mechanical Engineering,* January 1996, pp. 18–20; Chris Stylianides, "Animating an Integrated Job Shop/Flexible Manufacturing System," *International Journal of Operations & Production Management,* 15(8), 1995, pp. 63–72.

This chapter focuses on management decision making. As the opening vignette indicates, decision making in organizations is part of the management process, but increasingly managers are turning to technology to help them sift through vast amounts of information. Decision making, as this chapter shows, involves a complex mixture of knowledge, experience, creativity, and risk taking. More and more in organizations today, decision making is conducted in groups or teams, and it isn't confined merely to top management.

An important measure of the effectiveness of an individual manager, a management team, or a worker team is the quality of decisions reached. Indeed, some have argued that management simply *is* decision making and that the essence of managerial behavior is found by studying decision making.

Managers in every type of organization—business, hospital, government, education—make decisions every day involving competing goals and objectives, risk, uncertainty, and alternative courses of action. A **decision** is defined here as a conscious choice among analyzed alternatives followed by action to implement the choice. Thus, managerial decision making entails both a process and subsequent action. A **decision-making process** is a series of related steps or stages that lead up to an action, an outcome, and assessment.

In today's complex, information-rich organizations, managerial decision making is often a fragmented, rapid process. In the modern work environment it's becoming less likely that a single individual can process enough information to make the best decisions for the organization. Besides the vast amount of data available for most nonroutine decisions, managers respond to interruptions and unexpected events, and often find decision making to be a process that occurs over time rather than a single event. Managers must learn how to deal with a decision-making environment that emphasizes oral communication, brief meetings, incomplete information, and close approximations, with decisions often based on impressions, estimates, and personal experience. Decision making often reflects the manager's effort to make sense of the complicated environment, to attain some control over the uncontrollable, and to achieve some sense of order.

Managers in any organization must find, solve, and prevent problems. An organized approach to decision making—including a clear understanding of the current state of affairs, the historical basis for improving decisions, and the possible errors that can be made—enables managers to make better decisions and to reach personal and organizational goals. The TQM approach to the decision-making process is based on several fundamental assumptions: (1) decisions must be based on measurable facts, (2) decisions should focus on continuous improvement, and (3) teams of workers can often make better decisions than managers.

Management theorists have investigated decision making from many different perspectives and have developed a set of useful concepts to understand the phenomenon. Several of the more important concepts will be explored to increase your awareness of the complexity of this highly social process that involves reason and emotion, risk and uncertainty, and imagination and knowledge. Figure 5–1 presents these and other influencers of decisions that managers and workers make.

decision
A conscious choice among analyzed alternatives, followed by action to implement the choice.

decision-making process
A series or chain of related steps leading to a decision, its implementation, and follow-up.

FIGURE 5–1
The Decision-Making
Influencer Environment

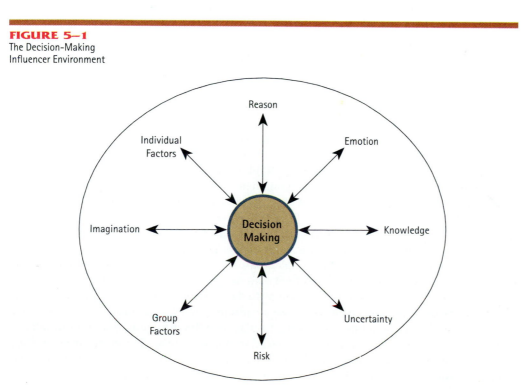

Decision making can be understood as a series of steps that run from clearly identifying a problem to implementing and assessing actions. Using such a systematic approach to decision making ensures that relevant information has been gathered, alternative choices have been considered, and possible consequences of actions are understood. This chapter describes a nine-step decision-making process for improving organizational effectiveness.

Individual decision making differs from group decision making. Each has its own set of strengths and weaknesses that a manager should understand to use the differing approaches effectively. Separate sections are dedicated to individual and group decision making.

The chapter concludes with an overview of information technology available to assist management decision making. Managers today are confronted with an overwhelming amount of data and information and a bewildering variety of tools to help them manage it. Quality-based management effectively uses information technology to ensure that the right information is available to the right people at the right time.

TYPES OF MANAGERIAL DECISIONS

Given that decision making is an entirely human process, it is fraught with complexities and ambiguities that are reflective of human beings themselves. By gaining some understanding of the different concepts that researchers have used to understand decision making, the practicing manager can often avoid difficulties. For example, a manager who is used to making decisions based on intuition may notice that many of his recent decisions are less effective than they used to be. If he is aware of the distinction between intuitive and systematic decision making, he may understand that his intuitions are based on personal experiences that may no longer be appropriate in a changed environment. Switching, at least temporarily, to a more systematic approach may very well lead to more effective decisions.

Following are just some of the more useful concepts that have been studied and applied to management decision making. On your own, think of some that might not be mentioned here, but that you can investigate in other management books.

Programmed versus Nonprogrammed Decisions

Decision making in an organization occurs during routine operations and in unexpected situations alike. Management thinker Herbert Simon (see Chapter 2) has distinguished between decision making under these different conditions:

programmed decision
A decision that is repetitive and routine, with a definite procedure developed for handling it.

Programmed Decision: If a particular situation occurs often, a routine procedure usually will be worked out for solving it. Decisions are programmed to the extent that they are repetitive and routine, and a definite procedure has been developed for handling them.

nonprogrammed decisions
Novel, unstructured decisions.

Nonprogrammed Decision: Decisions are nonprogrammed when they are unstructured. There is no established procedure for handling the problem, because it is either complex or extremely important. Such decisions deserve special treatment.

Managers in most organizations face many programmed decisions in their daily operations. Such decisions should be treated without expending unnecessary organizational resources. On the other hand, the nonprogrammed decision must be properly identified as such since this type of decision can involve significant risk and uncertainty. Table 5–1 gives examples of each type of decision in different kinds of organizations. It illustrates that programmed and nonprogrammed decisions require different kinds of procedures and apply to distinctly different types of problems.

Despite some managers' efforts to place all organizational processes under rigorous and invariant control regimens, variation, complexity, and ambiguity in the workplace are the rule rather than the exception. Much day-to-day variation can be accommodated with routine responses, yet a creative response or nonprogrammed decision of some sort is often needed. Nonprogrammed decisions involve searching for information and alternatives that lie outside the routine decision-making process. These decisions are often time-consuming and (unlike routine decisions) demand that workers be prepared to create alternative solutions, analyze them critically, and choose a course of action.

TABLE 5-1	TYPES OF DECISIONS	
	Programmed Decisions	Nonprogrammed Decisions
Type of Problem	Frequent, repetitive, routine, much certainty regarding cause-and-effect relationships	Novel, unstructured, much uncertainty regarding cause-and-effect relationships
Procedure	Dependence on policies, rules, and definite procedures	Necessity for creativity, intuition, tolerance for ambiguity, creative problem solving
Examples	*Business:* Periodic reorders of inventory	*Business:* Diversification into new products and markets
	University: Necessary grade point average for good academic standing	*University:* Construction of new classroom facilities
	Health care: Procedure for admitting patients	*Hospital:* Purchase of experimental equipment
	Government: Merit system for promotion of state employees	*Government:* Reorganization of state government agencies

Source: John M. Ivancevich and Michael J. Matteson, *Organizational Behavior and Management,* 3rd ed. (Burr Ridge, Il.: Richard D. Irwin, 1993), p. 584.

Many organizations now use computers and software to assist with complex, nonprogrammed decisions. With the goal of self-sufficiency, the U.S. Postal Service has embarked on a 10-year program to modernize, and in some cases radically alter, the way it manages and processes the mail. At the heart of this effort is the goal of automating virtually all of the letter mail in 1995. In support of this goal, a series of long-term planning models has been developed to help select equipment and plan for its use at the more than 250 general mail facilities throughout the nation. These models use linear programming and other heuristics to arrive at optimal solutions.[1]

Like the Post Office, manufacturing industries in the U.S. are turning to the use of analytical decision techniques to improve quality and productivity. Many have adopted an operations research information system (ORIS) to identify the type of data needed to address manufacturing concerns within specific areas. The ORIS methodology forces the collection of more and better data to aid in the routine, programmed decisions that can lead to more effective work flow.[2]

Programmed decisions that don't allow for flexibility aren't always useful for workers in manufacturing jobs either. Product design engineers are still often directed by management to create product assembly processes so simple that they require no input from assemblers on the factory floor. Although such a design may be valuable to an untrained customer assembling a product at home (e.g., a piece of home exercise equipment), the same attitude behind the design for a trained assembly worker reflects contempt for the ability of workers to make nonprogrammed decisions.

One company that has succeeded in employing an innovative form of Frederick Taylor's time-and-motion regimentation on the factory floor is New United Motor Manufacturing, Inc. (NUMMI), of Fremont, California. NUMMI is a joint venture between Toyota and General Motors. NUMMI has used the principles of scientific management to create a highly programmed process flow and to increase quality, productivity, and employee motivation at the same time. How does the company manage this? It does so by allowing the workers themselves to design the formal work standards and establish the programmed decisions. As University of Southern California Professor Paul Adler stated following a two-year study of the company, "Procedures that are designed by the workers themselves in a continuous, successful effort to improve productivity, quality, skills, and understanding can humanize even the most disciplined form of bureaucracy."[3]

Programmed and nonprogrammed decisions affect organizations daily. Sometimes managers need to react to events and make decisions. Other times they can anticipate changes and make decisions before they happen. This distinction is captured in two more decision types: proactive and reactive.

Proactive versus Reactive Decisions

Recall that *decision* has been defined as a conscious choice among analyzed alternatives. A decision made in anticipation of an external change or other conditions is called a **proactive decision**. Managers who utilize a systematic, proactive approach can prevent problems from developing.

proactive decision
A decision made in anticipation of an external change or other conditions.

A **reactive decision** is one made in response to external changes. Using a reactive approach, a city street department may wait for citizens to complain about poor street conditions before a crew is sent to repair pot holes. A manager may initiate action to correct product defects after customer complaints force him to do something. Rather than apply preventive maintenance (proactive), a machine shop manager may spend money only to repair broken machines (reactive).

reactive decision
A decision made in response to external changes.

Total quality management is based upon the conviction that it's better to be proactive than reactive whenever possible. Quality management recognizes that one person alone doesn't make things happen; whether one is the boss or out on the shop floor, success depends on a team. To help focus the endowed talents and virtues of subordinates, managers must first provide a vision; otherwise all decisions are reactive. Reactive decisions aren't necessarily made out of context, but rather without a context. The vision supplied by managers becomes a guidepost, allowing many levels of an organization to make decisions without consulting their superiors.[4]

Managerial vision provides the context for proactive decision making. If the vision is strong enough and communicated effectively, many employees will intuitively make decisions in support of that vision. Intuitive decisions are based on experience and are usually made in situations where there is little time for analysis. Systematic decision making should also conform to the managerial vision for the organization, but involves more time and prior data gathering. These two types of decision making are explored next.

Intuitive versus Systematic Decisions

intuitive decision making
A process of estimating or guessing to decide among alternatives.

Intuitive decision making involves the use of estimates, guesses, or hunches to decide among alternative courses of action. Most managers will admit that many of their decisions are influenced to a great extent by their "intuitions." The way that term is used here doesn't refer to something mysterious. Instead, intuition is merely the choices that seem reasonable to a manager based on experience. Nonetheless, decisions based purely on intuitions can be premature, unnecessary, and even counterproductive. For example, one common flaw with "merit" pay systems is that managers may falsely assume that they can determine meaningful individual differences among workers' performances. If these differences are determined more by personal opinion and human biases than by systematic data collection and analysis, the concept of merit may be lost. Such biased pay raise decisions can be destructive rather than productive in encouraging workers to perform at high levels.

systematic decision making
An organized, exacting, data-driven process for choosing among alternatives.

In contrast to intuitive decision making, **systematic decision making** is an organized, exacting, data-driven process, as represented by the comparisons in Table 5–2. Systematic decision making requires developing a clear set of objectives, a relevant information base, and a team-based, consensus-seeking sharing of ideas and creativity as well as exacting implementation and assessment.

It is the essence of the manager's job to make the decisions that guide day-to-day activities and chart the future course of the organization. W. Edwards Deming calls the systematic approach to decision making "management by fact." Management by fact is also known as "data-based decision making." Manufacturing, agriculture, and other industry sectors use sophisticated econometric analyses to improve productivity, quality, and competitiveness.[5] Not all organizations need this level of sophistication, but all can benefit from management by fact. Some variables to consider when using this approach are shown in Table 5–3.

Not all situations require systematic decision making. However, in all cases judgment is needed to determine when a decision could be intuitive or systematic. Neither approach is

TABLE 5-2	INTUITIVE VERSUS SYSTEMATIC DECISION MAKING
Intuitive	**Systematic**
My hunch is that we should improve customer support after we sell them our product.	Customer surveys have indicated that we need to improve postsale support.
This process is out of control and needs adjustment.	Control charts indicate that this process has been operating beyond the control limits for seven consecutive weeks. Therefore, something needs to be done.
My feeling is that this firm could benefit from TQM.	Based on success I've observed with TQM in firms similar to ours, we too could probably benefit from its principles and techniques.

the best in all situations. Some surprises will occur. At times managers must react quickly and intuitively. Sound intuition, however, is developed primarily from experience and training, as well as from practice in systematic decision making. For example, a service repair manager may have to react to an angry customer who is dissatisfied with a product. If the manager doesn't react quickly and appropriately, the customer may be lost. Yet the manager's reactive, intuitive decision will be better if it's based on training and experience with similar situations.

Later we'll see that a quality-based decision-making approach encourages employees to apply creativity to programmed and nonprogrammed, systematic and intuitive decisions alike. Continuous improvement in organizational performance requires creativity in making programmed decisions or in establishing work processes. Furthermore, business success demands constant attention to detecting and responding to changes in customer needs and competitive challenges from abroad. To respond adequately to changes in customer

TABLE 5-3	MANAGING BY FACT

- Identify the source of the material and as much as possible about the time and manner in which the information was collected.

- Don't be seduced by dramatic graphics or charts, or the appearance of sophistication in statistics or other data presentations.

- Don't succumb to the persuasiveness of the presenter's communication skills without retaining an appropriate level of skepticism about the content of the message.

- Always be wary of situations where the presenter has a vested interest in convincing you of the conclusions.

- Particularly in the case of survey research, consider how the data were compiled.

- Look for some level of statistical checks on the reliability, accuracy, and meaningfulness of findings whenever possible. In some cases, this may require an exploration of what is not reported.

- Learn to discern whether the data are being overinterpreted and overextended.

- Always consider the relevance and applicability of the results to your situation.

- Remember that the results of a single study, no matter how well done, should be used with extreme caution.

- Be cautious in making changes in response to simple data. There is often greater underlying complexity than meets the eye.

Source: Adapted from Stephen A. Rubenfeld, John W. Newstrom, and Thomas B. Duff, "Caveat Emptor: Avoiding Pitfalls in Data-Based Decision Making," *Review of Business*, Winter 1994, pp. 20–23.

needs and the global marketplace, employees at all levels within the organization should be able to use their knowledge and experience to make nonprogrammed decisions for the organization. But decision making should occur within a well-developed decision-making process. In the next section you'll learn about a decision-making process that managers and workers can follow to make creative, yet sound, organizational decisions.

THE DECISION-MAKING PROCESS

The decision-making process is a manager's mechanism for seeking some desired result. The nature and structure of the process influence how effective the decision outcome is likely to be in solving or preventing the problem. But note again that decision making is a *process* rather than a single, fixed event. In most decision situations, managers go through a series of steps or stages that help them identify the problem, develop alternative strategies, analyze those strategies, choose one among the alternatives, implement the choice, and assess the results. These stages aren't always rigidly applied, and feedback is typically conceived to be a part of each step. Identifying steps in the decision process is valuable since it helps the decision maker to structure the problem situation in a meaningful, systematic way. A variety of models can be used. Figure 5–2 shows the segments of one common progression of events that leads to a decision.

The basic steps in the figure's model are (1) establish specific goals and objectives, (2) identify and define the problem, (3) establish priorities, (4) determine causes of the problem, (5) develop alternative solutions, (6) evaluate the alternatives, (7) select a solution, (8) implement, and (9) follow up. The first seven steps are the **decision formulation** stages; the last two steps are the **decision implementation** stages.

Step 1: Establish Specific Goals and Objectives

Decision making is always done in the context of goals and objectives. We'll discuss the setting of goals and objectives more in the next two chapters. Here it's important to point out that all behavior is basically goal oriented.[6] Especially in organizations, goals and objectives are needed in each area where performance influences effectiveness. If goals and objectives are adequately established, they will dictate what results must be achieved and the measures that indicate whether they have been achieved. The establishment of goals and

decision formulation
The process of (1) identifying a decision opportunity or need, (2) collecting information, (3) from the information, developing alternative courses of action, and (4) selecting one of the alternatives.

decision implementation
The process to implement the alternative and then do follow-up to assess each of the implementation alternatives.

FIGURE 5–2
The Decision-Making Model:
A Sequence of Steps

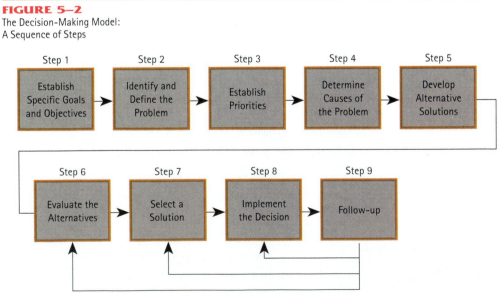

Feedback Paths

objectives binds people in the organization together. The firm's system of drawing people together is a crucial factor in its success.[7] Total quality management must be applied within a context of a set of customer-driven goals and objectives that involve all staff.[8]

Step 2: Identify and Define the Problem

Problems are defined as the realization that a discrepancy exists between a desired state and current reality. Thus problems become apparent when clear goals and objectives are established. How critical a problem is for an organization is measured by the gap between the levels of performance specified in the organization's goals and objectives and the levels of performance attained. For example, a product defect rate of 10 per million doesn't meet the famous "six sigma" quality standard established by Motorola, which allows for only three defects per million.

problem
The realization that a discrepancy exists between a desired state and current reality.

It's easy to understand that a problem exists when there is a gap between desired results and actual results. But certain factors often lead to difficulties in precisely identifying the problem. These factors are:

1. *Perceptual inaccuracies.* Individual attitudes, feelings, or mental models may prevent individuals from recognizing problems. For example, prior to 1968 the Swiss dominated the world of watchmaking. They had continuously improved their products and were constant innovators. Yet by 1980 their market share had collapsed from 65 percent to 10 percent. Why? They didn't perceive that world demand was changing from mechanical to electronic inner works. The Swiss themselves had invented electronic quartz movement. Yet when Swiss researchers presented the revolutionary idea to Swiss manufacturers in 1967, it was rejected. The new movement didn't fit their mental model of watches, so they couldn't see its potential for the future.

2. *Defining problems in terms of solutions.* This is really a form of jumping to conclusions. For example, prior to any research a quality engineer may state, "The excessive rework we're experiencing is due to bad supplies." Here the quality engineer is suggesting a solution before the problem has been adequately identified. The supplies may be of low quality, but there are other potential explanations of excessive rework, including poor employee training, out-of-date technology, or cumbersome process flow. Research needs to be conducted to identify the problem before solutions are suggested.

3. *Identifying symptoms as problems.* Some companies with ongoing quality problems blame their employees. They will argue that their employees simply lack appropriate motivation or interest in creating higher quality products and services. Other companies, such as AT&T, recognize low employee morale as a symptom and have acted to treat the symptom by correcting its underlying causes. Since AT&T introduced its Chairman's Quality Award in 1990, it has seen significant increases in quality across the company. That program is just one of many that have led the company to win half a dozen national quality awards, including the Baldrige Award, since 1988. That's when Robert Allen took over as CEO and started paying attention to TQM, customer service, and employee empowerment. Under Allen's leadership, AT&T has transformed itself from a rigid, hierarchical company, to a more open, bottom-up one. The company now invests $1 billion annually in training for employees. It learned that its former quality troubles weren't the lack of employee will, but rather due to its previously oppressive, top-down structure.[9]

Problems usually are of three types: opportunity, crisis, or routine. Crisis and routine problems present themselves; opportunities usually must be found. Opportunities await discovery. They often go unnoticed and eventually are lost by an inattentive manager. On the other hand, by their very nature, most crises and routine problems demand immediate attention. Thus a manager may spend more time handling problems than pursuing important new opportunities. Many well-managed organizations try to draw attention away from crises and routine problems and toward longer-range issues through planning activities and goal-setting programs that establish companywide priorities.

Step 3: Establish Priorities

All problems aren't created equal. Deciding whether to launch a new product in response to a competitor's move is probably a more significant decision than whether the employee lounge should be repainted. The process of decision making and solution implementation requires resources. Unless the resources an organization has at its disposal are unlimited, it must prioritize its problems. This means being able to determine each problem's significance, which involves considering three issues: urgency, impact, and growth tendency.

Urgency is defined as the amount of time available to solve a problem. Some companies have learned that urgent problems are best dealt with at their source. For example, Avcorp Industries, Inc., has improved its bottom line by ensuring that urgent decisions are made on the factory floor. This change has won the parts maker praise from its leading customer Bell Helicopter Textron, which accounts for 60 percent of Avcorp's roughly $5 million in annual sales. The company's delinquency on Bell's work orders has fallen to less than 1 percent from 18 percent in 1993. The new system is named "Red Flag," after the red flags and alarms workers raise when they meet a production snag or technology-related issue that could hinder a delivery commitment. When an employee raises a red flag, an alarm sounds at 30-second intervals until a supervisor comes to offer assistance.[10]

Impact refers to the seriousness of a problem's effect. Effects may be on people, sales, equipment, or any number of other organizational variables. Whether problem effects are short or long term and whether the problem is likely to create other problems are also impact-related issues.

Growth tendency refers to future consequences of a problem. A problem may currently be of low urgency and have little impact, but if it is allowed to go unattended, its consequences may become more severe over time. For example, a decision to cut back on routine preventive maintenance of plant equipment as a cost-cutting measure may not create a significant problem immediately; but over time, major difficulties may arise.

The more significant the problem as determined by its urgency, impact, and growth tendency, the more important it is that it be addressed. A critical part of effective decision making is determining problem significance. Another critical part is determining the problem's cause.

Step 4: Determine Causes of the Problem

It's usually ill-advised to determine a solution to a problem when its cause is unknown. Determining the cause of a problem is often best done by the employees who deal with it every day. One technique many firms are using to determine the cause of unsatisfied customers is to empower frontline service employees. Customer knowledge obtained by contact employees can be used to improve service in two ways: by facilitating the interaction with customers and by guiding the firm's decision making. Employees who have frequent contact with customers often have a better understanding of customer needs and problems than others in the firm. Research has shown that open communications between managers and contact employees can improve service quality.[11]

Step 5: Develop Alternative Solutions

Before a decision is reached, alternative solutions to the problem need to be developed. This step involves examining the organization's internal and external environments for information and ideas that may lead to creative solutions to a problem. Quality-based organizations use a practice known as *benchmarking* to identify and study other firms that perform effectively a process the benchmarking firm wants to improve. Health care organizations, for example, use a practice known as *clinical benchmarking* to collect and analyze data from a number of service providers to determine the most effective way to organize a process.[12]

Step 6: Evaluate the Alternatives

Once alternatives have been developed, they must be evaluated and compared. In every decision situation, the objective is to select the alternatives that will produce the most favorable outcomes and the least unfavorable outcomes. In selecting among alternatives, the decision maker should be guided by the previously established goals and objectives. The alternative-outcome relationship is based on three possible conditions:

1. **Certainty:** The decision maker has complete knowledge of the probabilities of the outcomes of each alternative.
2. **Uncertainty:** The decision maker has absolutely no knowledge of the probabilities of the outcomes of each alternative.
3. **Risk:** The decision maker has some probabilistic estimate of the outcomes of each alternative.

Decision making under conditions of risk is probably the most common situation. In evaluating alternatives under these conditions, statisticians and operations researchers have made important contributions to decision making. Their methods have proved especially useful in analyzing and ranking alternatives.

In evaluating alternative solutions, two cautions should be kept in mind. First, this phase of the decision-making process must be kept separate and distinct from the previous step—especially in a group decision-making context. When alternatives are evaluated as they are proposed, this may restrict the number of alternative solutions identified. If evaluations are positive, there may be a tendency to end the process prematurely by settling on the first positive solution. On the other hand, negative evaluations make it less likely for someone to risk venturing what may be the best solution.

The second caution is to be wary of solutions that are evaluated as being "perfect"—especially when the decision is being made under conditions of uncertainty. If a solution appears to have no drawbacks or if, in a group setting, there's unanimous agreement on a course of action, it may be useful to assign someone to take a devil's advocate position. The role of the devil's advocate is to be a thorough critic of the proposed solution. Research supports the benefits of devil's advocacy and the conflict a devil's advocate may cause, thus forcing a decision maker to reexamine assumptions and information.[13]

Step 7: Select a Solution

The purpose of selecting a particular solution is to solve a problem in order to achieve a predetermined objective. This means that a decision isn't an end in itself but only a means to an end. Although the decision maker chooses the alternative that is expected to result in achieving the objective, the selection of that alternative shouldn't be an isolated act. If it is, the factors that led to the decision are likely to be excluded. Specifically, the steps following the decision should include implementation and follow-up.

Unfortunately for most managers, situations rarely exist in which one alternative achieves the desired objective without having some impact on another objective. If one objective is optimized, the other is suboptimized. In a business, for example, if production is optimized, employee morale may be suboptimized, or vice versa. Or a hospital superintendent may optimize a short-run objective such as maintenance costs at the expense of a long-run objective such as high-quality patient care. Thus the interrelatedness of organizational objectives complicates the decision maker's job.

In managerial decision making, the decision maker can't possibly know all of the available alternatives, the consequences of each alternative, and the probability of these consequences occurring. Thus, rather than being an optimizer, the decision maker is a satisficer, selecting the alternative that meets a satisfactory standard. A **satisficer** is a person who accepts a reasonable alternative that isn't necessarily the optimal alternative. This isn't a negative comment on managerial decision making. Rather, it's a frank acknowledgment that searching for optimal solutions is usually time and cost prohibitive. Managers must be prepared to act on decisions that may, in fact, have some negative implications along with the positive results they are intended to achieve.

Step 8: Implement the Decision

Any decision is little more than an abstraction if it isn't implemented, and it must be effectively implemented to achieve an objective. It's entirely possible for a good decision to be hurt by poor implementation. In this sense, implementation may be more important than the actual choice of the alternative.

certainty
No element of chance, possible loss, or unpredictability.

uncertainty
The decision maker has absolutely no knowledge of the probabilities of the outcomes of each alternative.

risk
The chance of a possible loss, or unpredictability, in a decision.

satisficer
A person who accepts a reasonable alternative that isn't necessarily the optimal alternative.

In most situations, implementing decisions involves people. Thus, the test of a decision's soundness is the behavior of the people who put it into action or are affected by it. Although a decision may be technically sound, it can be undermined easily by dissatisfied employees. A manager's job isn't only to choose good solutions but also to transform such solutions into behavior in the organization. This is often accomplished by empowering employees to make decisions that affect work processes. For example, to avoid the apathy and atrophy brought on by the powerless assembly line mentality that some employees develop toward their jobs, Cellular One of Baton Rouge, Louisiana, adopted a continuous quality improvement (CQI) approach. Cellular One now involves each person in the organization in decision making and implementation of quality improvements.[14]

Step 9: Follow-up

Effective management involves periodic measurement of results. Actual results are compared with planned results (the objective). If deviations exist, changes must be made. If actual results don't meet planned results, changes must be made in the solution chosen, in its implementation, or in the original objective if it's deemed unattainable. If the original objective must be revised, then the entire decision-making process will be reactivated. The important point is that once a decision is implemented, a manager can't assume that the outcome will meet the original objective. Some system of control and evaluation is necessary to make sure the actual results are consistent with the original objectives.

Sometimes a decision's outcome is unexpected or is perceived differently by different people. Dealing with this possibility is an important part of the follow-up phase in the decision process. As Figures 5–2 and 5–3 show, the follow-up step results in feedback to other steps in the decision-making process. This feedback can result in different means of implementation, selection of different alternatives, or a revised evaluation of the various alternatives.

Summary of the Decision-Making Process

The nine-step decision-making process is an outline of how managers in the modern workplace spend much of their time. In an increasingly technological world, work has become less a matter of physical effort and more a matter of processing information, even in traditional "sweat" industries like agriculture and manufacturing. Yet, making effective, quality-based decisions requires more than just the ability to process information and then choose among and manage alternatives. A quality-based approach to decision making requires effective post-decision implementation, usually involving employees from various levels and functions of the organization.

No matter what steps are involved, decision making always involves people. Some decisions are made by individuals acting alone. More often in today's quality-based organizations, decision making occurs in groups. The next two sections explore how decision making by individuals differs from group decision making.

FIGURE 5–3
Follow-Up Portion of Decision
Making

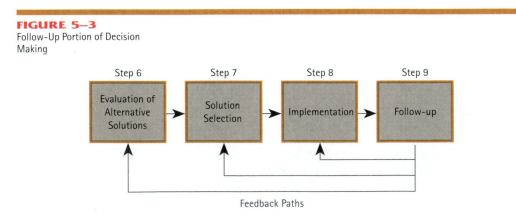

Feedback Paths

INDIVIDUAL DECISION MAKING

In today's workplace managers make a lot of decisions in groups, but many still must be made on an individual basis. To be an effective manager requires the ability to make individual decisions. This ability is enhanced by knowing some of the factors that influence individual decision making.

Several behavior factors influence the decision-making process. Some of these factors influence only certain aspects of the process, while others influence the entire process. Each behavioral factor may affect decision making and, therefore, must be understood if managers are to fully appreciate decision making as a process involving individuals in organizations. Figure 5–1 listed individual factors as an influence in the decision-making process. Figure 5–4 extends the individual factors, highlighting four key elements: values, personality, propensity for risk, and potential for dissonance.

Values

In the context of decision making, values are the guidelines a person uses when confronted with a situation in which a choice must be made. Most of an individual's enduring values are acquired early in life and are a basic part of the person's personality. Other values can be acquired in adulthood and are usually associated with group membership. In a quality-based organization, for example, the group values customer service, continuous improvement, and employee empowerment to make decisions. Values influence the decision-making process in the following ways:

❖   In establishing goals and objectives, managers must make value judgments regarding the selection of opportunities and the assignment of priorities.
❖   In developing alternatives, managers must make value judgments about the various possibilities.
❖   In selecting a solution, the values of the decision maker influence which alternative is chosen.
❖   In implementation, value judgments are necessary in choosing the means for implementation.

FIGURE 5–4
Individual Influencers
of Decision Making

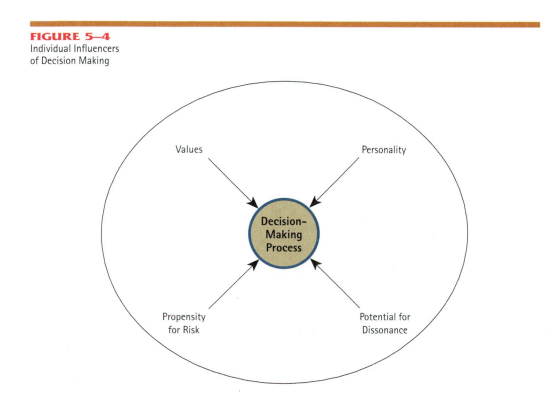

❖   In the follow-up stage, value judgments can't be avoided when corrective action is
    taken.

Values play a role throughout the decision-making process, so they need to be recognized by managers. Successful application of TQM starts with communicating the organization's values and beliefs. As these values and beliefs are diffused and adopted throughout the organization, they become a guidepost, enabling individual employees to make decisions that are in the interest of the organization.[15]

Personality

Decision makers are influenced by many psychological forces. One of the most important is the decision maker's personality, which is reflected in the choices made. Several studies have examined the effect of selected personality variables on the decision-making process.[16] These studies generally have focused on three sets of variables:

1. *Personality variables.* These include the individual's attitudes, beliefs, and needs.
2. *Situational variables.* These pertain to the external (physical and social) situations in which individuals find themselves.
3. *Interactional variables.* These pertain to the individual's momentary state as a result of the interaction of a specific situation with characteristics of the individual's personality.

The most important conclusions concerning the influence of these personality variables on the decision-making process are:

❖   It's unlikely that one person can be equally proficient in all aspects of the decision-making process. The results suggest that some people will do better in one part of the process, whereas others will do better in another part.
❖   Such characteristics as risk tolerance are associated with different steps of the decision-making process.
❖   The relation of personality to the decision-making process may vary for different people on the basis of such factors as gender and social status.

Significantly, this research has determined that the decision maker's personality traits combine with certain situational and interactional variables to influence the decision-making process.

Propensity for Risk

You probably know that decision makers vary greatly in their willingness to take risks. This specific aspect of an individual's personality influences decision making so strongly that it's broken out of other personality variables and considered separately. A decision maker with a low tolerance of risk will establish different objectives, evaluate alternatives differently, and select different alternatives from another decision maker with high risk tolerance in the same situation. The former will avoid decisions where risk is high; the latter will often seek more risky alternatives. Many people are bolder and more innovative and advocate greater risk taking in groups than when they're acting as individuals.

Risk propensity is also affected by whether potential outcomes are characterized in terms of losses or gains. This, in turn, depends on how the decision maker "frames" the decision. Framing refers to the decision maker's perception of the decision's possible outcomes in terms of gains or losses.[17] When the choice is perceived as being between losses, there is a greater propensity to take risks than when it is perceived as being between gains.

Potential for Dissonance

Much attention has been focused on the decision itself and on the forces and influences affecting the decision maker before the decision is made. But only recently has attention been given to what happens *after* a decision is made. Specifically, behavioral scientists are focusing attention on the occurrence of postdecision anxiety.

Such anxiety is related to what Festinger calls *cognitive dissonance.*[18] Festinger's cognitive dissonance theory states that there is often a lack of consistency or harmony among an individual's various cognitions (attitudes, beliefs, and so on) after a decision has been made. That is, there will often be a conflict between what the decision maker believes and the consequences of a particular decision. As a result, the decision maker will have doubts and anxiety about her choice. The intensity of the anxiety may be greater when any of the following conditions exists:

1. The decision is important psychologically or financially.
2. There are a number of foregone alternatives.
3. The foregone alternatives have many favorable features.

Any or all of these conditions are present in many decisions in all types of organizations. You can expect, therefore, that cognitive dissonance will affect many decision makers across many decision opportunities.

When dissonance occurs, individuals are likely to use any of the following methods to reduce their dissonance:

1. Seek information that supports the wisdom of their decision.
2. Selectively perceive (distort) information in a way that supports their decision.
3. Adopt a less favorable view of the foregone alternatives.
4. Minimize the importance of the negative aspects of the decision and exaggerate the importance of the positive aspects.

Although each of us may resort to some of this behavior in our personal decision making, a great deal of it could be extremely harmful in terms of organizational effectiveness. The potential for dissonance is influenced heavily by one's personality, specifically one's self-confidence and potential to be persuaded. In fact, all of the behavioral influences are closely interrelated and are only isolated here for purposes of discussion. For example, what kind of risk taker you are and your likelihood of experiencing dissonance following a decision are closely related. Both characteristics are strongly influenced by your personality, your perceptions, and your value system.

Cognitive dissonance theory holds that a person's desire to reduce dissonance is also related to the desire to appear consistent to oneself. But this desire for personal consistency isn't always a positive attribute for decision makers as it can lead to inflexibility. The modern decision-making environment calls for flexibility and adaptability. The desire to reduce cognitive dissonance becomes dysfunctional when it leads to what has been called **escalation of commitment**. This is an increased commitment to a previous decision despite contrary information. Research has shown that individuals will escalate their commitment to a failing course of action when they view themselves as responsible for the action. According to dissonance theory, this behavior results from the individual trying to demonstrate that the original decision was correct.[19]

escalation of commitment An increased commitment to a previous decision despite contrary information.

Before managers can fully understand the dynamics of the decision-making process, they must appreciate the behavioral influences on themselves and other decision makers in the organization when they make decisions. Understanding that a common response to cognitive dissonance is escalation of commitment to a bad decision should help managers change bad decisions and maintain flexibility.[20]

The individual forces discussed in this section are heightened in a group decision-making environment. Quality-based managers should carefully study the dynamics of group decision making because it's an important part of the continuous improvement process. In the next section you will learn about some forces affecting groups as they wrestle with decision making.

GROUP DECISION MAKING

In most organizations today, a great deal of decision making is achieved through teams, task forces, and committees. This tendency toward group or team decision making is due in part to organizations' increased complexity and to the large amount of information needed to make sound decisions. This is especially true for the nonprogrammed decisions that typically have the greatest uncertainty of outcome and require the most creativity. In most organizations it's unusual to find decisions on such problems being made by one individual. The complexity of many of these problems requires specialized knowledge in numerous fields, knowledge usually not possessed by one person. This requirement—coupled with the fact that decisions eventually must be accepted and implemented by many units throughout the organization—has increased the use of the team approach in the decision-making process.

Individual versus Group Decision Making

Considerable debate has centered on the relative effectiveness of individual versus group decision making. Groups usually take more time to reach a decision than individuals do. But bringing together individual specialists and experts has its benefits since the mutually reinforcing impact of their interaction often results in better decisions. In fact, a great deal of research has shown that consensus decisions with five or more participants are usually superior to individual decision making, majority vote, and leadership decisions.[21]

On the other hand, research has also found group decision making to be negatively influenced by such behavioral factors as pressure to conform (sometimes called "group-think"), a dominant personality type's presence in the group, "status incongruity" (whereby lower-status participants are inhibited by higher-status participants and acquiesce even though they believe that their own ideas are superior), and certain participants' attempts to influence others because these participants are perceived to be expert in the problem area.

Certain decisions (such as nonprogrammed decisions) appear to be better made by groups, whereas others appear better suited to individual decision making. Keep in mind the following points concerning group processes for nonprogrammed decisions:

1. In establishing goals and objectives, groups probably are superior to individuals because of their greater knowledge.
2. In developing alternatives, the groups can ensure a broad search in the various functional areas of the organization.
3. In evaluating alternatives, the collective judgment of the group, with its wider range of viewpoints, seems superior to that of the individual decision maker.
4. In selecting a solution, research has shown that group interaction and the achievement of consensus usually result in the acceptance of more risk than an individual decision maker would accept. In any event, the group decision is more likely to be accepted as a result of the participation of those affected by its consequences.
5. Implementation of a decision, whether or not made by a group, usually is done by individual managers. Thus, since a group can't be held responsible, the responsibility for implementation rests with the individual manager.

TQM-based organizations have evolved several forms of group decision making. One form that has been used effectively in a number of industries is the process improvement team.

Process Improvement Teams

process improvement team

The "working team" of a continuous improvement process consisting of anyone from the organization who can contribute to a problem's solution.

Process improvement teams are a key part of the total quality management culture. Such teams consist of employees from throughout the organization and are often made up of people from interacting functional areas (such as sales and marketing). Everyone on the team has equal status; no one is automatically appointed leader based on his or her position with the firm. As the Ethics Spotlight shows, Wainwright Industries uses the process improvement team approach to enhance the safety of its operation.

Process improvement teams are chartered by a manager who gives the team a well-defined problem to solve. In a TQM organization, no team is chartered without ensuring that team members have received training in basic team processes, and in the tools and techniques of quality management. Successful process improvement teams are usually limited to six to eight people. One person is appointed the leader, another the facilitator, and a third the recorder. The leader is responsible for activities like setting the agenda, arranging meeting times, and getting a room. The facilitator is charged with ensuring that the meetings stay focused on the problem and that everyone has an opportunity to be heard. The recorder takes the minutes and reports after each meeting to the manager who chartered the team.

ETHICS SPOTLIGHT

EMPLOYEE SAFETY IS FIRST AT WAINWRIGHT INDUSTRIES

Because of lack of support, managers have traditionally attributed variations in safety performance to variations in awareness. But any supervisor or team leader knows that accidents in the plant come primarily from the human element. The management challenge is to maximize the level of readiness for the workforce as a whole. The ethical challenge for managers is in deciding how much of a firm's resources should be devoted to the effort. Wainwright Industries has decided to make safety a priority in its plants.

"Safety is the first basic human need," claims Mike Simms, plant manager at Missouri's Wainwright Industries. "If you don't feel safe in your environment, how can you possibly do a good job?"

While many managers would agree on that assumption, companies that actually act on it represent a rarer breed. As its 1994 Malcolm Baldrige award attests, Wainwright is a special kind of company. Just ask Darel Schartman, loss control consultant for Traveler's Insurance, who handles the Wainwright account. He knew within five minutes of his first visit that Wainwright was different.

"For one thing, it was the cleanest facility I had ever been in and the employees seemed happy to be at work," Schartman recalls. "Their attendance rate is 99 percent daily. Besides, how many companies actually invite their insurance carrier in to look around and request their guidance and support?"

Wainwright provides metal stamping and assembly, CNC machining, and technical services for customers such as Ford, General Motors, McDonnell Douglas, IBM, ITT, and United Technologies.

Safety and quality have always been important at the family-owned business, which has 275 employees at two locations. As early as 1984, Wainwright began experimenting with such quality management initiatives as teamwork and employee involvement. Still, as Mike Simms admits, three or four managers continued to make most of the decisions. It wasn't until a change in corporate philosophy that safety moved to the forefront of all operations. He said, "In April 1991, the owners and I confessed that we had failed in our part of the bargain. We stood up in front of all the associates and told them we knew they were committed to us, but that we were still trying to make decisions for them. What we were really doing was trying to maintain control." That meeting marked a turning point for the company.

Management realized that the most important assets at the company were the employees, many of whom had worked there for years. The decision was made to prioritize safety—the most important concern of the employees—as the first and most important measurement category, followed by internal customer satisfaction, external customer satisfaction, quality, and business performance. Since that time, accidents have decreased by 72 percent; lost time due to accidents has decreased by 85 percent; and lost work days have gone down by 87 percent. Customer satisfaction ratings are at 95 percent and growing, profits are up, and workers' compensation costs have dropped to $13,000 from a 1990 payout of $92,600.

According to Simms, a safe environment is created by several factors: good training, safe work practices, properly guarded machinery, a clean work environment, a willingness to share information, teamwork, and management support. Wainwright spends, on the average, 7 percent of the annual payroll on training. Once hired, employees (called "associates" at Wainwright) receive training in team building, statistical process control, and problem solving. Courses are offered on-site during working hours, because management feels that the hour or two spent on training will more than repay itself in the long run.

Continuous improvement process suggestions are the primary method of employee participation in company decision making. Wainwright employees have surpassed a goal of 52 suggestions per year each, turning in, on average, 1.25 implemented suggestions per week. Each suggestion, regardless of the amount of money or time it saves, counts as one chance to win a prize at the end of the month. Safety suggestions count as three chances, to highlight their importance to the company. A computer randomly picks a name from the suggestion pool each month; the winner receives an $80 gift certificate.

One suggestion that has been implemented is to videotape a reenactment of all accidents, starring the employees who were involved and their group team leader. In the videos, the employee or employees describe what happened and, as closely as possible without creating a new hazard, reenact the circumstances of the accident. The group team leader or manager then discusses the cause of the accident, ways it could have been avoided, and any corrective action taken to ensure that a similar accident doesn't occur.

Simms says that every aspect of the business has benefited from the emphasis on safety. "We have never regretted our decision to empower our associates or place safety first," he said. "The mind-set here has become, 'How can I do it better?' rather than 'How can I fix it?' We take a proactive stand and it has paid off."

Sources: Adapted from S.L. Smith, "How a Baldrige Winner Manages Safety," *Occupational Hazards*, February 1995, pp. 33–35; Thomas R. Kraus, "Driving Continuous Improvement in Safety," *Occupational Hazards*, February 1995, pp. 47–50; "Steven L. Curtis, "Safety and Total Quality Management," *Professional Safety*, January 1995, pp. 18–20.

A key question for many organizations is whether teams need both a leader and a facilitator to be productive. If team leaders undergo intensive training in interpersonal skills, group decision making, and team dynamics, they can learn and integrate the skills necessary to both lead and facilitate process improvement teams. Even when facilitators are present, team members often look to team leaders to handle digressions and resolve conflicts because the team leader is the traditional authority figure. The presence of facilitators gives leaders license to become team members and participate in digressions, thus undermining the facilitator's ability to focus the group.

VLSI Technology in San Jose, California, makes the team leader–facilitator transition by training in-house management staff in group process skills. The training teaches supervisors, engineers, and other key employees how to facilitate problem-solving teams.[22]

The important points to remember about process improvement teams, no matter what structure you employ, is that they must have a clear goal, a time frame for the achievement of the goal, and human and other resources necessary to conduct a thorough search for alternative solutions. Empowering employees with the information and authority to make key operational decisions lies at the heart of a TQM-based organization. Not only does empowerment aid in boosting employee morale, but it also helps create better service to customers. What Managers Are Reading reviews two of the leading manuals on employee empowerment.

Decision making at both the individual and group levels requires creativity. In the next section we explore techniques for stimulating group creativity.

Techniques for Stimulating Creativity in Group Decision Making

If groups are better suited to nonprogrammed decisions than individuals are, then an atmosphere fostering group creativity must be developed. In this respect, group decision making may be similar to brainstorming in that discussion must be free-flowing and spontaneous. All group members must participate, and the evaluation of individual ideas must be suspended in the beginning to encourage participation. Still, a decision must be reached, and this is where group decision making differs from brainstorming.

When properly utilized, three techniques—brainstorming, the Delphi technique, and the nominal group technique—increase a group's creative ability to generate ideas, understand problems, and reach better decisions. Raising a group's creative capability is especially necessary when individuals from diverse sectors of the organization must pool their judgments to create a satisfactory course of action for the organization.

Brainstorming. In many situations, groups are expected to produce imaginative solutions to organizational problems. In such instances, brainstorming has often enhanced the group's creative output. **Brainstorming** includes a firm set of rules whose purpose is to promote the generation of ideas while at the same time avoiding members' inhibitions that face-to-face groups usually cause. The basic rules are:

❖ No idea is too ridiculous. Group members are encouraged to state any extreme or outlandish idea.

❖ Each idea presented belongs to the group, not to the person stating it. In this way, group members utilize and build on the ideas of others.

❖ No idea can be criticized. The session's purpose is to generate ideas, not to evaluate them.

Brainstorming is considered effective in advertising and various other fields. In some other situations, it has been less successful because there is no evaluation or ranking of the ideas generated. Thus the groups never really conclude the problem-solving process.

The Delphi Technique. The **Delphi technique** involves soliciting and comparing anonymous judgments on the topic of interest through a set of sequential questionnaires that are interspersed with summarized information and feedback of opinions from earlier responses.

The Delphi technique retains the advantage of having several judges while removing the biasing effects that might occur during face-to-face interaction. The basic approach has

brainstorming
A process whereby a group of individuals generate ideas according to a firm set of rules while at the same time avoiding the inhibitions that are usually caused by face-to-face groups.

Delphi technique
A process involving soliciting and comparing anonymous judgments on the topic of interest through a set of sequential questionnaires that are interspersed with summarized information and feedback of opinions from earlier questionnaires.

been to collect anonymous judgments by mail questionnaire from a specified set of individuals—members of a management team, for example. Staff members summarize the responses as the group consensus and feed this summary back to the original respondents along with a second questionnaire for reassessment. Based on this feedback, respondents independently evaluate their earlier responses. The underlying belief is that the consensus estimate results in a better decision after several rounds of anonymous group judgment. Although it's possible to continue the procedure for several rounds, research has shown that, typically, no significant changes occur after the second round of feedback.

The Nominal Group Technique (NGT). NGT has gained increasing recognition in health, social service, education, industry, and government organizations. The term **nominal group technique** was adopted by researchers to refer to processes that bring people together but don't allow them to initially communicate verbally. Thus the collection of people is a group nominally (in name only). In its present form NGT actually combines both verbal and nonverbal stages.

Basically NGT is a structured group meeting that proceeds as follows: a group of 7 to 10 individuals sit around a table but don't speak to one another. Talking to each other isn't permitted during the first stage of NGT. Rather, each person writes ideas on a pad of paper. After five minutes, a structured sharing of ideas takes place. Each person presents one idea. A person designated as recorder writes the ideas on a flip chart in full view of the entire group. This continues until all of the participants indicate that they have no further ideas to share. There is still no discussion.

The output of this phase is usually a list of ideas. The next phase involves structured discussion in which each idea receives attention before a vote is taken. Discussion includes asking for clarification and stating the degree of support for each idea on the flip chart. In the next stage, independent voting, each participant privately selects priorities by ranking or voting. The group decision is the mathematically pooled outcome of the individual votes.

Both the Delphi technique and NGT have excellent records of successes. There are two basic differences between them: (1) In the Delphi process, all communication between participants is by way of written questionnaires and feedback from the monitoring staff. In NGT, communication is direct between participants. (2) NGT participants meet face-to-face around a table, whereas Delphi participants are physically distant, never meet face-to-face, and are typically anonymous to one another.

Practical considerations, of course, often influence which technique is used. These considerations can include the number of working hours available, costs, and participants' physical proximity.

This brief overview of individual and group decision making should help you understand some of the forces that influence decision making. You also should have an appreciation of the differences between individual and group decision making, as well as an understanding of the different circumstances appropriate for each approach.

In the next section we examine in greater detail one of the dominant factors in modern decision making: information overload. Information is available to managers in greater volumes than ever before. The section below also explores some of the tools managers use to harness information.

> **nominal group technique**
> A process of bringing people together in a group to solve a problem. In the NGT participants aren't allowed to communicate verbally in the initial phase.

THE INFORMATION AGE

Businesses today have access to more information than ever before. The abundance of newspapers, journals, magazines, TV and radio programs, seminars, business and government reports, and the explosive growth of the Internet has led many commentators to label this the *Information Age.*[23] The sheer volume of information available presents a real challenge to business managers, raising important questions about the impact of information technology on the management of organizations. Understanding this impact becomes even more critical as organizations struggle to improve quality and competitiveness in the face of relentless challenges from foreign firms.[24] Obviously, every manager can't use all

available information. The challenge is to collect, store, and process the most relevant information to make more effective decisions.

One challenge facing organizations is to communicate useful information to managers in a timely fashion. Organizations must be able to make decisions quickly to keep pace with competition. Yet if an organization isn't prepared to handle a large volume of information, or if the information doesn't reach key decision makers, the volume of information and its speed of travel are of no value whatsoever. Two important points for managers to remember is that not all information is useful and useful information is better if it's widely shared.

Attributes of Useful Information

Not all information is appropriate for decision making. For information to be truly useful, it must be accessible, timely, relevant, accurate, verifiable, complete, and clear.[25] Table 5–4 summarizes these attributes. As the table shows, the requirements are fairly rigorous and may be difficult to meet. For instance, when information is needed quickly, accuracy may be sacrificed for speed; information obtained quickly may not be error free.

Information Sharing

A major problem facing organizations is the manner in which information is shared. Because of the abundance of data, much valuable information never reaches the person who can benefit from it the most. In such cases, decisions affecting billions of dollars may be based on bad information.

In today's economy, information—more than factories and products—is the key to growth and competitiveness. Some managers withhold information from workers because they're afraid employees will use the information against them or somehow share it with competitors. Unfortunately, workers can't respond to the need for continued improvement

TABLE 5-4	ATTRIBUTES OF USEFUL INFORMATION
Attribute	Description
Accessible	Information can be obtained easily and quickly.
Timely	Information is available when needed.
Relevant	Managers need the information to make a particular decision.
Accurate	Information is error free.
Verifiable	Information is confirmed.
Complete	All details needed are available.
Clear	Information is stated in such a way that no facts are misunderstood.

without information. Organizations that train people in the value of information and how to use it gain a competitive advantage over those failing to share information.

The key to sharing information is to put it in the hands of the people who can use it, in a form they can understand. For example, client/server technology is enabling the gas industry to reorganize and revolutionize the workplace so that teams of workers can work on the same task simultaneously. The result is unprecedented levels of efficiency and new highs in customer service. With client/server computing, PCs perform functions once handled only by mainframe computers. In October 1994, Southern Connecticut Gas began rolling out major client/server application systems. The company is using the approach for marketing–sales support, gas distribution–management systems, construction work in progress, and a full set of financial applications.[26] As the Workplace of Tomorrow shows, organizations can also benefit by sharing information with customers.

Another innovation allowing for the wide sharing of information is groupware. Groupware, such as Lotus Notes helps organizations build integrated work group and work flow systems. These systems include electronic mail (e-mail), scheduling, and group conferencing.[27] In the competitive groupware industry, powerful new additions to this type of software will continue throughout the 1990s. Netscape, for example, has recently been applied inside organizations to create Intranet, allowing workers with disparate computer platforms to share information.[28] These powerful new tools will create productivity enhancement opportunities for firms by expanding the ability to share vital information.

MANAGEMENT INFORMATION SYSTEMS

Organizations have been using computers to transform raw data into information for many years. As the need for information has accelerated, so has competition among businesses to use information to gain a competitive advantage. The quality of a manager's decision is directly related to the information available; the better the information, the better the decision. A **management information system (MIS)** combines computers and regular, organized procedures to provide managers with information needed in making decisions.

An MIS is critical for decision making in all aspects of management: organization and job design, human resource decisions, strategic planning, customer service, and so on. An MIS can also help reduce cost. For example, a study by Arthur D. Little Company suggests that electronic management and transport of patient information could lower U.S. health care costs by almost $30 billion.[29]

Any organization striving to achieve quality must make data-based decisions. Figure 5–5 shows that the TQM approach consists of both processes and people. The processes include the analytical procedures used to make decisions, such as inventory control, quality

management information system (MIS)
A combination of computers and regular, organized procedures to provide managers with information needed in making decisions.

FIGURE 5–5
Information for Quality
Decisions

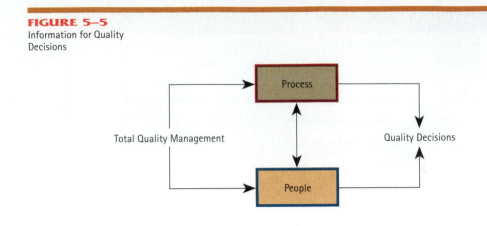

control, and product development. The people component of the model has been referred to as "internal customers," the employees of the organization. The objective is to provide internal customers with the information they need to perform their jobs. Employees can't be empowered without adequate information to make decisions and take action. In short, management information systems play a critical role in TQM programs by providing information needed to develop the best processes for decision making and by enabling internal customers to make decisions.

MIS Functions

A management information system is used to collect data, store and process those data, and then present useful and timely information to managers (Figure 5–6). This section discusses these functions.

Collection of Data. We've emphasized the massive amount of information available to organizations—personnel records, information about customers and competitors, sales and accounting data, and so on. The first function of an MIS is to determine the information needed to make decisions and to organize it into a database. A **database** is an integrated collection of data stored in one place for efficient access and information processing. A common database for all departments or units is a key to successfully implementing a TQM initiative.[30]

Data can be obtained from sources within and outside the organization. Generally, most data collected for an MIS come from internal sources such as company records or reports and information compiled by managers themselves. External sources include trade publications, customers, consultants, updated industry and market studies, and periodical and newspaper articles. Managers must specify the information they need to make decisions and identify the specific sources of that information.

database
An integrated collection of data stored in one place for efficient access and information processing.

FIGURE 5–6
Functions of an MIS

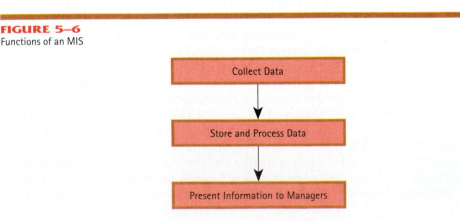

WORKPLACE OF TOMORROW

STATES REINVENT DEPARTMENT OF MOTOR VEHICLES OFFICES

A DMV officer uses a palmtop computer to issue a parking ticket.

More and more government organizations are implementing total quality management programs. President Bill Clinton and Vice President

Al Gore have set "reinventing government" as one of the major themes of their administration. Since they established that theme, governmental offices at the federal, state, and local levels have been using TQM to become more responsive to customers, and develop better working relationships among employees.

Most people have had experience with motor vehicle offices—either to get a driver's license or to have one replaced. Often, that experience involved waiting in long lines, only to be told by a surly employee that they couldn't help you. With TQM, the department of motor vehicles (DMV) offices of tomorrow might be quite different.

New technology is helping to pull the state DMV offices out of the Dark Ages. In Massachusetts, where the DMV was notorious for not answering the phone, reforms such as interactive phone banks and credit card fee payments have streamlined the process. Now, speeding tickets can be paid on the spot—by punching a credit-card number into a cellular phone.

Other innovations are on the way. Some states now use digital photo-imaging for license pictures, so photos can be stored on computers. That way, DMVs can renew or replace lost licenses by mail.

Florida and other states are talking to Time Warner, Inc., about creating an interactive cable channel that would provide information and testing for written driving tests and allow viewers to call up records, outstanding tickets, and renewal times. Using information provided by the channel, residents also could pay fees electronically or by touch-tone phone.

In fact, doing business with some DMVs soon may be as easy as using a bank card. Virginia, Washington, and California are planning to roll out ATM-style kiosks, made by the likes of AT&T and IBM, where drivers can transact DMV business. Eventually, licenses may have magnetic strips like credit cards that can be swiped through a machine to verify information. The goal of such changes, says Massachusetts Registrar of Motor Vehicles Jerold A. Gnazzo, is "to never see the customer again."

In the meantime, though, DMVs that have begun reengineering claim that customer satisfaction is way up. Partly, officials say, that's because employees themselves are more pleasant, since their workloads are lighter.

Source: Adapted from Pam Black, "Finally, Human Rights for Motorists," Business Week, May 1, 1995, p. 45; John Burbidge, "Three Tales of Participation at Work in Government," Journal for Quality & Participation, March 1995, pp. 20–23; Marc Hequet, "TQM at City Hall," Training, March 1995, pp. 58–64.

A growing concern has been raised about the quality of information found in databases. Consider the following:

❖ A survey by MIT researchers of information managers at 50 large companies reported that half of the managers believed their corporate information was less than 95 percent accurate, limiting its usefulness; nearly all of them said that databases kept by individual departments weren't good enough to use for important decisions.

❖ One airline made phantom bookings in its database of passenger reservations while installing a new software system. The software was fixed but the false reservations weren't, so planes were taking off partly empty for several months.

❖ A large manufacturer developed a database to consolidate all sales records by customer number. But salespeople created a new customer number for each sale, including sales to existing customers. A single customer, McDonnell Douglas Corp., was listed in the database under more than 7,000 customer numbers.[31]

Software has now been developed that uses statistical control to analyze big databases, detect inaccuracies, and ensure quality. Collecting data is only the beginning of a good MIS system. Data must also be efficiently stored and processed.

Storing and Processing of Data. Once created, a database must be stored and processed in a form useful to managers. Data are generally stored on magnetic tape or hard disks when mainframe computers are used and on hard disks, floppy (soft) disks, or CD ROMs when minicomputers or microcomputers are used.

Data for an MIS must be current, which requires periodic updating of the database. A computer operator or programmer can update the database manually by loading the appropriate tape or disk into the computer, which locates the data to be changed and makes the necessary changes. Systems also are available to automatically update data. In this case, the database is permanently connected to the MIS and the computer automatically makes changes as new data become available.

Once data are stored in the MIS, managers can use the data for decision making. Some data can be used in the form in which they're stored. But more often data must be processed to meet managers' specific information needs.

database management system (DBMS)
A computer software program that helps firms manage their data files.

A **database management system (DBMS)** is a computer software program that helps firms manage their data files. Such programs change information stored in data files, add new information, and delete information no longer needed. DBMS software can be used to sort and merge files, process data, and print reports. Some frequently used database programs include dBASE III PLUS, FaxPro, Oracle, Rapidfile, and PC-File.

Presenting Information to Managers. Processed data must be put in a form useful to managers. Verbal information can be presented in text format in the forms of reports, outlines, lists, articles, or books. Numerical information can be presented in table or graph format. Computer programs offer numerous graphic options. The most commonly used computer graphics are bar charts, pie charts, and graphs (Figure 5–7). More sophisticated products now include voice and video data as well.[32]

The specific information presented to managers varies depending on the task being performed. Low-level managers are concerned with decisions that control the company's day-to-day operations. Many of these decisions follow a predetermined set of procedures that lead to the desired outcome. These managers' needs can be met by typical data processing that generates routine records and statements. Mid-level managers are responsible for implementing plans made by top-level management. These tactical decisions require internal information and the processing and retrieval of data. An MIS can be useful in providing this type of information. For example, a manager may wish to evaluate how effectively a product is being produced. Volumes of data would be of little use in making this decision; the manager should specify the information needs. Finally, top-level managers are responsible for long-range strategic plans. For instance, top-level managers may make strategic decisions involving new product design, financial policies, and acquisition.

Computer Networks

computer network
A collection of computers connected in a manner that allows them to function individually and communicate with each other.

A management information system can include multiple computers connected to each other. A **computer network** is a collection of computers connected in a manner that allows them to function individually and communicate with each other. Computer networks usually include a mainframe or server as the foundation of the system. Other mainframes, servers, or microcomputers can communicate with the mainframe or server or with each other. Networks link computers within an office, across the country, or even worldwide—in which case the computers are linked by telephone lines or satellites.

local area network (LAN)
A system of telecommunications links that connects all computers in one company directly without telephone lines.

A **local area network (LAN)** is a system of telecommunications links that connect all computers in one company directly without telephone lines. Because computers in the network can communicate with one another, members of a firm can send information back and forth instantly. In late 1993, securities brokerage firm Machaira Group, Inc., installed its first LAN. Today, Machaira's brokers execute buy-and-sell orders electronically from their PCs, reducing time on each transaction and locking in good prices on fast-moving stocks while the customer waits on the telephone.[33]

decision support system (DSS)
An interactive information system that enables managers to gain instant access to information in a less structured format than an MIS.

DECISION SUPPORT SYSTEMS

Management information systems may not be adequate for many mid- and top-level management decisions. While an MIS provides information, the information may not be specifically tailored to managers' needs. A **decision support system (DSS)** is an interactive

FIGURE 5–7
Most Commonly Used
Computer Graphics

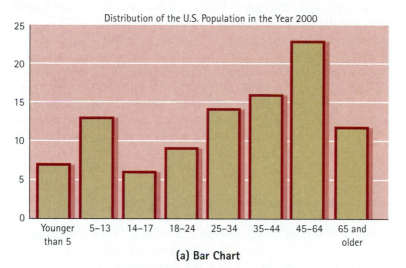

(a) Bar Chart

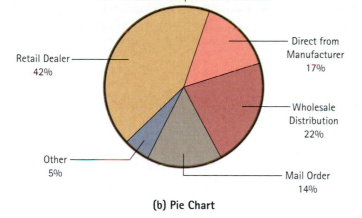

(b) Pie Chart

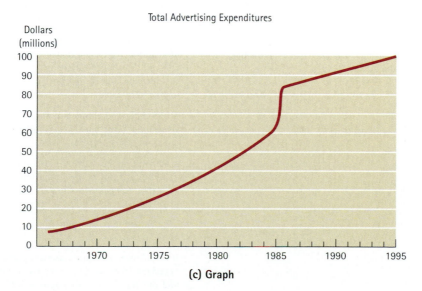

(c) Graph

information system that enables managers to gain instant access to information in a less structured format than an MIS. DSS software combines corporate information on past performance with what's currently taking place; it allows managers to work with large amounts of data not available otherwise. Through a DSS, managers can obtain information about the firm, competitors, and the business environment.

Decision support systems are growing increasingly user friendly. Some of the latest systems now use interactive, graphical interfaces to allow managers easy access to data.[34] The cost of a DSS interface can run as high as 60 percent to 70 percent of the total cost of building the system. It's important that the interface be adaptable to different users' needs and also communicate constant commands to the internal components of the DSS.[35] DSS use will increase as the interface between humans and computers becomes more friendly.

The main differences between an MIS and a DSS are summarized in Table 5–5. A DSS supports managerial skills at all levels of decision making by providing instant response to managers' information needs. Thus a DSS is a specialized MIS designed to improve the effectiveness of decisions.

An **executive information system (EIS)** is a user-friendly DSS designed specifically for executives. An EIS is easy to use and requires no knowledge of the computer. It consolidates the analysis provided by a DSS, interprets it in light of the organization's goals, and then presents it to executives in an easily understandable format. By moving a mouse or merely touching the screen, the user directs the computer to provide information. Executive information systems use big-screen, high-quality monitors and produce full-color displays. An EIS allows top-level managers to ask questions and receive immediate answers in the form of graphs, charts, and reports. Fidelity Investment's EIS, for example, eliminates the need to produce the firm's 45-page financial report on paper. The user can bring up infor-

executive information system (EIS)
A user-friendly DSS designed specifically for executives. It's easy to use and requires no knowledge of the computer.

TABLE 5–5	DIFFERENCES BETWEEN AN MIS AND A DSS	
Management Information Systems	**Decision Support Systems**
1. The main effect is on structured tasks where standard operating procedures, decision rules, and information flows can be reliably predefined.	1. The impact is on decisions in which there is sufficient structure for computer and analytic aids to be of value but where managers' judgment is essential.
2. The main payoff is an improving efficiency by reducing costs, turn-around time, and so on, and by replacing clerical personnel.	2. The payoff is in extending the range and capability of managers' decision processes to help them improve their effectiveness.
3. The relevance for managers' decision-making is mainly indirect; for example, by providing reports and access to data.	3. The relevance for managers is the creation of a supportive tool, under their own control, that doesn't attempt to automate the decision process, predefine objectives, or impose solutions.
	4. A DSS tends to be aimed at the less well structured, underspecified problems that upper managers typically face.
	5. It attempts to combine the use of models or analytic techniques with traditional data access and retrieval functions.
	6. It focuses on features that make it easy to use by noncomputer people in an interactive mode.
	7. It emphasizes flexibility and adaptability to accommodate changes in the environment and the decision-making approach of the user.

Source: Reprinted by permission from Page 106 of *Computer Information Systems for Business,* by V. Thomas Dock and James C. Wetherbe. Copyright © 1988 by West Publishing. All rights reserved.

mation on the monitor, save it in an assortment of formats, and manipulate it using a variety of programs. Many executives believe that their EIS is strategic to their organization's success as it allows for more informal decision making and reduces the time needed to make those decisions.[36] For example, Domecq Importers, Inc., an alcoholic beverage distributor, blended an array of client/server products to create an EIS that turns internal and external data into a budgeting and competitor analysis tool for strategic management of the company. The system has led to dramatic changes in the way Domecq executives plot their business strategies.[37]

If EISs are to become strategic management tools, the need to match specific executive decisions with critical success factors is essential. *Critical success factors* provide the framework for linking the most critical operational activities with key executive activities.[38]

Developing the DSS

Developing and implementing a successful DSS isn't easy. Organizations must spend time planning the DSS. The system's goal is user satisfaction and better-quality decisions. Users' needs are a major consideration in developing a DSS; failure to consider these needs is a leading cause of DSS failure. One study reported that previous user involvement influences satisfaction with DSS and perceived DSS benefits. Decision makers involved in designing and specifying their requirements were found to be more satisfied with their DSS and have stronger perceptions of DSS benefits.[39] Users' needs must be met in terms of both hardware and software. For instance, hardware may not deliver information fast enough or software may not provide information in a useful form for decision making. Both problems result in dissatisfaction with the DSS.

The true test of a DSS is whether it yields information that managers can use. If invalid assumptions are made in designing the system, it will yield invalid information. For instance, if a DSS is developed that doesn't take competitive actions into consideration, managers may be making decisions that inaccurately assume there are no competitors. In developing a DSS, two of the most difficult tasks are deciding which elements to include in the system and understanding how these elements interact with each other.

A DSS helps a manager make decisions by providing timely, raw information. Some information technologies go a step further, interpreting information and, essentially, making the decision. Such technologies are usually called expert systems or artificial intelligence.

Expert Systems and Artificial Intelligence

Computers do several things better than humans. They're faster and more accurate, they can run all day and all night, and they're often cheaper than humans. But humans can think—they're more innovative than computers and can change or adapt to different situations. Computer scientists have worked for years to combine computers' speed and accuracy with the human ability to reason, adapt, and make decisions.

Artificial intelligence allows computers to solve problems involving imagination, abstract reasoning, and common sense. Computer scientists are trying to empower computers to behave as though they could think by perceiving and absorbing data, reasoning, and communicating in ways similar to human behavior. The term **expert systems** describes the computer hardware and software capable of making decisions. Expert systems are computer programs that imitate human thinking and offer advice or solutions to complex problems in much the same way that a human expert does. For instance, expert systems are used to plan shipping schedules, provide financial advice to investors, and help managers respond to competing firms' actions. Most financial institutions use expert systems in such areas as lending, financial planning, trading, fraud detection, auditing, and production selection.[40]

Whereas decision support systems provide information to managers covering a wide range of factors, expert systems cover much smaller fields of knowledge. Expert systems comprised of facts are decision rules gathered from "experts" in a specific field. The user interacts with the system, each asking questions of the other. An expert system provides recommendations and explains the logic used to arrive at those recommendations. While expert systems are yet to make the logical decisions humans can make, the quality of these systems is rapidly improving.

artificial intelligence
A technology that allows computers to solve problems involving imagination, abstract reasoning, and common sense.

expert system
The computer hardware and software capable of making decisions.

TRENDS IN INFORMATION SYSTEMS

The amount of information available to managers will continue to increase dramatically, making information systems even more crucial to firms. The business sector's use of computers to process information is expected to continue to grow rapidly. Virtually no firm, regardless of size, will be able to function efficiently without a computer-based information processing system.

The amount of computer power a dollar can buy has grown a thousand times every two decades, and this rate shows no sign of slowing. The trend toward smaller, faster, and less costly computers will also continue, fueled by advances in three areas: smaller computer chips, new operating systems, and better, faster communications technology.

Smaller, portable computers such as notebooks, subnotebooks, and personal digital assistants are changing the way people in business use information systems. Notebook computers now are as essential as a briefcase for many business travelers. Salespeople, reporters, writers, managers, and others use the small computers to work on airplanes, commuter trains, and in hotels as they communicate with coworkers in other places. Salespeople often have computers in their cars for quick access to information. Many no longer come into the office, preferring instead to work out of their homes, a practice known as *telecommuting*.

Telecommuting

The Information Age makes it possible for more people to work at home, staying in touch with the office through telecommuting. Link Resources, a New York research firm, reports that 8.4 million Americans now telecommute.[41] *PC Magazine* predicts that by the year 2000 there will be 25 million telecommuters in the U.S.[42] Currently, 12 percent of AT&T's workforce has a telecommuting-related arrangement, with one in three managers working from a remote site on a regular or occasional basis.[43] Several large firms such as J.C. Penney, Travelers Insurance, and IBM allow some employees to work at home and communicate with the office through computer-based information systems.

While technology is making telecommuting more practical, there are still issues within the workplace, concerning decision making in particular, that make the transition difficult and slow. Most companies that use telecommuting are still in the early stages of adoption, and they are trying to determine which jobs are suitable candidates for telecommuting. For managers who are unsure of trusting employees who telecommute, close monitoring in the early stage can allay concerns. However, workers who are problems in the office will be problems at home.[44]

Telecommuting can help firms reduce costs by reducing the need for office space. Oldsmobile, for example, is eliminating 4 of 16 zone offices in 1995 and will replace 5 others with so-called *virtual zone offices*. The virtual office will be comprised of people working at home and linked together via laptop computers, modems, and cellular phones.[45]

With mobile computers (laptops, notebooks) now making up about 20 percent of PC sales, information systems managers are working to give remote users the same level of support and applications now available at desktop workstations. Early adopters of telecommuting advise drawing up a policy that establishes guidelines for handling remote workers and to start small with a few pilot programs.[46] Until information systems become more powerful, workers who telecommute still don't have all the benefits of workers in the office. For decision makers, access to critical databases is limited due to security concerns.

Telecommuting is possible because new technologies have enabled managers to access company databases from home. Going one step further, the Internet allows managers to access databases from around the world. It's the fastest-growing segment of the so-called Information Superhighway, and no discussion of information technology is complete without mentioning the Internet.

The Internet

Perhaps the most profound information-related development for business in the last few years is the explosive growth of the Internet. The Internet has been available for years to computer experts and hackers—people who stay up late into the night tapping away at their keyboards to the soft glow of the computer screen. It has only been in the last half-decade that the Internet has become available for business through such services as America Online, Prodigy, Compuserve, and others.

The most important and universal application for the Internet is still electronic mail (e-mail). E-mail enables users anywhere in the world to communicate over the Internet at a fraction of the cost of a long-distance telephone call.

In 1994, a new contender for the second most universal application firmly established itself: the World Wide Web (WWW). The WWW presents a consistent, intuitive interface to virtually all the information on the Internet while masking its underlying complexity. There are now over 30,000 Web sites, and the number is doubling every 53 days.[47] For business, the implications are immense: suddenly there is a new broadcast, publishing, and communications medium that reaches millions of the world's largest organizations and most wealthy people, and promises to make access easy for nontechnical people as well. Marketing is the main business application so far, especially for small firms.[48] According to BIS Strategic Decisions, $20 to $30 billion of business-to-business merchandise was sold through electronic catalogs in 1993.[49] In June of 1994, GM's Saturn began advertising on Prodigy.[50] Sony New Technologies coordinates different divisions and makes their products available to computer users on the WWW. Sony is developing an Internet access service called Sony Online. The strategy is to develop a direct marketing channel and bypass conventional retail distribution channels.[51]

Businesses create a presence on the WWW by establishing a "home page." These home pages can be linked to other databases and computers called "servers." People who visit a home page on the Internet can choose what other information they want by clicking their mouse button when their cursor is over highlighted text or graphics. The special hyper-text markup language (html) used to create home pages makes possible this point-and-click navigation of the web. If you have access to the web, Table 5–6 presents a list of business home page addresses.

The Internet affects decision making in that it offers the potential for worldwide information gathering and discussion groups. It's too early to determine what uses managers will make of the Internet in key business decision making. However, its vast potential requires that managers continue to seek ways to use it to develop competitive advantage.

TABLE 5–6	SELECTED HOME PAGE ADDRESSES
AT&T	http://www.att.com
Compaq	http://www.compaq.com
Cray Research	http://www.cray.com
Hewlett Packard	http://www.hp.com
IBM	http://www.ibm.com
Intel	http://www.intel.com
Microsoft	http://www.microsoft.com
J.P. Morgan	http://www.jpmorgan.com
University of Houston	htpp://www.uh.edu
Shoponline	http://www.shoponline.com
Fidelity Investment	http://www.fid–inv.com

Source: Adapted from "Internet," *Business Week*, May 22, 1995, p. 99; "Internet Directory," *The Wall Street Journal*, June 29, 1995, pp. B5–B12.

Information systems have become a major part of today's organizations. Without them, managers wouldn't have immediate access to useful information. When used properly, they can increase business efficiency, assist managers in decision making, and even think like experts. Information systems will play an ever-increasing role in the business world and in society.

SUMMARY OF LEARNING OBJECTIVES

COMPARE PROGRAMMED AND NONPROGRAMMED DECISIONS.
Decisions are programmed to the extent that they are repetitive and routine and a definite procedure has been developed for handling them. Decisions are nonprogrammed when they are novel and unstructured.

CONTRAST INTUITIVE AND SYSTEMATIC DECISION MAKING.
Intuitive decision making involves the use of estimates, guesses, or hunches to decide among alternative courses of action. Most managers will admit that many of their decisions are influenced to a great extent by their intuitions. Systematic decision making is an organized, exacting, data-driven process. Systematic decision making requires the development of a clear set of objectives; a relevant information base; a team-based, consensus-seeking sharing of ideas and creativity; and exacting implementation and assessment.

IDENTIFY AND EXPLAIN THE NINE STEPS IN THE DECISION-MAKING PROCESS.
(1) Establish goals and objectives. Decision making is always conducted in the context of goals and objectives. (2) Identify and define the problem. Problems are defined as the realization that a discrepancy exists between a desired state and current reality. (3) Establish priorities. Unless the resources an organization has at its disposal are unlimited, it must prioritize its problems. (4) Determine causes of the problem. It is ordinarily difficult and usually ill-advised to determine a solution to a problem when the problem's cause is unknown. (5) Develop alternative solutions. Before a decision is reached, alternative solutions need to be created and developed, and their potential consequences must be explored. (6) Evaluate alternative solutions. Once alternatives have been developed, they must be evaluated and compared. (7) Select a solution. The purpose of selecting a particular solution is to solve a problem in order to achieve a predetermined end. (8) Implement the decision. Any decision is little more than an abstraction if it isn't implemented. (9) Follow up. Effective management involves periodic measurements of results.

EXPLAIN THE DIFFERENCE BETWEEN INDIVIDUAL AND GROUP DECISION MAKING.
Individual decision making is subject to behavioral factors involving a person's values, personality, propensity for risk, and potential for dissonance. These forces are heightened in a group decision-making environment. Groups usually take more time than individuals to reach a decision. However, bringing together specialists in a group situation has benefits in that the mutually reinforcing effects of their interaction can result in better decisions. Research has shown that consensus decisions with five or more participants are usually superior to individual decision making, majority vote, and leader decisions.

DEFINE THE TERMS COGNITIVE DISSONANCE AND ESCALATION OF COMMITMENT.
Cognitive dissonance is the lack of consistency among a person's cognitions after a decision is made. The escalation of commitment is when there is an increased commitment to a previous decision despite contrary information.

DESCRIBE BRAINSTORMING, THE DELPHI TECHNIQUE, AND THE NOMINAL GROUP TECHNIQUE.
In the process of brainstorming, a group generates ideas according to a firm set of rules while at the same time avoiding the inhibitions that are usually caused by face-to-face groups. The Delphi technique involves soliciting and comparing anonymous judgments on the topic of interest through a set of sequential questionnaires that are interspersed with summarized information and feedback of opinions from earlier responses. The nominal group technique is a process of bringing people together but initially not allowing them to actually communicate verbally. At a later stage in the NGT process, structured discussion is encouraged and monitored.

EXPLAIN THE TEAM APPROACH TO DECISION MAKING IN A TQM ENVIRONMENT.
Through the use of steering teams, natural management teams, work teams, and process improvement teams, organizations can make decisions that result in continuous improvement of their operations. The steering team consists of top management (the people who establish the organization's strategic objectives). The natural management team consists of a manager and those managers or supervisors who report directly to her. Work teams consist of non-managerial employees and their manager or supervisor in a department or unit. Process improvement teams consist of anyone from the above-mentioned teams who may have knowledge about the problem. The process improvement team is the unit that sets out to make decisions that solve organizational problems within the context of organizationwide objectives.

EXPLAIN HOW AN MIS CAN HELP DECISION MAKING
Managers can use an MIS to gather, store, and process the information needed to make decisions.

EXPLAIN HOW A DECISION SUPPORT SYSTEM WORKS
A decision support system uses a user-friendly interface to enable managers to retrieve data from company databases. It also allows for rapid processing of data in graphical or text formats.

EXPLAIN THE BENEFITS AND COSTS OF TELECOMMUTING
Telecommuting allows companies to reduce overhead costs associated with office space and allows workers more time to be productive by eliminating long commutes. On the other hand, for security reasons, key data often aren't available to telecommuters, and many managers don't have training in managing people who aren't physically present.

REVIEW AND DISCUSSION QUESTIONS

Recall

1. Why is decision making sometimes called the essence of management?
2. Identify and connect the nine steps in making a decision.
3. Name the different types of decisions.
4. What are the three components of decision making in a TQM environment?

Understanding

5. Decision making occurs at both the individual and group levels in most organizations. Managers need to know the strengths and weaknesses of both approaches. Explain and provide examples of situations where managers should use individual or group decision making.
6. Why does decision making in a TQM environment focus on continuous improvement? Can't managers simply make one right decision that solves problems completely?
7. Decision making always ends with implementation and follow-up steps. Why are these so important to the process?

Application

8. Say you are the manager of 50 people in a department of a major retail discounter. You have recently received word that the customer service center has been receiving complaints about the quality of the goods in your department. How would you decide what to do with this information?
9. Much of what we believe about decision making has a historical basis, not just an experimental or research basis. Identify an important decision facing a local politician or national business figure. Then develop a list of goals and information associated with the particular decision. What information is the politician or businessperson likely to have that you lack? How might that person's goals differ from yours? How can a decision maker effectively combine many different people's goals or information?
10. Describe an experience where you have decided to stop doing business with a company. What led to this decision?
11. How can managers use an MIS to improve decision making?
12. What are the main considerations in the development of a decision support system?
13. What are the limitations of artificial intelligence and export systems?
14. How does telecommuting affect organizational decision making?

KEY TERMS

artificial intelligence, p. 141
brainstorming, p. 132
certainty, p. 125
computer network, p. 138
database, p. 136
database management, p. 138
decision, p. 117
decision formulation, p. 122
decision implementation, p. 122
decision-making process, p. 117

decision support system, p. 138
Delphi technique, p. 132
escalation of commitment, p. 129
executive information system, p. 140
expert system, p. 141
intuitive decision making, p. 120
local area network, p. 138
management information system, p. 135
nominal group technique, p. 133
nonprogrammed decision, p. 118

proactive decision, p. 120
problem, p. 123
process improvement team, p. 130
programmed decision, p. 118
reactive decision, p. 120
risk, p. 125
satisficer, p. 125
systematic decision making, p. 121
uncertainty, p. 125

CASE STUDY

Chrysler Builds Quality through Employee Empowerment

You should have Chrysler CEO Bob Eaton's problem. Demand for his company's cars, trucks, and minivans has been powerful. But the chief executive of Chrysler, the most profitable automaker in the world on a per vehicle basis, can't expand as fast as he wants in global markets because he can't find enough good people quickly enough. "For the first time in Chrysler's recent history," he laments, "we have the capital available, but we don't have enough engineers and managers to grow any faster abroad than we currently are, which is about 20 percent a year."

Only a few years ago Chrysler was near death. There's still much that needs improving, the company is gaining in productivity, but could do better. For example, it wants to catch up to Toyota, which leads the world in terms of worker's time needed to produce a car. "In the United States," says Eaton, "Ford is the most productive, we're next, and GM is last." The automotive consulting firm of Harbour & Associates calculates that Toyota requires 18 to 20 hours to assemble a car; Ford 24; Chrysler 28; and GM 32. Toyota also leads the world in quality, but Chrysler is catching up.

The company lately has turned out a fleet of hot-selling new cars: the four-door subcompact Neon; the Ram full-size pick-up, which even has a console up front that can be used as a desk for a portable computer; and the hand-built Viper convertible. In 1994, earnings rose 246 percent, to $3.7 billion, and sales were up 20 percent, to $52.2 billion, both far above previous records. The company full funded its pension plan after being in dangerous deficit since the 1950s, and 91,550 of Chrysler's 125,825 employees collected a profit-sharing bonus averaging $8,000, also an all-time high. Eaton says that in North American automotive operations alone, Chrysler undoubtedly out-earned General Motors, and possibly Ford. Unlike Chrysler, both its U.S. competitors get much of their profit from finance companies and other subsidiaries.

Given the performance, there might be some lessons to learn from Chrysler's comeback. When asked how Chrysler was able to be so successful, Eaton said, "If I had to use one word, it's empowerment. That is the biggest reason." Eaton, who ran GM's European operations out of Zurich before coming to Chrysler in 1992, added, "At GM, I didn't go a week without being involved in a product decision, but since I've been at Chrysler, I've basically never been involved in one."

Chrysler's innovation was to form so-called "platform teams." The company puts all the engineers and designers assigned to specific project together on a single floor, along with representatives of marketing, finance, purchasing, and even outside suppliers, and grant them considerable decision-making autonomy. Close contact keeps the team fast and efficient. As with many good ideas, the discovery of platform teams was serendipitous. When Chrysler acquired American Motors in 1988, it decided to keep AMC's corps of 700 engineers intact. Rather than reassign them to functional departments, such as steering or powertrain, it put them to work en masse developing the 1993 Grand Cherokee. Until then, industry practice called for designers to draw, engineers to fabricate, and manufactures to tinker—performing their operations in isolation and in sequence. When a design advanced from one department to the next, the process was known industrywide as "throwing it over the wall."

When Chrysler sets out to create a new model or revamp on old one, Eaton explains, it forms a team of about 700 people. A vice president acts as "godfather" to the group, but all of the actual work is defined by leaders below that rank, and the group organizes itself as it sees fit.

Eaton and a dozen senior managers meet with the leaders to sketch a vision for the vehicle and set aggressive goals: for design, performance, fuel economy, and cost. Basically, Eaton explains, management works out a contract with the team, after which it is turned loose. He said, "That contract simply sets out all the objectives we hope they achieve. Then they go away and do it, and they don't get back to us unless they have a major problem. And so far, they aren't getting into major problems. Now, if management became involved with them, inevitably we would give our opinion, and we would get our imprint upon it. It would become Chrysler's vehicle or Bob Eaton's vehicle. But because we stay out, of it, it becomes their vehicle, and they work much, much harder, with much more pride, and the success or failure is theirs. As a result, every single vehicle that we have done since I have been at Chrysler has come in below its total investment target and its cost-per-car target."

When disputes erupt, they are fought out decided by team members. Ideas, big and small, can come from anyone. When teams have power to create the car and responsibility to meet the budget, they do meet the budget. Because the teams are efficient and motivated to hold down costs, Chrysler has created a car from scratch for as little as $1.3 billion, which it generally costs its U.S. competitors a lot more. Says Maryann Keller, auto analyst at Furman Selz: "Chrysler is clearly the best of the American trio in empowerment, cost structure, and having the newest products."

When Chrysler was having problems with quality several years ago, Eaton made it a priority to be the company's No. 1 quality advocate. In the spirit of empowerment, he pushed responsibility for quality down to the plant level. He now makes monthly factory visits to reinforce the quality message. Throughout the ranks at Chrysler, Eaton has won praise for encouraging independence and initiative. "Eaton lets you run your business," said one vice president. Eaton is viewed throughout the company as a coach and a listener who eschews the trappings of power in favor of teamwork and consensus building.

Chrysler's swing to break-down-the-walls empowerment is nothing new or unique. Eaton says that everywhere he worked before—when he was at GM at home or abroad—everybody attempted to empower self-directed teams. "I've tried to do it a dozen times in my career," he said. "But it's never been as successful to the extent it is at Chrysler. And that's because there are no committees, no hierarchy outside the group. When decisions are made, they're made by somebody down in the organization how knows a helluva lot more about the issue than I do."

As Eaton surveys the auto market, he concludes that its success, like that of most everything else in the world, comes down to people. The biggest difference between Japanese and U.S. companies back in the 1970s he says, was that they were engaging their people, and we were not. "We're making tremendous progress in really involving all of our people," he says. "But we're not where we want to be yet. We've got a far more productive white-collar workforce in the United States than the Japanese have, but what we still don't have is a sufficiently productive blue-collar workers along now." For example, they are more involved in designing their own work and creating self-directed work teams.

Eaton said, "There's no magic. What will make all the difference in business will be how well you train your workforce—and how well you empower."

QUESTIONS

1. Empowerment refers to the practice of pushing decision making down to the employees who are involved with the work process. Do you think most blue-collar employees are readily receptive to this responsibility? What can a manager do to help them adjust to making decisions that affect the production process?

2. Team decision making requires building consensus before a decision is actually made and actions taken. What are some ways to build consensus in a team setting?

3. Not all decisions should be made by consensus. Describe some decisions that an automaker like Chrysler needs to make that shouldn't wait for consensus.

Sources: Adapted from: Eileen P. Gunn, "Empowerment That Pays Off," *Fortune*, March 20, 1995, pp. 145–146; Alex Taylor, III, "Will Success Spoil Chrysler?" *Fortune*, January 10, 1994; and Douglas Lavin, "Robert Eaton Thinks 'Vision' is Overrated and He's Not Alone," *The Wall Street Journal*, October 4, 1993, pp. A1, A6.

CASE STUDY

Dudley C. Jackson Employees Run the Show

How many presidents of wholesale distributors can leave their business for 14 days at a time and not worry about calling the office? Probably not too many. How many executives can afford to leave their company for 20 hours a week—sometimes longer—to participate in community affairs? Again, probably not too many. But Ken Jackson, the dynamic president and leader of Dudley C. Jackson, Inc. (DCJ), a specialty distributor in Helena, Alabama, is able to do both because he has entrusted much of the organization's decision making to its employees. Jackson spends about 20 hours a week offsite, lecturing to business groups and high school students, speaking about total quality management, and doing community services. He is able to be away from the office because he has decentralized decision making and created self-managing employees.

The idea behind employee self-management is for workers to become, to a large degree, their own managers. In attempting to use their human resources more fully, many organizations have moved beyond the mentality that managers make decisions and employees are simply expected to do what they're told. Self-management involves an increasing reliance on workers' creative and intellectual capabilities, not just their physical labor. This concept has been carried through successfully at Dudley C. Jackson.

DCJ was founded in 1949 by Dudley Jackson, now 83. He and his wife, Caroline, who have been married for 58 years, serve as co-chairmen of the board and still come to the office daily. The company has evolved from primarily providing lubrication equipment to a specialty distributor with expertise in three areas.

DCJ offers a full range of equipment to pump and apply coatings during production processes. Customers include wood furniture and cabinet manufacturers, and metal fabricators. The company also offers specialized pumping and dispensing systems for materials like ink, mastics, adhesives, and food products, as well as its original core business of lubrication equipment and systems. DCJ's major market areas as Alabama, Tennessee, Mississippi, and the Florida panhandle.

The company worked its way up to being named the 1993-1994 Alabama Productivity award winner by making two major moves. The first was the introduction in March 1991 of its See Excellence Everywhere (SEE) quality program. SEE challenges employees to look for ways of improving productivity and quality, not just in their individual work areas, but companywide. The statement attached to the program was, "Do the right thing, the right way, the first time, every time: From the customer's point of view."

In order to promote more effective communication within the company, DCJ restructured its management organization in November 1992. The result was to move from a traditional pyramid, management style to a "wheel" format, offering a direct line of communication between Jackson and DCJ's five operation managers.

The changes haven't gone unnoticed. They have helped to empower employees to the point where Jackson can spend 80 to 100 hours a month engaged in various community and civic activities. DCJ believes that, in order to implement a successful quality program, you've got to treat your employees as though they're your customers. At DCJ that philosophy has worked wonders. The company has virtually no turnover. Each employee has an average seniority of 10 years, with 19 of its 24 employees having five or more years experience with the company. Flex-time is encouraged, and the dress code is casual.

DCJ, which gives 5 percent of pre-tax profits to charity each year, also gives back to its employees via a retirement plan. Its 401K retirement program matches 50 cents on the dollar up to 5 percent of an employee's salary. However, in 1994 the company contributed $1.50 for each $1 saved by an employee.

Perhaps the biggest benefit president Ken Jackson bestows on his employees is the gift of empowerment. With Jackson removed from the business for up to 20 hours a week, his employees are empowered, and motivated, to make the major decisions. When he's not in the office, Jackson leaves word of where he'll be. However, his staff has never had the need to track him down.

"Our employees understand their level of empowerment in order to immediately address any dissatisfied customer," says Jackson. "Our primary focus is not on who is responsible for a problem, but rather on how we can prevent a recurrence. Our employees understand that their ideas will be considered."

Empowerment places responsibilities for spotting and solving problems squarely on the employees. "Empowerment is one step beyond involvement," says William C. Byham, co-author of *Zapp! The Art Lightning of Empowerment*. Involvement encourages supervisors to solicit comments from their workers and then act on those ideas considered viable. According to Byham, empowerment adds an imperative, as well as the element of shared responsibility. "Empowerment requires leaders to not just ask for suggestions, but to let employees make the decisions and then implement the actions necessary for change," he says.

Jackson explains that while he sets the company goals and provides the resources for them to be carried out, DCJ's employees are the ones who see to it that goals are met. "Most business have individuals who understand segments of the business better than the owner does," says Jackson. "The owner or general manager should be the person who gives the focus to where the business is going, develops the strategic plan, and knows the big picture. What I have is the version. The employees have the mission."

That mission is achieved best through empowerment. When employees are treated with respect and trust, they develop a sense of ownership and a belief that the company will give something back.

"You can't delegate overnight, and managers can't expect someone to run their business immediately," says Jackson. "First, you've got to let them make small decisions with a potential for failure, then large decisions, the really big decisions. If they fail, allow them to correct the situation and improve it themselves. Think of the confidence that gives them."

QUESTIONS

1. DCJ is a distributor with 24 employees, 19 of which have had more than five years experience with the firm. Do you think that the small number of employees and the relatively long time they have spent with the firm gives DCJ an edge in creating an empowered workforce? Explain.

2. What is the role of incentive systems in the creating of empowered workers?

3. Ken Jackson discusses the power of allowing employees to make increasingly responsible decisions. Explain how proceeding in this fashion affects both the employee and the manager.

Sources: Adapted from John R. Johnson, "Productivity Enhances Profitability," *Industrial Distribution*, February 1995, pp. 18–20; Howard Rothman, "The Power of Empowerment," *Nation's Business*, June 1993, pp. 49, 52; Frank Shipper and Charles C. Manz, "Employee Self-Management Without Formally Designated Teams: An Alternative Road to Empowerment," *Organizational Dynamics*, Winter 1992, pp. 48–61.

VIDEO CASE

Decision Making

In a global economy, sound business decisions depend on a number of important factors. The quality of managerial decisions can determine a company's success or failure. A recent study concluded that managers spend approximately 50 percent of their time dealing with the consequences of bad decision making.

In this video case study, two successful businesses—the Second City Theater in Chicago and Heavenly Ski Resort in Lake Tahoe—explore the following decision-making topics:

1. Managers make different decisions under different business conditions.
2. When managers take steps to explore and evaluate alternatives, it leads to more effective decisions.
3. All managers need to be aware of the many factors that can affect the decision-making process.

Broadly defined, decision making is a process of choosing among alternative courses of action. In the business world, this process takes place under varying conditions of certainty and risk. Decision making is more likely to be effective when approached in a series of steps that explore and evaluate alternatives.

1. Identify the problem.
2. Generate alternative solutions.
3. Evaluate the alternatives.
4. Select the best alternative.
5. Implement the decision.
6. Evaluate the decision.

To evaluate a decision, managers must gather information that can shed light on its effectiveness. Although most managers would prefer to follow all of these decision-making steps, time and circumstances don't always allow it. This decision-making process can also be influenced by other important factors such as intuition, emotion, stress, confidence, and risk propensity.

Second City has grown from its roots as a small "mom and pop" theater, to a large, internationally known corporate enterprise. Rather than investing all its resources into its immensely popular Old Town Chicago improv theater, the Second City has decided to translate its expertise into other ventures, such as television, corporate training, and other theaters in Toronto, suburban Chicago, and Detroit.

Heavenly Lake Tahoe accommodates nearly 750,000 skiers per year, and competes as one of eight large Tahoe-area resorts. Like the Second City Theater, managers at Heavenly must make decisions affecting the growth of the company in less than ideal conditions.

Although following the six decision-making steps may lead to a sounder decision-making process, theory doesn't always play out in practice. Management may follow some steps, but perhaps not all of

them, depending on the factors affecting the decision-making process. "Most of the managers are encouraged to make a decision right away and don't hold on to the problem. It's such a fast pace that I want them to just go on to the next thing and not hold the problem back. I've empowered them to pretty much make their own decisions," said Steve Jacobson, director of food and beverage at Heavenly.

Making people laugh takes a lot of hard work and courage, as well as creativity and insight. Decisions about artistic design don't always fit the mold of the decision-making model. Kelly Leonard, associate producer at Second City, said, "We did a show which was a parody of Our Town and it was at times brilliant and at times not. It got great reviews, it was very intricate in its knowledge of Our Town. However, it demanded a certain understanding of the play and of the Second City form to really get all the jokes. What we found is that though critics loved it and many of us loved it here, the audience didn't understand it. We tried an advertising campaign to support it, which to that time we had not advertised much and it didn't work and people wouldn't come. So we had to switch over the show."

Both the Second City Theater and Heavenly Lake Tahoe face the challenge of providing entertainment to consumers. In their day-to-day operations, both companies experience the need to make decisions in varying conditions of certainty, uncertainty, and risk. Both companies follow the steps of the decision-making model when feasible. Identifying a problem, generating alternatives, evaluating the alternatives, selecting the best alternative, implementing the decision, and evaluating the decision. Factors such as intuition, emotion and stress, and confidence or risk propensity can also have an impact on the decision-making process. Awareness of the nature of decision making, its important steps, and influential factors may help managers minimize the time they spend responding to the consequences of poor decision making. This can enable managers to spend more time maximizing opportunities for growth.

QUESTIONS

1. Decision making is described in the video as a series of steps. Do you agree with the six steps as outlined in the video? What additional procedures might be added to the process?
2. There are situations where decision making requires input from many people, and times when decisions have to be made by an individual. Describe a situation that would require wide input, and one where an individual should make a decision without outside input. How do these situations differ?
3. Managerial decision making is affected by something called "risk propensity." What does this term mean? How can managers improve their risk propensity?

APPLICATION EXERCISE

WHAT CAR BUYERS LOOK FOR IN A CAR

A study asked potential car buyers what characteristics are very important in their purchase decisions. The eight characteristics are:

1. Price: dollar amount of purchase.
2. Features: options (e.g., tape player, power controls, sports package).
3. Styling: exterior design and look.
4. Foreign origin: model bears a non-U.S. nameplate (e.g., Honda).
5. U.S. origin: model bears U.S. (Big Three) nameplate.
6. Reliability: record of absence of need for repair; low maintenance.
7. Safety: crash, repair, and survival record of the make.
8. Feel: interior features of the car (e.g., seating, controls).

First, rank each of the eight features in terms of their importance to you. Second, rank the items in terms of how you believe the typical American car purchaser would rate them. That is, which item would receive the most votes of "very important?" Which would be second, third, and so on.

Then compare your rankings with other class members' rankings. Next listen to the survey rankings provided by your teacher. Now divide the class up into groups of six to eight people. Use different techniques described in the chapter to try to reach group consensus on the most important features. Notice how your own decisions are influenced by decisions of others in the group. What values influence your and others' decisions? How do the different personalities in the group affect the ability to reach consensus?

	Your Ranking	Your Estimated Typical Ranking	Survey Ranking
1. Price			3
2. Features			7
3. Styling			6
4. Foreign origin			8
5. U.S. origin			5
6. Reliability			1
7. Safety			2
8. Feel			4

Actual survey ranking: 1.-3; 2.-7; 3.-6; 4.-8; 5.-5; 6.-1; 7.-2; and 8.-4.

Source: "Detroit May Be Missing the Mark that Matters Most," Survey of 1,250 adults conducted July 13–18, 1990, for *Business Week* by Louis Harris & Associates, Inc. Results should be accurate to within three percentage points. *Business Week*, October 22, 1990, p. 91.

CHAPTER 6

Planning

After studying this chapter, you should be able to:

❖ Define <u>planning</u> and discuss the characteristics of effective planning.

❖ Describe four characteristics of modern firms that underscore the need for planning.

❖ Discuss the benefits organizations gain by planning.

❖ Describe the steps in the planning process.

❖ Explain the following quality-based planning methods: (1) Plan, do, check, act (PDCA), (2) time-based planning, and (3) planning for continuous improvement.

❖ Describe quantitative measures for different types of business objectives.

❖ Compare quality-based planning with other approaches.

❖ Explain the advantages and disadvantages of decentralized planning.

❖ Discuss the primary planning objectives.

❖ Explain the difference between variable and moving budgets.

❖ Explain the difference between strategic, operational, and tactical planning.

CAI Successfully Launches Service Quality Program

In many organizations, quality initiatives have as their principal focus an improvement in service and operations. However, Canadian Airlines International's "Service Quality" program also was the basis for carrying out one of the largest employee training projects in North American business annals. Planning played a major part in the successful delivery of the training program. It helped organize tasks, kept people focused, and delivered the needed training to the right people at the right time.

CAI employees

In 1994, after a year and a half of preparation and training, CAI switched over its entire reservations, airport, cargo, and financial information systems to a new supplier. For those involved in planning, developing, and delivering the training to prepare CAI's employees, contractors, and suppliers, this was a major feat of logistics and coordination. The project scope included the following:

- ❖ The total transition project comprised 13,000 milestone events, with 50,000 tasks.
- ❖ 12,000 people attended training in a 96-day "window" for a total of 50,000 days of training.
- ❖ 26 classrooms were in use in Canada, London, Beijing, Tokyo, and Hong Kong.

The real beginning of this story was in 1990, when CAI was coming to terms with the impact of five recent mergers, which reformed the company. Routes, aircraft configurations, facilities, and collective agreements had to be standardized while management and many employees were resolving cultural differences and coping with staffing redundancies. To turn the situation around, a new strategy, called *service quality*, was adopted. The new focus on quality was aimed at enhancing service standards and reducing costs by regaining customer focus and improving core business processes.

The Employee Training and Development group played a key role in supporting the new strategy. Employees were provided with quality skills training and were brought together in teams to change the systems and processes they worked with. For the training group, this meant launching a whole new spectrum of services to deliver quality skills and assist improvement teams throughout the company. The overall result was a tremendous leap in customer approval ratings, as well as increased employee involvement in improvement initiatives and in the developing of a unified culture to provide quality service.

Because CAI had to keep running while the training progressed, a limited number of people could be released for training at any one time.

Even with training running in two shifts, some employees would be trained up to three months ahead of time. They would go back to using the existing system and then, on cut-over weekends, switch back and apply their new skills and knowledge while ensuring seamless customer service.

The training group's earlier involvement with quality improvement efforts meant that standardization of the basic processes was in place. In particular, a core "training for impact" strategy focused all development around analyzing and solving business problems. Until this time, training productivity had been measured by activity. That is, how many seats had been filled, how many courses given, and how many annual days of training delivered per employee. By moving away from routine activity-based training, CAI was able to install a regimen where each training activity was tested against the value added to customer service.

This shift in the measure of success affected the overall outcome of the transition training project. For example, with the training courses for the new airport reservations systems averaging three weeks each, it was daunting to consider the logistics of training over 4,000 agents. With the adoption of the training-for-impact strategy, the task became to identify those competencies that were needed to allow basic operation of the systems, leave out the "nice to know," and ensure employees weren't retrained in skills they already possessed. Each day of unnecessary training saved was equal to savings of 16 person-years of production plus 66 weeks of instructor time—or approximately $850,000.

Planning and executing the change effort at CAI was aided by the overall focus on customers. The focus on internal customers ensured the early and continuous involvement of future trainees. External customer focus provided a guiding hand when the volume and complexity of issues to be resolved became daunting.

Project planning also played a big part. In an organization whose operation is schedule driven, the urge to leap into action—and not be late—is constant. The significant amount of time spent on planning and reviewing the plan for completeness and connectivity to 25 other plans created some frustrations. However, this approach did ensure that the training plan coincided with the overall corporate plan and ongoing operations. The discipline to stick to the plan and a significant change process put a damper on endless requests for individual variations.

Source: Adapted from Rob Muller, "Training for Change," *Canadian Business Review,* Spring 1995, pp. 16–19; and Cecil Footer, "Tough Guys Don't Cuss," *Canadian Business,* February 1995, pp. 22–28.

How does an organization or a manager prepare for the future? Understanding and applying the basic principles of planning can help. This means continually looking ahead for opportunities and threats, and calculating the next move. Planning forces a firm to ask: What decisions need to be made today for us to be ready for tomorrow and the years beyond? In a total quality management environment, planning focuses on exceeding customer expectations, meeting competitive challenges, and committing to long-term organizational performance.

All organizations operate in uncertain environments. The opening vignette shows how Canadian Airlines used planning to organize a major training initiative. For an organization to succeed, management somehow must cope with, and adapt to, change and uncertainty. Planning is management's most valuable tool to help it adapt to change. If an organization doesn't plan, its position and fate will mostly be the result of chance. If management wishes to have any control over the firm's direction, it must plan. Otherwise it will have to rely on defensive reactions rather than proactive actions. Management will be forced to respond to current pressures rather than act to achieve the organization's long-term goals.

In one way or another, every manager plans. But the approach to planning, the manner of arriving at plans, and the comprehensiveness of planning can differ greatly from organization to organization. Formal planning distinguishes effective managers from ineffective ones.

If you wish to effectively manage the performance of individuals and organizations, you must understand the concept of, and the necessity for, planning. Planning is the part of the management process that attempts to define the organization's future.[1]

This chapter examines planning and its uses for modern organizations. There are different types of planning activity and different ways of putting plans together. You will gain an understanding of operational, tactical, and strategic plans, and then learn a six-step planning process. The chapter concludes with an overview of several planning methods, including those used in a quality-based organization.

WHAT IS PLANNING?

As technology expands, global competition heats up, and the speed of new product development increases. Planning can help a firm be more competitive in such a volatile environment. Planning enables a firm to respond to changing business demands, market conditions, and customer expectations. To be effective, planning must be flexible and responsive, and often should include input from persons throughout all levels of the organization. It should not be totally controlled by a few planners at the top of the hierarchy.

Chapter 5 introduced you to the central management function of decision making. Decision making can only be conducted within the context of company values, a mission statement, goals, and objectives. As noted in Chapter 1, *planning* is the process by which managers examine their internal and external environments, ask fundamental questions about their organization's purpose, and establish a mission, goals, objectives, and actions (Figure 6–1). Planning includes all the activities that lead to the definition of objectives and to the determination of appropriate courses of action to achieve those objectives.

Quality pioneer Armand Feigenbaum emphasized objectives and the actions necessary to achieve them when he defined planning as "thinking out in advance the sequence of actions to accomplish a proposed course of action in doing work to accomplish certain objectives."[2] Planning helps organizations achieve results. Ultimately, the true test of any manager is whether he is able to achieve results that are aligned with the values and mission of the organization.

Planning, at its best, means that decisions made today will produce useful results at a later date. The planning process is dynamic, involving many variables from the firm's internal and external environments, as well as the firm's central or core values. Usually, the planning process is systematic and, in leading organizations, involves people at all levels.

Planning Is Systematic

Planning, like decision making, is most effective when it's systematic. Consider a firm that brings together employees from several departments to form a team charged with updating

FIGURE 6–1
Planning Results in
Organizational Missions,
Goals, and Objectives

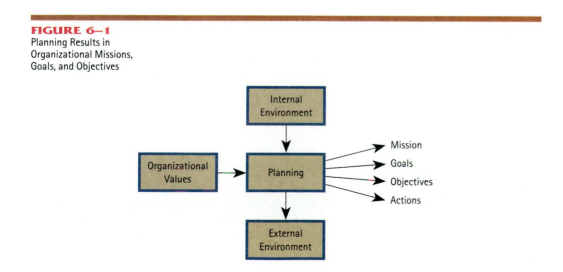

the firm's personal computers. As part of the planning process, the team considers costs and budgets, technical specifications, and the type and amount of hardware and software purchases and support. This part of the planning process leads to the development of a plan for a timely and cost-effective acquisition of personal computers. Final budgets, financing arrangements, delivery timetables, and operating policies are set. This systematic approach to planning is likely to result in effective action.

Planning Involves Everyone

Around the political world, large centralized states have succumbed to global pressures. No longer able to produce quality goods and services for its people, the Soviet Union broke apart at the end of 1991. The large, centralized bureaucracy that planned the production and distribution of goods and services in the former Soviet Union was not efficient enough to match world levels. And people of the former Soviet Union, with their access to information about the outside world, knew that countries with less centralized planning were able to offer more and better-quality goods and services. In a sense it was the decentralized control of the world's newest primary resource—information—that led to the demise of the world's largest centralized bureaucracy—the former Soviet Union.

centralized planning
System in which responsibility for planning lies with the organization's highest level.

decentralized planning
System in which responsibility for planning lies with workers and lower levels of the organization.

With **centralized planning**, responsibility for planning lies with the highest level of the organization. For the Soviets, this meant the central government. With **decentralized planning**, responsibility for planning lies with everyone, including workers and lower levels of the organization. In quality-based organizations, workers are called upon regularly to participate in the planning process and to implement the plan. Quality-based planning emphasizes worker involvement in determining objectives, the use of resources, and implementation.

Many organizations have found that moving from a centralized to a decentralized structure helped improve quality, productivity, and competitiveness. A number of speakers at the 1994 American Production and Inventory Control Society convention addressed the future of large organizations. Alvin Toffler, author of futurist books like *Future Shock* and *The Third Wave,* said that large organizations of all types must "demassify" because they can't effectively process all the information available today. Lumbering bureaucracies are being replaced by agile corporations better able to use information technology.[3]

The federal government of the United States, for example, is on the brink of serious decentralization. Although Democrats and Republicans have greatly different visions of government's role, both want to create a smaller, nimbler, more market-driven bureaucracy. A number of formerly federal programs will be shifted to states, cities, and counties. Washington's attempt at decentralization will give states more freedom to experiment with health care, welfare, and other services.[4]

On the other hand, decentralization isn't for everyone. Decentralized planning requires a well-developed communications network so that independent units don't spin out of control. For example, since taking over as chief agency officer at the Equitable Life Assurance, Joe Sequet has made changes that put the home office more firmly in control of what happens in the field. Reversing a company trend toward decentralization of field functions away from the home office, the changes wrought by Sequet create a more uniform way of recruiting, training, and supervising agents, and provide structure for greater field management interaction with executive management in the home office.[5]

Planning is central to competitiveness and quality for firms of all sizes and types in the global economy. The ability to allocate resources according to a plan ensures that firms are able to meet the new competitive challenges. The next section examines more closely some primary reasons planning is necessary.

WHY PLANNING IS NECESSARY

Planning is the process by which a firm links its decision-making process to its superordinate values and mission, and establishes goals and objectives. Planning puts purpose into action. Without planning, firms can only react to changes in the environment, technology, and customer demands. With careful planning, a firm can both anticipate and influence upcoming events.

Four characteristics of the modern organization underscore the need for planning: (1) pressure to reduce cycle times, (2) increased organizational complexity, (3) increased global competition, and (4) the impact of planning on other management functions.[6] Planning is one effective way that managers can address each of these characteristics, as we will describe next.

Pressure to Reduce Cycle Times

Cycle time reduction (CTR) has become a key goal for organizations. Cycle time refers to the length of time required to complete a process and to be ready to begin anew. For example, automobile manufacturers compete fiercely to reduce the new product development cycle time. Of the big three U.S. manufacturers, Chrysler has the fastest new product development cycle time, being able to create a new offering in 2.5 years. By comparison, Ford and General Motors cycle times are more than three years. Toyota leads the way with a new product development cycle time of two years.

cycle time reduction (CTR) Length of time required to complete a process and to be ready to begin anew.

High-performing, competitive organizations have realized that although in the past, economy of scale was key, today **economy of time** is key. Sam Walton said that everyone thought the success of Wal-Mart was a result of placing large stores in small towns and evolving to superstores in large cities (economies of scale). In reality, as he pointed out, the key was having faster inventory turns (economy of time). Like Wal-Mart, organizations of all types are putting significant planning effort into improving functionality, reducing time, and accommodating the needs of people who interact with the organization.[7]

economy of time Essentially, having faster inventory turns. In the past, organizations grew successful through sheer size (economy of scale); now they grow successful through speed (economy of time).

It's critical to note that managers shouldn't apply CTR merely to achieve blinding speed. Cycle time reduction in companies should be done in a way that simultaneously reduces costs and increases customer satisfaction. This relationship is expressed in Figure 6–2.

Increased Organizational Complexity

As firms and economies become larger and more complex, so does the manager's job. Few decisions made in a firm—research and development, production, finance, marketing—can be made independently of other decisions. More products and more services add to the complexity of managing the business. The more markets a firm competes in, the more products it offers, and the more competitors in the markets, the greater is the internal complexity. Formerly the Big Three auto firms—GM, Ford, and Chrysler—competed among themselves only. Now they compete among at least 30 major auto firms worldwide. In his book *The Fifth Discipline*, Peter Senge makes the point that to remain competitive in the global economy, organizations must learn to be comfortable with uncertainty and complexity. Managers must develop a capacity for thinking clearly and continuously about the unknown future.[8] Planning helps firms deal with complexity and uncertainty by providing a road map for change. With such a road map an organization can move with the forces of global competition without straying off course.

FIGURE 6–2
Cycle Time Reduction Leads to
Lower Costs and Improved
Customer Service

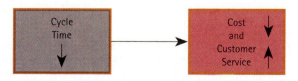

Source: James C. Wetherbe, "Principles of Cycle Time Reduction," *Cycle Time Research*, 1995, p. 1.

Increased Global Competition

New customers, new markets, and new parts of the world pose both opportunities and competitive threats to a firm. Planning is vital to survival in this expanded marketplace. In the last five years, Eastern Europe and satellites of the former Soviet Union have entered the global economy in a more meaningful way as restrictions have been lifted on trade and transportation. Smaller countries in Southeast Asia—Hong Kong, South Korea, Singapore, and Taiwan (the so-called *little tigers*)—have attempted to emulate Japan's manufacturing success. China, India, Vietnam, Latin America, and Africa pose similar market opportunities and competitive threats in the future.

A more diverse consumer population has created new markets. Firms have been able to expand their opportunities through the Hispanic, Asian, African-American, single-parent, and single-person markets. This diverse population has also created a challenge to traditional hiring and managing practices. Firms have had to reexamine and adjust their hiring, managing, and benefit plans.

The economic issue of global competition is forcing companies to become more flexible and client oriented, while demanding that they simultaneously lower costs.[9] Driven by global competition, businesses are being forced to change at an unprecedented rate. For those who are able to manage change effectively, it becomes the key to success. Every change represents an opportunity to increase the quality and competitiveness of the firm.[10] Planning is the key to ensuring an adequate business response to global competition.

Impact on Other Management Functions

Plans direct most other key organizational activities—organizing, managing, selling, training, promoting—so plans must be in place prior to a company's embarking on these activities. Unplanned activities can cause a firm to tamper with the system, to move in multiple, contradictory directions, and to give workers an unclear vision. Plans must cover this wide domain of subsequent organizational activities or else the firm will likely find itself adrift.

As we've seen, internal and external forces have made planning necessary for the modern organization's survival. The next section explains some specific benefits of planning.

BENEFITS OF PLANNING

Specific benefits of planning include (1) coordination of effort, (2) preparation for change, (3) development of performance standards, and (4) development of managers (Table 6–1).

Coordination of Effort

Management exists because the work of individuals and groups in organizations must be coordinated, and planning is one important technique for coordinating effort. An effective

TABLE 6-1	BENEFITS OF PLANNING
Benefit	Example
Coordinating efforts	Our firm gains competitive advantage based on a least-cost approach; thus our efforts are aimed at increasing productivity.
Preparing for change	We anticipate another oil embargo. Thus we're planning to produce smaller, gas-efficient cars.
Developing performance standards	We plan to develop cars that get 40 to 50 miles per gallon on the highway.
Developing managers	These performance standards will be difficult to achieve. Let's make sure our managers are adequately trained to reach them.

plan specifies goals and objectives both for the total organization and for each of its parts. By working toward planned objectives, each part contributes to and is compatible with the entire organization's goals.

Preparation for Change

An effective plan of action prepares an organization for change. The longer the time between completion of a plan and accomplishment of an objective, the greater the necessity to include contingency plans. Yet if management considers the change's potential effect, it can be better prepared to deal with it. History provides vivid examples of what can result from failure to prepare for change. The collapse of many banks, savings and loans, and airlines in the past decade is due in large part to lack of preparedness.

Development of Performance Standards

Plans define expected behaviors. In management terms, expected behaviors are **performance standards.** As plans are implemented throughout an organization, the objectives and courses of action assigned to each individual and group are the bases for standards, which can be used to assess actual performance. In some instances the objectives provide the standards. Managers' performance can be assessed in terms of how close their units come to accomplishing their objectives. In other instances the actions performed are judged by standards. A production worker can be held accountable for doing a job in the prescribed manner.

performance standards
In management terms, expected behaviors as defined by plans.

Some people in the training profession believe that the notion of "competencies" should be the basis of human resource management instead of performance standards. The idea is to define a set of competencies for each job in the organization—a list of things that the job holder must be able to do. These job-specific competencies become the basis for human resource planning, including screening, hiring, training, and compensating employees. This approach requires that managers

1. Define the mission of the job.
2. Describe the major outcomes required to achieve the mission.
3. Define performance standards for each major outcome.
4. Identify known barriers to achieving the performance standards.
5. Determine which barriers will be best overcome by training the worker.
6. Develop and deliver training.[11]

Through planning, management derives a basis for developing performance standards or competencies based on organizational goals and objectives. Without planning, performance standards are difficult to define, and those standards developed may be contrary to the organization's values and mission.

Development of Managers

Planning involves managers and workers in high levels of intellectual activity. Those who plan must be able to deal with abstract ideas and information. These ideas must be juggled in a variety of ways to produce a range of *what if?* questions and answers. Running these through the imagination helps managers be prepared in the event that any of the scenarios comes to pass.

Planning also involves managers in concrete action. Through planning, the organization's future can be improved if its managers take an active role in moving the organization toward that future. Thus, planning implies that managers should be proactive and make things happen, rather than be reactive and let things happen.

Through planning, not only do managers develop their ability to think futuristically, but also, to the extent that their plans lead to effective actions, their motivation to plan is reinforced. The act of planning sharpens managers' ability to think as they consider abstract ideas and possibilities for the future, and it reinforces the planning cycle as objectives are met through systematic actions. Thus both the result and the act of planning benefit the organization and its managers.

scope
The range of activities covered by a plan.

time frame
The period considered by a plan.

level of detail
The specificity of a plan.

strategic planning
Comprehensive, long-term, and relatively general planning. Focuses on broad, enduring issues to increase the firm's effectiveness.

operational planning
A focused, short-term, and specific form of planning that translates the broad concepts of the strategic plan into clear objectives for the short term.

tactical planning
On the continuum between the strategic and operational planning processes, a more specific form of planning than strategic planning.

single-use plans
Plans that have a clear time frame for their utility.

TYPES OF PLANNING

Although all effective planning focuses on the customer and on issues of quality and competitiveness, planning activities differ in scope, time frame, and level of detail. **Scope** refers to the range of activities covered by the plan. **Time frame** is the period considered by the plan, ranging from immediate/short-term to distant/long-term. **Level of detail** concerns the specificity of the plan. All plans must be specific enough to direct actual decisions, but multiple contingencies and uncertain futures require some plans to be more general than, for example, a mattress factory's production schedule for the coming month.

Strategic, Operational, and Tactical Planning

Strategic planning (detailed in Chapter 7) is comprehensive, long-term, and relatively general. Strategic plans focus on the broad, enduring issues for ensuring the firm's effectiveness and survival over many years. A strategic plan typically states the organization's mission and may describe a set of goals to move a company into the future. For example, it may establish a mission of world dominance in a particular product area, and set a goal to penetrate new markets based on targeted consumer research and development work.

Operational planning is focused, short-term, and specific. Operational planning translates the broad concepts of the strategic plan into clear numbers, specific steps, and measurable objectives for the short term. Operational planning requires efficient, cost-effective application of resources to solving problems and meeting objectives.

Tactical planning falls on the continuum between the strategic and operational planning processes. It's more narrow, intermediate-term, and specific than strategic planning. Tactics deal more with issues of efficiency than with long-term effectiveness.

The type of planning process followed is determined by the type of goals and/or objectives to be achieved by the plan. Broad, long-term goals require strategic planning; short-term, precise objectives demand operational planning.

Single-Use versus Standing Plans

Single-use plans have a clear time frame for their utility. For example, a task force may be established to plan the development of a new product. This single-use plan will include de-

The U.S. Constitution, an example of a standing plan, has guided Americans in making many decisions for over 200 years. Similarly, many businesses rely on standing plans to guide their future development.

tailed goals and objectives, but will become obsolete when the product has been developed. Then the organization will have no need to further consult this plan.

A **standing plan**, in contrast to a single-use plan, has ongoing meaning and applications for an organization. A good example is the U.S. Constitution. This standing plan for the organization of American government and jurisprudence has provided guidance for over 200 years. Management and leadership scholar Burt Nanus wrote, "The Constitution is a written description of the founding fathers' vision for the United States, setting a clear direction and defining values but not specifying how to get there."[12] Although many single-use plans (such as the Clinton administration's economic plan) have been developed within the parameters of the Constitution, the Constitution constantly controls the powers and discretion of government.

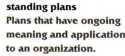
standing plans
Plans that have ongoing meaning and application to an organization.

STEPS IN THE PLANNING PROCESS

The **planning process** (Figure 6–3) is very much like the decision-making process studied in Chapter 5. It consists of six steps: (1) assess current conditions, (2) determine goals and objectives, (3) establish an action plan, (4) allocate resources, (5) implement, and (6) control. This six-step process does not distinguish among the different types of plans we've just discussed. Instead, it's generally applicable to all types of plans, differing only in the issues considered as well as in specificity, scope, and time frame. Throughout the discussion of these planning steps, we'll describe TQM tools and techniques. Later we'll examine other quality planning approaches.

planning process
A six-step process: (1) Assess current status. (2) Determine objectives. (3) Identify the actions required. (4) Allocate resources. (5) Assign responsibilities for implementation. (6) Control the planning decision.

Step 1: Assess Current Conditions

Before goals and objectives can be established, the current state of the firm must be assessed. In strategic planning, for example, this includes the firm's resources as well as market trends, economic indicators, and competitive factors. Strategic planning takes a broad view of the organization's internal and external environments.

In operational and tactical planning, a manager's assessment of current conditions focuses less on trends and more on hard information about cash flow, market share, employee turnover ratios, and so on. In contrast to strategic planning, operational planning focuses on more specific goals and objectives.

Effective quality-based planning is participative; that is, managers seek out information from a broad base of organizational constituencies to form a picture of the current situation. For example, a firm's assorted functional areas—sales, engineering, finance—may have competing definitions of the basic difficulties facing the organization. All these points of view must be considered to obtain a reliable assessment of the organization's internal and external operating environments. Using a TQM approach, managers may choose to utilize cross-functional teams to break down barriers between departments. Some quality management thinkers use the term *silos* to refer to isolated units or departments within an organization. Silos are impediments to the flow of information and obstructions to TQM-based participative planning.

Competitive benchmarking is another approach to assessing current conditions that's widely used among quality-based organizations. Benchmarking sets standards for perfor-

FIGURE 6–3
Steps in the Planning Process

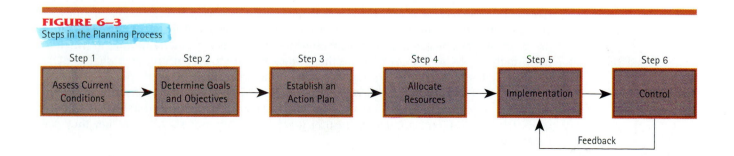

Step 1	Step 2	Step 3	Step 4	Step 5	Step 6
Assess Current Conditions	Determine Goals and Objectives	Establish an Action Plan	Allocate Resources	Implementation	Control

Feedback

Motorola brings in new ideas by "benchmarking" diverse organizations, such as, a neighborhood church. The company has also consulted kids in its search for innovation, resulting in its decision to make pagers available in several different colors.

mance based on what others have been able to achieve. Among TQM-based organizations, competitive benchmarking has become something of an obsession. For example, Motorola is one of the corporate leaders in applying the principles of quality management throughout the organization. Chris Galvin, president and COO, encourages people to strive to see things from a new angle and in a different light. Benchmarking is one tool that provides insights into new opportunities. At Motorola, no organization is too diverse to use as a benchmark. The company once benchmarked a neighborhood church to study its excellent customer service. Motorola also brings in kids to look at its products. When asked about Motorola's pager, one child said the color black was boring and that the company should offer different colors. The company had never even considered this simple idea, and now pagers are available in several different colors.[13]

Planners who use benchmarking are motivated by the knowledge that if they don't use this technique, other firms are likely to gain a competitive advantage. Once the internal and external environments have been assessed, the next step is to set appropriate goals and objectives.

Step 2: Determine Goals and Objectives

goals
Future states or conditions that contribute to the fulfillment of the organization's mission.

Once current conditions are assessed, goals and objectives can be set. Often these two terms are used interchangeably by managers, but it is useful to distinguish between them. **Goals** are defined as future states or conditions that contribute to the fulfillment of the organization's mission. More concrete and specific than a mission, goals express relatively intermediate criteria of effectiveness. They can also be stated in terms of production, efficiency, and satisfaction. Quality and productivity become workplace reality only when employees choose day-to-day behaviors that support the ideals and goals of the company. To achieve the goals of a business, employees must understand those goals as a framework in which to perform their jobs, something that tells them what tasks are to be performed at what level.[14]

Goals describe what is important to an organization and give its staff a sense of purpose. The first of Deming's 14 points of quality is "Create constancy of purpose toward improvement of product and service."[15] Quality organizations need leadership to establish goals that are difficult enough to inspire great effort, but not so difficult that they are unattainable.

REFLECTIONS BY PHILIP B. CROSBY

Planning

Those who would plan for something to happen inside organizations sometimes become so involved in the process and mechanics of creating a plan that they forget the obvious, and the results they obtain are not what they had hoped for. The obvious is that no plan works unless those who have to execute it understand their personal roles, and have had an opportunity to contribute some information to the creation of the plan. Simply, if plan requirements are not understood in detail, they can never be accomplished properly.

Elaborate computer-driven planning and control systems, such as PERT, have been created over the years in an attempt to make plans more comprehensive. Many companies now have planning departments that plaster the walls with diagrams and issue hourly status reports. But these approaches are often much like taking a physical several times a day rather than learning how to prevent illness. Prevention consists of taking actions that head off difficulty, rather than learning how to identify and treat it.

Recently I was involved in a video project for which we were planning to create a dozen sessions, each complementary to the others. We planned to market them through national advertising and allow people to call an "800" number and order the product by paying with a credit card. We resolved that we were going to use the project as an example of how to plan something so that each and every action was completed according to requirements the first time. There would be no wasted effort or money.

Rather than lay everything out on some process plan with a lot of arrows and diagrams we decided to bring the people involved together before any funds were expended. First we wrote a two-page description of the project, complete with the dates we would like to have it on the market. Then we invited the video producer, the advertising agency, the fulfillment house, the public relations person, the accounting firm, the members of Career IV staff who would be involved, and the studio people.

In an hour-long meeting, with plenty of time allotted, we laid out the project as we saw it and obtained agreement on the various completion dates. Each attendee was asked to think through their operation over the interval before the next meeting and return with suggestions and questions. We went around the room making certain we worked out the implementation details and wrote them carefully into a plan.

A great many preventive and money saving actions came out of that meeting. For instance, the studio people said that they could take my computer disk containing the scripts and transmit them directly to the teleprompters. We would also be able to make changes easily at their terminal. The advertising people learned that the box they had designed was not the best size for processing and packaging. The fulfillment people suggested that we hire a company of handicapped workers to do the packaging.

The result was a plan everyone understood, with clear and measurable requirements that everyone agreed to meet, and a completely hassle-free execution. The participants subsequently knew each other well enough to deal directly with one another when they had questions. Nothing had to be done over, except for a few takes during the video shoot.

Quality, after all, means conformance to the agreed requirements.

Objectives are short-term, specific, measurable targets that must be achieved to accomplish organizational goals. Figure 6–4 shows the distinction between goals and objectives with a hurdler who must clear a set of obstacles (hurdles) to get to the finish line. The hurdles can be seen as objectives on the way to the final goal (the finish line). For a concrete example, a firm seeking to have sales outlets in all major population centers (the goal) could state its current year's objective as "to open and begin operations in Chicago, Los Angeles, Louisville, and Milwaukee." Thus, just as goals are derived from the organization's mission, objectives are derived from the organization's goals.

objective
A specification of desired future conditions.

Objectives let workers and citizens know what's important. Objectives must be relevant, challenging, and focused. Management plans in order to determine the priority and timing of objectives. In addition, management must also resolve conflicts between objectives.

Priority of Objectives. It's entirely possible for an organization to have multiple goals and objectives contributing to its mission. In fact, some writers today insist that the old profit-centered enterprise needs to be replaced in a postindustrial society by "multipurpose" institutions that involve employees, customers, and the public as well as investors in establishing multiple goals.[16] For example, a hospital may pursue patient care, research, and training. Universities typically state three significant goals: research, teaching, and service. The existence of multiple goals and objectives places great pressure on managers not only to coordinate routine operations, but also to plan and allocate scarce resources.

FIGURE 6–4
Difference Between Goals
and Objectives

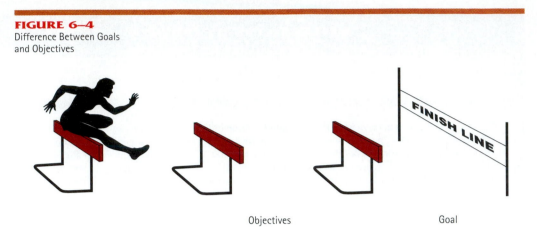

Objectives   Goal

The runner sets objectives to clear each hurdle on the way to his goal: Crossing the finish line first. This activity
is carried out within the context of a larger mission, winning the track meet for the team.

Managers always face alternative objectives, and they must establish priorities if they want to allocate resources in a rational way. Making decisions about the priority of objectives requires managers to distinguish between those that are mission critical, and those that aren't. The former are a higher priority. Once this distinction has been made, the manager might still be faced with the need to prioritize among the mission-critical objectives because time and resources won't allow them to all be accomplished at once. At this point, setting priorities may require the manager to seek input from others in the firm. Ultimately, however, the manager must set priorities for the firm and be prepared to carry them out.

Conflicts among Objectives. At any time, shareholders (owners), employees (including unions), customers, suppliers, creditors, and government agencies are all concerned with the operation of the firm. The process of establishing objectives and setting priorities must not overlook these interest groups, and plans must incorporate and integrate their interests. The form and weight to be given to conflicting objectives is a matter of managerial judgment. Common planning trade-offs managers face include:

1. Short-term profits versus long-term growth.
2. Profit margin versus competitive position.
3. Direct sales effort versus development effort.
4. Greater penetration of present markets versus developing new markets.
5. Achieving long-term growth through related businesses versus achieving it through unrelated businesses.
6. Profit objectives versus nonprofit objectives (that is, social responsibilities).
7. Growth versus stability.
8. Low-risk environment versus high-risk environment.

Management must consider the expectations of the diverse groups on whom the firm's ultimate success depends. For example, present and potential customers hold power over the firm. If they aren't happy with the price and quality of the firm's products, they withdraw their support (stop buying). Suppliers can disrupt the flow of materials to express disagreement with the firm's activities. Government agencies can enforce compliance with regulations. Managers must recognize these interest groups and their power to affect the firm's objectives.

Studies of objectives that business managers have set for their organizations confirm the difficulty of balancing the concerns of interest groups. These studies also suggest that the more successful firms consistently emphasize profit-seeking activities that maximize stockholder wealth. This is not to say that successful firms seek only profit-oriented objectives, but rather that such objectives are dominant.[17]

Measuring Objectives. Objectives must be clear, achievable, and measurable to be effective. In fact, many people believe that specific, measurable objectives increase the performance of both employees and organizations, whereas difficult objectives—if employees accept them—result in better performance than easier objectives. In practice, effective managerial performance requires establishing objectives in every area that contributes to overall organizational performance.

Effective planning requires measurements of objectives. A number of measurements exist to quantify objectives in some of the general areas of business.

Profitability objectives include the ratios of (1) profits to sales, (2) profits to total assets, and (3) profits to capital (net worth). Managers have a tendency to emphasize the ratio of profits to sales as an important measure of profitability. Both quantities in this ratio are taken from the income statement, which management generally regards as a better test of performance than the balance sheet.

Some managers believe that the true test of profitability must combine the income statement and the balance sheet. These managers use either the profit/total asset ratio or the profit/net worth ratio. Which of these two measures is preferred depends on whether the source of capital is an important consideration. The profit/total asset ratio measures management's use of all resources, regardless of origin (i.e., creditors or owners). The profit/net worth ratio measures how management used the owner's contribution.

The measures are not mutually exclusive. All three ratios are profitability objectives because each measures, and therefore evaluates, different yet important aspects of profitability.

The purposes of profit are to measure efficiency, to recover one cost element of being in business (return on invested capital), and to provide funds for further expansion and innovation. The minimum profitability is that which ensures the continuous stream of capital into the organization, given the inherent risks of the industry in which the organization operates.

Marketing objectives measure performance relative to products, markets, distribution, and customer service. They focus on prospects for long-run profitability. Thus well-managed organizations measure performance in such areas as market share, sales volume, number of outlets carrying the product, and number of new products developed.

Productivity objectives are measured with ratios of output to input. Other factors being equal, the higher the ratio, the more efficient is the use of inputs.

Some managers contend that the ratios of value added to sales and to profit are the superior measures of productivity. They believe that a business's objective should be to increase these ratios and that departments in the firm should be evaluated on the basis of these increases. The argument for value added is that it measures the increase in value of the purchased materials due to the firm's efforts, since value added is equal to the difference between the purchase price and the market value of materials and supplies. In this way, a firm's efficiency is measured directly. This measure of productivity also could be used for comparisons among a firm's individual departments.

Physical and financial objectives reflect the firm's capacity to acquire resources sufficient to achieve its objectives. Measurement of physical and financial objectives is comparatively easy since numerous accounting measures can be used. Liquidity measures, such as the current ratio, working capital turnover, debt/equity ratio, and accounts receivable, and inventory turnover can be used in establishing objectives and evaluating performance in financial planning.

Quality objectives have become increasingly important in organizations. As we have noted, Deming and Crosby have specified fundamental principles or guides for quality management. Another quality expert, Joseph Juran, has recommended 10 steps to quality improvement, with an emphasis on the sequence or process of achieving quality (Table 6–2).[18]

Deming, Crosby, and Juran offer a mix of goals and procedures that provide managers with guidance for planning. When businesses define their goals in terms of customer satisfaction, planning requires them to translate customer satisfaction into meaningful areas and measures. Parasuraman, Zeithaml, and Berry offer 10 dimensions of service quality that define customer satisfaction: access, communication, competence, courtesy,

TABLE 6-2	JURAN'S PLANNING OBJECTIVES

1. Build awareness for opportunities to improve quality.

2. Set specific goals for quality improvement.

3. Organize resources to meet the goals.

4. Provide worker training.

5. Conduct projects to solve quality problems.

6. Report on progress toward goals.

7. Give employees recognition.

8. Communicate results.

9. Keep score.

10. Maintain momentum by institutionalizing improvement as part of the regular systems and procedures for the company.

credibility, reliability, responsiveness, security, tangibles, and knowing the customer (Table 6–3).[19] These 10 dimensions provide management with key areas on which to concentrate to satisfy customer expectations. Quality derives from meeting or exceeding customer expectations on each dimension. The What Managers Are Reading segment discusses a popular book that tells managers to choose one of three possible "market disciplines": operational excellence, customer intimacy, or product leadership.

planning values
Underlying priorities that determine planning objectives and decisions.

Planning values are the underlying decision priorities that determine planning objectives and decisions. To be successful in the long term, quality programs must involve more than superficial, isolated behavioral changes. What is called for is a systemwide approach involving changes in a company's fundamental operations, beliefs, and values.[20] All units within an organization should adapt their objectives to the corporate goals. In fact, all aspects of the organization should revolve around the core values and beliefs.[21] International business leaders recognize that defining and implementing the right corporate values is a top priority for them and a vital influence on the success of their organizations. In the U.K., for example, a survey of leading companies shows that 80 percent of them have written statements of corporate values. The most important were people, competitiveness, customers, quality, and productivity. The lowest ranked were social responsibility and profitability.[22]

Harvard business professor David Garvin identified eight planning values that are the basis of a quality-based system: performance (primary operating characteristics, e.g., speed), features (supplements to performance), reliability (no malfunctioning or need for repair), conformance (to established standards), durability (product life), serviceability (speed and ease of repair, if needed), aesthetics (appeal to taste, looks, feel), and perceived quality (customer perception).[23]

Garvin's planning values highlight the difference between traditional and quality-based views. In the traditional view, quality meant the performance characteristics and the number of features available to the customer.

Regulated standards for products or practices are often used as planning values. But making plans that simply meet standards is a reactive approach to planning that doesn't motivate higher performance. Proactive, quality-based planning, on the other hand, involves setting objectives that add value by exceeding mandated standards or even setting standards of quality where none had previously existed. For example, innovative hiring or compensation plans, maternity and family leave programs, and financial support for ongoing education of workers at local colleges and technical schools are examples of proactive objectives that display quality-oriented planning values.

TABLE 6-3	MEASURES OF SERVICE QUALITY OBJECTIVES
Concept	How It Is Measured and Demonstrated
1. Access	Availability to customers
2. Communication	Providing clear descriptions to customers, answering their questions
3. Competence	Proven expertise at a task
4. Courtesy	Friendliness, respect for the customer
5. Credibility	Believability, meeting promises
6. Reliability	Error reduction
7. Responsiveness	Speed at meeting customer requests
8. Security	Maintaining customer safety and privacy
9. Tangibles	Physical appearance of workplace
10. Knowing the customer	Demonstrated capacity to listen to, respond to, and satisfy the customer

WHAT MANAGERS ARE READING

THE DISCIPLINE OF MARKET LEADERS
by Michael Treacy and Fred Wiersema

Customers are fed up with excellent products and services. What they want now must be exceptional, outstanding, even astonishing. How are firms, struggling to keep up with the latest consumer tastes, to compete? According to *The Discipline of Market Leaders*, the management techniques of total quality management, reengineering, and core competence don't go far enough in explaining what sustains the most competitive companies today. Instead, channeling energy to increase customer value year after year by focusing on three value disciplines determine company success:

- Operational excellence—reliable products at competitive prices with a minimum of fuss or inconvenience.
- Customer intimacy—knowing your customers so well you can provide "total solutions" for them instead of separate products or services.
- Product leadership—state-of-the-art products or services.

Upon hearing of the three disciplines, managers might get the idea that they will be successful if they get their people working on all three immediately. However, that would be the wrong approach. According to the authors, the worst thing you can do is forge ahead on all fronts without a clear focus, overcommitting resources and becoming unable to focus powerfully on any one of the three disciplines. The authors suggest the correct prescription is to:

- Provide the best offering in the marketplace by excelling in one of the value disciplines.
- Maintain threshold standards on the other tow dimensions of value that are important to your customers.
- Dominate your market by improving value, year after year.

Operationally excellent companies, such as McDonald's, Dell Computer, GE Appliances, and Price/Costco, excel by having different people consistently doing the same continuously refined steps. Companies destined to fail are those that let products and services proliferate in an attempt to be everything to every customer. Operationally excellent companies realize that unchecked growth in variety and service hurts efficiency.

Companies that practice the discipline of *customer intimacy* keep their customers because they do it better than anybody else. Powerful service groups, using institutionalized knowledge, provide the needed continuity. According to the authors, "a steady client is a lasting asset; a one-time client is a poor investment."

To practice *product leadership* you need eye-popping innovation because customers yawn at creeping newness. To develop successful new products, a company must shun "aimless experimentation and daydreams," say the authors. Innovative companies must get upstream of customer needs to anticipate what is coming next.

Source: Adapted from "How to Succeed in Business by Really Focusing," *Production*, May 1995, pp. 30-31; and Lou Wallis, "Staying Ahead of the Pack," *Across the Board*, April 1995, pp. 59–60.

Managers should establish planning values that are responsive to both the internal and external environments of the organization. Internal features are people, processes, and practices that promote quality and continuous improvement. External features relate to external customer satisfaction, such as product attributes that exceed expectations.

Once the organization's goals and objectives have been established, the next step is to develop an action plan.

Step 3: Establish an Action Plan

To achieve objectives, action plans are required. Actions need to be specified prior to implementation as part of the planning process.

actions
Specific, prescribed means to achieve the objective(s).

Actions are specific, prescribed means to achieve objectives. Actions determine success or failure in meeting objectives. Planned courses of action are called strategies or tactics, and are usually differentiated by scope and time frame as we have described. Whatever the name, a planned action is directed toward changing a future condition; that is, achieving an objective.

In some instances, managers have a choice among alternative actions. For example, productivity increases can be achieved through a variety of means, including improved technology, employee training, management training, reward systems, and improved working conditions. In such cases, managers must select the most effective alternative. Often several possible courses of action exist for top managers who are planning for the total organization. As the plan becomes more localized to a simple unit in the organization, the number of alternatives tends to become fewer yet more familiar.

The important point is that courses of action and objectives are causally related. That is, the objectives are caused by the courses of action. The intellectual effort required in planning involves knowing not only what alternatives will accomplish an objective but also which one is most efficient.

forecast
A prediction of future events based on past and current data.

Often, managers can test the effects of a course of action by **forecasting** (the process of using past and current information to predict future events). With a forecast, a firm attempts to determine the likely outcome of alternative courses of action. For example, a sales forecast would include past and current information about the firm's product, price, advertising, and cost of goods sold. External conditions to be measured include the price of competing products, the levels of consumer income, consumer credit interest rates, and other measures of local economic activity.

Forecasting models range from the subjective to the sophisticated. Forecasts based on brief, personal, subjective estimates are called hunches. For increasing sophistication, there are statistical studies of predicted consumer purchases (market surveys), historical analyses of past sales to convert into estimates of future sales (time-series analysis), and even more sophisticated models of a wide range of past, current, and predicted economic variables (econometric forecasting). Forecasts are used to predict hiring requirements, factory space needs, employee training expenditures, and health care costs, among other decisions important to the firm.

Of course, most successful action requires a commitment of organizational resources. The next section examines how managers make resource allocation decisions.

Step 4: Allocate Resources

resources
Financial, physical, human, time, or other assets of an organization.

"Total Factor Productivity" (TFP)
A measure of a firm's effectiveness in using its resources to create product values.

The fourth step in the planning process is allocating resources. **Resources** are defined as the financial, physical, human, time, or other assets of an organization. Resources are also known as *factors of production*. Highly productive firms use their capital, human, and material resources more effectively to create product values than do less productive firms. A measure of this effectiveness is known as **Total Factor Productivity** (TFP). Studies have shown that gains in the TFP of individual firms are directly related to the intensity of their investment in research and development, primarily to investments for product and process improvements.[24]

budget
A predetermined amount of resources linked to an activity.

Expenditure of resources is usually controlled by use of a budget. A **budget** is a predetermined amount of resources linked to an activity. For example, as part of the plan to bring a new product to market, a budget is likely to include salaries, materials, facilities, travel, and other resources. A good budget recognizes and allocates the needed resources to ensure implementation.

A close relationship exists between budgeting as a planning technique and budgeting as a control technique. After an organization has been engaged in activities for a time, actual results are compared with the budgeted (planned) results, which may lead to corrective action.

The complexity of the budget phase is shown in Figure 6–5. The sales forecast plays a key role, as is evident in its placement at the top of the chart. All other budgets are related to it either directly or indirectly. The production budget, for example, must specify the materials, labor, and other manufacturing expenses required to support the projected sales level. Similarly, the marketing expense budget details the costs associated with the sales level projected for each product in each sales region. Administrative expenses also must be related to the predicted sales volume. The projected sales and expenses are combined in the financial budgets, which consist of formal financial statements, inventory budgets, and the capital additions budget.

Forecast data are based on assumptions about the future. If these assumptions prove wrong, the budgets are inadequate. So financial budgets' usefulness depends mainly on

FIGURE 6–5
The Budgeting Process consists of actions and decisionsthat affect the entire organization.

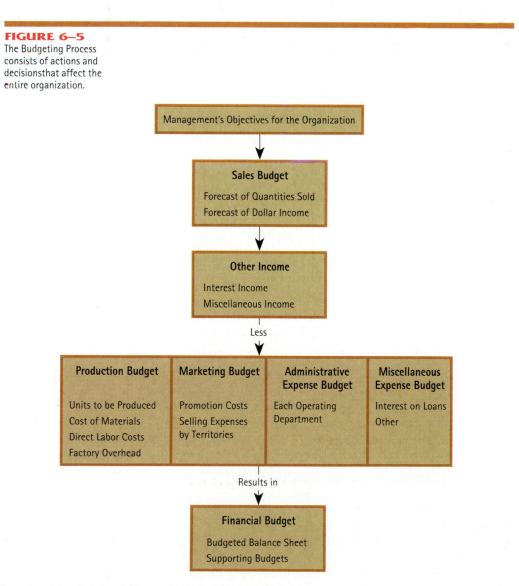

Source: James H. Donnelly, Jr., James L. Gibson, and John M. Ivancevich, *Fundamentals of Management*, 9th ed. (Burr Ridge, Il.: Richard D. Irwin, 1995), p. 191.

how flexible they are with regard to changes in conditions. Two principal means exist to provide flexibility: variable budgeting and moving budgeting.

variable budgeting
Provides for the possibility that actual output deviates from planned output.

Variable budgeting provides for the possibility that actual output deviates from planned output. It recognizes that variable costs are related to output, while fixed costs are unrelated to output. Thus, if actual output is 20 percent less than planned output, it doesn't follow that actual profit will be 20 percent less than that planned. Rather, the actual profit varies, depending on the complex relationship between costs and output.

moving budgeting
Preparation of a budget for a fixed period with periodic updating at fixed intervals.

Moving budgeting is the preparation of a budget for a fixed period (say, one year) with periodic updating at fixed intervals (such as one month). For example, a budget is prepared in December for the next 12 months (January through December). At the end of January, the budget is revised and projected for the next 12 months, (February through January). In this manner, the most recent information is included in the budgeting process. Premises and assumptions are being revised constantly as management learns from experience.

Moving budgets have the advantage of systematic reexamination; they have the disadvantage of being costly to maintain. Although budgets are important instruments for implementing a firm's objectives, they must be viewed in perspective as one item on a long list of demands for a manager's time.

Some experts have begun to question the value of budgets. The major criticism is that by strictly adhering to a planning process based solely on numbers and dollars, companies tend to overlook critical variables such as quality, customer service, and technological change. For example, technology management has become increasingly important in the modern age. Organizations have to be in a position to adapt to technological innovation. In order to do that, management must find a way to improve technological forecasting and to translate these forecasts into plans that enable the organization to maximize its opportunities to gain from technologies.[25] The payoff from dedicating resources to technological forecasting may not appear in short-term budgets. Managers should beware of resource allocation processes that don't allow for preparation for future change.

Information is also a resource that needs to be budgeted. Information is perhaps the most important resource in modern, knowledge-based organizations. Employees cannot be expected to help plan without full access to the company's information—cost and market data, product developments, and so on.

Quality-based organizations share information broadly. For example, David Kearns remade Xerox so that planning and decision making would occur at each level of the organization. After years of declining market share due to higher-quality Japanese products, Kearns established a new quality program based on the four planning values of competitive benchmarking, pushing responsibility down the organization hierarchy, emphasis on quality, and customer satisfaction. Today every department at Xerox is *expected* to know what organization in the world is the best at what that department does. And each department is expected to measure that competitor's performance, find out how it is being done, adopt the best practices for its own performance, and improve upon it—constantly. This downward push of information and responsibility goes right to the front-line workers. Under Kearns's leadership, management invited labor leaders in and gave them full information about the nature of the firm's challenge. According to John Foley, then vice president of personnel, "When we hired a production worker in the old days, we used to say crudely that we hired his hands and not his head. Very frankly, what we are finding out is that there is an awful lot in his head."[26]

Having an action plan is only part of the process of giving life to a plan. Effective managers should also have a strategy for implementing the action plan.

Step 5: Implement the Plan

implementation
The assignment of people and responsibilities for achieving a plan.

Implementation concerns the delegation of tasks, taking action, and achieving results. Without effective implementation, the four preceding steps are pointless. Implementation means using resources to put a plan into action. In some instances, such as small businesses and entrepreneurial ventures, the manager carries out each step of the planning process, including implementation. In most large organizations, however, the manager must implement plans through others, motivating them to carry out the plan, rewarding them for successful performance, and redirecting them when their actions lead to outcomes that differ from the objectives. Managers have three ways to implement plans through others: authority, persuasion, and policies.

Authority is a legitimate form of power in the sense that it accompanies the position, not the person. The nature of authority in organizations involves the right to make decisions and to expect subordinates to comply with those decisions. With authority, a manager can expect subordinates to carry out a plan so long as it doesn't require illegal or unethical behavior. Authority is often sufficient to implement simple plans, but a complex plan can seldom be implemented through authority alone.

Persuasion is a process of selling a plan to those who must implement it, communicating relevant information so individuals understand possible implications. Persuasion requires convincing others to accept a plan on its merits rather than on the authority of the manager. There is a danger involved with using persuasion. What happens if persuasion fails? If the plan is crucial, management must implement it by use of authority. It's usually good advice to managers that if they have failed once in the use of persuasion, they should limit its use in the future.

Policies are written statements that reflect a plan's basic values and provide guidelines for selecting actions to achieve objectives. When plans are expected to be rather permanent, policies are developed to implement them. Standard operating procedures (SOPs) are a typical example of formal guidelines used by workers and managers to make consistent decisions across consistent situations. Effective policies have these characteristics:

❖ *Flexibility.* A policy achieves a balance between rigidity and flexibility. In quality-based organizations, policies always leave some room for workers at all levels to exercise their discretion.

❖ *Comprehensiveness.* A policy must cover multiple contingencies. The degree of comprehensiveness depends on the scope of action controlled by the policy itself. Narrow issues require narrow policies.

❖ *Coordination.* A policy must readily coordinate among other decisions, teams, and departments. Activities must conform to the policy without building conflict across activities.

❖ *Clarity.* A policy must be stated clearly and logically. It must specify the aim of the action, define appropriate methods, and describe the limits of discretion provided to those applying the policy.

❖ *Ethics.* A policy must be ethical and responsive to cultural differences. This may be most difficult to follow when a firm is doing business in a foreign country if local standards are inconsistent with the firm's standards as developed in another country or society. Again, judgment must often be applied.

According to Crosby, the basic purpose of a policy should be "to perform exactly like the requirement or cause the requirement to be officially changed to what we and the customers really need."[27] Policies can sometimes be brief, enduring, and dramatic. For example, Nordstrom provides each employee with a brief, complete statement of policy (Figure 6–6). Other policies, such as a firm's overall personnel policy, are an ongoing concern for managers and employees. As a result, managers should seek to carefully define the process of policy development. For example, the question of who should be involved in policy development is one of the most important issues in personnel policy development. For many such policies, a cross-section of employees from the entire organization needs to be involved in the drafting of policies. Another issue in policy development is how and when to communicate new policies to employees. Managers must take care that policy development processes and the communication of policies to employees are clear and allow for appropriate feedback.[28]

Whereas a policy is a general guide to decision making, a **regulation** (or standard procedure) provides a set of instructions to implement the policy. For example, a policy of "employee empowerment" may translate into a procedure for team leaders where work process changes can only be instituted after a meeting with all affected employees, where

---

authority
The legitimate use or form of power stemming from the position, not from the person.

persuasion
The process of convincing workers of the value of a plan prior to implementation.

policies
Written statements that reflect a plan's basic objectives and provide guidelines for selecting actions to achieve the objectives.

regulation
A standard procedure providing a set of instructions to implement a policy.

FIGURE 6—6
Nordstrom's Employee Policy

> Our number one goal is to provide **outstanding customer service.**
>
> Set both your personal and professional goals high.
>
> We have great confidence in your ability to achieve them.
>
> Nordstrom Rules:
> **Rule #1: Use your good judgment in all situations.**
>
> There will be no additional rules.

the employees must approve any changes. Team leaders may also be trained to follow specific procedures in initiating the discussion, recording employees' recommendations, and documenting the approved changes.

The final step of planning is controlling the implementation.

Step 6: Control the Implementation

After completing the first five steps in the planning process, management must control the implementation. The firm must manage ongoing work activities to ensure that the intended objectives are met or, in some cases, adjusted. Controlling includes all managerial activities dedicated to ensuring that actual results conform to planned results. Figure 6–7 highlights the last two steps of the planning process. Note that the controlling step and the implementation step occur virtually simultaneously. As actions are undertaken to implement the plan, measurement of the effectiveness of those actions should provide immediate feedback. Managers should be careful not to make the mistake of waiting until their actions have been completed before they measure their effectiveness. The process of corrective actions based on measurement is known as **feedback.**

Managers must provide information that reports actual performance and permits comparison of the performance against standards. Such information is most easily acquired for activities that produce specific and concrete results; for example, production and sales activities have results that are easily identifiable and for which information is readily obtainable.

More will be said about control issues in Chapter 16. Here you should note that controlling results in a part of the planning function. People responsible for taking corrective steps when actual results are not in line with planned results must know that they are indeed responsible and that they have the authority to take action.

feedback
The process of corrective actions based on measurement.

FIGURE 6—7
Controlling the Implementation of a Plan

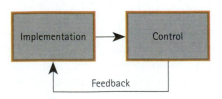

TOTAL QUALITY APPROACH TO PLANNING

Firms that use the total quality management approach employ a number of specific planning methods. This section examines three of those methods: the plan, do, check, act cycle; time-based planning; and planning for continuous improvement. These approaches form the basis for quality planning. Deming describes **quality planning** as the activity of (1) determining customer needs and (2) developing the products and processes required to meet those needs. Quality planning is required for every product and service within an organization, not only for goods and services sold to external customers. TQM planning stresses employee involvement, teamwork, and focusing the entire company on the customer. Many TQM-based companies have revised their operations to link work processes and business planning strategy to customers.[29]

Each of the quality approaches to planning discussed in this section emphasizes exceeding customer expectations, continuous improvement, and team-based problem solving. Additionally, although each of these planning approaches is based on a similar concept of quality, each is developed by a different thinker and has some unique aspects.

This section concludes with a look at control methods within a quality management environment. You will be introduced to several tools that quality-based organizations use to identify problems.

quality planning
The activity of (1) determining customer needs and (2) developing the products and processes required to meet those needs.

The Plan, Do, Check, Act Cycle

The **plan, do, check, act (PDCA)** planning process introduced the concept of planning as a cycle that forms the basis for continuous improvement. In the PDCA cycle (it's also called the *Shewart Cycle,* after its originator, Walter Shewart), the first step is to plan the quality improvement. Second, workers perform or produce a small version or batch of the procedure/product. Third, workers check the results of this pilot project. (The word *study* is sometimes used in place of *check* to reduce some of the negative ideas associated with checking work.) Fourth, workers implement the tested process. The PDCA cycle (Figure 6–8) is then repeated.

Employees at Cincinnati-based Procter & Gamble use the PDCA cycle to manage their environmental quality efforts. First, they develop a *plan* to remove pollutants from each stage of production, as well as from packaging and the final product. Next (*do*) they reduce discharges to the environment and correct other potentially harmful environmental defects. Then they *check* the results, using statistics, charting, and other measurement tools. Once the results are assessed, employees install permanent systems to maintain the quality improvement and to apply it to other aspects of the business (*act*). Using this technique, a Procter & Gamble pulp mill cut landfill dumpings by 75 percent; a coffee-processing plant in Missouri added a machine to compact chaff from coffee beans, cutting solids

Plan, do, check, act (PDCA)
A four-step cycle: (1) Plan the quality improvement. (2) Workers produce a small version or batch of the procedure/product. (3) Workers check the results of this pilot project. (4) Workers implement the complete process. Also called the "Shewart Cycle" after its originator, Walter Shewart.

FIGURE 6–8
PDCA Cycle

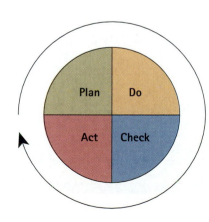

in sewage by 75 percent. New packaging cut 3.4 million pounds of waste in deodorant product cartons. As a result of PDCA, P&G's redesigned Crisco bottle uses 28 percent less plastic than the earlier bottle.[30]

Time-Based Planning

concept to customer
The period between the time a product is first considered and the time it is sold to the customer.

Speed can often determine the success or failure of a plan's implementation. The important period between the time a product is first considered and the time it's sold to the customer is called **concept to customer**. Speed in planning and delivering a product or service can be a strategic competitive advantage. All other things being equal, the prize (typically, market share) goes to the fastest firm. Further, paying attention to time usually forces the firm to look at other issues (e.g., design, staffing, and inspection) affecting products and services quality. For example, it's not uncommon for a product to lie idle during 90 percent of the time allocated for its assembly. Paying attention to production speed can lead to reductions in these idle periods. Not only are time-sensitive firms likely to deliver products to their customers faster than competitors; they're also likely to develop greater customer loyalty and to learn more about improving the production process itself.[31]

reengineering
Fundamental rethinking and radical redesign of business processes to achieve dramatic improvements in critical, contemporary measures of performance, such as cost, quality, service, and speed.

One important initiative currently popular in many organizations is reengineering. **Reengineering** has been defined as "the fundamental rethinking and radical redesign of business processes to achieve dramatic improvements in critical, contemporary measures of performance, such as cost, quality, service, and speed."[32] Reengineering was to a large extent responsible for the trend toward corporate "downsizing" or "rightsizing" that swept organizations around the world during the early to mid-1990s. Many layers of management have been excised from organizations in the interest of reducing the time it takes for organizations to accomplish goals. More layers of management mean more approvals, delays, and foul-ups.

WORKPLACE OF TOMORROW

HERE COMES THE HORIZONTAL ORGANIZATION

In the manic rush to devise principles by which to manage and motivate companies, it's increasingly difficult to tell the big idea from the fad. An idea, such as reengineering, is hailed as the next cure-all. A mass of companies jumps on the bandwagon chanting the new mantra, often without a clear plan. Inevitably, the approach works for some, but not for others.

Many managers have become shell-shocked and are skeptical of all new innovations. Through the maze of new ideas, however, a consensus is building around a model organization for perhaps the next 50 years—the horizontal organization. After more than half a century during which the hierarchical model was the dominant organizational structure, a new structure is beginning to emerge.

The horizontal organization focuses less on what it makes than on how it makes it. American Express Financial Advisors, for example, sells financial products, but its organizational redesign focused on how its financial planners sell its products, emphasizing building relationships with customers.

The horizontal corporation includes several potent elements: teams will provide the foundation of organizational design. They will not be set up inside departments, like marketing, but around core processes such as new product development. Process owners, not department heads, will be the top managers, and they may sport strange titles. GE Medical Systems, for example, has a "vice president for global sourcing and order to remittance."

Rather than focusing solely on financial objectives or functional goals, the horizontal organization emphasizes customer satisfaction. Work is simplified and hierarchy flattened by combining related tasks and eliminating work that doesn't add value. Information zips along an internal superhighway: the knowledge worker analyzes it, and technology moves it quickly across the corporation instead of up and down, speeding up and improving decision making.

The key virtue, says Pat Hoye, dealer-service support manager at Ford Motor, is that the horizontal organization is the kind of company a customer would design. The customer, after all, doesn't care about the service department's goals or the dealer's sales targets; he just want his car fixed right and on time. In the horizontal organization, the customer's goals are paramount.

As never before, management will make all the difference. Getting from the vertical to the horizontal organization is a huge management challenge. Unraveling lines of authority and laying out new ones can entangle a company. It's critical that processes be defined with adequate breadth which ensures that they span the company and include customers and suppliers. The challenge, almost by definition, is that you can't timidly test the idea in one corner of the organization. Nonetheless, ever larger numbers of organizations are taking up the challenge of becoming a horizontal organization.

Source: Adapted from Rajiv M. Rao, "The Struggle to Create an Organization for the 21st Century," *Fortune*, April 3, 1995, pp. 90–99; "After Reengineering, What's Next?" *Supervisory Management*, May 1995, pp. 1 and 6; and "Is a Horizontal Organization for You?" *Fortune*, April 3, 1995, p. 96.

On the whole, however, reengineering efforts have failed to achieve their desired objectives. Senior managers still complain that middle managers are entrenched, blocking necessary changes. And middle managers complain that senior managers have neither the vision nor the fortitude to take the enterprise through changes. To survive, managers must be willing to challenge their assumptions. There is a whole pattern of thought, a whole set of ideas and expectations, that must be let go. According to one of the original founders of the reengineering approach, to speed change in the organization, managers must:

1. Abandon perfectionistic organizational thinking, with its faith in an eternal, universally right way of doing things;
2. Trade in the airy abstraction of authority that comes from their title or office, for the messier reality of authority based on competence and ability; and
3. Broaden their age-old devotion to growth to include an equally old, but only recently rediscovered, devotion to service.[33]

The Workplace of Tomorrow discusses another organizational approach that is providing a challenge to managers' planning skills: the horizontal organization.

Another important initiative in current industry practice, as noted earlier, is called *cycle time reduction*. Cycle time reduction is concerned with reducing the time it takes for organizational processes, reducing costs, and increasing customer service. One of the key concepts in cycle time reduction is **the 3 percent rule.** This rule states that only 3 percent of the elapsed time for a process is actually needed to complete the activity. Insurance claim filing and handling is a good example: completing the claim physically may take only five minutes, but it often takes 30 days for the claim to be processed.[34]

Reengineering and cycle time reduction are two techniques planners use to reduce the time for key organizational processes. Both of these techniques recognize, however, that reducing the time it takes to complete processes is a never-ending challenge. That's why most organizations also use another form of planning that allows for the continuous improvement of the organization.

the 3% rule
A key concept in cycle time reduction that states that only 3 percent of the elapsed time for a process is actually needed to complete the activity.

Planning for Continuous Improvement

Effective planning and plans lead to quality outcomes and to continuous improvements in performance. Quality pioneer Joseph M. Juran notes three main negative outcomes resulting from a lack of attention to quality in the planning process:

❖ *"Loss of sales due to competition in quality."* In the United States this has affected almost any manufactured product, from TVs to lawn mowers to cars.

❖ *"Costs of poor quality, including customer complaints, product liability lawsuits, redoing defective work, products scrapped, and so on."* Like Crosby, Juran estimates that 20 to 40 percent of all costs of doing business are from redoing poor-quality work.

❖ *"The threats to society."* These include minor annoyances like home appliance breakdowns, as well as global disasters such as the Three Mile Island nuclear emergency, the Bhopal, India, poison gas release; and the Chernobyl, Ukraine, nuclear reactor explosion and contamination.[35]

Managers can minimize the possibility of negative outcomes by using quality-based planning methods and by establishing quality goals. The primary outcome of quality planning is customer satisfaction and delight. Juran's description of quality planning includes the following main points:

❖ Identify customers, both external and internal.
❖ Determine the customer's needs.
❖ Develop product features that satisfy customer needs.
❖ Establish quality goals that meet customers' and suppliers' needs at a minimum combined cost.
❖ Develop a process to produce the needed features.
❖ Prove that the process can meet the quality goals under operating conditions (i.e., prove process capability).[36]

Thus the focus of quality outcomes is on the customer—both external and internal customers. Changes in the workplace have helped create systems for continuous improvement in many organizations. For example, American Express made a significant change when it adopted a system built on customer-based transactions. The company created a comprehensive delivery sytem around its external customer requests that would support key customer transactions.[37]

The notion that customer expectations are a moving target underlies planning for continuous improvement. A new national economic indicator, the **American Customer Satisfaction Index** (ACSI) was introduced at Quality Forum X in 1994. The ACSI is intended to join the ranks of the consumer price index (CPI) and gross domestic product (GDP) as one of the leading indicators that business people use in their analyses and forecasts. ACSI, which will be updated quarterly, looks at seven sectors of the economy: manufacturing nondurables; manufacturing durables; transportation, communications, and utilities; retail; finance and insurance; services; and public administration and government. The ACSI uses a 100-point ranking.[38]

Some models of planning aim to identify and implement the "big hit," the one-time, massive change in the production process or in the product that reduces costs or improves the product in a significant fashion. Then no other changes or improvements are made until the next "big hit" occurs at the end of another planning cycle. But between planning cycles, the original improvements tend to erode. Eventually, the improvements erode enough to initiate another plan for improvement. In quality-based management, the planning cycle is continuous. Improvements typically are not dramatic, but they are consistent and incremental. There is no backsliding, no lulls, and no satisfaction with the status quo.

Quality-based planning is dynamic, continuous, and flexible, yet firmly wedded to the customer and continuous improvement. The value of planning lies in its ability to lower the overall cost of doing business by anticipating and responding to change in a systematic fashion. Planning is inherently quality based; it reduces the cost of doing business while also anticipating and satisfying customer needs.

Table 6–4 summarizes traditional and quality-based characteristics of planning. As you can see, the quality-based planning values emphasize the system as the source of organizational problems rather than the employees. Quality-based planning values regard the employee as an asset, and assume that a process can never be optimized, but rather needs to be improved continuously.

American Customer Satisfaction Index (ACSI) A leading indicator, introduced in 1994 and updated quarterly, that looks at seven sectors of the economy (manufacturing nondurables; manufacturing durables; transportation, communications, and utilities; retail; finance and insurance; services; and public administration and government).

TABLE 6–4   TRADITIONAL VERSUS QUALITY-BASED PLANNING CHARACTERISTICS

Traditional Characteristics	Quality-Based Characteristics
Quality is expensive to produce.	Quality lowers costs.
Inspection.	Defect-free goods don't need to be inspected.
Workers cause defects.	System causes defects.
Optimization by experts.	No process is ever optimized.
Standards, quotas, goals.	Eliminate standards, quotas.
Management by fear of layoff, job loss.	Drive out fear.
Employees are a cost.	Employees are an asset.
Buy from lowest cost vendor.	Buy on basis of lowest total cost.
High revenues – low costs = high profits.	Loyal customers = long-term profit.
Profit is best indicator of success.	Profit tells history, not the future.

Quality-based organizations use a number of different methods to control the implementation of a plan. The more popular methods include:

❖ *Pareto charts.* This tool enables managers to determine which of a vital few causes account for the majority of the problems. A Pareto chart is a bar chart that illustrates problem causes in order of severity by frequency of occurrence, cost, or performance.

❖ *Fishbone charts.* These are used to identify possible causes of a problem and isolate the most likely causes at a particular point in time. Construction of a fishbone chart doesn't solve a problem, but ensures that possible causes aren't overlooked and that managers don't apply "fixes" where they are not necessary.

❖ *Flow charts.* A flow chart is a diagram of the product or work flow through each process. Such a chart is used to (1) detect obvious redundancies and inefficiencies in the work flow, (2) identify places for data collection and control charts, and (3) set up channels of communicating control chart signals to help solve problems.

❖ *Run charts.* A run chart is a graph of data points in time order. These data points may be measurements, counts, or percentages of a product or service characteristic. Run charts can illustrate trends or cycles in the characteristic or can serve as a preliminary step to using control charts.

Examples of each of these quality control tools are given in the appendix.

Statistical process control (SPC) provides another set of tools that are commonly used to direct the implementation of a plan in a TQM-based organization. Using SPC, managers can determine whether variation in a system is within expected parameters (in which case they should leave it alone) or whether the variation is beyond expected parameters and in need of intervening action. SPC is explored in more detail in Chapter 16.

Planning, as a fundamental activity of managers, can cover any time span from short to long term. We have surveyed the steps involved in planning, some key quality planning tools and techniques, the benefits of planning, and other topics. These certainly don't cover all of the important issues associated with planning. However, this chapter has highlighted the fact that planning is an important management function. All organizational goals and objectives flow from planning. Without planning, organizations drift and react to environmental changes. Planning enables firms to act rather than merely react.

SUMMARY OF LEARNING OBJECTIVES

DEFINE PLANNING AND DISCUSS THE CHARACTERISTICS OF EFFECTIVE PLANNING.

Planning means that decisions made today will produce results at a later date. The planning process is dynamic, involving many variables that must be considered and linked in putting together the plan. Effective planning requires consistency in pursuing the plan's objectives and flexibility in its implementation. Planning, like decision making, must be proactive and systematic. Effective planning needs clear priorities and flexibility.

DESCRIBE FOUR FACTORS THAT UNDERSCORE THE NEED FOR PLANNING.

Four factors underscore the need for planning: (1) pressure to reduce cycle times on key organizational processes, (2) increased internal complexity of organizational processes, (3) increased external change in markets, and (4) the impact of planning on other management functions. A great deal of time often passes between the decisions and results. Careful planning can help a firm to control the expenditure of resources during this time period.

DISCUSS THE BENEFITS ORGANIZATIONS GAIN BY PLANNING.

The fact that most managers plan in some form is evidence of its importance in management. Four specific benefits of planning are (1) coordination of effort, (2) preparation for change, (3) development of performance standards, and (4) development of managers.

DESCRIBE THE STEPS IN THE PLANNING PROCESS.

The planning process consists of six steps: (1) assess the current state, (2) determine goals and objectives, (3) establish an action plan, (4) allocate resources, (5) implement the plan, and (6) control.

EXPLAIN THE FOLLOWING QUALITY-BASED PLANNING METHODS: (1) PLAN, DO, CHECK, ACT (PDCA), (2) TIME-BASED PLANNING; AND (3) PLANNING FOR CONTINUOUS IMPROVEMENT.

In the PDCA cycle, the first step is to plan the quality improvement. Second, workers perform or produce a small version or batch of the procedure/product. Third, workers check the results of this pilot project. Fourth, workers implement the tested process. The PDCA cycle is then repeated.

Speed in planning and delivering a product or service—time-based planning—can be a strategic, competitive advantage. Time is important in the planning cycle.

Planning for continuous improvement revolves around the notion that customer expectations are a moving target. There is no single, ultimate solution that will permanently meet customer demands.

DESCRIBE QUANTITATIVE MEASURES FOR DIFFERENT TYPES OF BUSINESS OBJECTIVES.

For the objective of profitability, possible quantitative measures include profit/sales ratio, profit/total assets ratio, and profit/capital ratio. For the objective of marketing, possible quantitative measures include market share, sales volume, rate of new product development, and number of outlets. For the objective of productivity, possible quantitative measures include output/labor costs ratio, output/capital costs ratio, and value added/profit ratio. For physical and financial objectives, possible quantitative measures include current ratio, working capital turnover, debt/equity ratio, accounts receivable turnover, and inventory turnover.

COMPARE QUALITY-BASED PLANNING WITH OTHER APPROACHES.

Quality-based planning differs from other approaches in its reliance on participative planning and statistical process control techniques, its emphasis on continuous improvement, and its focus on exceeding customer expectations. Other planning approaches may do one or more of these, but quality approaches use all of these principles for all organizational planning.

Statistical process control is a central feature of quality-based planning. Using simple statistical tools, quality-based managers know when to act to correct variation in their system. But, more important, they know when not to act.

EXPLAIN THE ADVANTAGES AND DISADVANTAGES OF DECENTRALIZED PLANNING.

Decentralized planning allows employees to make decisions and plan at all levels of an organization. This means people who are most deeply involved in specific processes have the responsibility to control and improve them. Decentralized planning can lead to a loss of control if lines of communication among business units are inadequate.

DISCUSS THE PRIMARY PLANNING OBJECTIVES.

Profitability objectives measure profitability of an organization. Some measures include profits/sales, profits/total assets, and profit/net worth. Marketing objectives measure performance relative to products, markets, distribution, and customer service. Productivity objectives are measured in ratios of output to input. Physical and financial objectives reflect the firm's capacity to acquire resources sufficient to achieve its objectives. Quality objectives refer to the organization efforts to exceed customer expectations.

EXPLAIN THE DIFFERENCE BETWEEN VARIABLE AND MOVING BUDGETING.

Variable budgeting recognizes that variable costs are related to output whereas fixed costs are unrelated. Therefore, it provides for the possibility that actual output deviates from planned output. Moving budgeting is the preparation of a budget for a fixed period, with periodic updating at fixed intervals.

EXPLAIN THE DIFFERENCES AMONG STRATEGIC, OPERATIONAL, AND TACTICAL PLANNING.

Strategic planning takes a long-term perspective; operational planning takes a focused, specific, short-term perspective; and tactical planning takes an intermediate-term perspective.

KEY TERMS

actions, p. 166
American Customer Satisfaction Index, p. 174
authority, p. 169
budget, p. 166
centralized planning, p. 154
concept to customer, p. 172
cycle time reduction, p. 155
decentralized planning, p. 154
economy of time, p. 155
feedback, p. 170
forecast, p. 166
goals, p. 160

implementation, p. 168
level of detail, p. 158
moving budgeting, p. 168
objective, p. 161
operational planning, p. 158
plan, do, check, act (PDCA), p. 171
performance standards, p. 157
persuasion, p. 169
planning process, p. 159
planning values, p. 164
policies, p. 169
quality planning, p. 171

reengineering, p. 172
regulation, p. 169
resources, p. 166
scope, p. 158
single-use plans, p. 158
standing plans, p. 159
strategic planning, p. 158
tactical planning, p. 158
the 3% rule, p. 173
time frame, p. 158
total factor productivity, p. 166
variable budgeting, p. 168

REVIEW AND DISCUSSION QUESTIONS

Recall

1. Name the elements of the quality planning process.
2. What are the important outcomes of planning?
3. What role did reengineering play in changing organizational structures?

Understanding

4. What is the difference between a plan and a decision? Which outcome or process do you feel is more difficult to do well on a consistent basis? Why?

5. Even with a carefully constructed plan, managers and workers are often required—or they demand—to change the plan. What would cause the people who made the plan to later want to change it? Are there good and bad reasons to change a plan? Who should best decide to make the change: those who made the plan or those who are putting the plan into action?

6. A senior manager has said: "It's not the plan, but the planning process that counts. A good plan can be filed away as soon as it is finished yet still produce all the important outcomes I desire." Explain.

7. Explain the benefits of planning for an organization involved in global competition.

Application

8. Prepare a 5- to 10-step action plan for writing a term paper for a college business course. Be sure to identify each step in the plan in such a way that you can be sure you know when you have completed the step. After putting the steps in order, date each step or deadline, using the current school term as the overall time frame, with the paper due the last day of class.

9. Prepare a short-term plan for the coming week's activities. After a brief assessment of the current status, name objectives, resources, and actions to be pursued. One week from now, review the implementation and success of your plan.

10. Interview a practicing manager (one with planning or budgeting responsibilities) to find out his or her thoughts on planning. How does planning help in performing the job?

CASE STUDY

Arthur Taylor Takes TQM to School

Arthur Taylor, president of Muhlenberg College since 1992, is no ordinary scholar. Although one of his titles is "Distinguished Professor," in fact he never completed the classwork for his doctoral degree. What he does bring to this one-time Lutheran seminary is more compelling than an advanced degree: Arthur Taylor's students are being schooled in every facet of total quality management (TQM), boldly applied to every facet of campus life from faculty training to student recruitment, fundraising, and career counseling.

Mr. Taylor became a TQM devotee in 1985. Charged with saving Fordham University's business school, he had to find a focus for the programs under him. He consulted with the late Dr. W. Edwards Deming, and his teaching staff began studying TQM with the quality expert. Within five years, the school was saved. Dr. Deming's method, well known in industry, was not widely applied in higher education. One of Deming's major premises is "drive out fear."

That premise resulted in the historic Muhlenberg Plan In. On February 3, 1993, classes were canceled for the day and every student, professor, secretary, gardener, technician, and other employee of the college was invited to the planning marathon. More than 1,000 attended, breaking into 32 concurrent sessions addressing such diverse concerns as new facilities versus green space, nurturing quality teaching, the college's role in students' social lives, internationalizing the curriculum, and environmental literacy.

It was quite a tour de force, Mr. Taylor recalls. "Deming always said, 'If you listen to the people doing the job, they will tell you how to do the job best.' So we invited them to do just that, and it was quite efficient—eliminated a lot of constant conferencing and consulting. In one day we knew what was on everyone's mind."

Mr. Taylor's relationship with Muhlenberg began in 1992 when the school's trustees called him, among other consultants, for advice. With declining enrollments and escalating costs creating a panic at private colleges across the country, Muhlenberg's leaders needed a plan. The college has been solvent for the last four decades, but its trustees had done little to position the school for the future.

Then in his seventh year as dean at Fordham, Mr. Taylor expected only to perform an objective assessment of Muhlenberg's situation. Instead, he fell in love with the institution. Since accepting the challenge of the presidency, Mr. Taylor has taken responsibility not only for the institution's financial future, but also for excellence in all areas. He presented his four-part mission in his inaugural speech in 1993—his plan to make Muhlenberg "truly distinctive among colleges." Taylor's plan has four primary components:

1. Continuous improvement in student focus.
2. Continuous improvement in the global experience of faculty and students.
3. Continuous improvement in the supremacy of teaching.
4. Continuous improvement in financial strength.

Under Taylor's plan, TQM transforms students into "customers" and ensures the quality of the academic "product" they've purchased. Their dorms, their security, even their relationships with each other are affected. "TQM is a religion," Taylor says. "It's a philosophy. It's not a technique."

Academic policies have been redesigned to encourage rather than inhibit student responsibility, recognizing alternatives to classroom learning as valued educational experiences. A student community-service initiative is being developed, faculty-student interaction is emphasized through new events created to foster such communication, and a climate of ownership of one's academic goals and efforts is being fostered.

Taylor has made it known that students need not schedule an appointment to see him. They can knock on his door—at the office or at home—whenever they need to talk to him. "And they do," he says, "at 3 AM sometimes. If they're troubled or afraid of something, we want them to know they don't have to worry; we'll push them forward."

Mr. Taylor has pledged to be creative about globalizing Muhlenberg. To that end, in addition to increased faculty and student experiences abroad, Taylor has created the College of Asian & Western Learning. The unique program is another direct result of the Plan In. As many as 400 students will receive an intense international education, including a full year of study in Japan.

TQM has profoundly affected faculty life at Muhlenberg, most notably in the creation of the Faculty Center for Teaching. Conceived by the faculty at one of their own seminars, the new center is a place where they can immerse themselves in "the scholarship of teaching," says Kathryn Wixon, associate professor of foreign languages and literatures. The center is operated and governed by faculty.

The financial strength of the institution is also beginning to improve under Taylor's leadership. With an endowment of only $38 million, 87 percent of Muhlenberg's $39.5 million budget comes from tuition and fees. To attract additional students, Saturday morning classes and library privileges for the entire family have been instituted. In addition, Taylor helped restructure the Board of Trustees, bringing in new people with "fresh enthusiasm and fresh funds." The rewards from the move were almost immediate: alumni contributions are up 20 percent from 1994, foundation funds have increased by 50 percent, and trustee giving has tripled. Within the next year, Taylor plans to start a true capital campaign.

TQM on campus is not unique to Muhlenberg. What's unique is the approach to planning and implementing that Arthur Taylor has spearheaded. The one-of-a-kind, all-college Plan In turned up many good ideas from forgotten corners of the institution. What would you tell your college or university president if you were invited to a Plan In?

QUESTIONS

1. What was the purpose of the Muhlenberg Plan In? What would you tell the president of your college or university of it held such a plan in?
2. What are some of the primary obstacles to implementing TQM in higher education?
3. Taylor has identified the students as his institution's primary customer. What problems do you think might be associated with viewing students as customers?

Source: Adapted from Mary Mihaly, "Arthur Taylor: Taking TQM to School," *Industry Week*, March 6, 1995, pp. 48–54; and "The Other Side Speaks," *Industry Week*, March 6, 1995, p. 52.

CASE STUDY

SGS-Thomson Microelectronics Plans for Bright Future

Pasquale Pistorio and SGS-Thomson Microelectronics NV epitomize the international electronics industry. As president and CEO of the semiconductor manufacturer, Pistorio leads a company of Franco-Italian origin with production and marketing efforts in Europe, North America, and Asia. In 1987, the Argate Briana, Italy-based company was formed by a merger of Thomson Semiconductors of France and SGS Microelectronics of Italy. It now produces discrete and integrated chip devices across a spectrum of electronics applications that touch all reaches of the world.

In March 1995, Pistorio announced revenues for fiscal 1994 at $2.645 billion, a 17.6 percent compound annual growth rate between 1987 and 1994, and a 30 percent increase from 1993's revenues. In 1987, SGS-Thomson's sales were in the range of $200 million per quarter, and losses were approximately $40 million per quarter. In contrast, in 1994 sales were more than $700 million for the fourth quarter with profits of more than $100 million. How did Pistorio take the company from a monthly money-loser to a world-class competitor? He did so through planning and determination to turn plans into actions.

Pistorio explained that there are three major guidelines that have helped SGS-Thomson to achieve its success: innovation, driven by the market through strategic alliances; globalization; and productivity through total quality management.

Innovation driven by the market is fundamental for any high-tech company where leading-edge technology and products are indispensable for world competitiveness. An even more competitive position can be obtained by increasing the productivity of R&D, Pistorio explained. SGS-Thomson has always strongly believed in the importance of innovation, and, consequently, of R&D—so much so that even in the most difficult years it never eliminated one person or cut one cent from its R&D investment.

Thanks to a well-balanced presence in all of the world's major markets, the company is well established and enjoys closer links with its customers in Europe, Asia/Pacific, Japan, and the Americas. Continuous efforts toward globalization have brought the company to increase its revenues outside Europe from the original level of 38 percent at the time of the merger to 54 percent in 1994.

Through the implementation of TQM, SGS-Thomson has set for itself the target of 15 percent increase in productivity per year, measured in sales per employee. In fact, since the merger it actually achieved a compound yearly productivity improvement of 15.5 percent, growing from $44,000 per employee in 1987 to $130,000 per employee in 1994. This improvement has been made possible by a solid TQM program, Pistorio acknowledged. This is evident in the company's firm belief in employee empowerment, the development of their potential through training, and their participation in the fact-based decision-making process.

Describing his management style, Pistorio said, "I used to define myself, in the Italian language, as 'manuale management.' This means 'a man with the hands on.' I'm not a very sophisticated thinker. I think that management you need essentially a few good, basic things. Number one, you need to understand, motivate, and drive people. This is the most important issue—choosing, motivating, and leading the people. The second thing you need is big, big dedication and hard work. At least I think I try to compensate for my intellectual limitations with hard work. And the third thing you need is a lot of good common sense. The rest may come from the books you read and the training seminars you attend."

Pistorio said his company is very dedicated to "bringing the culture and behavior of TQM down the ranks." He said, "We believe in timely, fast decision-making processes; we believe in decentralizing as much as possible—decision making at the lowest possible point close to the customer."

Above all, Pistorio said, "I think the major important style of management is that we believe very strongly in people, and we believe very much that you have to have the people motivated. Given the tools to perform, you will achieve success."

QUESTIONS

1. Pistorio has established a 15 percent per year growth target for his company. What would Deming say about such a numeric goal?
2. Do you think there are special challenges for international companies like SGS-Thomson in the implementation of a TQM philosophy? Explain.
3. How does TQM help a firm increase the productivity of its research and development function?

Source: Reprinted with permission from *Industry Week*, April 17, 1995, pp. 43–48. Copyright Penton Publishing, Inc., Cleveland, Ohio.

VIDEO CASE

Planning and Strategic Management at Ford Motor Company

Ford Motor Company, like the other two major automobile manufacturers in the United States, experienced difficult times during the early 1980s. Ford and the others had seen their market share severely eroded by better-quality cars from international competitors. Ford was able to weather the competitive storm, and has seen its fortunes rebound, through effective strategic planning.

Donald Peterson was Ford's CEO during the company's recovery period. To create an atmosphere of trust among employees, and between employees and management, Peterson and his fellow managers at Ford emphasized the use of employee teams to solve corporate problems. This emphasis, according to Peterson, was based on the assumption that employees want to contribute, and want to do the right thing.

As the environment at Ford began to change for the better, the leadership initiated a process to establish a strategic vision for the company. Out of this process came a written statement of the company's mission, values, and guiding principles (MVGP) that would provide strategic focus for all the company's employees. The mission is a definition of the purpose of the company. The key values were defined as people, process, and profits. The guiding principles are the code of conduct for Ford's people as they conduct the company's business worldwide.

Reflecting on how he was able to steer Ford through the thicket of intense competition, employee skepticism, and consumer dissatisfaction characterizing the early part of the decade, Peterson said, "As we were working through the extraordinarily difficult early 1980s, when we were losing so much money, we had many gatherings of our employees, talking about our problems and talking about what we had to do to solve them. And it became very clear that there was a pattern in these conversations of a request from people in the company to understand clearly what it is we stand for—what is the basic, core culture of this company. We set about the process of letting the people think about that very question. And then they in turn selected a team of themselves to continue the process in a series of meetings with top Ford executives to work out what we call our mission, values, and guiding principles."

In a video presentation to all Ford employees in 1985, Peterson introduced the MVGP statement. He explained that he wanted the statement to be a "basic platform" upon which the board and all Ford employees would stand together. Peterson told the video audience that he hoped all employees would understand and embrace what the statement meant, what was behind it, and what it would take to live the values and guiding principles in day-to-day work.

As a result of the broad acceptance of the MVGP statement, Ford has made employee involvement and teamwork a way of life at the company. People at all levels of the organization have learned new skills to help them contribute to the continuous improvement of quality. The Taurus project team, for example, is legendary for its efficiency in the design, development, manufacture, and marketing of the Ford Taurus. The new employee spirit was captured by chip-and-scratch coordinator Leon Garner when he said, "I look at each car as if I'm buying it."

The MVGP statement led to a renewed emphasis on quality throughout the company. Terry Holcomb, statistical process control coordinator in the trim department at Ford's Atlanta assembly plant, noted, "There's always room for improvement. The day that there's no room for improvement I guess I'll quit." Holcomb's plan won Ford's internal Q1 (the "Q" stands for "quality") award in 1991. One improvement that Holcomb's plant made during 1990 was in the placement of the moonroof control relay. The relay had been located behind the glove box and had interfered with the smooth functioning of the glove box door. Using a "management by facts" approach, Holcomb's team determined the best way to fix the problem. Their improvement lowered the plant's TGW (things gone wrong) rate from 18 in the second quarter of 1990, to just 2 in the first quarter of 1991.

Bob Anderson, the Atlanta plant manager, said, "When management and the workforce settle on a common goal, with that goal being productivity and quality, you end up with [that] result. But you've got to have that common goal and everyone willing to get behind that common goal." Harold Poling, chairman of the board and chief executive officer, summarized the impact of the MVGP statement on Ford's operations: "I think that if our employees recommit themselves to the basics of the business, which were the things that helped us achieve our success in the 80s, quality, product, cost, and employee relations and relations with our dealers and suppliers, then we'll be successful in the years ahead. It's a team effort and that's what we had in the decade of the 80s. And I'm confident that with that same teamwork we'll be successful in the decade of the 90s."

QUESTIONS

1. Ford is a complex organization with a highly diverse workforce and worldwide operations. Do you think it is possible that the statement of mission, vision, and guiding principles can be applied in all of the company's transactions? What are the limits of such a statement?

2. According to the video, Ford put together its MVGP statement through lengthy discussions with employees. Why do you think it was desirable for Ford executives to include employees in the drafting of the statement? Do you think this was the most *efficient* way to complete this project? Explain.

3. One of the reasons the automobile industry in America lost its competitive standing to foreign competition was that the internal organizational structure of each of the Big Three auto manufacturers had become stagnant. One lesson that has been learned by many companies in a variety of industries is that stagnation leads to competitive decline. Do you think a statement such as Ford's MVGP will help the company continue to change? Explain.

APPLICATION EXERCISE

TEAM PLANNING

As project development manager (PDM) for a $14 billion global high-tech communications firm, you are responsible for managing a team of engineers, marketing directors, manufacturing reps, legal staff, financial analysts, and other key personnel as they take an idea from the basic research and development stage to the market/sales stage. You have been assigned to lead a team that will soon pick up a project from research and development. As part of their efforts to train new PDMs, management has asked you to prioritize the list of activities your team will follow. The accompanying 16 steps are recognized as required to do the job. Read the following instructions, and complete this exercise in team planning.

INSTRUCTIONS

1. On your own, order the activities from first (1) to last (16) in the sequence you feel they need to be completed. Write your numbers in column 1.
2. As a team, agree on a sequence of activities. Record it in column 2.
3. The instructor will then provide an expert's list as to the recommended rank ordering. Write these numbers in column 3.
4. Compute your individual accuracy by calculating the absolute difference between the numbers in columns 1 and 3. Write these numbers in column 4. Then add the figures from column 4 to determine your personal score.
5. Compute your team accuracy using columns 2 and 3 to determine the score. Write these in column 5. Then add the figures in column 5 to determine your team score. Write the personal scores of other team members below, along with your team score.

Activity	1	2	3	4	5
Find qualified people to fill the team positions.	——	——	——	——	——
Measure team progress toward project goals.	——	——	——	——	——
Identify all the tasks needed to complete the project.	——	——	——	——	——
Develop your team strategy and major priorities.	——	——	——	——	——
Recognize and reward team performance.	——	——	——	——	——
Prepare team members for their responsibilities.	——	——	——	——	——
Gather and assess the facts of the current situation.	——	——	——	——	——
Establish the qualifications for each team position.	——	——	——	——	——
Take corrective action on project and recycle plans.	——	——	——	——	——
Lead and coordinate ongoing team activities.	——	——	——	——	——
Allocate the team operating budget.	——	——	——	——	——
Compare actual team results to original objectives.	——	——	——	——	——
Set team performance goals.	——	——	——	——	——
Define the scope and authority of each team position.	——	——	——	——	——
Decide on a basic course of action for the team.	——	——	——	——	——
Determine checkpoints for intermediate review.	——	——	——	——	——

Scores:

Your personal score

Your team score

CHAPTER 7

Strategy

After studying this chapter, you should be able to:

- ❖ Define strategic thinking and strategy.

- ❖ Explain the four components of the strategic planning cycle.

- ❖ Identify the three factors that go into developing a mission statement.

- ❖ Describe the cost-leadership, niche, and differentiation operating strategies.

- ❖ Discuss the four classifications of an organizational portfolio matrix.

- ❖ Explain the different strategic choices associated with the portfolio matrix.

- ❖ Explain how quality-based strategy differs from a traditional approach.

- ❖ Identify the components of the value chain.

- ❖ Identify Porter's five competitive forces.

- ❖ Explain what is meant by a SWOT analysis.

Merger Mania Strikes Again

The downsizing era that was the major cost-control strategy for American companies during much of the late 80s and early 90s has suddenly been replaced by a new wave of corporate megamergers. Between January and September 1995, more than $270 billion worth of mergers and takeovers had been announced, according to the Securities Data Company.

Chase Manhattan headquarters in New York City.

Many of the deals have been surrounded with the fanfare typical of a major sporting event. When Walt Disney Corporation announced it was about to acquire Capital Cities/ABC the media went crazy. This seemed like a return to the wild and crazy 80s when corporate deal making hit an all-time peak.

The Disney/ABC merger was followed closely by the announcement that Westinghouse, known more for appliances than entertainment, was going to acquire CBS. Other major deals have also occurred. One deal that consolidates the efforts of two major software companies is IBM's acquisition of Lotus. IBM was mainly interested in acquiring Lotus's celebrated Notes software, being unable to produce a competitive groupware product of its own. Kimberly-Clark paid $7 billion to acquire Scott Paper; drug maker Upjohn is merging with Sweden's Pharmacia in a $6 billion merger; railroad giant Union Pacific is paying $5.4 billion for Southern Pacific;

and Time-Warner has recently made a bid to purchase Turner Broadcasting System, Inc.

One of the largest mergers to occur, however, is that between venerable Chase Manhattan Bank and Chemical Bank. This merger creates a new entity that will be the largest U.S. bank, with over $297 billion in assets. When the merger is complete, the new Chase will have $20 billion in equity to invest, a sum exceeded by only three other banks in the world. The numbers are breathtaking. Although the combined banks would have assets that would rank only 21st in the world (behind a number of giant Japanese and European competitors), with more than $163 billion in overall deposits, and some 4 million consumer accounts, Chase will be the dominant retail banker in New York. Its $20 billion portfolio of credit-card balances will be fourth in the nation. It will be the global leader in emerging-markets underwriting and trading revenues. And, with $191 billion in loan syndications under its belt so far this year, the new Chase will be far and away the leader in that booming business.

By combining the two banking operations that compete directly in many markets, the new bank expects to cut 12,000 employees and $1.5 billion in annual expenses by the first quarter of 1999. But that's the easy part. The big question is: can the new megabank engineer lasting revenue gains from a combination unprecedented in its size and diversity, producing an organization that yields profit growth long after the excess costs have been wrung out? The early evidence doesn't point to an easy task. Both banks have been able to eke out only mediocre long-term results on their own. In addition, the merger is likely to reveal some difficult cultural barriers, and the new bank's retail operations face a market in revolution, where success increasingly depends less on size than on nimbleness and creativity.

Without question, however, the merger presents a major competitive challenge to wholesale banking competitors around the world. A top London foreign exchange specialist said that a merged Chase "will certainly be a stronger force." In retail banking, however, size is only a starting point. Experts predict that up to 450,000 jobs will disappear from the banking business in the next decades as banks increasingly go electronic. Paying attention to customers, segmenting markets, and serving each segment differently is what matters.

Is this new wave of mergers good for the U.S. economy? There's reason to be skeptical. The inevitable result of these mergers will be a new round of corporate downsizings and layoffs, as companies attempt to find cost savings. Moreover, the megacompanies may be tempted to take advantage of new-found market strength by raising prices.

But it may be that what used to be big is merely midsize when measured on a global stage. Perhaps the larger danger is that many of the benefits of size will prove to be illusory. While managers struggle to absorb their new acquisitions, they may be vulnerable to nimble entrepreneurs. For now, however, the very big rule.

Sources: Adapted from Michael J. Mandel, Christopher Farrell, and Catherine Yang, "Land of the Giants," *Business Week,* September 11, 1995, pp. 34–35; Kelly Holland and John Meehan, "Wow! That's Some Bank," *Business Week,* September 11, 1995, pp. 36–39; David Griesing, Michael Oneal, and Ronald Grover, "Time Warner Turner: Nice Script, But . . . ," *Business Week,* September 11, 1995, pp. 40–41.

strategic thinking

The determination of an enterprise's basic long-term goals and objectives, the adoption of courses of action, and the allocation of resources necessary for carrying out these goals.

strategy

A broad plan of action for pursuing and achieving the firm's objectives and satisfying its mission.

As a proactive and systematic approach to quality and competitiveness, any organization needs a strategy. A strategy is based on **strategic thinking**, which is defined as "the determination of the basic long-term goals and objectives of an enterprise, and the adoption of courses of action and the allocation of resources necessary for carrying out these goals."[1] Another characterization of strategic thinking is that it's "the pattern or plan that integrates an organization's goals, policies, and action sequences into a cohesive whole."[2] Essentially, strategic thinking is a process that results in an outcome called a **strategy** that is the basis for subsequent organizational decisions and actions. In practice, the development of strategy and a strategic plan involves taking information from the organization's internal and external environments and deciding on an organizational mission, goals, and operational strategies.

Traditionally, strategies have been established and managed by top-level managers of an organization. In contrast, for the modern organization, strategy development is not reserved merely for top management—strategy and management are important to all employees. Today, top managers are being encouraged to play the role of communicating the strategy to the organization. Managers need to keep the people of the enterprise continually re-inventing themselves in a way that is aligned with overall strategy. Everyone in the organization should be encouraged to keep looking at unusual sources for new technologies, and at unusual people for new ideas. Over the long haul, the point of strategic thinking is to invent new products and services, to create new businesses, and to hire talented people.[3]

In today's complex workplace, strategic planning has to account for unexpected events, randomness, and chaos. Chaos theory has been applied to numerous scientific disciplines over the past decade and has recently been used to understand the dynamics of organizations. Essentially, chaos theory says that predictions of the future could be enormously inaccurate with only small imprecisions in measurement of existing conditions. Weather phenomena are a good example of chaotic systems. How often have you noticed your local weather forecaster being embarrassingly wrong? Usually, they're wrong because some weather conditions are just too complex to measure with great accuracy.

The same thing is true in today's complex organizations and global economy. Managers like to be able to predict the future so they can better prepare for it. Chaos theory suggests there may be some inherent limitations in their ability to forecast the future accurately. Some have even argued that the long-term future is essentially unknowable. They think managers should recognize elaborate computer-modeled forecasts presented to them as a fiction. The purpose of such forecasts, these theorists claim, is to allay anxiety rather than perform any genuinely predictive function.[4] For example, who could have predicted the return to mergers and acquisitions as a competitive strategy? Yet, as the opening vignette shows, many large firms are using this approach to enhance their competitive position.

On the other hand, chaos theory provides a useful framework for understanding the dynamic evolution of industries and the complex evolution of individual companies within industries. By understanding industries and organizations as complex, perhaps chaotic, systems, managers can build better strategies.[5]

New organizational strategies and structures enable organizations to deal with complexity through constant learning and creativity. As Harvard Business School professor Rosabeth Moss Kanter stated, "New organizational models offer the best of both worlds—enough structure for continuity, but not so much that creative responses to chaos are stifled."[6] Strategic planning helps organizations create order out of chaos and complexity to accomplish results, high performance, high quality, and competitiveness, as Figure 7–1 illustrates.

This chapter focuses on developing and managing strategy in a highly competitive global economy. We'll first look at several important frameworks for strategic thinking. These frameworks are useful for understanding an organization and its environment. Next, we'll explore a four-step approach to developing a strategic plan: (1) assessing the organization's internal and external environments; (2) establishing a mission statement; (3) establishing goals and objectives; and (4) establishing an operating plan. We'll conclude by discussing how quality can be integrated into overall organizational strategy to improve competitiveness.

FIGURE 7–1
Strategic Planning Turns
Disorderly Chaos into Orderly
Results, High Performance,
High Quality, and
Competitiveness

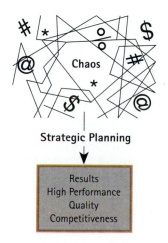

STRATEGIC THINKING FRAMEWORKS

As was mentioned, strategic thinking helps managers prepare for the future. In this section, we'll review several frameworks for organizing the vast amount of data and information available to managers.

Most organizations are a portfolio of businesses. For example, General Electric not only makes consumer electronics, but also runs the National Broadcasting Company (NBC), one of the world's largest television networks. Colleges and universities are typically organized around semiautonomous schools or colleges, each with several programs or departments. Managing such groups of businesses is made a little easier if resources and cash are plentiful and each business unit is experiencing growth and profits. Unfortunately, that's rarely the case.

Today, many firms use merger and acquisition as a means of improving their competitive position. However, the stakes in choosing the right businesses to acquire, and integrating them for optimal value and competitive advantage can be daunting. Some experts consider total shareholder return to be the most important performance measure. Others like to look at the trends in the total industry, or begin with customer attitudes.[7]

REFLECTIONS BY PHILIP B. CROSBY

Strategic Quality Management

The unscientific approach to philosophy concentrates on anecdotal discussion and usually relates to "who" and "why," Who created the universe and why?

The scientific approach to philosophy concentrates on "what" and "how," Plow the ground with this tool to plant seed.

The conventional approach to quality management is an unhappy combination of these two concepts. Rather than determining what's best for a particular company and a particular situation, people concentrate on learning what other companies did. Then they take what they've learned and change it around to suit themselves. The result is less than satisfactory because if something works, they never really know why.

Those responsible for making quality happen tend to assume that those who write or speak on the subject are all talking about the same things. Thus I hear people say that they combine the best of philosopher A with the best of philosopher B, adding a teaspoon from philosopher C. So a little Newton, some Franklin, and a slice of Voltaire make up a performance cocktail suitable for understanding how the price of gold is set.

A strategic quality management approach requires that subject's concepts be understood exactly the same by all involved. It wouldn't be practical, for instance, to have different accounting concepts in each department of an organization. No one would know what the other was talking about. No one would dream of a strategic accounting plan based on such unscientific thought. The who and why must be understood by top management before the what and how can be launched. Unless the strategy is approached in this way, the company will find itself searching fruitlessly for the mythical silver bullet that solves all problems.

Quality isn't something the temple priests can create for you. Swearing great oaths and offering blood sacrifices accomplishes little. Quality can't be delegated as we've noted before. That's why I've always referred to the "quality reformation" rather than "quality revolution."

Once I had a manufacturing line in my department that made coils for telephone switches. For years it had had a defect level of 4 percent. That number was accepted as the sort of worldwide standard in the company. I could never get much done about reducing it. Then I had the opportunity to appoint a new manager for that operation. I selected a young electrical engineer who had no experience in that area.

"We need to get the coils down to zero defects," I told her. "That's the world standard."

"OK," she said and went to work identifying specific causes of the defect rate. She built her workforce into a team that improved material handling, machine maintenance, worker training, and a dozen other things. They found, for instance, that many coils were damaged when they dropped off the end of the winding machine and fell onto the transfer ramp. They learned that it was possible to stack the finished goods in a way that nicked wires; they found that new workers weren't being properly oriented.

Within a few months the defect rate was under 1 percent and they were still pounding away at it. I sent the details and results of their work throughout the international operations of the corporation where they also had departments. Soon defect rates began to drop elsewhere and they stayed down, many at zero. Now anything less than defect-free is considered unacceptable.

That's what a worldwide quality strategy is all about. Define proper goals, help people reach them, and recognize their achievements.

To cut across these differences, some method is needed to help managers make difficult strategic choices about which businesses to add, which to keep, and which to jettison. One of the best known and most widely used methods is the business portfolio matrix developed by the Boston Consulting Group (BCG).

The Business Portfolio Matrix

The first step in this approach is to identify each division, product line, and so forth, that can be considered a business. These are **strategic business units (SBUs)**. An SBU is a product or service division within a company that establishes goals and objectives in harmony with the firm's overall mission and is responsible for its own profits and losses. Each SBU has four characteristics:

1. It has a distinct mission.
2. It has its own competitors.
3. It is a single business or collection of businesses.
4. It can be planned for independently of the other businesses of the total organization.

Thus, depending on the organization, an SBU could be a single product, product line, division, department, or agency. Once managers have identified and classified all the SBUs, they need some method of measuring their performance. This is the important contribution of the Boston Consulting Group's approach.

Using the BCG approach, an organization would classify SBUs in the business portfolio matrix (Figure 7–2). The business portfolio matrix depends on two business indicators of strategic importance. The vertical indicator, market growth rate, refers to the annual rate of growth of the market in which the product, division, or department is located. The horizontal indicator, relative market share, illustrates an SBU's market share. This indicator ranges from high to low relative share of the market. Based on these two axes, BCG has identified four distinct SBU classifications:

1. **Star.** An SBU that has a high share of a high-growth market is considered a star. Stars need a great deal of financial resources because of their rapid growth. When growth slows, they become cash cows and important generators of cash for the organization. For example, IBM acquired software maker Lotus to take advantage of the star status of LotusNotes, the exceedingly popular groupware application. IBM didn't have an application that could compete with Notes, and it recognized that the market for groupware would continue to grow.[8]

2. **Cash cow.** An SBU that has a high share of a low-growth market is labeled a cash cow. They produce a lot of cash for the organization but, since the market isn't growing, they don't require a great amount of financial resources for growth and expansion. As a result, the cash they generate can be used by the organization to satisfy current debt and to support SBUs in need of cash. Microsoft's operating systems division

strategic business unit (SBU)
A product or service division of a company that establishes goals and objectives in harmony with the organization's overall mission.

star Build - Innovate
A strategic business unit that has high market share in a high-growth market.

cash cow Hold
A strategic business unit with a high market share in a low-growth market.

FIGURE 7–2
Business Portfolio Matrix

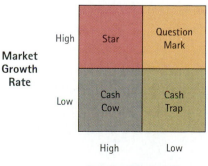

Relative Market Share

could be considered a cash cow with DOS and Windows. The market growth for new operating systems has stabilized, and Microsoft has a high share of that market.

question mark
A strategic business unit that has low market share in a high-growth market.

3. **Question mark.** When an SBU has a low share of a high-growth market, the organization must decide whether to spend more financial resources to build it into a star, or to phase it down or eliminate it altogether. Many times such SBUs require high amounts of resources just to maintain their share, let alone increase it. We mentioned IBM's purchase of Lotus in the star example. IBM's own groupware, called "WorkGroups," was a question mark for the company. Instead of putting more resources into building this business, which had a low share of a high-growth market, IBM purchased Lotus with its star groupware application LotusNotes.

cash trap
A strategic business unit that has low market share in a low-growth market.

4. **Cash trap.** When an SBU has a low share of a low-growth market, it may generate enough cash to maintain itself or it may drain money from other SBUs. The only certainty is that cash traps are not great sources of cash. Sears made a tough decision in the spring of 1993 to stop publishing its famous catalog. Tradition had been keeping the catalog alive, even though Sears' customers had been using it less. The catalog had become a cash trap. Management finally recognized that reality, overcame inertia built up by tradition, and axed the catalog.

Depending on whether SBUs are products, product lines, or entire divisions, an organization can have a number and combination of the preceding classifications. Once the relevant identifications have been made, the organization is faced with strategic choices.

Strategic Choices

Every organization can be analyzed using the BCG business portfolio matrix. This technique enables managers to put each SBU through some tough questions. Four alternative strategies can be taken with each SBU (Figure 7–3).

1. *Build.* If an organization has an SBU that it believes has the potential to be a star (probably it's a question mark at present), it would want to build that SBU. The organization may even decide to give up short-term profits to provide the necessary financial resources to achieve this objective. A firm should also build its current stars.

2. *Hold.* If an SBU is a successful cash cow, a key objective would certainly be to hold or preserve the market share so that the organization can take advantage of the positive cash flow.

3. *Harvest.* This objective is appropriate for all SBUs except those classified as stars. It focuses on increasing the short-term cash return without too much concern for the long-run impact. It's especially worthwhile when more cash is needed for investment in other businesses.

4. *Divest.* Getting rid of SBUs with low shares of low-growth markets is often a good move.

SBUs can change position in the business portfolio matrix. As time passes, question marks may become stars, stars may become cash cows, and cash cows may become cash traps. In fact, one SBU can move through each category as the market growth rate changes.

FIGURE 7–3
Alternative Strategies with SBUs

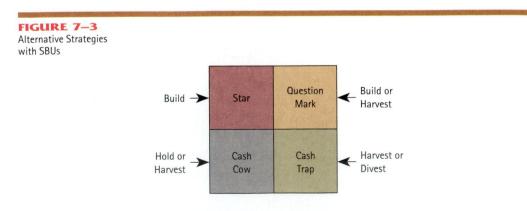

How quickly these changes occur is influenced by the industry's technology and competitiveness. This underscores (1) the importance and usefulness of viewing an organization in terms of SBUs and (2) the necessity of constantly seeking new ventures as well as managing existing ones.

A major criticism of the business portfolio matrix centers on its focus on market share and market growth as the primary indicators of profitability. One study found that using the BCG matrix actually decreased managers' ability to choose the more profitable project. Looking at managers in six countries over a five-year period, the study found that of those managers who had used the BCG matrix in their analysis of what businesses to invest in 87 percent selected the less profitable investment.[9]

Another caution that should be kept in mind when using the BCG matrix is that many complex concepts in strategic thinking are reduced to 2 × 2 arrays for the purpose of simplification. The 2 × 2 is the simplest from of array on which the value of more than one variable can be plotted on each of more than one axis. An important reason for the popularity of the 2 × 2 seems to be that any concept worth using in the world of business has to be reducible to a fairly stark and simple form. However, the apparent simplicity of the 2 × 2 is both a strength and a weakness. When it's used to display concepts thoughtfully distilled from the real world, it can be very powerful. When employed to explain a situation whose complexity must fit into four boxes, it can be dangerously misleading.[10] Although these criticisms are valid, thanks to the BCG model's power in assessing SBU's strategic position, it is used extensively by managers across all industries.

Porter's Five Forces

Harvard Business School economist Michael Porter has developed several useful frameworks for developing an organization's strategy. One of the most often-cited is the **five competitive forces** that determine industry structure. Porter's view is that in any industry the nature of competition is embodied in five competitive forces: (1) the threat of new entrants, (2) the threat of substitute products or services, (3) the bargaining power of suppliers, (4) the bargaining power of buyers, and (5) the rivalry among the existing competitors (see Figure 7–4).

five competitive forces
A view held by Harvard Business School economist Michael Porter that in any industry the nature of competition is embodied in five competitive forces.

FIGURE 7–4
The Five Competitive Forces that Determine Industry Competition

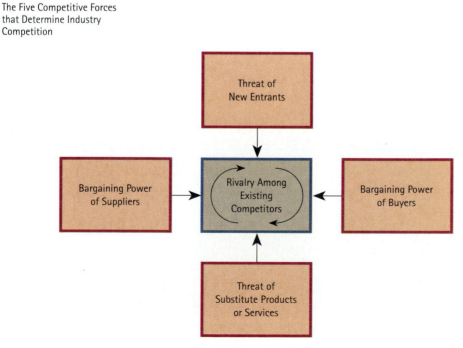

The strength of these five forces varies from industry to industry. However, no matter the industry, these five forces determine profitability because they shape the prices firms can charge, the costs they have to bear, and the investment required to compete in the industry. For example, the threat of new entrants limits the profit potential in an industry because new entrants seek market share by driving down prices, and thus driving down profit margins. Or, powerful buyers or suppliers bargain away profits for themselves. Managers should use the five forces framework to determine the competitive structure of an industry prior to making strategic decisions.

The Value Chain

value chain

All the activities an organization undertakes to create value for a customer.

Another important framework developed by Porter is known as the **value chain.** The value chain is all the activities an organization undertakes to create value for a customer. Figure 7–5 shows a typical value chain.

According to Porter, competitive advantage grows out of the way firms organize and perform the various activities of their value chain. To gain competitive advantage over rivals, a firm must either provide comparable buyer value but perform the activities of the value chain more efficiently (reducing costs), or perform the activities in a unique way that creates higher value and commands a premium price.

Strategy guides the way a firm organizes its value chain and performs the individual activities. Quality-based organizations understand their value chain not as a set of isolated functions or organizational silos, but as linked activities. Managers in the quality organization view the value chain as a system. Improvements to the system are usually made by teams of individuals representing the various activities.

Ford Motor Company, for example, has established a bold strategy called Ford 2000. This program is designed to help the automaker reduce excessive car and truck production costs. A major component of Ford 2000 is the breaking down of barriers between various activities in the value chain. In the context of the sweeping changes set in motion in 1993

FIGURE 7–5
The Value Chain

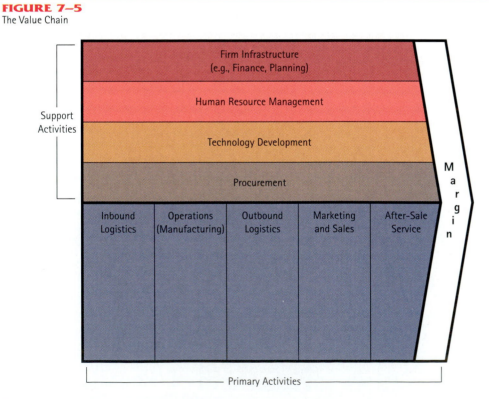

Source: Michael E. Porter, *The Competitive Advantage of Nations* (New York: The Free Press, 1990), p. 41.

by CEO Alex Trotman, the ability to see problems from a different angle and the willingness to speak out are prized traits in every employee.[11]

As another example of strategic thinking using the value chain, TRW, Inc., dramatically improved the quality and productivity of its fastener division by focusing on the procurement activity. Procurement is one part of the firm's value chain. TRW's new program uses a team approach to procurement. The company's managers used strategic planning to undertake this change effort, which called for a significant initial capital outlay. Only a long-term focus on value-chain improvement enabled the managers to know that their initial expenses would be recouped by reducing downtime and stabilizing process flow.[12]

These various frameworks are used by managers as part of strategic thinking. They are useful to narrow the range of issues considered, focusing on the forces and sources of competitive advantage. Another aspect of strategy development in a firm is strategic planning. In the next section we consider a process of planning that is best construed as a cycle that revolves around strategic thinking. It's important to remember that strategic thinking and strategic planning are concurrent, ongoing activities.

STRATEGIC PLANNING

Strategic planning is the process of examining the organization's environment, establishing a mission, setting desired goals and objectives, and developing an operating plan. During the strategic planning process, firms will typically ask themselves, "What do we want the future to be?" or "What must we do now to better ensure that the desired future is achieved?"

In the high-performance organization, strategic planning never ends. Either the organization is formulating a new strategy or it's implementing an existing one, assessing

strategic planning
The process of determining desired objectives or benchmarks and of developing ways to reach them. "What do we want the future to be? What must we do now to better ensure that the desired future is achieved?"

FIGURE 7–6
Relationship between the Organization's Strategic Plan and Operational Plans

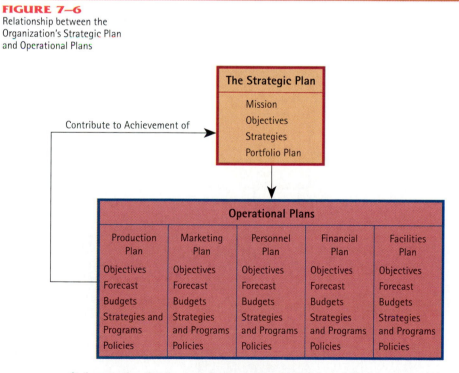

At the same time that the strategic plan provides direction for individual departments' plans, they are contributing to the success of the strategic plan.

Source: Adapted from James H. Donnelly, Jr., James L. Gibson, and John M. Ivancevich, *Fundamentals of Management*, 9th ed. (Burr Ridge, Il.: Richard D. Irwin, 1995), p. 198.

progress, and revising processes as needed. For example, a company president has the primary task of articulating the firm's strategy on a daily basis to employees, customers, the public, and others. Allied Signal's CEO Lawrence Bossidy uses the organization's strategy as a starting point to "coach people to win." He is a charismatic and persistent leader who exhorts his employees to focus on three core processes: strategy, operations, and human resources.[13]

Most managers in an organization don't directly develop the organization's strategic plan.[14] Those who are interested in the benefits and results of planning frequently aren't responsible for implementing the plan. It's a disparate activity, relying on inputs from some and interpretation by others. But managers may be involved in this process in two important ways: (1) they usually influence the strategic planning process by providing information and suggestions relating to their particular areas of responsibility, and (2) they must be completely aware of what the process of strategic planning involves as well as the results, because everything their respective departments do and the objectives they establish for their areas of responsibility should all be derived from the strategic plan.

In well-managed organizations, therefore, a direct relationship exists between strategic planning and the planning done by managers at all levels.[15] The focus of the planning and the time perspectives will, of course, differ. Figure 7–6 illustrates the relationship between the strategic plan and operational plans. It indicates that all plans should be derived from the strategic plan while at the same time contributing to the achievement of the strategic plan.

Strategic planning is best conceived as a cyclical process that is fueled by strategic thinking. Figure 7–7 shows the four major components of strategic planning, each informed by strategic thinking. The cyclical representation is best because it connotes that strategic planning never ends. Competitive organizations are always thinking strategically, and are frequently involved in one or more of the components of strategic planning. For example, many firms have five-year strategic plans. If they are competitive, they probably revise the plan every 18 months to two years.

The frameworks that were discussed in the previous section can help focus managers' thinking in the strategic planning process. For example, Porter's five forces help determine

FIGURE 7–7
The Strategic Planning Process

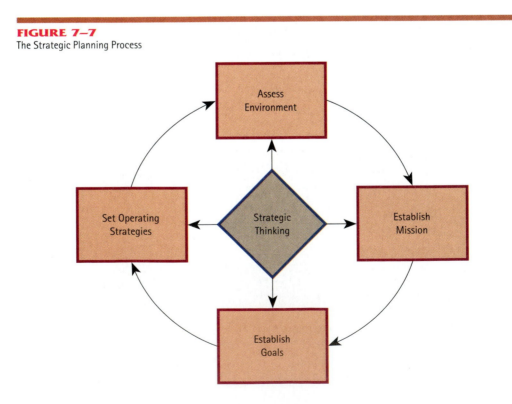

which elements of an organization's external environment to focus on, whereas the value chain helps in the analysis of a firm's internal environment. Now let's examine each component of strategic planning more closely.

The Environment

A strategy, plan, or mission for the future begins with an assessment of the current situation in which the company finds itself. A systematic, thorough analysis requires attention to four things: internal strengths and weaknesses, and external opportunities and threats. Such an analysis is often referred to as a **SWOT analysis** (**S**trengths, **W**eaknesses, **O**pportunities, **T**hreats). Historically, the SWOT analysis has provided managers with useful signals for strategic change.[16]

A company's strengths are usually derived from its financial, human, and other resources. The firm's financial assets include cash, securities, receivables, and other tangible resources usually presented on its balance sheet and other accounts. Human resources are less easy to evaluate, yet that this is a primary component of modern organizations. Human resources include the ideas, ingenuity, patents, and other intangible yet essential bases for competitiveness that only human beings can provide to an organization.

Externally, the company's business environment presents both threats and opportunities. An **opportunity** is anything that has the potential to increase the firm's strengths. For example, a pending reduction of trade barriers may allow a firm to increase its business in another country. A **threat** is anything that has the potential to hurt or even destroy a firm. For instance, a change in tax laws may portend ruin for a firm that specializes in using tax breaks that are to be eliminated by the change.

Key components of an organization's environment include the socio-cultural milieu, technological developments, economic conditions, and political climate. Each of these is explained in more detail below.

SOCIO-CULTURAL MILIEU - Change is constant in modern societies. Strategic planners, therefore, must be able to identify the changing cultural and social conditions that will influence the organization. Unfortunately, many organizations still don't consider the impact such changes will have or else they underestimate their impact. Managers need to be aware of developments in the socio-cultural environment. Many organizations use a technique known as **environmental scanning** to stay in touch with developments. This technique involves the acquisition and use of information about events and trends in an organization's external environment, the knowledge of which would assist management in planning the organization's future courses of action. Research has shown that organizations using this technique focus primarily on the competition, customer, regulatory, and technological sectors of their environment. Information is usually received from multiple, complementary sources.[17]

Another technique used by many firms is called **issues management**. This technique focuses on a single issue. One person is often assigned leadership on the issue and is responsible for strategic decisions on that issue.

Marketing organizations routinely used measurements of **customer-perceived value**—such as conjoint analysis and focus groups—to develop new products and services and improve existing offerings. Now, a few innovative companies are relying on techniques such as these to redesign key parts of their organizations. First, they obtain precise information on the needs and values of their internal and external customers. Then, they use this information to, among other things, tailor products and services to meet distinct market segment requirements. As a result, they not only see performance improve, but they have also given their customers the opportunity to define what customer satisfaction means. This allows firms to reduce costs and improve customer service, while increasing profitability.[18]

TECHNOLOGICAL DEVELOPMENTS - Changes in technology can influence an organization's destiny. Technological innovations can create new industries or vastly alter existing ones. Consider the personal computer's impact on management over the last 15 years. Communication and information technologies are also changing the rules of work.[19]

SWOT analysis
The process of examining a firm's internal and external environments for important strengths, weaknesses, opportunities, and threats.

opportunity
Anything that has the potential to increase the firm's strengths.

threat
Anything that has the potential to hurt or even destroy a firm.

environmental scanning
A technique used by management whereby information about events and trends in an organization's external environment are used in planning the organization's future courses of action.

issues management
A technique used by many firms in which one person is assigned leadership on a single issue and is responsible for strategic decisions on that issue.

customer-perceived value
The relative worth of a company's products or services as discerned by its customers. This information is used to tailor products and services to meet distinct market segment requirements, thus reducing costs and improving customer service while increasing profitability.

Telecommuting, for example, has led to "distributed work"—work activity conducted by teams of people separated from each other in time and space. Management of distributed work processes takes place using advanced communications technologies.[20] Strategic thinking helps managers anticipate technological changes, adapt to their implementation in the workplace, and exploit them for competitive advantage.

ECONOMIC CONDITIONS - As this book makes clear, the economy of the 1990s will be increasingly global and increasingly competitive. New players enter the worldwide economic game every day. New alliances form, new trading blocs come into existence, and new rules of fair competition are constantly being drafted and debated. The emerging global economy will create a more complex economic playing field than ever before. Stock markets run all night around the world. Major investment banks will monitor and issue buy and sell orders overnight on the international stock markets. Competitive advantage is gained by those firms with satellite and computer links to the world. In his book *Managing the Future,* management consultant Robert B. Tucker identifies ten driving forces behind changes that are revolutionizing business and world markets:[21]

1. Speed
2. Convenience
3. Demographics and Age Waves
4. Lifestyles
5. Choices
6. Discounting
7. Value Adding
8. Customer Service
9. Technology
10. Quality

Add to this list globalization and the delayering of corporations and you have defined a very dynamic economic environment. As a result of these forces, managers will need to make a wide variety of adjustments on a continuous basis if they want their companies to remain competitive into the 21st century. New companies will come into being, and old ones that don't adapt will die. This is an era of instant communication and fast-changing technologies. It's also an era of employee empowerment and changing global relationships and structures. Traditional ways of doing business are gone, along with comfortable relationships. If companies are going to achieve success, they must stay abreast of and adapt to changing economic conditions.[22] The What Managers Are Reading segment asserts that competing for the future requires developing "industry foresight."

POLITICAL CLIMATE - The political climate that propelled the United States into a world superpower no longer exists. Nations of the world no longer need to align themselves with one of two opposing economic giants. The collapse of the Soviet Union did bring an end to the Cold War that had kept the world on the edge of its nuclear seat since World War II. But the end to this political standoff has thrown the world into disarray as former Soviet satellites struggle for identity, ethnic animosities buried under the weight of the Russian bear rise up again in troubling frequency, and world trade battles rage over differing interpretations of fair play and justice. These and similar complex battles over scarce resources, differing value systems, and long-festering hatred will shape the political climate well into the next century. Business must be prepared for volatile, even revolutionary changes in geographic boundaries, contract and licensure regulations, and limitations on direct investment. As democracy rises around the world, expect much debate and even rancor as many long-oppressed people finally get an opportunity to flex their political muscles.

mission statement
A statement of the firm's long-term vision of what the firm is trying to become, which differentiates this firm from other firms. The mission provides direction and a sense of purpose to all employees.

Establishing a Mission

An organization's *mission* is its *raison d'être* (French for "reason for being"), the fundamental purpose it's designed to serve. The organizational **mission statement** answers the question "What is this organization's purpose?" for employees, customers, and other constituents.

WHAT MANAGERS ARE READING

COMPETING FOR THE FUTURE
by Gary Hamel and C.K. Prahalad

To find out if their business is competing for the future, professors Gary Hamel of the London School of Business and C.K. Prahalad of the University of Michigan ask senior managers three questions: first, what percentage of your time is spent on external rather than internal issues—understanding, for example, the implications of a particular new technology versus debating corporate overhead allocations. Second, of this time spent looking outward, how

much is spent considering how the world could be different in five or ten years, as opposed to worrying about winning the next big contract or how to respond to a competitor's pricing move? Third, of the time devoted to looking outward and forward, how much is spent in consultation with colleagues, where the objective is to build a deeply shared, well-tested view of the future, as opposed to a personal and idiosyncratic view?

As Prahalad and Hamel have learned, the answers to those questions typically conform to what they call the 40-30-20 rule. It's their experience that about 40 percent of senior executive time is spent looking outward, and of this time about 30 percent is spent peering into the future. And of the time spent looking forward, no more than 20 percent is spent trying to develop a collective view of the future. Thus, on average, senior management is spending less than 3 percent ($40\% \times 30\% \times 20\% = 2.4\%$) of its energy building a corporate perspective on the future.

In their book, *Competing for the Future*, Prahalad and Hamel assert that a

senior management team must devote 20 to 50 percent of its time over a period of months to develop a prescient and distinctive point of view of the future. It then must also be willing to revisit that point of view, elaborating and adjusting it as the future unfolds.

The vital first step in competing for the future is developing what the authors call industry foresight. This is defined as an understanding of the industry that is deeper than that of competitors. It is an understanding of the trends and discontinuities—technological, demographic, regulatory, or lifestyle—that could be used to transform industry boundaries and create a new competitive space. Industry foresight gives a company the potential to get to the future first and stake out a leadership position. Managers are reading Hamel and Prahalad's book to learn how to develop industry foresight and control the destiny of their business.

Source: Adapted from Gary Hamel and C.K. Prahalad, "Seeing the Future First," *Fortune*, September 5, 1994, pp. 64-70; Gary Hamel and C.K. Prahalad, *Competing for the Future* (Boston, Mass: Harvard Business School Press, 1994).

Whereas a strategy addresses ongoing goals and procedures, the firm's mission statement describes an even more fundamental rationale for its existence.

Some organizational theorists assert that organizational missions should be based on something even more abstract, an organizational vision. In other words, a mission statement should flow out of the vision. A true vision is a basic structure of the future that allows an organization the flexibility of means to build toward it. A vision is important because it helps the firm model strategic plans and provides a kind of touchstone for goal setting. It can be critical in a shifting industry by offering a hedge to reactive decision making. A vision keeps a firm focused on its superordinate, or long-term, goals.

A number of electric utilities, for example, have made visioning an integral part of their strategic planning process. They work from the top down to develop a picture of what they want their company to look like in the future. They communicate this vision throughout the organization to encourage buy-in from every employee.[23]

To establish a mission, a firm must take into consideration its history, distinctive competence(s), and environment.

HISTORY - For established firms, the mission should be consistent with what is known about the firm's history. This history includes accomplishments and failures, objectives and policies, decisions, employees, and more. An organization must assess its history to determine its current resource base, its image, and its various capacities. Odd as it may sound, many management consultants help organizations appreciate and use **organization stories**. Stories tell of experiences and events that transpired where the story-teller works. Within an organization, stories serve to legitimate power, to rationalize group behavior, and

organization stories
Within an organization, stories tell of experiences and events that transpired where the story-teller works. Stories legitimate power, rationalize group behavior, and reinforce organizational values, identity, and commitment.

to reinforce organizational values, identity, and commitment.[24] Before writing, human cultures relied on stories to convey the history of their culture to the young and to outsiders. Similarly, organizational stories convey the history of the organization to new employees and outsiders. Managers should review organizational stories when establishing a mission statement.

Start-ups and new ventures need a mission, too, but have no history upon which to base a long-term vision. Instead, such firms can look to the history of the industry they are part of, or to the history of the human needs and expectations they hope to satisfy through organized activity.

distinctive competence
A capacity that's unique to the firm and that's valued in the market.

DISTINCTIVE COMPETENCE - Although a firm is likely to be capable of doing many things, strategic success stems from the firm identifying and capitalizing on what it does best and also what customers desire. A **distinctive competence** is a capacity that's unique to the firm and that's valued in the market. For example, Eastman Kodak's CEO George M.C. Fisher, after a little more than a year at the helm, sold off the company's healthcare businesses and refocused it on its core imaging business. This renewed emphasis on imaging has led to development of digital imaging technology, which will be used in several promising new products. One promising new product is the CopyPrint station, which uses digital technology to make photo enlargements from ordinary prints.[25]

ENVIRONMENT - The business environment contains opportunities, constraints, and threats to the firm. Before a mission is articulated, these conditions must be analyzed and evaluated, as discussed above. The mission should be responsive to the organization's environment.

Characteristics of a Mission Statement

For quality-based organizations, the mission statement that results from the analysis of history, distinctive competence, and the environment must be (1) customer-focused, (2) achievable, (3) motivational, and (4) specific.

CUSTOMER-FOCUSED - Mission statements in quality-based organizations emphasize a customer focus. Many firms have faltered or failed because they continued to define themselves in terms of what they produced rather than in terms of who they served.

Quality-based organizations formulate strategy based on the premise that customer satisfaction and, better yet, customer delight and loyalty are necessary for enduring success. The reasons are many and fundamental. Finding new customers is far more expensive than keeping current customers. Dissatisfied customers not only fail to return to buy again, they are also likely (1) to decline to express the reasons for their dissatisfaction (which could be a source of learning and growth for the firm) and (2) to share their dissatisfaction with other potential customers. As Deming notes, "no one can guess the future loss of business from a dissatisfied customer."[26] Customers, not employees, are a firm's best salespeople.

Rubbermaid is a good example of a company that consistently produces customer delight. Virtually every product the company makes is popular, with 9 out of 10 new products rated a commercial success. In a survey of consumers, Rubbermaid was chosen the second most powerful brand in America in terms of product quality, concern for customer needs, consumer trust, and consumers' willingness to recommend the company. The fundamental new product strategy is to understand the definition of value through the eyes of the consumer.[27]

ACHIEVABLE - While a mission statement should be challenging, it must also be achievable. Unrealistic ambitions can exceed a firm's capabilities. Although it's important to ensure that goals are achievable, it's equally important to guard against setting your sights too low. Many organizations are now using what are called "stretch targets" to ensure the organization continues to reach beyond its current level of competitiveness. AlliedSignal's CEO Lawrence Bossidy is known for setting stretch targets, even for some of the company's more lackluster businesses. Over the long term, he aims to increase earnings by 15 percent per year. To reach that goal, the company must increase sales by 8 percent each year through 1997. Once Bossidy gets his people to agree on growth targets, it's up to them to seek and cultivate the right markets and products.[28]

MOTIVATIONAL - The mission must serve as a source of motivation at all levels. Effective mission statements have meaning to every employee, allowing each of them to translate the mission's words into their own motivation, and serving as a guide for decisions and actions.

Motivation affects the enduring effort of employees. Yet, as Crosby notes, "A company whose top management is committed to quality, with roots, does not suffer from uncertainty and bewilderment."[29] Crosby describes the "three phases involved in getting an organization or a person to be productive in the very best meaning of the word: conviction, commitment, and conversion."[30] Conviction means the employee is dedicated to the idea. Commitment describes the behavioral expression of the psychological conviction. Conversion means that the employee has rejected outdated, noncompetitive notions of success.

SPECIFIC - Quality-based strategies are specific. A mission statement must be clear enough to allow employees and customers to know in what business the firm competes as well as in what business it doesn't compete. Being specific in the mission allows employees to focus their energy and to be more productive, making the entire firm more profitable. Broad statements of value or goodness (e.g.,"the highest quality at the lowest price") do not make a good mission statement. By attempting to be all things to all people, a firm's energy is scattered, making the firm less able to develop distinctive competence and making it nearly impossible to please anyone. Since the 1980s, mission statements have found their place in a growing number of organizations. From corporations to community groups, these declarations are being used to give those organizations direction, purpose, perspective, and vision. Most mission statements are directed both inside and outside their respective organizations, providing a message to management, staff, clients, and prospects. When writing a mission statement, it's time for an organization to step back and reflect on what it's trying to do. It needs to focus on the fundamental elements that both define the organization and make the difference between its success and failure.[31]

A year-end 1994 study of the companies listed in the *Business Week* 1000, analyzing randomly selected firms across industrial groups, shows that having a mission statement significantly increases shareholder equity. In fact, the average return on stockholder's equity for firms with mission statements is 16.1 percent. The return for firms without mission statements is 9.7 percent.[32]

Table 7–1 on the following page provides the mission statements of three well-known companies. Can you spot their attention to the four characteristics we've just reviewed?

Establishing Goals and Objectives

A firm's mission must be further translated or reduced into meaningful goals, which specify in more concrete detail the firm's long-term aspirations. Organizational goals are the end points or targets stemming from the organization's mission. Goals define what the organization seeks to accomplish through its ongoing, long-run operations.

Effective goals are capable of being converted into precise actions and shorter-term objectives. Clear goals tell employees where they should direct their efforts, without creating doubt about the firm's intentions. Leaders in an organization set the tone by communicating not only what needs to be done, but also how it should be done. All leaders, at whatever level, must focus on the essential flow of the business processes in their area of responsibility. Leaders of high-performance organizations don't speak of the cost of quality; they speak of the price of poor quality. The high-performance organization leader trains the staff so they are able to achieve quality goals, and controls the processes to ensure consistent high quality. He or she also determines internal performance measures, which correlate highly with customer requirements.[33]

Goals facilitate management control, serving as standards against which the firm's performance will be measured. Clear goals and objectives help employees track progress by

TABLE 7-1	THREE CORPORATE MISSION STATEMENTS

Levi Strauss

We seek profitable and responsible commercial success creating and selling jeans and casual clothing. We seek this while offering quality products and service—and by being the leader in what we do. What we do is important. How we do it is also important. Here's how: by being honest. By being responsible citizens in communities where we operate and in society in general. By having a workplace that's safe and productive, where people work together in teams, where they talk to each other openly, where they're responsible for their actions, and where they can improve their skills.

Federal Express

Federal Express is committed to our PEOPLE-SERVICE-PROFIT philosophy. We will produce outstanding financial returns by providing totally reliable, competitively superior global air-ground transportation of high-priority goods and documents that require time-certain delivery. Equally important, positive control of each pack will be maintained utilizing real-time electronic tracing systems. A complete record of each shipment and delivery will be presented with our request for payment. We will be helpful, courteous, and professional to each other and the public. We will strive to have a satisfied customer at the end of each transaction.

Ben & Jerry's

Ben & Jerry's is dedicated to the creation and demonstration of a new corporate concept of linked prosperity. Our mission consists of three interrelated parts:

Product Mission—to make, distribute and sell the finest quality all-natural ice cream and related products in a wide variety of innovative flavors made from Vermont dairy products.

Social Mission—to operate the company in a way that actively recognizes the central role that business plays in the structure of society by initiating innovative ways to improve the quality of life of a broad community: local, national, and international.

Economic Mission—to operate the company on a sound financial basis of profitable growth, increasing value for our shareholders, and creating career opportunities and financial rewards for our employees.

Source: Adapted from R. Duane Ireland and Michael A. Hitt, "Mission Statements: Importance, Challenge, and Recommendations for Development," *Business Horizons*, May–June 1992, pp. 34–42.

providing precise targets and immediate feedback. An employee focused on customer satisfaction as a strategic goal has something to measure as an indicator of success.

Operating Strategies

operating strategy
A broad plan of action for pursuing and achieving a firm's goals and satisfying its mission.

After a mission and goals are specified, they must be put into action through an **operating strategy.** An operating strategy is a broad plan of action for pursuing and achieving the firm's goals and satisfying its mission. The competitive strategy model offers several alternative operating strategies.

COMPETITIVE STRATEGY MODEL - According to the competitive strategy model, organizations can develop distinctive competence in three ways: differentiation, cost leadership, and niche.

Differentiation.   In an effort to distinguish its products, a firm using the **differentiation strategy** offers a higher-priced product equipped with more product-enhancing features than its competitors' products. Differentiation strategy firms seek a premium price for their products and attempt to maintain high levels of customer loyalty. The firm markets and sells the product to a relatively small group of customers who are willing to pay a higher price for the premium features. This differentiation strategy (sometimes called a *premium strategy*) leads to relatively high-cost, low-volume production, with a high gross profit margin per item. Often advertising or marketing adds a perception of luxury that creates demand for the product due to the psychological value of buying and using it. Mercedes Benz cars, Ben & Jerry's ice cream, and Godiva chocolates are marketed under a differentiation strategy.

differentiation strategy
In this approach, a firm offers a high-priced product equipped with the greatest number of product-enhancing features, and sells the product to a relatively small group of customers who are willing to pay top dollar for premium features. Sometimes called premium strategy.

Cost Leadership.   In contrast to the differentiation strategy, the **cost-leadership strategy** means low costs, low prices, high volume, and low profit margins on each item. With this strategy, a cost leader attempts to attract a large number of customers with low prices, generating a large overall profit by the sheer volume of units sold. Examples of cost leaders are the U.S. Postal Service, McDonald's, and generic brand cigarettes produced by tobacco giants such as R. J. Reynolds. It's difficult, though not impossible, to be both lower cost and differentiated relative to competitors.[34] One company that has managed both is Saturn Corporation. Differentiation is a key competitive strategy that has been built in from Saturn's beginnings in 1985. First, Saturn sold the company instead of the car. Second, it developed a relationship with customers. In its first year, Saturn's advertisements centered on employee commitment and low price. Since then, Saturn has focused on the experience of its customers, emphasizing economy and quality at the same time.[35]

Niche.   The **niche strategy** involves offering a unique product or service in a restricted market (usually a geographic region). For example, Milwaukee-based Midwest Express Airlines employs a niche strategy. It offers luxury service, food, and seating, while using Milwaukee as its sole hub. The air carrier does not compete in all national markets: it does not serve Arizona, Utah, New Mexico, or the northwestern United States. The airline appeals primarily to a select group of business travelers, including those frustrated by crowded Chicago airports and willing to pay for premium service. Also, given its low-cost structure, Midwest Express doesn't need to charge a truly premium price. This operating strategy allows the airline to be profitable because of its niche.

Every organization must choose one of these market strategies, summarized in Figure 7–8. Although strategic planning doesn't guarantee success, it can increase the likelihood of achieving success. Integrating quality practice into overall corporate strategy gives firms a powerful source of competitive advantage.

QUALITY AND STRATEGY

The renewed emphasis on quality and competitiveness that has occurred among organizations over the past decade has strong implications for overall strategy. For instance, the drive to grow and expand, so common to businesses for most of the twentieth century, must be tempered by an ability to maintain contact with customers. Many organizations learned the hard way that bigger is not better if all contact with customers is lost. At the same time, companies have learned that customers, or "stakeholders," come in a variety of forms. There are internal and external stakeholders. One important internal stakeholder that has gone through cycles of neglect in American business is the employee. Today, quality-based organizations are focusing on employees as their most vital resource.

In this section, we'll be examining how quality fits into overall corporate strategy by focusing on implications for internal and external stakeholders. These stakeholders include employees, customers, suppliers, shareholders, and the community. As the Ethics Spotlight

cost-leadership strategy
A strategy of low price, high volume, and low profit margins on each item. With this strategy, a cost leader attempts to attract a large number of customers with low prices, generating a large overall profit by sheer volume of units sold.

niche strategy
A strategy that applies the premium strategy to a restricted market (usually a geographic region).

FIGURE 7–8
Competitive Strategy Model

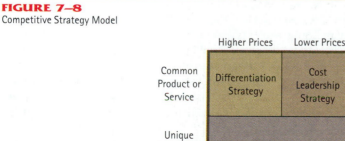

ETHICS SPOTLIGHT **ETHICS AND STRATEGIC PLANNING**

Corporate ethics isn't just a warm and fuzzy idea. It's a strategic management issue that should be considered in every facet of business decisions. An ethical organization expects, and communicates through work and deed, ethical behavior and fair treatment of all stakeholders.

Ethics and the moral obligations of management were an accepted component in the strategic planning process during the early development of corporate strategy as a field of study. The integrity of common purpose was a major theme during much of the early work in corporate strategy. But what impact does an organization's ethical behavior have on profitability? Research has shown that the equity market didn't punish American automobile manufacturers for the product recalls of the 1970s. However, other research has shown that a firm's reputation is an asset.

Managers face a number of difficulties in developing corporate ethics programs. These difficulties often arise from conflicting interests and priorities. Pressures may be both internal and external. Corporate ethics programs usually evolve from a combination of proactive and reactive policies. Nonetheless, it is of little dispute that trust, commitment, and common purpose on the part of stakeholders of a firm are essential to success. The argument for a strong commitment to ethics can be summarized in five statements:

1. The strategic decisions of any large-scale economic enterprise in a competitive global environment result in both benefits and harms. The harms, which include the discharge of employees, the termination of suppliers, the deterioration of environments, etc., cannot be avoided, although until recently they have been ignored.
2. It is the responsibility of the senior executives of the firm to distribute those benefits and allocate those harms among the stakeholders of the company. This can be done arbitrarily or thoughtfully. If it's done thoughtfully, then ethical principles offer the only form of analysis that's relevant.
3. Ethical principles offer the only form of analysis that's relevant for the distribution of benefits and the allocation of harms because they provide the only means of recognizing the interests and rights of each of the stakeholders and comparing those interests and rights through the use of known principles.
4. Stakeholders who believe that the benefits have been distributed through a process that recognizes their interests and rights, and that compares those interests and rights with those of other stakeholders through the use of known principles,

will develop trust in the direction of the firm.
5. Stakeholders who develop trust in the direction of the firm will show commitment to its future. Commitment to the future of a firm will ensure efforts that are both cooperative and innovative. Cooperating, innovative, and directed efforts on the part of all of the stakeholder groups will lead to competitive and economic success, however measured, for that firm over time.

This is a considerable departure from the existing paradigm that holds that the selection of a strategic posture within an industry and the leveraging of strategic resources across industries lead to competitive and economic success. The argument above is that the selection of the posture and the leveraging of the resources are not enough in a competitive global economy. Trust, commitment, and effort must be added to ensure cooperative and innovative acts on the part of all of the stakeholders. The argument is that strategic planning must be both analytical and ethical.

Source: Adapted from Jacquie L'Etang, "Ethical Corporate Social Responsibility: A Framework for Managers," *Journal of Business Ethics*, 1995, pp. 125–132; Larue Tone Hosmer, "Strategic Planning as if Ethics Mattered," *Strategic Management Journal*, 1994, pp. 17–34; David C. Selley, "Ethics as a Management Tool," *Canadian Business Review*, Summer 1994, pp. 41–43.

argues, including stakeholders in strategic thinking and planning is good policy from an analytical and ethical point of view.

Employees

Whereas the traditional view of strategy suggests that managers and shareholders are a company's most important asset, a quality-based view directs attention to the customers and nonmanagement employees. These stakeholders are highlighted in quality firms because they are critical in defining and adding value to the product or service.

Employees in the modern workplace are conceived differently from those at the turn of the century, as we have already noted. Increasingly, organizations are relying upon their own people as the source of new ideas, energy, and creativity. The modern knowledge worker requires a different management approach than the sweatshop laborer, as discussed in the Workplace of Tomorrow.

The traditional view of labor as a cost of production has been replaced in the quality-based strategy by a view of employees as a resource. The only sustainable competitive advantage for a firm in the global marketplace is its human resources. Although cash,

WORKPLACE OF TOMORROW

THE INFORMATED WORKPLACE

Early in the 20th century an organizational form—the functional hierarchy—was invented to meet the business challenges of increasing throughput and lowering unit costs. Business processes were divided into separate functions—manufacturing, engineering, sales, and so on. Other innovative features included mass-production techniques, the minute fragmentation of tasks, the professionalization of management, the growth of the managerial hierarchy to standardize and control operations, and the simplification and delegation of administrative functions to a newly contrived clerical workforce. Collectively, these components were incredibly successful; they came to define the modern workplace.

The industrial hierarchy rested on the premise that complexity could constantly be removed from lower-level jobs and passed up to the management ranks. That is, clerks and factory workers became progressively less involved in the overall business of a firm as their jobs were narrowed and stripped of opportunities to exercise judgment. Automation was a primary means of accomplishing this. Meanwhile the manager's role evolved as guardian of the organization's centralized knowledge base. His legitimate authority derived from being credited as someone fit to receive, interpret, and communicate orders based on the command of information.

In the brave new age of the information economy, this system cannot hold. Mass-market approaches have been forced to give way to a highly differentiated and often information-saturated marketplace in which firms must distinguish themselves through the value they add in response to customers' priorities. Information technologies now provide the means for generating such value with speed and efficiency.

Doing so means using the modern information infrastructure to cope with the complexities of a business outside a central managerial cadre. It's more efficient to handle complexity wherever and whenever it first enters the organization—whether during a sale, during delivery, or in production.

This approach is now possible because of the way the unique characteristics of information technologies can transform work at every organizational level. Initially, most people regarded computers in the workplace as the next phase of automation. But whereas automation effectively hid many operations of the overall enterprise from individual workers, information technology tends to illuminate them. It can quickly give any employee a comprehensive view of the entire business or nearly infinite detail on any of its aspects.

These new technologies informate as well as automate. They surrender knowledge to anyone with the skills to access and understand it. Information technologies can increase the intellectual content of work at all levels. Work comes to depend on an ability to understand, respond to, manage, and create value from information. Thus, efficient operations in the informated workplace require a more equitable distribution of knowledge and authority; the transformation of information into wealth means that more members of the firm must be given opportunities to know more and to do more.

Source: Adapted from Shoshana Zuboff, "The Emperor's New Workplace," *Scientific American*, September 1995, pp. 203–204.

---

equipment, facilities, and infrastructure can be quickly transferred, built, or acquired, human resources are not so easily or quickly developed. Strategic management of employees requires managers to dedicate time, money, and attention to their training and development. This not only increases workers' value; it also enhances their capacity for continuous improvement. In a global market, allowing a workforce to grow stagnant without ongoing training is to invite failure.

Managers must ensure that employees see value in the training they receive. With the rampant changes that are occurring in the modern economy, many employees are suffering from a malady known as **initiative burnout**. Whether it's total quality management, cycle time reduction, or business process reengineering, employees in many organizations have begun to feel that something new is coming around the corner every day.[36]

The prudent approach is to adopt a long-term strategy, and then build a sensible training program that helps employees develop skills that can be applied to problems throughout the organization. Employees want training that will help them make progress in their careers, but managers have to recognize that progress in modern organizations has been redefined. Career paths in the modern organization often don't follow the traditional "corporate ladder." In the customer-focused organization, employees spend more time moving along a horizontal ladder—doing projects with people from different departments in their organization—than climbing the vertical ladder.[37]

Much of the work in modern organizations involves collecting, organizing, and analyzing information. In short, professional work is knowledge work. To help the modern professional succeed requires not only training, but also an organizational structure conducive to

initiative burnout
That which occurs among employees who have experienced too many management initiatives (e.g., TQM, reengineering, cycle time reduction) in too short a time.

continuous learning. The main difference between training and learning is that training is often a group activity; learning is often more effective as an individual activity.[38] Managers who provide both training and a learning environment for employees will create more innovation, better service, and more efficient operations than competitors.

Although employees are a central part of a quality-based organization's resources, the main objective is satisfied customers.

Customers

Defining organizational strategy in terms of customer expectations is fundamental to the quality-based approach to strategic management. **Customers** are defined as the end users of the organization's products and/or services.

For some companies, a variety of customers or groups may use its products and services. For example, a hotel may rent single rooms to walk-up business customers, to tourists in small groups, or to a business manager of a professional organization who secures rooms for thousands of convention goers. Similarly, a household-goods moving firm may sell its full range of services to corporate clients at a discount for large volume, and at regular rates to single households that use only some of the firm's services (e.g., shipping but not packing of household goods). Careful identification of the firm's customers is essential.

How does a company find and develop loyal customers? There is no simple answer to this critical question. Happy customers return and refer other customers. Unhappy customers not only fail to return; they are likely to turn away other potential customers. One estimate is that one dissatisfied customer can produce 250 noncustomers (people who are indifferent, perhaps even hostile to a firm's product or service).[39] In a free-market economy, where customer choice and freedom are paramount, satisfied customers are the fundamental focus of any strategy.

At the Seventh Annual Customer Satisfaction and Quality Measurement Conference, Bradley Gale, founder of Customer Value, Inc., reported three stages of customer satisfaction in a quality-based organization: conformance quality, customer satisfaction and market-perceived quality, and customer value. The first stage represents the zero-defects approach of Phil Crosby. It's the stage at which a company is able to give the customer what the company has said it would provide. Stage two goes beyond conformance in creating an image of quality that is perceived by the marketplace. Stage three represents those companies that have gone beyond customer satisfaction to customer delight. In this stage, the customer will perceive overall value in the product, the company, and the shopping experience.[40]

Customers use the goods and services produced by a firm. Many firms, in turn, are customers of suppliers. Working with suppliers to ensure a steady flow of high-quality raw materials is vital to a firm's overall success.

Suppliers

Suppliers provide essential raw materials for the firm. The traditional view of suppliers is that a single supplier of any one raw material can threaten a firm's flexibility, especially its capacity to force price concessions by playing off two or more suppliers against one another.[41] This is compounded by a traditional view of purchasing as a low-cost function, where the business is awarded to the supplier offering the lowest cost per unit. The quality-based strategy focuses on developing long-term relationships with key suppliers, focusing on building partnerships, continuously improving product quality, and driving down costs. Special attention is devoted to eliminating defective parts and to involving the supplier in the design process for the firm's product(s). This type of relationship is the basis of such process innovations as just-in-time manufacturing.

A significant development in the automobile industry is the adoption of a set of minimal requirements for suppliers by the Big Three U.S. automakers. Called Quality Systems Requirements 9000 or QS 9000, the new quality requirements will be imposed on suppliers of production and service parts materials. QS 9000 is structured to enhance a company's quality system and requires a systematic managerial strategy. It also requires that suppliers

---

customers
End users of the firm's products and services.

maintain both short- and long-term business plans, perform feasibility reviews, maintain control plans from the part prototype through prelaunch to final part production, and adhere to strict process control requirements.[42]

Publicly traded firms have another set of constituents interested in the firm's performance: stockholders. While many stockholders are interested only in maximizing returns on their investment, most also realize that this is best accomplished through an effective quality strategy.

Stockholders

Stockholders are those who own a firm's stock. The traditional view of business in the United States has placed highest priority on satisfying stockholder expectations which, because of their exclusively financial interest, usually meant paying close attention to the quarterly report. This focus results in a heavy emphasis on short-term profit improvements, often realized at the expense of long-term investment.

In Japan, by way of contrast, stockholders and senior management are the first to suffer in bad business times. The traditional U.S. approach to a downturn in the business cycle has been to lay off workers first while the firm waits for customer demand to return. A 1980 NBC News White Paper, "If Japan Can, Why Can't We?" showed how Mazda of Japan, during an energy-cost-induced sales crisis, assigned engineers to selling jobs, to learning more about the customer, without layoffs.

A major responsibility of managers is communication with stockholders. Perhaps the most effective communicator is Warren Buffet, chairman of the investment firm Berkshire-Hathaway and one of the world's wealthiest people. Buffet is well known for his annual reports to shareholders. In fact, many people purchase Berkshire-Hathaway stock just to have an opportunity to read Buffet's message.

A quality-based organization typically uses a strategy of open books with employees and stockholders. Their commitment to communication helps everyone feel they are an important part of the organization. Good communication from managers to stockholders helps the latter understand the long-term strategy of the firm. This helps to align stockholders' interests with the strategic interest of the organization.

A final stakeholder of most organizations is the community. The community is an important stakeholder in that it defines the rules for legal business activity and is the source of many important resources for the organization's continued success.

Community

The *community* consists of private citizens plus government and other public or regulatory agencies. Traditionally, the community is dependent on the firm and is grateful for the salaries and taxes it pays and for its use of community suppliers and contractors. Many communities and states offer companies special inducements to bring their production to the community.

Environmental concerns are an increasingly important issue to companies in a multitude of industries. In the past, dirty air and water that resulted from heavy industrial production were often accepted as a cost of doing business. The community accepted pollution along with wages and purchases from the polluting firm. Today, many companies have adopted a new approach to the environment known as **total quality environmental management (TQEM)**. Interfirm teaming for environmental advantage, which is known as TQEM alliancing, initiates a cyclical or continuous approach to environmental improvement. It does so by forging strategic relationships among firms that can leverage each other's environmental weaknesses. It allows firms to take their environmental improvement initiatives beyond regulatory compliance and into proactivity, beyond pollution control to total pollution avoidance, and beyond profitability for a quantitative as well as qualitative bottom line, because firms will be integrating external as well as internal functions across different business domains.[43]

Not only must a firm act in a legal, ethical fashion with each stakeholder; the community also expects a strong sense of social responsibility from the firm. Further, most communities view the firm as needing to make a positive contribution to the community, beyond

stockholders
Those who own a firm's stock.

total quality environmental management (TQEM)
A continuous improvement approach to a company's environmental management practices. It involves forming alliances with other organizations for the purpose of working together to solve common problems.

Wetlands provide a habitat for waterfowl, improve water quality, recharge farm wells, and reduce flooding. Since 1990, as a member of the Partnership for Wetlands Preservation, Dow Chemical Corporation has shown its concern for the environment by financing the preservation and enhancement of more than 700,000 acres of wetlands in the United States and Canada. The company has also worked to save and restore more than 60,000 acres of endangered wetlands on or near their own property.

the firm's payroll, purchases, and taxes. The strategic quality-based view of the community as a stakeholder must also be long term.

Strategic thinking is the basis for forming an organization's strategy. Strategic formulation requires a firm to focus on its internal and external environments, and to search for opportunities and threats. Strategic implementation is the action step necessary to realize an organization's goals. A clear strategy is defined in terms of situation analysis, mission statement, goals, and operating strategies. Strategies are important at all levels of the organization, not just for top management.

Quality-based strategies reflect a shift from an internal to an external focus. Global economic changes have increased the role of information and knowledge-based work. Effective strategic responses to global competition include zero defects, benchmarking, time-based strategies, and continuous improvement.

Quality-based strategies are not always successful. A study of top American managers found that quality efforts most often failed due to misguided attempts to quickly achieve profitable results or other results not fundamentally built upon quality.[44] Quality efforts succeed best when the firm builds a coherent strategy aimed at improving quality. A survey of 584 companies in North America, Japan, and Europe found that firms with significant problems must build their quality efforts from the bottom up, beginning with training and teams; better-performing firms can focus on simplifying work procedures, training workers in problem solving, and building long-term relationships with suppliers; top-performing firms can further improve their quality through benchmarking and empowering trained workers to make important decisions.[45]

Quality-based strategies reflect a change from traditional economic, organizational, and managerial strategies. Table 7–2 summarizes the major differences between traditional and quality-based approaches to strategy.

TABLE 7-2	TRADITIONAL VERSUS QUALITY-BASED CHARACTERISTICS OF STRATEGY
Traditional	Quality-Based
Profit is primary goal.	Quality is primary goal.
Quarterly earnings growth is sought.	Customer satisfaction is sought.
Stockholders take precedence.	Customers take precedence.
Senior managers are key employees.	All employees are important.
In bad times, employees are cut.	In bad times, stock dividend is cut.
Capital is equity based.	Capital is debt based.
Absentee ownership.	Employee ownership.
Managers are cosmopolitan, mobile.	Growth is valued; managers are promoted from within.
Business portfolio is diversified.	Business portfolio is focused.
Top executives get stock options.	Gainsharing, ESOPs, Improshare.
Managers manage; workers work.	All employees manage.
There is secrecy concerning costs.	There is candor concerning costs.

SUMMARY OF LEARNING OBJECTIVES

DEFINE STRATEGIC THINKING AND STRATEGY.

Strategic thinking is the determination of the basic long-term goals and objectives of an enterprise, and the adoption of courses of action and the allocation of resources necessary for carrying out these goals. A firm's strategy conveys its basic sense of values to top management, to the public, to employees, to the world.

EXPLAIN THE FOUR COMPONENTS OF THE STRATEGIC PLANNING CIRCLE.

First, a situation analysis requires attention to the four elements of a firm's environment: internal strengths and weaknesses plus external opportunities and threats. Second, the mission states the organization's fundamental purpose. It answers the question, "Why are we in business?" Third, organizational objectives are the end points of the firm's mission and what it seeks through ongoing, long-run operations. With objectives, the mission is defined by a finer set of specific and achievable statements. Fourth, an operating strategy is a broad plan of action for pursuing and achieving the firm's objectives and satisfying its mission.

IDENTIFY THE THREE FACTORS THAT GO INTO DEVELOPING A MISSION STATEMENT.

In developing a firm's mission statement, managers should consider the firm's history, distinctive competencies, and environment.

DESCRIBE THE COST-LEADERSHIP, NICHE, AND DIFFERENTIATION OPERATING STRATEGIES.

The cost-leadership strategy means low prices, low costs, high volume, and low profit margins on each item. With this strategy, a cost leader attempts to attract a large number of customers with low prices, generating a large overall profit by the sheer volume of the units sold.

The niche strategy applies the premium strategy to a restricted market (usually a geographic area). From a quality-based view, it could be argued that the only relevant strategy is a niche strategy, where the firm sharply focuses on a specific segment of the customer base.

A differentiation strategy firm offers a higher-priced product equipped with the greatest number of product-enhancing features. Differentiation strategy firms seek a premium price for their products and attempt to maintain high levels of customer loyalty to the company. The firm then sells the product to a relatively small group of customers who are willing to pay top dollar for these premium features.

DISCUSS THE FOUR CLASSIFICATIONS OF AN ORGANIZATIONAL PORTFOLIO MATRIX.

A cash cow is a strategic business unit (SBU) with a high market share of a low-growth market. A star is an SBU with a high market share of a high-growth market. A cash trap is an SBU with a low market share of a low-growth market. A question mark is an SBU with a low market share of a high-growth market.

EXPLAIN HOW QUALITY-BASED STRATEGY DIFFERS FROM A TRADITIONAL APPROACH.

A quality-based strategy focuses on exceeding customer expectations, empowering employees with information and planning responsibility, and continuous improvement. The traditional management approach was to shut nonmanagement employees out of the planning process altogether. In addition, traditional management planned to offer the customer products that were produced in high volume with little variety. Quality-based firms are flexible and able to engage in short production runs to customize products for individual customers.

IDENTIFY THE COMPONENTS OF THE VALUE CHAIN.

A firm's primary activities consist of inbound logistics, operations, outbound logistics, marketing and sales, and after-sale service. A firm's support activities consist of firm infrastructure, human resource management, technology development, and procurement.

IDENTIFY PORTER'S FIVE COMPETITIVE FORCES.

The five competitive forces are the threat of new entrants, the threat of substitution, the bargaining power of suppliers, the bargaining power of buyers, and intra-industry forces.

EXPLAIN THE DIFFERENT STRATEGIC CHOICES ASSOCIATED WITH THE PORTFOLIO MATRIX.

There are four basic strategy alternatives: hold, harvest, build, or divest. A hold strategy should be used with cash cows. Harvest should be used as a short-term strategy with cash cows, question marks, and cash traps. A build strategy should be used with stars and question marks. A divest strategy should be used with cash traps.

EXPLAIN WHAT IS MEANT BY A SWOT ANALYSIS.

A SWOT analysis refers to the process of examining a firm's internal and external environments for important strengths, weaknesses, opportunities, and threats.

KEY TERMS

cash cow, p. 187
cash trap, p. 188
cost-leadership strategy, p. 199
customer-perceived value, p. 193
customers, p. 202
differentiation strategy, p. 198
distinctive competence, p. 196
environmental scanning, p. 193
five competitive forces, p. 189

initiative burnout, p. 201
issues management, p. 193
mission statement, p. 194
niche strategy, p. 199
operating strategy, p. 198
opportunity, p. 193
organization stories, p. 195
question mark, p. 188
star, p. 187

stockholders, p. 203
strategic business unit (SBU), p. 187
strategic planning, p. 191
strategic thinking, p. 184
strategy, p. 184
SWOT analysis, p. 193
threat, p. 193
total quality environmental management (TQEM), p. 203
value chain, p. 190

REVIEW AND DISCUSSION QUESTIONS

Recall

1. Explain the differences between a cash cow and a cash trap; between a star and a question mark.
2. What are the four components of strategic planning?
3. What are the characteristics of a mission statement?

Understanding

4. How can a firm prevent strategic objectives from becoming numerical quotas?
5. Who is responsible for strategy in a quality-based organization?
6. Explain the customer's role in strategic planning from a quality perspective.

7. Traditional firms have emphasized stockholders and their demands for increased profits, earnings per share, and stock price. How does a quality-based approach respond to stockholders?

Application

8. Write a mission statement for your business school. What are the key elements of the statement? Who are your customers?
9. Review the differentiation, cost-leadership, and niche strategies. Identify five national or global firms that use each strategy.
10. List the features that might appeal to a customer choosing among liquid refreshments (e.g., soft drinks, bottled water, milk).

CASE STUDY

Kiva Container Corporation's Small Business Strategy

If you run a small business, you run your life, control your destiny, and make a good living. That's the romance of running a small busi-

ness; it's also the myth. People who run a small business will tell you it's business, or the bank, that owns them. A small business invariably demands hard work and long hours that as often as not end in failure, not fortune.

With the proliferation of opportunities that accompany a globalizing economy, there arises a new set of hazards for small businesses. If current times carry one economic subtext, it's this: there are no simple businesses anymore. Hard work will always have its place, but today managerial dexterity, mental acumen, and sharp instincts often spell the difference between success and failure for small businesses.

Small businesses must struggle all the harder today for a variety of reasons, the most seminal one being that competition has intensified. It now comes from all quarters—and at an accelerating pace. At the end of World War II, the U.S. generated 40 percent of the world's gross domestic product. By the end of the century, America's share of world GDP should decline to little more than 20 percent. Combine that with falling trade barriers, large disparities in labor rates, and highly mobile capital, and you've got a recipe for economic trench warfare.

Kiva Container Corporation of Phoenix, Arizona, is a small business in the packaging industry. It makes boxes from both corrugated paper and cardboard, chiefly for manufacturers of consumer goods. Family run for three generations, Kiva produces a livelihood for 67 people, many of whom have been with the company for 15 years or longer. Ron Stafford and his son Ron started the business in 1957. Kiva is the Hopi name given to the meeting place where the Hopi conducted their commerce. In both form and spirit, Kiva container is tribal, binding three generations of the Stafford clan to it.

Over the past decade, Kiva has been buffeted by external forces, ranging from rising local taxes to increasing global competition. Even though times are tough, and the Staffords have had many offers from others interested in buying their business, they want to pass on the business in good health to future generations.

In today's interconnected world, Kiva remains a tortoise that nonetheless must move at a hare's pace. Kiva's sales in 1994 were about $10 million. The net margin in a typical year is a mere 5 percent. To boost that number, and to keep the top line from eroding, Kiva has pursued a two-pronged strategy. First, it has tried "to get as horizontal as possible," says Tom Stafford, executive vice president of sales. They have done this by offering a wide array of products and services to entice efficiency-minded customers with the promise of one-stop, one-invoice, shopping.

Second, Kiva has tried to produce more value-added product, much of it proprietary and even patented. That has meant moving fast to get ahead of the market in materials, by producing corrugated plastic containers, which can last 40 times longer than corrugated cardboard containers. Eight years ago the company opened a plant in Anaheim, California, to convert corrugated plastic into boxes.

Five years ago, Kiva Container made just four basic products and variations thereof. Since then, Kiva's product offerings have "grown 1000 percent," said Tom Stafford. A few years ago, the company lost several customers when they couldn't get everything they wanted from Kiva. "We have done a lot of things to get that business back," said Stafford.

Key to making the horizontal strategy work is the need to constantly innovate. Kiva has invested $50,000 in a CAD/CAM system to generate new designs quickly. Larger customers come looking for patentable designs. The potential payoff of Kiva is larger, but so is the up-front cost and attendant risk. Currently, Kiva is talking to half a dozen large customers, each of which could give it $1 million in business, based on a single proprietary design. But product innovation requires a lot of preliminary design and development work with no guarantee that it will yield a contract. Tom Stafford estimates that in the past year alone Kiva has spent $50,000 on product proposals that have resulted in zero sales. In fact, the Staffords assert that some customers come in, look at Kiva's ideas, and go elsewhere to have them executed. Kiva wants big customers because there is big operating leverage in the work—if they can get it.

At the same time, Kiva must keep pushing on related fronts. Attending trade shows has become more important than it used to be. But a large regional show can cost Kiva $25,000 to $30,000, and meanwhile, the number of shows has increased exponentially. Kiva has brought more consultants in and sent more employees to seminars—all to meet the market's expectations. Larger customers now insist that Kiva manufacture according to ISO 9000 standards—which for a box maker is overkill. But Kiva complies to meet its customers' expectations.

Today, most fast-growing small businesses are in the service sector. Although Kiva is a manufacturer, it is increasingly focusing on the service end of its business to win competitive advantage from bigger firms. Small business managers must continue to follow the small business strategy that allows them to be nimble, fast, and flexible. Small company innovation consistently exceeds that of large companies. Innovation and service are the keys to small businesses competing in a cutthroat global economy. Kiva Container has learned this lesson. If it continues to follow its small business strategy, the company will survive for a fourth generation of Staffords to manage.

QUESTIONS

1. Name some of the advantages that small businesses have over large businesses in adapting to increased global competition. Name some of the disadvantages.
2. What strategies can the Staffords use to lure large customers away from the larger packaging businesses?
3. Small businesses are faced with more global competition today than ever before. How can small business managers best prepare for an increasingly complex competitive environment?

Source: Adapted from Edward O. Welles, "There Are No Simple Businesses Anymore," *The State of Small Business*, 1995, pp. 66–79; Jenny McCune, "The Face of Tomorrow," *Journal of Business Strategy*, May/June 1995, pp. 50–55; Anna Brady, "Small Is As Small Does," *Journal of Business Strategy*, March/April 1995, pp. 44–46.

VIDEO CASE

A Conversation with Ben and Jerry

Ben & Jerry's Homemade Ice Cream, Inc., is unique because of the way Ben Cohen and Jerry Greenfield decided to organize and manage their company. Annual sales have increased to more than $120 million dollars since Ben & Jerry's was founded in the late 1970s. Commenting on his firm's remarkable record and his partner's contributions to that success, Jerry said, "What Ben brings is a real sense of experimenting, trying new things, no sense of failure whatsoever. Ben has often said that he would rather fail at something new than succeed at something that has already been done. I think another major thing that Ben brings is that he's never satisfied. So, no matter what we do he's always looking to improve it. I'm very good at routine things. I don't mind doing the same thing over and over again, which is good when you're trying to make ice cream. We didn't really regard ourselves as going into business or setting up a business or anything like that. We looked at ourselves as ice cream makers, having this little homemade parlor and doing it for two or three years and then doing something else. So we weren't looking at what form of legal structure we needed to put together for a business as it would grow and evolve over the years."

Ben corroborated Jerry's story about the pair's initial nonchalance about corporate legal form, stating: "I think we talked to some lawyer and he said we should form a corporation and so we did. The lawyer talked about sub S versus not sub S for a while and then we said which do you think we should do and he said not sub S and so we said OK."

Starting the company on a shoestring wasn't frightening to the young partners because they didn't have real high expectations. As Jerry put it, "We had $12,000. Sure it was our life savings and everything, but we didn't look at this as some huge thing that we were getting into. When we were getting into business it was a lark, something fun to do, to work together, to be our own bosses. The question of legal liability and putting together a corporation and stock and things like that wasn't on our minds."

A Ben & Jerry's stockholder meeting is something to behold. Their meetings aren't the stuffy, formal, technical number sessions of Wall Street. A Ben & Jerry's annual meeting is more like a county fair. One shareholder said, "It was like nothing I had ever seen before. It was part of a festival weekend that Ben & Jerry's was hosting. It was under a tent. The chairman of the board and many of the executives were in Bermuda shorts and T-shirts." You won't find many of the people complaining about that irreverence, however. Last year the value of Ben & Jerry's stock increased 150 percent and the company reported record earnings of $3.7 million.

Jerry points out that, despite the fun of the shareholder meetings, the company has always felt the same pressures as any other entrepreneurial firm, especially the pressure for more money. He said, "We always needed more money. It's funny how everybody keeps telling you you'll need more money and you don't think it's true but as you grow in your busness you need more money." Ben supported Jerry's remarks, stating, "We went public because we had a need to raise capital in order to expand. We went public just in the state of Vermont. It was the first ever just intrastate Vermont public stock offering. And the idea was that if we could make the members of the community as owners of the business as the business prospered the community would automatically prosper."

Ben & Jerry's has always been run with an exceedingly open management style. Ben pointed out that "all the accountants, lawyers and financial advisors were telling us we were crazy when we wanted to become a public held company and have to open our books to everybody. We said that's the only kind of business we want to run where we can open our books to everybody and be proud of it. You know they said you really ought to take venture capital because if you need more money the venture capitalists will give you more money and we realized that if we took venture capital that that would be a few rich people that would loan us a whole lot of money in order to get richer and what we wanted to do was we wanted to give the opportunity to the people of limited wealth to achieve some money. So we had a very low minimum buy—for $126.00 you could become an owner of Ben & Jerry's. At the end of the IPO, 1 out of every 100 Vermont families had bought stock in the company."

Ben & Jerry's is famous for its ice cream, but it's also famous for its overall business philosophy that encourages giving back to the community. The two founders spoke eloquently about their founding and guiding philosophy: "Ben and I are not really capable of looking at an accounting report and making a whole lot of sense out of it" said Jerry. "We can see if we're making money or not, if some expenses are out of line, or sales are out of line, but I'd say beyond that we don't have a very sophisticated take on financial matters here. That's not to say that financial information here doesn't get used, it just doesn't get used by us." Ben added, "Right, that's definitely true. The financial information gets used a lot and I encourage it. You know when our business was first starting out the financial advisors, the business pundits, the advisors and accountants were saying our concern for the community and our use of our company resources to improve the quality of life in the community was going to be our downfall. Now we're realizing that it's really those things that have driven our success. And what we have discovered is that there's a spiritual aspect to business just as there is to the life of individuals. As you support the community the community supports you back. It's really not so crazy."

QUESTIONS

1. Ben and Jerry began with low expectations for the company, and thus had little concern for the corporate legal form they adopted. What consequences can arise from choosing the wrong legal form when starting a business?

2. Ben and Jerry both commented that they have little sophistication for understanding the financial condition of their firm. What do you think are some of the absolutely essential financial considerations that any entrepreneur or business person must understand?

3. Ben & Jerry's has made its mark because it has a good product, but also because it has been a good corporate citizen. How do these two factors work in the company's favor?

APPLICATION EXERCISE

COMPUTER SOFTWARE, INC.

You have been asked to consult in determining the strategic design and organizational structure for a start-up firm selling personal computer software, in a national market, for home use. The software offerings of Personal Software, Inc. (PSI) include educational, entertainment, and home management packages. The firm intends to buy the software products from a variety of sources or license its development and production to manufacturers. The founder of PSI does not foresee basic product design nor manufacture in its activities. PSI has obtained or licensed a very good initial array of products and excellent financing. You have been asked to design a structure for 100 full-time people, including all support and clerical staff. No part-time staff should be included. Be sure to identify the number of people included in each group, office, department, region, and so on. Provide a clear organizational chart with title and reporting lines. Write a mission statement for this firm along with three specific strategic objectives.

PART 3

Organizing

CHAPTER 8

Organizational Structure and Design

After studying this chapter, you should be able to:

❖ Define the terms organizing and organizational structure.

❖ Determine when organizational structure is a problem.

❖ Explain how managers determine organizational structure.

❖ Compare scientific management and craftsmanship.

❖ Discuss the significance of work teams and quality circles.

❖ Discuss how authority can be delegated.

❖ List the most common bases for departmentalization.

❖ Explain the different dimensions of organizational structure.

❖ Compare mechanistic, organic, and matrix organizations.

❖ Discuss several emerging forms of organizational design.

The Organization of Tomorrow

The organization of tomorrow will be structured much differently from that of today. As the year 2000 draws closer, the organizations leading the way will be those that offer quality products, can adapt quickly to their customers' demands, and can accommodate environmental concerns. According to David Nadler, president of Delta Consulting Group, who represents such clients as AT&T, Xerox, and Corning, "CEOs feel that companies need to be structured in dramatically different ways." Although there is no agreement on exactly what this organization will look like, a picture of a flat, lean, high-performance workplace is emerging. By the year 2000, the average company will be smaller and employ fewer people; the traditional hierarchical organization will give way to other forms such as the network of specialists; the model of doing business will shift from making a product to providing customer service; and work itself will be redefined to include constant learning and more high-order thinking.

At a General Electric factory in Puerto Rico, 172 hourly workers, 15 salaried advisers, and 1 manager produce surge protectors that guard power stations and transmission lines against lightning strikes. Three layers, no supervisors, and no staff. A plant like this would typically employ about twice as many salaried people. But at the GE plant, each hourly worker is on a team with about 10 people that meet weekly. Each team "owns" some portion of the work—assembly, shipping, receiving, and so on. But team members come from all areas of the plant so that each team has representatives from all facets of operations. An adviser attends the meetings but sits in the back of the room, speaking up only if the team needs help.

Perhaps the biggest change taking place in organizations today is in the use of teams. The concept was discovered more than 40 years ago at the bottom of a coal mine in Yorkshire by a researcher from London's Tavistock Institute of Human Relations. Typically, as in the case of the GE plant, a team replaces the boss by controlling everything from schedules to hiring and, in some cases, even firing. Some teams are self-managed, meaning they are not directed by a manager. This trend toward empowering workers grew in America during the 1980s. Today about one in five U.S. employers operates self-managed teams. Some predict that by the year 2000, half of all

U.S. workers will be managing themselves as quality improvement programs spread across the country. The result: workers have the incentive and power to respond to customers' needs.

The Chrysler component plant in New Castle, Indiana, is a case in point. In the mid-1980s the firm was about to shut down its oldest plant, which was experiencing all sorts of problems. According to machine shopworker John Pennington, who earns $17.26 an hour, "If they wanted us to run five parts, we would run two. I missed work when I wanted to. We would drink coffee and just wait for the problem to get corrected." In 1986 Chrysler initiated self-management teams in a last-ditch effort to save the plant. Workers were renamed "technicians" and line supervisors became "team advisers"; time clocks were removed. Now 77 teams assign tasks, confront lazy workers, order repairs, and even alter working hours. Employees have taken ownership of the plant and absenteeism has dropped from 7 percent to below 3 percent. Most important, the number of defects per million parts made has fallen from 300 to 20, while production costs continue to drop.

Source: Adapted from Paul Shrivastava and Stuart Hart, " Greening Organizations—2000," *International Journal of Public Administration,* March 1994, pp. 607–635; Walter Kiechel III, "How We Will Work in the Year 2000," *Fortune,* May 17, 1993, pp. 38–52; Thomas A. Stewart, "The Search for the Organization of Tomorrow," *Fortune,* May 18, 1992, pp. 92–98; Joann S. Lublin, "Trying to Increase Worker Productivity, More Employees Alter Management Style," *The Wall Street Journal,* February 13, 1992, pp.= B1, B7; and Michael F. Dealy and Frederico DeAlmeida, "Changing Organizational Structure," *Fortune,* July 13, 1992, Advertisement Section.

Most managers believe that quality and competitiveness are two keys to success in our complex global environment. Organizations that can react to and control this constantly changing environment will survive. They must be designed so that workers are committed to quality and customers are satisfied.

This chapter presents the basic elements of organizing. It first discusses the concept of organizing and organizational structure (including some of its myths and problems). It then examines four decisions managers make in determining organizational structure: specialization of jobs, delegation of authority, departmentalization, and span of control. Next, the dimensions of organizational structure—formalization, centralization, and complexity—are presented. The final section covers organizational design, including mechanistic and organic models, the matrix design, and other systems.

ORGANIZING AND ORGANIZATIONAL STRUCTURE

In Chapter 1 we noted that the organizing function provides a structure of task and authority relationships that serves the purpose of improving quality. *Organizing* is the process of structuring both human and physical resources to accomplish organizational objectives. Thus organizing involves dividing tasks into jobs, delegating authority, determining the appropriate bases for departmentalizing jobs, and deciding the optimum number of jobs in each department.[1]

Developing a responsive organizational structure that is committed to quality is one of the most critical challenges facing managers today. Yet there is obviously a gap between what managers say and do, and this gap is particularly evident when linking quality performance with customer satisfaction.[2] Consider the following:

❖ 18 percent of U.S. firms report that senior management evaluates quality performance less than annually or not at all, compared to 2 percent for Japanese firms.

❖ 22 percent of U.S. companies regularly translate customer expectations into the design of new products or services, compared to 58 percent for Japan.

❖ 22 percent of U.S. firms report that technology is of primary importance in meeting customer expectations, compared to 49 percent for Japan.[3]

Large companies like Home Depot, Southwest Airlines, and Microsoft, despite their size, have succeeded because their organizations are nimble and respond quickly to changes in the market.[4] Many managers recognize that their organization is not responsive and flexible, that it doesn't move quickly when it must. But these same managers often attribute this problem to people—departments that cannot get along, uncommitted or unmotivated employees, or the inability to develop quality products in a timely fashion. These are clear symptoms of problems with organizational structure.

Organizational structure is the framework of jobs and departments that directs the behavior of individuals and groups toward achieving the organization's objectives. Organizational structure's contribution to the organization's performance is demonstrated each time a customer is satisfied. When customers are not satisfied, chances are great that the fault is with the organizational structure. Thus organizational structure provides an orderly arrangement among functions so that the organization's objectives can be accomplished effectively. Although the organizing function refers to decisions managers make, organizational structure reflects the outcomes of these decisions.

Organizational structure must be consistent with an organization's strategy. Strategic planning specifies *what* will be accomplished by *it* when; organizational structure specifies *who* will accomplish what and *how* it will be accomplished. Many organizations, unfortunately, try to implement a new strategy with an obsolete organizational structure. The result becomes the failed "initiative of the month." For instance, an organization may recognize a need to be "more market driven" or "more quality conscious." The result is a new program for customer satisfaction or quality improvement. But an organization doesn't simply *become* quality conscious. Rather it must develop an organizational structure that results in the behaviors that the strategy calls for. In developing an effective organizational structure, managers must be aware of several myths and avoid the problems associated with organizational structure.

> **organizational structure** The framework of jobs and departments that directs the behavior of individuals and groups toward achieving the organization's objectives.

Overcoming Myths about Organizational Structure

An effective organizational structure does not result from chance, luck, or historical accident. It is the responsibility of management to deliberately develop a structure that enhances the organization's overall strategy, taking into consideration factors such as competition and the environment. Managers, in attempting to implement a new program or directive, often encounter resistance to change. Over time, organizational structures become quite ingrained and resistant to change. This behavior is not consistent with an environment that is constantly changing and can place an organization in a weak position relative to competitors. For example, many U.S. firms have adopted total quality management programs to compete with Japanese firms. These programs required changing the basic structures of some organizations and they failed in cases in which an outdated structure was reinforcing behaviors contrary to TQM. To keep in step with the constantly changing environment, many organizations find themselves reorganizing on a regular basis.[5]

Managers must also recognize that there is no single best structure for an organization. What works at IBM may be different from what works at Apple or Compaq. The challenge managers face is to design the best structure for a specific organization, the structure that facilitates getting work done well. If structure actually impedes the completion of work and hence the achievement of the organization's objectives, managers have a problem. If a bank teller cannot respond to a customer's request because of the lack of authority, a problem exists in the bank's structure. Likewise if an assembly line worker does not have the knowledge or ability to perform a job effectively, the company has a problem in its structure. Often employees can't do quality work because the organization's structure gets in their way.

Detecting Problems in Organizational Structure

When is organizational structure a problem? Ultimately whenever work is not getting done well, there is likely to be a problem with organizational structure. Many factors or circumstances account for such problems. Conflicts between departments or groups within an organization suggest a structure problem. These conflicts may result from personality differences but more often they are attributable to differences in the departments' goals. For example, the marketing department is most concerned with sales and introducing new products, whereas the production department is concerned with quality control. Difficulty in coordinating work between departments, slowness in adapting to change, and ambiguous job assignments also indicate problems with organizational structure. If employees are asking what goals are most important or what work to concentrate on, organizational structure may be the underlying problem.

Structure problems can be disastrous for the organization. First, the organization becomes a collection of departments or independent groups pursuing their own goals rather than a coherent organization with a common goal. Second, the organization's structure begins to dictate its strategy rather than strategy dictating structure. When this happens, an organization's structure determines what it does, which violates an important principle of management: strategy should dictate structure. Finally, if structure is allowed to determine strategy, only strategies compatible with the existing organizational structure are acceptable. This approach severely limits the strategies that an organization can pursue effectively; it especially limits efforts toward innovation and change.

General Motors illustrates how structural problems can damage an organization. In 1979 GM dominated the U.S. market for cars and light trucks with a 46 percent share; 12 years later its share fell below 35 percent. Although many factors contributed to GM's problems—drop in demand for large cars, obsolete factories, poor quality, to name a few—all were symptoms of a nonresponsive organizational structure, one that is failing. Efforts to change GM's structure have been hampered by a stubborn middle-management bureaucracy and an uncooperative United Auto Workers union. In addition to eliminating 74,000 jobs (including thousands of white-collar jobs) and 21 factories, experts believe that GM needs to restructure its entire organization to survive. Restructuring may include doing away with six separate operating divisions—Buick, Pontiac, Chevrolet, Oldsmobile, Cadillac, and Saturn—a highly inefficient setup.[6] GM, along with IBM and Sears, lost a total of $32.4 billion in 1992, and dropped out of the 20 largest companies in stock market value. Even after showing strong earnings in 1994, IBM underwent major restructuring. CEO Louis Gerstner felt too much of IBM's earnings came from mainframes and other products in shrinking markets.[7] In all cases, the organization structure did not enable these firms to respond fast enough to changes in their markets.[8]

Perhaps the greatest influence on how workers perceive their work and how they behave is organizational structure. It is management's job to design an organizational structure that enables employees to do their best work and achieve the organization's objectives. The next section examines the fundamental considerations or decisions that determine organizational structure.

DETERMINING ORGANIZATIONAL STRUCTURE

Most of us have worked in some type of organization and we tend to think of structure in narrow terms: what is our own job task? Whom do we report to? How much responsibility do we have? Managers responsible for designing organizational structure must think in much broader terms that describe the entire structure itself, not just the jobs that comprise it. In determining which type of structure enables people to do their best work, managers make many decisions. The four major decisions pertain to specialization of jobs, delegation of authority, departmentalization, and span of control.

Figure 8–1 summarizes the choices managers can make regarding these decisions. In general, the structure of an organization falls on the same part of each continuum. In other words, an organization structured for workers to do highly specialized jobs will also tend to group jobs according to homogeneous or common functions, and assign to managers only a few workers with little authority. The following sections examine each of these decisions in greater detail.

FIGURE 8-1
Designing Organizational
Structure

Specialization of jobs:

   High _____ Low

Delegation of authority:

   Centralized _____ Decentralized

Departmentalization:

   Homogeneous _____ Heterogeneous

Span of control:

   Narrow _____ Wide

Specialization of Jobs

One of the manager's major decisions is determining how specialized jobs will be. Most organizations consist, to some degree, of specialized jobs, with workers performing different tasks. By dividing tasks into narrow specialties, managers gain the benefits derived from division of labor. These benefits include minimum training required for jobs consisting of only a few tasks and economic gains obtained when employees become highly efficient in those tasks, resulting in better-quality output.

SCIENTIFIC MANAGEMENT VERSUS CRAFTSMANSHIP - Frederick W. Taylor, a leading proponent of specialization, did much of his work in the late 1800s and early 1900s. [9] The environment then was characterized by a smokestack economy of assembly lines and blue-collar workers—many of whom were unskilled, illiterate immigrants. Taylor's system, the catalyst for the scientific management movement, required that tasks be broken down to the smallest element and that problem solving be elevated to managers. Taylor, through his time and motion studies, identified basic movements that minimize effort and maximize the output of lathe operators, iron workers, and bricklayers. This system has permeated our entire society. Specialization now applies to employees as diverse as airline pilots, nurses, and accountants. People learn a job routine and repeat the tasks over and over. If they experience problems, they must consult a supervisor or manager. Work or execution is clearly separate from thinking or planning.

It is not hard to understand why this system replaced the craftsmanship system, which for many years was considered the only alternative to scientific management. According to quality expert Joseph Juran, "Taylor's concept of separating planning from execution fitted our culture and, at the time, was very logical. You had a lot of immigrants . . . some of them were completely illiterate. And they were in no position, in his [Taylor's] opinion, to make decisions on how work should be done." [10] Craftsmanship is basically the opposite of scientific management. The craftsman is responsible for his own work; management only provides the means and facilities for the craftsman to perform the entire operation. Craftsmanship produces high-quality products but is expensive and results in low output. Table 8–1 shows each system's strengths and weaknesses. The development of the assembly line destroyed craftsmanship and gave way to scientific management and greater specialization. For many years, it has been assumed that scientific management's strengths outweigh the weaknesses of craftsmanship.

As we noted earlier, many of us think of organizational structure in terms of our own jobs. Specialization has in some instances inspired a "that's not my job" attitude, which has seriously hurt some organizations. The system that worked so well after World War II—when America flooded the world market with affordable domestic products—is not as effective in today's complex global economy. Many organizations are searching for an alternative approach.

TABLE 8-1	SCIENTIFIC MANAGEMENT VERSUS CRAFTSMANSHIP	
	Scientific Management	Craftsmanship
Strengths		
	High productivity	High skill
	Lower cost	High-quality output
	Higher wages	Pride in work
	Unskilled workers	High job interest
	Predictable scheduling	Control by worker
Weaknesses		
	Low morale and boredom	Low productivity
	Poor quality	Higher cost
	Lack of pride	Lower wages
	Low job interest	Poor control
	Control by managers	Scheduling problems

TEAMS AND QUALITY CIRCLES - Japan was the first nation to realize that the scientific management approach to specialization would work only in an expanding market. Once markets began to shrink, Japanese firms made quality an issue and invaded markets that for years were thought to be untouchable. Basically the Japanese approach was to attack what they called Taylorism. It seems somewhat unfair to credit Taylor solely with the entire system of scientific management since others took part in its development. But the Japanese identified Taylor's concepts of time and motion with their failures: high absenteeism, low morale, and poor-quality output. While some parts of the world were experiencing the benefits of specialization, Japan was experiencing its disadvantages. Other nations are now experiencing these same disadvantages and will also have to make changes if they hope to prosper.

One major problem Japan found with specialization is that many workers simply did not enjoy their jobs. Jobs were boring and workers performing a single task over and over lost sight of the larger picture, the finished product. In his seminars, Deming argues for the right of all people to have "joy in their work."[11] He argues equally hard for companies to make money, but believes that unless people enjoy their work, there will be little commitment to quality—and it is quality that produces greater profit. Deming views designing an organizational structure much like designing a good orchestra, where players are there to support each other. According to him, a business is "a network of people, materials, methods, equipment, all working in support of each other for the common aim."[12] Thus managers must determine the appropriate degree of specialization without creating a demotivating and demoralizing environment in which workers don't do their best work. This may have been easier for Japanese firms to accomplish because specialization had not become entrenched in their society.

Many organizations are modifying and redesigning jobs so that they can be performed by teams.[13] The most popular type is a *problem-solving team*, comprised of knowledgeable workers who gather to solve a specific problem and then disband.[14] A *work team*, as noted in Chapter 5, is a group of employees who work closely together to pursue common objectives.[15] Some organizations become *team-based*, using teams throughout the organization on a regular basis; others use teams more selectively. Some teams are directed by a manager whereas others are self-managed. The idea behind self-managed work teams is for workers to become their own managers, which increases reliance on their creative and in-

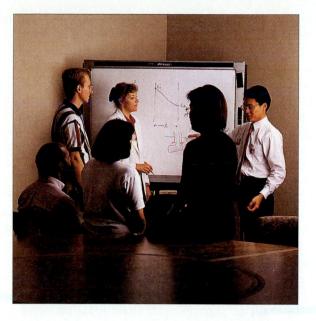

A Self-directed team of W. L. Gore "associates" works without the assistance of managers or bosses.

tellectual capabilities besides their physical labor. At W.L. Gore & Associates—a manufacturer of a wide range of electronic, medical, fabric, and industrial products—"associates" (the term *employee* is not used) work on self-directed teams without managers or bosses.[16] Regardless of which form is used, teams can move swiftly, flexibly, and effectively to produce innovative products. Team members learn each others' jobs and bring their ideas together, capitalizing on workers' creativity. When truly empowered, a work team can change bored and demoralized *workers* into innovative and productive *partners*. Johnsonville Foods was a pioneer in the use of self-managing teams to run a factory. Teammates were given the power to hire and fire members and to give bonuses to one another.[17]

In moving from a traditional form of organization to teams, managers are often asked to transform into team leaders. And this is not a simple process. Individuals thrust into this new role of team leader require behavioral skills—coaching, motivating, and empowering—and a change in mind-set. The skills needed most by team leaders are: the ability to admit they don't know everything; to know when to intervene with the team; to learn how to share power; to become focused in what they take on, not what they give up; and to get used to learning while on the job.[18] Making the transformation to this type of role does not come natural to everyone, but these skills can be learned.

Quality circles are based on the belief that the people who work with the process are best able to identify, analyze, and correct the problems in any given situation. They originated in Japan in 1962 and were expanded into a highly developed system by Japanese firms. A **quality circle** is a small group of people, usually fewer than 10, who do similar work and meet about once a week to discuss their work, identify problems, and present possible solutions.[19] Participation in the circle is voluntary and the workers establish a moderator or team leader to lead discussions. The group's findings and proposals are forwarded to management.

American firms began using quality circles in the mid-1970s and the concept grew in popularity during the next 15 years. Unfortunately some efforts to use quality circles failed because they were merely adaptations of the scientific management system. The aim of managers in some cases was to increase the productivity of workers, who refused to cooperate. But these failures resulted from how the approach was used rather than from flaws in the approach itself. Quality circles cannot simply be "installed" in an organization. The concept has been most successful when used as part of an organizationwide improvement effort. Quality circles are detailed in Chapter 16.

The extent to which jobs are specialized is a critical managerial decision. The important point here is that jobs vary considerably along the dimension of specialization. By

quality circle
A small group of people, usually fewer than 10, who do similar work and meet about once a week to discuss their work, identify problems, and present possible solutions.

changing the degree to which jobs are specialized, managers change the structure of the organization. Chapter 9 discusses job design in further detail.

Delegation of Authority

When designing an organizational structure, managers must also consider the extent to which authority will be distributed throughout the organization. As discussed in Chapter 5, *authority* is the organizationally sanctioned right to make a decision. Managers delegate (assign) certain tasks to others, simply because one person cannot get all the work done. When delegating authority, managers must weigh the pros and cons of decentralization and centralization and strike an appropriate balance for the organization.

decentralization
The process of distributing authority throughout the organization

centralization
The process of retaining authority in the hands of high-level managers, who make all the decisions.

DECENTRALIZATION AND CENTRALIZATION - Authority can be distributed throughout the organization or held in the hands of a few. **Decentralization** is the process of distributing authority throughout the organization. It delegates an organization member (historically a manager) the right to make a decision without obtaining approval from a higher-level manager. The authority to identify problems or issues and recommend solutions is delegated as well. In the strictest sense, decentralization represents one end of a continuum (Figure 8–1) in which the authority to make decisions is shared with all members of the organization. At the other extreme, **centralization** is the process of retaining authority in the hands of high-level managers, who make all the decisions.

REFLECTIONS BY PHILIP B. CROSBY

Elements of Organizing

One thing we all learn as we practice the art/science of management is that it is very hard to process information through a system. Once we get past the level where we see each employee several times a day, it becomes necessary to rely on other people or systems to get the word out.

When I started Philip Crosby Associates (PCA), I decided that we would have a way of working that guaranteed each associate all the information and direction they needed at all times. Traditionally, the way to attempt this is to have layers of supervision and pass things along, like a chain letter. However, supervisors, at all levels, only look up. They worry about their boss(es) more than about their employees. All of the bosses I worked for in the early stages of my career spent their time staying out of trouble and keeping us away from what was happening. Any information they were supposed to transmit was edited severely. Their main source of intimidation and control was that they knew more than their subordinates about what was going on. However, when we think that their bosses were doing the same thing, we realize that they were rather uninformed also.

I didn't want a system of supervision in PCA for the purpose of control. Rather we would set it up so people would have leaders who helped them. Management would take on the job of communicating with people. The quality improvement team would be responsible for recognition, and the supervisors would concentrate on supporting and helping associates. The key to it all would be openness; that is why we concentrated on the word associate rather than employee.

For the routine life of the company we set up a weekly newspaper (when there were only 30 associates) and monthly Family Council meetings. At that time everyone, including the switchboard operator, came to a session lasting about an hour where all was revealed. Anyone could ask anything or write it in so they didn't have to speak up. Management gave status reports; committees or teams revealed their status. A weekly informal newsletter took care of personal announcements.

We set up a Systems Integrity Board consisting of senior management. Every change that was going to be made was approved by this board, which then let everyone know about it. When you are operating 25 or so classrooms and teaching in several languages, just changing the words on one chart can cause chaos if it isn't managed. Procedural changes were accomplished by the procedures committee, which represented all departments. We held all company meetings on one day each month; the rest of the month was meeting-free. As a result of these efforts and more, the associates did not have to rely on their supervisors for general information, there were virtually no rumors (any that came up could be addressed at the Family Council), and everyone knew what was going on. Senior management was scheduled by the Quality Improvement Team to get around and see everyone regularly. The president had a dinner at each location every year to present awards and such, and we had an annual company black tie get-together. All of this was to let people know that it was all right for them to participate in running the company. And they did.

Decentralization has several advantages. Managers develop their own decision-making skills and are motivated to perform because advancement is related to performance. Managers can also exercise more autonomy, which increases job satisfaction and motivation, contributing to the organization's profitability. Hewlett-Packard attributes much of its success to decentralization, through which people and power were moved away from headquarters. While other major computer manufacturers like IBM and DEC were losing money, Hewlett-Packard made a healthy profit of $881 million in 1992.[20] Decentralization also has a number of disadvantages. It requires costly management training, and organizations can end up employing highly paid managers. Delegation also leads to extensive (and often stifling) planning and reporting procedures. Some managers find it difficult to make decisions even though they have the authority because the methods used to measure accountability are time-consuming and instill fear in the managers.

Many firms are decentralizing—a trend expected to continue throughout the decade. Some decentralized firms are thriving, like Motorola, General Electric, American Telephone & Telegraph, and United Parcel Service.[21] Others are feeling decentralization's drawbacks. KFC envisioned tastier foods and happier customers when it decentralized several years ago. But the firm's regional divisions failed to coordinate their efforts, resulting in so much redundancy that restructuring was a failure.[22] Aluminum Co. of America (Alcoa) found that customers' rejections increased and customer satisfaction decreased after the firm decentralized.[23] Other companies including Levi Strauss have experienced similar problems with decentralization—overlap in functions and a lack of coordination. Levi Strauss placed its order-processing system under centralized control after retailers complained that they had to work with multiple divisions, each with its own procedures.[24]

Peters and Waterman's book *In Search of Excellence* identifies eight attributes that characterize America's best-run companies.[25] One attribute is that excellent firms are both centralized and decentralized. They delegate authority all the way to the shop floor yet are fanatic about centralizing certain decisions they believe to be critical to the firm's core value. For instance, 3M is recognized for encouraging engineers to *bootleg* (borrow time, energy, and funds from other assignments to explore new product ideas). Yet a select group of engineers at 3M retains relatively tight control over funding new product development projects. In essence, what Peters and Waterman are describing is the coexistence of firm, centralized direction with adequate individual autonomy—a difficult balance for managers to strike. Some companies are decentralizing operations closest to the customer to remain responsive in the marketplace. Less visible internal functions (such as personnel or order-processing, as in the case of Levi Strauss) are centralized.

EMPOWERMENT - Some organizations have begun to empower workers to make decisions that typically have been made by superiors. **Empowerment** involves giving employees responsible for hands-on production or service activities the authority to make decisions or take action without prior approval.[26] For instance, a machine operator can stop production if a problem is detected, or a ticket agent can give a customer a refund without calling the supervisor. In talking about decentralization, we refer to the delegation of authority to other *managers*. Empowerment means that production, process control, and quality assessment become part of *everyone's* job and all individuals are given the ability and authority to take positive actions that will lead to high quality and performance. At Federal Express, for example, "all workers are routinely expected to take whatever initiative is required to fix problems and/or extend first rate service to a customer."[27]

Empowerment is at the heart of any total quality management program. It helps to accomplish many points advocated by leading quality experts. One of Crosby's 14 points is to define the type of training employees need to actively carry out their role in the quality improvement process.[28] Deming's points include removing barriers that rob workers of their right to pride of workmanship and making everyone responsible for the quality transformation.[29] The goal of employee empowerment is to stop trying to motivate workers with extrinsic incentives such as money and instead build a work environment that motivates them from within through intrinsic incentives such as pride in workmanship.[30] McGregor, with his familiar Theory X and Y, argued a similar case more than 30 years ago.[31]

empowerment
Giving employees who are responsible for hands-on production or service activities the authority to make decisions or take action without prior approval.

Empowerment is essential if employees are to make a total commitment to continuous quality improvement.

Workers' lack of literacy is a major drawback to quality programs and to the competitiveness of an organization. About 30 million Americans are functionally illiterate.[32] If companies want to be competitive and empower employees, they may need to educate them. At General Motors, for instance, workers are being asked to assemble the product, inspect it for quality, and fix any problems. With layers of supervisors being eliminated, assembly line workers are being asked to do many things they have never done before; basic education skills are a necessity. GM and many other organizations have developed education programs to teach workers to read, write, and perform other basic skills.

chain of command
The formal command that defines the lines of authority from the top to the bottom of the organization.

CHAIN OF COMMAND - The delegation of authority creates a **chain of command**, the formal channel that defines the lines of authority from the top to the bottom of the organization (Figure 8–2). As you can see, the chain of command is a series of superior–subordinate relationships from the highest position in the organization to the lowest.

The chain of command is the communication link among all positions in the organization. It specifies a clear reporting relationship for each person in the organization and should be followed in both downward and upward communication. Generally, no individual should report to more than one supervisor. However, modern organizations are empowering employees to communicate with a person outside the chain under special circumstances.

line position
Is in the direct chain of command and contributes directly to the achievement of the organization's goals.

LINE AND STAFF POSITIONS - The chain of command includes both line and staff positions. A **line position** is in the direct chain of command and contributes directly to achieving the organization's goals. In Figure 8–3 the president, the vice presidents of op-

FIGURE 8-2
Chain of Command

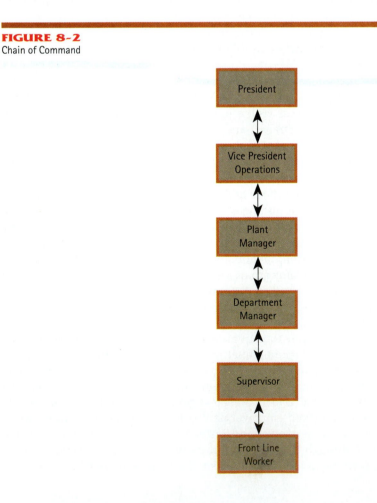

FIGURE 8-3
Differentiating between
Line and Staff Positions

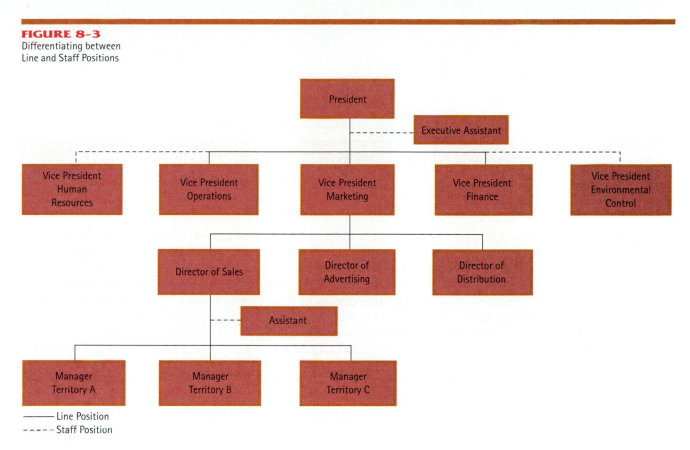

erations, marketing, and finance; the directors; and the sales managers are in line positions. **Staff positions** facilitate or provide advice to line positions. In Figure 8–3, the executive assistant, the vice presidents of human resources and environmental control, and the assistant to the director of sales are considered staff positions because they provide support to others.

Departmentalization

Departmentalization is the process of grouping jobs according to some logical arrangement. As organizations grow in size and as job specialization increases, it becomes more complex to determine how jobs should be grouped. In a very small organization like a mom-and-pop grocery store, the owner can supervise everyone. In a large grocery chain, managerial positions are created according to some plan so that the organization can run smoothly. As we said earlier, some jobs are so specialized that they are unhealthy, which, as we will see, is changing the way organizations group jobs. The most common bases for departmentalization are function, product, customer, and geographic.

FUNCTIONAL DEPARTMENTALIZATION - Grouping jobs together according to the functions of the organization is called **functional departmentalization**. Generally, businesses include functions such as production, finance, marketing, research and development, and human resources (Figure 8–4). This method's major benefit is that it establishes departments based on experts in a particular function, taking advantage of specialization. But specialization does not encourage communication across departments. Functional departmentalization works best when the environment the organization faces is stable and tight control over processes and operations is desired.

PRODUCT DEPARTMENTALIZATION - **Product departmentalization** groups jobs associated with a particular product or product line. It enables people working with a

staff position
A position that facilitates or provides advice to line positions.

departmentalization
The process of grouping jobs according to some logical arrangement.

functional departmentalization
Grouping jobs together according to the organization's functions.

product departmentalization
Grouping jobs associated with a particular product or product line.

FIGURE 8-4
Functional
Departmentalization

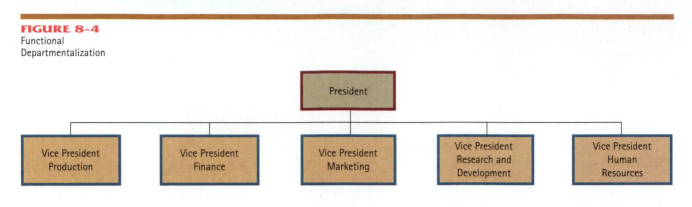

particular product to use their skills and expertise. Figure 8–5 illustrates how an organization groups jobs on this basis. Large organizations such as General Motors and Procter & Gamble have used this approach. The product manager may also draw on the resources of other organization members. Product departmentalization gives an organization the flexibility to develop specific strategies for different products and to grow or make acquisitions with relative structural ease. It has also been used by managers of multinational corporations with diversified product lines. But this type of grouping is expensive because it requires a manager for each product and runs the risk of duplicating effort among divisions.

**customer
departmentalization**
**Grouping jobs in a manner
that serves customers'
needs.**

CUSTOMER DEPARTMENTALIZATION - Organizations using **customer departmentalization** (Figure 8–6) group jobs in a manner that will serve customers' needs. Organizations that have extremely large customers or that serve diverse groups are most likely to use this approach. For example, a firm that sells defense systems to the government may group jobs based on customers. Banks typically departmentalize on the basis of consumer and commercial accounts. Customer departmentalization can be a costly method of grouping jobs if a large staff is required to integrate different departments' activities.

**geographic
departmentalization**
**Grouping jobs based on
defined territories.**

GEOGRAPHIC DEPARTMENTALIZATION - Grouping jobs based on defined territories is called **geographic departmentalization** (Figure 8–7). Such a structure is useful when an organization is widely dispersed and its customers' needs and characteristics vary greatly; organizations can respond to unique customer needs in the various regions more quickly. Geographic departmentalization is the most common form used by MNCs. Its major drawback is that it usually necessitates a large headquarters staff to manage the dispersed locations.

FIGURE 8-5
Product Departmentalization

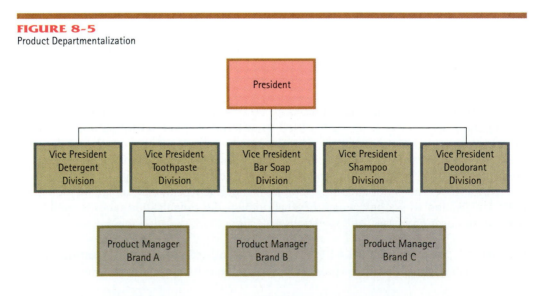

FIGURE 8-6
Customer Departmentalization

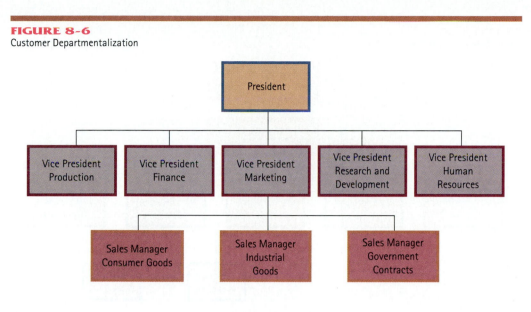

ALTERNATIVE FORMS OF DEPARTMENTALIZATION – As an organization evolves over time, it may use more than one method to group jobs. **Mixed departmentalization** involves grouping jobs using more than one basis. Figure 8–8 illustrates how a bank might mix product, customer, and geographic departmentalization. In reality, most groups organize departments using multiple bases.

Because departmentalization reinforces specialization, some organizations are trying to involve everyone in the decision process by breaking down the barriers that often divide departments. Steelcase, Inc., actually did away with formal departments. People work in multidisciplinary teams that encourage interaction. The physical facilities are also void of departments; they contain areas for teams to work and space for working on special projects. Executives are located in the center of the building, where everyone has equal access to them. This complex change took several years to implement but has been credited with cutting delivery cycles in half and dramatically reducing inventory.[33]

Some firms are abandoning departmentalization altogether and organizing around processes, as opposed to function, product, customer, or geography. **Process organization** involves basing performance objectives on meeting customer needs and identifying the processes that meet those needs. For instance, the processes that meet customer needs may be service quality or new product development. These processes, not departments, are

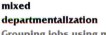

mixed departmentalization
Grouping jobs using more than one basis.

process organization
Organization that bases performance objectives on meeting customer needs and identifying the processes that meet those needs.

FIGURE 8-7
Geographic
Departmentalization

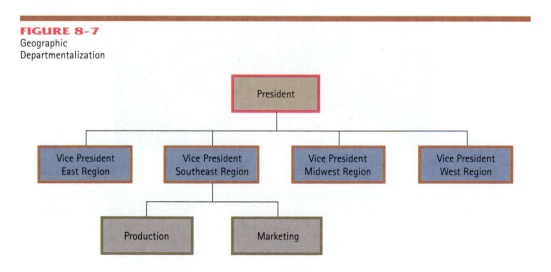

FIGURE 8-8
Mixed Departmentalization

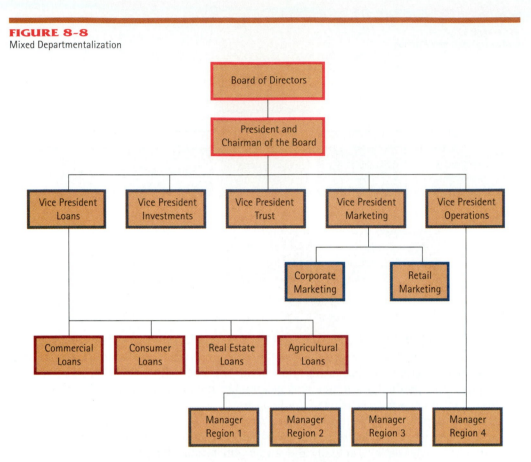

At Hallmark, jobs are organized around the new product development process, according to specific holidays.

used to organize the company. At Hallmark Cards, jobs are organized around the new product development process, according to specific holidays. There are teams for Christmas, Valentine's Day, and so on. Each holiday team includes artists, writers, lithographers, merchandisers, and accountants. Team members come from all over a 2-million-square-foot building so they can work together. Now one team works on a Mother's Day card; previously the card had to go from one large department to the next. The time it takes to develop new cards is cut in half. Between projects or teams, workers return to "center of excellence" for training or brief work assignments. Hallmark hopes any remaining signs of department structures eventually will disappear. [34]

Span of Control

Span of control refers to the number of people who report to one manager or supervisor. This is the final decision managers must make in designing organizational structure. The objective is to determine the optimal span of control, wide or narrow. A wide span of control (or flat organization) results in a large number of workers reporting to one supervisor; a narrow span (or tall organization) results in a small number. Figure 8–9 compares the two structures. In the first case, two supervisors each direct eight workers; the maximum span of control is eight. There are two levels of management: a president and the two supervisors. In the second case, four supervisors report to two department heads and each supervisor directs four workers. The maximum span of control is four, and there are three levels of management: a president, two department heads, and four supervisors.

No formula exists for determining the ideal span of control. The ideal number of people that one person can supervise depends on a variety of factors (Table 8–2). [35] As you can see, these factors could result in different spans of control for different managers in different organizations. Furthermore, spans of control could be different for managers at the same level in the same organization, depending on their experience or the nature of the jobs they are supervising. Consistent with some of the trends in organizational structure we have already discussed (teams, quality circles, empowerment, process organization), many organizations are widening their spans of control. The objective is to develop a flatter, more

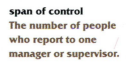

span of control
The number of people who report to one manager or supervisor.

FIGURE 8-9
Wide versus Narrow Span
of Control

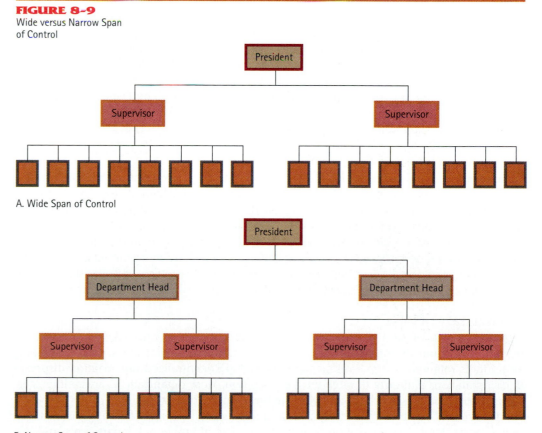

A. Wide Span of Control

B. Narrow Span of Control

TABLE 8-2	FACTORS TO CONSIDER IN DETERMINING THE SPAN OF CONTROL

1. *The competence of both the manager and the subordinates.* The more competent they are, the wider the span of control can be.

2. *The degree of interaction required among the units to be supervised.* The more the required interaction, the narrower the span of control must be.

3. *The extent to which the manager must carry out nonmanagerial tasks.* The more technical and job-related work the manager has to do, the less time is available to supervise others; thus the narrower the span of control must be.

4. *The relative similarity or dissimilarity of the jobs being supervised.* The more similar the jobs, the wider the span of control can be; the less similar the jobs, the narrower it must be.

5. *The extent of standardized procedures.* The more routine the subordinates' jobs are and the more each job is performed by standardized methods, the wider the span of control can be.

6. *The degree of physical dispersion.* If all the people assigned to a manager are located in one area and are within eyesight, the manager can supervise relatively more people than if people are dispersed throughout the plant or countryside at different locations.

responsive organizational structure in which decisions can be made without going through several levels of management.[36] It is also resulting in the layoffs of thousands of managers who are no longer needed, the subject of the Ethics Spotlight.

DIMENSIONS OF ORGANIZATIONAL STRUCTURE

The four organizational design decisions we have just discussed—specialization of jobs, delegation of authority, departmentalization, and span of control—determine the structure of organizations. Organizational structure provides the foundation upon which the organization functions. It also dramatically influences performance. Therefore, managers must be concerned with the entire structure and how it influences the organization. Three dimensions have been identified that enable managers to describe and understand the organizations' structure and measure differences between different organizations: formalization, centralization, and complexity.[37]

Formalization

formalization

The extent to which communications and procedures in an organization are written down and filed.

Formalization refers to the extent to which an organization's communications and procedures are written down and filed. A highly formalized organizational structure would be characterized by rules and procedures to prescribe members' behavior. Simple and routine tasks lend themselves to formalization; more complex and nonroutine tasks don't.

In general, organizations characterized by high specialization, little delegation of authority, functional departments, and narrow spans of control are more formalized. Scientific management, then, results in a high degree of formalization, whereas craftsmanship leads to less formalization. In this sense, organizations that empower workers reduce formalization.

Centralization

Centralization, as we said earlier, refers to how much the authority to make decisions is dispersed throughout the organization. In a highly centralized organization, decision-making authority is retained by top-level managers. A highly decentralized organization disperses decision-making authority throughout the operation. Most organizations are neither centralized nor decentralized, but somewhere in between the two extremes.

In terms of the four organizational structure decisions, centralization is the result of high specialization, low delegation of authority, the use of functional departments, and narrow spans of control.

ETHICS SPOTLIGHT ARE LAYOFFS NECESSARY?

The unprecedented restructuring taking place in corporate America hasn't been painless. As many organizations relentlessly downsize, thousands of employees are being laid off. Workplace Trends reported that in 1991 large corporations permanently cut 556,000 jobs, and the trend is continuing at a rapid pace. Through October of 1995, over 343,500 jobs were cut for the 10-month period. In total, over 43 million jobs have been lost in the United States since 1979. Many predict that the next decade will see even greater job cuts. This trend's impact on individuals, families, and society is profound:

- Allen Stenhouse—with a 24-year insurance career, a $50,000 income, a $279,000 condo, and a 14-year marriage—was laid off two days before Christmas. He divorced, lost his savings and his condo, and lives on Social Security and disability benefits.
- Gerald Feldman lost his $57,000-a-year job as director of finance and equipment administrator for a mid-size office equipment retailer. He receives $270 a week in extended unemployment benefits; his wife Claire earns $8 an hour working in collections for a retailer. They are four months behind in their mortgage payments and have received a notice of foreclosure.
- Sara Rutenberg, a Hollywood TV studio attorney, says she feels incredible anxiety about her job, her kids, and the declining value of her home. She worries about credit, layoffs, and medical bills.

Thousands of such people are losing much more than their jobs. They are losing their place in society, their optimism, and their self-esteem. Even corporate giants like IBM, General Motors, Procter & Gamble, and United Technologies have cut thousands of positions, producing deep social, psychological, and economic trauma. Many Americans, for the first time since World War II, feel that tomorrow may not yield a brighter future. According to a survey conducted by Deliotte and Touche, 81 percent responding listed employee morale as the top human resource issue.

Few people argue that corporations need to restructure, downsize, and cut costs in an effort to become more efficient and competitive. But some critics question the ethics of executives who allow overstaffing when times are good, yet impersonally cut thousands of jobs during recessions and restructuring; they say layoffs are nothing more than managers admitting they failed to plan. Not only are the individuals who lose jobs damaged, but workers who are spared are often left demoralized. Rights Associates, a counseling and outplacement firm, questioned human relations executives at 909 companies that have downsized. Seventy percent reported that workers who kept their jobs felt insecure about their future employment prospects.

Downsizing holds several other potential drawbacks. Layoffs can be very expensive, especially if the organization has to rehire in the future. As a result of layoffs, experience, skills, and loyalty leave the organization. According to a study conducted by the Wharton School of Business at the University of Pennsylvania, companies with a history of layoffs have trouble attracting new talent when needed. The same study also shows that more than a third of the downsizing companies had to use overtime or consultants later to do the job.

Some firms are committed to retaining their employees through restructuring efforts during good times and bad.

Even though losses reached $2.3 billion at Ford Motor Co., very few employees were released. Net income fell 12 percent at 3M, but employees who were willing to relocate could stay. Sales dropped 16 percent at Baldor Electric, but no layoffs occurred because the CEO believes that to build a good company, you have to get and keep the best people. Strategies for reducing the number of layoffs include instituting hiring freezes, restricting overtime, retraining or reassigning employees, switching to part-time work, sharing jobs, converting employees to consultants, giving unpaid vacations, shortening the work week, and reducing pay. Jack Welch, CEO or General Electric, feels worker skills have to be upgraded through intense and continuous training: "Companies can't promise employment, but we may be able to guarantee employability."

The continued restructuring of American organizations will bring more layoffs in the coming years. But managers responsible for downsizing must consider the long-term impact of layoffs on the organization. After all, an effective organizational structure should contribute to the organization's performance. According to Frank Popoff, CEO of Dow Chemical, when you lay people off, "You lose all the loyalty you've busted your butt to build. The quality of work you get from motivated workers is literally lightyears ahead of what you get from people who aren't well-motivated."

Source: Adapted from Louis Uchitelle and N. R. Kleinfield, "Downsizing Fraying America's Psyche," *Lexington Herald-Leader*, March 3, 1996, pp. A1, A10; J. Duncan Moore, Jr., "Morale Hits New Low," *Modern Health Care*, December 11, 1995, pp. 52–57; Gene Koretz, "Downsizing Isn't Down Enough," *Business Week*, December 4, 1995, p. 24; "Jack Welch's Lesson for Success," *Fortune*, January 25, 1993, pp. 86–93. Edmund Faltermayer, "Is This Layoff Necessary?" *Fortune*, June 1, 1992, pp. 71–86; Bruce Nussbaum, Ann Therese Palmer, Alice Z. Cuneo, and Barbara Carlson, "Downward Mobility," *Business Week*, March 23, 1992, pp. 56–63; and Brian O'Reilly, "Preparing for Leaner Times," *Fortune*, January 27, 1992, pp. 40–47.

Complexity

Complexity is defined as the number of different job titles and the number of different departments. As organizations grow, divide work, and create more departments, they become more complex. Because of the dissimilarities in the jobs of both individuals and departments, a complex organization is more difficult to manage than one with few job titles and departments.

High specialization, product departmentalization, customer departmentalization, geographic departmentalization, high delegation of authority, and narrow spans of control result in high complexity.

complexity
The number of different job titles and the number of different departments.

Organizations differ in terms of how much they're formalized and centralized as well as their degree of complexity. These differences result from managers' decisions concerning the organization's structure. No single structure is best for a particular organization. The purpose of structure is to reward and encourage behaviors that lead to accomplishing organizational objectives. Regardless of differences in how formalized, centralized, and complex organizations are, the critical issue is whether the organizational structure enables employees to do quality work. Perhaps the most important point is that managers must manage organizational structures over time and make changes in response to the changing environment.

ORGANIZATIONAL DESIGN

In this chapter we have noted that organizational structure is the framework of jobs and departments that directs the behavior of individuals and groups toward achieving an organization's objectives. Structure provides the foundation within which the organization functions, and managers must design an organizational structure that enhances the organization's overall strategy. Managers have many alternatives in developing an organizational structure. **Organizational design** is the process by which they develop an organizational structure. Since organizational structure is determined by specialization of jobs, delegation of authority, departmentalization, and span of control (Figure 8–1), organizational design includes coordinating these dimensions of organizational structure and deciding the extent to which the organization will be specialized, centralized, and so on.

Two extreme models of organizational design—the mechanistic model and the organic model—have provided much of the framework for understanding organizational design.[38]

The Mechanistic Model

In the early part of the 20th century, much theory and practice in management was guided by the nature of the work and the existing organizational structure at that time. That is, many organizations, seeking a high production level, relied on unskilled workers. Factory workers were highly specialized, and little authority was delegated. Thus the term **mechanistic organization** describes a rigid organization that attempts to achieve production and efficiency through rules, specialized jobs, and centralized authority.

organizational design
The process by which managers develop an organizational structure.

mechanistic organization
A rigid organization that attempts to achieve production and efficiency through rules, specialized jobs, and centralized authority.

WHAT MANAGERS ARE READING

REENGINEERING THE CORPORATION

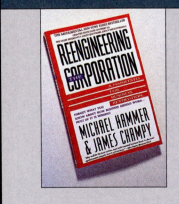

According to Michael Hammer and James Champy, authors of the best-selling book *Reengineering the Corporation,* "America's business problem is that it is entering the twenty-first century with companies designed during the nineteenth century." The book presents a new vision of how companies should be organized in order to succeed in the decade ahead.

Based on their experiences as consultants to a variety of organizations, Hammer and Champy show how some of the world's leading firms use principles of reengineering to save millions of dollars, achieve high levels of customer satisfaction, and speed up and make more flexible all aspects of their operations. The key to reengineering is abandoning the most basic notions on organizing that date back to Scientific Management. These theories—division of labor, control, and managerial hierarchy—no longer work in today's competitive global environment. In place of these ideas the authors offer the notion of process orientation, of concentrating on and rethinking end-to-end activities that create value for customers.

Source: Michael Hammer and James Champy, *Reengineering the Corporation* (New York: Harper Business, 1993).

Max Weber used the term *bureaucracy* to describe an organization based on a formal system of legitimate authority.[39] The major characteristics of Weber's bureaucracy describe the mechanistic mode:

❖ Tasks are divided into highly specialized jobs.

❖ Each task is performed according to a standardized set of rules that ensures uniformity.

❖ Each member of the organization is accountable to a single manager.

❖ Business should be conducted impersonally, and managers should maintain a social distance from workers.

❖ Employment and advancement should be based on technical qualifications, and workers should be protected from arbitrary dismissal.

As you can see, this represents an extreme type of organization—perhaps not the kind in which you have worked or would like to work. It is important, though, to view the mechanistic model as one end of a continuum, and see the organic model as the other. Neither is the ideal form of organizational design, and most organizations change over time. Later in this chapter we will look at other forms of more or less bureaucratic organizational design.

The Organic Model

The organic model of organizational design is in sharp contrast to the mechanistic model. The **organic organization** seeks to maximize flexibility and adaptability. Whereas the mechanistic model is rigid and bureaucratic, the organic model encourages greater utilization of human potential. The organic model deemphasizes specialization of jobs, status, and rank. Horizontal and lateral relationships are as important as vertical relationships.[40]

The organic organization provides individuals with a supportive work environment and builds a sense of personal worth and importance.[41] Thus managers in this organization encourage and motivate employees to reach their potential. This type of organization tends to be decentralized, and communication flows throughout the organization rather than through the chain of command. Departmentalization would be based on product and customer rather than on function.

The organic model describes a more human organization. You may have already decided that this is the best type of organization. It may look that way. Earlier in the chapter, we said that the best structure is one that facilitates getting the work done well. We also said that structure sometimes interferes with quality work. But this doesn't mean that everything about the mechanistic model is bad in all situations or that everything about the organic model is good in all situations. Remember, we're describing a continuum. Between these two extremes are many organizational designs—some we have yet to discover.

The Matrix Organization

The matrix design attempts to capture the strengths and reduce the weaknesses of both the mechanistic and organic designs. After more than 30 years of use, the matrix organization continues to elude definition. A **matrix organization** is a cross-functional organization overlay that creates multiple lines of authority and places people in teams to work on tasks for a finite period of time.[42] The functional departments are the foundation, and a number of products or temporary departments are superimposed across the functional departments. The result (Figure 8–10) is a dual, rather than singular, line of command. This form of organization could be thought to fall in the middle of the continuum, with mechanistic and organic organizations at the two extremes. Although the matrix organization was first developed in the aerospace industry, it is now used in all types of organizations, both private and public.

As Figure 8–10 shows, individuals or groups in each cell report to two managers. For instance, someone working in marketing on Product A would report to the Vice President-Marketing and Product Manager A. This arrangement is useful in speeding up innovation because each person's primary responsibility is to help produce what the organization sells. The key is to free people from bureaucratic constraints by empowering them to create winning ideas and products, while at the same time providing the structure needed to be

organic organizaton
An organization that seeks to maximize flexibility and adaptability. It encourages greater utilization of human potential and deemphasizes specialization of jobs, status, and rank.

matrix organization
A cross-functional organization overlay that creates multiple lines of authority and places people in teams to work on tasks for a finite period of time.

FIGURE 8-10
The Matrix Organization

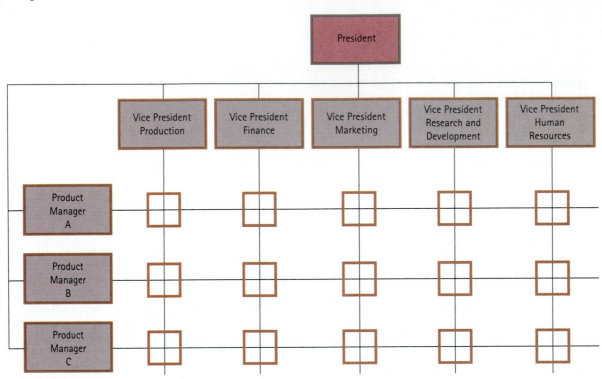

successful.[43] Frigidaire Co., owned by Swedish-based Electrolux since 1986, uses a matrix organization that functions as a team and focuses attention on the consumer. The matrix organization has helped Frigidaire to become increasingly competitive, flexible, and market-driven.[44]

Matrix organizations have increased in popularity as organizations have decentralized and adopted quality programs. They are most appropriate when coordination is needed in complex and uncertain environments.[45] Matrix organizations lead to efficient use of a specialized staff, offer timely response to a changing environment, enable technical specialists to interact with each other, free top-level management from day-to-day activities to spend more time planning, and encourage individual growth and development.[46] Since product or project groups are often employed with the matrix design, many organizations using teams and quality circles adopt this form of organization because of its flexibility and adaptability.

The matrix design has several drawbacks. Dow Chemical adopted a matrix organization in the 1960s to promote internal communication. But the matrix generated miles of red tape, scores of committees, and an even larger bureaucracy. Nonetheless Dow sticks with the matrix today and credits it with many of the firm's successes.[47] The matrix can lead to confusion because individuals or groups report to more than one superior. Several bosses may place conflicting demands on subordinates or struggle with each other for power, placing workers in a compromising position. In some cases, organizations find that groups take longer to make decisions than individuals. The matrix is also costly because additional managers and staff may be needed.[48]

Other Forms of Organizational Design

Many other forms of organizational design have been developed or are emerging in response to the rapidly changing environment. Increased global competitiveness, decentralization, buyouts and hostile takeovers, and the quality revolution are just a few of the factors causing organizations to search for new designs. This section looks at several additional forms of organizational design.

THE MULTIDIVISIONAL ORGANIZATION - The multidivisional (M-Form) organization has emerged in Western Europe and the United States during the past 50 years.[49] The **multidivisional organization** (Figure 8–11) is a high-performance organization whose operating units or divisions are partially interdependent. Thus each division's product is different from that of the other divisions. But all divisions share common endowments such as technology, skill, and information. Hewlett-Packard is divided into 50 semiautonomous divisions, one manufacturing hospital instruments, a second computers, a third hand-held calculators, and so on. Each division sells to slightly different customers and uses different manufacturing methods, but all share a common foundation in electrical engineering, use similar manufacturing methods, and depend on a central laboratory to supplement their research.

> **multidivisional organization**
> A high-performance organization whose operating units or divisions are partially interdependent.

This design attempts to strike a balance between autonomy for the divisions and control over them. The M-Form structure represents the ambiguity common in many organizations. That is, each division is partially independent yet partially dependent on the entire organization. IBM found that as a huge, centralized organization it simply could not react fast enough to changes in the competitive marketplace. With the M-Form, each division is expected to operate independently to maximize profits and is sufficiently autonomous to make timely decisions. But the M-Form only succeeds if divisions cooperate on things they share in common. The key is to make sure this cooperation does not stifle a division's creativity and performance. This is the delicate balance between centralization and decentralization.

THE NETWORK ORGANIZATION - A **network organization** is a flexible, sometimes temporary, relationship between manufacturers, buyers, suppliers, and even customers.[50] The design is dynamic in that the major components can be assembled or reassembled to meet changing competitive conditions. A major advantage of networks is that each member can concentrate on those activities it performs best. In the auto industry, everything from building factories to producing cars is getting cheaper as auto companies quit making parts and concentrate on designing cars.[51] Members are held together by contracts and pursuit of common goals, not by the more traditional hierarchy. The term *virtual corporation* has been used to describe a temporary network of independent organizations, linked by information technology, that come together quickly to exploit fast-changing opportunities.[52] A virtual corporation has neither a central office nor an organization chart; rather, it is a series of partnerships that will more than likely terminate once an opportunity is met. Similarly, a modular corporation consists of a hub surrounded by a network of the best suppliers in the world. The hub is the center of activities, such as research

> **network organization**
> A flexible, sometimes temporary, relationship between manufacturers, buyers, suppliers, even customers.

FIGURE 8-11
The Multidivisional (M-Form)
Organization

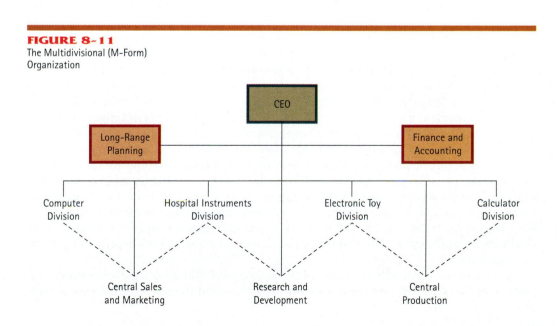

and development; the network is made up of outside specialists that make the parts, handle deliveries, and perform accounting activities.[53]

Some organizations have pushed networks to the point where barriers between the firm, its customers, and its competitors have almost disappeared. Rather than manufacturing the $3.4 billion worth of products it sells annually, Nike has established a network of subcontractors in China, South Korea, Taiwan, and Thailand. Each develops its own products, while Nike continually invests in research and development, providing subcontractors with the results. Even if subcontractors use this knowledge to make products for competitors, Nike feels it will benefit most of all from what subcontractors learn in the process. Nike can respond to changes in fashion faster than its rivals by rearranging the network.[54]

This design is gaining popularity not only in the United States but globally. Members can be added as needed when operating in a global context. For example, a firm entering a foreign country for the first time may add a broker or a trading company to the network. Members that are not performing or are no longer needed can be removed. Since members pursue their distinctive competencies, quality is enhanced. Organizations can also eliminate those activities or operations that can be done better by others.

Several other terms have been used to describe this emerging organizational design. Some refer to *spider webs*, with the center of the web functioning as the centralized organization. This center is connected to various members—each performing a specialized function, and all interconnected with each other—much like a spider web. Each member is able to tap into the organization's collective knowledge and expertise via the spider web. A *shamrock* has also been used to describe an organization based around the core of essential executives and workers, and supported by external contractors and part-time help. The Global Exchange examines the growth of global network organizations.

THE COMPLETE ORGANIZATION - Many different metaphors have been used to describe changes in modern organizations: *reengineering, paradigm shifting*, and *reframing*. The emerging organizations of the future have been described as lean, flexible, responsive, and perhaps above all else, highly competitive. Many of these attributes are captured in what Philip Crosby calls *completeness*, as characterized by the following:

❖ Policy is made by leadership with the consent of the governed.
❖ Requirements are provided in a way that everyone understands.
❖ Everyone keeps learning due to the availability of information and freedom of choice.
❖ Performance measurement is based on a culture of consideration.
❖ The organization's purpose is to help individuals be successful in every aspect of their lives.[55]

According to Crosby, modern communication systems will let management know and understand the will of the people. Because of this, misunderstandings will be avoided, special interest groups will be easily identified, and activities will be well thought out. At the chapter's start we said that an effective organizational structure enables workers to get the job done. Complete organizations are responsive structures committed to quality.

Many challenges remain; new forms of organizations will be developed to meet them. One challenge is designing quality-based organizations and implementing total quality management programs. The *spiral model* (Figure 8–12) integrates many concepts, practices, and philosophies of quality management, such as flexibility, completeness, and empowerment. The spiral indicates that quality implementation is continuous. From the center of the spiral comes the guiding vision of the organization, from which stems the foundational principles of culture, leadership, planning, and change management. The next layer includes the management dynamics of commitment, team building, performance management, and motivation. The final layer contains four implementation activities associated with quality management: vision, empowerment, evaluation, and continuous improvement. The spiral is divided into four slices, each representing these four activities.[56]

What will the organization of the year 2000 look like? Will it be a global network or a matrix organization? Will complete managers really respond to the will of the people? Will

GLOBAL EXCHANGE   GLOBAL NETWORK ORGANIZATIONS

A new form of organizational structure is changing the global business environment. This organization is delayered and downsized, and it operates through a network of market-sensitive business units. The success of these organizations comes from the ability to couple to, and decouple from, the networks of knowledge nodes. These entities, known as *network organizations,* originated over a decade ago but have recently been labeled the organizational structure of the future. The network's center or hub is a centralized staff of functional specialists managed in traditional ways. The extended network consists of a decentralized global structure of rotating members: one that designs the product, one that manufactures it and so on. The network's composition changes constantly to meet the organization's global needs. They will link, as needed, teams of empowered employees, consultants, manufacturers, suppliers, and customers. The structure of a global network organization is shown below.

Many factors explain the growing popularity of network organizations. Organizations designed in the 1950s and 1960s sought economies of scale through centralized planning and control. This organizational structure became obsolete in the 1980s when the forces of technology and globalization demanded both efficiency and effectiveness. A structure was needed that adapted quickly to innovations while at the same time controlling costs. Organizations were forced to search globally for new markets, minimize costs, maximize returns, specialize in those activities the organization does best, and farm out activities that could be performed more efficiently by others. The network structure enables organizations to concentrate on those things it does most efficiently and contract the remaining activities with other firms.

For example, BMW utilizes a global network organization. Any part of a BMW may come from another firm; about 55 to 75 percent of the total production costs at BMW come from parts contracted with other firms. BMW keeps abreast of technological developments through its own subsidiaries and partnerships with other firms. BMW Motor Sports Group, Advanced Engineering Group, and Motorcycle Group specialize in technologically advanced forms of automobile or motorcycle development and production. Each of these subsidiaries concentrates on engineering and design innovations; the objectives of these groups is to identify the best outside supplier for a specific technology. BMW also engages in joint ventures with Leowe Opta (electronics), the French firm Cecigram (new production technologies), and others.

Global competition in the 21st century will force managers, at least to some extent, to design global network organizational structures. Network structures facilitate lateral communication that is lacking in many organizational hierarchies. They also help managers and workers unleash creativity. The forces that have pushed many U.S. and foreign firms to adopt network forms of organizational structure are likely to intensify with the emergence of new global participants, like Eastern Europe. New foreign products will increase competition and new foreign markets will mean new opportunities. It is hard to imagine the traditional organization surviving in this environment.

Source: Adapted from Sirkka L. Jarvenpaa and Blake Ives, "The Global Network Organization of the Future," *Journal of Management Information Systems,* Spring 1994, pp. 25–57; Charles C. Snow, Raymond E. Miles, and Henry J. Coleman, "Managing 21st Century Network Organizations," *Organizational Dynamics,* Winter 1992, pp. 5–19; Ralph H. Kilman, "A Networked Company That Embraces the World," *Information Strategy: The Executive's Journal,* Spring 1990, pp. 23–26; and John B. Bush and Alan L. Frohman, "Communication in a Network Organization," *Organizational Dynamics,* Autumn 1991, pp. 23–36.

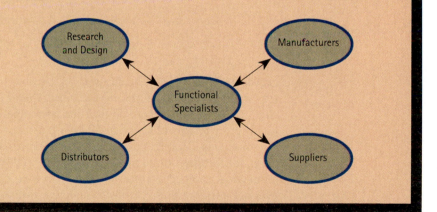

the spiral model represent how organizations develop a structure? Or will some new form of organization be developed? Anticipating and shaping the future is part of the excitement of management. And although we can't answer all these questions definitively, we do know that to survive, organizations of the future will be designed in such a way that workers are committed to quality and customers are satisfied.

THE WORKPLACE OF TOMORROW

As we noted at the outset of this chapter, the organization of tomorrow will be structured differently. Changes in organizational structure are now taking place at a rapid pace. The result will be flatter, highly decentralized organizations that bring firms closer to their

FIGURE 8-12
The Spiral Model

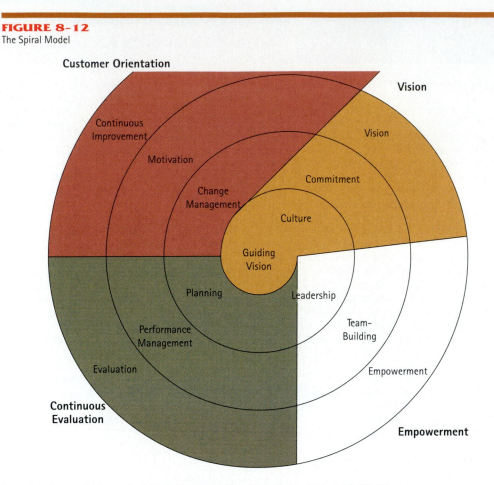

Source: Bruce Brocka and M. Suzanne Brocka, *Quality Management* (Homewood, Il.: Business One Irwin, © 1992), p. 50.

customers.[57] Successful businesses will be able to respond quickly to changes in the environment. And organizations cannot be customer oriented and responsive unless they know what their competitors are doing. Thus, benchmarking toughest competitors and working to identify key factors of success will be a must.[58]

Changing organization structures also means different jobs for managers. As organizations decentralize and empower teams, the middle manager will be replaced by the project manager. A project is a task with a beginning, a defined task (such as introducing a new product), and an end.[59] Project managers, unlike traditional managers, supervise a project for its duration. The career of a manager in this environment will be characterized by uncertainty, little job security, and more and more work done by teams addressing projects with a beginning and an end.[60] Managers of the future will have to be creative, on the edge of technology, willing to change, and constantly investing in new knowledge.

With all the changes taking place, many organizations are also learning that some things should never change. At IBM, it's service to the customer; at Disney, it's bringing happiness to people. Organizations increasingly are rediscovering their core values as they struggle to cope with change.[61] Successful companies will adapt to the changing world—this is a must—without losing their core values.

SUMMARY OF LEARNING OBJECTIVES

DEFINE THE TERMS ORGANIZING AND ORGANIZATIONAL STRUCTURE.

Organizing is the process of structuring both human and physical resources to accomplish organizational objectives. Organizational structure is the framework of jobs and departments that directs the behavior of individuals and groups toward achieving the organization's objectives.

DETERMINE WHEN ORGANIZATIONAL STRUCTURE IS A PROBLEM.

Whenever work is not getting done well, organizational structure is a problem. Conflicts between departments or groups within an organization suggest a structure problem. Difficulty in coordinating work between departments, slowness in adapting to change, and ambiguous job assignments also indicate problems with organizational structure.

EXPLAIN HOW MANAGERS DETERMINE ORGANIZATIONAL STRUCTURE.

Managers determine organizational structure by deciding the degree to which jobs are specialized; determining the extent to which authority is delegated; grouping jobs according to some logical arrangement; and determining the number of people who report to one manager.

COMPARE SCIENTIFIC MANAGEMENT AND CRAFTSMANSHIP.

Scientific management requires that tasks be broken down to the smallest element and that problem solving be elevated to managers. Taylor used time and motion studies to identify basic movements that minimize effort and maximize output. Craftsmanship is basically the opposite. Craftsmen are responsible for their own work, with management providing the means and facilities for the craftsmen to perform the entire operation.

DISCUSS THE SIGNIFICANCE OF WORK TEAMS AND QUALITY CIRCLES.

Many organizations are modifying and restructuring jobs so they can be performed by work teams. A work team is a group of employees who (1) work closely together to pursue common objectives and (2) can be directed by a manager or are self-managed. A quality circle is a small group of people who do similar work and meet regularly to discuss their work, identify problems, and present possible solutions.

DISCUSS HOW AUTHORITY CAN BE DELEGATED.

Authority can be delegated by decentralizing the organization, giving an individual (usually a manager) the right to make a decision without obtaining approval of a higher-level manager. Some organizations have begun to empower production workers to make decisions that typically have been made by managers.

LIST THE MOST COMMON BASES FOR DEPARTMENTALIZATION.

The most common bases for departmentalization are by function, product, customer, and geography. Some organizations use a combination of these, called mixed departmentalization, while some are actually doing away with the traditional departmental structure. Process organization groups jobs according to the processes that satisfy customer needs.

EXPLAIN THE DIFFERENT DIMENSIONS OF ORGANIZATIONAL STRUCTURE.

Three dimensions are used to compare organizations. Formalization refers to the extent to which procedures are written down and filed. Centralization is the extent to which authority is distributed throughout the organization. And complexity reflects the number of different job titles and different departments.

COMPARE MECHANISTIC, ORGANIC, AND MATRIX ORGANIZATIONS.

The mechanistic model represents one end of a continuum. It is a rigid organizational design that attempts to achieve production and efficiency through rules, specialized jobs, and centralized authority. The organic model (at the opposite end of the continuum) seeks to maximize flexibility and adaptability by encouraging greater utilization of human potential. The matrix organization falls in the middle of the continuum. It is a cross-functional organizational overlay that creates multiple lines of authority.

DISCUSS SEVERAL EMERGING FORMS OF ORGANIZATIONAL DESIGN.

The multidivisional organization is a high-performance organization whose operating units or divisions are partially interdependent. This design attempts to strike a balance between autonomy for the division and control over them. A network organization is a flexible, sometimes temporary, relationship between manufacturers, buyers, suppliers, customers, and others. The members can be changed rapidly to meet competitive challenges. In complete organizations, policy is made by leaders with the workers' consent, and requirements are provided in a way that everyone understands. The organization's purpose is to help individuals be successful in every aspect of their lives.

KEY TERMS

centralization, p. 218
chain of command, p. 220
complexity, p. 227
customer departmentalization, p. 222
decentralization, p. 218
departmentalization, p. 221
empowerment, p. 219
formalization, p. 226

functional departmentalization, p. 221
geographic departmentalization, p. 222
line position, p. 220
matrix organization, p. 229
mechanistic organization, p. 228
mixed departmentalization, p. 223
multidivisional organization, p. 231
network organization, p. 231

organic organization, p. 229
organizational design, p. 228
organizational structure, p. 213
process organization, p. 223
product departmentalization, p. 221
quality circle, p. 217
span of control, p. 225
staff position, p. 221

REVIEW AND DISCUSSION QUESTIONS

Recall

1. What are some common myths about organizational structure?
2. What is the difference between teams and quality circles?
3. What are the advantages and disadvantages of decentralization?
4. Distinguish between line and staff positions.
5. Compare the different forms of departmentalization with an emphasis on the strengths and weaknesses of each.
6. Contrast the various forms of organizational design using the mechanistic and organic models as opposite ends of a continuum.

Understanding

7. Why is organizational structure so critical to the success of organizations?
8. How does empowerment relate to total quality management?
9. In terms of organizational structure and design, how do you think the organization of the future will look?

Application

10. Think of recent purchases in which you, as the customer, were not satisfied. Did you hold the worker responsible? Could your dissatisfaction be attributed to problems with organizational structure and design? What could managers do to make sure other customers do not experience the same problem?

CASE STUDY

Johnson & Johnson Decentralizes

The 1980s have become known in business as the decade of financial restructuring. Takeovers, mergers, and acquisitions dominated business during this period. The 1990s are seeing a different kind of restructuring, as corporations try to make their organizations more decentralized, giving people more freedom to be creative and eliminating inefficiencies that have plagued many large firms. The real problem is not size, but the burden it places on the job of managing. According to management consultant Peter Drucker, "The Fortune 500 is over." Drucker doesn't mean that large corporations will all go out of business, but he believes they will begin to divide their assets and resources into smaller, more efficient, and more independent businesses. IBM is organizing into more autonomous units, GM is eliminating 74,000 jobs and closing 21 factories, and AT&T is contracting services like payroll, billing, and public relations, while laying off 40,000 workers.

Johnson & Johnson, with annual revenues of $15 billion, is a large organization with the best features of a small organization: focus, flexibility, and speed. CEO Ralph Larsen oversees 168 highly decentralized businesses in 53 countries, each focusing on health care, with annual sales from $100,000 to $1 billion. "Decentralization is the heart of Johnson & Johnson," he says. Larsen not only encourages each company's president to act independently, he expects them to. Marvin Woodall, president of tiny startup Johnson & Johnson Interventional Systems Co., doesn't spend much time at his parent company's headquarters. He prefers to run his small staff an hour away, and if he wants to go to Europe to check on operations there, he doesn't ask. Larsen also decides whom to hire, what products to produce, and whom to sell them to. Ultimately, Larsen and the other 165 presidents are accountable to executives at "headquarters," which some presidents visit as infrequently as four times a year. Only 1.5 percent of J&J's 82,700 employees work at headquarters, which doesn't actually manage but provides the capital and selects the people to run the businesses.

Johnson & Johnson was decentralizing long before it became fashionable in corporate America. Decentralization was pushed by Chairman Robert Johnson in the 1930s, when he encouraged Ethicon Inc. (manufacturer of sutures) and Personal Products Co. (feminine hygiene products) to operate independently. Since J&J has had over 50 years of practice, the company knows how to make decentralization work. But J&J also knows the importance of balancing autonomy and corporate structure—decentralization and centralization. Such a balance is difficult to achieve.

At the heart of Johnson & Johnson's management system is a diverse array of products ranging from familiar consumer goods like Band-Aids and baby powder to advanced care products for yeast infections and athlete's foot. Given all these different products, Larsen compares his job to an orchestra conductor's: providing inspiration and direction but assuring creative freedom. For instance, the company funded its Vistakon division hundreds of millions of dollars to start a new business making and selling disposable contact lenses. Today this business generates $250 million a year in sales. Larsen's job is not only to fund such ventures, but also to require that everyone in the organization focus on cutting costs and generating an acceptable return on investment. Thus each president has to think like an entrepreneur, counting every penny and spending only on projects that yield a satisfactory profit. That makes it critical for Larsen to select the right executives to run the 166 companies.

Decentralization is not without risks. Numerous businesses operating autonomously can result in duplication of function, increasing overhead. At J&J, overhead is 41 percent of sales, compared to 30 percent for more centralized Merck and 28 percent for Bristol-Myers Squibb, another competitor. Sales functions are also duplicated, as dozens of J&J sales representatives from different units call on large retailers like Wal-Mart and Kmart; big retailers prefer to reduce the number of contacts from suppliers. To cut duplication, Larsen has established employee teams called customer-support centers to work on-site with retailers to simplify distribution and ordering. Larsen has also pushed the different companies to reduce duplication in functions such as payroll, purchasing, distribution, and accounts payable. In addition, he presses hard to keep hiring from getting out of hand, another problem with decentralization.

Although decentralization does pose some problems, Larsen plans to stick with it. Since 1980 yearly profits have averaged over 19 percent. And as global competition intensifies, large organizations will have to be focused, stay close to the marketplace to come up with ideas, and encourage employees' creativity.

Source: Adapted from Brian O'Reilly, "J&J Is on a Roll," Fortune, December 26, 1994, pp. 178–192;" Joseph Weber, "A Big Company That Works," Business Week, May 4, 1992, pp. 124-32; Brian Dumaine, "Is Big Still Good?" Fortune, April 20, 1992, pp. 50-60; and Joseph Weber, "How J&J's Foresight Made Contact Lenses Pay," Business Week, May 4, 1992, p. 132.

QUESTIONS

1. How can organizational structure limit large organizations like Johnson & Johnson?
2. Why does decentralization seem to be working so well at J&J?
3. How does J&J balance centralization and decentralization?
4. Name some problems organizations are likely to face when decentralizing.
5. Could Johnson & Johnson be described as a multidivisional organization? Explain.

VIDEO CASE

Organizational Structure: Big Apple Bagels and the St. Louis Bread Company

In the past, a corporation was structured much like the military, with a formal chain of command and division of labor. Over time, many companies came to realize that the bureaucratic structure of the traditional corporation can often cause breakdowns in communication and lower efficiency.

Manufacturers of products in relatively unchanging in relatively unchanging environments often take a mechanistic approach to production. In such environments, employees strictly adhere to their job descriptions. However, companies that depend on their ability to continuously introduce innovations usually take a more organic approach, giving employees more room to make decisions and communicate outside the chain of command. Some companies may choose to radically modify or reengineer their structure.

Big Apple Bagels and St. Louis Bread Company are two rapidly growing businesses that share a similar market. However, the organizations are structured quite differently from one another. Whatever the structure, for an organization to be successful, it must be responsive to its customers. This operating principle runs a lot deeper than just making sure the right kind of cheese gets put on a turkey sandwich.

Many companies are finding that changing the way in which they are organized improves their responsiveness. For example, they may choose to simplify their structure and reduce the layers of management, thus reducing the layers in the chain of command. Another option is to widen the spans of control. The traditional organization has a tall structure and a narrow span of control. This means managers have few subordinates who report directly to them. A company with a flat organizational structure has a wide span of control with fewer reporting levels.

Many companies are empowering their employees and allowing them to make decisions on their own rather than insisting that they report to various levels of management. When Paul Stolzer opened the first Big Apple Bagel store in 1985, he had no idea that in the short span of seven years his small store would grow into a franchise that boasts 75 stores with more opening all the time. Stolzer said, "The stores have changed quite extensively over the years. We are actually a fourth- or fifth-generation store right now. Initially, the stores were set up as strictly bagel bakeries with a predominant product being bagels and cream cheese. We've progressed to a more aggressive stature, adding a few more dimensions to our operation in that we have dine-in facilities, a more extensive sandwich menu, and a very, very strong coffee program. We're still progressing. That's one thing that never ends."

One thing that hasn't changed is Big Apple Bagels' open-door policy. From top management to line workers, communication channels are wide open. Jim Lentz, director of training for the company said, "At Big Apple Bagels we have an open-door policy between the franchisee and the franchisor, and between the ultimate consumer and the franchisor in that we encourage people to come up with suggestions, new products, new ideas. We're never further than a phone call or a stop away. We're continually in the franchisee's stores to make sure that their operation meets our specifications."

In 1987, Ken Rosenthal opened his first St. Louis Bread Company store in Kirkwood, Missouri, with used baking equipment. Today, St. Louis Bread company operates over 50 stores in the St. Louis area, with stores opening in other midwestern markets as well. The growth happened quickly, forcing the company to change its organizational structure. Originally, it was a small store with 17 employees. When it became a large chain, employing over 1,000 people, a more traditional organizational structure was needed.

When a company is growing, it may need to use some of the concepts of reengineering. Reengineering entails the radical redesign of business processes to achieve major gains in cost, service, or time. For example, by mid-1992, St. Louis Bread was growing at a frantic pace. The partners decided it was time to slow down and take a breath. They began to realize that the opportunistic approach wouldn't work anymore.

They had reached a point where the controls and information systems they had in place were inadequate for a larger operation. New equipment was purchased to automate processes on the line. Thirty thousand dollar point of purchase cash registers were installed to track everything from sales per hour to sales per stockkeeping unit to sales by stores.

Doron Berger said, "The organization at St. Louis Bread Company is probably not atypical of many organizations. While we have a hierarchical structure in terms of someone is ultimately accountable for the results of the business, we do fight vigorously to maintain a flat organization. In other words, there aren't a lot of layers between the president-CEO and the people who are on the front lines. I think we have succeeded because of the effort we have put into that."

In November of 1993, Au Bon Pain, the dominant bakery/cafe chain in the country acquired St. Louis Bread Company. Au Bon Pain's stores were all in urban areas. St. Louis Bread Company would enable them to tap into the suburban market. David Hutkin said, "Our organizational structure has not changed dramatically. It really hasn't changed since the acquisition. We've continued to run the company very independent of the parent company, and we're still doing the same things as we were doing before."

A company like Big Apple Bagels is considered to be a boundaryless organization. In such an organization, the corporate structure is more horizontal than vertical. Boundaryless businesses are typically organized around core customer oriented processes, such as communication, customer contact, and managing quality. In order to enjoy the benefits a horizontal organization offers, four boundaries must be overcome:

- ❖ Authority
- ❖ Task
- ❖ Political
- ❖ Identity

Even a relatively boundaryless company has an authority boundary. Some people lead, others follow. To overcome problems that may arise, managers must learn how to lead and still remain open to criticism. Their "subordinates" need to be trained and encouraged not only to follow but also to challenge their superiors if there is an issue worth considering. As one Big Apple executive said, "I think there are some natural boundaries that occur between a franchisor and a franchisee, or an employee and an employer. What we try to do at Big Apple Bagels is to eliminate those boundaries by keeping the phone line open at all times as well as the fact that a lot of us have been franchisees as well as now being a franchisor so we know what it's like to sit on both sides of the table and to be able to talk to the franchisee from the standpoint of we were there at one time as well and we have that empathy for their position."

The task boundary arises out of the "it's not my job" mentality. A task boundary can be overcome by clearly defining who does what when employees from different departments divide up work.

The political boundary derives from the differences in political agendas that often separate employees and can cause conflict. This is closely related to identity boundary. The identity boundary emerges due to an employee tendency to identify with those individuals or groups with whom they have shared experiences, or with whom they share fundamental values.

To overcome the identity boundary, employees and management need to be trained to gain an understanding of the business as a whole and avoid the "us versus them" mentality. A good way to do this is by forming cross-functional teams, in which tasks are shared and cross training simply happens as a result of employee interaction.

The new boundaryless organization relies on self-managed work teams. It reduces internal boundaries that separate functions and create hierarchical levels. A horizontal corporation is structured around core, customer-oriented processes.

Lines of communication are open, allowing line-level employees to communicate their questions and concerns directly to those at the management and executive level. Not all organizations are structured the same way. There are factors to consider such as organizational size, culture, and production volume. These factors may indicate that under some circumstances, a tall organizational structure may be more appropriate than a flat structure. Companies in the future may change or alter the way they operate but customer satisfaction, quality, and efficiency will always be the primary goals.

QUESTIONS

1. If companies today are working so hard to break down boundaries, why is it that there are boundaries in the first place?

2. What are some new technologies that will help managers keep lines of communication open to employees? To customers?

3. The video mentions that St. Louis Bread Company had to use a more traditional organizational structure when it grew rapidly. Why do you think that was necessary? What do you think the company gains by adopting such a structure? What does it lose?

APPLICATION EXERCISE

STARTING A QUALITY CIRCLE

Could you use the quality team concept in your class? Using much of what we discussed in this chapter, let's take a stab at it. Call it quality circles if you like. (Actually, it will be difficult in this brief application to develop a quality circle.) First we will provide some guidelines. Then you can design a program to implement a quality team. The guidelines are: (1) participation is voluntary, (2) emphasis is on self-development and mutual development, (3) all team members will participate, and (4) the team will operate continuously.

A list of suggested steps follows. Propose how you would complete each step.

1. Stimulate interest.
2. Identify the issues.
3. Identify the areas for improvement.
4. Select team leaders.
5. Form teams.

CHAPTER 9

Job Analysis, Design, and Redesign

After studying this chapter, you should be able to:

List the steps in job analysis.

❖ Compare job descriptions and job specifications.

❖ Define the term job design.

❖ Evaluate the job specialization approach to job design.

❖ Discuss the concepts of job range and job depth.

❖ Explain how job redesign differs from job design.

❖ Contrast the different approaches to job redesign.

❖ Discuss the advantages of the team-based approach to job design and redesign.

Cincinnati Milacron: Designing Jobs for Today's Workers

Managers pay a whopping $1,000 to attend one of W. Edwards Deming's "Quality, Productivity and Competitive Position" seminars. The esteemed management consultant—now over 90 years old—is credited with teaching the Japanese how to produce top-quality goods. Yet he condemns the way workers are treated in America. Says Deming, "People want to work, but they want to take joy in their work. American managers still insist on managing people instead of the system—creating fear and mistrust in the workplace, removing joy, rewarding themselves at the top with bonuses and perks, punishing those at the bottom. It is destructive, and it prevents companies from functioning effectively as a system."

In 1992 Japanese politicians set off an intense debate when they blasted the American work ethic. Are American workers lazy, or are the jobs designed in a manner that encourages laziness and absenteeism? Deming believes the latter. In fact, by some measures, Americans are working harder than ever. The percentage of Americans working has increased steadily since 1948, and increased 77 percent for women. More Americans than ever hold two jobs; among families headed by married couples, 65 percent have two or more people working. But many people show up for work less than enthused, feel pressured, worry about losing their jobs, and are asked to do more for less money. Some experts feel it is time to look at work differently. Workers have changed, as has the work environment. Jobs must be designed to satisfy literate, independent-minded workers.

In 1991 Cincinnati Milacron, Inc., opened a small plant in Cincinnati, Ohio. Here workers in teams of two build an entire computer-controlled lathe by themselves. They don't punch timeclocks and they don't have supervisors. They are responsible for making the machine, installing it, and teaching customers how it is op-

erated. Absenteeism is almost zero, and workers feel like they are part of what they are doing. Although such a solution may still be the exception, it illustrates how workers respond when given a chance to participate in the workplace.

Cincinnati Milacron was one of 15 U.S. manufacturers of plastics machinery that dominated the market in 1980, when foreign-made equipment began flowing into the States. By 1985 foreign competition had captured half of the U.S. market. Cincinnati Milacron is now one of the five U.S. firms that survived the decade—partly because it adopted teamwork.

When business got so bad in 1983, workers at an Ohio plant realized they had to fight to save their jobs and the plant. They also knew the answer was to somehow change the way they worked so they made better, more competitive products. Up to then, products had been developed in the traditional method, passed sequentially from one department to another. In an effort to develop an improved injection molder, a team was organized to develop the machine simultaneously. Workers from manufacturing, marketing, engineering, purchasing, and inventory joined the nine-member team. The team reported directly to the vice president of plastics machinery to increase autonomy and reduce the bureaucracy. The approach was named Wolfpack, to signify that the people working on the project were a group, and that there would be an extremely aggressive approach taken to achieve ambitious goals. The new machine was delivered on schedule and on budget, and outsold Cincinnati Milacron's previous model by two to one. And perhaps more importantly, Toyota recently purchased several machines for its auto plants. Today, the emphasis on the formal planning process and on the planning document is disappearing. In its place is a more interactive process that makes use of the insights of those in contact with customers.

Source: Adapted from Stephen J. Wall and Shannon Rye Wall, "The Evolution (Not the Death) of Strategy," *Organizational Dynamics,* Autumn 1995, pp. 6–19; Gary S. Vasilash, "Cells in Cincinnati," *Production,* October 1995, pp. 38–40; Ronald E. Yates, "U.S. Management 'Doomed' to Failure," *The Orlando Sentinel,* January 19, 1992, pp. D1, D4; Bob Davis and Dana Milbank, "If the U.S. Work Ethic Is Fading, Alienation May Be Main Reason," *The Wall Street Journal,* February 7, 1992, pp. A1, A8; Ronald Yates, "Prophet of Boom," *Chicago Tribune Magazine,* February 16, 1992, pp. 14-22; and Charles Garfield, *Second to None* (Homewood, Ill.: Business One Irwin, 1992), pp. 168-69.

In Chapter 8 we discussed how some organizations are designing structures that empower workers to make their own decisions. Workers in America have changed greatly during the 20th century. They are more literate and they have different objectives in their work. People want interesting work, recognition for good work, the chance to work with others who respect them, an opportunity to develop skills, and a voice in the design of their jobs—they want to be heard. They are no longer satisfied to simply have a job, as few of today's independent-minded workers remember what it was like to be out of work during the Depression. Even fewer realize that prior to the Depression, unemployment insurance did not exist. In those days, people had no choice but to work, and do as they were told.

Work itself is also changing. Robots do much of the work in factories, replacing many traditional blue-collar jobs. And white-collar workers, once thought to be indispensable, are now losing their jobs regularly as firms decentralize. In July 1993, Procter & Gamble announced that it would cut 13,000 jobs by 1996 through restructuring and by closing 30 plants.[1] Organizations are being told that the front-line workers need more autonomy to make decisions. Organizations like Cincinnati Milacron are struggling to design—or redesign—jobs more suited to today's worker and the current work environment.

This chapter examines job design. First, we will discuss the steps involved in job analysis, including developing job descriptions and job specifications. Then we will present three different aspects of job design: job specialization, job range, and job depth. Next, approaches to job redesign will be examined, including job rotation, job enlargement, and job enrichment. Finally, we will discuss the team-based approach to job design.

JOB ANALYSIS

job analysis
The process of gathering, analyzing, and synthesizing information about jobs.

Prior to actually designing a job, the organization must determine the description of the job itself. **Job analysis** is the process of gathering, analyzing, and synthesizing information about jobs.[2] This time-consuming, complicated task is a vital input to job design decisions. Job analysis (1) specifies the task that must be accomplished to complete a job and (2) determines the skills and knowledge necessary to perform the tasks.[3] Table 9–1 lists some questions that may be answered through job analysis.

Job analysis is an ongoing process. As organizations evolve over time, missions and objectives change, as do conditions in the environment and the nature of the work. By analyzing and redesigning existing jobs, organizations can adapt to those changes and remain competitive. Many jobs have changed as a result of technology, global competition, and the pressure to produce quality products. Managers are learning that organizations are a collection of human beings that need to be developed and nurtured, not a collection of assets to be traded, manipulated, and motivated by fear (as the Ethics Spotlight relates). The essence of empowerment is providing workers with more latitude in their decisions, enabling them to improve quality. As we will see later, this also influences job design.

TABLE 9–1	QUESTIONS ANSWERED BY JOB ANALYSIS
Question	Possible Answers
What activities are required in a job?	Hand and body motions, use of equipment, services, communication with others.
What skills are needed to perform the activities?	Education, previous experience, licenses, degrees, or other personal characteristics.
What are the working conditions of the job?	Physical demands, degree of accountability and responsibility, extent of supervision, and other job environment factors.

ETHICS SPOTLIGHT   DRIVING OUT FEAR

Some say fear is a great motivation. This may have been true when the pyramids were built or in American "sweatshops" of the late 1800s. But today's work force is not made up of first-generation, uneducated laborers, and more and more managers are coming to the realization that individuals cannot perform their best unless they feel secure. One of Deming's most important points for integrating total quality into the organization is to drive out fear. Consider the following:

- Constantly being afraid of losing your job.
- Waking up each morning dreading going to work.
- Working in an environment that makes you feel afraid, insecure, and inadequate.
- Being fired for bringing a problem to management's attention.

- Having a boss who uses punishment to make sure you do as you are told.

Of course, the list could go on indefinitely. Unfortunately, many workers regularly experience these fears. And the consequences can be devastating to both the individual and the organization. Fear can lead to higher levels of stress, health and family problems, lower levels of performance, and general burnout. As a result, the organization suffers. Individuals do not perform at a high level, but rather show up for work and go through the motions. This attitude can become contagious as even the more enthusiastic workers become demotivated and fearful. Ultimately, quality suffers; quality is difficult to achieve unless workers feel secure. The economic loss to the organization is impossible to measure. To obtain quality, managers must develop a culture of openness in which individuals are not afraid to speak up, make a mistake, and so on.

Managers who use their power to create fear are not only behaving unethically; they are most likely not accomplishing their objectives. Workers may believe they will be punished if they do not perform, which of course generates fear. But fear impedes performance; it does not increase performance. On the other hand, managers can project an image of support and teamwork. It has been demonstrated repeatedly that rewarding individuals for good work is much more effective than the threat of punishment.

At Chevron, employee loyalty fell as the size of the workforce was reduced. But the company openly posts results of employee morale surveys and has vowed to improve them by developing a new relationship with workers.

Driving out fear is not a simple task. In some organizations, workers are skeptical because after being told they could speak up or that their jobs were secure, managers penalized or even fired a worker who spoke up. The only way to overcome fear and negative feelings that build up over time is to treat workers with dignity and respect; eliminating fear must start at the top.

Managers' actions must demonstrate that management by fear is no longer acceptable. A firm can do this by providing training, treating all workers fairly, and maintaining an atmosphere of teamwork. John Welch Jr., CEO of General Electric, made it clear in the firm's annual report who gets promoted and who doesn't. In short, he won't tolerate autocratic managers and has fired several at the highest levels of the company. Those managers who do not suppress and intimidate workers, and who perform, have a bright future.

Change cannot take place all at once. By maintaining a consistent atmosphere that is devoid of fear, managers stimulate cooperation and mutual respect. Eventually workers begin to trust and work as a team. In the long run they are much more positive about their jobs, their coworkers and supervisor, and the organization. At this point high quality can be achieved.

Source: Adapted from Edward Tuvin, "How Can We Get Out of the Mess We've Created," *Journal of Quality & Participation*, March 1995, pp. 90–96. Brian O' Reilly, "The New Deal," *Fortune*, June 13, 1994, pp. 44–52; W. Edwards Deming, *Out of the Crisis* (Boston: MIT Center for Advanced Engineering Study, 1986, pp. 59–62; Marshall Sashkin and Kenneth J. Kiser, *Total Quality Management* (Seabrook: Ducochon, 1991), pp. 29–30; Howard S. Gitlow and Shelby J. Gitlow, *The Deming Guide to Quality and Competitive Position* (Englewood Cliffs, N.J.: Prentice-Hall, 1987), pp. 130–38; and James C. Hyatt and Amal Kumar Naj, "GE is No Place for Autocrats, Welch Decress," *The Wall Street Journal*, March 3, 1992, pp. B1, B6.

Job analysis applies to all types of jobs. Job analysis began with factory jobs, an integral part of the scientific management movement. The purpose was to use objective data to determine the single best way to design work. But eventually job analysis made its way into office and clerical jobs, and today applies to management jobs as well. Job analysis is used to help design work that enhances employee performance, not to limit workers by determining the single best way to do things. In many instances, those directly involved in doing the work are participating in the job analysis. They are closest to the task and can provide excellent information about the job.

Steps in Job Analysis

A typical job analysis involves several steps (Figure 9–1). First, the job analyst must examine how each job fits into the overall organization. An overview of the organization and jobs provides a working picture of the arrangement of departments, units, and jobs. During this step, organization charts are used to examine the formal relationships among the firm's departments and units. The relationships among jobs are also examined. For example, when analyzing an assembly line job, the analyst would be interested in the flow of work to and from the assembly line worker. Since analyzing each job would be too costly and time consuming, the second step involves determining which jobs in the organization will be analyzed.

The third step involves collecting data on the jobs to be analyzed. Data are collected on the characteristics of the job, the behaviors and activities required by the job, and the employee skills needed to perform it. Several methods are used to collect job analysis data. Observation is used to collect data for jobs that require manual or standardized activities, such as assembly line work. Interviewing workers, often conducted along with observation, is probably the most widely used data collection method. Questionnaires and logs or diaries pertaining to job tasks, frequency of tasks, when the tasks are accomplished, and so on are also used to collect information. A questionnaire called the *Job Analysis Information Format* (Figure 9–2) can provide basic information for use with any method employed to collect analysis data. Information collected by the job analyst is then used to prepare job descriptions and job specifications, steps four and five.

job description

A written summary of the job, detailing the job's activities, equipment required to perform them, and the job's working conditions.

Job Descriptions and Job Specifications

The major output of job analysis is the job description. The **job description** is a written summary of the job: its activities, equipment required to perform the activities, and the

FIGURE 9–1
Steps in a Typical Job Analysis

FIGURE 9-2
Job Analysis Information
Format

Your Job Title _____   Code _____ Date _____

Class Title _____   Department _____

Your Name _____   Facility _____

Supervisor's Title _____   Prepared by _____

Superior's Name _____   Hours Worked _____ AM/PM _____ to AM/PM _____

---

1. What is the general purpose of your job?

2. What was your last job? If it was in another organization, please name it.

3. To what job would you normally expect to be promoted?

4. If you regularly supervise others, list them by name and job title.

5. If you supervise others, please check those activities that are part of your supervisory duties.

_____ Hiring	_____ Coaching	_____ Promoting
_____ Orienting	_____ Counseling	_____ Compensating
_____ Training	_____ Budgeting	_____ Disciplining
_____ Scheduling	_____ Directing	_____ Terminating
_____ Developing	_____ Measuring performance	_____ Other _____

6. How would you describe the successful completion and results of your work?

7. *Job duties*—Please briefly describe what you do and, if possible, *how* you do it. Indicate those duties you consider to be most important and/or most difficult.

   a. *Daily duties*—

   b. *Periodic duties* (Please indicate whether weekly, monthly, quarterly, etc.)—

   c. *Duties performed at irregular intervals*—

   d. How long have you been performing these duties?

   e. Are you now performing unnecessary duties? If yes, please describe.

   f. Should you be performing duties not now included in your job? If yes, please describe.

8. *Education.* Please check the blank that indicates the educational *requirements* for the job, not your *own* educational background.

   a. _____ No formal education required.   d. _____ 2-year college certificate or equivalent.

   b. _____ Less than high school diploma.   e. _____ 4-year college degree.

   c. _____ High school diploma or equivalent.   f. _____ Education beyond under-graduate degree and/or professional license.

   List advanced degrees or specific professional license or certificate required.

   Please indicate the education you had when you were placed on this job.

9. *Experience.* Please check the amount needed to perform your job.

   a. _____ None.   e. _____ One to three years.

   b. _____ Less than one month.   f. _____ Three to five years.

   c. _____ One month to less than six months.   g. _____ Five to 10 years.

   d. _____ Six months to one year.   h. _____ Over 10 years.

   Please indicate the experience you had when you were placed on this job.

10. *Skill.* Please list any skills required in the performance of your job. (For example, amount of accuracy, alertness, precision in working with described tools, methods, systems, etc.)

    Please list skills you possessed when you were placed on this job.

11. *Equipment.* Does your work require the use of any equipment? Yes No . If yes, please list the equipment and check whether you use it rarely, occasionally, or frequently.

Equipment	Rarely	Occasionally	Frequently
a. _____	_____	_____	_____
b. _____	_____	_____	_____
c. _____	_____	_____	_____
d. _____	_____	_____	_____

working conditions of the job. It helps the organization with a variety of activities, including planning, recruiting, and training. It also helps workers understand what a specific job entails and what jobs fit their particular skills and interests. Figure 9–3 shows a job description of a human resource manager.

Traditionally, a human resource manager was responsible for writing job descriptions. These job descriptions usually emphasize what employees should do, how they should think, and so on. In other words, they were for the most part prescriptive. Many organizations, in an effort to encourage more participation, now involve workers in developing their own job descriptions. By teaching workers how to write their own job descriptions and then having the employees and supervisors discuss and agree on a job description, workers must think about the best way to achieve desired outcomes. Rather than being prescriptive, this is an outcome-oriented approach to developing job descriptions. It is used by organizations interested in empowering workers to take control of their own jobs.

job specification
A written explanation of skills, knowledge, abilities, and other characteristics needed to perform a job effectively.

The **job specification** is a written explanation of skills, knowledge, abilities, and other characteristics needed to perform a job effectively. The job specification evolves from the job description. The key difference is that the job description describes factors about the

---

FIGURE 9–3
Job Descriptions of a Human
Resource Manager

JOB TITLE: HUMAN RESOURCE MANAGER   Department: HRM
                                                          Date: Jan. 1, 1996

General Description of the Job

Performs responsible administrative work managing personnel activities of a large state agency or institution. Work involves responsibility for the planning and administration of an HRM program that includes recruitment, examination, selection, evaluation, appointment, promotion, transfer, and recommended change of status of agency employees, and a system of communication for disseminating necessary information to workers. Works under general supervision, exercising initiative and independent judgment in the performance of assigned tasks.

Job Activities

Participates in overall planning and policymaking to provide effective and uniform personnel services.
Communicates policy through organizational level by bulletins, meetings, and personal contact.
Interviews applicants, evaluates qualifications, classifies applications.
Recruits and screens applicants to fill vacancies and reviews applications of qualified persons.
Confers with supervisors on personnel matter, including placement problems, retention or release of probationary employees,
    transfers, demotions, and dismissals of permanent employees.
Supervises administration of tests.
Initiates personnel training activities and coordinates these activities with work of officials and supervisors.
Establishes effective service rating system, trains unit supervisors in making employee evaluations.
Maintains employee personnel files.
Supervises a group of employees directly and through subordinates.
Performs related work as assigned.

General Qualifications Requirements

Experience and Training
    Should have considerable experience in area of HRM administration. Six-year minimum.
Education
    Graduation from a four-year college or university, with major work in human resources, business administration, or industrial
        psychology.
Knowledge, Skills, and Abilities
    Considerable knowledge or principles and practices or HRM selection and assignment of personnel; job evaluation.
Responsibility
    Supervises a department of three HRM professionals, one clerk, and one secretary.

job, while the job specification describes factors about the person. The job specification is useful in recruiting and selecting workers.

JOB DESIGN

After job analyses, job descriptions, and job specifications have been done, an organization can use their information to design and redesign jobs. **Job design** determines exactly what tasks must be performed to complete the work. Job design should structure job elements and duties to increase performance and satisfaction.

There is no one best way to design jobs. Managers enjoy an array of choices. The choice of job design involves making trade-offs based on different characteristics of the job. Some job designs emphasize structuring jobs so they are broken down into simple, repetitive tasks; others emphasize the enjoyment of the work. This section discusses three characteristics of job design: job specialization, job range, and job depth.

job design
A determination of exactly what tasks must be performed to complete the work.

Job Specialization

Scientific management and Taylor's work stimulated a great deal of interest in **job special-ization**, which breaks down work into smaller, more discrete tasks. The task specifies what is to be done, how it is to be done, and the exact time allowed for doing it.[4] Although specialization has been criticized because it leads to boredom and dissatisfaction, it made sense during the early 20th century, and some of its principles are still relevant today. When Henry Ford developed the moving assembly line for manufacturing cars in 1913, job specialization led to production efficiencies. Many products made today—ranging from

job specialization
Breaking down work into smaller, more discrete tasks.

REFLECTIONS BY PHILIP B. CROSBY

Job Design

My first job that let me move around the building was as a reliability engineer in a missile assembly area where I learned that the way to enjoy a job, and be considered useful at the same time, was to adjust the job so I would be comfortable with the things that interested me and I would be of the most value to the organization. I had discovered that most jobs are described by people who never actually perform them and have no idea of the reality involved. The layout of my job was to investigate problems found by the inspection and test functions during assembly and then classify the incidents as to seriousness, cause, and responsibility. With a code system I filled out these determinations on the bottom of a defect report. Then I was supposed to feed it to me IMB punch card system (obviously, this was a while ago) and go find another problem. However, I soon determined that nothing happened to this information after it went into the system except to be produced as a long, very heavy report for management to ignore.

So I began going to see the department I had determined to be responsible for causing the problem. This was pretty much limited to engineering, production, purchasing, marketing, and quality. Now and then the Navy, our customer, was the villain. There was always enough blame to go around.

When I visited them at the senior levels (although I certainly was not senior), I showed them the problem and asked what they wanted to do about it. I offered to help them

gather information or take action or both. They were always pleased with the offer and usually were surprised that the situation existed after all. I learned a great deal by participating in their analysis and evaluation. They assumed that I already knew as much as they did so they let me in on everything.

The result of all this was that we routinely began to get rapid corrective action that actually eliminated the problems. I began to publish a regular list of problems and the actions taken. Everyone wanted to be listed on the page that said the action was completed. The part of my job involved with causing this action to happen probably took 5 percent of my time. However, without that time investment, I would have just been another in a long line of frustrated trouble shooters. No action ever came out;of that list of problems published by the card machine.

The result of it all was that I was promoted to another job where I could help others work in the same way. I immediately redesigned that job to make it more effective and interesting. All this was done by doing; there were no corrections made on paper.

Jobs need not be defined so that they are limited as soon as they brush up against something else. It is reasonable to encourage overlap and innovation as long as the effect is to help the process move toward success. Most jobs are laid out to be too small; none that I ever saw were too big. The more unimportant they are, the longer the description of their content.

children's toys to this textbook to sophisticated computers—simply cannot be made by one individual; some degree of specialization is necessary.

Thus specialization is not the culprit it is often made out to be; the problem for organizations is identifying their appropriate degree of specialization. As we have noted in other chapters, the problems of boredom and absenteeism have plagued some companies and industries. It has long been assumed that managerial or white-collar jobs do not lend themselves to specialization—managers must think, create, and communicate. On the other hand, more and more organizations are designing jobs that enable all workers, including nonmanagerial or blue-collar staff, to be creative and enjoy their jobs. Later in the chapter, we'll discuss strategies for redesigning jobs to overcome the problems associated with job specialization.

Job Range and Depth

job range
The number of tasks a worker performs.

job depth
The amount of discretion a worker has in performing tasks.

Two other job characteristics are range and depth. **Job range** refers to the number of tasks a worker performs. A greater number of tasks takes longer for one individual to complete than fewer tasks. **Job depth** refers to the amount of discretion a worker has in performing tasks. Jobs designed with little depth are generally at lower levels of the organization.

Job specialization is closely related to the range and depth of jobs. Generally, more specialized jobs have low range and depth, such as assembly line workers or bookkeepers. They perform only a few tasks and have little discretion in performing them. On the other hand, less specialized jobs such as teachers or scientists have high range and depth. In service industries such as hotel and banking, the frontline workers who actually face the customers also have jobs with high range and depth, and can make or break the business.[5]

Job range and depth can be used to differentiate jobs within and between organizations. Within an organization, jobs can be designed with different ranges and depths. Generally, as a person moves higher up in the organization and assumes more responsibility, job range and depth increase. But even at the same level, a machine mechanic may have higher range and depth than a machine operator. And an assembly line job at a Ford plant may not have the same range and depth as an assembly line job at a Toyota plant.

As is the case with specialization, it is the manager's responsibility to design jobs with optimal range and depth. If an employee has too many tasks or too much discretion, the job will not be accomplished efficiently and performance will suffer. Conversely, workers performing a single task with no discretion become bored, which may also lead to poor performance.

JOB REDESIGN

In response to the limits of specialization, organizations began to redesign jobs to give workers more autonomy, while at the same time meeting organizational objectives for performance. Table 9–2 presents the results of a Gallup poll of American workers. As can be seen, interesting work and the opportunity to learn new skills are more important than high income or chances for promotion, though workers are fairly dissatisfied with the former aspects of their jobs. **Job redesign** refers to an organization's attempts to improve the quality of work and give workers more autonomy. Typically, job redesign attempts to improve coordination, productivity, and product quality, while at the same time responding to workers' needs for learning, challenge, variety, increased responsibility, and achievement.[6] Many firms are finding that workers with creativity are their greatest asset.[7] Job specialization is associated with the scientific management movement and gives employees the least amount of autonomy and may stifle creativity. This section covers several approaches to redesigning jobs (job rotation, job enlargement, job enrichment, and flextime) that gives workers more autonomy. The last section of the chapter covers team-based approaches associated with total quality management techniques, which provide workers with the most autonomy.

job redesign
Attempts by the organization to improve the quality of work and give workers more autonomy.

Job Rotation

job rotation
Systematically moving employees from one job to another.

The **job rotation** approach involves systematically moving employees from one job to another. Job rotation increases job range by introducing workers to more jobs and therefore

TABLE 9-2	WHAT IS MOST IMPORTANT TO WORKERS *(Percentage of American workers who believe certain aspects of their jobs are very important, and percentage who are completely satisfied with these aspects of their current jobs)*

	Very Important	Completely Satisfied
Good health insurance and other benefits	81%	27%
Interesting work	78	41
Job security	78	35
The opportunity to learn new skills	68	31
Annual vacations of a week or more	66	35
Being able to work independently	64	42
Recognition from coworkers	62	24
Having a job in which you can help others	58	34
Limited job stress	58	18
Regular hours, no nights or weekends	58	40
High income	56	13
Working close to home	55	46
Work that is important to society	53	34
Chances for promotion	53	20
Contact with a lot of people	52	45

*Reprinted with permission © *American Demographics* (August 1992). For subscription information, please call (800) 828-1133.

more tasks. The goal is to reduce worker dissatisfaction caused by job specialization and to increase interest and motivation.[8] For instance, workers in a tool factory may work on a machine one week, conduct stress tests the next, then pack orders, and so on. A variety of companies including Ford, Bethlehem Steel, and Western Electric have used this approach.

Job rotation's major drawback is that it does little to change the nature of the work itself. Rather than performing one task over and over again, a worker performs a variety of tasks. In both cases, the jobs are highly specialized so workers may grow bored or dissatisfied. Inefficiencies may also result since workers must be trained for several jobs. Because of these limitations, job rotation has not been entirely successful, but it is often used along with other approaches we will now discuss.

Job Enlargement

Job enlargement was organization's first attempt to actually redesign work. In a study of mass production jobs in auto assembly plants, researchers found that workers were dissatisfied with highly specialized and repetitive tasks.[9] Based on this assumption, the **job enlargement** approach increases the worker's number of tasks. For example, a job may be redesigned so that a worker responsible for performing four tasks is given eight tasks to complete, thereby increasing the job range. While job rotation involves moving employees from one job or task to another, job enlargement seeks to increase job satisfaction by increasing the number of tasks the worker performs, thereby reducing boredom and monotony.

Many organizations have implemented job enlargement programs, including American Telephone & Telegraph (AT&T) and Maytag. Although job enlargement requires additional training and may not remove all the boredom, many such programs have increased satisfaction. Unfortunately, job enlargement isn't always successful. If workers simply end

job enlargement
Increasing the number of tasks a worker performs.

WHAT MANAGERS ARE READING
THE FIFTH DISCIPLINE

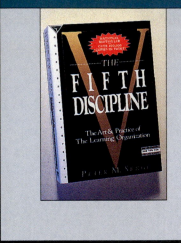

In his book *The Fifth Discipline*, Peter M. Senge advances a means of creating a "learning organization." He argues that in the long run, the only sustainable source of competitive advantage is the organization's ability to learn faster than competitors. Senge describes an organization in which jobs enable people to expand their capacity to create the results they truly desire, where new ways of thinking are nurtured, and where people continually learn to work together. Thus, the learning organization is more effective than the sum of its individual parts.

Many companies have adapted the disciplines of the learning organization, enabling members to think and work together more effectively. By mastering the disciplines, organizations rediscover how to focus on what really matters and how to bridge teamwork into creativity. The disciplines of the learning organization also free individuals of confining assumptions and mind-sets, enabling them to bring the most creativity to their jobs.

Source: Peter M. Serge, *The Fifth Discipline* (New York: Currency Doubleday, 1990).

GLOBAL EXCHANGE
JOB DESIGN AND THE GLOBAL ECONOMY

According to renowned economist Milton Friedman, the combination of political and technological changes throughout the world opens up a vast amount of low-cost labor. Indeed, it could lead to what Friedman calls another Industrial Revolution. But the news isn't good for everyone. As the United States, Mexico, and Canada put the final touches on the North American Free Trade Agreement, more American jobs may well go sough. In 1992, $13-an-hour workers at a North American Philips Corp. plant in Greenville, Tennessee, were laid off when the jobs were moved to Juarez, Mexico, where pay is $2 an hour. As global competition intensified during the 1980s, thousands of factory workers were laid off or suffered wage cuts as factories and jobs moved to foreign countries.

The 1990s is likely to see more of the same. The trend around the world is to create trading regions, such as the European Community and Pacific Rim. According to President Carlos Salinas of Mexico, the only way for North America to compete with these nations is to unite through the Free Trade Agreement. Meanwhile, countries such as China and Malaysia are rapidly increasing their exports. Unfortunately, this will all dramatically impact lower-skilled workers in the United States. For instance, Sears has cut 21,000 low skilled jobs since 1990.

But the news isn't all bad. Those who advocate free trade--like MIT economist Rudiger Dornbusch—argue that the loss of low-skilled jobs is bound to happen, especially in a world were cheap labor is plentiful. But is trade growth increases exports of quality goods, higher-paying jobs should be developed as lower-paying jobs are lost. Between 55 and 60 percent of Motorola's workers are employed in the United States. The cost of labor is a relatively small part of the cost of the product. Manfacturing plants are located close to the markets they serve. Major criteria for choosing a plant location include its proximity to the customers and the level of skill of the labor force. Motorola also learned that making high-quality products in a short time requires highly skilled workers and teamwork systems. To boost quality and productivity, jobs have been designed so that the 3,000 workers in Arlington Heights, Illinois, making cellular phones work in teams. One team discovered a way to reduce static, which causes defects as circuit boards for phones are produced. This discovery increased quality and gave Motorola an edge over foreign competitors.

Motorola's higher-skilled approach requires designing and redesigning jobs so that workers can unleash their creativity. Even companies in such labor-intensive industries as apparel are trying this approach. Russell, Levi Strauss, and Hanes have created teams of 30 to 50 workers to make an entire item. Then team members, not the managers or engineers, determine the best way to produce the garment. Levi's Blue Ridge, Georgia, plant converted entirely to teams, and defects fell from 2.6 percent of production to 1.9 percent within a year.

Some companies are learning the hard way that closing plants and moving jobs abroad is no always the answer. General Electric's motor division closed several plants and demanded that the remaining hourly workers accept and 11 percent pay cut and pass up scheduled raises. Althoug they pay cuts saved $25 million a year, both morale and productivity dropped dramatically. The division is restructuring again. This time teams of seven to eight workers rotate tasks and make daily decisions about their work. So far productivity gains have been better than average. GE's senior vice president for external and industrial relations says, "The biggest change in our thinking since 1988 is that we now see that the productivity available is really extraordinary."

up doing four boring tasks instead of two, it is unlikely that satisfaction will rise. The Global Exchange examines implications of global competition for job redesign and retraining workers.

Job Enrichment

Based on Herzberg's two-factor theory of work motivation (see Chapter 13), much work has been directed at changing jobs in more meaningful ways than was accomplished by job rotation or job enlargement. This theory's basic idea is that workers are motivated by jobs that increase their responsibility and feeling of self-worth.[10] **Job enrichment** attempts to give workers more control of their activities, addressing their needs for growth, recognition, and responsibility. Job enrichment increases not only the number of tasks performed (job range), but also job depth by giving workers more opportunity to exercise discretion over their work.

There are several approaches to job enrichment. Some managers redesign jobs to delegate more authority to workers, while others remove controls and assign new tasks to make the work as interesting as possible. This can be accomplished by redesigning jobs with some additional features, providing learning opportunities, giving workers control over resources and tasks, and letting workers schedule some of their own work.

One widely known method of job enrichment is the job characteristics approach, which looks at the job from the job holder's perspective and not the organization's.[11] The **job characteristics approach** (Figure 9–4) suggests that jobs should be redesigned to include important core dimensions that increase motivation, performance, and satisfaction, and reduce absenteeism and turnover.[12] These core dimensions include:

Skill variety: The degree to which the job requires a variety of different activities in carrying out the work, which involves a number of skills and talents.

job enrichment
Giving workers more control of their activities, addressing their needs for growth, recognition, and responsibility.

job characteristics approach
An approach suggesting that jobs should be redesigned to include important core dimensions that increase motivation, performance, and satisfaction, and reduce absenteeism and turnover.

FIGURE 9-4
The Job Characteristics Approach

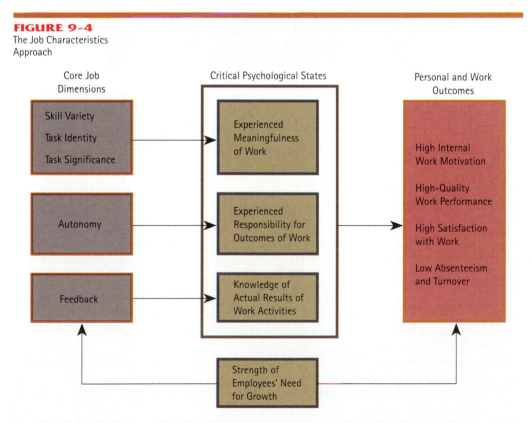

Source: Adapted from J. Richard Hackman and R. G. Oldham, "Motivation through the Design of Work: Test of a Theory," *Organizational Behavior and Human Performance*, August 1976, p. 256.

Carpenters build a duplex in Oakland, CA, in conjunction with the Urban Redevelopment Project and Laney College. Their job motivation and satisfaction largely depends on their sense of responsibility, the meaningfulness of the work, and a knowledge of the effectiveness of their efforts.

Task identity: The degree to which the job requires completion of a "whole" and identifiable piece of work—that is, doing a job from beginning to end with a visible outcome.

Task significance: The degree to which the job has a substantial impact on other people's lives or work—whether in the immediate organization or in the external environment.

Autonomy: The degree to which the job provides substantial freedom, independence, and discretion to the individual in scheduling work and in determining the procedures to be used in carrying it out.

Feedback: The degree to which carrying out work activities required by the job results in individuals obtaining direct and clear information about the effectiveness of their performance.

Presence of these core dimensions in a job is expected to create in workers three critical psychological states that are necessary for motivation and satisfaction:[13]

1. *Experienced meaningfulness:* The degree to which job holders experience work as important, valuable, and worthwhile.
2. *Experienced responsibility:* The extent to which job holders feel personally responsible and accountable for results of their work.
3. *Knowledge of results:* Job holders' understanding of how effectively they are performing their jobs.

The more these three states are experienced, the higher the motivation, performance, and satisfaction, and the lower the absenteeism and turnover.

As Figure 9–4 shows, three of the job dimensions—skill variety, task identity, and task significance—contribute to a sense of meaningfulness. Autonomy is directly related to feelings of responsibility. The more control workers feel they have over their jobs, the more they feel responsible. Feedback is related to knowledge of results. For workers to be internally motivated, they must have a sense of the quality of their performance. This sense comes from feedback.

Since different people have different capabilities and needs, managers should be aware of the potential for individual differences to affect how the job characteristics approach works. The final part of the model, called employee need-growth strength, suggests that people with a strong need to grow and expand their potential are expected to respond more strongly to the core job dimensions than those with low growth-need strength. For example, job enrichment will probably have less effect on a person without strong need for personal growth than on a person who values personal growth.

Managers must realize that job enrichment might change a job's skill requirements. Thus not everyone will necessarily be able to perform the enriched job, especially without additional training. And the organization may need to adjust its compensation rates for the enriched job because of the higher skill levels required.[14]

Before beginning a job enrichment effort, managers should complete at least two actions. First, the job in question needs to be thoroughly understood. Enrichment might not be feasible due to costs or other technological constraints. Second, individual preferences about enriched work should be considered. Do the employees want the work to be enriched? Obviously, accurate job descriptions and job specifications can greatly facilitate assessing these issues.

Flextime

Another approach to redesigning jobs lets employees have input in establishing their work schedules. **Flextime** is a schedule that allows workers to select starting and quitting times within limits set by management.[15] Rather than working the traditional eight-hour day, workers are given greater flexibility in deciding exactly when they will work. A person may work 10 hours one day and 6 another. Jobs designed using flextime include bank tellers, data entry clerks, lab technicians, engineers, and nurses.

Flextime programs have reportedly been successful in many instances. Over half the firms using them report such improvements as increased productivity, lower labor costs, and higher morale.[16] One study found that flextime reduces paid absence, idle time, and overtime pay.[17] Another study reported that satisfaction with the work schedules and with interactions improved significantly for both managers and nonmanagers.[18] Furthermore, companies are finding that flextime builds loyalty, and that employees are committed to making flextime work.[19]

Flextime is difficult to implement for production units with assembly lines and multiple shifts. Since work is largely machine controlled, it is a challenge to plan flexible work schedules. Flextime is also difficult to arrange for jobs that must be continuously covered like bus drivers or retail sales clerks. There can also be increased cost of heating and cooling buildings for longer workdays. It may not be possible to coordinate supervisor and subordinate work schedules, resulting in lack of supervision part of the time. Most workers may prefer similar hours—say 9 AM to 5 PM—leaving other times understaffed. Without supervision, some employees may abuse flexible scheduling. Thus, while flextime is appealing and some evidence suggests it has been successful, proper administration is needed to ensure success.

flextime
A schedule that allows workers to select starting and quitting times within limits set by management.

TEAM-BASED APPROACH TO JOB DESIGN AND REDESIGN

Throughout most of Europe, Asia, and most recently the United States, the concept of job design is being revolutionized. The thrust of this new approach is to place greater emphasis on worker autonomy and increased decision-making responsibility. This new form of job design goes beyond traditional job enrichment programs by empowering workers, often members of teams, to make their own decisions. At Amgen (a Thousand Oaks, California, biotech firm), teams are used for every job from product development to distribution. Sales have grown an average of 102.9 percent for four years, while annual profits have grown an average of 182.2 percent.[20] As we noted in Chapter 8, a team is a group of employees who work closely together to pursue common objectives; a team cannot be effective unless supported by the organization's basic structure. Figure 9–2 shows that team-based approaches to job design and redesign provide workers with the greatest autonomy, and is synonymous with total quality management. One of the most important benefits of the team-based approach is improved communication and coordination. People learn how other jobs are done and how to coordinate efforts to work together better.[21]

The use of teams has implications not only for organizational structure but also for the design of specific jobs. Working as a member of a highly motivated, self-directed work team is much different from performing several specialized tasks or performing jobs redesigned through job enrichment programs. While job enrichment gives workers more responsibility, they are still part of a large manufacturing group. Work flows from one person to another, each with a specific job to do. As a member of a work team, an individual participates in small group decisions. The group decides when to perform tasks, who will perform them, and so on. Many labels have been used to describe this approach, including Japanese management, TQM, and autonomous work groups. We will refer to it in general as a team-based approach. Table 9–3 compares various approaches to job design and redesign.

Teams also motivate workers by moving them sideways (laterally) instead of up. With fewer promotions to give out due to decentralization, many organizations are redesigning jobs and developing teams that enable employees to transfer back and forth among teams

TABLE 9–3	APPROACHES TO JOB DESIGN AND REDESIGN				
	Job Specialization	Job Rotation	Job Enlargement	Job Enrichment	Job Teams
Description	Breaks work down into small, more discrete tasks.	Systematically moves workers from one job to another.	Increases the number of tasks the worker performs.	Increases the number of tasks and gives workers more control over activities.	Group works together to complete an entire task.
Assumptions	Production efficiencies can be achieved through division of labor.	By providing more variety, specialization reduces worker dissatisfaction.	Workers are dissatisfied with highly specialized and repetitive tasks.	Giving workers more control meets their needs for growth, recognition, and responsibility.	Teamwork reduces boredom and increases satisfaction and quality.
Setting	Assembly line and mass production jobs.	Assembly lines and settings that can entail several different jobs.	Mass production, office, and clerical jobs.	Mass production, office, clerical, and managerial jobs.	Mass production, office, clerical, and managerial jobs.
Strengths	Workers master one job; training is minimized; useful if workers are unskilled or illiterate.	Can increase interest and motivation in the short run.	Can increase satisfaction and decrease boredom and monotony.	Provides growth and learning opportunities; redesigning jobs based on dimensions is important to workers.	Provides the most autonomy and opportunity for growth; empowers workers to make their own decisions.
Weaknesses	Can lead to boredom and absenteeism; little variety, responsibility, or growth.	Requires more training; doesn't change the nature of the work itself.	Requires more training; may not remove all the boredom from jobs.	Can change skill requirements, necessitating additional training; everyone may not be able to perform the enriched job.	Very difficult to implement; must overcome resistance; may be costly and time-consuming before benefits occur.

that make different products. This replaces the assembly line structure in which employees worked on one product. For instance, American Greetings Corporation redesigned 400 jobs into teams and asked workers and managers to reapply. All employees were guaranteed a job without a pay cut, and many moved laterally into a new type of work.[22] This process unleashes creativity and gives workers a change in tasks and a chance to work with different people without having to deal with the uncertainty of changing jobs or organizations.

When an organization decides to build teamwork into its structure, it must design or redesign jobs accordingly. It is easy to talk about team-based approaches but actually involving members of the organization in teamwork is difficult. Typically, developing teams involves redesigning jobs so that workers' (or teams') activities make up a whole or more complete task.[23] Although knowledgeable workers are critical to successful teams, individual skills are substantially leveraged through teamwork. Thus managers must provide employees with the knowledge and skills needed to perform tasks, but more importantly, they must create an atmosphere in which teamwork can prosper.[24] For the most part, this attitude or philosophy flows from the top down and creates a sense of group pride, good relations with co-workers, and a spirit of teamwork that brings out the best in worker performance.[25] Training team members within this context eliminates old, counterproductive ideas and signals workers that the spirit of teamwork permeates the organization.

Perhaps the most important aspect of designing jobs for teams is empowering workers so that they have greater control over their work. This basically means that jobs must be designed so that authority equals responsibility. By making individuals accountable for their actions, they become challenged to take responsibility for thinking, for implementing ideas, and for investing themselves in the organization.[26] Empowerment involves several conditions:

❖ Workers must believe their efforts can result in positive outcomes.
❖ Workers must have the knowledge and skills to do their jobs effectively.
❖ Work must be designed to form a "whole" job that is meaningful to the worker.
❖ Workers must have the authority to make decisions about the work on their own.[27]

Designing jobs that empower workers to make decisions about their work can help the organization as well as the individual. Chaparral Steel has become the world's lowest-cost steel producer. Management attributes this distinction to empowered workers who take the initiative, use their heads, and get the job done. In return, workers don't punch clocks, they set their own lunch hours and breaks, they park next to the CEO, and they share in company profits. Many workers have proposed innovations and ideas that have lowered costs dramatically.[28] At trucking firm Schneider National, everyone from drivers up is empowered to make decisions that improve operations. Each of the 9,000 drivers can earn a fifth paycheck every month based on performance, and Schneider National has become the industry leader.[29] Suggestions by empowered workers saved Eaton Corporation (manufacturers of gears, valves, and axles) $1.4 million in a year. For instance, one worker suggested how sandblasting welding electrodes rather than machining them would save $5,126 a year. Employees have earned $44,000 in credits at the factory store for such ideas.[30]

Although there has been much talk about teams, their use is still fairly uncommon in the United States. In 1990 it was estimated that less than 10 percent of the American workforce was organized into teams.[31] But organizations hesitate to adopt this approach for several reasons. Many executives and managers are simply reluctant to empower workers. Additionally, workers themselves have been reluctant to participate in teams, fearing that teams will reduce their freedom when, in fact, they should do just the opposite. Some workers simply do not want to accept accountability for their work, opting for an easier—yet more mediocre—job experience. The large bureaucratic structures of some organizations are not conducive to designing jobs in which workers set their own schedules and production goals, have access to formerly confidential information, vote on such issues as pay raises and new hires, and make other critical decisions. Some organizations try to implement teams, but either don't go far enough in empowering workers or don't give the concept long enough to work. When truly empowered, teams can turn bored employees into productive partners.

THE WORKPLACE OF TOMORROW

The job, as a way of organizing work, is slowly disappearing. Regular hours, specific duties, and standard pay no longer fit the type of work that is being done.[32] As technology continues to change, the conditions of mass production that created jobs years ago are also changing. Automated assembly lines no longer require workers to perform repetitive tasks. And as large organizations begin to outsource much of their work to smaller firms, the source of most jobs no longer exists.

In the future, it will be much more likely that a person will be hired for a particular project and assigned to that project's team.[33] When the task is completed, the team disbands and workers move on to the next project; the new project may even be with a different organization. In this type of job environment, individuals will have to stay abreast of current trends and technologies so that their skills are in demand.

Job security and loyalty are also becoming part of history. Workers can no longer expect to work for the same company for all, or even most, of their careers. IBM, once known for its commitment to keep employees for life, has reduced the size of its workforce from over 400,000 to about 250,000. And employees are feeling the crunch. In the period from 1980 to 1982, 79 percent of management and 75 percent of nonmanagement employees in the United States reported their job security was "good" or "very good." The figures for the period 1992 to 1994 dropped to 55 percent and 51 percent.[34] Some workers now find that they will have to accept "temporary" jobs. From 1991 to 1995, the number of temporary employees in the United States increased from 1.2 million to more than 2 million.[35]

Jobs in the workplace of tomorrow will be filled with people who can work without job descriptions. Rather than performing a specific set of duties, the workers of the future will be empowered to be self-managers. Their major task will be to focus on the customer and to perform whatever activities are needed to satisfy customers rather than doing a job.

SUMMARY OF LEARNING OBJECTIVES

LIST THE FIVE STEPS OF JOB ANALYSIS.
Job analysis involves examining the overall organization, selecting the jobs to be analyzed, collecting data on jobs, preparing the job description, and preparing the job specification.

COMPARE JOB DESCRIPTIONS AND JOB SPECIFICATIONS.
A job description is a written summary of the job. It details the job's activities, equipment required to perform those activities, and the job's working conditions. A job specification evolves from the job description. It's a written explanation of skills, knowledge, abilities, and other characteristics needed to perform a job effectively.

DEFINE THE TERM JOB DESIGN.
Job design determines exactly what tasks must be performed to complete the work. Job design should structure job elements and duties to increase performance and satisfaction.

EVALUATE THE JOB SPECIALIZATION APPROACH TO JOB DESIGN.
The job specialization approach to job design breaks down work into smaller, more discrete tasks. Specialization leads to production efficiencies and was useful when the assembly line was developed. Job specialization has been criticized for leading to monotony and boredom for workers, taking enjoyment out of the job.

DISCUSS THE CONCEPTS OF JOB RANGE AND JOB DESIGN.
Job range refers to the number of tasks a worker performs. Job depth refers to the amount of discretion a worker has in performing the tasks. Highly specialized jobs generally have low range and depth, while less specialized jobs have high range and depth.

EXPLAIN HOW JOB REDESIGN DIFFERS FROM JOB DESIGN.
Job redesign refers to the attempts of organizations attempts to improve the quality of work and give workers more autonomy. While job design determines exactly what tasks must be performed, job redesign is more concerned with how the tasks can be made interesting and challenging to workers.

CONTRAST THE DIFFERENT APPROACHES TO JOB REDESIGN.
There are several approaches to job redesign. Job rotation involves systematically moving workers from one job to another, but does little to change the nature of the work itself. Job enlargement increases the number of tasks performed by a worker, actually changing the work. However, workers may simply end up doing more tasks that they don't enjoy. Job enrichment gives workers more control of their activities, thereby addressing their needs for growth and recognition. Flextime enables workers to select their work schedules within limits set by management.

DISCUSS THE ADVANTAGES OF THE TEAM–BASED APPROACH TO JOB DESIGN AND REDESIGN.
Teams provide workers with the greatest amount of autonomy. Although job enrichment gives workers more responsibility, they are still part of a large manufacturing group. As a member of a team, an individual participates in small group decisions. By empowering team members so they have greater control over their work, managers challenge workers to take responsibility for thinking, implementing ideas, and investing themselves in the organization.

KEY TERMS

flextime, p. 253

job analysis, p. 242

job characteristics approach, p. 251

job depth, p. 248

job description, p. 244

job design, p. 247

job enlargement, p. 249

job enrichment, p. 251

job range, p. 248

job redesign, p. 248

job rotation, p. 248

job specialization, p. 247

job specification, p. 246

REVIEW AND DISCUSSION QUESTIONS

Recall

1. What steps are involved in job analysis, and what is the major output?
2. Explain the difference between job range and job depth.
3. Why do firms use job rotation?
4. What approach to job redesign represents the first attempt to actually redesign work? Why?
5. What are the core dimensions of the job suggested in the job characteristics approach?
6. What is empowerment? How does it relate to designing work teams?

Understanding

7. Why is job specialization often blamed for boredom and absenteeism?
8. Why did organizations begin to redesign jobs?
9. How do team-based approaches to job design and redesign differ from other approaches?

Application

10. Call a local company in your area and ask for a sample job description. Does it do a good job of explaining what the job entails? If you were looking for a job, would you find it complete and helpful?

CASE STUDY

Team-Based Job Design at Semco S/A

Semco S/A is Brazil's largest manufacturer of marine and food-processing machinery. Close to financial disaster in 1980, Semco is now one of Brazil's fastest-growing companies. The turnaround began in 1980 when Ricardo Semler became president and redesigned Semco's organizational structure and management style. When Semler started the process, the company had 11 layers of management; he reduced them first to eight, then six, and finally three. Since 1980 employment is up 700 percent and sales are up over 800 percent.

A big part of Semler's reorganization involved using a team-based approach to job design. Work teams run the show at Semco, setting their own time schedules and production goals, sharing information and profits, and determining how earnings are distributed, who gets hired, and who gets promoted. Some employees even set their own salaries. Semler himself leaves the company for months at a time, and the company does fine without him. He says it's all in the way the company is organized and jobs are designed.

How can the president leave and not be missed? By empowering workers and sharing information, power within Semco comes from the value one provides, not from hoarding information or having the largest office. According to Semler, when everyone has the same basis of information, the organization hierarchy tends to disappear. By publishing the balance sheet and all financials monthly on the bulletin board, everyone knows what the company is making. The result of such sharing of information is one of the few plants in the world where all workers have flextime. Everyone on the assembly line can come and go whenever they want, as they schedule their own time.

This might sound too good to be true. Wouldn't many workers cut out early and not show up at all? Not when you hire responsible adults, a basic assumption that Semco begins with. Employees are encouraged to contribute their best efforts to the organization and are rewarded for doing so. Semco has experienced very little abuse of the system. When people are treated as problem solvers and empowered to make decisions, Semco has found that they will solve problems one way or another.

Managers are encouraged to take the company in any direction they want. And practically no one stays in the same position for more than two or three years. Jobs are rotated drastically—a sales manager becomes a controller for rocket fuel propellants. Although this is a personal decision, most people request a change once they are ready to try something else.

Although everyone can't be in leadership positions, they are given the opportunity to make a lot of money without going into management. Many people make more than their bosses since they have specific skills that are difficult to find. Besides paying well, jobs are designed to be self-fulfilling so people can feel their work is worthwhile. One approach is to eliminate jobs that cannot be made fulfilling. Semco has no secretaries, no receptionists, and no assistants of any type. Everyone does their own work.

Few workers at Semco complain that they are not autonomous. In fact, some would like more structure in their jobs. But structure costs money, and workers have to approve the budget. Semler has cut the corporate budget every year. He predicts that his company will be about the same size in 20 years, but will generate much more business. The reason is that the company relies on its employees' brains and creativity. By using a team-based approach to job design, Semco hopes to increase productivity without adding layers of bureaucracy.

QUESTIONS

1. Why did Semler reduce the layers of management when he became president of Semco?
2. How does Semco use a team-based approach to job design?
3. Why is it important that information be shared among everyone?
4. How does Semco use job rotation?

5. Assess the importance of both pay and job fulfillment in a team-based approach such as Semco's.

Source: Adapted from Ricardo Semler, *Maverick* (New York: Warner Books, 1993); Michael Rigg, "Vision and Value: Keys to Initiating Organizational Change," *Industrial Engineering*, June 1922, pp. 12–13; Charles Garfield, *Second to None* (Burr Ridge, Il.: Business One Irwin, 1992), pp. 157–64; and Anthony A. Atkinson, "The Promise of Employee Involvement," *CMA Magazine*, April 1990, p. 8.

VIDEO CASE

Detroit Diesel Corporation: An Evolution of Tasks and Attitudes

Sitting around a table in one of the vendor conference rooms at Detroit Diesel, Jim Bachman, a Series 60 line trainer, and Jim Brown, UAW Local 163's shop chairman, recall an incident that highlights the extent of change in their plant. This example of shop floor activity illustrates to these two men, as well as to the 2,100 other hourly employees in the diesel engine plant, what it took to generate new employee attitudes toward both production quality and their jobs.

Through the efforts of employees and their union, the line was brought in house, in to the Detroit Diesel plant. (A liner is a foundry cast part that fits into the engine block.) The union and company negotiated an agreement that provided for job classifications to allow liner technicians to do their own inspection and job setting. The operations on the new line included hardening the part in the furnace, rough boring the center, cutting grooves on a turning machine, grinding to obtain the correct overall diameter, using a honing machine to obtain the correct inside diameter, into which the pistons will fit, and inspecting the final product.

Unexpectedly, the new liner jobs raised some quality issues because of the complex job assignments and the many different machining operations employees needed to learn. At first, a high level of scrap was generated, so to help improve the situation, full-time hourly trainers were put in the area to assist, teach, and maintain a focus on quality. Jim Bachman is one of these trainers.

Soon after the lines technicians began their jobs, one part of the work flow ran into a problem. As the liners came off the 100 percent gauge on the centerless grinder and moved on the next operation, the liners were found to be slightly undersized. The problem clearly had gone undetected for some time, and when Bachman finally spotted the deviation, the liner techs discussed what to do. Within minutes, the line was shut down.

With production halted, area superintendent Jack Zibell was informed of the trouble. After and intense 30 minutes searching for the source of the problem, the liner techs, engineers, union quality reps, and area manager withdrew from their hubble. Everyone had agreed that in incorrectly set grinding wheel was the culprit. This was fixed quickly, and production was started up. However, employees began voicing their skepticism regarding what would happen to the more than 900 defective liners that were in the plant at that time. Comments like, "Management doesn't care about the quality; watch, they'll send those parts out," were heard by the superintendent, union officials, and other managers. Zibell and the others involved decided that this was the time to make it clear that shutting down the line was the right thing to do and that quality was a critical part of everyone's job. Management took the eight liner technicians involved with the line shutdown and had them find the 24 "worst case" liners. These were put into engines and submitted to the toughest quality test, the 200-hour check, in which the engines were

placed under extreme conditions an run for 200 consecutive hours. To make sure that the employees knew that was taking place, each employee on the line was sent periodically to monitor the tests. When none of the "defective" liners failed, a second test of 100 hours was run in order to convince everyone that the defect had no impact on reliability.

Once the testing was complete, and even though not one of the liners had failed, the rest of the "defects" were scrapped because the potential for failure still existed. Employees were taken aback. This was not the "volume at all costs approach," but rather "quality at any cost." But even more dramatic to the liner techs was the fact that not once during the entire crisis had Zibell, the general superintendent, or Rob Tykal, the area manager, asked who had set up the faulty grinding wheel, nor had they attempted in any way to determine who was to "blame." Instead, Zibell, Tykal, and others were intent upon seeing that a group of engineers, liner techs, and union quality reps worked cooperatively to develop internal checks so that similar problems would not occur in the future anywhere on the line.

This approach to plant problems now typifies the expectations held for all employees, managers, and union members. Jobs and roles have changed. "Supervisors are expected to be coaches and part of the team," Jim Brown commented. Bachman agreed and added that "it used to be that people came in and did the same task, day in and day out. Now, people have multiple jobs and responsibilities. In my area, the liner group, people like to change jobs. They feel more important and better about themselves." In fact, one formal change in jobs came about when the union and management bargained a new contract that took 44 manufacturing job classifications and reduced them to 14. In early 1993, they reduced these further when they rolled three of the existing fourteen into a single classification. "There is a lot less 'it's not in my job classification!'" stated Brown. Not only have these changes affected the way problems are solved and the way jobs are done, but absenteeism has declined substantially while productivity, quality, and sales have all improved.

DETROIT DIESEL'S TRANSFORMATION

How did these changes come about at Detroit Diesel? It began over five years ago when Detroit Diesel's market share of diesel engines designed for the heavy duty truck market had fallen to an all-time low of 3.3 percent. With 700 employees on layoff, high absenteeism rates, and skepticism about the long-term viability of the organization as GM moved to sell it, Roger Penske bought an initial 60 percent share (quickly increased to 80 percent) of the organization. Penske, who also owns a manages to Penske Racing Team, which recently won its ninth Indianapolis 500, came into the organization with the philosophy, "Effort Equals Results." As he says, "People ask me today about what's different at Detroit Diesel. I can tell you that the first thing if the spirit and teamwork."

Teamwork takes place at all levels, much of it demonstrated by the cooperative working relationship of the top-level managers and the union officials, including Jim Brown. Brown says he was skeptical at first. However, in a meeting, he and Penske both agreed to a 100 percent working partnership based on trust, which would continue unless one of the parties violated that trust. It was then that Brown began to believe they could make it work. The largest change from the union standpoint is the strong role the union now plays at Detroit Diesel.

During the past five years, virtually everyone's job has changed, and with new skills now necessary for high performance, constant training takes place. To support the employees with the kind of training necessary for a change of this magnitude, Detroit Diesel and UAW Local 163 jointly funded and built a world-class training and fitness center connected to the plant. Jim Brown commented that now "the union is a partner in running the business and is involved in all decision making. This has clearly changed my job."

To make sure all employees share and understanding of the business side as well as a sense of why their jobs are important, Penske and Lud Koci, the president of Detroit Diesel, hold "Update Meeting" four times a year. With small groups of employees, this owner and his president present the corporate financial, marketing, and production information to their employees. They field questions, take suggestions, and make sure that the employees come away feeling like owners. The meetings run continually until all employees have been included. The increase in the company's market share to more than 26 percent and the projected 1993 increase in earnings have given employees, management, and the union something exciting to discuss. Shop chairman Brown commented that "the average employee in this plant probably knows as much about the business as the average executive in any other company."

A CONTINUING PROCESS

Back on the liner line where this story started, liner technicians recently became aware of some problems with the liner material as it came in from the supplier foundry. As Jim Bachman described it, "We sent some employees out to the foundry that makes the liners so that we could get an understanding of what they have to do to deliver a good product to us. In turn, they came out to our shop to see what we were running into on a day-to-day basis." This kind of activity has helped the employees at Detroit Diesel understand the importance of what they can contribute to the final product, to product quality, and to the overall success of Detroit Diesel.

Currently, as the technology for a new flywheel housing line is being designed, the employees on the existing production line are being asked to show the engineers what is good about the design of the line they work on and what is bad. The joint design team's job is to design out the bad parts. Once again, employees will contribute all their job knowledge to assure that, as a team, the newly designed production line will use technology effectively to assure both product quality and ergonomically appropriate jobs. This is what Penske means when he says that "the one who puts out the most effort gets the best results."

QUESTIONS

1. The Detroit Diesel case illustrates how the knowledge, skills, and abilities (KSAs) needed in a given class of jobs might change as the business strategy changes. What new KSAs in the liner technicians' jobs appear necessary because of the organizational need for high quality?
2. What types of training would be needed to support the change in job design described in the case?
3. Because the union and management have agreed to reduce the job classifications significantly, the content of each employee's job undoubtedly has been increased. What motivational impact would you expect from such a change?
4. Describe the current supervisory role at Detroit Diesel. What do you think the most critical skills for the production supervisors are?
5. What performance management techniques (discussed in Chapter 7) would be most effective in the situation described in the case? What balance between individual performance and group performance evaluation would you suggest?
6. Roger Penske has stated that "each employee in this firm is important as any other." What elements of work-life as described in the case suggest that Penske and his managers have followed through on this philosophy?

APPLICATION EXERCISE

DEVELOPING A JOB DESCRIPTION

The purpose of this exercise is to develop a job description for a job of your choice. Since the job description is the output of a systematic job analysis, you must select a job and obtain the needed information before developing the job description. You can select any job, perhaps one you've held, are holding now, or would like to hold. Here's a list of jobs for your convenience:

Airline pilot	Talk show host
Computer operator	Teacher
Golf coach	Retail clerk
Police officer	Intensive care nurse
Machine operator	Auto mechanic

Once you have selected a job, reread the material on job analysis. How can you obtain the information needed to write the job description? Try calling a company and talking with someone in that job or in the human resource department. Once you have all the information you need, use the following format to write the job description.

Job title: Give the job's title and other identifying information such as its wage and benefits classification.

Summary: In a brief one- or two-sentence statement, describe the job's purpose and what outputs are expected from someone holding it.

Equipment: Clear statement of the tools, equipment, and information required for effectively performing the job.

Environment: Give the job's working conditions, location, and other relevant characteristics of the immediate work environment such as hazards and noise levels.

Activities: Describe job duties, behaviors performed on the job, and social interactions associated with the work (for example, size of work group and amount of dependency in the work).

CHAPTER 10

Human Resource Management

After studying this chapter, you should be able to:

❖ Define human resource management (HRM).

❖ Explain how HRM is linked to strategic planning.

❖ List several sources from which job applicants are recruited.

❖ State the purpose of EEO programs and identify the three main factors that contributed to EEO's development.

❖ Describe the forecasting and planning aspects of human resource planning.

❖ List the typical decision steps in the human resource management selection process.

❖ Define training and learning.

❖ Compare some of the more popular methods of performance evaluation.

❖ Discuss the difference between direct and indirect compensation.

❖ Explain the comparable worth concept.

Hiring Right Makes Sense

Top-performing organizations invest much energy, time, and attention in the hiring and selection process. Fairfield Inn puts a potential job candidate through an average of 14 interviews. Finding the right person for the job is considered essential to perpetuate the best culture at Thomas Interior Systems, an office furnishings designer and reseller in Elmhurst, Illinois. The small firm has only 75 employees, but prides itself on having every worker become part of the quality-driven culture. Careful, intensive recruitment and selection like Fairfield Inn's and Thomas Interiors System's serve two purposes. First, the organization gains a close look at candidates' suitability, especially their fit with the culture. Second, attention to detail gives candidates plenty of opportunity to eliminate themselves if the culture doesn't feel right. Being rigorous, fair, and accurate in recruitment and selection minimizes the mistake of the wrong person being attracted and taking the job. Rigorous screening is expensive, but hiring the wrong people who do not fit a quality-based culture is also costly. Hiring, training, and initiating frequent recruitment and screening processes can cost over $50,000 for a single mid-level management position. Some examples of how serious hiring decisions are highlight this chapter.

Instead of hiring permanent employees, more firms are hiring temps or what is today referred to as complementary or contingent workers. Largely in response to downsizing, companies have hired contingent workers. Over 20 percent of the total increase in employment in 1994 came from temporary workers. KLA Instruments hires highly trained engineers for special projects. Previous experience, specific skills that can be used on projects, and willingness to undergo training are important in screening engineers. Since KLA needs engineers to step right into a project, selecting individuals who can contribute immediately is important.

A company that is working hard to find and hire international leaders for the 21st Century is Molex, Inc., a technology firm. Molex generates more than 70 percent of its approximately $1 billion annual sales outside the U.S. The firm screens American applicants in order to hire entry-level professionals who are fluent in at least one other language. The language requirement is an important part of the interview process. Multilingual competency is very important because of the firm's international plans and growth.

Molex career paths are developed for incoming professionals based on many factors including multilingual competency. In regions outside the U.S., hiring and selection includes an English language competency. An understanding of international issues and language competency are the key screening hurdles that Molex professional job applicants must pass in order to be seriously considered for employment.

Insurance company American General reduced annual turnover of its agents by over 20 percent with the use of a carefully constructed questionnaire administered to potential hires. Younkers, a department store in Iowa, cut staff turnover rates by 25 percent with a similar test. Hiring correctly, hiring the best, and following up on the hiring itself are the rules in organizations that care about quality. Hiring well just doesn't happen. It requires time, energy, and a commitment to recruitment and selection.

Source: Adapted from Gallian Flynn, "Contingent Staffing Requires Serious Strategy," *Personnel Journal,* April 1995, pp. 50-58; Charlene Marmer Solomon, "Navigating Your Search for Global Talent," *Personnel Journal,* May 1995, pp. 94-101; Suzanne Oliver, "Slouches Make Better Operators," *Forbes,* August 16, 1993, pp. 104-5; Jim Clemner, *Firing on All Cylinders* (Burr Ridge, Il.: Business One Irwin, 1992), pp. 148-49, 154-56; Michael Barrier, "Small Firms Put Quality First," *Nation's Business,* May 1992, pp. 22-32; Barbara Levin, "Chevron's HR Conference: Strategic Planning to Meet Corporate Goals," *HR Focus,* May 1992, p. 9; and Jay W. Spechler, *When America Does It Right* (Norcross, Ga.: Industrial Engineering and Management Press, 1988), p. 541.

Human resources are the key resource in creating a quality-oriented organization. This is obvious in firms such as Fairfield Inn, KLA Instruments, Molex Inc., and American General. Being recognized as an important person who is needed, respected, and listened to is an important part of belonging to an organization, a work team, or even an occupation group. Peters and Waterman's *In Search of Excellence* expresses a fundamental lesson about importance of human resources:

Treat people as adults. Treat them as partners; treat them with dignity; treat them with respect. Treat them—not capital spending and automation—as the primary sources of productivity gains... If you want productivity and the financial reward that goes with it, you must treat your workers as the most important asset.[1]

John E. Condon, past chairman of the board of the American Society for Quality Control, said it even more specifically: "People really do make quality happen."[2] The obvious importance of human resources in making quality happen and improving competitiveness provides human resource management (HRM) departments with a golden opportunity. Quality can serve as the primary goal that fosters a strategic HRM approach that can add value to an organization's products, services, and image.

This chapter addresses human resources practices, principles, and programs. It suggests that to improve quality and competitiveness, people must be the driving force. As the opening vignette, "Hiring Right Makes Sense," suggests, you must pay attention to people from the start. If you do not hire wisely, it will be almost impossible to instill the quality-is-first culture that is needed to compete effectively. In large, formal organizations such as General Motors and Procter & Gamble, a department usually guides the human resource program. But, even in a small organization, an action-oriented approach to people and their needs, goals, expectations, skills, knowledge, and abilities must be followed. The chapter discusses human resource management (HRM) in terms of the function, department, or activities that are concerned with accomplishing quality improvements and increased competitiveness by acquiring, retaining, developing, and properly utilizing the human resources—managerial and nonmanagerial.

human resource management (HRM) The process of accomplishing organizational objectives by acquiring, retaining, terminating, developing, and properly using the human resources in an organization.

HUMAN RESOURCE MANAGEMENT BACKGROUND

Human resource management (HRM) is a function performed in organizations that facilitates the most effective use of employees to achieve an organization's goals. The history of HRM departments can be traced to England from 1700 to 1785, where masons, carpenters, leather workers, and other craftspeople organized themselves into guilds. They used their unity to improve their work conditions.[3] These guilds became the forerunners of trade unions.

The field further developed with the arrival of the Industrial Revolution in the latter part of the 18th century, which laid the basis for a new and complex industrial society. In simple terms, the Industrial Revolution began with the substitution of steam power and machinery for time-consuming hand labor. Working conditions, social patterns, and the division of labor were significantly altered. A new kind of employee, a boss (who wasn't necessarily the owner as had usually been the case in the past), became a power broker in the new factory system. With these changes also came a widening gap between workers and owners.

The drastic changes in technology, the growth of organizations, the rise of unions, and government concern and intervention concerning working people resulted in the development of personnel departments. No specific date is assigned to the appearance of the first personnel department, but around the 1920s more and more organizations seemed to take note of and do something about the conflict between employees and management.[4] Early personnel administrators—called *welfare secretaries*—were hired to bridge the gap between management and operators (workers). In other words, they were to speak to workers in their own language and then recommend to management what had to be done to get the best results from employees.

For years the HRM function wasn't linked to the corporate profit margin or what is referred to as the *bottom line*. HRM's role in the firm's strategic plan and overall strategy was usually couched in fuzzy terms and abstractions. HRM was merely a tag-along unit with people-oriented plans; it was not a major part of the planning and strategic thinking process. Today, thanks to recognition of the crucial importance of people, HRM is increasingly a major player in developing strategic plans. Organizational plans and strategies are inextricably linked to human resource plans and strategies. HRM strategies must reflect clearly the organization's strategy with regard to people, profit, and quality improvement.[5] The human resource manager is expected to play a crucial role in improving employees' skills and the firm's profitability. In essence, HRM is now viewed as a "profit center" and not simply a "cost center."

A Model of Human Resource Management

So many factors influence workers' behavior and performance that a framework or a model can be used as a way to order everything. A model is simply a map that can help a manager or anyone see how the pieces, parts, and activities fit together. Figure 10–1 presents five main parts: some of the internal and external environmental forces, HRM activities, characteristics of people, and the two main outcomes discussed throughout the book (quality improvement and enhanced competitiveness).

Since so many HRM activities are practiced, only eight (noted by bullets in Figure 10–1) are covered in this chapter. Remember that organizations, by conducting HRM activities, attempt to find and keep the best-qualified human resources to accomplish their goal. Matching people and activities to improve quality and competitiveness is a top priority. Improper matching thwarts quality improvement.

EQUAL EMPLOYMENT OPPORTUNITY

Equal employment opportunity (EEO) refers to the employment of individuals in a fair and nonbiased manner. It has slowly become a societal priority and has needed legal and administrative guidelines to encourage action. Equal employment opportunity is usually couched in legal terminology, but it is also an emotional issue.[6] Employers have been ordered to develop employment policies that incorporate laws, executive orders, court decisions, and regulations to end job discrimination.

One approach used to reach the goal of fair employment is **affirmative action**. The goal of affirmative action is to urge employers to make a concerted effort to promote the

equal employment opportunity (EEO)
An umbrella term that encompasses all laws and regulations prohibiting and/or requiring affirmative action.

affirmative action
Programs designed to ensure proportional representation of workers on the basis of race, religion, or sex. If a company has a federal contract exceeding $50,000, it's required to have an affirmative action program. Firms can also voluntarily establish such programs.

FIGURE 10–1
A Model of Human Resource
Management Activities and
Outcomes

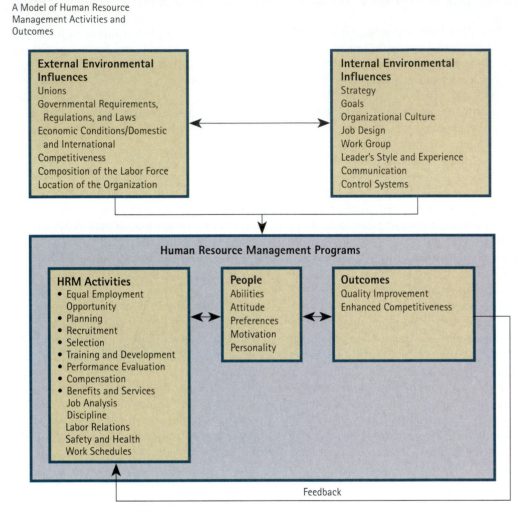

Human Resource Management Programs

External Environmental Influences
Unions
Governmental Requirements, Regulations, and Laws
Economic Conditions/Domestic and International Competitiveness
Composition of the Labor Force
Location of the Organization

Internal Environmental Influences
Strategy
Goals
Organizational Culture
Job Design
Work Group
Leader's Style and Experience
Communication
Control Systems

HRM Activities
• Equal Employment Opportunity
• Planning
• Recruitment
• Selection
• Training and Development
• Performance Evaluation
• Compensation
• Benefits and Services
  Job Analysis
  Discipline
  Labor Relations
  Safety and Health
  Work Schedules

People
Abilities
Attitude
Preferences
Motivation
Personality

Outcomes
Quality Improvement
Enhanced Competitiveness

Feedback

• Discussed in this chapter

hiring of groups of employees who were discriminated against in the past. Employers are asked under affirmative action to use at least in part the race, sex, or age of a person in reaching an employment decision.

A fair employment strategy and an affirmative action strategy are two approaches that appear to be in conflict. The courts, managers, and employees are involved in struggling to be fair and to correct past discrimination. However, controversy, debate, and frustration often occur when attempting to reconcile the two strategies.[7]

A number of important federal employment opportunity laws have been passed and used to improve the fairness of employment for employees.[8] Table 10–1 lists a sample of some of the major laws affecting equal opportunity employment.

The Civil Rights Act of 1991 increased the likelihood that employees will sue by making their discrimination cases easier to win and by making the damages they can be awarded more substantial.[9] Therefore it is in the organization's best interest for managers to develop policies and procedures that comply with the law. The best way to begin studying the relationship between HRM functions and the law is to devote time and attention to equal employment opportunity. No other regulatory area has so thoroughly affected HRM as EEO. EEO has implications for almost every activity in HRM: hiring, recruiting, training, terminating, compensating, evaluating, planning, disciplining, and collective bargaining.[10]

DIVERSITY SCOPE

THREE IMPORTANT QUESTIONS ABOUT AFFIRMATIVE ACTION

How Did Affirmative Action Begin?
In 1965 President Lyndon B. Johnson signed Executive Order 11246 that required "employers doing business with the federal government to develop affirmative-action plans to assure equal employment opportunity in their employment practices."

In a typical large corporation, affirmative action begins with adopting a strong policy of equal employment opportunity, followed by monitoring to identify possible discrimination.

Affirmative action was simply a commitment by a company that it would take positive steps to ensure it wouldn't discriminate. It has evolved from posting notices that declare a company won't discriminate to monitoring applicant pools to see that they're rich with women and minorities. This monitoring also helps the company see if its efforts are sufficient to attract all kinds of qualified people.

When problems are identified, companies establish employment goals that are targets designed to ensure that women and minorities are represented in all segments of the workforce. Many companies develop and implement programs that enable individuals to compete with others on as equal a footing as possible. These programs tend to center around recruitment, training, development, mentoring, family assistance—all designed to expand opportunities for qualified people.

Three main rationales for existing affirmative-action programs: Compensation for past discrimination, correction of current discrimination, and diversification as an end worth pursuing in and of itself.

What Is the Difference Between Affirmative Action and Diversity?
Affirmative action is quite different from diversity. Affirmative action is legally driven and is about trying to achieve equality of opportunity by focusing on specific groups. Diversity efforts focus on managing and handling the workforce you already have. One key difference is that managing and valuing diversity gives your organization a competitive advantage. "One is to right wrongs, the other is a strategic advantage and a business imperative," says Anita Rowe, partner at Gardenswartz & Rowe, a Los Angeles-based diversity consultant firm. Rowe sees diversity as much more inclusive than affirmative action.

You can view affirmative action and diversity management as a continuum. Nondiscrimination means the company will not discriminate. Affirmative action means the company will take positive steps to ensure that it doesn't discriminate. Then, you move into the next stage—proactively promoting a diverse and inclusive workforce. "This isn't necessarily because it's the legal thing to do or even the morally right thing to do, but because there's a legitimate business reason," says Rowe.

Does Affirmative Action Mean You Must Have Quotas?
No, quotas are illegal. The only exception to this is in specific legal cases where courts mandate them based on past active discrimination; quotas may be imposed only by judges. All guidelines and mandates regarding affirmative action state clearly that candidates must be qualified. Affirmative action simply encourages the development of ways to seek out and promote well-qualified candidates.

Source: Adapted from Carole Marmer Soloman, "Affirmative Action: What You Need to Know," *Personnel Journal*, August 1995, p. 61.

Employers set up equal employment opportunity (EEO) programs to prevent employment discrimination in the workplace and/or to take remedial action to offset past employment discrimination.[11]

The three main factors that led to the development of EEO were (1) changes in societal values, (2) the economic status of women and minorities, and (3) the emerging role of government regulation.

Societal Values and EEO

Throughout history, Western society has accepted the principle that people should be rewarded according to the worth of their contributions. When the United States became a nation, that principle was embodied in the American dream: the idea that any individual, through hard work, could advance from the most humble origins to the highest station, according to the worth of her or his contributions. In the United States success did not depend on being born into a privileged family; equal opportunity was everyone's birthright. To this day, the American dream, with its emphasis on merit rather than privilege, is widely accepted by the public.

Until the early 1960s it was not unusual for many people, while believing in the American dream of rewards based on merit, also to believe that African-Americans (and other minorities) had their "place"—a place largely cut off from rewards that the majority received. This apparent contradiction in beliefs was the U.S. dilemma as observed even in the 1940s by the distinguished Swedish economist, Gunnar Myrdal, in his studies of United States race

TABLE 10–1	A SELECTED SAMPLE OF FEDERAL LAWS
Law	**Provisions**
Equal Pay Act of 1963	Requires all employers covered by the Fair Labor Standards Act and others to provide equal pay for equal work regardless of sex.
Title VII of Civil Rights Act of 1964 (amended in 1972, 1991, and 1994)	Prohibits discrimination in employment on the basis of race, color, religion, sex, or national origin; created the Equal Employment Opportunity Commission (EEOC) to enforce the provisions of Title VII.
Age Discrimination in Employment Act of 1967	Prohibits private and public employers from discriminating against persons 40 years of age or older in any area of employment because of age; exceptions are permitted where age is a bona fide occupational qualification.
Equal Employment Opportunity Act of 1972	Amended Title VII of Civil Rights Act of 1964; strengthens EEOC's enforcement powers and extends coverage of Title VII to government employees, faculty in higher education, and other employers and employees.
Americans with Disabilities Act of 1990	Prohibits discrimination in employment against persons with physical or mental disabilities or the chronically ill; enjoins employers to make reasonable accommodation to the employment needs of the disabled; covers employers with 15 or more employees.
Civil Rights Act of 1991	Provides for compensatory and punitive damages and jury trials in cases involving intentional discrimination; requires employers to demonstrate that job practices are job related and consistent with business necessity; extends coverage to U.S. citizens working for American companies overseas.
Family and Medical Leave Act of 1993	Requires all employers with 50 or more employees to provide 12 weeks of unpaid leave for family and medical emergencies.
Uniformed Services Employment and Reemployment Rights Act of 1994	Protects the employment rights of individuals who enter the military for short periods of service.

relations for the Carnegie Corporation. African-Americans were often excluded from schools, public accommodations, jobs, and voting. Economic realities for blacks belied the ideals of the American dream.[12]

Economic Status of Minorities before 1964

Undeniable economic inequality helped focus national attention on employment as a specific area of discrimination. In the 1950s, unemployment figures for African-Americans were twice as high as for whites, and higher still among nonwhite youth. While African-Americans accounted for only 10 percent of the labor force, they represented 20 percent of total unemployment and nearly 30 percent of long-term unemployment. Moreover, in 1961 only one-half of African-American men worked steadily at full-time jobs, whereas two-thirds of white men did. African-Americans were three times as likely as whites to work less than full-time. Similar statistical differences existed for other minorities, such as Hispanics and Native Americans.[13]

The Government

The practice of managing human resources is regulated by government-initiated laws, regulations, and monitoring. Managers need to understand government's role and expectations in order to more effectively coordinate and direct human resources.

In organizations, much of the compliance burden has been directed to the HRM department. But every manager and employee has a compliance responsibility. The growth of equal employment opportunity has given employees specific rights in their relationship with their employers. Employee rights were not widely publicized or seen as front-page news prior to the early 1970s. Today employee rights and perceptions that something is wrong are taken very seriously. When employees perceive discrimination problems, it is difficult to work hard, to concentrate on quality principles, and to remain committed to the firm.

HUMAN RESOURCE PLANNING

Human resource planning is a two-step process that involves forecasting future human resource needs and then planning how to adequately fulfill and manage these needs. Figure 10–2 points out the activities involved in needs forecasting and program planning.

human resource planning (HRP)
Estimating the size and makeup of the future workforce.

FIGURE 10–2
The Human Resource Planning Process

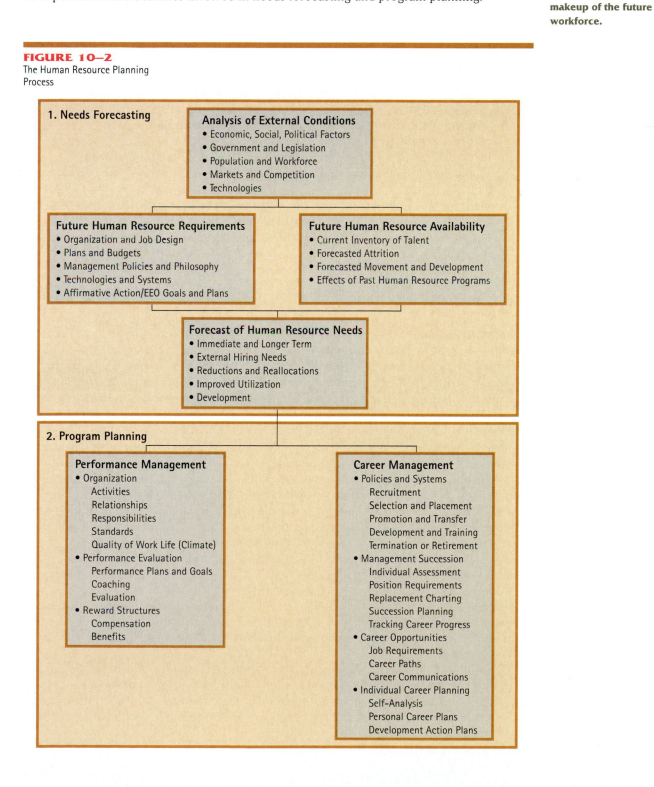

1. Needs Forecasting

Analysis of External Conditions
- Economic, Social, Political Factors
- Government and Legislation
- Population and Workforce
- Markets and Competition
- Technologies

Future Human Resource Requirements
- Organization and Job Design
- Plans and Budgets
- Management Policies and Philosophy
- Technologies and Systems
- Affirmative Action/EEO Goals and Plans

Future Human Resource Availability
- Current Inventory of Talent
- Forecasted Attrition
- Forecasted Movement and Development
- Effects of Past Human Resource Programs

Forecast of Human Resource Needs
- Immediate and Longer Term
- External Hiring Needs
- Reductions and Reallocations
- Improved Utilization
- Development

2. Program Planning

Performance Management
- Organization
  Activities
  Relationships
  Responsibilities
  Standards
  Quality of Work Life (Climate)
- Performance Evaluation
  Performance Plans and Goals
  Coaching
  Evaluation
- Reward Structures
  Compensation
  Benefits

Career Management
- Policies and Systems
  Recruitment
  Selection and Placement
  Promotion and Transfer
  Development and Training
  Termination or Retirement
- Management Succession
  Individual Assessment
  Position Requirements
  Replacement Charting
  Succession Planning
  Tracking Career Progress
- Career Opportunities
  Job Requirements
  Career Paths
  Career Communications
- Individual Career Planning
  Self-Analysis
  Personal Career Plans
  Development Action Plans

Human resource planning's major objective is determining the best use of the talent and skills available to accomplish what's best for the individual and the organization. As Figure 10–2 shows, needs forecasting involves four specific activities. The external market conditions must be studied, as well as the firm's future human resource requirements. The firm must determine if talented and skilled human resources are available.

Human resource planning also involves paying attention to the performance of the organization and the individual. Thus, evaluation, developing compensation and reward programs, and coaching are important planning activities. There's also the need to select, assign, develop, and manage the careers of individuals.

Human resource planning requires the linking of external analysis and scanning with human resource management. Techniques and activities must be carefully employed to accomplish the quality and competitiveness outcomes that a firm seeks. These techniques include the use of:

1. *Human resource inventories:* the skills, abilities, and knowledge that exist within the firm already.
2. *Human resource forecast:* the firm's future requirements in terms of numbers available, skill mix, and external labor supply.
3. *Action plans:* the recruitment, selection, training, orientation, promotion, development, and compensation plans used.
4. *Control and evaluation:* the monitoring system used to determine the degree of attainment of human resource goals.

Human resource planning involves the necessary activities that help managers reduce uncertainty about the future. For human resource plans, managers can make forecasts, plan so that change can be managed more efficiently, and display the role they play in properly managing human resources.

RECRUITMENT

recruitment
The set of activities an organization uses to attract job candidates with the abilities and attitudes needed to help the organization achieve its objectives.

Whenever human resources must be expanded or replenished, a recruitment plan must be established or set in motion. **Recruitment** is the set of activities an organization uses to attract job candidates with the abilities and attitudes needed to help the organization achieve its objectives. Recruitment requires a sound human resource planning system that includes personnel inventories, forecasts of the supply and demand of human resources, action plans, and control and evaluation procedures. The first step in recruitment is a clear specification of needs: number of people, skills mix, knowledge, and experience level. This information is especially important so that affirmative action goals and timetables for the recruitment and hiring of minorities can be met.

If human resource needs cannot be met within the company, outside sources must be tapped. Enron keeps a file on applicants who have sought employment with it over the past year. Even though these applicants were not hired, they frequently maintain an interest in working for a company with a good reputation and image. By carefully screening these files, some good applicants can be added to the pool of candidates.

Advertisements in newspapers, trade journals, and magazines notify potential applicants of openings. Responses to advertisements will come from both qualified and unqualified individuals. Occasionally a company will list a post office box number rather than provide the company name. Called *blind ads*, such advertisements eliminate the need to contact every applicant. But they do not permit a company to use its name or logo as a form of promotion. Some organizations effectively use their own employees in newspaper and magazine ads.

The college campus is a major source for recruiting lower-level managers.[14] Many colleges and universities have placement centers that work with organizational recruiters. Applicants read ads and information provided by the companies, and then they sign up for interviews. The most promising applicants are invited to visit the companies for more interviews.[15]

To find experienced employees in the external market, organizations use private employment agencies, executive search firms, and/or state employment agencies. Some private employment agencies and executive search firms are called *no-fee agencies*, which means that the employer pays the fee instead of the applicant. An organization is not obligated to hire any person referred by the agency, but the agency usually is informed when the right person is found.

The employees responsible for recruiting are faced with legal requirements. These requirements are enforced by laws administered by the Equal Employment Opportunity Commission (EEOC). The federal government attempts to provide equal opportunities for employment without regard to race, religion, age, sex, national origin, or disability, through Title VII of the Civil Rights Act of 1964 and the Equal Employment Opportunity Act of 1972.[16] These laws have broad coverage and apply to any activity, business, or industry in which a labor dispute would hinder commerce. The laws also cover federal, state, and local government agencies.

The hiring practices of airlines have been the subject of two important court decisions on recruitment. A bona fide occupational qualification (BFOQ) is a position taken by an employer that sex, race, or religion are valid criteria for making decisions about employees or job applicants. One decision held that female gender is not a BFOQ for the job of cabin flight attendant. Another held that an airline's policy that a flight attendant must be single is unlawful. No other female employees are subject to the policy, and there was no formal policy restricting employment to single male flight attendants. Another court ruled it illegal to fire a female employee for being pregnant and unmarried. A sex discrimination case against a New York law firm was settled, before a court ruling, when it agreed to recruit, hire, and promote women attorneys on the same basis as men.

Legal procedures regarding equal employment opportunities and recruitment are important to employers. Organizations must adjust to and work with these laws. Although adjustments are sometimes difficult, they seem to be a better alternative than long, costly court battles. Providing equal opportunities to all qualified job applicants makes sense both legally and morally. The vast majority of managers believe that all citizens have a right to any job they can perform reasonably well after a sufficient amount of training.

SELECTION

Selection is the process by which an organization chooses from a list of applicants the person or persons who best meet the criteria for the position available, considering current environmental and financial conditions. The selection process involves screening and making decisions. Firms such as Fairfield Inn and Holland America spend time and energy on their selection programs. Applicants are screened and the firm decides whether to extend a job offer. Job candidates also enter into the decision-making process by deciding whether the job offer fits their needs and goals. Traditionally, the enterprise is attempting to accurately assess the probability that the candidate will succeed in the job.

Organizations that emphasize quality require employees who are excellent problem solvers, who can apply statistical concepts, and who are team oriented. Identifying these abilities and personality characteristics must be done at the selection point. For example, because of the need to be team oriented, Motorola shows job applicants videotapes of problem-solving groups in action. Applicants are then asked to describe their reactions and how they would respond to the videotaped situations.[17]

The selection of people depends largely on organizational needs and legal requirements. Table 10–2 describes a few of the important legal guidelines affecting the selection step.

The actual selection process is a series of steps. It starts with initial screening and ends with the orientation of newly hired employees. Figure 10–3 presents each step in the process. A candidate can be rejected at any one of the nine steps. Recognizing human resource needs through the planning phase of staffing is the point at which selection begins. Preliminary interviews are used to screen out unqualified applicants. This screening often

selection
The process by which an organization chooses from a list of applicants the person or persons who best meet the criteria for the position available, considering current environmental conditions.

TABLE 10–2	SOME LEGAL GUIDELINES FOR THE SELECTION STEP IN STAFFING	
Selection Screening Steps	Legal Activities	Illegal Activities
Tests	Can be used if they have been validated	Cannot be used when there is no relationship between test results and performing the job
Interview information	To ask if a person is a U.S. citizen	To require citizenship or to ask proof of citizenship
	To ask about convictions for crime	To ask if a person has ever been arrested
Age	To require proof of age after hiring	To require a birth certificate
Racial identity	To keep records on racial and ethnic identity for purposes of reporting	To ask for race, creed, or national origin in application or interview

FIGURE 10–3
Typical Selection Decision Steps

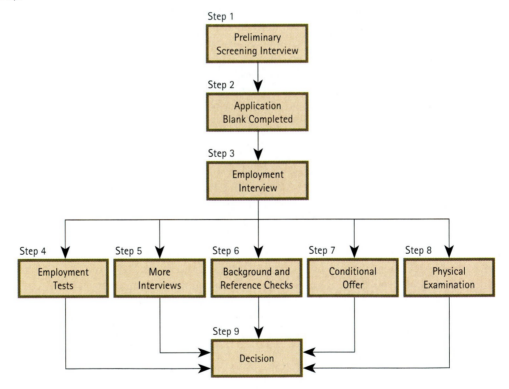

is an applicant's first personal contact with an organization. Applicants who pass the preliminary screening usually complete an application.

Screening Interviews

Interviews are used throughout the selection process. Interviewers usually first acquaint themselves with the job analysis information. Second, they review the application information. Third, they typically ask questions designed to give better insight into the applicants, and they add this information to that on the application.[18]

Three general types of interviews are used: structured, semistructured, and unstructured. In the *structured interview*, the interviewer asks specific questions of all interviewees. In the *semistructured interview*, only some questions are prepared in advance. This approach is less rigid than the structured interview and allows the interviewer more flexibility. The *unstructured interview* allows interviewers the freedom to discuss whatever they think can be important. Comparing answers across interviewees is rather difficult, however.

Some firms now use computers to administer structured employment interviews. Although this does not replace the face-to-face interview, the computer can provide a base of information about each applicant before the interviewer meets him. An applicant can typically complete a 100-question computer-aided interview in less than 20 minutes.[19]

The selection interview's goal is to obtain information for making an accept or reject decision. But in ethical terms, what is reasonable to ask? And what degree of self-disclosure is it legitimate to expect of job candidates? There is little research from an ethical standpoint to help answer these questions.[20]

Tests

Managers often complain that they have a problem hiring and retaining successful employees. Relying solely on intuition rather than finding objective procedures to select employees is not adequate. Subjective procedures are not very accurate in predicting how employees actually will perform the job. One method to improve upon intuition and subjective judgments is testing.[21] A *test* is a means of obtaining a standardized sample of a person's behavior.

A few of the advantages of valid selection tests (how well a test score predicts job success) and reliable selection tests (those that provide consistency of measurement) are:

1. Improved accuracy in selecting employees. Individuals differ in skills, intelligence, motivation, interests, needs, and goals. If these differences can be measured, and if they're related to job success, then performance can be predicted to some extent by test scores.
2. An objective means for judging. Applicants answer the same questions under test conditions. Then their responses are scored. One applicant's score then can be compared with the other applicants'.
3. Information on present employees' needs. Tests given to present employees provide data on their training, development, or counseling needs.

The U.S. Supreme Court made a landmark ruling relating to tests in the *Griggs* v. *Duke Power Company* case in 1971.[22] Six years earlier Duke Power had established a policy requiring job applicants to pass a number of tests and have a high school education to qualify for placement and promotion. A group of African-American employees challenged these requirements, arguing that they were denied promotions because of the testing policy. The Supreme Court ruled that neither the high school requirement nor the test scores showed a relationship to successful job performance.

Organizations using any test now must carefully examine how the scores are used. And test results must be validated. There must be statistical proof that test scores are related to job performance. But testing still can be an important part of the selection process.[23] It is also a major tool for making decisions.

An interesting method for making decisions is through the use of *impairment testing*.[24] A video game is used to measure the employee's ability to work. Both labor and management agree that the video testing doesn't violate the employee's privacy. In terms of cost, timeliness, and accuracy, video impairment testing is better than testing urine or blood samples.

The Factor One impairment test costs about $200 per employee. It can be used as often as desired. Factor One testing detects impairment of motor skills and eye-hand coordination rather than chemical metabolite. It provides information on whether an employee who's impaired should be working that day. The Factor One test operates on an IBM PC or compatible computer and takes about 30 seconds to complete. Video testing could be applied to fleet truck drivers before they are permitted to leave the dispatch center. Failure to pass the test would mean not being able to drive the truck. Such testing could decrease a company's liability exposure.

Impairment testing doesn't indicate the cause of impairment (e.g., drugs, insomnia, marital problems). It can miss recent illicit drug use. Also the test identifies people as impaired who aren't drug users and for all practical purposes are not performance impaired.

The Hiring Decision

After completion of the preliminary screening steps—evaluation of the job application information, interviewing, and testing (if it is used)—it is recommended that a reference check be conducted.[25] Checking with previous employers can provide important information. However, fear of defamation lawsuits has caused a growing number of organizations to provide no relevant information. Courts in most states have held that former and prospective employers have a "qualified privilege" to discuss an employee's past performance. In order to exercise the privilege, a previous employer must follow three rules: (1) the previous employer must determine that the prospective employer has a job-related need to know; (2) the previous employer may release only truthful information about the former employee; and (3) the previous employer may not release EEO-related information such as race, age, or ethnic background.[26]

TRAINING AND DEVELOPMENT

Training and development of human resources involve change: change in skills, knowledge, attitudes, and/or social behavior. To remain competitive, changes in these areas are needed. Maintaining technological superiority, teamwork, world-class quality performance, and social harmony among individuals who differ ethnically and skillwise depends on the ability to cope with changes. For example, due to technical and software advances, computer specialists have to be continually retrained.

Link to Performance

Training is, in short, an attempt to improve current or future employee performance. In most organizations that emphasize quality, training is done in problem solving, problem analysis, quality measurement and feedback, and team building. The following specific points are important to know about training:

- ❖ **Training** is the systematic process of altering employees' behavior to further organizational goals.
- ❖ **Development** is the acquisition of knowledge and skills that may be used in the present or future. It is a more long-term focus.[27]
- ❖ A **formal training program** is an effort by the employer to provide opportunities for the employee to acquire job-related skills, attitudes, and knowledge. In the case of total quality improvement programs at IBM, Motorola, and Xerox, all employees go through a formal training program.
- ❖ **Learning** is the act by which individuals acquire skills, knowledge, and abilities that result in a relatively permanent change in their behavior.
- ❖ A **skill,** introduced in Chapter 1, is any behavior that has been learned and applied. Therefore, the goal of training is to improve skills. Motor skills, cognitive skills, and interpersonal skills are targets of training programs.

Since training and development are forms of education, some findings regarding learning theory logically might be applicable. These principles can be important in the design of both formal and informal training and development programs.

In order to learn, a person must want to learn. In the context of training or development, motivation influences a person's enthusiasm, keeps attention focused on the activities, and reinforces what is learned. For example, if a person is not motivated to improve the quality of his work, little can be accomplished in a training or development program.

training
The systematic process of altering employees' behavior to further organizational goals.

development
The acquisition of knowledge and skills that may be used in the present or future.

formal training program
An effort by the employer to provide opportunities for the employee to acquire job-related skills, attitudes, and knowledge.

learning
The act by which individuals acquire skills, knowledge, and abilities that result in a relatively permanent change in their behavior.

Approaches and Programs

A University of Michigan study and a Hay Associates study found that the most profitable companies (based on the PIMS database) showed the greatest commitment to management and executive development.[28] A study of 300 Fortune service 500 and the top 100 Fortune international 500 companies also provided data. Of the 153 survey respondents, 64 percent represented Fortune 500 industrial companies, 25 percent represented service 100 companies, and 11 percent represented international 100 companies.

A survey of organizations indicated that total dollars budgeted for formal training in 1994 was about $51 billion. More than 47 million individuals received some type of formal training. Training experts suggest that more than $180 billion a year is spent on informal training.[29]

Called *human relations programs*, the earliest management programs designed to affect managerial attitudes were oriented toward individual development. Human relations programs were an outgrowth of the human relations movement, which fostered consideration of the individual in the operation of industry from the 1930s to the 1950s. The movement's rationale from the organization's point of view was that an employee-centered liberal supervisory style would lead to more satisfied employees. This, in turn, would reduce absenteeism, employee turnover, and strikes. Sometimes the style also increased performance.

PERFORMANCE EVALUATION

Performance evaluation is the systematic review of individual job-relevant strengths and weaknesses. Two processes are used in reviewing an individual's job performance: observation and judgment. Both processes are subject to bias or human error. It would be ideal to eliminate evaluation bias and measure only objective indicators of performance, such as number of units produced, cost of completing a unit, or the time to finish a unit. But objective indicators often measure factors beyond a person's control. Therefore subjective criteria such as a manager's rating of a subordinate are often used. It is the manager's rating where bias enters the picture since every rater is asked to observe and then make a judgment on the observations.

performance evaluation A postcontrol technique focusing on the extent to which employees have achieved expected levels of work during a specified time period.

Deming has called for the elimination of performance evaluation systems. He believes that it is detrimental to improving quality because it angers and alienates employees.[30] He condemns every form of performance evaluation. We believe these comments apply to poorly designed and implemented performance appraisal systems. But his across-the-board indictment is too encompassing. Because of performance appraisal's widespread use over an extended period of time, Deming's condemnation isn't likely to result in its elimination. Performance evaluation doesn't have to discourage quality or teamwork.[31]

Performance evaluation is a difficult process to implement. The problems of bias are hard to overcome. The evaluation itself appears to make raters and ratees uncomfortable. But in terms of HRM, formal evaluations can serve many purposes:

1. To make decisions easier involving promotion, transfer, pay raises, and termination.
2. To help establish training and development programs and evaluate their success.
3. To provide feedback to employees that points to strengths and weaknesses.
4. To predict whether recruitment and selection activities lead to attracting, screening, and hiring the best-qualified human resources.
5. To help determine what type of individual can be successful within the organization.

These five purposes can only be accomplished if the evaluation system used satisfies two requirements. It must be relevant to the job(s) being evaluated, and it must be accepted by the raters and ratees. Raters must believe in the importance of evaluation and feedback. Performance evaluation must be viewed as a significant part of the rater's job to motivate human resources. From the ratee's perspective, performance evaluation must be relevant, fair, used by raters familiar with ratees' job performance, and open to modification if flaws are detected. Evaluation systems also must be able to discriminate between good, average, and poor performers.

Performance Evaluation Methods

Managers usually attempt to select a performance evaluation procedure that will minimize conflict, provide ratees with relevant feedback, and help to achieve organizational objectives. Basically, managers must try to develop and implement a performance evaluation program that also can benefit other managers, the work group, and the organization.

As with most managerial procedures, there are no universally accepted methods of performance evaluation to fit every purpose, person, or organization. What is effective in IBM might not work in General Mills. In fact, what is effective within one department or one group in a particular organization might not be right for another unit or group within the same company. Only a few of the numerous evaluation methods can be presented. More detailed and complete presentations of performance evaluation methods are found in human resource management books.

GRAPHIC RATING SCALES - The oldest and most widely used performance evaluation procedure, the graphic scaling technique, has many forms. Generally, the rater is supplied with a printed form for each subordinate to be rated. The form lists a number of job performance qualities and characteristics to be considered. Rating scales are distinguished by: (1) how exactly the categories are defined, (2) the degree to which the person interpreting the ratings (e.g., the ratee) can tell what response was intended by the rater, and (3) how carefully the performance dimension is defined for the rater.

Each organization devises rating scales and formats that suit its needs. Table 10–3 is an example of the type of rating form used in many organizations.

RANKING METHODS - Some managers use a rank order procedure to evaluate all subordinates. Subordinates are ranked according to their relative value to the company or unit on one or more performance dimensions. This procedure usually identifies the best and worst performers, who are placed in the first and last positions on the ranking list. The next best and next poorest performers then are noted. This continues until all subordinates are on the list. The rater is forced to discriminate by the rank order performance evaluation method.

Some problems are associated with the ranking method. First, ratees in the central portion of the list likely will not be much different from one another on the performance rankings. A second problem involves the size of the group of subordinates being evaluated. Large groups are more difficult to rank than small groups.

DESCRIPTIVE ESSAYS - The essay method of performance evaluation requires that the rater describe each ratee's strong and weak points. Some organizations require each rater to discuss specific points, whereas others allow raters to discuss whatever they believe is appropriate. One problem with the unstructured essay evaluation is that it provides little opportunity to compare ratees on specific performance dimensions. Another limitation involves variations in raters' writing skills. Some simply aren't very good at writing descriptive analyses of subordinates' strengths and weaknesses.

RATING ERRORS - The numerous traditional performance evaluation methods each have problems and potential rating errors. The major problems and errors can be technical in the form of poor reliability, poor validity, little practicality, or rater misuse. In some situations, raters are extremely harsh or easy in their evaluations. These are called *strictness* or *leniency rater errors*. The harsh rater tends to give lower-than-average ratings to subordinates. The lenient rater tends to give higher-than-average ratings. These kinds of rating errors typically result because raters apply their own personal standards to the particular performance evaluation system being used. For example, the words *outstanding* or *average* may mean different things to various raters.

Rating errors can be minimized if:
1. Each dimension addresses a single job activity rather than a group of activities.
2. The rater can observe the ratees' behavior on a regular basis.

TABLE 10–3   TYPICAL GRAPHIC RATING SCALE

Name _____ Dept. _____ Date _____

	Outstanding	Good	Satisfactory	Fair	Unsatisfactory
Quantity of work Volume of acceptable work under normal conditions Comments:	❑	❑	❑	❑	❑
Quality of work Thoroughness, neatness, and accuracy of work Comments:	❑	❑	❑	❑	❑
Knowledge of job Clear understanding of the facts or factors pertinent to the job Comments:	❑	❑	❑	❑	❑
Personal qualities Personality, appearance, sociability, leadership, integrity Comments:	❑	❑	❑	❑	❑
Cooperation Ability and willingness to work with associates, supervisors, and subordinates toward common goals Comments:	❑	❑	❑	❑	❑
Dependability Conscientious, thorough, accurate, reliable with respect to attendance, lunch periods, reliefs, etc. Comments:	❑	❑	❑	❑	❑
Initiative Earnest in seeking increased responsibilities; self-starting, unafraid to proceed alone Comments:	❑	❑	❑	❑	❑

3. Terms such as *average* are not used on rating scales, since different raters react differently to such words.
4. The rater does not have to evaluate large groups of subordinates. Fatigue and difficulty in discriminating among ratees become major problems when large groups of subordinates are evaluated.
5. Raters are trained to avoid leniency, strictness, and other rating errors.
6. The dimensions being evaluated are meaningful, clearly stated, and important.

Halo error involves the rating of a single worker on several aspects of performance. When there is a significant halo error, a high correlation among the rater's scores across several performance areas exists. For example, a manager may be asked to rate an employee on quality, teamwork, finishing projects, and initiating projects. In general, a worker would be expected to be good in some of these areas and not so good in other areas, so the correlation among the ratings would be moderate to low. When halo error occurs, such a worker receives nearly identical ratings on all the performed areas.

COMPENSATION

compensation
The HRM activity that deals with every type of reward that individuals receive for performing organizational tasks.

Compensation is the HRM activity that deals with every type of reward that individuals receive for performing organizational tasks. It is basically an exchange relationship. Employees exchange their labor for financial and nonfinancial rewards. Financial compensation is both direct and indirect. *Direct financial compensation* consists of the pay an employee receives in the form of wages, salary, bonuses, and commissions. *Indirect financial compensation* (also called *benefits*) consists of all financial rewards that are not included in direct financial compensation, such as vacation and insurance. Figure 10–4 presents a number of direct and indirect forms of compensation.

Nonfinancial rewards like praise, self-esteem, and recognition also affect employees' satisfaction with the compensation system. Levels of employees' quality and quantity of productivity can be related to nonfinancial rewards as well. A more comprehensive study of compensation would include a special section on nonfinancial rewards.

From the employees' point of view, pay is a necessity in life. The compensation received from work is one of the chief reasons people seek employment. Pay is the means by which they provide for their own and their families' needs. For some people compensation may be the only (or certainly a major) reason why they work. Others find compensation a contributing factor to their efforts. But pay can do more than provide for employees' psychological needs. People's pay indicates their worth to an organization.

Compensation often equals 50 percent of the cash flow of an organization. For some service organizations, it is an even larger percentage. It may be the major method used to attract employees as well as a way to try to motivate them toward more effective performance. Compensation is significant to the economy. For the past 30 years salaries and wages have equaled about 60 percent of the GNP of the United States and Canada.

The quality improvement emphasis on teamwork and shared responsibility is usually better suited for team-based compensation and incentive systems. When individual merit pay systems create a competitive situation, they may be contrary to what quality improvement requires. Group, plant, and organizationwide systems seem more compatible with quality enhancement.

Compensation Objectives

The objective of the traditional compensation function is to create a system of rewards that is equitable to employer and employee alike. The desired outcome is an employee who is

FIGURE 10–4
Types of Compensation

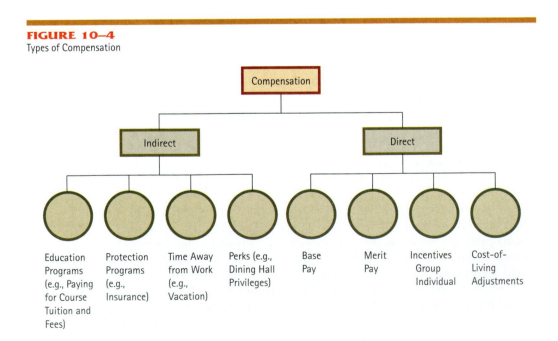

attracted to the work and motivated to do a good job for the employer. Patton suggests that compensation policy has seven criteria for effectiveness:

❖ *Adequate.* Minimum government, union, and managerial pay levels should be met.
❖ *Equitable.* Everyone should be paid fairly, in line with their effort, abilities, and training.
❖ *Balanced.* Pay, benefits, and other rewards should provide a reasonable total reward package.
❖ *Cost-effective.* Pay should not be excessive, considering what the organization can afford to pay.
❖ *Secure.* Pay should be enough to help employees feel secure and aid them in satisfying basic needs.
❖ *Incentive-providing.* Pay should motivate effective, productive work.
❖ *Acceptable to the employee.* Employees should understand the pay system and feel that it is reasonable for the enterprise and themselves.[32]

Pay can be determined absolutely or relatively. Some people have argued that a pay system set by a single criterion for the whole nation or the world (i.e., the absolute control of pay) is the best procedure. Since absolute pay systems are not used, however, the pay for each individual is set relative to the pay of others. Pay for a particular position is set relative to three groups:

❖ Employees working on similar jobs in other organizations (Group A).
❖ Employees working on different jobs within the organization (Group B).
❖ Employees working on the same job within the organization (Group C).

The decision to examine pay relative to Group A is called the *pay-level decision.* The objective of the pay-level decision is to keep the organization competitive in the labor market. The major tool used in this decision is the pay survey (discussed later in this chapter). The pay decision relative to Group B is called the *pay-structure decision.* The pay structure involves setting a value on each job within the organization relative to all other jobs. This uses an approach called job evaluation. The decision involving pay relative to Group C is called *individual pay determination.*

Compensation and Performance

Increasing payroll costs of the 1990s and competition in the global marketplace have caused managers throughout the world to search for ways to increase productivity by linking compensation to employee performance.[33] High performance requires much more than employee motivation. Employee ability and health, adequate equipment, good physical working conditions, effective leadership and management, safety, and other conditions all help raise employee performance levels. But employees' motivation to work harder and better is obviously an important factor. A number of studies indicate that if pay is tied to performance, the employee produces a higher quality and quantity of work.[34] Not everyone agrees with this. Some researchers argue that if you tie pay to performance, you destroy the intrinsic rewards a person gets from doing the job well.[35] Intrinsic rewards are powerful motivators, too, but research on them has been limited to only a few studies. The importance of money to employees varies among individuals. If the organization claims to have an incentive pay system but in fact pays for seniority, the motivation effects of pay will be lost. The key to making compensation systems more effective is to be sure that they are directly connected to expected behaviors.[36]

In sum, theorists disagree over whether pay is a useful mechanism to increase performance. Because of individual differences in employees and jobs, it seems more fruitful to redirect this research to examine (1) the range of behaviors that pay can affect positively or negatively, (2) the amount of change in worker behavior pay can influence, (3) the kinds of employees whom pay influences positively and negatively, and (4) the environmental conditions present when pay leads to positive and negative results.

It can be said that organizations view performance-based compensation programs as anything from a miracle cost-reallocation process to a time-consuming waste of resources.[37] All of these views have merit. To implement such a program, managers must keep in mind that a performance-based compensation system's goal is to develop a productive, efficient, effective organization that enhances both employee performance and motivation.[38] The pay for performance program must, therefore, be driven by performance-oriented systems and processes rather than by the organization's compensation system and processes.

Developing a system that shows employees that pay is tied to performance requires a number of managerial skills. First, managers must be able to allocate pay on the basis of merit. Any merit pay increase must be meaningful, not a token, if it is to be motivational. Second, managers must be willing to specifically discriminate in terms of rating and rewarding performance. Third, managers must communicate the pay system at the time of employment in terms of initial pay, expected long-term pay progressions, and pay adjustments.[39] The manager should also inform the employee what performance levels are required to obtain the pay increases. Finally, managers must have the ability to discuss the pay for performance linkage with subordinates.

The first step in the direction of creating a pay for performance work culture is to develop performance evaluation systems that are considered equitable, meaningful, and comprehensive by both managers and employees. Deming concludes that this is not possible to do with evaluation. When pay rewards cannot be linked to measurable performance, management has a problem. That is, if performance measures are poorly developed, employees will have difficulty perceiving the connection between pay and performance. Thus if compensation is to have any influence on motivation, it is crucial to develop accurate measures of performance.

Linking pay to performance has become simpler than was originally thought due to computer technology.[40] Modern spreadsheet programs used on personal computers enable us to take performance evaluation ratings and directly transform them into projected pay increases. These pay increases can be costed out accurately and subsequently tied to the firm's overall financial strategy. Note, however, that this linkage is predicated on a performance evaluation system that is in place and is adequately communicated to and accepted by employees.

Selected Methods of Compensation

Employees can be paid for the time they work (flat rates), the output they produce (individual incentives), or a combination of these two factors.

FLAT RATES – In the unionized firm where wages are established by collective bargaining, single *flat rates* rather than different rates are often paid. For example, all clerk typists might make $6.50 per hour, regardless of seniority or performance. Flat rates correspond to some midpoint on a market survey for that job. Using a flat rate doesn't mean that seniority and experience do not differ. It means that employers and the union choose not to recognize these variations when setting wage rates. Unions insist on ignoring performance differentials for many reasons. They contend that performance measures are inequitable. Jobs need cooperative effort that could be destroyed by wage differentials. Sales organizations, for example, pay a flat rate for a job and add a bonus or incentive to recognize individual differences.

Choosing to pay a flat rate versus different rates for the same job depends on the objectives established by the compensation analyst. Recognizing individual differences makes the assumption that employees are not interchangeable or equally productive. By using pay differentials to recognize these differences, managers try to encourage an experienced, efficient, and satisfied workforce.

individual incentives
A form of compensation in which the employee is paid for units produced.

INDIVIDUAL INCENTIVES – Perhaps the oldest form of compensation is the **individual incentive** plan in which the employee is paid for units produced. Individual incentive plans take several forms: *piecework, production bonuses,* and *commissions*. These methods seek to achieve the incentive goal of compensation.[41]

Straight piecework usually works like this. An employee is guaranteed an hourly rate (often the minimum wage) for performing an expected minimum output (the standard).

For production over the standard, the employer pays so much per additional piece produced. This is probably the most frequently used incentive pay plan. The standard is set through work measurement studies as modified by collective bargaining. The base rate and piece rate may emerge from data collected by pay surveys.

A variation of the straight piece rate is the differential piece rate. In this plan, the employer pays a smaller piece rate up to the standard and then a higher piece rate above the standard. Research indicates that the differential piece rate is more effective than the straight piece rate, although it is much less frequently used.[42]

Production bonus systems pay an employee an hourly rate. Then a bonus is paid when the employee exceeds the standard, typically 50 percent of labor savings. This system is not widely used.

Commissions are paid to sales employees. Straight commission is the equivalent of straight piecework and is typically a percentage of the item's price. A variation of the production bonus system for sales is to pay salespeople a small salary and commission or bonus when they exceed standards (the budgeted sales goal).

Individual incentives are used more frequently in some industries (clothing, steel, textiles) than others (lumber, beverage, bakery) and more often in some jobs (sales, production) than others (maintenance, clerical). Individual incentives are possible only in situations where performance can be well specified in terms of output (sales dollars generated, number of items completed). In addition, employees must work independently of each other so that individual incentives can be applied equitably. Digital Equipment Company (DEC) uses an incentive system to reward whistleblowing. The Ethics Spotlight illustrates that ethics is a global issue that must be carefully considered in human resource management matters.

Are individual incentives effective? The research results are mixed.[43] Most studies indicate they do increase output though other performance criteria may suffer. For example, in sales, straight commissions can lead to less attention being paid to servicing accounts. Working on hard-to-sell customers may be neglected because the salesperson will elect to sell to easy customers. There is also evidence of individual differences in the effect of incentives on performance.[44] Some employees are more inclined to perform better than others. This should not be a surprise since we know that people have different motivations to work.

Each individual-oriented pay plan is attacked by advocates of teamwork and employee involvement-oriented plans. The encouragement of teamwork is assumed to be virtually impossible with the traditional plans for compensating excellent individual performance[45]—a position expressed again and again by Deming and many of his followers.

GAINSHARING INCENTIVE PLANS - **Gainsharing plans** are companywide group incentive plans. Their goal is to unite diverse organizational elements behind the common pursuit of improved organizational effectiveness by allowing employees to share in the proceeds.[46] The system has proven to be exceptionally effective in enhancing organizationwide teamwork. Gainsharing plans that use cash awards and have been in place for at least five years have shown productivity ratio improvements resulting in labor cost reductions of 29 percent.[47]

Since 1983 more and more companies have been implementing gainsharing plans using a formula that establishes a bonus based on improved productivity. Gainsharing rewards are normally distributed on a monthly or quarterly basis.[48] The factors that dictate a gainsharing plan's success include (1) company size, (2) age of the plan, (3) the company's financial stability, (4) unionization, (5) the company's technology, and (6) employees' and managers' attitudes. A gainsharing plan is expensive to administer, so projected benefits must be weighed against costs.

Linking pay to group performance and the creation of team spirit are two reasons cited for gainsharing's rising popularity.[49] For gainsharing to succeed, it must be supported by management. Management must also understand what gainsharing can and can't accomplish in order to optimize this type of group-based incentive program.

The traditional forms of gainsharing—the Scanlon Plan, Rucker Plan, and Improshare—are differentiated by their performance measures.[50] These are organizational systems for

gainsharing plans
A compensation system based on a companywide incentive system that results in the sharing of rewards caused by improved productivity, cost reductions, or improved quality.

ETHICS SPOTLIGHT

GLOBAL ETHICS: WORLD-CLASS EXPECTATIONS

An interim meeting of the CAUX round table in Tokyo.

Global ethics is becoming a concern for many business managers. As companies conduct more and more business around the globe, assumptions about what is ethical in business transactions or handling human resource management problems are put to the test. Defining ethical behavior in a domestic setting is very difficult. However, when one considers ethical behavior in another country, the complexity increases dramatically.

The Caux Round Table brings together leaders from Europe, Japan, and the United States. Their mission: To focus attention on global corporate responsibility in the belief that the world business community plays a role in improving economic and social conditions. The group has developed world standards to increase ethical behavior. The standards are based on two principles: the concept of human dignity and the idea of living and working together for the common good to enable mutual prosperity.

Where does a company begin in instilling a global ethics perspective? The CAUX Round Table suggests:

1. Think about the company's mission and values.
2. Clearly articulate those values. Define and communicate a code of ethical behavior.
3. Remember that cultural differences dictate flexibility and sensitivity.
4. Develop training in which employees learn and apply the company's values.
5. Create performance appraisal systems that reinforce the ethical behavior the company demands.
6. Communicate ethical behavior examples wherever and whenever possible.

H. B. Fuller Company, manufacturers of adhesives and other specialty chemicals, practices the six-step Caux Round Table principles. The St. Paul, Minnesota-based, company pursued buying a subsidiary from a European adhesive manufacturer. The European company was interested in H. B. Fuller's bid but didn't like the image of many American firms that had massive layoffs once a purchase of firms was completed. H. B. Fuller's management was able to show a record of concern for people, care in handling human resource problems, and an ability to work closely with employees in difficult times. H. B. Fuller was able to show that its corporate culture valued human resources. The European company accepted H. B. Fuller's bid for the subsidiary and turned down 11 other bids. H. B. Fuller found that ethical behavior domestically and globally stem from corporate values that are communicated and understood by employees.

Source: Adapted from Charlene Marmer Solomon, "Put Your Ethics to a Global Test," *Personnel Journal*, January 1996, pp. 66–74; Dawn Anfuso, "Colgate's Global HR Unites Under One Strategy," *Personnel Journal*, October 1995, p. 49; and Sallie Hughes, "Taking on the Bad Guys," *Mexico Business*, February 1995, pp. 13–17.

sharing benefits (paid in the form of cash bonuses) for improved productivity, cost reductions, or improvements in quality.[51] America's first gainsharing plan was set up in 1935 by the Nunn-Bush Shoe Company in Milwaukee. Today gainsharing plans are found in all types of organizations. Most plans, however, are at large, unionized manufacturers in the Midwest.

Lincoln Electric Plan.   The most successful gainsharing or productivity-sharing plan at a single company is the Lincoln Electric Plan. Lincoln is a manufacturer of arc welding machinery and electric motors in Cleveland, Ohio. Domestic sales totaled $385 million in 1992.[52] The company claims that its impressive profits stem from an inspired work force and entrepreneurial management ideas. Lincoln's gainsharing plan was developed by James F. Lincoln, who headed the company for 50 years and wrote the book *Incentive Man-*

Lincoln Electric claims one key to its success is a highly motivated workforce. Under Lincoln's unique compensation system, employees are paid only for what they individually produce, receive no paid vacation time, and can't be laid off after two years of employment.

agement. With a workforce of 2,500, the company has a mere 3 percent annual turnover, including retirements. Employees are paid only for what they individually produce. There are no paid holidays and no unions. Promotions are based on merit, job reassignments must be accepted, and overtime is mandatory. The basic compensation system at Lincoln rests on the following principles: (1) All compensation is based on piecework. (2) There are no perquisites for managers. (3) After two years of employment, the worker can't be laid off. (4) There is no mandatory retirement. An average Lincoln line employee makes $45,000 per year.

An advisory board of several executives and about 30 employees reviews and makes suggestions for company improvements. The firm has a stock purchase plan in which about two-thirds of the employees participate; they now own about one-third of the total stock. The stock is privately traded and not sold on any exchange. Employees hire replacements for vacancies in their work group. The company basically subcontracts the work to the work group, using past performance and time studies as standards of performance. When these standards are beaten, the employees share generously in the gains. This bonus isn't used as a substitute for adequate wages for Lincoln Electric, but is an enhancement for a job well done.

The Equal Pay Act

Today U.S. women working full-time earn only about 70 to 75 percent of what men earn.[53] Historically it was felt that women worked sporadically to bring in money for luxuries. The Virginia Slims opinion poll of 1990 found that women and men work for the same primary reason.[54]

The Equal Pay Act (1963) amending the Fair Labor Standards Act is the first antidiscrimination law relating directly to women. The act applies to all employers and employees covered by the fair Labor Standards Act, including executives, managers, and professionals. The Equal Pay Act requires equal pay for equal work for men and women. It defines equal work as employment requiring equal skills, effort, and responsibility under similar working conditions.[55]

Under the Equal Pay Act, an employer can establish different wage rates on the basis of (1) seniority, (2) merit, (3) performance differences (quantity and quality of work) and (4) any factor other than sex. Shift work differentials are also permissible. But all these exceptions must apply equally to men and women. Since passage of the act, the female–male earnings gap has narrowed slightly. And, between 1979 and 1987, the narrowing of the gap reflected increases in earnings per hour rather than in number of hours worked.[56] In an effort to close the remaining earnings gap, there has been a growing movement in the past few years to have the widely accepted concept of equal pay for equal jobs expanded to include equal pay for comparable jobs. Thus, for young people entering the workforce today, there is practically no difference between wages for men and women within a single job; the male/female wage discrepancy is heavily generational.

Comparable Worth

comparable worth
A concept that attempts to prove that individuals who perform jobs requiring similar skills, efforts, and responsibilities under similar work conditions should be compensated equally.

The doctrine of comparable worth (sometimes called pay equity) is not a position that provides that women and men be paid equally for performing equal work. **Comparable worth** is a concept that attempts to prove and remedy the allegation that employers systematically discriminate by paying women employees less than their work is intrinsically worth, relative to what they pay men who work in comparable professions. The term *comparable worth* means different things to different people. Comparable worth relates jobs that are dissimilar in their content (for example, nurse and plumber) and contends that individuals who perform jobs that require similar skills, efforts, and responsibilities under similar work conditions should be compensated equally.[57]

Advocates of comparable worth depend primarily upon two sets of statistics to demonstrate that women employees are discriminated against by employers. First, they point to statistics that show that women earn from 59 to 88 percent less than men overall.[58] Second, women have tended to be concentrated in lower-paying, predominately female jobs. In spite of the fact that more women are entering the workforce, about one-fourth of all women employed in 1988 worked in three job categories: secretarial/clerical, retail sales, and food preparation and service.[59]

As for the issue of comparable worth, in a five-to-four decision on June 9, 1984, the Supreme Court ruled that a sex discrimination suit can be brought under the 1964 Civil Rights Act on a basis other than discrimination based on "equal or substantially equal work."[60] The suit involved Washington County, Oregon, prison matrons claiming sex discrimination because male prison guards, whose jobs were somewhat different, received substantially higher pay. The county has evaluated the males' jobs as having 5 percent more job content than the females' jobs, and paid the males 35 percent more. On July 1, 1984, the state of Washington began wage adjustment payments to approximately 15,000 employees. For example, women in female-dominated jobs now receive $4.17 more per week. This was the first of several adjustments aimed at eliminating state pay disparities between male and female jobs by 1993.[61]

BENEFITS AND SERVICES

benefits
Indirect financial compensation consisting of all financial rewards not included in the direct financial compensation package.

Indirect financial compensation, called **benefits** and services, consists of all financial rewards that are not included in direct financial compensation. Unlike pay for performance programs and incentive plans, benefits and services are made available to employees as long as they are employed by the organization. Annual surveys suggest that about 75 percent of all U.S. workers say that benefits are crucial to job choice. If limited to only one benefit (beyond cash), 64 percent say that health care is most important.[62]

Employee benefits and services are part of the rewards of employment that reinforce loyal service to the employer. Major benefits and services programs include pay for time not worked, insurance, pensions, and services like tuition reimbursement.

This definition of benefits and services can be applied to hundreds of programs. There is a lack of agreement on what is or is not to be included, the purposes to be served, responsibility for programs, the costs and values of the various elements, the units in which the costs and values are measured, and the criteria for decision making. Compensation decisions with respect to indirect compensation are more complex than decisions concerned with wages and salaries.

Benefits Required by Law

The programs offered in work organizations today are the product of efforts in this area for the past 60 years. Before World War II, employers offered a few pensions and services because they had the welfare of employees at heart or they wanted to keep out a union. But most benefit programs began in earnest during the war, when wages were strictly regulated.

The unions pushed for nonwage compensation increases, and they got them. Court cases in the late 1940s confirmed the right of unions to bargain for benefits: *Inland Steel* v. *National Labor Relations Board* (1948) over pensions, and *W. W. Cross* v. *National Labor Relations Board* over insurance. The growth of benefit programs indicates how much unions have used this right. In 1929 benefits cost employers 3 percent of total wages and salaries; by 1949 the cost was up to 16 percent and in the 1970s it was nearly 30 percent. By 1990 costs of benefits and services totaled about 50 percent.[63]

Additional Benefits and Retirement Plans

In addition to benefits required by the law (such as unemployment insurance, social security, and workers' compensation), many employers also provide other kinds of benefits: compensation for time not worked, insurance protection, and retirement plans. There are many differences in employers' practices regarding these benefits. The most widely used benefits include paid vacations, holidays, and sick leave, life insurance, medical insurance, and pension plans.

CHILD CARE - Two fairly recent additions to benefits packages are child care and elder care. Nearly 50 percent of today's workers are women and as many as 70 percent of these women have children under age six at home. The Bureau of the Census reports that working mothers pay about $15.1 billion per year for child care while they work. The U.S. Dept. of Labor states that in 1995 more than 80 percent of the women between the ages of 25 and 44 will be working outside the home at least part-time. This suggests that child care programs will become a necessity.

Regardless of these facts, only a small number of U.S. employers offer child care assistance to their employees.[64] Child care needs and preferences are very diverse. Of seventy-seven companies who reported providing child care, approximately half provide financial assistance, typically through a dependent care option. The Internal Revenue Service Code permits up to $5,000 of employee payments for dependent care expenses to be excluded from an employee's annual taxable income.[65]

One company that offers child care assistance is Boehringer Ingelheim Corporation, a pharmaceutical firm whose highly trained, skilled workforce is 45 percent female.[66] Its child care plan, begun in 1987, covers six different areas: (1) up to eight weeks unpaid leave after the birth or adoption of a child, (2) an Internal Revenue Code Section 129 flexible spending account for child care expenses, (3) reimbursement of up to $1,000 for adoption fees, (4) a half-hour accommodation time for employees with preschool- or school-age children, (5) provision of child care information, and (6) support of a child care consortium of employers.

ELDER CARE - People age 65 or older will comprise 23 percent of the U.S. population by 2050.[67] Recent research shows that at least 20 percent of all employees already provide assistance to one or more elderly relatives or friends. On average, these employees spend between 6 and 35 hours per week providing this care. At least 50 percent of these employees also have children at home. The burden falls most heavily on the working woman who traditionally took care of elderly relatives and did not work outside the home. Employees who are also caregivers to seniors experience the following problems: missed work (58 percent), loss of pay (47 percent), and less energy to do their work well (15 percent).

SPECIAL ISSUES IN HUMAN RESOURCES

The HRM topics already discussed affect quality enhancement. Each topic is important and must be properly managed to ensure the efficient use of human resource abilities, skills, and experience. In addition, however, three special issues—AIDS, sexual harassment, and substance abuse—have become significant in the workplace.

AIDS in the Workplace

There are many reasons why a company should be knowledgeable about and have a plan to deal with acquired immune deficiency syndrome (AIDS). There is the moral reason that people are dying and organizations are likely to be involved by simply being a part of society. Today about every 54 seconds, another person is infected with the AIDS virus. As of 1993, the fifteenth year of the AIDS epidemic, there have been approximately 500,000 cases of AIDS in the United States.[68] AIDS is the leading cause of death of men between 24 and 35 years old. The law of probability suggests that AIDS will enter every workplace eventually. Individuals, work groups, and departments will feel the tragedy of AIDS.

The vast majority of employers haven't provided AIDS education for employees. One firm that has put an AIDS training program in place is Teledyne, Inc., of Boston. The computer science firm is providing all 3,500 U.S.-based employees with seminars that cover virus transmission, how HIV infection develops, unusual precautions in first aid, and supervisor's legal responsibilities.[69]

The 1992 Americans with Disability Act (ADA) protects individuals with a disability (e.g., AIDS) from being discriminated against in terms of hiring, advancement, compensation, training, or other conditions of employment. Under the ADA, employers may require employee physicals only if the exams are clearly job specific and consistent with business necessity and then only after an offer of employment has been made to a job applicant.[70]

A major concern of organizations is finding a balance between the rights of a person with AIDS and co-workers' rights to a healthy, safe environment. Education, counseling, and safety are the keys to minimizing the impact AIDS will have on an organization. Assuming individuals are knowledgeable about AIDS is not warranted. Misperceptions at all levels of organizations are commonplace. Typically most companies fail to develop an AIDS awareness program until it suffers its first case or a number of AIDS cases. Taking the initiative is overdue in the United States, especially when AIDS has resulted in the deaths of over 250,000, mostly young, Americans in 15 years.

Sexual Harassment

According to public opinion polls, the majority of American women believe they have experienced sexual harassment on the job. As the law has evolved, two types of conduct have been found to constitute sexual harassment in violation of Title VII of the Civil Rights Act. The first type, originally identified in 1977, is the designated *tangible job benefit*, also known as *quid pro quo harassment*. This form of harassment occurs when an employee's career path is directly impacted by a supervisor's unwelcome requests for sexual favors or other sexual advances.

A second type of sexual harassment is a *hostile work environment*. The elements necessary for proving a hostile work-environment-related sexual harassment claim are stated by a New York State case:

A person would have to show that (1) he or she belongs to a protected group (i.e., female or minority group); (2) he or she was subject to unwelcome sexual harassment as defined above; (3) the harassment complained of was based upon his or her membership in the protected class; and (4) the harassment complained of affected the terms, conditions, or privileges of his or her employment.

The creation of a work environment in violation of Title VII can occur in many ways depending on the size of the workforce, managers' sensitivity to sexual harassment, and the dynamics of the workplace.

As Clarence Thomas's 1991 Supreme Court hearings confirmed, sexual harassment cases are difficult to unravel. Often they involve one person's word against another's. The nation watched as Anita Hill described a series of incidents she found offensive. Clarence Thomas denied that the incidents occurred. Thomas was eventually confirmed to the Supreme Court seat, but the hearings were a catalyst in sexual harassment becoming a major concern across the United States.

Sexual harassment can cause lasting emotional damage, depression, and reduced productivity. Each of these consequences is costly to individuals and organizations. One study estimated that the cost to the federal government resulting from sexual harassment over a two-year period was about $267 million.

The number of sexual harassment complaints filed with the Equal Employment Opportunity Commission (EEOC) has dramatically increased from 3,456 in 1981 to 12,000 in 1993.[71] Since most victims don't file with the EEOC, these figures represent only some of the incidents. As the problem continues, managers are advised to develop a program to combat sexual harassment. Typically a company-based program involves (1) development of a sexual harassment policy and complaint resolution procedure, (2) training managers to implement the policy and procedure, (3) educating employees to recognize and confront harassment, (4) providing follow-up care after harassment incidents, and (5) monitoring the workplace for awareness of and compliance with sexual harassment policies.[72]

E. I. Du Pont de Nemours & Company has acquired a reputation as a progressive firm in terms of HRM training on sexual harassment. In 1981 the company prepared and delivered a program to educate managers about the law and sexual harassment. This original program was expanded to include everyone in the firm. A program called "A Matter of Respect" was launched in 1988. To date, about 70,000 of Du Pont's 95,000 U.S. employees have completed the workshop. Each session is led by male and female instructors who examine, critique, and role play real-life situations. Video vignettes are also discussed and analyzed. The discussions are designed to help participants examine their own attitudes. Participants also talk to each other and learn that different viewpoints are held and that misunderstandings can easily emerge.[73]

Under Du Pont's policy (which employees firmly believe), reported harassment incidents are fully investigated immediately. The rights of both the accuser and the accused are protected at all times. If the investigation reveals that harassment has occurred, disciplinary action in line with the seriousness of the circumstance is immediately meted out. Some Du Pont harassers have been reprimanded; others have been terminated. Du Pont's program has been such a success that it now markets "A Matter of Respect" to other companies.

The seriousness of sexual harassment and why it must be dealt with through policies, increased awareness, and training are captured by a statement of the U.S. Merit Protection Board:

> *Victims pay all the intangible emotional costs inflicted by anger, humiliation, frustration, withdrawal, dysfunctional family, and other damages that can be sexual harassment's aftermath. Victims of the most severe forms of harassment, including rape, can face not only severe emotional consequences, but also the possibility of a life-threatening disease. Some victims may leave jobs for one with a lower career path in order to escape the sexual harassment.*[74]

Due to its trauma and potential impact, sexual harassment demands prompt managerial action. It is impossible for a worker to pay attention to the quality of production or service when harassment is occurring. Corrective action is required because of the need to protect the rights of every worker. It is also required because the law (although it's gray in some areas) indicates that employers are liable for sexual harassment. In fact, employers may also be responsible for the acts of their employees. For example, where an employer (or an employer's agents) knows or should know of the harassment and fails to take immediate and corrective action, the employer may be held liable. Sending a clear message that sexual harassment of any form will not be tolerated is a recommended course of action.[75]

Substance Abuse

Substance abuse is a major problem that may impact the safety, productivity, and image of organizations.[76] An American Management Association survey indicates that about 75 percent of major U.S. companies now engage in drug testing.[77] Most major corporations also conduct pre-employment substance abuse testing. Like many forms of testing, substance abuse screening has passionate opponents. Claims that it is inaccurate, an invasion of privacy, and demeaning are well articulated. But so long as there are estimates that any firm with more than six employees has a substance abuser, testing is likely to continue. It is also estimated that substance abuse costs U.S. industry over $100 billion annually because of lost productivity. Substance abusers are absent 2.5 times more days than nonabusers, file five times the number of medical claims and workers' compensation claims, and have four times as many on-the-job accidents. Clearly programs and policies are needed to reduce the burden of substance abuse.

Management's most powerful tool to combat substance abuse is an informed, educated workforce. Detecting substance abuse or a related problem requires careful observation and proper training. Signs of possible substance abuse include:

❖ Difficulty in recalling instructions.
❖ Frequent tardiness and absence.
❖ Numerous restroom breaks.
❖ Extended work and lunch breaks.
❖ Difficulty in getting along with coworkers.
❖ Increased off- and on-the-job accidents.
❖ Dramatic change in personality.[78]

Can managers be good observers and diagnosticians? Sometimes. But patterns of behavior suggesting substance abuse could also be caused by family problems, workplace stress, or physical health problems. Drugs taken on the job is illegal, while having family problems isn't.

The controversy about substance abuse detection and testing is likely to continue unabated. The need is for a policy and program that (1) explains the company's philosophy on substance abuse, (2) describes the firm's policy on testing, (3) implements a discipline and rehabilitation program, (4) communicates the program to all employees, and (5) educates managers on how to enforce a fair substance abuse policy and program.[79] The foundation of an effective approach to preventing substance abuse is a clear, coherent program. Certainly substance abuse is unacceptable in the workplace. Therefore employers must reserve the right to test even though they'll probably exercise the right sparingly. Dealing fairly with substance abuse problems sends a positive message to employees and customers.

SUMMARY OF LEARNING OBJECTIVES

DEFINE HUMAN RESOURCE MANAGEMENT (HRM).
Human resource management (HRM) is a function performed in organizations that facilitates effective use of employees to achieve organizational goals.

EXPLAIN HOW HRM IS LINKED TO STRATEGIC PLANNING.
HRM is a crucial part of the strategic plan of most organizations. People are the core ingredient in any firm. Thus HRM approaches and activities focus on people. As a result, the strategic plan introduces the people-focused approach of HRM.

LIST SEVERAL SOURCES FROM WHICH JOB APPLICANTS ARE RECRUITED.
Job applicants are recruited from advertisements, college campuses, employment agencies, search firms, word-of-mouth, and current employee references.

STATE THE PURPOSE OF EEO PROGRAMS AND IDENTIFY THE THREE MAIN FACTORS THAT CONTRIBUTED TO EEO'S DEVELOPMENT.
Equal employment opportunity (EEO) consists of all the laws and regulations pro—and/or requiring affirmative action. The three

major factors that contributed to EEO were (1) changes in societal values, (2) the economic status of women and minorities, and (3) the emerging role of government regulation.

DESCRIBE THE FORECASTING AND PLANNING ASPECTS OF HUMAN RESOURCE PLANNING.

Any manager who's involved with performing management functions and who's concerned about quality and competitiveness must plan carefully and engage in forecasting. Whether the best people will be available to do the job is always an issue. Finding, attracting, and using the most talented and skilled people in the right numbers is the essence of human resource planning. Human resource inventories, forecasts, and evaluations are part of the tool kit used to conduct efficient planning.

LIST THE TYPICAL DECISION STEPS IN THE HUMAN RESOURCE MANAGEMENT SELECTION PROCESS.

The steps can include a screening interview, completion and review of an application, a formal interview with the supervisor, tests, background checks, and a physical exam.

DEFINE TRAINING AND LEARNING.

Training is the systematic process of altering employees' behavior to improve the accomplishment of organizational goals. Learning is the art by which people acquire skills and knowledge that result in a relatively permanent change in their behavior.

COMPARE SOME OF THE MORE POPULAR METHODS OF PERFORMANCE EVALUATION.

Remember that Deming is a loud opponent of any type of performance evaluation. But his extreme view is not widely followed in the question of whether performance evaluation should be conducted. Rating scales are perhaps the most popular evaluation method since they are easy to use. Typically a score is circled or a box is checked as a rater reviews 8 to 10 traits. In the ranking method the rater ranks individuals on each of a list of characteristics. No method has universal approval because they all have weaknesses.

DISCUSS THE DIFFERENCE BETWEEN DIRECT AND INDIRECT COMPENSATION.

Direct compensation consists of an employee's pay in the form of wages, salaries, bonuses, and commissions. Indirect financial compensation (called benefits) typically includes vacation, various types of insurance, health club privileges, and so on.

EXPLAIN THE COMPARABLE WORTH CONCEPT.

Comparable worth relates jobs that are dissimilar in content. It contends that individuals who perform jobs that require similar skill, effort, and responsibility under similar work conditions should be compensated equally.

KEY TERMS

affirmative action, p. 263
benefits, p. 282
comparable worth, p. 282
compensation, p. 276
development, p. 272
equal employment opportunity
 (EEO), p. 263

formal training program, p. 272
gainsharing plans, p. 279
human resource management
 (HRM), p. 262
human resource planning (HRP),
 p. 267
individual incentives, p. 278

learning, p. 272
performance evaluation, p. 273
recruitment, p. 268
selection, p. 269
training, p. 272

REVIEW AND DISCUSSION QUESTIONS

Recall

1. Why has HRM become a more prominent part of organizational strategic plans in the past decade? Do you expect HRM to remain a top priority in the next decade? Why?
2. What are the advantages and disadvantages associated with various forms of testing: intelligence, skills, substance abuse?

Understanding

3. Distinguish between the two recognized forms of sexual harassment. Which form is less difficult to substantiate? Why?
4. Group compensation plans appear to be better suited for firms attempting to create a quality-oriented culture. Does this mean that individual compensation plans will become extinct? Why?
5. Why would managers resist Deming's plan to eliminate performance evaluation? Use practical managerial reasons to develop your response.

6. What has been the impact of EEO on diversity in the workforce?
7. If employers used the notion that workers must perform "reasonably well," would this enhance or inhibit quality productivity as it relates to world markets?

Application

8. Outline a sound AIDS awareness policy that would properly educate workers.
9. Interview an HRM contact in a large firm. Determine what type of testing program exists and how the test results are used.
10. Search literature and determine what type of group performance evaluation approaches are available. Critique the usefulness to managers of at least two approaches.

CASE STUDY

The Mirage Hotel: A Human Resource Volcano

At the Mirage Hotel—a top-quality facility—in Las Vegas, the management team values human resources. The concerns of quality and the concerns for people stand out in many areas.

With 3,054 rooms and 7,000 employees, the Mirage is one of the largest hotels in the world. There are 89 other casinos/hotels in Las Vegas—each with its own brand of service vying for the best employees and customers who come back again and again. These 7,000 employees are the key to the Mirage's image as a top-quality hotel. In the hotel industry, employee turnover reaches a staggering 60 percent annually. But the Mirage's turnover rate is only about 19 percent. Why is there a whopping 41 percent difference between the Mirage's average and the industry's average?

The answer appears to center on employees who like to work at the Mirage and the customers who like to be around pleasant, thoughtful, respectful people. Mirage employees, from the clerk to the director of operations, display a pride, a sense of belonging, and a commitment to their work. They like it, and they project this warmth and spirit for their customers.

The Mirage Resort's Chairman Stephen Winne calls the office of human resources "the department." It's the department that recruits the best workers, makes their training a business priority, and keeps them motivated. It's the department that ensures friendly desk clerks, helpful clerks, and efficient maids.

As a place of employment, the Mirage has an excellent reputation for concern about employees. When the hotel opened, an intensive screening process was put into place. An aggressive recruitment campaign generated 57,000 applications for the original 6,500 job vacancies. Once people are hired at the Mirage, they go through an intensive training and orientation program. All new employees must successfully master the 10 essential Mirage job tasks. The 10 tasks were developed by analyzing jobs, customer satisfaction, and service. The Mirage spends $2 million annually on the 10–task training program. Arte Nathan, vice president for human resources, is the person behind the quality and the people-are-first culture that have emerged at the Mirage.

One of Arte Nathan's innovations with a human resource emphasis is called the Mirage Employee Services Center. Employees can file health insurance claims, receive payroll information, deposit checks directly, and receive other services at the Center. Arte wants employees to feel that they, like the casino and hotel customers, receive service from the hotel. He takes pride in ensuring that employees are satisfied so they can deliver service that results in customer satisfaction.

Work at the Mirage is done with thousands of customers streaming in and out each day. The 7,000 employees, like the thousands of customers, can become lost in the hectic shuffle. To create a more cohesive feeling, Mirage management decided to create 20-person teams. The Mirage is loaded with these employee teams that have their own leaders. The team is the anchor for the employee and provides a feeling of cohesiveness. Each team wears a different color. Team spirit is highlighted by these different badge or lapel colors.

The employee cafeteria—an excellent facility—serves the same food that hotel guests eat. Employee meals are free, and they can eat as many meals as they like. Again, building employee satisfaction is an important part of how the Mirage does business.

The Mirage has concluded that employees are the first link in the chain of creating a friendly, cooperative, and productive atmosphere for customers. This philosophy not only is expressed, but is also practiced. Customers appear to like the Mirage, and people like to work in the hotel and casino. The connection between effective human resources practices and quality is one reason why the volcano at the front entrance erupts exactly on time and the Mirage earns over $250 million per year.

Arte Nathan and other managers applied the "customer-is-a-top-priority" thinking to Mirage employees. It's a simple notion that most firms miss in developing programs. The Mirage makes it and keeps it as a top priority in a very competitive business in a city filled with competitors.

QUESTIONS

1. There is tremendous competition for business in Las Vegas. How could another casino and hotel compete effectively against the Mirage?
2. Should the Mirage really be so proud of a 19 percent annual turnover rate?
3. Do you agree with the concept of developing employee satisfaction programs, which, if effective, will lead to customer satisfaction and better business?

Source: Adapted from Bill Leonard, "HR Policies Ensure the Mirage Won't Vanish," *HR Magazine*, June 1992, pp. 85, 87, 91.

VIDEO CASE

Human Resources Management

What is it about a company that allows it to attract the best employees? The first thing that usually comes to mind for most people is salary. Salary can be an effective lure to top talent, but benefits are also important when a candidate considers a position with a company. In most organizations, benefits make up a significant part of the total compensation paid to an employee. These benefits can include a variety of health insurance plans, retirement options, and life insurance choices. Employee benefits also include sick days, vacation days, holidays, and personal days. Typically, the human re-sources department of an organization administers the benefit plans. The size of the human resources department can vary considerably depending on the size of the company, but one thing all human resources departments have in common despite their size is the need to manage large amounts of data that can be regularly updated and organized.

Efficient management of human resources data is crucial to containing costs and to providing the best possible service to employees. The computerized database is one tool HR departments commonly use to manage employee benefit information. Information systems that use databases organize data into fields. Each field contains specific information such as name, address, health insurance options, or available vacation days. Several fields make up a record. Generally, there is one record per employee. The database can be sorted by fields so that specific information on an individual employee can be extracted and analyzed alongside data from other individuals. This allows an organization to track information on a group of employees, such as total vacation days available.

Databases can be used by both large and small organizations since they can exist on large mainframes or personal computers. Two organizations that have found unique ways of using information systems for human resources management are Hewitt Associates and USX Corporation.

Hewitt Association manages defined benefit programs such as 401(k) or other retirement plans for large companies. The company uses sophisticated technology and a customer-service orientation to excel in its industry. Account representative Laurie Caputo explained Hewitt's approach to customer service, "Whenever a call comes through to me as a representative on the phone, I feel the most important thing that I can impart to a person is personalized service and my complete attention during that call. I also want to provide accurate information. I consider myself an extension of their benefits office and the client, so it's very important that when they talk to us they get the sense that we care about them and that we are really part of their team."

Giving the right answers, performing transactions quickly and accurately, and providing professional counsel—for Laurie Caputo, these are the keys to keeping benefit plan participants and clients satisfied. Laurie is an account representative in Hewitt Associates' benefit center, a modern communications facility that lets participants find information on defined benefit, defined contribution, and flexible benefits programs. Through an interactive voice response system and a staff of account representatives, participants can get information, make transactions, and enter personal data. Brenda Sural, Hewitt's voice response system consultant said, "Voice response provides an automated method of communicating with the plan. For the participants it's great because it provides a convenient and confidential method of getting information. When we sit down with a client to define a voice response system, we'll look very carefully at any printed material that they give to employees as well as study their plan features so we can customize a voice response system that's unique to them."

The voice response system is designed for ease of use by callers who are not necessarily familiar with the technology. A plan participant calls the voice response system and gets a professionally recorded message, which is actually a digitized audio file that is retrieved based on the caller's input. The system is linked to a mainframe database, and before any information is provided, the caller must pass security. When a caller enters the voice response system, they are first asked for their employer ID number, and a four- to six-digit personal identification number. The computer treats the voice response unit as an input device, such as a computer terminal. The caller uses a Touch-Tone phone to answer the questions and navigate through the system. When a more personal touch is needed, participants can be connected to an account representative.

When a call reaches an account representative, that representative's screen displays how far into the voice response system the caller had journeyed. Thus, if the caller had already passed security, the representative would have the caller's name and account information already displayed on the screen. Account representatives'

computer terminals are linked directly to Hewitt Associates' mainframe. A graphical user interface makes it easy for them to perform transactions, and offers the capability of running two different applications simultaneously, a function known as *multitasking*. One use of multitasking is the online help feature. When an account representative needs more information, the help feature provides information for whatever application is on the screen. The representative doesn't have to search through a list of choices. The system also uses a real-time database, meaning that any information that is retrieved is up to date. Any updates made to the participant's records by the account representative occur instantly, and a letter confirming the change is automatically sent the same day.

Hewitt Associates uses information technology to provide cost effective solutions to defined benefits management for large corporations. The use of sophisticated voice response systems and databases and a focus on customer service enable Hewitt to save its clients money while making a profit. As the next example shows, some companies are using technology to let employees help themselves to important human resources data.

USX, one of the largest steel companies in the United States, also turned to computer technology to help its employees better plan their retirement investments. Bob McMaster, manager of USX's benefits information management system, said, "Basically we were looking for a better way to communicate information and benefits to employees. With the changing environment people are retiring at an earlier age. We wanted them to have the ability to see what the effects on an earlier pension would be."

To address this concern, USX installed an interactive retirement planning application in multimedia kiosks throughout the company. At each kiosk, employees enter their Social Security number and a personal identification number to retrieve their retirement plan data directly from a host computer. A graphical interface and audio prompting make navigation easy. Employees can input personal savings information, and obtain 401(k), and Social Security projections along with their company pension plan. After projecting through retirement, the employee can print out the results and go back and review their assumptions. McMaster said, "The employees realize that this is truly a benefit for them. We have had 85 percent of our employees actually use the system at the kiosk. Many people, of course, return time and again to update their information."

According to McMaster, the benefits from an information systems approach to human resources management can include:
- ❖ Cost savings.
- ❖ Better service for employees.
- ❖ Instant access to personnel data.
- ❖ Easy updating.

In summary, databases provide a useful tool for organizing and managing employee benefit and personal data. Fields in a database are used to group similar types of data such as last name, ZIP code, or telephone numbers. Sorting data by fields allows a human resources department to track specific types of data that can be useful in budgeting and controlling costs. A well-organized database can be instantly accessed and updated. Whether an organization uses a mainframe or personal computers, a database offers an efficient way for a human resources department to manage personnel data. As human resources management costs rise with the increasing price and number of benefit options, information systems that are well implemented can offer a way to contain costs and provide better employee service.

QUESTIONS

1. Most of us have had some experience with voice response technology in registering for school, contacting a local government office, or elsewhere. What have you found to be some of the limitations of such a system? How could these limitations be overcome with enhanced or additional technology?

2. People that call Hewitt Associates can speak with an account representative if their questions aren't answered by the voice response system. Do you think Hewitt should do away with this option? Explain your answer.

3. Employee benefit plans have become more complex, allowing companies the flexibility of tailoring plans to meet individual needs. What are the advantages of this increasing complexity? What are some of the disadvantages? How did USX Corporation respond to the complexity of benefit plans?

4. USX Corporation allows employees to retrieve their retirement plan and determine what payments they can expect when they retire. Explain some potential pitfalls of the approach taken by USX.

APPLICATION EXERCISE

RECRUITMENT ACTIONS

An important HRM activity outlined at this chapter's start involves recruitment (attracting applicants to fill job vacancies). As the chapter says, hiring the right person is vital to accomplishing an organization's quality goals.

SETTING UP THE EXERCISE

1. Divide the class into groups of five or six.
2. Read "Hire the Right Person Recruitment Pool" and answer the questions.
3. Read "Finding the Right Person" and answer the questions.
4. Reconvene the entire class and discuss what the groups concluded.

HIRE THE RIGHT PERSON RECRUITMENT POOL

The objective of this part of the exercise is to review various sources of job candidates. Finding individuals who are team players, interested in quality, and hard working is important. List two internal (within-the-firm) sources of job candidates and at least three external sources of job candidates.

1. Internal source: _____
   Likelihood of finding the right person and why: _____
   _____

2. Internal source: _____
   Likelihood of finding the right person and why:
   _____

3. External source: _____
   Likelihood of finding the right person and why:
   _____

4. External source: _____
   Likelihood of finding the right person and why:
   _____

5. External source: _____
   Likelihood of finding the right person and why:
   _____

   ❖ Which source would be best for finding the most qualified job candidates?
   ❖ Why should a combination of internal and external sources be used to find the best candidates?

   ❖ In the sources identified, which is the best for finding minority candidates? Why?

FINDING THE RIGHT PERSON

Developing a profile of job candidates is needed before a final selection decision is made. Exhibit 10–1 indicates the kind of profile information needed to determine whether a job candidate is quality oriented. How would you develop the most accurate profile of each of the needed characteristics?

❖ Which of the characteristics will be difficult to assess during the recruitment and selection phase? Why?

❖ What are some legal considerations that should be followed in collecting information via an interview, test, or personal references?

EXHIBIT 10–1	JOB APPLICANT PROFILE			
Characteristics	Interview	Test	Personal References	Other
• Self-motivation				
• Interpersonal abilities				
• Communication abilities				
• Adaptability				
• Ability to work as part of a team				
• Experience with statistical quality techniques and tools				
• Attitude about quality				

PART 4

Leading

CHAPTER 11

Group Dynamics and Team Building

After studying this chapter, you should be able to:

❖ Describe the various types of informal and formal groups typically found in organizations.

❖ Explain how the four stages of group development influence the creation of an effective group.

❖ Discuss various characteristics of groups, including role-making, group norms, and cohesiveness.

❖ Describe the three parts of the model of effective small group interaction.

❖ List the activities needed to develop team-driven companies.

❖ Discuss some of the problems encountered when building teams.

Work Teams *Work*

A team-based decision in a Florida medical center reduced its turnaround time for routine tests by 70 percent (to 48 minutes), reduced a diagnostic procedure from 40 steps to 8, and reduced the number of hospital staff that come in contact with a patient from 27 to 13.

Sales & Marketing magazine surveyed sales forces and found that some of the best sales results come from firms using a team-based approach. United Parcel Service, Procter & Gamble, RJR Nabisco, General Electric, and Times Mirror are successful companies that emphasize the collective expertise of teams in solving customer problems. To promote group efforts, some firms have dropped individual incentives, replacing them with compensation that encourages teamwork. Even sports, like paintball, are being used by major corporations to provide new, exciting, and fun ways to develop teams, decrease stress, and raise morale.

An aging Chrysler plant in Indiana, a candidate for closing in the 1980s, was marked by absenteeism, grievances, and defects. In 1986 the union and Chrysler adopted a team approach. Workers became "technicians." Some supervisors

Skylab 4

left; those who remained became advisers to the teams. Absenteeism dropped 60 percent. The number of grievances fell from over 1,000 per year to 33 in 1991. Defects per million parts shrank from 300 to 20, an improvement of over 90 percent.

Government agencies as well as the private sector have reaped the benefits of teamwork. NASA saved over $12 million by reducing the thickness for its space shuttle thermal blankets, based on a suggestion from a quality team. At an Air Force base in California, savings of over $3.3 million in three years resulted in gainsharing distributions to workers of close to $1.7 million. And the transportation–service department of Salt

River Project (SRP), a water and electric utility in Arizona, began a move toward self-directed work teams after 90 years of traditional management. Now team members interact directly with customers, dealing with both positive and negative feedback.

Pitney Bowes, in Stamford, Connecticut, trained workers in needed basic communication skills, shifted to compensation based on skills rather than seniority, and organized self-managed teams of workers. Teams chose their own members, set production goals, and arranged schedules with little management control. Despite job losses, inventories declined 50 percent and output per square foot rose 50 percent.

Source: Adapted from Catherine Petrini and Rebecca Thomas, "A Brighter Shade of Team Building," *Training Development,* November 1995, p. 9; Charles Retts, "From Hierarchy to High Performance," *Training Development,* October 1995, pp. 30–33; Timothy D. Schellhardt, "Managing: 'Theory P' Stresses How Departments Interact," *The Wall Street Journal,* December 13, 1991, p. B1; Timothy D. Schellhardt, "Managing: Coordinated Team Efforts Show Winning Results," *The Wall Street Journal,* December 17, 1990, p. B1; Charles Manz, as cited in Joann S. Lublin, "Trying to Increase Worker Productivity, More Employees Alter Management Style," *The Wall Street Journal,* February 13, 1992, p. B1; Erika Penzer, "Making a Federal Case for Quality," *Incentive* 165, no. 8 (August 1991), p. 30; and Mark Alpert, "Pitney Bowes: Jumping Ahead by Going High Tech," *Fortune,* October 19, 1992, p. 113.

Groups are a common and necessary form of collective action. Armies, sporting teams, bridge clubs, and church choirs are everyday examples of collective behavior known as a group. As we all recognize, there is a power in group behavior that is unmatched by individual action. An organization may ignore an individual's demand for a salary increase. The same demand made by a union for a general membership wage increase, if it is ignored, could cripple the organization's productive capacity. For these reasons, it is natural and important for people to learn the dynamics of group behavior. This chapter describes types of groups, how they function, and what factors are likely to turn any group into a highly effective component of the organization.

CATEGORIES OF GROUPS

group
Two or more people who engage in purposeful collective action.

Much of the daily work of organizations is performed by groups. A **group** is defined as two or more people who act together to accomplish a goal. From an organizational perspective, there are two categories of groups: the informal group and the formal group. All other types of groups or teams are variants of these two basic forms of collective behavior.

Informal Groups

informal group
Two or more people who engage in voluntary collective activity for a common purpose. Informal group actions are generally not recognized by the organization.

An **informal group** arises when two or more people engage in voluntary collective activity for a common purpose. Informal group actions generally aren't recognized by the organization. Examples of such groups include friendship groups and interest groups.

FRIENDSHIP GROUPS - A friendship group is a collection of people with like values or beliefs who get together for a common purpose—possibly just to have fun!

INTEREST GROUPS - An interest group is a collection of people addressing a specific subject. An example would be five people from different walks of life who meet regularly to discuss art and attend plays.

While not directly related to work organizations, informal groups are found in all organizations. Our ability to join one or more informal groups is greatly enhanced when we regularly interact with diverse groups of people. Most large organizations fit this description quite well. Large organizations increase our exposure to many different informal groups that we might join. With an informal group, the "joining" part is often rather casual.

Formal Groups

formal groups
Two or more people who engage in organizationally required actions for a common purpose. The term formal designates a permanent entity with prescribed organizational roles.

Groups are formal to the extent that membership is based on the employee's position in an organization. **Formal groups** consist of two or more people who engage in organizationally required actions for a common purpose. They're a permanent part of the organization. A marketing department is an example of a formal group. The role definition and membership requirements for a formal group are quite explicit. Thus to maintain membership in the marketing department, a marketing manager may have to reach targeted sales goals for assigned products.

WORK GROUPS ~ Within a formal group, such as a customer relations department, there are many work groups. A **work group** is defined as two or more people in a work organization who share a common purpose. This common purpose is usually the completion of a task. The work group is the smallest formal organizational personnel arrangement. As such, a work group represents the most basic level of collective work activity. In a department, it is possible to find many work groups. To govern the relationship between the group and the organization, the group has assigned reporting relationships, a formal leader, and, often, specific instructions to guide task completion. For many years the formal work group with external supervision was the mainstay of productive effort in organizations.

WORK TEAMS ~ The term *work team* describes a special type of organizational work group. The primary difference between a work team and a work group is the way in which they are governed. Generally, teams are self-managing and have a great deal more decision autonomy than work groups.

Teams have become a widespread business phenomenon in recent years. Success stories of the team concept include product development at Chrysler with the new Viper sports car as well as the use of cross-functional and cross-national work teams at Ford and Mazda.[1] These examples highlight the advantages of using self-managing cross-functional teams to decrease product development time and/or increase overall product quality. Because effective work teams can be a valuable asset to a firm, people who can successfully facilitate team interactions play an increasingly important role in organizations throughout the world.[2] Although historically the use of teams has tended to be most prevalent in Japanese firms, the team approach seems to be gaining momentum in the United States as well.[3] More than 20 years ago management expert and professor Edward Lawler estimated that about 150 manufacturing plants in the United States used some sort of self-managing team approach. In 1990 he estimated about 7 percent of the manufacturing firms in the United States used a team approach.[4] In 1992 team expert Charles Manz estimated that 40 to 50 percent of all workers would be employed in self-managing teams by the end of the century.[5] For example, by 1989 about 20 percent of General Electric's 120,000 U.S. employees were working under some form of team concept.[6]

work group
An organized collection of workers responsible for a task or outcome.

Like effective work teams in the business world, auto-racing crews take pride in quick response and quality assurance.

A major advantage of the work team concept is quick response time. But another obvious advantage is that the team can be a source of quality assurance at every step of the production process. Self-directed teams typically handle job assignments, plan and schedule work, make production-related decisions, and take action on problems, all with minimal direct supervision.[7] The team's self-regulating nature allows for greater error detection and correction on the spot rather than at the end of the assembly line. In today's highly automated assembly facilities, almost every workstation has a switch within easy reach that the worker can use to stop the assembly line when something is wrong. Stopping the assembly line was far more difficult 20 years ago and required managerial intervention. Because it was more trouble in the past to correct errors on the spot, most errors just slipped through. Immediate error correction means that fewer defects make it through final assembly, which yields higher-quality products. Because of the recent increased concern for quality, this approach may mean that a modern assembly line has to be "down" as much as 20 percent of the time.[8] In a sense, commitment to quality has its price—it means that both organizational systems and work groups must be structured to produce quality. Thus procedures, methods, and practices of both the organization and its work groups must be physically and psychologically attuned to production requirements. To do so, teams have become a focal component in delivering quality medical services, solving sales problems, and making factories more productive.

Teamwork allows one employee to compensate with his or her strength for another employee's weakness. Everyone on a team has a chance to contribute ideas, plans, and figures; but anyone may expect to find some of his best ideas submerged by consensus of the team. A good team has a social memory. As a collective, the team should be able to "remember" the contributions of individuals for the good of the group. Over time, contributing members play a major role in shaping the group's activities.

REFLECTIONS BY PHILIP B. CROSBY

Groups and Quality Teams

At one time I worked in a "matrix" organization. As a product line quality department manager I reported to the Quality Division director and obtained trained people from his functional departments. He gave me advice and technical direction.

My other boss was the program director who was responsible for the product and also supervised engineering, manufacturing, finance, planning, and several other departments as they worked on his program. He gave me money.

Many people had a problem with being on two charts, with two bosses, even though they had different missions. It didn't bother me because I saw them in different roles and made certain that I kept them informed enough to leave me alone. Communication has to be forced—people will not usually seek it out on their own.

These teams were set up to accomplish a task and then disbanded when the task was complete. Inside the operations special teams would be established to attack a specific problem. They were short-lived and existed only until the problem was resolved completely. This rarely took more than a few weeks. Other groups were brought together for the purpose of communications, such as quality improvement, and they lasted much longer.

It took me a while to learn that just because something is worthwhile, it does not have permission to become fat and inefficient. This was important because it was possible to have meetings going on at all times—there were enough teams about. (I wrote a chapter on this in *Quality without Tears,* showing that one executive only had a single day in which to work each year.)

In my organization, which contained about 1,000 people, we set up some rules for team meetings of all sorts. First, an agenda had to be published at least a day ahead of time. Second, all meetings had to be held standing up, and to this end we removed all the chairs from our conference rooms. No one believed we did this, and folks came from far away just to watch. But we did, and the meetings were short and effective. The message was that it does not take long for prepared people to discuss a subject, come to a conclusion, and then agree on some action. What takes long is being unstructured and having unlimited time. Those groups we disbanded.

We learned to do as much work as possible within the organization as it was set up, without adding any other blocks anywhere.

Teams are not without problems; the team building process is often flawed from the start. People often try to form and implement teams without a plan, based on emotion instead of common sense.[9] Employees need time to get accustomed to the idea of teams, and it is a mistake for management to demand acceptance. Team members need to know why teams are being used, and where each of them fit into the process. If employees feel teams are being used to reduce the size of the workplace or to make them do more work, they will sabotage the process. The team approach is certain to fail when managers do not set up a supportive environment.[10] And all too often, firms are finding that team leaders eventually resort to human nature and refuse to share authority with the rest of the team.[11]

QUALITY CIRCLES - The **quality circle,** introduced in Chapter 8, is a group of employees who meet to brainstorm about how to improve quality and cost control in the workplace. Quality circles differ from work teams in terms of membership, the type and frequency of problems handled, authority to implement decisions, and the group's relationship to the organization.[12] Whereas work teams are at the core of the organizational structure, quality circles are supplemental. Participation in quality circles may be voluntary or members may be appointed, depending on the organization. Membership in quality circles is often cross-disciplinary and agendas usually focus on technical or procedural quality problems. Whereas work teams typically deal with problems as they arise, on a continual and informal basis, quality teams usually turn over responsibility for implementing solutions to problems to management. Quality circles can evolve into self-managed teams, but this is atypical.[13]

Within the past 20 years, many American manufacturing firms have embraced quality circles in an effort to respond to worker concerns over the quality of work life, to improve product quality, and to mimic one visible aspect of Japanese success. But the use of quality circles alone is ineffective—and even frustrating and counterproductive—without a companywide commitment to quality management. As W. Edwards Deming notes, quality circles "can thrive only if management will take action on the recommendation of the circle."[14] Reporting on the use of quality circles in a Japanese auto parts plant, Deming found that effective communication by management fostered a positive team spirit, intense loyalty, and high motivation. He noted extensive use of visual communications in the plant in the form of posters, signs, and graphs.[15]

quality circle
Volunteer group of employees who meet to brainstorm about how to improve quality and cost control in the workplace.

STAGES OF GROUP DEVELOPMENT

Now that we've gone over the different kinds of groups, we can examine how groups develop in a four-stage process of forming, storming, norming, and performing (Figure 11–1). Group development describes the progression from a collection of people literally tossed

FIGURE 11–1
Stages of Group Development

together for a common purpose to a well-functioning whole whose effectiveness has stood the test of time.

Stage 1: Forming

forming
The early stage of group development when members begin to know each other's strengths and weaknesses.

Forming is the actual beginning of the group, when members get to know one another and understand each other's abilities and deficits. In the formation stage, the collection of people quickly comes together as a functioning unit. Members temporarily accept formation rules and orders in an effort to initiate the group. With the process under way, formal group functions are defined and the beginnings of hierarchy emerge. Sometimes formal organizational task requirements dictate group purpose. Often a formal leader is appointed to facilitate group development.

Stage 2: Storming

storming
The stage of group development when the group addresses inherent conflicts and develops solutions that keep the group focused on its work.

As the name suggests, this is the most tumultuous stage of development. **Storming** refers to the group's coming to grips with inherent conflicts and developing solutions that keep the group focused on its work. During this stage members learn to accept individual differences as the beginnings of a collective "group personality" emerge. This collective viewpoint is the result of sharing common work, values, and purpose. Along with personality emergence comes informal vying for power or control of the group. Also, specialization through subgroups begins to develop. Group members negotiate roles that are needed for effective group functioning and members adopt those roles.

Stage 3: Norming

norming
The stage of group development when the group develops norms or unwritten codes of conduct for group behavior.

During the **norming** stage the group charts out its long-term vision of group purpose and how it will function over time. The agreement among members of the long-term vision is referred to as developing **shared values**. The group's norms are the unwritten guides to behavior. Conformity to norms is enforced through rewards and sanctions. Members who adhere to norms reap the benefits the group has to offer such as status, affiliation, and personal growth. Deviance from group norms may subject the member to punishment, humiliation, or ostracism.

shared values
Beliefs, attitudes, or actions that are commonly agreed upon and understood by group members. Shared values are an invisible and unspoken guide to daily behavior within the group and to interaction outside the group.

Stage 4: Performing

performing
The stage of group development when the group functions to its fullest potential toward goal attainment.

The group is now at the **performing** stage in which the group functions as a highly effective unit. During this stage, a group that has remained together for a long period of time fine-tunes group functioning. Group members carefully redefine group roles as needed. They decide how best to balance needs of the group and the organization. At this stage the group is most able to develop the skills of members, recruit new members, and perform the group's work at a high level.

Some short-term groups have to disband and merge members into other task groups. Some authors consider this "ungrouping" process a separate stage. By the performing stage, all individuals have learned their roles in the group. The more effective the group, the quicker the group reaches the performing stage of development.

At each stage the group is confronted with increasingly difficult decisions. One of the greatest challenges is how best to reward individual contribution and still maintain the group's integrity. In fully mature groups, individual efforts have been well integrated into specific group functions. Over time, the group's success or failure becomes evident. This is largely determined by how well the group performs its assigned functions and contributes to the organization's overall effectiveness.

CHARACTERISTICS OF GROUPS

An effective group is one that fully utilizes the abilities of members in the attainment of group goals. Groups continue to be effective as long as the group can elicit contributions from members. Another way of thinking about the relationship between a member and the group is as a type of *exchange*. The group member gives time, energy, knowledge, and ability, while the group provides the member with need satisfaction. Group membership holds the potential to satisfy several basic human needs. Individual member needs that are met through group involvement include need for achievement, need for affiliation, and need for power.[16] Members of a group that has successfully attained a specific goal are encouraged to know that goal attainment would have been impossible without their efforts. Likewise, successful group members interact. For many individuals, group membership at work is their primary attachment to other people. Table 11–1 identifies 10 characteristics of effective groups.

Like the need for affiliation, the need for power can be fulfilled in a socially acceptable manner at work. Work group hierarchy allows some group members a degree of control over other group members' activities. People are accepted into the group, their behavior is scrutinized, and they are encouraged or discouraged based on group members' evaluation of them. The group leader or a designated leader may derive a real sense of personal power because of these types of valuative activities. But beyond these issues of group functioning are other more enduring issues. For example, how does an effective group continue to function at high levels over time? What mechanisms sustain the group even as high-performing members leave the group?

Role Making in Groups

All work groups are defined by roles that members in the group perform and by the hierarchy or status of these roles. As discussed in Chapter 1, a *role* is a set of shared expectations regarding a member's attitude and task behavior within the group. At the most basic level, a group will have two roles: leader and member.

The greater the group's task complexity, the more roles will emerge. Group member agreement about the role to be performed is referred to as the **sent role**. The sent role is in essence the formal requirements of the role within the group. The **received role** is the role recipient's understanding of what the sent role means. In other words, the sent role may be received differently by different people. The **enacted role** is the manner in which the received role is expressed or redefined by the individual assuming the role.[17] This is how formal group expectations are transmitted, filtered, and processed for action by the role

sent role
The role expectations "sent" by group members regarding an individual's attitudes, beliefs, or behaviors.

received role
The role recipient's understanding of what the sent role means.

enacted role
The manner in which the role recipient actually expresses or redefines the received role.

TABLE 11–1	CHARACTERISTICS OF EFFECTIVE GROUPS

1. Group roles and expectations are understood by all group members.

2. Group members have developed a good working relationship.

3. Group members are attracted to the group and are loyal to the leader.

4. Members have a high degree of trust and confidence in one another.

5. Group activities such as decision making and problem solving occur in a supportive atmosphere.

6. The group leader's role is to create a supportive atmosphere in which group work occurs. The leader should (1) seek information from group members about decisions that will affect them and (2) provide information that they need to do their jobs better.

7. The group should attempt to develop each member's full potential.

8. An atmosphere that encourages members to influence each other should be maintained. Influence assures that new ideas enter the group and that dominant personalities work to the group's betterment.

9. The process for selecting a group leader should be based on the qualities that the individual brings to the group that encourage a supportive and open atmosphere.

10. Communication among members and the leader should be encouraged. If problems exist, free and open communication will bring problems to the surface.

Source: Adapted from Rensis Likert, *New Patterns of Management* (New York: McGraw-Hill, 1961), pp. 162–78.

occupant. We all have different backgrounds, values, education, and beliefs about how the job should be done. All these factors are brought to the forefront during role creation and enactment processes.

PROBLEMS IN ROLE MAKING - Role creation with groups is not without its share of problems. Common problems include role conflict, role ambiguity, and role overload.[18]

role conflict
Incompatibility between a role's requirements and the individual's own beliefs, attitudes, or expectations.

Role conflict represents the incompatibility between the role's requirements and the individual's own beliefs or expectations. Remember, we all assume multiple roles in many different aspects of our lives. For example, a worker could simultaneously hold the roles of mother, wife, devoted church leader, manager, and engineer. It is easy to see that many of these different roles have required behaviors that may conflict with one another.

Such internal conflict can come from a variety of sources. One source, *interrole conflict*, occurs when two different types of roles collide. A manager may have to fire an employee who is also a friend and the coach of his son's Little League team. The friend part of him doesn't want to fire the man, but his job requires him to do so. *Intrarole conflict* occurs when two similar roles come in conflict—for example, when your boss tells you to increase productivity and your workers are pushing for better working conditions. In this example, you are simultaneously a subordinate and a superior. Further, you believe that the organization needs greater productivity and also that the work rules make for dissatisfied and unmotivated workers. *Intersender conflict* occurs when contradictory messages come from the same source. Your boss preaches that quality is the most important aspect of your work. However, he insists on hiring low-skilled workers who can't fully utilize the robotics that are a major determinant of quality in the company. *Person-role conflict* occurs when an individual's beliefs are in direct conflict with the requirements of his or her role. For example, you know that a product batch is defective and shipping the products could possibly cause consumer injury and increase liability for the firm. You've also received a memo from your boss insisting your job is to help build sales volume by expediting the shipment of as many products as possible. You know shipping the product is wrong but you feel compelled to make your volume quota.

role ambiguity
A situation in which a role's actual behavioral requirements aren't clear. The role recipient doesn't understand what his actions or responsiblities are in his job.

In **role ambiguity**, role requirements are not clear. In general, role ambiguity results when the role occupant is not sure how to fulfill role requirements. Simple routine roles rarely generate ambiguity. In a routine role, such as an assembly line job, role requirements are specific or decision criteria are simple. Professional roles present a greater chance of role ambiguity. Managers often face a technical situation that they are not trained to fully understand, and they must decide to rely on a subordinate's judgment. The ambiguity for the manager is whether to consult a staff specialist (which might waste time) or go with the subordinate's judgment. The manager knows full well that he'll be held responsible regardless of a positive or a negative outcome.

role overload
A situation in which the role recipient is overwhelmed by the job's requirements.

Role overload is a condition where a task's demands overwhelm the role occupant's ability to perform the task. Too much, too little, or conflicting information may surpass the role occupant's ability to perform the task at a satisfactory level. With the emphasis on "lean organizations" and the corresponding reduction of America's white-collar workforce, it's very likely that role overload will be a common contributory symptom of role stress reported by those who remain.

Role conflict, role ambiguity, and role overload are all potential problems that can decrease a group's effectiveness. Managers must recognize the potential problems that can undermine a group's overall performance.

Group Norms

group norms
A set of expectations about how people are to act.

Group norms define the borders of acceptable member behavior. Usually within-group behavior is thought of as a positive force in group productivity. But norms can actually have a negative effect on group output. Take, for example, the restriction of output. A work group might easily produce 25 units an hour. yet if the group's strategy is to suppress output, then the norm enforces lower effort and lower output. Norms represent a form of control over intermittent or random behaviors by group members—be they positive or negative behaviors. However, norms are not developed for all situations or circumstances that the group might encounter, but only for those that hold some importance for the group. The group uses rewards and sanctions to encourage acceptance of the norm. Group members who adhere to the norm may receive praise or recognition for their devotion to group norms. Completing a project ahead of schedule may be rewarded with a Friday afternoon off.

Member acceptance of a norm is referred to as **conformity**. Conformity is important because it creates a system of shared values among both veteran group members and newcomers to the group. On the one hand, newcomers may be amazed by group performance or behavioral expectation.[19] New members quickly learn to meet group expectations if they want a good standing in the group. On the other hand, veteran members of the group help create and enforce group norms. Without group norms, the group's expectations would be vague at best. For this reason, groups with clear normative expectations are more effective at attaining group goals and in the process create greater member satisfaction than groups with comparatively limited normative guidance. Table 11–2 lists the purposes of common group norms and provides examples of situations where the norms are enforced. Group norms are communicated in one of four ways:

❖ By explicit statements by the group leader.
❖ By explicit statements by group members.
❖ By critical events in the group's history.
❖ From past group experiences.[20]

> **conformity**
> **The process by which members adopt group norms, roles, and behaviors.**

Most often group norms develop through efforts of the group leader. The leader communicates the group's wishes and values to new members and reinforces them with existing members. But the leader may not always be present in a norm-signaling situation. In this instance, co-workers may communicate the conformity to the group norm. For example, a member of the counter crew at a fast-food restaurant observes a co-worker's negative attitude toward customers. He might quickly take the worker aside and remind her that if the customer complained, the entire crew could be reprimanded for her poor attitude. If the rude worker fails to alter her inappropriate customer behavior, she might be shunned by other crew members until her behavior improved.

Another impetus for the development of group norms is a critical event in the group's history. Say, a group representative is outmaneuvered in a staff meeting to the group's disadvantage. This could force a group norm to develop regarding how ideas are presented to other groups to ensure a successful outcome for the group.

TABLE 11–2 CREATING NORMS IN ORGANIZATIONS	
Purpose of a Norm	Example in a Work Group
1. To facilitate group survival	The group informally sets productivity goals for the group to do a fair day's work but not much more.
2. To make work expectations clear	When overtime is available, rather than just asking who wants to work overtime and possibly being unfair, a seniority list is used to indicate who had it last and who is now eligible.
3. To help the group avoid embarrassment	Employees might be reprimanded in private and rewarded in public.
4. To express the group's basic values	A group of truck drivers might make it clear that drinking and partying are fun and normal but being convicted of driving under the influence will result in expulsion from the group.

Source: Adapted from Daniel C. Feldman, *Academy of Management Review* 9, no. 1 (1984), pp. 47–53.

Cohesiveness

cohesiveness
A measure of a group's ability to work well together. Cohesiveness is expressed through the group's ability to do its work effectively, attract new members as needed, influence one another, and maintain the group's integrity over time.

A group has **cohesiveness** to the extent that (1) the group can do its work effectively, attract new members when necessary, and maintain the group over time, and (2) members are able to influence one another.[21] Cohesiveness is a way of describing how well the group functions. Highly cohesive groups are good problem solvers. Further, in both work and social situations, members of cohesive groups interact more than people in less cohesive groups do.

By developing interaction skills, cohesive groups set the stage for greater success in social influence attempts. Social influence regulates deviation from accepted norms.[22] Group members can gang up on an individual member who is acting in ways the group believes conflict with group norms. For example, over a period of weeks, task group members on an auto assembly line might notice that one group member's "quality emphasis" is slipping. Each group member may pick a different time or example to encourage the deviant worker to rethink how he does his job. This type of positive social influence may well make the deviant worker aware of his actions and bring him closer to the group norm. But if the worker's behavior is intolerable to the group, the social influence may be shifted toward the group leader—perhaps to force the leader to fire the worker for nonconformity to the quality norm.

groupthink
The suppression or ignoring of countervailing ideas that represent a threat to group consensus or unanimity.

Group decision making is not without some degree of risk. Group norms and conformity tendencies may actually suppress opposing or contrary perspectives. Irving Janis called this concept groupthink. **Groupthink** is "a mode of thinking that people engage in when they are deeply involved in a cohesive in-group, when members' strivings for unanimity override their motivation to realistically appraise alternative courses of action."[23] Groupthink has been given as an explanation for the decision making that led to the Kennedy administration's disastrous 1961 Bay of Pigs invasion. In essence, groupthink means the suppression or ignoring of countervailing ideas that represent a threat to group consensus or unanimity. Unfortunately, when the group is wrong, group consensus doesn't mean very much in the long run. It is important to note, however, that within the same group, groupthink can occur during one decision-making situation and not another.[24]

Cultural Diversity

Groups are increasingly characterized by cultural diversity. Whether at work, at school, or during leisure time, cultural diversity exists in groups whose members differ from each other in important characteristics such as gender, age, ethnic background, disability status, religious affiliation, and lifestyle. The greater the number of these characteristics that are present, the more culturally diverse the group. As U.S. organizations turn to women and minorities to fill an estimated 83 percent of the jobs that will open up in the 1990s, cultural diversity in the workforce will reach an unprecedented high.[25] The growing globalization of organizations also contributes to increased diversity.

WHAT MANAGERS ARE READING

MANAGING WORKFORCE 2000

In their book *Managing Workforce 2000: Gaining the Diversity Advantage*, David Jamieson and Julie O'Mara point out the workplace challenges created by diversity. Not only do employees have ethnics and gender differences; they have differing skill and educational levels, ages, physical abilities, cultural backgrounds, lifestyles, values, and needs. The challenge to managers is to deal effectively with these differences, and to use them as a springboard to higher achievement.

The authors identify four management strategies for effectively managing the diverse workforce: matching people and jobs; managing and rewarding performance; informing and involving people; and supporting lifestyles and life needs. The authors illustrate how organizations such as Apple Computer, Federal Express, and McDonald's use these skills to deal with changes in the workforce.

Source: David Jamieson and Julie O'Mara, *Managing Workforce 2000* (San Francisco: Jossey-Bass Publishers, 1991).

Proactive management of cultural diversity can be a competitive advantage. At Ameritech, a Black Advocacy Panel reviews corporate policy on affirmative action and works to improve diversity at top levels.

Cultural diversity has several implications for groups. The varying rules and customs about relationships between genders, social class, or some other different group complicate interactions between group members. Research has generally shown that groups with a substantial degree of cultural diversity are not able to solve complex problems as effectively as homogeneous groups.[26] Many managers overlook the relationship between quality management and effective group interaction in a culturally diverse workplace. To interact productively in a diverse group it is necessary to respect other cultures and create new ways of integrating diverse groups and to expand the range of acceptable behaviors for accomplishing goals while maintaining quality standards.[27]

Managing diverse groups has become a critical challenge in corporate America, as firms that do not include diversity as part of their business plan will be at a competitive disadvantage.[28] For instance, one study found that firms receiving Department of Labor recognition for exemplary affirmative action programs are better able to recruit, develop, and maintain human resources, providing a competitive advantage.[29] Several approaches have been used to enhance cooperation and communication among culturally diverse groups, including: multicultural workshops; female and minority support groups and networks; managerial reward systems based on managers' ability to train and promote women and minorities; fast-track programs targeted at women and minorities who demonstrate exceptional potential; and mentoring programs pairing women and minorities with senior managers.[30] At Ameritech, for example, the Black Advocacy Panel was formed to review corporate policy on affirmative action and works to improve diversity at top levels.[31]

A MODEL OF EFFECTIVE
SMALL GROUP INTERACTION

Research on group dynamics indicates that group effectiveness is best understood using a model that describes the inputs, processes, and outputs of group interaction.[32] *Group input* consists of group structure, group strategies, leadership, and rewards. The structure of the group includes the members' personalities and abilities plus the overall size of the group. The group structure dictates what the group can accomplish. The group strategy clarifies, among several action plans, the one that the group intends to use to achieve its goals. For example, a group that wants to increase quality may use a strategy that intentionally slows down the production process to allow workers more time to complete their tasks. The final inputs are leadership and rewards. The leadership of the group must support and facilitate the group's overall strategy and goals, provide resources, communicate vertically, and reward performance.

Rewards are one motivation for a group member to work in unison with the group. Although extrinsic rewards such as money and promotions are important on an individual level, group rewards serve as a powerful motivating force. Group recognition may be equally important to an individual. We have all seen sporting events where a player on the winning team reports an incredible feeling of accomplishment even though her individual contribution to winning the final game was minor. And the images at NASA mission control of a successful spacecraft landing tell a similar story of pride in group membership and achieving a difficult goal. Similarly, on an everyday level, work groups revel in their daily successes, knowing that their contributions made a difference. Table 11–3 presents a model of small group interaction.

The inputs define how the *group process* of the work group will unfold. Three separate processes occur in all work groups: influence, group development, and decision making. The process of *influence* is a necessary and important part of the overall well-being of the group. Particularly in autonomous work groups or self-managing work groups, mutual influence allows all members access to change other members' minds or challenge unrealistic assumptions. But not all influence is productive. "Social loafing" and "free riding" occur when one group member does less work than others, knowing full well that his contribution will be hidden in the group effort.[33] Mutual influence should be viewed as inevitable and healthy. *Group development* describes the process of activities, interactions, and sentiments that occur as time passes. A major part of group development is the attachment and identification to the group. For example, wearing union jackets or company clothing outside of the work environment indicate pride and group identity. Further, members quickly learn that not all groups are equal. Those groups that provide an opportunity for enjoyable and productive work are valued by members and nonmembers alike.

Quality products, reasonable quantity, and satisfied group members are all *group outputs*. From a managerial perspective, it is important to think about the human component of quality as a quite different concept than the statistical notion of quality. In an environment where groups are the primary productive unit, quality is largely a function of how well the group interacts on a continual basis. Similarly, a group that has been recognized

TABLE 11–3	A MODEL OF SMALL GROUP INTERACTION

Inputs ⟶	Processes ⟶	Outcomes
Group structure	Influence	Group performance
Group strategies	Development	Quality
Leadership	Decision making	Quantity
		Quality of group life
		Integrity of the group in the future

Source: Adapted from Marilyn E. Gist, Edwin A. Locke, and M. Susan Taylor, "Organization Behavior: Group Structure, Process, and Effectiveness," *Journal of Management* 13, no. 2 (1987), pp. 237–57.

TO TEAM OR NOT TO TEAM: THAT IS THE QUESTION

Over the past decade the team concept has been an important component of many effective organizations. Successful use of teams requires a well-articulated plan. Redesigning the organization to house the team concept is a five-step process. First, organize the physical work setting to support group activity. Second, create organizational structures and job designs that promote skill expansion and cooperation of interdependent tasks. Third, pay people enough so that lack of money is not a constant irritant. Fourth, attract and select the best employees. Fifth, clearly communicate high expectations to new employees. But the key is to view these five steps as an integrated system that produces high-quality products with minimal resources.

With the introduction of the restyled Accord in the early 1980s, Honda Motor Company became a dominant competitor in the U.S. auto market. Over the past decade Honda's success has included being the first Japanese firm to build cars in the United States, the first Japanese automaker to enter the luxury car market (Accura), and the first Japanese automaker to produce the best-selling car in the United States (Accord). Honda's success in the U.S. market has been attributed to its reliance on Japanese management techniques used at its Marysville, Ohio, production facility. The centerpiece of the Japanese management philosophy is the team concept. The team concept was used for decision making from the shop floor to the executive offices.

Recently Honda's sales have slowed. Consumers complain that Hondas are bland, underpowered vehicles. These complaints seem somewhat ironic considering Honda's longstanding involvement in international Grand Prix auto racing. While still successful, Honda recognized that it may have outgrown the traditional Japanese management team concepts. Nobuhiko Kawamoto, Honda's president since 1990, expressed concern that Honda has gotten conservative and sluggish. It suffers from group decision-making paralysis. Too many voices yield slow decisions. The solution appears to be more centralized decision making.

During the same time period, Hewlett-Packard (HP) experienced problems similar to Honda's. These problems were manifest in an inability to bring new products to market in a timely manner. The demon seed was a decentralized cluster of three dozen committees that oversaw the development of all new products. This formal group decision-making structure included too many different groups with too many decisions, resulting in slow new-product development. CEO John Young engineered a sweeping management reorganization to quickly get products into consumers' hands. The reorganization cut many middle management jobs. Removing two entire layers of management reduced costs and time-to-market. HP found that rather than eliminating the team concept, what it needed was more groups rather than fewer groups. But each group would be smaller, more flexible, and more responsive to market requirements. HP formed a structure of smaller groups that were much closer to the action. In this way, HP management pushed decision making to the lowest levels. Smaller design teams linked to purchasing, production, and marketing were formed to develop new products. Results include a successful new matchbox-sized Kittyhawk disk drive. Unlike Honda, HP solved its decentralization problems with more streamlined decentralization rather than less. In the past, popular wisdom held that jobs could be designed either to maximize productivity or to maximize employee satisfaction. The great potential of teams is that this trade-off may be avoided in designing work. However, while diversity is a great side benefit of work teams, how they impact the bottom line is the real incentive for companies to use them.

Source: Adapted from Michael A. Campion and A. Catherine Higgs, "Design Work Teams to Increase Productivity and Satisfaction," *HR Magazine*, October 1995, pp. 101–107; "How Team Work Can Pay Off," *Black Enterprise*, June 1995, p. 234; Clay Chandler and Paul Ingrassia, "Just as U.S. Firms Try Japanese Management, Honda Is Centralizing," *The Wall Street Journal*, April 11, 1991, p. 1; Robert D. Hof, "From Dinosaur to Gazelle," *Business Week*, special edition, "Reinventing the Corporation," 1992, p. 65; and Ernesto J. Poza and M. Lynne Markus, "Success Story: The Team Approach to Work Restructuring," *Organizational Dynamics* 8 (Winter 1980), pp. 3–25.

for producing high-quality products is also likely to be collectively satisfied with life at work. A final group outcome is cohesiveness. For all practical purposes, the highly effective group is one with high levels of outcomes. The Global Exchange takes a closer look at the effectiveness of teams.

IMPLEMENTING WORK TEAMS

One strong theme that runs throughout the Deming quality philosophy is the need for teams and teamwork. According to Deming, teamwork is needed throughout the company. The aim of a team is to improve the input and the output of any stage of operations.[34]

Teams are an essential part of a lean production system in which workers are directly employed in producing products, while fewer supervisors, inspectors, and planners oversee workers. In the lean production system, smaller, "strong" teams are responsible for and able to control the entire production process. Adopting a team approach, Corning Glass eliminated one management level at its corporate computer center, substituting a team adviser for three shift supervisors. This saved $150,000 annually and raised the quality of customer service. Corning found increases in autonomy and responsibility among workers, who experienced more meaningful and productive work.[35] In another instance, a change to automation led to a shift from a functional organizational design to self-managed teams in an insurance firm. This change required the company to reorganize to support organizational goals, not simply work unit goals. A 24-month follow-up report found improved work structure, flows, and outcomes.[36]

Three main features of self-managed teams include (1) extensive worker control over operating decisions, especially those traditionally made by supervisors, foremen, and quality inspectors; (2) high levels of feedback from the work itself (e.g., self-charting, on-line computerized reports); and (3) cross-training so each worker can perform many functions (i.e., job despecialization).[37]

Developing Team-Driven Companies

Consulting group McKinsey & Company has identified a plan for developing flatter, team-driven companies.[38] The McKinsey Plan includes the following:

❖ *Organize around processes rather than task.* Performance objectives should be based on customer needs such as service. The processes that meet those needs should be the major components of the company.

❖ *Flatten the hierarchy by grouping subprocesses.* Teams should be arranged in parallel, with each doing many steps in a process, not a series of teams with each doing a few steps.

❖ *Give leaders responsibility for processes and process performance.* Self-managed teams are responsible for multiple tasks. Team members possess a set of skills relevant to the groups' tasks, and have discretion over the methods of work, task schedules, assignment of members to different tasks, compensation, and feedback about performance for the group as a whole.[39]

❖ *Link performance objectives and evaluation of all activities to customer satisfaction.* Everything should be driven by the customer; successful performance also means customers have been satisfied.

❖ *Assign performance objectives to teams, not individuals.* This makes teams the focus of organizational performance and design. Individuals cannot continuously improve quality and work flows.

❖ *Assign managerial tasks to teams as much as possible.* Workers' teams should be responsible for activities such as hiring, evaluating, and scheduling.

❖ *Emphasize the need for workers to develop several competencies.* In a team-driven company, only a few specialists are needed. Productivity can be increased by asking the team to take on more difficult tasks and asking team members to serve as consultants to other teams.[40]

❖ *Train team members on a just-in-time, need-to-perform basis.* Information should go directly to those who can use it in their jobs. Trained and empowered workers know how to use information.

❖ *Put team members in touch with customers.* Field trips and spots on problem-solving teams can bring team members closer to customers. Knowledge of customer needs are then reflected in team work.

❖ *Reward skill development and team performance.* Performance evaluation should focus on team achievements rather than individual achievements. It is counterproductive to talk about teamwork while evaluating and rewarding individuals.

As you can see, in a team-driven organization, work is designed around customers, not tasks. Senior managers are responsible for processes that are critical to satisfying customers. Self-directed work teams make decisions regarding hiring, scheduling, and so on. (The Ethics Spotlight examines how teams can go too far.) Fewer people are needed between senior managers and work teams, and their job is to facilitate, not control. This, in part, explains why so many mid-level management positions are being phased out in companies today.

ETHICS SPOTLIGHT **WHEN TEAMS GO TOO FAR**

Much has been written about the value of work teams, yet many firms remain reluctant to implement them. In the early 1990s self-managed work teams accounted for about 7 percent of the workforce. Self-managed work teams bring a new voice to the decision process. But greater decision-making input isn't always required or even wise. Relatively simple or routine jobs are not likely candidates for self-managed teams. When the task is sufficiently complicated, self-managed work teams have proven highly successful. Perhaps the greatest benefit of self-managed work teams is their ability to quickly solve problems where they originate. In essence, self-managed work teams provide the group with real-time control over work decisions. But regardless of the task or purpose of the team, most successful work teams share the characteristic of high-quality facilitation.

Common decisions that confront self-managed work teams include rewards, reprimands, task assignments, work scheduling, and performance evaluation. Normally group governance is achieved through a democratic process. A leader is elected from the group's membership and conflicts are resolved through unanimity. Although they have little formal training in management, team leaders are responsible for monitoring group activities and representing the group to other parts of the organization. All this sounds rather idyllic, but self-managing is still controlling other people's behavior. Rather than external control imposed by a formal management group, control is achieved through internal group consensus monitored by an internal process with a designated team leader serving as a facilitator.

Recently Peters Control Inc. organized all production workers into 20 ten-member, self-managed work teams. Each team leader reviews his team's quarterly sick leave report, which also includes year-to-date absences. While reviewing the absenteeism report for the control systems group, the team leader was reminded that Jon Anders had been absent a total of 5 to 10 working days in each of the past three quarters. At the team's next quality circle meeting he discussed the issue with all team members present. All agreed that other team members had to work more or harder to compensate for Jon's absences. The team leader asked Jon what he thought about the situation. Jon responded with a statement and a question: "Isn't my work above average? At least, that's what my [team-based] performance evaluation indicated! And, have I exceeded my allowable number of sick leave days? If I haven't exceeded my allowable sick leave days, I'm just using a benefit that I'm entitled to." Jon's reply wasn't defensive but factual. Indeed, most who knew him well sensed that he really was sick.

After the meeting several team members expressed regrets about how Jon had been treated. Clearly they believed that he had done nothing to warrant a reprimand by the team. Embarrassed for being singled out for what clearly was a disciplinary action by the self-managed team, Jon kept to himself as much as possible. But he confided to a close friend that this type of situation never happened with the traditional management structure. Jon believed that self-managed teams can create as many problems as they solve.

Source: Adapted from Kristin K. Reiste and Al Hubrich, "How to Implement Successful Work Teams," *National Productivity Review*, Autumn 1995, pp. 45–55; Greg Burns, "The Secrets of Team Facilitation," *Training and Development*, June 1995, pp. 46–52; Brian Dumaine, "Who Needs a Boss," *Fortune*, May 7, 1990, pp. 52–60; Charles Manz and Henry Sims, *Superleadership: Leading Others to Lead Themselves*: (Englewood Cliffs, N.J.: Prentice Hall, 1989), and David Barry, "Managing a Bossless Team: Lessons in Distributed Leadership," *Organizational Dynamics*.

Overcoming Resistance to Teamwork

The transition to teams isn't always easy. Certain environmental and technological conditions are more likely to be conducive to team development. For example, a newly built plant with a just-hired work force (a "greenfield" operation) can be more open to teams than an established plant with long-employed workers. Also a still-developing, uncertain technology may lend itself to the team concept more than a rigid, sequential technology. In either case, effective leadership can help teamwork succeed.[41]

Many problems encountered when building teams include: confusing team building with teamwork; haphazard team planning; starting teams before assessing team needs; training team members individually; and not making teams accountable.[42] Team members also have a tendency to become so intent on some of the group's issues, they forget effective team processes.[43] Team members have to be trained not only to get along, but also to work together as a team. A system for planning team work must be developed. First, team needs should be defined; then team members should be trained as a team. Teams must also be accountable for what they've learned in training and what they do at work. Teams flourish when managers make room for spontaneity, value speaking out, encourage intellectual exchange, and select self-motivated people.[44]

In addition, delegating more responsibility to teams can mean fewer managers. Middle management is often the primary target for staff reduction when the team approach is implemented. A shift to teams and flatter organizations may reduce managers' opportunities for advancement. Yet an emphasis on seniority in some Japanese firms often provides managerial opportunities for a significant percentage of employees. At Kobe Steel, for instance, about 95 percent of all employees are promoted to a managerial job during the course of their career.[45]

Opponents of quality work teams have even gone to court to challenge their use.[46] The International Association of Machinists (IAM) and the United Auto Workers (UAW) have severely criticized worker involvement in teams, arguing that teams undermine labor unions' traditional role. Teams, they claim, threaten a union's very existence by posing a long-term threat to workers' job security and other union benefits. Teams resolving grievances, disciplining workers, and awarding pay raises threaten traditional labor union power and roles.

The quality management approach to teamwork can be summarized as follows: (1) empower workers to solve problems and make decisions, (2) cultivate the natural sense of pride in doing a good job, (3) view management as the process of creating an organizational system made up of self-managed teams, and (4) share the financial successes resulting from the use of the team method via formal organizational recognition and rewards. The introduction of quality management programs does not appear to have an adverse effect on teamwork.[47] Teams are a primary source of continuous improvement and a cornerstone of quality management.

THE WORKPLACE OF TOMORROW

Organizations will increasingly utilize groups as they continue to downsize. Work at many companies, at least those that remain after outsourcing, will require workers to be even more empowered. Job security is diminishing and pay raises do not come as frequently. While not a panacea, the team-based approach overcomes some of these shortcomings by making jobs more interesting; workers see a larger picture and are motivated by co-workers.[48]

In the years ahead, workers will also be evaluated more and more as a group. Performance will be based on group productivity, and group members will be expected to improve their skills and help others perform better. Rewards will be based on group performance rather than individual performance, and the entire group will be held accountable for its actions. Teams will establish their own identity by devising their own name and by promoting personal relationships.[49] In short, the emphasis in groups will be promotiong cooperative teamwork.

The workplace of tomorrow will be even more diverse than today's. By the year 2000, white males will represent 45 percent of the workforce, a drop from the current 51 percent. Yet human resource experts estimate that only 3 percent to 5 percent of U.S. corporations are diversifying their workforces effectively.[50] As corporate leaders begin to realize the impact of diverse groups on their organizations, their commitment to diversity will become much stronger. This means increased resources allocated for diversity training—for recruiting, training, and retaining qualified workers with diverse backgrounds. Managers will learn that a diversified workforce will be a major asset in the 21st century.

SUMMARY OF LEARNING OBJECTIVES

DESCRIBE THE VARIOUS TYPES OF INFORMAL AND FORMAL GROUPS TYPICALLY FOUND IN ORGANIZATIONS.

Informal groups include both friendship groups and interest groups. As the name implies, we join friendship groups to interact with people with whom we share common ideas or values. Interest groups include people who share common interests or ideas but aren't necessarily friends. Political group affiliation exemplifies an interest group where members express similar beliefs and interests but might not be friends.

EXPLAIN HOW THE FOUR STAGES OF GROUP DEVELOPMENT INFLUENCE THE CREATION OF AN EFFECTIVE GROUP.

The four stages of group development are forming, storming, norming, and performing. Forming is the actual beginnings of the group, when the members get to know one another and understand each other's abilities and deficits. During storming, the group comes to grips with inherent conflicts and develops solutions that keep it focused on its work. Norming is the group process of charting out the group's long-term vision and purpose. In this stage rewards, sanctions, and rules of behavior are established. Performing is the stage where the group works like a well-oiled machine. Group members understand their role in the group and perform their job effectively.

DISCUSS VARIOUS CHARACTERISTICS OF GROUPS, INCLUDING ROLE MAKING, GROUP NORMS, AND COHESIVENESS.

Role making (the process of developing the various roles of group members) consists of understanding role development and role communication. Group norms define the borders of acceptable member behavior. Positive group member behavior is rewarded; negative group member behavior is sanctioned or punished. Cohesiveness connotes the group's ability to attract new members, maintain itself over time, and influence its members.

DESCRIBE THE THREE PARTS OF THE MODEL OF EFFECTIVE SMALL GROUP INTERACTION.

Group input consists of group structure, group strategies, and leadership. *Group processes* consist of influence, development, and decision making. *Group output* consists of group performance (quality, quantity, quality of group life, and the integrity of the group in the future).

LIST THE ACTIVITIES NEEDED TO DEVELOP TEAM-DRIVEN COMPANIES.

The following activities are necessary for developing team-driven companies: organize around processes rather than tasks; flatten the hierarchy by grouping sub-processes; give leaders responsibility for processes and process performance; link performance objectives and evaluation of all activities to customer satisfaction; assign performance objectives to teams, not individuals; assign managerial tasks to teams as much as possible; emphasize the need for workers to develop several competencies; train team members on a just-in-time, need-to-perform basis; put team members in touch with customers; and reward skill development and team performance.

DISCUSS SOME OF THE PROBLEMS ENCOUNTERED WHEN BUILDING TEAMS.

Problems encountered when building teams include confusing team building with team work; haphazard team planning; starting teams before assessing team needs; training team members individually; and not making teams accountable.

KEY TERMS

cohesiveness, p. 302	groupthink, p. 302	role conflict, p. 300
conformity, p. 301	informal group, p. 294	role overload, p. 300
enacted role, p. 299	norming, p. 298	sent role, p. 299
formal group, p. 294	performing, p. 298	shared values, p. 298
forming, p. 298	quality circle, p. 297	storming, p. 298
group, p. 294	received role, p. 299	work group, p. 295
group norms, p. 300	role ambiguity, p. 300	

DISCUSSION AND APPLICATION QUESTIONS

Recall

1. What are the basic differences between a group and a team?
2. Define role ambiguity, role conflict, and role overload.
3. Name ways you would avoid possible obstacles to team success.

Understanding

4. How are the terms *conformity, cohesiveness,* and *norms* used in group development?
5. *In Search of Excellence* authors Peters and Waterman describe the need for each worker to feel simultaneously like an important individual and like a member of an organization. They call this a sense of "duality," wanting to experience both individuality and integration with the whole. What's your belief about this issue?
6. The traditional view of the group has been that management must control the group's tendency to restrict production and even to protect poor performers. The quality-based team approach effectively reverses those assumptions. How do you explain this change of perspective on work groups or teams?

Do traditional views still apply in some countries, industries, or firms?

7. The model of small group interaction could be described as a "systems" view of group interaction. Explain what it means to describe group interaction as a system.

Application

8. Select a department in an organization (e.g., human resources, sales, or accounting) and describe how the model of small group interaction discussed in this chapter influences group interaction in that organization.
9. Examine your past experiences as a member of a group and discuss your experiences with role conflict, role ambiguity, and role overload.
10. Discuss how the term *storming* can apply to a specific group development situation. Be specific, and provide an example of a real organizational situation.

Workers then trained suppliers in SPC, continuous flow manufacturing, and the design of work experiments to improve quality.

Education became an investment, not a cost. "Ownership" of the education function moved from the educational staff function to the customers—IBM managers who told the education staff what was needed, what worked, and what didn't work.

Training focused on quality information and processes as well as on specific, job-related training. With this two-pronged approach, workers received fundamental training in quality ideas, theories, and techniques plus help with improving specific concerns and processes on the job. The mix of theory and practice helped increase revenue per employee 35 percent from 1986 to 1989.

QUESTIONS

1. How might a team be involved in the benchmarking process?
2. Recommend some things that management could do to get workers to think in terms of team success rather than individual success.
3. What are the basic training needs of a team?

Source: H. G. Eyrich, "Benchmarking to Become the Best of the Breed," *Manufacturing Systems*, April 1991, pp. 40-47; Karen Bemowski, "Big Q at Big Blue," *Quality Progress*, May 1991, pp. 17-21; Brad Stratton, "Four to Receive 1990 Baldrige Awards," *Quality Progress*, pp. 19-21; and *Margaret Kaeter*, "Quality Training," *Quality*, March 1991, pp. 15-25.

CASE STUDY

IKEA

Swedish furniture retailer IKEA ("eye-key-ah") moved into the American market in 1985, bringing a unique approach to selling furniture. IKEA not only provides customers with tape measures, catalogs, pencil, and paper; it also provides them with child care and free diapers, and lends them roof racks for carrying furniture home on their car roofs. By 1989 IKEA's $350 of sales per square foot was triple that of traditional furniture stores.

But while in some ways IKEA helps customers shop, it also cuts costs by making customers pick out their merchandise, then pull unassembled pieces off the racks in the warehouse, and finally haul the pieces to their cars. By 1989 IKEA's U.S. sales reached $130 million, contributing to the furniture giant's $3 billion in global sales.

IKEA first opened its doors in Sweden in 1953. Founder Ingvar Kamprad combined his initials with those of his farm (Elmtaryd) and parish (Agunnaryd) to form the unique name. Now with over 89 stores in 21 countries, IKEA is recognized by its bright blue-and-yellow buildings. A media blitz of catalogs and billboards gets its word out. The key to adapting to foreign ownership is keeping the lines of communication open. IKEA established a global international telecommunication (IT) steering board made up of seven IT managers, who set technical standards for the company's operation around the world.

The key to foreign ownership is keeping the lines of communication open. IKEA established a global international telecommunications (IT) steering board made up of seven IT managers, who set technical standards for the company's operations around the world.

IKEA has a fundamental value: to offer well-styled, high-quality, reasonably priced home furnishings within the context of a comfortable—even pleasurable—shopping experience. IKEA has 1,800 suppliers in 45 countries; about 90 percent of the inventory is exclusive, conceived in Sweden by 20 in-house designers. Customers get immediate value, not family heirlooms. "You get what you pay for," says the editor of a bargain buyer newsletter. "IKEA sells mass-market merchandise that's good design at inexpensive prices. But it's not going to last forever."

IKEA's no-nonsense, low-price approach satisfies customers with immediate gratification in a business where deliveries can often take six weeks. And salespeople don't pressure. Instead, customers can test product samples on the floor. Not all products are in stock. IKEA's U.S. president admits, "Not having enough merchandise in stock is our No. 1 problem. Also, Nos. 2 and 3." And sales assistance is scarce. Yet, as one customer concludes, "It's probably the best value for the quality it offers."

One way IKEA cuts costs is to cut space. Buying in volume from low-cost manufacturers around the world, IKEA saves on shipping and warehouse costs by packing components in flat boxes; even pillows and comforters are compressed and vacuum-packed. This low-space packaging saves 20 to 30 percent of the cost of the product. Prices are breathtakingly low on everything every day in every location—25 to 50 percent lower than comparable quality elsewhere. Bookcases sell for $39, sofa beds for $149, and sets of dishes for $13. Their global top-seller is a two-foot-by-four-foot rag rug.

IKEA follows four fundamental principles:

❖ *Satisfy universal customer needs*, not only with products, but also with services. Products designed to save space and services designed to help parents with young children while they shop are popular around the world.

❖ *Listen to customers for local concerns.* Americans like water fountains at the front of the store and ice for beverages. And larger American cars need larger parking spots and more room to maneuver through a parking lot. In America, cars come to the loading dock, while Europeans take products to their cars.

❖ *Start small and expand slowly.* IKEA used the New York and Los Angeles areas as its two primary U.S. markets, but began outside the big cities to test its ideas in towns like Pittsburgh and Burbank.

❖ *Build support systems for local stores.* The New York and Los Angeles markets have separate support systems. As one IKEA executive says, "You have to organize yourself very close to the customer. You can't support stores in Los Angeles in the right way from the East Coast."

IKEA Cooks, a new store that focuses on one home furnishing segment at a time, opened in Manhattan in September 1995. For the grand opening, the store was filled with cookware and kitchen cabinets. In early 1996 the store was redesigned with a totally new theme.

QUESTIONS

1. Identify reasons why people would and wouldn't like to shop at IKEA.
2. Can inexpensive products be described as "quality" products? Can a company provide customers with limited services and be considered a "quality" company?
3. Do Americans perceive products differently because they're judged to be Scandinavian in design or production? What are some features customers associate with Scandinavian products?

Source: Adapted from Dawn Wilensky, "IKEA N.Y.'s Ever-Changing Face," *Discount Store News*, October 2, 1995, pp. 6–37; Anne Stuart, "My Owner Lies Over the Ocean," *CIO*, October1, 1995, p. 39; Janet Blamford, "Why Competitors Shop for Ideas at IKEA," *Business Week*, October 19, 1990, p. 88; Barbara Solomon, "A Swedish Company Corners the Business," *Management Review*, April 1991, pp. 10–13; and Diane Harris, "Money's Store of the Year," *Money*, December 1990, pp. 144–150.

VIDEO CASE

Groups and Teams at Southwest Airlines

If most work situations have one thing in common it's probably the use of groups and teams to achieve goals. In fact, one of a supervisor's primary responsibilities is to ensure that their group or team works together effectively. For a supervisor to be an effective leader of a group or team it's important to understand how these units operate in the workplace. Supervisors should also note the general characteristics of groups and teams and be familiar with some basic guidelines that will make their group or team work more effectively.

Southwest Airlines is one example of a company the knows the value of groups and teamwork because its operations depend on them. As the nation's seventh largest domestic airline, Southwest is the only airline to ever win the coveted triple crown based on statistics from the department of transportation, Air Travel, and Consumer Reports. The latter honor recognized Southwest as having the best reported on-time performance of a major airline since the inception of the award in 1987. The report also recognized Southwest for having the best baggage handling record and the fewest customer complaints for 1992.

Chris Wahlenmaier, station manager for Southwest, said, "It's vital to our operation to have groups to respond to the various functions that we require as an operation as vast as ours to get the job done well and to do it as productively as we do. We have to break our workers down into groups as we have ramp agents that respond to a taxiing air craft when it comes in. For example, we've got our operation agents that put together weight and balance forms for us so that the aircraft is properly loaded."

A group is simply defined as two or more people who interact with one another, are aware of one another, and think of themselves as being a group. A company is in and of itself a very large group, but most employees cluster into smaller groups. These groups can be categorized in one of many ways. A "task group" is a group set up to carry out a specific activity then disband when the activity is completed. A committee formed to develop a company wide safety policy is one example of a task group.

A "functional group," on the other hand, is one that fulfills an organization's ongoing needs by performing a particular function—ramp agents, pilots groups, and customer service agents are some examples of functional groups at Southwest. A Southwest ramp agent group is a good example of a function oriented group. It was set up by management to carry out a specific function. In this case, to taxi an airplane to the gate, load and unload the plane, and prepare the plane for departure. The group varies in size depending on availability but always consists of at least two people.

Laura Rollheiser, supervisor of ramp agents, said, "The technical side of turning around a plane is you figure you only have like at least fifteen to twenty minutes. It starts with the lead agent who plans the load and gets the gate set up. When the plane pulls into the gate there's one guy flagging him in, there's another one ready to chock, there's another one pulling off the belt. That's teamwork to the max. You can't beat that. It's just everybody is so good at what they do here and they all know what they're supposed to do and that's why we can have such a quick turn time. I mean it's just that efficient."

While a group is simply two or more people interacting with each other, a team is a group of people with a diverse set of backgrounds who bring their individual talents and experience together to achieve a common goal. When Southwest lands a plane it relies on teamwork from a variety of work groups to complete the turnaround. Before landing, the pilot contacts the station operations department for gate parking position. At this time, the pilot will request assistance from maintenance personnel if service is needed. After the plane lands and is safely parked at the terminal the fueling personnel fuel the aircraft. Ramp agents begin unloading luggage, air mail, and air freight. The provisioning agents retrieve waste and recyclable material off the aircraft and restock the galleys with beverages, snacks, and other supplies. Once all customers, luggage, air freight, air mail, and provisions are securely loaded on the aircraft the operations agent completes the weight and balance calculations. Finally the ramp agents push the aircraft away from the terminal, disconnect the push back and tow bar from the aircraft, and direct the pilot to the taxi way for departure to the next destination.

This teamwork approach requires the work groups to constantly interact so they can achieve the common goal landing the plane and preparing it for it's next destination. Southwest is so effective in it's use of teamwork that it leads the industry in plane turnaround by averaging an astounding 15 minutes from landing to departure. The industry average is nearly double that.

Another example of teamwork is demonstrated when representatives from various areas of the company come together to achieve a common goal. Southwest utilized this approach with several cross-functional committees which were set up to help the airline tackle a variety of objectives. The culture committee which looked for ways to enhance employee morale is one example.

So how can supervisors capitalize on the potential benefits of teams and work groups? One important step is to make sure all members of the group understand the group's objectives and responsibilities. Lou Freeman, supervisor of pilots, described how Southwest creates effective teams, "Southwest empowers all of it's employees to make decisions on a ground level, basically. If you're doing the job and a situation comes up where you have to make a call, Southwest lets you make that call without being second guessed later on. As long as you make a call in good faith it's okay."

Besides communicating the expectations of the company, the supervisor should also keep the group or team informed about what's happening in the organization and any changes that may be planned in the future. This lets members know that they're important to the organization. Supervisors should also support the group or team when it wants to bring legitimate concerns to higher management. But they must be careful to do so without cultivating an us-versus-them mentality. Chris Wahlenmaier offered his observations on the role of supervisors at Southwest: "As supervisors, we try to lead by example. We try to be out there with employees. If there's a job that needs to be done we want to be working along side of them. Show them that we're there for them in whatever capacity that may be. That's what our function is to do and we're there for them all the time."

To make the most of a work group or team's potential the supervisor must not be afraid to draw on the diversity of strength and experiences from all members. To help stimulate high-quality performance from their group or team, a supervisor should help the other members achieve their personal best. They can do this by coaching employees and encouraging them. Knowing when to let members solve problems on their own and when to pull them back on track. Bob Rushlow, maintenance superintendent, talked about this balancing act: "Most of the time at Southwest here in our maintenance department the mechanics handle most of the things that come up. If something happens where we are on an extended delay, I personally get involved at times. I have a night supervisor that gets involved on our night problems. If need be we get everybody in the company involved to fix an airplane if it's a severe enough problem."

Rewarding a group or team for a job well done is an extremely important motivator, but the supervisor should be sure to recognize the entire group or team effort not just individual achievements. James Story, manager of ramp operations, spoke about Southwest's recognition system:"We try and commend the employees on a daily basis. When a job is done well, we make a point to go and tell an agent that you have done an excellent job and we appreciate it. Doing that goes a long way in recognizing an agent and when it comes time for them to put out that extra effort, they do so because they feel like they are appreciated. They feel like they are part of something."

Groups and teams are a very effective way of utilizing the strengths and experiences of many employees to achieve a variety of goals. This not only helps the company but also serves as a tremendous motivator. In fact members of groups and teams tend to take on more responsibility and are generally more enthusiastic about their work. In most cases it's up to the supervisor to see that group and team members realize their maximum potential. They can do this by understanding the different types of groups that operate in the work place: task and function oriented groups, as well as formal and informal groups. Supervisors should understand the dynamics of team work and the basic guidelines that help make a work group or team more effective.

When supervisors effectively utilize the inherent potential of their groups and teams they will help their organization reach and surpass many of its goals. The use of work groups and teams has helped Southwest prosper in a highly competitive industry. In a time when several other airlines have been forced to declare bankruptcy, Southwest has remained profitable every year since 1972. Southwest has also been cited as one of the ten best companies to work for in America. Chris Wahlenmaier, said,"Southwest is famous for recognizing employees just through small gifts or whatever. Employees will get stuff through the mail or they get a birthday card on their birthday from the company. It's little things like that that say 'thank you for what you do' because they're the ones that make the difference. And as long we're telling them 'thank you' and 'we appreciate what you've done for Southwest Airlines and our customers' we're going to continue to win triple crowns like we've done in the past ."

QUESTIONS

1. This video tape discussed the virtues of work groups and teams. Managers who use the team approach should structure rewards for teams rather than individuals. Discuss some possible ways managers can recognize and reward groups and teams.
2. Define work group. Explain the difference between a task group and a functional group.
3. Define a work place team.

APPLICATION EXERCISE

FLEXIBLE WORK SCHEDULES

In the national operations department of a large insurance firm, 120 information associates (IAs) and five section supervisors work in five sections in the department that processes customer files, written and phone inquiries, and billing checks. IAs handle customer claims from all over the United States; they read mail requests, and access and file information. Most of it is done at video display terminals. The department operates on a 40-hour schedule, from 8:30 AM to 5 PM, central time, Monday through Friday, 52 weeks a year, with nine holidays.

Of the 120 IAs, 99 are women; 42 of the women are single parents. The typical IA is 27 years old with over two years in the department and a high school diploma. Their average pay is $395 per week with an above-average benefits package. (The 1994 U.S. average is about $410 in salary plus an additional 40 percent in benefits.) In the past year 28 IAs were hired to replace workers who quit; another 8 were needed to replace fired workers who had poor performance and/or attendance records.

Daily absenteeism averages 7 percent; it is higher than 7 percent on Fridays and Mondays, but lower at midweek. Employees are allowed four days of paid absence before they are judged to be absent without pay. Few IAs exceed this four-day limit, although over 75 percent of IAs use all four days. Four to eight IAs are late by 20 minutes or more each day; requests for discretionary time off during the day are common. A new hire costs about $6,900 to locate (with ads in the newspaper), interview, hire, train, and bring up to speed, based on the company's own analysis of its historic costs of hiring.

Some employees have proposed a schedule with more flexible work hours (FWH). The basic considerations for FWH include: band hours (earliest start and latest finish times for each workday; e.g., 5 AM and 8 PM); core hours (times when all IAs must be present e.g., 10 AM and 2 PM); the days and hours of the possible workweek; banking (storing up work hours in exchange for later time off); the degree of employee choice and variability in scheduling hours; and supervisor's role in managing these features (e.g., scheduling, record keeping).

You've been asked to develop a proposal that satisfies the needs of the company and its employees. State your general strategy, specific priorities, and recommended plan of action to address these concerns. You may be asked to represent one side and negotiate an agreement.

CHAPTER 12

Motivation

After studying this chapter, you should be able to:

❖ Define motivation.

❖ Explain the process of motivation.

❖ Compare content, process, and reinforcement theories of motivation.

❖ Describe Maslow's hierarchy of needs, Herzberg's two-factor theory, and McClelland's achievement–motivation theory.

❖ Discuss expectancy, equity, and reinforcement theories of motivation.

❖ Discuss the advantages of goal setting.

❖ Identify the attributes of effective goals.

❖ Describe some motivational tools and techniques used in a quality management system.

Compensating for Competitive Performance

At Technology Solutions (a computer systems integration firm that uses artificial intelligence, telecommunications, and imaging technology), high sales results parallel the high pay for project managers. Technology Solutions pays an annual cash compensation package of almost $300,000, compared with about $170,000 for the industry average. Managers can lose up to 25 percent of their base salary if their sales don't match the industry's 18 percent growth rate. But meet that rate, and stock option incentives kick in, resulting in a real "carrot and stick" compensation system.

A high school in Michigan awarded straight-A students with free reserved parking, concert tickets, college tuition credits, free meals, records, watches, and school jackets. Even students with C grades earned jewelry store discounts, items at local restaurants, and free tickets to sports events. One critic said, "We're basically paying kids for expected performance." Since 1981, a New York Foundation has offered to pay the college tuition for thousands of financially needy or at-risk students, contingent only upon their completing high school.

High turnover of women in sales positions prompted S.C. Johnson of Wisconsin to restructure its basic sales jobs. Johnson changed the jobs in response to complaints about boring work, slow career progress, and a sense of not fitting in with the company. Territories were changed to reduce travel time, meaning less time away from home for salespeople. Sales staff were also given more freedom to negotiate prices. "They're staying because we made the jobs more doable and more interesting," says an S.C. Johnson vice president.

Incentives are behind just about every effort to boost sales and productivity. Florida-based accounting firm Riggs, Storey, Fulmer, & Ingram increased its revenue an average of 35 percent three years in a row by compensating partners solely on what they produce. The maker of Frookies cookies offers a cash bonus to salespeople who surpass their previous year's sales, with tiers built in to reflect the market competition and to provide even higher possible bonuses. A small firm, Leegin Leather, spent $400,000 to take its sales team, team associates, and spouses to Hawaii as a reward for getting customers to place last-quarter sales by November 30, to allow time for production during the holiday rush. National Leisure Group of Boston spent about $1,000 on each salesperson who produced $1 million in net sales for the firm; rewards included entertainment on the town, plaques, and recognition at company events.

In 1988 Portland-based Oregon Steel Mills went public. Once nearly worthless, in three years the stock made almost 100 employees into millionaires. After 17 years with the company, a bookkeeper went from raising her son alone in a mobile home to living in a half-million dollar home on a golf course and net worth of over $1.25 million. A mill supervisor and a clerk married and retired with a nest egg of $2.5 million. All of this came about from 100 percent employee ownership in the mill, with 20 percent of pretax profits going to profit sharing.

Source: Adapted from Stuart Kahan, "Good Grades = More Dollars," *Practical Accountant,* February 1995, pp. 63–64; Richard S. Teitelbaum, "Companies to Watch: Technology Solutions," *Fortune,* July 27, 1992, p. 97; Suzanne Alexander, "For Some Students, the Value of Learning Lies in Dance Tickets and Parking Passes," *The Wall Street Journal,* January 29, 1992, p. B1; "Companies Try to Stop Exodus of Women, Minorities," *Milwaukee Journal,* January 12, 1992, p. D5.1; Susan Greco, Christopher Caggiano, and Michael P. Cronin, "What Motivates a Salesperson Most?" *Inc.,* January 1992, p. 98; and Dana Milbank, "Newly Rich: Here Is One LBO Deal Where the Workers Became Millionaires," *The Wall Street Journal,* October 27, 1992, p. A1.

motivation
The set of forces that initiate behavior and determine its form, direction, intensity, and duration.

People work for many different reasons: to survive, to achieve personal goals, to feed their families, to be respected. They may excel at their jobs for other reasons: for pride of workmanship; because of ability; out of a sense of obligation; for personal, peer, and social recognition; or to make a customer happy. Just as there are many reasons for motivation, there are also many theories to explain it. **Motivation** is the set of forces that initiate behavior and determine its form, direction, intensity, and duration. So what should a manager know about motivation? For one thing, most theories of work performance include motivation as a central concept. If managers are concerned with increasing productivity or quality, they must be concerned with motivation.[1]

THE IMPORTANCE OF MOTIVATION

Why focus on worker motivation? The American labor force grew by almost 3 percent in the 1970s; in the 1990s this growth will be less than 1 percent. In 15 years, through the early 1990s, the number of high school graduates declined over 25 percent. The once popular view that computers and technology would make workers obsolete has been replaced by a realization that business still needs an educated workforce. Rather than seeking input and a competitive edge from a small number of key, top-level workers, companies must find ways to actively elicit the participation of all employees', to motivate all employees to greater levels of quality performance.[2]

To achieve organizational goals, managers must understand basic human nature. What motivates a person to work hard? What does a person want or need from work? Once this central question is answered, a reward system can be designed to satisfy these wants and needs. Although this may sound easy, it is not.

ASSUMPTIONS ABOUT HUMAN NATURE

Before we begin our discussion of motivation, let us review several important assumptions about human nature. Managers, like most of us, have very specific attitudes and beliefs about what makes people tick. Like most other aspects of life, different people have different assumptions about human nature. To a large degree, these assumptions dictate what we expect to see and what we actually see. In essence, assumptions are a theoretic frame of reference against which we compare our daily human interactions. If we assume that most blue-collar workers are disinterested in their work, we might interpret some workers' low performance as confirmation of this lack of interest even though the correct interpretation might be that they were poorly trained. McGregor's two contrasting explanations of human nature have been widely used to understand and shape managerial practices. His sets of assumptions (called Theory X and Theory Y) describe diametrically opposed views of managerial direction and control.[3]

Motivation

The business of getting people to do something enthusiastically and of their own initiative is very complex unless we come upon the proper chord. Tom Sawyer was able to convince his peers that painting a fence was so much fun that they paid for the privilege of joining him. Life is much easier in fiction. I have always encouraged people to write articles and books that would help others understand and progress. But getting as article out of someone who is not a dedicated writer is way on the other side of pulling teeth. It is more like pulling ribs; some people just are not tilted that way. Finding subjects for them to write about is no help. They still procrastinate.

One year I challenged myself to see if we could get 25 articles out of our organization. I announced that there would be a "writer's weekend" held the following year. Those who had published an article, contracted for a book, or done something similar would be invited along with their spouses. Oh yes, the event would be held in Bermuda. Attendance would be limited to 25 couples (the first published), and there would be guest speakers from the writing field, including an agent.

Suddenly the writing activity began to pick up. Our marketing folks had volunteered to assist in placing articles and soon we were beginning to see some in print. By request, writing classes were held in the evenings and workshops were conducted by experienced writers. In that 13-month period 28 articles were published, and 30 more appeared later as a result of that activity. The routine flow, some years later, in consistent. It is felt to be just something that professionals do.

The Bermuda weekend went off on schedule and everyone had a wonderful time. Ownership of the organization changed right after that so there were no more events, but that made no difference. Once people found out what writing was all about, they created their own energy.

The best motivation is one that helps people do something worthwhile that they would like to do anyway. When my children were young we had a posted rule by the swimming pool that no flotation devices were permitted. Only swimmers could enter the pool. As a result every child in the neighborhood learned to swim early in life. I taught many of them personally. It is not difficult when they choose to learn.

When we can communicate with others in a way that helps them make the choice that is best for them, we are being useful. When we aim it at something that is best for us, and not for them, we are not being useful.

The whole purpose of communication is to be useful.

Theory X states that workers are passive (if not lazy) and in need of direction and control. Thus workers need external management through the use of force, persuasion, rewards, and punishment. McGregor described Theory X as the traditional view of direction and control.

Theory Y asserts that workers are eager to learn, responsible, and creative. McGregor believed that workers' capacities to learn are great and their abilities are underutilized. If given the autonomy, workers are quite capable of self-direction and self-control. And the reward system must be supportive of increased employee participation.

THE MOTIVATION PROCESS

According to behavioral scientists, effective worker performance requires motivation, ability, and a reward system that encourages quality work.[4] In a general sense Figure 12–1 describes the psychological relationship between motivation, behavior, reward, and feedback. A person's motive or motivation is characterized as a need-based state of arousal. Need deprivation increases our state of arousal or search to reduce the need deficit. At work, the term *behavior* refers to the specific work or task action that results from this need-deficit-induced arousal. And finally, rewards are the direct consequence of our behavior. Feedback is knowledge produced about the cause-and-effect sequence that either stimulates or suppresses future states of arousal, depending on our level of need satisfaction.

A reward is an attractive or desired consequence. Rewards can be either intrinsic or extrinsic. **Intrinsic rewards** (the intangible psychological results of work that are controlled by the worker) are inherent in the job and occur during performance of work. A task might be intrinsically motivating because it results in a feeling of accomplishment. Intrinsic rewards can have significant, yet often underestimated, impact on job satisfaction,

intrinsic rewards
Intangible psychological results of work that are controlled by the worker.

FIGURE 12–1
A Model of Motivation.

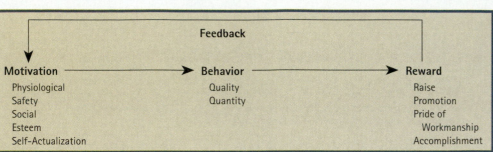

extrinsic rewards
Results of work that are externally controlled.

ability
A measure of a worker's skill, competence, and/or genetic characteristics.

which, as we will see, is closely linked to motivation. **Extrinsic rewards** are administered by another party and occur apart from the actual performance of work. An example of an extrinsic reward is a paycheck.

To be motivated, workers must also be able to do the job. **Ability** is the worker's physical and mental characteristics required to perform the task successfully. Management must do everything it can to continually develop each worker's ability through training.

MOTIVATION THEORIES

Over the years many people have attempted to develop theories to describe how motivation affects work behavior. Theories of worker motivation attempt to explain people's inner workings, initiatives, and aspirations. We will look at the three basic types of motivation theories in this chapter: content, process, and reinforcement.

Content Theories of Motivation

content theory
A theory of motivation defining motivation in terms of need satisfaction (also called need theory). The ability to satisfy a need is a motivating force that leads to a behavioral response.

hierarchy of needs
A motivational theory that people have five basic needs arranged in a hierarchy (physiological, safety, social, self-esteem, and self-actualization), developed by Abraham Maslow.

Content theories (also called *need theories*) are based on the idea that people are driven to meet basic needs that produce satisfaction when they're met. These theories include Maslow's hierarchy of needs, Herzberg's two-factor theory, and McClelland's achievement motivation theory.

MASLOW'S HIERARCHY OF NEEDS - Abraham Maslow's motivation theory, commonly referred to as the **hierarchy of needs** (Figure 12–2), is based on two key assumptions. First, different needs are active at different times, and only needs not yet satisfied can influence behavior. Second, needs are arranged in a fixed order of importance called a *hierarchy*.

According to Maslow's theory, behavior is triggered by a need *deficit* that drives the individual to reduce the tension it creates. Tension leads to behavior that will potentially satisfy the need. For example, a new baby in the family means a greater financial burden. As a result, the worker increases work effort to ensure a promotion and raise. In Maslow's theory, the idea that a satisfied need can't influence behavior is called the *prepotency* of the need. This prepotency (urgency that the unmet need exerts) influences behavior. In our example, the as yet unmet need for a promotion and raise has high prepotency. Until the need is satisfied, the unmet need is said to influence behavior. Furthermore, as soon as a lower-order need is satisfied, a higher-order need emerges and demands satisfaction.

Maslow identified five categories of needs:
- *Physiological needs*, such as food, air, and water.
- *Safety needs*, such as freedom from fear or harm.
- *Social needs*, such as friendship, camaraderie, and teamwork.
- *Self-esteem needs*, meaning acceptance of self as having value.
- *Self-actualization needs*, the fulfillment of potential and personal growth.[5]

FIGURE 12–2
Maslow's Hierarchy of Needs

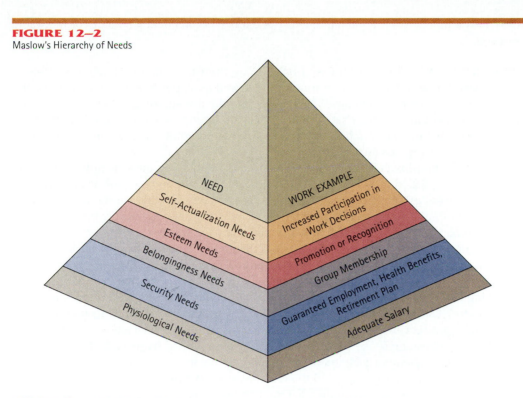

Source: Adapted from Abraham H. Maslow. "A Theory of Human Motivation." *Psychological Review 50* (1943), pp. 370–96.

The hierarchy of needs gives managers a straightforward way of understanding how various work conditions satisfy employee needs. Certain basic conditions of employment (such as pay) satisfy physiological needs. Safety needs are met by safe work conditions and job security. Social needs are satisfied by interaction and communication with fellow workers. And finally, work that is fulfilling can satisfy self-esteem and self-actualization needs.

Although Maslow's ideas were a welcome relief from the emphasis on abnormal behavior that dominated the psychology of the day, they are not without some potential pitfalls. First, Maslow himself recognized that the hierarchy is not a stair-step approach. Human needs are multiple and they often occur simultaneously in modern society. It may make more sense to think about higher-order needs (such as esteem and self-actualization) as one set and lower-order needs (such as physiological, safety, and social needs) as another set. Using just these two categories, we can see that it is certainly possible for several needs to influence our behavior at any given time. Second, we have to consider the relative level of the need that is present at a given time. Being thirsty is a relative concept. If you're in a desert and have no water, the prepotency of the need will influence 100 percent of your behavior. But if you're mildly thirsty all morning but you're writing the weekly report, your behavior may be more determined by a deadline than your thirst. Third, Maslow's theory describes needs as internal; it says nothing about the environment's effect on behavior. How are needs determined? For example, the need for new clothes may be determined by comparing our clothes with those worn by friends, models, or prestigious people. Functionally our clothes may be fine but by comparison to our friends' clothing, they might look old or out of style. So what might be considered a lower-order need for clothing becomes translated into a higher-order need for self-esteem. The referent for our need deficit is not internal but rather is external. In other words, the definition of need for new clothing is determined through other people, society, education, and religion—the external environment.

To a large degree, Maslow's ideas help us understand that everyone has basic needs that must be satisfied. One way to satisfy these needs is through work. But the complexity of the need satisfaction process makes simple prescription problematic. Maslow's need hierarchy describes a model of basic human needs but offers little practical guidance for motivating workers.

HERZBERG'S TWO-FACTOR THEORY - Prior to Frederick Herzberg's research, job satisfaction and dissatisfaction were often viewed as opposite ends of a single continuum. Thus many managers believed that the greater the amount of any good condition, the greater the amount of worker satisfaction. Managers further believed that eliminating bad conditions would result in job satisfaction. But Herzberg found that not being satisfied is different from being dissatisfied.

Herzberg and his colleagues were interested in identifying those factors that caused workers to be satisfied with their work. To investigate this idea, Herzberg designed a study in which data were gathered from accountants and engineers. Herzberg asked participants in the study to think of times when they felt especially good and especially bad about their jobs. Each participant was then asked to describe the conditions or events that caused those good or bad feelings. Of particular interest was the finding that the participant identified different work conditions for each of the two feelings. That is, while the presence of one condition (e.g., fulfilling work) made the participants feel good, the absence of that condition (fulfilling work) did not make them feel bad. Consequently, Herzberg postulated that motivators lead to satisfaction, but their absence does not necessarily lead to dissatisfaction.

Herzberg discovered two factors that separately explained satisfaction and dissatisfaction. Factors whose presence prevent dissatisfaction are called **hygiene factors** or maintenance factors. Hygiene or maintenance factors refer to aspects of work that are peripheral to the task itself and more related to the external environment (the **job context**). The term *hygiene factor* is linked to the finding that the absence of readily available rest rooms led to worker dissatisfaction. Hygiene factors include:

❖ Company policy and administrative practices.
❖ Technical supervision by the manager.
❖ Interpersonal relations with the supervisor.
❖ Worker salary, job status, and job security.
❖ The worker's personal life.
❖ Physical conditions of the work setting (e.g., air conditioning).

Factors whose presence lead to satisfaction are called **satisfiers** or, simply, motivational factors. These factors can produce high levels of motivation when they're present. Motivational factors relate directly to the **job content** (the specific aspects of a job). They include:

❖ Achievement.
❖ Recognition.
❖ Advancement.
❖ The task or work itself.
❖ The worker's potential for personal learning or growth.
❖ The worker's responsibility for results.[6]

Figure 12–3 presents Herzberg's two-factor theory.

Motivational and maintenance factors are often distinguished by the fact that motivational factors are *intrinsic,* whereas maintenance factors are *extrinsic.*

At the time of Hertzberg's study, his ideas were considered groundbreaking. Herzberg and his colleagues challenged traditionally accepted ideas about the causes and nature of job satisfaction. But when the two-factor theory was tested in other organizations, researchers found little support for the theory. Controversy over Herzberg's findings centers on three areas:

❖ *Method of data collection:* The information was collected via a potentially biased, structured interview format.
❖ *Individual differences:* Individual differences were discovered to affect the two factors. For example, some workers avoid advancement.
❖ *Limited sample:* Conclusions were based primarily on studies of professionals (i.e., engineers and accountants), whose tasks differ significantly from other kinds of workers.[7]

hygiene factor
In Herzberg's two-factor theory, the aspects of work that are related to the external environment and not the work itself.

job context
Factors external to the job. For example, a unionized work force applies union contract rules to all jobs.

satisfier
In Herzberg's two-factor theory, factors (such as decision-making autonomy) that can lead to satisfaction.

job content
A specific aspect of the job. For example, job variety is a content factor.

FIGURE 12–3
Herzberg's Two-Factor Theory

Motivators	Hygiene Factors
Achievement	Pay
Challenge	Supervision
Responsibility	Physical Work Conditions
Recognition	Rules, Regulations, Policies
Autonomous Decisions	Benefits

Low .... Hi   Low .... Hi
　　Satisfaction　　　　　　Dissatisfaction

Herzberg's motivational factors correspond to Maslow's higher-order needs, while his maintenance factors correspond to lower-order needs. Interestingly, Maslow and Herzberg both provide evidence that the value of the work itself can contribute to worker motivation.

MCCLELLAND'S ACHIEVEMENT MOTIVATION THEORY – Another psychologist, David McClelland, paid further attention to the potential of work itself to motivate.[8] McClelland's approach is different, however, in that he focused on the need for achievement in individuals rather than in the general population of workers. McClelland believed that a person's unconscious mind is the key to his or her particular needs. In his own words, "If you want to find out what's on a person's mind, don't ask him, because he can't always tell you. Study his fantasies and dreams. If you do this over a period of time, you will discover the themes to which his mind returns again and again. And these themes can be used to explain his actions."[9]

McClelland believed that by showing subjects a picture and then asking them to write a story to describe what's happening in the picture and what the probable outcome would be, the story would reveal the writer's needs and motives. McClelland identified three primary needs: need for achievement, need for affiliation, and need for power. Like Maslow's need theory, McClelland's theory suggests that people vary in the degree to which their motive for behavior is determined by any one or a combination of these needs.

The **need for achievement** is a measure of a person's desire for clear, self-set, moderately difficult goals, with feedback given based on goal achievement. High achievers are seen as self-starters, goal-oriented, or full of task initiative, all of which are typically valued by firms.

The **need for affiliation** is the desire to work with others, to interact with and support others, and to learn the lessons of life through the experiences of others. A pronounced desire for social acceptance can be a powerful motivating force in our daily lives. Work organizations are important social institutions, bringing people in contact with one another on a regular basis. The need for affiliation is Maslow's social need applied to the individual.

The **need for power** is a desire to have influence and control over others. This need can be an important determinant of behavior. People dominate one another in many socially acceptable ways. People are submissive to the dominance of police, managers, tour guides, and others. It is natural and often informative to allow other people control over an aspect of our lives. Many people seek jobs that afford them the opportunity to fulfill a basic need in a socially acceptable manner, and success at many jobs actually requires people to be forceful and capable of exerting their will over others. In these positions, people with a high need for power will outperform those with a low need for power.

McClelland's work fits well with Herzberg's view of achievement as a motivator and with Maslow's concept of higher-order need satisfaction as a source of motivation. In addition, McClelland's research moves beyond basic or lower-level needs as explanations for

need for achievement
A measure of a person's desire for clear, self-set, moderately difficult goals, with feedback given based on goal achievement.

need for affiliation (n Aff)
The desire to work with others, to interact and support others, with a concern for their growth and development. An individual version of Maslow's hierarchical social need.

need for power (n Pow)
A desire to have influence and control over others, to have impact.

behavior. Maslow, Herzberg, and McClelland all recognize the importance of achievement and social relations as motivational factors. But only McClelland moves one step beyond by adding an additional dimension, the need for power. As we will see, the need for power can be an important explanation for human behavior.

MANAGERIAL APPLICATION OF NEED THEORIES ‒ McClelland's needs for achievement and affiliation and Herzberg's intrinsic motivators—responsibility, personal growth, and the work itself—are consistent with quality expert W. Edwards Deming's belief that motivation and worker commitment come from pride of workmanship and the joy of work. But managers often underestimate employees' need for achievement. A climate of achievement in the workplace can be cultivated in several ways. First, work that is challenging and gives the employee a sense of responsibility is motivational. Second, managers can identify and recognize individual employees' contributions rather than simply attributing a firm's success to managers. Need theories also form the basis for the more complex explanations of human behavior provided by process theories of motivation.

Process Theories of Motivation

process theory
Theories of motivation supporting the belief that motivation is a rational cognitive process internal to the individual rather than an external process.

Process theories describe cognitive processes and decisions that help predict subsequent behavior. These theories include equity and expectancy. Whereas need theories view motivation as subconscious and instinctive, process theories view motivation in terms of workers' explicit thought processes (cognitions) and conscious decisions to select and pursue a specific alternative (choice). Thus, according to process theory, a worker is likely to consider a variety of methods, weighing each method in terms of how attractive its expected outcomes might be, before engaging in an activity. The two major process theories are expectancy theory and equity theory.

EXPECTANCY THEORY ‒ Victor H. Vroom developed an expectancy theory of motivation sometimes referred to as *VIE theory*. In a nutshell, expectancy theory describes the process people use to evaluate (1) the likelihood that their effort or expenditure will yield the desired outcome and (2) how much they want the outcome. In this theory, motivation is based on three factors that determine the degree of effort to put forth.[10]

expectancy
The probability that a person's effort will lead to a satisfactory level of job performance.

The first factor in VIE theory is the expectancy that effort will lead to desired results or a first-order outcome. In most work situations a first-order outcome would be a personal belief that you can complete the job within some range of success. **Expectancy** is the individual's subjective assessment that effort will produce the desired results or a first-order outcome. This is the "can do" (perceived capability) component of an employee's approach to work. Expectancy is a probability assessment rated between 0 (certain to not produce results) and 1.0 (certain to produce results).

valence
In expectancy theory, the value or importance the individual places on a second-order outcome. For example, if a person doesn't want a promotion because it would bring more responsibility, then promotion has a low valence.

The second factor in VIE theory is the **valence** or value of the outcome to the individual (i.e., the rewards). Valence represents the outcome's desirability to the individual. Desirable rewards encourage effort; undesirable rewards discourage effort. A valence can range from negative to positive depending on whether the individual believes the outcome is personally undesirable or desirable.

instrumentality
In expectancy theory, the subjective probability that satisfactory job performance will lead to other desired outcomes such as pay increases or promotion.

A third factor in the theory is the **instrumentality** of successful task performance in leading to a second-level outcome or a desired reward. If a first-level outcome is successful completion of your job or working at an above-average level of performance, a second-level outcome might be a raise or a promotion. So the instrumentality of a task is the employee's assessment of how instrumental or likely it is that successful task performance will be rewarded with a raise. Thus instrumentality is a measure of the correlation between performance and rewards, which is scored from −1.0 (performance of the behavior will definitely prevent the worker from receiving the reward) to +1.0 (performance will definitely produce the reward for the worker). Figure 12–4 presents the expectancy theory.

We can use a mathematical representation of the expectancy theory process. The valence of the potential reward, the instrumentality of the performance linked to the reward, and the expectancy of achieving the reward determine the level of effort. Then the values

FIGURE 12–4
Expectancy Theory

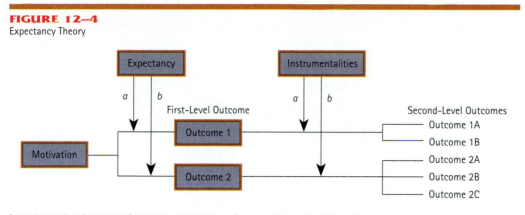

Source: Adapted from Fred Luthans, *Organizational Behavior*, 6th ed. (New York: McGraw-Hill, 1992), p. 163.

are multiplied to produce a force to perform for each effort. Presumably the actual level of effort will be determined by the highest VIE score.

The actual determination of the VIE score can be complicated. For example, the levels of possible effort are often infinite rather than discrete (effort versus no effort). The employee may not have an accurate idea of expectancy. (That is, she may not know if her efforts will produce the level of performance needed to earn a reward.) Also the employee may be uncertain about how performance will be rewarded. If so, the instrumentality for each level of effort cannot be determined.

For limited, discrete choices of effort (e.g., attend or not attend) and known instrumentalities (e.g., a score of 95 on an exam will guarantee the student an A grade), the calculations are simple and the research is generally supportive of expectancy theory.[11] Expectancy theory is, for the most part, of limited, practical daily value for managers. Nevertheless, it does provide a general guide to the factors that determine the amount of effort a worker puts forth. Expectancy theory also helps explain how a worker's goals influence his efforts. The theory's utility for managers is that VIE theory suggests a complex thought process that individuals use in the process of becoming motivated.

The following pointers can be inferred from the insights offered by expectancy theory:

1. *Ask what outcomes workers desire.* Workers often prefer rewards that differ from management's assumptions. For example, for some workers in dual-career families, health care benefits may be irrelevant if the spouse's employer already provides them. Also, time off for child and elderly parent care may be preferred over bonuses, promotions, and job transfers to new locations.

2. *Break down effort-performance barriers.* Providing workers with tools, information, and an effective production support system will help translate effort into performance.

3. *Clarify and communicate instrumentalities.* Workers who know that performance will lead to rewards are more likely to work hard. For those rewards that are controlled by management (e.g., bonuses and promotions), management must let workers know the performance level required to achieve these rewards.

4. *Develop meaningful self-administered rewards.* Intrinsic rewards have a perfect instrumentality correlation (−1.0 or 1.0) and require no management action to award them. For example, developing pride of workmanship builds a self-motivated worker.

EQUITY THEORY ~ J. Stacy Adams' equity theory concerns the worker's perception of how she is being treated. In particular, equity theory is based on the assessment process workers use to evaluate the fairness or justice of organizational outcomes and the *adjustment process* used to maintain perceptions of fairness. The concepts of fairness and equilibrium (internal balance) are central to equity theory. The basic idea in equity theory is that an employee first considers her input (effort) and then her outcomes (rewards).

Next the employee compares her personal ratio of effort to reward to the ratio of a referent. The referent is usually another employee doing basically the same work, some standard ratio based on a fair day's work, or another employee at approximately the same level in an organization.[12]

reference ratio
In equity theory, a person compares the ratio of his job inputs to his job outcomes and then makes a similar comparison for an identical worker. The ratio for the comparison referent is called the reference ratio. For example, a person compares his job effort to his pay and then makes the same comparison for the person working next to him. In an equitable situation, the two ratios are identical.

This ratio of a comparison person's input to outcome is called a **reference ratio** (Table 12–1). If the employee believes that his input-to-outcome ratio is lower than the reference ratio, he can (1) reduce his effort or (2) seek higher rewards to bring his input-to-outcome ratio in line with the reference ratio. Conversely, if the employee's ratio is higher than the reference ratio, she can increase her effort or reduce her rewards. If Georgia feels that she's overrewarded for her work, she might feel guilty. To reduce this tension, she could work harder or find more work to do. Her actions would reflect the need to adjust her internal state of fairness. Likewise, John (an underrewarded worker) is off-balance in the opposite direction. He too would seek an equity adjustment. If no pay increase appeared to be forthcoming, theory suggests that he'd decrease his effort to again create an equitable outcome.

Note that a worker's inputs and outcomes need not be in exact balance to one another as long as the reference ratio imbalance matches the worker's ratio. That is, a worker may feel that she is working very hard, but may not feel unfairly treated as long as her comparison workers are also working very hard. Many workers are willing to work hard as long as the burden is shared. Equity theory helps to account for workers' feelings of mistreatment by highly paid managers. This issue is explored further in the Global Exchange on the following page.

Reinforcement Theory

operant conditioning (or reinforcement theory)
Skinner's theory that behavior is a function of its consequences. Behavior is contingent upon reinforcement. Behavior that's reinforced will be repeated.

Reinforcement theories view motivation largely in terms of external factors and describe the conditions under which behavior is likely to be repeated. Reinforcement theory's view of motivation is different from content and process theories' views. Both process and content theories consider motivation to be a function of either internal needs or internal cognition. On the other hand, **operant conditioning** (also called **reinforcement theory**) views motivation as largely determined by external factors. Our experience with past situations dictates or guides future behavior. Noted psychologist B. F. Skinner stated that behavior is a function of its consequences.[13] Behaviors that have positive consequences are likely to be repeated and those that have negative consequences are likely to be avoided in the future. According to reinforcement theory, workers are motivated by the consequences of their

TABLE 12–1	THE EQUITY THEORY REFERENCE RATIO

Equity Model

$$\frac{O_p}{I_p} = \frac{O_o}{I_o}$$

O_p = Worker's perception of own outcome.

I_p = Worker's perception of own inputs.

O_o = Worker's perception of another worker's outcome.

I_o = Worker's perception of another worker's input.

RESTORATION OF EQUITY

Underreward	Overreward
1. Ask for raise.	1. Try to get raise for other workers.
2. Lower inputs.	2. Raise inputs.
3. Rationalize why you get less than others.	3. Rationalize why you get more than others.
4. Change your comparison worker.	4. Change your comparison worker.

Source: Adapted from Ramon Aldag and T. Stearns, *Management*, 2nd ed. (Cincinnati, OH: South-Western, 1991), pp. 422–23.

GLOBAL EXCHANGE   MOTIVATION AND CEO COMPENSATION AROUND THE WORLD

Left to right: Ben Cohen, Robert Holland (Ben & Jerry's CEO), Jerry Greenfield.

The levels of pay for workers, managers, and executives vary around the world. In some countries, workers' pay is but a small fraction of top managers' salaries. In other countries, the gap between workers' and top managers' pay is much narrower. Annual total compensation for American chief executive officers (CEOs) averaged over $3.8 million in 1992—far higher than the compensation of CEOs in Japan, France, Italy, Canada, Germany, Hong Kong, and Switzerland.

Research linked higher CEO pay to higher performance; CEO's at small and midsize companies earn much less than CEO's at large companies. Much of American CEOs' pay is in the form of benefits and long-term incentives like stock options. Stock options are not treated as an expense for the firm nor are they treated as immediate taxable income for the executive.

So are such incentives "pay?" The Economist concludes, "Such complexity, combined with the secrecy surrounding nearly all option and bonus schemes, makes them look more like a conjurer's sleight of hand than a spur to corporate competitiveness."

As a point of comparison, Japan's top-paid CEO earned $6.3 million, whereas the top-paid American CEO (Thomas Frist of Hospital Corporation of America) received total compensation of $127 million. Even more revealing, average compensation for a Japanese CEO was $872,646 in 1991—a mere 25 percent of the average for American CEOs. Even CEOs of poorly performing American firms were compensated handsomely. For another comparison, let us examine the relationship of the CEO's salary to the average worker's salary. In Japan the CEO makes about 32 times the average worker's pay. But in the United States the gap is considerably larger. In fact, the average CEO in an American firm is compensated 157 times more than the average worker in the company.

Presumably the rationale for increasing compensation packages to CEOs in American companies is motivation. Salary plus incentives can make the CEO rich. Usually compensation is tied to the firm's financial performance. The better the company's performance, the greater the CEO's total compensation. But critics of this motivational strategy conclude that it may not motivate the CEO toward achieving short-term gain to grab the compensation incentives but not add any sustainable wealth to the organization. In essence, as a motivational strategy, contemporary CEO compensation packages in U.S. firms may have two drawbacks. First, most CEO compensation schemes reward in the short term (most yearly but often in five years or less). Some argue that this is far too short a time horizon to adequately assess the net value of the CEO's strategic management. Second, substantial CEO compensation may motivate the CEO in the short term but may alienate workers and stockholders. Workers see all their gains in efficiency going to CEO compensation.

In 1992, the ice cream maker Ben & Jerry's limited CEO pay to seven times the lowest worker's pay. Although originally Ben and Jerry believed that forming a link between what the CEO may earn and what the lowest-paid worker earns would reduce much of the workers' feeling of inequity or disenchantment, the policy has generated a great deal of controversy within the organization. Still in 1994 the highest executive salary was under $160,000—low for a $150 million company.

American CEOs who decry unfair trade and feisty unions sound much less credible when they earn multimillion-dollar tax-protected compensation packages. For some firms, belt-tightening and "lean production" does not seem to apply to the executives.

Source: Adapted from Kevin J. Sigler and Joseph P. Haley, "CEO Pay and Company Performance," *Management Finance*, Volume 21, Issue 2, 1995, pp. 31–41; "CEO Pay at Large vs. Small Companies," *HR Focus*, December 1995, p. 16; "Paying the Boss," *The Economist*, February 1, 1992, p. 13; Carrie Dolan, "Many Companies Now Base Workers' Raises on Their Productivity," *The Wall Street Journal*, November 15, 1985; and John A. Byrne, "Executive Pay: The Party Ain't Over Yet," *Business Week*, April 26, 1993, pp. 56–64.

work behavior. In the process of experiencing rewards at work, workers often see a link between their own actions (i.e., their behaviors) and the reward (i.e., the consequences of their behavior). For example, a manager rewards workers at a plant that has reduced the number of accidents in the plant by holding a company-paid picnic for the workers and their families.

The basis or method used to distribute rewards or disincentives as well as the nature of the rewards and disincentives themselves profoundly influence behavior. Rewards may be made on a contingent or noncontingent basis. **Contingent rewards** are distributed based

contingent rewards
Rewards distributed based on a specific preceding behavior.

noncontingent rewards
Rewards that aren't linked to any specific behavior.

reinforcement
The process of using contingent rewards to increase future occurrences of a behavior.

positive reinforcement
The process of providing rewards contingent upon desired worker behavior.

negative reinforcement
Behavioral reinforcement occurring when an unpleasant consequence is withdrawn when the desired behavior occurs.

punishment
The process of administering an undesirable consequence for an undesirable behavior.

hot stove rule
A punishing experience reinforces future behavior. The hot stove is a good teacher—once burned, we're likely to avoid being burned in the future.

extinction
The process of nonreinforcement of a behavior. Simply by ignoring the behavior or not reinforcing it, the behavior will dissipate over time.

on a specific, preceding behavior. For example, a sales clerk may receive a free weekend trip for having the highest sales in her department for the preceding quarter. **Noncontingent rewards** are not linked to any specific behavior. For example, a paid holiday may be available to all staff regardless of their level of performance. A newly hired worker and a worker with 20 years of experience with the company receive the same reward.

INCREASING THE BEHAVIOR - Reinforcement is the process of using contingent rewards to increase future occurrences of a specific behavior. Reinforcement occurs in one of two ways. **Positive reinforcement** occurs when a positive consequence (reward) is applied to a desired behavior. Positive reinforcement increases the frequency of the particular behavior that it follows. *Positive* refers to the nature of the consequence; *reinforcement* refers to the strengthened likelihood of the subsequent behavior. For example, a fruit picker receives $2 for each bag of fruit she picks. **Negative reinforcement** occurs when an unpleasant consequence is withdrawn when the desired behavior occurs. For example, a manager stops criticizing an employee when he achieves the daily production quota.

DECREASING THE BEHAVIOR - Two approaches are suggested to decrease a current behavior: punishment and extinction. **Punishment** is the process of administering an undesirable consequence for an undesirable behavior. Punishment holds many negative connotations for many people. But remember that punishment is a naturally occurring phenomenon in the learning process.[14] For example, a child who falls off a bicycle learns quickly to maintain balance. The famous **hot stove rule** suggests that being burned by a hot stove provides an example of punishment at the most general level and in its most vivid form.[15] The hot stove rule suggests that nature is a good teacher. Nature teaches us that punishment should be swift, intense, impersonal, and consistent, and should provide an alternative.[16] Reduced to its basic components, punishment provides the recipient with useful information. As with all reinforcement, the objective is the association of the behavior with its consequence.

Although the term *punishment* is often objectionable, the concept is widely applicable to work settings. At work, punishment occurs continually. A worker drops a box on his big toe and breaks the toe. In the future he'll exercise greater care or risk more physical injury. Although few people would disagree about the informational content in the preceding example, it still doesn't fit our concept of punishment. We think of punishment as being yelled at or being passed over for promotion due to poor performance. Regardless of the form punishment takes, it is still the same process of applying an unpleasant consequence contingent upon the occurrence of an undesired behavior.

A second way to decrease an undesired behavior is through **extinction** (the process of nonreinforcement of a behavior). Or, more simply put, if the behavior is unrewarded, its occurrence will diminish over time. For example, an employee who tells off-color jokes at meetings could be rewarded for the behavior with laughter. But not laughing at the jokes (i.e., removing the reward) could eliminate the joke telling in the future.

Figure 12–5 shows how application and withdrawal of contingent consequences can be applied to desired and undesired behaviors to produce reinforcement.

FIGURE 12–5
Contingencies of Reinforcement

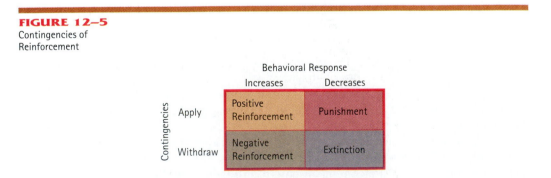

To be effective, positive reinforcement, negative reinforcement, punishment, and extinction must be applied on a contingent basis. That is, the consequence of the behavior must be known by the worker prior to the expression of the behavior. Without this contingency, the behavior's consequence may actually reinforce a variety of behaviors, not all of them desirable. Frequently, trial and error is necessary to determine if a consequence (i.e., possibly a reward) truly reinforces a target behavior.

The nature of the reward also helps to determine the reinforcement's efficacy. Not all rewards produce a reinforcing effect. Some workers prefer some rewards that other workers may want to avoid. For example, one worker may desire overtime hours because she wants the extra income, whereas another worker may not want the additional income, given the work required. Thus "rewarding" overtime hours only to productive workers may punish rather than reinforce productivity.[17] For a reward to qualify as a reinforcer, the reward must increase the frequency of the worker's behavior. Managers use rewards hoping to motivate employees, to influence them to perform better.

MANAGERIAL APPLICATIONS OF REINFORCEMENT - Several factors can influence reinforcement's effectiveness. These principles help to ensure conditions of optimum reinforcement.

❖ *Immediate reinforcement:* Reinforcement should coincide as closely as is practical with the completion of the target behavior.
❖ *Reinforcement size:* The larger the amount of reinforcer that is delivered after occurrence of a target behavior, the more effect the reinforcer will have on that behavior's future frequency.
❖ *Relative reinforcement deprivation:* The more deprived a person is of the reinforcer, the more effect it will have on future occurrence of the target behavior.[18]

GOAL SETTING: AN APPLIED MOTIVATION THEORY

One of the most widely researched theories of human behavior is goal-setting theory. Simply put, **goal-setting theory** states that people who set goals outperform those who don't set goals.[19] The organizational process of goal setting deals with (1) aligning personal and organizational goals and (2) rewarding goal attainment. Goal-setting principles are evident in such popular programs as management by objective (MBO) and self-management.

goal-setting theory
The belief that people who set goals outperform people who don't set them.

Advantages of Goal Setting

Goals help workers to translate general intentions into a specific action. Goals, introduced in Chapter 6, are targeted levels of performance set prior to work. Goal-setting research emphasizes the role of conscious intentions in work.[20] That is, people with goals perform at higher levels than people without goals. Goals can help to:

❖ Direct attention and action.
❖ Mobilize effort.
❖ Create persistent behavior over time.
❖ Lead to strategies for goal attainment.[21]

Attributes of Effective Goals

In general, employees need to feel that working to achieve the goal is in their own best interest, not just the manager's interest. Employees also need support for their efforts, including time, tools, information, and other resources needed to do the job. Finally, employees must feel confident that their work will be rewarded.

Five goal attributes enhance the potential for goal acceptance and enduring goal commitment.[22] **Goal acceptance** is a psychological embracing of the goal as the worker's own aspiration; **goal commitment** is a behavioral follow-through, meaning persistent work effort to achieve the goal.

goal acceptance
A psychological embracing of the goal as the worker's own aspiration.

goal commitment
Behavioral follow-through (persistent work effort to achieve the goal).

1. *Goal specificity.* Specific goals are more effective than ambiguous ("do your best") goals. Specific goals include four elements: action verb, outcome, deadline, and cost.[23] The verb (e.g., *increase, complete, reduce*) establishes the action to be followed. The outcome is expressed in terms of a single measurable result (e.g., quarterly sales of $250,000, a completed report, increased hiring of minority job applicants). The deadline establishes the time (e.g., hour, day, shift) when the goal should be achieved. The cost identifies the resources to be consumed in reaching the goal.

2. *Goal difficulty.* Difficult but attainable goals lead to higher performance than easy goals. What constitutes a difficult but attainable goal is based on relevant data, knowledge, and skills. If an employee is new and her skills are untested, the manager and employee might use historical data from similar past cases to assign a goal. An operational definition of a goal's ease or difficulty will often be established by looking at the worker's or team's prior performance record. In some cases, new tasks require employees to set a difficult goal without benefit of a historical baseline. For example, in designing the first personal digital assistant (PDA), Apple had no historical records to use as a baseline. Determining a challenging goal for completing the design required original, creative thinking.

3. *Goal feedback.* Feedback can occur at three levels: (1) in setting the goal ("What should I aim for?"), (2) in ongoing feedback after the goal is set and work commences ("How am I doing?"), and (3) in evaluating the final result ("How did I do?").

   In establishing an appropriate goal, the worker and manager need to exchange information on their aspirations, skills, schedules, and other work priorities. Ongoing feedback keeps the worker focused. Finally, a manager's feedback when a goal is met ("You met the goal under difficult circumstances. That's a great job you did!") maintains the worker's faith in the goal-setting process.

4. *Participating in goal setting.* Employees need to be involved in and have control over setting their own goals. Allowing workers to be involved in the goal-setting process encourages a higher degree of commitment to meeting those goals. Early research in goal setting emphasized assigned goals over worker participation.[24] But more recent research suggests that active employee participation in setting goals can be more effective.[25] Employees can be involved in the goal-setting process to a greater or lesser extent, depending on their experience and skill. For inexperienced employees, management helps clarify task expectations by assigning goals based on relevant data and knowledge. These clarified task expectations are called *assigned goals*. For more experienced employees, the manager and the employee exchange information and jointly establish goals. This process produces *interactive or negotiated goals*. Finally, veteran, well-trained workers can set their own goals with little or no input from the manager, resulting in *self-set goals*.

5. *Competition.* Sometimes the worker's or work group's goal is defined in terms of exceeding the performance of another worker or work group. This form of competition within the firm can increase the goal's specificity and difficulty. Finding a relevant competitive standard can be the most productive way to facilitate performance initiated by goals. Disadvantages can also arise from competition. When one team's performance depends upon the performance of another team, cooperation rather than competition is necessary.

QUALITY MANAGEMENT AND MOTIVATION

John Wallace, CEO of the 1990 Malcolm Baldrige Award-winning Wallace Company, said this about worker motivation:

> Basically, I think all of your people want to do the very best job they can. I hear a lot of people say: "Well, this quality movement will never work because the people don't

want to do a good job." I disagree because I still think that once people feel like a pro-gram is real and that the organization and its leadership are serious, then you'll get folks to buy in.[26]

Positive Assumptions about Employees' Work Ethic

As McGregor noted some 30 years ago, worker behavior is often a product of managerial assumptions, attitudes, and behavior toward the worker. Treat a worker with respect and dignity, and you engender trust and cooperation. If you treat a worker like a dumb replaceable machine, then don't be surprised when the worker unplugs his work brain at shift's end regardless of the circumstances or the cost to the organization. Known as the *Pygmalion effect,* or self-fulfilling prophecy, increasing a manager's expectations of subordinates' performance actually improves performance.[27]

Comparing the Big Three U.S. auto producers (GM, Ford, and Chrysler) to the Japanese transplants (e.g., Diamond-Star Illinois and NUMMI in California) on the number of work rules contained in each contract, we find some interesting facts. Work rules limit worker autonomy and discretion. Both autonomy and discretion can be important ways of involving workers in improving quality. We find the Big Three are far more rule-bound and oriented toward Theory X management. With fewer rules and limits on employee autonomy, the transplants follow the Theory Y approach more closely. Quality can best be attained by involving all members of the organization. This is achieved only with a quality system design (which is management's responsibility) and a highly trained and involved workforce.

A firm committed to the principles of quality management frames its core question about how to motivate employees something like this: how do we enable workers to feel a natural sense of pride in their work and to be self-motivated? This approach to motivation is based on the assumption that employees inherently want to do a good job. In the quality management view, employees are assets, not liabilities. Negative assumptions about employees' desire to do a good job ("If you don't watch them every minute, they're sure to slack off.") are seen as counterproductive. These negative assumptions can lead to a system where employees are motivated by fear. For example, when attempts were made to unionize minimum-wage workers at a plant in Louisiana, the workers were more frightened by the threat of losing their jobs than by the possibility of continuing to live in near-poverty. As one employee, a 32-year-old single parent, said, "It's so awful there, and I do want my life to get better. But I can't lose this job."[28]

In the quality-based approach to managing employees, management's primary responsibility in terms of employees' performance is to create and maintain a motivation system that supports each employee's natural ambition and pride of workmanship.[29] Quality expert Philip B. Crosby claims that employees who work for money alone are loyal to money, not the organization. He says that most employees also work for fulfillment, appreciation, and the social companionship provided by work.[30]

Tools and Techniques

In the quality management firm, the manager's primary role in motivating employees is (1) to stabilize the system and (2) to remove obstacles that prevent "natural," intrinsic motivation from occurring. This role requires the use of quality tools and techniques, such as charting, pay for performance, flexible rewards, flexible working hours, self-managed work design, and job enrichment.

charting
A technique used to measure the frequency of a worker's target behavior over time.

CHARTING - Before goals are set, management must identify desirable and undesirable work behaviors and then measure the frequency of these behaviors over time. One technique for accomplishing this is called **charting**. In charting, a process called **pinpointing** is used to identify **target behaviors** (behaviors that either contribute to or detract from the organization's quality aims). Goals can then be set based on data gathered in the charting process.

Charting (Figure 12–6) provides an accurate measure of behavior and a visual impression of the impact of the intervention. In the figure, the target behavior is the speed of the

pinpointing
The identification of quality-based target behaviors.

target behaviors
Behaviors that either contribute to or detract from the organization's quality aims.

FIGURE 12–6
A Chart of Phone Response
Effectiveness

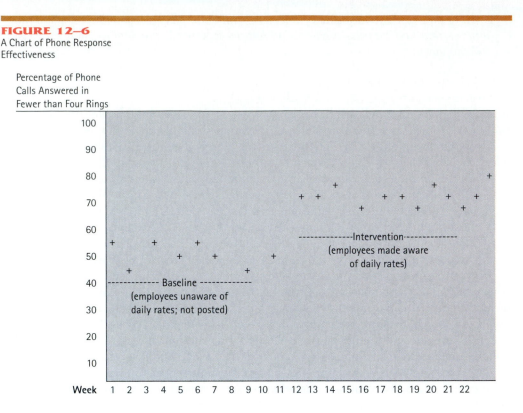

Percentage of Phone
Calls Answered in
Fewer than Four Rings

baseline

The portion of a behavioral chart that measures work behavior before any effort is made to change the worker's behavior.

intervention period

The portion of time posted on the behavioral record chart that follows the introduction of a change.

event counting

An enumeration of a behavior (e.g., number of times that safety goggles are worn) within a given time period.

time sampling

A series of observations or checks throughout the specified time period, usually to see if the behavior was occurring (or not occurring) at the time of the check.

output counting

A measure of results of a targeted process.

response to a ringing telephone. The first portion of the chart, the **baseline**, measures the behavior before any change has been implemented. After goal setting occurs, the baseline is used as a comparison to judge the success of the intended change in work behavior. The second part of the chart concerns the **intervention period** (the portion of the time or the behavioral record chart following the introduction of a change).

Target behaviors can be measured in three ways:

❖ **Event counting** records instances of a behavior (e.g., number of times that safety goggles are worn) within a given time period.

❖ **Time sampling** consists of a series of observations or checks throughout the specified time period, usually to see if the behavior was occurring (or not occurring) at the time of the check. For example, was the employee wearing safety goggles when she was observed?

❖ **Output counting** measures the products of the target behavior. Examples of outputs to be counted include measures of customer satisfaction, the number of orders shipped, and the number of packages delivered on time. One travel agency surveys customer reactions to gauge agents' the effectiveness of in serving agents clients.[31]

PAY FOR PERFORMANCE - Pay for performance is an application of positive reinforcement. Under this compensation plan, worker performance is measured, with higher levels of performance resulting in higher pay.

There are many forms of pay for performance. For example, many salespeople are paid on commission: that is, the more product the salesperson sells, the more money he earns. Many firms use pay for performance only for managers. Still, a study of 172 large firms showed that 67 percent of the firms with pay for performance plans that involved all employees had significant productivity gains, whereas less than 40 percent of those that offered the incentives only to top managers had such productivity gains.[32]

With pay for performance plans, performance must be clearly measured and monitored to see that it is consistent with the firm's fundamental goals; otherwise performance is likely to be misdirected. Many factories once found output easy to measure by simply counting finished products, but they often found that paying workers only for the number of finished products resulted in poor quality. And, in some industries, such as automobile sales, pay for performance has led to high-pressure sales tactics that ultimately alienate customers, as is shown in the Ethics Spotlight.

One form of pay for performance—profit-sharing—comes highly recommended by quality experts. Profit-sharing allows workers to share in the success of their efforts. Profit-sharing can be as simple as a bonus based on the company's profitability (as Ford did several years ago by giving all production line workers an average bonus of about $3,000). Profit-sharing can also allow workers to buy stock in the company at a reduced price. Both approaches make quality work a form of investment. The better the quality of the product, the greater the sales. The greater the sales, the greater the return to stockholders and/or the greater the rise in the stock's value, and the greater the bonus. Profit-sharing provides a direct link between performance and pay. Deming[33] and Crosby[34] agree that profit-sharing is the best form of merit pay. In answer to the question of whether a factory worker and the CEO receive an equal share, Deming says, "Well, why not? Certainly."

In one case, consultants worked with employees of a midsized manufacturing firm and set the following compensation incentive objectives: (1) provide extra compensation to motivate high levels of performance, (2) provide additional compensation contingent on the firm's overall profit performance, (3) avoid increased fixed compensation costs, (4) vary payout to reflect both company performance and individual contribution, (5) introduce contingent pay to all organizational levels, and (6) integrate compensation with the performance appraisal program. This new plan produced dramatic results. For instance, employees worked overtime on December 31 to meet performance standards. Almost two-thirds of

ETHICS SPOTLIGHT | ONE PRICE FITS ALL

Buying a car has always been a complex, nerve-racking experience. Next to the purchase of a home, the car is the most expensive purchase an individual is likely to make. Due to the pressure of price, need for technical knowledge about performance and fuel economy, and environmental issues such as environmentally friendly air conditioners and low-pollution engines, the decision to purchase a car is downright tough! But add to this complex decision process a high-pressure salesperson, and it is enough to make you get into your old car and drive away happy with what you have.

All this complexity has not gone unnoticed by automakers. In fact, market research indicates that consumer satisfaction with the entire car purchase is abysmally low. At the heart of the consumer discontent is negotiating price with the salesperson. Common tactics include *low-balling* (quoting a unrealistically low price), the *slam dunk* (where you agree to pay sticker price or above-

sticker, which assures a high dealer profit), and *stealing the trade-in* (where the dealer makes additional profit on your trade-in by giving you much less than it warrants). These common techniques breed suspicion and contempt for auto dealers and salespeople.

In an effort to remedy the situation, the auto industry it trying a new customer-friendly way to sell cars called *no-haggle pricing*. No-haggle pricing's origin as a sales technique is commonly attributed to the Saturn Motor Company, which essentially doesn't discount from sticker price. Recently, Ford followed suit by offering all three models of its popular Escort for one price, $9,999. But there's more to it than just putting the price in the car window and sticking to that price when the customer wants to haggle. To be successful, dealers who use this pricing strategy must redesign their compensation systems to reinforce the change. Generally, salespeople are put on salary or, if they resist, they're sometimes fired. To take the place of salespeople, greeters are hired to assist customers. When the customer is ready

to purchase, she's directed to a sales manager who closes the deal.

This new approach has resulted in lower overall margins for dealers. New profit per unit has decreased to about 7 percent. But there's a bright side to lower profit. Volume is up substantially. A dealer that was selling about 30 new cars per month now sells 90. Accompanying the increased volume is need for greater service. During the same period for those dealers using no-haggle pricing, profits from service operations rose 50 percent.

But does no-haggle pricing represent a shift in the ethical treatment of the auto-buying public? Some believe that it is nothing more than an attempt by dealers to reduce costs (e.g., salespeople's commission) and simultaneously increase volume and service work.

Source: Adapted from Arlena Sawyers, "No-Haggle Pricing Going Full Throttle," *Advertising Age*, March 22, 1993, p. S10; Neal Templin, "Ford Expands 'One Price' Plan for Its Escorts," *The Wall Street Journal*, March 12, 1992, p. B1: and David Woodruff, "What's This—Car Dealers with Souls?" *Business Week*, April 6, 1992.

the employees earned a bonus of 7.5 percent of their base salary; several earned 15 percent bonuses.[35]

Another form of pay for performance, *skill-based pay*, is based on the range, depth, and type of an employee's particular skills, rather than on skills listed in the job description.[36] Skill-based pay systems allow workers to increase their base pay by learning new job skills. This generally means that the worker must become proficient in several or all jobs in her work area. Once the worker has qualified for a new job, her base pay increases. Skill-based pay schemes benefit both the employee (through greater compensation) and the organization (through greater work flexibility and depth of work knowledge).

material reward
A reward with financial value (e.g., cash, stock, stock options).

symbolic rewards
Tangible and intangible rewards with psychological impact.

social rewards
Rewards that come from interpersonal behavior and enhance personal self-efficacy.

task rewards
Rewards that are related to the work itself, such as the nature, design, and allocation of specific work assignments in terms of job responsibilities, autonomy, task-generated feedback, and scheduling control.

FLEXIBLE REWARDS - Rewards can be classified as material, symbolic, social, and/or task (Table 12–2). Providing workers with flexibility in their choice of rewards can be a powerful motivation application. A recent survey of over 10,000 workers found that 97 percent want to become actively involved in their work, and expect flexible rewards.[37] Flexible rewards were also found to be critical success factors in a study of insurance agent effectiveness.[38]

Material rewards (e.g., cash, stock, stock options) have financial value. They're inherently flexible to some degree because they allow the employee to choose how the money is spent. **Symbolic rewards** have psychological impact and can be either tangible (a trophy) or intangible. **Social rewards** (such as praise) come from interpersonal behavior and enhance personal self-efficacy. **Task rewards** relate to the work itself. They include the nature, design, and allocation of specific work assignments, in terms of job responsibilities, autonomy, task-generated feedback, and scheduling control.

FLEXIBLE WORKING HOURS - Flexible working hours is another motivation application. What constitutes a typical workweek? Eighty years ago an American worker might have been expected to work six 12-hour days. Today most American employees put in a 5-day, 40-hour week. But some firms offer 4-day, 10-hour shifts. In Japan most workers work 5 days a week (45 hours). In Europe the typical work week is, in some cases, only 35 hours.

Not only has the length of a typical work week changed, the schedule for those hours has changed for many employees. Some are allowed flexibility in meeting their required number of work hours each week. In addition, some workers are allowed flexible arrangements for maternity leave, family care responsibilities, and balancing peak-load and off-peak times of the year.

TABLE 12–2   WORK REWARDS

Material Rewards
Direct: Cash, wage, raise, bonus, sales commission, piece-rate pay, stock options, profit-sharing plan, retirement plan.

Fringe: Health plan, free meals, vacation, passes to sports events, retirement plan, convention trips, free company products or discounts, use of company facilities, company car, expense reimbursement, club membership.

Symbolic Rewards
Plaques, jewelry, certificates, office art or accessories, gold watch, trophy, increased office size, corner office, promotion, new title.

Social Rewards
Praise, recognition, compliments, acknowledgments, pat on the back.

Task Rewards
Enriched job, preferred task assignments, job rotation, new job responsibilities, improved work conditions, flexible work hours, early release, freedom to do personal work on company time, extended breaks.

For many two-income families, time can be a more powerful source of motivation than money. Aetna is one company that has responded to changing workforce demands and staff's need for more accommodating work schedules.[39] It now allows six-week maternity leaves. In the Aetna health claims department, 40 percent of all workers are on *flextime*, which allows them to choose their own starting and ending hours of work. In just a few years the number of part-time employees rose from 700 to 1,200; and many employees *telecommute* (work out of the home using telecommunications, especially personal computers and modems) and share jobs.

SELF-MANAGED WORK DESIGN – Allowing employees to have input into the pace of work, scheduling, and task structure is motivational because it focuses on the outcome—quality. Too often, efficiency has been emphasized. Workers adapt by doing what they can. This may mean putting in three screws where five were required. Self-managed work design implies that the worker can best control the pace of the work.

JOB ENRICHMENT – Job enrichment (which we discussed in Chapter 9) is the enhancement of "natural" motivation inherent in a task. In one study, engineers were more motivated by a "technical challenge than the opportunity for career advancement."[40] This recent study is entirely consistent with a stream of academic research collectively known as *task design theory*. Task design theory suggests that increasing the job variety, job autonomy, job identity, and feedback from the job leads to increases in motivation and satisfaction.[41] These task characteristics can be naturally motivating aspects of work. Their ability to increase employee involvement and commitment should not be overlooked.

Motivated workers are a key element for continuous quality improvement. We have traced the development of the theoretic basis for a theory of work motivation. Both content and process theories of motivation are useful in understanding the basis for worker behavior. To be effective in the long run, managers must do more than memorize theory. Understanding motivation theory should help managers draw the linkage between organizational goals and individual needs. By asking the simple question: what does this worker want from the job? the manager can use applied motivational concepts such as goal setting to meet both individual needs and organizational goals.

WHAT MANAGERS ARE READING   HIGH-INVOLVEMENT MANAGERS

P articipative management has gained widespread popularity in modern organizations. Different approaches such as job enrichment, gainsharing, and self-managing work teams all share the goal of increasing employee involvement and motivation, subsequently leading to higher quality, productivity, and performance. In his book *High-Involvement Management,* Edward E. Lawler III discusses the major approaches to participative management, how they work, and their strengths and weaknesses. He also shows how to implement these approaches and how to deal with problems companies have experienced using them.

Participation plays a key role in motivation. Lawler points out that participation in decisions can affect motivation, though the relationship is complex. Research does suggest that participation can affect motivation under certain conditions. When workers participate in decisions about target performance levels and goals, they have more commitment to achieve those goals. Participation can also affect motivation to produce a high-quality product when workers have input into how the work is done, methods used, and how day-to-day activities are performed. Finally, when tied to performance in ways employees can understand and influence, financial rewards can enhance motivation.

Source: Edward E. Lawler III, *High Involvement Management,* (San Francisco: Jossey-Bass Publishers, 1991).

THE WORKPLACE OF TOMORROW

Motivating employees in the workplace of the future will be a challenge to managers. Workers will often be members of teams, empowered to make decisions that were once the domain of managers. In this environment, the role of the manager will be more that of a "coach" than a "cop," giving workers the freedom to express themselves. In fact, at many companies a new breed of manager is reshaping the way workers are motivated. These managers coach rather than command, prod rather than push, and empower rather than order.[42]

Participation in decisions made in an organization can have a positive impact on motivation.[43] In the workplace of tomorrow, workers will be given interesting tasks and participate in decisions about how to perform the tasks. This results in high intrinsic motivation because people feel responsible for how well the work is performed. People will be motivated to do high-quality work because it will satisfy their need to feel good about the work for which they are responsible.

Organizations will also establish a connection between participative management and financial rewards through gainsharing plans. These plans basically tie rewards to performance; employees share in the success of the organization by distributing profits back to those responsible for creating them.[44] Sharing in the financial success of an organization also has a positive impact on motivation, and stimulate and sustains long-term job performance.[45] Gainsharing is also useful in organizations utilizing teams. Behlen Manufacturing, for instance, uses a combination of base pay, an employee stock ownership program, and gain-sharing bonuses to align individual and company goals and reward effective teamwork.[46]

SUMMARY OF LEARNING OBJECTIVES

DEFINE MOTIVATION.

At a general level, motivation is the set of forces (e.g., needs) that initiate behavior and determine its form, direction, intensity, and duration.

EXPLAIN THE PROCESS OF MOTIVATION.

Motivation can be defined as a process to satisfy basic human needs. For example, Maslow believed that people engage in specific behaviors to satisfy lower-order as well as higher-order needs. The process model (Table 12–1) shows how needs influence behavior. Behavior leads to some level of reward. (Poor performance leads to lower levels of the reward than does high performance.) Finally, feedback is the reinforcement component of the model. If a specific need-driven behavior is reinforced with a reward, the behavior is likely to be repeated.

COMPARE CONTENT, PROCESS, AND REINFORCEMENT THEORIES OF MOTIVATION.

Content (or need-based) theories are based on the idea that people are driven to meet basic needs that, when they're met, produce satisfaction. An example is Maslow's theory of motivation. Process theories of motivation describe the cognitive processes and decisions that help predict subsequent behavior. Equity theory is an example of a process theory of motivation. Reinforcement theory views motivation largely in terms of external factors that (1) elicit behavior responses and (2) describe the conditions under which the behavior is likely to be repeated. B.F. Skinner's theory of operant conditioning is such a theory.

DESCRIBE MASLOW'S HIEARCHY OF NEEDS, HERZBERG'S TWO-FACTOR THEORY, AND MCCLELLAND'S ACHIEVEMENT–MOTIVATION THEORY.

Maslow was the first psychologist to discuss a hierarchy of needs or an ordering of need importance. These needs range from lower-level needs (like the need to eat when hungry) to higher-level needs (such as the need to achieve our fullest potential). Herzberg's two-factor theory suggests that satisfaction and dissatisfaction at work come from different sources. He believed that hygiene factors in the work environment can cause dissatisfaction when they aren't present in sufficient quantity. But by themselves they can't cause satisfaction. The same can be said for satisfiers. Too little decision-making latitude can cause decreased satisfaction, not dissatisfaction. McClelland's achievement motivation theory states that motivation is need-determined, based on three universal needs: need for achievement, need for affiliation, and need for power.

DISCUSS EXPECTANCY, EQUITY, AND REINFORCEMENT THEORIES OF MOTIVATION.

Expectancy theory is a cognitive theory of motivation. Sometimes called VIE theory, expectancy theory describes the process people use to evaluate (1) the likelihood that their effort or expenditure will yield the desired outcome and (2) how much they want the outcome in the first place. While somewhat cumbersome in practice, expectancy theory focuses our attention on motivation as a rational decision process. Equity theory is a process theory based on the concept of fairness. In inequitable situations, we must first restore equity. For example, if we believe we are underpaid, we may reduce our effort in order to restore equity. Equity theory predicts that people who are overrewarded tend to work harder. But remember that equity is a relative concept. Equity determinations are usually made by comparing ourselves to those close by, not to some national database. Reinforcement theory suggests that behavior is a function of external reinforcement of previous behavior. We tend to repeat behaviors we've been rewarded for and avoid behaviors that we've been punished for.

DISCUSS THE ADVANTAGES OR GOAL SETTING.
Goals can help to (1) direct attention and action, (2) mobilize effort, (3) create persistent behavior over time, and (4) lead to strategies for goal attainment.

IDENTIFY THE ATTRIBUTES OF EFFECTIVE GOALS.
First is goal specificity (a set, specific goal). Second is goal difficulty. Difficult goals provide more internal motivation and lead to higher performance than easy goals do. Third, goal feedback lets people know how they are proceeding toward goal attainment. Fourth, workers' participation in goal setting leads to greater commitment and ultimate goal attainment. Finally, competition often leads to a higher level of task performance.

DESCRIBE SOME MOTIVATIONAL TOOLS AND TECHNIQUES USED IN A QUALITY MANAGEMENT SYSTEM
Charting provides a visual image of the degree of proximity toward a target. Time sampling consists of a series of observations made during a fixed time period to gauge whether a target will be met. Output counting measures the products of the target behavior. How many were produced, what was the defect rate, how many were shipped? In addition, several pay schemes are used to increase interest and rewards for extra performance. These include pay for performance, flexible rewards, flexible working hours, self-managed work design, and job enrichment.

KEY TERMS

ability, p. 318
baseline, p. 330
charting, p. 329
content theory, p. 318
contingent rewards, p. 325
event counting, p. 330
expectancy, p. 322
extinction, p. 326
extrinsic rewards, p. 318
goal acceptance, p. 327
goal commitment, p. 327
goal-setting theory, p. 327
hierarchy of needs, p. 318
hot stove rule, p. 326

hygiene factor, p. 320
instrumentality, p. 322
intervention period, p. 330
intrinsic rewards, p. 317
job content, p. 320
job context, p. 320
material reward, p. 332
motivation, p. 316
need for achievement, p. 321
need for affiliation, p. 321
need for power, p. 321
negative reinforcement, p. 326
noncontingent rewards, p. 326
operant conditioning, p. 324

output counting, p. 330
pinpointing, p. 329
positive reinforcement, p. 326
process theory, p. 322
punishment, p. 326
reference ratio, p. 324
reinforcement, p. 326
satisfier, p. 320
social rewards, p. 332
symbolic rewards, p. 332
target behaviors, p. 329
task rewards, p. 332
time sampling, p. 330
valence, p. 322

REVIEW AND DISCUSSION QUESTIONS

Recall
1. What are the components of a basic model of motivation?
2. What are the differences between Theory X assumptions about human nature and Theory Y assumptions?
3. What are the factors in Herzberg's two-factor theory?
4. What are the characteristics of an effective goal?

Understanding
5. What does it mean to say that content theories of motivation are need-based and process theories of motivation are determined by human cognition?

6. Define the terms equity and inequity. Describe a work situation that is equitable and one that is inequitable.
7. What motivates you at work? Is it pay or other factors?
8. How can fear be used as a motivator? Can fear motivate people? How do managers develop the capacity to use fear to motivate workers?
9. Why do managers look for motivated workers?

Application
10. In describing a specific work situation, illustrate how a manager might use the principles of a content theory of motivation to motivate workers.

CASE STUDY

Motivating the Sales Force at Hewlett Packard

Hewlett Packard (HP), the computer firm based in Cupertino, California, uses several methods to motivate its sales force. The "must-win" program spotlights the salesperson for the best sales approach and attitude in each region every quarter. The winners receive many prizes, including a plaque engraved with their name and accomplishments and a $500 cash award. Winners are also invited to appear with Manuel Diaz, director of sales and marketing, in an interactive telemeeting. Via HP's television studio and satellite hookup, top salespeople talk about their achievements with sales teams at over 80 sales offices.

Sales quality manager Jeff Williams says programs like this are important because "they cause sales management to turn their attention to critical sales rep behavior such as leadership, teamwork, and a positive, winning attitude." These qualities lead to a long-term competitive advantage.

HP uses several other annual recognition programs to motivate the sales force. The 100 Percent Club recognizes members of the sales force that reach 100 percent of their sales goals. Membership in the President's Club is awarded to the top 100 employees worldwide (85 salespeople and 15 district sales managers). The main reward of the President's Club is a three-day trip to a luxury resort for winners and their spouses. Here they interact with upper management, including CEO Lewis Platt and HP founders Dave Packard and Bill Hewlett. This demonstrates that outstanding performance is recognized by top management as well as peers.

The team approach used at HP is also a motivational tool. HP empowers salespeople to manage accounts, represent the entire company, and manage customer relationships. This results in higher quality work, personal fulfillment, and career growth. In addition, products are reaching the customer much faster.

Although it is difficult to measure the effectiveness of these motivation techniques, they seem to be working. Salespeople like the trips and rewards, but most of all, they like the recognition by peers and upper management.

QUESTIONS
1. Why is motivating the sales force important at HP?
2. What type of rewards does HP use to motivate the sales force?
3. Which particular theory or theories of motivation explain the methods used by HP to motivate its sales force?

Source: Adapted from Stratford Sherman, "Secrets of HP's 'Muddled' Team," *Fortune*, March 18, 1996, pp. 116–118; Melissa Campanelli, "The Secrets of America's Best Sales Forces," *Sales & Marketing Management*, January 1992, pp. 93–95; and Cate Corcoran, "HP Chief Promises to Get Units Working Together," *InfoWorld*, August 31, 1992, p. 94.

VIDEO CASE

Employee Motivation at Tellabs, Inc.

It's important to understand the reasons why effective managers must be concerned with employee motivation. After identifying some of the factors contributing to motivation, this video looks at how Tellabs, Inc., has successfully applied motivation theory.

Tellabs is based in the Chicago area, but is internally known for its telecommunications products and services. However, recently the company gained fame when its stock increased 1,683 percent over a five-year period, making Tellabs the best performing stock at that time on the New York Stock Exchange, the American Stock Exchange and Nasdaq. Tellabs was founded in 1975 by a group of engineers brainstorming at a kitchen table, and grew from 20 employees with annual sales of $312,000 to 2,600 employees with annual sales of $494 million in 1994. Tellabs currently designs, manufactures, markets, and services voice and data transport and network access systems.

One of the principal reasons for Tellabs' remarkable success has been its ability to motivate its workforce. In simple terms, employee motivation refers to an employee's willingness to perform in his or her job. Effective managers must be concerned with motivating employees toward common goals that will improve the success of the company. At Tellabs, a motivated workforce has enhanced the quality of its products and services.

Tellabs' manager of quality, Joe Taylor, explains what's behind the company's motivated workers: "In the past 10 years we've found that to improve our quality we had to invest in our employees through training programs. Specifically, they have the tools and the resources now to make a difference within our processes in the factory and provide us with process improvements."

A motivated workforce contributes to increased quality in goods and services, greater efficiency in work processes, and improved customer service. Grace Pastiak said, "When I look at the improvements that Tellabs has made since implementing just-in-time and Total Quality Commitment, by far the biggest gain has been exciting employees to do their best and giving them the opportunity to implement their own ideas."

At its core, motivation results from an individual's desire to satisfy personal needs or goals. Every person has a set of needs or goals that influences their behavior. Abraham Maslow postulated that needs can be placed in a hierarchy and that as each need level in the hierarchy is satisfied, the person will concentrate on meeting needs at the next level.

Frederick Herzberg, conducted a study in the 1960s that concluded that factors pertaining to the work itself, such as achievement, recognition, and responsibility, tended to actually motivate employees. Other factors, such as supervision, pay, and company policies, might increase job satisfaction, but not necessarily employee motivation.

A third approach to motivation, developed by Douglas McGregor, involves two opposing theories about the nature of human behavior. Theory X holds that some employees are lazy or unwilling to work unless motivated by negative factors such as threats and constant supervision. Theory Y holds that employees want to work and do a good job and are motivated best by incentives, responsibility, and ownership of their work.

Maslow's hierarchy, Herzberg's factors, and McGregor's theories suggest that it's in a company's best interest to offer employees adequate rewards and to appeal to their pride of workmanship. At

Tellabs, many employees say that the entrepreneurial atmosphere nurtured by managers makes them feel good about themselves. So Tellabs clearly takes a Theory Y approach.

Effective managers help create a work environment that encourages, supports, and sustains improvement in work performance. At Tellabs, managers have implemented job rotation systems and a cadre of high performance teams to help enrich jobs and create an innovative working environment. Another innovation at Tellabs to ensure a high level of employee motivation is high performance teams.

Some companies may use a combination of motivation theories. In 1992, Tellabs presented its corporate goals, known as Strategic Initiatives, to its employees. The corporate mission statement emphasized the company's goals quality, customer satisfaction, profits, growth, its people, and its corporate integrity.

Tellabs' total compensation plan includes an Employee Stock Option Plan and retirement investments, such as 401(k). Also employees receive an annual bonus based on the company's productivity.

At Tellabs, employee motivation and performance are enhanced by an atmosphere in which employees are openly told they are valued and trusted. Managers encourage calculated risk taking and innovation. They empower workers through cross-functional teams so that they are able to identify problems and develop effective solutions.

Tellabs' Career Development System trains internal candidates for key management positions, while its competitive compensation plan shares the wealth, contributes to employee satisfaction, and encourages peak performance.

QUESTIONS

1. McGregor's Theory X and Theory Y have totally different views of the typical worker. Which of the two theories do you think managers should adopt? Explain. Describe how adopting theory X would affect a manager's behavior toward employees. Do the same for Theory Y.

2. What are some of the potential pitfalls of using employee empowerment as a motivational device in the workplace?

3. Herzberg's theory says workplace factors lead to employee motivation. What are some workplace factors not mentioned in the video that could affect employee motivation?

APPLICATION EXERCISE

TIME FOR A RAISE

You need to make salary decisions for the eight team leaders you manage. Each team leader currently earns about $32,000 per year. You have $16,000 for salary increases. Each team leader's work record and personal background are described below.

	INDIVIDUAL DECISIONS		GROUP DECISIONS	
	Scale	Raise	Scale	Raise
Adamson	____	____	____	____
Berkowitz	____	____	____	____
Colombo	____	____	____	____
Dierdorff	____	____	____	____
Epplington	____	____	____	____
Forrestal	____	____	____	____
Gonzalez	____	____	____	____
Harris	____	____	____	____

Employee	Quantity	Absent	Team	Quality	Late
Adamson 7/$31,600/HS/26	38.65	10	Very good	Very good	3
Berkowitz 3/$31,750/BS/25	34.59	4	Very good	Very good	0
Colombo 4/$32,000/BS/26	38.74	3	Good	Good	2
Dierdorff 6/$31,600/11th/24	37.51	0	Very good	Excellent	5
Epplington 3/$31,700/BS/25	36.03	0	Excellent	Excellent	4
Forrestal 4/$31,750/BS/27	38.61	6	Good	Good	3
Gonzalez 5/$32,000/BS/26	35.23	4	Good	Very good	2
Harris 5/$31,800/HS/24	37.94	6	Good	Good	1

Listed beneath the team leader's name are her or his years with the company (not necessarily in this job), current salary, highest degree or grade of education, and age. *Quantity* of work ranges from 0 (lowest) to 40 (highest). *Absent* counts number of sick and personal days taken in the past year. *Team* evaluates the cohesiveness, cooperation, and spirit of the team leader's group. *Quality* reflects the defects in a team's quantity of work. Both team and quality range from poor to fair to good to very good to excellent. *Late* is the percentage of team projects (about 50 per year) completed after the agreed-upon deadline.

INSTRUCTIONS

Rate the performance (using the following point scale) and write the dollar raise you've chosen for each team leader. In your class group, discuss your individual decisions and make a group decision for each team leader's raise. Write your group's ratings and/or raises on the board, as directed.

4.0 Excellent (meets or exceeds all standards/expectations).
3.0 Very good (meets all standards/expectations).
2.0 Good (generally meets standards/expectations).
1.0 Fair (often fails to meet standards/expectations).
0.0 Poor (fails to meet generally accepted standards/expectations).

CHAPTER 13

Leadership

After studying this chapter, you should be able to:

❖ Distinguish between leaders and managers.

❖ Explain the relationship between leadership and power.

❖ Compare the theories of trait, behavioral, and situational leadership.

❖ Describe the theory of transformational leadership.

❖ Define self-leadership and discuss the societal trends that contributed to its development.

❖ Describe the various behavioral and cognitive self-management strategies.

❖ Explain how a business can develop a self-leadership culture.

Leadership in Transition

Successful organizations are guided by people with vision. Over time, IBM has been blessed with exactly that type of leadership. Thomas Watson, Sr., built IBM's business through the continual development of punch card technology. With this technological innovation, IBM (nicknamed Big Blue) became synonymous with successful big business. But Watson's lack of vision about the influence of the next technology—the computer—nearly cost IBM dearly.

Louis V. Gerstner, Jr.

Fortunately, his son, Thomas Watson, Jr., had the youthful energy and foresight to envision the potential impact of the general-purpose computer in business applications. The passing of the reins from father to son was largely an internal decision at IBM. Although not totally convinced of the computer's role in general-purpose data processing, Thomas Watson, Sr., stepped aside as chairman and CEO of IBM. Thomas Watson, Jr., quickly pushed for computer development based on the firm's existing strength—punch card technology. His innovative coupling of punch card technology (a field IBM dominated) as a computer input medium gave IBM a competitive advantage in the early years of computing. One thing is sure: Thomas Watson, Jr., had a good understanding of the marketplace and the vision to interpret the computer's role in IBM's future.

For the next three decades IBM dominated the direction and technical standards in the computer industry. IBM frequently used its position in the industry to ward off the threat of competitive inroads into its market share. But over the past decade IBM's position as the industry leader has eroded. Its early 1990s market position worsened with IBM reporting a $4.97 billion loss in the last quarter of 1992. Unlike earlier years when external threats were handled internally, IBM's CEO John Akers found board members and major stockholders pushing for his resignation. Akers finally was forced by pressure from the board of directors to step down as chairman and CEO of IBM.

Just as IBM's success can be attributed to leadership, so apparently can blame for failure be laid at the leader's feet. Who will lead IBM out of the dark path of loss, toward the light of profit? After Akers' pressure cooker resignation, the IBM board did the unthinkable for IBM—it went outside of IBM's executive ranks to select a new CEO. Louis V. Gertsner, Jr., former RJR Nabisco CEO, was handed the reins of Big Blue. This move suggests that no longer can corporate executives expect to internally resolve their problems through managing better. IBM's market share declined from 30 percent in 1985 to 19 percent in 1991. Promoting from within wasn't the answer—new leadership from outside became the clarion call.

How is Gerstner doing? By all indications, he should be happy. IBM had a net profit of nearly $3 billion in 1994, the best year since 1990. But 68 percent of the profits came from high-end products like mainframes and minicomputers, products for which demand has peaked and markets are dwindling. So, despite such success, some critics are wondering if Gerstner really does have a vision—a long-term growth strategy for the largest computer company in the world. Gerstner's response: he is remaking the business to become a leader in the emerging field of networked computing and electronic commerce. In his vision, communications rather than computing is the key; it will involve everything from multimedia PCs to the Internet.

Leadership is visionary action. In troublesome times, it can be hard for leaders to make major changes—often because they are just too committed to the past or simply don't have any more ideas. New views of the competitive world often come from outside the corporation. Boards recognize that change requires new vision. IBM's board broke with past practices and selected an outside CEO. And early in 1996, the computer giant's share price skyrocketed 42 percent to around $119; Wall Street experts are predicting shares will hit $140 by year end.

Source: Adapted from Ira Sager, "It's Hot! It's Sexy! It's . . . Big Blue?" *Business Week,* March 4, 1996, p. 39; Ira Sager, "The View From IBM," *Business Week,* October 30, 1995, pp. 142–150; Ira Sager and Amy Corteso, "IBM: Why the Good News Isn't Good Enough," *Business Week,* January 23, 1995, pp. 72–73; Stephen Baker and Maria Mallory, "IBM after Akers," *Business Week,* February 8, 1993, pp. 22–24; "Akers Quits under Heavy Pressure; Dividend Is Slashed," *The Wall Street Journal,* January 27, 1993, A1–A3; Carole J. Loomis, "King John Wears an Uneasy Crown," *Fortune,* January 11, 1993, pp. 44–46; and George Anders, Eben Shapiro, Michael Miller, and Laurence Hooper, "IBM's Pick Is Talented But Some See Flaws in His Record at RJR," *The Wall Street Journal,* March 25, 1993, p. A1.

Advocates of total quality management, such as W. Edwards Deming, Philip B. Crosby, and J. M. Juran, maintain that quality improvements are the responsibility of senior-level managers. The challenges of global competitiveness and quality place a heavy emphasis on managers to provide the type of leadership for workers that yields continuous improvement and customer satisfaction. Increased worldwide competition requires innovative strategies that emphasize quality products or services. This requires leadership. Although profound changes—in training, statistical skills, and responsibility, for example—are needed among the workforce, none of these are likely to occur without quality-based leadership. This chapter describes how effective leaders provide vision, direction, and meaning to organizational activities.

Our understanding of effective leadership has evolved and matured considerably over the years. One traditional vision of leadership was General Patton barking commands from a tank turret with the troops surrounding him eagerly awaiting orders. A contemporary view of leadership is Mary Kay Ash awarding a pink Cadillac to top saleswomen. Both leaders had a vision of the future, mobilized resources, and motivated people to join them in their quest.

But as society, people, and situations change, so must leaders' actions change. Gone are the days of blind obedience to leaders. Contemporary leadership is based on participation. Our review describes this journey from autocratic to more participative and democratic styles of leadership. In the end, the goal of effective leadership is the production of a high-quality product or service.

Traditional models of leadership have been tested and many doubts have been raised about their capacity to produce a competitive, quality-based workforce for the 21st century. The trend in leadership styles is toward more participative and consultive leadership and away from the dogmatic, authoritative approaches of yesteryear. Since leaders have always been expected to be able to both manage and anticipate change, most models of leadership require the effective leader to have a vision. A **vision** is a clear sense of the or-

vision
A clear sense of the organization's future.

ganization's future. Without vision, leaders have nowhere to lead workers. Without an understanding of the global demands of the market, leaders are not likely to be successful. With this in mind, **leadership** is defined as the process of influencing other people to attain organizational goals.[1]

leadership
The process of exerting influence over people.

LEADERS AND MANAGERS

Are leaders and managers different? Noted Harvard psychologist Abraham Zaleznick thinks so.[2] He believes managers focus on demands and constraints of the moment rather than more far-reaching matters. Unlike leaders, managers must deal with internal daily production concerns. Often managers seem more concerned with "getting things done" than with "getting the right things done." At the worst, managing is reduced to little more than people processing and product massaging. In the process, managers sometimes show little concern for the customer or the product's final use. Unfortunately, this may translate into getting the product out the door regardless of quality. This preoccupation with what Zaleznick calls *process* orientation leads to mediocrity. For the manager, the goal becomes preserving the status quo.

Zaleznick believes that, unlike managers, leaders are bored with routine or, as Tom Peters puts it, they "thrive on chaos" and seek innovative and novel solutions. Rather than have a concern for process, the leader is concerned with *substance*. For a leader, substance is everything. The manager asks, What is the best way to consistently maintain quality and meet production targets? The leader asks an entirely different question: for a particular product, what is quality and how will the definition change in the future? The difference between managers and leaders is based upon what they do. Managers deal with the pressures of the moment. The manager is concerned with the process surrounding the work flow. The leader is concerned with providing meaning or purpose in work for employees and creating meaning in the product for customers.

Lee Iacocca's transformation of Chrysler is an example of how a leader can create vision and meaning for both workers and customers. Chrysler workers believed that they were part of the solution to problems facing the auto industry. They were creating the new Chrysler corporation. What followed is history. Certainly the firm's customers believe that Chrysler created in its minivan a new alternative to the gas-guzzling station wagon that fit the needs of the family and the environment. Iacocca's strategic vision of new products, new markets, and new ways of creating quality and value for the consumer became a reality. Workers produced a better, higher-quality product—not just because of technology, but because they believed they could. The results were dramatically increased customer demand and profitability.

Leadership is both an individual property and a process. As an individual property, leadership is a combination of personal attributes and abilities such as vision, energy, and knowledge. As a process, leadership is the individual's ability to create a shared vision of the future. Creating a shared vision requires the leader to set goals, motivate employees, and create a supportive and productive culture in the organization. Indeed, in many instances it is difficult to separate the individual from the process. This is because the leadership process is an extension of the leader's personality and ideas. Collectively then, individual leadership properties and the leadership process influence employee behavior.

POWER AND LEADERSHIP

Influencing the behavior of others is at the core of leadership. To accomplish this, leaders use their **power**, which is, simply, the ability to get people to do something they otherwise wouldn't do.[3] Managers usually have several sources of power at their disposal. The following section summarizes a number of sources of power within organizations.[4]

power
The capacity to influence people.

REWARD POWER - Reward power is the manager's ability to allocate organizational resources in exchange for cooperation. Reward power is probably the most widely used form of power. Rewards controlled by managers include pay raises, promotions, bonuses, and recognition.

COERCIVE POWER - Coercive power, sometimes referred to as *punishment power*, is the opposite of reward power. Coercive power is the manager's ability to apply penalties when an employee fails to cooperate. For example, an employee who exhibits inappropriate behavior or violates company policy might be given a "below-average" performance evaluation or even be passed over for promotion. But punishment power can generate fear and distrust among employees, as the Ethics Spotlight shows. These negative aspects of punishment must far outweigh the benefits before punishment can be successfully used to alter an employee's behavior.

EXPERT POWER - Expert power is based on an individual's technical or expert knowledge about a particular area. Expertise may be in the form of experience, information, or advanced education. Special knowledge allows an individual to persuade others

---

ETHICS SPOTLIGHT

THE USE OF PUNISHMENT POWER AT GENERAL ELECTRIC

When an employee is so troubled by a company's actions that he blows the whistle, will the employee be congratulated or condemned? How will society react? How will the employer react? Can a firm drive out distrust and fear by its leadership practices?

After several visible ethical scandals, including a 1985 conviction for altering time cards of engineers on a government project, General Electric made a concerted effort to increase employee awareness of ethical concerns. CEO Jack Welch became a strong advocate of voluntary disclosure of corporate wrongs. Welch, a globally admired leader of a firm with over $60 billion in annual sales and more than a quarter-million employees, found that his emphasis on profits had interfered with ethical compliance. To improve this situation, company-produced videos and seminars created an atmosphere that encouraged employees to identify and report wrongdoings by the company. But when employee Chester Walsh detected at $42 million fraud, GE's ethical policy came under scrutiny. On the one side, Walsh claimed that the real ethic at General Electric was to punish whistle-blowers (employees who find breaches of ethics and then report them), while on the other side, GE management pointed the finger at Walsh, saying he was motivated by a federal law that allows him (as the whistle-blower) to claim up to one-quarter of the $70 million set-

tlement levied against GE. GE claimed the law encouraged Mr. Walsh to allow the corruption to grow so he could profit from the size of the settlement.

General Electric, a major supplier to the government and foreign trade, was big enough to merit its own investigation unit at the U.S. Justice and Defense departments. About 20 percent of 60 investigations of GE began with whistle-blowers. GE whistle-blowers say that GE's intense effort to be profitable was at the root of the problem. GE counters with the claim that a confidential toll-free phone number for reporting ethics violations, along with forms and alternative channels for letting management know where practices are questionable, provides a leadership culture of openness and receptiveness to whistle-blowers. Former GE employees, whistle-blowers themselves, claim otherwise. One woman, pointing out unfair billing practices to management, found herself ostracized rather than eliminated. Another employee, reporting time card fraud and overcharging one government work, claims he was dismissed for his effort.

One GE lawyer explained the pressure on GE to balance integrity with an emphasis on making its profit numbers: "To make sure that every time we give a performance message—make your number—we also give a compliance measure." In Philadelphia in 1985, in response to a threat that "heads would roll" if costs were not contained, GE managers illegally charged $800,000 in cost overruns to a phony research account to be

paid by the U.S. Department of Defense. U.S. attorney Ed Zittlau said, "The managers feared for their jobs. From their point of view, the mischarging looked like the lesser of two evils."

Fear and greed drive some GE managers: fear of losing their jobs for below-par performance, greed for healthy bonuses for meeting goals. A manager can double a $200,000 annual salary if profit goals are met.

Is there any way out of this conflict of interest? General Motors attempted to drive out fear by shifting responsibility for measuring work from managers to workers, while keeping most of the other work mechanisms in place. By reducing the levels and numbers of white-collar, midlevel managers charged with inspection, and by encouraging innovation to improve work and save production jobs threatened by market failure, GM's California New United Motor Manufacturing Inc. (NUMMI) plant showed phenomenal success where once workers and management had witnessed only declining quality and profitability. GE now evaluates people on what it calls *boundarylessness* to weed out those who obstruct the free flow of ideas.

Source: Adapted from Stratford Sherman, "How Tomorrow's Best Leaders Are Learning Their Stuff," *Fortune*, November 27, 1995, pp. 64–70; Amal Kumar Naj, "Internal Suspicions: GE's Drive to Purge Fraud Is Hampered by Workers' Mistrust," *The Wall Street Journal*, July 22, 1992, pp. A1, A4; Steven Pearlstein, "Contracting: Bringing a Breach of Ethics to Light," *Washington Post*, national weekly edition, July 27–August, 1992, pp. 21–22; and "Manufacturing Management: Return of the Stopwatch," *The Economist*, January 23, 1993, p. 69.

to do as she wishes. The advertising executive who has developed many successful campaigns is sought after for advice and so has expert power.

RERFERENT POWER – Referent power arises from an individual's personal characteristics that are esteemed by others. Referent power stimulates imitation and loyalty. Thus people we admire have referent power. When someone we admire asks us to do something, we are more inclined to do it than if someone we don't admire makes the request. We also emulate the admired person's behavior in the hope that by doing so, we will be as successful as he or she is.

LEGITIMATE POWER – Legitimate power accompanies certain positions within an organization. Managers and supervisors have legitimate power, and can assign various tasks to subordinates. The use of legitimate power to direct, reward, discipline, and control workers is called authority. Authority is the leader's formal power granted by membership in the organization.

PERSONAL POWER – Personal power consists of both expert and referent power, or a combination of both.[5] A sense of personal power comes from a belief that one can reach his or her goals in his or her own way; a sense of personal power is communicated by developing authority, accessibility, assertiveness, a positive image, and solid communications skills.[6]

MODELS AND THEORIES OF LEADERSHIP

Leadership is one of the most studied aspects of management. A tremendous variety of research, terms, and values underlie leadership definitions, theories, and findings. Three widely accepted historical models have evolved through the 20th century. Trait theory, the first attempt to describe effective leaders in a systematic fashion, focuses on a *trait* such as a physical or personality attribute of the leader. Studies of trait theory led to the behavioral model. Behavioral models focus on (1) the work itself and (2) worker attitudes. Behavioral models, in turn, led to contingency models of leadership. **Contingency leadership models** state that the leader's behavioral style must be contingent on the situation if the leader is to be effective. Contingency models emerged as two different approaches: (1) fit the leader to the situation and (2) fit the decision to the situation. Subsequent leadership theorists have sought alternative explanations for effective leadership, including visionary leadership and substitutes for leadership.

> **contingency leadership models**
> Leadership theories that assert that the specific leadership behavioral style must be contingent on the situation if the leader is to be effective.

Trait Theory of Leadership

Today we tend to notice effective leaders—Herb Kelleher of Southwest Airlines, Geraldine Laybourne of Nickelodeon, Robert Goizueta of Coca-Cola, the late Sam Walton of Wal-Mart—and ask what personal characteristics make them effective. This question is at the root of the **trait theory of leadership**, which identifies effective leaders in terms of certain physical and psychological attributes (e.g., intelligence, height, articulateness). Trait-based leadership approaches focus on traits of those who emerged or assumed power as the leader and on traits of those leaders considered to be effective.

> **trait theory of leadership**
> An early attempt to describe effective leaders in a systematic fashion that focuses on the leader's physical and personality attributes.

One review of 12 leadership studies revealed conflicting results. Nine studies supported the idea that leaders were taller than followers, although two studies found the reverse to be true. The same study concluded that leadership ability is associated with the person's judgment and verbal skills.[7] Edwin Ghiselli notes that, within a certain range, intelligence is an accurate predictor of leadership effectiveness.[8] But leaders who are much more intelligent or much less intelligent than their followers will not be effective. Also Ghiselli's findings suggest that leader initiative, self-assurance, decisiveness, and maturity, among other traits, are important for leader success. A 1992 survey of 750 leading American companies identified the most preferred skills or characteristics of an ideal MBA. These qualities were oral and written communication skills (preferred by 83.5 percent of respondents), leadership (79.7

percent), analytical skills (75.3 percent), the ability to work in teams (71.4 percent), and the ability to manage rapid change (65.9 percent).[9]

A study of 21 less effective leaders established that leaders who failed to be promoted (or were fired or forced to retire) were more insensitive, abrasive, arrogant, and intimidating; excessively ambitious; and unable to delegate, staff effectively, or adapt to bosses with different styles. By contrast, the more effective leaders were more direct yet diplomatic, and were flexible at dealing with others.[10] Another study found that specific technical skills or knowledge of the work group's task were related to leader success.[11] Flexibility is also a valuable leader trait. With modern flexible manufacturing systems, firms stress a greater variety of superior product features, factories that can produce a range of products, and rapid product innovation to meet changing customer tastes. This is a broader definition of *quality* than reliable products, conformance, and just-in-time delivery.[12]

Trait theory constitutes an important yet incomplete approach to leadership. Not all effective leaders are tall or exceptionally smart. Serious cultural differences exist; some attributes seen as positive in some cultures are seen as negative in others. For example, American leadership practices have tended to endorse direct, forceful leaders. Not all successful leaders are dominating, extroverted, or self-confident. The trait approach is a simple—perhaps too simple—method for trying to identify or predict effective leadership. Yet at the same time it presents an appealing potential explanation for the effectiveness of people like Sam Walton and Lee Iacocca. The Diversity Scope examines some differences in leadership characteristics of men and women.

But trait theory generally ignores the workers. Lists of traits also fail to give weight to the relative importance of the many possible traits. (For example, is decisiveness more important than intelligence?) Many trait studies were of small numbers of leaders, which lim-

DIVERSITY SCOPE   MEN AND WOMEN AS LEADERS

Do differences in leadership traits exist between men and women? While this subject has been debated a great deal, with mixed opinions, certain style differences have been identified by Dr. Judy Rosener. She has found that through socialization, men and women are taught differently. Thus, while both men and women make good—and bad—leaders, it is important to understand the different leadership styles they use. The most effective leader will combine the positive traits of both men and women and use them appropriately.

CHARACTERISTICS ATTRIBUTED TO MEN

Lead by Command and Control. This works best in the military, but has drawbacks when managing across gender lines.

Encourage Rewards for Services Rendered. This is the traditional reward system, much like the old barter system. Creating more flexibility in what an organization rewards is very important in helping a diverse group of workers to find success.

Rely on Positional Power. As males have held many of the power positions, it is not surprising that they derive power from their position. This is a poor strategy with highly acculturated employees, but works well in other cultures.

Follow a Hierarchical Structure. Historically, leaders have relied on lines of authority in getting the job done. As TQM has gained popularity, the end result is a flatter organization, and it may become more difficult to follow a hierarchical structure.

Action Orientation. Aggressive, take-charge managers have succeeded in the past, and will succeed in the future, though an overly aggressive stance turns workers off.

Think Analytically. Leaders with this trait have a great track record, especially when combined with intuitive thinking.

CHARACTERISTICS ATTRIBUTED TO WOMEN

Share Power and Information. Power, to some extent, stems from position and in-

formation, and can be used to influence others. Women are skilled at maintaining power through relationships, and are more willing to share power than men.

Enhance Self-Worth of Others. Female leaders tend to build their co-workers' esteem. This is a trait that builds employee commitment and is essential in managing a diverse group.

Encourage Participation. This is a powerful and important characteristic of a leader. Employees feel motivated when they know they are part of the organization and that their opinions count.

Get Others Excited About Their Work. Female leaders place great emphasis on process as well as product; they want to enjoy the journey. This trait is useful because it helps employees find intrinsic value in their work.

Source: Adapted from Judy B. Rosener, "The Valued Ways Men and Women Lead," *Human Resources*, June 1991, p. 149; Judy B. Rosener, "Ways Women Lead," *Harvard Business Review*, November/December 1990, pp. 119–125; and Lee Gardenswartz and Anita Rowe, *Managing Diversity* (Burr Ridge, IL: Business One Irwin, 1993), pp. 356–361.

Linda Alepin, vice president of business development at Amdahl, a multibillion-dollar supplier of mainframes and other products, has led that company's turn-around efforts since it was hit hard by the collapse of the mainframe market in 1993. As leader of the turn-around, Linda's job is market-oriented. She describes her role as "to keep two to three steps ahead of the company. I'll find the project, find a sponsor, align it with the company's direction. Mainly, I've got to stay ahead of the curve." ("Amdahl Jumps out of the Box," by Bill Kelly, *Journal of Business Strategy*, May–June 1995, pp. 22–28.)

ited the studies' ability to generalize, especially across cultures and countries. Most of all, trait theory studies were inconsistent in their findings and in their value to management. Trait theory does suggest that some value can be found in attention to both the task and the workers. The deficiency of trait theory in explaining significant variance in leadership effectiveness, as well as some of its useful findings, has led to the behavioral style models of the leader.

Behavioral Models of Leadership

As research shifted away from the idea that leaders are endowed with certain characteristics, it moved toward the notion that different leaders have or could develop different leadership styles. This approach, known as the behavioral style, defines leader effectiveness in terms of *leader behaviors*—what the leader *does*—rather than in terms of traits the leader *possesses*.

TASK-ORIENTED AND PEOPLE-ORIENTED STYLES - In the **behavioral style model**, effective leaders focus both on the work and on workers' attitudes and expectations. A **task-oriented behavioral style** consists of behaviors such as setting goals, giving directions, supervising worker performance, and applauding good work. Since Frederick W. Taylor's time, there has been regular attention to the leader as a task-driven manager. Yet attention to task alone was insufficient. Thus there evolved a **people-oriented behavioral style**. It consists of behaviors such as showing empathy for worker needs and feelings, being supportive of group needs, establishing trusting relationships with workers, and allowing workers to participate in work-related decisions. According to Philip B. Crosby, "The future executive can go all the way through undergraduate business school and graduate business school without receiving a course on how to help the employee. It's always 'systems and programs analysis,' not how do we help the person do the job, how do we help people."[13]

JOB-CENTERED AND EMPLOYEE-CENTERED LEADER BEHAVIORS - Studies conducted at the University of Michigan focused on job-centered and employee-centered leader behaviors.[14] These two categories of leader behaviors represent directions that are either task oriented or people oriented. At first, an employee-centered leader was found to be effective, but the original study did not separate cause and effect. Did an employee-centered leader produce good work, or did good work produce an employee-centered leader? More careful subsequent research found that whereas employee-centered leaders did create more positive worker attitudes, job-centered leaders achieved higher worker productivity.[15] Figure 13–1 summarizes leader behavioral styles.

behavioral style model
The leadership theory that focuses on (1) the work and (2) workers' attitudes and expectations.

task-oriented behavioral style
Leadership behaviors such as setting goals, giving directions, supervising worker performance, and applauding good work.

people-oriented behavioral style
The aspect of leadership theory consisting of behaviors such as showing empathy for worker needs and feelings, being supportive of group needs, establishing trusting relationships with workers, and allowing workers to participate in work-related decisions.

FIGURE 13-1
Leader Behavioral Styles

	Task-oriented	People-oriented
Ohio State Studies	Initiating Structure	Consideration
Michigan Studies	Job-Centered Authoritarian	Employee-Centered Democratic

INITIATING STRUCTURE AND CONSIDERATION - The Ohio State studies, conducted at the University beginning about 50 years ago, identified initiating structure and consideration as task- and people-oriented behavioral styles, respectively.[16] Leaders emphasizing initiating structure usually follow a behavioral pattern: they insist that workers follow rigid work methods, insist on being informed of worker behavior, push workers for greater efforts, and make detailed decisions for the workers, concerning what work is to be done and how it is to be done. Leaders emphasizing consideration appreciate a job well done, stress high morale, treat workers as their equals, and are friendly and approachable. Subsequent studies generally found that leaders who score high on both behaviors are more effective than leaders scoring low on these behavioral styles.

Leaders were not found to be consistently effective despite a consistent, well-trained, and focused set of task- or people-oriented behaviors. Some workers did not respond well to task-oriented leaders. There were times when people-orientation helped task performance and times when it detracted from task performance. Dissatisfaction with behavioral style theories' ability to explain effective leadership led to the third phase in traditional leadership approaches, namely contingency or situation-based leadership effectiveness models, which we'll discuss shortly.

At Wal-Mart, managers employ a combination of people-oriented management with task skills and modern technology. Visiting senior managers ask employees, "Is there anything we can do for you?" as they simultaneously track task performance via a computer terminal that provides sales figures by store and department, measures labor hours and inventory losses, and compares these numbers with data for previous time periods, other stores or sales districts, as well as the national standards for Wal-Mart.[17]

LEADERSHIP GRID - Robert R. Blake and Anne Adams McCanse developed the Leadership Grid as a vehicle for leader behavior assessment and development. Using a series of questionnaires and structured seminars, the Leadership Grid technique assesses leadership orientation. The Leadership Grid incorporates both task orientation (concern for production) and people orientation (concern for people) into a two-dimensional matrix grid (Figure 13-2). Concern for people and concern for production are each arrayed along a nine-point continuum. A person with a high concern for people and low concern for production would be represented by the (1,9) cell of the matrix.

In the reverse situation, a person with a high degree of concern for production and a low concern for people would rate the (9,1) cell. In the midrange position is the person who is moderate on both dimensions, represented by the (5,5) cell. An individual rated at the top on both dimensions would be in the (9,9) cell. This technique demonstrates that it is likely that both orientations are more or less present in all managers rather than there being distinct or different leader behaviors. Leaders must be able to demonstrate concern for both people and production.

Further, Blake and McCanse believe that the (9,9) cell, which represents high people orientation and high task orientation, is the preferred style. The rationale for their belief is that a leader not only must support the worker, but also must structure the work setting toward task achievement. Finally, a series of seminars are used to guide the leader more toward the (9,9) orientation. A positive feature of the Leadership Grid is the recognition that both types of leader behaviors are important and that people have different orientations or predisposi-

FIGURE 13–2
The Leadership Grid

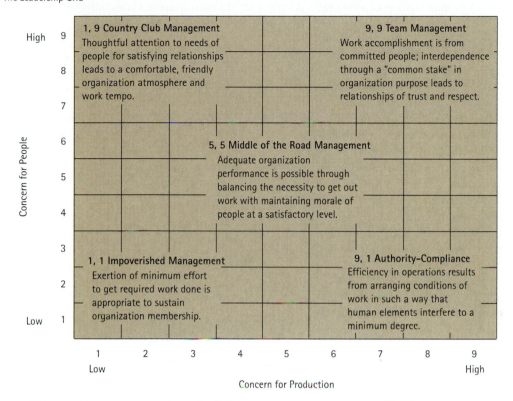

Source: The Leadership Grid© Figure from *Leadership Dilemmas—Grid Solutions*, by Robert R. Blake and Anne Adams McCanse (Houston: Grid Publishing Company), p. 29. Copyright © 1991, by Scientific Methods, Inc. Reproduced by permission of the owners.

tions that they bring to the management process. A negative feature of this approach is the assumption that leader behaviors can be readily changed through seminar participation. As we will see, this is not a common assumption among management scholars.

Contingency Models of Leadership

According to **situational theories of leadership**, the appropriate leader behavior is the one that best fits the constraints of a specific situation. An effective leader exhibits the leader behavior that matches the situation's demands. Leader effectiveness is contingent on displaying behavior appropriate to the situation's demands. In this context, situational leadership theories (1) identify important leadership situations and (2) suggest various leadership behaviors that increase worker satisfaction and productivity.

Two contrasting explanations of leadership situational effectiveness have emerged. One fits the leader to the situation; the other fits the leader's behavior to the situation. The first approach assumes the leader's behavioral style is relatively fixed or not easily changed. In this approach the best advice is to find the situation where the leader is most effective and avoid those situations where the leader is least effective. Is this always possible? Probably not! But the idea has merit. If we can find the situation where a manager's dominant leadership style is most effective, both leader and follower are best served. An example of this approach to situational leadership is Fiedler's LPC theory, which will be discussed below.

The second approach makes the assumption that both the leader's decisions and the work situation are relatively fluid and subject to change. This perspective removes the assumption of a rigid leadership style that nothing can change. This approach views managers as adaptive and able to respond effectively to different people and different situations. An example of this approach is the Vroom-Jago model, which we will explain later.

situational theories of leadership
Theories in which the appropriate leader behavior is the one that best fits the constraints of a specific situation.

Both approaches to situational leadership hold merit and have research support. But the second approach of fitting the decision to the situation appears to offer a more realistic view of human nature. Leaders face people with different personalities, abilities, and motivations. To assume that a leader would treat them all alike is simplistic at best.

Fiedler's LPC theory
A two-step theory in which the leader is adjusted to the situation. The first step is to measure and determine the leader's behavioral style. The second step is to find or create a situation that would be conducive to the leader's fixed style.

FIEDLER'S LPC THEORY - Fiedler's fit-the-leader-to-the-situation approach (known as **Fiedler's LPC Theory**) was one of the first widely embraced situational leadership theories.[18] In this theory, the leader's behavioral style first had to be measured and determined. Next, a situation had to be found or created that would be conducive to the leader's fixed style. Fiedler found that for particularly difficult work conditions (poor relationships with workers, little power over workers, and an unstructured task) or relatively undemanding work situations (good relationships with workers, high power over workers, and a clearly structured task), the effective leader needed to be task oriented. In mixed (not easy, not difficult) situations, a people-oriented style worked best (Figure 13–3).

Fiedler measured a leader's style using an instrument that identified the leader's least preferred co-worker (LPC). The LPC measures the leader's behavioral style in terms of task orientation and people orientation. With this measure, a leader who identified his LPC in terms critical of the worker's task initiative and accomplishment was described as task oriented. If the leader identified the LPC in relatively positive terms (that is, the leader preferred not to work with this person but found little to criticize), the leader was described as people oriented. This relatively unique method of assessing a leader's style has been questioned, although Fiedler's research showed an improvement over noncontingent approaches to leadership.

path-goal leadership theory
Theory based on the expectancy theory of motivation. The leader's role is to help the worker engage in organizational activities that lead to rewards that the worker values.

PATH-GOAL THEORY OF LEADERSHIP - House and Mitchell's **path-goal leadership theory** is based on the expectancy theory of motivation. The role of the leader is twofold: (1) clarify for the follower the path by which an individual can achieve personal goals (salary increases and promotions) and organizational outcomes (increased productivity and profitability) and (2) increase rewards that are valued by the follower. In a sense, the leader facilitates the organizational learning process. To do this, the leader engages in behaviors that help followers better understand how their actions are linked to organizational rewards. Effective leaders help workers engage in behaviors that lead to rewards they value. In essence, the leader motivates the follower toward outcomes valued by the individual and the organization.

FIGURE 13–3
Fiedler's Analysis of Situations in Which the Task- or Relationship-Motivated Leader Is More Effective

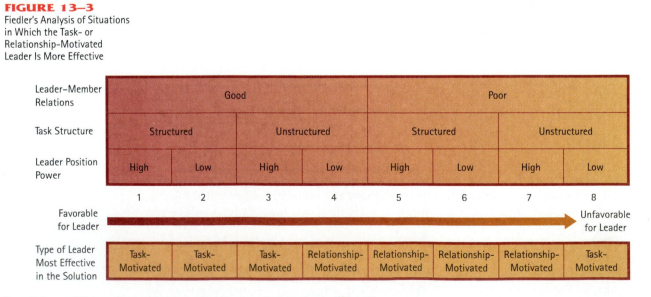

Leader–Member Relations	Good				Poor			
Task Structure	Structured		Unstructured		Structured		Unstructured	
Leader Position Power	High	Low	High	Low	High	Low	High	Low
	1	2	3	4	5	6	7	8

Favorable for Leader →→→→→→→ Unfavorable for Leader

| Type of Leader Most Effective in the Solution | Task-Motivated | Task-Motivated | Task-Motivated | Relationship-Motivated | Relationship-Motivated | Relationship-Motivated | Relationship-Motivated | Task-Motivated |

Source: D. Organ and T. Bateman, *Organizational Behavior*, 4th ed. (Homewood, Ill.: Richard D. Irwin, 1990), p. 558.

Path-goal theory identifies four types of leader behaviors:
1. *Directive behavior.* The leader makes clear task expectations by setting goals, structuring work flow, and providing feedback through regular performance feedback. This leader behavior is similar to the traditional leader behavior known as initiating structure.
2. *Supportive behavior.* The leader demonstrates concern for the follower and, when problems occur, is ready and willing to offer advice or just listen. Supportive behavior is the same as the traditional leader behavior known as consideration.
3. *Participative behavior.* The participative leader actively seeks ideas and information from workers. Participative behavior implies that followers actually participate in making decisions that affect them. For participative style to be effective, workers must perceive that their participation is meaningful and will be used by management.
4. *Achievement behavior.* Achievement leadership translates into setting expectations and task goals at a high level. This involves making the job challenging but not impossible to accomplish.

These four behaviors form a repertoire of meaningful actions that a leader might exhibit under different work situations. The theory also suggests that leaders have the ability to increase rewards that are valued by the follower. Leaders are effective to the extent that they can motivate followers, influence their ability to perform, and increase their job satisfaction. The model specifies that a follower's attitudes and behaviors are influenced by two factors: leader behaviors and situational factors. Followers' attitudes and behaviors include their level of job satisfaction and their ability to perform their task. Situational factors (sometimes referred to as environmental factors) include task requirements, the work group, and the formal authority structure. Personal characteristics of the follower include locus of control and perceived ability.

Path-goal theory prescribes which leader behaviors are likely to be effective with different situational constraints. Leaders are expected to change their behavior toward the follower when situational changes occur. From the workers' perspective the leader behaviors must be seen as facilitating or enabling workers to accomplish both immediate task goals and their own personal goals.

The theory suggests that the following match between leader behaviors and the situation results in effective leadership. For example, the directive behavior is suggested for situations that require more task structuring, monitoring, and feedback. Directive behavior may be particularly appropriate for a new employee with limited job experience. The supportive style might be suitable in a situation where workers know the job well and are experiencing delays or "client conflict" and just need to know that they're doing the right thing. Participative behavior is appropriate for workers who know their jobs well enough to make meaningful contributions to decisions that affect themselves and their department.

Finally, achievement behavior is suitable in situations where high performance is in the best interest of both the employee and the organization. A sales department compensated on a commission basis would provide an opportunity for achievement-oriented leader behavior. Here achievement-oriented leader behavior sets high sales expectations that, when they're met, yield the sales department greater financial rewards. Achievement-oriented leadership works best when the followers have a high need for achievement.

In summary, path-goal leadership theory views the leader as the vital link between the organization and the individual. Leaders need to motivate workers to understand how their work efforts are tied to valued salary increases, promotions, praise, recognition, and respect. Figure 13–4 presents the path-goal theory.

VROOM-JAGO MODEL - Victor Vroom and Arthur Jago enhanced the widely respected Vroom and Yetton situational leadership theory.[19] In the **Vroom-Jago model**, the ever-changing nature of work situations requires the leader to develop a variety of behavioral responses or decisions and apply them to the different situations as they occur. Leadership is a series of assessments of the situation by the leader. Vroom and Jago believe the results of these assessments guide the leader toward the appropriate leadership style for

Vroom-Jago model
A theory in which the ever-changing nature of work situations requires the leader to develop a variety of behavioral responses or decisions and apply them to the different situations as they occur.

FIGURE 13–4
Path-Goal Theory

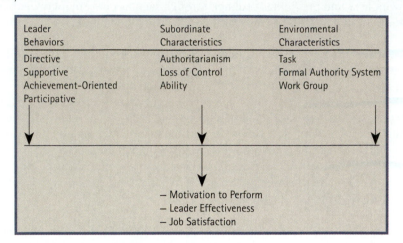

Leader Behaviors	Subordinate Characteristics	Environmental Characteristics
Directive	Authoritarianism	Task
Supportive	Loss of Control	Formal Authority System
Achievement-Oriented	Ability	Work Group
Participative		

— Motivation to Perform
— Leader Effectiveness
— Job Satisfaction

Source: Robert J. House and Terrence Mitchell, "Path-Goal Theory of Leadership," *Journal of Contemporary Business,* Autumn 1974, pp. 81–97.

the situation. The leadership style ranges from autocratic to consultative to group-centered (Figure 13–5). Figure 13–6 illustrates questions and decision rules used to determine which leadership style is appropriate for a given situation. As in path-goal theory, the assumption is that people are flexible and can adapt to different situational constraints.

The autocratic decision is task-oriented and should be used when work conditions are simple or favorable to the leader. For example, when the information needed to make a decision is known to the leader, the workers are sure to support the leader's decision, and the decision's time frame is short, then the leader could be autocratic. In some cases, the leader might have more time to make and implement the decision. Then the leader might invest time in consulting with workers and developing their capacity to make later decisions themselves.

But if the leader lacks important information, doubts the work group's likelihood of accepting an autocratic decision, and needs time to develop group commitment, a group-centered decision is required. Here the leader acts in a people-oriented fashion. When the conditions are unclear but not difficult, a consultative decision style is appropriate.

Both of these approaches showed significant evidence and garnered support from other researchers, but weaknesses and inconsistencies led other researchers to seek alternative explanations of effective leadership. By this stage in the development of leadership research, it was clear that simple models of behavior or the situation were insufficient in capturing the nature of effective leadership. Attempts to identify additional external, task structural, or personal characteristics, including environmental uncertainty, well-structured

FIGURE 13–5
Vroom and Jago's Fit the Leader Decision to the Situation: Alternative Leadership Styles

Style	Explanation
AI	*Autocratic.* Solve the problem yourself using the information you have.
AII	*Less autocratic.* Obtain the needed information from workers; then solve the problem yourself. Workers provide information but not alternatives.
CI	*Consultative.* Share the problem with workers individually (but not as a group), seeking suggestions and possible alternatives. Solve the problem yourself.
CII	*More consultative.* Share the problem with workers as a group, seeking suggestions and possible alternatives. Solve the problem yourself.
GII	*Group decision.* Share the problem with workers as a group, seeking suggestions and possible alternatives. Attempt to reach a consensus and be willing to accept and implement the workers' solution.

FIGURE 13–6
Vroom and Jago's Fit the Leader Decision to the Situation: The Questions and Decision Rules (Styles refer to Figure 14–5)

Question	Decision Rule
A	*Is there a quality standard that makes one alternative superior to another?* If yes, go to B; if no, go to D.
B	*Do I have enough information to make a good decision?* If yes, go to D; if no, go to C.
C	*Is the problem structured?* If yes, go to D; if no, go to D.
D	*Must workers accept my decision if they are to implement it effectively?* If A and D are no, choose Style AI. If A is no and D is yes, go to E. If A and B are yes, and D is no, choose Style AI. If A, B, and D are yes, go to E. If A is yes, B is no, C is yes, and D is no, choose Style AII. If A is yes, B is no, C is yes, and D is yes, go to E. If A is yes, B is no, C is no, and D is no, choose Style CII. If A is yes, B is no, C is no, and D is yes, go to E.
E	*If you make the decision alone, are workers likely to accept your decision?* If A is no and D and E are yes, choose Style AI. If A is no, D is yes, and E is no, choose Style GII. If A, B, D, and E are yes, choose Style AI. If A, B, and D are yes and E is no, go to F. If A is yes, B is no, C and D are yes, and E is no, go to F. If A is yes, B is no, C and D are yes, and E is yes, choose Style AII. If A is yes, B and C are no, and D and E are yes, choose Style CII. If A is yes, B and C are no, D is yes, and E is no, go to F.
F	*Do workers share the firm's goals?* If yes, choose Style GII. If A is yes, B is no, C is yes, D is yes, and E and F are no, go to G. If A is yes, B is no, C is no, D is yes, and E and F are no, choose Style CII.
G	*Is conflict among workers likely among preferred solutions?* If yes, choose Style CII. If no, choose Style CI.

tasks and charismatic leadership models, have produced limited success in explaining effective leadership.

The traditional phases or developments were marked by (1) attempts to remedy shortcomings in previous and current models of leadership with (2) increasingly more sophisticated models that better predicted or explained leadership effectiveness, and (3) a model of the leader as a dominant, essential force in actively directing individual workers or groups or teams of workers.

LIFE CYCLE THEORY - Another situational approach to leadership is **life cycle theory**, in which the follower's maturity is the basis for choice of leadership style.[20] Specifically, this model assumes there is no all-purpose leadership style, and leader behavior is comprised of two independent parts: directive behavior and supporting behavior.[21] As followers become more mature, leader behavior moves from directive to supporting.

life cycle theory
This model assumes there is no all-purpose leadership style, and leader behavior is comprised of two independent parts: directive behavior and supporting behavior.

Substitutes for Leadership

In many work situations traditional approaches to leadership are ineffective or sometimes just not possible. Kerr and Jermier believe that situational characteristics can reduce the need for traditional leadership.[22] They identify three situational characteristics that include characteristics of the subordinate, the task, and the organization. These characteristics can act as either neutralizers or substitutes for leadership.

In certain situations, leader behavior can be neutralized by an organizational characteristic. A **neutralizer** is any situation that prevents the leader from acting in a specified way.[23]

neutralizer
Any situation that prevents the leader from acting in a specified way.

For example, a union contract may require that all union members in the organization receive the same raise regardless of job performance. This situation neutralizes the leader's ability to reward or reinforce positive behavior as well as to sanction negative behavior. In essence, the leader can't reward top performers at a higher rate than low performers.

In other situations, **substitutes for leadership** replace the need for traditional leadership. New employees often require more direct, task-oriented leader behaviors. But training and education can reduce the need for task-oriented leader behaviors. In this manner, training and education serve as substitutes for leadership. Figure 13–7 gives examples of other neutralizers and substitutes for leadership.

substitutes for leadership
Illustrates the idea that other factors in the work environment can and do cause workers to behave in a certain manner. The leader can use these factors to guide work behavior when direct leadership is neither desirable nor possible.

transformational leadership
An approach to leadership based on changing workers' basic values and attitudes about their jobs. The transformational leader encourages worker participation in decisions and challenges workers to help the leader create the future organization one day at a time.

transactional leadership
A leadership approach in which leaders appeal to the workers' rational exchange motive.

TRANSFORMATIONAL LEADERSHIP

Early in the chapter we distinguished between leaders and managers. We also discussed trait theory—an early theory suggesting leaders have certain characteristics that could be identified or may be developed for those deficient in the trait. Today most management scholars use the terms *managing* and *leading* to refer to two different processes. But for many years trait theory took a back seat to behavioral and situational explanations of leadership.

Several theorists use the term **transformational leadership** to describe an inspirational form of leader behavior based on modifying followers' beliefs, values, and ultimately their behavior. Bass refers to this process as leadership that creates "performance beyond expectations."[24] Lee Iacocca transformed Chrysler not just by changing products but also by changing the attitudes of both workers and customers. Similarly Larry Quadracci's inspirational leadership transformed a small midwestern printer, Quad Graphics, into a highly profitable national corporation. Home Depot, after three years of sagging stock prices, has hired back Pat Farrah, one of the founders and a self-proclaimed "radical," who was given much of the credit for the retailer's initial success; stock shot up 28,000 percent since the company went public in 1981.[25]

In contrast, **transactional leadership** is more closely related to both behavioral and situational leader behaviors. Transactional leaders appeal to workers' rational exchange mo-

---

FIGURE 13–7
Substitutes for Leadership and for Task-Oriented and Consideration Leader Behaviors

Substitute or Neutralizer	Consideration	Initiating Structure
Subordinate Characteristics		
1. Experience, ability, training		Substitute
2. Professional orientation	Substitute	Substitute
3. Indifference toward rewards offered by the organization	Neutralizer	Neutralizer
Task Characteristics		
1. Structure, routine task		Substitute
2. Feedback provided by task		Substitute
3. Intrinsically satisfying task	Substitute	
Organization Characteristics		
1. Cohesive work group	Substitute	Substitute
2. Low position power (leader lacks control over organizational rewards)	Neutralizer	Neutralizer
3. Formalization (explicit plans, goals, areas of control)		Substitute
4. Inflexibility (rigid, unyielding rules and procedures)		Neutralizer
5. Leader located apart from subordinates with only limited communication possible	Neutralizer	Neutralizer

Source: Gary A. Yuki, *Leadership in Organizations* (Englewood Cliffs, N.J.: Prentice Hall, 1989), pp. 108–12.

tive. Workers exchange labor for wages. Leaders help clarify the path from effort to reward. For the worker, this is a form of self-interested exchange—do this and you get rewarded. For the leader, it is a process of keeping workers riveted to organizational goals. Both transactional and transformational leadership are valid approaches to leadership.

Transformational leadership helps us to realize that leaders who transform organizations are unique and individually different. As you recall, early trait theorists were unsuccessful in identifying physical attributes and personality types needed for effective leadership. But transformational leadership research holds the promise that individual qualities are a critical element in transforming an organization. Successful companies often have bold, dominant leaders who guide, inspire, and create a vision of the future. Roberto Goizueta of Coca-Cola, Steve Jobs in the early years of Apple Computer, and Lee Iacocca of Chrysler are examples of people who made the leadership difference.

Do leadership traits exist? Sure they do! But can we teach people these traits and expect them to go out and transform organizations? Certainly not! But neither are real leaders born. Leadership needs certainly more than a common set of traits. And don't assume that leaders just pop up periodically. Leadership is personal and situational, and it requires an investment and, undoubtedly, some luck.

SELF-LEADERSHIP

Two societal trends will greatly impact future leadership approaches.[26] First, a highly educated workforce in a democratic society will seek greater decision-making participation and other forms of power sharing.[27] Second, a highly competitive world economy has led to the necessity for increased cost-cutting measures. The United States uses more middle managers than foreign competitors do. The result has been a permanent reduction in the white-collar workforce. Both trends make a shift toward greater worker control more likely in the future.

Shifting societal trends requires new leadership strategies. For effective leadership in the future, two things must occur. First, leaders must engage in behaviors that actively encourage workers to gain control over their work destiny. This means power sharing and requires a confident, secure leader as well as willing, able workers. Second, workers need to develop the requisite self-control strategies such as self-management and self-leadership. New leadership approaches to managing increasingly competitive markets will, of necessity, increase worker participation in the decision-making process. As we noted earlier, this means more democratic rather than authoritarian leaders.

Thanks to innovative leadership, Lincoln Electric, in Cleveland, Ohio, has earned a reputation for product quality. Lincoln's leadership system assumes workers are self-motivated. Workers can rearrange tasks, and any improvement in quality of output earns the worker more money, so both the employee and the company benefit from such an approach. Teamwork and reliability are rewarded, with some employees doubling their base pay with incentive compensation. There are about 100 employees for each manager; employees are graded on their ability to work without a supervisor.[28]

Self-leadership is a management philosophy that encompasses a systematic set of behavioral and cognitive strategies that lead to improved performance and effectiveness.[29] This philosophy encourages individual employees to develop their own work priorities that are consistent with organizational goals. What happens to the manager in the self-leadership process? Interestingly, rather than abdicating control, the manager must actively encourage the development of self-leadership capabilities in subordinates.

But this may not be as easy as it sounds. While many believe that workers would jump at the chance for more control, some actually resent it. Why would this be? Mainly fear of the unknown. For a long time workers have been encouraged to complete their work according to procedures and standards designed by their managers or specialists. With the self-leadership approach, workers are asked to assume new responsibilities. Often workers believe they are untrained or unable to accomplish this new role successfully. One way to increase worker self-control is to use empowerment to overcome worker resistance or fear.

self-leadership
The philosophy and a systematic set of behavioral and cognitive strategies for workers leading themselves to higher performance and effectiveness.

REFLECTIONS BY PHILIP B. CROSBY

Leadership and Quality

When I was running my first production operation, I wanted very much to be a good leader. For this reason I read everything I could on the subject and watched closely how others handled their responsibilities. It wasn't long before I was certain that I knew a great deal about being a leader. We were running a three-shift operation six days a week, and I made certain that I was up to date on all data and personnel changes. I met with my staff each morning and spent a great deal of time with all people.

One of my children became ill at this time and was forced to spend a few days in the hospital. We wanted to make certain that she was not alone, so the family divided the 24-hour day into segments. I came over during the day but my assigned segment was 8 PM to midnight. This let me do my office work while she dozed or watched TV, and I could still get some sleep before going to work.

The second night, when my uncle relieved me, I decided to drop by the plant on the way home to check in on our third shift. As I walked into the normally bustling plant I realized that things were different during that period. It had been a long time since I worked that shift.

The people were delighted to see me, and I spent 30 minutes or so just wandering around seeing what was happening. One of the operators motioned me over to her workstation and pointed out that they were out of components "again." The stockroom was locked on the third shift and not enough parts had been left.

"It happens all the time," she noted.

The superintendent grabbed me to have a cup of coffee with the members of the quality team who were having a 15-minute stand up meeting. They were having a hard time obtaining customer information concerning new products that were being delivered. Requests to the quality engineering department were not gaining any response.

Before I left, I had picked up six different problems that were not being properly addressed by the rest of the operation. The next morning I brought these to the attention of my staff and asked them for action. No one know anything about the problems I had brought them, but they agreed to respond more promptly. The quality engineering manager and the production control supervisor thought that the complaints were overstated. However, at my urging they agreed to get into the situation.

Two nights later I repeated my visit and found that a few things had been fixed, but that the people had no feeling that they were receiving much support. They also gave me five more assignments. At the next morning's staff meeting I stated that I was tired of being an errand boy and that we needed to make the third shift, and second one too, equal in all respects to the first. I handed them a schedule in which we would all take turns visiting these activities. I also brought the shift superintendents in so they could voice their discomfort. I told the quality engineering manager privately that he was going to wind up running the third shift if things did not improve quickly.

It all worked out for the best. Our output rose while our problems dropped to almost nothing. I heard later that they thought I was a great leader. But it was thanks to a sick child, not to proper leadership thinking. I never let my people go lonely again.

---

self-management
An individual's capacity to arrange and control personal activities and reources, including goalsand rewards, without an external force.

role modeling
Leader's primary vehicle for encouraging self-leadership.

As noted in Chapter 8, *empowerment* is the process of providing workers with the skills, tools, information, and, above all, the authority and responsibility for their work. Worker empowerment gives workers direct control over many aspects of their work. Self-leadership transfers control of directing individual work behavior from the manager to the worker. Leadership becomes an internal process. Real empowerment involves the worker's commitment to **self-management**, which is the use of work strategies that help to control daily activities in order to achieve organizational goals.

The manager's role in the self-leadership organization is to encourage workers to develop self-control skills. By self-control, we mean their ability to control their own work destiny in both the short term and the long term. Self-leadership deemphasizes external forms of control. The primary vehicle leaders use to encourage self-leadership is **role modeling**, a process by which leaders exhibit behaviors that they expect other employees to follow. For example, leaders need to set goals for themselves in a manner that their employees can observe. Although the idea of role modeling seems simple, in reality it seldom happens. For role modeling to be successful, it must be apparent to the worker that the manager is demonstrating a work behavior that she'd like the employee to emulate. Second, the worker needs to see some connection between adopting the behavior and achieving positive outcomes. Research also suggests that workers are most likely to emulate the behavior of successful managers.[30] Figure 13–8 compares behaviors of traditional and self-managing leaders.

FIGURE 13–8	Traditional Leader Behaviors	Self-Managing Leader Behaviors
Comparing Traditional and Self-Managing Leader Behaviors	Organization: Structures own and subordinates' work	Encourages self-reward
	Domination: Restricts or limits the discretion of individuals or groups	Encourages self-observation
	Production: Sets standards for task performance	Encourages self-goal setting
	Recognition: Expresses approval or disapproval of behavior	Encourages self-criticism
	Integration: Promotes group cohesion and reduces group conflict	Encourages self-rehearsal
	Communication: Provides, seeks, and exchanges information with group members	Acts as a role model by exhibiting appropriate behavior
		Fosters the development of a culture that nourishes and supports self-leadership

Source: Adapted from Charles C. Manz and Henry P. Sims, *Superleadership: Leading Others to Lead Themselves* (Englewood Cliffs, N.J.: Prentice Hall, 1989); Chester A. Schriescheim, Robert House, and Steven Kerr, "Leader Initiating Structure: A Reconciliation of Discrepant Research Results and Some Empirical Tests," *Organizational Behavior and Human Performance* 15 (1976), pp. 297–321; and Robert Lord, R. J. Foti, and C. L. DeVader, "A Test of Leadership Categorization Theory: Internal Structure, Information Processing, and Leader Perceptions," *Organizational Behavior and Human Performance* 34 (1984), pp. 343–78.

APPLICATIONS OF SELF-LEADERSHIP

Self-leadership involves the use of behavioral and cognitive self-management strategies designed to improve performance and effectiveness. First, we'll look at some behavioral self-management strategies—employees' observable, measurable self-initiated methods to improve their work performance. Then we'll examine two cognitive self-management strategies. Figure 13–9 lists various strategies.

Some of these methods may sound familiar. In fact, maybe you already practice some or all of these self-management strategies. Complete Figure 13–10's questionnaire to find out.

Behavioral Self-Management

Behavioral self-management is a set of strategies that help people gain greater control over their lives. Common behavioral self-management strategies include self-set goals, self-observation, self-reward, self-cueing, self-administered rewards, and self-designed jobs.

With **self-set goals**, the initiative for setting the goal and the level of the goal itself comes from the worker, not the manager. Self-set goals are consistent with the firm's overall goals and are based on the worker's commitment to the firm's goals. Self-set goals free the manager from a traditional supervisory duty and empower workers with a greater sense of personal control. This autonomous approach to goal setting is recommended as a matter of ethics, not just effectiveness.[31]

behavioral self-management
The process of managing overt, measurable physical activities.

self-set goals
Goals that result when both the initiative for setting a goal and the level of the goal itself come from the worker, not the manager.

FIGURE 13–9	Behavioral Self-Management	Cognitive Self-Management
Strategies for Two Types of Self-Management	Self-set goals	Opportunity Building
	Self-observation	Positive Self-talk
	Self-rewards	
	Self-cueing	
	Self-designed jobs	

Source: Adapted from Charles C. Manz, *Mastering Self-Leadership: Empowering Yourself for Personal Excellence* (Englewood Cliffs, N.J.: Prentice Hall, 1992).

FIGURE 13–10
Are You a Self-Leader?

Score yourself on how often you would do the following. 10 = 100%, 0 = 0%

_____ 1. Propose specific goals for your activities.

_____ 2. Reward yourself for doing a good job.

_____ 3. Refuse to reward/punish yourself for a poor job.

_____ 4. Make lists of things to do that day, week, or month.

_____ 5. Check off complete items on the daily or weekly list.

_____ 6. Keep an after-the-fact record of your daily activities.

_____ 7. Organize your day or week in your head while doing some other activity.

_____ 8. Rehearse the steps and sequence of an activity before you do it.

_____ 9. Ask people you work with to set goals for themselves.

_____ 10. Find great pleasure simply in knowing you've done a good job.

_____   Your average score

Calculate your average score and compare your score with those of other people in your class.

---

self-observation
The process where a worker monitors her own behavior, noting actions, events, or outcomes.

Self-observation is a process in which a worker monitors his own behavior and notes actions, events, or outcomes. The self-leadership philosophy assumes that workers can monitor their own behavior. Self-observation includes keeping performance records. For example, a package delivery worker might keep a notebook recording the time of each delivery. Self-observation increases worker empowerment and autonomy.

Deming and other quality experts emphasize the need to eliminate piecework incentive systems, inspectors, time clocks, and exhaustive audits or observations of worker behavior. Self-observation enables a person to answer the question How am I doing? without having to ask a supervisor.

self-reward
The process of a worker monitoring, evaluating, and applying a reward or disincentive for her own performance.

With **self-rewards** (also called _self-administered rewards_), a worker monitors, evaluates, and applies a reward or disincentive for her own performance. Self-awards enable the individual to personally recognize that a performance milestone has been surpassed. An example is rewarding yourself with a break only after completing a major portion of the assigned task. Another type of self-reward is recognizing the naturally rewarding aspect of the work itself—for example, reminding yourself that it feels good to do your best or that it is intrinsically rewarding to clear your desk of pending cases each day. Although these ideas have a simplistic edge, they get back to basics and are powerful motivators. The worker decides the measure and worth of an activity rather than adhering to a universal definition. Self-administered rewards add meaning and purpose to work. In essence, the worker knows what she is supposed to do, does it, and then pats herself on the back or rewards herself with a break.

self-cueing behavior
The process of planning or making arrangements for an activity prior to its performance.

When a mechanic lays out the necessary tools prior to commencing work, he is practicing **self-cueing** (the process of planning or making arrangements for an activity prior to its performance). This practice helps to prevent defects from occurring during the execution stage. One type of self-cueing, **behavioral rehearsal**, involves practicing an activity under simulated or controlled conditions. For example, the night before a meeting with a customer, a sales team might conduct a role play in which some members of the sales team play the role of the customers and ask appropriate questions, giving the sales team a chance to rehearse their answers.

behavioral rehearsal
The practice of an activity under simulated or controlled conditions.

self-designed jobs
Jobs in which workers are allowed to propose and design work process changes.

Self-designed jobs allow workers to propose and design work process changes, rather than simply imposing external constraints on them. This can result in a personal sense of competence, self-control, and purpose. At the Federal Express facility in Memphis, Tennessee, in response to the problem of late-arriving and mislabeled packages, management implemented a system called minisort. But the minisort process was inefficient and unpopular among workers. One worker observed, "If you got on someone's nerves, they sent you to minisort." So a team of 12 workers was appointed to solve the problem. The team cut minisort staff from 150 to 80 workers (saving $30,000), clarified minisort tasks, and implemented prevention measures, which cut the number of packages sent to minisort in the first place from 10,000 to 4,000 per night. In four months the number of late packages dropped from 4,300 to 432. The team's work actually cut their own wages, yet as one worker said, "For management to listen to me, that's important."[32]

Cognitive Self-Management

Not all self-management strategies are observable and measurable. In **cognitive self-management**, the individual worker creates mental images and thought patterns that are consistent with the firm's goals. Two cognitive self-management strategies are opportunity building and positive self-talk.

Opportunity building is the process of seeking out and/or developing new possibilities for success. An oft-told marketing story involves two shoe salespeople sent to sell shoes in a foreign country. The negative thinker told the firm's headquarters, "Opportunities nonexistent. Nobody here wears shoes." The positive thinker said, " Opportunities unlimited. Nobody here wears shoes." Thus an obstacle may be converted to an opportunity by the way we perceive and define the problem.

Positive self-talk is the process of creating mental imagery that reinforces a worker's sense of self-esteem and enhances efficacy.[33] For example, a customer service agent, upon dealing with an angry customer, reminds herself that she has been successful in calming and satisfying angry customers in the past by listening for important words or phrases used by the customer. By maintaining her self-confidence, the agent is using positive self-talk to help her manage a difficult situation.

DEVELOPING A SELF-LEADERSHIP CULTURE

The development of an effective self-leadership culture begins with a commitment from the top levels of management. One extensive study found that pessimism, stagnation, and barriers to the use of basic total quality methods were due to the lack of a leadership style consistent with statistical process control.[34] In this case, the leadership emphasis was on

cognitive self-management
A mental process that includes the creation of images and thought patterns consistent with the firm's goals and behaviors.

opportunity building
The process of seeking out and/or developing new possibilities for success.

positive self-talk
The process of creating mental imagery that reinforces a worker's sense of self-esteem and enhances efficacy.

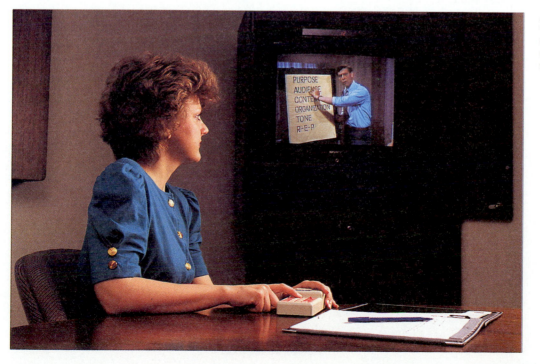

An Aetna employee views a training video. Training is often used to develop employee's self-management skills.

quick fixes and crisis management, rather than on continuous improvement methods. Three keys to developing a self-leadership culture are sharing information, training, and reinforcement.

SHARING INFORMATION ‑ Self-managed workers need a great deal of information. Many traditional management secrets must become part of their information base. Workers need information concerning costs and profits if they are to set goals and commit to certain actions. When they're informed, workers become more willing to accept responsibility for their actions. In addition, open communication sends a message to employees that they are respected and trusted.

TRAINING ‑ Training in the use of self-management strategies might focus on improving communication skills, team building, or developing the various self-management strategies discussed in this chapter. Training helps to reinforce managerial policy statements at all levels of an organization. Managers may feel threatened by the idea of a self-managed workforce, so in addition to training, they also need assurance that they will continue to have an important role in organizational success.

REINFORCEMENT ‑ In addition to sharing information and conducting training programs, the administration of performance rewards can help to reinforce the use of self-management behaviors. For instance, a "team player" or "star performer" award might be issued to an employee who demonstrates outstanding self-leadership ability.

Leadership Challenges

Critical global issues confront the economy and firms as we face the 21st century.[35] The most effective managers will be those who understand leadership as a broad, empowering tool, and who have a special capability to develop self-managed leadership in others. Figure 13–11 shows a model of the quality management approach to leadership.

The quest for quality implies a new kind of business leadership. Effective leadership in the future will more likely than not mean leading others to lead themselves. Workers will

FIGURE 13–11
Quality Management
Leadership Model

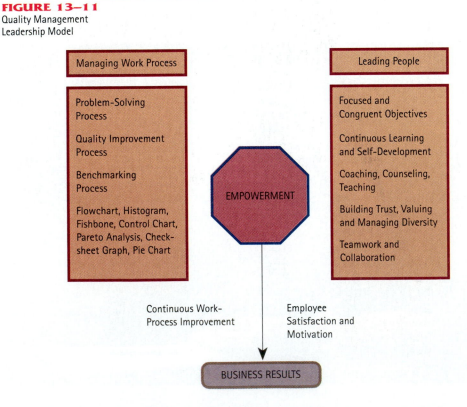

WHAT MANAGERS ARE READING

LEADERSHIP AND THE NEW SCIENCE

In her book *Leadership and the New Science*, Margaret J. Wheatley writes that our assumptions about effective leadership are grounded in seventeenth-century physics. Since science has changed so much, she argues that we need to explore what has become known to us in the twentieth century in learn-

ing about and leading organizations. Wheatley investigates concepts that have emerged from this "new science" that are changing our understanding of the universe. These concepts are applied to a number of leadership challenges including:

- How can we find order in a chaotic world?
- How is order different than control?

- How can we create more participative, open, and adaptive organizations?
- How can we reconcile individual autonomy and organizational control?
- What leads to organizational growth and self-renewal instead of decline and death?

Source: Margaret J. Wheatley, *Leadership and the New Science* (San Francisco: Berrett-Koehler Publishers, 1992).

---

have to develop skills in self-management. Workers who develop self-management skills are better able to control the pace and flow of their work. To facilitate this process, effective leadership in the future must encourage employees to develop self-leadership skills. A summary of some challenges future leaders will face follows:

- ❖ Increasing global competition.
- ❖ Emphasis on speed, service, and information.
- ❖ Lean and flexible work demands for more value-added labor and reduced indirect labor costs.
- ❖ Need to employ untrained, unskilled, and disenfranchised employees.
- ❖ Fewer low-skilled jobs available as more low-skilled workers enter the market.
- ❖ Increasing gaps (1) between elite, skilled employees with lifetime employment and a working underclass with limited skills and few employment options and (2) between knowledge-intensive, highly educated employees and labor-intensive, unskilled employees.
- ❖ Employee demands for greater participation. Shift to teams, skill-based pay, and cooperation with the firm.
- ❖ Further expansion of information technologies. Flatter, decentralized organizations with greater employee need for self-management.

Empowering workers through self-leadership is a good start but may not be enough when competitive position has eroded. Visionary transformational leadership may be required to resuscitate a poorly performing organization. IBM's new chairman, Louis Gertsner, Jr., faces tremendous challenges in the coming years. For IBM to regain competitive ground in the computer industry, he must communicate his vision for IBM to employees, customers, and competitors. Gertsner must transform how IBM thinks about itself and how consumers view IBM. The transformational leadership of Thomas Watson, Jr., in the 1950s was the cornerstone of IBM's success for the next three decades. If IBM is to reconstitute the Big Blue of yesteryear, Louis Gertsner, Jr., must craft a new vision for IBM in the year 2000 and beyond.

Managing Cultural Diversity

Another major challenge facing leaders today is managing a diverse workforce. In 1987, the Hudson Institute published *Workforce 2000: Work and Workers for the 21st Century*.[36] This landmark study opened the eyes of corporate America to the reality that dramatic changes are taking place in the workforce. The study projected that 25 million people would join the American workforce between 1987 and the year 2000; only 15 percent of these new workers would be white males, almost 61 percent would be women, and 29 percent would be minorities (minority women were counted twice).

As a result, employers will have to train, manage, and motivate a workforce composed of individuals with widely varying backgrounds and perspectives.[37] In the past, managers had to decide how to manage a predominantly white, male workforce. Managing diversity requires various activities related to recruiting, hiring, and effective use of people from different cultural backgrounds.[38] Programs must be developed to promote both the awareness of cultural differences and positive attitudes toward these differences. Human resource managers must develop bias-free systems to recruit, train, and promote individuals from diverse backgrounds. Work itself will also have to be restructured since it has been structured in terms of men in the past.[39] For instance, this will include more flextime so women can bear children and still advance their professions; about half the workforce is comprised of women.

Any leader that sincerely values cultural diversity must make it safe for everyone in the organization to talk about differences. This means a change for those organizations that have been denying differences exist while meeting EEO or affirmative action guidelines. Valuing diversity looks at the multicultural workforce from a positive perspective rather than from a defensive position. Valuing diversity views people as having equal rights while being different, and encourages the open discussion of these differences of gender, age, ethnicity, physical ability, and so on.[40] Diversity awareness training programs can help bring these differences out into the open and identify the unique characteristics and talents of diverse individuals that are a resource for the organization.

Both total quality management (TQM) and managing diversity offer potential for increasing an organization's competitiveness, and both face challenges when managers attempt to implement them. But when used in combination, the two are better managed and their benefits increase.[41] Both stress empowerment or involvement of employees, both represent changes in the normal way of doing things, and both require long-term commitment on the part of the organization. When managing cultural diversity is integrated with TQM, some of the significant challenges that organizations face when implementing TQM are successfully addressed. For instance, one of the major challenges managers face when implementing TQM programs is changing the culture of the organization. When TQM and managing diversity are used in tandem, managers are more likely to succeed in changing the culture of the organization.

While cultural diversity brings stimulation, challenge, and energy, it does not always lead to harmony.[42] A mix of genders, cultures, and alternative lifestyles can lead to conflict and misunderstanding. The job of the manager is to create an environment where differences are appreciated and where a group of diverse individuals work productively together. This is a formidable challenge, but organizations that meet this challenge face a brighter future.

THE WORKPLACE OF TOMORROW

Frank Loscavio's crew rebuilt a Jamaican power plant in 6 months rather than the normal 22. Nickelodeon's Gerry Laybourne helps nourish creativity with one new idea after another, such as redesigning the work space to stimulate creativity. Richard Semler has made Semco into the ultimate flexible company; six people share his title of CEO. Jack Stack, head of engine manufacturing firm SRC, teaches factory workers everything he knows about the financials of the firm.[43] While each may be unique in his own way, these leaders share at least one characteristic—they are unconventional. And unconventional leadership styles may work best as organizations embrace the concepts of reengineering, teamwork, and empowerment.

Effective leaders in the future will be employee-centered, putting people first. By placing the interests of their people above their own, leaders gain loyalty and motivate workers. They will listen to subordinates, and will thereby be properly informed, enabling leaders to make good decisions. As noted at the outset of the chapter, leaders and managers are different. Effective leaders stress relationships with others, values and commitment; articulate a vision of what the organization can be in the long run; move the organization in new directions, rejecting the status quo; communicate why things are done; favor risk and change; and generate a feeling of value and importance in work.[44] This will be indicative of leaders in the workplace of the future.

The mix of skills needed to be an effective leader is changing. Leaders need *technical skills*, which include specialized knowledge, analytical ability, and the ability to use tools and techniques of the discipline. They also need *conceptual skills*, the ability to see the enterprise as a whole and recognize how the various parts of the organization interact. Finally, leaders need *human skills*, the ability to work effectively as a group member to build cooperative effort.[45] Leaders will continue to make use of these skills, with greater emphasis on human skills such as communication and team-building. Successful leaders will be those that navigate among conflicting goals of the organization and steer a winning course.[46]

SUMMARY OF LEARNING OBJECTIVES

DISTINGUISH BETWEEN LEADERS AND MANAGERS.
Managers are concerned with the pressures of the moment. For the manager, efficient use of resources may be of more immediate concern than quality. Leaders are concerned with long-term visionary concepts: what is quality today and what will consumers want tomorrow?

EXPLAIN THE RELATIONSHIP BETWEEN LEADERSHIP AND POWER.
Leadership requires the exercise of power. Every leader has a base of power, but for any two leaders, the power base may be quite different. This chapter identified five bases of power: (1) power based on the ability to reward others for compliance, (2) power based on the ability to punish others for noncompliance (coercive power), (3) power based on expertise in a particular functional area such as engineering, (4) power based on personal characteristics (referent power), and (5) power based on the position in the organization (legitimate power).

COMPARE THE THEORIES OF TRAIT, BEHAVIORAL, AND SITUATIONAL LEADERSHIP.
The trait theory of leadership seeks to identify traits and skills effective leaders should possess. Behavioral theorists identified behaviors that effective leaders should exhibit. Early research identified two types of behaviors: task-centered leader behaviors and people-centered leader behaviors. Situational leadership theory emphasizes that situational constraints can influence leader effectiveness. For example, situational influences in path-goal theory include characteristics of the subordinate and characteristics of the task.

DESCRIBE THE THEORY OF TRANSFORMATIONAL LEADERSHIP.
Transformational leadership describes an inspirational form of leader behavior based on modifying followers' beliefs, values, and ultimately their behavior. Lee Iacocca at Chrysler Corporation is an example of a transformational leader.

DEFINE SELF-LEADERSHIP AND DISCUSS THE SOCIETAL TRENDS THAT CONTRIBUTED TO ITS DEVELOPMENT.
Self-leadership is a management philosophy that encompasses a systematic set of behavioral and cognitive strategies that lead to improved performance and effectiveness. In essence, self-leadership gives people more control over their work. Two societal trends have made self-leadership possible in work settings. First, today's workers are better educated than workers of previous generations. They bring better skills to the workplace. Second, a more competitive marketplace requires greater efficiency. Efficiency can be improved by giving workers more control over their work.

DESCRIBE THE VARIOUS BEHAVIORAL AND COGNITIVE SELF-MANAGEMENT STRATEGIES.
Behavioral self-management includes self-set goals, self-observation, self-rewards, self-cueing, and self-designed jobs. Behavioral self-management conditions workers to use environmental information and work control strategies to help pace and control their work. Cognitive self-management includes two strategies: opportunity building and positive self-talk. Cognitive self-management strategies foster mental self-images and thought patterns aimed at goal attainment.

EXPLAIN HOW A BUSINESS CAN DEVELOP A SELF-LEADERSHIP CULTURE.
Top management commitment is necessary to build a strong self-management culture. In addition, to encourage the growth of self-management throughout the organization, management must develop a management system that shares information and ideas, continually trains workers, and reinforces or rewards the positive gains derived from self-management.

KEY TERMS

REVIEW AND DISCUSSION QUESTIONS

Recall

1. What is the difference between a leader and a manager?
2. Identify several bases of power. What do you believe is the most common basis of power for a manager?
3. What are the two most common types of leader behaviors?

Understanding

4. What general purpose underlies the path-goal theory of leadership?
5. Can an individual be both leader and manager? If so, describe the process by which both activities can emerge in the same person.

6. Identify a managerial situation that illustrates a neutralizer and another situation that illustrates a substitute for leadership.
7. What actions should managers take to develop self-leadership skills in their subordinates?

Application

8. Assume that you work as manager of a customer service department in a large retail store. Describe three naturally occurring rewards that are likely to be inherent in that type of job.
9. Describe two situations that would call for two very different leadership behaviors.
10. In your own words, describe three challenges that leaders of large corporations will face in the coming decade.

CASE STUDY

SAS: Business Class Means Quality

Jan Carlzon built SAS, the Scandinavian-based airline, into a world-class airline favored among business people. Yet, as the world evolved, SAS found itself in an awkward position. Once it was protected by a generous government subsidy and fare protection in the highly regulated Western European market. In the early 1990s Western Europe was uniting, privatizing, and facing new competition from the United States. The same business pressures that bankrupted Pan American, TWA, and Eastern (once the most recognized American carriers around the world) brought American, Delta, and United into Europe. And SAS could easily see itself next in line.

In the price-regulated era, SAS had carved itself a solid niche among the favored business travelers, where price was less an object than service, meals, and scheduling. And SAS employees earned a unique status as well, leading to high labor costs. For example, although wages among technical people were competitive at $18 to $22 per worker, SAS could only count on 1,300 to 1,400 hours of work from its mechanics each year (20 percent less on the night shift) versus almost 2,000 hours for the typical American airline, a 30-percent plus cost advantage for the American carriers.

SAS provided first-line workers with an unusually high level of freedom to make decisions, all driven by the need to serve customers best. Carlzon often described SAS as an inverted pyramid, where customers were on top, followed by front-line workers, with Carlzon working for all of them at the bottom of the upside-down chart. But changing airline competition, with new players and reduced regulations, called for a new response to keep its market share.

SAS responded with a twofold strategy. First, SAS continued to focus on the business traveler, while second, it built bridges by developing partnerships with similar carriers around the world, to beat the Americans at their own game. The American game also meant the "hub and spoke" strategy. (The U.S. domestic market had grown by use of a system where fliers are sent to hubs—massive centers for transferring passengers—and then sent out again through one of the spokes.) SAS found it necessary to use the hub-and-spoke method on a global basis. Previously cut off from the U.S. domestic market by an absence of connections through New

York's JFK International Airport, SAS worked around that blockage with a partnership with Continental, only to see that carrier declare bankruptcy. Nonetheless, Carlzon defended the partnership on the basis of increased revenues and reduced costs for SAS. "The Continental deal is worth $20 million a year net. What would have been the downside if we didn't do it?"

Partnerships also meant turning cost centers such as mechanical services into profit centers, where partners could pool services, personnel, and other costs, while providing opportunities for both partners to benefit from increased customer service and scheduling. The European Quality Alliance (EQA) included SAS, Finnair, and Austrian. Links followed with Nippon (Japan), a British carrier, Canadian Airlines International, and Spanair (a Spanish charter carrier).

SAS also employed sophisticated monitoring systems to alert pilots to developing problems. Pilots could then radio ahead to alert mechanics, who could begin the repair process by assembling parts before the plane even hit the shop. As a result, morning readiness for all fleets was over 99 percent and the availability of planes after unscheduled maintenance exceeded SAS's goal of 95 percent by 1.5 percentage points. At most cities, flight regularity reached 100 percent, meaning no canceled revenue-generating flights.

SAS also achieved efficiency with the mechanical staff. The number of technical employees per plane was reduced from 42 to 32, with a target of 30, while flight hours per employee (a measure of productivity) increased from 57 to 71 in the late 1980s, with a target of 75 flight hours per employee.

SAS is also pushing its cargo operations hard into the former Eastern Bloc countries. While the demand for goods is growing, one of the biggest impediments SAS faces is a decaying infrastructure—physical structures are deteriorating and outdated, pilferage is rampant, and automation is nonexistent.

Carlzon believes firmly in doing 100 things 1 percent better, as compared to 1 thing 100 percent better, meaning continuous improvement. To do this, SAS leaders were expected to share information and then responsibility with each worker. According to Carlzon, this makes an empowered worker. "An employee without information can't take responsibility. With information, he cannot avoid taking it."

Source: Adapted from Douglas W. Nelson, "SAS on Steady Course," *Air Transport World,* September 1995, pp. 109–110; Ken Shelton, "People Power," *Executive Excellence,* December 1991, pp. 7–8; Henry Lefer, "How SAS Keeps 'Em Flyin'," *Transport World,* November 1991, pp. 68–74; and Joan M. Feldman, "SAS: Playing Partners," *Air Transport World,* pp. 102–6.

QUESTIONS

1. What is Jan Carlzon's vision or strategy for SAS?
2. Why is cost cutting such a big part of SAS's strategy?
3. In what ways has SAS used self-leadership concepts to empower workers?

VIDEO CASE

Leadership at Marshall Industries

An organization must have leadership at every level in order to succeed. Leaders must tailor their leadership skills based on their assessment of their tasks and their followers. At Marshall Industries, one of the top five electronics distributors in North America, leaders include the founder and the president of the company, as well as the warehouse manager and an entry level warehouse employee. The diversity of these leaders' skills illustrates that different skills are appropriate to each situation within an organization.

Managers need to understand essential definitions and concepts related to leadership in the work place. Leadership is providing direction, energizing others, and obtaining commitment to a cause. For leadership to take place a group must have a task, job, or assignment to be performed or a quality to be achieved, one or more leaders, and, of course, followers.

The skills and behaviors of effective leaders vary with the nature of the job to be done, the behavior of the followers, and the leader's style and behavior. Leadership situations within organizations are usually a combination of: Visionary/Pathfinding, Problem Solving, and Implementing.

Marshall Industries is one of the largest electronics distributors in the United States. The company has enjoyed tremendous success over the past 10 years. During this time, Marshall has evolved away from a results-oriented, internally competitive mode of employee accountability toward a team-centered focus on quality through continuous process improvement. New demands have been made upon Marshall's existing leadership, and new leaders have emerged at all levels of the company.

Gordon Marshall, the founder and chief executive officer of Marshall Industries, exemplifies the characteristics of the Visionary/Pathfinder leader. Visionary/Pathfinder leaders usually emerge at the top level of an organization. Their leadership role is to create a vision of future possibilities and influence others to share it. Gordon Marshall faced perhaps his biggest leadership challenge at an unusual point in his career. As he stated, "I came back to the company in February of 1982. I was semi-retired. The company was losing money, so I decided to come back and see if I could fix it."

Several years after his return, Marshall spotted an article about W. Edwards Deming's quality principles—an article that would eventually have a major impact at Marshall Industries. Marshall said, "The things that really hit me, struck me as being so fundamental. One: Listen to the voice of the customer. Two: Improve the quality of your product or service and then have a process that continues to improve those things on a ongoing basis. Three: Do it right the first time and take the cost out of the process so you can become the lowest cost producer. Produce the highest quality and do the best job of servicing the customer."

Robert Rodin, the president and chief operating officer of Marshall Industries, remembers the beginnings of Gordon Marshall's vision. Rodin said, "About three and a half years ago Gordon read an article on Dr. Deming and his 14 points and he showed it to myself and Dick Bently. While very concise, it was difficult to understand and we began to really wrestle with the concepts. We met with some people and we attended the Deming four-day seminar and began to get a picture of what this possibly could mean for the company."

Gordon Marshall's leadership role as Visionary/Pathfinder was to point out a possible way to go and to mobilize commitment. The Visionary/Pathfinder leaves it to others to study, refine, and implement their vision. Rodin has functioned in a dual leadership role at Marshall Industries. He's shared the role of Visionary/Pathfinder with Gordon Marshall, but he's also been the Problem Solver and Implementer of strategies and practices that will realize the initial vision. As he put it, "In the past, in my role in the company I was really focusing a lot on administrative details, refereeing, cheerleading, and making sure our company was dealing with the fires of the day. Our thinking was basically short term. In the new system, my responsibilities are very different. We're not in a functional organization where the job of everybody who works for me is to make me happy, but rather to build the best process to achieve our mission. So, in this new role, I have to facilitate continuous improvement and eliminate barriers. I have to provide vision into the future in the strategic nature of our business and work with our employees very frequently on a peer level to understand and make sure that they understand their jobs and find ways that I can facilitate continuous improvement and innovation for them."

Leadership occurs not just at the top management level of an organization but wherever there is a group or team task. That means almost any organizational situation. Warehouse manager Mike Lelo is another leader at Marshall Industries. His leadership role is that of Problem Solver. Like president Rodin, Lelo tailors his leadership role to the situation and to the behavior of his followers. Lelo said, "Marshall deals with over 200 suppliers and 200,000 parts companies. We have about 30,000 customers. To operate this whole thing, we have to employ about 140 people. I'll never go out and say this is exactly how this is to be done because, guess what, it changes again everyday. There are things that are going to be different. I could never get out and be involved in such detail in every department where I'm directing everybody what to do. I have them come back to me and say this is what I am doing. Then we'll analyze something, think about it, and make sure we're doing the right things. But I'll never say 'Go out and do this.'

"The moment a person is hired at Marshall's they go through an orientation that shows them all about the company in general. When they come into the warehouse, we don't just say 'Go into the first department that you're assigned to and that's where you're going to stay when you work here.' We tour the whole facility, we show them all the operations and how they interconnect—how receiving sends parts to storage, how storage goes to picking and special handling, and so forth. And they start to see the whole wheel that's spinning."

Lelo is not concerned with conceiving or implementing a vision for Marshall Industries' future, but with solving immediate and incipient problems that occur in the company's central warehouse. As Mike Lelo and his followers address and solve these problems his style is supportive and facilitative. He helps them articulate goals and the paths to obtain those goals. His followers are self assured. Lelo's leadership style seems to work because of his good interpersonal relationships with his team members as well as their acceptance of responsibility and their maturity. His relationship-based style of leadership works well at the warehouse at Marshall Industries with it's eager, mature supervisors.

At Marshall Industries, leaders include Gordon Marshall, a Visionary/Pathfinder, Robert Rodin a Visionary/Pathfinder and Implementer, and Mike Lelo, an Implementer and Problem Solver. Their leadership skills differ, but each is appropriate to their specific leadership challenge. Each has found that the needs of the organization have shaped their leadership style and each can expect that the demands of leadership will demand additional changes in the future.

QUESTIONS

1. Recall and explain the different leadership styles discussed in this video.
2. Do you think that leadership should be primarily undertaken by managers?
3. Identify and discuss several Visonary/Pathfinder leaders. What is their vision? Who are the Problem Solvers and Implementers of that vision?

APPLICATION EXERCISE

PERSONNEL AND PRODUCTION

You have been manager of the Galesburg plant, Consumer Products Division, of the Dallinc Corporation for the past three years. During your tenure, despite an aging physical plant, you've shown a profit increase each year that exceeded the corporate average.

One technique you brought to Galesburg from your previous job is self-managed goal setting. It has worked—you believe—to your advantage at Galesburg. Although it took time to develop this system throughout the plant, the effort appears to have been worth it. Despite initial resistance from some managers (especially senior, autocratic types), you've found first a begrudging acceptance and, for most managers, by now a general acceptance.

Carole Samson was hired as your personnel director three months ago, moving from another city and another corporation. As a matter of courtesy and practice, you delayed asking Carole for formal goals for herself and her department until she had time to learn more about the job and to perhaps hear about your self-managed goal system. Last week in a brief note to Carole, you suggested that she think about setting goals for the coming six-month budget period. Carole wrote back:

While I will be at corporate headquarters this week, I want to respond to your request for goals for myself and my department. While I see a need for goals in production and sales, I do not see how they apply to a cost center like personnel. Last week, for instance, my staff was busy studying the new OSHA regulations and also collecting an attitude survey of team leaders. There seems to be a strong interest in a day care center and more training in computer software, so I'll have to attend to these issues shortly. And next week we begin work with the controller's office preparing for the upcoming contract negotiations; the new high-performing team concept has greatly complicated our negotiating strategy, especially since no one fully understands how it fits into our bargaining agreement. We have to schedule a meeting to explain the new fringe benefits to the exempt (nonunion) staff. And the monthly safety inspection keeps things hectic, especially with the new OSHA requirements.

So you see, I think we are too busy putting out fires and coping with the new "diverse" workforce to consider setting goals. The old rules of union and management, of traditional personnel practices have all changed. We have a tough enough time getting things done without spending more time setting goals. Take a close look at our department and I think you'll agree.

If you check the personnel department, you'll probably also agree with my request for two new staff assistants at the C-II level to help us keep up with these new demands. My goal is to staff the department adequately and increase our budget to respond to the changing demands on personnel. I'd be happy to discuss these goals when I return. I hope you find my response to be helpful, given the unique problems facing the department.

In the same batch of mail, you had a note from Ann Rodwick, your production manager. The note was attached to a goal-setting statement from one of her team leaders, Paul Aguilar. Paul's goal statement said simply:

For the six-month period, produce 80,000 finished units within budgeted costs of $1,525,000.

Ann's note said:

Paul is ambitious (he has reduced costs 3 percent, but unless he gets a handle on quality control, he'll be in trouble on this one. And he has been having a tough time with the new computerized recordkeeping system. Worse, unless he has the new Pace line installed by the third month of the six-month period, he'll never make this goal. And his turnover is getting worse; maybe he's been pushing his team too hard to meet these goals. But, bottom line, this is the level of output we are pushing Paul to achieve. Any ideas?

You have meetings with Carole and Ann scheduled for tomorrow morning.

QUESTIONS

1. What do you plan to say to them?
2. Do you have any specific constructive advice?
3. Prepare some notes to outline your thinking. Then be ready to discuss this thinking with your class team for 20 minutes. Specifically, discuss the following issues: (1) Are goal-setting concepts applicable to all departments? (2) What specific direction do you intend to set for the Personnel Department and the Production Department?

Source: This exercise was adapted from one originally written by Henry P. Sims as The Bill Minder Case.

CHAPTER 14

Interpersonal and Organizational Communication

After studying this chapter, you should be able to:

- ❖ Define communication.

- ❖ Describe the communication process.

- ❖ Discuss the role of communication in organizations.

- ❖ Contrast the different types of interpersonal communication.

- ❖ Identify the three formal channels of organizational communication.

- ❖ Explain the significance of informal communication.

- ❖ List the barriers to organizational communication.

- ❖ Discuss how organizations can facilitate communication.

Inspiring Worker Involvement

As we have said many times throughout the text, total quality management is changing American business. Companies are devoting themselves to customer satisfaction and continual improvement in their products and processes. In many cases, achieving total quality involves a major shift in how workers think about their jobs. In the most extreme case, workers who once viewed their job as pleasing the boss must shift 180 degrees to view their job as pleasing the customer. Communication is a key to a successful shift in the way workers think about their jobs. An organization will benefit greatly by motivating its employees in quality improvement efforts.

Globe Metallurgical employee.

According to Charlotte Scroggins, vice president for communications for the American Productivity and Quality Center in Houston, companies with successful quality processes all emphasize communication. "They always include communication as a critical link to employees, suppliers, customers, shareholders, and the media. Communication is one of the things that must be present in order to achieve a successful quality process." In short, quality cannot be achieved without communication. Under scientific management, managers and supervisors told workers what to do; total quality management necessitates an open dialogue between workers and managers.

Globe Metallurgical, Inc., manufacturer of silicon metal and ferrosilicon products for the auto industry, began a TQM program in 1985. The program's purpose was to shift the firm's emphasis from inspecting each shipment in order to en-

sure that the firm met customer specifications, to an emphasis on continual improvement of each step in the process.

Previously, hourly workers were never included in the decision-making process. Instead they were told what was going to be done. This time Globe decided a dynamic communication process was needed to build understanding between management and workers. To get workers to buy into the quality improvement effort, committees and teams were formed to examine how the company works. Plant committees and quality circles met daily to search for ways to improve quality and cut cost. The company attempted to implement each idea that came out of a quality circle or committee.

The process has paid off for Globe Metallurgical, which won the Malcolm Baldrige National Quality Award in 1988. CEO Arden Sims attributes much of Globe's recent success to improved communication and the respect of employees, which enabled the firm to transform successfully. Today Globe leads the industry in terms of sales growth, profit growth, quality, productivity, and costs.

Source: Adapted from K. N. Anand, "Which Comes First: The Chicken or the Egg?" *Quality Progress,* May 1995, pp. 115–118; Jane Easter Bahls, "Managing for Total Quality," *Public Relations Journal,* April 1992, pp. 16–20; Bruce Rayner, "Trial-by-Fire Transformation: An Interview with Globe Metallurgical's Arden C. Sims," *Harvard Business Review,* May-June 1992, pp. 116–29; and Teri Lammens, Alessandra Bianchi, and Susan Greco, "The Calendar Method," *Inc.,* February 1991, p. 78.

Communication is perhaps the single most important factor in establishing quality in an organization.[1] The view that communication is critical to organizational excellence dates back at least to 1938, when Chester Barnard wrote his famous book *The Functions of the Executive.*[2] In it, Barnard described one of the major responsibilities of executives as developing and maintaining a system of communication. Organization members must solve increasingly complex problems. Through effective communication, individuals can overcome barriers, work through problems, and achieve the organization's goals.

While a father relaxed on the couch listening to a tape, his four-year-old son and two-year-old daughter asked him if they could wash their fire truck in the family room. He answered, "Sure, just put a towel under the truck and be sure to keep the water on the towel," and put the headphones back on. But when he got up to change the tape, the laughter from the other room—and what he thought was splashing water—was overwhelming. Checking on the kids, he found the carpet completely drenched with water. His question: "What do you think you're doing?" Their answer: "You said to keep the water on the towel and we did." Unfortunately, they had poured dozens of buckets of water on the towel. It took a week to dry the carpet, the floor, and the room beneath the floor.

Whether we're in the role of parent, child, student, worker, or whatever, each of us has had a similar experience. While we often recover—the carpet dried out and everyone survived—communication breakdowns can have negative consequences. Problems between spouses, families, and even nations can often be traced to communication failures. Likewise, many problems in organizations can be attributed to poor communication.

Communication is an important part of the leadership function; managers cannot be effective leaders if they cannot communicate. Successful leaders have visions of greatness. Leaders don't create budgets; they set direction.[3] That is, they have a clear picture of what they want the organization to be, and they communicate that vision to other members of the organization. When President John F. Kennedy said, "We will put a man on the moon before the end of the decade," Americans clearly understood his vision, and thousands of individuals devoted themselves to making his vision a reality.

This chapter's topic is interpersonal and organizational communication. First, we discuss the nature and scope of communication. Then, we examine various types of interpersonal and organizational communication. Finally, we look at barriers to organizational communication and strategies for facilitating communication.

THE NATURE AND SCOPE OF COMMUNICATION

The term *communication* is fairly common. Most of us have used it in one way or another to describe our interactions with others. Historical figures are often compared by their ability to communicate. TV, radio, and newspapers are referred to as communication media (the plural of *medium*); the telephone and computer are called communication devices. Unfortunately, communication is often taken for granted, though in fact it is a complex activity.[4] Failure to understand this complexity often leads to problems with communication.

communication
The exchange of information between a sender (source) and a receiver (audience).

Communication is defined as the exchange of information between a sender (source) and a receiver (audience). If meaning is not shared, communication has not taken place. A production worker stopped her machine to fix it because it was making defective products. The foreman came by and ordered: "Run it," so she turned the machine back on. When asked to explain her behavior, the worker replied, "He ordered me to make defectives."[5] The foreman surely didn't mean to order the worker to make defective products, but that's the message that was communicated. The Ethics Spotlight illustrates how one such communication breakdown resulted in a crisis for Sears.

As companies throughout the United States and other parts of the world move toward total quality management (TQM), they are wrestling with an important aspect of TQM: communicating quality in the organization. Many TQM efforts are unsuccessful because organizations do not understand how to communicate quality.[6] Effective communication is the cornerstone of quality management. The way we perceive and talk to each other at work— about quality, job tasks, changes taking place, or other issues—is a major determinant of the organization's success. Communication also sets the tone for success of individuals and teams.[7] At the University of Michigan Hospitals, the work of a group of head nurses was redesigned using the team concept; communication was the most difficult and challenging part of team development.[8] Poor communication, on the other hand, reduces quality, weakens productivity, and leads to anger, lack of trust, and cynicism.[9] Despite the importance of

---

ETHICS SPOTLIGHT | THE WRONG MESSAGE AT SEARS

When Sears, Roebuck & Co. Chairman Edward A. Brennan pressured auto repair centers to boost profits, he apparently didn't realize the message he was sending. But on June 11, 1992, Brennan found out that perhaps the wrong message was communicated. On that day the California Dept. of Consumer Affairs accused Sears of systematically overcharging auto repair customers at its 72 Sears Tire & Auto Centers in that state and proposed revoking the company's license to operate the centers.

A growing number of consumer complaints had spurred the consumer affairs department to conduct a year-long undercover investigation. It found that its agents were overcharged nearly 90 percent of the time, by an average of $223. "This is a flagrant breach of trust and confidence the people of California have placed in Sears for generations," said Jim Conran, the department's director. "Sears has used trust as a marketing tool, and we don't believe they've lived up to that trust." He was referring to one of the company's advertising slogans, "You can count on Sears."

On June 15, four days after California's charges, New Jersey accused six Sears auto centers, along with five unrelated repair shops, of doing unneeded work. Other states, including Florida, Illinois, New York, and Alabama, also began studying California's action.

What caused one of the nation's most respected retailers to wind up in such a mess? Critics believe the trouble started in 1990 when Sears had a 40 percent drop in earnings and a 60 percent drop in net income for its merchandise group (including the auto centers and appliances). Brennan started a shake-up, slashing costs by $600 million, renovating the company's 868 stores, and pushing new everyday low prices. In 1990, Sears standardized compensation of auto service employees nationwide, introducing commissions and by-the-job pay rates in some areas. Conran, of the California consumer affairs department, said complaints began soon after Sears established a quota of parts and repair sales for every eight-hour shift. Crew members who failed to meet the quotas had work hours reduced or were transferred. Attorneys for former Sears auto employees, government investigators, and law enforcement officials feel that these policies add up to a system of fraud. According to Ray Liebaum, a deputy attorney general in California, "There was a deliberate decision by Sears management to set up a structure that made it totally inevitable that the consumer would be oversold."

Sears emphatically denied any wrongdoing and said it would appeal California's delicensing action before an administrative judge and in the courts if necessary. The attorney representing Sears in the California case, Dirk Schenkkan, accused the consumer affairs department of beating up on Sears to boost its own standing at a time when its funding was threatened by California budget cuts. A statement by Sears said the California investigation was "very seriously flawed and simply does not support the allegations. The service we recommend and the work we perform are in accordance with the highest industry standards."

Nonetheless on June 21, 1992, Sears settled charges with New Jersey by agreeing to pay $200,000 for a study of auto-repair standards and an additional $3,000 in penalties. But the big blow came a few months later on September 2, when Sears agreed to pay an estimated $15 million to settle charges in California and 41 other states, as well as settlement of 19 related class action lawsuits. The California settlement alone will cost the firm $8 million. Denying any charges, Sears agreed to refund $50 to affected consumers for up to five repair services. Sears also agreed to pay the state of California $1.3 million for reimbursement of legal fees and $1.5 million to establish an auto repair training program. Sears could potentially pay over $46 million, but officials don't expect all eligible customers to apply for refunds. The damage to Sears' reputation and loss of goodwill is impossible to measure.

Source: Adapted from Julia Flynn, Christina Del Valle, and Russell Mitchell, "Did Sears Take Other Customers for a Ride?" *Business Week*, August 3, 1992, pp. 24–25; Gregory A. Patterson, "Sears Will Pay $15 Million Settling Cases," *The Wall Street Journal*, September 3, 1992, p. A4; Kevin Kelly and Eric Schine, "How Did Sears Blow This Gasket?" *Business Week*, June 29, 1992, p. 38; and Tung Yin, "Sears Is Accused of Billing Fraud at Auto Centers," *The Wall Street Journal*, June 12, 1992, pp. B1, B6.

communication, most CEOs of top U.S. companies acknowledge that they are not spending enough time on employee communication.[10]

The Communication Process

Communication can be described as a process in which a message is encoded and transmitted through some medium to a receiver who decodes the message and then transmits some sort of response back to the sender. It is through the communication process that the sharing of a common meaning takes place. As Figure 14–1 shows, communication begins with a **sender**, a person, group, or organization that has a message to share with another person or group of persons.

In organizations, executives, managers, workers, departments, and even the organization itself can be the source of a message. Executives must communicate with the board of directors, top-level managers, as well as groups and individuals outside the organization such as stockholders, regulators, and customers. Managers must communicate with managers in other departments, superiors, subordinates, customers, and suppliers. Workers must communicate with superiors, customers, and each other. Clearly we could go on and on. The point is that every organization member is a source with a message to communicate to internal and external parties.

A **message** is an idea or experience that a sender wants to communicate. Messages can be communicated both verbally and nonverbally. For instance, a manager may want to communicate a process to a worker. This can be done in many ways: explaining the process, illustrating it, or providing a written explanation. The critical issue is that the message is presented in a way that the intended meaning will be conveyed by the manager.

To convey meaning, the sender must **encode** the message by converting it into groups of symbols that represent ideas or concepts. Encoding translates ideas or concepts into the coded message that will be communicated. We use symbols (languages, words, or gestures) to encode ideas into messages that others can understand. When encoding a message, the sender must use symbols that are familiar to the intended receiver. A person with a message to communicate should know the audience and present the message in language that the audience can grasp. A computer company developing a sales presentation targeted at a nontechnical audience should ensure that its presentation is written and delivered using words and graphics familiar to that audience. In referring to concepts, the sender should use the same symbols that the receiver uses to refer to those concepts, and should avoid using symbols that can have more than one meaning.

To relay the message, the sender must select and use a **medium of transmission** (a means of carrying an encoded message from the source to the receiver). Ink on paper, vibrations of air produced by vocal cords, and electronically produced airwaves such as radio and TV signals are examples of transmission media. If a sender relays a message

sender
A person, group, or organization that has a message to share with another person or group of persons.

message
An idea or experience that a sender wants to communicate.

encode
To convert a message into groups of symbols that represent ideas or concepts.

medium of transmission
A means of carrying an encoded message from the source to the receiver.

FIGURE 14–1
The Communication Process

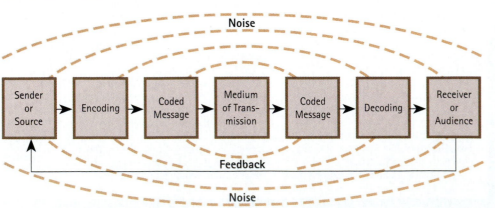

through an inappropriate medium of transmission, the message may not reach the right receivers. Organizations use memos, meetings, reward systems, policy statements, production schedules, and many other mediums to communicate with members. Some may not always be appropriate. Deming, for instance, thinks some reward systems such as individual ratings send an inappropriate message; they emphasize individual competition and place artificial limits on performance.[11]

Decoding is the process by which the receiver interprets the symbols (coded message) sent by the source by converting them into concepts and ideas. Seldom does the receiver decode exactly the same meaning that a sender encoded. When the receiver interprets the message differently from what the sender intended, the cause may be **noise** (interference that affects any or all stages of the communication process). Noise has many sources, such as competing messages, misinterpretation, radio static, faulty printing, or use of ambiguous or unfamiliar symbols. Yelling at a subordinate may result in noise, even though the manager uses familiar words to convey the message. Noise may be present at any point of the communication process.

Feedback is the receiver's response to the sender's message. During feedback, the receiver becomes the source of a message that is directed back to the original source, who then becomes a receiver. Thus communication can be viewed as a circular process, as Figure 14–1 shows. But feedback may not take place immediately. For instance, a consumer products manufacturer may advertise the benefits of a product (the message), but the consumer may not actually purchase the product (feedback) until some time after receiving the source's message. In organizations, feedback is necessary for two-way communication. Quality can best be achieved when people in organizations communicate with each other and work cooperatively. It is often nonmanagers who are closest to production problems, suppliers, and customers. If they do not have the capacity to provide feedback, managers will miss out on valuable information.

The communication process has a **channel capacity**, a limit on the volume of information that it can handle effectively. Channel capacity is determined by the least efficient component of the communication process. With verbal communications, there is a limit to how fast a source can speak and how much a receiver can decode. If a manager transmits more than one message, the communication process may not be totally effective because the audience (receivers) may not be able to decode all the messages at the same time, especially if they are inconsistent. For instance, a manager at a branch bank tells all new tellers that customers are important, and also tells them to close their windows early so they can balance their windows and get out of the bank on time. The result is longer lines at closing times, and the new tellers don't get the message that customers are important.

Selecting a Communication Medium

Media selection is a critical aspect of effective communication. A *communication medium* is a conduit or channel through which data and meaning are conveyed.[12] Communications media include face-to-face, telephone, and written communication. Managers must determine which media to use in sending and in receiving information. Suppose, for instance, a

decoding
The process by which the receiver interprets the symbols (coded message) sent by the source by converting them into concepts and ideas.

noise
Interference that affects any or all stages of the communication process.

feedback
The receiver's response to the sender's message.

channel capacity
The limit on the volume of information that a channel can handle effectively.

TABLE 14–1	ALTERNATIVE COMMUNICATION MEDIA	
Oral	Written	Nonverbal
Face-to-face	Letters	Touch
Telephone	Computer printouts	Eye contact
Speeches	Electronic mail	Body language
Video conferencing	Memos	Time
Intercom	Bulletin boards	Space

sales manager wants to communicate a new compensation plan to the selling force. How should the new plan be communicated? What media should be used? Would letters, memos, oral presentations, telephone calls, or some other medium work best? The answers to these questions will likely affect the success of the new compensation program. Table 14–1 lists assorted media choices.

media richness
Media's capacity to convey data.

One factor that has been stressed in choosing media is the **media richness** (media's capacity to convey data).[13] One medium may be richer than another; that is, one medium may have a greater capacity to carry data than another. Data-carrying capacity refers to the degree to which a medium can effectively and efficiently convey data.[14] Thus the best medium can be determined by its richness or effectiveness.

Several criteria are used to evaluate a medium's richness: the medium's capacity for timely feedback; its capacity for multiple uses, such as audio and visual; the extent to which the message can be personalized; and the variety of language, such as natural and body language, that can be used.[15] Face-to-face is the richest medium because feedback is the fastest, both audio and visual cues can be used, the message is personal, and a variety of languages can be used. Conversely, formal numeric media such as computer printouts are the least rich because feedback is very slow and data-carrying capacity is limited to visual information.

Suppose the sales manager decides the most effective way to inform the selling force about the new compensation plan is through face-to-face communication. The meaning of the spoken word, the rate, pitch, and force of the verbal message, and facial expressions can all combine to give a single, powerful message. Each salesperson will have the opportunity to see the manager, hear the message, interpret it, and give and receive feedback. This seems to be the best way to ensure the new plan's success. Unfortunately there are thousands of salespeople in several countries throughout the world. Face-to-face communication is simply not possible.

In addition to richness, several other factors must be considered in selecting a communication medium. First, cost must be weighed against the medium's speed of transmission and its overall effectiveness. A telephone call, for instance, may be the fastest and most effective medium when speed is critical in communication, even though a letter would be much less expensive. Some messages have a greater impact when delivered in person. Communicating a promotion personally, or both in person and by letter, may convey the maximum impact. Second, the purpose of the communication influences the media choice. To communicate technical or quantitative information, a written report may be most effective. Third, the extent to which interaction is necessary should be considered when selecting a medium. A performance review could be in writing, but a face-to-face meeting would allow for questions, feedback, and understanding. Finally, the receiver's capabilities also influence which medium is selected. A receiver that tends to forget oral communication may need written reminders providing documentation for the future.

In summary, media choice depends on the situation's requirements. Some situations may call for oral communication, some for written, and others for a combination. Always select a communication medium that conveys the intended message to the target audience.

The Role of Communication in Organizations

Throughout this book we have discussed several functions of management, including planning, organizing, and leading. Controlling will be discussed in the next part of the book. We have also emphasized the importance of quality. Management is largely a profession that functions through the vehicle of communicating with people—most good managers are good communicators. Indeed, managers need technical, analytical, and conceptual skills (see Chapter 1) to perform their functions and develop a culture that is conducive to quality. But communication is an essential part of all other management functions and processes. Put another way, "The job of the manager is, ultimately, communication, regardless of how varied or specialized the activity of the moment might be."[16]

Many managers stress open communication as a means of improving organization effectiveness and quality. The goal of constantly improving quality can only be achieved if it supersedes differences, jealousies, competition between individuals and departments, and turf battles.[17] Open communication requires more than maintaining open offices. It also involves managers' accessibility to workers, day-to-day interaction with employees, and breaking down barriers and resistance to change. If an organization decides to implement quality teams, communication is essential. Resistance to the change should be expected. Here communication helps people deal with change, work through it, and adapt to the new way of doing things, whether it be quality teams or some other change. In short, communication pervades every aspect of the organization, every individual, team, or department, and each external relationship with customers, suppliers, and competitors. The organization cannot achieve its goals without open, two-way communication.

INTERPERSONAL COMMUNICATION

Individuals spend a great deal of time in organizations interacting with each other. **Interpersonal communication** is communication between two people, usually face-to-face.[18] Other communication media (such as the telephone or the computer) can also be used to communicate interpersonally. Through interpersonal communication we develop and maintain human relationships—the basic social units of any organization. Thus interpersonal communication is the fundamental building block of organizational communication.

Interpersonal communication Communication between two people, usually face-to-face.

It is extremely difficult for one individual to accomplish much within an organization.[19] This was the basic message President Bush sent the American public during his 1992 Republican Party presidential nomination acceptance speech. He attributed much of his administration's ineffectiveness to the Democrat-controlled Congress. Critics replied that the problem wasn't Congress, it was the president's inability to communicate with Congress. They added that President Reagan, the "great communicator," had his way with the

---

REFLECTIONS BY PHILIP B. CROSBY

Interpersonal and Organizational Communication

One Monday morning, while taking a break at a conference, I wandered over to the golf practice range. I realized that the man hitting balls out of the practice sand trap was one of the world's premier golfers. He had just won the previous PGA tournament, in fact. I edged over and stood watching in awe as he pounded ball after ball up near the pin.

Then he decided to rest for a few moments and climbed out of the bunker. He walked over to me and we shook hands and chatted. He asked about my game.

"Inconsistent is the word," I said. "I get six or seven pars in a round and the rest are not worth mentioning. Do you have any suggestions?"

"Hit a thousand balls a day," he said. "I haven't found any other way."

"Don't you have something you could sell me?" I asked. "How about some new clubs, or a pair of pants, or a ball warmer, or a magic glove?"

He laughed and patted me on the shoulder.

"You left out motivation classes for the caddies," he said. "You know as well as I do that you are responsible for your own game. If you can par six or seven holes, you can par them all." He went back to work.

The truest form of communication is participation. I have noticed that many managers try to tell their people something without being an example of it themselves. This is particularly true of quality. Executives in particular think that they can spend some money and buy what is called TQM. This consists of a bunch of techniques, tools, and classes intended to change the way people work. But the communication is not real. Management commitment cannot be demonstrated by anything else except the management being committed, in person.

I decided to take the advice of this obviously dedicated professional. Hitting a thousand balls a day is a little past my activity level, but I did take some lessons and began to work the game more seriously, to make certain that I was lined up and set up properly. I thought about things. All of this didn't take any more time, but it certainly had its effect on my game. My handicap now is the lowest it has been for 25 years.

Communication is getting the message to the areas that need it in a way that will be accepted and implemented. That requires both credibility of presentation and integrity of content.

Don't try to sell something you don't believe.

same Democratic Congress for eight years. Only through successful interpersonal communication can anything be accomplished in an organization. This can be upsetting to a powerful organizational member such as President Bush or the CEO of a large corporation. Individuals must eventually realize that power is based on the ability to influence others, and communication enables one individual to influence the behavior of others.

Oral Communication

oral communication
Communication using the spoken word to transmit a message.

Oral communication takes place when the spoken word is used to transmit a message. Conversations can take place in person, via telephone, or through some other mechanism that allows individuals to speak to one another. Oral communication enables prompt, two-way interaction between parties. Many meetings and conferences that involve people from different locations, even different parts of the world, are conducted using TV hookups so participants can interact personally. Perhaps the major benefit of this type of communication is that ideas can be interchanged and prompt feedback can be provided. Questions can be addressed, positions and issues debated, and a plan for action or resolution established. Oral communication that takes place in person also allows the use of gestures, facial expressions, and other emotions such as tone or voice.

Oral communication, because of its immediacy, can result in poor communication. If, for instance, a person becomes angry, noise enters the communication process. Messages that are not clearly encoded may also fail to communicate the intended idea. A hurried manager may give an oral instruction or initiative without thinking about the outcome. (Recall what happened when the foreman instructed the factory worker to turn the machine on.) While feedback is immediate, it may also be without thought, reducing the quality of the communication. Individuals often feel the need to respond immediately in a face-to-face meeting, when in fact they should take some time to prepare a well-thought-out response.

Written Communication

written communication
Transmitting a message through the written word.

Transmitting a message through the written word is called **written communication**. This type of communication can help eliminate the problem we just discussed. Written messages allow a manager to think about the message, reread it several times, and perhaps get others to review the message before it's transmitted. The receiver can take time to read the message carefully and accurately. Written messages are also more permanent than oral, providing a record of the communication. Whether it's a long report or a short memo, written communication can be referred to in the future as needed. Managers often find it necessary to document their decisions for legal reasons.

Despite the advantages of written communication, managers generally prefer to communicate orally. Written communication takes more time to prepare and does not allow interaction or immediate feedback. Managers rely on two-way communication to resolve problems quickly. It takes much longer to get ideas on paper, to distribute them to others, and to receive written responses; a telephone call or meeting is quicker. Written communication, by its formal nature, may also discourage open communication. E-mail, a form of written communication, is more timely and allows quick response, perhaps explaining its popularity.

Nonverbal Communication

nonverbal communication
Intentional or unintentional messages that are neither written nor spoken.

All intentional or unintentional messages that are neither written nor spoken are referred to as **nonverbal communication**.[20] Examples include vocal cues, body movements, facial expressions, personal appearance, and distance or space. A certain look or glance, seating arrangements at a meeting, or a sudden change in voice tone can communicate a strong message. Nonverbal messages can be powerful, depending on the situation. Silence, for example, has been described as a tremendous communication device.

The difficulty with nonverbal communication is that the receiver must know the specific background or frame of reference of the source to accurately decode the message. For example, on her first day of work a new employee witnesses her boss screaming at a coworker. She's shocked, and asks the co-worker if this happens often. He explains that the boss is a great guy and a great manager, will do anything for you, and happens to yell all the time. Now she has a different perspective. On the other hand, imagine if a manager who is known to be cool and calm and rarely changes expressions glares at someone in a meeting.

Managers must recognize that nonverbal communication can occur unintentionally. After being on the job for about three months, a computer programmer had come to the conclusion that his supervisor didn't like him. He was so concerned he decided to look for another job, but he decided to talk to his supervisor before he quit. He told the supervisor, "Obviously I did something to upset you." The manager looked at him without emotion, told the programmer he was doing a great job and could expect a nice raise at his six-month review, and offered no other explanation. Managers have to understand the potential of nonverbal communication and realize that unintentionally they may be sending the wrong message.

Nonverbal communication is important to multinational companies (MNCs) operating in a foreign country. People in different countries and cultures have different sets of nonverbal symbols and meanings. Nonverbal cues such as touch, body language, and personal distance are used differently across cultures. For instance, a study of how often couples in coffee shops touched reported that couples in San Juan, Puerto Rico, touched 180 times an hour; couples in Paris, France, 110 times; in Gainesville, Florida, twice per hour; and in London, England, once.[21] Managers encounter difficulty interpreting nonverbal communication while working in foreign countries. Likewise they are uncertain what nonverbal messages they may be transmitting. A business deal in Japan can fall through if a foreign executive refuses a cup of green tea during a visit to a Japanese firm.[22] Representatives working in a foreign country should be given adequate training in the nonverbal customs of the country. The Diversity Scope looks at this issue.

DIVERSITY SCOPE   NONVERBAL COMMUNICATION IN THE GLOBAL ENVIRONMENT

When American firms conduct business in foreign countries, they often find they underestimate the significance of nonverbal communication. In some cultures, the verbal message is not as important as the nonverbal message. Managers accustomed to communicating through reports, contracts, and other written and verbal communication may be at a disadvantage in a foreign country. In Japan, for instance, true intentions are often disguised by an agreeable smile. Japanese people realize when they are being taken in, but foreigners may not.

Time has different meanings in different countries. In the United States a delay in responding to a communication is generally taken to mean that the issue is not important to the other party. The amount of time a person is kept waiting for a meeting indicates the importance of the person or subject. For instance, a salesperson kept waiting for several hours may get discouraged because this suggests the purchasing manager isn't interested in the product. In some foreign countries this is viewed much differently. In Latin America the time a person is kept waiting means very little. In Japan a lengthy delay of weeks or months doesn't mean the party has lost interest. Americans must have patience or risk a breakdown in communication. Giving a person a deadline in the Middle East is viewed as rude and demanding.

The connotations associated with greetings and body motions vary across countries. While it is traditional to shake hands in America, the palms of hands touch and the head is nodded for greeting in India. It is also considered rude to shake hands with a woman in India. The traditional form of greeting in Japan is bowing; in Latin America it's a hearty embrace and friendly slap on the back. Arm gestures are used for emphasis in Latin America, the raised eyebrow means "yes" in the Middle East, and a forefinger to the nose means "me" in Japan. Kissing is considered offensive in India and is not seen on TV, in movies, or in public places.

Space also has different meanings throughout the world. In the United States office size indicates an individual's relative status. Executives tend to have the largest corner office. As stature in the organization decreases, so does office size. The French locate offices according to activities and interests; the supervisor is usually found in the middle of subordinates to improve communication. What is considered crowded in America is seen as spacious in Arab and Spanish cultures.

Shapes, sizes, and colors also convey different meanings. In Japan, pine, bamboo, or plum patterns are positive, as are muted shades. Cultural shapes such as Buddha and combinations of black, dark gray, and white have negative overtones. Round or square shapes are acceptable in the Middle East, while symbols such as the six-pointed star or raised thumb are avoided. Europeans favor white and blue, while black generally has negative overtones. These differences have implications for dress, product and package design, and various forms of communication such as advertising.

Source: Adapted from James C. Simmons, "A Matter of Interpretation," *American Way*, April 1983, pp. 106–11; E. T. Hall, "The Silent Language in Overseas Business," *Harvard Business Review*, May–June 1960; and "The Art of Lying," *World Press Review*, November 1985, p. 10.

Empathic Listening

You have been reading this book that we have written for some time. Reading and writing are both forms of interpersonal communication, but they are not the only ones. Speaking and listening are other forms. We all have a lot of experience speaking, but perhaps listening is the one form of communication that we have the least experience with. In his best-selling book *The 7 Habits of Highly Effective People*, Stephen Covey suggests that the key to effective listening is to seek first to understand, then to be understood.[23] Covey describes *empathic listening* as listening with the intent to understand. This is not easy—it requires looking at an issue from another person's point of view. It requires listening not only with your ears, but with your eyes and your heart as well.

Studies have found that 70 to 80 percent of our waking life is spent communicating on some level. Of this time, 45 percent is spent listening.[24] Unless someone listens, communication cannot take place. For instance, retail bankers have found that practicing active listening skills enables them to identify their clients' financial goals.[25] Fortunately, listening is a skill that can be learned and improved. By avoiding barriers to effective listening and by developing listening skills, we can all become empathic listeners.

Distractions such as interruptions, telephone calls, and unfinished work are a major barrier to effective listening.[26] Creating an environment free of such distractions will improve listening. Many listeners also take detours during a communication. For instance, if someone mentions a word that brings out certain emotions, we become distracted and tune out the message. Many receivers also begin to debate a point, thinking ahead and planning a response. You're likely to miss the message in this case.

It is not easy to listen, but we can all start by taking time to listen. Relax, try to close out other distractions, and give both your mental and physical attention to the other person. Help the other person relax by assuming a nonthreatening listening posture, maintaining eye contact and a warm facial expression. This demonstrates that the listener is interested in what is being said.

Communication can also be improved by giving and requesting constructive feedback. If people say what they think others want to hear, feedback is of limited value. Honest feedback can be used to determine if the listener understood the intended message. Effective listeners focus on the message's meaning, postpone judgments until the communication is complete, actively respond to the speaker, and avoid focusing on emotionally charged words.[27]

Effective and empathic listening takes time and practice. Listening with empathy puts you on the same level with another person. It's difficult to listen when you don't understand the other person. Effective listening is not a passive exercise; it is an active skill that requires full participation. Good listeners take notes, ask questions, and are totally attentive

---

WHAT MANAGERS ARE READING

THE 7 HABITS OF HIGHLY EFFECTIVE PEOPLE
by Stephen R. Covey

In his book *The 7 Habits of Highly Effective People*, Stephen R. Covey presents an integrated approach for solving personal and professional problems. Covey believes these habits distinguish the happy, healthy, and successful from those who fail or must sacrifice happiness for success. He outlines a step-by-step process for living with fairness, integrity, honesty, and human dignity. These principles give an individual the security needed to adapt to change, and the wisdom to take advantage of the opportunities that change creates.

Habit 1 is to be proactive, or to take responsibility for your own life. Habit 2 is to begin with the end in mind, or to start with a clear understanding of your destination. Habit 3 is to put first things first, meaning to organize and execute around priorities. Habit 4 is to think win-win, which means to seek mutual benefits in human interactions. Habit 5 is to seek first to understand, then to be understood. This habit involves empathic communication, or listening with the intent to understand. Habit 6 is to synergize, or use all of our skills in concert to reach greater heights. Habit 7 is to sharpen the saw, or to practice and renew all habits. The seven habits build on each other; you cannot achieve 2 without 1, and so on.

Source: Stephen R. Covey, *The 7 Habits of Highly Effective People* (New York: Fireside, 1990).

to what is being said.[28] Although listening may not come naturally to all of us, with practice we can become better listeners and reap the benefits of effective communication.

Organizations using quality teams find that conflicts are often brought into the open. Some mechanism must be established to deal with these conflicts. One solution is to create a forum for active listening in which disagreements are resolved through constructive discussions.[29] Unresolved conflicts can have a negative impact on work group productivity.

ORGANIZATIONAL COMMUNICATION

We noted earlier that individuals and groups must communicate effectively for organizations to be successful. This section examines formal and informal channels of organizational communication and their impact on the communication process. It is the manager's job to ensure that effective, efficient channels are available to facilitate communication. Figure 14–2 illustrates the forms of organizational communication, both formal and informal. Managers must understand these forms as well as barriers to organizational communication and how to remove them.

Formal Channels of Communication

Formal channels of communication are the official paths prescribed by management. These formal channels generally follow the organization's chain of command. Information can be communicated downward, upward, or horizontally, and can be oral, written, or nonverbal.

DOWNWARD COMMUNICATION - Information flows down the organizational hierarchy from managers and supervisors to subordinates through **downward communication**. As Figure 14–2 shows, this communication follows the formal lines of authority prescribed by the chain of command. Downward communication generally involves job instructions, manuals, policy statements, memos, motivational appeals, and other forms of formal instruction or feedback. Downward communication is not always adequate because workers need more information than just job instructions. They also need to know, for instance, what other members of the organization are doing. Nevertheless downward communication is important because lack of communication from superiors can leave workers misinformed, feeling disconnected, and less satisfied with their jobs.

downward communication **Information that flows down the organizational hierarchy from managers and supervisors to subordinates.**

FIGURE 14–2
Formal and Informal Channels of Communication

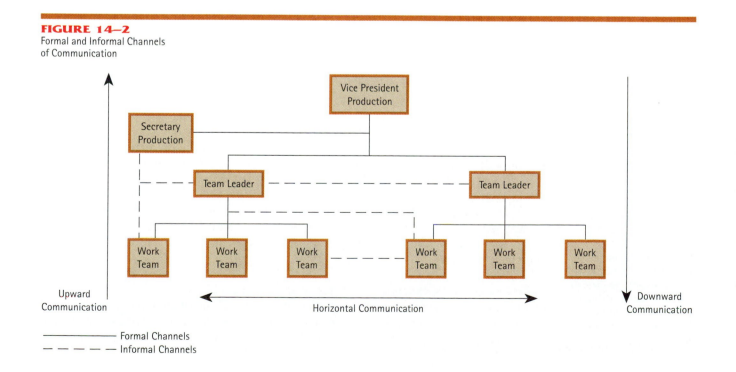

- ——————— Formal Channels
- — — — — — Informal Channels

One problem managers face is deciding which and how much information to communicate to subordinates. Too much information, especially if it is irrelevant, is eventually ignored. Every Friday some salespeople find dozens of reports and summaries in their mailboxes—much of it useless—and begin to ignore the material. Unfortunately, some of it may be valuable. Managers who wish to empower workers must provide quality information that can enable workers to improve. This may also require communicating information that was once considered only for managers, such as financial and performance data.

upward communication
Information that flows up the organization from the subordinates to supervisors and managers.

UPWARD COMMUNICATION - Information that flows up the organization from subordinates to supervisors and managers is called **upward communication**. This type of communication is necessary for managers to evaluate the effectiveness of downward communication. It also enables workers to feel they are a meaningful part of the organization. Many types of messages are communicated upward, including suggestions for improvements, feelings about the job or the organization, problems or grievances, requests, and responses to downward communication. Many workers face a dilemma concerning what they should communicate to superiors. In any event, upward communication should be encouraged, as it is a means of driving fear out of the organization (one of Deming's 14 points for quality). A factory worker must not be afraid to tell the supervisor that the machine is making defective products.

Obviously, information is not effective unless it is accurate. Upward communication is often distorted in one way or another to be made more acceptable to managers. Workers may be reluctant to report problems if they think managers will blame them. Managers should create an environment in which workers feel comfortable reporting good news and bad. Empowered workers are more likely to report accurate information than less powerful or fearful employees. Managers can demonstrate that upward communication is valued by replying or acting promptly and positively.

Robert W. Galvin, former CEO of Motorola, emphasized the need for both downward and upward communication in developing a total quality management program.[30] The goal of Motorola (and many other firms) is *total customer satisfaction*. This requires (1) a good information flow in the company and (2) quality information available to everyone involved in making decisions. At Motorola workers aren't fearful of communicating problems upward. Galvin's philosophy is that problems and mistakes are part of innovation and constant improvement; they just shouldn't be made before the customer's eyes.

horizontal communication
Messages that flow between persons at the same level of an organization.

HORIZONTAL COMMUNICATION - Messages flow between persons at the same level of the organization through **horizontal communication**. This includes staff meetings, face-to-face interactions, and sharing of information through memos and reports. Horizontal communication is needed to coordinate the activities of diverse but independent units or departments. For instance, the manager of marketing and sales needs to communicate with the manager of production to avoid understocking or overstocking the product. At Johnson Controls, two of its facilities, one in Reynosa, Mexico, and the other in McAllen, Texas, must communicate with each other as part of the firm's total quality commitment.[31]

Traditionally, horizontal communication took place more among managers than nonmanagers. But as organizations have begun to utilize work teams and quality circles, workers from different units or departments are often called together to work on a project or problem. Many organizations are placing increasing emphasis on horizontal communication. In their book *Re-inventing the Corporation*, John Naisbitt and Patricia Aburdene observe, "The top-down authoritarian management style is yielding to a networking style of management, where people learn from one another horizontally, where everyone is a resource for everyone else, and where each person gets support and assistance from many different directions."[32]

grapevine
An informal communication channel that cuts across formal channels of communication and carries a variety of facts, opinions, rumors, and other information.

Informal Channels of Communication

Not all organizational communication follows the official chain of command. One informal channel of communication is the grapevine. The **grapevine** cuts across formal channels of communication and carries a variety of facts, opinions, rumors, and other information. All organizations, large or small, have grapevines; it is futile for managers to try to eliminate this informal channel. Conversely, communications must be managed effectively so that the grapevine is not the main source of information.[33]

While grapevines don't always have negative consequences, they are frequently troublesome to managers. A middle manager once learned of an impending transfer when she received a telephone call from a real estate agent in another part of the country. She eventually found that the real estate agent's contact at corporate headquarters learned about the transfer and passed it on to the realtor. Unfortunately, the woman's supervisor had yet to tell her about the transfer. The grapevine can also be the source of harmful rumors and gossip, and is especially dangerous if manipulated by managers to communicate with employees instead of using normal, open channels to communicate.[34] Managers can control this to some extent by communicating accurate, timely information, by maintaining and cultivating open channels of communication in all directions, and by moving quickly to dispel rumors and correct inaccurate information.

Despite its limitations, the grapevine offers an abundance of operating data, generates corporate memory, and can communicate important insights with speed and economy.[35] As organizations move toward the new paradigm of flat, borderless, and globally dispersed network organizations, informal communication—more than ever before—provides an important source of needed information.

Communicating Quality in Organizations

Effective communication is vital to the success of total quality programs, especially when directed to audiences inside the organization.[36] Communication is often the least understood and most poorly managed aspect of TQM efforts. Whether we're talking about participative management, empowerment, or teamwork, today's decentralized organizations require effective communication.[37] The main elements of total quality efforts are process, people, customers, and leadership. To do the right things right the first time, individuals and teams must have clear, measurable data to make sound decisions.[38]

How do you communicate quality? The leader's vision must be clearly articulated and communicated to workers. Organizational change cannot work unless effective communication influences individual behavior change, but in such a way that the organization enjoys maximum benefit from the change. Communication should be aligned horizontally with the organization's product-making and service-delivery processes, and vertically with the company's objectives. In this way, members of the organization see how their actions are related to each other and how they are progressing toward achieving the objectives.[39] Managers can communicate total quality in the organization by following these guidelines:

❖ Make involvement the goal.
❖ Provide a plan of action.
❖ Develop a document with guidelines.
❖ Provide an example of TQM in action.
❖ Use existing internal communication channels.
❖ Arm management to deliver the total quality message.
❖ Report process achievements as well as results.
❖ Celebrate.[40]

The principles embodied in the seven Malcolm Baldrige National Quality Award categories are directly applicable to communication. These guidelines help define communication's critical role in a high-quality, customer-oriented organization. A study of Baldrige Award winners and members of the Baldrige Board of Examiners reported that communicators' most important duties in a total quality environment are encouraging employee involvement and empowerment; encouraging proactive management of customer relationships; determining customer requirements; and benchmarking companywide and function-by-function performance against competitive and best-in-field performance measures.[41]

Open and frequent communication is necessary for a successful quality program.[42] Communication is at the heart of both Crosby's and Deming's 14 points. In Crosby's case, management commitment, quality improvement teams, quality awareness, employee education, goal setting, and recognition all require effective communication. As for Deming's points, constancy of purpose, constant improvement, institute training and leadership, driving out fear, and breaking down barriers between departments can't be accomplished without effective communication. Still, perhaps more than anything, sharing information and feedback are the nucleus of total quality efforts—and both require effective communication.

BARRIERS TO ORGANIZATIONAL COMMUNICATION

Communication isn't always effective. Breakdowns occur for many reasons. Some can simply be attributed to poor habits—lack of preparation or vague directions. Barriers such as these can be overcome without too much difficulty if the communicator is willing to work at it. Other barriers can be much more difficult to overcome. For instance, a survey conducted at General Motors' Saginaw Division found that lack of trust between management and labor was resulting in poor communication throughout the division. General Motors started a new two-way communication program to share information and rebuild trust. The program was a huge success, but took several years to get results.[43] This section examines common barriers to organizational communication.

Personal Characteristics

One major barrier to organizational communication is the personal makeup of the parties involved. People have attitudes about work-related matters, conditions in the world, their personal life, and communication in general. Some individuals have defensive attitudes and interpret messages as an order or threat. Some people simply have incompatible personalities. Others feel inferior or threatened, become defensive in an attempt to cover up their feelings, and respond aggressively. Constantly being on the offensive is an obstacle to communication.

source credibility
The receiver's confidence and trust in the source of the message.

Another problem involves the parties' credibility. **Source credibility** refers to the receiver's confidence and trust in the source of the message. If the receiver has little or no faith in the source, it will be difficult for the two parties to communicate. Individuals lose credibility when they pass along inaccurate information or fail to follow through with directives or initiatives. New leaders are often greeted with a sense of excitement and hope by other members of the organization. But if they make promises they don't keep—pay raises, new offices, lower taxes, and so on—they lose their credibility and their ability to communicate effectively.

Several other personal characteristics can inhibit communication. Some individuals tend to be disorganized, which carries over to their communication efforts. Poor listening habits on the part of the receiver are also a communication barrier. Some people, rather than listening, are thinking ahead to how they will respond and do not receive the message. Receivers may also have certain predispositions and tune out the communicator because the message is not consistent with their beliefs. Finally individuals may be biased due to age, gender, looks, or some other factor, and these biases inhibit the communication process. Such biases are especially alarming as the workforce becomes more diverse.

Frame of Reference

Individuals have different backgrounds and have had many different experiences that shape the meanings they assign to words. There is a great deal of difference between you or I saying, "I'm starved," as we head to a restaurant, and a child who hasn't eaten in 10 days uttering the same words. We have a different *frame of reference* so we may have difficulty achieving common understanding. When a parent tells a child, "I never had so many toys when I was a kid," the child may find it difficult to understand because the parent and the child have different frames of reference. Likewise, if a supervisor and a subordinate or two co-workers have different backgrounds and experiences, organizational communication may suffer.

A related problem in communication concerns people blocking out information they aren't comfortable with. **Selective perception** occurs when people screen out information that is not consistent with their beliefs or background. When people receive information that conflicts with what they believe, they tend to ignore it or distort it to make it conform to their beliefs. Managers, for instance, generally analyze problems based on their frame of reference. In other words, a sales manager analyzes a problem from the sales point of view, whereas an environmentalist analyzes problems based on a different set of beliefs.

Conflicting frames of reference and selective perception can hamper organizational communication in various ways. As individuals move up the organizational hierarchy, for instance, they may develop different frames of reference. A salesperson, who is concerned with closing the deal, may attach different meanings to words from those of a sales manager, who must be concerned with cost control and other management issues. Likewise an individual in the production department may have a different frame of reference from a marketing staffer. This can reduce the effectiveness of upward, downward, or horizontal communication.

One challenge faced by organizations implementing total quality management programs is breaking down barriers between individuals and departments. Because traditional organization structure encourages competition among individuals, units, departments, or divisions, these entities develop their own frames of reference.[44] This makes it difficult for people to communicate and work together toward the same goal. In the worst scenario, individuals only care about their own job and their own department's performance. A worker is rewarded for reaching a production quota, while quality control and customer satisfaction are somebody else's problem. Under these circumstances, effective communication is difficult, and the organization's overall performance is likely to suffer.

Resistance to Change

All organizations go through change, whether it be a new TQM program, new leadership, or new owners. Change is a constant in today's organizations. Yet no matter how innocuous or even beneficial, there is a human tendency to resist change.[45] Change triggers rational and irrational emotional reactions because it involves uncertainty. People resist change for several reasons: they fear the loss of something they value; they mistrust management; they view the change differently from those initiating it; or they have low tolerance for change.[46] Whatever the reason, resistance to change is a significant barrier to communication.

A major bank's CEO felt that change was needed because of branch managers' lack of interest in doing anything other than making loans and administration; the managers had little interest in other management issues confronting the bank. The CEO decided to schedule monthly meetings with all bank officers, including branch managers, to discuss broad issues like the bank's overall goals, personnel policy, productivity, strategies, and compensation programs. But the meetings were disappointing—nothing more than a forum for one-way communication from the CEO to those present at the meeting. The number of meetings was increased, and the CEO asked for individual reports on how to deal with management problems and issues. The results of this approach were even more disappointing. The reports demonstrated a clear lack of communication between the CEO and the branch managers.

FACILITATING ORGANIZATIONAL COMMUNICATION

Although some barriers to communication cannot be completely removed, organizational communication can be facilitated in several ways. By understanding the barriers and striving to be better communicators, individuals can improve the communication process. In some cases this may be relatively simple, perhaps breaking a few bad habits. In other ways this can be a long, ongoing, demanding process.

selective perception
People screening out information that isn't consistent with their beliefs or background.

Developing Communication Skills

Perhaps the best way to facilitate communication is to develop the skills needed to be a better communicator. Both managers and nonmanagers need to develop communication skills. Managers must improve their ability to understand workers and to be understood. With more individual responsibility, workers must also be able to communicate effectively.[47] Individuals can acquire these skills through managerial training programs in communication.

We have already discussed the importance of *listening* in effective communication. A good communicator listens with *empathy*. By understanding the feelings of others, the communicator can anticipate how a message will be decoded. And by encouraging *feedback*, the communicator can determine whether the message was properly decoded. The use of *simple language* can also facilitate communication. Complex language and the use of confusing or misleading terms introduces noise into the communication process. Good communicators also *question* others, asking for ideas and suggestions, thus encouraging participation. They *initiate* new ideas and calls for action, and *evaluate* ideas of others, offering insightful summaries.

Minimizing Resistance to Change

As we said, many workers resist change, which is a major barrier to communication. By minimizing resistance to change, managers can help facilitate the communication process. Otherwise change will be poorly implemented and result in no change at all or a very short-term, superficial change. In some instances organizations are worse off after the change effort fails because of the resulting miscommunication and lack of trust.

Managers have several methods to minimize resistance to change.[48] One way is to deal with change before it occurs through education and communication. Preparing people for change helps cut down on resistance. Also, having people affected by the change participate in it will increase their commitment to the change. Being supportive when change is being implemented is critical. Support can be shown by being understanding, being a good listener, and going to bat for subordinates on important issues. Reducing resistance to change can also be accomplished through negotiation and agreement. Regardless of which method is used, managers responsible for implementing change must overcome resistance to change to facilitate effective communication and a successful change effort. An organization is more likely to adapt to change if it has many means of two-way communication that reach all levels and that all employees can understand.[49]

Communicating with a Diverse Workforce

Managers increasingly face the prospect of communicating with a diverse workforce, which makes communicating more difficult. To facilitate communication in such an environment, managers must be aware of diversity and understand its value.[50] Differences in gender, race, culture, and the like can influence how people interpret (decode) messages. A good communicator should be aware of an individual's background and experiences, and anticipate the meaning that will be attached to different messages.

The globalization of the world's economy has placed increased emphasis on cross-cultural communication. Whenever two parties have different cultural backgrounds, communication breakdowns may result. People often tend to communicate based on their own background or culture. Thus, they are more likely to send a message that is not intended or misinterpret a message they are receiving when communicating with someone from another culture. Effective listening skills are especially important for individuals involved in cross-cultural communication.

Communicating with an increasingly diverse workforce is critical to an organization's viability.[51] This isn't a question of civil rights or affirmative action, which are something different. It concerns the demands a diverse workforce places on the communication skills of managers and coworkers. This requires the skills in listening, empathy, feedback, and language already discussed. It also requires skills in understanding other cultures plus the ability to overcome hidden biases and stereotypes about other people.

In Phoenix, Arizona, the Honeywell Diversity Council works to create a workplace that values individual differences and strengths.

Communication Audit

The communication audit is a useful tool for managers to use in understanding and improving organizational communication. A **communication audit** is a systematic method for collecting and evaluating information about an organization's communication efforts. Such an audit can:

❖ Provide information about communication behavior in the organization.

❖ Provide a means for diagnosing discontent or revealing problems in communication.

❖ Provide a clear picture of current communication patterns and determine those aspects that may be most affected by change.

❖ Provide a before-and-after picture of organizational communication in relation to change.[52]

communication audit
A systematic method for collecting and evaluating information about an organization's communication efforts.

There are no black-and-white guidelines for conducting a communication audit. Information can be collected from both managers and workers via surveys, interviews, observing operations, and reviews of formal and informal reports and procedures used in communicating. Organizations use many different formats when conducting a communication audit. The Baldrige Award guidelines offer one set of standards for measuring the quality of communication.[53] These guidelines can be used to conduct an audit of all communication activities of the organization. (Appendix 1 reviews the guidelines.) An organization can use such information to compare its communication activities with those of the best-managed companies in America.

A total quality communication audit can be used to assess communications activities in a total quality context (see Table 14–2). The process begins by identifying policies that relate to the communication area being studied. Then the objectives of the communication activities must be identified as well as the channels or media used to reach these objectives. Finally, the overall quality communication system must be evaluated. The main benefit of the audit is comparing communication objectives to actual performance.[54]

As firms in the next decade struggle with such issues as global competition, downsizing, reorganization, and so on, communication in organizations is taking on increased significance. Effective communication characterizes successful organizations, whereas poor communication leads to such problems as lower quality and productivity, anger, and mistrust. Through effective communication, individuals can solve complex problems and achieve the goals of the organization.

TABLE 14–2	A COMMUNICATOR'S ROLE IN A TOTAL QUALITY CULTURE

1. Encouraging employee involvement and empowerment.

2. Proactive management of customer relationships.

3. Determining customer requirements.

4. Benchmarking companywide and function-by-function performance against competitive and best-in-field measures.

5. Providing counsel and support to executive management.

6. Counseling management and developing public responsibility plans.

7. Recognizing employees for their quality contributions.

8. Promoting and supporting the quality education process.

9. Establishing and promoting companywide quality values.

10. Facilitating the total quality planning process.

Source: Karl J. Skutski, "Conducting a Total Quality Communication Audit," *Public Relation Journal*, September 10, 1992, pp. 29–32.

THE WORKPLACE OF TOMORROW

As technology advancements move at ever-faster speeds, talk about the information revolution also grows.[55] Whether or not all predictions about the growth of information will come true, one challenge facing managers in the workplace of tomorrow will be to effectively communicate with employees and customers. As information technology changes, the way communication is accomplished and managed is also becoming obsolete.[56]

A major key to success in this changing environment is a broad set of communication skills and the ability to quickly size up and work with all types of people.[57] Technology has replaced staffs; flatter organizations with fewer managers have replaced pyramids with many managers; teams have replaced the worker. The result is a critical need for cross-functional or horizontal communication. Listening is as important as speaking. As firms continue to downsize, reengineer, and move to the team concept, communication will be essential to overcome some of the damage in organizations caused by such changes.

Leaders of organizations are becoming more sophisticated in learning that communication is the link between strategy and results.[58] In other words, strategy dictates all activities of an organization, even communication. In the workplace of tomorrow, the most effective communications will take into account the overall business strategy and the environment in which they operate.

SUMMARY OF LEARNING OBJECTIVES

DEFINE COMMUNICATION.
Communication is the exchange of information between a sender and a receiver. If meaning isn't shared, communication hasn't taken place.

DESCRIBE THE COMMUNICATION PROCESS.
Communication is a process in which a message is encoded by a sender and transmitted to a receiver through some medium. The receiver decodes and interprets the coded message. Because of interference or noise in the communication process, the receiver seldom decodes the exact meaning that the sender intended.

DISCUSS THE ROLE OF COMMUNICATION IN ORGANIZATIONS.
Communication is an essential part of all management functions. Managers largely function by communicating with people. Most managers stress open communication to improve the organization's quality and effectiveness.

CONTRAST THE DIFFERENT TYPES OF INTERPERSONAL COMMUNICATION.
Interpersonal communication is communication between two people. It can be oral, written, or nonverbal. Oral communication makes use of the spoken word and enables prompt, two-way interaction

between parties. Transmitting a message via written word allows the manager to think about the message before it is sent, and gives the receiver a chance to read the message carefully. Written messages also provide a permanent record. Nonverbal communication includes vocal cues and body movements. Nonverbal messages can be powerful, but are often difficult to interpret.

IDENTIFY THE THREE FORMAL CHANNELS OF ORGANIZATIONAL COMMUNICATION.

Information flows down the organization from managers and supervisors to subordinates through downward communication. Information flows up the organization from subordinates to supervisors and managers through upward communication. Messages flow between persons at the same level of the organization through horizontal communication.

EXPLAIN THE SIGNIFICANCE OF INFORMAL COMMUNICATION.

Informal communication does not follow the organization's official chain of command. Informal channels such as the grapevine communicate facts, opinions, rumors, and other information. Although they do not always have negative consequences, they can be the source of misinformation and harmful gossip.

LIST THE BARRIERS TO ORGANIZATIONAL COMMUNICATION.

Barriers include the personal characteristics of the parties involved; conflicting frames of reference and selective perception (screening out information that people are not comfortable with); and rational and irrational reactions triggered by change.

DISCUSS HOW ORGANIZATIONS CAN FACILITATE COMMUNICATION.

An organization can facilitate communication by helping members develop important communication skills, including listening, empathy, feedback, and the use of simple language. Resistance to change can be minimized by preparing individuals for change, thereby reducing another barrier to communication. Managers must also learn to communicate with a diverse workforce. Finally, a communication audit can identify problems with and improve the communication process.

KEY TERMS

channel capacity, p. 371	grapevine, p. 378	nonverbal communication, p. 373
communication, p. 368	horizontal communication, p. 378	oral communication, p. 373
communication audit, p. 383	interpersonal communication, p. 373	selective perception, p. 381
decoding, p. 371	media richness, p. 372	sender, p. 370
downward communication, p. 377	medium of transmission, p. 370	source credibility, p. 380
encode, p. 370	message, p. 370	upward communication, p. 378
feedback, p. 371	noise, p. 371	written communication, p. 373

REVIEW AND DISCUSSION QUESTIONS

Recall

1. What is the meaning of the term communication?
2. What are the advantages and disadvantages of oral, written, and nonverbal communication?
3. What is the grapevine? How can managers control this channel of communication?
4. Why does communication sometimes break down? What are some common barriers to communication?
5. What skills are necessary for effective communication?
6. How can managers minimize resistance to change?

Understanding

7. Describe the communication process, providing an example of each component.

8. Why is communication critical to organizations implementing total quality management programs?
9. Why are all three formal channels of communication important in organizations?

Application

10. Select an ad that you're familiar with. Discuss it in relation to the communication process. Who is the source? What is the message? What is the medium of transmission? How did you decode the message? What was your response or feedback to the message? Was there any noise present in the communication process?

CASE STUDY

Matsushita Acquires MCA

When a company is acquired by foreign ownership, the new culture must be communicated to employees. Managers and nonmanagers alike need to know about the new company's history, portfolio, and business strategy. Any merger or acquisition can be potentially troublesome for employees, who are often fearful and uncertain of changes taking place. But when a foreign company acquires a domestic firm, the potential is even greater. During the transition that typically includes layoffs and restructuring, clashes due to cultural differences are also likely to occur. Damage to employee morale and productivity can be extensive.

Many firms fail to communicate to employees the new company's culture and the changes taking place. Managers may be spending their time dealing with details of the merger or acquisition, and simply fail to take time to communicate with employees. Some firms hold off on communicating anything until all details are finalized. Because of a lack of communication through formal channels, the grapevine becomes the source for employees to learn about the new parent company. Unfortunately, much of this information can be inaccurate and result in more fear and uncertainty.

When Matsushita Electric Industrial Co. Ltd. of Japan purchased MCA Inc., employee communication became a priority. The new parent company assured everyone that it would be business as usual at MCA. The president of both MCA and Matsushita wrote letters to all employees with this reassurance. A communication plan was also developed to integrate the MCA companies, which included Spencer Gifts, Putnam Publishing, the Curry Co., and Universal Studios. Up until this point, MCA did not have a formal communication program.

The communication program developed at MCA included several aspects. A team was created to manage the transition. The team was made up of executives from human resources, benefits, finance, legal, and corporate communications. The team's goal was to make the employee the customer of transition communication. Employees were interviewed to determine their information needs. A

newsletter, video presentations, and programs were developed to communicate to employees what MCA and Matsushita were about. Company meetings were held so employees could get their questions answered in person and be reassured about their jobs. Employees also learned that they were an important part of a team working all over the world.

In no time, MCA has become the pride of Matsushita. Recent films from MCA's Universal Pictures like *Jurassic Park* and *The Flintstones* recorded impressive profits, whereas other firms in the Matsushita empire are not doing as well. But another challenge faces the giant company—unrest among managers at MCA, who want to take greater control of the entertainment company.

QUESTIONS

1. Why is communication important when a company is acquired by a foreign firm?
2. What can be done to control the grapevine when one firm is acquired by another?
3. Why did MCA need a formal communication program after being purchased by Matsushita?
4. What were the benefits of the communication plan developed by MCA?

Source: Adapted from Robert Neff, "Tradition Be Damned," *Business Week*, October 31, 1994, pp. 108–112; Neil Gross, "Matsushita's Urgent Quest for Leadership," *Business Week*, March 8, 1993, p. 52; Karin Ireland, "Marketing a Foreign Acquisition," *Personnel Journal*, November 1991, pp. 96–102; and Karin Ireland, "Communication after the Foreign Acquisition of MCA," *Personnel Journal*, November 1991, p. 99.

VIDEO EXERCISE

Oral and Nonverbal Communications

In the "Oral and Nonverbal Communications" video, a junior person in a company is given an assignment to make a persuasive presentation to an executive board. The video follows her over a period of 48 hours as she prepares for her presentation. Communication principles are described demonstrated throughout the video.

For this exercise, watch the video and try to list the effective communication techniques described and demonstrated. After the

video, make a list of all the techniques on the board and place them into categories.

Next discuss the merits of the various points made in the video. For example, how effective is it to use notes as the person in the video does? What are some good alternatives?

Finally, after the tips for effective communications have been listed and categorized, discuss how you can develop the skills needed for effective communications.

APPLICATION EXERCISE

The president of a large corporation wishes to inform all employees that the organization has decided to implement a TQM program. The president would also like to encourage all employees to participate fully and dedicate themselves to the total quality effort. This first communication is critical in getting the program off on the right foot and in generating enthusiasm throughout the organization.

The following message was developed:

Although our company has done a good job, it simply hasn't been good enough. Faced with increasing competition from foreign firms, we have to reduce our costs and increase our output. The company has decided to implement a total quality management program. You may have heard of similar programs at other organiza-

tions. Total quality programs are based to a large extent on the work of Dr. Deming. I have attached his 14 points for your information.

As the president, I would like to call on you to cooperate fully in this important effort. Your future and the future of the company depend upon our ability to improve quality. The division heads will be in communication with each of you shortly as our quality initiative gets under way. Thank you in advance for your cooperation.

Did the president accomplish the objectives of the communication? Why?
Does the president demonstrate good communication skills?
Does this message encourage feedback?
Rewrite the message to meet the objectives and overcome any problems you detected.

PART 5
Controlling

CHAPTER 15

Control Systems

After studying this chapter, you should be able to:

❖ Describe the red bead experiment and explain its message to managers.

❖ Describe the three elements of the control process.

❖ Define total quality control.

❖ Explain workers' role in total quality management.

❖ Explain management's role in total quality management.

❖ Contrast statistical process control with total quality control.

The Red Bead Experiment

Before he died in 1993, W. Edwards Deming used a vivid exercise to illustrate the use and misuse of controls in managing quality. The so-called red bead experiment is designed to show that worker inability to meet performance objectives is often a function of the system, not of worker laziness or lack of skill.

The exercise begins with a large container of 4,000 beads—800 red and 3,200 white. Deming provides participants (typically, six are selected) with paddles, each containing 50 holes for collecting beads. The participants represent workers, and the paddles are their tools. The workers' task is to dip the paddle into the container of beads and then remove it with each hole containing a bead—red or white. Deming first demonstrates the work process. Dipping the paddle into the bucket he inevitably produces at least a few red beads. (Given that red beads constitute 20 percent of the beads in the container, statistically we'd expect 10 red beads per 50 beads produced.)

Deming then puts the workers to the task. Each worker, in turn, dips the paddle into the container and withdraws 50 beads. This is production—very simple, yet very frustrating. Deming sets a production quality standard of 2 red beads per 50 beads produced (8 fewer than the expected 10). This standard is the basis for a quality control system. Deming then serves as the foreman inspecting the results of each "production run." The bead production system thus has a production process, a standard, and a supervisory review process.

As foreman, Deming evaluates each worker according to the quality control standard of no more than 4 percent red beads (2 of 50) among the white beads on the paddle. He proceeds to reward, promote, reprimand, and even ridicule and fire workers based on their conformance to this standard. When a worker succeeds at meeting the goal, Deming praises her; he may offer the lucky worker a raise, even a promotion. When a worker produces more than 2 red beads per 50, Deming criticizes him harshly for failing to meet the control standard. In this fashion, Deming illustrates the pointlessness of a merit system in which workers' performance is due to normal variation within management's system, not their individual ability.

In the red bead experiment, few of the workers' attempts to meet the production goal are satisfactory. Since 20 percent of the beads in the large container are red, random samples of beads will, on average, contain 20 percent red beads. While workers can produce some paddles with two or fewer red beads, the average expected will be 10 red beads (20 percent of 50) per production run. Over the long run, no worker can consistently produce fewer than 10 red bead "defects" and no worker will achieve the standard on a regular basis.

Deming points out that it would be a waste of management time to find out why Worker X produced more beads than Worker Y. The difference between their performance, he points out time and again, is simply normal variation within the system created by management. The important point is that any process can be looked at in the same way. Although usually workers have more control over the outcome of their work, any process is subject to normal variation that affects even the best workers.

People involved in this exercise soon realize both its parallels with actual work situations—setting goals, trying hard, motivating, reprimanding—and its futility. The only way to lower defect rates is to lower the number of red beads in the bowl. Workers know the number of red beads is the problem, but they can't change the process. As a result of this exercise, most people realize that exhorting workers to try harder is not the answer to more effective organizations. They learn that it is the system that needs improvement.

Source: Adapted from W. Edwards Deming, *Out of the Crisis* (Cambridge, Mass.: Center for Advanced Engineering Study, Massachusetts Institute of Technology, 1986), pp. 109-112; Ronald Yates, "Prophet of Boom," *Chicago Tribune*, February 16, 1992, pp. 14-22; Rafael Aguayo, *Dr. Deming: The Man Who Taught the Japanese about Quality* (New York: Fireside Books, 1990), pp. 53-58; and Ellen Earle Chaffee and Lawrence A. Sherr, *Quality: Transforming Postsecondary Education* (Washington, D.C.: ERIC Clearinghouse on Higher Education, 1992).

The red bead experiment described in the opening vignette illustrates that the production system must be designed and managed to effect quality, rather than to create difficult or impossible expectations for workers. It is management's responsibility to design the system so that workers can succeed.

Control is a fundamental management responsibility, closely linked with the planning and organizing processes. It also has an important impact on motivation and team behavior. Control is both a process (e.g., working to keep things on schedule) and an outcome (e.g., the product has met standards). In traditional terms, the controlling function includes all activities the manager undertakes in attempting to ensure that actual results conform to planned results (see Chapter 6).

Like many management terms, control has different meanings to different people so an individual's concept of control often reflects a personal perspective. Statisticians may think of control in terms of numbers (variances, means, errors, control limits); engineers think of control in terms of specifications, monitoring, and feedback; and managers think of controlling the activities, attitudes, and performance of subordinates. Despite these differing approaches to control, there are some characteristics of all organizations that must be controlled: production and operations, financial resources, human resources, and organizational change and development (Figure 15–1).

FIGURE 15–1
Managers Must Control Four
Characteristics of
Organizations

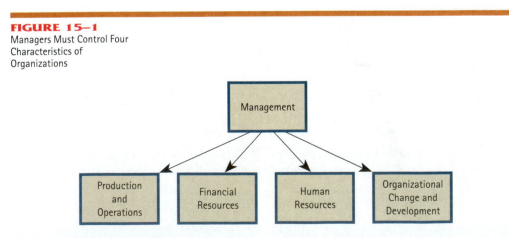

After planning or making a decision, managers must deploy organizational resources to achieve specific goals or objectives. (See Chapters 5 and 6 for models of decision making and planning.) Even though decision making and planning are conducted systematically and with accurate information, unexpected circumstances may yet arise. Unforeseen events may occur in the social, economic, political, or natural environment. Thus, managers must be prepared to redirect organizational activities toward desired ends. To do this, they need an understanding of the elements of control.

ELEMENTS OF CONTROL

What elements define a control system? **Control** is a process used (1) to evaluate actual performance, (2) to compare actual performance to goals, and then (3) to take action on the difference between performance and goals.[1] Quality statistician Walter Shewhart elaborated these three elements within the control process under the concepts of specification, production, and inspection.[2] (See Figure 15-2.)

control
The process of maintaining conformance of the system.

❖ *Specification* is the statement of the intended outcome. Control requires the specification of a standard. A standard is an operationally defined measure used as a basis for comparison. Specification fully describes the preferred condition, which may take the form of a goal, standard, or other carefully determined quantitative statement of conditions.

❖ *Production* means making the product or delivering the service. Shewhart defines this element as the work required to achieve objectives. It's important to note that this applies as much to service as to manufacturing.

❖ *Inspection* is a judgment concerning whether the production meets the specifications. Inspection determines whether corrective actions need to be taken.

Clear specification of a performance standard requires an **operational definition**. An operational definition converts a concept into measurable, objective units.[3] For example, the concept of weight can be operationally defined in terms of grams, pounds, or another standard measure. These measures are not subject to personal interpretation. In contrast, the concept of heavy can be interpreted differently by different people. For some, six ounces is heavy; for others, six pounds is heavy. Says Deming, "An operational definition puts communicable meaning into a concept. Adjectives like 'good,' 'reliable,' 'uniform,'

operational definition
A definition that converts a concept into measurable, objective units.

FIGURE 15-2
Steps in the Control Process

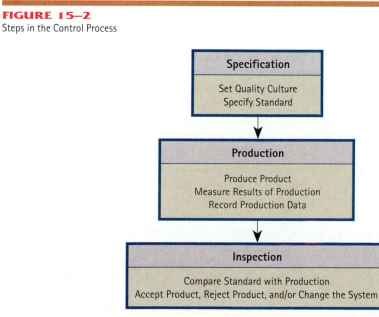

'round,' 'safe,' and 'unemployed' have no communicable meaning until they are expressed in operational terms. An operational definition is one that reasonable men agree on."[4]

To illustrate the importance of operational definitions, Deming tells the story of the "wrinkled" auto instrument panel. A manager of an auto manufacturing plant told him the reported defect rate in an auto instrument panel was 35 to 50 percent per day. The defect in question was "wrinkles" in the panel. When Deming examined this rate, he found that each inspector had his own visual perception of what constituted a wrinkle. Deming resolved the defect rate problem by working with the inspectors to develop an operational definition of wrinkle. As a result, the defect rate dropped to 10 percent in less than one week.[5]

The process of setting performance standards must begin with a strategy, conveyed in terms of operationally defined measures. Operational measures underlie the control process. Not only do they control operations through finished-product or after-service inspections; they also enable workers to evaluate processes as they are occurring.

Production and operations are controlled by performance standards. Standards determine the activity or outcome to be measured.[6] Control of production and operations requires measurement to identify deviation from standards. Through measurement and assessment, workers can find possible improvements within the product or process and indicate where to initiate change.[7] The act of measuring errors or defects often has an immediate, direct effect on reducing them.

It is important to point out that control applies to all types of organizations, not just manufacturing. Businesses that provide a service must also be concerned with controlling their operations and the quality of their work. One of the principal ways in which service organizations control performance is through employee training. Small and large firms alike have recognized the importance of giving employees the knowledge and information they need to serve customers. Home Depot, the hardware and home repair discounter, has made an art of empowering employees to exceed each customer's expectations. As a result, the company has established a service reputation that prompted Wal-Mart CEO David Glass to remark, "They're running the best retail organization in America today."[8] Home Depot doesn't conduct extensive marketing surveys, but relies on its associates who are trained to ask customers what they want and expect.

Birkenstock Footprint Sandals, a small California distributor of cork-heeled sandals, has found similar success with empowerment. Company managers have found that a small employee empowerment project begun in 1989 has snowballed into broad performance and productivity gains. In January 1993, the company hired its first full-time trainer to further advance its commitment to employee empowerment as a means of controlling quality and productivity.[9]

Inspection in traditionally managed companies typically occurred at the end of production or the provision of a service. Quality management discourages this type of inspection. In fact, the third of Deming's 14 points states, "Cease dependence on mass inspection." As Deming puts it, "Routine 100 percent inspection to improve quality is equivalent to planning for defects, acknowledgement that the process has not the capability required for the specifications."[10] Quality-based firms used statistical sampling techniques concurrent with the production process to ensure that most products or service encounters exceed performance specifications.

When statistical sampling indicates a deviation from specifications, corrective action may be necessary. People undertaking corrective actions must know that they're responsible and must have the authority to effect change. Job descriptions that have specific, operationally defined performance objectives are necessary to control performance. Responsibilities that fall between the jobs of two individuals should be avoided. For the control function to be most effective, operationally defined objectives, clear authority, and accurate information are requisite.

In the next two sections we will examine different techniques managers use to control organizational behavior and performance. You will learn about three different types of control: preliminary, concurrent, and feedback. Next, you will learn about three approaches to quality control: total quality control, statistical process control, and total quality management. As you read about and discuss these different approaches to organizational control, notice how quality control shifts management's focus from the worker as the source of de-

---

REFLECTIONS BY PHILIP B. CROSBY

Control and Quality

A football coach carefully planned and then studied the statistics of the games his team had played. In each of the past three contests, he noted, they had scored the same number of touchdowns as the opposing team but had lost the game because two extra point attempts had been blocked. As a result of these data, he decided that they should spend more time learning how to block the kicks the opponents attempted after they scored touchdowns.

Most of the practice that week was spent on this effort and the team was rewarded the following game by being able to block three extra points. Even though they lost the game 18 to 7, they were encouraged by their success and began to devote all of their time to kick blocking. Soon they were denying their opponents that one point seven and eight times a game. They scored no touchdowns of their own but were brilliant in accomplishing their chosen goal. they never won another game or made another point, and the coach was fired. This is an example of being carried away by the concepts of containment and measurement.

It was some time later, and in a new profession, before it began to dawn on the coach that the best system for containing extra points was to keep the other team from scoring touchdowns. A defense based on prevention achieved more than one focused on a single point.

This sort of discovery happens regularly. A city commission found that improved street lighting reduced crime rates more than extra police; a person with a weight problem found that a new, much more accurate scale had no effect on the weight loss program. We must be careful not to confuse the systems of measurement with the setting of goals. Keeping neat records of overspending is not the way to manage money.

The instruments on a car's dashboard are examples of control charts. Their purpose is to assist the operator in managing the vehicle. They control nothing in themselves; they just display what's happening, and they haven't changed much in 50 years. This is also true of statistical control charting.

Just as automobile drivers are successful when they are carefully trained, understand the requirements of operation, and are responsible for their own actions—so workers are successful when the same conditions exist. When they are directed to do useless work, or limited in their communications, then they fail.

All that comes from management. When management depends on focused systems rather than people, it pays the price.

---

fects to the system as the source of such problems. This subtle shift has helped many once-outpaced American companies—such as U.S. automakers—regain competitive standing in the global marketplace.[11]

TYPES OF CONTROL

Management has numerous control methods at its disposal. Each has strengths and limitations. Managers must decide what type of control system to employ in different situations. Some control techniques have very specific, limited application. Nonetheless, all control techniques must be economical, accurate, and understandable.

The techniques managers use to control production and operations can be classified under three main types: preliminary control, concurrent control, and feedback control. Figure 15–3 illustrates each of the types which we will detail next.

Preliminary Control

Preliminary control focuses on preventing deviations in the quality and quantity of resources used in the organization. For example, human resources must meet the job requirements as defined by the organization: employees must have the physical and intellectual capabilities to perform assigned tasks.[12] Materials used in production must meet acceptable levels of quality and must be available at the proper time and place. Capital must be on hand to ensure an adequate supply of plant and equipment. Financial resources must be available in the right amounts and at the right times.

Preliminary control procedures include all managerial efforts to increase the probability that actual results compare favorably with planned results. From this perspective, policies are important means for implementing preliminary control since policies are guidelines for future actions (see Chapter 6). It's important to distinguish between *setting*

preliminary control
Control method focusing on preventing deviations in the quality and quantity of resources used in the organization.

FIGURE 15–3
The Controlling Function

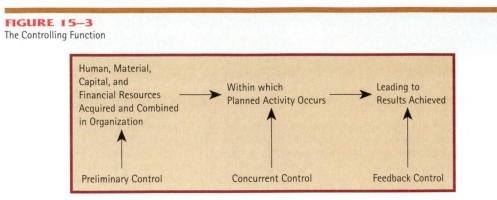

Source: James H. Donnelly, Jr., James L. Gibson, and John M. Ivancevich, *Fundamentals of Management*, 9th ed. (Burr Ridge, Il.: Richard D. Irwin, 1995), p. 273.

policies and *implementing* them.[13] Setting policy is included in the planning function (see Chapter 6), whereas implementing policy is part of the control function.[14] Similarly, job descriptions are aspects of the control function because they predetermine the activity of the jobholder.[15] At the same time, however, we must distinguish between defining and staffing the task structure. Defining jobs is part of the organizing function (see Chapter 9); staffing them is part of the controlling function.

Management needs to be concerned with preliminary control of processes in four areas: human resources, materials, capital, and financial resources.

HUMAN RESOURCES - The organizing function defines the job requirements and predetermines the skill requirements of jobholders. These requirements vary in degree of specificity, depending on the nature of the task. Preliminary control of human resources is achieved through the selection and placement of managerial and nonmanagerial personnel.[16] Figure 15–4 shows the steps involved before a person actually begins to work at a firm. Each step along the way, including placement, is a preliminary control step during which the potential worker's skills, abilities, and attitudes are assessed for his or her qualifications for a given position.

Candidates for positions must be recruited from inside or outside the firm, and the most promising applicants must be selected based on matching skills and personal characteristics to the job requirements. The successful candidate must be trained in methods and procedures appropriate for the job. Most organizations have elaborate procedures for providing training on a continual basis.

WHAT MANAGERS ARE READING

GUIDE TO QUALITY CONTROL
by Kaoru Ishikawa

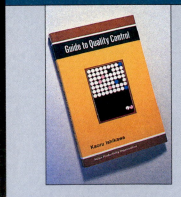

*G*uide to Quality Control is a comprehensive source for quality control techniques written by Kaoru Ishikawa. Dr. Ishikawa is a widely recognized and honored writer in quality control. This book has been used around the world to introduce managers to quality control practices, and is regarded among the best on this subject. Many large companies use the book as part of their in-house training.

Ishikawa wrote the book to be used as a guide rather than a detailed handbook. It includes instructions for making and reading graphs, Pareto diagrams, histograms, scatter diagrams, and other control techniques. Though the book has been used for classroom teaching and training, it is also suitable for self-study.

Source: Kaoru Ishikawa, *Guide to Quality Control* (White Plains, NY: Krauss International Publications, 1982).

FIGURE 15—4
Preliminary Control of Human
Resources

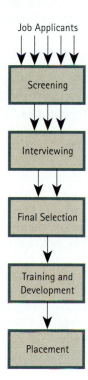

Appropriate attention to preliminary control of human resources ensures that the organization will have a match between its needs and individual skills, abilities, and attitudes. With increasing emphasis on information and knowledge as the primary focus of global business, the search, selection, and placement of people is an increasingly vital function. Where human resource professionals had been relegated to staff support in the past (typically, under the rubric *personnel*), many firms today have line positions for human resources. This significant shift reflects the growing awareness that competitive advantage can be gained through proper screening and development of people. In their human resource planning, managers should distinguish between procedures designed to obtain qualified subordinate managers (staffing) and those designed to obtain qualified nonmanagers and operatives (selection and placement). Although basic procedures and objectives are essentially the same, the distinction is important because managerial competence is a fundamental determinant of the organization's success.

MATERIALS — The raw materials that are converted into a finished product must conform to quality standards *before* they are used in the production process. At the same time, a sufficient inventory or delivery system must be maintained to ensure a continuous inflow of raw materials so the manufacturer can meet customer demand. The techniques of inventory control are discussed in Chapter 16; at this point, we are concerned only with controlling incoming materials.

Numerous methods that use statistical sampling to control the quality of materials have been devised. These methods typically involve inspection of samples rather than an entire lot. Thus, statistical methods are less costly, but there's a risk of accepting defective material if the sample is nonrandom or, by chance, contains none of the defective items.

We won't provide a complete discussion of statistical sampling procedures in this text. However, the essence of the procedure can be described. As an example, suppose management establishes a standard that it will accept no more than a 3 percent defect rate from a supplier. The incoming material would be inspected by selecting random samples and calculating the percentage of defective items in the sample. Based on this sample, managers must make a decision to accept or reject the entire order or to take another sample. This method is not perfect. Based on the sampling technique, managers could reject an entire lot even though the overall defect rate is less than 3 percent, or they may accept a lot even though the defect rate is greater than 3 percent. The control system used is based on balancing the relative costs of these two types of potential error.[17] We'll say more about the role of statistics in control later in this chapter.

capital budget
An intermediate and long-run planning document that details the alternative sources and uses of funds.

CAPITAL - The acquisition of capital reflects the need to replace existing equipment or to expand the firm's productive capacity. Managers of this process are often faced with complicating factors such as financial risk and uncertainty about potential outcomes.[18] Capital acquisitions are controlled by establishing criteria of potential profitability that must be met before the proposal is authorized. Such acquisitions ordinarily are included in the **capital budget**, an intermediate and long-run planning document that details the alternative sources and uses of funds. Several major imperatives are driving managers to wager money on capital budgets: customer service, quality, productivity, and capacity expansion.[19] Managerial decisions that involve the commitment of present funds in exchange for future funds are termed **investment decisions**. The methods that serve to screen investment proposals are based on economic analysis. Below are a number of widely used capital control methods. Each involves formulating a standard that must be met to accept the prospective capital acquisition.

investment decisions
Managerial decisions that involve the commitment of present funds in exchange for future funds.

payback method
Calculates the number of years needed for the proposed capital acquisition to repay its original cost out of future cash earnings.

THE PAYBACK METHOD - This is the simplest method of capital control. The **payback method** calculates the number of years needed for the proposed capital acquisition to repay its original cost out of future cash earnings. For example, a manager is considering implementing new information technology that would reduce labor costs by $20,000 per year for each of the four years of the new technology's expected life. The cost of the technology is $40,000. If we use the Clinton Administration's proposed 36 percent marginal tax rate on corporations with taxable income over $10 million, the additional after-tax cash inflow from which the machine's cost must be paid is calculated as follows:

Additional cash inflow before taxes (labor cost savings)		$20,000
Less: Additional taxes		
Additional income	$20,000	
Depreciation ($40,000/4)	$10,000	
Additional taxable income	$10,000	
Tax rate	0.36	
Additional tax payment		$ 3,600
Additional cash inflow after taxes		$ 16,400

The payback period can be calculated as follows:

$40,000/$16,400 = 2.44 years.

The proposed new information technology would repay its original cost in about two and one-half years; if the predetermined standard requires a payback of three years or less, the information technology would be an appropriate investment.

The payback method suffers many limitations as a standard for evaluating capital resources. It doesn't produce a measurement of profitability. More important, it doesn't take into account the time value of money; that is, it doesn't recognize that a dollar today is worth more than a dollar at a future date. Other capital control methods do include these important considerations. The primary reason for using the payback method is that in situations where the technology changes rapidly and new products become obsolete quickly, corporations should look for investment opportunities that pay back within a short period of time.

rate of return on investment
One alternative measure of profitability, consistent with methods ordinarily employed in accounting.

RATE OF RETURN ON INVESTMENT - One alternative measure of profitability, consistent with methods ordinarily employed in accounting, is the simple **rate of return on investment.** Using the preceding example, the calculation would be as follows:

Additional gross income		$20,000
Less: Depreciation ($40,000/4)	$10,000	
Taxes	$ 3,600	
Total additional expenses		$13,600
Additional net income after taxes		$ 6,400

The rate of return is the ratio of additional net income to the original cost:

$6,400/$40,000 = 16%

The calculated rate of return would then be compared to some standard of minimum acceptability, and the decision to accept or reject would depend on that comparison. In this case, if the standard rate of return were 10 percent, the purchase of the information technology would be a good investment. The measurement of the simple rate of return has the advantage of being easily understood. It has the disadvantage of not including the time value of money. The discounted rate of return method overcomes this deficiency.

DISCOUNTED RATE OF RETURN - The **discounted rate of return** is a measurement of profitability that takes into account the time value of money. It is similar to the payback method, only cash inflows and outflows are considered. The method is widely used because it is considered the correct method for calculating the rate of return. Based on the preceding example,

discounted rate of return
A measurement of profitability that takes into account the time value of money.

$40,000 = $16,400/(1 + r) + $16,400/(1 + r) 2 + $16,400/(1 + r) 3 + $16,400/(1 + r) 4, r = 23%.

The discounted rate of return (r) is 23 percent, which is interpreted to mean that a $40,000 investment repaying $16,400 in cash at the end of each of four years has a return of 23 percent.

The rationale of the method can be understood by thinking of the $16,400 inflows as cash payments received by the firm. In exchange for each of these four payments of $16,400, the firm must pay $40,000. The rate of return—23 percent—is the factor equating cash inflows and present cash outflow. This rate of return can be compared to a company minimum standard to determine its acceptability.

FINANCIAL RESOURCES - Adequate financial resources must be available to ensure payment of obligations arising from current operations. Materials must be purchased, wages paid, and interest charges and due dates met. The principal means of controlling the availability and cost of financial resources is budgeting—particularly cash flows and working capital budgets.

These budgets anticipate the ebb and flow of business activity when materials are purchased, finished goods are produced and inventoried, goods are sold, and cash is received.[20] This operating cycle results in a problem of timing the availability of cash to meet obligations. The simple relationship between cash and inventory is shown in Figure 15–5 on the next page. When inventories of finished goods increase, the supply of cash decreases as materials, labor, and other expenses are incurred and paid. As inventory is depleted through sales, cash increases. Preliminary control of cash requires that cash be available during the period of inventory buildup and be used wisely during periods of abundance. This requires the careful consideration of alternative sources of short-term financing during inventory buildup, and alternative short-run investment opportunities during periods of inventory depletion.

Managers use certain ratios to control financial resources. For example, the control standard may be stated in the current ratio (the ratio of current assets to current liabilities), and a minimum and a maximum set. The minimum ratio could be set at 2:1 and the maximum at 3:1, which would recognize the cost of both too little and too much investment in liquid assets. The control would involve corrective action taken when the actual current ratio deviates from the standard. Other financial ratios contributing to control of financial resources include the acid-test ratio, inventory turnover, and average collection

FIGURE 15–5
The Relationship between
Cash and Inventory

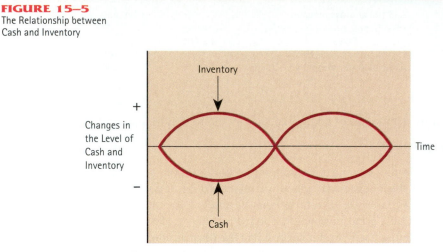

Source: James H. Donnelly, Jr., James L. Gibson, and John M. Ivancevich, *Fundamentals of Management,* 9th ed. (Burr Ridge, Il.: Richard D. Irwin, 1995), p. 280.

period. These ratios are discussed in greater detail in the section on feedback control methods.

Concurrent Control

concurrent control

Monitoring ongoing operations to ensure that objectives are pursued.

Concurrent control monitors ongoing operations to ensure that objectives are pursued. The standards guiding ongoing activity are derived from job descriptions and from policies resulting from the planning function. Concurrent control is implemented primarily by the supervisory activities of managers. Through personal, on-the-spot observation, managers determine whether the work of others is proceeding in the manner defined by policies and procedures.[21] Delegation of authority provides managers with the power to use financial and nonfinancial incentives to effect concurrent control.

direction

The acts of managers when they (1) instruct subordinates in the proper methods and procedures and (2) oversee subordinates' work to ensure that it's done properly.

Concurrent control consists primarily of actions of supervisors who direct the work of their subordinates. **Direction** refers to the acts of managers when they (1) instruct subordinates in proper methods and procedures and (2) oversee subordinates' work to ensure that it's done properly.

Direction follows the formal chain of command, since the responsibility of each superior is to interpret for subordinates the orders received from higher levels. The relative importance of direction depends almost entirely on the nature of the tasks performed by subordinates. The supervisor of an assembly line that produces a component part requiring relatively simple manual operations may seldom engage in direction. On the other hand, the manager of a new product research unit must devote considerable time to direction. Research work is inherently more complex and varied than manual work. So it requires more interpretation and instruction.

Directing is the primary function of the first-line supervisor, but at some point every manager in an organization engages in directing employees. The direction given should be within the stated organizational mission, goals, and objectives (see Chapters 6 and 7). As a manager's responsibilities grow, the relative time spent directing subordinates diminishes as other functions become more important.

The scope and content of directing vary according to the nature of the work being supervised. In addition, a number of other factors determine differences in the form of direction. For example, since direction is basically a process of personal communications, the amount and clarity of information are important factors. Subordinates must receive sufficient information to carry out the task and they must understand the information they receive. On the other hand, too much information and detail can be distracting.

The tests of effective direction are similar to the tests of effective communication. To be effective, a directive must be reasonable, understandable, appropriately worded, and consistent with the organization's overall goals. Whether these criteria are met isn't the manager's decision. Rather, it's the subordinate who decides. Many managers have assumed that their directives were straightforward and to the point only to discover that their subordinates failed to understand or to accept them as legitimate.

Feedback Control

Feedback control methods focus on end results. Corrective action is directed at improving either the resource acquisition process or the actual operations. This type of control derives its name from its use of results to guide future actions. A simple illustration of feedback control is a thermostat, which automatically regulates the temperature of a room (Figure 15–6). Since the thermostat maintains the preset temperature by constantly monitoring the actual temperature, future results (activation of heating or cooling units at time x) are directly and continually determined by feedback (room temperature at time $x - 1$). Room temperature at time x then feeds back to control the heating and cooling units at time $x + 1$, and so on. The feedback control methods employed in business organizations include budgets, standard costs, financial statements, quality control, and performance evaluation.

This section outlines two feedback control methods widely used in business: financial statement analysis and standard cost analysis.

FINANCIAL STATEMENT ANALYSIS - A firm's accounting system is a principal source of information managers can use to evaluate historical results. Periodically, the manager receives a set of financial statements that usually includes a **balance sheet** and **income statement**. These financial statements summarize and classify the effects of transactions in assets, liabilities, equity, revenues, and expenses—the principal components of the firm's financial structure.[22] The balance sheet describes an organization's financial condition at a specified point in time. The income statement is a summary of an organization's financial performance over a given time period.

A detailed analysis of the financial statement's information enables management to determine the adequacy of the firm's earning power and its ability to meet current and long-term obligations. Managers must have measures of and standards for profitability, liquidity, and solvency. Whether a manager prefers the rate of return on sales, on owner's equity, on total assets, or a combination of all three, it's important to establish a meaningful norm—one that's appropriate to the particular firm, given its industry and stage of growth. An inadequate rate of return negatively affects the firm's ability to attract funds for expansion, particularly if a downward trend over time is evident.

The measures of **liquidity** reflect the firm's ability to meet current obligations as they become due.[23] The widest known and most often used measure is the **current ratio** (the ratio of current assets to current liabilities). The standard of acceptability depends on the particular firm's operating characteristics. Bases for comparison are available from trade associations that publish industry averages. A tougher test of liquidity is the **acid-test ratio**, which relates only cash and near-cash items (current assets excluding inventories and prepaid expenses) to current liabilities.

feedback control
A type of control where corrective action is directed at improving either the resource acquisition process or the actual operations.

balance sheet
Describes an organization's financial condition at a specified point in time.

income statement
A summary of an organization's financial performance over a given period of time.

liquidity
Reflects the firm's ability to meet current obligations as they become due.

current ratio
The ratio of current assets to current liabilities.

acid-test ratio
Relates only cash and near-cash items (current assets excluding inventories and prepaid expenses) to current liabilities.

FIGURE 15–6
Feedback Control Regulates Room Temperature through a Thermostat

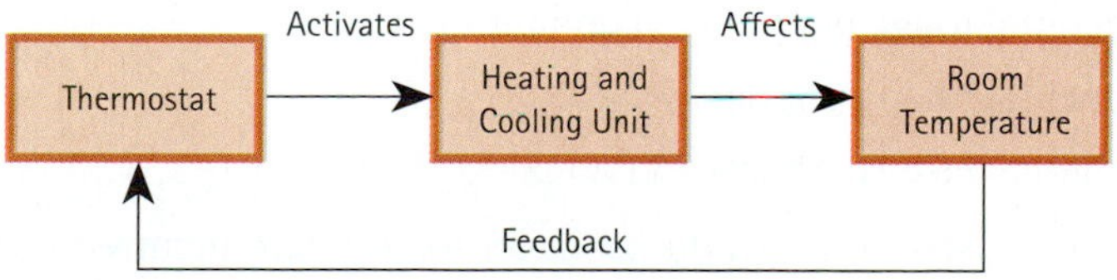

The relationship between current assets and current liabilities is an important one. Equally important is the composition of current assets. Two measures that indicate composition and rely on information found in both the balance sheet and income statement are the **accounts receivable turnover** and the **inventory turnover**. The accounts receivable turnover is the ratio of credit sales to average accounts receivable. The higher the turnover, the more rapid the conversion of accounts receivable to cash. A low turnover would indicate a time lag in the collection of receivables, which in turn could strain the firm's ability to meet its own obligations. Appropriate corrective action might be tightening of credit standards or a more vigorous effort to collect outstanding accounts. The inventory turnover also facilitates the analysis of appropriate balances in current assets. It's calculated as the ratio of cost of goods sold to average inventory. A high ratio could indicate a dangerously low inventory balance in relation to sales, with the possibility of missed sales or a production slowdown. Conversely, a low ratio might indicate an overinvestment in inventory to the exclusion of other, more profitable assets. Whatever the case, the appropriate ratio must be established by the manager, based on the firm's experience within its industry and market.

Another financial measure is **solvency**, the ability of the firm to meet its long-term obligations—its fixed commitments. The solvency measure reflects the claims of creditors and owners on the firm's assets. An appropriate balance must be maintained—a balance that protects the interest of the owner yet doesn't ignore the advantages of long-term debt as a source of funds. A commonly used measure of solvency is the ratio of net income before interest and taxes to interest expense. This indicates the margin of safety; ordinarily, a high ratio is preferred. However, a very high ratio combined with a low debt-to-equity ratio could indicate that management hasn't taken advantage of debt as a source of funds. The appropriate balance between debt and equity depends on many factors. But as a general rule, the proportion of debt should vary directly with the stability of the firm's earnings.

Firms also use *debt ratios* to assess the amount of financing being provided by creditors. Two popular debt ratios are the **debt/equity ratio** and the **debt/asset ratio**. The debt/equity ratio is a measure of the amount of assets financed by debt compared to that amount financed by profits retained by the firm and investments (stocks and other securities). The debt/asset ratio is an expression of the relationship of the firm's total debts to its total assets.

STANDARD COST ANALYSIS ‐ Standard cost accounting systems are considered a major contribution of the scientific management era. A **standard cost system** provides information that enables management to compare actual costs with predetermined (standard) costs. Management can then take appropriate corrective action or assign to others the authority to take action. The first use of standard costing was to control manufacturing costs. In recent years, standard costing has also been applied to selling, general, and administrative expenses.[24] Here we discuss standard manufacturing costs.

The three elements of manufacturing costs are direct labor, direct materials, and overhead. For each of these, an estimate must be made of cost per unit of output. For example, the direct labor cost per unit of output consists of the standard usage of labor and the standard price of labor. The standard usage derives from time studies that fix the expected output per labor hour; the standard price of labor is fixed by the salary schedule appropriate for the kind of work necessary to produce the output. A similar determination is made for direct materials. Thus, the standard labor and standard materials costs might be as follows:

Standard labor usage per unit   2 hours

Standard wage rate per hour $5.00

Standard labor cost $(2 \times \$5.00)$ $10.00

Standard material usage per hour   6 pounds

Standard material price per pound $.30

Standard material cost $(6 \times \$.30)$ $1.80

The accounting system enables the manager to compare incurred costs and standard costs. Today, cost accounting practices are undergoing significant changes to keep pace

---

accounts receivable turnover
The ratio of credit sales to average accounts receivable.

inventory turnover
The ratio of cost of goods sold to average inventory. Facilitates the analysis of appropriate balances in current assets.

solvency
The firm's ability to meet its long-term obligations, its fixed commitments.

debt/equity ratio
A measure of the amount of assets financed by debt compared to that amount financed by profits retained by the firm and investments (stocks and other securities).

debt/asset ratio
An expression of the relationship of the firm's total debts to its total assets.

standard cost system
Provides information that enables management to compare actual costs with predetermined (standard) costs.

with the rapidly evolving manufacturing environment. **Activity-based accounting**, a new system of cost accounting based on activity, has been advocated by many academicians and practitioners. Its underlying principle is that activities consume resources and products consume activities. (See Chapter 5.) The labor costs of supporting departments can be traced to activities by assessing the portion of each person's time spent on each activity, which can then allow for restatement of departmental cost in activities and their associated costs. Activity costs then are traced to the product based on the amount of activity volume each product consumes. The overall impact is more accurate product costs information.

activity-based accounting
Analyzes all organization activities that consume resources.

Summary of Types of Control

In the three types of control we just examined, the focus of corrective action differs (Figure 15–7). Preliminary control methods are based on information that measures some attribute or characteristic of resources; corrective action focuses on resources. Concurrent control methods are based on information related to ongoing processes; corrective action is focused on these processes. The focus of corrective action associated with feedback control is not that which is measured (i.e., results). Rather, feedback control provides information concerning the quality and/or effectiveness of resources and processes.[25]

QUALITY CONTROL TECHNIQUES

The total quality movement has brought with it a set of tools and techniques for controlling organizational processes. Three approaches in particular—total quality control, statistical quality control, and total quality management—are in wide use in a broad spectrum of industries. These approaches are all similar in their focus on exceeding customer expectations as a central value. Another central value is a focus on the system (in contrast to the traditional focus on the worker) as the source of most production or service errors or defects.

Figure 15–8 contrasts the traditional model of control and a quality-based control model. As you can see, in the traditional approach training for workers is not included, management inspects the results of production, and failure to meet production specifications results in worker reprimands. In contrast, in the quality-based control model worker training is included, workers inspect the results of production during the production process, and failure to meet production specifications results in revision of the system.

Any comprehensive quality control program includes the use of statistics. Whether an organization's primary focus is service or manufacturing, statistical tools can provide insights that lead to process improvements. Managers who intend to implement a broad program of continuous improvement through quality control should learn the basics of statistics.

FIGURE 15–7
The Three Types of Control

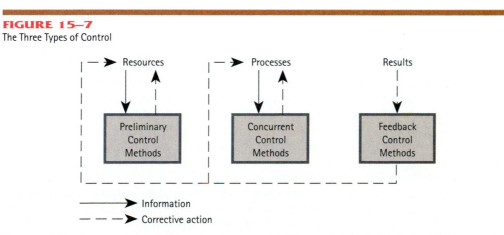

Source: James H. Donnelly, Jr., James L. Gibson, and John M. Ivancevich, *Fundamentals of Management*, 8th ed. (Burr Ridge, Il.: Richard D. Irwin, 1992), p. 265.

FIGURE 15–8
Models of Traditional and
Quality–Based Control

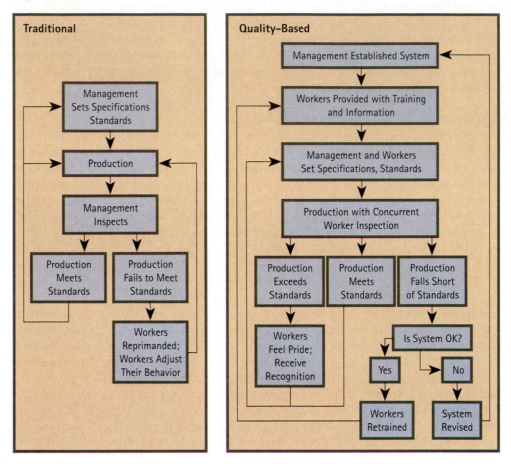

Statistical Process Control (SPC)

statistical process control
A method of implementing quality control before the final inspection stage. It relies on statistical tools to control variation within given processes.

The use of statistical process control has long played an important role in business and industry.[26] **Statistical process control (SPC)** is based on two assumptions: (1) nature is imperfect and (2) variability exists everywhere in systems. Therefore, probability and statistics play a major role in understanding and controlling complex systems. Charts, diagrams, and graphs are conceptual tools managers can use to summarize statistical data, measure and understand variation, assess risk, and make decisions. **Statistics** is defined as "that branch of applied mathematics which describes and analyzes empirical observations for the purpose of predicting certain events as a basis for decision making in the face of uncertainty."[27]

statistics
That branch of applied mathematics that describes and analyzes empirical observations for the purpose of predicting certain events as a basis for decision making in the face of uncertainty.

Statistical process control has traditionally been employed in manufacturing environments. For instance, LaRoche Industries' Geneva nitrogen plant, a producer of low-density ammonium nitrate for industrial explosives, faced operating problems that threatened a plant shutdown. Before starting capital-intensive overhauls, the firm used statistical process control to gain a better handle on plant operations and to assess the impact of changes in various process parameters. LaRoche found a way to make process improvements that saved nearly $300,000 a year by reducing raw material consumption and improving production yields.[28] Statistical process control can also be applied outside the classic manufacturing environments such as project office functions.[29]

descriptive statistics
A computed measure of some property of a set of data, making possible a statement about their meaning.

Statistics come in two varieties: descriptive and inferential. **Descriptive statistics** are a computed measure of some property of a set of data, making possible a statement about its meaning. An example of a descriptive statistic is the average (mean) time it takes to answer the telephone in the customer service department. Other descriptive statistics include the mode (the most common data point) and the median (the point at which 50 percent of the other points lie above and 50 percent below). Mean, median, and mode are also often referred to as measures of central tendency.

Inferential statistics are computations done on a set of data, or among several sets of data, that are designed to facilitate prediction of future events, or to guide decisions and actions. An example of an inferential statistic might be the correlation of the average time the customer service department takes to answer the telephone with customer attitudes about the organization. It might be found that faster average response time is correlated with increased customer satisfaction. In that case, this statistic would be a catalyst to action centered on reducing telephone response time.

inferential statistics
Computations done on a set of data, or among several sets of data, that are designed to facilitate prediction of future events or to guide decisions and actions.

Variation exists in any process. Because of this, no two products or service encounters are exactly alike. The control of quality is largely the control of variation. The job of statistical process control is to limit this variation within an acceptable range. So how do we determine what is acceptable variation?

There are two types of variation in any system: random and nonrandom. Random variation is often referred to as the "normal" variation of a system. Random variation potentially affects all components of a process. Nonrandom variation is not considered to be part of the normal cause processes of a system. This type of variation leads to unpredictable outcomes, something management wants to eliminate.

Random and nonrandom variation are explained in turn by two different types of causes: common and special. **Common cause variation** is just the random variation in a system and, typically, can't be completely eliminated. Managers should work to minimize the range of common cause variation as part of their continuous improvement process. *Range* refers to the extreme upper and lower measures of a variable. But, given the assumption that the perfect system isn't likely to be achieved, managers need to be aware that some common cause variation is likely to remain.

common cause variation
The random variation in a system. Typically, it can't be completely eliminated.

Special cause variation, on the other hand, is due to some *external* influence upon a system. This could be anything from drug abuse by workers to earthquakes. Managers want to eliminate special cause variations to the extent possible. In our examples, this would be done by screening workers and offering drug abuse counseling, or by locating in areas not prone to earthquakes. A **stable system** is one that has eliminated special cause variation and is subject only to the unavoidable (yet reducible) common cause variation.

special cause variation
Variation within a system that is due to some external influence.

stable system
A system that has eliminated special cause variation and is subject only to the unavoidable common cause variations.

Without getting into the mathematics, SPC involves statistical sampling and the use of graphs to determine acceptable variation. Samples of an important variable within a process are collected and its values are plotted on a graph, usually a control chart. Using *standard deviation* (a standard measure of variation around a mean), upper and lower control limits can be established. Typically, these limits are set at three standard deviations above and below the mean. Based on statistical theory, this should account for over 99 percent of all data points. In other words, assuming the data points are normally distributed, 99 percent will fall within three standard deviations above or below the mean. Figure 15–9 shows a normal curve (also called a *bell-shaped curve*) the mean, and three standard deviation units from the mean in each direction. As you can see, the area of the curve encompassed by these points accounts for 99 percent of the data. The normal curve is a mathematical abstraction useful in describing a set of natural events. It isn't a law of nature, but it has proven to be useful in describing a wide range of phenomena. Managers who find a data point that's beyond the three standard deviation units above or below the mean can be confident that they have an unexpected event and that intervening action may be necessary.

Using SPC, managers can determine whether variation in a system is within expected parameters or whether the variation is beyond expected parameters. Any system, over a period of time, will experience some variation on a critical measure around an average (mean) value. Using statistical techniques (techniques that are quite simple, but won't be explored here) managers can establish upper and lower *control limit* values around the mean that define normal variation. System performance within these control limits is said to be subject to common cause variation. Managers shouldn't take action to correct common cause variation.

FIGURE 15–9
The Normal Curve

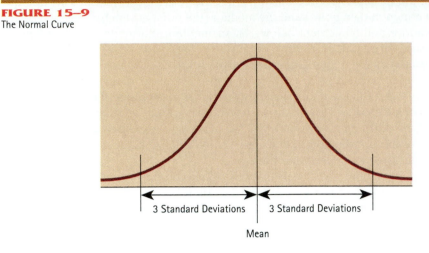

3 Standard Deviations | 3 Standard Deviations

Mean

On the other hand, system performance that goes beyond either the upper or lower control limits is possibly due to special cause variation. Managers who detect special cause variation in their system should take corrective action.

As an example, consider a firm that wants to establish quality control over one of its key suppliers. One critical measure may be the percentage of orders that are delayed each week. To develop a baseline, the company may randomly sample 100 orders each week from this supplier for, say, 20 weeks to develop a mean percentage of orders that are delayed. With these data, it's possible using well-tested statistical methods to establish upper and lower control limits. The range of values within these limits would be the range of expected variation due to common causes. If the mean percentage of delays during the 20-week baseline period is .06 and the upper and lower control limits are .11 and .01, respectively, then any subsequent weeks where the percentage of delays is between these values is probably due to common cause variation (e.g., traffic conditions, worker absences, misplaced orders).

However, if for several weeks the manager notices that the percentage of delays is above .11 (or below .01), a special cause may be operating and action may need to be taken. Some possible special causes are (1) the supplier was bought out and is under new management and (2) a trucker strike is delaying deliveries. Quality-based managers use statistical measures to know when key processes are affected by special cause variation and need immediate attention.

control chart

A record of the targeted activity over time, with established upper and lower tolerances or control limits.

Figure 15–10 shows a control chart based on the preceding scenario. A **control chart** is a record of the targeted activity over time, with established upper and lower control limits. Control charts are an important tool in statistical process control used to determine if a process is behaving as intended or if there is some unnatural variation.[30] The horizontal axis is divided into units of weeks, and the vertical axis into units of percentage of orders delayed. The upper and lower control limits, as well as the mean, are based on the 20-week baseline period during which these measures were taken. As you can see from the plotted data points, weeks 1 through 7 are within the upper and lower control limits and their deviation from the mean can be attributed to common cause variation. However, weeks 8 through 10 are beyond the upper control limit. A prudent manager would watch closely for a continuation of this trend, which may indicate a special cause is operating. According to statistical methods, a run of seven straight data points beyond the control limits would indicate a need for intervention.

One company that has become famous for its quality transformation provides its workers with extensive training on basic SPC. Motorola's famous "six sigma" quality program is named for a statistical term that expresses its companywide goal of less than about three defects per million for each product it produces. Compare that figure to the average American company, which operates at three or four sigma or about 67,000 to 6,200 defects per

FIGURE 15—10
Control Chart of Delayed
Orders

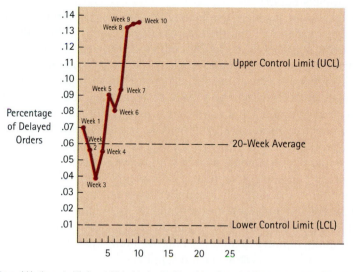

Note: Weeks 1 through 7 are within the control limits established during the 20-week baseline period. Weeks 8 through 10 show a consistent run beyond the upper control limit and suggest that a special cause variation may be at work.

million. Motorola workers train at Motorola University where they learn how to use statistical tools to control their processes. When the company conducted a survey of 100,000 of its workers to determine if they felt the quality tools and training were useful, it found that most of them thought it was, but that it wasn't happening fast enough. This from a group that management had traditionally thought to be resistant to change.[31]

Banc One CEO John McCoy was named 1992 Banker of the Year by the newspaper *American Banker* in part because of his bank's superior customer service. Each quarter, Banc One surveys 35,000 customers to find out what they expect from the company. Statistical data are compiled to direct managerial focus. One result of these surveys is that nearly 60 percent of Banc One's 1,377 branches are open on Saturday, and 20 percent are open on Sunday.[32] McCoy directed these changes based on statistical analysis of the survey data.

The practice of quality management in any type of organization—whether it's service, manufacturing, retail, nonprofit, or something else—can benefit from applying statistical methods to organizational processes or customer expectations. Although statistical techniques are common to most quality management environments, each manager must decide how best to apply these techniques to his or her own organization. What's common across organization types is the fundamental purpose of quality control—to minimize variation.

SPC is the most narrowly focused of the approaches to quality control discussed in this section. It's concerned primarily with quantitative measures of performance, and doesn't address the issue of how to achieve performance improvements. Total quality control and total quality management focus on worker and manager behavior as well as techniques for controlling organizational performance through their activities.

Total Quality Control (TQC)

In traditional production management, quality control consisted of assigning the last person on the assembly line the responsibility of ensuring that the product worked. Today, quality control begins at the beginning; that is, quality control is maintained from the design process through manufacturing, sale, and use of the product. The sum of all these efforts is called total quality control. The principles of total quality control can be applied equally well to either products or services. Customers will always seek products and services of consistently high quality. To understand how total quality control can transform an organization, consider that each worker within a company can be viewed as providing a product or service for some other individual, and that the product or service can be evaluated using the tools of total quality control.[33]

Armand Feigenbaum is often credited with coining the term *total quality control* (TQC).[34] TQC represents a more comprehensive form of quality control than SPC, although it recommends using statistics to improve quality. According to Feigenbaum, "**Total quality control** is an effective system for integrating the quality-development, quality-maintenance, and quality-improvement efforts of the various groups in an organization so as to enable marketing, engineering, production, and service at the most economical levels which allow for full customer satisfaction."[35] In a recent interview, Feigenbaum maintains that companies achieve competitive advantage by providing quality products and services based upon world-class work processes.[36] To practice TQC is to develop, design, produce, and service a quality product that's economical, useful, and always satisfactory to the customer.[37]

The fundamental purpose of total quality control is to manufacture products or deliver services that meet the level of quality demanded by customers. TQC's emphasis is on customer satisfaction. Feigenbaum identifies several TQC benchmarks for the 1990s: quality is what the customer says it is; quality is a way of managing; quality and innovation are mutually dependent; quality requires continuous improvement; and quality is implemented with a total system connected with customers and suppliers.[38]

According to Feigenbaum, there's no such thing as a permanent quality level. Demands and expectations for quality are constantly changing. A distinction of good management is personal leadership in mobilizing the knowledge, skill, and positive attitudes of everyone in the organization to recognize that what they do to make quality better helps to make everything in the organization better. Quality is also essential for successful innovation for two reasons. The first reason is the rapid speed of new product development. The second is that when a product design is likely to be manufactured globally, where international suppliers must be involved in every stage of development and production, the entire process must be clearly structured.[39]

In a quality-based system, control is a conscious, positive, preventive stance created in the system. TQC begins with planning—planning that's aimed at preventing quality problems. The concerns addressed by quality planning include:

1. Establishing quality guidelines.
2. Building quality into the design.
3. Procurement quality.
4. In-process and finished product quality.
5. Inspection and test planning.
6. Control of nonconforming material.
7. Handling and following up on customer complaints.
8. Education and training for quality.[40]

As we mentioned, TQC is similar to total quality management in its customer-focused approach to control. Total quality management uses both the techniques and ideas of SPC and TQC, but goes further in its involvement of workers in the quality process. TQM's main progenitor, W. Edwards Deming, is a familiar name in a wide range of industries and organizational types. Deming has become required reading for managers searching for total quality. His TQM philosophy includes specific guidelines for organizational control. On the other hand, Feigenbaum, the main figure behind TQC, is less widely known and studied. His program for quality improvement is familiar primarily to quality engineers.

Total Quality Management (TQM)

Total quality management (TQM), the generic name given to the Deming approach to quality-based management, is heavily oriented toward treating the *system* as the primary source of error or defects in manufacturing or service work. We have already examined many elements of Deming's management philosophy throughout this text, summarized primarily in

total quality control
An effective system for integrating the quality-development, quality-maintenance, and quality-improvement efforts of the various groups in an organization so as to enable marketing, engineering, production, and service at the most economical levels that allow for full customer satisfaction.

his 14 points. Additionally, we saw in this chapter's opening vignette how Deming demonstrates the folly of controlling processes through worker reprimands or rewards when they're operating within normal system variation.

Although quality management uses a myriad of statistical techniques to control processes, there are also some fundamental lessons for control from a human psychology perspective. Deming stresses in his 14 points such things as "pride of workmanship," "self-improvement," and "drive out fear." These are all elements of the "softer" side of management (the nonquantitative side) but equally important to master. Managers who only use SPC are likely to ignore the need for pride in workmanship that most workers share. Thus, the *total* in total quality management requires managers to be familiar with a wide range of facts about the workplace, both those that can be described mathematically and those that can't. Figure 15–11 describes the benefits that accrue to an organization from paying attention to these nonquantitative aspects of a TQM approach.

Let's examine just a few of the important elements of TQM. You'll learn about the worker's role and the manager's role in a TQM environment.

THE WORKER'S ROLE IN TQM - In their book *In Search of Excellence*, consultants Tom Peters and Bob Waterman illustrate the importance of personal worker control in quality.[41] They describe an experiment designed to determine the effect of loud, disturbing noise on performing a mental task. The experimental group was provided a button it could press to eliminate the noise. The control group had no such button. In performing the mental task, the experimental group achieved five times the productivity rate and only 20 percent of the error rate of the control group. The significant point of this experiment is that, although the experimental group performed better, no one in the experimental group ever touched the button. Subjects who merely believed they had personal control over their working conditions achieved higher productivity and greatly reduced error rates compared to those who

FIGURE 15–11
Total Quality Management
Model

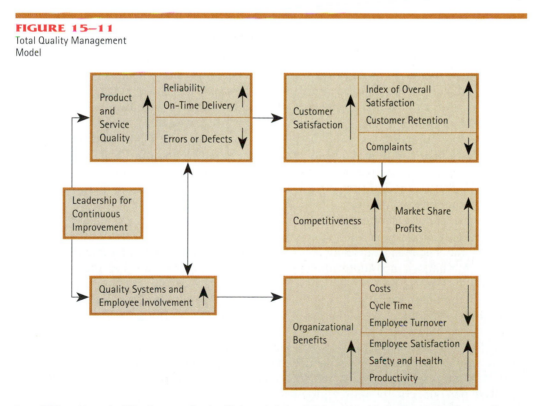

Source: U.S. General Accounting Office, *Management Practices: U.S. Companies Improve Performance through Quality Efforts*, GAO/NSIAD-90-190, May 1991, p. 15.

Personal Environment RH Modules, or PEMS—the small vertical devices positioned at the corners of the desk—give employees greater control over their work environment, allowing them to alter variables such as temperature, light level, sound level, and even fragrance at their workstations.

didn't believe they had control. A personal sense of control, not reduced noise, explained the difference between the two groups.

To enhance workers' sense of personal control, Johnson Controls of Milwaukee, Wisconsin, has developed an office product it calls "Personal Environments RH Modules" (PEMS). These modules enable workers to control the temperature, light level, sound level, and even fragrance at their workstations. Investigators from Rensselaer Polytechnic Institute (RPI) in Troy, New York, studied the effect of PEMS workstations used by 500 employees at the West Bend Mutual Insurance Company in West Bend, Wisconsin. The RPI researchers found a 2 percent increase in productivity in workers who used PEMS. West Bend executives think the increase in productivity attributable to the workstations is more like 6 to 8 percent. Terry Weaver, vice president at Johnson, remarked, "The groundbreaking aspect of this study is that for the first time there is hard evidence that workers are more productive when they can control their environment."[42]

Japanese management expert Mikio Katano also recommends that managers place a high value on workers. A production engineer with Toyota Motor Corporation's Motomachi factory, Kitano has been counseling factory managers to slow down in their application of automation. Kitano is not antitechnology, but he does oppose machines that needlessly overcomplicate processes. "The key to productivity is simplicity," he says. "Men control machines, not the other way around." As quoted in Karen Lowry Miller, Kitano emphasizes that when workers feel they have control over a discrete section of the assembly line, they develop a sense of pride and autonomy.[43]

As the Global Exchange on the next page shows, not only are Japan and America discovering the virtues of allowing workers to control the processes for which they are responsible; Mexican workers have also achieved higher quality and productivity levels through increased personal control of work processes.

Deming provides an example of successful worker quality control in the production of stockings. Managers with the stocking company first recognized a problem in production

GLOBAL EXCHANGE

MAQUILADORAS: MEXICAN WORKERS PRACTICE TOTAL QUALITY

Most discussions about global quality leaders focus on Japan, Germany, and other industrial powerhouses. Seldom does one associate Mexico with world-class industrial production. But that's changing. Mexico's fast-growing border plants, known as maquiladoras, have adopted quality as a way of life. Maquiladoras were first established in 1965 after the United States tightened its immigration rules and Mexican farm laborers were no longer able to find seasonal work in California. As the maquiladora program was originally conceived, U.S. companies would establish "twin plants" on each side of the Mexican border. The plant on the U.S. side would manufacture parts and ship them to the Mexican plant for assembly. Since the inception of this system, the tradition for the maquiladora was associated with this type of basic assembly and rough manufacturing work. Despite low-quality production, the attraction of low-wage labor ensured that U.S. companies would use the program. Roughly 650,000 workers are employed by maquiladoras.

Today, low wages are not enough of an attraction to keep U.S. companies interested in the maquiladora program. Maquiladora workers typically make $2.00 per hour today: their functional counterparts in East Asia might earn that much in an entire day. In fact, in the early 1980s, two-thirds of the existing maquiladora plants had packed up and moved to Asia. Managers of the surviving maquiladoras realized that their competitive niche no longer was cheap labor. They realized that they need to provide high-quality labor as well.

Leon Opalin Mielniska, vice president at Banco Nacional de Mexico (BANAMEX) in Tijuana, explained the transformation that's occurring in maquiladora management. "In Mexico, we are improving our manufacturing by investing in our labor and improving our human resources."

Proving this point, Shure Brothers' Juarez facility uses a cross-functional TQM team known as the "Paradigm Busters" to improve the manufacturing process of the company's top-selling microphone products. The team is made up of seven Mexican and three American Juarez employees. After training in fundamental quality concepts, the team implemented a set of changes to improve processes. When the results were assessed, the team not only had cut manufacturing steps from 349 to 96 and lowered production time from 32 days to just 2 days, it had also recommended significant product design improvements. James Furst, vice president of total quality at Shure Brothers, said, "We've had other TQM in Mexico that really makes it take off."

Turnover at the Shure Brothers' Tijuana plant plummeted from 8 percent per month to 1 or 2 percent after TQM was introduced. At the same time, the Paradigm Busters were able to cut the workforce on one product form 56 to 29 people. Furst explained, "When we changed the working atmosphere by empowering people, they changed their work habits."

And the Shure Brothers' story isn't unique. Another example of the Mexican turn to quality is at Mattel's MABAMEX facility in Tijuana. Plant workers run a just-in-time assembly line on which workers themselves control the line's speed. Workers move the line forward when they are satisfied with the quality of the product.

The Mexican plants of U.S. industrial giants Ford, General Electric, and IBM match and often surpass their U.S. counterparts in productivity and quality. Although pay in Mexico is about one-sixth the U.S. level, productivity grew at twice the U.S. rate from 1988 to 1993. Companies now regularly benchmark the maquiladoras against Asian competitors. "We run our Mexican factories with basically the same premise as in the U.S.," says James Meyer, senior vice president at Thompson Consumer Electronics, Inc., of Indianapolis. "They use state-of-the-art, expensive, very modern equipment. These are not high-volume sweatshops."

As these examples show, involving workers in the TQM transformation and allowing them a measure of control over their work processes is effective in maquiladoras. Using this approach, Mexico has been able to develop a new competitive niche by combining low wages with high quality.

Source: Adapted from Candice Siegle, "Maqs Are Back," *World Trade*, August 1995, pp. 22–26; Martha H. Peak, "Maquiladoras: Where Quality Is a Way of Life," *Management Review*, March 1993, pp. 19–23; and Douglas Harbrecht, Geri Smith, and Stephen Baker, "The Mexican Worker: Smart, Motivated, Cheap—And a Potent New Economic Force to Be Reckoned With," *Business Week*, April 19, 1993, pp. 84–92.

costs when they faced a situation where costs were soon to exceed revenues. Management hired a statistician to help them diagnose their problem. The statistician recommended that the company send 20 supervisors to a 10-week training course to learn techniques for charting the number of defective stockings. When the supervisors returned, they were asked to apply some of the principles they had learned.

In all but two cases, defects fell within statistically established control limits with a mean defect rate of 4.8 percent per production worker (called "loopers" in the stocking business). Next, individual loopers were charted. Management found (1) an excellent looper whose skills were passed on to others by training them, (2) a looper who improved markedly with eyeglasses, and (3) a looper whose performance changed dramatically after charting. One of the loopers remarked, "This is the first time that anybody ever told me that care mattered." Within seven months, the mean number of defects dropped to 0.8 percent. Instead of 11,500 stockings rejected each week, only 2,000 were rejected.[44]

A quality-based system of control must be built on worker trust and pride of workmanship, which provides a basis for worker self-control.[45] In this quality-based view, control must be seen as an internal, individual process before it can result in an external process. Control becomes an internal quality guide practiced by all employees rather than an external set of rules applied by managers. Juran defines self-control as "A means of knowing what the goals are . . . a means of knowing what the actual performance is . . . a means for changing the performance in the event that performance does not conform to goals and standards."[46]

Using standards, workers have a quality-based strategy for determining those activities necessary and harmful to quality. Activities are built around the standards; irrelevant, redundant, or non-value-added activities are eliminated.

Although workers play an important role in implementing a TQM approach, management has the responsibility of leadership. In most organizations, workers below the managerial level are unlikely to lead a revolution in organizational philosophy. It's up to management to steer the ship. Managers must create the vision for the organization. This is no different in a TQM environment or a scientific management environment. What's different is the behavior of managers.

MANAGEMENT'S ROLE IN TQM - Quality-based management believes control of work processes is effected first by the work force, then by automation, then by managers, and finally by upper managers. Upper management is responsible for creating the system; workers are trained to maintain control. Thus a quality-based approach locates control at the lowest levels of the firm—the workers on the line who provide the service.[47]

The traditional managerial control function has focused on supervision during the production process. Supervision has been widely practiced as a traditional method of keeping an eye on workers—looking for mistakes. Some managers have even resorted to using information technologies to eavesdrop on employees. Procter & Gamble, for example, examined workers' phone records to search for possible leaks of sensitive information. This type of practice has debilitating effects on performance and is ethically questionable. In some cases, the corporate trend toward downsizing and rightsizing has led workers lower down in the corporate hierarchy to tell bosses only what they think they want to hear, even resorting to lying. Extreme pressure to perform can lead to improper behavior.

To control the ethical practices within corporations, many firms are creating high-level positions for "ethics officers." Their responsibility is to control behavior that runs against an organization's mores and values. As the Ethics Spotlight shows, ethics officers can find a home in TQM-based organizations.

The responsibility for quality control ultimately rests with management. However, managers must also promote worker self-management or "quality-mindedness" practices, as Armand Feigenbaum refers to it.[48] To further employee self-management, managers must develop worker participation programs and policies. With knowledge of the company's costs and goals, workers can practice control with minimal supervision. Management's job is to ensure that workers have the knowledge, the tools, and the power to prevent problems from arising. Managers must also encourage employee suggestions and cost consciousness by recognizing and implementing worker quality improvement decisions. And, if there are problems, management should give workers the first opportunity to solve them.

Managers need patience to transform their organizations using the principles and tools of total quality management. If a manager grows frustrated too soon with the lack of worker understanding or motivation to become involved in the new philosophy, she may not give it a chance to work.[49] As a 1991 Ernst & Young survey found, companies that fail with TQM are those that haven't provided their workers with the information and training they need to be effective.[50] Managers must realize this. Most workers want responsibility and control over their work. Most will understand and accept a new approach to their work if management demonstrates commitment to improving the system. That means workers need to be trained in the tools and techniques of TQM, SPC, and TQC. They need to be empowered to control their work processes. And they need to be encouraged constantly to develop pride in their work and their organization. These elements of quality are the least quantifiable, but no less important.

ETHICS SPOTLIGHT

ETHICS OFFICERS CONTROL ORGANIZATIONAL BEHAVIOR

A new movement is taking place across corporate America. Stung by bad press and public outrage over several highly publicized cases of unethical behavior, large organizations are calling in a new breed of professional to control things. Not that the new "ethics officers" could have prevented Ivan Boesky from insider trading, or stood in the way of the broad misdealings of the Bank of Credit and Commerce International (BCCI). Nonetheless, corporations that have ethics officers on staff find them useful and are employing them to handle increasingly complex issues. While some of the first ethics officers had a policing mentality, today's ethics officers see their charge as communicating standards and changing the corporate culture.

Textron's Bell Helicopter unit started its ethics program in 1987 with ethics ombudsmen. The ombudsmen operated at a lower level than today's ethics officers. The Textron ombudsmen, for example, handled only ethics infractions and employee complaints. Based on their early success, Textron has expanded its ethics program to include a full-time ethics officer, Richard Greaves. His job includes addressing worker complaints on issues from expense accounts to possible misconduct by colleagues. Mr. Greaves also provides training sessions on ethical decision making, coordinates meetings for a senior management ethics committee, and monitors broader corporate ethics issues.

Sheena Carmichael of Crime Concern believes that the route to preventing theft and crime within a company lies through formalizing or operationalizing its ethics. Companies should begin by conducting ethical audits, face-to-face interviews to find out the gaps in perceptions and values between management and staff; and then put in place appropriate structures—a senior member of staff as ethics officer and ombudsman, a helpline, thorough training, regular opportunities for debating ethical issues and ways of monitoring effectiveness.

Five years ago, few corporations had ethics officers. Today, 15 to 20 percent of big companies have them. An ethics officer typically holds a title from director to vice president and earns $90,000 to $200,000 per year. In most cases, ethics officers report directly to the company's chief executive.

One effective tool that ethics officers use to control employee behavior is an ethics hotline. At Raytheon Corporation, ethics officer Paul Pullen receives some 100 cells a month. Around 80 percent involve issues he can resolve on the spot or refer to appropriate departments in the company. Another 10 percent of the callers are simply looking for advice. But, on the average, about 10 callers per month report a serious ethical lapse that Pullen must discuss with senior management. Pullen says, "Most people have high standards, and they want to work in an atmosphere that is ethical. The complaints come from all levels, and they are typical of what you would find in any business: possible conflicts of interest, cheating on timecards, cheating on expense reports."

As Pullen notes, most workers prefer to work in an environment that has high ethical standards. Total quality management recognizes the need for worker control over work processes. It follows that if workers can control, at least to some extent, the ethical environment they work in, they can be more productive. At least that's the reasoning behind the growing trend toward corporate ethics officers.

Source: Adapted from Beverly Geber, "The Right and Wrong of Ethics Officers," *Training*, October 1995, pp. 102–109; Anita Vande Vliet, "To Catch a Thief," *Management Today*, October 1995, pp. 70–74; Juli Amparano Lopez, "More Big Businesses Set Up Ethics Officers," *The Wall Street Journal*, May 10, 1993, p. B1; and Kenneth Labich, "The New Crisis in Business Ethics," *Fortune*, April 20, 1992, pp. 167–76.

THE WORKPLACE OF TOMORROW

The control process is becoming increasingly important in a global economy where product quality is a requirement for long-term survival. Many companies continue, for instance, to adopt statistical process control (SPC) because they realize it is a powerful tool for improving quality; other companies institute SPC because their customers require it. Suppliers to the big three auto companies are required to show proof of using SPC in their manufacturing operations, and will not get the business without it.[51] Driven by tougher customer standards, more steelmakers are investing heavily in SPC.[52] This trend is expected to continue in the years ahead as companies strive to improve quality and tailor production capabilities to customer requirements.

In today's competitive environment, it will be difficult to determine how extensive a company's control system should be. Managers are faced with a dilemma: they are under intense pressure to cut costs and be more competitive, yet they are expected to implement total quality control systems and thereby improve product quality. These conflicting trends may be resolved in the workplace of tomorrow through a balanced view of control systems. This view recognizes that there are costs of having too much control in an organization, and costs of having too little control.[53] The key to the future will be to minimize the company's total cost of control by utilizing those controls that are most appropriate for the risks the company faces.

SUMMARY OF LEARNING OBJECTIVES

DESCRIBE THE RED BEAD EXPERIMENT AND EXPLAIN ITS MESSAGE TO MANAGERS.

The red bead experiment illustrates the problems associated with attempts to control worker behavior with rewards and disciplinary actions. The system, not the workers, is responsible for the prevailing defect rate. The experiment demonstrates that the system must be designed and managed to bring about quality, rather than to create difficult or impossible expectations for workers.

DESCRIBE THE THREE ELEMENTS OF THE CONTROL PROCESS.

The three elements of control are specification, production, and inspection. Specification fully describes the preferred condition, a goal, standard, or carefully determined quantitative statement of conditions. Production means acting to meet the specifications (i.e., making the product). Inspection is a judgment as to whether the product meets the specifications. Appropriate follow-up actions must then be taken, based on the findings of the inspection.

DEFINE TOTAL QUALITY CONTROL

Total quality control is an effective system for integrating the quality-development, quality-maintenance, and quality-improvement efforts of the various groups in an organization so as to enable marketing, engineering, production, and service at the most economical levels that allow for full customer satisfaction.

EXPLAIN THE WORKERS' ROLE IN TOTAL QUALITY MANAGEMENT.

Control should be primarily in the hands of the workers, and not in the hands of a supervisor or an outside or final inspector. Management's job is to ensure that workers have the knowledge, tools, and power to prevent problems from arising. A quality-based system of control must be built on worker trust and pride of workmanship, which provides a basis for worker self-control. In this quality-based view, control is an internal process before it can result in an external process. The responsibility for planning, implementing, and maintaining control ultimately rides with management. The effective application of control and of achieving quality rests more on the effective use of self-management practices. Control becomes an internal quality guide, practiced by all employees, rather than an external set of rules applied by managers to workers. Successful control must be recognized and rewarded.

EXPLAIN MANAGEMENT'S ROLE IN TOTAL QUALITY MANAGEMENT.

The traditional managerial control function has focused on supervision during the production process. Supervision has been widely practiced as a traditional method of keeping an eye on workers, looking for special causes of variation. Traditional management has used technology to monitor and intimidate workers. In contrast, quality-based management believes control is effected first by the workforce, then by automation, then by managers, and finally by upper managers. Upper management is responsible for the system; workers are then judged capable of effecting control. Thus a quality-based approach locates control at the lowest levels of the firm—with information technology and the workers.

CONTRAST STATISTICAL PROCESS CONTROL WITH TOTAL QUALITY CONTROL.

Statistical process control (SPC) focuses on the use of statistics to identify and understand production and operations. SPC isn't concerned with how to resolve problems in systems. Total quality control (TQC) focuses on customer expectations to control production and operations. Although it recognizes the importance of statistics, it also sees the importance of worker involvement with the quality improvement process.

KEY TERMS

accounts receivable turnover, p. 400
acid-test ratio, p. 399
activity-based accounting, p. 401
balance sheet, p. 399
capital budget, p. 396
common cause variation, p. 403
concurrent control, p. 398
control, p. 391
control chart, p. 404
current ratio, p. 399
debt/asset ratio, p. 400

debt/equity ratio, p. 400
descriptive statistics, p. 402
direction, p. 398
discounted rate of return, p. 397
feedback control, p. 399
income statement, p. 399
inferential statistics, p. 403
inventory turnover, p. 400
investment decisions, p. 396
liquidity, p. 399
operational definition, p. 391

payback method, p. 396
preliminary control, p. 393
rate of return on investment, p. 396
solvency, p. 400
special cause variation, p. 403
stable system, p. 403
standard cost system, p. 400
statistical process control, p. 402
statistics, p. 402
total quality control, p. 406

REVIEW AND DISCUSSION QUESTIONS

Recall

1. What is a stable system? Who is responsible for creating and maintaining a stable system?
2. Describe the differences between preliminary, concurrent, and feedback control.
3. What are the differences between traditional control and quality control?

Understanding

4. Explain the role of statistics in quality control.
5. Why does the red bead experiment work so well to highlight the system as the source of error in work processes?

6. Who is responsible for achieving and maintaining control in an organization?
7. Do you think that all variation within a system can be eliminated by comprehensive preliminary control?
8. Why do workers seem to perform at higher levels when they have personal control of their work processes?

Application

9. Design and implement a statistical measure to assess your arrival time for class each day.
10. Think of ineffective controls that you have experienced in school, at work, or in other aspects of your life. How were they ineffective? How might they have been improved?

CASE STUDY

Whirlpool Lets Customers Control Product Design

Manufacturing consultant Earl Hall has remarked that "The global markets of the 21st-century will demand the ability to quickly and globally deliver a high variety of customized products." Futurist Alvin Toffler has coined the term *prosumer* (a concatenation of *producer* and *consumer*) to signify the consumer's increasingly important role in the design of products and services. Some have projected that the time is rapidly approaching when consumers will play a role in the design of all of the major items they consume. Some companies are already riding this wave of change.

Whirlpool is a familiar name in the home appliance business. But the industry giant found itself faced with a dilemma even senior managers couldn't resolve. On the surface, it seemed simple enough—company surveys had determined that consumers wanted a cooking range with controls that were easy to clean. Whirlpool engineers responded to the survey, proposing that the company use modern touch-pad controls like those on microwave ovens. Touch-pad controls can be cleaned with one swipe of a damp cloth. The problem was, the idea of push-button controls flew in the face of industry wisdom. Earlier models with push-button controls had not sold well in stores, while consumers chose ovens with knobs they could grasp and turn.

Rather than reject the results of its consumer study, the company decided to follow consumers' wishes to the letter. It designed a touch-pad controlled range and, during roll-out, monitored consumer reaction every step of the way. At the company's Benton Harbor, Michigan, headquarters, consumer volunteers played with computer simulations of the new controls, and marketers tested prototypes with passersby in nearby shopping malls.

The result of all this effort is a range with a touch-pad control system so easy to use it doesn't require a manual. The user simply turns on the oven in a simple series of steps. The new range hit the sales floor in 1992 and became one of Whirlpool's hottest-selling models.

This example of bringing the customer into the design process is one of the ways in which Whirlpool involves the consumer in controlling corporate behavior. Each year the company sends its Standardized Appliance Measurement Satisfaction (SAMS) survey to 180,000 households, asking people to rate all of their appliances on a number of attributes. If the survey finds that a competitor's product ranks higher, Whirlpool engineers tear it apart to find out why.

In addition to the survey, the company pays hundreds of consumers to "use" computer simulations of potential products at the company's Usability Laboratory. Engineers record consumer reactions on videotape.

Vice president John Hamann explained that consumers' expectations aren't immediately clear. For example, one SAMS survey showed that people want clean refrigerators. After analyzing this and asking more questions, Whirlpool found that consumers don't want refrigerators that are easy to clean, but rather refrigerators that look clean. The company promptly designed refrigerators with stucco-like fronts that hide fingerprints.

Whirlpool uses consumer data to differentiate its products from those of its chief competitors (Maytag and Electrolux). Since 1982, the company has nearly tripled in size to become the world's largest major appliance manufacturer. And the company has plans for continued expansion. CEO David Whitwam is confident that consumer research methods will lead to big gains overseas. This confidence has already been justified in European microwave oven sales. Until recently, fewer than one-third of European households had microwaves. But Whirlpool's consumer research showed that more families would buy them if they performed more like conventional ovens. In late 1991, Whirlpool introduced the VIP Crisp, a microwave model strictly for European markets. It contains a broiler coil for top browning and a unique dish that sizzles the underside of the food. The Crisp is now Europe's best-selling microwave.

Bringing the customer into the process of product design is another fundamental element of total quality control. Determining what customers are willing to purchase before bringing a product or service on line ensures a market. However, consumer demand is constantly shifting, and companies such as Whirlpool that use sophisticated techniques to bring the consumer into the design of new products on a continuous basis will stay out front in the global economy.

QUESTIONS

1. What type of control is displayed by the Whirlpool SAMS survey?
2. Whirlpool managers are interested in controlling product design. What kind of questions do you think the SAMS survey asks? List 10 questions that you think would help in the design of new home appliances.

3. Develop a means for measuring and assessing responses to your questions in Question 2. What type of statistics will help the most? Would you use descriptive or inferential statistics?

Source: Adapted from Sally Solo, "How to Listen to Consumers," *Fortune,* January 11, 1993, p. 77; William H. Davidow and Michael S. Malone, *The Virtual Corporation* (New York: HarperCollins, 1992); and Alvin S. Toffler, *The Third Wave* (New York: William Morrow, 1980).

VIDEO CASE

Planning and Controlling at Marshall Industries

Planning and controlling are essential to the study of people and behavior within an organization and crucial to achieving quality management. It's a process of continually refining all product and process elements to satisfy and exceed customer expectations. Rapid technological change, the new global economy, shifting financial markets, dynamic political change, and culturally and ethnically diverse workplaces all impact managerial decision making at ever-increasing rates. That's why its critical to understand the processes of planning and controlling and how they affect the goal of total quality in an uncertain and ever changing environment.

For a business to be successful, it must have a firm understanding of the loop between planning and controlling. This video takes a look at how the planning and control loop works during a typical day at Marshall Industries, a leading distributor of industrial electronic components and semiconductors based in the Los Angeles area.

Gordon Marshall, the founder of Marshal industries, shares his philosophy in building a successful company: "I want to create a company that I would like to work for. If you ask yourself that, then that sets certain criteria for how you want to be treated, how you want to be looked upon, how you want to be supported, how you want to be talked to, and so forth. The other thing that I want to do is not ever give a person a reason to fail. In other words, I would give him everything he needed to succeed. I would never want him to come to me and say, 'You wouldn't let me do this, therefore, I failed.'"

Until recently, Marshall was a large but traditionally organized company that was facing increased competition in a rapidly changing technological environment. To respond, Marshall initiated a sea of change in its organizational culture. The planning changes began strategically with Marshall making a massive commitment to advanced computerization of its entire system. The control system also changed, Marshal shifted over time from a command and control orientation to a competitive team system.

Richard Bentley, executive vice president, commented on this shift in management style: "When we made the shift and took everybody off of basically 100 percent commission to a salaried program, we weren't sure what the results were going to be. And since then we have had almost continuous record months and record quarters, and our sales are at an all-time high."

There are two key components to planning: strategic and operational. Strategic planning identifies the objectives and programs that shape the destiny of the organization. Operational planning looks at tactics or actions to carry out a strategy.

Similarly, there are two major methods for implementing and measuring control: control systems and control orientations. Controlling is the process that aligns employee performance to help meet strategic goals. Control systems help managers recognize deviations in processes so they can either correct or take advantage of them.

Organizational control refers to managerial methods to direct individual performances to fulfill organizational plans. The classical approach was command and control. In this orientation, managers establish target rewards and penalties. Marshall's management team got rid of its commissioned sales plan in order to build a stronger team ethic within its sales force. Robert Caldarella, general manager of corporate sales, commented on this shift in control orientation at Marshall: "You'll always get self-motivated people who do things for themselves under a commission plan. With the elimination of the plan, you encourage team work, you get people offering suggestions, and being motivated by just watching teams grow and mature into a force."

A control orientation common among government contractors is called conformance. Under this orientation, rigorous specifications are preestablished that the supplier must conform to. Teams at Marshall have to concern themselves with everything from the accuracy of the bar-coded part numbers to rigid shipping deadlines and packaging specifications.

What is more typical of Marshall is a third managerial control orientation called competitive team. In this approach to control, teams share information to enhance competitiveness with other firms—an approach that is gaining worldwide acceptance.

Of course the customer is the ultimate influence on the loop between planning and control. Robert Rodin, Marshall's president, said, "We realized when we built our organization around listening to the voice of the customer that we weren't aligning ourselves to bring them answers and to help them. We were trying to close them. Changing to a customer orientation has had a fundamental change in the way we interface, from the way we pick up our telephone to the way we interact with our customers and suppliers."

Another example of strategic planning at Marshall was the decision to introduce robotics on the warehouse floor. Along with that came the introduction of PITs or process improvement teams, involving workers in different jobs throughout the warehouse. The company also changed its emphasis from production quantity to production quality.

One aspect of operational planning crucial to Marshal's warehousing operations is called just-in-time planning. Mike Lelo, warehouse manager, explains how it works at Marshall: "Just recently we had a situation in which we had a late delivery. It hit our warehouse at approximately 5:30 PM. And with some of the programs we have in place we were able not only to receive this shipment and do a normal verification to ensure that it was right, we were able to store it on our automated system, have the sales order already on the system allocated to those parts and get it back off the automated system, picked, labeled, bagged, tagged, and special handled to our packaging department, up to manifest station and shipped out the door for a Saturday delivery. Having a whole system working together and people who knew what they were doing it went right through without a hitch."

In this ongoing loop, good controlling is just as critical as smart planning. Marshall president Rob Rodin uses control systems to minimize deviations in operational processes. He said, "We've tried to take all of these strategies and operationally define them. We talk about adding value. For a customer we may say, 'Mr. customer we want to add value.' The customer defines that for us. We want the shipment zero days late, one day early. As soon as we understand operationally what adding value means, then we use scientific method to measure and keep track of our performance."

Managers study variations and deviations to adjust controls and refine planning. They also consult regularly with customers to add value that exceeds customer expectations. The planning and control systems Marshall Industries has successfully initiated is all part of a continuous loop in which the objective is not a fixed goal, but a continuous refining and improving of the entire organizational system. Learning basic planning and control techniques gives today's manager the extra edge in a competitive global economy where quality is the ultimate measuring stick.

QUESTIONS

1. What is the difference between operational and strategic planning? Explain the difference in the context of a retail store operation.
2. Organizational control refers to the methods managers use to direct employees toward organizational goals. What control techniques are common in the classical approach? How does that approach differ from what is found in quality-based organizations?
3. This video talked about the "planning-control loop." What does this mean?

APPLICATION EXERCISE

Hibson's is a department store in a large, suburban mall. You have been asked to assist management with a program for 19 full-time sales associates (SAs) in a section of the store. Sales associates are responsible for providing customer service in the store, ensuring customer satisfaction, and making sales. Observations, anecdotal information, and a review of industry standards of sales dollars generated by each sales associate have convinced management and the associates that they are underperforming. Management and the SAs are looking to you for help in finding a solution.

Local market conditions are stable, with competition from a variety of retail stores. Advertising, pricing, and other marketing issues are outside the domain of your work; all of you agree that SA performance, not marketing, is the issue. Sales associates receive above-the-industry average base compensation. An individual-based commission plan was attempted six months ago; the SAs asked management to drop the program when they decided that it caused dysfunctional competition among the SAs, who recognize the need for a more fluid team approach to sales, sales support, and customer satisfaction. That also led to a behavioral survey.

In the survey, assistant managers and the SAs collected observational measures, carefully recording and then classifying SA behaviors. The associates were involved in the study; in fact, they helped self-record and collect the data. Measures were made for all shifts over a representative sales month. Management and the associates agree that the measures are fair and accurate. Behavior was classified as: (1) selling (conversing with customers, assisting with selecting and fitting, registering sales, and completing charge slips), (2) stock support work (arranging and displaying merchandise, tagging and replenishing stock, and packing and unpacking stock), (3) other work-related behavior (giving directions, taking returns, checking credit, answering questions, etc.), (4) idle time (socializing and not working), and (5) absence from the work area. Sales data for each associate has been recorded for each shift. Direct measures of customer satisfaction were not collected. Management will provide you with the full records of these measures shortly. You are not familiar with the specific results of the survey.

Outline your basic plan for effecting change. Include problem definition, standards, measures, controls, an action plan, and recommended follow-up.

Source: Fred Luthans, *Journal of Applied Psychology* 66 (1981), pp. 314–23; and Fred Luthans, *Journal of Organizational Behavior Management* 7 (1985), pp. 23–35.

CHAPTER 16

Managing Production and Operations

After studying this chapter, you should be able to:

❖ Define production and operations.

❖ Discuss the evolution of modern manufacturing.

❖ Explain the role of production and operations managers.

❖ Compare traditional company organizations with cellular organizations.

❖ List the factors that should be considered in selecting a site.

❖ Evaluate computerization's effects on production and operation management functions.

❖ Explain the importance of productivity and quality.

❖ Discuss the importance of safety to productivity and quality.

Flexible Manufacturing—
The Next Frontier

In their book *The Machine That Changed the World,* a group from MIT's International Motor Vehicle Program showed how Japanese automobile companies were much leaner than U.S. auto manufacturers. The book's major message was that while American car companies in the 1970s and 1980s were still using production techniques developed by Henry Ford in 1913, the Japanese were using a new system of *lean manufacturing.* This system involved using less of everything, including inventory, labor, factory space, and investment. Car company executives attributed the Japanese firms' success to lower labor costs. But in 1982 Honda opened the first Japanese plant in the United States and paid U.S. wages; Honda still had lower labor costs than other U.S. plants.

Since then, the world of auto making—and that of many other products—has changed. American manufacturing firms have improved quality dramatically in recent years. In many instances, this has been accomplished by imitating ideas pioneered by the Japanese. Chrysler, for instance, after studying Honda, has cut $1 billion a year in costs. Many U.S. firms are manufacturing better-quality products with fewer workers and less inventory in less time. In many industries Japanese firms are no longer far ahead of U.S. companies. But while the quality gap has been

Assembly line at GM in Lordstown, Ohio.

reduced, the world's best companies are gearing up for the next frontier—flexible manufacturing.

Through a flexible manufacturing system (FMS), a single factory turns out a wide variety of products with computer-controlled robots. The idea behind this system is fairly simple. By reading the market more quickly, manufacturing many different products on the same line, and switching from one to another instantly and at lower costs, a firm can respond to customers quickly and economically. New products reach markets faster, product improvements are made faster, and competitors are left to catch up. Many experts feel flexibility will be the key to competitiveness in the coming decade. Japan and the United States are racing once again, and Japan is ahead. According to Aleda Roth, a manufacturing expert at Duke University, "Most American companies are a generation behind—as far behind as they were on quality." The Japanese take product quality as a given. Without durability, conformance to customer specifications and on-time delivery, a firm can't survive. The Japanese focus is on more and better product features, flexible factories, expanded customer service, and more new product introductions.

Many top U.S. companies (including General Electric, Figgie International, and Motorola) are working hard to develop FMS. General Motors has upgraded its Lordstown, Ohio, plant for flexible manufacturing. There, more cars can be built on one assembly line—450,000 a year—than anyplace else in the world. Robots and other machinery can easily be reprogrammed to build a wide mix of cars to meet changing demand. Workers have also been retrained to handle a variety of tasks instead of repeating a few rote tasks over and over.

Source: Adapted from Erle Norton, "Small, Flexible Plants May Play Crucial Role in U.S. Manufacturing," *The Wall Street Journal,* January 13, 1993, pp. A1–A2; Thomas A. Stewart, "Brace for Japan's Hot New Strategy," *Fortune,* September 21, 1992, pp. 62–74; Bradley A. Steitz, "Detroit's New Strategy to Beat Back Japanese Is to Copy Their Ideas," *The Wall Street Journal,* October 1, 1993, pp. A1, A10; and James B. Treece and Patrick Oster, "General Motors: Open All Night," *Business Week,* June 1, 1992, pp. 82–83.

Businesses strive for the perfect blend of management and machinery. Creating and maintaining that balance is the production and operations manager's task. The job hasn't been easy. In the 1970s double-digit inflation plus a recession dealt heavy blows to industry in the United States and the rest of the industrial world. Consumers could no longer afford to buy as much so they wanted goods that would last. The cost of money soared, and financing the growth of companies became very expensive. Millions of employees lost their jobs. Vulnerable in key areas such as automobiles, textiles, machine tools, and steel, the United States gradually lost market share to competitors from Japan, Germany, Korea, and other nations.

To recapture markets, top management asked production and operations managers to increase production, improve quality, and cut costs. There is much work to be done to complete a turnaround. And technology, competition, products, and worker skills have changed so much in the past 20 years that the production and operations manager's job requires a wide range of analytical and communication skills. These managers must understand sophisticated technology, delegate more, and forfeit some decision-making power. Everything used to be mechanical; now it is more sophisticated, computerized, and modern.[1] As this chapter's opening vignette illustrates, flexible manufacturing will be a key to future competitiveness.

This chapter portrays how production and operations managers do their jobs. We start by describing production and operations, and then give a brief history of manufacturing. We next discuss the production and operations manager's various responsibilities, including organizing the production process, planning site location and layout, controlling materials, purchasing, inventory, and production scheduling. Other topics covered include using technology such as computers and robots, increasing productivity while maintaining quality control, and maintaining safety for employees, consumers, and the environment.

DEFINING PRODUCTION, MANUFACTURING, AND OPERATIONS

production
The total process by which a company creates finished goods or services.

Many people confuse the terms *production, manufacturing*, and *operations*. **Production** is the total process by which a company produces finished goods or services. This process might involve the work, ideas, and plans of the design engineers as well as the production manager, plant manager, plant superintendent, and their crews plus any other department actually involved with bringing forth the product. Table 16–1 illustrates different types of businesses, products, and the processes involved. Production isn't limited to the manufacture of goods; it applies to both the service and manufacturing sectors of the economy. For example, a company might produce shampoo and cream rinse for hair, which are manufactured goods; another company might operate a chain of hair salons, which produce a service. The word *production* can also be used to name the total amount of product brought forth, as in the statement "Total production increased by 20 percent in 1990."

	TABLE 16-1	PRODUCTION PROCESSES FOR DIFFERENT ORGANIZATIONS	
Organization	Inputs	Production Processes	Outputs or Products (Type)
Magazine publisher	Information in various forms (written, verbal, and photo or art pictorials), labor, energy, capital, ink, paper, tools, equipment, technology	Planning, budgeting, scheduling, design and layout, writing, editing, typesetting, art and photo preparation, management control, printing, folding, cutting, binding, shipping on time	Magazines (non-durable goods)
Hair-styling salon	Clients, hair knowledge, skills, information, hair care supplies, tools, technology, equipment, labor, energy, capital, water	Planning, budgeting, scheduling, materials ordering and handling, design, hair preparation, washing, conditioning, coloring, styling, meeting schedules, maintaining customer satisfaction (quality control)	Personal hair care (service)
Steel conduit manufacturer	Steel, chemicals, labor, energy, capital, tools, technology, equipment, water, location	Planning, budgeting, scheduling, materials ordering and handling, metal processing, labor organization, employee relations and safety, quality control, forming, cooling, storage and distribution, meeting schedules	Steel wire and pipe products (durable goods)

Manufacturing refers only to the physical process of producing goods; services are not manufactured. The word *manufacturing* comes from the ancient Latin words *manu* (hand) and *factor* (create or make)—in other words, handmade. In ancient Rome distinguishing between machine-made and handmade was not an issue; all goods were handmade. If someone sang for the Romans, it was a service; if someone crafted a brand new jar for storing olive oil, it was a manufactured good, something created by the work of hands.

Operations are the functions needed to keep the company producing and delivering. They're literally any function or series of functions enacted to carry out a strategic plan. In a firm such as Ford Motor, operations usually include purchasing, materials management, production, inventory and quality control, maintenance and manufacturing engineering, and plant management. Operations' importance cannot be overstated if firms—and nations—are to be successful. The tasks involved in producing and delivering a product or service are the value-added elements that build individual, corporate, social, and national wealth.[2] Figure 16–1 shows the activities managed by operations in the traditional plant.

manufacturing
The physical process of producing goods. (Services are not manufactured.)

operations
The functions needed to keep the company producing and delivering. Literally any function or series of functions enacted to carry out a strategic plan.

THE EVOLUTION OF MODERN MANUFACTURING

Until the 19th century, manufacturing was done largely by hand. Modern manufacturing can be traced from its origins in the use of fuel energy and mass production to today's technological innovations being developed throughout the world. A brief discussion of this evolution will help us understand the role of the production and operations manager.

Early Innovations

Several early innovations were crucial in manufacturing's development. Specifically, the use of fuel energy, scientific management, and mass production paved the way for modern manufacturing.

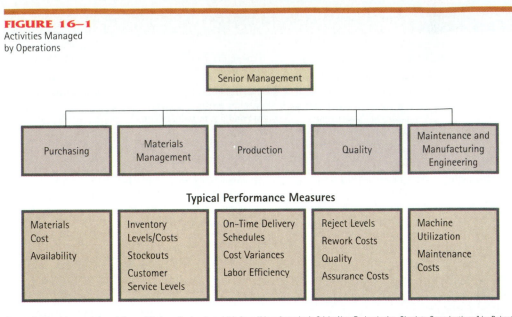

FIGURE 16–1
Activities Managed
by Operations

Source: Reprinted by permission of *Harvard Business Review*. An exhibit from "Manufacturing's Crisis: New Technologies, Obsolete Organizations," by Robert H. Hayes and Ramchandran Jaikumar, September–October 1988. Copyright © 1988 by the President and Fellows of Harvard College; all rights reserved.

FUEL ENERGY ‑ Fuel energy made it possible to use large machinery in factories; large machinery made mass production possible. In the United States steam-powered mills of the 19th century were the first indication of the industrial growth to follow.

SCIENTIFIC MANAGEMENT ‑ As the 20th century began managers became interested in improving production of individuals and of the total organization. Frederick W. Taylor, the father of scientific management, pioneered the use of scientific methods to improve productivity.[3] The essence of his philosophy was that scientific laws govern how much a person can produce per day and that management's function is to discover and use these laws in operating productive systems.

Taylor's approach was not greeted with universal approval. Some unions feared scientific management because it was rigid; unions played almost no role in Taylor's setup of jobs; and they had little idea of Taylor's ultimate goal. In some cases managers embraced Taylor's time study and incentive plans but ignored the need to organize and standardize the work to be done. The result was poorly designed production operations and overworked employees.[4] Despite critics and inept use, Taylor's philosophy and work helped shape work flow systems, incentive packages, and the design and arrangement of jobs. His principles of scientific management are still part of the procedures used in production and operations.

mass production
A system permitting the manufacture of goods in large quantities.

assembly line
A moving conveyor belt that carries work from on workstation to the next.

MASS PRODUCTION ‑ The use of assembly lines and the division of labor—each worker does one small, specialized part of the work—brought about **mass production**, which permits the manufacture of goods in large quantities. Around 1913 a significant breakthrough occurred—the establishment of the moving assembly line for manufacturing Ford cars. In the mass production of early Fords, one worker attached the headlamps, another attached the hood, and so on. Each worker performed one function on each and every car as its chassis came down a moving conveyor belt (**assembly line**). The belt carried work from one workstation to the next. Ford's assembly line began at the entrance to a long shedlike factory building and emerged bearing finished cars at the other end. When a finished auto emerged at the end of the assembly line, workers had given *form utility* to the materials used. Form utility is the value added by giving useful form to materials. A formed car is indeed more useful than a pile of parts!

Standardization of parts was another essential factor in the development of mass production. At Ford each headlamp was exactly the same size and was connected to the same spot on identical car frames as they came down the assembly line. Thus one worker could attach headlamps over and over rather quickly and easily with a standard level of quality because the parts were standardized.

Some workers and social critics complained about the "human machines" who moved their arms and hands over and over again, in the same motions, to the rhythms of the inescapable assembly line. Silent film star Charlie Chaplin even imitated and mocked them in his movie *Modern Times*. But mass production and the assembly line were here to stay. No significant business operation could afford to ignore their technological advances. Their tremendous production capacity would eventually make the United States the most productive and richest nation in the world. Today, innovations continue to take place with the assembly line, such as the computer-controlled and automated paint line of Automotive Moulding Co. (a supplier of exterior components) at its LaGrange, Georgia, plant.[5]

Industrialization and America's Postwar Supremacy

During the 1920s many nations of the world became increasingly industrialized and some of them increasingly competitive. By World War II, Japan and Germany were well-developed industrial nations, but they needed raw materials and markets. With its superior production and manufacturing achievements—coupled with the fact that its production capacity was not destroyed or badly damaged—the United States emerged from World War II as the leader in production and manufacturing.

During the 1950s, 60s, and most of the 70s, American goods and services were the most sought after in the world. The holds of cargo planes and ships carried American cars and trucks, mechanical and electrical parts, chemicals, commodities, clothing, medicines, food products, toys, soft drinks, and recordings to every major port in the world. In those planes' and ships' passenger compartments, American services and technical know-how were being exported too. Doctors, nurses, dentists, X-ray technicians, teachers, broadcasters, engineers, agricultural advisers, and hundreds of other specialists carried their know-how to foreign markets. Soon the workers, entrepreneurs, and governments of those markets began to respond in kind. As Europe and Japan recovered from the war's devastation, they rebuilt their industries. They began to export goods and services, competed with each other, and created an industrial and marketing basis for competing in world markets.

Consumerism and Planned Obsolescence

In the expansion of the late 1950s and the 60s the pace of life—and the pace of production and consumption—escalated with unimagined speed. Salaries rose, prices increased, production rates climbed. By the 70s new and unexpected pressures appeared. Uneasiness and dissatisfaction began to spread. Americans became disillusioned with leadership at national, local, and even trade and labor union levels. With disillusionment came cynicism. Manufacturers talked of planned obsolescence—goods made to last only a short period of time so consumers would have to buy again. Consumers began to question both quality and prices of products and services. Critics also questioned the facilities being used for manufacturing; many factories were old, outdated, inefficient, and dirty.

In addition to leadership, quality, and facility problems, the pressures to produce more and faster made pride of accomplishment all but impossible. Goods and services were in such demand that the prevailing cries were "Never mind about the details—it's got to get out!" and "If there's anything wrong with it, they can send it back!" And they did. In the 1940s products might be returned once in a while; by the mid-70s corporations maintained whole departments solely to handle returns of defective items.[6]

Made in America versus Global Competition

The decline in confidence in once-invincible "made in America" products became a critical issue. The manufacturing community developed a new interest in what production and operations managers do and how to improve it. Today American firms are searching for new ways to manufacture and deliver quality goods and services.

The book *Made in America* starts with the statement, "To live well, a nation must produce well."[7] In the United States fears of economic decline have been linked to the nation's inability to manage production and operations efficiently over the past two decades. Critics claim that America does not produce as well as it should or as well as some other nations (e.g., Germany, Japan, and Korea) do. The Global Exchange on this page examines how U.S. productivity stacks up with the rest of the world.

Why must the United States find new manufacturing methods? Traditional mass production methods have been changing as other countries, such as Germany and Japan, have used alternatives successfully. For example, the Japanese auto industry's success is based on a system different from Detroit's. The Japanese make products that are different in color, shape, and weight for each market segment. They have had to develop manufacturing technologies, job designs, and work flows that allow them to reduce production volume while increasing their speed in bringing new products to market. The Japanese emphasize quality, service, and cost.

GLOBAL EXCHANGE   THE GLOBAL PRODUCTIVITY CHALLENGE

Women sort apricots in a factory in Malatya, Turkey, an area that is one of the world's largest producers of apricots.

—

Says General Electric CEO Jack Welch, "For a company and for a nation, productivity is a matter of survival." Basically, rising productivity means a higher standard of living for a nation. For over 120 years productivity in manufacturing, farming, mining, construction, and transportation has risen in developed countries at an annual rate of 3 to 4 percent. These gains have meant a great deal to these nations and their citizens—increases in disposable income and purchasing power, better education and health care, and more leisure time. In recent years, however, productivity growth in the United States has fallen below this trend that held for most of the 20th century. Thus far in the 1990s, there have been signs of resurgence, with growth of 1.6 percent.

U.S. manufacturing and services rank first in productivity throughout the world. In 1990 the average American worker produced $45,000 worth of goods and services, compared to $37,850 for the average German worker and $34,500 for Japanese workers, who work more hours per year. To retain the world's highest standard of living, American factories, stores, and offices must continue to be the most productive in the world.

Even though America's workers are the world's most productive, the nation's lead is eroding. U.S. productivity is improving more slowly than ever before and slower than its rivals'. Despite efficiency improvements and cost containments of recent years, the United States lags behind nations such as Germany, Japan, Britain, and France in productivity growth. Nations like Korea and Taiwan are also making big gains in productivity, raising their competitive position in the world. And although American business does a good job increasing productivity by cutting inputs like labor, firms need to improve outputs by investing in people and innovation. Finally, productivity growth has been stagnant in the largest section of the economy—services. Many are concerned that unless these trends are reversed, America's standard of living will fall.

No one knows for sure why America's productivity growth has stagnated. As a result of takeovers, process redesign, and downsizing, American manufacturing is more productive than ever. The problem is that American factories are not increasing output as much as this increased efficiency would allow. The more corporate America tries to increase productivity, the more elusive that goal becomes. From 1980 to 1990 U.S. industrial output rose only three-quarters as fast as manufacturing productivity, compared to Japan where both industrial output and productivity grew in tandem. U.S. manufacturers not only cut payrolls, they also cut capital spending and research. One result, for instance, is that on average, a machine tool in an American factory is seven years older than one in Japan; but new computer-controlled tools are much better than older equipment.

Businesses have learned how to cut costs or inputs. But to improve America's productivity problems, outputs must also be increased. The huge federal deficit, a major source of disinvestment, is one place to start. The government must also develop policies that encourage capital formation, research, training, education, and entrepreneurship. Investments must also be made in workers. Not only are educated and highly trained people more productive; they also attract better jobs.

Source: Adapted from Alfred F. Smith III, "U.S. Productivity: Down, But Not Out," *AMA Banking Journal*, February 1994, pp. 21–22; Thomas A. Stewart, "U.S. Productivity: First But Fading," *Fortune*, October 19, 1992, pp. 54–57; Peter F. Drucker, "The New Productivity Challenge," *Harvard Business Review*, November–December 1991, pp. 69–79; and Karen Pennar, "The Productivity Paradox," *Business Week*, June 6, 1988, pp. 100–2.

Henry Ford's comment, "The customer can have any color as long as it's black," is often quoted to illustrate that Ford didn't understand his customers. But according to Peter Drucker, few people understand what Ford was actually saying: flexibility costs time and money, and the customer won't pay for it.[8] General Motors, by offering customers both colors and annual model changes at no additional cost, was able to beat Ford.

Today most manufacturers have learned to do what GM did in the mid-1920s, and some have gone even further in combining flexibility and standardization. Yet some manufacturing people continue to think, like Henry Ford, you can have standardization at low cost or flexibility at high cost, but not both. The successful factory of the future will have both at low cost. Put another way, craftsmanship has returned. Consumers will order high-quality products to their specifications. But instead of being made by hand, the products will be produced in flexible, high-tech factories.

How to increase flexibility and speed product development is a top priority of all managers, especially those in production and operations. Compaq, Boeing, Merck, Microsoft, Honda, 3M, and Toyota are known for their ability to develop, manufacture, and market what consumers want, when they want it, at an affordable price for a specific group of customers. Typically these innovative product developers are global, and 35 to 70 percent of their sales come from outside their home market.[9]

In the search for new and better manufacturing methods, production and operations managers are playing more significant roles in their organizations. As markets and technologies globalize, these managers increasingly need to understand foreign customers' needs, preferences, and price limitations. The basis for successful global competition lies in the successful adaptation of the production and operations functions of American business. Unless production and operations can restore the stature of goods and services made in the United States, the economic quality of American life is likely to suffer. Products that cannot compete in the global market in terms of quality and price are unacceptable for the future of U.S. business.

THE ROLE OF THE PRODUCTION AND OPERATIONS MANAGER

Production and operations managers are responsible for producing the goods that business needs to sell. There are many kinds of production and operation systems, just as there are many kinds of products—goods and services—wanted by people in the marketplace. Production and operations vary in size from a single person in a very small company like family-owned baker L'Madiellenes to thousands of employees in a huge multinational corporation such as Procter & Gamble.

The production goals of every business focus on producing products—and producing the best, the fastest, and at the least cost. Thus the production and operations manager must produce with effectiveness and efficiency while maintaining quality control. Richard Bodine, president of Bodine Corporation, knows about speed, efficiency, and effectiveness. He manufactures assembly lines for organizations. His firm is now working on an electro-mechanical system that will assemble 2,400 alkaline batteries per hour. Bodine manufactures about 30 machines a year at a rate that is fast, efficient, and results in high quality.[10]

A production and operations manager's job is to see that the operations necessary to achieve the company's production goals are carried out. To do this, these managers oversee a number of company operations. Typical functions include:

Product planning.

Site location and layout.

Inventory control.

Purchasing and materials management.

Manufacturing and production.

Production control.

Quality control.

Plant management.

In moderate-sized firms, the production and operations manager is often a vice president who reports directly to top management; managers or supervisors representing the preceding functions report to the production and operations manager.

Production and operations managers have product planning responsibilities such as preparing forecasts, schedules, and budgets in collaboration with top management, finance, and marketing. In start-up operations, they oversee site location and layout. They also oversee the hiring, training, and development of personnel for departments involved with production and operations. Working with all other departments in the company—especially marketing, physical distribution, warehousing, and shipping—is important as well.

Organizing the Production Process

Chapter 9 presented different ways to organize, depending on needs, types of production, strengths and weaknesses of company managers, and the like. Titles vary also. The inventory control manager in one company may be called the purchasing and inventory control manager in another company. Knowing the exact titles and type of organization in place enables managers to have appropriate expectations and communicate effectively. Production and operations managers must fit into different types of organizations.

TRADITIONAL ORGANIZATIONS - The organization chart in Figure 16–2 follows the traditional or job-shop form. It gives each manager a specific area of authority and responsibility; but it can also pit managers against each other. For example, if a purchasing manager has budgeted $50,000 for a quantity of a specific part and the inventory control manager must order them on a rush basis for $60,000, the purchasing manager's responsibility and authority are subordinated to the inventory manager's needs. Andy Grove (CEO of Intel, the world's largest semiconductor company) believes that companies structured the traditional way will have a difficult time thriving in the future.[11]

Figure 16–2 shows typical departments in this type of organization and some common measures used in judging departmental performance. For example, the quality manager's performance would be appraised on the basis of costs, defect levels, and rework costs.

CELLULAR ORGANIZATION - In the past decade more and more companies have begun to use a cellular organization. Here workers cooperate in teams (cells) to manufacture total products or subassemblies. Each cell is responsible for the quality and quantity of its products. Each has the authority to make adjustments to improve performance and product quality. Figure 16–3 illustrates how, in the cellular arrangement, machines are arranged to handle all the operations needed to assemble the products. The parts follow a path through each cell to final assembly.

The basic difference between the cellular and the traditional organization is that workers in the cells are all responsible for their output. The linear competitiveness of the traditional structure is avoided. Instead each individual is pressured to perform so that the group will succeed. Cells tend to be tightly self-monitoring and self-correcting. In a cellular organization companies tend to have much smaller staffs overall, with middle management positions reduced and lean management numbers at the top.

PROCESS AND PROJECT MANUFACTURING - How a company organizes may be related to the type of manufacturing carried on. *Process manufacturing*, for example, is carried on in various forms. This type of manufacturing applies various processes, or methods, to change materials into finished goods.

❖ The *assembly process* puts parts together to form whole products, such as cars and trucks.

❖ The *continuous process* uses mass production techniques to make many items of one kind, such as roller bearings, nuts, or bolts.

FIGURE 16–2
Traditional Manufacturing
Organization

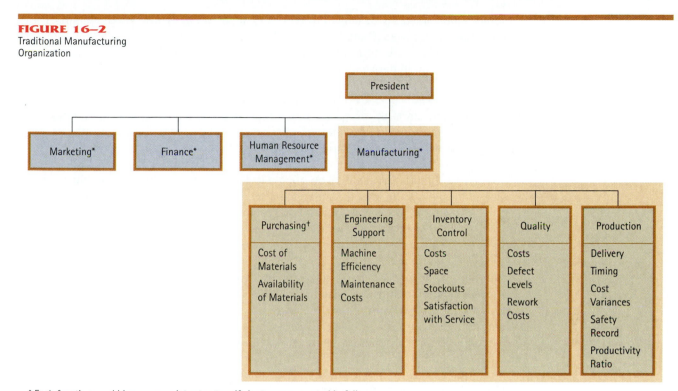

* Each function would have a complete structure if chart were presented in full.
† Examples of performance measures are shown below each departmental grouping.

FIGURE 16–3
Cellular Manufacturing Layout

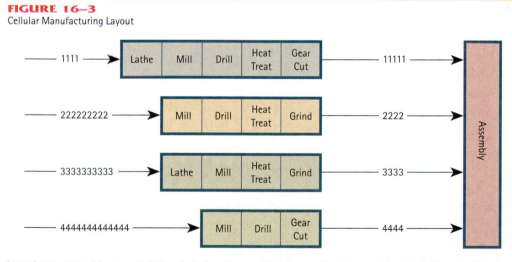

❖ *Intermittent processing* uses one process for a batch of goods, and then changes processes to produce goods having some differences from the earlier batches (e.g., stainless steel restaurant kitchen drainboards and fitted metal cabinets).

❖ The *analytic process* breaks down materials into components to extract the parts needed, as in oil refining and smelting.

❖ The *synthetic process* brings items together to create an entirely different product. For example, in the synthetic fabric industry and the rubber industry, materials are changed by chemical and heat processes before being formed.

❖ The *extractive process* removes a product from raw material, as in coal mining.

Project manufacturing usually involves very large projects for which materials and workers must be removed. There is no assembly line or workstation layout within a factory or shop; the product is built in place. Examples include the building of large ships, large printing presses, and high-rise offices.

Planning Site Location and Layout

When a company starts up or opens a new branch, the production and operations manager is heavily involved in planning the site location and layout. Company officers, engineers, and heads of departments add their ideas and lists of requirements.

SITE SELECTION - A site may be bought or leased with or without a building already in place. If the site is to be leased, all managers involved should make their plans and submit their needs to a commercial or industrial real estate broker. The broker then submits a list of properties available in the area within the price range required. Sites may come with a "build to suit" lease or may be a turnkey location whose building and interior facilities are already completed.

The type of business dictates the kind of facility. Service sector businesses often require small office facilities in heavy-traffic areas convenient to customers or to the electronic communications and other services the business itself requires. Heavy industry, on the other hand, requires vast space near ship operations as well as transportation to market. A production and operations manager's plan for site location considers most if not all of the following factors:

❖ Economies of cost or other economic advantages for land, buildings, or units.
❖ Taxes, insurance, and other costs.
❖ Proximity to related industries and suppliers, warehouses, and/or service operations.
❖ Availability of an appropriate labor force, considering such factors as quality and cost.
❖ Availability of economical transportation for materials and supplies as well as for finished goods.
❖ Proximity to market for goods.
❖ Air and water conditions.
❖ Proximity to plentiful, economical energy services.
❖ Climate and environment that's in line with the industry's needs and is amenable to employees' lifestyle.
❖ Ample space for current and future needs of firm.
❖ Proximity to such employee needs as housing, schools, mass transportation, religious facilities, day care, shopping, and recreational facilities.
❖ Community receptiveness.

Some site choices may be based on the overriding advantages of one factor, such as availability of labor or market, or low cost of land. In recent years, for example, many American companies have chosen to locate in Mexico because of the low costs of facilities, land, and labor. Clothing manufacturers have settled in Korea and Taiwan because of abundant cheap labor. Another increasingly popular production site is eastern Europe. Major changes in the business climate and a large untapped market have made the former Soviet Union, Poland, Hungary, and other central and eastern European countries intriguing options for joint ventures and new plants.

SITE LAYOUT - Just as it dictates the kind and location of facility, the type of business will determine the layout of the site selected. For each kind of business, production and operations managers must meet different needs. Different kinds of production require varying space for assembly lines, workstations, or other specific arrangements for work layouts.

The manager must plan the layout in detail before the site is chosen. The plan must account for the needed square footage, work areas, office and conference areas, storage, and shipping needs. To draw up specific plans, managers use templates, models, drawings, and the latest computer techniques.

The case of a small manufacturer in a Chicago suburb illustrates how site layout decisions are made. After carefully considering a number of sites, management decided on the suburban Chicago location, which had around 100,000 square feet of interior space plus three recessed loading docks and one enclosed loading dock. The company distributes finished goods by direct mail and in private-label batches for other companies. All finished goods are transported by truck from the facility. The interior layout required office space for top management, finance, marketing, design and pattern making, conferences, order handling, customer service, billing, accounting, and personnel management. In addition, the firm needed work areas for cutting, assembling, sewing, finishing, labeling, storing, and packing and shipping. Due to humidity and extreme temperatures, all interior work and storage areas required heating and air-conditioning. At least one enclosed loading dock was required for shipping in subzero temperatures or heavy rain and snow. The shape and layout of the building chosen was well suited to the company's particular kind of assembly process.

Managing Materials, Purchasing, and Inventory

Materials management, purchasing, and inventory control cover the planning, ordering, and internal storage and distribution of supplies and materials needed for production. Other names used for these areas include *material handling, procurement, supply room management,* and *inventory management.*

Some variations occur in the way authority and responsibility are organized. In some companies the purchasing department purchases every good or service bought from outside sources. In others the purchasing function covers only those materials and supplies used in the actual production process.

In large companies the materials manager may oversee the functions of purchasing and inventory control, or inventory control may be part of production control, depending on its scope. Inventory control may handle only inventory of components and subassemblies, or it may cover all inventories—of supplies, raw materials, components, and subassemblies, and even finished products.

In recent years two important systems have been created to handle materials management and inventory control. Just-in-time (JIT) inventory control and materials requirements planning (MRP) have greatly refined the degree to which materials and inventory control can be managed and scheduled.

The just-in-time inventory control approach was developed by Taiichi Ohno at Toyota Motor Company of Japan.[12] **Just-in-time (JIT) manufacturing** requires that the exact quantity of defect-free raw materials, parts, and subassemblies are produced just-in-time for the next stage of the manufacturing process. This concept extends backward to suppliers and forward to the final customer. JIT's goal is to match the output of manufacturing with market demand, eliminating waste.[13]

An efficient JIT system can result in low inventories of purchased parts and raw materials, work in process, and finished goods. It saves warehouse and work area space while lowering the costs of carrying large inventories. Reducing inventory can also expose other production problems. A sometimes tardy supplier can be covered if the firm carries a large inventory. Smaller inventories spotlight the efficiency of all sources. A delinquent supplier will be replaced.

In today's economy, it is common for many customers to expect next-day delivery, even on hard-to-locate parts and materials.[14] National Semiconductor has reduced its delivery time 47 percent, cut distribution costs 2.5 percent, and increased sales by 34 percent using a JIT system.[15] When production and parts deliveries are organized on a JIT basis, quality is critical. Defective parts slow the process and defeat the very purpose of JIT. As noted in Chapter 1, *zero defects* (ZD) is a performance standard developed by Philip B. Crosby to address some organizations' attitudes that mistakes are human and acceptable.[16] By committing themselves to avoiding errors, people can move closer to the goal of zero defects. ZD's aim is to build quality into a product and eliminate costly inspections after production. Jaguar, for instance, reduced assembly line defects by 80 percent in two years.[17] Team-based

just-in-time (JIT) manufacturing

A system requiring that the exact quantity of defect-free raw materials, parts, and subassemblies are produced just in time for the next stage of the manufacturing process.

work groups and quality management are generally part of JIT manufacturing. Because JIT systems have little margin for error, both upstream workstations and suppliers outside the organization must deliver on time in the right quantity with no defects.

Since JIT systems have little finished goods inventory, machine breakdowns are costly. Thus careful attention to maintaining efficient equipment becomes a high priority. Machines must be in top working order to fulfill the JIT demands. A top-quality repair team that can move into immediate action must be available if JIT is to work effectively.

materials requirements planning (MRP)
A computer-driven system for analyzing and projecting materials needs and then scheduling their arrival at the work site at the right time.

Materials requirements planning (MRP) is a computer-driven system for analyzing and projecting materials needs and then scheduling their arrival at the right work site at the right time in the right quantities.[18] MRP works closely with the master production schedule (which we'll discuss shortly) and takes into account such variables as lead time in ordering.

MRP focuses on "getting the right materials to the right place at the right time." In most cases, making "right" decisions requires a computer to handle all of the materials and components involved. The MRP program analyzes data from inventory, the master production schedule, and the bill of materials. The output includes inventory status, planned order timing, and changes in due dates because of rescheduling.

MRP is used in companies involved in assembly operations. Firms that produce large volumes of tools, generators, turbines, appliances, and motors are particularly attracted to MRP. It is also useful in companies that order a high number of units.

Together JIT and MRP provide a system that saves time and dollars. They have helped managers control the amount of inventory required to keep production moving smoothly. With JIT and MRP, suppliers of parts and subassemblies can plan in much closer time tolerances. In very large operations, such as the Detroit auto assemblies, nearby suppliers are actually hooked up by computer to follow the progress of assembly line work. From this vantage point, their trucks can arrive nearly at the moment the materials are needed. Lead times on orders are greatly reduced, and costs of storing inventory drop sharply.

Scheduling

The production, or manufacturing, manager is responsible for the company's main goal: producing goods in the amounts and sequence planned and on schedule. This function is critical to the firm's success. Three elements of management—planning, organizing, and controlling—can be clearly seen in the production manager's tasks. Planning the use of labor, facilities, and materials for fulfilling the production schedule is a complex, ongoing task. The manager will usually have more than one product to plan for, with the resultant needs for changes in materials, production processes, energy, and labor.

A *master production schedule* must be created. It will show when the manager plans to produce each product and in what quantities. The production manager is responsible for meeting the dates, quantities, and cost commitments on the schedule. The master schedule will affect the efforts and success of every department in the company. Therefore it should also reflect the needs of the finance, marketing, shipping, and all other departments.

Production managers must plan for flexibility to be able to change from one process to another on short notice. They may use a number of tactics to meet emergencies or make changes in the plan. Requesting overtime, hiring temporary workers, cross-training workers so they can do more than one job, and many other methods are available.

program evaluation and review technique (PERT) chart
A graphical system for tracking the events that must take place to accomplish a task.

Flexibility as well as adherence to schedule can be achieved with the use of the **program evaluation and review technique (PERT) chart**. PERT was developed in the 1950s from the joint efforts of Lockheed Aircraft, the U.S. Navy Special Projects Office, and the consulting firm of Booz Allen & Hamilton. They were working on the Polaris missile project and wanted to provide the United States with an advantage over what was then the Soviet Union in time of completion.

An important part of PERT is the construction of a chart, a graphical system for tracking events that must take place to accomplish a task. A PERT chart is one of the most effective tools of modern management. To create one, five steps are followed:

1. Break the project to be accomplished into events or completed actions; label each with the amount of time needed to do it.

2. List the first event of the task.
3. List the event that follows the first one; draw a line with an arrow from the first event to the next one, showing the sequence. (If two events follow, draw arrows to both events to show that one event leads to two, or even more, events.)
4. Chart all the events needed to complete the project in the same way, to completion.
5. Label the arrows with the amount of time it takes to complete each activity.

Figure 16–4 presents a PERT chart for the replacement of a machine in a manufacturing plant. The letters represent the activities necessary to replace the machine. The numbers in the circles represent completed activities, called events; number 1 is the origin of the project. For instance, B represents securing bids and awarding contracts; 3 represents that bids have been secured and contracts awarded. Each activity is also assigned an expected time for completion; removing existing equipment is expected to take two weeks.

As Figure 16–4 shows, some activities must be completed before others, while some can be completed simultaneously. The prerequisites are shown in the figure. For example, specifications must be prepared and old equipment must be removed before painting. All activities must be accomplished before the final event, rescheduling production. The longest path from start to completion of the project in terms of time needed to complete the activities is called the *critical path*. In this case, the critical path is 1-2-3-6-7-8, which takes 20 days. Thus the project cannot be completed in less than 20 days.

The PERT chart can be used to track exactly where a product or project is in its development and what needs to be done next to keep it on its path. Bottlenecks can be identified and corrected. For example, if the third event in a sequence always involves a delay, the production manager can identify the problem and make changes as needed.

The PERT chart is only as good in planning as its user's ability to identify all the steps in a chain of events. Because it helps break down the production tasks into clearly separate segments, PERT also helps to identify needs and uses for computerized manufacturing programs, temporary workers, and overtime techniques. This breakdown is helpful in the current climate of rapid change in production techniques, numbers of products, and kinds of new products. The public presents an ever-ready market for newer, more appealing products; getting the products to the consumer is up to the production staff. In the recent past

FIGURE 16–4
Example of a PERT Chart

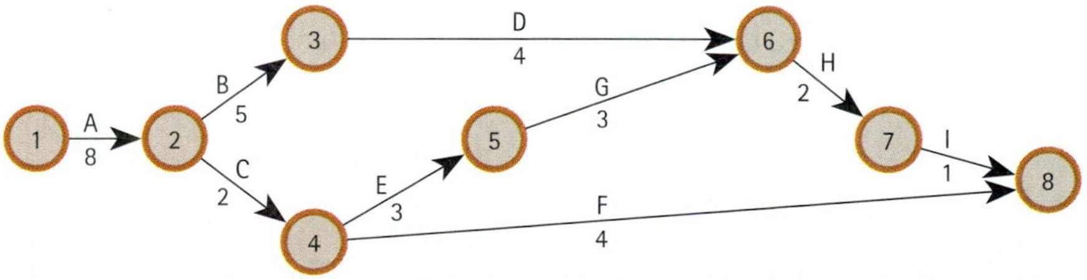

Activity	Description	Completion Time (Days)	Prerequisites
A	Prepare Specifications	8	None
B	Secure Bids and Award Contracts	5	A
C	Remove Existing Equipment	2	A
D	Train Operators for New Machine	4	A, B
E	Electrical Modifications	3	A, C
F	Paint	4	A, C
G	Install Machine	3	A, C, E
H	Test Machine	2	A, B, D
I	Reschedule Production	1	A, B, D, H

companies could expect to bring out a new product line or new models in the line no more frequently than every year. Now in many industries new products are inserted into the master schedule—and from there into the marketplace—as fast as they can be designed.

PRODUCTION TECHNOLOGY

computer-aided design (CAD)
The use of computers to draw plans for a product or service.

computer-aided engineering (CAE)
The use of computers to plan engineering processes and test designs.

Increased production is achieved not only through efficient planning; computers have added flexibility and speed to the production process. **Computer-aided design (CAD)** is the use of computers to draw plans for a product or service. CAD programs offer smart analysis functions that can speed up the development cycle for new products.[19] Over 84 percent of U.S. manufacturers responding to a survey by the National Association of Manufacturers indicated that they employ CAD.[20] **Computer-aided engineering (CAE)** is the use of computers to plan engineering processes and test designs. Many large companies are using CAE up front to greatly shorten product development cycles and save on the cost of developing models or prototypes.[21] CAD and CAE have enabled the development of millions of new designs. Designs can be drawn, extended, contracted, added to, or taken from—all within the computer. Engineers can test designs for function and stress and try out variations without the cost or risk of building models or samples. Drafters using CAD can perform many of these tasks once the initial design is developed. The computer does much of the calculation and the drawing in two or three dimensions as needed.

CAD has been used to design products ranging from buildings to potato chips. Dimension Measurement System Inc. has developed a technology that uses CAD to produce suits made to measure. Light is projected onto a prospective buyer from three directions, and digital cameras capture images from various angles. A computer processes these inputs to get three-dimensional contours of the body. These measurements are sent to a CAD pattern maker made by Microdynamics Inc. The pattern maker modifies standard patterns for individual measurements, the CAD data are downloaded to an automatic fabric cutter, and workers sew the garment.[22]

computer-aided manufacturing (CAM)
The use of computers for controlling the operation of traditional, modified, and electronic machines, including robots.

Computer-aided manufacturing (CAM) includes the use of computers for controlling the operation of traditional, modified, and electronic machines, including robots. CAD/CAM systems make it easier for plants to make a wide variety of products and undertake production-line changeovers in short periods of time.[23] The Marlboro McLaren Mercedes Formula One racing team designed a car in only three months using CAD/CAM.[24] In Japan the Fujitsu plant in Akashi was using robots effectively in the 1980s. The plant specializes in sheet metal manufacture, producing more than 100,000 parts each month for 1,500 different products. The production order, specifying the parts, the number, and the materials to be used, is given to the main computer. The computer then selects the most efficient way to make the parts and creates a layout for the automated shear machines and punch presses to follow. The Fujitsu plant is estimated to be 40 percent more productive with the CAM system, saving approximately $10,000 worth of material a month.

Robotics

robot
A computerized, reprogrammable, multifunctional machine that can manipulate materials and objects in performing particular tasks.

In the United States the auto industry is the best-known user of robots for manufacture. A **robot** is a computerized, reprogrammable, multifunctional machine that can manipulate materials and objects in performing particular tasks. Robots paint, sand, test, and weld car parts; robots track individual cars on the assembly line and perform dozens of repetitive, exacting, unwieldy, or dangerous tasks.[25]

In 1988 approximately 51 percent of robots in operation in the United States were used in the auto industry. By 1995 that percentage fell to about 26 percent as robot usage increased in the service sector and other areas. But robots will probably continue to play a significant role in auto production. According to the Robotic Industries Association, U.S.-based robotics firms booked more orders—3,742 robots—in the first quarter of 1995 than in any previous quarter.[26]

The ability to manipulate other objects makes a robot unique compared to other kinds of computerized machinery. Toshiba Corp. uses robots to manipulate the numerous controls on oscilloscopes (engineers' instruments for testing the performance of electronic devices). This lets human engineers concentrate on less tedious and more creative work.[27] Robots also can perform the same tasks, such as welding a piece in place over and over again, hundreds and hundreds of times, without becoming tired or being endangered, as human workers would be in the same function. Robots are therefore used especially in situations that are too repetitive or dangerous for human beings. For example, a robot can be more efficient, consistent, and cost-effective than its human counterpart in the task of opening and closing a car door thousands of times. In applying acid to the surface of metal parts, a robot can perform at a constant pace for thousands of hours without danger or exhaustion.

From the early, simple machines like automated mail delivery carts to the sensor-monitored "intelligent" machines of today, robotics has made a rapid ascent. An estimated 33,000 robots are currently at work in American industry, most of them in the auto, appliance, aerospace, chemical, electronics, food processing, home furnishings, pharmaceuticals, and textiles manufacturing areas. Technologies such as machine vision and tactile sensing promise to expand robot use in service industries such as education, health care, security, and training and development.

Flexible Manufacturing Systems

Robots and other computerized machines programmed to switch fairly easily from producing one kind of product to another can be grouped in a **flexible manufacturing system (FMS)**. Parts and materials flow to the operation by automated equipment, and finished products are removed automatically. Their flexibility allows FMS to be used for just-in-time inventory control projects as well as for small batches of customized parts or products without raising costs drastically. The type of flexibility a company should emphasize depends strongly on the competitive environment of the industry.[28]

flexible manufacturing systems (FMS)
A grouping of robots and other computerized machines programmed to switch fairly easily from producing one kind of product to another.

The National Bicycle Industrial Co., a subsidiary of Japanese electronics giant Matsushita, has used FMS with great success. Robots, computers, and people work together to make production flexible and responsive.[29] With 20 employees and a design-smart computer, the firm can produce any of 11,231,862 variations of 18 models of racing, road, and mountain bikes in 199 color patterns and about as many sizes as there are people. Production doesn't start until an order is placed. But within two weeks, the customer is riding her personalized bike.

National Bicycle designs and manufactures the bicycle to fit the customer's size, shape, and strength. The bicycle store mails or faxes the specifications to the firm. A computer operator punches the data into a microcomputer. The bicycle is bar coded for one customer. The bar code is fed into the computer that instructs a robot where on the frame to build or what color the bicycle should be painted. The customer's name is imprinted on the frame. A custom-made, personalized bike brings many smiles to a happy customer. Personalized, flexibly manufactured bicycles sell for $545 to $3,200, compared with $250 to $510 for standard bicycles.

IMPROVING QUALITY

Computers, JIT systems, production schedules, and robots are all used in production and operations to improve quality, cost, service, and productivity. Improvements in productivity and quality have long-term effects on a firm's success.

The term *quality* and its implications are now very important throughout the industrialized world. Germans brag about their cars' quality. The Swiss praise the quality of their watches. The quality of Italian marble and tile work sets the standard for everyone in that industry. At times quality refers to workmanship or an evaluation such as the Good Housekeeping Seal of Approval. From the consumer's perspective, quality is best described as "perceived excellence." It is what a person requires from the product or service. Thus quality is the conformance to customer requirements. This involves finding out what the customer wants, writing it down, training everyone to accomplish it, and then delivering it to the customer on time.[30]

The perception of quality generally depends on how well the product or service meets the evaluator's specifications and requirements. In judging the quality of a Honda Accord or a Pontiac Bonneville, a car buyer may compare the vehicles on performance, features, reliability, aesthetics, and other requirements before making the purchase decision. Whether the buyer purchases a second Honda or a Pontiac three years later will depend on how well the first car meets his expectations of quality.

As we discussed earlier in this chapter, the quality of American goods—unquestioned before and just after World War II—slipped in the 1960s, 70s, and 80s. Many reasons have been advanced for this. The postwar economic boom created a seemingly ever-expanding market as demand for goods and services rose. Consumers—looking for the latest models in cars, cameras, tape recorders, and televisions—bought more and faster. Technological change accelerated and business hurried to keep pace, while workers complained they had no time or authority to maintain quality. In the midst of plenty, imperfections in the production process began to erode consumers' confidence and industry's optimism.

As American-made goods no longer were seen as top-quality, foreign competitors' products began to gain acceptance as meeting top-quality standards. In major markets (cars, steel, electronics), this loss of sales cut deeply into the U.S. economy.

Greater competition increases the importance of high quality. For example, foreign competitors—Toyota, BMW, Daimler-Benz, and Volvo—have stimulated the American auto industry's current quality improvements. Meanwhile the Japanese are again redefining and expanding the notion of quality. Their newest concept is called *miryokuteki hindshitsu*: making cars that are more than reliable—cars that fascinate, bewitch, and delight.[31] Japanese engineers are now working to give each car a special look, sound, and feel without sacrificing reliability. They call this the "second phase of quality."

Former Chrysler chairman Lee Iacocca didn't surrender the auto market to the Japanese—or to the Germans, French, Italians, or Swedes. He claimed, "Our cars are every bit as good as the Japanese." And recent recalls of Japanese products, including cars, do raise questions about consistency of quality. Four electronic giants—Sony, Matsushita Electric, Pioneer Electronics, and Toshiba—recalled hundreds of thousands of color TV sets in 1990.[32] Seiko Epson recalled laptop computers that smoked. Toyota had to recall thousands of luxury Lexus cars in the United States because of defects in the cruise control mechanism and in a brake light. Nissan recalled nearly 38,000 cars in Japan. Nonetheless, while Honda Motor Co. recalled one car for every 24 it sold in 1991, both Ford and Chrysler recalled more than three fourths of those they sold.[33] These recalls underscore the principle that working on quality is a continual process. If a product is manufactured correctly in the first place (zero defects), there won't be a recall.

Consumer pressure, lost market share, good business thinking, and competition, then, all motivate companies (whatever their nationality) to focus on quality.

Managing Quality Control

The quality control manager may be responsible for defining standards with exact specifications or for issuing guidelines regarding exact specifications set by an outside agency. Standards are set by hundreds of regulating agencies such as the federal Food and Drug Administration (FDA) and Bureau of Standards. These standards affect color, size, shape, taste, texture, durability, and many other properties of goods produced in the United States. From toothpaste to rocket fuel, American products are tested and standardized to a greater degree than any others in the world. Government contracts can be lost and consumer purchasing can fall rapidly if standards are not met.

The quality control manager must select or devise procedures to test the quality of products, establish troubleshooting procedures, pinpoint causes of any defects in products, and correct any problems rapidly to minimize losses. Customer complaints or returns of defective products must also be analyzed so that necessary corrections can be made.

Complaints and returns from customers can build up and result in lost customers and sales. Therefore a quality control expert must develop a system that reduces the chances that low-quality products or services get to the customers. A four-step program can help keep the perception of poor quality from being associated with the company.

Step 1: Define quality characteristics. The first step involves defining the quality characteristics desired by the customer or client; this means finding out what customers want. Examining customer preferences, technical specifications, marketing suggestions, and competitive products provides necessary information. Customer preferences are extremely significant since repeat sales likely depend on a reasonable degree of customer satisfaction. A Rolex watch customer wants accuracy, a long service life, and style. But a Timex watch customer has other quality standards and preferences. The Timex keeps reasonably accurate time and sells at a much lower price than the Rolex. The quality characteristics of Rolex watches meet and depend on different customer preferences than the quality characteristics of Timex watches.

Step 2: Establish quality standards. Once the quality characteristics have been defined, the next step is to establish the desired quality levels. Quality standards serve as the reference point for comparing the ideal to what actually exists. Standards for factors such as size, color, weight, texture, accuracy, reliability, time of delivery, and support are set by management.

The cost of achieving and sustaining a specific level of quality must be estimated and compared to the cost of potential rejections. Figure 16–5 represents what is often called the *quality funnel principle*: the closer to the start of the production process, the lower the cost of rejection. As the product or service progresses through the process, more resources are invested; the greater the amount of resources invested, the higher the cost of rejection. The greater cost is incurred when the customer or client is the source of rejection. In that case the cost of processing the complaint and the cost of lost goodwill are added to the cost of resources. For example, complaints about Ford's Pinto were costly in the form of lost repeat sales, customer lawsuits, and recalls to repair defective parts.

In 1979 Crosby's book, *Quality Is Free*, introduced the quality program he established at ITT.[34] Crosby challenged the notion that quality reduces the bottom line. Rather, quality is free, but suffers from the lack of an obvious method of measurement. He argues that the real costs that detract from the bottom line are the costs of inspection and fixing problems plus all other costs associated with not doing jobs right the first time. Nonconformance to customer requirements wastes money. By stating the standards of management in a way that no one can misunderstand them—zero defects—quality becomes the goal of everyone in the organization.

FIGURE 16–5
The Quality Funnel Principle

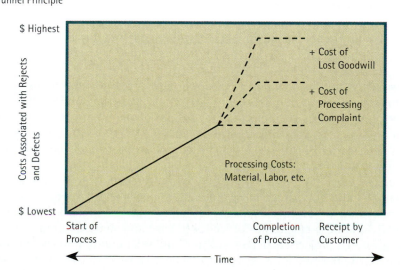

Source: David Bain, *The Productivity Prescription: The Manager's Guide to Improving Productivity and Profits.* © 1982. Reprinted with permission of McGraw-Hill, Inc.

In 1987 the International Organization for Standardization published the ISO-9000 series of quality standards. The ISO standards are international guidelines for the design and development, production, final inspection and testing, installation, and servicing of products, processes, and services.[35] To register, a company must document its quality systems and go through a third-party audit of its manufacturing and customer service processes.[36] ISO-9000 is evidence of a global movement toward quality. Although only 621 U.S. firms had registered for ISO-9000 as of 1993, these standards have gained widespread acceptance in Europe. Approximately 20,000 firms from European Community countries are registered under ISO-9000. A growing worldwide acceptance of ISO-9000 and the feeling that registration will be required to do business in Europe and elsewhere are expected to increase the number of U.S. companies that adopt the standards.

Step 3: Develop quality review program. The methods for quality review, where and by whom reviews will be reported and analyzed, and other review procedures must be formalized. One important decision involves how many products will be checked for quality. Will all products be inspected or only a representative sampling? The greater the number of products inspected, the greater the costs associated with quality review. Representative sampling is less costly but creates (1) the risk that more low-quality products will get into customers' hands, (2) a greater likelihood that customer goodwill can be tarnished, and (3) the need to decide on what number of defects or poor-quality products will be acceptable.

Sampling procedures can take many forms. Some organizations use a random spot check. A random selection of the product is inspected for quality. When a formal random spot check is used, the results can be meaningful and can provide adequate control. Other forms of sampling plans using statistical analysis are also available.[37] Decisions about which plan to use involve making inferences about the entire procedure, based on samples. Representative sampling presupposes that defective products will occasionally slip through the quality check network.

Step 4: Build quality commitment. A commitment to quality among an organization's work force has three ingredients:

❖ *Quality focus.* From top management to operating employees, all employees must sincerely believe that quality of all outputs is the accepted practice. Satisfying customer or client quality needs must be the goal of all employees.
❖ *Quality intelligence.* Employees must be aware of the acceptable quality standards and how those standards can be met.
❖ *Quality skills.* Employees must have the skills and abilities to achieve the quality standards set by management.

Employees' commitment to producing the high-quality output is imperative.[38] It can be obtained with motivational programs. The numerous approaches include job enrichment, goal setting, positive reinforcement, and team development. Participative management (an approach with many adherents) involves employees in important management decisions.

Benchmarking

American industry today is competing globally, as companies worldwide are eyeing global markets rather than relying on domestic markets. The United States must sell abroad to pay for the goods and services it purchases abroad and for the money it has borrowed from abroad. To compete successfully for foreign markets, the United States must explore foreign innovations such as the Japanese auto industry's as well as manufacturing technologies being developed abroad.

For decades American businesses largely ignored technological innovations coming from foreign labs and companies. Most production and operations experts scoffed at Korean steel-processing procedures, Japanese inventory systems, Swedish assembly line team concepts, and Taiwanese electronics procedures. But today more and more U.S. managers are scanning foreign projects, activities, and innovations. Importing ideas and methods of potential benefit is becoming an accepted practice. At Xerox, for example, every department is expected to conduct a global search for the firm or organizational unit that performs its function best. This performance level then becomes the target for Xerox.

Companies taking a leadership role today set standards based on their best competitors or best industry practices.[39] This process is referred to as *benchmarking*. As we noted in Chapter 4, benchmarking is the continuous process of measuring a firm's goods, practices, or services against those of its toughest competitors. The main themes of benchmarking are improving operations, purchasing, services, quality, and marketing systems, and reducing the time to market.[40] Benchmarking is perfectly legal and enables a firm to establish operating goals and productivity objectives based on the best practices in the industry. Successful benchmarking requires three fundamental activities:

❖ Know your operation and assess its strengths and weaknesses. This involves documenting work process steps and practices and defining the critical performance measurements used.

❖ Know industry leaders and competitors. Capabilities can be differentiated only by knowing leaders' strengths and weaknesses.

❖ Incorporate the best and gain superiority. This involves emulating and surpassing the strengths of the best.[41]

There are several different types of benchmarking, including internal, functional, and competitive. *Internal benchmarking* involves comparing divisions within an organization. *Functional benchmarking* involves studying the best companies for a particular function, regardless of their industry. *Competitive benchmarking* is the measurement of direct competitors' activities. Many companies use one or more of these benchmarking techniques. Manco, Inc., manufactures tape, weather stripping, and mailing supplies. Manco studies service leaders to learn their standards and emulate their strengths. Not only does Manco benchmark its major competitor (3M); it also studies other service leaders like Wal-Mart. And other leading firms like P&G benchmark against Manco.[42]

Quality Circles

As noted in Chapter 8, quality circles are based on the belief that the people who work with the process are best able to identify, analyze, and correct the problems in any given production situation. Popularized in Japan in 1962, they were expanded into a highly developed system by Japanese firms. Quality circles usually consist of 10 or fewer people working in a related area. They meet about once a week and discuss the flow of work, its problems, and potential solutions. Participation in the circle is voluntary, and the workers establish a moderator or team leader to lead discussion. The group's findings and proposals are forwarded to management.

Experience with quality circles suggests that several preconditions are required for success. First, those involved must be intelligent. They must know how to use statistics and work design analyses. They must know the technical aspects of the job. Second, management must trust the participants enough to provide them with confidential cost information (from competition). Third, participants must be dedicated to working together as a team. They must have a team spirit, since groups, not individuals, are rewarded for success. Fourth, quality circles work best as part of what is called *total quality control*. This philosophy follows three principles: (1) The goal is to achieve a constant and continual improvement in quality year after year. (2) The focus extends beyond the actual product or service that a firm provides, to every process in the organization (e.g., finance, accounting, research and development). (3) Every employee bears responsibility for quality improvement.

Implementing total quality control involves the same steps used to develop the quality control system. But the breadth of the quality focus—that every employee is responsible—and the challenge of continual improvement require extra effort.

The extra effort has paid off in the Metal Stamping Division of Irvin Industries, Inc., of Richmond, Kentucky. After receiving quality improvement training, the firm declared that quality was a must and that each quality circle would set a goal of zero defects. Each Irvin employee has accepted the goal and is working to achieve zero defects.[43] Quality circle improvements have resulted in many cost savings, a reduced injury rate, and increased morale.

Quality is also important in services. If a plastic surgeon performs a poor-quality surgical procedure on a patient's face, permanent disfiguration can result. Businesses trying to provide quality service need to use every single step of the process applied to product quality control.

Service quality is of concern at the former Soviet Union's Aeroflot Airlines.[44] Described as the world's biggest airline, Aeroflot carries about 5 million passengers annually. Statistics and glossy promotion booklets boast of excellent services to and from 99 countries. In reality, Aeroflot's reputation among most Eastern European and Western passengers is that it provides the poorest service of any world-class airline: overbooked flights, long lines to make reservations, poor or no food service, shortages of trained flight attendants, and old equipment. As the former Soviet Union moves toward a market-driven economy, the airline must totally overhaul its view of service quality and delivery to be competitive in the international marketplace. To accomplish this, Aeroflot has teamed up with British Airways to launch a new international airline called Air Russia.[45] (Services are detailed in the next chapter.)

Quality Control versus Quality Management

In this section we have discussed several techniques for controlling quality. We also noted that it is the production and operations manager's job to improve (or manage) quality. Unfortunately concepts of quality control and quality management are often confused. This confusion is the source of many problems that organizations encounter with quality programs or total quality management. Some firms find that quality is a long-run commitment and abandon quality initiatives. Plagued by poor earnings, McDonnell Douglas Corp. embraced TQM, only to drop the program in less than two years, declaring it a failure.[46] A study conducted by Ernst & Young found that many businesses waste millions of dollars on quality-improvement strategies that don't improve performance.[47] In part these failures can be attributed to the presence of quality control with the absence of quality management.

Quality *control* is based on statistical actions and techniques that contain or reduce the nonconformances of processes by applying a series of screens.[48] This involves applying statistical techniques to control a process. This chapter's appendix summarizes seven common statistical tools. The key issue in quality control is understanding the variability in key measures of a product or service. First, variability is controlled with specified limits; then it is reduced further.

In contrast, quality *management* is a commitment to run the entire organization based on prevention, so there is nothing to screen out.[49] Quality management includes quality control as one of its functions, but also includes other activities like benchmarking, continuous improvement, and quality teams. While quality control was developed to contain non-

---

conformances within a manufacturing process using statistical tools, quality management attempts to eliminate the nonconformance (zero defects).

Quality control remains an effective way to run a manufacturing process, but it is not a management system. Quality control's weakness is that it cannot be totally effective all the time, so errors are acceptable. It is management's job to create a culture of prevention in an organization. This function cannot be delegated to technicians or workers. The idea is to help all in an organization to concentrate on doing their job right the first time. Without quality management, an organization's efforts to improve or control quality are likely to fail.

IMPROVING PRODUCTIVITY

The rate at which goods and services are created (output per labor-hour worked) is called productivity. In a healthy economy, productivity must be high and also steadily increasing. One common measure of productivity, *labor productivity*, is expressed in dollars of output (adjusted for inflation) per hour worked. Another important factor in output is technology and how employees use it. Labor and technology combined generate the outputs that are priced and sold to consumers.

Amid increasing labor, material, and opportunity costs plus uncertain world events, fast technological change, and shifting investment policies, a firm's productivity must continually increase for it to stay in business. The challenge facing managers and nonmanagers in firms of all sizes is immense. Ignoring either quality or productivity improvements is likely to result in lost markets, layoffs, foreclosures, and general business decay. Because the labor force will increase slowly in the 1990s, America will need 2 percent annual productivity gains for decent economic growth.[50] Consumers are demanding more quality, and companies need to improve the output per labor and technological input. This will require U.S. industries to take the offensive and invest in new technology and world-class production equipment.[51]

From a manager's perspective, a motivated employee works hard, sustains that pace, and is self-directed toward meeting challenging goals. Productivity improvement can only occur through such motivated employees. A quality circle program, a total quality control system, and a productivity improvement strategy all need motivated employees to implement and sustain them.

In their book *In Search of Excellence*, Thomas Peters and Robert Waterman point to the success of companies that have put the responsibility for quality on every employee and backed it up with management commitment to job security, meaningful profit sharing, and recognition. They cite companies such as Dana Corporation, a midwestern manufacturer of propeller blades and gearboxes. Through the leadership of then chairman Rene McPherson, Dana Corporation became the number 2 Fortune 500 company in returns to investors. McPherson points out:

> *Until we believe that the expert in any particular job is most often the person performing it, we shall forever limit the potential of that person, in terms of both his own contribution to the organization and his own development. Consider a manufacturing setting: Within their 25-square-foot area, nobody knows more about how to operate a machine, maximize its output, improve its quality, optimize the material flow, and keep it operating efficiently than do the machine operators, materials handlers, and maintenance people responsible for it. Nobody.[52]*

This attitude, according to Peters and Waterman, is expressed in one way or another by the best of the American corporations. At Delta it's the "Family Feeling;" at Hewlett-Packard the "HP Way" and "Management by Wandering Around." The authors define the attitude as "tough-minded respect for the individual and the willingness to train him, to set reasonable and clear expectations . . . and to grant him practical autonomy to step out and contribute directly to his job."[53]

MAINTAINING SAFETY FOR EMPLOYEES, PRODUCTS, AND THE ENVIRONMENT

A productivity and quality improvement strategy and motivated workers are key ingredients for business success. But these can be diminished if the company shows little regard for the environment or sacrifices safety. It is important to improve productivity and quality without jeopardizing the well-being and future of the employees or the environment.

Employee and Product Safety

Chapter 3 had a detailed discussion of social responsibility. Here we will view this issue in relation to the operations and production areas, where many of the most potentially hazardous materials, processes, and products are found. Although safety is part of every employee's responsibility, corporate responsibility for safety is most often delegated to the production and operations manager. Employee safety is mandated by a number of government regulations and laws; the production and operations manager is responsible for implementing these regulations in the plant. Compliance costs time, work, and money that must be provided for in schedules and budgets. Production and operations managers should realize that unsafe practices and contamination of the environment can implicate them through their failure to practice sound management.

Johnson & Johnson, maker of bandages and other health care products, is intent on being known as the number 1 firm in safety.[54] When any workplace accident causes death or a fracture, injury, or burn resulting in at least one lost day of work, the head of the company unit involved must file a written report to top management within 24 hours. The head must then travel to company headquarters in New Brunswick, New Jersey, and personally explain to a top-level committee what went wrong. Johnson & Johnson slashed its annual lost workday incidence per 100 workers from 1.81 to 0.14 in eight years (1981–89). Corporate workers' compensation expenses now average about $50 billion annually.[55] It pays to be as safe as possible.

Not only must employees have safe working conditions, the goods produced must be safe for the consumers who ultimately buy them. Product safety is the specific responsibility of the quality control department. Growing consumer consciousness of the issue has increased efforts to make accident-proof products. Automatic testing devices tug and pull plastic eyes and noses on toy rabbits to make sure they won't come off in eager two-year olds' mouths. Medicine bottles are made tamperproof, and sharp products such as paring knives bear brightly colored labels to prevent consumers from cutting themselves accidentally.

The United States regulates production more than any other nation. Compliance, a production cost, has become increasingly expensive. The increased expenditures show that most companies and employees at all levels have begun to take safety issues seriously. Consumer accidents receive greater attention and investigation today than they did a decade ago.

Monsanto, the fourth largest chemical producer in the United States, has developed a program to promote safety and help clean up the environment. Table 16–2 reproduces its pledge.

Globalization of Environmental Pollution

In 1992 leaders from 170 countries met in Rio de Janeiro for the U.N. Conference on Environment Development, which focused international concern on some alarming issues. The atmosphere's ozone layer is thinning. The U.S. National Aeronautics and Space Administration, along with scientists from several institutions, reported that the ozone layer over some regions, including the northernmost parts of the United States, Canada, Europe, and Russia, is depleted by as much as 50 percent.[56] Sulfur dioxide pumped into the air by manufacturing and power plants mixed with air has created rain with a high acid content (acid rain), which damages forests and lakes. Of the 6,750,000 square miles of the earth's original forests, only about 40 percent remains. Global forest destruction extends from the U.S. Pa-

TABLE 16–2	THE MONSANTO PLEDGE

- Reduce all toxic releases, working toward a goal of zero.

- Ensure that no Monsanto operation poses undue risk to employees and communities.

- Work to achieve sustainable agriculture through new technology and practices.

- Ensure groundwater safety—making our technical resources available to farmers dealing with contamination, even if our products are not involved.

- Keep our plants open to our communities, bringing the community into plant operations. Inform people of any significant hazard.

- Manage all corporate real estate to benefit nature.

- Search worldwide for technology to reduce and eliminate waste from our operations, with the top priority being not making it in the first place.

Source: *Business and Society Review*, Spring 1990, p. 66.

cific Northwest to the tropical forests of Brazil and Malaysia.[57] In the former Soviet Union, millions breathe toxic air while factories pump sewage into lakes and toxins into the air.[58] The Ethics Spotlight on the next page examines the threat the Commonwealth of Independent States (CIS) poses to the rest of the world.

Individuals, firms, the government, and special-interest groups are trying to solve these problems. Many firms are making products and containers that can be recycled, slowing the need for more and bigger landfills. In addition to making products that can be recycled, some firms educate consumers and encourage them to recycle. Lyondell Petrochemical (a major refiner in Houston) has started making gasoline from used motor oil.[59] The United States and Mexican governments are working together on the pollution problem inside Mexico's border with the United States, where some factories burn tires for fuel; the region has been described by the American Medical Association as a "virtual cesspool."[60] Economists working for the United Nations and the Environmental Defense Fund are trying to link countries with vastly different economies and environmental laws into a single pollution control system.[61] These are just a few examples, and the results may seem small in comparison to the size of the problem, but they're steps in the right direction. It will take the ongoing participation of every individual and firm plus cooperation from all nations' governments to reverse the current threats to our environment.

In recent years a number of great American companies have surrendered their leadership to foreign competitors.[62] Most recently IBM has gone from industry leader to crippled giant, struggling to restructure itself to be more flexible and responsive. To survive and prosper in the future, firms will have to develop and maintain advanced production technology. To improve productivity, General Electric is investing $70 million in its 40-year-old Appliance Park—five mammoth factories near Louisville, Kentucky. Although GE is taking a major risk overhauling its old machines, chairman John Welch knows he has no choice.[63]

THE WORKPLACE OF TOMORROW

Tomorrow's production and operations environment will continue to benefit from innovations in assembly line techniques, lean manufacturing, and flexible manufacturing. For instance, Hotpoint Ltd., the United Kingdom's leading manufacturer of home laundry products, has integrated product verification and testing as its final assembly line step. By eliminating the intermediate shuttling of complete units to and from remote testing stations, Hotpoint reduces time and labor costs from work-in-process and lessens the potential

ETHICS SPOTLIGHT   A NEW THREAT FROM THE EAST

The Cold War is over; communism is dead. But after 74 years of mismanagement, the Soviet regime has left behind a legacy of environmental damage that threatens much of the world and requires billions of dollars for cleanup. Consider the following:

- Lenin Steelworks in Magnitogorsk, Russia, discharges enough pollution to foul the air over 4,000 square miles, twice the area of Delaware.
- Economic planners, in the process of irrigating arid farmland, nearly drained the Aral Sea.
- Rain drips into the reactor wreckage at Chernobyl, threatening to cause another nuclear reaction.
- Hundreds of factories are pouring waste (including heavy metals, salts, carcinogens, and oil products) into the Neva River, which provides drinking water for St. Petersburg, Russia.

The Soviet empire once spanned one-sixth of the earth. The environmental problems it left equal it in magnitude. Soviet industry was built without regard for the environment. Says a spokeswoman for the Washington, D.C.-based Natural Resources Defense Council, "If we don't deal with [Commonwealth of Independent States] environmental problems now, we won't have to worry about dealing with economic problems." Germany and France are pushing the world's leading industrial nations to pledge billions of dollars in environmental aid besides the $24 billion in economic assistance they have already promised.

Russia and the other former Soviet republics need help not only with cleanup, but also in stopping ongoing environmental destruction. A Western diplomat in Moscow describes CIS as a "big polluting machine." Cars pollute the air with leaded gasoline and their lack of catalytic converters. CIS households, with smaller homes and fewer appliances, use 90 percent less energy than do Western households, but factories and the oil and gas industries produce vast wastefulness and environmental nightmares. Designed without the environment in mind, manufacturing uses more than four times as much energy per unit of GNP as in the United States. Malfunctioning old equipment, lack of spare parts, poor workmanship, and shabby repairs regularly produce immense blowouts, leaks, and spills in the oil and gas industry throughout the former Soviet Union.

A horrendous disaster occurred in March 1992 near Tashkent, the capital of Uzbekistan, when drillers struck oil at a well in the Fergana valley oilfields but could not control the flow. Oil shot hundreds of feet into the air, filling the sky with black slime and smoke for 62 days. After a month, Uzbek officials called in Oklahoma-based Cudd Pressure Control, Inc., to seal off the well. Before it was finally controlled in early May, the well threw out as much as 6.2 million barrels of oil, which soaked into nearby cotton fields or burned off into the air. Uzbek officials never said how severe the damage was, and neither did the U.S. Environmental Protection Agency, which sent a technical team to the site at the Uzbek government's request. Experts estimate the oil spill to be some 24 times the amount spilled by the Exxon Valdez in Alaska. Loss from this well alone cost the Uzbeks around $130 million while creating untold environmental damage.

The Fergana valley spill, while the worst reported, is but one of many disastrous incidents in recent years. One blowout near the Caspian Sea blazed for a year before it was controlled. A gas pipeline explosion several hundred miles south of Moscow resulted in 607 deaths when sparks from passing trains ignited a leak. In western Siberia a break in a rusted oil line leaked 3 million barrels of oil into the ground and caused 27 wells to be shut down. Moscow officials have admitted that in 1989, 26,000 ruptures occurred, spilling 4.3 million barrels of oil.

Over 370,000 miles of oil and gas pipelines cross through the former Soviet Union. Many stretches of pipeline, as well as compressors, need to be repaired or replaced. Some German consultants estimate that principal gas lines are leaking almost 10 percent of their annual production, and local connecting networks are losing up to 40 percent of their load. That loss far exceeds Germany's entire yearly gas requirement. Leaking pipelines are said to have cost the former Soviet republics some $8 billion in oil and gas revenues in 1991.

The biggest danger to the outside world lies in the CIS nuclear energy program. Its 37 reactors provide 12 percent of the Commonwealth's energy, but at least 15 are poorly designed and should be taken out of operation. Their slowness to cool during emergencies can cause the core to explode, which happened at the Chernobyl plant in 1986. The aftermath was felt throughout Europe. Nearly $180 million of agricultural products had to be destroyed in Poland, Germany, Austria, and Hungary; herds of reindeer were destroyed in Finland, Sweden, and Norway; and in Britain, some 1,350 miles away, sale of sheep was banned until radioactive isotopes they may have consumed while grazing had dissipated. The radioactive contamination that fell on Europe is expected to cause about 6,000 more cancer deaths in the next 50 years. Over 2.5 million acres of farmland in Ukraine and Belorussia were never properly cleaned, and radioactive food occasionally shows up in markets.

Even if other nations provide financial aid, the responsibility for the cleanup falls on the business and citizens of the former Soviet Republics. But first, the CIS must stop the pattern of environmental abuse that has been taking place for years.

Source: Adapted from Richard C. Morais, P. Pietsch, and Christoph von Schoeller, "Blowout," *Forbes*, July 20, 1992, pp. 65, 68; Paul Hofheinz, "The New Soviet Threat: Pollution," *Fortune*, July 27, 1992, pp. 110–14; and Associated Press, "Sewage Is Found Pouring into River Used for Russian City's Drinking Water," *Herald-Leader* (Lexington, Ky.), September 17, 1992, p. A8.

of material handling damage.[64] At General Electric's Appliance Park in Louisville, Kentucky, self-directed work teams made up of factory employees determine how to run an assembly line. After a $47 million loss in 1993, the manufacturing facility made a $44 million profit in 1994.[65]

As we noted at the outset of the chapter, lean manufacturing and flexible manufacturing are changing the way products are made. In the workplace of tomorrow, product development cycles will shorten, and lean manufacturing will replace mass production. Lean manufacturing is characterized by an emphasis on product quality, an integrated approach to the various aspects of manufacturing, reliance on subcontractors to produce a greater portion of the value added, and an emphasis on speed in order processing, production, and delivery. According to Chrysler's François Castaing, the companies that will win product development competition in the future will be those that quickly and inexpensively design automobiles that create intense passion.[66] The same could be said for most industries. In an increasingly competitive global economy, quick, lean, worker-empowered manufacturing will be the key to long-run survival. Lean manufacturing can increase productivity, reduce costs, shorten lead time, and enhance customer partnerships.[67] Benchmarking will increasingly be used in pursuit of world-class product quality. Flexible manufacturing will play a key role in achieving such quality.

SUMMARY OF LEARNING OBJECTIVES

DEFINE PRODUCTION AND OPERATIONS.
Production refers to the total process by which a business creates finished goods or services. Operations refers to the functions needed to keep the company producing. Functions such as purchasing, materials management, production, inventory and quality control, and maintenance are included. The process and functions needed to produce and/or deliver goods or services make up the production and operations management function.

DISCUSS THE EVOLUTION OF MODERN MANUFACTURING.
Fuel energy, scientific management, and mass production were crucial to manufacturing's development. As the United States became increasingly industrialized, American goods were sought throughout the world. But confidence in American goods declined as foreign competitors began making better-quality products. Today American firms are scanning the globe to search for new and better production methods.

EXPLAIN THE ROLE OF PRODUCTION AND OPERATIONS MANAGERS.
Production and operations managers are responsible for producing the products that business needs to sell. Typical functions include product planning, site layout and location, inventory control, purchasing and materials management, manufacturing and production, production control, quality control, and plant management.

COMPARE TRADITIONAL COMPANY ORGANIZATIONS WITH CELLULAR ORGANIZATIONS.
The traditional organization emphasizes specialists in areas linked to manufacturing. Cellular organizations have a layout in which workers are grouped into what is called a cell. Groupings are determined by the operations needed to perform work for a set of similar items. In the cellular arrangement, units are completed by a team. The layout speeds up the assembly from start to finish.

LIST THE FACTORS THAT SHOULD BE CONSIDERED IN SELECTING A SITE.
Many factors should be considered including cost of land or buildings; insurance and taxes; proximity to related industries and other important facilities or services; availability and cost of labor; availability of transportation; proximity to market for goods; air and water conditions; proximity to energy resources; climate and environment consistent with needs; space for expansion; proximity to employees' needs such as housing and schools; and receptiveness of the community.

EVALUATE THE EFFECTS OF COMPUTERIZATION ON PRODUCTION AND OPERATION MANAGEMENT FUNCTIONS.
The computerization's effects have been significant in terms of speed, efficiency, and productivity. CAD and CAE have enabled tremendous flexibility and experimentation. The computer has become a major tool that must be understood by all production and operations employees.

EXPLAIN THE IMPORTANCE OF PRODUCTIVITY AND QUALITY.
Improvements in productivity and quality have long-term effects on the success of organizations. Ignoring either quality or productivity improvements is likely to result in lost markets, layoffs, foreclosures, and general business decay. Consumers are demanding more quality, and companies need to improve the output per labor and technological input.

DISCUSS THE IMPORTANCE OF SAFETY TO PRODUCTIVITY AND QUALITY.
Corporate responsibility for employee safety is often delegated to the production and operations manager. Product safety is the specific responsibility of the quality control department. Pollution, global warming, toxic waste, and preserving the earth's forests are all concerns. The corporation expects the production and operations unit to oversee environmental matters. Environment-friendly technologies are needed in all areas, especially manufacturing. Production and operations units will be asked to work more on minimizing pollution while still contributing to a firm's profit margins.

KEY TERMS

assembly line, p. 420
computer-aided design (CAD), p. 430
computer-aided engineering (CAE), p. 430
computer-aided manufacturing (CAM), p. 430
flexible manufacturing systems (FMS), p. 431

just-in-time (JIT) manufacturing, p. 427
manufacturing, p. 419
mass production, p. 420
materials requirements planning (MRP), p. 428

operations, p. 419
production, p. 418
program evaluation and review technique (PERT) chart, p. 428
robot, p. 430

REVIEW AND DISCUSSION QUESTIONS

Recall

1. What are the functions of production and operations?
2. When is project manufacturing used? Give an example of project manufacturing.
3. What are the advantages and disadvantages of just-in-time inventory?
4. List some responsibilities of the production manager and operations manager.
5. What is PERT? How is a PERT chart created?
6. How can quality and productivity be improved?

Understanding

7. Trace the evolution of modern manufacturing, highlighting the significant events along the way.

8. If you were going to open a fast-food restaurant like McDonald's, what factors would be important in selecting a site and a site layout?
9. How have computers improved the production process? Give several examples of how computers are used in manufacturing.

Application

10. Review a daily newspaper for one week. Cite examples of American businesses concerned about environmental pollution and safety. Also cite examples of concerned non-American firms.

CASE STUDY

Kao Responds to Demand

Kao Corporation is Japan's largest soap and cosmetics company and the world's sixth largest, with annual sales exceeding $5 billion. The corporate philosophy at Kao is that everyone must contribute their intelligence to achieve the corporate purpose of developing and using innovative technologies to create products that offer real consumer value. According to James Abegglen, chairman of Gemini Consulting-Japan, no company can match the flexibility of Kao's distribution. Goods can be delivered within 24 hours to any of 280,000 shops, whose average order is only seven items. This capability is based on a world-class information system and a wholly owned network of wholesalers. This control enables Kao to get hot-selling items on store shelves faster and to keep smaller inventories than competitors.

Kao's objective is to maximize the flexibility of the entire firm's response to demand. This requires not only flexible manufacturing, but also an information system that links all aspects of the business: sales and shipping, production and purchasing, accounting, R&D, marketing, stores' cash registers, and salespeople's hand-held computers.

Many firms in America and elsewhere rely on point-of-purchase data in determining production requirements. A manager generally receives information on the previous day's sales. At Kao, managers see daily sales, stock, and production figures. They can learn about a competitor's sale within a day and make necessary adjustments. When introducing a new product, information from 216 retailers is combined with a test-marketing program called the Echo System. This system uses focus group interviews and consumer responses

through calls and letters to measure customer satisfaction faster than surveys do. Within two weeks of introduction, Kao knows if a product will be successful, who's buying it, whether the packaging is effective, and what needs to be changed. Response to the factory is immediate, and flexible manufacturing allows for instant changes.

Kao's system basically eliminates the lag between a purchase and feedback about the purchase to the factory. This makes Kao less dependent on keeping a finished goods inventory. It also allows the firm to smooth out production levels and increase variety without increasing stock. In 1987 Kao made 498 products, and inventory averaged 9.2 percent of sales. Today Kao makes 564 products, and inventory is down to 8.6 percent.

Flexibility at Kao comes not only from manufacturing, but also from information. A flexible factory is of little use if it can't be exploited. Kao knows what's selling and can respond to this information at the factory quickly.

QUESTIONS

1. How does Kao stress flexibility?
2. Why is information so important to Kao?
3. How can Kao respond to customer demand more effectively than some manufacturing firms?

Source: Adapted from "Kao Corp." *Computerworld*, August 21, 1995, pp. 552–557; Thomas A. Stewart, "Brace for Japan's Hot New Strategy," *Fortune*, September 21, 1992, pp. 62–74; Masayoshi Kanabayashi, "Japan's Top Soap Firm, Kao, Hopes to Clean Up Abroad," *The Wall Street Journal*, December 17, 1992, p. B4; and "A Time for Mutual Respect and Understanding," *Fortune*, July 27, 1992, pp. S16–S17.

VIDEO CASE

Washburn Guitars: Processing and Scheduling

A poorly scheduled job breeds chaos. In business, work flow equals cash flow, and work flow is driven by the schedule. In an ideal situation the schedule is followed, jobs are completed on time, the shop stays busy, and the pace remains steady. But what if changes need to be made at a moment's notice? What if a special order needs to be filled quickly? What if extra time is needed to set up a special job? All of these factors change the schedule whether you're producing bicycles, bagels, bass guitars, or bank statements.

Effective production scheduling will make a company more competitive. The successful job shop is one that is designed to handle changes quickly and without loss of time of disruption to the operation.

Washburn guitars produces 115,000 instruments annually. These range from acoustic and electric guitars and basses to mandolins and banjos. At its Chicago plant, Washburn produces about 15 top-of-the-line electric guitars each day. Its instruments are played by musicians like David Gulmore of Pink Floyd, Joe Parry of Arrowsmith, Darryl Smith of the Rolling Stones, Graham Parker, and Gregg Allman.

Grover Jackson, a world-renowned guitar designer, oversees operations at the Chicago plant. The production process at Washburn might be described as a *synthetic system*. This means that the materials used to build each guitar undergo many physical changes from start to finish. Scheduling each of these operations is important to ensure that there's an even flow through production, with minimum bottleneck occurring and with the numbers of each model to meet demand.

Production schedules vary from nearly continuous batches all the way down to custom, special order, and one-of-a-kind instruments. Collectively, this process could be called *intermittent process*, meaning the production runs are short and the machines are changed frequently to produce different pieces.

Sometimes scheduling can be affected by *priority rules*. Scheduling priority may be based on such criteria as first come first served, earliest due date, and shortest operating time. For example, at Washburn, the production of a popular, more expensive guitar may take precedence over the manufacturing schedule of a less expensive item.

Another prioritizing factor relates to the length of time needed to produce a given guitar model. Occasionally, Washburn gets rush orders from big-name musicians on concert tours. Brady Breen, Washburn's production/facilities manager, said, "Very often a musician will need a piece at the drop of a hat. If it's been stolen we need to replace those. If it's been broken and it's repairable they send it to us and we repair it. If it's not, we need to build them another one to keep the artist with his instrument."

Since manufacturing different guitar components for a variety of models requires frequent new setups of critical machinery, scheduling work is important at Washburn. The company uses a system known as *flexible manufacturing* since the production machine can perform multiple tasks or jobs, and can produce a variety of products. The same machine builds guitar necks, drills holes for the fret board, body, and electronics, and handles this task for a variety of different models. Chris Nichols, Washburn's process engineering the less cost per part you're going to obtain. I work all the employees around this to make sure we do whatever we have to do to make this 100 percent available.

The production of an electric guitar begins with the gluing and shaping of the wood to make the guitar's body. Next, the hardware and electronics components are assembled. This consists of pick ups, tuning keys, the bridge, wiring, and strings. Everything is tested at the point of assembly before it is shipped.

The rotation and availability of parts in stock can also affect production scheduling. At Washburn it generally takes 90 days to purchase the parts for a new model. The introduction of a new model means new parts and new production specifications. Currently, Washburn produces its line of acoustic guitars overseas. But there are plans to move the entire production operation, acoustic and electric, to a new 120,000-square-foot facility in Nashville, Tennessee. Breen explained, "In an effort to expand our existing production there have been considerations to move to Nashville where we would have the liberty of building a larger structure customized to our specifications and take advantage of the labor pool, which is considered to be the center of the guitar making industry."

Today more information systems are available than ever before and new production technologies are being developed at a fast pace. Managers of the future will need to have a strong knowledge of the links between the scheduling of work, the production process, and how they impact market demand and customer satisfaction. The company with the most effective production schedule is going to be better able to provide the customer with the right product at the right time for the right place. So whether you're making cars, computers, copiers, or cheeseburgers, good scheduling will make a big difference in the success of your business.

QUESTIONS

1. Explain what is meant by a *synthetic system*. Explain how priority rules can affect a production process.
2. Explain what is meant by *flexible manufacturing*.
3. How can the concepts of the production process covered in this case be transferred to a service environment?

APPLICATION EXERCISE

In 1989 the MIT Commission on Industrial Productivity published a book entitled Made in America. The book emphasized that some U.S. industries and products have lost 50 percent or more of their share of world markets since 1960. Which of these industries do you think have lost this share? (Check yes or no.)

	Yes	No	Coming Back
Automobiles			
Cameras			
Microwave ovens			
Machine tools			
Optical equipment			
Color TV sets			
Stereo equipment			
Steel			
Copiers			
Commercial aircraft			

Every industry should be checked yes except for commercial aircraft. Each of the other U.S. industries or products listed has lost 50 percent or more of the world market since 1960. The decline of the manufacturing or production part of business is one reason why market share has dwindled.

In which of the above industries do you think the United States has made a comeback? (Check the coming back column.) To verify your answer, go to the library and research these industries.

Also select a single industry, like commercial aircraft, and research it thoroughly, answering the following questions:

1. Has the United States gained or lost market share in this industry since 1990?
2. Is quality a critical factor in this gain or loss? Explain.
3. What production and operations techniques (e.g., JIT, flexible manufacturing, CAD/CAE/CAM, benchmarking) are used in this industry by leading competitors?
4. What must production and operations managers do to maintain and increase market share in this industry?

CHAPTER 17

Managing Services

After studying this chapter, you should be able to:

❖ Define service.

❖ Discuss the concept of tangibility as it relates to goods and services.

❖ List four characteristics that distinguish services from goods.

❖ Explain the significance of service quality and productivity.

❖ Discuss how service organizations can improve quality and productivity.

❖ Describe when an organization has a performance culture.

❖ Discuss the components of peak performance.

❖ Explain how organizations can encourage peak performance.

Elk Mountain Ranch

"**T**he mountains, the sky, and the log walls seem to suggest that all is well with the world, and that there's enough time for everything." At least that's what they say at Elk Mountain Ranch. Nestled among aspen and evergreen on Little Bull Creek in the San Isabel National Forest, Elk Mountain Ranch is Colorado's highest at 9,535 feet. With a breathtaking view of snow-capped peaks, the ranch is a nature lover's and photographer's paradise.

Upon arrival, guests at the ranch are welcomed by a friendly staff eager to please. Since the ranch is relatively small—only 30 guests a week—individual attention and activities tailored to the groups' particular interests are the order of the day. You'll never get lost in a crowd or wait in lines at Elk Mountain Ranch.

On the first night of their stay, guests meet in the main lodge for a traditional meal of turkey and all the trimmings. After dinner, hosts Tom and Sue Murphy greet another new group of people who have come from miles away. Though Tom and Sue have done this many times before, they know each person is looking for a unique experience. Boldly, Tom states the goal of the staff at Elk Mountain Ranch: "We want this to be the best vacation you ever had."

Tom and Sue Murphy are not selling a tangible good like a car or a pair of jeans; they are selling a service. Services are products that involve human effort and are therefore somewhat different from goods. Quality services often require quality efforts from people, and there is a high cost to poor quality service. One bad trail ride, one rude wrangler, one disgruntled guest, and Tom and Sue fail to reach their bold goal.

When asked the most important part of his job, Tom doesn't hesitate—it's managing people. With a staff of about 20 wranglers, activities directors, cooks, housekeepers, and maintenance workers, it is imperative that each person know his or her responsibilities. Tom and Sue know these people are the critical link to a great vacation. The mountains and the streams are tangible evidence of a beautiful vacation, but the extra effort of a wrangler on a trail ride or an activities director with a child is what ultimately makes for the best vacation ever.

Keeping the staff motivated to perform at a high level at all times is not easy. These are people, not machines. And they are young, a long way from home, and removed from the pleasures of everyday life. They work long hours, take little time off, and perform a variety of roles. After a long day on the trail, wranglers show up to entertain guests at the evening square dance. Likewise, after preparing another gourmet meal, the cooks head out on a late-night hayride, ready to sing with the group.

Nothing is too small a detail at Elk Mountain Ranch. Host Sue Murphy washes clothes because one family is planning on a second week of travel throughout Colorado. An overnight camping trip, long-awaited by an eight-year-old girl is cancelled due to a bad storm. Tom Murphy pitches a tent back at the ranch, and a little girl goes home saying "This was the best vacation I ever had." Elk Mountain Ranch sells memories like these.

It isn't easy week after week, sending another group of guests away this happy. And a new group of guests is a new challenge, and summer goes on, and a tired staff has to reach down, once more, and help the guests see "that all is well with the world, and that there's enough time for everything."

Source: Elk Mountain Ranch brochure; Interview with Tom Murphy; and the best vacation ever, to Elk Mountain Ranch.

Most organizations today are aware that the service they offer to their customers is a significant source of competitive advantage. Even manufacturing companies, whose primary activity is the production of a tangible good, must be concerned with the way they interact with customers of that good. Customer satisfaction measurement and management has the overall objective of satisfying—perhaps even delighting—customers. Exceeding customer expectations is now widely recognized as an effective route to strategic, market-driven organizational behavior.[1] The cost of failing to meet customers' expectations of service quality is high in terms of lost customers, bad publicity, or responses needed to rectify customer complaints and win back lost customers.

Managing services has become a critical issue as service firms face many of the same challenges manufacturing firms have experienced—particularly increased competition and consumer demands for better quality. Some experts have pointed to parallels between the U.S. decline in manufacturing and these current challenges facing service firms.[2] The future of service businesses depends upon their ability to deliver quality services. The best service organizations are managed differently from their competition.

This chapter examines how services are managed. First we discuss the nature and importance of services. Then we examine characteristics that distinguish services from other goods. Next we present a scheme for classifying services. Then we look at quality and productivity in service organizations and issues related to developing and managing services. Finally we discuss developing a performance culture.

THE NATURE AND IMPORTANCE OF SERVICES

service
An intangible product that involves human or mechanical effort.

A good is a tangible product that consumers can physically possess. A **service** is an intangible product that involves human or mechanical effort.[3] Another way to think about a service is that it's instantaneously perishable; the transaction and consumption occur at the same time. In contrast, a product can be stored and used at some point in time after the transaction between buyer and seller. Most workers in the U.S. today are employed in some type of service organization. Table 17–1 shows America's largest service firms.

Few products can be classified as a pure good or pure service; most products contain both tangible and intangible elements. When you order your favorite meal in a restaurant, you're purchasing a tangible product. Yet we often compare and evaluate restaurants on their quality of service. This is an important point. Any business, whether it's primarily in-

TABLE 17-1	AMERICA'S TEN LARGEST SERVICE FIRMS		
Rank	Name	Industry	Sales (millions)
1	American Telephone & Telegraph	Telecommunications	$65,101
2	Enron	Natural gas	14,126
3	Time Warner	Entertainment	13,070
4	Fleming	Wholesale	12,937
5	Supervalu	Wholesale	10,632
6	MCI Communications	Telecommunications	10,562
7	McKesson	Wholesale	10,345
8	Sprint	Telecommunications	9,230
9	Sysco	Wholesale	8,892
10	Marriott	Hotels	8,865

Source: *Fortune*, May 31, 1993, p. 206.

volved in manufacturing or mining, or any other process, typically also provides services to a customer. Many businesses that had traditionally conceived of themselves as manufacturers are building competitive advantage around customer service. For example, according to William Toller, CEO of Witco Chemical Company, satisfying the customer is no longer the ultimate business virtue. He said companies must go beyond satisfaction and create customer loyalty. To create loyalty among Witco customers, Toller said his company looks for those things that customers perceive as adding value to their relationship with the company. This allows Witco to focus on the critical few issues that affect both the company's performance for customers and for profitability.[4]

Figure 17–1 illustrates the concept of tangibility on a continuum ranging from pure goods to pure services. Salt or some other staple good is an example of a pure good. A consultant is an example of a pure service. Products falling in the middle have a mix of both tangible and intangible elements. Though most products are neither a pure good nor a pure service, one element usually predominates, and this is the basis for classifying a product as a good or service. Air travel is considered a service because it is generally intangible. Pilots, jets, and airports, however, are tangible. As we will show later, these tangible elements are important in managing services.

FIGURE 17–1
A Continuum of Product Tangibility

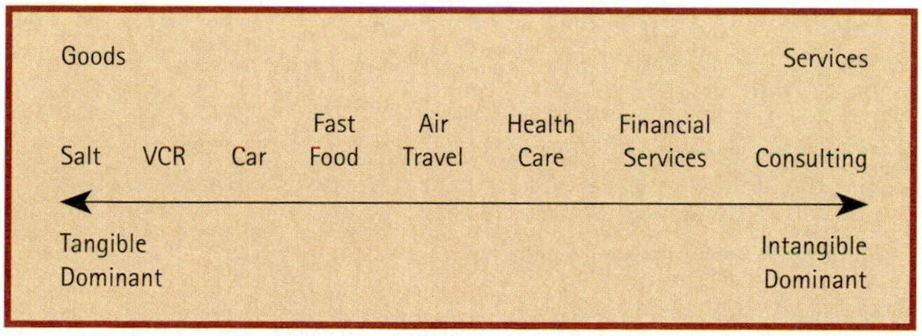

Services are an important part of the American economy. Service industries account for about 70 percent of the U.S. gross national product.[5] Today, the service sector occupies a full 76 percent of the American workforce (86 percent if employees performing service functions in manufacturing firms are included). It's estimated that for the period between 1990 and 2000 , about nine out of ten jobs will be service related.[6] Several service industries—including insurance and retailing—face intense competition, some from foreign firms. Nonetheless service jobs are expected to grow faster than jobs in other sectors of the economy. The Global Exchange examines foreign competition in service industries.

CHARACTERISTICS OF SERVICES

We must recognize several important characteristics of services. These characteristics affect the manner in which services are produced and managed. Production and management of cars, for instance, is somewhat different from production and management of financial services. This is because financial and other services are distinguished by four characteristics: intangibility, inseparability of production and consumption, perishability, and heterogeneity. Later in the chapter we will examine how these characteristics influence the management of services.

GLOBAL EXCHANGE   **SERVICES UNDER ATTACK**

The world economy has become dominated by services. They now account for about 70 percent of the gross national product and most of the new jobs created in the industrial countries of the world. Nearly 8 of 10 workers in the United States alone are employed by service companies.

The United States is the world's services leader, with 150 companies in the Global Service 500. But with the slowing global economy and rising foreign competition, America is undergoing its next wave of restructuring, this time in the service sector. In the past few years jobs have been lost in many service industries, including banking, insurance, retail, and airlines. Until recently services have been sheltered from competition and had little incentive to increase productivity. But deregulation and foreign investment are challenging the status quo in many service industries. This has led some experts to warn U.S. service companies to prepare for a dramatic change.

Just as the smokestack economy of the 1980s underwent great changes, service industries in the 1990s will strive for increased productivity. And although many experts point to the creation of new jobs as one or the service economy's strengths, this is in fact a symptom

of the inefficiencies that plague many service firms. They have hired new workers while neglecting technology and economic efficiency. The result if a bloated, vulnerable economy. Even though service workers hold nearly 80 percent of the jobs in private industry, the service sector must make those workers more productive to remain competitive. An increased standard of living depends on such a productivity improvement.

Conventional wisdom held that services were immune to foreign competition. People claimed that while cars, TVs, and microwaves could flow freely across national borders, insurance, hotels, and banking could not. Unfortunately this is not the case. The United States is the world's richest market for services, so for multinational firms looking to expand, it offers great opportunities. Foreign competition is forcing domestic service firms to rethink how they do business. Every day, for instance, seven Boeing 747s loaded with inexpensive carnations and roses fly into the United States from Columbia. The prices help florists as well as low-overhead flower outlets. Retail florists have seen their share of the $12.7 billion cut-flower market drop from over 75 percent 10 years ago to about 50 percent today, and it's still falling.

Most foreign investment has been in

the nonfinancial segment of the service sector, such as retail and wholesale trade, business services, and hotels. Notable foreign acquisitions include:

- MCA by Matsushita (Japan) for $7.9 billion.
- Columbia Pictures by Sony (Japan) for $4.7 billion.
- Holiday Inn by Bass PLC (Great Britain) for $2.2 billion.
- Federated and Allied Department Stores by Campeau (Canada) for 11.2 billion.
- Farmers Group Insurance by B.A.T. Industries (Great Britain) for $5.1 billion.
- First Maryland Bancorp by Allied Irish Banks (Ireland) for $1.1 billion.

Such foreign direct investment may not appear to be much of a threat. Foreign buyers are not likely to run off with the assets of U.S. service companies. But foreign firms' increasing presence in American markets will force U.S. service firms to respond to heightened competition through quality and productivity.

Source: Adapted from Stephen S. Roach, "Services under Siege—The Restructuring Imperative," *Harvard Business Review.* September–October 1991, pp. 82–91; Joshua Levine, "Halloween Boo-quets, Anyone?" *Forbes,* October 26, 1992, pp. 206–8; and Nora E. Field and Ricardo Sookdeo, "Introducing a New List," *Fortune,* August 26, 1991, pp. 166–70.

Intangibility

The major feature that distinguishes services from other products is that they cannot be physically possessed. **Intangibility** is the quality of not being able to be assessed by the senses of sight, taste, touch, smell, or hearing. Intangibility is especially important because the other three unique characteristics of services are derived from this trait. Think of some services we have discussed or some you have purchased lately. Can you touch or feel them? Usually not. Services such as hair cuts, banking, medical exams, and the like cannot be physically possessed like a tangible good.

Because services are intangible, they are difficult for customers to evaluate. If you have a physical exam, the best outcome is a clean bill of health. But how do you know you had a thorough physical? A physical exam cannot be evaluated in the same manner as a tangible product. A car can be taken for a test drive, the tires kicked, and an opinion formed.

Although it is hard to evaluate a service, it is not impossible. Before selecting a physician, you could visit her office, look at the facilities, talk to nurses and doctors, and observe the clinic's atmosphere. These are *tangible cues*—they are used to evaluate an intangible service. This also illustrates that many services have a tangible element, just as goods have an intangible element. Airlines have pilots and planes, banks have tellers and facilities, and clinics have doctors and nurses. Management of these tangible elements is critical to the success of services.

intangibility
The quality of not being able to be assessed by the senses of sight, taste, touch, smell, or hearing.

Inseparability of Production and Consumption

Services are also characterized by **inseparability** of production and consumption, meaning they are produced and consumed at the same time. Goods can be carefully designed, produced, and consumed at a later date. This is not the case for services. Inseparability has two important implications. First, the *service provider* plays a critical role in delivery of services and may in fact be the service. Service providers play a critical role in services in that customers will often associate the service provider with the service. Insurance agents, bank tellers, hair stylists, flight attendants, and many other occupations represent the entire business to a customer. Many service organizations have implemented extensive training programs to ensure that these key employees have the skills needed to deal with customers. For example, Canadian Airlines International's "Service Quality" program was also the means for carrying out one of the largest employee training projects in North American business history. Employees were provided with quality skills training and brought together in teams to change the systems and processes they work with.[7]

A second implication is that because production and consumption occur simultaneously, the *customer* also has an important role in service delivery.[8] Most services cannot be performed unless the customer is present or directly involved in the production process. The customer must be present to get a hair cut, fly on a plane, or see a movie. In some cases the customer actually shares part of the responsibility for delivering services. Many gas buyers pump their own gas, bank customers operate automatic teller machines (ATMs), and (as Figure 17–2 illustrates) some restaurant customers even cook their own meals. (Note how the price increases if the house chef cooks the steak.) Similarly, a sightseer who interacts with local residents is involved in the production and consumption of a city's tourism services. Likewise a patient must tell a doctor the symptoms of an illness before treatment can be prescribed.

Because customers are so involved in service transactions, these **critical service encounters** are an excellent opportunity for businesses to gain feedback on their performance. A critical service encounter is one where customers are likely to be forming opinions about the overall quality of the business. Frontline service employees most often manage these critical service encounters and are an important source of information about customers. Customer knowledge obtained by contact employees can be used to improve service in two ways: by facilitating the interaction with customers, and by guiding the firm's decision making. Employees who have frequent contact with customers often have a better understanding of customer needs and problems than others in the firm. Research has shown that open communication between managers and customer service employees improves customer service quality.[9] Research has also shown that the warmth of

inseparability
A situation in which services are produced and consumed at the same time.

critical service encounter
A service encounter where customers are likely to be forming opinions about the overall quality of the business.

FIGURE 17–2
Customer Involvement in the
Production of Services

The Butcher Shop
STEAKHOUSE

THE STEAKS

The Butcher's Special Cuts
14 oz Filet Mignon
20 oz Ribeye
25 oz Strip (Bone On)
24 oz Top Sirloin
28 oz T-Bone
20 oz Shish-ke-bab

THE PRICE

$16.95 If You're the Chef,
Two Bucks Extra for the House Chef.
Steak Dinner for Two $11.50 Per Person
By Sharing A Steak

THE CHICKEN

MARINATED CHICKEN BREASTS
*Two boneless breasts of chicken
marinated in our special sauce
and grilled over the
open charcoal pit.* $12.95

All Entrees served with baked potato, salad and bread.

THE EXTRA
Sauteed Mushrooms $4.25
*Sauteed in butter, garlic, wine
and seasoning. Served sizzling
in a hot skillet.
Enough to share.*

THE DESSERTS
Katie's Delight $3.50
*Layers of whipped cream,
cream cheese, and fudge
pudding, then topped with
chocolate chips, and pecans*

Cheesecake $3.50

A 15% gratuity will be included on checks for parties of seven or more.
Other Locations: Chicago, Memphis, Little Rock, Knoxville

communication style from the service provider to the customer can affect customer perception of service quality. Results from 83 participants in a simulated bank interview experiment indicated that the warmth of the service personnel contributed to a high-quality service rating, and increased the future confidence of dealing with the bank.[10]

Because customers often play an active role in producing services, the service customer also must have the ability, skill, training, and motivation needed to engage in the production process. The service encounter can't be completed unless customers have the skills needed to participate in the transaction. This makes management of services even more complex. A TV is poor quality because it's made that way; a bank may be poor quality because the customer never learned how to use the ATM card.

Perishability

Perishability results from the inseparability of production and consumption; it means that unused service capacity can't be stored and used at a later date. As we noted in Chapter 16, manufacturing firms use inventory control methods to resolve this problem. Service organizations can't handle this problem in the same way. If a movie theater is half empty for the matinee, seats can't be stored for the crowded evening show. Services must be produced and consumed simultaneously; any unused capacity is wasted.

Many service organizations have tried to deal with this problem through pricing. Airlines offer deep discounts, knowing that unused capacity can't be recovered. Movie theaters drop prices for the matinee. In some cases the bulk of a firm's service activities must be performed at one point in time. Accounting firms are busiest in April when taxes are due. Heating repair firms can't handle all the calls they get on the first cold day of fall. Because services cannot be stored, such fluctuations in demand are a challenge to managers. In part, the explosion in the temporary help industry in the U.S. over the past few years is a response to fluctuating demand for services. Many businesses need to hire people who have strong customer service skills for only a portion of the year. Temporary agencies are able to provide well-trained people who help companies meet their peak demand challenges. Using temporary help allows managers to avoid laying off people, or having employees idle during nonpeak periods.

perishability
Unused service capacity can't be stored and used at a later date.

Heterogeneity

Robots are fairly consistent in their performance, but services are often performed by humans—and people are not always consistent. **Heterogeneity** refers to the inconsistency or variation in human performance. Two different service providers can be inconsistent in their performance, as can a single provider from one service encounter to another. For example, you may have a favorite hair stylist whom you feel performs better than anyone else. But on a given day, even your favorite stylist may be inconsistent, for one reason or another, and do a below-par job. Services are simply more difficult to standardize than tangible goods.

heterogeneity
The inconsistency or variation in human performance.

For example, service quality in the hotel and restaurant industry contains elements that are tangible and intangible. Hotels frequently have standardized procedures regarding reservations, front-desk procedures, and checkout. For a restaurant, intangible and standardized components include the amount of time a customer must wait before being seated, when dirty dishes are cleared, and when the check is presented. As with tangible and standardized output, restaurants may have strict specifications about these activities. At the least, a firm that has established specifications that are closely aligned with its customers' desires has a quality advantage over organizations that haven't accurately identified customers' wishes.[11]

CLASSIFYING SERVICES

It is important to develop a classification scheme for services. Not only do such schemes help managers understand customer needs; they also provide insights into the management of services.[12] For instance, a categorization scheme for services answers questions such as:

❖ Does the customer have to be present to initiate or terminate the service transaction?
❖ Does the customer have to be present for the service to be delivered?
❖ Does the customer participate in the service transaction?
❖ Is the customer or target of the service changed in some way after the service transaction is completed?
❖ Is there a high degree of labor intensiveness?
❖ How much skill is required of the service provider?

Answers to such questions help managers enhance service quality. Consider taking a car to an auto repair shop. If customers have to drop off the car to initiate the service, their satisfaction with the service will be determined, to some extent, by their interactions with the personnel, their success in explaining their problem, and getting satisfactory results. On the other hand, using an ATM card requires little contact with the bank. The ATM must work and the transaction must be satisfactory, but how the money gets into the machine—the process—is of little interest to customers.

Table 17–2 provides a scheme for classifying services. Services are classified according to the type of market or customer (consumer or organizational) they serve. This distinction is important because the buying decision process differs between organizations and consumers. Consumers purchase (and consume) services to satisfy personal needs and wants. Industrial services are used (1) to produce other goods and services or (2) in an organization's ongoing operation. For example, both consumers and organizations need insurance, accounting services, and perhaps lawn care. But the nature of these needs is usually quite different between the two groups. An accountant may help consumers prepare their income tax returns, whereas an organization must maintain a complex set of records for tax purposes.

Services are also classified by degree of labor intensiveness. Many services—including repairs, education, and hair styling—depend heavily on the knowledge and skills of service providers. Other services, such as telecommunications, gyms, and public transportation, rely more on equipment. Labor-intensive (people-based) services are generally more heterogeneous than are equipment-based services. Consumers tend to view providers of people-based services as the service itself. As we said earlier, flight attendants represent an airline to many people. Consequently, service providers must pay special attention to the selection, training, motivation, and control of employees. Labor-intensive services are especially difficult to standardize.

Managers of labor-intensive services must be on guard for *employee burnout*. Customer service representatives are particularly susceptible to burnout because they are often required to deliver high levels of service quality while caught in the stressful position of perceiving that their organization cannot or will not meet a customer demand. Service representatives typically work long hours, lack autonomy, bear responsibility without authority, have insufficient resources and guidelines to handle problems, face demanding quotas, and often endure manager apathy. The results of a survey offer clear evidence of burnout's consequences for customer service representatives. The higher the level of burnout, the lower the employee's job satisfaction and organizational commitment. Burnout reduces the employee's energy and leads to reduced efforts at work. Managers

TABLE 17–2	CLASSIFICATION OF SERVICES
Category	Examples
Type of market	
Consumer	Life insurance, car repairs
Organizational	Lawn care, management consulting
Degree of labor intensiveness	
Labor based	Repairs, executive recruiting
Equipment based	Public transportation, air travel
Degree of customer contact	
High contact	Hotels, health care
Low contact	Dry cleaning, motion pictures
Skill of the service provider	
Professional	Legal counsel, accounting services
Nonprofessional	Taxi, janitorial
Goal of the service provider	
Profit	Financial services, overnight delivery
Nonprofit	Government, education

should view burnout as a result of stressful work environment. They can alleviate the problem by creating a work culture that supports, recognizes, and rewards customer service representatives.[13]

The third way to classify services is by degree of customer contact. Health care, hotels, real estate agencies, and restaurants are examples of high-contact services. With high-contact services, actions are generally directed toward individuals. The consumer must be present during production; in fact, the consumer must often go to the production facility. The service facility's physical appearance may be a major factor in the consumer's overall evaluation of a high-contact service. With low-contact services (such as repairs, dry cleaning, and mail services) customers generally do not need to be present during service delivery. (For example, consumers do not wait at a dry cleaner while their clothes are being laundered.) As a result, physical appearance is not as important for low-contact facilities.

A fourth way to classify services is by the service provider's level of skill. Professional services tend to be more complex and more highly regulated than nonprofessional services. In the case of a doctor's physical exam to diagnose a medical problem, consumers often don't know what the actual service or its cost will be until the service is completed because the final product is situation specific. Also doctors and surgeons are regulated by laws and by professional associations. Even less-skilled service providers, such as airline pilots, undergo extensive training and retraining, and must comply with a host of regulations and policies. However, clerks in the concession stands of movie theaters need lower skill levels to carry out their jobs.

Finally, services can be classified according to the service provider's goal: profit or nonprofit. There are several differences between profit and nonprofit services. The objectives of nonprofit organizations are not stated in financial terms, and the benefits of nonprofit services are not measured by profit or return on investment. In addition, nonprofit organizations usually have two audiences: clients and donors. A public school system is targeted to families with school-age children but also relies on the general public for support through taxes. Many nonprofit services, such as legal aid, are targeted to low-income segments. Public perceptions of nonprofit organizations impact their ability to raise funds, as the Ethics Spotlight shows.

QUALITY AND PRODUCTIVITY IN SERVICE ORGANIZATIONS

Two major challenges facing service organizations are to improve quality and productivity. Service quality improvement centers on the quality theme of exceeding customer expectations. Service providers are taught to listen to customers, and to go beyond their expressed needs to deliver service that also meets tacit or implicit needs. For example, the best service organizations help customers determine what they want by giving them options and examples of what will help them achieve their objectives. Good clothing stores don't just have racks of clothing and fitting rooms, but also helpful employees that can assist the customer in designing a wardrobe.

Service productivity is also a major issue for managers. It goes far beyond merely asking employees to work harder. Service productivity improvements most often come from designing a better system, one that takes advantage of the skills of the people in the organization. The best companies know that real productivity gains come from challenged, empowered, excited, rewarded teams of people. Yet, not all companies are rushing ahead to manage their businesses this way. Two reasons why teams have not caught on are that teams aren't easy to manage and that results are not measurable or tangible.[14] These issues will be discussed more fully below.

Service Quality

Only the customer can judge the quality of services. Thus **service quality** is the conformance of the service to customer specifications and expectations.[15] To a medical clinic's administrators, service quality is often viewed as physicians' credentials; consumers, however,

service quality
A service's conformance to customer specifications and expectations.

ETHICS SPOTLIGHT   SCANDAL AT UNITED WAY OF AMERICA

Months after the scandal erupted at United Way of America (UWA), local United Way organizations are still feeling the impact. On February 28, 1992, allegations of lavish spending and mismanagement forced UWA President William Aramony to resign. Though the unethical behavior may be limited to Aramony himself, the affair has tarnished the long-time charity's image. Says Robert O. Bothwell, executive director of the National Committee for Responsive Philanthropy, "The scandal has tarred and feathered United Way's motherhood-and-apple-pie image." It has also raised some serious questions about fundraising. Should Corporate America promote employee payroll deductions for charities? Is there adequate oversight of charity organizations by board of directors and outside auditors?

UWA's problems are well documented. Aramony received an annual compensation package of $463,000, flew first-class, and routinely hired family and friends for jobs at United Way affiliates. Since then United Way has tried desperately to restore public trust. Elaine L. Chao, former deputy secretary of the U.S. Dept. of Transportation, was hired as president and vowed, "The old way of doing things has got to change." Representatives from local United Ways have been placed on UWA's board. New financial controls were initiated to calm local affiliates, which protested the national organization's problems by holding back dues.

Just how much trust has been restored is unclear. In 1991 the 2,000 local United Way organizations raised $3.17 billion, an increase of 1.9 percent from 1990. Many local organizations do not expect to do as well in 1992, but attribute reductions to the weak economy. In the meantime there is a growing trend toward letting donors direct their contributions to specific causes and groups. Some of the largest United Way organizations in New York and Los Angeles are rethinking the way funds are distributed.

The scandal has also opened Corporate America's door to other charities. Some large firms like Citibank and Nike have included Earth Shore, an environmental group, as another option in giving through payroll deduction. At American Telephone & Telegraph, employees in New York can also use payroll deductions for Black United Funds. In Massachusetts, Polaroid and Lotus Development let workers donate to Community Works. And almost everyone agrees that firms that permit charity drives should eliminate arm twisting, which is resented by most employees.

Charity organizations are at a critical juncture. Government cuts and increased unemployment place a heavy burden on charities. Modern charity organizations need to go back to the basics: what is our mission, who is our customer, and are we meeting their expectations? Public trust in charities in general has declined, according to a survey conducted by Independent Sector. If this trend continues, United Way and other charities face a difficult future.

Source: Adapted from Ron Stodghill H, Christina Del Valle, Greg Sandler, and Lois Thernien, "United They Stand?" *Business Week*, October 19, 1992, p. 40; Pamela Sebastian, "Unemployment and Unforgotten Scandal Work against United Way Campaigns," *The Wall Street Journal*, October 21, 1992, pp. B1, B12; and Susan B. Garland, "Keeping a Sharper Eye on Those Who Pass the Hat," *Business Week*, March 16, 1992, p. 39.

are more concerned with waiting time and interactions with doctors and staff members than with where doctors obtained their degrees.[16] We are moving into a time when service organizations do not merely produce, they perform; and customer value is the focus of competitive advantage.[17] Service organizations must determine what benefits customers expect to receive and must then develop service products that meet those expectations. Performing the wrong functions for customers isn't service quality. Only by meeting customer expectations on a consistent basis can an organization deliver service quality.

True service quality rarely goes unnoticed. But providing service quality is easier said than done. Evidence of poor service is increasing: planes are late, restaurants provide slow or inefficient service, sales clerks are rude. Such occurrences have led humorists to call poor service a growth industry.[18]

To improve the quality of its services, a service provider must first understand how consumers judge service quality. Intangibility makes service quality hard to evaluate. Because the service itself is intangible, consumers generally make quality judgments based on *how* the service is performed. Several studies have reported that reliability is the most important determinant of service quality.[19] Building a zero-defects culture is as important in service industries as manufacturing. But doing it right the first time is more difficult for services because of (1) the inseparability of production and consumption and (2) heterogeneity. Table 17–3 lists some of the criteria customers use to judge service quality.

There is an increasing number of service quality measurement instruments now available for customer service managers. One instrument that managers have applied to a number of service settings, including higher education, is called SERVQUAL.[20] SERVQUAL

TABLE 17–3	CRITERIA USED TO JUDGE SERVICE QUALITY
Criteria	**Examples**
Reliability: Consistency in performance and dependability.	Accuracy in billing. Keeping records correctly. Performing the service at the designated time.
Tangibles: Physical evidence of the service.	Physical facilities. Appearance of personnel. Tools or equipment used to provide the service.
Responsiveness: Employees' willingness or readiness to provide service.	Mailing a transaction slip immediately. Calling the customer back quickly. Giving prompt service (e.g., setting up appointments quickly).
Assurance: Employee's knowledge and ability to convey trust and confidence.	Knowledge and skill of contact personnel. Company name or reputation. Personal characteristics of contact personnel.
Empathy: Caring and individualized attention to customer.	Learning customers' specific requirements. Providing specialized individual attention. Consideration for the customer.

Source: Adapted from Leonard L. Berry and A. Parasuraman, *Marketing Services; Competing through Quality* (New York: Free Press, 1991), p. 16; A. Parasuraman, Valerie A. Zeithaml, and Leonard L. Berry, "A Conceptual Model of Service Quality and Its Implications for Future Research," *Journal of Marketing*, Fall 1985, p. 47; and A. Parasuraman, Valerie A. Zeithaml, and Leonard L. Berry, "SERVQUAL: A Multiple-Item Scale for Measuring Consumer Perceptions of Service Quality," *Journal of Retailing*, Spring 1988, p. 23.

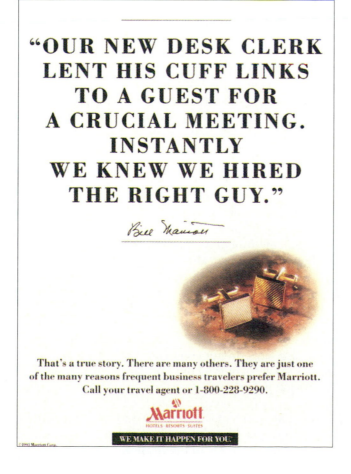

Service quality is not an accident. At Marriott, employees are the critical link to the customer.

WHAT MANAGERS ARE READING

SERVICE AMERICA!

—

According to Karl Albrecht and Ron Zemke, authors of *Service America!*, an intense interest in the quality of service is shaking the business world. The authors argue that times have changed, and we no longer live in Industrial America. We live in Service America, where firms must perform rather than produce, and where even physical products are distinguished by the quality of the service accompanying them.

Service America! illustrates how service managers can turn a company in the service field into a customer-driven and service-oriented business. The key to service management is managing the thousands of "moments of truth," which are the critical incidents where customers come into contact with the organization and form lasting impressions about the quality of service. One bad experience or negative moment of truth can wipe out all of a customer's good impressions about a company, and vice versa. Albrecht and Zemke present techniques that have been used by organizations to successfully manage these moments of truth. Included is a workable approach for instilling service excellence into every niche of the organization.

Source: Karl Albrecht and Ron Zemke, *Service America!* (Burr Ridge, IL: Dow-Jones-Irwin, 1985).

is a survey instrument designed to measure expectations and evaluations of service quality by consumers. The survey provides feedback on two to three dozen specific areas of service. Each area is categorized into five determinant factors, and a score is created for each determinant. The determinant scores are averaged to generate an overall service quality score.[21]

Some industries have developed their own measurement instrument that allows managers to compare their service rating with others in the industry. For example, dining consumers determine which restaurants meet their quality and value standards using an instrument known as DINESERV. Restaurateurs who fail to measure up will soon see declining customer counts as guests switch to competing restaurants. The DINESERV tool is a reliable, relatively simple tool, for determining how consumers view a restaurant's quality. The 29-item questionnaire comprises service-quality standards that fall into five categories: (1) assurance, (2) empathy, (3) reliability, (4) responsiveness, and (5) tangibles. By administering the DINESERV questionnaire to guests, a restaurant manager can get a reading on how customers view the restaurant's quality, identify where problems are, and determine how to solve them. DINESERV also provides managers with a quantified measure of what consumers expect in a restaurant.[22]

One danger of measurement instruments used to assess service quality is that they can become ends in themselves. Customer satisfaction managers have a tendency to become more concerned with simply measuring customer satisfaction then actually using the resulting information to improve service quality.[23] Quality-based managers use customer feedback on service quality to improve operations on a continuous basis.

Service quality is difficult to improve. In some cases companies simply do not recognize that service quality problems exist. Many dissatisfied customers never complain to the company. For example, in a survey of airline passengers, a consumer group of 100,000 frequent fliers ranked airline food lowest among 14 airline services. But passengers usually do not complain to airline companies about the food.[24] Service quality is also difficult to manage. One airline employee may interact with hundreds of customers every day. Managers can't possibly observe each of these encounters and evaluate the quality of services especially if unhappy customers do not complain.[25] Nonetheless studies have shown that customers tell twice as many people about bad service experiences as they do about good ones.[26] Customers left unhappy, whether they complain or not, may destroy a service organization.

Service quality is not an accident. It definitely can be nurtured and improved through total organizational commitment. First, managers must take quality seriously. Without commitment to quality at the highest levels of the organization, lower-level employees cannot be expected to follow suit. Next, all employees must be committed to quality. Organizations must develop specific service guidelines that are communicated to employees and enforced by management. Finally, high-quality service must be recognized and rewarded. Washington, D.C.-based corporate travel business Travelogue, Inc., generates $40 million a year in revenues. Travelogue competes against travel industry giants like American Express and Carlson Travel by providing highly personalized service at no extra cost. Above all else, owner Osman Siddigue and his people are polite and accommodating.[27]

In any service organization the front-line workers—bank tellers, flight attendants, receptionists—are the most critical resource. Part of what a service firm sells is its employees.[28] A rude flight attendant is a rude airline; an incompetent receptionist is an incompetent doctor's office. Unfortunately these front-line employees are often the organization's least-trained and lowest-paid members. Before it can improve service quality, a firm must realize that its employees are the critical link to the service customer.

Service Productivity

According to Peter Drucker, managers' single greatest challenge is to raise knowledge and service workers' productivity.[29] This involves getting the most out of people. Like manufacturing productivity, **service productivity** is the output per person per hour. Productivity improves in services when the volume or value of output increases relative to the volume or value of inputs. This can be accomplished by working employees harder; recruiting and training more productive workers; reducing worker turnover; buying more efficient equipment; automating the tasks performed by service employees; eliminating bottlenecks in the production and delivery of services that lead to downtime; and standardizing the process and the services output.[30]

service productivity
Output per person per hour.

Productivity in the service sector has shown little growth in recent years.[31] Because it is nearly twice as large as the manufacturing sector, the low productivity growth in services pulls down the national average. Nonetheless capital spending in services has increased steadily for several years. Some economists suggest that service productivity is understated because no data are available for services that employ about 70 percent of the people in service jobs.

The major way to improve service productivity is to invest in people.[32] Frederick W. Taylor used the term *working smarter* to describe a means for increasing productivity without working harder or longer. Working smarter is critical in service jobs. Productivity can be increased by defining the service task and eliminating unnecessary work. Since services are often human performances or at the very least involve humans, service workers must be trained and retrained; continuous learning must be part of productivity improvements.

The **critical success factors** approach to boosting productivity of service workers directs managers to determine those things that must go right to succeed in achieving goals and objectives. The method itself has three stages: (1) list goals and objectives; (2) identify the critical success factors necessary to achieve the goals and objectives; and (3) suggest ways in which the critical success factors are to be measured. Generalized notions of productivity make little sense in a service environment. For example, whereas the number of pages typed is easy to see and count as output, the relationship that a secretary creates between the manager and the outside world is an outcome that's difficult to measure. The context-specific nature of productivity requires an understanding of how a knowledge worker achieves goals and objectives. Once the nature of productivity is understood, measuring it becomes a much simpler task.[33]

critical success factors
Those things that must go right to achieve goals and objectives.

Some organizations, as a result of increased competition and a stagnant economy, have attempted to increase productivity by doing more with less. This involves trimming the number of workers and increasing the remaining employees' efficiency through training and labor-saving technology. New technology provides tools corporations need not only to automate existing processes and leverage resources, but also to redefine what work gets done and how it gets done. For example, in managing the accounts receivable process only large firms may be able to justify the cost of in-house, technology-based productivity enhancements. An alternative is to outsource all or part of a firm's operations to computer services firms, commercial finance companies, and banks. The best path to implementing an effective automated solution varies, but a broad range of technology applications can deliver new levels of productivity and customer service.[34]

Under the pressure of international competition, businesses are intent on improving productivity and service in the realization that they have entered the high-performance era. In some ways, offices are like manufacturing plants. White-collar productivity can be measured and improved. Waste can be eliminated. A reliable method of work organization, with service standards for every activity and a favorable work environment, must be established. There has to be a willingness on the part of management to change the organization, to train employees to manage the system, and to encourage them to think and act like owner-managers.[35] Research by the National Center on the Educational Quality of the Workforce has shown that an educational increase of 10 percent among workers in the service sector increases productivity by an average of 11 percent.[36]

DEVELOPING A PERFORMANCE CULTURE

Obviously performance is important for all businesses, but performance is especially important for service businesses. Service businesses do not *produce*, they *perform*; they don't sell things, they sell performances. And these performances are often labor intensive, meaning the service is a human performance. The human performance is the actual product that customers buy. If human effort is unresponsive and incompetent, so is the product. The majority of complaints that come into Toyota or IBM are aimed at products; the majority of complaints that come into Delta or Citicorp are aimed at people.

Service productivity and efficiency, as we already noted, can be increased by investing in people. One such investment is developing a performance culture. An organization has a **performance culture** when everyone can do his or her best work. Managers are responsible for developing a culture in which service employees have the training, knowledge, and freedom to meet customers' needs. Many organizations make the claim that they are "customer-driven," but, as we will soon see, it takes much more than rhetoric or good intentions to develop a performance culture.

performance culture
A work situation where everyone can do his or her best work.

The Components of Peak Performance
A customer walked into a post office and asked to buy 10 rolls of stamps and counted out $320. After looking in his drawer, the employee said he could only sell the customer sheets. The customer explained that sheets would cause a great deal of unnecessary work for his assistant and that rolls were exactly what he needed and wanted. The employee said that if he sold him 10 rolls he would have none left in his drawer. "That's great," the customer said. "You're having a good day. You've sold out."

The employee then told the customer that it was policy that he couldn't sell all of his rolls because he wouldn't have any for other customers later in his shift. The customer noted that a recurring fantasy of every businessperson he knew was to sell out. The employee then suggested that he buy four rolls, come back later (perhaps in disguise) and buy three more and so on.[37]

We can learn several important lessons from this story. First, customer satisfaction was not the organization's objective. Second, a company policy stopped the employee from doing his job. Third, the customer was penalized by a policy he knew nothing about until he engaged in the transaction.

On the first hot day of May a woman with a 1983 model car found that the air conditioner was broken. Even though the car was over 10 years old, it had only been driven 35,000 miles, had never had a single problem, and would cost over $20,000 to replace. So, deciding to get the car repaired, she took it to the dealership where she bought it. The dealer agreed that the car was in great shape and was worth repairing, gave her a ride to work, and promised the car for later that day.

The problem was diagnosed as a faulty o-ring that was causing the freon to leak out. Though the part was inexpensive, the labor bill was over $100. The car was ready as promised, and the air conditioner worked like a charm—for two days. Unfortunately, the mechanic missed the real problem, a more serious one with the condenser. When the woman returned, the man working at the counter offered to put the amount already paid toward replacing the condenser, but the customer did not want to invest another $400 in the car even though it was in good shape. The employee asked her, "What would you like us to do?" She replied: "Refund my money." She left with a check five minutes later.

There is something to be learned from this scenario also. First, the service department at this dealership was customer oriented. Second, service quality is delivering what you promise when you promise it. And third, even though some problems cannot be prevented, organizations can recover from them. Recovery training should be employed to teach service workers how to make decisions on their own and to help them develop an awareness of customers' concerns.[38] Without the authority, the ability, and a sense of the customer's feelings, the service employee wouldn't have refunded the money.

The first episode illustrates an organization that lacks the culture to enable employees to perform at their best. The second episode illustrates a peak performance. The postal worker was operating at a minimum, the worker at the service garage at a maximum. Interestingly both workers chose to do what they did. But in one case the worker voted in favor of the customer—probably because leaders of that organization had established a performance culture.

The foundation of all peak performances and the development of a performance culture is **discretionary effort**, the difference between the minimum amount of effort a worker must expend to keep from being penalized (acceptable performance) and the maximum amount a person can bring to a job.[39] Discretionary effort is that effort over which workers have the most control and over which managers have the least control. As Figure 17–3 shows, jobs highest in discretionary effort are customer contact jobs and knowledge jobs. As we move from the manufacturing sector to the service sector, the discretionary content of jobs increases. Assembly line workers don't bring much discretionary effort to

discretionary effort
The difference between the minimum amount of effort a worker must expend to keep from being penalized and the maximum amount a person can bring to a job.

FIGURE 17–3
Discretionary Effort
Component of Different Jobs

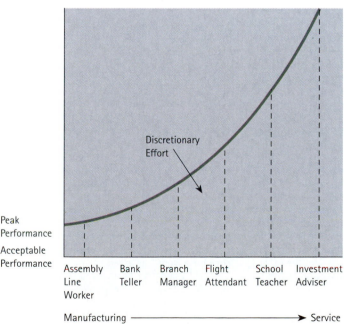

their jobs because machines dictate workers' output. Teachers or consultants, on the other hand, bring a great deal of discretion to their jobs.

Peak performance (the highest level of performance a worker can achieve) is the sum of acceptable performance and discretionary effort.[40] Returning to our two episodes, workers become or fail to become peak performers when their work requires discretionary effort, the "choose-to-do" part of their job and not the "have-to-do" part of their job—acceptable performance. Thus discretionary effort is the common denominator of peak performance, and the critical element for managers who wish to develop a high-performance culture in their organizations.

Achieving Peak Performance

Naturally firms want to encourage peak performance. But this is quite difficult because discretionary effort—the key to achieving peak performance—is not easily controlled by managers. Some service workers are satisfied with acceptable performance, which their customers come to accept. But the reality of today's highly competitive global economy is that acceptable performance is not acceptable. There may be little difference between products offered by various banks, such as checking accounts, auto loans, and savings accounts. But one bank may provide better service than another. When services are the same, a firm wins or loses with service. The challenge facing managers is to unleash workers' discretionary effort.

Empowering employees to make decisions and take action without management's approval increases the likelihood that discretionary effort will be exercised. Employees who fear the consequences of making a mistake or who, because of policies, cannot make a decision on their own, are less likely to exercise discretion. The postal worker couldn't sell the stamps in rolls because of a policy, and either didn't care about the customer or (more likely) was afraid to break the policy. Service managers have begun to empower workers

---

REFLECTIONS BY PHILIP B. CROSBY

Managing Services

I had a chat with two hotel managers in an airplane. They were anxious to tell me about their service program that ensured that guests were getting what was needed. They worked for the same chain and were one their way to a corporate management meeting. They planned to present the results of their jointly developed program to this session.

The key to their program was an assistant manager at a desk in the hotel lobby. In each room was a tent card stating that the hotel had a "quality hot line." If guests had a problem they punched the hot line number on their telephone and the assistant manager answered. If she was off on a mission, then the call would be transferred to the front desk. The call and its result were logged into the computer system and the resident manager could have an instant printout. They had some of these with them.

Guests' most common complaint referred to the time it took for room service. The second most common had to do with items in the room, such as towels, being missing or inadequate. One hotel averaged 23 calls per day on the hot line; the other averaged 34. The number range was pretty standard over the six months that the program had been in effect.

"We're really giving our guests great service," said one manager. "They get their problem fixed within 20 minutes and we have a goal of 15 minutes by the end of this year."

I said it appeared to me that the same problems happened over and over. There didn't seem to be much effective corrective action. What they had was a very expensive way of fixing things temporarily. They were crestfallen and repeated the story to make certain that I had not misunderstood.

"How about installing that system on this airplane," I asked. "If we run out of gas, we can call a hot line and they'll send some up. I think I wouldn't like that."

"What would you suggest?" one said.

"Prevention, prevention, prevention. Use each problem as a way of learning how to never let it happen again. Guests really don't want to talk to the hot line. They would prefer to just go about their business."

They were disappointed.

"You're saying that what we call service is just another name for rework?" he asked.

"True," I said. "The best way to serve your customers is to not make them part of the problem."

and encourage them to exercise discretion, realizing this has a positive impact on service quality and customer satisfaction. But empowerment alone does not ensure that a performance culture is created.[41] Managers must be committed to developing a responsive organizational structure that encourages performance, and employees must be motivated and committed to the organization's goals. This means taking extra care in hiring workers and paying close attention to matters of personality and psychology (matching the right worker with the right job). It also means giving employees adequate authority, providing them with more training and linking at least part of their pay with customer satisfaction.[42]

MANAGEMENT COMMITMENT ‑ In Chapter 8 we said that an appropriate organizational structure reinforces and rewards behaviors that accomplish the organization's goals. It is management's job to articulate these goals and develop a structure that facilitates achieving them. If managers aren't committed to customers, workers are likely to behave in the same way. Thus managers must identify performances that enhance the organization's efficiency and effectiveness. In many service organizations managers and workers alike spend an inordinate amount of their time, energy, and resources performing activities that aren't critical. Managers must identify those activities that are most critical and focus the organization's attention on being the best in the world at these activities.[43]

Managers should also tie rewards directly to performance that enhances the work's efficiency and effectiveness. Recognition should be given to individuals who perform beyond the acceptable level. Employees should be encouraged to participate with management in defining goals and standards against which individual performance can be judged. In short, if there is no incentive to perform above acceptable levels, individuals likely perform at minimums rather than maximums. Managers must be fully committed to a performance culture; their every action must clearly demonstrate this commitment to subordinates. The worst thing a manager can do is talk performance culture but take actions that convey a much different message to workers. Achieving competitive success through people involves fundamentally altering how one thinks about the workforce and the employment relationship. It means achieving success by working with people, not by replacing them or limiting the scope of their activities. It entails seeing the workforce as a source of strategic advantage, not just as a cost to be minimized or avoided. Firms that take this different perspective are often able to successfully outmaneuver and outperform their rivals.[44]

EMPLOYEE COMMITMENT ‑ By now it is clear that services are much different from goods. In many instances the service is a human performance. Unfortunately the front-line worker is often the lowest-paid and least-trained member of the organization. With new technologies in banking—automatic teller machines, direct deposit of pay checks, direct withdrawal of bills and other payments—we rarely have to go into a bank. This has led some bankers to conclude that service encounters with the bank are becoming less important when the opposite is actually true. With all this technology, a customer only visits a bank personally with a special problem or need. Service contact personnel at the bank now take on increased significance as machines complete the more routine tasks. The same can be said for many other services.

Organizations can encourage employee commitment by investing in service workers. Most performance cultures are characterized by a high degree of training. Workers are not only trained to perform their job; they are trained to solve problems, to deal with irate customers, and to deal with other members of the organization. Knowledge is important— knowledge of how one job fits into the overall scheme of the organization, knowledge of other jobs, knowledge of the organization's goals, and knowledge of the customers. The conditions under which quality service can be provided must also be present. When a service worker needs operational support or advice to help a customer, the support must be readily available. Without training, knowledge, and support, a worker cannot be truly empowered. Unfortunately some managers believe empowerment merely means telling workers that they are free to make decisions. Training and knowledge are also needed to make the right decisions.

THE WORKPLACE OF TOMORROW

Services are America's largest business category, and one of the brightest spots in the economy. Whereas manufacturers and retailers struggled to grow in the late 1980s and early 1990s, services firms rapidly expanded in sales, employment, and number of establishments.[45] Service businesses do, however, face several challenges in the years ahead. Research has indicated that there are significant aspects of service operations that will have to be addressed in order to meet the serious productivity and competitiveness challenges that service firms face today and in the future. Many of the challenges found in the service sector stand today where manufacturing challenges stood early in the twentieth century. The composite view of the service sector of the U.S. economy is a fractured one. Certain service industries show a clear sign of strengthening productivity while others remain in a stagnant or progressively declining state.[46]

Another challenge facing service organizations is to increase service quality. Research conducted by Xerox Canada revealed that as the business environment in the 1990s has become more complex, customers are demanding enhanced access and responsiveness from their business partners and suppliers. According to Xerox's research, there must be an understanding on the vendor's part that the customer's time and energy are valuable commodities.[47] The first step in the journey to service excellence is to make an organizational commitment to service quality. The commitment to service excellence is a cultural issue, which is the reason it's so hard to implement. Organizations should survey customers to determine what they want, and then take a hard look at their business processes to determine where they come up short. If there are gaps between the expectations and perceptions of customers and the services provided by organizational processes, action should be taken to narrow, and ultimately close them. Often, the reasons that services don't measure up to the expectation of customers reside deep within the organization's processes that have been changed, fixed, patched, and modified without regard for the impact on the customer.[48]

Building a culture of high performance in services requires that managers lead by example, provide adequate training, and offer rewards for good performance. Research has shown that the behavior of managers has a large impact on the performance of the organization. Having a rude boss, for example, is a major factor in employee productivity and motivation. According to OPTUM, a 24-hour phone service that answers consumer questions about health issues, workers whose bosses treat them poorly are five times as likely as other employees to report physical problems such as sleep troubles, headaches, and upset stomachs.[49] A supportive environment that drives out fear of making mistakes is necessary for

NationsBank has improved productivity and quality by using a participative and bottom-up approach to reengineering.

high performance. At the same time, people should be encouraged to learn from their mistakes, and to come up with ways to do better the next time they're in a similar situation. Research has also shown a strong correlation between employee commitment to the organization and the degree to which managers allow them to make decisions and participate in planning.[50]

NationsBank has benefited from its commitment to a high performance organizational culture. While pursuing an agressive acquisitions strategy, the company has been able to control expenses and improve customer satisfaction through the systematic application of reengineering principles in five of its centers of international operations. By using a strongly participative and bottom-up approach to reengineering, NationsBank has achieved consistent productivity and quality gains companywide, while remaining sensitive to the needs of employees and customers at every location.[51]

The benefits from frequent, sincere appreciation can be seen on the bottom line of nearly every measurable corporate attribute, including productivity, sales, product and service quality, and customer satisfaction. Yet, by concentrating only on outstanding performers, most companies recognize less than 5 percent of their workforce, often with rewards that don't reinforce their award-winning behavior.[52] High performing companies create ways to recognize all employees who contribute to the firm's overall success. From simple programs such as prizes for the best suggestions of the week to more complex volume or customer satisfaction rating criteria, profit and nonprofit organizations alike can benefit from recognizing employee contributions.

SUMMARY OF LEARNING OBJECTIVES

DEFINE SERVICE.

A service is an intangible product that involves human or mechanical effort.

DISCUSS THE CONCEPT OF TANGIBILITY AS IT RELATES TO GOODS AND SERVICES.

Consumers can physically possess a tangible good. A service cannot be physically possessed because it is intangible. Most products are neither a pure good nor pure service, but a mix of tangible and intangible elements. One element usually predominates, which is the basis for classifying a product as a good or service.

LIST FOUR CHARACTERISTICS THAT DISTINGUISH SERVICES FROM GOODS.

Services can be distinguished from goods by intangibility (services cannot be assessed by senses of sight, taste, touch, smell, or hearing), inseparability of production and consumption (services are produced and consumed at the same time), perishability (unused capacity cannot be stored and used at a later date), and heterogeneity (inconsistency or variation in human performance).

EXPLAIN THE SIGNIFICANCE OF SERVICE QUALITY AND PRODUCTIVITY.

Service quality and productivity are at the heart of many service management strategies. Service quality is the conformance of the service to customer specifications and expectations. Only by meeting customer expectations on a consistent basis can an organization deliver service quality. Productivity in services is the output per person per hour. A major challenge facing service organizations is to raise service workers' productivity.

DISCUSS HOW SERVICE ORGANIZATIONS CAN IMPROVE QUALITY AND PRODUCTIVITY.

Service quality can be improved only when managers take quality seriously. But all employees must be committed to quality. Organizations must develop specific guidelines that are communicated to employees and enforced by management. High-quality service must be recognized and rewarded. The major way to improve service productivity is to invest in people. Defining the service task, eliminating unnecessary work, and training service workers must be part of productivity improvements.

DESCRIBE WHEN AN ORGANIZATION HAS A PERFORMANCE CULTURE.

An organization has a performance culture when everyone can do her best work. Managers are responsible for developing a culture in which service employees have the training, knowledge, and freedom to meet customers' needs.

DISCUSS THE COMPONENTS OF PEAK PERFORMANCE.

Peak performance—the highest level of performance a worker can achieve—is the sum of acceptable performance and discretionary effort. Acceptable performance is the minimum amount of effort needed to not be penalized. Discretionary effort is that effort over which workers have the most control and managers have the least control.

EXPLAIN HOW ORGANIZATIONS CAN ENCOURAGE PEAK PERFORMANCE.

Peak performance can be achieved by empowering workers to make decisions and take action without management's approval. Managers must be committed to developing a responsive organization structure that encourages peak performance. Employees must be motivated and committed to the organization's goals.

KEY TERMS

critical service encounter, p. 451
critical success factors, p. 459
discretionary effort, p. 461
heterogeneity, p. 453

inseparability, p. 451
intangibility, p. 451
peak performance, p. 462
performance culture, p. 460

perishability, p. 453
service, p. 448
service productivity, p. 459
service quality, p. 455

REVIEW AND DISCUSSION QUESTIONS

Recall

1. What is a service? Name five different services.
2. What characteristics distinguish services from goods?
3. Describe a classification scheme for services, giving an example for each category.
4. What is service quality? How can it be improved?
5. Explain what is meant by a performance culture.
6. How do you calculate peak performance? Define each component of the formula.

Understanding

7. Explain how a manager may use a classification of services.
8. Why is service productivity important to our economy? How can efforts to improve service productivity reduce service quality? Give an example.
9. What makes an individual perform at the minimum? What can an organization do to encourage workers to perform at maximums?

Application

10. If an airline president asked you to put together a program for improving service quality, how would you respond? Be sure to explain why your program would improve service quality.

CASE STUDY

British Airways

The spirit of airline competition in the 1990s can probably be best described as service or else. Having lost billions of dollars in recent years, carriers are desperate to raise fares, and some feel better service will make higher fares possible. So rather than competing on price, airline companies are focusing on service. At the top of the heap stands British Airways, named in *Euromoney* magazine's annual poll of business travelers as the airline providing the best service.

In 1991 British Airways' profits were an industry-high $496 million. Its average revenue per passenger, $396, was also among the best in the industry. In terms of passengers carried and passenger miles flown, British Airways has become the world's largest international airline. All this from the airline that lost an industry-record $1 billion in 1982.

When Sir Colin Marshall took over as CEO of British Airways in early 1983, the company was the laughingstock of the industry. Comedians referred to the company, known by its initials BA, as "Bloody Awful." Employee morale had hit rock bottom; thousands of employees had just been laid off, and those remaining were embarrassed to work for the worst airline in the world. Since then, Colin Marshall has changed the company from one that seemed to disdain customers to one that strives to please them. Marshall's first challenge was to restore pride. To send a clear message to both employees and potential customers, he ordered newly designed uniforms for all personnel. The fleet of planes was also repainted with bright stripes and the motto "To fly, to serve." With this motto, the service era was born at British Airways.

Words alone do not guarantee quality service, so Marshall launched a major campaign to change employees' attitudes toward service. He surmised that many passengers, especially those traveling on business, desired better service from airlines. Marshall required that all BA employees attend a two-day seminar called "Putting People First." Its purpose was to put airline employees in the customers' shoes. Employees were asked to think about some of their own bad experiences with service.

Obvious problems—dull, tasteless food, poor cabin service, cramped leg room—were remedied immediately. But Marshall also scrutinized the less obvious details. For example, research had shown that passengers like to be called by name, so BA employees spent several months observing passengers on flights from London to Glasgow and Manchester. When ticket agents addressed passengers by name, customer satisfaction scores went up approximately 60 percent. Now BA agents call customers by name whenever possible. Troubleshooters who speak several languages were placed at London's Heathrow Airport to provide passenger assistance. Booths were set up at JFK Airport in New York City for BA passengers to videotape comments about service. Flights were scheduled for the convenience of customers, not the airline.

BA also changed its Concorde service. Marshall decided to treat the firm's seven Concordes, which were losing money, as a symbol of a revitalized airline. The planes were redecorated, and prices were raised substantially. The new price is 30 percent higher than first-class fares on a conventional jet. But because the Concorde can cross the Atlantic Ocean in half the time it takes other jets, BA developed a new advertising theme to emphasize time's importance to business travelers. As a result the Concorde began flying at over 60 percent occupancy (the breakeven point) on its transatlantic routes.

Then in early 1989 BA invested $40 million to improve first-class service. Video terminals were installed at each seat, and cabin interiors were redesigned. A new wine cellar offers an improved selection; first-class passengers may eat when they wish.

These changes are all part of Colin Marshall's service imperative, and managers from other service industries are taking note. Marshall himself likes to recall the famous Twentieth Century Limited, the train that ran from New York to Chicago. Conductors would pay passengers $1 for every minute the train was late, no matter who or what was to blame. With all the air traffic delays and weather problems, it would be tough for airlines to make the same offer. But, as Marshall says, "We could promise to make the delays completely painless with concentrated service attention. Think how many customers you could acquire for life if and when the guarantee is cheerfully, quickly and easily paid."

Today, British Airways' marketplace performance unit tracks some 350 measures of performance, including aircraft cleanliness, punctuality, technical defects on aircraft, customers' opinions on British Airways' check-in performance, the time it takes for a customer to get through when telephoning a reservations agent, and customer satisfaction with in-flight and ground services. The unit's overreaching mission is to act as a surrogate for customers in assessing the airline's performance.

QUESTIONS

1. Why did Colin Marshall have to change employees' attitudes toward service?
2. How did British Airways use research to help serve customers better?
3. Why would a passenger pay 30 percent more to fly on a Concorde than to fly first-class on a conventional jet?
4. How does the marketplace performance unit help ensure service quality?

Source: Adapted from Steven E. Prokesch, "Competing On Customer Service: An Interview with British Airways' Sir Colin Marshall, *Harvard Business Review*, November–December 1995, pp. 110–112; "Measuring Performance Through Customers' Eyes," *Harvard Business Review*, November–December 1995, pp. 108–109; Paula Dwyer, "British Air: Not Cricket," Business Week, January 25, 1993, pp. 50–51; "British Investment in USAir Approved," Lexington, (K.Y.) *Herald-Leader*, March 16, 1993, p. B3; Stewart Toy, Andrea Rothman, and Paul Dwyer, "Air Raid," *Business Week*, August 24, 1992, pp. 54–61; Richard D. Hylton, "United to BA: Take Off," Fortune, September 7, 1992, p. 9; "Best and Worst in the Air," *Parade Magazine*, June 7, 1992, p. 8; and Keneth Labich, "The Big Comeback at British Airways," *Fortune*, December 5, 1988, pp. 163–74.

VIDEO CASE

Managing Services

The service sector of the U.S. economy now comprises over 70 percent of the gross national product. More people work in the service sector than any other sector of the economy. This is in contrast to the early part of the 20th century when most people were employed in agriculture, and to the middle part of the century when the majority of Americans worked in manufacturing. The U.S. economy has only for the past several decades been predominately a service economy.

A service economy creates a range of challenges for managers that are vastly different than those in a manufacturing economy. In manufacturing, managers are concerned with production and operations. In a service economy, managers' focus shifts more to customer satisfaction.

One service company that has established itself as a leader in the area of customer satisfaction is Kinko's. Like many businesses, Kinko's started out as a small idea. In 1970, Kinko's founder Paul Orfalea began his own business selling basic school supplies and copies to students at the University of California, Santa Barbara. The first Kinko's store was so small that the copy machine had to be wheeled out to the sidewalk to allow customers in the store.

Today, Kinko's is the leading retail provider of document copying and business services in the world. There are more than 830 branch offices in the United States and in Canada, Japan, The Netherlands, and South Korea. Kinko's offers a wide range of business services in a one-stop shopping atmosphere. Customers can choose from full- and self-service copying, color and oversize copies, binding, computer services, electronic document distribution, fax, overnight mailing services, and passport photos. Many branch offices offer videoconferencing facilities.

Service companies like Kinko's know that poor customer service results in unhappy customers and lost sales. Research has shown that an unsatisfied customer will, on average, tell 9 to 10 others about their bad experience. Studies have also shown that it costs five times as much to get a new customer as to keep an existing one.

How can a company satisfy customers? It's not easy. Services can't be standardized the way tangible products can. Customers themselves often find it difficult to articulate what a good service encounter is like. Often, such intangibles as atmosphere, friendliness of staff, and cleanliness are cited by customers as important to their satisfaction.

Kinko's has learned to provide the services its customers want. In the 1970s, the company geared its services toward college students and professors. In the late 1980s, Kinko's shifted its focus to meet the growing needs of the small business and home office market.

Besides adjusting to changing market needs, Kinko's trains its employees to satisfy customers. As one Kinko's manager put it: "Our primary objective is to take care of the customer. We are proud of our ability to serve him or her in a timely and helpful manner, and to provide consistency and quality at a reasonable price." Each store manager is responsible for ensuring that employees stay focused on service quality. Kinko's managers stress store-wide commitment to quality.

Kinko's managers are also concerned about employee productivity. In the service sector, productivity is difficult to define. For Kinko's, it means employees who are prepared to meet the needs of every customer who comes in the door. These needs must be met effectively and efficiently, without sacrificing quality or diminishing customer satisfaction.

To ensure each employee is able to meet the challenge, Kinko's is dedicated to worker training. A series of comprehensive training courses held at the company's central office is designed to help employees develop necessary skills. In addition, employees are constantly offered training on new equipment and services. To check on the quality of service in each store, Kinko's uses a "mystery shopper" program. Quality monitors posing as regular customers shop at a Kinko's location and rate the quality of service on 29 variables.

Overall, the approach Kinko's uses to managing service quality has been successful. Employees work together as a team to create quality for each customer. Kinko's has been recognized as one of the top service companies in the United States. The company's emphasis on training, and its dedication to quality will help the company thrive in the competitive copying industry.

QUESTIONS

1. What are some of the different issues a manager focuses on in a service as opposed to a manufacturing business?
2. Besides the friendliness of staff, store atmosphere, and cleanliness, what are some things customers look for in service companies?
3. Discuss good and bad service encounters that you've had. What made the good ones good and the bad ones bad? What are some common mistakes companies make that seem to be easily correctable?

APPLICATION EXERCISE

The purpose of this exercise is to evaluate a service you have recently purchased or experienced, and make some suggestions as to how it can be improved. Refer back to the material in the chapter as you complete the exercise.

Select the service to be evaluated (e.g., airline, insurance, hair cut) and list it here.

Now circle the number that represents your level of agreement with each of the following statements.

	Strongly Disagree				Strongly Agree	
1. The service is consistent in performance and dependability.	1	2	3	4	5	6
2. The tangible tools or facilities used to provide the service are in good working order and have a neat appearance.	1	2	3	4	5	6
3. Workers are willing and ready to provide service.	1	2	3	4	5	6

4. The workers are knowledgeable and trustworthy.   1   2   3   4   5   6

5. The workers care about customers and provide individual attention.   1   2   3   4   5   6

Now let's assess the service. Items circled 1 or 2 show poor performance; 3 or 4 show middle-of-the-road or average performance; 5 or 6 show good performance. For each item not marked 5 or 6, how can this service be improved?

Item 1

Item 2

Item 3

Item 4

Item 5

CHAPTER 18

Managing Organizational Change

After studying this chapter, you should be able to:

- ❖ Explain why individuals resist change in organizational settings.

- ❖ Describe the different types of change agents.

- ❖ Define survey feedback and explain how it's used.

- ❖ List the six areas used in the chapter's framework for managing change.

- ❖ Compare the depth in team building and empowerment

techniques.

- ❖ Describe why it's hard to reshape an organization's culture.

- ❖ Explain the types of diagnosis techniques available to managers.

- ❖ Explain the technique of force-field analysis.

- ❖ Describe foresight-led change.

- ❖ Define what is meant by a stretch target.

Honda Changes Design Tactics to Create New Civic

Redesigned Honda Civic

It should have been a time of triumph for Ron Shriver. The Honda engineer, then 33 years old, had just helped launch the all-new 1992 Civic at the company's East Liberty (Ohio) factory. Already, car magazines and enthusiastic buyers were showering praise on the spunky subcompact. *Car & Driver* magazine said, "Honda has achieved the pole position in the small car sweepstakes."

But instead of celebrating, Shriver was worried. Slick new features on the Civic such as rear-seat heat vents and a beefier engine had hiked costs just as auto sales were slumping in the U.S. and Japan. American car buyers were balking at sticker prices that topped out at $15,000. Honda Motor Company's profit margins, already razor thin, looked as if they would disappear. So, even as the first 1992 model-year Civics were hitting the road, Shriver put together a 12-member team that would spend the next 18 months scouring Honda's U.S. suppliers and its Ohio factory workers for ideas to make the next Civic cheaper to build.

Shriver didn't know it at the time, but back in Japan, Honda executives from president Nobuhiko Kawamoto on down had reached the same conclusion: The rising yen meant Honda could no longer afford to overengineer its car line. Kawamoto assigned Hiroyuki Itoh, the Civic's chief engineer, the task of putting together his own team—one that within months would merge with Shriver's U.S. crew to collaborate on an all-out battle to wring costs out of the Civic.

It was not an easy alliance. For the first time, U.S. engineers and marketers were given the opportunity to have a say in shaping a new model from its earliest designs. The car maker also worked far harder than ever before with U.S. suppliers, and had to relax some of its vaunted engineering standards. Perhaps most important, Japanese engineers used an unprecedented number of money-saving suggestions from factory workers and suppliers on both sides of the Pacific.

The new Civic is the first Honda model entirely conceived and executed since Kawamoto shook up the company in the early 1990s. For 20 years, Honda's renowned R&D engineers had always dictated new designs. Success bred arrogance: Even in Japan, sales and manufacturing teams were only consulted after designs were nearly set. When disagreements arose, the engineers had the final word. And the U.S. unit has no say over any but cosmetic changes. "We always did what we wanted, thinking it was the right thing," says Kawamoto, a 27-year R&D veteran who took over Honda's top job in 1990. "But we had to see that profits wouldn't keep growing."

So, soon after the fifth-generation Civic debuted in 1992, Kawamoto ordered Itoh to begin by revamping Honda's design process itself. Because Honda's R&D specialists in the past hadn't sought input early enough from manufacturing, factories had rarely had time to test designs to minimize capital investment. Kawamoto also knew that Honda had to work earlier with suppliers to eke out production efficiencies.

Itoh's first step was to end the engineering dictatorship. Early that year, he put together a seven-member redesign team that united Japanese executives from engineering, manufacturing, purchasing, quality, and sales from day one—and all had equal say. Soon after Itoh formed his team, Shriver and a group of Ohio employees flew to Tokyo to outline their plans to ferret out excess costs in the U.S. "We received input from the factory much earlier," Itoh said. "We wanted to get sales thinking, 'How can we sell this?' and the factory thinking, 'How can we make this?'"

The result was a host of money-saving manufacturing tricks that Honda hopes customers won't notice. Although none brought huge savings individually, collectively they add up to a bundle. Whereas the old Civic sported a complicated trunk hinge that made it easy to retrieve luggage, the new model returns to a simpler, traditional hinge that's cheaper to make, if not quite as convenient. Elsewhere, the dashboard and the inner door trim are made from one molded piece each, instead of two or more, which simplifies manufacture. And the cloth on the rear seats, which get less wear, has 30% fewer threads.

Still, Japanese designers and engineers sometimes accepted new ideas only after a struggle. For instance, one East Liberty paint shop employee had a suggestion to simplify the design of front and rear plastic bumper covers, or fascias. On the old Civic, the front fascia had two separate air inlets and a bottom section that had to be individually masked before painting. In the summer of 1992, when Itoh and 10 Honda executives made a fact-finding trip to Ohio, the worker proposed building the fascias with removable grills that wouldn't need masking. But the executives, cautious because Japanese consumers are very picky about paint, nixed the idea.

Unfazed, the Ohio plant worker persisted with her idea. She countered with several alternatives, which executives presented at later meetings. Eventually, Itoh accepted a compromise. The front fascia would have only one easily masked opening, while the rear would require no masking. Honda's annual savings: $1.2 million in the U.S. alone. Honda's engineers "weren't accustomed to hearing from the factory so early on," says the worker whose idea was finally accepted. "They had to get over the shock."

The U.S. sales team also pitched in. The Civic's air conditioning and sound systems had always been dealer-installed options. Dealers charged what they could get, typically $1,200 to $1,500. Now, however, air conditioning will be installed at the factory, for just $850. Audio systems will see similar savings.

Has this massive change effort at Honda been successful? It's too soon to tell. However, Shriver, Itoh, and the members of their redesign team had better not stand still. Despite the dollar's recent recovery, many analysts expect the yen to continue its decades-long upward trek. And with Detroit steadily improving its small cars—while straining to maintain a $2,000 per car price advantage—Honda's entry-level sedan is under more competitive pressure than ever before.

Sources: Adapted from Edith Hill Updike, David Woodruff, and Larry Armstrong, "Honda's Civic Lesson," *Business Week,* September 18, 1995, pp. 71, 73, 76; Larry Armstrong, Kathleen Kerwin, and Bill Spindle, "Trying To Rev Up: Can Japan's Carmakers Regain Lost Ground?" *Business Week,* January 24, 1994, pp. 32–33.

Change is a topic very much on the minds of managers today. Most would agree that the pace of change is forever increasing, leaving less and less time to think about decisions before they're made. Indeed change is a major factor that managers have to deal with. Claims that we are in a period uniquely characterized by change, however, are probably overstated. Humans have always dealt with more change than they could handle. Events force themselves upon us unexpectedly. Great minds think of new ways of organizing society, science, or the arts. Revolutions overthrow political order.

In the context of organizations, change has always occurred. Perhaps what makes managers today believe their era to be unique is that much of modern organizational change is driven by market competition. In previous decades, when large American firms had little competition there was little reason to create organizational change. The economic picture is far different today. Global competition that gives consumers more choices is a major driver of organizational change. This driver wasn't present for most of the twentieth century. In fact, truly global competition is probably a phenomenon that has become real only in the last 20 years.

Global competition requires that managers think of ways to change their organization continuously to gain competitive advantage. As the opening vignette shows, it's just not acceptable anymore to adopt industrywide changes as they occur. Today, managers must try to determine what the future is going to be like and then change their organization in the present to prepare for that future. Industry foresight is required to help managers position their organization to be competitive in the global marketplace of 5, 10, and even 25 years into the future.[1]

In the past decade, managers have led the following organizational changes:

* The workforce has changed significantly. Many organizations have downsized to become leaner, with less middle management and fewer layers in the corporate hierarchy.
* Networking technologies have been implemented to increase worker productivity.
* Flexible work systems have enabled a number of companies to meet the needs of an increasingly professionalized workforce.
* Employee training has helped workers adapt to and thrive in new work environments that are increasingly diverse.
* Reengineering in organizations has reduced steps in work processes, and forced organizations to focus on their core competencies.
* Quality management has given the worker more power in the workplace, including involvement in decision making and planning, and customer satisfaction.

The changes taking place in American business and industry can be summarized into four elements: (1) globalization of competition; (2) delayering of organizations; (3) growth of computerization and computer networks; and (4) the emergence of the information highway. As a result of these changes, managers will need to make a wide variety of adjustments if they want their companies to remain competitive into the 21st century. New companies will come into being, and old ones that don't change themselves will die. This is an era of instant communication and fast-changing technologies. It's an era in which customers demand quality and value. It's also an era of employee empowerment and changing global relationships and structures. Traditional ways of doing business are gone, along with comfortable relationships. It's hard to let go of systems and habits that have developed over a lifetime, but if companies are going to achieve and maintain success, they must continuously reinvent themselves.[2]

In the past decade, many companies have tried to remake themselves into better competitors. Their efforts have gone under many banners: total quality management, reengineering, right sizing, restructuring, and cultural change. In almost every case, the goal has been the same: to cope with a new, more challenging market by changing the way business is conducted. A few of these change programs have been very successful. A few have been utter failures. Most fall somewhere in between with a distinct tilt toward the failure end of the scale. The lessons learned from these failures will be relevant to more and more organizations as the business environment becomes increasingly competitive. One lesson that has been taken away is that change involves numerous phases that, together, usually take a long time to complete. A second lesson is that critical mistakes in the management of any of the phases can have a devastating impact on the success of the change effort.[3]

This chapter discusses some forces of change. It also presents frameworks and models that can serve as blueprints for ordering managerial thinking about change. They serve as a guide for first diagnosing and then managing change. In addition, various intervention methods are discussed in terms of change. Finally, the ever-present cultural and structural factors that make or break change interventions are discussed.

CHANGE FORCES

Today's organizational domain includes unpredictable and uncontrollable domestic and international forces. New developments in mergers and acquisitions, regulation, privatization, downsizing, union–management collaboration, high-involvement participation, plant closings, reengineering, managing culturally diverse workers, and environmental protection occupy managers' time. These and many other forces from outside and inside the organization demand attention.

Organizations around the world have been experiencing increasingly rapid change for much of the second half of the twentieth century. With the globalization of markets, worldwide telecommunications, and increasingly rapid and efficient travel over the past decade, the need for organizations to continuously reinvent themselves is greater than ever. The average U.S. business lasts only about 40 years. Complex and rapid changes in the world's economic and social climates heighten the threat to the survival of organizations. Organizations that learn to search creatively for the future can transform themselves when they confront the chaos of a constantly changing competitive environment.[4] Figure 18–1 shows three strategies for change that managers can choose among in their quest for competitiveness. Restructuring leads to a smaller organization, reengineering and continuous improvement to a better organization, and transformation or reinvention to a different organization.

For organizations to survive continuous transformation or reinvention, there has to be some factor that binds people together. It is a firm's system of drawing its people together for a common purpose that is the one crucial factor to success. Changes in the workplace have helped create unifying systems for continuous improvement in several firms. For example, American Express made a significant change when it adopted a system built on customer-based transactions. The company created a comprehensive delivery system around

FIGURE 18–1
The Quest for Competitiveness

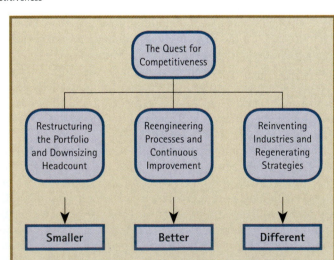

Source: Gary Hamel and C. K. Prahalad, *Competing for the Future* (Boston, Mass.: Harvard Business School Press, 1994), p. 15.

its external customer requests that would support key customer transactions. Motorola provides another example of an exceptional company whose success is largely a result of its systematic approach toward implementing change. In Motorola's case, the unifying factor wasn't individual customer transactions, but rather the use of a common language to help unify its people.[5]

Internal Forces

Internal change forces are pressures that come from a worker, a group, or a department. Sometimes the pressure is the cost of producing a microchip or car. For example, unit cost increases; therefore, pricing the product at a reasonable amount to make a sale is a force that may signal a need for change. If the product costs too much to produce, it can't be priced competitively.

Poor worker morale over some inequity in the reward system could be an internal pressure point that a manager becomes aware of and must address. Although attitudes may be difficult to observe directly, increased grievance rates, absenteeism, or turnover may suggest poor or decreasing morale. Identifying internally driven forces for change is sometimes difficult. Is the poor morale caused by the culture, the structure, or the manager, or does the worker bring this attitude to work? It's a difficult question to answer.

Regardless of changes in an organization's environment, mission, or structure, employee satisfaction and quality of work life remain significant concerns for most organizational change and development efforts. Although morale and motivation are not often the impetus for such change programs, they are almost always tied inextricably to the problems that have manifested themselves. One of the most effective tools a manager has for understanding and diagnosing the issues involved is the organizational survey. Surveys can be done through questionnaires or through interviews. They help managers stay in touch with the forces of change that are at work among employees. Staying in touch with these forces allows them to be managed and turned to positive outcomes.[6]

internal change forces Forces for change that occur within the organization, such as communication problems, morale problems, and decision-making breakdowns.

External Forces

External (outside-the-organization) forces can be a signal that change is needed. Government regulations such as the Americans with Disabilities Act (ADA) of 1992 or affirmative action requirements could suggest the need to change a firm's work area layout or recruitment and selection program. Skyrocketing health care costs, now totaling over $800 billion annually, suggest that organizations may need to change their health care coverage program or the type of fringe benefits provided to employees.

Market competitors and how they reward employees, distribute products, service customers, or form alliances with foreign partners may signal the need to change. Foreign competitors often play by different rules that American firms must learn to cope with or change if they're to survive.

The wave of cultural diversity sweeping across America is a powerful external force that necessitates change. Integrating and utilizing the talents of a more diverse workforce, and effectively rewarding this culturally diverse workforce will require changes in attitude, interpersonal interaction, and perception. Changes in managers' cultural awareness are also needed. As the Diversity Scope shows, this external change has led to increased stress levels for managers.

RESISTANCE TO CHANGE

Any change, no matter how clearly beneficial to employees and the organization as a whole, will meet with and often be sabotaged by resistance. The failure of many recent large-scale efforts at corporate change can be traced directly to employee resistance. Total quality management (TQM) is an example. The evidence shows that a large number of firms that have attempted to apply TQM in their organization have gained little in their competitive position as a result of their change efforts. Many reengineering efforts have also fallen short of expectations.[7] A major reason for these disappointing results is employee resistance to change.

DIVERSITY SCOPE

NEW MULTICULTURAL WORKPLACE RAISES MORALITY ISSUES

—

- Deciding whom to appoint to a challenging new position in Europe, a manager passes over an Asian employee and gives the job to a white male. He worries that there may be some prejudice in his own judgment.
- Because she wants to see more minorities in visible positions, a manager promotes a slightly less qualified minority candidate over a majority candidate, all the while feeling guilty.
- A male manager hesitates to hug a longtime employee who has just lost her mother.

Worry, guilt, indecision—these are the symptoms of managers under stress. All of the managers in the situations above are facing circumstances in which their usual modes of coping are not sufficient. Earlier in their careers, issues concerning multicultural interaction were not as worrisome. In that earlier era, a manager's first concern was to take decisive action, not to spend time puzzling over the subtleties of race relations. Back then, a manager was reasonably clear about the goal of promoting the best-qualified individual no matter what. A man could touch a woman co-worker in a nurturing manner without fear of being inappropriate. However, today the climate in the workplace has changed, and issues of race and gender, indeed of multiculturalism, are in the foreground of many managerial decisions. This new climate at work creates uncertainties and stresses for both managers and employees.

Of course, all managerial life entails some stress. Time stress, role stress, career stress, and interpersonal stress are all common examples. Today, in addition, people find themselves placed increasingly under a previously unidentified form of stress: the discomfort they feel when they face a situation in which, because of the presence of multicultural factors, their usual modes of coping are insufficient. This form of stress can be called "diversity stress."

Diversity stress exists wherever cultures clash: in mixed race settings, in settings where women work alongside men, in companies that employ an international workforce. In fact, diversity stress can exist in any situation where beliefs and values differ. Diversity stress is a type of morality stress. Morality stress occurs when managerial decisions are shrouded in ambiguity and competing moral principles, and people are uncertain how to behave. Often, in multicultural type situations, managers are apprehensive about the consequences of their actions. Contemplating their alternatives under a situation in which moral issues are involved and there is no clear path to resolution, they experience morality stress, which is exacerbated by the manager's organizational role.

When managing a multicultural workforce, managers face several moral dilemmas. One such dilemma is the need to show special consideration for special circumstances, while at the same time treating people fairly and impartially. Another moral dilemma is the need to deceive and the need to tell the truth. For instance, under circumstances in which they are required to fill a job with a woman or minority, managers often feel that they must tell the new job holder that they were the best person for the job.

Finally, managers face the moral dilemmas inherent in the need to compete aggressively while competing within standards of fair competition. In the competition to attract the best employees and to meet governmental standards, for example, being racially "correct" is one way to come out ahead. In one company, this dilemma surfaced in the following situation: a Spanish-speaking employee from South America was tapped by the company personnel manager to do some translating. A few weeks later the company's payroll manager informed the employee that she had been requested to change the employee's race classification in their system from White to Hispanic. The employee

questioned whether the company was just trying to make a quota and was personally uncomfortable with the change: "Just because I am Spanish speaking doesn't mean I am Hispanic, does it?"

Certainly, today the culture of business has changed to the point where many managers now recognize diversity issues in their everyday decisions. Managers working in modern multicultural work environments must weigh competing demands under circumstances in which there is no obvious resolution. They are often uncertain about what behaviors are appropriate in what circumstances. They feel a moral obligation to act in accord with some moral standard, yet are not always clear about what that standard is. In any particular situation, they may not be clear whether their own moral standard or that of the company should take precedence. Furthermore, managers may not be comfortable seeking out others to discuss either the particular situation or the moral standard.

Broadly speaking, there are two ways that organizations will deal with diversity stress in their cultures. One is to develop a power culture in which one group dominates and all others are subject to it. In this organization, ambiguities will be ignored. Homogeneity will be the main value. All diverse cultures will be subordinated to one "common" culture.

The alternative mode is to develop a consensual organization based on the diversity of cultures represented. In such an organization, valuing cultural differences is the moral imperative. In this organization the effective individual will be educated about multicultural influences and will be able to monitor his own reactions to diversity stress with some objectivity. Both individuals and management will be sensitive to issues of clustering. The organization itself will strive to resolve ambiguities around values.

Sources: Adapted from Rae Andre, "Diversity Stress as Morality Stress," *Journal of Business Ethics*, June 1995, pp. 489–496; J.A. Waters and F. Bird, "The Moral Dimension of Organizational Culture," *Journal of Business Ethics*, 1987, (6), pp. 15–22.

Self-Interest

Some individuals resist change because they have a personal self-interest in the way things are done. They enjoy the work flow or their position—and change threatens these. For example, working in an office affords individuals an opportunity to interact socially, compare work situations, and examine problems with others.

Habit

The comfort of working the same way day after day has a certain appeal to people. For many individuals, life is a pattern of getting up, going to work, coming home, and going to bed. People become accustomed to sameness; they get in the habit of doing tasks a certain way. Changes in personnel, work flow, structure, or technology threaten the continuation of a pattern or set of habits.

Fear

Change introduces uncertainty and a degree of fear. People fear having to learn a new way or to become accustomed to a new leader, and possibly failing. Employees are sometimes provided with an opportunity to relocate and take a different, better-paying job in the firm. But this change is considered risky and introduces the possibility of failing.

Peer Pressure

Peers often apply pressure to resist change. For example, peers may resist the introduction of automation because they assume, sometimes correctly, that fewer workers will be needed to perform the job. These peers can pressure colleagues who might otherwise emotionally and personally support automation and its potential to improve productivity.

Bureaucratic Inertia

Large government institutions, educational institutions, and business organizations have a built-in resistance because of the traditional rules, policies, and procedures. The refrain is: "This is how we've done things for years." Why change? The Big Three auto manufacturers had a degree of bureaucratically built-in resistance to the smaller Japanese cars that arrived in the 1970s. These smaller, more gas-efficient cars caught the attention of American consumers—especially after the gas shortages of 1973. But the Big Three simply didn't respond in a timely or aggressive fashion. They each were steeped in traditional thinking about small cars—especially Japanese autos.

Figure 18–2 (an implementation analysis guide developed by consultant David A. Nadler) provides a quick look at three distinct areas that are concerned with resistance to change, control, and power. As an implementation diagnosis device, this form provides an indication of 12 implementation action steps. Managers using the guide can provide their own assessment of how good or how poor action has been in these 12 areas.

Inflexible rules, policies, and procedures preclude the use of adaptive changes in any organization. Bureaucracy, red tape, and traditionally built-in ways of conducting business are difficult to overcome. Often managers know they're in a bureaucratic maze, but it's difficult to wrestle through the barriers, delays, and stonewalling that can become common. As Philip B. Crosby's Reflections discusses, the idea of doing things right the first time was not met with enthusiasm by managers. The idea initially met barriers of resistance and stonewalling.

REDUCING RESISTANCE TO CHANGE

Before changes in organizations can be made, overcoming or reducing resistance and encouraging and building support for changes is needed. According to Andersen Consulting's Terry Neill, head of Andersen Consulting's worldwide change management effort, winners out-execute competitors rather than out-strategize them. Neill translates an old French saying, "Change is a door that can only be opened from the inside." As Notre Dame football coach Lou Holtz puts it: "It's not my job to motivate players. They bring extraordinary motivation to our program. It's my job not to demotivate them." W. Edwards Deming believes all workers have a pride of workmanship. It's management's job to remove the impediments to pride of workmanship, leaving room for workers to empower themselves.[8] There are no simple, always-perfect prescriptions for reducing resistance, but six options may prove useful.

Education and Communication

Explaining in meetings, through memos, or in reports why change is needed is especially helpful when there's resistance because of a lack of information. Open communica-

FIGURE 18-2
Implementation Analysis
Guide

	Implementation Practices	Rating	Comments/Explanation
Shaping Political Dynamics	1. Getting the support of key power groups.		
	2. Using leader behavior to support the direction of change.		
	3. Using symbols and language.		
	4. Building in stability.		
Motivating Change	5. Creating dissatisfaction with the status quo.		
	6. Participation in planning and/or implementing change.		
	7. Rewarding needed behavior in transition and future states.		
	8. Providing time and opportunity to disengage from current state.		
Managing the Transition	9. Developing and communicating a clear image of the future state.		
	10. Using multiple and consistent leverage points.		
	11. Using transition management structures.		
	12. Building in feedback and evaluation of the transition.		

Rating is an assessment of the general quality of action in each implementation practice area.

Scale:
5 = Very Good
4 = Good
3 = Fair
2 = Poor
1 = Very Poor

Summary Ratings

Motivation	Transition	Political	Overall

Source: Michael L. Tushman, Charles O'Reilly, and David A. Nadler, *The Management of Organizations* (New York: Harper & Row, 1989), p. 502.

tion helps people prepare for the change. Paving the way, showing the logic, and keeping everyone informed lowers resistance. This option is usually time consuming. The emphasis of a communications plan should be proactive rather than reactive. All messages should be consistent and repeated through various channels such as videos, memos, newsletters, e-mail, and regular meetings.[9]

Participation and Involvement

Bringing together those to be affected to help design and implement the change likely will increase their commitment. Empowerment of employees, attention to the customer, and customization of the quality program to company culture play a part in every company's quality efforts. Successful quality programs are heavily focused on effecting behavioral change throughout an organization. At 3M, for example, quality teams and standards pervade the entire organization: safety, environmental, marketing, customer relations, and the manufacturing facility.[10]

REFLECTIONS BY PHILIP B. CROSBY

Managing Organizational Changes

"I had this idea," I remarked at a staff meeting back in 1961. "We spend a lot of time and money checking and finding and fixing. Why don't we concentrate on getting things done right the first time? Then we won't have to check, find, and fix?"

As I looked around the room, expecting to see an enthusiastic response to this marvelous though, I experienced instant disappointment. They gave me that "poor soul" look as if I had suggested we pop in for lunch on Saturn. Instantly I knew how Galileo had felt.

"That would cost a fortune, Phil," said the engineering director.

"People would be very upset if we demanded they do everything right every time. We would have psychos on our hands and a strike too," said the personnel director.

"I can't believe your serious," said our quality expert. "Our acceptable quality expert. "Our acceptable quality levels are at 1 percent now, and that's very rigid. I'd need more inspectors if we're going to not have any defects."

"The employees are just not capable of doing that kind of work," said the production manager. "The school systems don't teach them good hand skills."

"I was thinking that we could train people more than we do. As far as I can see they're capable of doing great work," I replied. "I think the problem is that we've set up a process of doing work and then doing it over."

"That's the way everyone does it," replied the marketing manager. It has been that way for years, and it has been that way because that's the best way to work."

There was a finality to the statement and everyone seemed to nod at that moment for emphasis. Later I realized that each of them was thinking of the drastic revisions that would be necessary in their personal professional lives if these ground rules changed. Doing it right means that requirements must be clear; it means that people must be trained; it means that responsibility must be dropped down the organization chart; it means that some departments won't be as large as they were before; it means going against the conventional wisdom.

I was thinking that such a policy would make things easier. Everyone else was thinking it would be harder.

From this I learned in the final consideration that people aren't against change just because it's change. After all, they alter their own lives regularly. They change personal suppliers, such as restaurants; they change friends; they move; they get new clothes; they do all these things and more without even thinking of them as change. But in these cases they're the ones who are instigating the action.

In business life, when others start making things different, change is much more threatening. We may not understand the limits of what's going to happen. We may have not strings on it. We may, well, feel threatened. After realizing this I began taking care to explain the concepts of zero defects in a less terminal way, sort of easing into it until the group began to come up with the idea themselves. That way they could see how it would affect them and determine that it would make their lives easier, not harder.

Facilitation and Support

Being supportive is an important management characteristic when change is implemented. Managers must be supportive (e.g., show concern for subordinates, be good listeners, go to bat for subordinates on important issues) by providing training opportunities and helping to facilitate the change. Behaviors exhibited by leaders and managers can have an effect on employees' attitudes and perceptions about their work and their organization. Research conducted during a change effort in the marketing and sales division of an international pharmaceutical firm showed that different types of behaviors for managers and senior managers were significantly related to employee attitudes and perceptions.[11] Managers need to behave in ways that show commitment to the change and support for employees while they are learning to deal with the change.

Negotiation and Agreement

Resistance can be reduced through negotiation. Discussion and analysis can help managers identify points of negotiation and agreement. Negotiated agreement involves giving something to another party to reduce resistance. For example, convincing a person to move to a less desirable work location may require paying a bonus or increasing monthly salary. Once this negotiation agreement is reached, others may expect the manager to grant similar concessions in the future.

Manipulation and Co-optation

Manipulation involves the use of devious tactics to convince others that a change is in their best interests. Holding back information, playing one person against another, and providing slanted information are examples of manipulation. *Co-opting* an individual involves giving him a major role in the design or implementation of the change. For example, Exide Electronics is committed to improving quality in all facets of the organization by focusing on the customer and involving employees in the process. Its continuous improvement process implemented in its Raleigh (North Carolina) Plant Operation is known as the "correct action process." The process, implemented in 1992 and still in place today, consists of steering committees that oversee the process, work cells that run the daily business, corrective action teams that work on quality issues and continuous improvement, and task teams that work on special projects. Through this massive employee involvement (co-optation) the Raleigh Plant Operation was able to support an 11 percent increase in sales while achieving a 4 percent decrease in overall materials and operating costs.[12]

Explicit and Implicit Coercion

In using explicit and/or implicit coercion, managers engage in threatening behavior. They threaten employees with job loss, reduced promotion opportunities, poor job assignments, and loss of privileges. The coercion is intended to reduce a person's resistance to the man-age-ment-initiated change. Coercive behavior can be risky because it can generate bad feelings and hostility.[13]

Table 18–1 on the next page lists these six options for reducing the commonly found resistance to change and when it's appropriate to use each one. As illustrated, each of the options has advantages and disadvantages.

Companies that are successful in implementing change report much greater employee commitment to initiatives, smaller productivity fluctuations during implementation, and significantly shorter implementation timelines. Managers who want to overcome resistance to change must collect data to identify the relative strength of each factor that is causing the resistance and how it varies by stakeholder group.[14]

A FRAMEWORK FOR MANAGING CHANGE IN ORGANIZATIONS

Many frameworks can be useful for managing change and change processes. Figure 18–3 provides a process-oriented model for managing change that emphasizes six distinct stages in which managers must make decisions. Stage 1, the forces for change, has already been discussed in terms of internal and external factors.

Distinguished psychologist Kurt Lewin introduced the notion of three stages in the change process: unfreezing, changing, and refreezing. The unfreezing phase is designated as Stage 2 in Figure 18–3. Managers must recognize that change is needed or that the present state is inadequate. Recognition is easy if the magnitude of the problems (such as market share losses, more equal employment opportunity discrimination suits, rising turnover, or declining profit margins) are significant. Unfortunately, the indicators that change is needed aren't always dramatic. A loss here and there, a complaining group of customers, a disgruntled technician, or a lost contract isn't always an indication that change is necessary.

Some companies have adopted a new technique for helping managers recognize the need for change. The technique is known as the sense-and-respond (SR) model. The SR model involves sensing change earlier and responding to it faster. According to Steve Haeckel of the IBM Advanced Business Institute, the SR model requires managers to be very good at conceptual thinking.[15] That means managers must be able to think broadly and to entertain two or more (possibly contradictory) ideas about issues at the same time. The SR model requires that managers build an organizational context that delegates operational decision making and the design of adaptive systems to the people or teams

TABLE 18–1	METHODS FOR REDUCING RESISTANCE TO CHANGE			
Approach	Involves	Commonly Used When...	Advantages	Disadvantages
1. Education and communication	Explaining the need for and logic of change to individuals, groups, and even entire organizations.	There is a lack of information or inaccurate information and analysis.	Once persuaded, people will often help implement the change.	Can be very time consuming if many people are involved.
2. Participation and involvement	Asking members of organization to help design the change.	The initiators do not have all the information they need to design the change, and others have considerable power to resist.	People who participate will be committed to implementing change, and any relevant information they have will be integrated into the change plan.	Can be very time consuming if participants design an inappropriate change.
3. Facilitation and support	Offering retraining programs, time off, emotional support, and understanding to people affected by the change.	People are resisting because of adjustment problems.	No other approach works as well with adjustment problems.	Can be time consuming and expensive, and still fail.
4. Negotiation and agreement	Negotiating with potential resisters; even soliciting written letters of understanding.	Some person or group with considerable power to resist will clearly lose out in a change.	Sometimes it is a relatively easy way to avoid major resistance.	Can be too expensive if it alerts others to negotiate for compliance.
5. Manipulation and *co-optation*	Giving key persons a desirable role in designing or implementing change process.	Other tactics will not work or are too expensive.	It can be a relatively quick and inexpensive solution to resistance problems.	Can lead to future problems if people feel manipulated.
6. Explicit and implicit coercion	Threatening job loss or transfer, lack of promotion, etc.	Speed is essential, and the change initiators possess considerable power.	It is speedy and can overcome any kind of resistance.	Can be risky if it leaves people angry with the initiators.

Source: Reprinted by permission of the *Harvard Business Review*. An exhibit from "Choosing Strategies for Change," by John P. Kotter and Leonard A. Schlesinger (March–April 1979). Copyright © 1979 by the President and Fellows of Harvard College; all rights reserved.

FIGURE 18–3
Framework for Managing
Change

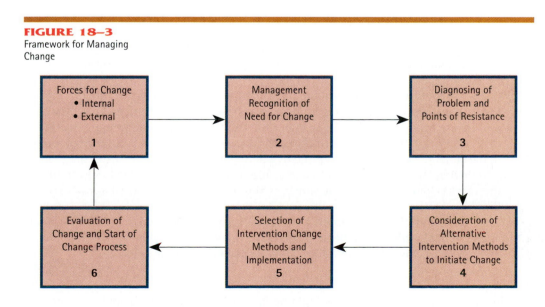

accountable for producing results. The SR corporation encourages all employees to be alert to changes in the environment and to act on those changes to improve the competitive position of the company.[16]

Stage 3 emphasizes diagnosis. A sound diagnosis can provide invaluable information that helps unfreeze when problems are identified. Diagnosis can also clarify the problem and suggest what changes can solve it. Diagnosis can be conducted using a variety of techniques.

When companies embrace TQM, quality becomes management's top priority. The primary concern for all managers is the assurance that the quality of the products or services provided meets the highest standards. Effective TQM programs assure that customers' needs are identified early in the process of designing and producing a product or service. It permeates every aspect of the organization: research and development, marketing, sales, and service. Successful TQM programs encourage people to make significant changes in the manner in which they perform their jobs, look at projects, and deal with subordinates, colleagues, bosses, and customers.[17]

Another popular diagnosis strategy developed by Lewin is known as force field analysis. This technique is a means of diagnosing situations and analyzing the various change strategies that can be used in a particular situation.

Once a manager determines that there's a gap between what's happening in the organization and what they'd prefer to be happening, then force field analysis becomes a useful tool. Before undertaking any change strategy, it's useful for managers to determine what they have working in their favor (driving forces) and what forces are working against them (restraining forces). Driving forces are those forces affecting a situation that are pushing in a particular direction; they tend to initiate a change and keep it going. In terms of improving productivity in an organization, words of praise from a manager, effective reward systems, and a high level of employee involvement in decision making are examples of driving forces.

Restraining forces are those forces that act to restrain or decrease driving forces. Low morale, anger, or inadequate work tools are examples of restraining forces. Equilibrium is the point at which the sum of the driving forces is equal to the sum of the restraining forces.

To understand these concepts, imagine that you manage a fast-food restaurant. If you decide to initiate a TQM program in the restaurant some of the driving forces might be customer demand, competition, cost pressures, government regulations, and franchise policies. Some of the restraining forces might be lack of resources, low employee morale, low employee skill level, employee resistance to change, or lack of knowledge about TQM. Figure 18–4 illustrates the relationship between driving forces and restraining forces in this scenario.

In utilizing force field analysis for developing a change strategy, there are a few guidelines that can be used:

1. If the driving forces far outweigh the restraining forces in power and frequency in a change situation, managers interested in driving for change can often push on and overpower the restraining forces.

2. If the reverse is true, and the restraining forces are much stronger than the driving forces, managers interested in driving for change have several choices. First, they can give up the change effort, realizing that it will be too difficult to implement. Second, they can pursue the change effort, but concentrate on maintaining the driving forces in the situation while attempting, one by one, to change each of the restraining forces into driving forces or somehow to immobilize each of the restraining forces so that they are no longer factors in the situation. The second choice is possible, but very time consuming.

3. If the driving forces and restraining forces are fairly equal in a change situation, managers probably will have to begin pushing the driving forces, while at the same time attempting to convert or immobilize some or all of the restraining forces.[18]

Stage 4 is the selection of a change intervention strategy. We'll discuss several strategies later, including survey feedback, team building, empowerment, and foresight-led change.

FIGURE 18–4
Driving and Restraining Forces
in Fast-Food Restaurant
Example

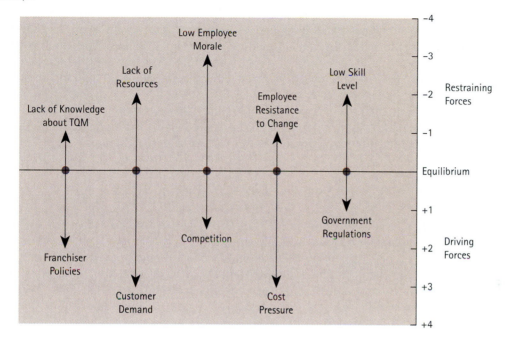

After evaluating the pros and cons of various change techniques, one or some combination of alternatives should be selected and then implemented (Stage 5). Implementation often isn't given enough consideration in attempts to bring about lasting change (refreezing).

Stage 6 in the change model points to evaluation and starting the process again. Managers want to learn whether changes have occurred and if so, what has been accomplished. Is the profit margin improved? Has morale improved? Have customers returned to our brand? It's hard to measure change over time because there are often many uncontrollable changes that influence effects of the original change effort. In the middle of a structural change, a new government regulation may have been passed that directly affects employees in the units undergoing change. Suppose the regulation means that employees must now file additional government paperwork. But employees have continually complained about paperwork. Now, with the new regulation, there's even more paperwork. Did the structural change cause the lower morale that now exists or was it the new regulation? It would be hard to say what lies behind the lower morale.

Generally it's agreed that measuring skills, attitudes, and values before, during, and after change is difficult.[19] But there are attempts to measure reactions (Did you like the change program?), learning (What was learned?), and outcomes (Is quality of output higher, lower, or about the same?).

Based on years of research and attempts to measure changes in reaction, learning, behavior, and outcomes, some general guidelines are useful:

1. Measurements should be conducted over a period of time. Soon after change has occurred, participants may be generally excited and interested because they're being asked for responses. Conducting measurement over a period of time will identify lag effects, extinction effects, and long-term results.

2. When possible, compare groups that have undergone change and those that haven't faced change. Comparisons are a form of internal benchmarking—how does a unit that was changed compare on outcomes or behavior with a unit that wasn't changed?

3. Don't rely only on quantitative measures such as cost, profit, units produced, or defective units. What do participants say? How do participants look? What do participants do without being asked? These types of qualitative measures provide insight into effects of change.

These useful guidelines can be applied to both small and major changes. Unfortunately too many organizations bypass or weakly address Stage 6 because evaluation is difficult. But since change is a continual process, starting over requires feedback. The evaluation step can, if done properly, provide feedback that influences Stage 1; that is, it becomes an internal-based force for change.

Introducing a change to an organizational culture that fosters and encourages total quality management can benefit from using the guidelines in Figure 18–3. This type of major change would need to incorporate each of the six stages just outlined.

TYPES OF CHANGE AGENTS

change agent
An individual or team of people whose main responsibility is to initiate, suggest, and even force change efforts within an organization.

A **change agent** is an individual or team of individuals whose responsibility is to practice the stages suggested in Figure 18–3. Typically an outsider (consultant) or someone from inside the organization heads up the change effort. Whether an outsider, insider, or combination change agent leader is best hasn't been determined and may depend on the situation. But four types of change agents have been identified: outside pressure (OP), people-change-technology (PCT), analysis for the top (AFT), and organizational development (OD).[20]

Outside Pressure (OP)

outside pressure (OP)
change agent
An individual or group not employed by a firm that pressures the firm to change.

The **outside pressure (OP) change agent** is an individual or group that isn't regularly employed by the firm but that still applies pressure on the firm to change. For example, the structural changes engulfing society over the past couple of decades have transformed the world from a corporation-centered and manufacturing-based order (the mass production era) to that of a predominantly service-based, technology, and information-driven system (the knowledge-service era). In the mass production era, people made their career choice about the time they graduated from high school and then stuck with it. Today, organizations know that to survive into the next century, they must obtain high performance from their workers. As a result, organizations are continually eliminating nonproductive functions and constantly reassessing, reshuffling, and retraining staff. Intelligent career/life planning in the knowledge-service era necessitates ongoing assessment, decision making, problem solving, and creating opportunities.[21] Because of societal changes, organizations must change the career paths they create for people. The topic of changing career paths is one in which modern managers are very interested. The "What Managers Are Reading" section briefly reviews two books about this topic.

People-Change-Technology (PCT)

people-change-technology
Change agents that use behaviorally oriented change techniques.

The **people-change-technology** change agent attempts to bring about change via various behaviorally oriented techniques. To be successful in the long term, quality programs must involve more than superficial, isolated behavioral changes. What is called for is a systemwide approach involving changes in a company's fundamental operations, beliefs, and values. Resistance to change will also be reduced if employees understand how the changes will increase the effectiveness of the organization and ultimately lead to more job security and more meaningful work.[22]

Organizational Development (OD)

Organizational development focuses on longer-term change that impacts the firm's culture. OD change programs and specific interventions are often headed up by outside consultants. They help plan and implement the change, occasionally help evaluate changes, and help the manager become involved with all aspects of the change process.

FIGURE 18–5
How Much Management
Involvement in Change?

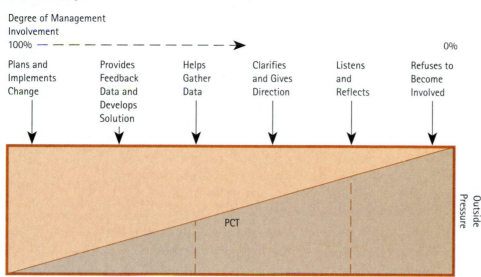

Source: Robert E. Callahan, C. Patrick Fleenor, and Harry R. Knudson, *Understanding Organizational Behavior: A Managerial Viewpoint* (Columbus, Ohio: Charles E. Merrill, 1986), p. 415.

Which change agent(s) should be used to introduce a total quality management program or a quality of work life program? To some extent the answer rests with the issue of involvement. How much involvement of the change agent is needed to start, sustain, and evaluate the change program? Figure 18–5 illustrates the relationship between the amount of involvement needed from a firm and the type of change agent. As the figure shows, the greater the outside pressure, the less is the need for direct management involvement in creating change. Some managers have even successfully invented an outside pressure to change their organization.[23]

INTERVENTION METHODS

The term **intervention** is used to describe a method, technique, or means to manage change effectively to improve an individual, group, organization, or all of these. An intervention can respond to forces for change or can create forces that provide the impetus for employees to accept change more readily. The various types of intervention can be placed in four categories: individual, group, intergroup, or organizational change.

    The type of intervention selected depends on the diagnosis, cost, time available, organization culture, management's confidence in the anticipated results, and depth preferred. **Depth of intervention** is defined as the degree of change that the intervention is intended to bring about.[24] A shallow intervention seeks mainly to provide information that's helpful to make improvements. A manager coaching a subordinate is an example of shallow intervention. A deep intervention is intended to bring about psychological and behavioral changes that are reflected in improved job performance. Sensitivity training is an example of deep intervention. With deep interventions, caution and the use of qualified experts should be top requirements.

    Moderate-depth interventions such as team building are intended to alter attitudes and perceptions. Different perspectives are presented and analyzed with the result being better understanding, more tolerance of other viewpoints, and modification of negative stereotypes.

    Only five intervention methods will be discussed in this text. However, many more methods are available for use in stimulating changes in people, structure, and technology.

intervention
The method, technique, or means used to change a structure, behavior, or technology.

depth of intervention
Depth is defined as the degree of change that the intervention is intended to bring about.

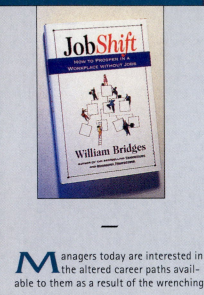
Again, as is often the case, there's no single method that's perfect or effective in every situation or case.

Survey Feedback

survey feedback
An organizationally focused, shallow intervention method that involves top management, data collection, data interpretation, and feedback of findings to employees, which result in the development of action plans.

Survey feedback is an organizationally focused, shallow intervention method. It's shallow because it doesn't attempt directly to effect psychological or behavioral changes. This method is typically conducted in four stages.[25] First, a change agent works with top management to design the questions to be used in a survey. This is the planning stage. Second, data are collected from a sample or an entire unit population (department, division, organization). Data may be collected using a survey questionnaire, interviews, historical records, or some combination of data collection techniques. Third, the change agent categorizes, summarizes, and interprets the survey-collected information and prepares reports. Fourth, employees are given feedback, meetings are held to discuss the findings, and action plans for overcoming identified problems are developed and implemented.

Survey feedback is a popular intervention method. It's efficient and participatory, and it provides much job-relevant information. Top management's endorsement and involvement are needed to help the survey feedback approach achieve its goals.

Team Building

team building
A moderate-depth intervention that attempts to improve diagnosis, communication, cooperation, and the performance of members and the overall team.

Teamwork is essential for continuous quality improvement. An effective team communicates well, cooperates, stimulates its members, and provides recognition and rewards them. **Team building** is a moderate-depth intervention that attempts to improve diagnosis, communication, cooperation, and the performance of members and the overall team. Be careful not to confuse team building with the widespread use of teams in quality-based organizations. Team building is the term used to refer to helping work groups perform at a higher level. It isn't focused on solving workplace problems through teams, but rather in making a team out of what might be a desultory work group.

The specific aims of team building intervention include setting goals and priorities, analyzing the group's work methods, examining the group's communication and decision-making processes, and examining interpersonal relationships within the group.[26] As each

Employees spray "silly string" in a team-building game.

of these aims is undertaken, the group is placed in the position of having to recognize explicitly each group member's contributions (both positive and negative).[27]

The process by which these aims are achieved begins with *diagnostic* meetings. Often lasting an entire day, the meetings enable all team members to share with other members their perceptions of problems. If the team is large enough, subgroups engage in discussion and report their ideas to the total group. These sessions are designed for expression of all members' views and to make these views public. In this context diagnosis emphasizes the value of open confrontation of issues and problems that were previously discussed in secrecy.

Identifying problems and concurring on their priority are two important initial steps. But a *plan of action* must be agreed on. The plan should call on each group member, individually or as part of a subgroup, to act specifically to alleviate one or more problems. If, for example, an executive committee agrees that one problem is a lack of understanding of and commitment to goals, a subgroup can be appointed to recommend goals to the total group at a subsequent meeting. Other team members can work on different problems. For example, if problems are found in the relationships among the members, a subgroup can initiate a process for examining each member's role.

Team building also is effective when new groups are being formed. There are often problems when new organizational units, project teams, or task forces are created. Typically such groups have certain characteristics that may be altered if the groups are to perform effectively. For example, the following combination of characteristics will lead to problems:

1. Ambiguity about roles and relationships.
2. Members having a fairly clear understanding of short-term goals.
3. Group members having technical competence that puts them on the team.
4. Members often paying more attention to the team's tasks than to the relationships among team members.

In such a case, the new group will focus initially on task problems but ignore the interpersonal relationship issues. By the time relationship problems begin to surface, the group can't deal with them, and performance begins to deteriorate.

To combat these tendencies, a new group should schedule team building meetings during the first weeks of its life. Meetings should take place away from the work site; one- or two-day sessions often suffice. The format of such meetings varies, but essentially their purpose is to enable the group to work through its timetable and members' roles in reaching the group's objectives.[28] An important outcome of such meetings is to establish an understanding of each member's contribution to the team and of the reward for that contribution. Although reports on team building indicate mixed results, the evidence suggests that group processes improve through team building efforts.[29]

Empowerment

An important part of changing an organization to a TQM approach is empowering managers and workers. As noted earlier, empowerment is a process that increases people's involvement in their work (design, flow, interactions, decision making). Empowerment can occur for individuals or for groups (teams).

Empowerment involves far more than giving employees greater decision-making ability. At its most practical level, empowerment is recognizing and releasing into the organization the power that people already have in their wealth of useful knowledge and internal motivation. Research has shown that there are three simple keys to successful employee empowerment:

1. Open and candid sharing of information on business performance with all employees.
2. More structure (rather than less) as teams and employee groups move into self management.
3. Replacing the organizational hierarchy with teams.[30]

However, not all companies are rushing ahead to manage their business through the use of employee teams. Two reasons why teams have not caught on at some companies is that teams are not easy to manage and the results are not easily measurable.[31]

Ultimately, achieving competitive success through people involves fundamentally altering how one thinks about the workforce and the employment relationship. It means achieving success by working with people, not by replacing them or limiting the scope of their activities. It entails seeing the workforce as a source of strategic advantage, not just as a cost to be minimized or avoided. Firms that take this different perspective are often able to successfully outmaneuver and outperform their rivals.[32]

Over the long term, workers are motivated by a sense of achievement, recognition, enjoyment of the job, promotion opportunities, responsibility, and the chance for personal growth. Worker motivation and performance are tied directly to the style of management that's applied and to the principles of positive or negative reinforcement. One characteristic of a quality management approach is employee empowerment. Employees at all levels of the organization are involved in planning and problem solving in areas related to their work.[33]

Foresight-Led Change

In their book, *Competing for the Future*, Gary Hamel and C.K. Prahalad argue that most organizations don't spend enough time thinking about the future of their industry and their business. In fact, they state that organizations, typically, fall under the "40/30/20 rule." This rule reflects their finding that about 40 percent of senior executive time is spent looking outward (i.e., outside the business). Of that time spent looking outward, only 30 percent is spent peering three or more years into the future. And of that time spent looking into the future, only about 20 percent is spent attempting to build a collective view of the future. Thus, on average, senior management spends less than 3 percent of its energy (40% x 30% x 20% = 2.4%) building an organizational perspective of the future.[34]

To compete effectively for the future, organizations must develop what Hamel and Prahalad call **industry foresight**. According to them, "industry foresight is based on deep insights into the trends in technology, demographics, regulation, and lifestyles that can be harnessed to rewrite industry rules and create new competitive space."[35] They distinguish

industry foresight
Beliefs about an industry based on deep insights into the trends in technology, demographics, regulations, and lifestyle that can be harnessed to rewrite industry rules and create new competitive space.

Setting stretch targets helped railroad and shipping company CSX save millions of dollars in capital expenditures by eliminating "loafing" locomotives and railcars.

this term from the more commonly used "vision." They don't like that term because it connotes unreality and intangibility.

Foresight-led change involves looking into the future, determining what the future is likely to be like, and then using that insight to change the organization in the present. Another term that has been used to describe this "pull" approach to change (as in pulling the organization into the future) is called **stretch targets.**

Stretch targets reflect a major shift in the thinking of top management. Executives are recognizing that incremental goals, however worthy, invite managers and workers to perform the same comfortable processes a little better every year. The all-too-frequent result: mediocrity. Stretch targets require big leaps of progress on such measures as inventory turns, product development time, and manufacturing cycles. Imposing such imperatives can force companies to reinvent the way they conceive, make, and distribute products. Table 18–2 provides guidelines on setting stretch targets.

For CEO John Snow of CSX, the $9.5 billion-a-year railroad and shipping company, stretch targets were a natural extension of his business approach. In 1991, CSX's return on capital hovered well below its capital charge in the range of 10%. Snow's bold goal: to make sure CSX would earn the full cost of capital by 1993 and thereafter. As Snow predicted, the stretch target he established forced managers to look hard at the railroad's core problem—the fact that the company's fleet of locomotives and railcars sat loafing much of the time at loading docks and seaport terminals. Raising the company's return on capital would mean working the massive fleet far harder than had ever been attempted.

Having set the target, Snow then got out of the way. The strategy proved to be a winner. Since 1991, while handling a surge in business, CSX has eliminated from its rolling stock 20,000 of its 125,000 cars—enough to form a train stretching from Chicago to Detroit. That

stretch targets
A "pull" approach to organizational change that uses foresight to determine what the future is likely to be and then using that insight to change the organization in the present.

TABLE 18–2	GUIDELINES FOR SETTING STRETCH TARGETS

- Set a clear, convincing, long-term corporate goal. Example: Earning the full cost of capital.

- Translate it into one or two specific stretch targets for managers, such as doubling inventory turns.

- Use benchmarking to prove that the goal—though tough—isn't impossible and to enlist employees in the crusade.

- Get out of the way: let the people in the plants and labs find ways to meet the goals.

caused capital expenditures for supporting the fleet to shrink from $825 million a year to $625 million. CSX is now earning its full cost of capital.[36]

For most of the twentieth century, change management was orchestrated in organizations on the basis of what has been called the **strategy-structure-systems doctrine.** The doctrine took hold as organizations increased in size and complexity, leading senior managers to delegate most of the operating decisions to division-level managers. Senior managers then recast their own jobs as defining strategy, developing structure, and managing the systems required to link and control the company's parts.

This approach to management has been successful for more than 50 years. It has enabled central managers to maintain contact with increasingly far-flung operations. But, while senior managers saw these increasingly sophisticated systems as necessary links to operations, those at the operational level felt them to be burdens too often calling them to heel.

Today, top-level managers at some of the most successful organizations are creating organizational change by reconnecting with the people of the organization. They have set out to shore up systems-based communications with actual physical encounters with the people that make the organization run on a daily basis. Leaders such as Asea Brown Boveri's (ABB) Percy Barnevik are beginning to articulate management's challenge to engage the unique knowledge, skills, and abilities of every individual in the organization. They are developing a management philosophy based on a more personalized approach that encourages a diversity of points of view and empowers employees to contribute their own ideas.[37]

As managers pay more attention to organizational culture, they need to have some insight into how it can be shaped and managed. In the next section, we'll explore some ways that managers can shape and manage organizational culture.

strategy-structure-systems doctrine
Senior managers for much of the twentieth century have described their jobs as defining strategy, developing structure, and managing the systems.

RESHAPING CULTURE AND STRUCTURE

The intervention methods available to managers for implementing change are impressive. But their impact is often limited by two aspects of organizations: culture and structure. Interventions can be attempted at either a shallow or deep level, but, ultimately, culture and structure significantly influence what changes occur.

Cultural Reshaping

The culture of organizations are rooted in the national cultures of their countries of origin. Since organizational culture consists of rules, rituals, and procedures, creating an ideology that helps direct employees' everyday experience and customs, it influences how change is received and coped with in terms of outcomes. History informs us that as U.S. firms expanded overseas, host nations' national cultures, a diverse workforce, and new competitors helped shape internal cultures. Changing the internal organizational culture of a domestic or international firm is extremely difficult, if not impossible. Reshaping, altering, or modifying long-standing rules, procedures, rituals, and ideology is a better way to present change objectives.

As Compaq Computer learned from its reshaping in the early 1990s, there are five keys to creating cultural change:

1. **Provide a clear vision and decisive leadership:** When Compaq's Eckhard Pfeiffer took over as CEO in 1991, he exhorted people "to compete for marketshare across the entire spectrum" of the PC industry. "That was a simple change," he recalls. "But such a strategic shift is so radical that "you have to communicate it a hundred times or more. It doesn't sink in the first few times."

2. **Change the old guard:** Six senior Compaq executives quit soon after Mr. Pfeiffer became CEO. He trimmed nearly 20 percent of the workforce during the first year.

3. **Tackle many problems at the same time:** During the first year after he assumed Compaq's number one job, Mr. Pfeiffer unveiled a new line of bargain-priced machines and also mounted an assault on the small-business and home-PC markets. In addition, he overhauled the manufacturing process and expanded abroad.

4. **Change how the company's employees are judged and rewarded:** Make sure management's compensation is tied to the new corporate goals.
5. **Have full backing from the board, along with full accountability:** Board support is absolutely essential in a turnaround because "you don't have a guarantee that it is going to be a winner," Mr. Pfeiffer noted. "We have seen many attempts that didn't work out."[38]

Employees are socialized into a firm's culture by a wide variety of practices. Shared meals, rituals, dress codes, and group membership result in socialization. By encouraging extensive interaction among employees, organizations help them become more attuned to the culture.

To reshape cultures to fit employees' mood and thinking, managers have moved toward a reward system that focuses on individual and group contributions to productivity rather than seniority, loyalty, and friendships. To counter the potentially negative consequences of individually based merit pay rewards, an increasing number of firms are using company-wide or group-based profit sharing and bonus plans.

Changes in society and in perceptions among employees have pointed out some significant inequities in distribution of rewards, opportunities to learn new skills, and power within organizations.[39] The widely publicized golden parachutes that in many cases overrewarded senior managers involved in mergers and acquisitions, and managers' large paychecks have alienated many employees, lowering their productivity and commitment. Encouraging and practicing more equity within the culture can, if done effectively, result in positive attitudes and feelings being transmitted during employees' socialization.

Where cultural features support past ineffective or failed strategies, they can constrain change. Generating change involves (1) understanding the powerful force of culture, (2) aligning culture with positive ethical and equitable values, and (3) devising sound reward, education, and socialization systems. In a growing number of firms, managers realize that reshaping culture requires reshaping structures.

Structural Reshaping

Structural reshaping requires an understanding of power, authority, and personal interactions in organizational settings. The organization blueprint is the organization chart. Unfortunately charts present a firm's structure as fixed and rigid. This, of course, isn't how most real interactions occur. Firms must use a dynamic approach to structure so that they can respond to changing conditions. Viewing the structure as temporary, fluid, and flexible is more compatible with today's world than establishing a set structure and using it for an extended period of time.

As changes become more intense and rapid, and as competition becomes more innovative, managers must be more responsive and astute at modifying their structures. Table 18–3 summarizes how key environmental forces affect firms' structures. The technological

TABLE 18–3	ENVIRONMENTAL CHANGE AND STRUCTURE		
Environmental	Pressure to Improve	Capabilities	Controls
Efficiency	Timing and productivity	Automate, just-in-time	Centralize, specialize
Customer responsiveness	Quality and service	Customize, differentiate	Networking, delayering
Technological change	Innovation and speed	Build skills, invest in R&D	Flatten pyramid, decentralize

Source: Adapted from Charles J. Fombrum, *Turning Points* (New York: McGraw-Hill, 1992), p. 215.

change force is ever present as new ideas are turned into innovative products. Competition in technology has become fierce and revolves largely around such features as product quality, production costs, and the ability to deliver products in a timely manner.

To derive the highest quality, managers must stimulate line employees' cooperation, problem-solving ability, and commitment. This means more employee involvement in decision making. Use of teams such as quality circles is a structural change that has been a response to the need for higher quality. Generating a bottom-up flow of ideas is easier with a decentralized structure.

The disintegration of large, tightly centralized bureaucratic structures continues. Large organizations still exist, but with reshaped structures. Such reshaping in structures proves that progressive managers are eliminating layers of administrators, decentralizing decision making, encouraging employee involvement, and improving communication. These processes are easy to state but often difficult to implement because of old fixed cultural norms, policies, rituals, and ideology. The productivity loss due to fixed, rigid, and culturally bound structures is incalculable. We can safely assume that these structures are costly in terms of lost efficiency, customers, and global competitiveness.

A TOTAL QUALITY CHANGE APPROACH

To achieve change and to convert to total quality management (TQM), there must be organizationwide changes in attitudes, communication, employee involvement, and commitment. This is a large undertaking in any organization. Bringing about a TQM change is difficult but can be made easier by understanding resistance to change and how to overcome resistance. Too often managers are aware of resistance barriers but don't address fear, inertia, or self-interest factors.

The Chief Executive Officer: A Key Player

The power to make change happen is often largely vested in management. It's management that must show the way, articulate the vision, and show by example that total quality is mandatory. Improved communications initiated by management must be a top priority. Merely inundating workers with quality information isn't the best approach. Communication must be a two-way process. Everyone must have an opportunity to make inputs into the TQM change and strategy. As the Workplace of Tomorrow segment shows, despite empowering employees, which is central to TQM, managers must maintain some controls.

The chief executive officer must communicate that she's making a commitment to achieve total quality in everything that's done in the organization. The CEO must commit to establish a companywide communications program that involves managers and workers. The communication must include the following:

❖ What's meant by total quality management.
❖ Why it's important.
❖ How it will be accomplished.
❖ Why the CEO is involved and committed.
❖ What benefits will be achieved.

Management must be prepared for resistance to change of any normal pattern or set of procedures. A TQM change represents a change in culture, and it may take a number of years to become effective and ingrained. Even though TQM can be initiated by managers, it must be practiced by everyone in the organization.

Although the benefits of quality management techniques have been widely publicized and the achievements of exemplary companies lauded, there is also a darker side to the quality revolution. Many companies that have embarked on the quality journey have given up during the early stages of implementation. In fact, a McKinsey and Company survey

MANUFACTURING BUILDS CHANGE THROUGH LEARNING

Deep within Wabash National Corporation's sprawling truck-trailer factory, 80 workers crowd into a lunchroom before the start of their 3 PM shift. David Graves hands out production schedules, introduces a new employee, and asks whether there are any questions. "If not, let's go build some trailers," he shouts.

Wabash National may sound more like a bank than a truck-trailer company. But as its competitors struggle to survive, the decade-old upstart shows that it's possible to build a globally competitive company from scratch in a stodgy industry. Wabash gained its edge by making customized trailers and innovative products for fast-growing companies such as Federal Express and Schneider National, Inc.

From the "walk and talk" interview in which job applicants get a glimpse of the frenetic factory pace to a profit-sharing plan that gives employees 10 percent of after-tax earnings, Wabash encourages workers to go all out. The company's retirement plan contributions are based not just on profit but on profit margins. Every quarter, Chairman Donald Ehrlich stands on a stack of plywood to give employees details of the company's latest record performance—and to exhort them to do even better.

At Wabash, new employees soon learn they should take classes and participate in efficiency teams—or their careers will wither. Two 25-cents-an-hour pay raises are awarded only after completion of two sets of courses, taken on employees' own time. Today, there are classes for workers who want to be welders and for recent immigrants to learn English. Ehrlich has also added a course in business basics. Now, workers can learn the difference between an operating expense and a capitalized expense. The backbone of the system is a series of classes in areas such as business economics, statistical process control, and the just-in-time inventory system.

Despite the emphasis on teamwork, Wabash leaves little doubt who is boss. Under its attendance policy, workers rack up a penalty point for being even one minute late; 20 points within 12 months can lead to dismissal. Any worker can suggest a new team, but management retains control by appointing team members and clearing expenditures. "We can't have 3,000 people going in different directions based on their own opinions," says Ehrlich. "There is a hierarchy." And increasingly in the future, that hierarchy will be based on the knowledge and skills workers use to add value to the workplace.

Sources: Adapted from Robert L. Rose, "A Productivity Push At Wabash National Puts Firm On a Roll," *The Wall Street Journal*, July 7, 1995, A1, A6.

found that two out of every three quality management programs stall in terms of failing to deliver tangible improvements in performance.[40]

The reasons for these dropouts vary: initiators frequently fail to carry their fellow managers with them; companies are disappointed by the results; quality programs unleash forces that top managers view as uncontrollable and potentially destructive; and incoming CEOs regard long-established quality improvement programs as barriers to change and constraints upon their authority.[41]

Nonetheless, the effectiveness of quality management techniques is evident from the remarkable business turnarounds that companies such as Motorola, Xerox, and Ford Motor Company have achieved. In all these companies, quality management programs have been successful not just in improving product and service quality in terms of their consistency, performance, timeliness, and robustness, but also in improving competitive and financial performance, enriching the jobs of employees, and transforming corporate cultures.

Integrating a quality management program within an organization, and achieving consistency between goals and performance measures is one of the most important tasks of upper management in managing the quality process. Once a goal has been achieved, then the company can shift its focus to the next priority. This building block approach has produced concrete results for some companies and many are now adopting it. At Hewlett-Packard, CEO John Young promoted the single goal of a tenfold reduction in warranty expenses. A similar single, sequential goal approach is central to Motorola's quality management program where quality targets are constantly updated with new standards as the old standards are surpassed.[42] The Global Exchange explains how Deutsche Telekom CEO Ron Sommer also used this incremental approach to achieving quality.

Achieving quality in the workplace is a long-term challenge for managers of any type of organization. One of the most difficult obstacles to overcome is not giving up too early in the implementation process. For those companies that have made quality a part of their day-to-day operations, it has been worth the struggle.

GLOBAL EXCHANGE

DEUTSCHE TELEKOM IN NEED OF RADICAL TRANSFORMATION

Ron Sommer is a man in a hurry. As new CEO of Deutsche Telekom he has to ignite a competitive spirit in workers long coddled by Germany's biggest monopoly, lay the groundwork for massive cost-cutting, prod the company to serve customers it long took for granted, and woo investors. To add to his long list of trouble, all this massive change must be completed by January 1, 1998, when the European Union is scheduled to throw open its doors to unfettered competition in telecommunications.

The key event will come in the summer of 1996 when Deutsche Telekom will begin privatizing in a $10 billion stock offering. If it succeeds, Sommer will have the capital he needs to make the company a viable competitor. If it fails, the company will continue to be owned by the government and be in a difficult position to engineer the necessary changes for long term success.

Sommer may have to cut up to 60,000 jobs, a quarter of Telekom's workforce. And that's just the beginning. After privatization, he'll have to raise profits enough to cover $86 billion in debt and pay a dividend. He may have to slash prices in half to meet competition. On top of all that, he has to begin offering the state-of-the-art services in multimedia that global corporations demand. Once deregulation takes place, Sommer will face rivals that have a 10-year head-start operating in deregulated markets.

"The company has an extremely high level of knowhow," Sommer says, "but it needs to be more customer friendly." Sommer's strategy is an attack on all fronts. First, he is working to secure regulatory approval for joint ventures with France Télécom and Sprint, key to meeting his goal of generating 20 percent of sales from international business by 1999.

Inside Telekom, Sommer is sending clear signals that the company must gear up to compete on price and service. Weeks into the job, he announced a 30 percent price cut for calls to North America. Telekom also cut prices on leased lines to mobile phone operators by up to 50 percent. Under Sommer's prodding, branch managers are trying to speed up service by up to 50 percent. It currently takes 12 days to hook up new phones. The goal is to provide next-day hookup.

Sommer has told managers that he wants Telekom to generate the brand awareness of a Coca-Cola or IBM. "I want us to be recognized as a great company," he says. But changing the company's image will never work unless Sommer can motivate his employees to flourish in a deregulated environment. That's like moving a mountain. Still, Sommer's no-nonsense approach is setting the tone for his senior executives, who must meet new performance criteria or be prepared to step aside.

In this heated atmosphere of radical corporate change, every step Sommer takes is critical. Nonetheless, time and again, Sommer has achieved stellar results with a simple philosophy, "It's not about magic. You just have to do it."

Sources: Adapted from Karen Lowry Miller, et al., "The Toughest Job in Europe," *Business Week,* October 9, 1995, pp. 52–53; Daniel Benjamin, "Some Germans Fear They're Falling Behind in High-Tech Fields," *The Wall Street Journal,* April 27, 1994, A1, A7.

SUMMARY OF LEARNING OBJECTIVES

EXPLAIN WHY INDIVIDUALS RESIST CHANGE IN ORGANIZATIONAL SETTINGS.

Reasons include self-interest, habit, fear, peer pressure, and bureaucratic inertia. The inertia exists because of people holding on to old ways of conducting business.

DESCRIBE THE DIFFERENT TYPES OF CHANGE AGENTS.

Outside pressure is an individual or group that doesn't work for the firm but exercises influence over how the firm is operated. People-change technology change agents attempt to bring about change by altering people's behavior directly through behaviorally oriented techniques. Organizational development change agents attempt to change behaviors of the entire organization through intervention methods that affect most individuals in the firm.

DEFINE SURVEY FEEDBACK AND EXPLAIN HOW IT'S USED.

Survey feedback is an organizationally focused, shallow intervention method that typically follows a four-step sequence. First, a questionnaire is designed after consulting with top management. Second, data are collected from a sample or population. Third, survey data are categorized, summarized, interpreted, and used in a report. Fourth, informational feedback is given and action plans for solving problems are developed.

LIST THE SIX AREAS USED IN THE CHAPTER'S FRAMEWORK FOR MANAGING CHANGE.

A framework that can be used to manage change includes six steps: identifying forces for change, recognizing the need for change, diagnosing the problem(s) and points of resistance, considering possible alternative intervention methods, selecting methods of intervention and implementation, and evaluating change and restarting the process.

COMPARE THE DEPTH IN TEAM BUILDING AND EMPOWERMENT TECHNIQUES.

Team building is considered to be of moderate depth, while empowerment techniques such as delegation, increased participation in decision making, worker evaluation of managers, and self-managed work teams can range from moderate to deep intervention.

DESCRIBE WHY IT'S HARD TO RESHAPE AN ORGANIZATION'S CULTURE.

Culture is so historic, embedded, and pervasive that it's usually not considered amenable to change. At best, the rituals, procedures, and ideology or segments of culture are discussed in terms of reshaping.

EXPLAIN THE TYPES OF DIAGNOSIS TECHNIQUES AVAILABLE TO MANAGERS.

Tools of diagnosis include interviews, questionnaires, observations, and unobtrusive measures (e.g., the wear and tear on a rug or chair). Each method has advantages and disadvantages.

EXPLAIN THE TECHNIQUE OF FIELD ANALYSIS.

Force field analysis is a technique by which a manager defines the driving and restraining forces of change, and assigns a value to each based on the degree to which each force can influence the change process.

DESCRIBE FORESIGHT-LED CHANGE.

Foresight-led change helps managers prepare for the future. It involves looking into the future, determining what the future is likely to be like, and then using that insight to change the organization in the present.

DESCRIBE WHAT IS MEANT BY A STRETCH TARGET.

Stretch targets require big leaps of progress for organizations. This reflects a major shift in management thinking, recognizing that incremental changes allow workers to perform the same comfortable processes year after year.

KEY TERMS

change agent, p. 484
depth of intervention, p. 485
industry foresight, p. 488
internal change forces, p. 475

intervention, p. 485
outside pressure change agent, p. 484
people-change-technology, p. 484
strategy-structure-systems doctrine, p. 490

stretch targets, p. 489
survey feedback, p. 486
team building, p. 486

REVIEW AND DISCUSSION QUESTIONS

Recall

1. What do employees fear when a change is being considered?
2. Explain how outside pressure can be so significant that it blocks or encourages changes within a firm.
3. Why is neutrality important in third-party peace-making interventions?

Understand

4. Why is survey feedback considered a shallow change intervention?

Application

5. Conduct your own diagnosis of a situation at your school, at home, or at work. Based on your diagnosis, what kind of change is needed?

6. Review some OD and training literature. Look at the most recent five years of a journal such as *Training, Training and Development,* or *Organizational Dynamics.* How many articles or pages in the most recent five-year period are directed to evaluating change programs? Why do you think this is the case?
7. Interview two or three human resource managers. Ask what framework or method their firms use to manage change.
8. How do managers develop industry foresight? How can you be better prepared to manage your own career in the future?
9. Use force-field analysis to analyze the potential for changing your major field of study. What are the driving forces? What are the restraining forces?
10. Set a stretch target in your own life. What steps can you begin to take to achieve the stretch target?

CASE STUDY

From Start-Up to Major Corporation: Michael Dell Deals with Change

It may be hard to believe, but Bill Gates isn't the only prodigy in computerdom enjoying an astounding summer. On August 17, Michael Dell, who pioneered the direct marketing of computers 12 years ago in his University of Texas dorm room, announced that Dell Computer had scored record sales and earnings for the quarter ended July 31. Sales hit $1.2 billion for that period, up 52 percent from the same three months in 1994. Profits of $65 million, up 128 percent were helped by a 44 percent surge in sales to corporations and the government, the high-margin customers that account for three-quarters of Dell's business. The results exceeded expectations; shares of Dell stock rose $1.25 to reach $74.25 that day.

This performance is a far cry form 1993 when Dell Computer's stock price plummeted from $49 in January of that year all the way to $16 by July. The company seemed to be unraveling. A widely publicized spat with a Kidder Peabody analyst who questioned the company's currency trading and its accounting practices had embarrassed Dell. The chief financial officer had resigned, leaving a management void. Worst of all, Dell had scrapped all its new lines of notebook computers because of poor production planning. This meant sitting on the sidelines of the fastest-growing segment of the PC market for more than 12 months. Says Michael Dell of that period: "I felt a gradual panicking. There was a period when every piece of news I heard got worse and worse." At one point that summer, as he and new chief financial officer Tom Meredith rushed through Heathrow Airport to catch a plane to Ireland, Meredith told

Dell he saw a silver lining in the notebook disaster—it had revealed that the company's information systems and management had not kept pace with its rapid growth.

Like the kid in junior high who comes back from summer vacation a foot taller than the rest of the class, Dell Computer's rapid rise had left it a gangly, dysfunctional mess. Sales had shot up from $546 million in fiscal 1991 to $2 billion in 1993 (the company's fiscal year ends in January). Growth had been pursued to the exclusion of all else, but no one knew how the numbers really added up. Says Dell, "One of the things that is confusing and almost intoxicating when you are growing a business is that you really have little way of determining what the problems are. You had different parts of the company believing they were making their plan, but when you rolled up the results of the company, you had a big problem. It was symptomatic of not understanding the relationship between costs and revenues and profits within the different lines of the business." Translation: the company couldn't track profits and losses by product type, which is a little like running a business using an abacus instead of a computer.

What Dell did as he began to see the wheels fly off his nine-year-old company was seek older, outside help—of the managerial kind. From companies like Motorola, Hewlett-Packard, and Apple Computer, Dell assembled a team of experienced executives. The key recruit: vice chairman Mort Topfer, 58, who headed Motorola's land mobile products division before leaving for Dell in June 1994. The youngest of the company's new senior managers is ten years older than the CEO, who in February 1995 celebrated his 30th birthday.

Growing too fast has pushed countless young entrepreneurs over the edge. So it's no small achievement that, despite his tender years, Michael Dell is now the CEO with the longest tenure of anyone running a major PC manufacturer.

It seems startling that it was a 19-year-old who stumbled upon the possibilities of customizing PCs, but Michael Dell has always been precocious. At age 12, Dell, the son of an orthodontist and a Paine Webber stock broker, devised a stamp auction that netted him $1,000. During his last year in high school he made $18,000 selling papers for the now defunct Houston Post and bought his first BMW—cash down. Obviously Dell was no simple delivery boy. He had figured out that the most likely newspaper subscribers were newlyweds or families who had just moved. So he tracked down sources like the city marriage license bureau and put together a targeted mailing list on his first computer, an Apple IIe.

Little did his Houston neighbors know that this foray into direct marketing was a sign of much bigger things to come. As a freshman at the University of Texas at Austin in 1983, Dell noticed that retail salesmen of computers often knew less about the PCs they were hawking than their customers did. He figured he could offer better service over the phone—as well as better prices, by selling dealers' excess inventory by mail. Over spring break the following year, Dell told his parents he wanted to quit school. In what is certainly one of the more extraordinary father–son conversations of its kind, his father asked him what he wanted to do. "Compete with IBM," Dell replied. He never did earn his degree in biology, but he was on his way to building a fortune worth $615 million in Dell stock alone.

The best evidence that Michael Dell's management style has changed over the years is his ability to share power with the team of elders he brought in. He is crafting a unique relationship with Motorola veteran Mort Topfer. The vice chairman is pushing the company to new focus on process and discipline.

Topfer's managerial skills complement those of his boss. Dell has an instinctive feel for technology and marketing, whereas Top-

fer is an operations guy with a penchant for detail. What's more, Dell has delegated an enormous amount of responsibility to Topfer, whom he often describes as his co-CEO.

Within weeks of his arrival, Topfer reoriented the company's business plan for the second half of 1994. He has since instituted multiyear planning. While Dell Computer already had a total quality management program in place, Topfer brought a Motorola-line intensity to the effort. One key target: the company's ability to share information internally. Now, financial information such as sales, profits, and inventory is available five to ten days after the close of a fiscal quarter, versus the 30 days it took in 1993. At Motorola, the norm is two to three days.

To really get a sense of Dell's newfound maturity, you must look at his relationships with the other senior managers he's brought in over the past couple of years. Dell used to go through executives like a hot knife through butter. In the past two years, however, he has assembled an impressive crew and allowed these new hires great latitude in running their businesses.

Given Dell's desire to make the transition from a small, high-growth outfit to a bit but nimble multibillion-dollar corporation, it's not surprising that the new management coterie is made up of refugees from bigger companies. The new management team has done far more than simply rejigger product lines; it's also turning around the corporate culture. One new recruit, Richard Snyder from Hewlett Packard, has a clear vision of what he intends to import from his old company: "I think the word is 'discipline.' It's very easy to have everything be urgent and important. But you can't be in that mode for long without burning out." His definition of discipline embraces such standard goals as meeting financial commitments all the way down the organization, but it also includes the kind of soft goals emphasized at H-P, such as respect for the individual. That shift just may make Dell Computer a kinder, gentler place to work. Explains Snyder, "Younger companies don't have that kind of culture yet. We want to get the turnover rate down. You can't be very competitive if you keep losing people."

Dell insiders say the company isn't the only thing that's changed. The boss is different too. He seems to have learned more than just management techniques from his elders. Although Dell himself may not acknowledge the change, long-time employees say he exudes a quiet confidence that was lacking before.

QUESTIONS

1. Why do you think Michael Dell needed to call on senior managers to help him run his company when he didn't need any help getting it started?

2. As many entrepreneurs discover, there is a vast difference between start-up ventures and mature organizations. What are some of the major differences? How does organizational change differ in each type of organization?

3. From the perspective of the individual entrepreneur, such as Michael Dell, what is the greatest personal change one must make in order to be an effective manager when the company goes from start-up to mature firm? Can you identify any other corporate leaders who have been able to stay with the company through this transition? Can you identify some who weren't able to stay with the company?

Sources: Adapted from Rahul Jacob, "The Resurrection of Michael Dell," *Fortune*, September 18, 1995, pp. 117-128; Scott McCartney, "Michael Dell—and His Company—Grow Up," *The Wall Street Journal*, January 31, 1995, pp. B1; Peter Burrows and Stephanie Anderson, "Dell Computer Goes Into the Shop," *Business Week*, July 12, 1993, pp. 138-140.

VIDEO CASE

Managing Change and Developing Organizations at Marshall Industries

The manager's job increasingly requires knowing how to manage change. But most change efforts fail because of inadequate preparation and attention to process. On the other hand employees want and seek change they see as improving their lives. They resist change when they doubt its usefulness. Marshall Industries is one of the five largest distributors of industrial electronic components in America. From its warehouses and corporate offices near Los Angeles, Marshall supplies 30,000 computer-related customers in the United States and Canada with a broad range of semiconductors, connectors, tool kits, and work stations. How did the management of Marshall Industries diagnose, plan, and implement useful changes? How did they overcome resistance to change? And how did they measure and modify the changes? This video examines those questions, focusing on Marshall's so-called "Red Letter Days" when major systems and organizational structure systems are changed, overhauled, revised, or, in one case, completely done away with.

One common way of labeling phases of change in human behavior are unfreezing, changing, and refreezing. Unfreezing involves initiating actions and attitudes to help employees see that change is in fact needed, and in their best interest. Sometimes this means helping people learn that the old way no longer works. The manager's goal is to instill an openness to change. The second phase involves actually making the change and changing behavior. Refreezing means reinforcing the changes made. Ideally, the newly created and desired behavior will become a natural, self-reinforcing pattern over time. Continuous improvement calls for continuous cycles of change. Successful managers know that nothing ever stays frozen.

Robert Rodin, Marshall Industries' president, commented on his company's approach to managing change: "We plan our approach. We do a little trial, we study the results of that trial, and then we act on it. We then continually cycle through that over and over again. Improvement continually is one of the goals, but innovation is the breakthrough that gets us to a new learning curve and allows us to be a better company."

But how does a manager recognize when change is necessary? Many businesses flourish on the principle that if it's not broken, don't fix it. Obvious change is called for when results are not in line with expectations, or staff morale is low, or the bottom line is sinking lower. Some companies miss signals for change when they neglect to monitor both their internal and external environments.

Marshall's director of quality, Jacob Kuryan, said, "Primarily trying to live our mission statement has really helped us reduce waste in our system. Let me give you an example. By making employees think about how they add value to the customer has allowed each and every individual at Marshall Industries to focus on customer service. If you don't know how to do something, you can't accomplish it. If you can't learn on a daily basis about customer requirements, about people, about what affects and motivates people, then you can't improve it. The only way to acquire customer knowledge is to be able to invite it from outside your organization and maybe examine your organization through an entirely different set of lenses."

Once a need for change is acknowledged, one process for diagnosing and planning for change is called "force field analysis." This process identifies and assesses the strength of forces driving change and those which are restraining it. From force field analysis managers can take action regarding which forces to change, who to do it, when, and how. It's important to decide in advance how success will be determined. Rodin said, "We realized that we were going to go through an awful lot of changes over the last four years. So we set a schedule together because people get nervous in a company when there's a lot of changes. Every 90 days we met with our executive team. Every two weeks we had a conference call. In this way people got to expect regular communications. But they weren't done in a haphazard way—it was predictable."

There's nearly always a learning period when change is introduced and implemented. During this period there may be a strong desire to return to the old ways of doing things. To stabilize change, management must be ready to increase support, encouragement, and resources to help people weather the transitional storm and internalize their newly learned behaviors. Monitoring change means creating objective standards and goals with reasonable time tables while retaining the flexibility to adjust to surprises and setbacks. Using these guideposts, a successful manager knows when the broken machine has been fixed in order to terminate change. How do these principles work in a real world environment? Managers at Marshall have gone through each phase of change repeatedly on "Red Letter Days" when major systems and organizational structures are changed.

Robert Rodin explained the concept of Red Letter Days: "We would always brief people on the Fridays before the conference calls and frequently roll out these programs on a Monday. After every meeting the field operations knew that they would have a meeting the following Monday. After every conference call the field knew that they would be updated that evening. And in this predictable way people didn't have a chance to come up with a lot of rumors, and nervous sensation about what might happen in the event that some special meeting was planned in the middle of a time that they weren't expecting."

Although in-depth year-long preparations were made, the sales division and its 500 sales people nationwide will never forget the day that individual commissions were abolished and replaced with quarterly bonuses based on overall company performance. Robert Caldarella, general manager of corporate sales said, "I remember the day we cut over to the incentive plan and moved away from the commission plan. Sales people came forward with their problem accounts, saying, 'Geez, I don't really think that this is a great account for us,' or 'I really don't think that this is a good Marshall account.' They became honest with themselves and they became honest with us as managers. Now we are one organization with people aligned in one direction."

Another Red Letter Day at Marshall was when automated retrieval machines went on line in the warehouse—an example of technology impacting both people and their task. Adrian Quintana, Jr., warehouse supervisor, said, "I think there was a lot of fear and uncertainty coming down here not knowing what working with an automated system was going to be like. Fear that it was going to eliminate a lot of jobs. You know they always hear that automation eliminates a lot of human jobs. But once we got down here and became accustomed to it and learned the system people found that it didn't eliminate jobs, it actually created new jobs. And I like working with the automated system. I think it's been really interesting learning the automation and it's eliminated a lot of the human errors that came from the conventional type environment."

On December 7th, 1995, Marshall implemented its biggest single change: new computer software for its operating and financial systems. Richard Bentley, executive vice president, said, "The computer change is probably the one that sticks most in my mind because I couldn't sleep and I came back in and it was like 4:00 in the morning here, which means the east coast was coming up. As the company came across the country and the machine was still running we felt very good and we were able to conduct business. So that's probably what sticks in my mind the most."

Marshall Industries, like most dynamic companies, is in a constant state of change. What sets it apart is how its managers approach change from the inside out, and from the bottom up. Marshall's management is very aware that they are part of an interrelated, interactive system where change is not random, but planned and anticipated. Caldarella said, "There are a couple of stories that we use commonly to teach our organization how to think about processes and systems within organizations. The first one is the hamburger story. It's a busy day and you've been working very hard in the morning. At noon you have to go out to lunch. You drive up to the hamburger stand and you tell them you're having a really busy day and need your lunch really quick and he says 'Hey no problem,' and then the hamburger doesn't come for an hour. When you walk out the door you don't give the waiter or the waitress a tip.

Whose fault was it that the hamburger was late? There could be any number of reasons why the hamburger was late. But the one that you punish was that waiter or the waitress. So the lesson that we teach, using that example, is that when you look at why something went wrong you have to understand the process. You have to look at the people, method, equipment, materials, and the environment—all those factors that fall into that category to understand what you have changed to improve that process."

The people at Marshall have learned to expect change. Although sometimes stressful, they know first hand how change is essential to success and survival. Donald E. Elario, Jr., vice president of operations, said, "Continuous improvement goes hand in hand with everything. It's everybody's role. It doesn't stop for anybody or anything. It's not just for operation, it's not just for automation. It's for sales, it's for accounting, it's for fixed assets, it's for everybody. Continuous improvement means you are truly never satisfied with whatever level you reach and one secret that we found is that's the way we function. No matter what we do we continue to look. As we're implementing the present, we're looking to the next and to the future and it just never stops. It absolutely never stops."

QUESTIONS

1. One method of changing an organization is unfreeze, change, refreeze. Explain this approach.
2. What techniques can a manager use to ensure that organizational changes are permanent?
3. What is the purpose of Marshall's Red Letter Days?

APPLICATION EXERCISE

The Beacon Aircraft Co.

OBJECTIVES

1. To illustrate how forces for change and stability must be managed in organizational development programs.
2. To illustrate the effects of alternative change techniques on the relative strengths of forces for change and forces for stability.

THE SITUATION

The marketing division of the Beacon Aircraft Co. has gone through two reorganizations in the past two years. Initially its structure changed from a functional form to a matrix form. But the matrix structure didn't satisfy some functional managers. They complained that the structure confused the authority and responsibility relationships.

In reaction to these complaints, the marketing manager revised the structure back to the functional form. This new structure maintained market and project groups, which were managed by project managers with a few general staff personnel. But no functional specialists were assigned to these groups.

After the change some problems began to surface. Project managers complained that they couldn't obtain adequate assistance from functional staffs. It not only took more time to obtain necessary assistance; it also created problems in establishing stable relationships with functional staff members. Since these problems affected their services to customers, project managers demanded a change in the organizational structure—probably again toward a

matrix structure. Faced with these complaints and demands from project managers, the vice president is pondering another reorganization. He has requested an outside consultant to help him in the reorganization plan.

THE PROCEDURE

1. Divide the class into groups of five to seven who will take the role of consultants.
2. Each group identifies the firm's driving and resisting forces. List these forces below.

Driving Forces	Resisting Forces
_____	_____
_____	_____
_____	_____
_____	_____
_____	_____
_____	_____
_____	_____
_____	_____

3. Each group develops a set of strategies for increasing the driving forces and another set for reducing the resisting forces.
4. Each group prepares a list of changes it wants to introduce.
5. The class reassembles and each group's recommendations are presented.

Source: Adapted from K. H. Chung and L. C. Megginson, *Organizational Behavior* (New York: Harper & Row, 1981), pp. 498–99. Reproduced with permission.

PART 6

Growth, Technology, and Innovation

CHAPTER 19

Entrepreneurship and Growth

After studying this chapter, you should be able to:

❖ Explain the term <u>entrepreneur.</u>

❖ Discuss the risks associated with becoming an entrepreneur.

❖ Explain people's motivation to become entrepreneurs.

❖ Describe the phases of the four-stage growth model.

❖ Discuss the important features of a business plan.

❖ Explain why it's valuable to carefully prepare a business plan.

❖ Discuss the role of entrepreneurship in the global economy.

Getting Started with Less: Today's Entrepreneurs Use Outsourcing

Not long ago, one couldn't get started in an entrepreneurial venture without a major capital investment, lots of skills, and the ability to do everything required to deliver a product or service. Today, entrepreneurs are finding that they are able to get new ventures started with much less by outsourcing much of their work.

Outsourcing is defined as the selective, short-term use of one or more contractors or consultants to assist in the accomplishment of a business function. Payroll services, tax compliance, employee benefits, and claims administration are the most commonly outsourced services. Now, small companies also are outsourcing a growing list of other major and minor functions, including equipment maintenance, manufacturing, sales representation, internal auditing, and accounting.

Take Innovative Medical Systems, Inc., for example. Tom Asacker's firm sells devices for preventing sleep apnea, as well as specialized mattresses designed to prevent bedsores. Drop by the company in Manchester, N.H., however, and you won't see a whole lot of manufacturing going on. You will see the firm's 25 employees involved in final assembly, quality assurance, strategic marketing, and customer service. All other

Frank Casale (right) greets participants at an Outsourcing Leadership Forum.

activities, including manufacturing of subassemblies, product design, computer networking, payroll administration, and direct mailing and advertising, are conducted by outsiders.

"We practice outsourcing both strategically and by necessity," says the 39-year-old Asacker. "I believe I improve my quality and responsiveness to the market by outsourcing to experts the things that I'm not expert at. And if I can get to the market fast with the highest-quality products using outsourcing, I've won for the long term, too."

Winning is what outsourcing is all about. Small firms such as Asacker's are making outsourcing both popular and profitable. In fact, small firms that do a lot of outsourcing tend to be more flexible, and are able to bring new products to market faster than their counterparts that do everything in-house. According to a Coopers & Lybrand study of nearly 400 small companies with median revenues of $6.5 million and median employment of 66 people, two-thirds use outsourcing. The study also found that the companies that used outsourcing had revenues, sales prospects, and growth rates that significantly exceeded those of firms that didn't use outsourcing.

"Initially, outsourcing was something that very large companies did that were in trouble; it was a controversial move," says Frank Casale, executive director of the Outsourcing Institute, a New York City company that provides information and runs seminars on outsourcing. "Now it's more accepted as a strategic-management tool for use by businesses of all sizes as compared with a last-second maneuver by a company that has run out of choices."

Business owners and experts agree that outsourcing can help small businesses focus more on what they do best—their core competencies. It also enables them to have the other functions performed by companies whose core competence is that function. Thus, tasks from administrative paperwork to product design are performed at a higher level of quality and usually at less cost than if a single firm tried to do them all.

Casale said, "Small companies now want to have as small a workforce as possible, be able to turn on a dime, and have access to world-class resources." Many small businesses have moved from outsourcing solely peripheral tasks to contracting out multiple functions that they depend upon for success.

Black Rock Ventures is a company that's nearly invisible but has generated roughly $10 million in sales in its first year of operation. One secret to its success is that the company, maker of the Killer Bee golf driver, is a prototype of the small "virtual company" (a company that makes heavy use of outsourcing). Black Rock contracted with a New Jersey company to design the Killer Bee, uses five marketing agencies around the country for its TV infomercials and other promotional activities, and has two Asian companies produce the club components and two American contractors assemble them. A local company handles telemarketing, order fulfillment, and customer service.

"We basically spend our time managing our vendors and planning our strategic direction," says Larry Hoffer, Black Rock's general manager and one of its five full-time employees. Hoffer admits that when the company grows it may have to bring more functions in-house. However, he said, "we don't want to grow this beyond probably 20 employees. We'll leave all the messy stuff to outside people."

Today's entrepreneurs still need to have a lot of skills, capital, and knowledge to start a new business venture. But, unlike years ago, they can get started without knowing how to do every step in the business process. Many small businesses have learned to focus on their strength, and contract with another firm to help them with other business functions. This trend is likely to continue, and those entrepreneurs who are able to form broad and complex partnerships with other firms will be the ones most likely to succeed.

Source: Adapted from Dale D. Buss, "Growing More by Doing Less," *Nation's Business,* December 1995, pp. 18-20; "Virtual Companies, Real Profits," *Nation's Business,* December 1995, p. 21.

E ntrepreneurship is one of the four pillars of a free enterprise society: land, labor, capital, and entrepreneurship.[1] The word *entrepreneurship* is derived from a 17th-century French word, *entreprendre,* which was defined as a person who undertook the risk of a new enterprise. Richard Cantillon, a French economist of Irish descent, popularized the concept of entrepreneurship in economics. In 1755 he described an entrepreneur as a person who pays a certain price for a product to resell it at an uncertain price, thereby making decisions about obtaining and using resources that consequently assume the risk of enterprise.[2]

The entrepreneur can be considered to be a creator. For our purposes, an **entrepreneur** is a person who

assumes the major risks of creating incremental wealth by making an equity, time, and/or career commitment of providing value to a product or service. The product or service itself may or may not be new or distinct, but value is added by an entrepreneur.[3]

This definition emphasizes (1) the creation of incremental wealth, (2) providing value, and (3) taking risks. It can fit the individual entrepreneur, collective entrepreneurship, or corporate intrapreneurship. Henry Ford (who created the assembly line process for automobiles and took risks at introducing this technology) was an entrepreneur. Art Fry (who invented the Post-It Note and worked diligently to make his discovery known) is an entrepreneur who operates within 3M, a large corporation. Anita Roddick (who launched the Body Shop to use naturally based ingredients to make cosmetics) is an entrepreneur. Steven Jobs and Stephen Wozniak (who created Apple Computer) are entrepreneurs. It can even fit the new breed of entrepreneur who sits in the center of a web of organization, brought together to deliver a product or service. As the opening vignette discusses, this type of virtual organization makes heavy use of outsourcing to create customer value.

Entrepreneurship has emerged in the 1990s as an important source of new jobs, new wealth, and new careers. Major corporations are attempting to capture the entrepreneurial spirit in the organization as a whole. Entrepreneurs are viewed by many as the individuals who can give the economy the boost it needs to compete globally, create new products and jobs, and initiate new forms of business. Around the world, emerging economies are also relying upon entrepreneurs to raise the standard of living. For example, newly created small businesses in the Czech Republic have played a major role in the transition to a market economy. An essential element in the Republic's emerging economy is the spontaneous motivation of private citizens to use their own capacity and resources in organizing their livelihoods.[4]

Estonia, another former republic of the Soviet Union, is growing wealth through entrepreneurship. The government there encourages the development of a private sector economy. It believes that the keys to growth and overcoming the many factors that inhibit its economy are the entrepreneur and a supportive environment.[5]

Today, if there's one clear message that's accepted, it's that new jobs are being created in much greater numbers in entrepreneurial firms. The Fortune 500 giants that we so often hear about aren't the new job creators.

This chapter looks at entrepreneurs and their growing role in global business and management transactions. The chapter examines the uniqueness of entrepreneurship, entrepreneurs, and how management principles are used by individuals who are responsible for job creation.

entrepreneur
A person who assumes the major risks of creating incremental wealth by making an equity, time, and/or career commitment of providing value to a product or service. The product or service itself may or may not be new or distinct, but value is added by the entrepreneur.

THE ENTREPRENEURIAL ENVIRONMENT

A nation's environment has a significant impact on the level of entrepreneurship. The United States has long held values and practiced traditions that encourage entrepreneurship. For example, the writings of 19th-century social critic Ralph Waldo Emerson emphasized concepts such as self-reliance, independence, and self-determination. Individual entrepreneurship as a part of the American experience is stated as follows:

Americans believe that their country is great because it is good; . . . they believe it is good because it is entrepreneurial. And so the controversy over what entrepreneurs are is far more than a debate about how to run a business. It is about how to lead and who is to lead. It is a discussion, as discussions about business always are, about what Americans are.[6]

Horatio Alger's writings discussed the triumphant individual hero who won riches and rewards by hard work, creative thinking, self-determination, faith, and some good luck. Alger's rags-to-riches stories personified freedom and creativity. His book titles (*Bound to Rise, Luck and Pluck*, and *Sink or Swim*) captured the spirit of entrepreneurship. These stories gave the country a noble ideal—an environment in which imagination and effort resulted in rewards.

The importance of an environment for entrepreneurship is not lost on modern leaders. Newt Gingrich, Speaker of the U.S. House of Representatives, believes that when human beings are liberated to become entrepreneurs, their self-interest becomes harnessed to the needs of the marketplace. The more freedom created for entrepreneurs to please customers, the greater the opportunity that one will have the chance to buy what one wants and live in the manner in which one chooses to live.[7]

In today's rapidly shrinking world, the big creative ideas pioneered by American entrepreneurs travel quickly to foreign lands. In the hands of global competitors, these ideas can undergo modification and improvement. Ideas, technology, and creativity travel and migrate overseas. As ideas migrate overseas, the resources needed to implement these ideas migrate as well. Workers in other parts of the world are usually cheaper than workers in the United States. This results in underbidding American labor.

An example of how new ideas diffuse around the world is the case of solid state transistors. Americans invented the solid state transistor in 1947. In 1953 Western Electric licensed the technology to Sony for $25,000—and the rest is history. A few years later RCA licensed several Japanese companies to make color TVs—and that was the beginning of the end of color TV production in America. In 1968 Unimation (a U.S. firm) licensed Kawasaki Hearing Industries to make industrial robots. The Japanese took the technology, kept improving it, and now are the robot-manufacturing leaders of the world. Americans have seen this pattern occur again and again with videocassette recorders, basic oxygen furnaces, microwave ovens, integrated circuits, and automobile stamping machines.

To compete in the changing environment, collective entrepreneurship must be added to the country's love affair with individual entrepreneurship. Collective entrepreneurship involves close working relationships among many different people at all stages of the invention, implementation, marketing, and modification processes. Individual skills must be integrated into a group. The collective group learns about each other, and the group's overall capacity becomes something greater than the sum of its parts.

The U.S. environment isn't likely to discourage the notion of a rags-to-riches story. Individual entrepreneurs will continue to be written about and used as role models. There's also likely to be more attention paid to group or collective entrepreneurship. As more firms embrace an entrepreneurial philosophy, human resources professionals must challenge conventional thinking about effective organizational development practices. Entrepreneurship involves a process of value creation in which an individual or team brings together a unique package of resources to exploit an opportunity. Human resource programs must adapt to reflect an orientation toward innovation and risk taking, long-term planning, results over process, flexibility, and active employee participation.[8]

A number of other ingredients point to the continual growth of an entrepreneurial environment around the world. Large firms, facing stiff new competition, are searching for innovative ways to survive and respond. To survive, large firms must recruit and retain the best human resources. However, today more and more of the brightest are deciding to start their own firms or to join small firms. An entrepreneurial career is now a viable alternative that college graduates are seriously considering. Thus competition for the best and the brightest—or the entrepreneurial-oriented—will rise.

CORPORATE ENTREPRENEURSHIP

The term *intrapreneurship* was coined by Gifford Pinchot in his book *Intrapreneuring*.[9] In his view, intrapreneurs are like corporate commandos who form teams (skunkworks) that use company resources to work on their own pet projects. They make things happen in spite of bureaucracy. Pinchot describes the corporate entrepreneur (intrapreneur) as someone who violates policy, ignores the chain of command, defies established procedures, and may come up with a new product or service. Management's challenge is to create a supportive environment that sustains these intrapreneurs' enthusiasm. Here we'll define an **intrapreneur** as someone inside an organization who pursues an innovation and champions it over a period of time. The What Managers Are Reading segment discusses a book that helps managers learn to think like entrepreneurs.

Art Fry, the 3M engineer who invented Post-It Notes, is an example of a corporate entrepreneur. He first thought of semisticky paper as a church choir director and wanted to have page markers for hymnals that would neither damage the books nor slip out easily.[10] He worked on the idea during his spare time. After years of experimenting, he finally came upon a glue and a pad concept with tear-off edges. Today hundreds of millions of dollars of Post-It Notes are sold.

Research into the effectiveness of corporate intrapreneurship suggests that it may be a generally effective means for improving long-term company financial performance. Moreover, the results of this research indicate that corporate intrapreneurship is a particularly effective practice among companies operating in hostile environments.[11] Corporate entrepreneurship can be summarized in five types: administration, opportunist, acquisition, imitative, and incubative. The use of a champion—someone who takes a leadership role—is important for each type.

Administrative Entrepreneurship

In administrative entrepreneurship the champion supports research and development and provides or helps secure needed resources to develop ideas and move them from the lab to the market. The administrative champion may be in the R&D unit or be a manager in another unit who views the idea or concept as important enough to invest his time, energy, or creativity. The Sony Walkman was invented by an R&D team at Sony, but a marketing team championed the Walkman system and pushed it to where it's now the industry standard.

Opportunist Entrepreneurship

Providing freedom to champions to seek and take opportunities is how firms such as Tupperware, Mary Kay Cosmetics, and insurance company A. L. Williams & Associates (ALW) operate. ALW's 200,000-person sales force sells more term insurance than any other firm in

intrapreneur
A person inside an organization who pursues an innovation and champions it over a period of time.

administrative entrepreneurship
This type of entrepreneurship is exhibited by the champion who supports research and development and provides or helps secure needed resources to develop ideas and move them from the lab to the market.

opportunist entrepreneurship
Exhibited by companies that allow employees to seek and take new opportunities that help the company.

WHAT MANAGERS ARE READING

HOW TO THINK LIKE AN ENTREPRENEUR
by Michael B. Shane

This book provides valuable insight on how to become a successful entrepreneur. Written in a simple and straightforward manner, the book advises aspiring entrepreneurs on how to get needed information and how to use it. Relying on his experience and wisdom, Michael B. Shane tells his readers how to use information instead of money as the essential tool to build an entrepreneurial business. According to Shane, new business ventures today often don't revolve around money, but around information.

In addition, the book provides insights into negotiating, planning, evaluating the competition, and creating a business plan with the three fundamental "Ms" of successful entrepreneurship—Marketing, Management, and Money. The decision-making process is identified by three categories of business decisions: (1) superficial decisions, (2) gut decisions, and (3) knowledge decisions.

The 140-page book also emphasizes that the customer is the source of success, security, and independence for the entrepreneur. Successful entrepreneurs must commit themselves to the customer above all else. Behind every successful entrepreneur there are happy, satisfied customers who are the driving force in the business.

Although the title of the book invites the attention of entrepreneurs, it contains lessons that carry a message to the management and CEOs of every large or small business operation.

Source: Adapted from Michael B. Shane, *How to Think Like an Entrepreneur* (White Plains, N.Y.: Bret Publishing, 1995), "How to Think Like an Entrepreneur," *National Public Accountant*, April 1995, p. 13.

the United States. Individuals join the firm as training reps. After they complete the company licensing and training program and observe field training sales transactions, they become reps. By selling and obtaining more training, the individuals continue to be promoted and earn more incentives. ALW isn't just selling insurance—it provides opportunities for salespeople to become financially independent. Sales personnel are able to build their own businesses.

acquisition entrepreneurship
A strategy whereby firms court other firms that have knowledge, ideas, or promising products.

Acquisition Entrepreneurship

Some firms encourage a strategy to court other firms that have knowledge, ideas, or promising products. General Electric, IBM, Motorola, and others have created joint ventures or new subsidiaries, or have added innovative product lines to their portfolios through acquisitions. In spite of some uncertainty, acquiring other firms or establishing new joint ventures requires entrepreneurial thinking and action.

imitative entrepreneurship
This form of entrepreneurship takes advantage of and extends the use of other firms' ideas, products, and technologies.

Imitative Entrepreneurship

This form of entrepreneurship takes advantage of and extends the use of other firms' ideas, products, and technology. The Japanese are experts at this form of entrepreneurship. They've studied American products, found ways to improve on them, produced them at a lower cost, and exported them to American markets. The VCR is an example of Japanese imitation. It was invented in the U.S., but is now manufactured almost exclusively by Japanese and other Asian firms.

One company that has tried very hard to prevent imitation of its product is Slick 50. Slick 50 is an oil additive that is touted by its users to have amazing restorative properties for a car's engine. The ingredients in Slick 50 are a closely guarded secret. Not even the current CEO knows entirely what's in the product. Other companies have tried to analyze the chemical composition of Slick 50, but so far none have been successful in reproducing it.[12]

incubative entrepreneurship
This type of entrepreneurship involves subjecting a new idea, technology, or innovation to experimentation and testing.

Incubative Entrepreneurship

The incubative version of entrepreneurship involves subjecting a new idea, technology, or innovation to experimentation and testing. Does it really work? Is it good? What risks are involved? The incubative champions are considered a semiautonomous new venture development unit that can either take the product from development to market or stop it from moving.

The classification system to describe corporate entrepreneurship (*intrapreneuring*, in Pinchot's words) shows that opportunities to be self-reliant and creative can exist in most firms. The challenge for corporations is to attract, retain, reward, and support the individuals who can move products from the idea stage to commercialization. A firm's entrepreneurial environment will have a lot to do with whether successful innovations occur. Large companies are becoming smaller, more responsive to change, and more tolerant of champions who challenge the routine pattern of doing business. Global competition will probably encourage even more of the five types of corporate entrepreneurship.

Joseph Schumpeter, a classical economist, said the job of the entrepreneur is "creative destruction." In a word, the entrepreneur is the one who overcomes the status quo, disregards the nay-sayers, and forges wealth out of the ore of opportunity. Entrepreneurs disrupt the economic equilibrium. They are driven by a vision of success that propels them over obstacles, around dead ends, and, for those who persevere, a place at the table of success which already seats the likes of Benjamin Franklin, Thomas Jefferson, Tom Watson, Bill Gates, Phil Knight, and other American heroes who took an idea and turned it into a successful business. In the next section, we'll examine the question: what is an entrepreneur?

WHAT IS AN ENTREPRENEUR?

Entrepreneurs create a business to build for growth and profit. They usually use a deliberate, planned approach that applies strategic management concepts and techniques. Entrepreneurs are also highly innovative, creating new products and markets, and applying creative strategies and ways of managing.

Bill Gates, cofounder of Microsoft, is an example of an innovative, growth-oriented entrepreneur. When IBM was fast developing its first personal computer in 1980, it asked 24-year-old Bill Gates to quickly write a software program that would provide the PC with an operating system. Believing his small company wasn't up to the task, Mr. Gates declined and suggested a competitor. But within days he reconsidered. He then found a Seattle programmer who had written a program called Q-DOS (the "Quick and Dirty Operating System") and bought the program's exclusive rights for $50,000. Mr. Gates gave the software a new name, MS-DOS, purchased a tie, flew to IBM's PC headquarters, and secured a contract.

That bit of luck and ingenuity put Mr. Gates and his company, Microsoft Corp., on the map. MS-DOS became the industry standard for personal computers. Its successors, Windows and Windows 95, are the operating systems used by about 80 percent of all PCs sold in the United States and provides Microsoft with half its yearly revenues. But unlike many software firms, Microsoft's fortunes aren't solely reliant on one product.

Observers attribute Mr. Gates's success to his technical genius, limitless energy, obsessive perfectionism, shrewd negotiating abilities, and business acumen. Unlike many founders of computer firms, he possesses the rare combination of technical genius and professional management skills that enabled his company to make a smooth transition from a fledgling start-up to a professionally managed, fast-growing firm.

At Microsoft's headquarters in Redmond, Washington, Mr. Gates leaves management tasks to skilled, professional managers while he focuses on technology, setting the company's strategic direction, and overseeing all major product development projects. A tall, bespectacled Harvard University dropout, he's a demanding taskmaster who sets rigorous standards for his programmers. His typical workday runs from 9:30 AM to midnight. The company's attitude emphasizes challenge and informality. Many of the 1,500 employees wear jeans and gather frequently for picnics and parties. Although programmers could earn more elsewhere, turnover is less than 10 percent, well below the industry average.

Because Microsoft is so dominant in the software industry, competitors—and sometimes computer company clients—complain about Mr. Gates's intimate knowledge of many companies' products and long-term strategy that are necessary in developing operations software for a major product. Some claim a conflict of interest exists. Others wonder whether Microsoft, involved in so many projects, has spread itself too thin. But its success shows no signs of ebbing. Mr. Gates is fast pursuing his vision—to bring computing power "to the masses."[13]

What are some of the motives that drive Mr. Gates and other entrepreneurs like him? This is a difficult question to answer, since each entrepreneur is driven by his own set of motives. Some, like John McCormack of Visible Changes, are immigrants or children of immigrants who are motivated by the promise of the American Dream. Others are motivated by the thrill of building a business. Still others are motivated by the dream of big profits. Not least are those who are motivated by a genuine desire to make a difference. Don't forget that founders of great nonprofit organizations such as the Salvation Army or the United Way were also entrepreneurs.

Today's nonprofits are increasingly run by people with backgrounds in management and entrepreneurship rather than clinical work. They increasingly resemble the corporations that help fund their work. Such ventures are headed by a new breed of entrepreneur known as the **social entrepreneur.**[14] The basic challenges faced by social entrepreneurs are the same as their for-profit counterparts. Each has some measure of risk taking.

social entrepreneur
One who manages a nonprofit organization and who has a background in management and entrepreneurship rather than clinical work. These organizations increasingly resemble the corporations that help fund their work.

Risks of Entrepreneurship

At least during the enterprise's early stages, the entrepreneur works in the domain of a small business. In launching a small business, the entrepreneur usually faces substantial *risk* (the chance of not knowing a decision or action's outcome). Popular mythology has it that starting a small business is extremely risky. One of the most common statements of this belief is that 8 of 10 new small businesses fail within a few years of their founding. Like a lot of other popular myths, this one is wrong. Outright failures of small businesses are in fact remarkably rare—if failure is defined, reasonably enough, as a business closing that results in losses to creditors either because the firm files for bankruptcy or because it simply closes its doors without paying its debts.

The confusion comes in mixing up business failures with business dissolutions. Lots of small companies go out of business for reasons that probably shouldn't be called "failure." The owner may have gotten bored, for instance, may be disappointed with the returns, or may simply want to try a greener pasture. If an entrepreneur closes one business and starts another one that is more successful, that's more reason for celebration than concern.

Two Dun & Bradstreet Corp. economists, Joseph W. Duncan and Douglas P. Handler, offered an even more encouraging statistic in a study published in 1994: almost 70 percent of all companies that started operations in 1985 were still active nine years later.[15]

Table 19–1 lists 15 reasons for business success or failure.[16] These reasons are from 20 studies that identified three or more variables as contributing factors to business success rates.

Although the risk of failure has been overstated, many entrepreneurs face significant *financial risk* as they typically invest most if not all their financial resources in the business. They take a *career risk* when leaving a secure job for a venture with a highly uncertain future. They also incur *family and social risks* because starting and running a business requires 60- to 80-hour work weeks that leave little time for family and friends. Demands of entrepreneurship often strain marriages and friendships. Entrepreneurs also assume a *psy-*

TABLE 19–1	FIFTEEN REASONS FOR BUSINESS SUCCESS OR FAILURE

Capital. Businesses that start undercapitalized have a greater chance of failure than those with adequate capital.

Record Keeping and Financial Control. Firms that do not keep updated accurate records and lack adequate financial controls have a greater chance of failure than those that do.

Industry Experience. Start-ups managed by people without prior industry experience have a greater chance of failure than those managed by people with such experience.

Management Experience. Start-ups managed by people without prior management experience have a greater chance of failure than those with experienced management.

Planning. Start-ups that do not develop specific business plans have a greater chance of failure than those with such plans.

Professional Advisors. Start-ups that do not use professional advisors have a greater chance of failure than those that use them.

Education. People without any college education who start a business have a greater chance of failing than people with one or more years of college education.

Staffing. Organizations that cannot attract and retain quality employees have a greater chance of failure than those that are more successful and retain quality in this regard.

Product/Service Timing. Firms that select products or services that are too new or too old have a greater chance of failure than firms that select products or services that are in the growth stage.

Economic Timing. Firms that start up during a recession are more apt to fail than those launched during an expansion period.

Age. Younger entrepreneurs are more likely to fail than older ones.

Partners. A business started by one person has a greater chance of failure than a business started by more than one person.

Parents. Start-up owners whose parents did not own a business have a greater chance of failure than those whose parents owned a business.

Minority. Minorities have a greater chance of failure than nonminorities.

Marketing. Start-up owners without marketing skills have a greater chance of failure than those with marketing skills.

chological risk—the risk of a deep sense of personal failure if the business doesn't beat the odds and succeed.

Taking on such risk requires a substantial level of motivation. Research has indicated that entrepreneurs are motivated by a number of factors. Some of these are reviewed in the next section.

Motivations of Entrepreneurs

Given entrepreneurship's sizable risks plus time and energy requirements, why do so many individuals take the entrepreneurial plunge? While potential costs are high, rewards can also be substantial. Entrepreneurs launch businesses because of one or more entrepreneurial motivations: independence, personal and professional growth, a superior alternative to a dissatisfying job, income, or security.

NEED FOR INDEPENDENCE - "Being my own boss" is a powerful motivator for many entrepreneurs who seek the freedom to act independently in their work. As heads of businesses, they enjoy the autonomy of making their own decisions, setting their own work hours, and determining what they'll do and when they'll do it.

Over the past 30 years, Bill Tobin has started 12 businesses, and they have all been successful. His social life, especially his interest in boating, has always been intertwined with his work. Today, Tobin has an office on his yacht. It houses a Compaq Presario 850C and an IBM Think-Pad with video capabilities, a cellular phone, and a cellular fax machine. With his yacht, Tobin spends about three months a year sailing and working in the Caribbean. The yacht serves as one of four offices he uses to run his current venture, PC Gifts and

One common attribute of entrepreneurs is the need for independence, typified by Bill Tobin who maintains his office on his yacht.

Flower, a shopping service on the Internet that he built in partnership with IBM.[17] This is the type of independence many entrepreneurs seek.

NEED FOR PERSONAL AND PROFESSIONAL GROWTH - The challenges of building a business inevitably involve individual growth. To succeed, an entrepreneur must be able to cope with risk, uncertainty, and stress, to handle many different interpersonal relationships, and to manage a business with limited resources. Many individuals become entrepreneurs to experience this growth and the fulfillment gained from building a business into a purposeful, productive entity. Perhaps the most crucial lesson of entrepreneurship is that one develops a sense of purpose that propels one forward.[18] This sense of purpose can bring meaning to the entrepreneur's life outside the business as well.

NEED FOR A SUPERIOR ALTERNATIVE TO A TYPICAL JOB - Many entrepreneurs establish businesses as an alternative they perceive as superior to a dissatisfying job. Despite frequent criticisms of the so-called Generation X, it's America's first computer generation, and it's beginning to combine technology and human freedom in ways that promise to restore the U.S. to economic leadership. A survey conducted in December 1993 asked people if starting a business was part of the American Dream. The results showed that 18- to 29-year-olds responded more positively than any other age group. That same group responded more negatively when asked if the American Dream meant owning a home or having a financially secure retirement. A February 1995 poll by Opinion Research Corp. found that 54 percent of those 18 to 34 were extremely or very interested in starting their own businesses, compared with only 36 percent of those 35 to 64. A survey was conducted at Marquette University in Milwaukee, Wis., in which it was found that nearly 10 percent of Americans 25 to 34 are actively working on starting a business, a rate nearly three times higher than that for any other age group.[19]

A 1995 Gallup Poll found that almost 70 percent of teenagers would like to start a business someday, compared with 50 percent of adults. And business programs to teach teens the fundamentals of entrepreneurship, almost unheard of five years ago, are cropping up in school and after-school courses, as well as summer camps.[20] High school students enrolled in entrepreneurship courses across Canada can now tap into "Planning for Success," an interactive, multi-media-based learning resource developed under the sponsorship of the Canadian Bankers Association. Using CD-ROM technology, the program is designed to close the gap between computer games and the world of new-venture planning.[21] These numbers indicate strongly that young people are seeking alternatives to typical jobs through entrepreneurship.

NEED FOR INCOME - Many entrepreneurs are enticed by the hefty profits that a highly successful business can provide, although the odds of such considerable success are slim. Others are motivated by making their own money in business. But, surprisingly, many entrepreneurs don't rate money as a primary motivator for starting a business. A survey of Inc. 500 entrepreneurs, for example, ranked money fourth in importance (behind frustration, independence, and controlling one's life).

NEED FOR SECURITY - Given the substantial risks and uncertainty of entrepreneurship, personal security may seem an unlikely motivator. But in a time of much corporate downsizing and layoffs, some entrepreneurs view running their own business as a more secure alternative, especially those in the middle and latter stages of their corporate careers. Knowing how to start and run a business gives one the ability to take action in the face of uncertainty. Sometimes just knowing what actions to take, whether or not they are successful, can provide a sense of security. As the Workplace of Tomorrow segment states, many middle managers who lost their jobs to corporate downsizing are finding refuge in entrepreneurship.

Entrepreneurial Characteristics

A number of studies have been conducted to determine whether entrepreneurs distinctly differ in personality and other characteristics from managers and the public at large. Drawing generalizations from this research is hard because studies differ in their definitions of entrepreneur.

Assuming a general definition of entrepreneur, some research support exists for a number of characteristics.[22] Studies have found that entrepreneurs possess a significantly greater need for independence and autonomy than do managers. Other studies have pictured the entrepreneur as having a substantial need to achieve and a tolerance of ambiguity—the ability to handle uncertain situations. Many entrepreneurs also have high energy and endurance, substantial self-esteem, and a strong dominance (a need to take charge, control, and direct others). Several studies also found that the entrepreneur has a lower need for social support compared to managers. She has high achievement values and a strong need for power and influence. The entrepreneur has an internal focus of control and resists subordination.[23] She's not a team player or joiner. Figure 19–1 uses the results of surveys and interviews to develop a composite list of entrepreneurial characteristics. In the next section we'll look at how entrepreneurs use their personal characteristics and skills to guide the growth of their companies.

THE STAGES OF BUSINESS GROWTH

There are no perfect models on how to succeed as an entrepreneur outside or inside an organization. Taking an idea, working with it, and eventually turning it into a business or product usually isn't an orderly process. The steps through the process are often unplanned and often are outside the entrepreneur's total control. The entrepreneurship process is frenetic, often unpredictable, challenging, and exciting all at the same time. The sequence of events is different for each product or service for each entrepreneur.

An idea's movement from something a person thinks up to a functioning business can be thought of as a four-stage model. David Holt's concise, informative model highlights activities in each of four distinct growth stages (Figure 19–2).

FIGURE 19–1
Characteristics of Successful
Entrepreneurs

Self-confident and optimistic	Energetic and diligent
Able to take calculated risks	Creative, need to achieve
Respond positively to challenges	Dynamic leader
Flexible and able to adapt	Responsive to suggestions
Knowledgeable of markets	Take initiatives
Able to get along well with others	Resourceful and persevering
Independent-minded	Perceptive with foresight
Versatile knowledge	Responsive to criticism

Source: John A. Hornaday, "Research about Living Entrepreneurs," in *Encyclopedia of Entrepreneurship,* ed. Calvin A. Kent, Donald L. Sexton, and Karl H. Vesper (Englewood Cliffs, N.J.: Prentice-Hall, 1982), p. 28. Adapted with permission.

FIGURE 19–2
The Four-Stage Growth Model

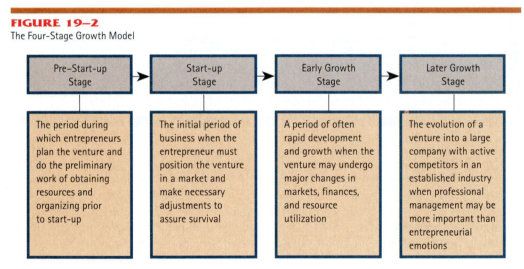

Source: Adapted from David H. Holt, *Entrepreneur* (Englewood Cliffs, N.J.: Prentice Hall, 1992), p. 104.

pre–start-up stage
The stage of entrepreneurship that involves asking fundamental questions about the potential of a business idea.

Pre–start-up Stage

Michael Dell, by working part-time and thinking about business, thought that his low-cost, direct-sales PC business was possible. He saw a gap or recognized a need and thought that his clone could fill it.

Asking questions about the potential of the product or service is part of the prestart-up stage. Is the product good? Is the product needed? Four sets of analyses are relevant no matter what the new venture will be. Figure 19–3 presents these four essential prestart-up activities: defining the business concept, analyzing the product market, planning the financing, and pre–start-up implementation. If the business is complex, the last of the pre–start-up activities can be extensive.

The four pre–start-up activities point out the need to do (1) product research patent searches to see if others already have filed patents, (2) market research to determine if a market exists, (3) financial analysis that includes making realistic forecasts of profits and cash flow, and (4) the necessary hiring, establishment of an inventory, advertising, and work needed to establish an accounting and payroll system.

FIGURE 19–3
Four Essential Pre–Start-Up
Activities

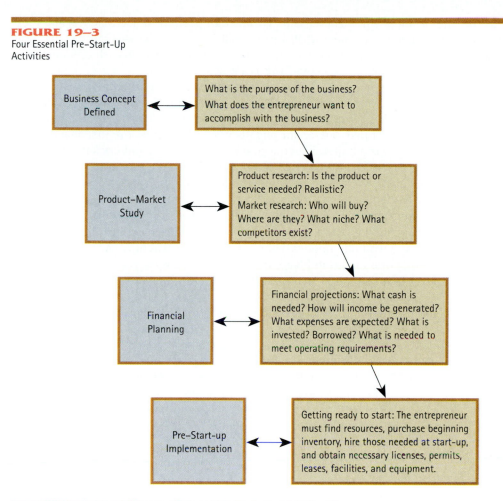

Business Concept Defined ↔ What is the purpose of the business? What does the entrepreneur want to accomplish with the business?

Product–Market Study ↔ Product research: Is the product or service needed? Realistic?

Market research: Who will buy? Where are they? What niche? What competitors exist?

Financial Planning ↔ Financial projections: What cash is needed? How will income be generated? What expenses are expected? What is invested? Borrowed? What is needed to meet operating requirements?

Pre–Start-up Implementation ↔ Getting ready to start: The entrepreneur must find resources, purchase beginning inventory, hire those needed at start-up, and obtain necessary licenses, permits, leases, facilities, and equipment.

Source: Adapted from David H. Holt, *Entrepreneur* (Englewood Cliffs, N.J.: Prentice Hall, 1992), p. 105.

One of the key variables in a new-venture start-up is the industry in which it intends to conduct business. All entrepreneurs should take the time to undertake an investigation of opportunities and threats in their industry. A strategic position in a growing, dynamic, and healthy industry can go a long way toward ensuring a successful venture. On the other hand, a weak position in a mature industry may sound a death knell before it even opens its doors.[24]

The entrepreneur also must be careful to select a compatible management team, since there is likely to be a good deal of stress in the early stages of building the company. In addition, the entrepreneur should produce carefully considered pro forma financial statements, including sales forecasts, income statement, balance sheet, and cash flow, to get some indication of the amount of capital that will be needed to run the business, and the amount of sales that will be needed to make a profit.

Start-up Stage

This is the initial period of opening the doors and doing business. During the start-up stage the entrepreneur takes action to meet the objectives set in the prestart-up stage. Examples of objectives in terms of sales, growth, and position are:

Sales: To attain monthly sales volume as forecasted in the prestart-up stage.

Growth: To increase monthly sales by at least 5 percent each month during the first year of business.

Position: To capture at least 10 percent of the market share at the medium-priced end of the market within 15 months of starting the business.

start-up stage
The initial period of opening the doors and starting to do business.

Ideally the business will meet its sales, growth, and position objectives. Meeting these objectives, however, may not mean that a profit will be earned. Losses are usually more common in the first year of a business. Does the business have enough cash or financial resources to cover variable and fixed costs? This is a crucial question.

One notable entrepreneur who has been involved in starting up companies at vastly different ages is J.R. Simplot. Known to his friends as Mr. Spud, Simplot made his first fortune in the potato business. Simplot's family moved to Idaho in 1904, when he was an infant. At fourteen, he dropped out of the eighth grade and built his first machine for processing potatoes. It was a boiler that cooked up scrap potatoes and horsemeat, the final product of which he used to feed his hogs. The boiler helped him prepare mass quantities of food through a tough winter, and in the spring he sold his pigs for a profit of some $7,000, a tidy profit at the time.

The next machine that grabbed Simplot's attention was an automatic potato sorter. Then still in his teens, Simplot and a partner ordered one of the machines. Simplot owned a 50 percent share and won the other half in a coin toss. That machine gave him a monopoly on the fast sorting of potatoes in Idaho, and Simplot was on his way to his first million. Today his potato empire supplies McDonald's with more than 50 percent of its french fries.

But the millions he earned from that start-up wasn't the end of J.R. Simplot's entrepreneurial exploits. At 86 years old, he is emerging as one of the single biggest winners in semiconductor technology. Through mind-boggling gains in the stock of Micron Technology, his high-tech fortune has suddenly ballooned to the point where it's clearly exceeded only by the likes of Microsoft cofounders Bill Gates and Paul Allen. Simplot's stake in Micron grew by $2.5 billion over 24 months. (That's $5 million every working day!) He now owns 21 percent of Micron, and plays a big role in the governance of the company.[25] J.R. Simplot followed the first rule of all successful start-ups—set clear goals and act to achieve them.

Early Growth Stage

early growth stage
The stage of new business development where a growth spurt can be expected.

Once the venture is positioned, successful businesses will have an early growth spurt. In some ventures the spurt is small and slow; other businesses' spurt is dramatic and rapid. Compaq Computer reached $1 billion in annual sales within five years after it was started, faster than any company in history. On the other hand, Coca-Cola's growth was slow and steady. Atlanta pharmacist John J. Pemberton invented Coca-Cola in 1886. His bookkeeper, Frank Robinson, named the product after two ingredients: kola nuts and coca leaves. By 1891 Atlanta pharmacist Asa G. Chandler bought the company for $2,300. Today annual sales are over $6 billion.

Most entrepreneurs don't know exactly where or how big the growth spurt will be when they start the business. Although Mr. Pemberton invented Coca-Cola, his unique product's success was enjoyed by those who bought him out. Entrepreneurs don't always accurately assess market demand, market changes, and resource needs. Managing sales, costs, and resources carefully is important in the early growth stage.

Later Growth Stage

later growth stage
The stage of a maturing business where growth has slowed and new competitors have entered the market.

In the later growth stage the growth rate is usually slower. Active domestic and international competitors frequently enter the market. Often companies that reach this stage sell stock to the public to raise funds. Also the entrepreneur may be replaced with a professional manager or team. Perhaps the most publicized change in an organization's top team took place at Apple Computer. In 1985 Apple cofounder Steven Jobs lost out in a power struggle to John Sculley, a professional manager who had been hired away from Pepsi-Cola to work with Jobs.

Managing growth became a significant challenge for Empress International, Ltd., a frozen-seafood distributorship out of Port Washington, N.Y. With sales exploding from $64 million in fiscal 1992 to $108 million in fiscal 1995, the company was feeling growing pains. Despite the rapid growth in sales, for example, only five new employees were added to the firm, giving it a total of only 30.

Although sales were going great, company president Joel Kolen says, the company found that uncontrolled growth can be dangerous. Systems of operation that had remained largely unchanged over the years since the company was founded by Kolen's father in 1953 simply weren't efficient enough to ensure sustained growth and continued success. To give the company a chance to catch up with sales, Kolen decided to hold fiscal 1996 sales relatively stable. This "breather" gives the company a chance to update operating systems.

The company has hired a chief financial officer to establish systems for analyzing and managing data, the market, inventory, and cash flow. In addition, the company is updating its physical facilities. The main power source has been converted from electricity to natural gas, and the company is boosting storage capacity. In addition, there are plans to increase the sales staff by 10 to 20 percent to accommodate the growth.[26]

The four-stage growth model illustrates that attention needs to be directed to different factors at each stage. During the prestart-up stage attention should be on the business concept, the product or service, financial plans, and implementation activities. The start-up stage requires that attention be directed at positioning. At the early growth stage proper management of sales, costs, and resources is important. During the later and usually slower growth stage, making the transition from an entrepreneur-managed business to a professionally managed business is the focus of attention. At all stages, it's important for the business firm to behave ethically. As the Ethics Spotlight discusses, ethical management is the key to success for Inland Steel.

ETHICS SPOTLIGHT — INLAND STEEL COMPETES ETHICALLY

In today's society, the survival of a business often depends on whether it has a good name. Whether a business will earn a good reputation largely depends on its ethics. Ethics can therefore be a do-or-die dilemma for any company. Inland Steel has made its good name through an insistence on ethical practices—both internal and external. The culture of ethics at Inland is the result of company chairman Bob Darnall. Darnall insists that Inland set high ethical standards to build long-term customer relationships.

"You have to stand for something," says Darnall about the ethics of companies. His own firm has a history of standing for high ethical principles; they are important to Inland's identity. Inland's leaders didn't "hide behind legalities or regulations or cite 'corporate needs' or some other 'overriding concerns' when they were faced with difficult ethical issues," Darnall explains. "They measured their actions against a higher standard: their own concept of right and wrong, their own view of their responsibilities—to Inland, yes, but also to society."

"Our people are our most important resource and will be treated with dignity and respect," Inland states in its corporate philosophy. That means sharing business information with them in good times and in bad, in sickness and in health. When it's had to reduce its workforce, Inland has taken the time to inform its employees why it's laying people off. Its severance and employee-assistance program went "far beyond the norm, providing months of financial assistance, up to two years of insurance and benefit coverage, and an extensive job-placement program," Darnall says. Likewise, Inland managers now share all the company's financial data with union leaders in the partnership agreement negotiated in 1993.

High ethical standards have helped give Inland the discipline it needs to build strong partnerships with customers over the long term. In boom times, the high prices on the spot market have tempted Inland to make some fast money rather than continuing to ship to strategic customers at lower contractual prices. Inland has stuck by its long-term partners.

Steelmakers often are tempted to promise customers more than they actually can deliver. "Time after time, we've had to say to our customers, 'No, we can't do that, we can't do everything you want,'" Darnall says. Making promises it can't keep damages any company's long-term credibility with its customers, the financial community, and others. A trust-worthy firm is one that does what it says it will do.

Steelmakers who prove trustworthy can develop close ties to their customers. Some customers have eliminated parts of their organization and handed over those responsibilities to Inland. "These customers are willing to make themselves vulnerable, because they trust us and understand the economic benefits of the business link," Darnall says. Mistrust between steel suppliers and users, and between management and labor, is always a competitive disadvantage. The ethical discipline of doing unto customers and employees as you would have them do unto you is good business in the long run.

The same is true of the community-at-large—and the world we live in. "Environmental leadership will prove to be good business," Darnall says. In the 1980s, Inland spent $90 million for a wastewater-recycling system that "went beyond what was mandated," Darnall says. It also spent $15 million to replace air-pollution-control equipment at a melt shop not because EPA required it but mainly because it improved the work environment—and the productivity of the workers there.

Source: Adapted from Bryan Berry, "A Higher Standard," *Iron Age New Steel*, September 1995, p. 2; Maureen Patterson, "Ethics is Good Business," *Buildings*, September 1995, pp. 33–37.

ENTREPRENEURSHIP AND THE BUSINESS PLAN

Creating and building a successful enterprise requires, above all, effective planning. As research clearly indicates, poor management and management inexperience are the primary causes of new-venture failure.[27] To be specific, 9 of every 10 closings have been attributed to inadequate management.[28]

But before we begin we should briefly discuss the critical first step that precedes planning, the first entrepreneurial task. This first step is the *entrepreneur decision*, specifically deciding whether to purchase an established business or to become an entrepreneur.

Making the right decision requires a clear understanding of entrepreneurship and the requirements for success. Above all, the decision should be based on an accurate self-assessment of individual skills, abilities, and shortcomings. This is so because initially the entrepreneur *is* the business. He makes all the decisions, initiates critical business relationships, and performs the management functions. The entrepreneur's strengths and limitations directly and profoundly affect the enterprise.

Many management observers agree that success requires certain entrepreneurial attributes. The entrepreneur must be motivated to make a profit because profitability (not self-fulfillment, independence, or other motivations) is essential for survival. The entrepreneur must be an effective planner, organizer, problem solver, and decision maker, and must be able to manage people well. Experience in the business is vital as are talents for getting along with people and handling stress. The entrepreneur must have nerve, be prepared to bounce back from inevitable setbacks, and be willing to devote long hours to the business.

Of the four management functions, planning probably contributes the most to new-venture performance. Planning provides a well-thought-out blueprint of action for the critical first months of the new business. This activity is vital because when resources are slim in the early days of the business, mistakes can be costly or even fatal. Careful planning reduces the chances of major mistakes; it also forces the entrepreneur to examine the business's external environment, competition, potential customers, strengths, and limitations.[29] But despite the importance of planning, many entrepreneurs don't like to plan because they believe planning hinders their flexibility.[30]

Writing a business plan is perhaps the most difficult task for new entrepreneurs, but also one of the most essential. For many entrepreneurs, writing a business plan is similar to having dental problems: it's very painful and often requires repeat visits for follow-up work. The major difference is that a trip to the dentist usually ends quietly, knowing that you'll probably be back within a year. Completing the business plan, however, can result in a feeling of exhilaration as your idea has come alive in the words and numbers.

A **business plan** is a road map for starting and running your business. To many, it's also a sales document, since you'll use the business plan to convince bankers, venture capitalists, family, friends, and even yourself to invest in your business. In fact, there are seven good reasons that you should write a business plan if you want to be an entrepreneur:

business plan

The entrepreneur's road map. The business plan contains descriptions of the company, its founders, the product, and its potential markets, as well as financial projections about the company's expected future performance.

1. **To sell yourself on the business:** This is a "reality check." The most important stakeholders in any business venture are the founders. The founders must be convinced that the business idea is sound so they develop a passion to make it a reality.
2. **To obtain bank financing:** Since the bank failures of the 1980s and 1990s, it's more necessary than ever for entrepreneurs to have a sound business plan if they're seeking bank financing. Getting bank money may be tougher now than it has been in a long time. A well-written, well-researched business plan can make the difference between getting the money needed to start the business and being rejected.
3. **To obtain investment funds:** For many years, the business plan has been the price of admission to the venture capital evaluation process. Rare is the private investor who will provide the seed capital a new business requires based merely on an oral presentation. Even if you do get to talk with a venture capitalist about your idea, you'll be required at least to submit financial pro formas in writing.
4. **To arrange strategic alliances:** Many small companies seek alliances with larger companies to get some of their expertise in key areas, or to offer their services.

Despite the corporate need for many such services, there usually are more vendors than needed. To help them select who they'll work with, large corporations usually want to see business plans of prospective small business partners.

5. **To obtain large contracts:** When small companies are seeking substantial orders or ongoing service contracts from major corporations it helps to have a business plan to convince the corporation of the long-term prospects of the small company. Through a business plan, corporate decision makers can see that the small company expects to be in business three years, five years, and more into the future. The business plan helps convey a feeling of partnership and commitment.

6. **To attract key employees:** A new business start-up will need talented, flexible people who are willing to take the risks associated with a new venture. Even in today's volatile job environment, many key executives are drawn to jobs with large corporations. A written business plan can assure prospective employees that the entrepreneurs have carefully thought through key issues facing the company and have a plan for dealing with them.

7. **To motivate and focus the management team:** As small companies grow and become more complex, a business plan helps the management team stay focused on the same goals. Many companies lose their way when they begin to grow. Management, including the founding entrepreneur, needs to plan growth to ensure the business has cash flow to pay the bills, people to handle the volume of work, and goods to meet the demand they've created.

Perhaps the hardest part of writing a business plan is getting started. Staring at a blank sheet of paper or computer screen can be a daunting image for many energetic entrepreneurs. The task of writing the business plan is made easier if it's broken into discrete chunks that can be woven together at the end. The plan should be anywhere from 10 to 40 pages, and it should be written with a clear idea of its intended audience. The following features are commonly included in business plans:

1. **Cover Page:** A cover page serves several purposes. It's the place where you include not only the company's name and business address, but also the name and telephone number of a main contact. The cover page should also include a warning that the business plan contains confidential material and is not to be copied or otherwise transmitted. It might also include a copy number, to indicate to readers that you keep track of each copy in existence. The cover might even include a photo of your product or service. It could also include the corporate logo.

2. **Table of Contents:** This should be detailed, with page numbers of each section provided. Some bankers and investors have a preferred way of reading a business plan that may not involve starting at the beginning and reading straight through. Many, for example, want to start by reading the financial projections. The business plan is more attractive to them if it's easy to find the material they're interested in.

3. **Executive Summary:** Many entrepreneurs forget to include an executive summary in their business plans. However, this is an essential component. The executive summary says in one or two pages everything that's important to say about the new venture. It's the single most important part of the plan because most investors turn to it early in their reading for a sense of the business idea.

4. **The Company:** This section includes discussion about the company's strategy and management team. It should include information about where the company will be located, the qualifications of the management team, and a little about the history and current competitive environment of the industry in which the business will compete. It should also include statements about how the company will differentiate itself from competitors, and why its strategy is unique.

5. **The Market:** In this section, the entrepreneur must conduct research to determine who will buy the product or service to be offered. It should also include analyses that project what percent of this market will buy the products or services offered by the new venture. In addition, this section usually includes an overview of competitors, their strategies, and their vulnerabilities.

6. **The Product/Service:** Here is where the entrepreneur discusses the product or service to be offered. If the new business is being formed around a product idea, the item should be described in great detail, and a picture should be provided. If the venture is being organized to perform a service, the process should be described in great detail.

7. **Sales and Promotion:** In this section, the entrepreneur describes the strategy that will be used to inform prospective customers about the new business. What types of advertising will be used? How will sales be completed? These and other questions let potential investors know whether the entrepreneur has thought about how transactions will be completed.

8. **Finances:** The financial plan is second only to the executive summary in terms of importance to the business plan. In the basic **financial pro forma** documents—the sales forecast, income statement, cash flow statement, and balance sheet—the entrepreneur lays out how the business will pay its bills and make a profit. Many investors turn immediately to the financial statements to determine whether a business plan has merit. Experienced professionals can usually tell at a glance if the entrepreneur has tried to be honest in making the assumptions behind the numbers, or whether pie-in-the-sky projections are based on wishful thinking. It's sound advice to the entrepreneur to be exceedingly conservative when making cost and sales projections. Generally, worst-case scenarios should be used.

9. **Appendices:** The appendices can include anything from brochures about the business or competitor businesses, newspaper or magazine clippings about the industry, resumes from the company principals, or other relevant documents. The table of contents should include a descriptor and page reference number for each item in the appendix.[31]

> **financial pro formas**
> Essential financial documents that project the company's sales, profits, and cash flow.

The business plan is a guide to the business that lets the reader understand the mission, goals, and objectives of the new venture. Prior to start-up, the business plan helps the entrepreneur decide if the business can be profitable, and what it will take to make it profitable. Too often, entrepreneurs fall in love with their business idea and charge ahead with no plan, only to discover later after much expense that there's no market for their product or service. Once a business plan has been judged feasible, it can establish the direction the new venture should take in order to grow and the methods it will need to use to manage that growth. It's also a vital source of information as the entrepreneur seeks investors, strategic partners, or clients.

No one denies that writing a business plan is a difficult chore. But if the task is organized properly, and if the information is gathered and sorted in advance, the time it takes to do the writing can be minimized. It's not a job that can be completed in a weekend, but it's one that entrepreneurs must tackle seriously if they're to ensure the best chance for achieving the goals of the business.[32]

ENTREPRENEURSHIP AROUND THE WORLD

Entrepreneurship flourishes in the United States, but it's also becoming an increasingly important economic driver around the world. As statist economies continue to discover the wealth-creating power of free markets, more and more people are starting their own businesses. The most striking example of this change to free markets is the downfall of the former Soviet Union. What had been a stagnant economy under the control of a centralized authority, has been opened to tap the dormant creative energies of the Russian people. Research has found that the average Russian entrepreneur is male with an average age of 34 years. For most, their current business venture is their first one. Russian entrepreneurs are energetic, independent, competitive, and self-confident.[33]

Some of the former Soviet satellite states, such as Poland, Azerbaijan, East Germany, and others are attempting to create an economic context that supports entrepreneurship. Many are encouraging private and foreign investment to ensure that entrepreneurs have access to the capital they need to start their businesses. Some are using government subsidies as a means of easing the difficulties of the new business start-up.

In January 1990, the newly democratic Polish government introduced a draconian plan for a market economy. Most observers expected the plan to spur reform through the restructuring of large state enterprises. When it failed to do so, they criticized it. But the plan

GLOBAL EXCHANGE

U.S. ENTREPRENEUR USES LETTER-OF-CREDIT FINANCING TO CONDUCT GLOBAL BUSINESS

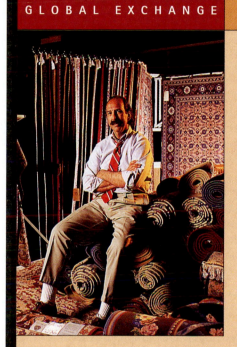

Roy Maloumian had an idea: why not manufacture hand-loomed rugs inspired by world-famous designs and sell them at a fraction of the cost of the museum-quality originals? Maloumian's family had been in the Oriental rug business for more than 35 years, so he knew the only way to do it was to blend low-cost production with high-quality merchandise.

Where could he find this blend? The People's Republic of China. But how would he finance the purchase of the rugs from China since, unlike a big company, he didn't have a lot of available cash? The answer, he found, was a letter of credit.

A letter of credit is like a loan. Instead of lending you money, a bank "lends" you its stability and creditworthiness and receives a fee instead of interest. The safest type is the irrevocable letter of credit. That's what Maloumian uses when his company, Tianjin–Philadelphia Carpet,

deals with its supplier in Tianjin, a seaport in northeast China.

"Letters of credit enable a small company like ours to compete very successfully abroad against much larger companies that have an internal source of funds," he says. "It puts us on an equal basis with these companies from the supplier's point of view."

When Maloumian needs a letter of credit, he applies with his Philadelphia bank. The application contains the foreign company's sales terms and lists the documents the overseas supplier must present to the bank for it to pay—or "honor"—the letter.

Documentation needed to complete the transaction includes a bill of exchange, which is like a check drawn on when the goods are delivered; a bill of lading; an insurance policy or certificate of insurance; a consular invoice, which varies by country; and a commercial invoice. Poorly completed documents usually mean delays.

After the bank approves Maloumian's application, it issues the letter of credit for the U.S. dollar value of the product he's purchasing, thus committing the bank to pay the foreign company when all of the letter's conditions have been met. The letter is sent, usually by telex, to the foreign company's bank, known as the "advising bank" because it advises the foreign company that the letter has been issued on the company's behalf. In this case, the other bank was the Bank of China's office in Tianjin.

If the letter of credit's terms are satisfactory to the supplier, he starts making the goods and preparing the necessary documents. Next, the supplier completes the order and gives it to a shipper while he sends the document to his bank before the letter of credit expires. That bank then forwards the documents to Maloumian's bank for payment. If everything is in order, Maloumian's bank pays the amount due and charges his firm's account.

Since Maloumian has a line of credit with his bank, he requests that payment be drawn from it to cover the amount taken out of his company's account. After the payment is made, Maloumian's bank sends the documents to his freight broker so that the merchandise can be cleared through U.S. Customs and trucked to Tianjin–Philadelphia's headquarters.

Importers like Maloumian should remember that banks assume only credit risk in a letter-of-credit transaction. They assume no liability for the merchandise represented by the letter, for the authenticity of documents provided by the foreign supplier, or for the financial responsibility of the foreign shipper. To protect themselves, entrepreneurs must understand the terms of sale offered by their foreign supplier and be comfortable with its reputation and solvency.

All letters of credit are issued under strict rules established by the International Chamber of Commerce. The rules are known as the Uniform Customs and Practices for Documentary Credits, or the UCP. In 1993, the UCP was revised under ICC Publication 500. For a copy, see your bank or a local library. It explains the responsibilities of all parties to a letter-of-credit transaction.

While letters of credit may seem complicated at first, they're also extremely useful. By using banks in international transactions, small-business owners—who don't have a lot of cash or can't have someone on site with an overseas supplier—can have the best of both worlds: They can take advantage of larger markets and can avoid much of the risk in dealing with strangers thousands of miles away operating under laws that may be vastly different from U.S. laws.

Source: Adapted from Len Karpen, "Your Company's Ticket Abroad," *Nation's Business*, August 1995, p. 47; Anne B. Fisher, "Raising Capital for a New Venture," *Fortune*, June 13, 1994, pp. 99–101.

succeeded in encouraging entrepreneurship, which now appears to be the main force driving economic reform in Poland. The formerly communist economy, where shortage of goods and services was routine, meant that liberalization would unleash consumer demand and present entrepreneurial opportunity. Polish entrepreneurs were better able than the large state enterprises to meet the new consumer demand.[34]

In contrast, the Ukraine adopted economic reform measures that favored continued administrative regulations over entrepreneurship. As a result, economic reform in that nation has been disappointing.[35]

One of the most important elements of these efforts to develop a culture of entrepreneurship is education. As you can imagine, people who are used to having their lives regulated and controlled by a central authority have some difficulty understanding the fundamentals of organizing and managing a profitable business. People in these newly free markets will need time to develop the work ethic, citizenship values, legal rules, and other elements of free economies that we take for granted.[36]

Beyond the emerging new economies of the former Soviet Union, several areas of the globe have a hyperentrepreneurial environment where business activity dominates daily life. Such areas as Hong Kong, Singapore, and Taipei have created economic contexts that are highly supportive of entrepreneurship. Other Asian nations, such as the People's Republic of China, are making efforts to encourage entrepreneurship. As the Global Exchange states, one U.S. entrepreneur used a creative approach to finance his business ventures in the PRC.

Singapore has created a national development model based on government entrepreneurship and technological development. This mixture has led some to call Singapore a nation of "technopreneurship."[37] In this model, foreign multinational corporations continue to be an integral driving force in economic growth and a conduit for technology transfer. The country will face new challenges in the future as the economies of India and China open up.

SUMMARY OF LEARNING OBJECTIVES

EXPLAIN THE TERM ENTREPRENEUR.

An entrepreneur is a person who assumes the major risks of creating incremental wealth by making an equity, time, and/or career commitment of providing value to a product or service. The product or service itself may or may not be new or distinct, but value is added by the entrepreneur.

DISCUSS THE RISKS ASSOCIATED WITH BECOMING AN ENTREPRENEUR.

Nothing is certain about business. Risks include loss of financial investment, losing a job, psychological strain and stress, and family pressure. Since entrepreneurs work long hours, there's also the risk of losing contact with friends.

EXPLAIN PEOPLE'S MOTIVATION TO BECOME ENTREPRENEURS.

There's no specific or universal set of motivations. In general, people are motivated because of such factors as desire for independence, personal and professional growth, a more rewarding job, higher income, and job security.

DESCRIBE THE PHASES OF THE FOUR-STAGE GROWTH MODEL.

The four-stage growth model involves prestart-up, start-up, early growth, and later growth. The prestart-up stage involves planning, organizing, and obtaining resources. The start-up stage focuses on positioning the venture. In the early growth stage adjusting to changes

and appropriately using resources are important. During the later growth stage professional managers are often needed to handle the usually slower rate of growth.

DISCUSS THE IMPORTANT FEATURES OF A BUSINESS PLAN.

A business plan should consist of nine essential components: cover page, table of contents, executive summary, description of the company, overview of the market, description of the product or service, sales and promotion strategies, financial statement, and appendices.

DISCUSS THE ROLE OF ENTREPRENEURSHIP IN THE GLOBAL ECONOMY.

Entrepreneurship has begun to emerge in many of the formerly centralized economies of Eastern Europe. It will take many years, however, before these economies develop the cultural values that support entrepreneurship. Countries in Asia, in contrast, have hyperentrepreneurial cultures that encourage new venture start-ups.

EXPLAIN WHY IT'S VALUABLE TO CAREFULLY PREPARE A BUSINESS PLAN.

The business plan serves as a framework to help conduct the needed functions of managing the business. It can also serve as an organized, formal document that leaders can review. Decisions on whether lenders will provide funds are often based to some extent on the quality and persuasiveness of the business plan.

KEY TERMS

REVIEW AND DISCUSSION QUESTIONS

Recall

1. Present the major sections of a business plan.
2. Where did the term *entrepreneurship* originate?
3. What are the growth model's four stages?
4. What are the motivations for becoming en entrepreneur?

Understanding

5. What are the reasons for encouraging entrepreneurs to write a business plan? Why do many entrepreneurs resist writing a business plan?
6. Why might people be attracted to attempt to start their own businesses?

7. Can a large company such as Du Pont or Procter & Gamble encourage entrepreneurship? Explain.
8. What role does a nation's "economic environment" play in the level of entrepreneurial activity?

Application

9. Make a list of several business ideas you might want to pursue. Make another list of the obstacles to starting your own business. How can you overcome these obstacles?
10. Locate three entrepreneurs: one who's over 50 years old, one who's a woman, and one who's an immigrant to America. Ask them why they became entrepreneurs. Prepare a report on their answers and your own interpretation.

CASE STUDY

Can Entrepreneurship Be Taught?

Can entrepreneurship be taught? That's the question that many of the leading business schools in the United States hope to answer in the affirmative. A large number of business schools are now offering entrepreneurship programs to both graduate and undergraduate students. The number of universities that teach entrepreneurship has grown from 16 in 1971 to well over 370 undergraduate and graduate programs in 1993.

The University of Houston College of Business Administration, for example, is in the third year of its unique entrepreneurship program for undergraduate students. Offered through the Department of Marketing and Entrepreneurship, the six-course program is offered to 30 students each year. Each student in the program must first traverse a rigorous selection process, including intensive interviews with faculty and entrepreneurs who teach in the program. The six-course sequence includes an introduction to entrepreneurship, revenue, cost, legal forms of business, business plan development, and business plan implementation. The first entrepreneurship class graduated in May 1995. Of the 30 students in the program, 12 had started businesses by the time they graduated.

Another school that has developed a strong reputation for entrepreneurship is Babson, located near Boston, Mass. Babson's Price Institute for Entrepreneurial Studies has a long tradition of helping its students achieve their entrepreneurial dreams. One such student is Michael Healey, president of PC-Build Computers. His story is typical of many new ventures.

On the first of the month, Michael Healey hid from his landlord. The rent was due on office space for PC-Build Computers, the brand-new company he was starting with fellow Babson College student Robert Lofblad.

They didn't have the money. In fact, when the partners rented the space, they knew they wouldn't have the money—not yet. But in three days, the Douglass Foundation would announce its prize for best student business plan at Babson.

Lofblad and Healey had a great plan: they would sell build-it-yourself computer kits to the hobby market. They thought it was a sure bet to win the prize money. They had to win—or go out of business before making their first sale.

On the fourth of the month, the winner was announced: PC-Build. Healey picked up the check and marched straight down the street into the business district of Wellesley, Mass. He put the $3,000 down as a deposit and picked up the keys to the office. He and Lofblad were in business.

"Basically, we started with nothing," says Healey, 31. Nothing but the lessons they learned at Babson, one of the best business school for entrepreneurs in the world.

Three years later, Jeffrey Timmons, one of Healey's professors, is using the PC-Build case as a classroom exercise for the annual SEE, the weeklong Symposium for Entrepreneurship Educators held at Babson. PC-Build has now expanded into Hartford, Conn. Healey expects the new location to start pumping revenues right away. "We made all our mistakes with the original office in Massachusetts," he says.

To fund this latest growth, Healey and Lofblad took on a couple of new investors, including Steve Spinelli, one of the founders of Jiffy Lube International Inc., who cashed out and became a full-time professor of entrepreneurship at Babson. Spinelli was one of the role models who inspired Healey to start PC-Build.

Today, the company employs 22 people, has annual revenues of $3.2 million, and is growing. Healey and Lofblad have a strategy to cash out in their seventh year.

A graduate of the University of Massachusetts at Amherst, Healey first worked in New England as a project manager for Siemens-Nixdorf, one of Europe's largest computer makers. When his division was downsized, he went to graduate school to learn how to become an entrepreneur. Babson taught him how to get the resources he would need; how to find customers; and how to survive in order to thrive.

"They taught me how to have a thick skin," says Healey. "Nothing offends me anymore."

"Let me tell you what we can't do," says Bill Bygrave, director of Babson Center for Entrepreneurial Studies. "We can't make people into entrepreneurs if they don't have the basic drive, energy, and a strong sense of what it takes to run a business. But give me someone who has those basic skills, and we'll make him into a much better entrepreneur."

The Price Institute for Entrepreneurial Studies, a sponsor of the annual SEE, has based its program on the conviction that entrepreneurs can make excellent teachers. As its mission statement asserts, "Successful entrepreneurs are, by necessity and natural inclination, superior learners and superior teachers; they do this every day." Price calls for schools to use real entrepreneurs in the classroom to create "an intellectual and practical collision between academia and the real world."

The UCLA MBA program also offers coursework in entrepreneurship. Its program also uses real entrepreneurs to teach the courses. One student who benefited from this approach is David Janes, Jr.

After earning his undergraduate degree in 1984, Janes went to work at the family business, California Manufacturing Enterprises. A science whiz, he had to round out his background before he could realize his dream of becoming an entrepreneur. Janes knew what he needed to learn: marketing, operational management, and finance. But he also sought exposure to savvy veterans of the entrepreneurial wars. At UCLA's MBA program, he found what he was looking for.

When accepted into the management program, "I was scared of computers," he says. "I would not be competent unless I had more training. I sought out partners at school; you cannot be successful without partners. I took classes in every topic, from human resources to finance. You've got to be a Renaissance person when you're running your own business."

Four days a week, he attended classes. On the fifth day, he would visit local companies, talking to entrepreneurs about the challenges they faced. He visited businesses in other countries, touring facilities in Mexico, the former Soviet bloc, and Japan.

"I tried to leave every facility with one idea," says Janes. At the Japanese electronics giant Matsushita Electric, he saw how employees who found defects were presented with a red apple. The modest reward system created a company in which every worker was in a frenzy to uncover product flaws.

After graduation, Janes returned to the family business, manufacturing spare parts for jet engines. He wanted to spin off his own division. One day, a staffer brought in a smashed snowboard. He had spent $600 to buy it, then destroyed it in just one hard afternoon on the slopes. "A group of us looked at it and said, 'Hey, we could build that,' Janes recalls. "We dissected it and found it was within our capabilities."

It was an epiphany. Janes had the product and manufacturing know-how to make it happen. He studied the snowboard market

and saw it was bursting with potential. "In 1991, snowboarding was not yet a craze but was in a growth stage," he says. He decided to become a player.

Janes and his engineers developed a unique snowboard with a durable capped edge. In 1992, he landed his first customer, a brand name company that placed a $500,000 order. In three years, 5150 Sports Inc. of Corona, Calif., has become a $14 million company. It manufactures snowboards for other firms and sells its own label to the retail market.

Every day, Janes, 33, applies the lessons he learned at UCLA: recruit the best people you can find; manage your company's growth; and, what one of his professors called the No. 1 job of the entrepreneur, never run out of cash.

David Janes, Michael Healey, and countless other young entrepreneurs have benefited from the training they received in business school entrepreneurship programs. Many schools are now rushing to introduce substantial entrepreneurship programs into their business school curriculums. But their levels of commitment vary greatly. To determine which programs truly make entrepreneurship a priority, investigate the following areas:

1. Find out whether entrepreneurship is a mainstream activity or a sideline. Get more specific information by asking follow-up questions such as: how many professors of entrepreneurship teach full-time? Are MBA students required to study entrepreneurship?

2. Request a catalog and count the number of courses in entrepreneurship. Are they offered just once a year or every term?

3. Talk to both students and graduates about the effectiveness of the program.

Above all, look at the school's graduates. Are they equipped with the tools they need to be successful entrepreneurs? Although many traits of successful entrepreneurship can't be taught, business schools believe they can provide basic training for success. Their ultimate measure of whether they've acheived that goal is graduates who start new ventures.

QUESTIONS

1. Do you think that entrepreneurship can be taught in the classroom? Explain your answer.

2. Many entrepreneurship programs in business schools use a team teaching approach, combining regular faculty with entrepreneurs. What do you think is the reason for using this approach?

3. Do you think a formal entrepreneurship program in business schools should be designed to help existing entrepreneurs or to create new ones? Can a single school serve both of these functions?

Sources: Adapted from: "Baylor's Business Program Ranked in the Top 25 Nationally," *Baylor Business Review*, Fall 1995, p. 17; "Choosing the Best," *Success*, September 1995, p. 25; Katherine Callan and Michael Warshaw, "The 25 Best Business Schools for Entrepreneurs," *Success*, September 1995, pp. 37–43.

QUESTIONS

1. What are some common problems foreigners experience when attempting to start companies outside their home country?

2. Do you think it's easier, in general, for foreigners to start businesses in the U.S. than for Americans to start businesses abroad? Explain.

3. How can the World Watch Society help countries become more friendly to business?

Sources: Adapted from Brad Glosserman, "Upstart Coffee Beans Gamble Pays Off," *Japan Times Weekly International Edition*, September 18–24, 1995, p. 16; Paul Wonnacott, "Merchandise Trade in the APEC Region," *World Economy*, 1995, pp. 33–51.

VIDEO CASE

Small Business and Entrepreneurship

Mountain biking, one of the fastest growing sports in America both recreationally and competitively, is debuting in the 1996 summer Olympics. It's roots began to spread in the late 1970's. And as Mountain biking grew so did one of the premier companies in the cycling business: Specialized Bicycle Components. Specialized Bicycle is one the industry's rags-to-riches stories. To appreciate the entrepreneurial spirit that started the company, and still guides it today, it's important to understand the company's goals, its position in the cycling industry, the unique characteristics of the business, Specialized Bicycle's approach to it, and the connection between foreign and domestic operations and the company's critical strategy for success.

Specialized Bicycle Components' headquarters is in Morganville, California at the southern tip of Silicon Valley. This area is a Mecca for both micro and mainframe computers, and for cycling. Today Specialized holds a 65 percent share of all mountain bikes sold with 6,000 retailers in 25 countries and approximately 200 employees in the U.S.

Specialized Bicycle's founder and president Mike Sinyard was a young cyclist touring Europe in 1974 with about $700 in his pocket and a lot more free time when he fortuitously met some Italians. His passion and admiration for the Italian high-quality handle bars led him to invest his remaining dollars to become an importer on a shoestring. Back in America Sinyard's first company catalog was hand written. He tried working at other jobs to get working capital to import parts, but a friend finally convinced him that climbing to success meant getting capital from others. In this case, advance payment from dealers. Given Mike's credit history his other approach to raising capital was to get everything cash on delivery, or COD.

Dealers recognized the quality of Mike's parts and, in those days, communication in the cycling community was based largely on word of mouth. As one dealer put it, "Other suppliers could wait for payment, but with Mike if we didn't pay him we knew he wouldn't eat." Sinyard recalled those early days, "What I found in doing business really is that if you work with people, with being very genuine and very straight with people, then people will accept you."

Specialized Bicycle's first manufactured product was a tire. Designing a tire was the turning point in the business. The tire was lightweight, sturdy, and lasted a lot longer than any existing tire available to the consumer. This was the first implementation of Sinyard's philosophy of moving the innovation and quality of racing technology to the consumer. The tires were a success, in large part because Specialized focused on doing it right. Sinyard said, "We really kind of pointed out how important the tires are on the bike. This is the most important square inch of the bicycle and that's the square inch that's touching the ground."

Today Specialized is the top seller of cycling tires. In 1980 the company introduced it's first mountain bike, the Stump Jumper. At $750 it was an immediate success. Today it remains the company's flagship bike although the model line has expanded and the technology has produced lighter, faster, and safer bikes. After a visit to the far east in 1975 manufacturing was moved to Taiwan. Only Specialized Bicycle's top of the line model is still manufactured in the United States.

Chris Murphy, director of marketing-bikes explained the company's marketing strategy, "Customers don't buy the second or third or fourth best brand when they spend $600.00. Our bikes range from $269 to $5000. There's a certain threshold where people say: 'I'm not settling for second best. I'm into the sport. I know exactly what I want. I want these features and I want the best bike out there.' And so if you expect to compete in that image/perception price point, your cutting-edge image is critical." Accessories are a major player in the company's success, including, tires, helmets, lights, water bottles, shoes, and clothing.

Research and testing at the Morganville headquarters also plays an important role. A key element of success at Specialized is innovation. Chris Murphy said, "We're involved in this sport. We ride, we go to the races, we're there with the racing teams. We hope we can identify the trends a little quicker and come back and say 'We need to take a look at this. We need to study this. And let's do more homework on this.' I think that what really has set us apart in the last 20 years is going out and finding something really fast and coming back and saying, 'Okay is this something?, Are we in? Ah, forget it,' and moving on to something else and deciding where we should go."

Recently Specialized has gotten involved in land access issues by hiring a full time coordinator to track public issues and legislative actions. Linda DuPriest, advocacy coordinator, explained, "My role as advocacy coordinator is to deal with social issues that affect the bicycle business or social issues opportunities for the bike industry such as mountain bike trail advocacy and access issues, teaching responsible, ethical, back country use to mountain bikers. Communicating to mountain bike consumers and dealers about the importance of behaving yourself on a trail."

It's a highly competitive marketplace. Specialized Bicycle's competitors include Trek, Cannondale, GE and a host of small customized manufacturers. Most of the competitors are also looking to both foreign and domestic collaborators. Gearing, shocks, handlebars, and stems and frames are some of the components provided by collaborators.

The company's philosophy or goals are clearly stated in the lobby on a stone plaque: Customer Satisfaction, Quality, Innovation, Teamwork, Profitability. Specialized Bicycle's healthy position in an industry faced with tight profit margins exerts pressure to continually find something that is lighter, faster, and sturdier. It's an industry where the players look for ways to expand the overall market. It's also an industry populated by a small network of innovators. Specialized is committed to expanding a market that's maturing and becoming crowded with competitors. The company is one that can't be separated from its president and founder, and his employees seem to be from the same mold. From Sinyard on down everyone has a passion for cycling.

Employees are the customers. Specialized Bicycle's strategy is Sinyard's strategy. Sinyard is very good at defining what it takes to create an environment for success. He has a vision for success, knows his limits, and seeks people with enthusiasm and passion. He said, "Part of the creative process is just trying new things and challenging people to do new things. And even if you do something that doesn't work you learn something from it and that's one of the things I really encourage people to do is take a risk and make it happen. Take a risk and if you make a mistake that's fine just learn from it and continue moving."

QUESTIONS

1. What does the narrator of this video mean when he says that Specialized is a company that can't be separated from its president and founder?

2. How crucial do you think Sinyard's "people skills" were to the start up of his company.

3. What strategies does Specialized pursue to stay abreast of trends in the cycling industry?

APPLICATION EXERCISE

EVALUATING YOUR SKILLS TO START AND OPERATE A BUSINESS
Think about a business that you might like to start and operate. Any business can benefit from a person's skills and experience in a number of areas. This brief self-assessment exercise is intended to promote serious thinking about experience and skill. As the chapter suggests, many businesses fail due to lack of managerial know-how; that is, skills and experience are lacking and the consequence is not being prepared for the day-to-day challenges of starting and/or operating a business.

Your type of business:

Circle or place an X on the spot on the scale that best describes your experience. Place the number that's closest to indicating your experience in the last column.

Skill	Much Experience	Some Experience	Little Experience	Rate Your Experience
Planning	3	2	1	
Accounting	3	2	1	
Establishing financial and accounting systems	3	2	1	
Selling	3	2	1	
Advertising	3	2	1	
Purchasing	3	2	1	
Recruiting and selecting human resources	3	2	1	
Coaching	3	2	1	
Motivating	3	2	1	
Evaluating human resources	3	2	1	
Organizing	3	2	1	
Production	3	2	1	
Quality control	3	2	1	
Quality improvement	3	2	1	
Quality assessment	3	2	1	
Computer use	3	2	1	
Other:	3	2	1	

In which areas do you lack experience? Don't be discouraged if you lack experience in any of these areas. Various sources of information can help you become knowledgeable before you enter into a business. Sources include books, seminars, training programs, businesspeople, business consultants, Small Business Administration courses, college courses, and adult education courses.

CHAPTER 20

Technology and Innovation

After studying this chapter, you should be able to:

❖ Define technology, innovation, and technology transfer.

❖ Discuss how technology implementation fits into a company's technology strategy.

❖ Describe the managerial skills needed for managing technology.

❖ Discuss the differences in technology-driven transfer, market-driven transfer, and product-and-process improvement transfer.

❖ Describe the different methods of international technology transfer.

❖ Describe some important steps to take to manage creativity effectively.

❖ Describe in historical terms whether the United States has ever had technology policies in various sectors of business and industry.

❖ Discuss the advantages and disadvantages of a national technology policy.

Sun Microsystems Keeps Creativity Flowing

The computer and telecommunications industries world wide are perhaps the most competitive arenas in which to conduct business. New ventures are continuously entering with aggressive strategies, novel technologies, and brilliant leaders. Old stalwart companies find their economies of scale strategies of the past no longer effective. To be a player in these industries means constant innovation, high quality, and a guiding vision of the future.

Sun Microsystems is led by 41-year-old CEO Scott McNealy. For more than a decade, McNealy has led the company by preaching the gospel of network computing—the idea that the true value of computers is realized when they're hooked together in networks. For years that message has been heeded by high-end users on Wall Street and in engineering firms. But the mainstream business market with their desktop computers didn't hear McNealy's message. That was before the explosion of the Internet and its potential for business was realized.

For the past several years, businesses have been tripping over themselves to get on the net. Now Sun's mantra, "The Network is the Computer," has begun to resonate and be heard around the world. Its Java programming language has created excitement among the cyberspace set. Java was officially released on January 12, 1996. But word of what it would portend had been circulating months in advance. Java is a programming language that enables the creation of tiny applications called "applets" that race across the Internet's World Wide Web and run on any computer platform. Programmers have already created applets for everything from animation to transmitting electronic ticker tape.

McNealy is not the prototype leader of a Silicon Valley firm. You won't find him burying himself in the arcana of computer code. Nor do you find a history of climbing the corporate ladder

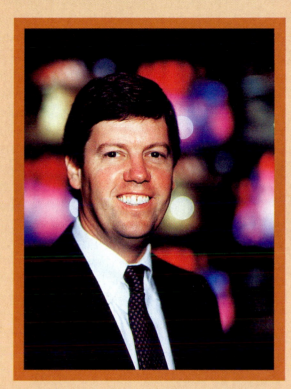

Scott McNealy

through a series of engineering jobs. McNealy studied economics at Harvard University and earned his MBA at Stanford. His passions are hockey and golf, and he's famous inside the company for sophomorish pranks and quick one-liners. Typical of his wit is his assessment of Microsoft's Windows and MS-DOS as "whipped cream on a road apple."

Following his MBA at Stanford, McNealy served a couple of stints in manufacturing jobs at FMC Corporation and minicomputer maker Onyx Systems. In 1982, he got a call from former Stanford classmate Vinod Khosla asking him to join Khosla and computer designer Andreas Bechtolsheim in starting Sun. McNealy's manufacturing skills enabled the young company to keep up with wild demand as sales soared from $9 million in 1983 to $39 million in 1984.

After Khosla left in a dispute with Sun's board, McNealy was named CEO at the young age of 30. Although he says he dislikes being labeled as brash, that is the adjective that follows him around. At Sun's Mountain View, California, headquarters, he has built a corporate culture based on his own motto: "Kick butt and have fun." The company has become famous for its aggressive marketing and juvenile antics staged around headquarters. Each April Fool's Day, scores of photographers converge on Sun headquarters to record the elaborate pranks that engineers play on McNealy and other executives. Once, for example, the engineers built a golf course hole in McNealy's office—complete with water hazard and green.

McNealy participates in the pranks. He has played general at an intramural squirt-gun war. The humor, which is turned on everyone including McNealy, has an important effect: It binds the company and helps employees live with their demanding jobs. "His humor and ability to raise a crowd to its feet is in many respects exactly what you need in a CEO and leaders in today's industry," says Thomas J. Meredith, a former Sun treasurer.

A good example of how McNealy's style promotes innovation and creativity inside Sun is Java itself. Without McNealy's stubborn commitment to Java, it never would have gotten off the ground. The idea behind Java was introduced to McNealy in 1990 when he asked a departing engineer to write a memo on how Sun could improve itself. The engineer wrote that it should create a software system for portable devices. McNealy was so impressed that he persuaded the engineer to stay on at Sun and do it.

McNealy gave the new project, code named Green, total independence and served as its chief cheerleader. Once, with the team burning out, he dropped in for a demonstration. The team only had a shaky prototype, but McNealy turned morale around when he exclaimed: "This is the greatest thing I've ever seen."

McNealy's style has led to a spirit of innovation and creativity at Sun that has suddenly vaulted the company into a competitive position that will allow it to take on the likes of Microsoft and Intel. Its Java programming language is the result of McNealy's dogged pursuit of computing as networking, and his ability to get others excited about that vision. But McNealy knows that Java isn't the last word in computing and networking, and he continues to push Sun to its limits to be the first to create the next important technology.

Sources: Adapted from Robert D. Hof, Kathy Rebello, and Peter Burrows, "Scott McNealy's Rising Sun," *Business Week,* January 22, 1996, pp. 66–73; Robert D. Hof and John Verity, "Now, Sun Has to Keep Java Perking," *Business Week,* January 22, 1996, p. 73.

Imagine a world where nearly everyone has access to the Internet, and to virtually unlimited cable television channels in their homes. Imagine a world where over 50 percent of all workers work out of their homes. Imagine a world where the greatest art, music, literature, and scientific discoveries are available to you at the touch of a button. Although that world doesn't exist yet in reality, it exists in the minds of technological leaders, such as Microsoft's Bill Gates. Gates is currently building his home of the future that will feature artwork tailored to individuals. As you enter a room, the room will sense your presence and display your chosen artwork, play your favorite music, and adjust the lighting to your desired level. It will display your personal newspaper, featuring the types of stories you find interesting gleaned from publications around the world. As Gates predicts in his book *The Road Ahead,* advances in computing, telecommunications, and other technologies will continue to radically change the way we live, work, and play.[1]

As discussed in the opening vignette, Sun Microsystems is poised to help create the future based on its commitment to networked computing. Sun succeeded by linking creativity and innovation to a sound strategy.

This chapter discusses technology and innovation in the context of current conditions and future expectations. There's no longer a pronounced technology gap between the

United States and other first-world nations. Instead of discussing a gap, it's more accurate to consider competition, technology changes, the development of technology strategy, and the need to manage technology. Chapter 1 clearly introduced competitiveness. Here we must consider competitiveness in the context of technology and innovation.

TECHNOLOGY AND INNOVATION: WHAT DO THEY MEAN?

Technology is defined many different ways depending upon a person's background. The engineer defines technology as specialized knowledge applied to achieving a practical purpose. The origin of the word *technology* gives insight into its meaning. It's derived from the Greek words *techne* (meaning art or craft) and *logos* (signifying discourse or organized work). The practice of technology is an art or craft, as distinguished from science, which is precise and is based on established theoretical principles. Technology is then applied as interpreted by the engineer, but it's not necessarily based on science.

Other general interpretations of technology are:

❖ The physical combined with the intellectual or knowledge processes by which materials in some form are transformed into outputs used by another organization or subsystem within the same organization.[2]

❖ A body of knowledge about the means by which we work on the world, our arts, and our methods… It can be studied, codified, and taught to others.[3]

Perhaps the clearest view of technology is that it involves human activity. Thus a good way to define **technology** that captures the importance of human activity is to state that it's the totality of the means people employ to provide comfort and human sustenance.[4] The motive for "bringing about technology" is the desire to obtain more or better things for people.

Innovation is defined as the generation of a new idea and its implementation into a new product, process, or service. It can lead to national economic growth, increased employment, and creation of profit. Innovation is a cumulative process of numerous decisions, ranging from idea conception to the development of technology. However significant technological invention may be, it doesn't constitute innovation if it creates no growth and profit. For example, Panhandle Eastern Corporation (PEC) has found dial-up videoconferencing to be a valuable tool for tackling time-sensitive issues, making it possible for executives, managers, and engineers to meet face-to-face in a matter of minutes. When the company installed its videoconferencing network two years ago, it did not realize just how much the technology would transform the way it manages its 34,000-mile interstate gas pipeline. An already-significant player in the North American gas transportation industry, PEC has used videoconferencing to help it embark on more projects to fuel its growth.[5] Videoconferencng is a significant innovation for PEC.

Figure 20–1 presents a model of the innovation process. This model displays innovation as a sequential process that can be divided into functionally separate but interacting stages. The bringing together of technological capabilities and market needs concisely describes the innovation process. Innovation includes the technical, design, manufacturing, management, and commercial activities involved in the marketing of a new (or improved) product or the commercial use of a new (or improved) process or piece of equipment. Be careful to note that technology innovation doesn't just occur within existing companies. Many new businesses have been created that take advantage of advances in information technologies. One new business, called "Agile Web," has been created by Lehigh University's Ben Franklin Technology Center and 19 companies in eastern Pennsylvania to test and demonstrate the tangible benefits of agility. The Agile Web will demonstrate how a group of small- to medium-sized member companies acting as a single business entity can provide one-stop shopping. For example, a customer could contact a member company or Agile Web CEO Ted Y. Nickel to outsource the design, prototyping, or manufacturing of a subassembly. Nickel matches the job's requirements with the capabilities of the vendors, then

technology
The totality of the means employed by people to provide comfort and human sustenance.

innovation
The generation of a new idea and its implementation into a new product, process, or service, leading to national economic growth, increased employment, and creation of profit.

FIGURE 20–1
Interactive Model of the
Innovation Process

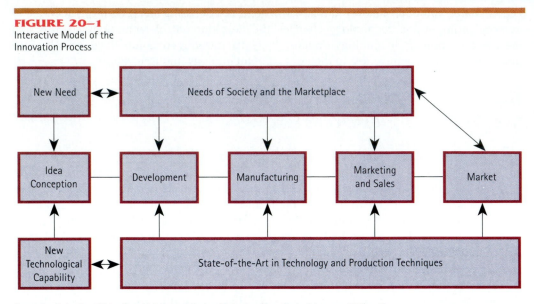

Source: Roy Rothwell and Walter Zegueld, *Reindustrialized and Technology* (Essex, England: Longman, 1985), p. 50.

configures the best available project team. The customer receives a single proposal, point of contact, and inclusive price.[6] The Agile Web uses technology and a virtual organization design to offer innovative services.

There are inevitably myriad opportunities for intrepid entrepreneurs to apply emerging technologies in new ways to add value for businesses or consumers. Certainly there have been a vast number of companies that have appeared in an attempt to provide services for the Internet. Others have used technology to create computer-generated graphics for movies. Steve Jobs's company Pixar scored big during the 1995 Christmas season with its hit movie Toy Story. The entire movie was done in stunningly realistic computer-generated graphics.

TECHNOLOGY AND COMPETITIVE ADVANTAGE

Since the early 1980s U.S. leadership in technology and innovation has been challenged by Japan, Germany, and newly industrialized countries such as South Korea, Taiwan, and Hong Kong. Contributing to these nations' economic success have been large investments in research and development, coupled with the development of an infrastructure that facilitates the incorporation and use of new technologies. Competition from newly industrialized countries is expected to intensify in the next few decades.[7]

It was probably inevitable that the *technology gap* that the United States enjoyed for decades would end. It's extremely difficult to sustain competitive advantage in any industry in the global economy. However, several factors internal to the U.S. economy have hastened its reduced competitiveness, such as R&D expenditures, fewer invention patents than in previous years, and a decrease in basic research. Diminishing U.S. technology and innovation strength actually began in the late 1960s. Several industries, created and dominated by U.S. firms, were taken away by foreign competitors who first offered low-cost, low-end products, then provided a growing array of better-quality products, and finally put out a broad range of higher-value and sometimes radically new products.[8] It happened first in the steel, automotive, and machine tool industries. Today competitors are taking away high-technology markets (e.g., electronics, medical equipment, and robotics) from American firms.

The fastest-growing industries in the United States are now high-tech ones. High-tech industries generally:

❖ Invest more heavily in manufacturing technology than do other manufacturing industries.
❖ Support higher compensation to production workers than other industries.

In the 1980s the United States, Japan, and Europe moved resources toward the manufacturing of high-value, technology-intensive goods and away from more labor-intensive goods.[9] Of seven industries that make up the high-tech cluster, three U.S. industries—scientific instruments, pharmaceuticals, and aircraft—gained global market share in the 1980s. Figure 20–2 compares the seven industries.

Another transformation that has occurred in the manufacturing sector is mass customization of products. This approach attempts to give each customer what she desires in a manufactured product. Note how this approach differs from that of Henry Ford's assembly line where every customer could choose any color Model T they wanted, as long as it was black.

Mass customization will continue to grow as a factor in competitive advantage in the U.S. and the global economy. It will be facilitated by widespread adoption of computer-integrated manufacturing and flexible manufacturing systems, which will offer great flexibility in switching over from one set of instructions to another on a fairly routine and limited range of choices. Mass customization will be made practical by the combination of several things. First, computer-assisted manufacturing will soon be augmented by virtual reality. Second, the technology that will allow virtual design will be readily integrated with

FIGURE 20–2
U.S. Global Market Share by
High-Tech Industry

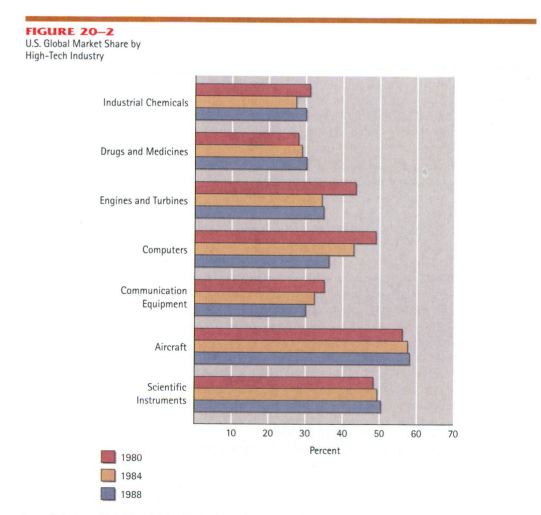

Source: "Technology and Global Competitiveness," *Engineering Management Review,* Spring 1992, p. 54.

A hotel guest works on a computer in his room. Many hotels have installed modem-ready network connections in hotel rooms so that business guests can tap into their office computers. In the future, hotels may have to invest heavily in telecommunications technology—an unprecedented business opportunity.

automation in the factory to create the prototype one wants. Third, at the technical level, the traditional means of manufacturing are now being augmented in new directions.[10]

Another key to manufacturing success in the future is in delivering products or services faster than one's competitors can. Quick response manufacturing (QRM) means reducing lead times—both the time to bring new products to market and time to manufacture an existing product from its raw materials—and can result in an enterprise that simultaneously achieves low cost, high quality, and rapid delivery. Two benefits of QRM are increased competitive advantage through newer technology and increased customer satisfaction.[11]

A country's home market is often thought of as the destination for its manufactured output. For obvious reasons—including proximity to the customer and common language—selling at home is easier than selling overseas. But in today's global economy the most competitive product in terms of price, quality, and ability to meet consumers' needs is winning sales regardless of its manufacturing origin. Historically the U.S. economy hasn't been oriented toward serving foreign markets. Its sheer size provided businesses with large domestic markets that supported their operations. The American manufacturer had little incentive to investigate, develop, and implement technologies that fit overseas markets.

Differences in macroeconomic conditions, as well as government trade and technology policies, affect the use of technology and innovation to spur international trade, competitiveness, and economic development. These are definitely important factors. But this chapter focuses on the role that management can and should play in building and sustaining competitive advantages on the basis of technology. A debt-laden economy, a confused political involvement, unfavorable regulatory policies, and a short-term-only profit perspective won't help a business in global competition. A number of U.S. firms succeed in technology and innovation competition around the world. Management lessons can be learned from them.

TECHNOLOGY FORECASTING: THE S-CURVE

A company's competitive position depends to some degree on its leadership in one or more applications of technology. Even for companies that aren't technological leaders, keeping up on trends is an important means of avoiding technological ignorance and sur-

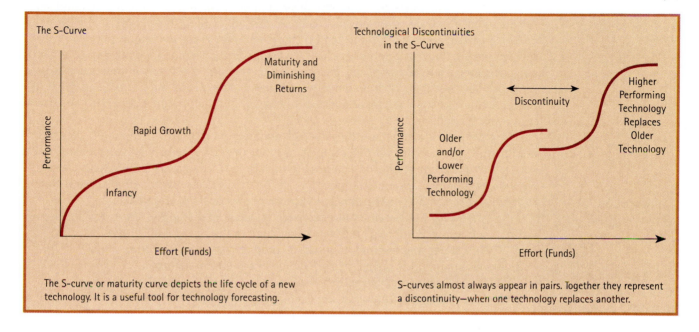

The S-curve or maturity curve depicts the life cycle of a new technology. It is a useful tool for technology forecasting.

S-curves almost always appear in pairs. Together they represent a discontinuity—when one technology replaces another.

prises. Uncertainty about future impacts of an innovation comes from several sources, and it doesn't disappear even after a new technology is introduced commercially. Much of the difficulty is connected to the fact that new technologies typically come into the world in a very primitive condition. Their eventual uses emerge during an extended improvement process that expands their practical applications.[12]

Technology forecasting is the art of determining the direction and impact of a new technology in the interest of creating or sustaining competitive advantage. A useful framework for technology forecasting is the S-curve, which graphs the relationship between effort put into improving a product or process and the firm's results from making the investment.[13] The **S-curve** shows the life cycle of a particular product or process. Figure 20–3 presents a pair of S-curves. It shows how one technology eventually outperforms another previously higher-performance technology. At the point of maturity in one curve, a discontinuity exists. It's at this point that opportunities or innovations enter the picture. For example, IBM outpaced Smith Corona in the office by developing electric typewriters and then computer-based word processors.

As new technologies are developed, new demands are placed on industries. For example, in order to compete successfully in the future, hotels may have to invest heavily in telecommunications technology. There is an unprecedented business opportunity for hotels.[14] Over time, investment in telecommunications will allow hotels to provide lucrative business services. Hotel owners must begin to plan now for how they're going to accommodate the needs of their business guests of the future. Many hotel chains already boast business services such as fax machines, copiers, and computers. Others have already installed modem-ready network connections in hotel rooms so that business guests can tap into their office computer. Future services will likely include video conferencing capability from a guest's room, printers in the room, Internet connections, and other advances.

Retailers are also faced with a vast array of new technologies. One school of thought is that a retailer should replace technologies faster because each new technology has a quicker payback. That is a good business strategy because the purpose of the technology, when it is implemented and managed correctly, is to continue to drive costs down and move productivity up. According to retailers, the hottest new technologies are related to connecting to vendors (EDI), product imaging, document imaging, executive information

technology forecasting
The art of determining the direction and impact of a new technology in the interest of creating or sustaining competitive advantage.

s-curve
A technology-forecasting tool that graphs the relationship between effort put into improving a product or process and the firm's results from making the investment.

systems, and handheld radio frequency terminals.[15] Retailers shouldn't wait until they get to the top of the S-curve to implement the next technological advance.

Another advance in retail is so-called *data mining*. This rapidly evolving area of data analysis directly supports key retail initiatives in micromarketing and micromerchandising. Advances in hardware and software technologies are making the analysis of enormous amounts of consumer data more realistic. Retailers now have an opportunity to explore this new technology to gain competitive advantage and offer the goods that each individual consumer wants. By applying data mining techniques over various time segments of purchase histories, it is possible to define activities that are more likely to drive shopper behavior.[16] This focused analysis of consumer behavior can help retailers establish an advantage over competitors.

Managers must decide how they'll attack competitors who are attempting to create discontinuities and how they'll defend their own advantages. That is, managers must decide what's the right technology and when is the right time to change or hold onto the technology. As a technology approaches the top of its S-curve, it takes greater effort or more funds to produce even small positive changes in product or process performance.

Richard Foster has provided the following managerial guidelines for assessing when a current technology is approaching its maturity limit or the top of the S-curve.

1. There's increasing discomfort about the productivity of system developers.
2. Development costs are increasing, and delays are more common.
3. Innovation and creativity actively wane.
4. Disharmony and poor morale are evident among the developers.
5. Across-the-board improvements become rare.
6. There are wide differences in technology and spending among competitors who use the same technology, with little or no apparent effects.
7. Frequent changes in the management team seem to have no impact on technology productivity.
8. Smaller competitors in select niches and/or supposed weaker competitors start succeeding with radical approaches that everyone else said couldn't work.[17]

Answers to these indicators of obsolescence require observation, interpretation, and questioning customers, vendors, and competitors. The S-curve presents a framework for helping to select the long-term technology portfolio a firm needs to successfully compete. The management of discontinuities shown in the S-curve analysis can help identify areas where the firm could take advantage of technology changes.

AN INTEGRATED TECHNOLOGY MANAGEMENT FRAMEWORK

The speed of technological change, the shifting competitive approaches in the global economy, and the importance of quality suggest that managers can benefit from a framework for thinking about these issues. Managers have a crucial role to play in integrating competitive actions, considering strategic issues, and understanding the opportunities associated with discontinuities. Fusing technological issues and management practice is important because these concepts can't operate in isolation. Technology needs to be properly managed.

Figure 20–4 presents a framework for managing technology that starts with the concept of quality. It's the quality requirement that starts the technology management process. Three distinct phases stand out in the framework: assessment, position taking, and policy formation. The assessment phase suggests that management should assess industry and the environment, determine the baseline (starting point) or anniversary date or start of the firm's present technology, assess new and emerging technologies, and determine how the firm conducts the transfer (commercialization) of technology.

The second phase of the framework—position taking—involves the activities traditionally emphasized in management; that is, deciding what investments will be made in various technologies. How much resources will be committed in the short and long runs? The sec-

FIGURE 20—4
The Integrated Technology
Management Framework

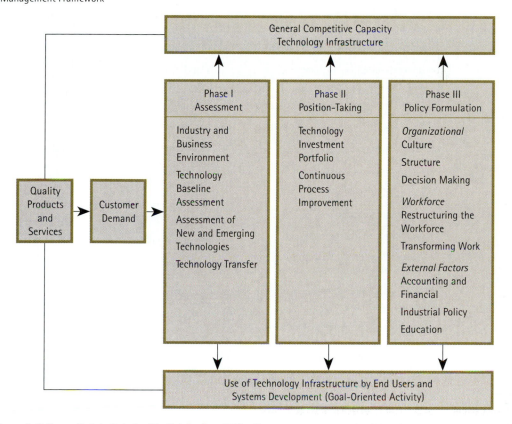

Source: Rod F. Monger, *Mastering Technology* (New York: Free Press, 1988), p. 38.

ond major decision involves continuously improving the technological infrastructure. Since technology, like all systems, suffers entropy (a winding down of its effectiveness) continuous improvement activities must be applied. Rubbermaid, for example, regularly ranks among the most admired companies in the U.S. A recent study of consumer brands ranked Rubbermaid second among the 150 largest consumer-product companies in such categories as product quality, likeability, and consumer trust. The company now averages more than one new product introduction a day, and nine out of ten of these meet or exceed internal criteria for return on assets. CEO Wolf Schmitt says Rubbermaid accomplishes this remarkable rate by focusing on continuous innovation based on continuous learning.[18]

The framework's third phase concerns the formulation of management policies oriented toward internal and external factors. Balancing organizational and workforce factors is important. All factors have to be integrated so that a technology strategy can be formulated, implemented, and monitored. Organizational, workforce, and external environmental issues must be addressed. Perhaps one of the most crucial areas involves the managerial workforce. What types of managerial skills are needed if a firm is to remain competitive and able to take advantage of technology?

The Managerial Skills Needed

Research has indicated that leadership, technical, and administrative skills are needed to effectively operate in today's technology-oriented firms.[19] There is, of course, no single set of skills, but rather a mix. A study of engineering managers suggests that the kind of skills in Table 20–1 are important in high-tech situations. These are similar to the types of skills discussed throughout the text. But note that more than technical skills are being suggested. This study found that experiential learning is the most prevalent mode of skill development.

TABLE 20-1	SKILL INVENTORY OF THE TECHNICAL MANAGER	
Leadership Skills	**Technical Skills**	**Administrative Skills**
Ability to manage in an unstructured work environment	Ability to manage the technology	Attracting and holding quality people
Clarity of management direction	Understanding technology and trends	Estimating and negotiating resources
Defining clear objectives	Understanding market and product applications	Working with other organizations
Understanding the organization	Communicating with technical personnel	Measuring work status, progress, and performance
Motivating people		
Managing conflict	Fostering innovative environment	Scheduling multidisciplinary activities
Understanding professional needs	Unifying the technical team	Understanding policies and operating procedures
Creating personnel involvement at all levels	Aiding problem solving	Delegating effectively
Communicating (written and oral)	Facilitating trade-offs	Communicating effectively both orally and in writing
Assisting in problem solving	System perspective	Minimizing changes
Aiding group decision making	Technical credibility	
Building multidisciplinary teams	Integrating technical, business, and human objectives	
Credibility	Understanding engineering tools and support methods	
Visibility	Planning and organizing multifunctional programs	
Gaining upper management support and commitment		
Action orientation, self-starter		
Eliciting commitment		
Building priority image		

Note: Inventory is based on engineering managers' responses to the survey question: "What skills do you see as crucial for effective role performance in your field as engineering manager?"

Source: Hans J. Thambain, "Developing the Skills You Need," *Research, Technology, Management,* March–April 1992, p. 43.

The presentation and discussion of the integrated technology management framework provide three premises that we'll consider as we proceed in the discussion:
1. The goal of technology systems is to produce quality products and services.
2. Technology shouldn't be managed alone, but must be managed as an infrastructure that's interrelated.
3. Continuous improvement must be made in technology to remain competitive.

The framework suggests that management's major responsibility is to build an infrastructure (including people, methods, policies, and management practice) that's appropriate to the enterprise's competitive needs. The framework uses as its starting point the quality of products or services.

TECHNOLOGY STRATEGY

Occasionally, the failures of some businesses to meet technical challenges from domestic and global competitors have been managerial failures. At various points managers of failed and failing firms didn't allocate resources needed to remain technologically competitive, failed to take timely advantage of S-curve-type discontinuities, and failed to support and reward people in a manner that's congruent with innovation. Accomplishing these tasks isn't easy. It requires a skilled manager who understands technology, innovation, and the interrelatedness of organizational units and components. Prior to the early 1980s the management of technology concentrated on R&D functions. Now a much broader, integrated view prevails. Manufacturing and process technology and the entire new-product development technology transfer processes are being studied.

There's now a realization that technology practices vary among firms and that some practices are more clearly associated with commercial success than others. These differences in practices can translate to competitive advantages. For example, Unilever didn't get where it is today by ignoring R&D. Like many other successful global companies, Unilever recognizes that R&D must be an integral part of business. Unilever believes in a balanced research program, ranging from exploratory science, where research brings in new knowledge from the academic world, to multifunctional teams working to bring an innovative product to market in the fastest possible time. Unilever also believes that innovation is key to international competitiveness; it's essential that global companies establish a world-class science base. Finally, the company believes that R&D must be an integral part of the business. However, research must be measured using business, not academic, yardsticks.[20]

Implementing Technology Strategy

The importance of managing technology has been generally accepted by practitioners. But too little attention has been paid to the notion of strategic use and implementation of technology. Together with the overall strategy, the technology strategy defines how a company can most effectively invest its technology resources to achieve sustainable competitive advantage.[21]

Planning a firm's technology strategy is a four-step process involving:

❖ Technology situation assessment (a scan of the internal and external environments beyond the depth of the traditional business portfolio mix).
❖ Technology portfolio development (determining the relative importance of the technology and the relative position of the firm's investment in a technology).
❖ Integration of technology and overall firm strategies.
❖ Setting technology investment priorities.[22]

The significance of a technology strategy is that it links a firm's technology goals to its overall business strategy. Thus technology must be planned and managed so that it's consistent with and supportive of the overall strategy. In order to plan the use of information technology, managers need a conceptual understanding of currently available information technology and how it relates to the strategic use of information within organizations. Business and organizational priorities must be set and communicated, because taking full advantage of information will inevitably restructure functional responsibilities within the firm. Global operations elevate information technology decisions to critical importance.[23]

Competition in the global economy is a matter of sheer survival for firms in many industries. For example, many steel companies in India, including Tata Steel, have experienced increased global competition in recent years. Tata Steel focused on its competitive strategy, research and development, and human aspects to boost its competitive position. With rapid technological change in the steel industry the world over, it's essential for operating steel plants to review, modernize, and update their facilities from time to time in order to remain competitive. Tata Steel came up with a strategy that has helped it retain its edge. In a three-phase modernization plan, new technology was gradually introduced. This has allowed Tata Steel to become one of the least expensive steel companies in the world in terms of hot metal costs, and has a clear advantage over other major integrated producers.[24]

Firms must not only have clearly stated overall strategies; they must also possess technologies that are efficient and profitable. A business strategy that's successfully implemented to use the technology available is desirable. Strategic use of technology is needed to build and sustain a competitive advantage. A survey of industry-leading companies shows that they go through a five-step process to balance their people, processes, and technology components to make their business more competitive. The process includes: (1) examining today's position, (2) setting goals, (3) making plans, (4) committing to the plan, and (5) doing it in small steps. The process also helps identify areas in need of improvement before making capital investments. Those in the survey found that following this process produces high-impact changes at minimal cost.[25]

Many commentators attribute Japan's success in the consumer electronics industry to its superior technology management practices. But a more compelling view is that U.S. firms considered TV a mature business (at the top of the S-curve) whereas the Japanese viewed it as a high-tech growth (discontinuity in the S-curve) business. This difference in strategic thinking led to different time horizons, investment priorities, and approaches to new product and process development—in essence, entirely different technology strategies.[26] The Japanese advantage in consumer electronics since 1986 was built over the course of decades and resulted from strategies that were dramatically different from those adopted by their technology-rich and resource-rich U.S. competitors.

A similar pattern of strategy differences is revealed in analyzing the videocassette recorder (VCR). The firms that succeeded in bringing the VCR to market used a "learning by trying" strategy that permitted innovation over a period of time through a gradual series of incremental product improvements.

The most striking feature of U.S. firms that failed to compete in technology-oriented industries is that many of them possessed superior technological capabilities. Xerox had a decade's technological lead in personal computing and failed. GE spent millions of dollars in technologically developing factory automation, but was outperformed by much smaller Fanuc. These and other commercial activities begin with what strategic steps are taken. As the What Managers Are Reading segment indicates, Microsoft Corporation's success is attributable primarily to its strategic moves.

WHAT MANAGERS ARE READING

BILL GATES CONTEMPLATES "THE ROAD AHEAD"

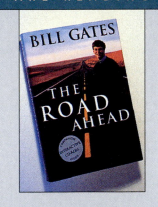

After a long wait and many delays Bill Gates, chairman and CEO of software giant Microsoft Corporation, finally released his book *The Road Ahead.* Gates' book became an instant bestseller as managers rushed to learn what the technology guru had to say about the future.

In his book, Gates looks ahead to show how emerging technologies will transform work and leisure. He believes Western culture is on the brink of changing the way it works, learns, and communicates. Just as the personal computer revolutionized the way we work, the tools of the information age—which are becoming everyday reality—will transform the way we make choices about almost everything.

Gates' book isn't all forward looking, however. Some of the most interesting material concerns the early strategies Microsoft used to grow rapidly. Gates, and his partner Paul Allen, had a vision of microcomputers being in every workplace and home long before the major computer manufacturers did. Their goal was to supply the operating system software for all of these computers without getting directly involved in making or selling hardware. Microsoft licensed its operating system software to the hardware manufacturers at extremely low prices. Gates and Allen believed that their money would be made through volume.

The strategy worked. Within three years all competing operating systems for PC or PC-compatible machines had virtually disappeared. Today, Microsoft's operating systems run on over 85 percent of all the personal computers in the world. The only exceptions are Apple's operating system, which runs on its products alone. In 1983, Microsoft announced that it was developing a graphical interface called "Windows." That product went on to also become a success, followed years later by "Windows 95," which was released in 1995 with as much fanfare as any new product has ever had.

Managers are reading *The Road Ahead* as much for the insights on the future of technology as for the incredibly successful strategic moves Microsoft used to become a global software power. Bill Gates is one of America's richest people, and his simple story of success through strategic brilliance is captivating and inspiring.

Sources: Adapted from Bill Gates, *The Road Ahead* (New York: Viking, 1995); Erick Schonfeld, "Bill Gates, Part I: The Book is Late," *Fortune*, February 20, 1995, pp. 17–18.

Clarity of focus and consistency of strategic technology implementation seem vital for successfully transferring technology to the marketplace. Maidique and Hayes say, "Even a superficial analysis of the most successful high technology firms leads one to conclude that they are highly focused."[27] Today's innovative companies focus resources by concentrating on fewer projects and spending more time on gut engineering and strategy. During the recession of 1990–1991, sales growth at 3M company in St. Paul, Minnesota, was relatively flat. Although new product contribution to the bottom line was a solid 25 to 27 percent, new initiatives were required. To speed time to market for new products, the company established the Corporate Time Compression Committee. The committee was successful in reducing time-to-market for new products by 50 percent.[28]

Strategic application of information technology is helping businesses in a wide range of industries gain competitive advantage through better knowledge of customer wants. For example, getting close to customers is a big issue today in the pharmaceuticals industry, which is undergoing great changes as more of its business comes from very large customers with a keen eye on value: managed health care organizations. It's also a big issue in other industries. Eli Lilly & Company recognizes that information technology is going to play a large role in helping it stay ahead of the competition and has even changed its corporate mission statement to reflect that information technology will be a key factor in delivering health care solutions. Eli Lilly thinks technology will help it play a broader role in disease management, helping improve patient care while controlling health care costs.[29]

Decision Making and Technology

As discussed in Chapter 5, explanations of decision making range from normative prescriptive models to behavioral anchored models. Normative models suggest that decisions about technology should be based on a comprehensive, quantitative analysis. The decision maker should scan a range of technology options, calculate the consequences of each, evaluate the consequences, and then select an option that satisfies a preselected decision rule. In some circumstances the rule may be to maximize expected value, while in other cases it may be to minimize expected loss. The decision rule in many cases is to maximize net present value.

Mintzberg, Simon, Quinn, and other management scholars suggest that in practice the normative model isn't feasible. Technology-oriented decision making often involves incomplete information, limited available resources, and lack of good competitor information. The normative model just doesn't fit the world faced by technology managers and strategists.

The path to successful technology assessment, position taking, and policy formulation is filled with uncertainty, successes, and failures. Added to these barriers are demands for high R&D spending to remain competitive. One of the most important decisions about technology involves the notion of transferring it from a basic form to an applied form; that is, commercializing the technology.

NEW PRODUCT DEVELOPMENT AND TECHNOLOGY TRANSFER

Although no single set of **new product development (NPD)** activities or steps can be defined that will be appropriate for all firms, it's possible to develop a general framework that applies across industries. Successful firms within an industry are likely to focus on certain essential NPD activities that allow them to achieve the best possible results within the constraints of the market. Compared to their competitors, top performers consistently put more strategic emphasis on each of the following activities: customization, new product introduction, design innovation, product development cycle time, product technological innovation, product improvement, new product development, and original product development.[30] Some are moving toward a system that moves new products through a series of stages and decisions to continue or discontinue. This system, known as the stage-gate system, is described in the Workplace of Tomorrow element.

new product development The set of steps or activities a firm uses to develop new products and services.

WORKPLACE OF TOMORROW

MANY COMPANIES USING STAGE-GATE SYSTEM FOR NEW PRODUCT DEVELOPMENT

New products fail at an alarming rate. An estimated 46 percent of the money that corporations spend on the conception, development, and launch of new products is spent on losers—products that fail commercially, or projects that are canceled prior to launch. Now there's a new process—the stage-gate system—which is driving new products to market quickly and successfully. Although pioneered in Canada by companies such as DuPont-Canada, Northern Telecom, and the Royal Bank, stage-gate processes have found international acceptance, and are now used in leading companies around the world such as Exxon, Procter & Gamble, Carlsberg Breweries, Corning, Kodak, Hoechst-Celanese, Polaroid, and Lego.

What is a stage-gate process? It's simply a template or road map for driving new product projects from idea through to launch and beyond. It breaks the product innovation process into stages—typically five or six—with each stage comprising a set of parallel, cross-functional activities. Between stages are gates: these gates open or close the door for projects to move to the next stage. Gates are the "quality control check points" in the process, where senior management reviews the quality of the project and decides whether to continue spending on it.

Sounds simple, but stage-gate processes are much more complex than the brief description above implies:

- Each stage specifies the required actions, including the detail, on how to do each task as well as various best practices. These stages thus prescribe the play-by-play game plan, which, if adhered to by the team and leader, all but guarantees success.
- The gates make the process work: they specify the deliverables or the desired results of each stage, and hence expectations for project teams

and leaders are clear. Gates mean tough go/kill and prioritization decisions based on solid criteria, so that the truly meritorious projects are funded, and the mediocre ones culled.

Stage-gate processes have profound effects on the way a firm manages new product projects. Implementing a stage-gate process goes beyond reengineering in that it significantly alters the innovation process, building in best practices. Stage-gate thus increases not only efficiency of the process (for example, faster times-to-market), but also effectiveness in terms of new product success rates. Research into dozens of firms that have adopted stage-gate processes reveals major improvements in performance: improved teamwork; less recycling and re-work; improved success rates; earlier detection of failures; a better launch; and even shorter cycle times (by about 30 percent).

The reason stage-gate processes work is that they are a systematic way of building best practices and critical success factors into a firm's new product development methodology. The common denominators of successful product development have been identified in numerous studies of new product winners:

A unique, superior product—Superior and differentiated products—ones that deliver unique benefits and superior value to the customer—are the number one driver of success and product profitability. Their success rates are reported to be three to five times higher than for me-too, reactive, and ho-hum products with few elements of differentiation.

A strong market orientation—A thorough understanding of customers' needs and wants, the competitive situation, and the nature of the market are essential components of new product success. This tenet is supported by virtually every study of product success fac-

tors. Not only does a strong customer focus improve success rates and profitability, but it also leads to reduced cycle time.

Predevelopment work (the homework)—Homework is critical to winning. Countless studies reveal that the steps that precede the actual design and development of the product make the difference between winning and losing. Successful firms spend considerably more time and money on vital up-front activities.

Sharp and early product definition—How well the project is defined prior to entering the development stage is a vital success factor. Some companies undertake excellent product and project definition before the door is opened to a full development program.

A true cross-functional team effort—Product innovation is very much a team effort. Product development projects must be organized as a cross-functional team with members from R&D, engineering, marketing, operations, finance, and so on.

Focus and sharp project selection decisions—Most companies suffer from too many projects and not enough resources to mount an effective or timely effort on each. This stems from a lack of adequate project evaluation and prioritization, with negative results.

The quest for new product access continues, simply because new products are so important to corporate prosperity and even survival. With new products introduced in the last five years now representing more than 50 percent of corporate sales and increasing, it is imperative that the conception, development, and launch process work well. Stage-gate approaches are what many companies are turning to.

Sources: Adapted from Robert G. Cooper, "How to Launch a New Product Successfully," *Cost & Management*, October 1995, pp. 20–23; Robert G. Cooper, *Winning at New Products: Accelerating the Process from Idea to Launch* (Reading, Mass: Addison-Wesley, 1993).

technology transfer
The process of applying knowledge.

Even when an organization understands the importance of integrating the technology and overall business strategy, the problem of developing new commercial products is a daunting task. **Technology transfer** can occur from one unit in a firm to another unit, from the lab to the marketplace, or from a developed country to a developing country. Transfer can occur from government, academic, and research organizations to private industry.

Bell & Howell's electronic auto parts catalog.

There's no transfer unless, and until, technical knowledge (i.e., a new machine or information) has been put to use.

Technology-Driven Transfer

A **technology-driven transfer** is one in which new technology can create market opportunities. At the early stages of the development of a new product or service, there's technological competition. It becomes a race between those pushing for improvements in existing technologies and others committed to developing a new technology. Usually in technology-driven development this change is evolutionary.

When a new product isn't yet tried in the market, there are few competitors or supporters. Visionaries, or those who see the future and are related to the business, are usually the risk takers.

One company that has excelled in innovation is Xerox. Its Palo Alto Research Center (PARC) has been the site of many innovations, such as laser printing, personal workstations, and others. John Seeley Brown, chief scientist and corporate vice president, is the director of PARC. Brown makes a distinction between invention and innovation. He says that one can't manage invention, but it is possible to create an environment in which invention is more likely to occur. To be an innovator, one must carry the inventions to the marketplace.[31]

One invention that PARC missed transferring to the marketplace is the graphical user interface (GUI) popular on most personal computers running today. Steve Wozniak and Steve Jobs, when they created the first Apple computer in their garage, developed their own version of the GUI they had seen at PARC. Apple went on to make GUI an essential part of the operating system for each computer it made. Within 10 years, most IBM and compatible machines were using Microsoft's Windows, a GUI much like the Apple interface. PARC's inability to recognize the commercial potential of its GUI interface provides a good example of the importance of being able to move from invention to innovation.

Market-Driven Transfer

In a **market-driven transfer,** customers express a need for a technology and the firm finds the technology to meet that need. In most cases the primary driver of transfer for commercialization purposes is that a need exists.[32] The task is to find the best technology to meet the need. A technology can be applied in several different markets. Sometimes the transfer from the lab or pilot phase to a new market can be dramatic. For example, application of the heart pacemaker, which was first discovered in 1928 to its first use in 1960, brought hope to many heart patients.

technology-driven transfer
The new technology that can create market opportunities.

market-driven transfer
Customers express a need for a technology and the firm finds the technology to meet that need.

In the 1980s at the suggestion of General Motors, Bell & Howell set out to modernize the auto parts catalog. Bell & Howell was faced with developing the technology that would result in a product that would process accurately a large volume of data and improve response time and electronic image quality. Then it was faced with applying the technology to meet market needs. This generated a host of technologies such as infrared touch screens, optical disk storage devices, and networking. Failures, mounting costs, and maintenance were problems to overcome. Bell & Howell had a culture that encouraged persistence, experimentation, and innovation. The result of the effort, attention on focusing, and seeing the value-added potential was the development of a market-driven transfer product, an electronic auto parts catalog.

Product-and-Process Improvement Transfer

product-and-process improvement transfer Improvements in the existing technology that result in a better product or process that meets customer needs.

In a **product-and-process improvement transfer,** improvement in existing technology leads to a better product or process that meets customer needs. Once a concept using a new technology has proven itself in the market, competition shifts to quality, price, performance, and features. In today's rapidly changing competitive environment, cost effectiveness and consistently high output quality are no longer enough to ensure corporate success. A company's business processes must also be more responsive and flexible than those of its competitors. Innovative ways must be sought continuously to provide technology to support motivated, adaptable work groups dedicated to meeting or exceeding customers' requirements in the shortest possible time.[33]

The pace of technological diffusion depends on a variety of technological and economic factors not directly linked to the product or service. For example, the facsimile (FAX) machine boom was possible because of telephone system technology; the VCR relies on the widespread use of TV sets. The Internet and the emerging global telecommunications "infostructure" pose new opportunities and threats to businesses. Firms are using the Internet to improve innovation, production, sales, and service processes. Lower communications and coordination costs impact business practices and strategies. Widespread use of the Internet will dramatically reduce transaction costs, leading to a growth in electronic commerce and productivity.[34]

For example, the impact of the information superhighway on retailing is possibly very significant, depending on the retail product, service, and market. The situation is still emerging and very dynamic. Retailers need to think about the different sort of marketplace that is served by the information superhighway. The traditional components of value in retailing are content, context, and infrastructure. In the electronic marketplace, these components are separated, creating new opportunities to add value for customers. Retailers who think about and plan for these changes may be the industry leaders of tomorrow.[35]

As a product, process, or service approaches maturity, the market begins to be saturated and new markets and new applications give way to a replacement of previous-generation products or services. Demand for hotel services has reached this stage. There are still opportunities for innovation (e.g., bounce-back weekends, hotel-entertainment packages, hotel-tour packages), but the innovations come from pushing package improvements or modifying previous packages for hotel guests.

A troublesome mistake a manager can make is to conclude that no improvement—technological or otherwise—can be made in a product or process. Industries that were thought to have reached their zenith can be revived suddenly if improvements have made their products easier to use and more obviously valuable to customers. Such is the case with the American robotics industry. Once thought to be a sure-bet career choice, robotics engineers didn't find many places of employment after an initial flurry of activity in the late 1970s and early 1980s. Since then, many manufacturing firms have gotten away from robotics.

That may now be changing, however. At the 1994 Robotics Industry Forum at Disney World in Orlando, Fla., the robotics people themselves seemed startled to report that industry growth is on the upswing. Net new orders from North American manufacturers to June 1994 were 4,355 robots, for example, totaling $383.5 million for U.S.-based robotics companies. This beat the numbers for the first half of 1993 by nearly 20 percent in units and 25 percent in dollars. Robotics Industries Association president Guy Potok attributed this growth to robots that are more functional, reliable, and easy to use.[36]

Robots are even appearing in service industries. For example, it used to be that when a patient missed a meal at Good Samaritan Hospital in Cincinnati, nurses often had to interrupt their work and rush down to the kitchen for the tray. Now the nurses can call the food service and request that SAM bring it up. Short for self-directed automated machine, SAM is a robot—a cordless, programmable courier that keeps going until its 24-volt battery needs to be recharged. SAM rents for $4,500 a month.[37]

Speed and quality of incremental innovations are critical to the success of product-and-process-driven market transfer. A vice president for science and technology at IBM concisely stated speed's importance:

> *Most development work is done just one step ahead of manufacturing... One cannot overestimate the importance of getting through each turn of the cycle more quickly than a competitor. It takes only a few turns for the company with the shortest cycle time to build up a commanding lead.*[38]

The emphasis on speed shouldn't lessen the importance of quality. Flawed products or poor services are worse than being late.[39] But being first to market new products, to use a new process, or to provide a new service means that the firm potentially can participate in the most profitable portion of the product life cycle. Incremental product innovation is a critically important competitive factor in some established industries. Firms in the cardiac pacemaker industry, for example, often benefit by bringing incremental innovations to market even though the new products may cannibalize the sales of existing profitable products. The more often an industry incumbent was the first to introduce important incremental innovations, the greater its market share in the industry.[40]

Continuously improved products, processes, and services don't just appear. They must be managed in a way that they become competitive advantages. Benchmarking (making comparisons between the technology in your company and others) is important. Product, process, and service comparisons can point out strengths, weaknesses, and competitive advantages. Xerox invented the art of photocopying. It was the only copier company making a profit in this business. Xerox didn't stay focused on copiers and instead became involved in the computer industry. Japanese firms such as Ricoh and Epson focused on copiers and benchmarked Xerox. As a result, Xerox's market share went from 90 percent in the early 1970s to about 20 percent in the late 1970s.

Benchmarking allows management to make comparisons in a real-time (current and most up-to-date) manner. Using benchmarking, performance gaps can be identified, action plans to make improvements can be established, and recalibrating the goals for the product, process, or service can be monitored.

Technology-driven and market-driven transfers of commercial technology occur early in the life of new technologies. At this early point, value lies in the matching of technology and market needs and being early to market with a high-quality technology. Product-and-process-improvement challenges occur later in the life cycle, when value comes from executing product, process, quality, or service improvements sooner than others do.

International Technology Transfer

The increasing globalization of business has brought more attention to the concept of international technology transfer. **International technology transfer (ITT)** is the process of applying knowledge across geographical or national boundaries. Transfers of product, process, or service technologies across national boundaries is a common phenomenon. But differences in national cultures, economic infrastructures, political systems, laws, and social norms create challenges for ITT.[41]

ITT can occur via many formal and informal methods. One method involves individuals from foreign nations studying in a host country obtaining knowledge that they can eventually bring back to their home country. There are also government-to-government agreements for ITT. Examples include agricultural programs for building farm technologies, nuclear engineering programs, and space research programs. Other modes of ITT include

international technology transfer (ITT)
The process of applying knowledge across geographical or national boundaries.

foreign direct investment, turnkey projects, trade in goods and services, contracts, licensing agreements, R&D programs in foreign countries, employment of local nationals by foreign firms (e.g., Americans working in the Georgetown, Kentucky, Toyota plant), and industrial espionage. Cultural variations across nations and organizational culture-based differences between firms involved in ITT are two of a number of factors that can influence whether any mode of transfer succeeds.[42]

In recent years three modes of ITT have grown in importance: licensing, joint ventures, and espionage.

licensing
A business arrangement that permits a firm or individual to use another firm's patents, copyrights, blueprints, and technology.

LICENSING - A business arrangement that permits a firm or individual to use another firm's patents, copyrights, blueprints, and technology is called a license. For a small firm that has limited capital or management expertise for entry into the global market, **licensing** is a good alternative. One risk of licensing is that a licensor may lose its competitive edge to a licensee over time. There's also the possibility that once the licensee has the technology, it can restrict the licensor's access to the market.

joint venture
The creation of an alliance between two companies to produce or market a product or service.

JOINT VENTURES - A **joint venture** is the forming of a partnership between a domestic and a foreign company to produce or market a product or service. This is a popular way to compete globally. Partners divide the activities in the value chain on a worldwide basis. Historically firms from developed countries formed alliances with firms in less developed countries to gain market access. Today more and more alliances involve firms from developed countries that join together to serve a region or the entire world. All U.S. auto companies have alliances with Japanese companies and, in several cases, with German, Swedish, Italian, French, and Korean companies to produce cars for sale in the United States.

Reasons for forming an alliance include learning about technology, gaining access to a distribution system, or to meet government requirements for local ownership. The companies that have had the most success in acquiring technology are in Japan and Korea, where joint ventures have been encouraged and supported by their governments.

espionage
The attempt to obtain competitors' technology by illegal means.

ESPIONAGE - Never before has there been such an intense effort to obtain competitors' technology. For example, French intelligence agents conducted **espionage** operations against the overseas offices of IBM and Texas Instruments.[43] Two Koreans were arrested by the FBI in Houston after allegedly paying $40,000 for blueprints of Dow Chemical's polymer plant in LaPorte, Texas.[44] A former Merck and Schering-Plough employee was sentenced to nine years in prison for attempting to see the formulas for medicines Ivernection and Interferon.[45]

The Freedom of Information Act is routinely used to obtain information that competitors submit to the U.S. government. Increasingly business executives have taken action to acquire a competitor's technology using methods previously considered unethical. Competitors want to know about company plans, R&D projects, product development, and key personnel changes. Besides top business executives gathering data on competitors, some governments have played a more prominent role recently. For example, the Japanese Ministry of International Trade and Industry (MITI) conducts or commissions study groups, committees, and reports that focus on technologies, the potential for technology transfer, and trends in international competition. MITI uses its intelligence reports to cajole Japanese executives to respond to emerging trades and foreign competition.

In addition to MITI, Japanese industry collects technology information through one of the large *sogo shoshas* (trading companies). A typical *sogo shosha* (e.g., Itoman Ltd., Mitsuri & Co. Ltd., or Sumitomo Corporation) has thousands of employees stationed in more than 100 overseas offices.[46] They send in a daily average of 100,000 pieces of information they've gathered. Each piece of information is coded, screened, and stored in a database.

The Japanese technology intelligence network is so extensive because of Japan's lack of success historically in the area of basic research. The Japanese are well aware of this shortcoming and have countered this problem with a network of information and technology intelligence. Because of technology's value, espionage is such a problem that security measures must be taken to slow down the transfer of important knowledge.

A NATIONAL TECHNOLOGY POLICY: MODEST CONSIDERATIONS

The United States is behind Asia and Europe in a number of areas and losing the technology war in other areas. Is there enough concern for the United States to adopt a national technology policy? One side states that in a free market economy the government should keep its hands off the technology policy area. Government has no theory or approach that can provide guidance in technology. But others claim that the laissez-faire approach will bankrupt America. The commercialization of technology is where competitive battles will occur.

Examination of America's history reveals that the United States has had technology policies in defense, medicine, and agriculture. The government hasn't kept its hands out of these areas. Think of the land grant acts for railroads, the creation of land grant universities via the Morrill Act, the protection of the steel industry via tariffs, many spin-offs from defense technologies into commercial products, and a broad support program for medical technologies. For years the U.S. government has been involved in policy formulation and intervention. As the Ethics Spotlight indicates, the U.S. government is concerned about the strategy of Microsoft.

The evidence suggests that some form of U.S. government stimulus and support for technology commercialization will occur.[47] If the United States is to compete with Japan, Germany, and other technologically advanced nations, it will eventually need much more cooperation and coordination among industry, academia, nonprofit institutions, and the government. Federal support of commercial technologies exists in nations that compete with the United States—France, Japan, Germany, and Taiwan.

The construction of the U.S. information infrastructure over the coming years will escalate the controversy surrounding the role of government. Already, congress has dealt with such issues as censorship on the Internet, the auctioning of radio and TV bandwidth, and the challenge of making basic services available to the poor, rural, and disadvantaged people of the country.

Some people, such as Bill Gates, argue that the new information infrastructure is best left to competitive capitalism. They argue that government interference will lead to roadblocks on the information superhighway. In fact, they argue that the highway itself will lead to an era of "friction-free capitalism" when electronic commerce will take place with electronic money at the speed of light.

It's not likely that capitalism will ever be totally friction free, however. Even now, several decades since the Internet was born, security remains elusive, and only a small percentage of the population use it regularly. It's not likely that the majority of commerce will take place over the information superhighway without some form of government involvement.

CREATIVITY AND INNOVATION

Today, business is at the crossroads of a new era driven by decreasing innovation cycles and increasing globalism. This new era will be marked by continuous and often unpredictable change. As we enter the new age, a few companies have found ways to put themselves in front of the pack; but none are masters of change. None have yet become agile enterprises that thrive in the new unpredictable and usually uncontrollable economic environment.[48] One way to achieve the agility necessary to remain competitive into the next century is through the creativity of individuals. Firms must learn to encourage, support, and harness the creative potential of every employee.

Creativity is defined as the ability to bring something new into existence. Creativity has a flavor of something that's mysterious or subversive. For example, economist Joseph Shumpeter referred to entrepreneurship as "creative destruction." Creative destruction means the ability to move beyond current processes, designs, and practices even though they may be working well. It means creating a culture of innovation, where new ideas have a place to develop and grow into tomorrow's success stories. Although much has been

creativity
The ability to bring something new into existence.

ETHICS SPOTLIGHT   MICROSOFT'S STRATEGY UNETHICAL?

Some people think that Microsoft Corp. is out of control. They claim it has a monopoly in the PC-operating systems market and owns about 75 percent of the office suite market. Market forces just aren't working to keep the company in check. These critics believe that the effect the Microsoft monopoly will have on the computer industry and markets is to reduce innovation, eliminate competition, and increase prices. They don't want to let Microsoft continue down its path unchallenged.

The basic fear is that Microsoft's practice of bundling and tying in as many new functions and product areas into its operating system is putting the squeeze on other companies and reducing competition. Areas such as utilities, database management systems, word processors, spreadsheets, electronic mail, presentation graphics, project management, communication software, compilers, development tools, accounting packages, and gateways to proprietary networks (including The Microsoft Network) are all candidates for bundling. Critics contend that if Microsoft is not stopped from its bundling strategy, software companies will abandon these markets and users will be left completely dependent on Microsoft. If that happens, the competitive forces necessary for innovation and technological advances will vanish.

Corporate information systems managers are getting nervous because Microsoft is using its dominance of PC operating systems to leverage and dominate other aspects of software from desktop applications to mission-critical, on-line applications. The existence of a vital third-party software market gives users a free choice. Many of Microsoft's customers are questioning if the company is acting in their best interests as it attempts to eliminate competition.

Currently, there is nothing to stop Microsoft from providing interface and design information on its PC operating system to its own applications group before the company provides it to its partners and competitors. This may be smart business, but critics say it's unethical and unfair—and it may be illegal under antitrust laws.

Without being forced to, though, Microsoft is not about to change its disclosure policies. So where are the limits? Can Microsoft decide to withhold information from its competitors indefinitely? Can it make interfaces exclusively available to the Microsoft applications group while a dependent user and vendor community sits and waits?

There is nothing—no government agency and no consent decree—to prevent this from happening. In the past, IBM, Eastman Kodak Co., and other dominant vendors have been forced to reveal interface information to their competitors. Why is the Microsoft situation different? Microsoft has literal control of the survival of other companies playing in the same markets because of its PC-operating system dominance. Once those companies have been overtaken, users will be left with no place to turn.

The critics contend that Microsoft likes to predatorily preannounce products to "freeze out" other companies from successfully selling products. That's what Microsoft has been accused of doing to Borland's TurboBasic and Turbo C products. Some may argue that this is just good strategy. It's OK, they argue, for a company with sales of $5 billion-plus, with pretax profits of $2 billion-plus, pretax margins approaching 40 percent and an annual growth in earnings of 55 percent to knowingly and intentionally freeze the market through vaporware announcements.

Microsoft got to where it is today with good products and talented employees. No one can take that away from it. However, some critics argue today that that dominance has now veered out of control, and it is to the detriment of the market and the entire industry. They want the U.S. Department of Justice to rein in Microsoft. Stopping Microsoft's acquisition of Intuit, Inc., was a good first action, the critics contend. But there are other actions they want the Justice Department to pursue as well. They believe that Microsoft should be required to separate its operating system groups and applications groups. The government should force the firm to operate its planned Network Service Division as a separate unit during the suit. A healthy market depends on growth, innovation, and fair competition. Microsoft's critics believe that will result only if Microsoft is brought under control.

Sources: Adapted from Martin A. Goetz, "Is Microsoft Out of Control? The Government Has to Stop Microsoft Now," *Computerworld*, June 19, 1995, pp. 107–108; Mark Cuban, "Why Microsoft Should Be Left Alone," *Computer Reseller News*, July 31, 1995, p. 18.

---

written on the topic, it's not clear that managers understand how to manage the dynamics of innovation to ensure the continual generation of new ideas. In this era of rapid change, with customers demanding tailored goods and service, continuous innovation will be a matter of business survival.[49]

In Silicon Valley—the high technology corridor of Southern California—firms that aren't able to create a culture of innovation don't last long. With each firm that perishes, a new one rises up to take its place. This process, known as flexible recycling, can result in novel reconfiguration of knowledge and human capabilities. The versatile "ecosystem" of Silicon Valley facilitates the process of flexible recycling and can be viewed as the enduring dimension of business activity in this unique economic domain.[50] This is creative destruction working at the level of the firm. As the Global Exchange explains, U.S. companies have an edge over international competitors in software innovation.

Earlier in this chapter we defined innovation as the generation of a new idea and its implementation into a new product, process, or service leading to the growth of the na-

GLOBAL EXCHANGE | SOFTWARE INNOVATION: AMERICA VERSUS EUROPE

What distinguishes commercial software developers in the U.S. and Europe? Who develops software better? These are critical questions in determining international competitiveness. Today, an increasing percentage of the software dollar is spent on commercial software products rather than customized software and services. And the stakes are high—the U.S. runs an $18 billion trade surplus in software with Europe alone. Of the world's top 100 independent software companies, 86 are U.S. based. The remaining companies are scattered in Britain (6), Germany (3), Netherlands (2), Israel (2), and France (1). Is there something unique that American software developers do to achieve this success?

Following are five differences that researchers have found between American and European firms. The first three observations address the important question of U.S. competitive advantage in software. The last two observations represent management and marketing issues:

1. THE HACKER PROFILE
Many American software firms have a culture that is influenced, if not dominated, by the hacker ethos—the creative, experimental individuals who depend on their intuition and wizardry to solve problems, rather than disciplined methodology-based approaches. Hackers are often not schooled in computer disciplines. In contrast, the hacker profile is less common outside of America. There, developers are carefully selected from among the ranks of university graduates. The European profile makes for a more mature, well-trained software professional. This is superior for the ongoing release cycles as the software grows—though perhaps at the expense of innovation.

2. RISK AND OWNERSHIP
America's packaged software culture is a highly entrepreneurial culture, fostered with risk (venture) capital. In contrast, the Europeans complain of the dearth of venture capital. Related to risk is reward sharing. Most key American software developers have a stake in their firm through ownership or stock options. Research indicates that far fewer European firms share ownership with their employees. As a result, there are fewer motivational rewards.

3. THE WORKWEEK
American entrepreneurial technology firms have a strong tradition of extended, perhaps excessive, work hours. In American software companies, key developers work, on average, 45 hours per week during normal periods and 60 hours during crunch periods. The European software scene is more tranquil. There, developers work, on average, just over 40 hours per week during normal times and just under 50 hours per week during crunch periods.

4. FAR FROM THE CUSTOMER
The bulk of software customers—in numbers and in influence—are in the United States. This leads to two problems for non-American firms: An image problem and a related substantive problem. The image problem stems from American businesses' reluctance and distrust of software from non-American firms—even from such software heavyweights as Britain. The substantive problem is having to traverse great distances and time zones to get to know one's customers.

5. KNOW THE WORLD
American developers lag in software designed for the global marketplace, particularly when it comes to departing from software that's strictly in English. In contrast, non-American developers are very attuned to these issues. Converting software from one spoken language to another is called localization. By modularizing all language-related components, software is less costly to localize.

So, who develops software better? Managers in successful software firms outside the U.S. compare and model themselves after the Silicon Valley model in many conscious and unconscious ways. For example, it seems that most software firms have developed a number of common organizational characteristics, such as flat organizational hierarchies and casual dress codes.

Although well-run firms have bloomed outside the U.S., they don't explain the imbalance in competitive outcomes. The root of the competitive difference in packaged software may lie in a combination of the first three of the above-mentioned observations (hacker profile, risk and ownership, and workweek).

Source: Adapted from Erran Carmel, "Entrepreneurial Technologists May Have the Upper Hand in Global Software Competition," *Research-Technology Management*, November/December 1995, pp. 10–11.

---

tional economy and the increase of employment, as well as the creation of profit. Innovation is a process. Creativity is the generation of something new—an idea, a process, or even a technique or style.

Creative Individuals

What are the attributes of creative people, those who bring new things, thoughts, or behaviors into existence? Einstein, Mozart, Hemingway, and Degas are considered creative. They possessed special traits and attributes. Creative people are flexible, self-motivated, and sensitive to problems; they are original thinkers, are able to concentrate, can think in terms of images, and have little fear of failure.[51]

Table 20–2 presents various characteristics of creative people that have appeared in the literature and have been discussed. This, like any list of characteristics, isn't definitive or very predictive. In general, the available research suggests that personality characteristics

TABLE 20–2		SELECTED CHARACTERISTICS OF CREATIVE PEOPLE
1.	Knowledge	Creative people spend a great number of years mastering their chosen field.
2.	Education	Education doesn't increase creativity. Education that stresses logic tends to inhibit creativity.
3.	Intelligence	Creative people don't necessarily have high IQs. The threshold for IQ is around 130. After that, IQ doesn't really matter. Creative people have been found to possess the following intellectual abilities: sensitivity to problems, flexibility in forming associations between objects, thinking in images rather than words, and synthesizing information.
4.	Personality	Creative people are typically risk takers who are independent, persistent, highly motivated, skeptical, open to new ideas, able to tolerate ambiguity, self-confident, and able to tolerate isolation. They also have a strong sense of humor and are hard to get along with.
5.	Childhood	Creative people have usually had a childhood marked by diversity. Experiences such as family strains, financial ups and downs, and divorces are common occurrences.
6.	Social habits	Contrary to stereotypes, creative people aren't introverted nerds. Creative people tend to be outgoing and enjoy exchanging ideas with colleagues.

Source: Based in part on Robert G. Godfrey, "Tapping Employees' Creativity," *Supervisory Management*, February 1986, pp. 16-20; and "Mix Skepticism, Humor, a Rocky Childhood—and Presto! Creativity," *Business Week*, September 30, 1985, p. 81.

and motivation are more important than intelligence levels in identifying creative people in a group.

Some strategies for creative thinking are listed below:

1. Use analogies.
2. Ask provocative questions.
3. Think in terms of possibilities.
4. Reward original thinking.
5. Become a creative reader.
6. Learn to listen carefully.
7. Study the process of innovation.
8. Be receptive to the unexpected.
9. Don't fall into the "one right answer" trap.[52]

Managing Creative People

Since creativity is difficult to isolate and pinpoint, we might conclude that managing creativity is a lost cause. But the opposite is true in that managers are fascinated by managing creativity in organizations. Attempting to manage creativity is important because it can lead to gaining a competitive advantage. Creativity is a resource that must be nurtured, supported, and rewarded for a firm to remain competitive. The new generation of workers appears to be concerned about locating organizations that support individual creativity, allowing people to find new ways to work, interact, and succeed.

Many firms have discovered that business process innovation can come from within and without. For example, until Aqualon management and union employees redesigned their workplace in 1992, tossing out traditional boss/employee roles in favor of autonomous work teams, the water-soluble polymer maker was in danger of being shut down by corporate parent Hercules, Inc. The redesign has boosted the company's return on capital from about 1 percent to 25.4 percent. Today, Aqualon's high-performance teams not only run the plant by committee, but they've redesigned nearly every process in the company. Worker-led changes have increased productivity as well.[53]

STEPS TO MANAGE CREATIVITY EFFECTIVELY - Organizations such as 3M, Hewlett-Packard, and the joint venture partnership of Microelectronics and Computer Corporation (MCC) find that recognizing and rewarding creativity are essential.[54] Encouraging experimentation and removing all sanctions for failure are important. James Burke, CEO of Johnson & Johnson, said, "We won't grow unless you take risks...Any successful company is riddled with failures. There's just no other way to do it."[55]

Harvard professor Rosabeth Moss Kanter's book, *The Change Masters*, presents steps *not* to use if creativity and innovation are to be encouraged (Table 20–3).[56]

Table 20–4 shows how a manager can enhance people's creativity. The exact steps to encourage new ideas, to provide clear objectives, or to provide recognition will depend to some extent on the manager's style, the creative attributes of the people making up the team, and the organization's culture. There are no universal prescriptions that always work with young and old workers, men and women, immigrants and U.S.-born workers, racially mixed work groups, or intellectual geniuses and average-intelligence employees.

Because they have very different dynamics from traditional business hierarchies, teams require very different managerial structures, roles and responsibilities, performance measurements and rewards, and training programs. Perhaps nowhere is the vast potential of teams—and the difficulties in realizing that potential—as apparent as in new product development. By cutting across the functional boundaries of research, design, operations, marketing, and sales, teams avoid the handoffs, downtime, and poor communication that have traditionally impeded product development. Mercer Management Consulting, Inc., has found four factors critical to the successful use of teams in new product development:

1. Appropriate team leadership, membership, evolution, and dynamics.
2. Appropriate team type.
3. Strong team sponsorship from senior management.
4. Organizational linkages and support systems.

TABLE 20–3   KANTER'S 10 RULES FOR STIFLING INNOVATION

1. Regard any new idea from below with suspicion because it's new, and because it's from below.

2. Insist that people who need your approval to act first go through several other levels of management to get their signatures.

3. Ask departments or individuals to challenge and criticize each other's proposals. (This saves you the job of deciding; you just pick the survivor.)

4. Express your criticisms freely, and withhold your praise. (That keeps people on their toes.) Let them know they can be fired at any time.

5. Treat identification of problems as signs of failure, to discourage people from letting you know when something in their area isn't working.

6. Control everything carefully. Make sure people count anything that can be counted frequently.

7. Make decisions to reorganize or change policies in secret, and spring them on people unexpectedly. (That also keeps people on their toes.)

8. Make sure that requests for information are fully justified, and make sure that it is not given out to managers freely. (You don't want data to fall into the wrong hands.)

9. Assign to lower-level managers, in the name of delegation and participation, responsibility for figuring out how to cut back, lay off, move people around, or otherwise implement threatening decisions you have made. And get them to do it quickly.

10. And above all, never forget that you, the higher-ups, already know everything important about this business.

Source: Rosabeth Moss Kanter, *The Change Masters* (New York: Simon & Schuster, 1983), p. 101.

TABLE 20–4	SELECTED PRESCRIPTIONS FOR FOSTERING ORGANIZATIONAL CREATIVITY

1. *Develop an acceptance of change.* Organization members must believe that change will benefit them and the organization. This belief is more likely to arise if members participate with their managers in making decisions and if issues like job security are carefully handled when changes are planned and implemented.

2. *Encourage new ideas.* Organization managers, from the top to the lowest-level supervisors, must make it clear in word and deed that they welcome new approaches. To encourage creativity, managers must be willing to listen to subordinates' suggestions and to implement promising ones or convey them to higher-level managers.

3. *Permit more interaction.* A permissive, creative climate is fostered by giving individuals the opportunity to interact with members of their own and other work groups. Such interaction encourages the exchange of useful information, the free flow of ideas, and fresh perspectives on problems.

4. *Tolerate failure.* Many new ideas prove impractical or useless. Effective managers accept and allow for the fact that time and resources will be invested in experimenting with new ideas that don't work out.

5. *Provide clear objectives and the freedom to achieve them.* Organization members must have a purpose and direction for their creativity. Supplying guidelines and reasonable constraints will also give managers some control over the amount of time and money invested in creative behavior.

6. *Offer recognition.* Creative individuals are motivated to work hard on tasks that interest them. But, like all individuals, they enjoy being rewarded for a task well done. By offering recognition in such tangible forms as bonuses and salary increases, managers demonstrate that creative behavior is valued in their organization.

High-performance teams in new product development add value by allowing a complex, highly collective activity to be managed and executed with innovation and speed. High performance is achievable, however, only if the critical support elements are in complete alignment from the start.[57]

Chapter 19 discussed intrapreneurship. These corporate commandos need an environment like that prescribed in Table 20–3. As our coverage of intrapreneurship made clear, there's no one best culture or reward system that works every time. The search for finding the right mix of people, culture, and rewards to encourage and support creativity and innovation is difficult, but is likely to continue unabated. The cost of stifling or stamping out creativity can be going out of business. Managing creativity is certainly a strategic mission that has short- and long-term consequences for organizations, individuals, and society.

Big companies have a difficult challenge to eliminate bureaucracy and foster the kind of creativity and innovation that leads to success. Research has shown that small-company innovation rate per employee far exceeds that of large companies. On the other hand, approximately two out of three small businesses fail in their first five years. Typically, this is because most small businesses start without any strategy, mission, or planning whatsoever. The message for the manager, then, is to think small, yet combine that with a manageable, nimble strategy that keeps the company from making crucial mistakes.[58]

Creativity Training

Creative employees are vital in today's competitive world, but they aren't sufficient. A firm needs to encourage creativity and also must renew people's creative spirit and instinct. Can people be trained to be creative? Some firms believe that training is an effective way to keep creativity alive. One survey suggests that about 25 percent of all U.S. companies employing over 100 people offer creativity training to employees.

Most creativity training techniques fall into four categories: *fluency techniques* are designed to stimulate the generation of ideas; *excursion sessions* push the mind to illuminate ideas; *pattern breakers* force thinkers to restate problems in novel ways; and *shake-up exercises* (games) help loosen up groups and make them more receptive to unusual ideas.[59]

The oldest fluency technique is brainstorming. A group of people fire off as many ideas as possible. The premise is that a group will produce a far greater number of ideas than an individual can. Judgment on every idea is deferred. Criticism is forbidden until ideas are evaluated later in the session.

A newer fluency concept is *brainwriting*. Employees write down their ideas on slips of paper with no identification of the originator. Then they exchange the slips of paper and attempt to build upon each others' insights. *Mindmapping* is a fluency approach involving drawing a primary idea at the center of the paper. New or related ideas are represented as vines growing in all directions.

An excursion technique is called a *forced relationship*. Polaroid managers from different departments used this technique. The creativity facilitator asked the managers to look at a number of paintings and to describe what they saw. Managers were then asked to "force-fit" their impressions about the paintings—to the task of figuring out how to improve interdepartment harmony.

Excursion exercises are intended to take a person's mind away from a problem so the unconscious mind can mull it over. Pattern breakers, however, keep the problem in focus, but in a different light. Synectics (a Cambridge, Massachusetts, creativity consulting firm) asks clients to take a stroll with an instant film camera and then uses the snapshots as prompts. A group returned with pictures of a glass jar, a household wash product, and a Federal Express package. The photo of the glass jar triggered a discussion about how to sell a service.

Shake-up exercises use games or team activities to help individuals laugh or relax. First Chicago Bank employs role-playing games—replete with funny costumes—and outdoor activities. Kodak uses a "humor room" stocked with games, objects (juggling balls and toy robots), and Monty Python movies. Groups of employees use the room to conduct meetings and also to relax.

Despite the growing popularity of creativity training, some believe that it's just a flaky fad. Like all fads, the creativity training boom is expected by critics to soon pass. A more serious concern is whether evidence derived using rigorous evaluation methods suggests that creativity training actually makes a difference. Are trained employees more creative than nontrained employees? To date, there's little evidence that creativity training improves performance, innovation development, or technological development.

SUMMARY OF LEARNING OBJECTIVES

DEFINE TECHNOLOGY, INNOVATION, AND TECHNOLOGY TRANSFER.

Technology is the totality of the means employed by people to provide comfort and human sustenance. Innovation is the generation of a new idea and its implementation into a new product, process, or service, leading to national economic growth, increased employment, and creation of profit. Technology transfer is the process of applying knowledge.

DISCUSS HOW TECHNOLOGY IMPLEMENTATION FITS INTO A COMPANY'S TECHNOLOGY STRATEGY.

Technology implementation involves the manner in which technology is introduced into the organization. Technology strategy involves decisions about what technologies to invest in and how to introduce those technologies into the workplace. Thus, technology implementation is a subset of overall technology strategy.

DESCRIBE THE MANAGERIAL SKILLS NEEDED FOR MANAGING TECHNOLOGY.

The skills often cited aren't much different from those required in any management situation: leadership, technical, and administrative skills.

DISCUSS THE DIFFERENCES IN TECHNOLOGY-DRIVEN TRANSFER, MARKET-DRIVEN TRANSFER, AND PRODUCT-AND-PROCESS IMPROVEMENT TRANSFER.

Technological discoveries in a lab or through basic research can create market opportunities. The technology in essence drives the demand for the product, service, or process. In market-driven transfer, a customer need exists. The task is to find the best technology to meet the need. Product-and-process improvement transfer centers on improving technology. Even the car, after years on the market, is continually being improved by innovative firms. Today improvements in technology are occurring in terms of quality enhancement and speed from the lab to the market.

DESCRIBE THE DIFFERENT METHODS OF INTERNATIONAL TECHNOLOGY TRANSFER.

The different methods of international technology transfer (ITT) are: licensing, joint venture, and espionage. Licensing is an arrangement whereby an individual or company obtains the rights to use another firm's patents, copyrights, blueprints, and technology for commercial purposes. A joint venture is the forming of a partnership between a domestic and a foreign company to produce or market a product or service. Espionage is the acquisition of information about another company's products or services by illegal means.

DESCRIBE SOME IMPORTANT STEPS TO TAKE TO MANAGE CREATIVITY EFFECTIVELY.

There's no one best set of steps. Some of the more reasonable steps to take include encouraging experimentation among workers, permitting on-the-job interaction among workers, tolerating failures, providing clear objectives and the freedom to achieve them, and offering recognition for good effort and performance.

DESCRIBE IN HISTORICAL TERMS WHETHER THE UNITED STATES HAS EVER HAD TECHNOLOGY POLICIES IN VARIOUS SECTORS OF BUSINESS AND INDUSTRY.

This hotly debated, politically charged notion of a national technology policy is likely to continue for years. The United States has, in fact, had technology policies in the fields of defense, medicine, and agriculture. These policies have resulted in laws, the formation of government agencies, the commercialization of technology, and the emergence of entire new industries. Some form of government intervention in technology issues will probably continue in the United States. Four likely areas of government involvement include climate setting, surveying, coordinating, and gap filling.

DISCUSS THE ADVANTAGES AND DISADVANTAGES OF A NATIONAL TECHNOLOGY POLICY.

A national technology policy is a statement of the government's role in development of a nation's technology infrastructure. Some critics claim government should stay out of the picture and let market forces determine the evolution of information technologies. Others claim that market forces will not lead to the poor, rural, and disadvantaged being connected to the information superhighway. This will create disparities in opportunities that market forces alone can't overcome.

KEY TERMS

creativity, p. 545
espionage, p. 544
innovation, p. 529
international technology
    transfer (ITT), p. 543
joint venture, p. 544

licensing, p. 544
market-driven transfer, p. 541
new product development, p. 539
product-and-process improvement
    transfer, p. 542
s-curve, p. 533

technology, p. 529
technology forecasting, p. 533
technology transfer, p. 540
technology-driven transfer, p. 541

REVIEW AND DISCUSSION QUESTIONS

Recall

1. How can a joint venture be used to acquire technology from a competitor?
2. What's the difference between creativity and innovation?
3. What is meant by the term technology gap?
4. What are the primary support activities in the value chain analysis?

Understanding

5. What are the arguments against having the federal government state and oversee a national technology policy?
6. Why is it difficult to determine whether creativity training offers anything of value to a firm?
7. Explain the S-curve and how it can be used as a guide for technology forecasting.

8. What steps are practiced by firms attempting to develop a coherent technology strategy?

Application

9. Visit a business, office, or factory and take note of the technologies being used. Which of these technologies originated in the United States? You'll need to do some library work to trace the history of the technologies you observed.
10. The chapter mentions that over 700 national laboratories exist in the United States. Many have had military missions. But as the world changes, these labs now must find private-sector partners and be concerned about commercializing technology. Identify a lab that's commercializing technology. What's it now doing?

CASE STUDY

Apple Computer Struggles to Survive

The year was 1984. George Orwell had written ominously of that year. His novel of the same name centered on a society in which individuality and personal expression were prohibited. Against the

backdrop of that foreboding image of society, Apple Computer projected itself as the hip young company that would stand fast against the leveling tendencies of corporate monsters like IBM. Its famous television commercial of a hammer-wielding olympic runner smashing the image of Orwell's big brother ran only one time. But that one time was during the 1984 Super Bowl, which was being watched by more than 43 million viewers around the world. Two days later, Macintosh computers were launched.

Apple proclaimed its Macintosh line to be the future of computing. Computers "for the rest of us" is how the company introduced its first Macs. They featured an easy to use graphical user interface and a push-button mouse. What the Mac lacked in raw computing power, it made up for in pure appeal. Mac enthusiasts sprouted overnight. The new machines were friendly, fun, and, more important, they weren't IBM.

Today, Apple, the very icon of postindustrial high-tech America, is up for sale to several bidders and has lost its hip image. What happened to this once-thriving Silicon Valley giant? There are many answers to that question. One lesson that can be learned from the Apple experience and applied to other industries is that cutting-edge products alone don't guarantee growth.

Apple Computer's woes should put to rest the powerful management myth that product innovation alone will succeed in the marketplace. Everyone knows that Microsoft's Windows 95 looks a lot like the 10-year-old Macintosh operating system. Yet, Apple is in trouble while Microsoft prospers. What else does a company need besides innovative products? The answer is effective business design.

Apple's proprietary, hardware-focused business design failed to meet key priorities of business customers who wanted open systems, minimum hardware costs, and the broadest possible range of business software. Apple's Macintosh is like Sony's Betamax VCR technology, a winning technology but a losing business design.

Some of the currently successful firms in the computer industry provide a stark contrast to Apple's business design. Hewlett-Packard, for example, hasn't provided products significantly different from those of its competitors. However, it has crafted a powerful business design that addresses new customer priorities. Hewlett-Packard built global business solutions for its global customers. Another computer industry success story, Sun Microsystems, built networking solutions for its business customers. As of this writing, Sun is poised to purchase Apple.

Apple probably began its demise during the height of its success. In 1985, the Macintosh was a hit and the company was prospering. That year, the company's board began debating the idea of allowing third-party manufacturers to produce Apple "clones," as was common with IBM machines. Every time the board came close to making a decision, however, it got scuttled.

When Apple finally decided to license its technology and allow the manufacture of clones, Microsoft's Windows operating system was everywhere. Apple executives insisted that Apple would claim 20 percent of the world's market share within five years. Again, however, Apple executives were unable to make a firm decision. To date, Apple has licensed its technology to just four small manufacturers who shipped a total of 200,000 units in 1995—a mere fraction of Apple's 4.5 million units shipped. Apple's worldwide market share never has reached the 20 percent promised. In fact, the company is struggling to maintain 10 percent.

If Apple survives it will undoubtedly have to change its business design, jettison assets, and remake itself into a smaller company. It already has plans to narrow its focus to market segments where it's traditionally been strong. Such a move would mean relinquishing the hope of ever again becoming the industry leader. The company has hinted that it may leave the low-end PC race. It has its eye on the Internet where the company holds some technological advantages. But it will run up against an everincreasing number of companies providing Internet services.

QUESTIONS

1. Why would Apple have been better off if it had licensed its technology to third-party manufacturers sooner than it did?
2. The case argues that Apple will have to radically change its strategy if it is to survive. What are some of the impediments to strategy change that Apple is likely to encounter?
3. What strategies do you think would be useful for Apple to gain market share over the next three to five years?

Sources: Adapted from Adrian J. Slywotzky and David Morrison, "Insights from a Falling Apple," *The Wall Street Journal*, January 29, 1996, p. A14; Kathy Rebello, Peter Burrows, and Ira Sager, "The Fall of an American Icon," *Business Week*, pp. 34–42.

VIDEO CASE

Managing Technology and Innovation at Nucor Steel

During the first half of the 20th century, the United States built a manufacturing empire around the steel output of midwestern cities. However, over the last 25 years the steel industry in the United States has collapsed. Today, the midwestern region that had been the backbone of the steel industry is referred to as "the rust belt," because of all the shuttered factories. It's not that the global demand for steel has declined, quite the opposite. What has happened is the technology of steelmaking advanced beyond what was being used in American plants, and they were no longer competitive. During the 1970s and 1980s, the Japanese built their own steel manufacturing empire on the strength of their newer, more productive steel factories.

Today, one innovative American company is managing to reverse the trend toward Japanese steel with a bold new approach that is raising eyebrows throughout the steel industry. Nucor Steel, a division of Nucor Corporation, opened a new steel plant in 1989 in the rural town of Crawfordsville, Indiana. Nucor started a revolution in steel manufacturing in this unlikely setting with the world's most technologically advanced mill.

The idea behind the Crawfordsville plant was to construct the steel mill economically. Doing so allowed Nucor to reduce its labor requirements. Once the factory was built, the company also developed an internal culture that had not previously been a part of the American steel industry, eliminating much of the inefficient bureaucracy that had paralyzed American steel mills. The steelmaker has decentralized decision making so much that plant managers run almost every aspect of the business. And the company rewards its employees for performance. Steelworkers at the plant are eligible for productivity and quality bonuses that are typically 130 to 150 percent of base pay. That can give the nonunionized workers total pay of up to $50,000 per year.

The Nucor plant, which is relatively small by industry standards, is known as a "mini-mill." But it isn't small in terms of productivity. It was designed to produce 800,000 tons of finished strip steel each year from scrap metal. The plant accomplishes this feat through the aid of two major technological advantages: continuous casting equipment and computer integrated manufacturing. The mill is the first continuous thin slab cast, flat roll steelmaking facility in the world. It allows Nucor steel to transform molten metal into hot band in one uninterrupted operation.

This innovation dramatically shortens the traditional production process, saving valuable time, manpower, and resources. The other technological advantage is the unprecedented level of computer integrated manufacturing (CIM) and management which had only previously been applied in other industries and in small portions of other steel plants. The Nucor steel mill provided an opportunity to employ a CIM system from the start-up. Plant general manager Keith Busse remarked, "When you look at how productive a facility like this is, it's almost frightening. We're producing a hot rolled ton of steel in seven-tenths of a man-hour. And we produce a cold rolled ton of steel in 1.2 man-hours. When you compare that to the integrated industry, we're looking at enormous productivity differences." The industry average is over four worker-hours per ton.

Nucor's CIM system controls the plant at three levels: machine setup, process control, and business information. These levels are linked together, and data are transferred from computer to computer throughout the entire process beginning with the order entry. Information concerning the order goes to production scheduling, then to the hot mill, the cold mill, shipping, and finally invoicing. The CIM system tells employees throughout the plant how to handle each slab, strip, or coil of steel at each stage of the process. The Nucor process includes 11 interactive databases, 1,500 programs, and a million lines of COBOL code. The CIM system helps Nucor establish optimum production schedules. It also lets the company serve its customers better by being able to tell them where their order is at any stage of the production process.

Nucor's production process is known as a "pull system," since it produces steel only in response to specific customer orders. Each order "pulls" the steel through the production process. This approach eliminates the need to inventory finished steel in anticipation of customer orders. The production begins at the scrap yard, which maintains a computer-monitored inventory. The scrap yard crew reads the order on the computer monitor and begins the production by feeding high-quality scrap into one of two 150-ton electric furnaces. The electric charge melts the scrap into hot molten steel, the steel is then moved into a ladle, and into the continuous caster. The caster produces a hot slab two-inches thick by 52-inches wide. Next the slab moves to a computer-controlled, gas-fired soaking furnace where it is heated to 2,000 degrees, at which point it can be rolled. From there, the slab proceeds on to the finishing mill.

One mill operator in a pristine computer operating room known as "the pulpit" controls the entire mill from the time the scrap enters the furnace until the finished coils exit the plant on the other end. Finished coils of 10 to 24 tons are bar-coded for computer tracking when they leave the plant. About half of the plant's steel is sold as hot band coils directly from the hot mill. The rest is sent to a cold mill next door for further finishing, including pickling, tempering, cold rolling for thickness reduction, and annealing for stress reduction.

Each workstation in the cold mill has its own computer terminal that provides processing instructions. Determining the best production schedule is vital for peak efficiency and minimizing setup time. Even the overhead crane operators benefit from the CIM system. They have radio-frequency terminals that help them find coils and tell them where to move them. After they move the coils, they enter updated locations and schedules.

As a result of their success, the Crawfordsville plant was a model for a new plant in Hickman, Arkansas. At Hickman, Nucor has continued to decentralize decision making, giving its plant managers a high level of autonomy. Hickman plant manager Rodney B. Mott says that "Hickman operates like a separate company." Mott has a big say in his plant's expansion plans. In the spring of 1994, for example, he installed a second $50 million caster, which turns liquid metal into bands of steel, nearly doubling the Hickman plant's capacity, to 36,000 tons per week.

That doesn't mean that headquarters isn't paying attention. Frequent telephone conversations with the central office in Charlotte, North Carolina, are common. And almost every measurable aspect of each plant's performance is reported throughout the company. That, in turn, leads to plenty of competition among the plants. "There's a lot of little sibling rivalries going on," Mott acknowledged.

Because of the success of Nucor's new mini-mills, Mott and other plant managers have been sought by other American steel companies to help them turn around their operations. But Mott has steadfastly refused such offers, even when the positions paid more money. The reason? "I'd still be taking orders," he said. That would be quite a change from Nucor, where the usual advice Mott gets from his boss is "trust your gut." It's not always easy to do, but that's the way decisions are made at Nucor. And it's the combination of decentralized decision making and bold new technologies that has made Nucor a force to be reckoned with in the international steel industry.

QUESTIONS

1. Nucor Steel has become competitive in the international steel industry through technology and innovation. What do you think the company needs to do to maintain its momentum and continue to be competitive into the next century?

2. Nucor has effectively applied computer integrated manufacturing (CIM) to its production processes. What steps do you think the company had to take to ensure employees are able to make full use of the CIM system? What ongoing steps do you think the company should be taking to ensure that its workers use the system to full advantage?

3. A major issue in organizational control is whether decision making should be centralized or decentralized. Nucor uses a decentralized approach, devolving a significant amount of authority to plant managers. What are some of the advantages of this approach? What are some of the disadvantages?

Source: Wendy Zellner, Robert D. Hof, Richard Brandt, Robert Baker, and David Griesing, "Go-Go Goliaths," *Business Week*, February 13, 1995, pp. 64–70.

APPLICATION EXERCISE

THE FARMER'S LAND

Objective:

To encourage students to think creatively about a problem.

Procedure:

Provide each participant with a handout illustrating the shape of a piece of land (see figure below). Explain the task: to subdivide a farmer's property upon his death into four pieces of equal size and shape for distribution to his four offspring. All land given to each offspring must be adjoining itself. The following is the key.

QUESTIONS

1. What previous experiences have you had that made it harder or easier for you to solve this problem?
2. What general problem type is this? What other problems are like this?
3. What general principle(s) could you use to help solve similar future problems?

Source: Adapted from N. R. F. Maier, Problem Solving and Creativity in Individuals and Groups (Belmont, Calif.: Brooks/Cole, 1970), pp. 96–97.

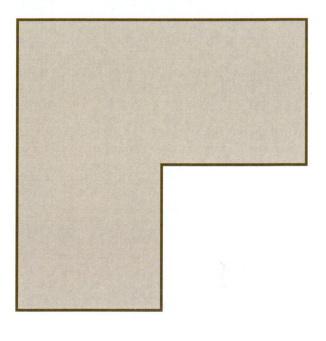

Appendix B

Seven Tools of Quality Control

The following seven tools—flow charts, run charts, control charts, fishbone diagrams, Pareto charts, histograms, and scatter diagrams—are basic components of statistical quality control.

FIGURE B–1
Flow Chart

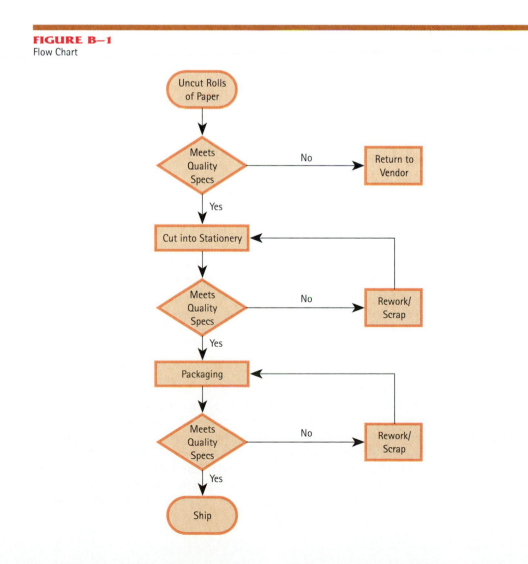

Flow Charts

Flow charts are used to provide a visual description of the steps in a process or work activity. The sequence of events that makes up the process is shown. Generally, flow charts begin with inputs, show what takes place to transform these inputs, and end with outputs. Flow charts are especially helpful in visualizing and understanding how things are currently being done and how they can be done differently to improve the process. Figure B–1 shows an example of a flow chart.

Up to two awards may be given in each category each year. Award recipients may publicize and advertise their awards. In addition to publicizing the receipt of the Award, recipients are expected to share information about their successful quality strategies with other U.S. organizations.

Companies participating in the Award process submit applications that include completion of the Award Examination.

Award Examination Review

The Award Examination is based upon quality excellence criteria created through a public–private partnership. In responding to these criteria, each applicant is expected to provide information and data on the company's quality processes and quality improvement. Information and data submitted must be adequate to demonstrate that the applicant's approaches could be replicated or adapted by other companies.

The Award Examination is designed not only to serve as a reliable basis for making awards but also to permit a diagnosis of each applicant's overall quality management.

All applications are reviewed and evaluated by members of the Malcolm Baldrige National Quality Award Board of Examiners. When Board members are assigned to review applications, business and quality expertise is matched to the business of the applicant. Accordingly, applications from manufacturing companies are assigned primarily to Board members with manufacturing expertise, and service company applications are assigned primarily to those with service expertise. Strict rules regarding real and potential conflicts of interest are followed in assigning Board members to review applications.

Core Values and Concepts

The Award Criteria are built upon these core values and concepts:
- Customer-driven quality.
- Leadership.
- Continuous improvement.
- Full participation.
- Fast response.
- Design quality and prevention.
- Long-range outlook.
- Management by fact.
- Partnership development.
- Public responsibility.

Brief descriptions of the core values and concepts follow.

Customer-Driven Quality

Quality is judged by the customer. All product and service attributes that contribute value to the customer and lead to customer satisfaction and preference must be addressed appropriately in quality systems. Value, satisfaction, and preference may be influenced by many factors throughout the customer's overall purchase, ownership, and service experiences. This includes the relationship between the company and customers—the trust and confidence in products and services—that leads to loyalty and preference. This concept of quality includes not only the product and service attributes that meet basic requirements. It also includes those that enhance them and differentiate them from competing offerings. Such enhancement and differentiation may include new offerings, as well as unique product–product, service–service, or product–service combinations.

Customer-driven quality is thus a strategic concept. It is directed toward market share gain and customer retention. It demands constant sensitivity to emerging customer and market requirements, and measurement of the factors that drive customer satisfaction. It also demands awareness of developments in technology, and rapid and flexible response to customer and market requirements. Such requirements extend well beyond defect and error reduction, merely meeting specifications, or reducing complaints. Nevertheless, defect and error reduction and elimination of causes of dissatisfaction contribute significantly to the customers' view of quality and are thus also important parts of customer-driven quality. In addition, the company's approach to recovering from defects and errors is crucial to its improving both quality and relationships with customers.

Leadership

A company's senior leaders must create clear and visible quality values and high expectations. Reinforcement of the values and expectations requires their substantial personal commitment and involvement. The leaders must take part in the creation of strategies, systems, and methods for achieving excellence. The systems and methods need to guide all activities and decisions of the company and encourage participation and creativity by all employees. Through their regular personal involvement in visible activities, such as planning, review of company quality performance, and recognizing employees for quality achievement, the senior leaders serve as role models reinforcing the values and encouraging leadership in all levels of management.

Continuous Improvement

Achieving the highest levels of quality and competitiveness requires a well-defined and well-executed approach to continuous improvement. Such improvement needs to be part of all operations and of all work unit activities of a company. Improvements may be of several types: (1) enhancing value to the customer through new and improved products and services; (2) reducing errors, defects, and waste; (3) improving responsiveness and cycle time performance; and (4) improving productivity and effectiveness in the use of all resources. Thus, improvement is driven not only by the objective to provide better quality, but also by the need to be responsive and efficient—both conferring additional marketplace advantages. To meet all of these objectives, the process of continuous improvement must contain regular cycles of planning, execution, and evaluation. This requires a basis—preferably a quantitative basis—for assessing progress, and for deriving information for future cycles of improvement.

Full Participation

Meeting the company's quality and performance objectives requires a fully committed, well-trained, and involved workforce. Reward and recognition systems need to reinforce full participation in company quality objectives. Factors bearing upon the safety, health, well-being, and morale of employees need to be part of the continuous improvement objectives and activities of the company. Employees need education and training in quality skills related to performing their work and to understanding and solving quality-related problems. Training should be reinforced through on-the-job applications of learning, involvement, and empowerment. Increasingly, training and participation need to be tailored to a more diverse workforce.

Fast Response

Success in competitive markets increasingly demands ever-shorter product and service introduction cycles and more rapid response to customers. Indeed, fast response itself is often a major quality attribute. Reduction in cycle times and rapid response to customers can occur when work processes are designed to meet both quality and response goals. Accordingly, response time improvement should be included as a major focus within all quality improvement processes of work units. This requires that all designs, objectives, and work unit activities include measurement of cycle time and responsiveness. Major improvements in response time may require work processes and paths to be simplified and shortened. Response time improvements often "drive" simultaneous improvements in quality and productivity. Hence it is highly beneficial to consider response time, quality, and productivity objectives together.

Design Quality and Prevention

Quality systems should place strong emphasis on design quality—problem prevention achieved through building quality into products and services and into the processes through which they are produced. Excellent design quality may lead to major reductions in "downstream" waste, problems, and associated costs. Design quality includes the creation of fault-tolerant (robust) processes and products. A major design issue is the design-to-introduction cycle time. To meet the demands of ever-more-rapidly-changing markets, companies need to focus increasingly on shorter product and service introduction time. Consistent with the theme of design quality and prevention, continuous improvement and corrective actions need to emphasize interventions "upstream"—at the earliest stages in processes. This approach yields the maximum overall benefits of improvements and corrections. Such upstream intervention also needs to take into account the company's suppliers.

Long-Range Outlook

Achieving quality and market leadership requires a future orientation and long-term commitments to customers, employees, stockholders, and suppliers. Strategies, plans, and resource allocations need to reflect these commitments and address training, employee development, supplier development, technology evolution, and other factors that bear upon quality. A key part of the long-term commitment is regular review and assessment of progress relative to long-term plans.

Management by Fact

Meeting quality and performance goals of the company requires that process management be based upon reliable information, data, and analysis. Facts and data needed for quality assessment and quality improvement are of many types, including: customer, product and service performance, operations, market, competitive comparisons, supplier, employee-related, and cost and financial. Analysis refers to the process of extracting larger meaning from data to support evaluation and decision making at various levels within the company. Such analysis may entail using data individually or in combination to reveal information—such as trends, projections, and cause and effect—that might not be evident without analysis. Facts, data, and analysis support a variety of company purposes, such as planning, reviewing company performance, improving operations, and comparing company quality performance with that of competitors.

A major consideration relating to use of data and analysis to improve competitive performance involves the creation and use of performance indicators. Performance indicators are measurable characteristics of products, services, processes, and operations the company uses to evaluate performance and to track progress. The indicators should be selected to best represent the factors that determine customer satisfaction and operational performance. A system of indicators tied to customer and/or company performance requirements represents a clear and objective basis for aligning all activities of the company toward common goals. Through the analysis of data obtained in the tracking processes, the indicators themselves may be evaluated and changed. For example, indicators selected to measure product and service quality may be judged by how well they correlate with customer satisfaction.

Partnership Development

Companies should seek to build internal and external partnerships, serving mutual and larger community interests. Such partnerships might include those that promote labor-management cooperation such as agreements with unions, cooperation with suppliers and customers, and linkages with education organizations. Partnerships should consider longer-term objectives as well as short-term needs, thereby creating a basis for mutual investments. The building of partnerships should address means of regular communication, approaches to evaluating progress, means for modifying objectives, and methods to accommodate to changing conditions.

Public Responsibility

A company's customer requirements and quality system objectives should address areas of corporate citizenship and responsibility. These include business ethics, public health and safety, environment, and sharing of quality-related information in the company's business and geographic communities. Health, safety, and environmental considerations need to take into account the life cycle of products and services and include factors such as waste generation. Quality planning in such cases should address adverse contingencies that may arise throughout the life cycle of production, distribution, and use of products. Plans should include problem avoidance and company response if avoidance fails, including how to maintain public trust and confidence. Inclusion of public responsibility areas within a quality system means not only meeting all local, state, and federal legal and regulatory requirements, but also treating these and related requirements as areas for continuous improvement. In addition, companies should support—within reasonable limits of their resources—national, industry, trade, and community activities to share nonproprietary quality-related information.

Criteria Framework

The core values and concepts are embodied in seven categories, as follows:

1.0 Leadership.
2.0 Information and analysis.
3.0 Strategic quality planning.
4.0 Human resource development and management.
5.0 Management of process quality.
6.0 Quality and operational results.
7.0 Customer focus and satisfaction.

The framework connecting and integrating the categories is given in the figure on page 36. The framework has four basic elements:

Driver Senior executive leadership creates the values, goals, and systems, and guides the sustained pursuit of quality and performance objectives.

System System comprises the set of well-defined and well-designed processes for meeting the company's quality and performance requirements.

Measures of Progress Measures of progress provide a results-oriented basis for channeling actions to delivering ever-improving customer value and company performance.

Goal The basic aim of the quality process is the delivery of ever-improving value to customers.

The seven Criteria categories shown in the figure are further subdivided into Examination Items and Areas to Address. These are described below.

Baldrige Award Criteria
Framework (Dynamic
Relationships)

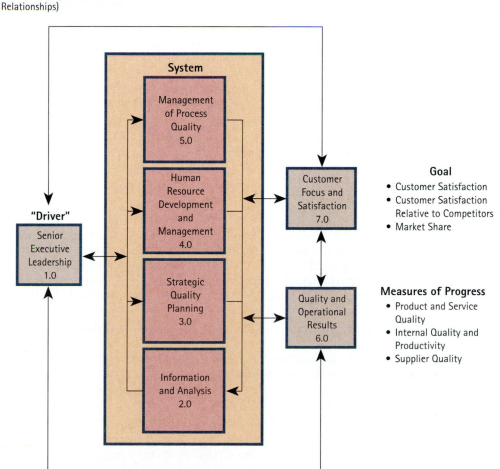

EXAMINATION ITEMS - In all, there are 28 Examination Items among the seven Examination Categories. Examination Categories each contain two or more Examination Items. Each Item focuses on a major element of an effective quality system. All information submitted by applicants is in response to the specific requirements given within these Items. Each Item is assigned an Examination point value. Item titles and point values are enumerated on page 35.

Linkage of the Award Criteria to Quality-Related Corporate Issues

INCREMENTAL AND BREAKTHROUGH IMPROVEMENT - Use of nonprescriptive, results-oriented Criteria and key indicators are intended to focus on *what* needs to be improved. This approach helps to ensure that improvements throughout the organization contribute to the organization's overall purposes. In addition to supporting creativity in approach and organization, results-oriented Criteria and key indicators encourage "breakthrough thinking"—openness to the possibility of major improvements as well as incremental ones. However, if key indicators are tied too directly to existing work methods, processes, and organizations, breakthrough changes may be discouraged. For this reason, analysis of operations, processes, and progress should focus on the selection and value of the indicators themselves. This will help to ensure that indicator selection does not unwittingly contribute to stifling creativity and preventing beneficial changes in the organization.

Benchmarks may also serve a useful purpose in stimulating breakthrough thinking. Benchmarks offer the opportunity to achieve significant improvements based on adoption or adaptation of current best practice. In addition, they help encourage creativity through exposure to alternative approaches and results. Also, benchmarks represent a clear challenge to "beat the best," thus encouraging major improvements rather than only incremental refinements of existing approaches. As with key indicators, benchmark selection is critical, and benchmarks should be reviewed periodically for appropriateness.

FINANCIAL PERFORMANCE - The Award Criteria address financial performance via three major avenues: (1) emphasis on quality factors and management actions that lead to better market performance, market share gain, and customer retention; (2) emphasis on improved productivity, asset utilization, and lower overall operating costs; and (3) support for business strategy development and business decisions.

The focus on superior offerings and lower costs of operation means that the Criteria's principal route to improved financial performance is through requirements that seek to channel activities toward producing superior overall value. Delivering superior value—an important part of business strategy—also supports other business strategies such as pricing. For example, superior value offers the possibility of price premiums or competing via lower prices, which may enhance market share and asset utilization, and thus may also contribute to improved financial performance.

Business strategy usually addresses factors in addition to quality and value. For example, strategy may address market niche, facilities location, diversification, acquisition, export development, research, technology leadership, and rapid product turnover. A basic premise of the Award Criteria is that quality principles support the development and evaluation of business decisions and strategies, even though many factors other than product and service quality must be considered. Examples of applications of the Criteria to business decisions and strategies include:

❖ Quality management of the information used in business decisions and strategy—scope, validity, and analysis.
❖ Quality requirements of niches, new businesses, and export target markets.
❖ Quality status of acquisitions—key benchmarks.
❖ Analysis of factors—societal, regulatory, economic, competitive, and risk—that may bear upon the success or failure of strategy.
❖ Development of scenarios built around possible outcomes of strategy or decisions including risks of failures, probable consequences of failure, and management of failure.
❖ Lessons learned from previous strategy developments—within the company or available through research.

The Award Criteria and evaluation system take into account market share, customer retention, customer satisfaction, productivity, asset utilization, and other factors that contribute to financial performance. However, the Criteria do not call for aggregate financial information such as quarterly or annual profits in evaluation of applications for Awards. This exclusion is made for several reasons—technical, fairness, and procedural:

❖ Short-term profits may be affected by such factors as accounting practices, business decisions, write-offs, dividends, and investments.

❖ Some industries historically have higher profit levels than others.

❖ The time interval between quality improvement and overall financial improvement depends upon many factors. Nor would this interval likely be the same from industry to industry or even for companies in the same industry.

❖ The Award Criteria measure performance relative to rigorous, customer-oriented, company-performance criteria. Though improved quality may improve a company's financial performance, its financial performance depends also on the quality performance of competitors—which the Award process cannot measure directly. The inclusion of aggregate financial indicators in evaluations would place at a disadvantage many applicants in the most competitive businesses.

❖ Financial performance depends upon many external factors, such as local, national, and international economic conditions and business cycles. Such conditions and cycles do not have the same impact on all companies.

❖ Some companies would not participate in the Award process if required to provide more detailed financial information.

INVENTION, INNOVATION, AND CREATIVITY ‐ Invention, innovation, and creativity—discovery, novel changes to existing practices or products, and imaginative approaches—are important aspects of delivering ever-improving value to customers and maximizing productivity. Although the state of technology may play a key role in corporate involvement in research leading to discovery, innovation and creativity are crucial features in company competitiveness and can be applied to products, processes, services, human resource development, and overall quality systems.

The Award Criteria encourage invention, innovation, and creativity in all aspects of company decisions and in all work areas:

❖ Nonprescriptive criteria, supported by benchmarks and indicators, encourage creativity and breakthrough thinking as the channel activities toward purpose, not toward following procedures.

❖ Customer-driven quality places major emphasis on the "positive side of quality," which stresses enhancement, new services, and customer relationship management. Success with the positive side of quality depends heavily on creativity—usually more so than steps to reduce errors and defects, which tend to rely more on well-defined quality techniques.

❖ Human resource utilization stresses employee involvement, development, and recognition, and encourages creative approaches to improving employee effectiveness, empowerment, and contributions.

❖ Continuous improvement and cycles of learning are integral parts of the activities of all work groups. This requires analysis and problem solving everywhere within the company.

❖ Strong emphasis on cycle time reduction in all company operations encourages companies to analyze work paths, work organization, and the value-added contribution of all process steps, thus fostering change, innovation, and creative thinking in how work is organized and conducted.

❖ Strong emphasis on cycle time and design encourages rapid introduction of new products and services, including those based on new concepts emerging from research areas.

❖ Quality and quality improvement requirements are deployed to all work units, including research, development, and other groups that have responsibility for addressing future requirements. For such groups, measures and indicators are expected to reflect quality, productivity, and effectiveness appropriate to the exploratory nature of their activities.

❖ Focusing on future requirements of customers, customer segments, and customers of competitors encourages companies to think in terms of attributes and, hence, innovative and creative ways to serve needs.

Appendix B
Seven Tools of Qualilty Control

The following seven tools—flow charts, run charts, control charts, fishbone diagrams, Pareto charts, histograms, and scatter diagrams—are basic components of statistical quality control.

FIGURE B–1
Flow Chart

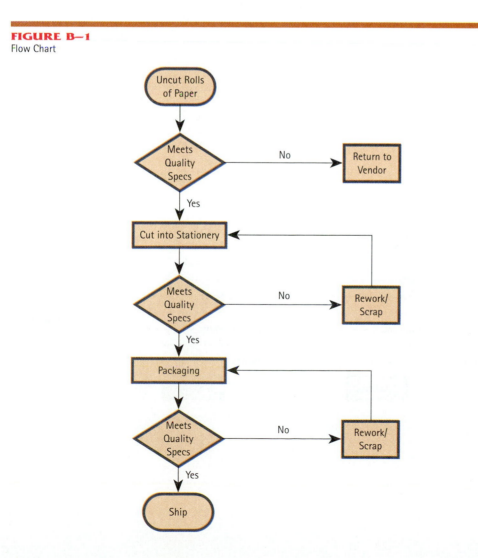

Flow Charts

Flow charts are used to provide a visual description of the steps in a process or work activity. The sequence of events that makes up the process is shown. Generally, flow charts begin with inputs, show what takes place to transform these inputs, and end with outputs. Flow charts are especially helpful in visualizing and understanding how things are currently being done and how they can be done differently to improve the process. Figure B–1 shows an example of a flow chart.

Run Charts

Run charts are used to plot measurements taken over specific time intervals such as a day, week, or month. Usually the quantity measure is plotted on the vertical axis, and time is on the horizontal axis. The run chart can be used to determine how something is changing over time and whether problems are taking place at certain periods of time. For instance, Figure B–2's run chart shows that the number of defective units produced goes up as the day progresses. This might suggest that workers grow fatigued as the day progresses.

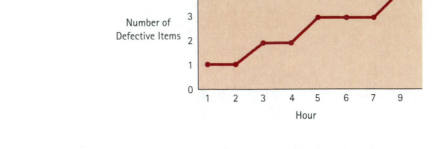

Control Charts

Control charts show the result of statistical process control measures for a sample, batch, or some other unit. Such charts can be used to study variation in a process and to analyze the variation over time. A specified level of variation may be acceptable, but deviation beyond this level is unacceptable. For instance, in Figure B–3 lower and upper limits are specified for the diameter of a component used in manufacturing computers. Measurements above or below these limits for a sample of parts initiate a search for the cause of the variation.

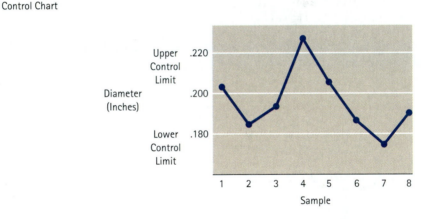

Fishbone Diagrams

Fishbone diagrams, also called cause and effect diagrams, look like a fishbone. The problem, such as a defect, is defined as the effect. Events that contribute to the problem are called causes. The effect is the "head" of the fishbone, while the causes are the "bones" growing out of the spine (Figure B–4). The fishbone chart can be used to see how different causes occur and lead to a problem. Once the causes are identified, corrective measures can be implemented.

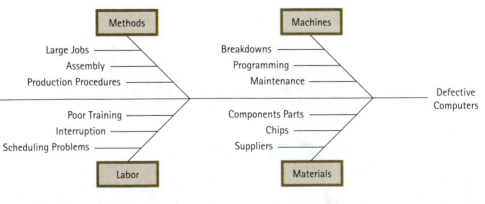

FIGURE B–5
Pareto Chart

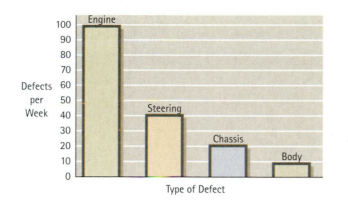

Pareto Charts
Pareto charts are used to display the number of problems or defects in a product over time. Pareto charts are fairly simple to construct, displaying the results as bars of varying length. Figure B–5 shows the number of defective cars for each type of error. The basic premise of the Pareto chart is that only a few causes account for most problems.

FIGURE B–6
Histogram

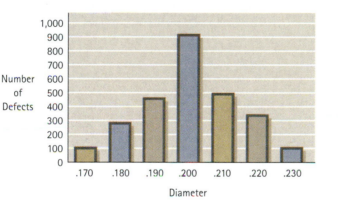

Histograms
Histograms (also called bar charts) show the frequency of each particular measurement in a group of measurements. Figure B–6 shows the frequency of defects of a component part for varying diameters. This information is useful in analyzing the variability in a process.

FIGURE B–7
Scatter Diagram

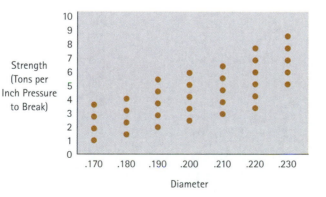

Scatter Diagrams
Scatter diagrams show the relationship between two characteristics or events. For instance, Figure B–7 shows the relationship between strength and diameter for samples of wires. By measuring these two variables and plotting the results, we can observe how one variable changes as the other changes. In this case strength increases with diameter.

Glossary

A

Ability   A measure of a worker's skill, competence, and/or genetic characteristics.

Accounts receivable turnover   The ratio of credit sales to average accounts receivable.

Acid-test ratio   Relates only cash and near-cash items (current assets excluding inventories and prepaid expenses) to current liabilities.

Acquisition entrepreneurship   A strategy whereby firms court other firms that have knowledge, ideas, or promising products.

Actions   Specific, prescribed means to achieve the objective(s).

Activity-based accounting   Analyzes all organization activities that consume resources.

Administrative entrepreneurship   This type of entrepreneurship is exhibited by the champion who supports research and development and provides or helps secure needed resources to develop ideas and move them from the lab to the market.

Affirmative action   Programs designed to ensure proportional representation of workers on the basis of race, religion, or sex. If a company has a federal contract exceeding $50,000, it's required to have an affirmative action program. Firms can also voluntarily establish such programs.

Analytical skill   The ability to use specific approaches or techniques in solving managerial problems.

Artificial intelligence   A technology that allows computers to solve problems involving imagination, abstract reasoning, and common sense.

Assembly line   A moving conveyor belt that carries work from one workstation to the next.

Authority   The right to give orders must accompany responsibility. The legitimate use or form of power stemming from the position, not from the person. The organizationally sanctioned right to make a decision.

B

Balance sheet   Describes an organization's financial condition at a specified point in time.

Baseline   The portion of a behavioral chart that measures work behavior before any effort is made to change the worker's behavior.

Behavioral rehearsal   The practice of an activity under simulated or controlled conditions.

Behavioral self-management   The process of managing overt, measurable physical activities.

Behavioral style model   The leadership theory that focuses on (1) the work and (2) workers' attitudes and expectations.

Benchmarking   The continuous process of measuring a firm's goods, practices, and services against those of its toughest competitors and leading firms in other industries.

Benefits   Indirect financial compensation consisting of all financial rewards not included in the direct financial compensation package.

Bounded rationality   A decision approach that recognizes decision making's boundaries or limits in terms of available resources.

Brainstorming   A process whereby a group of individuals generate ideas according to a firm set of rules while at the same time avoiding the inhibitions that are usually caused by face-to-face groups.

Budget   A predetermined amount of resources linked to an activity.

Business plan   The entrepreneur's road map. The business plan contains descriptions of the company, its founders, the product and its potential markets, and financial projections about the company's expected future performance.

C

Capital budget An intermediate and long-run planning document that details the alternative sources and uses of funds.

Cash cow A strategic business unit with a high market share in a low-growth market.

Cash trap A strategic business unit that has low market share in a low-growth market.

Centralization The relationship between centralization and decentralization is a matter of proportion; the optimum balance must be found for each organization. The process of retaining authority in the hands of high-level managers, who make all the decisions.

Centralized planning System in which responsibility for planning lies with the organization's highest level.

Certainty No element of chance, possible loss, or unpredictability.

Chain of command The formal command that defines the lines of authority from the top to the bottom of the organization.

Change agent An individual or team of people whose main responsibility is to initiate, suggest, and even force change efforts within an organization.

Channel capacity The limit on the volume of information that a channel can handle effectively.

Charting A technique used to measure the frequency of a worker's target behavior over time.

Cognitive self-management A mental process that includes the creation of images and thought patterns consistent with the firm's goals and behaviors.

Cohesiveness A measure of a group's ability to work well together. Cohesiveness is expressed through the group's ability to do its work effectively, attract new members as needed, influence one another, and maintain the group's integrity over time.

Common cause variation The random variation in a system. Typically, it can't be completely eliminated.

Communication The exchange of information between a sender (source) and a receiver (audience).

Communication audit A systematic method for collecting and evaluating information about an organization's communication efforts.

Communication skills The ability to communicate in ways that other people understand, and to seek and use feedback from employees to ensure that one is understood.

Comparable worth A concept that attempts to prove that individuals who perform jobs requiring similar skills, efforts, and responsibilities under similar work conditions should be compensated equally.

Compensation The HRM activity that deals with every type of reward that individuals receive for performing organizational tasks.

Competitiveness The degree to which a nation can, under free and fair market conditions, produce goods and services that meet the test of international markets while simultaneously maintaining or expanding the real incomes of its citizens.

Complexity The number of different job titles and the number of different departments.

Computer-aided design (CAD) The use of computers to draw plans for a product or service.

Computer-aided engineering (CAE) The use of computers to plan engineering processes and test designs.

Computer-aided manufacturing (CAM) The use of computers for controlling the operation of traditional, modified, and electronic machines, including robots.

Computer network A collection of computers connected in a manner that allows them to function individually and communicate with each other.

Computer skills The ability to use computer software applications and have a conceptual understanding of how computers work.

Concept to customer The period between the time a product is first considered and the time it is sold to the customer.

Conceptual skills Visualizing how each part of an organization fits and interacts with other parts to accomplish goals and objectives.

Concurrent control Monitoring ongoing operations to ensure that objectives are pursued.

Conformity The process by which members adopt group norms, roles, and behaviors.

Content theory A theory of motivation defining motivation in terms of need satisfaction (also called *need theory*). The ability to satisfy a need is a motivating force that leads to a behavioral response.

Contingency leadership models Leadership theories that assert that the specific leadership behavioral style must be contingent on the situation if the leader is to be effective.

Contingent rewards Rewards distributed based on a specific preceding behavior.

Continuous improvement A component of quality-based decision making that results in constant, incremental improvements in organizational processes.

Control The process of maintaining conformance of the system.

Control chart A record of the targeted activity over time, with established upper and lower tolerances or control limits.

Controlling A function of management that makes sure that the organization's actual performance conforms with the performance that was planned for it.

Cost-leadership strategy A strategy of low-price, high-volume, and low-profit margins on each item. With this strategy, a cost leader attempts to attract a large number of customers with low prices, generating a large overall profit by sheer volume of units sold.

Countertrading Complex bartering agreements between two or more parties.

Creativity The ability to bring something new into existence.

Critical service encounter A service encounter where customers are likely to be forming opinions about the overall quality of the business.

Critical success factors Those things that must go right to achieve goals and objectives.

Cultural Diversity Differences both within and between cultures.

Culture A system of behavior, rituals, and shared meaning held by employees that distinguishes the group of organization from other similar units.

Current ratio The ratio of current assets to current liabilities.

Customer departmentalization Grouping jobs in a manner that serves customers' needs.

Customer-perceived value The relative worth of a company's products or services as discerned by its customers. This information is used to tailor products and services to meet distinct market segment requirements, thus reducing costs and improving customer service while increasing profitability.

Customers End users of the firm's products and services.

Customs and entry procedures Inspection, documentation, and licensing of goods entering a country.

Cycle time reduction The length of time required to complete a process and be ready to begin anew. Cycle time reduction has become a key goal for organizations.

D

Database An integrated collection of data stored in one place for efficient access and information processing.

Debt/asset ratio An expression of the relationship of the firm's total debts to its total assets.

Debt/equity ratio A measure of the amount of assets financed by debt compared to that amount financed by profits retained by the firm and investments (stocks and other securities).

Decentralization The process of distributing authority throughout the organization.

Decentralized planning System in which responsibility for planning lies with workers and lower levels of the organization.

Decision A conscious choice among analyzed alternatives, followed by action to implement the choice.

Decision formulation The process of (1) identifying a decision opportunity or need, (2) collecting information, (3) from the information, developing alternative courses of action, and (4) from the alternatives, selecting one alternative.

Decision implementation The process to implement the alternative and then do follow-up to assess each of the implementation alternatives.

Decision-making process A series or chain of related steps leading to a decision, its implementation, and follow-up.

Decision support system An interactive information system that enables managers to gain instant access to information in a less structured format than an MIS.

Decisional roles The roles assumed by managers that establish them as decision makers after receiving interpersonal and informational input. Other decisional roles include entrepreneur, disturbance handler, resource allocator, and negotiator.

Decoding The process by which the receiver interprets the symbols (coded message) sent by the source by converting them into concepts and ideas.

Delphi technique A process involving soliciting and comparing anonymous judgments on the topic of interest through a set of sequential questionnaires that are interspersed with summarized information and feedback of opinions from earlier questionnaires.

Deontological ethics An approach to ethics that assumes certain ethical ideals are universal; that is, they apply in all situations regardless of the consequences.

Departmentalization The process of grouping jobs according to some logical arrangement.

Depth of intervention The degree of change that the intervention is intended to bring about.

Descriptive statistics A computed measure of some property of a set of data, making possible a statement about their meaning.

Development The acquisition of knowledge and skills that may be used in the present or future.

Differentiation strategy In this approach, a firm offers a high-priced product equipped with the greatest number of product-enhancing features, and sells the product to a relatively small group of customers who are willing to pay top dollar for premium features. Sometimes called premium strategy.

Direction The acts of managers when they (1) instruct subordinates in the proper methods and procedures and (2) oversee subordinates' work to ensure that it's done properly.

Direct ownership Purchasing of one or more business operations in a foreign country.

Discipline Obedience and respect help an organization run smoothly.

Discounted rate of return   A measurement of profitability that takes into account the time value of money.

Discretionary effort   The difference between the minimum amount of effort a worker must expend to keep from being penalized and the maximum amount a person can bring to a job.

Distinctive competence   A capacity that's unique to the firm and that's valued in the market.

Division of work   Specialization of labor is necessary for organizational success.

Dominant culture   An organization's core values that are shared by the majority of employees.

Downward communication   Information that flows down the organizational hierarchy from managers and supervisors to subordinates.

Duty   A tax on an import or export.

E

Early growth stage   The stage of new business development where a growth spurt can be expected.

Ecology   The branch of natural science devoted to the relationship between living things and their environment.

Economy of time   Essentially, having faster inventory turns. In the past, organizations grew successful through sheer size (economy of scale); now they grow successful through speed (economy of time).

Embargo   A prohibition of the import or export of certain goods.

Empowerment   Giving employees who are responsible for hands-on production or service activities the authority to make decisions or take action without prior approval. The process of providing workers with the skills, tools, information, and, above all, the authority and responsibility for their work.

Enacted role   The manner in which the role recipient actually expresses or redefines the received role.

Encode   To convert a message into groups of symbols that represent ideas or concepts.

Entrepreneur   A person who assumes the major risks of creating incremental wealth by making an equity, time, and/or career commitment to provide value to a product or service. The product or service itself may or may not be new or distinct, but value is added by the entrepreneur.

Environmental analysis   The monitoring of external environmental forces to determine the firm's opportunities and threats.

Environmental diagnosis   The process of making managerial and strategic decisions by assessing and interpreting data collected in the environmental analysis.

Environmental scanning   A technique used by management whereby information about events and trends in an organization's external environment are used in planning the organization's future courses of action.

Equal employment opportunity (EEO)   An umbrella term that encompasses all laws and regulations prohibiting and/or requiring affirmative action.

Equity   Fairness that results from a combination of kindliness and justice will lead to devoted and loyal service.

Escalation of commitment   An increased commitment to a previous decision despite contrary information.

Espionage   The attempt to obtain competitors' technology by illegal means.

Esprit de corps   Harmonious effort among individuals is the key to organizational success.

Event counting   An enumeration of a behavior (e.g., number of times that safety goggles are worn) within a given time period.

Exchange control   A limit on how much profit a foreign-based firm can return to its home country.

Executive information system   A user-friendly DSS designed specifically for executives. It's easy to use and requires no knowledge of the computer.

Expectancy   The probability that a person's effort will lead to a satisfactory level of job performance.

Expert system   The computer hardware and software capable of making decisions.

Exporting   Selling of domestic goods to a foreign country.

External environment   All factors such as laws, competition, technology, social-cultural norms and trends, and ecology that may affect the organization directly or indirectly.

Extinction   The process of nonreinforcement of a behavior. Simply by ignoring the behavior or not reinforcing it, the behavior will dissipate over time.

Extrinsic rewards   Results of work that are externally controlled.

F

Feedback   The receiver's response to the sender's message.

Feedback control   A type of control where corrective action is directed at improving either the resource acquisition process or the actual operations.

Fiedler's LPC theory   A two-step theory in which the leader is adjusted to the situation. The first step is to measure and determine the leader's behavioral style. The second step is to find or create a situation that would be conducive to the leader's fixed style.

Financial pro formas   Essential financial documents that project the company's sales, profits, and cash flow.

First-line management   Managers, also known as supervisors, office managers, or foremen, who coordinate the work of others who aren't managers (subordinates).

Five competitive forces   A view held by Harvard Business School economist Michael Porter that in any industry the nature of competition is embodied in five competitive forces: (1) the threat of new entrants, (2) the threat of substitute products or services, (3) the bargaining power of suppliers, (4) the bargaining power of buyers, and (5) the rivalry among the existing competitors.

Flexible manufacturing systems (FMS)   A grouping of robots and other computerized machines programmed to switch fairly easily from producing one kind of product to another.

Flextime   A schedule that allows workers to select starting and quitting times within limits set by management.

Forecast   A prediction of future events based on past and current data.

Formal group   Two or more people who engage in organizationally required actions for a common purpose. The term *formal* designates a permanent entity with prescribed organizational roles.

Formalization   The extent to which communications and procedures in an organization are written down and filed.

Formal training program   An effort by the employer to provide opportunities for the employee to acquire job-related skills, attitudes, and knowledge.

Forming   The early stage of group development when members begin to know each other's strengths and weaknesses.

Functional departmentalization   Grouping jobs together according to the organization's functions.

G

Gainsharing plans   A compensation system based on a companywide incentive system that results in the sharing of rewards caused by improved productivity, cost reductions, or improved quality.

General Agreement on Tariffs and Trade (GATT)   An agreement setting rules of conduct for fair and equitable international trade.

Geographic departmentalization   Grouping jobs based on defined territories.

Global corporation   A corporation operating as if the world were a single market, with corporate headquarters, manufacturing facilities, and marketing operations throughout the world.

Goal   A targeted level of performance set in advance of work.

Goal acceptance   A psychological embracing of the goal as the worker's own aspiration.

Goal commitment   Behavioral follow-through (persistent work effort to achieve the goal).

Goal-setting theory   The belief that people who set goals outperform people who don't set them.

Grapevine   An informal communication channel that cuts across formal channels of communication and carries a variety of facts, opinions, rumors, and other information.

Gross domestic product (GDP)   The measure of output attributable to all factors of production (labor and property) physically located within a country.

Gross national product (GNP)   The market value of an economy's final goods and services produced over a one-year period.

Group   Two or more people who engage in purposeful collective action.

Group norms   A set of expectations about how people are to act.

Groupthink   The suppression or ignoring of countervailing ideas that represent a threat to group consensus or unanimity.

H

Heterogeneity   The inconsistency or variation in human performance.

Hierarchy of needs   A motivational theory that people have five basic needs arranged in a hierarchy (physiological, safety, social, self-esteem, and self-actualization), developed by Abraham Maslow.

Horizontal communication   Messages that flow between persons at the same level of an organization.

Hot stove rule   A punishing experience reinforces future behavior. The hot stove is a good teacher—once burned, we're likely to avoid being burned in the future.

Human resource management (HRM)   The process of accomplishing organizational objectives by acquiring, retaining, terminating, developing, and properly using the human resources in an organization.

Human resource planning (HRP)   Estimating the size and makeup of the future work force.

Hygiene factor   In Herzberg's two-factor theory, the aspects of work that are related to the external environment and not the work itself.

I

Imitative entrepreneurship   This form of entrepreneurship takes advantage of and extends the use of other firms' ideas, products, and technologies.

Implementation   The assignment of people and responsibilities for achieving a plan.

Income statement   A summary of an organization's financial performance over a given period of time.

Incubative entrepreneurship   This type of entrepreneurship involves subjecting a new idea, technology, or innovation to experimentation and testing.

Individual incentives   A form of compensation in which the employee is paid for units produced.

Industry foresight   Beliefs about an industry based on deep insights into the trends in technology, demographics, regulations, and lifestyle that can be harnessed to rewrite industry rules and create new competitive space.

Inferential statistics   Computations done on a set of data, or among several sets of data, that are designed to facilitate prediction of future events or to guide decisions and actions.

Informal group   Two or more people who engage in voluntary collective activity for a common purpose. Informal group actions are generally not recognized by the organization.

Informational roles   The roles assumed by managers that establish them as the central point for receiving and sending nonroutine information.

Infrastructure   Communications, transportation, and energy facilities that mobilize the country and also indicate its economic condition.

Initiative   One of the greatest satisfactions is formulating and carrying out a plan.

Initiative burnout   That which occurs among employees who have experienced too many management initiatives (e.g., TQM, reengineering, cycle time reduction) in too short a time.

Innovation   The generation of a new idea and its implementation into a new product, process, or service, leading to national economic growth, increased employment, and creation of profit.

Inseparability   A situation in which services are produced and consumed at the same time.

Instrumentality   In expectancy theory, the subjective probability that satisfactory job performance will lead to other desired outcomes such as pay increases or promotion.

Intangibility   The quality of not being able to be assessed by the senses of sight, taste, touch, smell, or hearing.

Internal change forces   Forces for change that occur within the organization, such as communication problems, morale problems, and decision-making breakdowns.

Internal environment   The factors within an enterprise (such as employees, structure, policies, and rewards) that influence how work is done and how goals are accomplished.

International business   Performance of business activities across national boundaries.

International management   Performance of the management process in an international business setting.

International monetary fund (IMF)   Founded in 1944, it promotes cooperation among member nations by eliminating trade barriers.

International technology transfer (ITT)   The process of applying knowledge across geographical or national boundaries.

Internet   An "internetwork" comprised of thousands of computer networks at businesses, universities, government agencies, and libraries that are connected via phone, fiber-optic, or other high-capacity lines.

Interpersonal communication   Communication between two people, usually face-to-face.

Interpersonal roles   The figurehead, leader, and liaison roles assumed by managers that subsequently enable them to perform informational and decisional roles.

Intervention   The method, technique, or means used to change a structure, behavior, or technology.

Intervention period   The portion of time posted on the behavioral record chart that follows the introduction of a change.

Intrapreneur   A person inside an organization who pursues an innovation and champions it over a period of time.

Intrinsic rewards   Intangible psychological results of work that are controlled by the worker.

Intuitive decision making   A process of estimating or guessing to decide among alternatives.

Invention   A new product or service that hasn't yet been put into commercial use.

Inventory turnover   The ratio of cost of goods sold to average inventory. Facilitates the analysis of appropriate balances in current assets.

Investment decisions   Managerial decisions that involve the commitment of present funds in exchange for future funds.

Issues management   A technique used by many firms in which one person is assigned leadership on a single issue and is responsible for strategic decisions on that issue.

J

Job analysis   The process of gathering, analyzing, and synthesizing information about jobs.

Job characteristics approach   An approach suggesting that jobs should be redesigned to include important core dimensions that increase motivation, performance, and satisfaction, and reduce absenteeism and turnover.

Job content   A specific aspect of the job. For example, job variety is a content factor.

Job context   Factors external to the job. For example, a unionized workforce applies union contract rules to all jobs.

Job depth The amount of discretion a worker has in performing tasks.

Job description A written summary of the job, detailing the job's activities, equipment required to perform them, and the job's working conditions.

Job design A determination of exactly what tasks must be performed to complete the work.

Job enlargement Increasing the number of tasks a worker performs.

Job enrichment Giving workers more control of their activities, addressing their needs for growth, recognition, and responsibility.

Job range The number of tasks a worker performs.

Job redesign Attempts by the organization to improve the quality of work and give workers more autonomy.

Job rotation Systematically moving employees from one job to another.

Job specialization Breaking down work into smaller, more discrete tasks. A written explanation of skills, knowledge, abilities, and other characteristics needed to perform a job effectively.

Joint venture A partnership between a domestic firm and a firm in a foreign country. The creation of an alliance between two companies to produce or market a product or service.

Just-in-time (JIT) manufacturing A system requiring that the exact quantity of defect-free raw materials, parts, and subassemblies is produced just in time for the next stage of the manufacturing process.

L

Later growth stage The stage of a maturing business where growth has slowed and new competitors have entered the market.

Leadership The process of influencing other people.

Leading A function of managers who, by directing and motivating, influence organization members to perform in ways that accomplish the organization's objectives.

Learning The act by which individuals acquire skills, knowledge, and abilities that result in a relatively permanent change in their behavior.

Level of detail The specificity of a plan.

Licensing An agreement through which one firm (the licensor) allows another firm (the licensee) to sell the licensor's product and use its brand name. A business arrangement that permits a firm or individual to use another firm's patents, copyrights, blueprints, and technology.

Life cycle theory A situational approach to leadership in which the follower's maturity is the basis for choice of leadership style.

Line position In the direct chain of command and contributes directly to the achievement of the organization's goals.

Liquidity Reflects the firm's ability to meet current obligations as they become due.

Local area network (LAN) A system of telecommunications links that connects all computers in one company directly without telephone lines.

M

Management The process undertaken by one or more persons to coordinate other persons' activities to achieve high-quality results not attainable by any one person acting alone.

Management information system (MIS) A combination of computers and regular, organized procedures to provide managers with information needed in making decisions.

Management level The right to act and use resources within specified limits as a result of vertical specialization of the management process.

Managers The individuals who guide, direct, or oversee the work and performance of other individuals or nonmanagers.

Manufacturing The physical process of producing goods. (Services are not manufactured.)

Market-driven transfer Customers express a need for a technology and the firm finds the technology to meet that need.

Mass production A system permitting the manufacture of goods in large quantities.

Material reward A reward with financial value (e.g., cash, stock, stock options).

Materials requirements planning (MRP) A computer-driven system for analyzing and projecting materials needs and then scheduling their arrival at the work site at the right time.

Matrix organization A cross-functional organization overlay that creates multiple lines of authority and places people in teams to work on tasks for a finite period of time.

Mechanistic organization A rigid organization that attempts to achieve production and efficiency through rules, specialized jobs, and centralized authority.

Media richness Media's capacity to convey data.

Medium of transmission A means of carrying an encoded message from the source to the receiver.

Message An idea or experience that a sender wants to communicate.

Middle management Managers, also known as departmental managers, plant managers, or directors of operations, who plan, organize, lead, and control other managers' activities and who themselves are subject to a supervisor's managerial efforts.

Mission statement   A statement of the firm's long-term vision, of what the firm is trying to become, that differentiates this firm from other firms. The mission provides direction and a sense of purpose to all employees.

Mixed departmentalization   Grouping jobs using more than one basis.

Motivation   The set of forces that initiate behavior and determine its form, direction, intensity, and duration.

Multidivisional organization   A high-performance organization whose operating units or divisions are partially interdependent.

Multinational company (MNC)   An organization conducting business in two or more countries.

Multinational market group   An agreement by two or more countries to reduce trade and tariff barriers between them.

N

National technology policy   The policy of a national government concerning domestic development of technology infrastructure.

Natural management team   A management team consisting of a manager and people directly reporting to her who are also managers or supervisors.

Need for achievement   A measure of a person's desire for clear, self-set, moderately difficult goals, with feedback given based on goal achievement.

Need for affiliation   The desire to work with others, to interact and support others, with a concern for their growth and development. An individual version of Maslow's hierarchical social need.

Need for power   A desire to have influence and control over others, to have impact.

Negative reinforcement   Behavioral reinforcement occurring when an unpleasant consequence is withdrawn when the desired behavior occurs.

Network organization   A flexible, sometimes temporary, relationship between manufacturers, buyers, suppliers, even customers.

Neutralizer   Any situation that prevents the leader from acting in a specified way.

New product development   The set of steps or activities a firm uses to develop new products and services.

Niche strategy   A strategy that applies the premium strategy to a restricted market (usually a geographic region).

Noise   Interference that affects any or all stages of the communication process.

Nominal group technique   A process of bringing people together in a group to solve a problem. In the NGT partici-

pants aren't allowed to communicate verbally in the initial phase.

Noncontingent rewards   Rewards that aren't linked to any specific behavior.

Nonprogrammed decision   Novel, unstructured decisions.

Nonverbal communication   Intentional or unintentional messages that are neither written nor spoken.

Norming   The stage of group development when the group develops norms or unwritten codes of conduct for group behavior.

O

Objective   A specification of desired future conditions.

Operant conditioning (or reinforcement theory)   Skinner's theory that behavior is a function of its consequences. Behavior is contingent upon reinforcement. Behavior that's reinforced will be repeated.

Operating strategy   A broad plan of action for pursuing and achieving a firm's goals and satisfying its mission.

Operational definition   A definition that converts a concept into measurable, objective units.

Operational planning   A focused, short-term, and specific form of planning that translates the broad concepts of the strategic plan into clear numbers, specific steps, and measurable objectives for the short term.

Operations   The functions needed to keep the company producing and delivering. Literally any function or series of functions enacted to carry out a strategic plan.

Opportunist entrepreneurship   Exhibited by companies that allow employees to seek and take new opportunities that help the company.

Opportunity   Anything that has the potential to increase the firm's strengths.

Opportunity building   The process of seeking out and/or developing new possibilities for success.

Oral communication   Communication using the spoken word to transmit a message.

Order   Both material things and people should be in their proper places.

Organic organization   An organization that seeks to maximize flexibility and adaptability. It encourages greater utilization of human potential and deemphasizes specialization of jobs, status, and rank.

Organization   An administrative and functional structure that can be as small as a one-person operation or as large as more than 1 million employees.

Organizational design   The process by which managers develop an organizational structure.

Organizational structure   The framework of jobs and departments that directs the behavior of individuals and groups toward achieving the organization's objectives.

Organization stories   Within an organization, stories tell of experiences and events that transpired where the storyteller works. Stories legitimate power, rationalize group behavior, and reinforce organizational values, identity, and commitment.

Organizing   The function of management that assigns the tasks identified during planning to individuals and groups within the organization so that objectives set by planning can be achieved. The process of structuring both human and physical resources to accomplish organization objectives.

Output counting   A measure of results of a targeted process.

Outside pressure (OP) change agent   An individual or group not employed by a firm that pressures the firm to change.

P

Path-goal leadership theory   Theory based on the expectancy theory of motivation. The leader's role is to help the worker engage in organizational activities that lead to rewards that the worker values.

Payback method   Calculates the number of years needed for the proposed capital acquisition to repay its original cost out of future cash earnings.

Peak performance   The highest level of performance a worker can achieve.

People-change-technology   Change agents that use behaviorally oriented change techniques.

People-oriented behavioral style   The aspect of leadership theory consisting of behaviors such as showing empathy for worker needs and feelings, being supportive of group needs, establishing trusting relationships with workers, and allowing workers to participate in work-related decisions.

People skills   The ability to work with, communicate with, and understand others.

Performance culture   A work situation where everyone can do his or her best work.

Performance evaluation   A postcontrol technique focusing on the extent to which employees have achieved expected levels of work during a specified time period.

Performance standards   In management terms, expected behaviors as defined by plans.

Performing   The stage of group development when the group functions to its fullest potential toward goal attainment.

Perishability   Unused service capacity can't be stored and used at a later date.

Persuasion   The process of convincing workers of the value of a plan prior to implementation.

Pinpointing   The identification of quality-based target behaviors.

Plan, do, check, act (PDCA)   A four-step cycle. The first step is to plan the quality improvement. Second, workers produce a small version or batch of the procedure/product. Third, workers check the results of this pilot project. Fourth, workers implement the complete process.

Planning   The function of management that determines an organization's objectives and establishes the appropriate strategies for achieving those objectives. The process by which managers examine their internal and external environments, ask fundamental questions about their organization's purpose, and establish a mission, goals, and objectives. Planning includes all activities that lead to defining objectives and determining appropriate courses of action to achieve those objectives.

Planning process   A six-step process: (1) Assess current status. (2) Determine objectives. (3) Identify the actions required. (4) Allocate resources. (5) Assign responsibilities for implementation. (6) Control the planning decision.

Planning values   Underlying priorities that determine planning objectives and decisions.

Policy   A written statement that reflects a plan's basic objectives and provides guidelines for selecting actions to achieve the objectives.

Positive reinforcement   The process of providing rewards contingent upon desired worker behavior.

Positive self-talk   The process of creating mental imagery that reinforces a worker's sense of self-esteem and enhances efficacy.

Power   The capacity to influence people.

Preliminary control   Control method focusing on preventing deviations in the quality and quantity of resources used in the organization.

Prestart-up stage   The stage of entrepreneurship that involves asking fundamental questions about the potential of a business idea.

Proactive decision   A decision made in anticipation of an external change or other conditions.

Problem   The realization that a discrepancy exists between a desired state and current reality.

Process improvement team   The "working team" of a continuous improvement process consisting of anyone from the organization who can contribute to a problem's solution.

Process organization   Organization that bases performance objectives on meeting customer needs and identifying the processes that meet those needs.

Process theory   Theories of motivation supporting the belief that motivation is a rational cognitive process internal to the individual rather than an external process.

Product-and-process improvement transfer   Improvements in the existing technology that result in a better product or process that meets customer needs.

Product departmentalization Grouping jobs associated with a particular product or product line.

Production The total process by which a company creates finished goods or services.

Productivity The rate at which goods and services are created. An estimate of output per labor-hour worked.

Program evaluation and review technique (PERT) chart A graphical system for tracking the events that must take place to accomplish a task.

Programmed decision A decision that is repetitive and routine, with a definite procedure developed for handling it.

Punishment The process of administering an undesirable consequence for an undesirable behavior.

Q

Quality The totality of features and characteristics of a product or service that bear on the ability to satisfy stated or implied needs.

Quality circle A small group of people, usually fewer than 10, who do similar work and meet about once a week to discuss their work, identify problems, and present possible solutions. Volunteer group of employees who meet to brainstorm about how to improve quality and cost control in the workplace.

Quality planning The activity of (1) determining customer needs and (2) developing the products and processes required to meet those needs.

Question mark A strategic business unit that has low market share in a high-growth market.

Quota A limit to the amount of a product that can leave or enter a country.

R

Rate of return on investment One alternative measure of profitability, consistent with methods ordinarily employed in accounting.

Rationality A logical, structured approach to decision making.

Reactive decision A decision made in response to external changes.

Received role The role recipient's understanding of what the sent role means.

Recruitment The set of activities an organization uses to attract job candidates with the abilities and attitudes needed to help the organization achieve its objectives.

Reengineering The fundamental rethinking and radical redesign of business processes to achieve dramatic improvements in critical, contemporary measures of performance, such as cost, quality, service, and speed.

Reference ratio In equity theory, a person compares the ratio of his job inputs to his job outcomes and then makes a similar comparison for an identical worker. The ratio for the comparison referent is called the reference ratio. For example, a person compares his job effort to his pay and then makes the same comparison for the person working next to him. In an equitable situation, the two ratios are identical.

Regulation A standard procedure providing a set of instructions to implement a policy.

Reinforcement The process of using contingent rewards to increase future occurrences of a behavior.

Remuneration Employees should be paid fairly in accordance with their contribution.

Resources Financial, physical, human, time, or other assets of an organization.

Risk The chance of a possible loss, or unpredictability, in a decision.

Robot A computerized, reprogrammable, multifunctional machine that can manipulate materials and objects in performing particular tasks.

Role A behavior pattern expected of an individual within a unit or position. A set of shared expectations, among group members, regarding a member's attitude and task behavior within the group.

Role ambiguity A situation in which a role's actual behavioral requirements aren't clear. The role recipient doesn't understand what his actions or responsibilities are in his job.

Role conflict Incompatibility between a role's requirements and the individual's own beliefs, attitudes, or expectations.

Role modeling Leader's primary vehicle for encouraging self-leadership.

Role overload A situation in which the role recipient is overwhelmed by the job's requirements.

S

S-curve A technology-forecasting tool that graphs the relationship between effort put into improving a product or process and the firm's results from making the investment.

Satisficer A person who accepts a reasonable alternative that is not necessarily the optimal alternative.

Satisficing The process of finding, accepting, and implementing the alternative that best meets certain minimum goals.

Satisfier In Herzberg's two-factor theory, factors (such as decision-making autonomy) that can lead to satisfaction.

Scalar chain Subordinates should observe the formal chain of command unless expressly authorized by their respective superiors to communicate with each other.

Scope The range of activities covered by a plan.

Selection The process by which an organization chooses from a list of applicants the person or persons who best meet the criteria for the position available, considering current environmental conditions.

Selective perception People screening out information that isn't consistent with their beliefs or background.

Sender A person, group, or organization that has a message to share with another person or group of persons.

Self-cueing behavior The process of planning or making arrangements for an activity prior to its performance.

Self-designed jobs Jobs in which workers are allowed to propose and design work process changes.

Self-leadership The philosophy and a systematic set of behavioral and cognitive strategies for workers leading themselves to higher performance and effectiveness.

Self-management An individual's capacity to arrange and control personal activities and resources, including goals and rewards, without an external force.

Self-observation The process where a worker monitors her own behavior, noting actions, events, or outcomes.

Self-reward The process of a worker monitoring, evaluating, and applying a reward or disincentive for her own performance.

Self-set goals Goals that result when both the initiative for setting a goal and the level of the goal itself come from the worker, not the manager.

Sender A person, group, or organization that has a message to share with another person or group of persons.

Sent role The role expectations "sent" by group members regarding an individual's attitudes, beliefs, or behaviors.

Service An intangible product that involves human or mechanical effort.

Service productivity Output per person per hour.

Service quality A service's conformance to customer specifications and expectations.

Shared values Beliefs, attitudes, or actions that are commonly agreed upon and understood by group members. Shared values are an invisible and unspoken guide to daily behavior within the group and to interaction outside the group.

Single-use plans Plans that have a clear time frame for their utility.

Situational theories of leadership Theories in which the appropriate leader behavior is the one that best fits the constraints of a specific situation.

Skill An ability of proficiency in performing a particular task.

Social entrepreneur One who manages a nonprofit organization and who has a background in management and entrepreneurship rather than clinical work. These organizations increasingly resemble the corporations that help fund their work.

Social responsibility A firm's practices with other parties such as customers, competitors, the government, employees, suppliers, and creditors.

Social rewards Rewards that come from interpersonal behavior and enhance personal self-efficacy.

Solvency The firm's ability to meet its long-term obligations, its fixed commitments.

Source credibility The receiver's confidence and trust in the source of the message.

Span of control The number of people who report to one manager or supervisor.

Special cause variation Variation within a system that is due to some external influence.

Stable system A system that has eliminated special cause variation and is subject only to the unavoidable common cause variations.

Stability and tenure of personnel People need time to learn their jobs.

Staff position A position that facilitates or provides advice to line positions.

Standard cost system Provides information that enables management to compare actual costs with predetermined (standard) costs.

Standard of living Gross National Product per capita, which takes into account a nation's GNP in relation to its population.

Standing plans Plans that have ongoing meaning and application to an organization.

Star A strategic business unit that has high market share in a high-growth market.

Start-up stage The initial period of opening the doors and starting to do business.

Statistical process control A method of implementing quality control before the final inspection stage. It relies on statistical tools to control variation within given processes.

Statistics That branch of applied mathematics that describes and analyzes empirical observations for the purpose of predicting certain events as a basis for decision making in the face of uncertainty.

Steering team A team consisting of top management (the people who establish an organization's strategic goals and objectives).

Stockholders Those who own a firm's stock.

Storming The stage of group development when the group addresses inherent conflicts and develops solutions that keep the group focused on its work.

Strategic Alliance A combination of the resources of two firms in a partnership that goes beyond the limits of a joint venture.

Strategic business unit (SBU) A product or service division of a company that establishes goals and objectives in harmony with the organization's overall mission.

Strategic planning The process of determining desired objectives or benchmarks and of developing ways to reach them. "What do we want the future to be? What must we do now to better ensure that the desired future is achieved?" Comprehensive, long-term, and relatively general planning. Focuses on broad, enduring issues to increase the firm's effectiveness.

Strategic thinking The determination of an enterprise's basic long-term goals and objectives, the adoption of courses of action, and the allocation of resources necessary for carrying out these goals.

Strategy A broad plan of action for pursuing and achieving the firm's objectives and satisfying its mission.

Strategy–structure–systems doctrine Senior managers for much of the twentieth century have described their jobs as defining strategy, developing structure, and managing the systems.

Stretch targets A "pull" approach to organizational change that uses foresight to determine what the future is likely to be and then using that insight to change the organization in the present.

Subordination of individual interests to the general interest Resolving the tug of war between personal and organizational interests in favor of the organization is one of management's greatest difficulties.

Substitutes for leadership Illustrates the idea that other factors in the work environment can and do cause workers to behave in a certain manner. The leader can use these factors to guide work behavior when direct leadership is neither desirable nor possible.

Survey feedback An organizationally focused, shallow intervention method that involves top management, data collection, data interpretation, and feedback of findings to employees which result in the development of action plans.

SWOT analysis The process of examining a firm's internal and external environments for important strengths, weaknesses, opportunities, and threats.

Symbolic rewards Tangible and intangible rewards with psychological impact.

Systematic decision making An organized, exacting, data-driven process for choosing among alternatives.

T

Tactical planning On the continuum between the strategic and operational planning processes, a more narrow, intermediate-term, and specific form of planning than strategic planning.

Target behaviors Behaviors that either contribute to or detract from the organization's quality aims.

Task-oriented behavioral style Leadership behaviors such as setting goals, giving directions, supervising worker performance, and applauding good work.

Task rewards Rewards that are related to the work itself, such as the nature, design, and allocation of specific work assignments in terms of job responsibilities, autonomy, task-generated feedback, and scheduling control.

Team A group of employees who work closely together to pursue common objectives. A work group committed to quality practices and outcomes.

Team building A moderate-depth intervention that attempts to improve diagnosis, communication, cooperation, and the performance of members and the overall team.

Technical skills The ability to use specific knowledge, techniques, and resources in performing work.

Technological innovation All those activities translating technical knowledge into a physical reality that can be used in a societal scale.

Technology The accumulated competence to provide goods and services for people. The totality of the means employed by people to provide comfort and human sustenance.

Technology-driven transfer The new technology that can create market opportunities.

Technology forecasting The art of determining the direction and impact of a new technology in the interest of creating or sustaining competitive advantage.

Technology transfer The process of applying knowledge.

Telecommuting A practice made possible by the Information Age whereby people no longer come into the office, preferring instead to work out of their homes.

The 3 percent rule A key concept in cycle time reduction that states that only 3 percent of the elapsed time for a process is actually needed to complete the activity.

Threat Anything that has the potential to hurt or even destroy a firm.

Time frame The period considered by a plan.

Time sampling A series of observations or checks throughout the specified time period, usually to see if the behavior was occurring (or not occurring) at the time of the check.

Top management A small cadre of managers, usually including a CEO, president, or vice president, that is responsible for the performance of the entire organization through the middle managers.

Total quality control An effective system for integrating the quality-development, quality-maintenance, and quality-improvement efforts of the various groups in an organization so as to enable marketing, engineering, production, and service at the most economical levels that allow for full customer satisfaction.

Total quality environmental management (TQEM) A continuous improvement approach to a company's environmental management practices. It involves forming alliances with other organizations for the purpose of working together to solve common problems.

Total quality management (TQM) A management approach to long-term success through customer satisfaction, based on the participation of all members of an organization in improving processes, products, service, and the culture in which they work.

Trading company A link between buyers and sellers in different countries.

Training The systematic process of altering employees' behavior to further organizational goals.

Trait theory of leadership An early attempt to describe effective leaders in a systematic fashion that focuses on the leader's physical and personality attributes.

Transactional leadership A leadership approach in which leaders appeal to the workers' rational exchange motive.

Transformational leadership An approach to leadership based on changing workers' basic values and attitudes about their jobs. The transformational leader encourages worker participation in decisions and challenges workers to help the leader create the future organization one day at a time.

U

Uncertainty The decision maker has absolutely no knowledge of the probabilities of the outcomes of each alternative.

Unity of command Each employee should receive orders from only one superior.

Unity of direction The efforts of everyone in the organization should be coordinated and focused in the same direction.

Upward communication Information that flows up the organization from subordinates to supervisors and managers.

Utilitarian ethics An approach to ethics that assumes that ethical judgments depend upon the consequences of an action. A familiar utilitarian measure is that an action is good if it results in the greatest good for the greatest number.

V

Valence In expectancy theory, the value or importance the individual places on a second-order outcome. For example, if a person doesn't want a promotion because it would bring more responsibility, then promotion has a low valence.

Value chain All the activities an organization undertakes to create value for a customer.

Values Convictions that a specific mode of conduct is personally or socially preferable to another mode of conduct.

Virtue ethics An approach to ethics that assumes professional norms to be the measure of ethical status. If an act is appropriate within professional norms, it is considered to be ethically good or right.

Vision A clear sense of the organization's future.

Vroom-Jago model A theory in which the ever changing nature of work situations requires the leader to develop a variety of behavioral responses or decisions and apply them to the different situations as they occur.

W

Work group An organized collection of workers responsible for a task or outcome.

Work team A team of nonmanagerial employees and their manager or supervisor in a department or unit.

World Bank Formed in 1946, it lends money to underdeveloped and developing countries for various projects.

Written communication Transmitting a message through the written word.

Z

Zero defects (ZD) A concept proposed by Philip Crosby whereby management believes that no defects are acceptable. A performance standard developed by Philip B. Crosby to address the attitude of organizations that mistakes are human and acceptable.

Endnotes

Chapter 1

1. *Global Competition: The New Reality, Report of the President's Commission on Industrial Competitiveness*, Vol. II (Washington, D.C.: U.S. Government Printing Office, 1985), p. 6.
2. William Echikson, "Luxury Steals Back," *Fortune*, January 16, 1995, pp. 112–119.
3. *The Corporate Guide to the Malcom Baldrige National Quality Award: Proven Strategies for Building Quality into Your Organization* (Burr Rdige, IL: Business One Irwin, ASQC Quality Press, 1992), p. 11.
4. The Straining of Quality", *The Economist*, January 14, 1995, pp. 55–56.
5. Paul D. Larson and Ashish Sinha, "The TQM Impact: A Study of Quality Managers' Perceptions," *Quality Management Journal*, Spring 1995, pp. 53–66.
6. Ross Johnson and William O. Winchell, *Management and Quality* (Milwaukee, Wis.: American Society for Quality Control, 1989).
7. This definition is provided by the American Society for Quality Control, Milwaukee, Wis., no date, p. 2.
8. David A. Garvin, "Competing on the Eight Dimensions of Quality," *Harvard Business Review*, November-December 1987, pp. 101–9.
9. W. Edwards Deming, *Out of the Crisis* (Cambridge, Mass.: MIT Center for Advanced Engineering Study, 1982), p. 31.
10. Philip B. Crosby, Quality without Tears (New York: McGraw-Hill, 1984), p. 12.
11. Robert R. Morton, "Using GEMI's Environmental Self-Assessment Procedure (ESAP) to Evaluate Environmental Performance," *Total Quality Environmental Management*, Autumn 1994, pp. 75–84.
12. Robert F. Hartley, *Marketing Mistakes* (Columbus, Ohio: Grid, 1976), pp. 59–70.
13. Brian Dumaine, "The New Non-Manager Managers," *Fortune*, February 22, 1993, pp. 80–84; and "A Checklist of Qualities That Make a Good Boss," *Nation's Business*, November 1984, p. 100.
14. Charles M. Farkas and Phillippe De Backer, "There Are Only Five Ways to Lead," *Fortune*, January 15, 1996, pp. 109–112.
15. See Robert L. Katz, "Skills of an Effective Administrator," *Harvard Business Review*, September-October 1974, pp. 90–102.
16. "Microsoft's Other Dynamo," *Business Week*, January 8, 1996, p. 53.
17. "Trying to Climb the Corporate Ladder? Without Basic Computer Skills, You Risk Falling Off, Survey Reports," PR *Newswire*, January 20, 1988.
18. Del Marth, "Keeping All the Lines Open," *Nation's Business*, October 1984, pp. 85–86.
19. Bill Gates, "What I Learned From Warren Buffett," *Harvard Business Review*, January-February 1996, pp. 148–152.
20. Henry Mintzberg, *The Nature of Managerial Work* (Englewood Cliffs, N.J.: Prentice-Hall, 1980).
21. Henry Mintzberg, "The Manager's Job: Folklore and Fact," *Harvard Business Review*, July-August 1975, pp. 49–61; Jay W. Lorsch, James P. Baughman, James Reece, and Henry Mintzberg, *Understanding Management* (New York: Harper & Row, 1978), p. 220; and Neil Synder and William F. Glueck, "How Managers Plan—The Analysis of Managers' Activities," *Long-Range Planning*, February 1980, pp. 70–76.
22. Peter F. Drucker, *Management: Tasks, Responsibilities, Practices* (New York: Harper & Row, 1973), p. 17.

Chapter 2

1. Carol J. Loomis, "Dinosaurs," *Fortune*, May 3, 1993, p. 72.
2. Alonzo L. McDonald, cited in Alan M. Kantrow, "Why History Matters to Managers," *Harvard Business Review*, January–February 1986, p. 82.
3. Peter F. Drucker, *The Practice of Management* (New York: Harper & Row, 1954), p. 37.
4. Peter F. Drucker, *Post-Capitalist Society* (New York: Harper-Collins, 1993), p. 72.
5. Bruce Brocka and M. Suzanne Brocka, *Quality Management*, (Burr Ridge, IL: Business One Irwin, 1992), pp. 64–71.
6. W. Edwards Deming, *Out of the Crisis*, 2nd ed. (Cambridge, Mass.: MIT Center for Advanced Engineering Study, 1986).
7. Francis J. Gouillert and James N. Kelly, *Tranforming the Organization* (New York: McGraw-Hill, 1995), pp. 4–5.
8. A comprehensive analysis of Taylor is found in Charles D. Wrege and Ronald G. Greenwood, *Frederick W. Taylor: The Father of Scientific Management* (Burr Ridge, IL: Business One Irwin, 1991), p. 131.
9. Lyndall Urwick, *The Golden Book of Management* (London: Newman Neame. 1956), pp. 72–79.
10. Frederick W. Taylor, *Principles of Scientific Management* (New York: Harper & Row, 1911), pp. 36–37. Also see Claude S.

George, Jr., *The History of Management Thought* (Englewood Cliffs, N.J.: Prentice-Hall, 1968); and Edwin A. Locke, "The Ideas of Frederick W. Taylor: An Evaluation," *Academy of Management Review,* January 1982, pp. 14–24.

11. Other important contributors to classical organization theory include James De Mooney and Alan C. Reiley, who wrote *Onward Industry* (New York: Harper & Row, 1931), and Lyndall F. Urwick, who wrote *The Elements of Administration* (New York: Harper & Row, 1943).

12. Fritz J. Roethisberger and William J. Dickson, *Management and the Worker* (Cambridge, Mass.: Harvard University Press, 1931), p. 24.

13. Stephen R. G. Jones, "Worker Interdependence and Output: The Hawthorne Studies Reevaluated," *American Sociological Review,* April 1990, pp. 176–90.

14. Jim Tompkins, *The Genesis Enterprise* (New York: McGraw-Hill, 1995), pp. 7–11.

15. D.S. Pugh, D.J. Hickson, and C.R. Hinings, *Writers on Organizations* (London: Sage, 1985), pp. 103–6.

16. Ludwig von Bertalanffy, "The History and Status of General Systems Theory," *Academy of Management Journal,* December 1972, p. 411.

17. Chester I. Barnard, *The Functions of the Executive* (Cambridge, Mass.: Harvard University Press, 1938), p. 65.

18. Robert Kreitner, *Management* (Boston: Houghton Mifflin, 1992), p. 56.

19. Stratford Sherman, "The New Computer Revolution," *Fortune,* June 14, 1993, pp. 56–63, 66–71, 74–77, 80–81; and Daniel Fisher, "Compaq Squares off with Clones," *Houston Post,* June 16, 1992, pp. 1C, 10C.

20. "This Year, Servers Will Be King," *Business Week* January 8, 1996, p. 94.

21. Steven Cavaleri and Krzysztof Obloj, *Management Systems: A Global Perspective* (Belmont, CA: Wadsworth, 1993), pp. 6–10; Fremont E. Kast and James E. Rosenzweig, "General Systems Theory: Applications in Organizations and Management," *Academy of Management Journal,* December 1972, pp. 447–65; and Daniel Katz and Robert L. Kahn, *The Social Psychology of Organizations* (New York: John Wiley & Sons, 1966), p. 47.

22. Kast and Rosenzweig, "General Systems Theory," p. 463.

23. See Fred Luthans, "The Contingency Theory of Management: A Path Out of the Jungle," *Business Horizons,* June 1973, pp. 63–72; and Harold Koontz, "The Management Theory Jungle Revisited," *Academy of Management Review,* April 1980, pp. 175–88.

24. James Kim, "Employees Call Shots," *USA Today,* April 10, 1992, p. 4B.

25. Todd May, Jr., "Surprising Help from the Crash," *Fortune,* January 18, 1988, pp. 68–76.

26. Patricia M. Carey, "Getting Ready for NAFTA," *International Business,* October 1992, pp. 42–51.

27. Lester Thurow, *Head to Head* (New York: Morrow, 1992), pp. 56–57.

28. "The Uruguay Round … and Round," *The Economist,* January 23, 1993, p. 68.

29. John Case, *From the Ground Up* (New York: Simon & Schuster 1992), pp. 45–46.

30. William G. Ouchi, *Theory Z: How American Business Can Meet the Japanese Challenge* (Reading, Mass: Addison-Wesley, 1981).

31. Michael E. Porter, *The Competitive Advantage of Nations* (New York: The Free Press, 1990), p. 101.

32. Michael E. Porter, "The Rise of the Urban Entrepreneur," *Inc.,* July 1995, pp. 104–119.

Chapter 3

1. Steve Brooks, "Playing Without Rules," *Restaurant Business,* May 20, 1995, pp. 44–52.

2. Edgar H. Schein, *Organizational Culture and Leadership* (San Francisco: Jossey-Bass, 1984), p. 58.

3. T.A. Deal and A.A. Kennedy, "Culture—A New Look Through Old Lenses," *Journal of Applied Behavioral Science,* November 1983, p. 50.

4. Yoram Mitki and A.B. Shani, "Cultural Challenges in TQM Implementation: Learning from the Israeli Experience," *Journal of Administrative Sciences,* 12(2): 1995, pp. 161–170.

5. Lim Bernard, "Examining the Organizational Culture and Organizational Performance Link," *Leadership & Organization Development Journal,* 16(5): 1995, pp. 16–21.

6. Stephen M. Shortell, et al., "Assessing the Impact of Continuous Quality Improvement/Total Quality Management: Concept versus Implementation," *Health Services Research,* June 1995, pp. 377–401.

7. James M. Higgins, "Innovate or Evaporate," *The Futurist,* September/October 1995, pp. 42–48.

8. Julianne G. Mahler, "Evolution of a Quality Management Program," *Public Productivity & Management Review,* Summer 1995, pp. 387–396.

9. K.L. Gregory, "Native-View Paradigms: Multiple Cultures and Culture Conflicts in Organizations," *Administrative Science Quarterly,* September 1983, pp. 359–376.

10. G.S. Saffold III, "Culture Traits, Strength, and Organizational Performance: Moving Beyond 'Strong' Culture," *Academy of Management Review,* October 1988, pp. 546–558.

11. Mike Maremont, "Blind Ambition," *Business Week,* October 23, 1995, pp. 78–92.

12. Anthony Sampson, Company Man (New York: Times Business, 1995), cited in William Glasgall, "The Dinosaur in the Gray Flannel Suit," *Business Week,* October 30, 1995, p. 19.

13. David Jamieson and Julie O'Mara, *Managing Workforce 2000* (San Francisco: Jossey-Bass, 1991), pp. 28–29.

14. Xian-Zhong Xu and G. Roland Kaye, "Building Market Intelligence Systems for Environmental Scanning," *Logistics Information Management,* 8(2): 1995, pp. 22–29.

15. Bill Richardson, "The Politically Aware Leader: Understanding the Need to Match Paradigms and Planning Systems to Powerful, Turbulent Fields Environment," *Leadership & Organization Development,* 16(2): 1995: pp. 27–35.

16. Marianne Wilson, "Diversity in the Workplace," *Chain Store Age Executive,* June 1995, pp. 21–23.

17. Rosalia J. Costa-Clark, "Understand the Law When Developing Diversity Programs," *Human Resources Professional,* July/August 1995, pp. 25–28.

18. Patricia M. Carey, "Creating a New Generation of Black Technocrats," *Black Enterprise,* August 1995, pp. 140–142.

19. Tom Dunkel, "Affirmative Reaction," *Working Woman,* October 1995, pp. 39–43.

20. Anthony Lewis, "Court Says No to Different Experience," *Houston Chronicle,* March 29, 1996, p. 36A.

21. "Change or Perish: Labour's Response to Market Realities," *Crossborder Monitor,* September 13, 1995, pp. 1, 9.

22. Thomas Allison, "The Contingent Workforce," *Occupational Outlook Quarterly,* Spring 1995, pp. 45–48.

23. Arlene A. Johnson, "The Business Case for Work-Family Programs," *Journal of Accountancy,* August 1995, pp. 53–58.

24. Iaso Yamada, "A Sharp Increase of Positive-Minded Young Employees," *Japan 21st,* June 1995, pp. 5.

25. Rowena Rees, "Commonsense Campaign Tackles Work-Related Illness," *Works Management,* July 1995, pp. 18–19.

26. Duane Daugherty, "The General Duty Clause," *Supervisory Management,* October 1995, p. 5.

27. David Chapman and Gavin Johnson, "Safety First," *Management-Auckland,* September 1995, pp. 112–113.

28. National Bureau of Labor Statistics. Economy at a Glance. Located at World Wide Web site: http://stats.bls.gov:80/eag.table.html.

29. Karen Pennar, "Is the Nation-State Obsolete in a Global Economy?" *Business Week,* July 17, 1995, pp. 80–81.

30. Kenichi Ohmae, "Putting Global Logic First," *Harvard Business Review,* January-February 1995, pp. 119–125.

31. Kenichi Ohmae, op cit., p. 122.

32. Patricia M. Carey, "Getting Ready for NAFTA," *International Business,* October 1992, pp. 42–51.

33. Lester Thurow, *Head to Head* (New York: Murrow, 1992), pp. 56–57.

34. Norman S. Fieleke, "The Uruguay Round of Trade Negotiations: Industrial and Geographical Effects in the United States," *New England Economic Review,* July/August 1995, pp. 3–11.

35. Norio Komuro, "The WTO Dispute Settlement Mechanism: Coverage and Procedures of the WTO Understanding," *Journal of World Trade,* August 1995, pp. 5–95.

36. Grant D. Aldonas, "The World Trade Organization: Revolution in International Trade Dispute Settlements," *Dispute Resolution Journal,* July-September 1995, pp. 73–79.

37. Darryl K. Taft, "Judge Jackson Signs Microsoft Consent Decree in 20 Minutes," *Computer Reseller News,* August 28, 1995, p. 228.

38. David Schneider, "Like a Sieve," *Scientific American,* September 1995, p. 42.

39. Milton Friedman, *Capitalism and Freedom* (Chicago: University of Chicago Press, 1962).

40. Milton Friedman, "The Social Responsibility of Business Is to Increase Its Profits," *New York Times Magazine,* September 1970, pp. 33, 122–126.

41. S. Prakash Sethi, "A Conceptual Framework for Environmental Analysis of Social Issues and Evaluation of Business Response Patterns," *Academy of Management Review,* January 1979, p. 313.

42. Ibid, p. 66.

43. H. Gordon Fitch, "Achieving Corporate Social Responsibility," *Academy of Management Review,* January 1976, p. 45.

44. "Economics: Focus 'How Do You Mean Fair?'" *The Economist,* May 29, 1993, p. 71.

45. Beverly Geber, "Unethical? Who me?" *Training,* October 1995, p. 104.

46. "Do corporate executives think ethics matter?" *HRMagazine,* October 1995, p. 90.

47. "Consumers Eager to Know Values that Guide Business Decisions," *Marketing News,* November 6, 1995, p. 5.

48. Tuomo Takala and Outi Uusitalo, "Retailers' Professional and Professio-Ethical Dilemmas: The Case of Finnish Retailing Business," *Journal of Business Ethics,* November 1995, pp. 893–907.

49. G. Laczniak, "A Framework for Analyzing Marketing Ethics," *Journal of Macromarketing,* 1: 1983, pp. 7–18.

Chapter 4

1. Kenichi Ohmae, *The Borderless World* (New York: HarperPerennial, 1991), p. 10.

2. Lloyd Dobyns and Clare Crawford-Mason, *Quality or Else* (Boston: Houghton Mifflin, 1991), pp. 36–37.

3. Abraham H. Maslow, *Eupsychian Management* (Homewood, Il: Richard D. Irwin, 1965), pp. 264–265.

4. Amanda Bennett, "The Chief Executives in Year 2000 Will Be Experienced Abroad," *The Wall Street Journal,* February 28, 1989, pp. A1, A7.

5. Dobyns and Crawford-Mason, p. 237.

6. "Argentina Starts to Count Again," *Fortune,* February 22, 1993, pp. 102–4.

7. Amy Borrus, Joyce Barnathan, Bruce Einhonr, and Stewart Toy, "China's Gates Swing Open," *Business Week,* June 13, 1994, pp. 52–53.

8. Louis Kraan, "The Risks Are Rising in China," *Fortune,* March 6, 1995, pp. 179–180.

9. Sharon Moshavi, Pete Engardio, Shekhar Hattangadi, and Dave Lindorff, "India Shakes off Its Shackles," *Business Week,* January 30, 1995, pp. 48–49.

10. Lawrence G. Franko, "Global Competition II: Is the Large American Firm an Endangered Species?" *Business Horizons,* November-December 1991, pp. 14–22.

11. Stewart Toy, Susan Chandler, Robert Neff, and Margaret Dawson, "Flying High," *Business Week,* February 27, 1995 pp. 90–91.

12. Ian Katz, "It's Carnival Time for Investors," *Business Week,* March 13, 1995, pp. 53.

13. James Treece, Kathleen Kerwin, and Heidi Dawley, "Ford," *Business Week,* April 3, 1995, pp. 94–104.

14. Jean-Pierre Jeannet and Hubert D. Hennessey, *Global Marketing Strategies* (Boston: Houghton Mifflin, 1992), pp. 16–17.

15. Carla Rapoport, "A Tough Swede Invades the U.S.," *Fortune,* June 29, 1992, pp. 76–82.

16. John S. McClenahen, "How U.S. Entrepreneurs Succeed in World Markets," *Industry Week,* May 2, 1988, pp. 47–49.

17. Joseph V. McCabe, "Outside Managers Offer Packaged Export Expertise," *Journal of Business Strategy,* March–April 1990, pp. 20–23.

18. *Statistical Abstract of the United States,* 1995, p. 814.

19. Ibid, p. 814.

20. Mike McNamee, Susan B. Garland, and Richard S. Dunham, "Are You Better Off Now . . . ," *Business Week,* March 4, 1996, pp. 34–36.

21. Monci Jo Williams, "Rewriting the Export Rules," *Fortune,* April 23, 1990, pp. 89–96.

22. "Japan's Big Appetite for American Foods," *Parade,* June 7, 1992, p. 8.

23. Jerry Flint, "Baby Steps," *Forbes,* April 13, 1992, p. 92.

24. William J. Holstein and Kevin Kelly, "Little Companies, Big Exports," *Business Week,* April 13, 1992, pp. 70–72.

25. Joshua Levine, "The Rabbit Grows Up," *Forbes,* February 17, 1992, pp. 122–27.

26. Shelley Neumeier, "Why Countertrade Is Getting Hotter," *Fortune,* June 29, 1992, p. 25.

27. Matt Schaffer, "Countertrade as an Export Strategy," *Journal of Business Strategy,* May–June 1990, pp. 33–38.

28. Harris Collingwood, "GM Goes Trucking to China, *Business Week,* January 27, 1992, p. 41.

29. Edith Updike and Laxani Nakarmi, "A Movable Feast for Mitsubishi," *Business Week,* August 28, 1995, pp. 50–51.

30. Stratford Sherman, "Are Strategic Alliances Working?" *Fortune,* September 21, 1992, pp. 77–78.

31. James B. Treece, Karen Lowry Miller, and Richard A. Melcher, "The Partners," *Business Week,* February 10, 1992, pp. 102–7.

32. Bart Ziegler, "Light in the East," *Lexington Herald-Leader* September 23, 1990, pp. D1, D5.

33. Kazuo Nukazawa, "Japan and the USA: Wrangling toward Reciprocity," *Harvard Business Review,* May–June 1988, pp. 42–52.

34. Nancy J. Adler, *International Dimensions of Organizational Behavior* (Boston: Kent, 1986), pp. 10–11.

35. "McDonald's Comes to Mohammed," *Lexington Herald-Leader,* December 15, 1994, p. A17.

36. "Tires Recalled So They Don't Tread on Allah," *Lexington Herald Leader* July 25, 1992, p. A3.

37. Harris and Moran, p. 391.

38. John Byrne, Dean Foust, and Lois Therrien, "Executive Pay," *Business Week,* March 30, 1992, pp. 52–58.

39. Robert H. Doktor, "Asian and American CEOs: A Comparative Study," *Organizational Dynamics,* Winter 1990, pp. 46–56.

40. Byrne, Foust, and Therrien, pp. 52–58.

41. Joann S. Lublin, "Younger Managers Learn Global Skills," *The Wall Street Journal,* March 31, 1992, p. B2

42. *Statistical Abstracts of the United States,* 1992, pp. 830–31.

43. Chip Walker, "The Global Middle Class," *American Demographics,* September 1955, pp. 40–46.

44. Louis S. Richman, "Global Growth is on a Tear," *Fortune,* March 20, 1995, pp. 108–119.

45. Vern Terpstra, *International Marketing,* 4th ed. (Hinsdale, Il: Dryden, 1987), pp. 18–19.

46. Richard C. Morais, "Saber Rattling," *Forbes,* March 1, 1993, p. 49.

47. Sak Onkvisit and John J. Shaw, "Marketing Barriers in International Trade," *Business Horizons,* May–June 1988, pp. 64–72.

48. Louis J. Murphy, "Negotiations Are at Work in Geneva to Conclude the Uruguay Round," *Business America,* September 23, 1992, p. 12.

49. Ann H. Hughes, "United States and Canada Form World's Largest Free Trade Area," *Business America,* January 3, 1989, pp. 2–5.

50. Robin Gaines, "FTA Provides Vehicle for Driving into the Future," *Business America,* January 29, 1989, p. 5.

51. Blayne Cutler, "North American Demographics," *American Demographics,* March 1992, pp. 38–42.

52. Gaylon White, "Run for the Border," *Express Magazine,* Summer 1991, pp. 10–13.

53. Kenneth H. Bacon, "With Free-Trade Pact about Wrapped Up, the Real Battle Begins," *The Wall Street Journal,* August 7, 1992, pp. A1, A4.

54. Amy Borrus, "A Free-Trade Milestone, with Many More Miles to Go," *Business Week,* August 24, 1992, pp. 30–31.

55. Louis Richman, "How NAFTA Will Help America," *Fortune,* April 10, 1993, pp. 95–102.

56. Phil Davies, "Europe Unbound," *Express Magazine,* Spring 1992, pp. 16–19.

57. Bill Javetski and Silvia Sansoni, "The Finance Vigilantes Are Closing In," *Business Week,* January 30, 1995, pp. 46–47.

58. Shawn Tully, "Europe 1992," *Fortune,* August 24, 1992, pp. 136–42.

59. Stewart Toy, John Templeman, Richard A. Melcher, John Rossant, and Stanley Reed, "Europe's Shakeout," *Business Week,* September 14, 1992, pp. 44–51.

60. Fred S. Worthy, "Where Capitalism Thrives in China," *Fortune,* March 9, 1992, pp. 71–75.

61. Louis Kraur, "The Death of Hong Kong," *Fortune,* June 26, 1995, pp. 118–132.

62. Joyce Barrathan, Pete Engardio, Lynne Curry, and Bruce Einhorn, "China: The Emerging Economic Powerhouse of the 21st Century," *Business Week,* May 17, 1993, pp. 54–65.

63. Louis Kraur, "Singapore Connection," *Fortune,* March 4, 1996, pp. 172–183.

64. Brian Brenner, Edith Updike, Larry Armstrong, and James B. Treece, "Japan's New Identity," *Business Week,* April 10, 1995, pp. 108–119.

65. Paul Hofheinz, "Russia 1993," *Fortune,* January 25, 1993, pp. 106–8.

66. Rose Brady, Deborah Stead, Richard A. Melcher, Gail E. Scharer, and David Greising, "Why Yeltsin May Prevail," *Business Week,* April 5, 1993, pp. 34–5; and Peter Galuszk, Deborah Stead, and Karen Lowry Miller, "Yeltsin Pushes All His Chips into the Pot," Business Week, October 4, 1993, p. 54.

67. Craig Mellow, "Russia," *Fortune,* April 17, 1995, pp. 145–151.

68. Betsy McKay, "Caddies Supplant Communism as GM Sells Autos in Moscow," *Advertising Age,* June 15, 1992, p. 10.

69. Rick Tetzeli, "Eastern Europe Is One Hot Market," *Fortune,* January 26, 1994, p. 14.

70. "The Quality Glossary," *Quality Progress,* February 1992, pp. 20–29.

71. Marshall Sashkin and Kenneth J. Kiser, *Total Quality Management* (Seabrook, Md.: Docuchon, 1991), p. 26.

72. Andrew Kupfer, "How American Industry Stacks Up," *Fortune,* March 9, 1992, pp. 30–46.

73. "Conversations for the 90s: The Search for Superior Performance," *Harris Trust and Savings Bank,* 1992, pp. 1–19.

74. Robert C. Camp, "Learning from the Best Leads to Superior Performance," *Journal of Business Strategy,* May–June 1992, pp. 3–6.

Chapter 5

1. Ahmad Jarah, "Equipment Selection and Machine Scheduling in General Mail Facilities," *Management Science,* August 1994, pp. 1049–1068.

2. John Gum and James A. Chisman, "An Operation Research Information System," *Computers and Operations Research,* December 1994, pp. 1115–1127.

3. Paul S. Adler, "Time-and-Motion Regained," *Harvard Business Review,* January-February, 1993, pp. 97–108.

4. Ronald Yates, "Total Quality Leadership," *Vital Speeches of the Day,* January 15, 1995, pp. 211–213.

5. C.A. Knox Lovell, "Econometric Efficiency Analysis: A Policy-Oriented Review," *European Journal of Operational Research,* February 2, 1995, pp. 452–461.

6. Paul Hersey and Kenneth Blanchard, *Management of Organizational Behavior* (Englewood Cliffs, N.J: Prentice-Hall, 1993), p. 19.

7. D. Keith Denton, "Creating a System for Continuous Improvement," *Business Horizons,* January/February 1995, pp. 16–21.

8. John J. McManus, "The Theology of Total Quality Management," *Management Sciences,* December 1994, pp. 14–15.

9. Regina Eisman, "Eyes on the Prize," *Incentive,* January 1995, pp. 43–47.

10. Robert Melnbardis, "A Factory Takes Off," *Canadian Business,* November 1994, pp. 44–45.

11. Sandy Jap, "The Employee's Viewpoint of Critical Service Encounters," *Stores,* January 1995, pp. RR4–RR6.

12. Susan K. Bellile, "Benchmarking Sets Standards for Clinical Improvements," *Health Care Strategic Management,* February 1995, pp. 15–16.

13. R.A. Cozier and C.R. Schwenk, "Agreement and Thinking Alike: Ingredients for Poor Decisions," *Academy of Management Executive,* February 1990, pp. 69–74.

14. Shawn P. Steward, "Power to the People," *Cellular Business,* November 1994, pp. 70–72.

15. Ronald Yates, "Total Quality Leadership," op cit.

16. P.A. Renwick and H. Tosi, "The Effects of Sex, Marital Status, and Educational Background on Selected Decisions," *Academy of Management Journal,* March 1978, pp. 93–103; A.A. Abdel Halim, "Effects of Task and Personality Characteristics on Sub-ordinates' Responses to Participative Decision Making," *Academy of Management Journal,* September 1983, pp. 477–484.

17. Glen Whyte, "Decision Failures: Why They Occur and How to Prevent Them," *Academy of Management Journal,* August 1991, pp. 23–31.

18. Leon Festinger, *A Theory of Cognitive Dissonance* (New York: Harper & Row, 1957), Chapter 1.

19. B.M. Staw, "The Escalation of Commitment to a Course of Action," *Academy of Management Review,* October 1981, pp. 577–587.

20. For example, see Staw, "Escalation of Commitment to a Course of Action," op cit.; and Max H. Bazerman and Alan Appelman, "Escalation of Commitment in Individual and Group Decision Making," *Organizational Behavior and Human Decision Processes,* Spring 1984, pp. 141–152.

21. Richard A. Guzzo and James A. Waters, "The Expression of Af-fect and the Performance of Decision-Making Groups," *Journal of Applied Psychology,* February 1982, pp. 67–74; D. Tjosvold and R.H.G. Field, "Effects of Social Context on Consensus and Majority Vote Decision Making," *Academy of Management Journal,* September 1983, pp. 500-506; and Frederick C. Miner, Jr., "Group Versus Individual Decision Making: An Investigation of Performance Measures, Decision Strategies, and Process Losses/Gains," *Organizational Behavior and Human Decision Processes,* Winter 1984, pp. 112–124.

22. Sue Longmann-Czeropski, "Follow the Leader," *Quality Progress,* December 1994, pp. 47–49.

23. Bell, Daniel, "The Coming of Post-Industrial Society," (New York: Basic Books, 1973).

24. Kim, Irene, "The Virtual Engineer: Brainpower to Go," *Chemical Engineering,* October 1995, pp. 35–43.

25. V. Thomas Dock and James C. Wetherbe, *Computer Information Systems for Business* (St. Paul, Minn: West, 1988), p. 36.

26. Alan P. Crawford, "No Computer Is an Island," *American Gas,* November 1994, pp. 24–27.

27. Susan Concilla, "Groupware Competition Targets Lotus Notes Market Dominance," *Info Canada,* January 1995, pp. IC15, IC17.

28. Barbara Darrow, "Lotus Builds on Groupware," *Computer Reseller News,* January 9, 1995, pp. 3, 8.

29. Vernon M. Danielson, "Critical Care in Medical Facility Commu-nications Design," *Consulting-Specifying Engineer,* February 1995, pp. 62–64.

30. Frederick Stodolak and Joseph Carr, "Systems Must Be Compat-ible with Quality Efforts," *Healthcare Financial Management,* June 1992, pp. 72–77.

31. William M. Bulkeley, "Databases Are Plagued by Reign of Error," *The Wall Street Journal,* May 26, 1992, pp. 62–63.

32. Charlotte Dunlap, "Incite Works to Bring Voice, Data, Video to LAN," *Computer Reseller News,* January 23, 1995, p. 48.

33. Jennifer DeJong, "The Right Connections," *Inc.,* Winter 1994, pp. 48–54.

34. Sukumar Rantham and Michael V. Mannino, "Tools for Building the Human-Computer Interface of a Decision Support System," *Decision Support Systems,* January 1995, pp. 35–59.

35. Chetan S. Sankar, Nelson F. Ford, and Michael Bauer, "A DSS User Interface Model to Provide Consistency and Adaptability," *Deci-sion Support Systems,* January 1995, pp. 93–104.

36. Jeffrey P. Stamen, "When Will EIS Deliver?" *Chief Executive,* April 1992, pp. 24–34.

37. Mitch Betts, "Domecq Imports Successful Management Tool," *Computerworld,* October 24, 1994, p. 49.

38. Mark S. Van Clieaf, "Strategy and Structure Follow People: Improving Organizational Performance through Effective Exec-utive Search," *Human Resource Planning,* 1992, pp. 33–46.

39. Tor Guimaraes, Magid Igbaria, and Ming-Te Lu, "The Determinants of DSS Success: An Integrated Model," *Decision Sciences,* March-April 1992, pp. 409–430.

40. Tom Bridge and Yuri Y. Lin, "Expert Systems in Banking," *Cana-dian Banker,* July-August 1992, pp. 20–35.

41. Ronald Henkoff, "Why Every Red-Blooded Consumer Owns a Truck," *Fortune,* May 29, 1995, pp. 86–100.

42. "Internalizing Technology," *American Advertising,* Winter 1994/1995, pp. 8–15.

43. Susan B. Sears, "The Telecommuting Connection," *Credit World,* January/February 1995, pp. 6–8.

44. Paul Korzeniowski, "Telecommuting—A Driving Concern," *Busi-ness Communications Review,* February 1995, pp. 45–48.

45. Jennifer J. Laabs, "Oldsmobile Replaces Zone Offices with Vir-tual Offices," *Personnel Journal,* February 1995, p. 12.

46. Jean S. Bozman, "Out of Sight Not Out of Mind," *Computerworld,* December 26, 1994, pp. 60–61.

47. Amy Cortese, et al., "Cyberspace," *Business Week,* February 27, 1995, pp. 78–86.

48. Jeffrey Ubois, "CFOs in Cyberspace," *CFO: The Magazine for Se-nior Financial Executives,* February 1995, pp. 65–70.

49. Kelly Shermach, "Business Marketers Are Heavy Users of Inter-active Catalogs," *Marketing News,* January 16, 1995, p. 15.

50. Betsy Spethmann and Eric Hollreiser, "Brand Builders," *Brandweek,* February 20, 1995, pp. 18–19.

51. Mark Berniker, "Sony Online Debuts Internet Site," *Broadcasting & Cable,* February 20, 1995, p. 51.

Chapter 6

1. Charles W. Thomas, "Learning from Imagining the Years Ahead," *Planning Review,* May/June 1994, pp. 6–10.

2. Feigenbaum, *Total Quality Control* (New York: McGraw–Hill, 1961), p. 134.

3. Donald Davis, "The Age of Decentralization," *Manufacturing Sys-tems,* January 1995, p. 6.

4. Howard Gleckman and Susan B. Garland, "Downsizing Govern-ment," *Business Week,* January 23, 1995, pp. 34–39.

5. Carole King, "Equitable Tightens Reins on Agencies," *National Underwriter,* January 9, 1995, pp. 7–8.

6. John M. Ivancevich, James H. Donnelley, Jr., and James L. Gib-son, *Management: Principles and Functions,* 5th ed. (Burr Ridge, IL: Richard D. Irwin, 1989), pp. 69–70.

7. James C. Wetherbe, "Principles of Cycle Time Reduction: You Can Have Your Cake and Eat It Too," *Cycle Time Research,* 1995, pp. 1–24.

8. Mary Driscoll, "Never Stop Learning," *CFO,* February 1995, pp. 50–56.

9. "Aligning the Process with the People," *Chief Executive,* March 1995, pp. 8–13.

10. John H. Zimmermann, "The Principles of Managing Change," *HR Focus,* February 1995, pp. 15–16.

11. Timm J. Esque and Thomas F. Gilbert, "Making Competencies Pay Off," *Training,* January 1995, pp. 44–50.

12. Burt Nanus, *Visionary Leadership* (San Francisco, Calif: Jossey-Bass, 1992), p. 8.

13. Laura Rubach, "Total Quality Forum IV Speakers Focus on Change," *Quality Progress*, February 1995, pp. 47–50.

14. Joy Riggs, "Empowering Workers by Setting Goals," *Nation's Business*, January 1995, p. 6.

15. W. Edwards Deming, *Out of the Crisis* (Cambridge, Mass: Massachusetts Institute of Technology Institute for Advanced Engineering Study, 1986), p. 24.

16. William E. Halal, *The New Capitalism* (New York: John Wiley & Sons, 1986), p. 201.

17. For relevant discussions of these and related management problems, see M.L. Gimpl and S.R. Daken, "Management and Magic," *California Management Review*, Fall 1984, pp. 125–136; R.T. Pascale, "The Paradox of Corporate Culture: Reconciling Ourselves to Socialization," *California Management Review*, Winter 1985, pp. 26–41; and Frederick D. Sturdivant, *Business and Society* (Burr Ridge, Ill: Richard D. Irwin, 3rd Edition, 1985).

18. See Joel E. Ross, *Total Quality Management* (Delray Beach: St. Lucie Press, 1993), p. 3.

19. A. Parasuraman, Valerie A. Zeithaml, and Leonard. L. Berry, "A Conceptual Model of Service Quality and Its Implications for Future Research," Working paper 84–106 (Cambridge, Mass: Marketing Science Institute, 1984), pp. 13–14.

20. Judith A. Neal, et al., "From Incremental Change to Retrofit: Creating High Performance Work Systems," *Academy of Management Executive*, February 1995, pp. 42–54.

21. David I. Silvers, "Vision—Not Just for CEOs," *Management Quarterly*, Winter 1994/1995, pp. 10–14.

22. John Humble, David Jackson, and Alan Thomson, "The Strategic Power of Corporate Values," *Long Range Planning*, December 1994, pp. 28–42.

23. David A. Garvin, "Competing on the Eight Dimensions of Quality," *Harvard Business Review*, November-December 1987, pp. 101–109.

24. Alden S. Bean, "Why Some R&D Organizations Are More Productive Than Others," *Research-Technology Management*, January/February 1995, pp. 25–29.

25. Richard M. Cyert and Praveen Kumar, "Technology Management and the Future," *IEEE Transactions on Engineering Management*, November 1994, pp. 333–334.

26. R. Marshall and M. Tucker, *Thinking for a Living: Education and the Wealth of Nations* (New York: Basic Books, 1992), pp. 94–95.

27. Philip B. Crosby, *Quality Is Free* (New York: The New American Library, Inc., 1979), pp. 176–177.

28. Marjorie A. Beasley, "Developing and Applying Effective Personnel Policies," *Food Management*, March 1995, p. 42.

29. Ann M. Thayer, "Chemical Companies Extend Total Quality Management," *Chemical & Engineering News*, February 27, 1995 pp. 15–23.

30. Karen Bemoski, "Carrying on the P&G Tradition," *Quality Progress*, May 1992, p. 24.

31. George Stalk, Jr., and Thomas M. Hout, *Competing against Time: How Time-Based Competition Is Reshaping Global Markets* (New York: The Free Press, 1990).

32. Michael Hammer and James Champy, *Reengineering the Corporation* (New York: HarperCollins Publishers, Inc., 1993), p. 32.

33. James Champy, *Reengineering Management*, (New York: Harper Business, 1995).

34. James C. Wetherbe, "Principles of Cycle Time Reduction: You Can Have Your Cake and Eat It Too," *Cycle Time Research*, 1995, pp. 1–24.

35. J.M. Juran, *Juran on Quality Planning* (New York: The Free Press, 1988), pp. 1–2.

36. J.M. Juran, "The Quality Trilogy," *Quality Progress*, August 1986, pp. 19–24.

37. D. Keith Denton, "Creating a System for Continuous Improvement," *Business Horizons*, January/February, 1995, pp. 16–21.

38. Gary S. Vasilash, "Quality: Better Than Ever," *Productivity*, January 1995, p. 8.

Chapter 7

1. Alfred Chandler, *Strategy and Structure* (New York: McGraw-Hill, 1962), p. 7.

2. Hill and Jones, *Strategy* (Boston: Houghton Mifflin, 1992), p. 7.

3. Robert M. Randall, "Putting the Wow Back in Strategy and Marketing," *Planning Review*, May/June 1995, pp. 20–22.

4. Anita van de Vliet, "Order from Chaos," *Management Today*, November 1994, pp. 62–65.

5. David Levy, "Chaos Theory and Strategy: Theory, Application, and Management Implications," *Strategic Management Journal*, Summer 1994, pp. 167–178.

6. Rosabeth Moss Kanter, "The Best of Both Worlds," *Harvard Business Review*, November/December 1992, pp. 9–10.

7. "Planning the Deals that Generate Value and Gain Advantage," *Mergers & Acquisitions*, March/April 1994, pp. 14–22.

8. Amy Cortese and Ira Sager, "Gerstner at the Gates," *Business Week*, June 19, 1995, pp. 36–38.

9. J. Scott Armstrong and Roderick J. Brodie, "Effects of Portfolio Planning Methods on Decision Making: Experimental Results," *International Journal of Research in Marketing*, January 1994, pp. 73–84. For criticism of this research, see Robin Wensley, "Making Better Decisions," *International Journal of Research in Marketing*, January 1994, pp. 85–90. For Armstrong and Brodie's reply to this criticism, see J. Scott Armstrong and Roderick J. Brodie, "Portfolio Planning Methods," *International Journal of Research in Marketing*, January 1994, pp. 91–93.

10. Tony McCann, "The Rule of 2×2," *Long Range Planning*, February 1995, pp. 112–115.

11. Ida Picker, "Devine Providence at Ford," *Institutional Investor*, March 1995, pp. 55–58.

12. Doug Smock, "New TRW Strategy Boosts Plant Uptime," *Plastics World*, April 1995, pp. 32–38.

13. Noel M. Tichy and Ram Charan, "Lawrence A. Bossidy," *Harvard Business Review*, March/April 1995, pp. 68–78.

14. David M. Reid, "Where Planning Fails in Practice," *Long Range Planning* 23, no. 2 (1990), pp. 85–93.

15. G. David Wallace, "America's Leanest and Meanest," *Business Week*, October 5, 1987, pp. 78–84.

16. Mike Partridge and Lew Perrin, "Assessing and Enhancing Strategic Capability: A Value-Driven Approach," *Management Accounting-London*, June 1994, pp. 28–29.

17. Ethel Auster and Chun Wei Choo, "How Senior Managers Acquire and Use Information in Environmental Scanning," *Information Processing & Management*, September/October 1994, pp. 607–618.

18. Ken Toombs and George Bailey, "How to Redesign Your Organization and Match Customer Needs," *Planning Review*, March/April 1995, pp. 20–24.

19. Pat McLagan and Christo Nel, "The Dawning of a New Age in the Workplace," *Journal for Quality & Participation*, March 1995, pp. 10–15.

20. Charles E. Grantham and Larry E. Nichols, "Distributed Work: Learning to Manage at a Distance," *Public Manager*, Winter 1994/1995, pp. 31–34.

21. Michael P. Wynne, "Ten Trends That Will Change the Way You Lead," *Association Management,* March 1995, pp. 40–44.

22. Howard Isenberg, "The Second Industrial Revolution: The Impact of the Information Explosion," *Industrial Engineering,* March 1995, p. 15.

23. Thomas R. Kuhn, "Seeing Where You Want to Go," *Electric Perspectives,* January/February 1995, pp. 22–28.

24. Mark L. McConkie and R. Wayne Boss, "Using Stories as an Aid to Consultation," *Public Administration Quarterly,* Winter 1994.

25. Mark Maremont, "Kodak's New Focus," *Business Week,* January 30, 1995, pp. 62–68.

26. W. Edwards Deming, *Out of the Crisis* (Cambridge, Mass: MIT Center for Advanced Engineering Study, 1986), p. 175.

27. Tim Stevens, "Where the Rubbermaid Meets the Road," *Industry Week,* March 20, 1995, pp. 14–18.

28. Shawn Tully, "So, Mr. Bossidy," *Fortune,* August 21, 1995, pp. 70–80.

29. Deming, *Out of the Crisis,* p. 120.

30. Philip B. Crosby, *Running Things: The Art of Making Things Happen* (New York: McGraw Hill, 1986) pp. 78–80.

31. "This Month's Focus: The Mission Statement," *Manager's Magazine,* February 1995, pp. 30–31.

32. Charles A. Rarick and John Vitton, "Mission Statements Make Cents," *Journal of Business Strategy,* January/February 1995, pp. 11–12.

33. Peter Wickens, "Why 'How' is as Crucial as 'What,'" *People Management,* March 23, 1995, pp. 38, 39.

34. Michael E. Porter, *The Competitive Advantage of Nations* (New York: The Free Press, 1990), p. 38.

35. Karen Bemowski, "To Boldly Go Where So Many Have Gone Before," *Quality Progress,* February 1995, pp. 29–33.

36. John Guaspari, "A Cure for 'Initiative Burnout,'" *Management Review,* April 1995, pp. 45–49.

37. Arno Penzias, "New Paths to Success," *Fortune,* June 12, 1995, pp. 90–93.

38. Richard McDermott, "Designing and Improving Knowledge Work," *Journal for Quality & Participation,* March 1995, pp. 72–77.

39. George Stalk and Thomas M. Hout, Competing Against Time: How Time-Based Competition is Reshaping Global Markets, New York: Free Press, 1990.

40. Chad Rubel, "It All Comes Down to How Good Your Missiles Are," *Marketing News,* March 27, 1995, p. 7.

41. See Rafael Aguayo, *Dr. Deming: The American Who Taught the Japanese about Quality,* Secaucus, N.J.: Carol Publishing Group, 1990, p. 86.

42. Stephen Marquedent, "QS 9000: Quality Regs for Suppliers," *Quality,* March 1995, p. 26.

43. Katherine O'Dea and Katherine Pratt, "Achieving Environmental Excellence through TQEM Strategic Alliances," *Total Quality Environmental Management,* Spring 1995, pp. 93–108.

44. Jack Szwergold, "Why Most Quality Efforts Fail," *Management Review,* August 1992, p. 5.

45. Gilbert Fuchsberg, "Total Quality Is Termed Only Partial Success," *The Wall Street Journal,* October 1, 1992, p. B7.

Chapter 8

1. Hugh C. Willmott, "The Structuring of Organizational Structures: A Note," *Administrative Science Quarterly,* September 1981, pp. 470–74.

2. Jerry Bowles, "Is American Management Really Committed to Quality?" *Management Review,* April 1992, pp. 42–45.

3. *International Quality Study* (American Quality Foundation and Ernst & Young, 1991), pp. 16–23.

4. Wendy Zellner, Robert D. Hof, Richard Brandt, Stephen Baker, and David Greising, "Go-Go Goliaths," *Business Week,* February 13, 1995, pp. 64–70.

5. Tom Peters, *Thriving on Chaos* (New York: Alfred A. Knopf, 1987), p. 467.

6. James Treece, "Doing It Right, Till the Last Whistle," *Business Week,* April 6, 1992, pp. 58–59.

7. Ira Sager and Amy Cortese, "IBM: Why the Good News Isn't Good Enough," *Business Week,* January 23, 1995, pp. 72–73.

8. Carol J. Loomis, "Dinosaurs?" *Fortune,* May 3, 1993, pp. 36–42

9. Frederick W. Taylor, *Principles of Scientific Management* (New York: Harper & Row, 1911).

10. Scott Madison Paton, "Joseph M. Juran—Quality Legend: Part III," *Quality Digest,* March 1992, pp. 49–58.

11. Lloyd Dobyns and Clare Crawford-Mason, *Quality or Else* (Boston: Houghton Mifflin, 1991), p. 56.

12. Dobyns and Crawford-Mason, p. 60.

13. Marshall Sashkin and Kenneth J. Kiser, *Total Quality Management* (Seabrook, Md.: Ducochon, 1991), p. 118.

14. Brian Dumaine, "The Trouble With Teams," *Fortune,* September 5, 1994, pp. 86–92.

15. Charles Garfield, *Second to None* (Homewood, IL: Business One Irwin, 1992), p. 164.

16. Frank Shippes and Charles C. Manz, "Employee Self-Management without Formally Designated Teams: An Alternative Road to Empowerment," *Organizational Dynamics,* Winter 1992, pp. 48–61.

17. John A. Byrne, "Management," *Business Week,* September 18, 1995, pp. 122–132.

18. Susan Cominiti, "What Team Leaders Need to Know," *Fortune,* February 20, 1995, pp. 93–100.

19. "The Quality Glossary," *Quality Progress,* February 1992, pp. 20–29.

20. Julia Pitta, "It Had to Be Done and We Did It," *Forbes,* April 26, 1993, pp. 148–52.

21. G. Christian Hill and Ken Yamada, "Motorola Illustrates How an Aged Giant Can Remain Vibrant," *The Wall Street Journal,* December 9, 1992, pp. A1, A14.

22. Gilbert Fuchsberg, "Decentralized Management Can Have Its Drawbacks," *The Wall Street Journal,* December 9, 1992, pp. B1, B8.

23. Dana Milbank, "Restructured Alcoa Seeks to Juggle Cost and Quality," *The Wall Street Journal,* August 24, 1992, p. B4.

24. Fuchsberg, pp. B1, B8.

25. Thomas J. Peters and Robert H. Waterman, Jr., *In Search of Excellence* (New York: Warner Books, 1982), pp. 15-16.

26. Sashkin and Kiser, p. 67.

27. Tom Peters, *Thriving on Chaos* (New York: Knopf, 1988), p. 292.

28. Philip B. Crosby, *Quality Is Free* (New York: Mentor, 1979), p. 238.

29. W. Edwards Deming, *Out of the Crisis* (Boston: MIT Center for Advanced Study, 1986), pp. 23–24.

30. V. Daniel Hunt, *Quality in America* (Burr Ridge, IL: Business One Irwin, 1992), pp. 24–25.

31. Douglas McGregor, *The Human Side of Organizations* (New York: McGraw-Hill, 1960), pp. 33–34.

32. Krystal Miller, "At GM, The Three R's Are the Big Three," *The Wall Street Journal,* July 3, 1992, pp. B1, B6.

33. Garfield, pp. 4–5.

34. Thomas A. Stewart, "The Search for the Organization of Tomorrow," *Fortune,* May 18, 1992, pp. 92–98.

35. Robert D. Dewar and Donald P. Simet, "A Level-Specific Prediction of Spans of Control Examining the Effects of Size, Technology, and Specialization," *Academy of Management Journal,* March 1981, pp. 5–24.

36. Rahul Jacob, "The Struggle to Create an Organization for the 21st Century," *Fortune,* April 3, 1995, pp. 90–99.

37. Richard S. Blackburn, "Dimensions of Structure: A Review and Reappraisal," *Academy of Management Review,* January 1982, pp. 59–66.

38. Tom Burns and G. M. Stalker, *The Management of Innovation* (London: Tavistock, 1961).

39. Max Weber, *The Theory of Social and Economic Organization,* trans. A. M. Henderson and Talcott Parsons (New York: Oxford University Press, 1947).

40. C. R. Gullet, "Mechanistic vs. Organic Organizations: What Does the Future Hold?" *Personnel Administration,* 1975, p. 17.

41. Rensis Likert, *The Human Organization* (New York: McGraw-Hill, 1967).

42. Robert C. Ford and Alan W. Randolph, "Cross-Functional Structures: A Review and Integration of Matrix Organization and Project Management," *Journal of Management,* June 1992, pp. 267–94.

43. Martin K. Starr, "Accelerating Innovation," *Business Horizons,* July-August 1992, pp. 44–51.

44. Richard Jaccoma, "Smart Moves in Hard Times," *Dealership Merchandising,* January 1992, pp. 164–67.

45. Paul R. Lawrence, Harvey F. Kolodny, and Stanley M. Davis, "The Human Side of Matrix Organizations," *Organizational Dynamics,* September 1977, p. 4.

46. Stanley M. Davis and Paul R. Lawrence, *Matrix* (Reading, Mass.: Addison-Wesley, 1977).

47. "Dow Draws Its Matrix Again—and Again, and Again," *The Economist,* August 5, 1989, pp. 55–56.

48. Stanley M. Davis and Paul R. Lawrence, "Problems of Matrix Organizations," *Harvard Business Review,* May–June 1978, pp. 131–42.

49. Much of this discussion is based on William G. Ouchi, *The M-Form Society* (Reading, Mass.: Addison-Wesley, 1987), pp. 23–25.

50. Charles C. Snow, Raymond E. Miles, and Henry J. Coleman, "Managing 21st Century Network Organizations," *Organizational Dynamics,* Winter 1992, pp. 5–19.

51. Alex Taylor III, "The Auto Industry Meets the New Economy," *Fortune,* September 5, 1994, pp. 52–60.

52. John Byrne, Richard Brandt, and Otis Port, "The Virtual Corporation," *Business Week,* February 8, 1993, pp. 98–102.

53. Shawn Tully, "The Modular Corporation," *Fortune,* February 8, 1993, pp. 106–15.

54. "Why Networks May Fail," *The Economist,* October 10, 1992, pp. 83–84.

55. Philip Crosby, *Completeness: Quality for the 21st Century* (New York: Dutton, 1992), p. 73.

56. Bruce Brocka and M. Suzanne Brocka, *Quality Management* (Burr Ridge, IL: Business One Irwin, 1992), pp. 49–50.

57. Hal Lancaster, "Managers Beware: You're Not Ready for Tomorrow's Jobs," *The Wall Street Journal,* January 24, 1995, p. B1.

58. Charles Ames, "Sales Soft? Profits Not? It's Time to Rethink Your Business," *Fortune,* June 26, 1995, pp. 143–146.

59. Thomas A. Stewart, "The Corporate Jungle Spawns a New Species: The Project Manager," *Fortune,* July 10, 1995, pp. 179–180.

60. Walter Kiechel III, "A Manager's Career in the New Economy," *Fortune,* April 4, 1994, pp. 68–72.

61. James C. Collins, "Change is Good—But First, Know What Should Never Change," *Fortune,* May 29, 1995, p. 141.

Chapter 9

1. Gabriella Stern, "P&G Will Cut 13,000 Jobs, Shut 30 Plants," *The Wall Street Journal,* July 16, 1993, p. A3.

2. John M. Ivancevich, *Human Resource Management* (Burr Ridge, IL: Richard D. Irwin, 1992), p. 172.

3. Ricky W. Griffin, Task Design: *An Integrative Approach* (Glenview, IL: Scott, Foresman, 1982), p. 91.

4. Frederick W. Taylor, *The Principles of Scientific Management* (New York: Harper & Row, 1911), p. 21.

5. Ronald Henkoff, "The Best Service Workers," *Fortune,* October 3, 1994, pp. 110–122.

6. J. Barton Cunningham and Ted Eberle, "A Guide to Job Enrichment and Redesign," *Personnel,* February 1990, pp. 56–61.

7. Alan Farnhaum, "How to Nurture Creative Sparks," *Fortune,* January 10, 1994, pp. 94–100.

8. Allan W. Farrant, "Job Rotation Is Important," *Supervision,* August 1987, pp. 14–16.

9. Charles R. Walker and Robert H. Guest, *The Man in the Assembly Line* (Cambridge, Mass.: Harvard University Press, 1952).

10. Frederick Herzberg, B. Mausner, and B. Snyderman, *The Motivation to Work* (New York: John Wiley & Sons, 1959).

11. J. Richard Hackman, "Work Design," in *Improving Life at Work,* eds. J. Richard Hackman and J. L. Suttle (Santa Monica, Calif.: Goodyear, 1976), pp. 96–162.

12. J. Richard Hackman and Greg R. Oldham, *Work Redesign* (Reading, Mass.: Addison-Wesley, 1980), pp. 77–82.

13. Hackman and Oldham, pp. 72–77.

14. Michael A. Champion and Chris J. Barger, "Conceptual Integration and Empirical Test of Job Design and Compensation Experiments," *Personnel Psychology,* Autumn 1990, pp. 525–54.

15. Edward E. Lawler, *Pay and Organization Development* (Reading, Mass.: Addison-Wesley, 1981).

16. David A. Ralston, William P. Anthony, and David J. Gustafson, "Employees Love Flextime, But What Does It Do to the Organization's Productivity?" *Journal of Applied Psychology,* May 1985, pp. 272–79.

17. C. W. Proel Jr., "A Survey of the Empirical Literature on Flexible Work Hours: Character and Consequences of a Major Innovation," *Academy of Management Review,* October 1978, pp. 837–53.

18. Randall B. Dunham and John L. Pierce, "The Design and Evaluation of Alternative Work Schedules," *Personnel Administrator,* April 1983, pp. 67–75.

19. Sue Shellenbarger, "Employees Take Pains to Make Flextime Work," *The Wall Street Journal,* August 18, 1992, p. B1.

20. Andrew Erdman, "How to Keep That Family Feeling," *Fortune,* April 6, 1992, pp. 95–96.

21. Edward E. Lawler, *High-Involvement Management* (San Francisco: Jossey-Bass, 1991), p. 37.

22. Joan E. Rigdon, "Using Lateral Moves to Spur Employees," *The Wall Street Journal,* May 26, 1992, pp. B1, B5.

23. Marshall Sashkin and Kenneth J. Kiser, *Total Quality Management* (Seabrook, Md.: Ducochon, 1991), p. 140.

24. V. Daniel Hunt, *Quality in America* (Burr Ridge, IL: Business One Irwin, 1992), pp. 38–39.

25. Joseph A. Petrick and George E. Manning, "How to Manage Morale," *Personnel Journal,* October 1990, pp. 83–88.

26. Stephen L. Perlman, "Employees Redesign Their Jobs," *Personnel Journal,* November 1990, pp. 37–40.

27. Kenneth W. Thomas and Betty A. Velthouse, "Cognitive Elements of Empowerment: An 'Interpretive' Model of Intrinsic Task Motivation," *Academy of Management Review,* October 1990, pp. 666–81.

28. Brian Dumaine, "Unleash Workers and Cut Costs," *Fortune,* May 18, 1992, p. 88.

29. Myron Magnet, "Meet the New Revolutionaries," *Fortune,* February 24, 1992, pp. 94–101.

30. Thomas F. O'Boyle, "A Manufacturer Grows Efficient by Soliciting Ideas from Employees," *The Wall Street Journal,* June 5, 1992, pp. A1, A5.

31. Charles Garfield, *Second to None* (Burr Ridge, IL: Business One Irwin, 1992), p. 179.

32. William Bridges, "The End of the Job," *Fortune,* September 19, 1994, pp. 6–74.

33. Walter Kiechel III, "A Manager's Career in the New Economy," *Fortune,* April 14, 1994, pp. 68–72.

34. Brian O'Reilly, "The New Deal," *Fortune,* June 13, 1994, pp. 44–52.

35. James Aley, "The Temp Biz Boom: Why It's Good," *Fortune,* October 16, 1995, pp. 53–55.

Chapter 10

1. Tom Peters and Robert Waterman, Jr., *In Search of Excellence* (New York: HarperCollins, 1982), p. 64.

2. David E. Bowen and Edward E. Lawler III, "Total Quality-Oriented Human Resource Management," *Organizational Dynamics,* Spring 1992, pp. 29–41.

3. Henry S. Gilbertson, *Personnel Policies and Unionism* (Boston: Ginn, 1950), p. 17.

4. Henry Eilbert, "The Development of Personnel Management in the United States," *Business History Review,* Autumn 1959, pp. 345–64.

5. Jennifer J. Laabs, "Eyeing Future HR Concerns," *Personnel Journal,* January 1996, pp. 28–37.

6. David P. Twomey, *Equal Employment Opportunity Law* (Cincinnati, OH: South-Western Publishing, 1994).

7. L. E. Wynkter, "Business and Race: Multiculturalism Stalls at the National Divide," *The Wall Street Journal,* January 19, 1994, pp. B1–B2.

8. Charlene Marmer Solomon, "Affirmative Action: What You Need to Know," *Personnel Journal,* August 1995, pp. 57–67.

9. Ann C. Wendt and William M. Slonaker, "Discrimination Reflects on You," *HR Magazine,* May 1992, pp. 44–47.

10. *Equal Employment Opportunity Manual for Managers and Supervisors* (Chicago, IL: Commerce Clearing House, 1992).

11. Robert D. Freedman and David E. Bader, "EEO Insights: Managers and Employees Come Together," *HR Focus,* April 1992, p. 19.

12. Gunnar Myrdal, *An American Dilemma: The Negro Problem and American Democracy* (New York: Harper & Row, 1944).

13. Charles Silverman, *Crisis in Black and White* (New York: Random House, 1964).

14. Luis R. Gomez-Mejia, *Fostering a Strategic Partnership Between Operations and Human Resources* (Scarsdale, NY: Work In America Institute, 1994).

15. Carl Quintanilla, "The Old College Try," *The Wall Street Journal,* February 27, 1995, p. R8.

16. Twomey, *op. cit.,* pp. 1–4.

17. Bowen and Lawler, "Total Quality-Oriented," pp. 29–41.

18. Joan E. Rigdon, "Talk Isn't Cheap," *The Wall Street Journal,* February 27, 1995, p. R13.

19. "HR Managers Have the Most Common Causes of Poor Candidate Selection," *Personnel Journal* (July 1995), p. 25.

20. Clive Fletcher, "Ethical Issues in the Selection Interview," *Journal of Business Ethics,* 1992, pp. 361–67.

21. Scott L. Martin and Loren P. Lehnen, "Select the Right Employees through Testing," *Personnel Journal,* June 1992, pp. 47–51.

22. Bently Baranabus, "What Did the Supreme Court Really Say?" *Personnel Administrator,* July–August 1971, pp. 22–25.

23. Todd J. Maurer and Ralph A. Alexander, "Methods of Improving Employment Test Critical Scores Derived by Judging Test Content: A Review and Critique," *Personnel Psychology* (Winter 1992), pp. 727–762.

24. Cory R. Fine, "Video Tests Are the New Frontier in Drug Detection," *Personnel Journal,* June 1992, pp. 152–61.

25. A. J. Whitcomb, "Predicting Performance with Letters of Recommendation," *Public Personnel Management* (Spring 1993), pp. 81–90.

26. M. Brown, "Reference Checking: The Law Is On Your Side," *Human Resource Measurements* (supplement to Personnel Journal), December 1991, pp. 4–5.

27. William Fitzgerald, "Training versus Development," *Training & Development,* May 1992, pp. 81–84.

28. Albert A. Vicere and Virginia T. Freeman, "Executive Education in Major Corporations: An International Survey," *Journal of Management Development,* 1990, pp. 5–16.

29. "1994 Industry Report," *Training,* October 1994, p. 30.

30. Jim M. Graber, Robert E. Breisch, and Walter E. Breisch, "Performance Appraisals and Deming: A Misunderstanding?" *Quality Progress,* June 1992, pp. 59–62.

31. "Performance Appraisal: The Case against a Traditional Tool," *The Maryland Workplace,* Spring 1992, pp. 2–3, 10.

32. George T. Milkovich and J. M. Newman, *Compensation* (Burr Ridge, IL: Irwin, 1993), p. 98.

33. B. J. Dewey, "Changing to Skill-Based Pay," *Compensation and Benefits Review* (January–February 1994), pp. 38–43.

34. Peter V. Leblanc, "Pay for Work: Reviving an Old Idea for the New Customer Focus," *Compensation and Benefits Review* (July–August 1994), pp. 5–14.

35. Joel M. Stern and G. Bennett Stewart III, "Pay-For-Performance: Only the Theory Is Easy," *HR Magazine* (June 1993), pp. 48–49.

36. Andrew G. Spohn, "The Relationship of Reward Systems and Employee Performance," *Compensation and Benefits Management* 6 (Winter 1990), pp. 128–32.

37. Victoria A. Hoevemeyer, "Performance-Based Compensation: Miracle or Waste?" *Personnel Journal,* July 1989, pp. 64–68.

38. Ibid.

39. Stern and Stewart, *op. cit.*

40. John L. Petersen, *The Road to 2015* (Corte Madera, CA: Waite Group Press, 1994), pp. 7–9.

41. Frederick S. Hills, *Compensation Decision Making* (Chicago: Dryden Press, 1994).

42. Carla O'Dell, *People, Performance, and Pay: America Responds to the Competitiveness Challenge* (Scottsdale, Ariz.: American Compensation Association, 1986), p. 108.

43. Milkovich and Newman, *op. cit.,* pp. 10–12.

44. Timothy L. Ross, Larry Hatcher, and Ruth Ann Ross, "The Incentive Switch," *Management Review* 78, no. 5 (May 1989), pp. 22–26.

45. Bowen and Lawler, *op. cit.,* p. 38.

46. Jay R. Schuster and Patricia K. Zingheim, "Improving Productivity through Gainsharing: Can the Means Be Justified in the End?" *Compensation and Benefits Management* 5, no. 3 (Spring 1989), pp. 207–10.

47. Jerry McAdams, "Alternative Rewards: What's Best for Your Organization?" *Compensation and Benefits Management* 6, no. 2 (Winter 1990), pp. 133–39.

48. Dennis Collins, Larry Hatcher, and Timothy J. Ross, "The Decision to Implement Gainsharing: The Role of Work Climate, Expected Outcomes, and Union Status," *Personnel Psychology,* Spring 1993, p. 79.

49. Steven E. Markham, K. Dow Scott, and Beverly L. Little, "National Gainsharing Study: The Importance of Industry Differences," *Compensation & Benefits Review,* January–February 1992, pp. 34–45.

50. David Beck, "Implementing a Gainsharing Plan: What Companies Need to Know," *Compensation & Benefits Review,* January–February 1992, pp. 21–33.

51. S. E. Gross and J. P. Bacher, "The New Variable Pay Programs: How Some Succeed, Why Some Don't," *Compensation and Benefits Review* (January–February 1993), pp. 51–56.

52. Telephone conversation with assistant to Lincoln Electric CEO Richard S. Sabo, August 23, 1993.

53. Employment and Earnings, Bureau of Labor Statistics, U.S. Department of Labor, Tables 73, 79, October 1994.

54. Bickley Townsend and Kathleen O'Neil, "American Women Get Mad," *American Demographics,* August 1990, pp. 26–29, 32.

55. A. L. Otten, "People Patterns," *The Wall Street Journal,* April 15, 1994, p. A1.

56. "Low-Paid, with Children," *The Economist,* July 31, 1993, p. 26; Horrigan and Markey, "Recent Gains in Women's Earnings."

57. Greg Hundley, "The Effects of Comparable Worth in the Public Sector on Public/Private Occupational Relative Wages," *Journal of Human Resources,* Spring 1993, pp. 319–340.

58. Barry Gerhart, "Gender Differences in Current and Starting Salaries: The Role of Performance, College Major, and Job Title," *Industrial and Labor Relations Review* 43 (April 1990), pp. 418–33.

59. "Women in Sales are Closing the Earnings Gap," *Personnel Journal,* July 1995, p. 28.

60. William J. Heisler, W. David Jones, and Philip O. Barnham, Jr., *Managing Human Resources Issues: Confronting Challenges and Choosing Operations* (San Francisco: Jossey-Bass, 1988), p. 77.

61. Robert Buchele and Mark Aldrich, "How Much Difference Would Comparable Worth Make?" *Industrial Relations,* Summer 1985, pp. 222–33.

62. "Controlling the Costs of Employee Benefits," *The Conference Board,* 1992, p. 8.

63. J. E. Santora, "Employee Team Designs Flexible Benefits Program," *Personnel Journal,* April 1994, pp. 30–39.

64. "UAW–GM Child Care Center Hosts Slumber Parties," *Personnel Journal,* April 1995, pp. 28–29.

65. Cynthia D. Fisher, Lyle F. Schoenfeldt, and James B. Shaw, *Human Resource Management* (Boston: Houghton Mifflin, 1993), p. 612.

66. "To Attract Employees, Companies Help with the Kids," *Employee Benefit Planning Review* 43, no. 8 (February 1989), pp. 68, 70.

67. "Stride Rite Halts Its Elder-Care Program," *Personnel Journal,* September 1995, p. 11.

68. Nancy L. Brever, "Emerging Trends for Managing AIDS in the Workplace," *Personnel Journal,* June 1995, pp. 125–134.

69. Brever, *op. cit.,* p. 129.

70. Helen Elkiss, "Reasonable Accommodation and Unreasonable Fears: An AIDS Policy Guide for Human Resource Personnel," *Human Resource Planning,* March 1992, pp. 183–189.

71. Jennifer J. Laubs, "What to Do When Sexual Harassment Comes Calling," *Personnel Journal,* July 1995, pp. 42–53.

72. Kelly Flynn, "Preventive Medicine for Sexual Harassment," *HR Focus,* March 1991, p. 17.

73. Chris Lee, "Sexual Harassment: After the Headlines," *Training,* March 1992, pp. 23–31.

74. Jeffrey P. Englander, "Handling Sexual Harassment in the Workplace," *The CPA Journal,* February 1992, p. 14.

75. Jonathan A. Segal, "Seven Ways to Reduce Harassment Claims," *HR Magazine,* January 1992, pp. 84–86.

76. Nicholas J. Caste, "Drug Testing and Productivity," *Journal of Business Ethics,* April 1992, pp. 301–6.

77. Eric Rolfe Greenberg, "Test-Positive Rates Drop as More Companies Screen Employees," *HR Focus,* June 1992, p. 7.

78. Laura A. Lyons and Brian H. Kleiner, "Managing the Problem of Substance Abuse … Without Abusing Employees," *HR Focus,* April 1992, p. 9.

79. Martha Zetlin, "Corporate America Declares War on Drugs," *Personnel,* August 1991, pp. 1 and 8.

Chapter 11

1. David Woodruff, "The Racy Viper Is Already Winning for Chrysler," Business Week, November 4, 1991, pp. 36–38; and James B. Treece, "How Ford and Mazda Share the Driver's Seat," *Business Week,* February 10, 1992, pp. 94-95.

2. Greg Burns, "The Secrets of Team Facilitation," *Training & Development,* June 1995, pp. 46–52.

3. James P. Womack, Daniel T. Jones, and Daniel Roos, *The Machine That Changed the World* (New York: HarperCollins, 1991), p. 92.

4. Edward E. Lawler, "The New Plant Revolution Revisited," *Organizational Dynamics,* Autumn 1990, pp. 5–14. Lawler estimated the number of plants as "somewhere between 300 and 500" (p. 9).

5. Charles C. Manz, as cited in Joann S. Lublin, "Trying to Increase Worker Productivity, More Employers Alter Management Style," *The Wall Street Journal,* February 13, 1992, p. B1.

6. Lawler's 1980 estimate comes from personal communication, 1990. The 1990 estimate is from his keynote speech at the Self-Management Conference, University of North Texas, Denton, Texas, September 1990. See also *Business Week,* July 10, 1989, p. 59.

7. Cathy Felts, "Taking the Mystery Out of Self-Directed Work Teams," *Industrial Management,* March/April 1995, pp. 21–26.

8. Personal communication with production manager, Diamond Star Motors, Normal, IL, September 1991.

9. Jim Temme, "Team Formation: Don't Just Hope for Success, Plan for It Step by Step," *Plant Engineering,* July 10, 1995, pp. 126, 122

10. Jill L. Sherer, "Tapping into Teams," *Hospitals & Health Networks,* July 5, 1995, pp. 32–36.

11. Kenneth Labich, "Elite Teams," *Fortune,* February 19, 1996, pp. 90–99.

12. Henry P. Sims, Jr., and James W. Dean, Jr., "Beyond Quality Circles: Self-Managing Teams," *Personnel,* January 1985, pp. 25–32.

13. Esther R. Ruffner and Lawrence P. Ettkin, "When a Circle Is Not a Circle," *Advanced Management Journal* 52, no. 2 (1987), pp. 9–15.

14. W. Edwards Deming, *Out of the Crisis.* (Boston: MIT Center For Advanced Engineering Study, 1986), p. 137.

15. Deming, *Out of the Crisis,* p. 47.

16. David McClelland, *The Achieving Society* (Princeton, N.J.: Van Nostrand, 1961). Also see David McClelland and David H. Burnham, " Power Is a Great Motivator," *Harvard Business Review* March-April 1976, pp. 100–10.

17. George Homans, *The Human Group* (New York: Harcourt, Brace, 1950).

18. Robert L. Kahn, D. M. Wolfe, Robert P. Quinn, J. D. Snock, and R. A. Rosenthal, *Organizational Stress: Studies in Role Conflict and Role Ambiguity* (New York: John Wiley & Sons, 1964).

19. Meryl Reis Louis, "Surprise and Sense-Making: What Newcomers Experience in Entering Unfamiliar Organizational Settings," *Administrative Science Quarterly* (June 1980), pp. 226–51.

20. Daniel Feldman, "The Development and Enforcement of Norms," *Academy of Management Review* 9, no. 1 (1984), pp. 47–53.

21. Dennis Organ and Thomas Bateman, *Organizational Behavior* (Plano, Tex.: Business Publications, 1986), p. 473.

22. Marvin Shaw, *Group Dynamics: The Psychology of Small Group Behavior* (New York: McGraw-Hill, 1971), pp. 192–204.

23. Irvin Janis, *Groupthink,* 2d ed. (Boston: Houghton Mifflin, 1982), p. 9.

24. Christopher P. Neck and Gregory Moorhead, "Group think Remodeled: The Importance of Leadership, Time Pressure, and Methodical Decision-Making Procedures," *Human Relations,* May 1995, pp. 537–557.

25. Shirley A. Hopkins and Willie E. Hopkins, "Organizational Productivity 2000: A Work Force Perspective," *SAM Advanced Management Journal,* Autumn 1991, pp. 44–48.

26. Warren E. Watson, Kumar Kamalesh, and Larry K. Michaelson, "Cultural Diversity's Impact on Interaction Process and Performance: Comparing Homogeneous and Diverse Task Groups," *Academy of Management Journal,* June 1993, pp. 590–602.

27. Audrey K. Charlton and Jerry D. Huey, "Breaking Cultural Barriers," *Quality Progress,* September 1992, pp. 47–49.

28. James B. Strenski, "Stress Diversity in Employee Communications," *Public Relations Journal,* August/September 1994, pp. 32–35.

29. Peter Wright, Stephen P. Ferris, Janine S. Hiller, and Mark Kroll, "Competitiveness Through Management of Diversity: Effects on Stock Price Valuation," *Academy of Management Journal,* January 1995, pp. 272–287.

30. Catherine Ellis and Jeffrey A. Sonnenfeld, "Diverse Approaches to Managing Diversity," *Human Resource Management,* Spring 1994, pp. 79–109.

31. Michele Galen and Ann Theresa Palmer, "Diversity: Beyond the Numbers Game," *Business Week,* August 14, 1995, pp. 60–61.

32. Marilyn Gist, Edwin A. Locke, and M. Susan Taylor, "Organizational Behavior: Group Structure, Process, and Effectiveness," *Journal of Management* 13, no. 2 (1987), pp. 237–57.

33. S. G. Harkins, B. Latane, and K. Williams, "Social Loafing: Allocating Effort or Taking It Easy?" *Journal of Experimental Social Psychology* 16 (1985), pp. 457–65.

34. Deming, *Out of the Crisis,* p. 107.

35. Madeline Weiss, "Human Factors: Team Spirit," *CIO* 2, no. 10 (July 1989), pp. 60–62.

36. Lee W. Frederiksen, Anne W. Riley, and John B. Myers, "Matching Technology and Organizational Structure: A Case in White Collar Productivity Improvement," *Journal of Organizational Behavior Management* 6, no. 3–4 (Fall–Winter 1984), pp. 59–80.

37. Raymond Dreyfack, *Making It in Management, the Japanese Way* (Rockville Center, N.J.: Farnsworth, 1982), pp. 159–60.

38. Adapted from Thomas A. Stewart, "McKinsey's Plan," *Fortune,* May 18, 1992, p. 96.

39. This observation was made by Richard Hackman, as cited in Charles C. Manz and Henry P. Sims, Jr., "Leading Workers to Lead Themselves: The External Leadership of Self-Managing Teams," *Administrative Science Quarterly* (March 1987), p. 106.

40. Glenn M. Parker, *Team Player and Teamwork: The New Competitive Business Strategy* (San Francisco: Jossey-Bass, 1990), p. 145.

41. Deming, *Out of the Crisis,* p. 107.

42. Adapted from Gregory E. Huszczo, *Training for Team Building, Training and Development Journal* 44, no. 2 (February 1990), pp. 37–43.

43. Michael Pacanowsky, "Team Tools for Wicked Problems," *Organizational Dynamics,* Winter 1995, pp. 36–51.

44. Harold J. Leavitt and Jean Lipman-Blumen, "Hot Groups," *Harvard Business Review,* July/August 1995, pp. 109–116.

45. Dreyfack, *Making It in Management, the Japanese Way,* p. 155.

46. Philip A. Miscimarra, *Employee Involvement and the Law: Outstanding Issues.* Chicago, April 6, 1992.

47. Jackie Coyle-Shapiro, "The Impact of a TQM Intervention on Teamwork: A Longitudinal Assessment," *Employee Relations,* Vol. 17, ISS-3, 1995, pp. 63–74.

48. Brian O'Reilly, "The New Deal," *Fortune,* June 13, 1994, pp. 44–52.

49. Dean Tjosvold, *Teamwork for Customers* (San Francisco: Jossey-Bass Publications, 1993), pp. 74–75.

50. Faye Rice, "How to Make Diversity Pay," *Fortune,* August 8, 1994, pp. 78–86.

Chapter 12

1. Craig Pinder, *Work Motivation* (New York: Scott Foresman, 1984), p. 8.

2. "Increasing Labor Shortages Give More Power to Workers," *Milwaukee Journal,* January 7, 1990, p. 6D.

3. Douglas McGregor, *The Human Side of Enterprise* (New York: McGraw-Hill, 1960), pp. 33–58.

4. Lyman W. Porter and Edward Lawler, *Managerial Attitudes and Performance* (Burr Ridge, IL: Richard D. Irwin, 1968), p. 17.

5. Abraham H. Maslow, *Motivation and Personality* (New York: Harper & Row, 1954).

6. Frederick Herzberg, Bernard Mausner, and Barbara Bloch Snyderman, *The Motivation to Work* (New York: John Wiley, 1959).

7. See Robert J. House and Lawrence A. Wigdor, "Herzberg's Dual Factor Theory of Job Satisfaction and Motivation: A Review of the Empirical Evidence and a Criticism," *Personnel Psychology* 20 (Winter 1967), pp. 369–89. Also, Joseph Schneider and Edwin A. Locke, "A Critique of Herzberg's Classification System and a Suggested Revision," *Organizational Behavior and Human Performance* 6 (1971), pp. 441–58.

8. David C. McClelland, *The Achieving Society* (Princeton, N.J.: Van Nostrand, 1963).

9. David C. McClelland, *Motivational Trends in Society* (Morristown, N.J.: General Learning Press, 1971), p. 5.

10. Victor H. Vroom, *Work and Motivation* (New York: John Wiley & Sons, 1964).

11. Hugh J. Arnold, "A Test of the Multiplicative Hypothesis of Expectancy-Valence Theories of Work Motivation," *Academy of Management Journal*, March 1981, pp. 128–41.

12. J. Stacy Adams, "Inequity in Social Exchange," in *Advances in Experimental Social Psychology*, vol. 2, L. Berkowitz, ed. (New York: Academic Press, 1965).

13. B. F. Skinner, *Contingencies of Reinforcement: A Theoretical Analysis* (New York: Appleton-Century-Crofts, 1969).

14. Albert Bandura, *Principle of Behavior Modification* (New York: Holt, Rinehart, and Winston, 1969).

15. G. Strauss and L. Sayles, Personnel: *The Human Problems of Management* (Englewood Cliffs, N.J.: Prentice Hall, 1967).

16. R. D. Arvey and J. M. Ivancevich, "Punishment in Organizations: A Review, Propositions, and Research Suggestions," *Academy of Management Review* 5 (1980), pp. 123–32.

17. M. E. Schnake and M. P. Dumler, "Some Unconventional Thoughts on Punishment: Reward as Punishment and Punishment as Reward," *Journal of Social Behavior and Personality* 3 (1989), pp. 89–107.

18. Ibid.

19. Edwin A. Locke and Gary P. Latham, *A Theory of Goal Setting and Task Performance* (Englewood Cliffs, N.J.: Prentice Hall, 1990).

20. E. A. Locke and G. P. Latham, *Goal Setting: A Motivational Technique That Works* (Englewood Cliffs, N.J.: Prentice-Hall, 1984).

21. E. A. Locke, K. M. Shaw, L. M. Saari, and G. P. Latham, "Goal Setting and Task Performance: 1969–1980," *Psychological Bulletin* 90 (1981), pp. 125–52.

22. J. R. Hollenbeck and H. J. Klein, "Goal Commitment and the Goal-Setting Process: Problems, Prospects, and Proposals for Future Research," *Journal of Applied Psychology* 72 (1987), pp. 212–20; and J. R. Hollenbeck, J. R. Williams, and H. R. Klein, "An Empirical Examination of the Antecedents of Commitment to Difficult Goals," *Journal of Applied Psychology* 74 (1989), pp. 18–23.

23. J. M. Ivancevich and M. T. Matteson, *Organizational Behavior and Management* (Burr Ridge, IL: BPI/Irwin, 1990), pp. 164–66.

24. G. P. Latham and G. A. Yukl, "A Review of Research on the Application of Goal Setting in Organizations," *Academy of Management Journal* 18 (1975), pp. 824–45.

25. Lorenzi, 1989, op cit. G. S.-Y. Change and P. Lorenzi, "The Effects of Participative versus Assigned Goal Setting on Intrinsic Motivation," *Journal of Management* 9 (1983), pp. 55–64.

26. From an interview in Robert C. Hill and Sara M. Freedman, "Managing the Quality Process: Lessons from a Baldridge Award Winner. A Conversation with John W. Wallace, Chief Executive Officer of the Wallace Company," *Academy of Management Executive* 6, no. 1 (1992), p. 80.

27. Helen Rheem, "Effective Leadership: The Pygmalion Effect," *Harvard Business Review,* May/June 1995, p. 146.

28. Ron Suskind, "Threat of Cheap Labor Abroad Complicates Decisions to Unionize," *The Wall Street Journal,* July 28, 1992, pp. A1, A6.

29. W. Edwards Deming, *Out of the Crisis* (Cambridge, Mass.: Center for Advanced Engineering Study, Massachusetts Institute of Technology, 1986).

30. Crosby, 1986, pp. 17–20.

31. *The Wall Street Journal,* April 10, 1990, p. 1.

32. Labor letter, *The Wall Street Journal,* May 5, 1992, p. A1.

33. Cited in Dana Wechsler Linden with Vicki Contavespi, "Incentivize Me, Please," *Forbes*, May 27, 1991, pp. 210–11.

34. Crosby, pp. 141, 191.

35. J. R. Bratkovich and B. Steele, "Pay for Performance Boosts Productivity," *Personnel Journal,* January 1989, pp. 78–86.

36. "New Ways to Pay," *The Economist,* July 13, 1991, p. 69.

37. Jay Hall, "Americans Know How to Be Productive If Managers Will Let Them," *Organizational Dynamics,* Winter 1994, pp. 33–46.

38. Kay L. Keck, Thomas W. Leigh, and James G. Lollar, "Critical Success Factors in Captive, Multi-Line Insurance Agency Sales," *Journal of Personal Selling & Sales Management,* Winter 1995, pp. 17–33.

39. Carol Hymowitz, "As Aetna Adds Flextime, Bosses Learn to Cope," *The Wall Street Journal,* June 18, 1990, pp. B1, B5.

40. Mark Alpert, "The Care and Feeding of Engineers," *Fortune*, September 21, 1992, pp. 86–95.

41. J. R. Hackman and G. Oldham, "Development of the Job Diagnostic Survey," *Journal of Applied Psychology* 60 (1975), pp. 159–70. Also see J. R. Hackman and E. E. Lawler, "Employee Reactions to Job Characteristics," *Journal of Applied Psychology* 55 (1971), pp. 259–86.

42. Geoffrey Brewer, "The New Managers," *Incentive,* March 1995, pp. 30–35.

43. Edward E. Lawler III, *High Involvement Management* (San Francisco: Jossey-Bass Publishers, 1991), p. 31.

44. Wayne A. Hochwarter, "When to Use and When Not to Use Gainsharing Programs," *Supervision,* June 1995, pp. 8–11.

45. Thomasina R. Stenhouse, "The Long and Short of Gainsharing," *Academy of Management Executive*, February 1995, pp. 77–78.

46. Donald J. McNerney, "Case Study: Team Compensation," *Management Review,* February 1995, p. 16.

Chapter 13

1. R. Tannenbaum, I. R. Weschler, and F. Massarik, *Leadership and Organization* (New York: McGraw-Hill, 1961), p. 24.

2. Abraham Zaleznick, "Leaders and Managers: Are They Different?" *Harvard Business Review,* 1977, pp. 31–42; Abraham Zaleznick, "Real Work," *Harvard Business Review,* 1989, pp. 52–64; Abraham Zaleznick, *The Managerial Mystique* (New York: Harper & Row, 1989), pp. 1–42.

3. Robert Dahl, "The Concept of Power," *Behavioral Science* 2, 1957, pp. 201–15.

4. John R. P. French, Jr., and Bertram Raven, "The Bases of Social Power," in *Studies in Social Power,* ed. Dorwin Cartright (Ann Arbor: University of Michigan Press, 1959), pp. 150–67.

5. Kenneth A. Gutierrez and Brian H. Kleiner, "Enhancing Personal Power in Organizations," *Agency Sales Magazine,* March 1995, pp. 52–56.

6. Patricia Haddock, "Communicating Personal Power," *Supervision,* July 1995, p. 20.

7. Ralph M. Stogdill, "Personal Factors Associated with Leadership," *Journal of Applied Psychology,* January 1948, pp. 35–71.

8. Edwin E. Ghiselli, "Managerial Talent," *American Psychologist,* October 1963, pp. 631–41.

9. Charles C. DuBois, "Portrait of the Ideal MBA," *The Penn Stater,* October 1992, p. 31.

10. Morgan W. McCall and Michael M. Lombardo, "What Makes a Top Executive?" *Psychology Today,* February 1983, pp. 26–31.

11. Ralph Katz, "Skills of an Effective Administrator," *Harvard Business Review,* October–November 1974, pp. 90–101.

12. Thomas A. Stewart, "Brace for Japan's Hot New Strategy," *Fortune,* September 21, 1992, p. 63.

13. Philip B. Crosby, Running Things: *The Art of Making Things Happen* (New York: McGraw-Hill, 1986), p. 23.

14. Rensis Likert, *New Patterns of Management* (New York: McGraw-Hill, 1961).

15. N. C. Morse and Edward Reimer, "The Experimental Change of a Major Organizational Variable," *Journal of Abnormal and Social Psychology* 52 (1956), pp. 120–29.

16. Edwin A. Fleishman and James G. Hunt, eds., *Current Developments in the Study of Leadership* (Carbondale, IL: Southern Illinois Press, 1973), pp. 1–37.

17. Bill Saporito, "A Week Aboard the Wal-Mart Express," *Fortune*, August 24, 1992, p. 79.

18. Fred E. Fiedler and Martin M. Chemers, *Leadership and Effective Management* (Glenview, IL: Scott, Foresman, 1974).

19. Victor Vroom and Art Jago, "Decision Making as a Social Process: Normative and Descriptive Models of Leader Behavior," *Decision Sciences*, 1974, pp. 743–70.

20. Paul Hersey and Kenneth H. Blanchard, *Management of Organizational Behavior*, 3rd edition (Englewood Cliffs, N.J. Prentice-Hall, 1977).

21. O. M. Irgens, "Situational Leadership: A Modification of Hersey and Blanchard's Model," *Leadership & Organizational Development Journal*, 16, no. 2, (1995), pp. 36–39.

22. Steven Kerr and John M. Jermier, "Substitutes for Leadership: Their Meaning and Measurement," *Organizational Behavior and Human Performance*, December 1978, pp. 375–403.

23. Gary A. Yukl, *Leadership in Organizations* (Englewood Cliffs, N.J.: Prentice Hall, 1989), pp. 108–12.

24. J. M. Burns, *Leadership* (New York: Harper & Row, 1978), pp. 1–52; Bernard M. Bass, *Leadership: Performance Beyond Expectations* (New York: Free Press, 1985), p. 43; and Bernard M. Bass, "Leadership: Good, Better, Best," *Organizational Dynamics*, 1985, pp. 26–40.

25. Patricia Sellers, "Can Home Depot Fix Its Sagging Stock?" *Fortune*, March 4, 1996, pp. 139–146.

26. The material on self-leadership has been adapted from Henry P. Sims, Jr., and Peter Lorenzi, *The New Leadership Paradigm: Social Learning and Cognition in Organizations* (Newbury Park, Calif.: Sage, 1992).

27. Marshall Sashkin, "Participative Management Remains an Ethical Imperative," *Organizational Dynamics*, Spring 1986, pp. 62–75.

28. W. Baldwin, "This Is the Answer," *Forbes*, July 5, 1982, p. 52.

29. Charles C. Manz and Henry P. Sims, Jr., *Superleadership* (New York: Berkeley, 1990), pp. xviii.

30. Howard Weiss, "Subordinate Imitation of Supervisor Behavior: The Role of Modeling in *Organizational Socialization*," *Organizational Behavior and Human Performance* 19 (1977), pp. 89–105.

31. M. Sashkin, "Participative Management Is an Ethical Imperative," *Organizational Dynamics* 12 (1984), pp. 5–22.

32. Martha T. Moore, "Sorting Out a Mess," *USA Today*, April 10, 1992, p. 5B.

33. H. B. Braiker, "The Power of Self-Talk," *Psychology Today*, December 1989, p. 23. See also D. D. Burns, *The Good Feeling Handbook* (New York: William Morrow, 1989).

34. Gervase R. Bushe, "Cultural Contradictions of Statistical Process Control in American Manufacturing Organizations," *Journal of Management* 14, no. 1 (1988), pp. 19–31.

35. See M. Porter, "Why Nations Triumph," *Fortune*, March 12, 1990, pp. 94–98. Also, J. Dreyfuss, "Get Ready for the New Work Force," *Fortune*, April 23, 1990, pp. 165, 168, 172, 176, 180–81.

36. William B. Johnston and Arnold E. Packer, *Workforce 2000: Work and Workers for the 21st Century* (Indianapolis, Ind.: Hudson Institute, 1987).

37. Patricia W. Hamilton, "What a Changing Work Force Means for Business," *D&B Reports*, January–February 1992, pp. 20–23.

38. Taylor H. Cox and Stacy Blake, "Managing Cultural Diversity: Implications for Organizational Competitiveness," *Academy of Management Executive*, August 1991, pp. 45–56.

39. Tim Turner, "A Woman for All Seasons: An Interview with Betty Friedan," *Hemispheres*, August 1993, pp. 19–23.

40. Charles Garfield, *Second to None* (Burr Ridge, IL: Business One Irwin, 1992), pp. 286–91.

41. R. Roosevelt Thomas, Jr., *Beyond Race and Gender* (American Management Association, 1991), pp. 163–66.

42. Lee Gardenswartz and Anita Rowe, *Managing Diversity* (Homewood, IL: Business One Irwin, 1993), p. 4.

43. Jaclyn Fierman, "Winning Ideas from Maverick Managers," *Fortune*, February 6, 1995, pp. 66–80.

44. F. A. Manske, Jr., *Secrets of Effective Leadership* (Memphis, TN: Leadership Education and Development, Inc., 1987).

45. Robert L. Katz, "Skills of an Effective Administration," *Harvard Business Review*, September–October, 1974, pp. 23–35.

46. Thomas A. Stewart, "The Nine Dilemmas Leaders Face," *Fortune*, March 18, 1996, pp. 112–113.

Chapter 14

1. V. Daniel Hunt, *Quality in America* (Burr Ridge, IL: Business One Irwin, 1992), p. 186.

2. Chester Barnard, *The Functions of the Executive* (Cambridge, Mass.: Harvard University Press, 1938).

3. Frank M. Corrado, *Getting the Word Out* (Burr Ridge, IL: Business One Irwin, 1993), p. 10.

4. E. A. More and R. K. Laird, *Organisations in the Communications Age* (Sidney, Australia: Pergamon Press, 1985), p. 1.

5. W. Edwards Deming, *Out of the Crisis* (Cambridge, Mass.: Center for Advanced Engineering Study, Massachusetts Institute of Technology, 1986), p. 78.

6. Charlie Quinby, Lynd Parker, and Arnold N. Weimerskirch, "How, Exactly, Do You Communicate Quality?" *Quality Progress*, June 1991, pp. 52–54.

7. Robert K. Cooper, *The Performance Edge* (Boston: Houghton Mifflin, 1991), p. 70.

8. Sharon Vanriper, Diana Cprek, and Maureen Thompson, "Building an Empowered Work Team," *Nursing Management*, June 1995, pp. 48F–48J.

9. D. L. Kanter and P. H. Mirvis, *The Cynical Americans, Living and Working in an Age of Discontent and Disillusion* (San Francisco: Jossey-Bass, 1989).

10. "CEOs Say They Neglect Employee Communications," *Public Relations Journal*, May 1990, p. 13.

11. Marshall Sushkin and Kenneth J. Kiser, *Total Quality Management* (Seabrook, Md.: Ducochon Press, 1991), pp. 74–75.

12. Stephen R. Axley, "Managerial and Organizational Communication in Terms of the Conduit Metaphor," *Academy of Management Review*, July 1984, pp. 428–37.

13. Sim B. Sitkin, Kathleen M. Sutcliffe, and John R. Barrios-Choplin, "A Dual-Capacity Model of Communication Choice in Organizations," *Human Communications Research*, June 1993, pp. 563–98.

14. Richard Daft and Robert H. Lengel, "Information Richness: A New Approach to Managerial Behavior and Organization

Design," in *Research in Organizational Behavior*, ed. Barry N. Staw and Larry L. Cummings (Greenwich, Conn.: JAI Press, 1984), pp. 196–97.

15. Richard Daft, Robert H. Lengel, and Linda Klebe Trevino, "Message Equivocality, Media Selection, and Manager Performance: Implications for Information Systems," *MIS Quarterly* 1 (1987), pp. 353–64.

16. Richard K. Allen, *Organizational Management through Communication* (New York: Harper & Row, 1977), p. 2.

17. Howard S. Gitlow and Shelly J. Gitlow, *The Deming Guide to Quality and Competitive Position* (Englewood Cliffs, N.J.: Prentice-Hall, 1987), p. 147–48.

18. Gary L. Kreps, *Organizational Communication* (New York: Longman, 1986), pp. 53–54.

19. K. Weick, *The Social Psychology of Organizing* (Reading, Mass.: Addison-Wesley, 1969).

20. Cheryl Hamilton and Cordell Parket, *Communicating for Results* (Belmont, Calif.: Wadsworth, 1990), p. 127.

21. S. M. Jourard, *Disclosing Man to Himself* (Princeton, N.J.: Van Nostrand, 1968).

22. Ted Holden and Suzanne Woolley, "The Delicate Art of Doing Business in Japan," *Business Week*, October 2, 1989, p. 120.

23. Stephen R. Covey, *The 7 Habits of Highly Effective People* (New York: Fireside, 1990), p. 237.

24. John R. Ward, "Now Hear This," *IABC Communication World*, July 1990, pp. 20–22.

25. John Churchill, "The Banker as Financial Counsellor," *Canadian Banker*, January/February 1995, pp. 36–37.

26. Marjorie Brody, "Listen Up! Do You Really Hear What People Are Saying," *American Salesman*, June 1994, pp. 14–15.

27. Patricia Buhler, "Managing in the 90s: The Other Component of Communication—Listening," *Supervision*, May 1992, pp. 19–20, 26.

28. Carol Birkland, "Huh? Or the Art of Good Communication," *Fleet Equipment*, January 1992, pp. 36–37.

29. Larry D. Lauer, "How to Manage Internal Conflict," *Nonprofit World*, November/December 1994, pp. 46–48.

30. Kenneth R. Thompson, "A Conversation with Robert W. Galvin," *Organizational Dynamics*, Spring 1992, pp. 56–69.

31. Kambiz Farahmand, Raul Becerra, and Juan Ramon Green, "ISO 9000 Certification: Johnson Controls' Inside Story," *Industrial Engineering*, September 1994, pp. 22–34.

32. John Naisbitt and Patricia Aburdene, *Re-inventing the Corporation* (New York: Warner Books, 1985), p. 62.

33. Timothy Galpin, "Pruning the Grapevine," *Training and Development*, April 1995, pp. 28–33.

34. William W. Hull, "Beating the Grapevine to the Punch," *Supervision*, August 1994, pp. 17–19.

35. Polly LaBarre, "The Other Network," *Industry Week*, September 19, 1994, pp. 33–36.

36. Tom Varian, "Communicating Total Quality inside the Organization," *Quality Progress*, June 1991, pp. 30–31.

37. Cooper, p. 5.

38. Les Landes, "Total Quality & Communications: Principles and Opportunities," *Executive Speeches*, January 1991, pp. 19–25.

39. Quinby, Parker, and Weimerskirch, pp. 52–54.

40. Varian, pp. 30–31.

41. Karl J. Skutski, "Conducting a Total Quality Communications Audit," *Public Relations Journal*, April 1992, pp. 32, 29–31.

42. Jean L. Farinelli, "Motivating Your Staff," *Public Relations Journal*, March 1992, pp. 18–20.

43. Patrick J. McKeand, "GM Division Builds a Classic System to Share Internal Information," *Public Relations Journal*, November 1990, pp. 24–26, 41.

44. Sushkin and Kiser, p. 30.

45. Anne B. Fisher, "Making Change Stick," *Fortune*, April 17, 1995, pp. 121–130.

46. John P. Kotter and Leonard A. Schlessinger, "Choosing Strategies for Change," *Harvard Business Review*, March–April 1979, pp. 106–16.

47. Richard G. Charlton, "The Decade of the Employee," *Public Relations Journal*, January 1990, pp. 26, 36.

48. Kotter and Schlessinger, p. 112.

49. Thomas A. Stewart, "Rate Your Readiness to Change," *Fortune*, February 7, 1994, pp. 106–110.

50. Eleanor Davidson, "Communicating with a Diverse Workforce," *Supervisory Management*, December 1991, pp. 1–2.

51. "Public Relations Must Pave the Way for Developing a Diversified Workforce," *Public Relations Journal*, January 1992, pp. 12–13.

52. More and Laird, p. 163.

53. Skutski, pp. 32, 29–31.

54. Michael S. Hunn and Steven I. Meisel, "Internal Communication: Auditing for Quality," *Quality Progress*, June 1991, pp. 56–60.

55. Howard Gross, "Promises, Hopes, and Hyperbole: Adoption of New Information Technologies," *IEEE Transactions on Professional Communication*, June 1995, pp. 118–122.

56. Mitch Kozikowski, "Bring the Craft of PR into the Reality of Today," *Communication World*, April 1995, p. 23.

57. Cliff McGoon, "What Role Should We Play Today," *Communication World*, August 1994, pp. 12–16.

58. Gary F. Grates, "Communication in the Second Half of the Nineties: Strategy—Not Creativity—Drives Everything," *Communication World*, April 1995, pp. 16–19.

Chapter 15

1. Joseph M. Juran, *Juran on Leadership for Quality: An Executive Handbook* (New York: Free Press, 1989), p. 145.

2. Walter A. Shewhart, *Statistical Method from the Viewpoint of Quality Control* (Washington, D.C.: Graduate School, U.S. Dept. of Agriculture, 1939), p. 1.

3. W. Edwards Deming, *Out of the Crisis* (Cambridge, Mass.: Center for Advanced Engineering Study, Massachusetts Institute of Technology, 1986), Chapter 9, esp. pp. 276–77.

4. Ibid, pp. 290–91, 294.

5. Ibid.

6. Michel Perigord, *Achieving Total Quality Management* (Cambridge, Mass.: Productivity Press, 1990), Chapter 8.

7. Ibid, p. 121.

8. Patricia Sellers, "Companies That Serve You Best," *Fortune*, May 31, 1993, pp. 74–88.

9. Howard Rothman, "The Power of Empowerment," *Nation's Business*, June 1993, pp. 49, 52.

10. Deming, *Out of the Crisis*, p. 28.

11. Kathleen Kerwin and David Woodruff, "Is Detroit Pulling Up to Pass?" *Business Week*, January 11, 1993, p. 63.

12. See John M. Ivancevich and William Glueck, *Foundations of Personnel*, 5th ed. (Burr Ridge, IL: Richard D. Irwin, 1992).

13. Peter Lorange and Declan Murphy, "Considerations in Implementing Strategic Control," *Journal of Business Strategy*, Spring 1984, pp. 27–35.

14. George Schreyogg and Horst Stenman,"Strategic Control: A New Perspective," *Academy of Management Review,* January 1987, pp. 91–103.

15. Luis R. Gomez Mejia, Henry Tosi, and Timothy Hinkin,"Managerial Control, Performance, and Executive Compensation," *Academy of Management Journal,* March 1987, pp. 51–70.

16. Ivancevich and Glueck, *Foundations of Personnel,* Chapter 2.

17. Joel G. Siegel and Matthew S. Rubin,"Corporate Planning and Control through Variance Analysis," *Managerial Planning,* September–October, 1984, pp. 33–36.

18. Michael R. Walls,"Integration Business Strategy and Capital Allocution: An Application of Multi-Objective Decision Making," *Engineering Economist,* Spring 1995, pp. 247–266.

19. Joseph Spiers,"The Most Important Economist Event of the Decade," *Fortune,* April 3, 1995, pp. 33–40.

20. Frank Collins, Paul Munter, and Don W. Finn,"The Budgeting Games People Play," *Accounting Review,* January 1987, pp. 29–49.

21. Lawrence L. Stenmetz and H. Ralph Todd, Jr., *First-Line Management,* 3d ed. (Burr Ridge, IL: Richard D. Irwin, 1986).

22. Burton A. Kolb and Richard DeMong, *Principles of Financial Management,* 2d ed. (Burr Ridge, IL: Richard D. Irwin, 1988); and Diane Harrington and Brent D. Wilson, *Corporate Financial Analysis,* 2d ed. (Burr Ridge, IL: Richard D. Irwin, 1986).

23. Avi Rushinek and Sara F. Rushinek,"Using Financial Ratios to Predict Insolvency," *Journal of Business Research,* February 1987, pp. 74–77.

24. Ralph H. Garrison, *Managerial Accounting: Concepts for Planning, Control, Decision Making,* 5th ed. (Burr Ridge, IL: Richard D. Irwin, 1988).

25. Stephen G. Green and M. Ann Welsh,"Cybernetics and Dependence: Reframing the Control Concept," *Academy of Management Review,* April 1988, pp. 287–301.

26. Lynne B. Hare, Roger W. Hoerl, John D. Hromi, and Ronald D. Snee,"The Role of Statistical Thinking in Management," *Quality Progress,* February 1995, pp. 53–60.

27. Gabriel A. Pall, *Quality Process Management* (Englewood Cliffs, N.J.: Prentice-Hall, 1987), p. 94.

28. Mark Bryson,"Experimental Design Boosts Production Yields," *Chemical Engineering,* July 1995, p. 155.

29. Kevin M. Barry,"Measuring Continuous Improvement in a Project Office," July 1995, pp. 19–21.

30. Chuen-Sheng,"A Multi-Layer Neural Network Model for Detecting Changes in the Process?" *Computers & Industrial Engineering,* January 1995, pp. 51–61.

31. Lloyd Dobyns and Clare Crawford Mason, *Quality or Else* (Boston: Houghton Mifflin, 1991), Chapter 6.

32. Sellers,"Companies That Serve You Best," p. 76.

33. Thomas Pyzdek, *What Every Manager Should Know about Quality* (New York: Marcel Dekker, 1991), p. 3.

34. A.V. Feigenbaum, *Total Quality Control* (New York: McGraw-Hill, 1991); Mary Walton, *The Deming Management Method* (New York: Perigree, 1986), pp. 122–30; and Kaoru Ishikawa, *What Is Total Quality Control?* (Englewood Cliffs, N.J.: Prentice Hall, 1985), pp. 90–94.

35. Feigenbaum, *Total Quality Control,* p. 5.

36. "Whole System Change," *Executive Excellence,* July 1995, pp. 13–14.

37. Ishikawa, *What Is Total Quality Control?* p. 44.

38. Feigenbaum, *Total Quality Control,* p. 828.

39. Ibid, pp. 828–33.

40. Pyzdek, *What Every Manager Should Know about Quality,* pp. 3–4.

41. Thomas J. Peters and Robert H. Waterman, *In Search of Excellence* (New York: Harper & Row, 1982).

42. "Productivity from Control," *Nation's Business,* June 1993, p. 38.

43. Karen Lowry Miller,"The Factory Guru Tinkering with Toyota," *Business Week,* May 17, 1993, pp. 95–97.

44. Deming, *Out of the Crisis,* pp. 380–87.

45. Juran, *Juran on Leadership for Quality: An Executive Handbook,* Chapter 5.

46. Ibid., pp. 147–48.

47. Ibid., pp. 148–50.

48. Feigenbaum, *Total Quality Control,* pp. 204–9.

49. See George E. Wollner,"The Law of Producing Quality," *Quality Progress,* January 1992, pp. 35–40.

50. Gilbert Fuchsburg,"Total Quality Is Deemed Only Partial Success," *The Wall Street Journal,* October 1, 1992, pp. B1, B7.

51. Chris Rauwendaal,"Statistical Process Control in Extrusion," *Plastics World,* March 1995, pp. 59–64.

52. John Schriefer,"The Rewards of Quality," *Iron Age New Steel,* April 1995, pp. 3–32.

53. Dana R. Hermanson and Heather M. Hermanson,"The Internal Control Paradox: What Every Manager Should Know," *Review of Business,* Winter 1994, pp. 29–32.

Chapter 16

1. Alicia Swasey and Carol Hymowitz,"The Workplace Revolution," *Wall Street Journal Reports,* February 9, 1990, p. R6.

2. Vincent A. Mabert,"Operations in the American Economy: Asset or Liability," *Business Horizons,* July–August 1992, pp. 3–5.

3. Samuel Huber, *Efficiency and Uplift* (Chicago: University of Chicago Press, 1964).

4. Richard B. Chase and Nicholas J. Aquilano, *Production and Operations Management: A Life Cycle Approach* (Burr Ridge, IL: Richard D. Irwin, 1989), pp. 19–20.

5. "Automated Line Offers Consistency and Flexibility," *Modern Paint & Coatings,* July 1995, p. 24.

6. Erwin S. Stanton, *Reality-Centered People Management: Key to Improved Productivity* (New York: AMACOM, 1982).

7. Joseph H. Boyett and Henry P. Conn, *Workplace 2000* (New York: E. P. Dutton, 1991), pp. 23–27.

8. Peter F. Drucker,"The Emerging Theory of Manufacturing," *Harvard Business Review,* May–June 1990, pp. 94–102.

9. Gery Reiner,"Lessons from the World's Best Product Developers," *The Wall Street Journal,* August 6, 1990, p. A12.

10. Gary Slutsker,"Struggling against the Tide," *Forbes,* November 12, 1990, pp. 312–14.

11. Ani Hadjian,"Andy Grove: How Intel Makes Spending Pay Off," *Fortune,* February 22, 1993, pp. 56–61.

12. William J. Stevenson, *Production and Operations Management* (Burr Ridge, IL: Richard D. Irwin, 1990), p. 624.

13. Peter Turnbull, Nick Oliver, and Barry Wilkinson,"Buyer-Supplier Relations in UK Automotive Industry," *Strategic Management Journal,* February 1992, pp. 159–68.

14. Sal Aliotta,"Do You Really Want to Distribute?" *Industrial Distribution,* March 1995, p. 88.

15. Ronald Henkoff,"Delivering the Goods," *Fortune,* November 28, 1994, pp. 34–37.

16. Philip B. Crosby, *Quality Is Free* (New York: McGraw-Hill, 1979), pp. 200–1.

17. Mark Maremont, Thane Peterson, and Lori Bongiorno, "These Repair Jobs Are Taking a Little Longer than Expected," *Business Week,* April 27, 1992, pp. 117–21.

18. Michael Fredericks, "MRP Into the Next Century," *Logistics Focus,* June 1995, pp. 36–37.

19. Tim Studt, "CAD Systems Get Even Smarter, Speed Up Product Development," *R&D,* April 1995, pp. 25–27.

20. William H. Miller, "CADs Becoming Universal," *Industry Week,* February 20, 195, p. 22.

21. Robert Mills, "The Inevitability of CAE," *Computer-Aided Engineering,* July 1995, p. 4.

22. Fleur Templeton, "May Tailor? Kind of a By-the-Numbers-Type—But Good," *Business Week,* May 11, 1992, p. 101.

23. James Aaron Cooke, "Agility Counts! Part IV," *Traffic Management,* August 1995, pp. 27–31.

24. Barbara Schmitz, "Under-the-Wire Designs," *Computer-Aided Engineering,* July 1995, p. 8.

25. Mark Hornung and Richard A. Moran, *Opportunities in Microelectronic Careers* (Lincolnwood, IL: NTC Group, 1985), pp. 27–28.

26. "A Robot Revolution," *Modern Materials Handling,* July 1995, p. 13.

27. Fleur Templeton, "A Dial-Twisting Robot That Keeps Testing Gear Honest," *Business Week,* July 6, 1992, p. 65.

28. David M. Upton, "What Really Makes Factories Flexible?" *Harvard Business Review,* July/August 1995, pp. 74–79.

29. Susan Moffat, "Personalized Production," *Fortune,* October 22, 1990, pp. 132–35.

30. Philip B. Crosby, *Completeness: Quality for the 21st Century* (New York: E. P. Dutton, 1992), p. 116.

31. David Woodruff, "A New Era for Auto Quality," *Business Week,* October 23, 1990, pp. 84–96.

32. "Epidemic of Recalls Embarrasses Japanese Electronics Industry," *Houston Post,* March 29, 1990, p. A10.

33. Neal Templin, "Despite Big 3's Claims of Higher Quality, Japanese Still Boast Fewer Safety Recalls," *The Wall Street Journal,* March 24, 1992, pp. B1, B10.

34. Crosby, 1979, pp. 101–7.

35. Marion Mills Steeples, *The Corporate Guide to the Malcolm Baldrige National Quality Award* (Burr Ridge, IL: Business One Irwin, 1992), p. 312.

36. Cyndee Miller, "U.S. Firms Lag in Meeting Global Quality Standards," *Marketing News,* February 15, 1993, pp. 1, 6.

37. Sherie Posesorski, "Here's How to Put Statistical Process Control to Work for You," *Canadian Business,* December 1985, p. 163.

38. Allen E. Puckett, "People Are the Key to Productivity," *Industrial Management,* September–October 1985, pp. 12–15; and Philip E. Atkinson and Brian W. Murray, "Managing Total Quality," *Management Services,* October 1985, pp. 18–21.

39. William R. Landwehr, "Focus on Benchmarking," *Plant Engineering,* June 5, 1995, pp. 120, 118.

40. Gary Beasely and Joseph Cook, "The 'What,' 'Why,' and 'How' of Benchmarking," *Agency Sales Magazine,* June 1995, pp. 52–56.

41. Robert C. Camp, "Learning from the Best Leads to Superior Performance," *Journal of Business Strategy,* May–June 1992, pp. 3–6.

42. Charles Garfield, *Second to None* (Burr Ridge, IL: Business One Irwin, 1992), pp. 215–17.

43. "Quality Circles: A Worthy Tool to Use under the QIP Umbrella," *Quality Update,* Fall 1990, pp. 26–29.

44. Anatoly Brylov, "Aeroflot Taking the Dollar under Its Wing," *Business in the USSR,* September 1990, pp. 38–39.

45. Richard Melcher and Rose Brady, "Soviet Breakup? Coup? That's Minor Turbulence," *Business Week,* February 17, 1992, pp. 70–72.

46. Jay Matthews and Peter Katel, "The Cost of Quality," *Newsweek,* September 7, 1992, pp. 48–49.

47. Gilbert Fuchsberg, "Total Quality Is Termed Only Partial Success," *The Wall Street Journal,* October 1, 1992, pp. B1, B7.

48. Crosby, *Completeness,* p. xv.

49. Ibid.

50. Joseph Spiers, "Productivity Looks Promising," *Fortune,* March 9, 1992, pp. 21–22.

51. Edmund Faltermayer, "Invest or Die," *Fortune,* February 22, 1993, pp. 42–52.

52. Thomas J. Peters and Robert H. Waterman, Jr., *In Search of Excellence: Lessons from America's Best-Run Companies* (New York: Harper & Row, 1982), p. 249.

53. Ibid., p. 239.

54. Albert R. Karr, "The Corporate Race Belongs to the Safest," *The Wall Street Journal,* July 5, 1990, pp. B1, B5.

55. Tom W. Ferguson, "Job Injury Burden Could Disable Some Companies," *The Wall Street Journal,* July 10, 1990, p. A17.

56. Michael D. Lemonick, "The Ozone Vanishes," *Time,* February 17, 1992, pp. 60–63.

57. Nancy C. Morey and Robert V. Morey, "Business and the Environment in the 21st Century," *Business Forum,* Winter 1992, pp. 51–55.

58. Paul Hofheinz, "The New Soviet Threat: Pollution," *Fortune,* July 27, 1992, pp. 110–14.

59. Caleb Solomon, "Refiner Begins Making Gasoline from Used Oil," *The Wall Street Journal,* February 11, 1992, pp. B1–B2.

60. Dianna Solis and Sonia L. Nazario, "U.S., Mexico Take on Border Pollution," *The Wall Street Journal,* February 25, 1992, pp. B1, B8.

61. Jeffrey Taylor, "New Rules Harness Power of Free Markets to Curb Air Pollution," *The Wall Street Journal,* April 14, 1992, pp. A1, A4.

62. Dori Jones Yang and Andrea Rothman, "Boeing Cuts Its Altitude as the Clouds Roll In," *Business Week,* February 18, 1993, p. 25.

63. Zachary Schiller, "GE's Appliance Park: Revise, or Pull the Plug?" *Business Week,* February 8, 1993, p. 30.

64. "Forward Conveyor Speed Testing at Hotpoint," *Material Handling Engineering,* August 1995, p. 76.

65. Norman C. Remich, Jr., "A Kentucky Thoroughbred That Is Running Strong," *Appliance Manufacturer,* July 1995, pp. GEA3–GEA6.

66. Bradford Wernle, "How Chrysler Builds on the 20% Solution," *Advertising Age,* April 3, 1995, pp. s-7, s-12.

67. Joseph C. Day, "The Power of Lean," *Chief Executive,* March 1995, pp. 50–51.

Chapter 17

1. Paula M. Saunders, Robert F. Scherer, and Herbert E. Brown, "Delighting Customers by Managing Expectations for Service Quality: An Example from the Optical Industry," *Journal of Applied Business Research,* Spring 1995, pp. 101–109.

2. James Brian Quinn and Christopher E. Gagnon, "Will Services Follow Manufacturing into Decline?" *Harvard Business Review,* November–December 1987, pp. 95–103.

3. Steven J. Skinner, *Marketing* (Boston: Houghton Mifflin, 1990), p. 631.

4. Joan O. Fredericks and James M. Salter, "Beyond Customer Satisfaction," *Management Review,* May 1995, pp. 29–32.

5. *Statistical Abstracts of the United States,* 1992, p. 429.

6. Gustavo Vargas and Shasem H. Manoochehri, "An Assessment of Operations in U.S. Service Firms," *International Journal of Operations & Production Management,* 1995, 15(1), pp. 24–37.

7. Rob Muller, "Training for Change," *The Canadian Business Review,* Spring 1995, pp. 16–19.

8. Peter K. Mills and James H. Morris, "Clients as `Partial' Employees of Service Organizations: Role Development in Client Participation," *Academy of Management Journal,* December 1986, pp. 726–35.

9. Sandy Jap, "The Employee's Viewpoint of Critical Service Encounters," *Stores,* January 1995, pp. RR4–RR6.

10. Choy L. Wong and Dean Tjosvold, "Goal Interdependence and Quality Marketing Services," *Psychology & Marketing,* May 1995, pp. 189–205.

11. Carol A. Reeves and David A. Bednar, "Quality as Symphony," *Cornell Hotel & Restaurant Administration Quarterly,* June 1995, pp. 72–79.

12. Christopher H. Lovelock, "Classifying Services to Gain Strategic Marketing Insights," *Journal of Marketing,* Summer 1983, pp. 9–20.

13. Jagdip Singh, Jerry R. Goolsby and Gary K. Rhoads, "Employee Burnout and Its Implications for Customer Service Representatives," *Stores,* April 1995, pp. RR8–RR9.

14. John Hagerman, "Teams and Measurable Results," *CMA Magazine,* March 1995, p. 6.

15. Leonard L. Berry, David R. Bennett, and Carter W. Brown, *Service Quality: A Profit Strategy for Financial Institutions* (Burr Ridge, IL: Dow Jones-Irwin, 1989), p. 26.

16. Stephen W. Brown, "Building Quality into Service Calls for More than Just 'Smile Training,'" *Marketing News,* September 26, 1988, p. 16.

17. Karl Albrect, "Total Quality Service," *Quality Digest,* January 1993, pp. 17–19.

18. Gregg Fields and Joan Chrissos, "Service without a Smile a Growth Industry," *Herald-Leader* (Lexington, Ky.), October 4, 1987, pp. A1, A14.

19. Leonard L. Berry and A. Parasuraman, *Marketing Services* (New York: Free Press, 1991), p. 15–16.

20. Elizabeth Anderson, "High Tech v. High Touch: A Case Study of TQM Implementation in Higher Education," *Managing Service Quality,* 1995, pp. 48–56.

21. John Chidchester, "Tailoring Your Survey," *Credit Union Management,* April 1995, pp. 30–31.

22. Pete Stevens, Bonnie Knutson, and Mark Patton, "DINESERV: A Tool for Measuring Service Quality in Restaurants," *Cornell Hotel & Restaurant Administration Quarterly,* April 1995, pp. 56–60.

23. Scott M. Broetzmann, et al., "Customer Satisfaction: Lip Service or Management Tool?" *Managing Service Quality,* 1995, pp. 13–18.

24. Monci Jo Williams, "Why Is Airline Food So Terrible?" *Fortune,* December 19, 1988, pp. 169–72.

25. Thomas C. Keiser, "Strategies for Enhancing Service Quality," *Journal of Services Marketing,* Summer 1988, pp. 65–70.

26. Patricia Sellers, "How to Handle Customers' Gripes," *Fortune,* October 24, 1988, pp. 88–100.

27. Tatiana Pouschine, "In the Shadows of American Express," *Forbes,* October 26, 1992, pp. 154–59.

28. A. Parasuraman, "Customer Oriented Corporate Cultures Are Crucial to Services Marketing Success," *Journal of Services Marketing,* Summer 1987, pp. 39–46.

29. Peter F. Drucker, "The New Productivity Challenge," *Harvard Business Review,* November–December 1991, pp. 70–79.

30. Curtis R. McClaughlin and Sydney Coffey, "Measuring 'Productivity' in Services," in *Managing Services,* ed. Christopher H. Lovelock (Englewood Cliffs, N.J.: Prentice Hall, 1992), pp. 395–96.

31. C. Jackson Grayson, Jr., and Carla O'Dell, *American Business: A Two-Minute Warning* (New York: Free Press, 1988), pp. 36–38.

32. Drucker, "New Productivity Challenge," pp. 70–79.

33. Christine V. Bullen, "Productivity CSFs for Knowledge Workers," *Information Strategy: The Executive's Journal,* Fall 1995, pp. 41–20.

34. Michael J. Roche and Mary Porter, "Technology Provides Competitive Edge," *Corporate Cashflow,* July 1995, pp. 30–34.

35. Andrea R. Gaedeke, "In the Office," *Manager's Magazine,* July 1995, pp. 25–26.

36. Regina Eisman, "Higher Education, Higher Output," *Incentive,* July 1995, p. 15.

37. James H. Donnelly, Jr., and Steven J. Skinner, *The New Banker* (Burr Ridge, IL: Dow Jones-Irwin, 1989), pp. 33–34.

38. Christopher W. L. Hart, James L. Heskett, and W. Earl Sasser, Jr., "The Profitable Art of Service Recovery," *Harvard Business Review,* July–August 1990, pp. 148–56.

39. Donnelly and Skinner, *The New Banker,* pp. 21–24.

40. Ibid., pp. 21–26.

41. Scott W. Kelley, "Discretion and the Service Employee," *Journal of Retailing,* Spring 1993, pp. 104–26.

42. Ronald Henkoff, "Finding, Training & Keeping The Best Service Workers," *Fortune,* October 3, 1994, pp. 110–122.

43. James Brian Quinn, Thomas L. Doorley, and Penny C. Paquette, "Technology in Service: Rethinking Strategic Focus," *Sloan Management Review,* Winter 1990, pp. 79–87.

44. Jeffrey Pfeffer, Toru Hatano, and Timo Santalainen, "Producing Sustainable Competitive Advantage Through the Effective Management of People," *Academy of Management Executive,* February 1995, pp. 55–72.

45. Fanglan Du, Paula Mergenbagen, and Marlene Lee, "The Future of Services," *American Demographics,* November 1995, pp. 30–47.

46. Gustavo Vargas and Shasem H. Manoochehri, "An Assessment of Operations in U.S. Service Firms," *International Journal of Operations & Production Management,* 1995, 15(1), pp. 24–37.

47. "Xerox Canada, Ltd., Offers Seamless Customer Service in New Brunswick," *Telemarketing,* June 1995, pp. 54.

48. Tom Harvey, "Service Quality: The Culprit and the Cure," *Bank Marketing,* June 1995, pp. 24–28.

49. Regina Eisman, "Are Mean Managers Making You Sick?" *Incentive,* July 1995, p. 10.

50. Christo Boshoff and Gerhard Mels, "A Causal Model to Evaluate the Relationships Among Supervision, Role Stress, Organizational Commitment, and Internal Service Quality," *European Journal of Marketing,* 1995, 29(2): 23–42.

51. Marilyn Sczech and Dennis Attenello, "NationsBank Reengineers to Achieve Leadership in International Services," *National Productivity Review,* Spring 1995, pp. 89–96.

52. Sue Glassock and Kimberly Gram, "Winning Ways: Establishing an Effective Workplace Recognition System," *National Productivity Review,* Summer 1995, pp. 91–102.

Chapter 18

1. Gary Hamel and C.K. Prahalad, *Competing for the Future* (Boston, Mass: Harvard Business School Press, 1994), p. 73.

2. Howard Isenberg, "The Second Industrial Revolution: The Impact of the Information Explosion," *Industrial Engineering,* March 1995, p. 15.

3. John P. Kotter, "Leading Change: Why Transformation Efforts Fail," *Harvard Business Review,* March/April 1995, pp. 59–67.

4. Tom Broersma, "In Search of the Future," *Training & Development,* January 1995, pp. 38–43.

5. D. Keith Denton, "Creating a System for Continuous Improvement," *Business Horizons,* January/February 1995, pp. 16–21.

6. Allan H. Church, Anne Margiloff, and Celeste Coruzi, "Using Surveys for Change: An Applied Example in a Pharmaceuticals Organization," *Leadership & Organizational Development Journal,* 1995, 16(4), pp. 3–11.

7. Barry K. Spiker and Eric Lesser, "We Have Met the Enemy…", *Journal of Business Strategy,* March/April 1995, pp. 17–21.

8. Tom Peters, "Be Hyper-Active," *Incentive,* June 1995, p. 39.

9. Timothy Galpin, "Pruning the Grapevine," *Training & Development,* April 1995, pp. 28–33.

10. Barbara Kanegsberg, "Quality Strategies '95: Cultural Revolution," *Chemical Marketing Reporter,* April 1995, pp. SR3–SR5.

11. Allan H. Church, "Managerial Behavior and Work Group Climate as Predictors of Employee Outcomes," *Human Resource Development Quarterly,* Summer 1995, pp. 173–205.

12. Sarah Wenzel and Jude Panetta, "Accelerating Momentum for Change," *Hospital Material Management Quarterly,* May 1995, pp. 10–17.

13. Perry Pascarella, "Resistance to Change: It Can Be a Plus," *Industry Week,* July 27, 1987, p. 45ff.

14. Ronald F. Recardo, "Overcoming Resistance to Change," *National Productivity Review,* Spring 1995, pp. 5–12.

15. Robert M. Randall, "The Sense-and-Respond Model," *Planning Review,* May/June 1995, pp. 43–44.

16. Stephan H. Haeckel, "Adaptive Enterprise Design: The Sense-and-Respond Model," *Planning Review,* May/June 1995, pp. 6–13.

17. Arthur R. Pell, "What Makes TQM Succeed?" *Managers Magazine,* February 1995, pp. 26–27.

18. Paul Hersey and Kenneth H. Blanchard, *Management of Organizational Behavior* (Englewood Cliffs, NJ: Prentice Hall, 1993) pp. 368–369.

19. Kate Lademan, "Measuring Skills and Behavior," *Training & Development,* November 1991, pp. 61–66.

20. Noel Tichy, "How Different Types of Change Agents Diagnose Organizations," *Human Relations,* December 1975, pp. 771–79.

21. David Borchard, "Planning for Career and Life: Job Surfing on the Tidal Waves of Change," *Futurist,* January/February 1995, pp. 8–12.

22. Judith A. Neal, et al., "From Incremental Change to Retrofit: Creating High-Performance Work Systems," *Academy of Management Executive,* February 1995, pp. 42–54.

23. John P. Kotter, "Leading Change: Why Transformation Efforts Fail," *Harvard Business Review,* March–April 1995, pp. 59–67.

24. Roger Harrison, "Choosing the Depth of Organizational Intervention," *Journal of Applied Behavioral Science,* 1970, pp. 181–202.

25. Wendell L. French and Cecil H. Bell, Jr., *Organizational Development: Behavioral Science Interventions for Organizational Improvement* (Englewood Cliffs, N.J.: Prentice-Hall, 1990), p. 170.

26. An excellent framework for developing a team-building program is provided by Cynthia Reedy Johnson in "An Outline for Team Building," *Training,* January 1986, pp. 48ff.

27. Richard L. Hughes, William E. Rosebach, and William H. Glover, "Team Development in an Intact, Ongoing Work Group," *Group and Organizational Studies,* June 1983, pp. 161–81.

28. For other strategies for team building effectiveness, see Paul S. George, "Team Building without Tears," *Personnel Journal,* November 1987, pp. 122ff.

29. Kenneth P. deMeuse and S. Jay Liebowitz, "An Empirical Analysis of Team-Building Research," *Group and Organizational Studies,* September 1981, pp. 357–78.

30. W. Alan Randolph, "Navigating the Journey to Empowerment," *Organizational Dynamics,* Spring 1995, pp. 19–32.

31. John Hagerman, "Teams and Measurable Results," *CMA Magazine,* March 1995, p. 6.

32. Jeffrey Pfeffer, Toru Hatano, and Timo Santalainen, "Producing Sustainable Competitive Advantage Through the Effective Management of People," *Academy of Management Executive,* February 1995, pp. 55–72.

33. John W. Kennish, "Motivating with a Positive, Participatory Style," *Security Management,* August 1994, pp. 22–23.

34. Hamel and Prahalad, op cit., p. 4.

35. Ibid, p. 76.

36. Shawn Tully, "Why to Go for Stretch Targets," *Fortune,* November 14, 1994, pp. 145–155.

37. Christopher A. Bartlett and Sumantra Ghoshal, "Changing the Role of Top Management: Beyond Systems to People," *Harvard Business Review,* May–June 1995, pp. 132–142.

38. JoAnn S. Lublin and Alex Markels, "How Three CEOs Achieved Fast Turnarounds," *The Wall Street Journal,* July 21, 1995, pp. B1, B12.

39. Edward E. Lawler, *Ultimate Advantage* (San Francisco: Jossey-Bass, 1992).

40. G. Sharman, "When Quality Control Gets in the Way," *The Wall Street Journal,* February 24, 1992, p. A16.

41. R. Krishnan, et al., "In Search of Quality Improvement: Problems of Design and Implementation," *Academy of Management Executive,* 1993, 7(4), pp. 7–20.

42. Ibid, pp. 12–13.

Chapter 19

1. David H. Holt, *Entrepreneurship* (Englewood Cliffs, N.J.: Prentice-Hall, 1992), p. 3.

2. Richard Cantillon, *Essae sur la nature du commerce en general,* translated by H. Higgs, (London:, Macmillan, 1931), pp. 47–49, 53, 151–153.

3. This definition is a modified version of one offered by Robert C. Ronstadt, *Entrepreneurship: Text, Cases, and Notes* (Dover, Mass.: Lord, 1984), pp. 32–33.

4. Vladimir Benacek, "Small Businesses and Private Entrepreneurship During Transition: The Case of the Czech Republic," *Eastern European Economics,* March/April 1995, pp. 38–75.

5. K.R. Blawatt, "Entrepreneurship in Estonia: Profiles of Entrepreneurs," *Journal of Small Business Management,* April 1995, pp. 74–79.

6. Roger Kaplan, "Entrepreneurship Reconsidered: The Anti-management Bias," *Harvard Business Review,* May–June 1987, p. 89.

7. Dennis Kimbro, "Let Us Create Wealth," *Success,* July/August 1995, pp. 48–52.

8. Foard F. Jones, Michael H. Morris, and Wayne Rockmore, "HR Practices that Promote Entrepreneurship," *HRMagazine,* May 1995, pp. 86–91.

9. Gifford Pinchot, *Intrapreneuring* (New York: Harper & Row, 1985).

10. Hollister B. Sykes, "Lessons from a New Venture Program," *Harvard Business Review,* May–June 1986, pp. 69–74.

11. Shaker A. Zahra and Jeffrey G. Covin, "Contextual Influences on the Corporate Entrepreneurship-Performance Relationship: A Longitudinal Analysis," *Journal of Business Venturing,* January 1995, pp. 43–58.

12. Anne Reifenberg, "How Secret Formula for Coveted Slick 50 Fell into Bad Hands," *The Wall Street Journal,* October 25, 1995, pp. A1, A6.

13. Bill Gates, *The Road Ahead,* (New York: Viking, 1995).

14. Jerr Boschee, "Social Entrepreneurship," *Across the Board,* March 1995, pp. 20–25.

15. "The Most Dangerous Game?," *Nation's Business,* September 1995, p. 20.

16. Robert N. Lussier, "Startup Business Advice from Business Owners to Would-Be Entrepreneurs," *Sam Advanced Management Journal,* Winter 1995, pp. 10–13; Robert N. Lussier, "A Nonfinancial Business Success Versus Failure Prediction Model for Young Firms," *Journal of Small Business Management,* January 1995, pp. 8–20.

17. Bill Tobin, "Entrepreneurship Ahoy," *Inc.,* August 1995, p. 87.

18. Peter Metcalf, "Lessons Learned," Inc., April 1995, pp. 35–36.

19. Randall Lane, "Computers Are Our Friends," *Forbes,* May 8, 1995, pp. 102–108.

20. Maggie Jones, "Smart Cookies," *Working Woman,* April 1995, pp. 50–52.

21. Judy Margolis, "Getting Down to Business Via CD-ROM," *Canadian Banker,* January/February 1995, pp. 12–14.

22. Donald L. Sexton and Nancy Bowman, "The Entrepreneur: A Capable Executive and More," *Journal of Business Venturing,* 1(1): 1985, pp. 129–140.

23. Janice Langan-Fox and Susanna Roth, "Achievement Motivation and Female Entrepreneurs," *Journal of Occupational and Organizational Psychology,* September 1995, pp. 209–218.

24. Kathleen Allen, *Launching New Ventures* (Chicago, IL: Upstart Publishing Company, Inc., 1995), p. 83.

25. Andrew E. Serwer, "The Simplot Saga," *Fortune,* November 27, 1995, pp. 69–86.

26. Joel Kolen, "Knowing When to Take a Breather," *Nation's Business,* November 1995, p. 6.

27. For example, see *USA Today,* March 13, 1987, p. 13.

28. Dun & Bradstreet, *Business Failures Record* (New York: Dun & Bradstreet Business Economics Department, 1986), pp. 1–10.

29. See Erik Larson, "The Best-Laid Plans," Inc., February 1987, pp. 60–64; and Bruce G. Posner, "Real Entrepreneurs Don't Plan," *Inc.,* November 1985, pp. 129–35.

30. Richard L. Osborne, "Planning: The Entrepreneurial Ego at Work," *Business Horizons,* January–February 1987, pp. 20–24.

31. David E. Gumpert, *Creating a Successful Business Plan,* in William D. Bygrave, ed., *The Portable MBA in Entrepreneurship,* (New York: John Wiley & Sons, Inc., 1994) pp. 113–138.

32. Kathleen Allen, op cit., pp. 423–438.

33. Robert D. Hisrich, and Mikhail V. Grachev, "The Russian Entrepreneur: Characteristics and Prescriptions for Success," *Journal of Managerial Psychology,* 10(2): 1995, pp. 3–9.

34. Simon Johnson and Gary Loveman, "Starting Over: Poland After Communism," *Harvard Business Review,* March/April 1995, pp. 44–57.

35. A. Sekarev, "Ukraine: Crisis on the Basis of a Vague Economic Policy," *Problems of Economic Transition,* January 1995, pp. 40–56.

36. Newt Gingrich, "Renewing American Civilization," *Futurist,* July/August 1995, pp. 10–14.

37. H.K. Tang and K.T.Yeo, "Technology, Entrepreneurship and National Development: Lessons from Singapore," *International Journal of Technology Management,* 10(7): 1995, pp. 797–814.

Chapter 20

1. Bill Gates, *The Road Ahead* (New York: Viking Penguin, 1995), see especially Chapter 10.

2. C. L. Herlin and M. Roznowski, "Organizational Technologies: Effects on Organizations' Characteristics and Individuals' Responses," in *Research in Organizational Behavior,* ed. Larry L. Cummings and B. M. Staw (Greenwich, Conn.: JAI Press, 1985), p. 47.

3. F. Berniker, "Understanding Technical Systems," paper presented at Symposium on Management Training Programs: Implications of New Technologies, Geneva, Switzerland, 1987, p. 10.

4. Robert Fisher, *Science, Man, & Society* (Philadelphia: W. B. Saunders, 1975), pp. 5–7.

5. Michele Jachim, "Meeting On a Moment's Notice," *American Gas,* November 1995, pp. 38–39.

6. Debra Haverson, "Agility Tightens the Supply Chain," *Midrange Systems,* August 11, 1995, p. 30.

7. "High Technology," *Business Week,* January 11, 1993, pp. 78–82.

8. Joseph G. Morone, *Winning in High-Tech Markets* (Cambridge, Mass.: Harvard Business School Press, 1992), p. 1.

9. "Technology and Global Competitiveness," National Science Board, Science & Engineering Indicators (Washington, D.C.: U.S. Government Printing Office, 1991), pp. 133–40.

10. Joseph F. Coates, "Customization Promises Sharp Competitive Edge," *Research-Technology Management,* November/December 1995, pp. 6–7.

11. Robin Yale Bergstrom, "Speed . . . The Next Battlefield," *Production,* August 1995, pp. 60–61.

12. Nathan Rosenberg, "Why Technology Forecasts Often Fail," *Futurist,* July/August 1995, pp. 16–21.

13. Richard N. Foster, *Innovation: The Attacker's Advantage* (New York: Summit Books, 1986), p. 31.

14. Daniel Prosser, and Don O'Neal, "Two Views on Telecommunications," *Hotel & Motel Management,* October 16, 1995, pp. 36–38.

15. Dennis A. Conforto, "Competing with Retail Technologies," *Chain Store Age Executive,* November 1995, p. 120.

16. Barry Mason, "Data Mining: Exploring the Unknown," *Discount Merchandiser,* October 1995, pp. T58–T60.

17. Richard N. Foster, *Innovation: The Attacker's Advantage* (New York: Summit Books, 1986), pp. 214–217.

18. "Rubbermaid: Another Day, Another Product," *Chief Executive,* July/August 1995, pp. 12–13.

19. Hans J. Thamhain, "Developing the Skills You Need," *Research, Technology, Management,* March–April 1992, pp. 42–47.

20. "Unilever Seeks Competitiveness through R&D," *British Food Journal,* 97(3): 1995, pp. 40–41.

21. Chris Pappas, "Strategic Management of Technology," *Journal of Product Innovation Management,* Spring 1984, pp. 30–35.

22. Four suggested steps, ibid., p. 34.

23. John Teresko, "IT Leadership: CEO's Toughest Role," *Industry Week,* September 18, 1995, p. 53.

24. Amit Chatterjee and Tridibesh Mukherjee, "Staying Ahead of Global Competition: The Tata Steel Strategy," *Journal of General Management*, Autumn 1995, pp. 71–88.

25. Linda Stasko, "Computers Alone Are Not Always a Solution," *Machine Design*, September 28, 1995, pp. 73–80.

26. Richard S. Rosenbloom and William J. Abernathy, "The Climate for Innovation in Industry: The Role of Management Attitudes and Practices in Consumer Electronics," *Research Policy*, Spring 1980, pp. 209–25.

27. Modesto A. Maidique and Robert B. Hayes, "The Art of High Technology Management," *Sloan Management Review*, Winter 1984, p. 19.

28. Tim Stevens, "Tool Kit for Innovators," *Industry Week*, June 5, 1995, pp. 28–34.

29. Tom Trainer, "Listening to Your Customers," *Informationweek*, September 18, 1995, p. 236.

30. Roger J. Calantone, Shawnee K. Vickery, and Cornelia Droge, "Business Performance and Strategic New Product Development Activities: An Empirical Investigation," *Journal of Product Innovation Management*, June 1995, pp. 214–223.

31. Barbara Ettorre, "A Talk with Xerox's Top Scientist," *Management Review*, February 1995, pp. 9–12.

32. The discussion of market-driven transfer and process-and-product improvement transfer is based and draws upon William G. Howard, Jr., and Bruce R. Gluck, *Profiting from Innovation* (New York: Free Press, 1992), pp. 19–30.

33. Fred Hewitt, "Business Process Innovation in the Mid-1990s," *Integrated Manufacturing Systems*, 6(2): 1995, pp. 18–26.

34. Ajit Kambil, "Electronic Commerce: Implications of the Internet for Business Practice and Strategy," *Business Economics*, October 1995, pp. 27–33.

35. Bernard F. Mathaisel and Jeff Kvaal, "Information Superhighway: Road to the Future," *Chain Store Age Executive*, September 1995, pp. 42–44.

36. Cheryl Pellerin, "Growth, Change and Bright Horizons," *The Industrial Robot*, 22(1): 1995, pp. 34–35.

37. Charlotte Snow, "Technology Keeps Food Costs on Diet," *Modern Healthcare*, October 9, 1995, pp. 92–94.

38. R. E. Gomory, "From the Ladder of Science to the Product Development Cycle," *Harvard Business Review*, November–December 1989, p. 102.

39. Joseph T. Visey, "The New Competitors: They Think in Terms of Speed-to-Market," *Academy of Management Executive*, May 1991, pp. 23–33.

40. Catherine M. Banbury and Will Mitchell, "The Effect of Introducing Important Incremental Innovations on Market Share and Business Survival," *Strategic Management Journal*, Summer 1995, pp. 161–182.

41. For an excellent discussion of strategies for international technology transfer, see Robert T. Keller and Ravi R. Chinta, "International Technology Transfer: Strategies for Success," *Academy of Management Executive*, May 1990, pp. 33–43.

42. Ben L. Kedia and Rabi S. Bhagat, "Culture Constraints on Transfer of Technology across Nations: Implications for Research in International and Comparative Management," *Academy of Management Review*, October 1988, pp. 559–71.

43. Jay Peterzel, "When Friends Become Moles," *Time*, May 1990, p. 50.

44. Bob Sablatura and Jim Dalgleish, "Businessmen Arrested for Allegedly Trying to Buy Dow Trade Secrets," *Midland Daily News*, August 1, 1988, p. 1.

45. William M. Carley, "How the FBI Snared Two Scientists Selling Drug Company Secrets," *The Wall Street Journal*, September 5, 1991, p. 1.

46. E. M. Goodman, "The Japanese Information-Gatherers," *Research, Technology, Management*, July–August 1992, p. 47.

47. Lewis M. Branscomb, "Toward a U.S. Technology Policy," *Issues in Science and Technology*, Summer 1991, pp. 50–55.

48. Rick Dove, "Agile Practice Reference Models," *Production*, July 1995, pp. 16–19.

49. Tom Hardy, "Innovation and Chaos," *Journal of Business Strategy*, May/June 1995, pp. 7–10.

50. Homa Bahrami, and Stuart Evans, "Flexible Re-Cycling and High-Technology Entrepreneurship," *California Management Review*, Spring 1995, pp. 62–89.

51. E. Raudsepp, "Profile of the Creative Individual," *Creative Computing*, August 1983, p. 62.

52. Ted Pollock, "Mind Your Own Business," *Supervision*, January 1995, pp. 21–23.

53. Carol Hildebrand, "Of Human Bonding," *CIO*, May 15, 1995, pp. 31–36.

54. Lee Tom Perry, *Offensive Strategy* (New York: Harper Business, 1990), p. 169.

55. W. Guzzardi, "The National Business Hall of Fame," *Fortune*, 1990, p. 19.

56. Rosabeth Moss Kanter, *The Change Masters* (New York: Simon & Schuster, 1983), p. 101.

57. Joyce Ranney and Mark Deck, "Making Teams Work: Lessons from Leaders in New Product Development," *Planning Review*, July/August 1995, pp. 6–12.

58. Anna Brady, "Small Is As Small Does," *Journal of Business Strategy*, March/April 1995, pp. 44–46.

59. Thomas Kiely, "The Idea Makers," *Technology Review*, January 1993, pp. 32–40.

Photo Credits

Part 1

Opener, p. 1: The Archive. p. 3: © Kip Brandage/Woodfin Camp & Associates. p. 16: Courtesy of Dell Computers. p. 19: Courtesy of Microsoft. p. 31: The Bettmann Archive. p. 51: William Johnson / Stock Boston. p. 57: Louisa Preston. p. 66: Richard Howard / Offshoot Stock. p. 71: Bonnie Kamin. p. 89: The Archive. p. 99: Ed Kashi. p. 106a: Courtesy of Xerox. p. 106b: Louisa Preston. p. 107: Louisa Preston.

Part 2

Opener, p. 113: Courtesy of Canadian Airlines International. p. 115: Sam Ogden. p. 131: Courtesy of Wainwright Industries. p. 134: Louisa Preston. p. 137: Elena Dorfman / Offshoot Stock. p. 151: Courtesy of Canadian Airlines International. p. 158: Jonathan Wallen. p. 160: Courtesy of Motorola. p. 165: Louisa Preston. p. 183: Index Stock Photography. p. 195: Louisa Preston. p. 204: Courtesy of Dow Chemical.

Part 3

Opener, p. 210: James Schneph. p. 211: Brian Smith. p. 217: Courtesy of W.L. Gore & Associates. p. 224: James Schneph. p. 228: Louisa Preston. p. 241: Rob Kinmouth. p. 243: Courtesy of Lotus. p. 250: Louisa Preston. p. 252: Bonnie Kamin. p. 261: David Dempster / Offshoot Stock. p. 280: Courtesy of the Minnesota Center for Corporate Responsibility. p. 281: Courtesy of Lincoln Electric.

Part 4

Opener, p. 291: Courtesy of Louis V. Gerstner, Jr. p. 293: Courtesy of NASA. p. 295: Nubar Alexanian / Woodfin Camp & Associates. p. 303: Courtesy of Ameritech. p. 315: Bonnie Kamin. p. 325: Courtesy of Ben & Jerry's. p. 333: Louisa Preston. p. 339: Courtesy of Louis V. Gerstner, Jr. p. 357: Courtesy of Aetna. p. 367: Courtesy of Globe Metallurgical.

Part 5

Opener, p. 388: Roger Mastroianni. p. 389: Bonnie Kamin. p. 394: Louisa Preston. p. 408: Courtesy of Johnson Controls. p. 417: Sims/Boynton Photography. p. 422: Robert Frerck / Odyssey. p. 436: Louisa Preston. p. 447: Roger Mastroianni. p. 457: Courtesy of Marriott. p. 464: Courtesy of Nations Bank. p. 471: Bonnie Kamin. p. 486: Louisa Preston. p. 487: Bob Daemmrich / Stock Boston. p. 489: Courtesy of CSX.

Part 6

Opener, p. 499: Courtesy of Sun Microsystems. p. 501: Courtesy of The Outsourcing Institute. p. 505: Louisa Preston. p. 509: Russ Schleipman / Offshoot Stock. p. 519: Sal Di Marco Jr. / Black Star. p. 527: Courtesy of Sun Microsystems. p. 530: Jon Riley / Tony Stone Worldwide. p. 538: Louisa Preston. p. 541: Courtesy of Bell & Howell.

Name Index

Recardo, Ronald F., E-18
Reece, James, E-1
Reed, Stanley, E-4
Rees, Rowena, E-3
Reeves, Carol A., E-17
Reid, David M., E-6
Reifenberg, Anne, E-19
Reiley, Alan C., E-2
Reimer, Edward, E-13
Reiner, Gary, E-15
Reiste, Kristin K., 307n
Remich, Norman C., Jr., E-16
Renwick, P.A., E-5
Rheem, Helen, E-12
Rhoads, Gary K., E-17
Rice, Faye, E-11
Richardson, Bill, E-2
Richmann, Louis S., 486n, E-4
Rigdon, Joan E., E-8, E-9
Rigg, Michael, 258n
Riggs, Joy, E-6
Riley, Anne W., E-11
Roach, Stephen S., 448n
Robinson, Frank, 514
Roche, Michael J., E-17
Rockmore, Wayne, E-18
Roddick, Anita, 503
Roethisberger, Fritz J., E-2
Rokeach, Milton, 87
Ronstadt, Robert C., E-18
Roos, Daniel, E-10
Rosebach, William E., E-18
Rosenberg, Nathan, E-19
Rosenbloom, Richard S., E-20
Rosener, Judy B., 344n
Rosenthal, R.A., E-11
Rosenzweig, James E., E-2
Ross, Joel E., E-6
Ross, Ruth Ann, E-9
Ross, Timothy J., E-10
Ross, Timothy L., E-9
Rossant, John, E-4
Roth, Aleda, 417
Roth, Susanna, E-19
Rothman, Andrea, 467n, E-16
Rothman, Howard, E-14
Rothman, John R., 147n
Rothwell, Roy, 530n
Rowe, Anita, 344n, E-13
Roznowski, M., E-19
Rubach, Laura, E-6
Rubel, Chad, E-7
Rubenfeld, Stephen A., 121n
Rubin, Matthew S., E-15
Ruffner, Esther R., E-11
Rushinek, Avi, E-15
Rushinek, Sara F., E-15

S
Saari, L. M., E-12
Sablatura, Bob, E-20

Sabo, Richard S., E-10
Sager, Ira, 340n, E-6, E-7
Salinas, Carlos, 250
Salter, James M., E-16
Sampson, Anthony, E-2
Sandler, Greg, 456n
Sankar, Cheton S., E-5
Sansoni, Silvia, E-4
Santalainen, Timo, E-17
Santora, J. E., E-10
Saporito, Bill, E-13
Sashkin, Marshall, 243n, E-4, E-7, E-8, E-13
Sasser, W. Earl, Jr., E-17
Saunders, Paula M., E-16
Sawyers, Alena, 331n
Sayles, L., E-12
Schaffer, Matt, E-3
Scharer, Gail E., E-4
Schein, Edgar H., E-2
Schellhardt, Timothy D., 294n
Scherer, Robert F., E-16
Schiller, Zachary, E-16
Schine, Eric, 369n
Schlessinger, Leonard A., 481n, E-14
Schmitt, Wolf, 535
Schmitz, Barbara, E-16
Schnake, M. E., E-12
Schnieder, David, E-3
Schoenfeldt, Lyle F., E-10
Schonfeld, Erick, 538n
Schreyogg, George, E-15
Schriefer, John, E-15
Schriescheim, Chester A., 355n
Schumpeter, Joseph, 506
Schuster, Jay R., E-10
Schwenk, C. R., E-4
Scott, K. Dow, E-10
Scroggins, Charlotte, 367
Sculley, John, 514
Sczech, Marilyn, E-17
Sears, Susan B., E-5
Sebastian, Pamela, 456n
Segal, Jonathan A., E-10
Sekarev, A., E-19
Sellers, Patricia, E-13, E-14, E-15, E-17
Selley, David C., 200n
Semier, Ricardo, 258n
Semler, Richard, 360
Senge, Peter M., 3, 155, 250n
Serewr, Andrew E., E-19
Sethi, S. Prakash, E-3
Sexton, Donald L., 512n, E-19
Shane, Michael B., 505n
Shani, A. B., E-2
Shapiro, Eben, 340n
Sharman, G., E-18
Shaw, James B., E-10
Shaw, John J., E-4
Shaw, K. M., E-12
Shellenbarger, Sue, E-8

Shelton, Ken, 363n
Sherer, Jill L., E-10
Shermach, Kelly, E-5
Sherman, Stratford, 336n, 342n, E-2, E-3
Sherr, Lawrence A., 390n
Shewhart, Walter A., E-14
Shipper, Frank, 147n
Shippes, Frank, E-7
Shortell, Stephen M., E-2
Shrirvastava, Paul, 212n
Shuttle, J. L., E-8
Siegel, Joel G., E-15
Sigler, Kevin J., 325n
Silverman, Charles, E-9
Silvers, David I., E-6
Simet, Donald P., E-8
Simmons, James C., 375n
Simon, Herbert, 42, 118, 539
Simplot, J. R., 514
Sims, Arden, 367, 368n
Sims, Henry P., Jr., 307n, 355n, 364n, E-10, E-11, E-13
Singh, Jagdip, E-17
Sinha, Ashish, E-1
Sitkin, Sim B., E-13
Skinner, B. F., 324, E-12
Skinner, Steven J., E-16, E-17
Skutski, Karl J., 384n, E-14
Slutsker, Gary, E-15
Slywotzky, Adrian J., 553n
Smith, Adam, 82
Smith, Alfred F., 422n
Smith, Brian, 212n
Smith, Emily T., 92n
Smith, Geri, 409n
Smith, S. L., 131n
Smock, Doug, E-6
Snee, Ronald D., E-15
Snock, J. D., E-11
Snow, Charles C., 233n, E-8
Snow, Charlotte, E-20
Snyder, Neil, E-1
Snyderman, B., E-8
Solis, Dianna, E-16
Solo, Sally, 414n
Solomon, Barbara, 310n
Solomon, Caleb, E-16
Solomon, Charlene Marmer, 262n, 265n, 280n, E-9
Sonnenfeld, Jeffrey A., E-11
Sookdeo, Ricardo, 448n
Spechler, Jay W., 262
Spethmann, Betsy, E-5
Spiers, Joseph, E-15, E-16
Spiker, Barry K., E-18
Spindle, Bill, 472n
Spohn, Andrew G., E-9
Stack, Jack, 360
Staffold, G. S., III, E-2
Stalk, George, Jr., E-6, E-7
Stalker, G. M., E-8

Company Index

Subject Index